D1629056

Huck

Sustainable Development Goals

Sustainable Development Goals

Article-by-Article Commentary

by

Winfried Huck

Assistant Editor

Jennifer Maaß

2022

Published by
Nomos Verlagsgesellschaft mbH & Co. KG, Waldseestraße 3-5, 76530 Baden-Baden, Germany,
email: vertrieb@nomos.de

Co-published by
Verlag C.H.Beck oHG, Wilhelmstraße 9, 80801 München, Germany,
email: bestellung@beck.de

and

Hart Publishing, Kemp House, Chawley Park, Cumnor Hill, Oxford, OX2 9PH, United Kingdom,
online at: www.hartpub.co.uk

Published in North America by Hart Publishing,
An Imprint of Bloomsbury Publishing 1385 Broadway, New York, NY 10018, USA
email: mail@ hartpub.co.uk

ISBN 978 3 8487 6077 0 (NOMOS Print)
ISBN 978 3 7489 0206 5 (NOMOS ePDF)
ISBN 978 3 406 75351 0 (C.H.BECK)
ISBN 978 1 5099 3404 1 (HART)

First Edition 2022

Preface

The initial idea to write this book arose after the unanimously taken resolution of the United Nations General Assembly in September 2015, which formulated a Global Agenda with 17 goals and 169 sub-goals, unparalleled to date in form and scope. After publishing some papers and giving presentations, amongst others, in Cagliari, Cologne, Frankfurt, Havana, Mumbai, Naples, Pune, I submitted a proposal to the publishing house C.H. Beck, Munich, to write a legal commentary on precisely this resolution. However, my proposal was forwarded to Nomos Publishing House, Baden-Baden, who quickly took up the idea, and took the lead in coordinating C.H. Beck and Hart, despite the fact that a legal commentary with the focus set on a non-binding resolution could well be a hard-selling and therefore difficult product from a publisher's point of view. Nevertheless, when outlining the exposé in 2018/2019, the overwhelming impact within the legal matrix was highlighted and the concept could solidify.

The idea of such a book then gained weight from the questions that Duncan French and Louis J. Kotzé quite precisely formulated in the introduction to their book 'Sustainable Development Goals – Law, Theory and Implementation' (2018), addressing, amongst others, the question: 'How are such Goals [...] interpreted and implemented going forward, both at the international and domestic levels, in legislative, policy and importantly, judicial fora?'

I was fortunate to deepen my ideas and preparations for this book during my research stay at the Lauterpacht Centre for International Law (LCIL) at the University of Cambridge between May and July 2019. There I met many brilliant colleagues who inspired me personally greatly and who also spurred on my work on this book. In particular, I would like to acknowledge in an alphabetical order: Eyal Benvenisti, John Barker, Mihaela Barnes, Muin Boase, Marie-Claire Cordonier Segger, Gerard Conway, Markus Gehring, Joanna Gomula, Nartnirun Junngam, Avidan Kent, Paul Komba, Natalie Nunn, Hu Ren, Pablo Salas, Michele Saporiti and Isabel Staudinger. The unique atmosphere took the concept of this book steps further. Joanna Gomula opened the door initially to the LCIL, she was so kind to invite me to participate on a workshop on ASEAN in 2017, and she supported the idea of returning, for which I am deeply grateful.

Furthermore, in this academic but also personal context, I would like to mention the following colleagues in an alphabetical order who have motivated me, sometimes unconsciously, in my endeavours to achieve the outcome of this book: Daniele Amoroso, Paolo Farah, Stephen Hardy, Massimo Iovane, Markus Krajewski, Fulvio Palombino, Alicia Elias Roberts, Adriana di Stefano, Valentina Vadi and Giovanni Zarra. My gratitude is also owed to my home institution, the Ostfalia University of Applied Sciences, Wolfenbuettel, and all the people who supported me in granting a sabbatical to begin research at Cambridge University.

With the publication of this book, I reveal my immodest aim to present a manageable version of the SDGs for legal practice, which makes it possible to bring together the Global Agenda 2030 and the SDGs framed by it, with their respective legal context on different levels. The aim is to link international, European and national legal practice, to examine facts for their sustainability and to prepare the legal foundations of the Global Agenda 2030 in such a way that they become legally manageable and applicable in practice. This book, which begins with a general introduction, explains theory and practice and is generally dedicated to the practice that may accrue from the gradually yet vigorously growing implications and impacts of the SDGs on policies and areas of public and private law.

The more general exposition underlying the introduction could serve as a more universal basis for the interpretation and applicability of the SDGs in different frameworks of a broader legal array. To facilitate understanding of the interpretive approach in the second section, I provide here only a brief insight to illustrate the working method. Deemed useful,

Preface

the focus is on a systematic approach that provides additional content for each objective of the SDGs, framed by the following structure:

- Background and Origin
- Scope and Dimensions
- Interdependences
- Jurisprudential Significance
- Conclusion

To sum it all up, I have attempted to provide a concise, systematic review and analysis with a holistic legal perspective of how and to what extent the SDGs are becoming a legal norm, not through the UN, but rather through the reception of many other international organisations and public and private entities that are applying these SDGs as something earnestly valuable with a binding character that ought to be followed.

Over the past years, I have enjoyed working with many students and research assistants, but rarely have I experienced such enthusiastic motivation as with my team, which was composed of many students and post-graduates, most of whom worked with me for only a short period of time, and yet helped to move this project forward in an extraordinary way. I owe a huge debt of gratitude to my fantastic team, mostly graduates of my own faculty. The joint work started in 2020 and continued throughout 2021 with several people who merit mention.

The following people have contributed to this book in a vast and at the same time most different way, for which I owe them my sincere gratitude and it is the least to name them to acknowledge their excellent work, and I do so in alphabetical order:

- Ahmed Tahar Benmaghnia
- Guntram von Ehr
- Sarah Maylin Heß
- Susanna Hesko
- Aria Jalal-Gündüz
- Jennifer Alexandra Katharina Maaß
- Saparya Sood
- Alexander Schulte
- Marc-Anthony Walter

The excellent work of Jennifer Maaß during the entire course of the project should be highlighted. While writing her dissertation at the SWPS University in Warsaw, she, at the same time, remarkably co-led and structured this project. Her outstanding talents in project management, language and legal research, coupled with stunning accuracy, far exceeded my expectations. Without her, this book would most likely not have been ready for print in its current form and content.

I would also like to express my sincere thanks to Dr Wolfgang Lent of C.H. Beck, Munich, for the first encouraging feedback and Dr Matthias Knopik of Nomos Publishing House and the cooperating publishers for their trust in me, and above all, for the productive conversations promoting this publication.

Without any doubt, I have to finally admit that all mistakes in this book are entirely mine.

Comments would be greatly appreciated, and please write to w.huck@ostfalia.de.

Braunschweig, January 2022   *Winfried Huck*

CONTENTS

List of Abbreviations

10YFP	10-Year Framework of Programmes on Sustainable Consumption and Production Patterns
AAAA	Addis Ababa Action Agenda
AAAQ	Availability, Accessibility, Acceptability and Quality
AB	Appellate Body
ABS	Access and Benefit Sharing
ACCC	Aarhus Convention Compliance Committee
ACE	ASEAN Centre for Energy
ACERWC	African Committee of Experts on the Rights and Welfare of the Child
ACHPR	African Commission on Human and Peoples' Rights
ACHR	American Convention on Human Rights
ACommHR	African Commission on Human Rights
ACP	African Caribbean Pacific Group
ACP EPA	Economic Partnership Agreements with the African, Caribbean and Pacific States
ADB	Asian Development Bank
AfCHPR	African Commission on Human and Peoples Rights
AFINUA	Action Framework for Implementation of the New Urban Agenda
AFTA	ASEAN Free Trade Area
AG	Advocate General
AI	Artificial Intelligence
AIIB	Asian Infrastructure Investment Bank
AJIL	American Journal of International Law
ALDFG	Abandoned, List or otherwise Discarded Fishing Gear
ALI	American Law Institute
AoA	Agreement on Agriculture
APAEC	ASEAN Plan of Action for Energy Cooperation
APEC	Asia-Pacific Economic Cooperation
ASEAN	Association of Southeast Asian Nations
AsianJIL	Asian Journal of International Law
ASIL	American Society of International Law
ATCA	US Alien Tort Claims Act
AU	African Union
AUDA-NEPAD	African Union Development Agency - NEPAD
BBC	British Broadcasting Corporation
BIT	Bilateral Investment Treaty
BJIL	Berkeley Journal of International Law
BMJ	British Medical Journal

List of Abbreviations

BPOA	Barbados Programme of Action for the Sustainable Development of Small Island Developing States
BRI	Belt and Road Initiative
BVerfG	Bundesverfassungsgericht (German Federal Constitutional Court)
BvL	File/register number for proceedings on the concrete review of norms to the German Federal Constitutional Court
BvR	File/register number for proceedings on constitutional complaints as well as on municipal constitutional complaints to the German Federal Constitutional Court
CADE	Convention against Discrimination in Education
CAF	Development Bank of Latin America
CAFTA	Central American Free Trade Agreement
CAFTA-DR	Dominican Republic-Central America Free Trade Agreement
CAI	China-EU Investment Agreement
CAP	Common Agricultural Policy
CBAM	Carbon Border Adjustment Mechanism
CBD	Convention on Biological Diversity
CBDR	Common But Differentiated Responsibilities
CBDRRC	Common But Differentiated Responsibilities and Respective Capabilities
CCP	Common Commercial Policy
CDRI	Global Coalition for Disaster-Resilient Infrastructure
CEDAW	Convention on the Elimination of Discrimination against Women
C-EENRG	Cambridge Centre for Environment, Energy and Natural Resource Governance
CERCLA	Comprehensive Environmental Response, Compensation, and Liability Act
CERD	Committee on the Elimination of Racial Discrimination
CERES	Coalition for Environmentally Responsible Economies
CESCR	Committee on Economic, Social and Cultural Rights
CESR	Center for Economic and Social Rights
CETA	Comprehensive Economic and Trade Agreement
CFP	Common Fisheries Policy
CFS	Committee on World Food Security
CFS-FFA	CFS Framework for Action for Food Security and Nutrition in Protracted Crisis
CFS-RAI	CFS Principles for Responsible Investment in Agriculture and Food Systems
CFS-VGGT	CFS Voluntary Guidelines on the Responsible Governance of Tenure of Land, Fisheries and Forests
CGPJ	Consejo General del Poder Judicial [General Council of the Judiciary of Spain]

CIDA	Canadian International Development Agency
CIL	Customary International Law
CISDL	Centre for International Sustainable Development Law
CITES	Convention on International Trade in Endangered Species of Wild Fauna and Flora
CJA	Coroners and Justice Act
CJEU	Court of Justice of the European Union
CKGR	Central Kalahari Game Reserve
CMS	Convention on Migratory Species
CMW	Convention on the Protection of the Rights of All Migrant Workers and Members of their Families
CO_2	Carbon dioxide
CoP	Conference of the Parties
Covid-19	Coronavirus Disease 2019
CRC	Convention on the Rights of Children
CRE	Conférence permanente des Recteurs, Présidents et Vice-Chanceliers des Universités européenes [Standing Conference of Rectors, Presidents and Vice-Chancellors of the European Union]
CRED	Centre for Research on the Epidemiology of Disasters
CRPD	Convention on the Rights of Persons with Disabilities
CRS	Common Reporting Standards
CSD	Commission on Sustainable Development
CSIR	Council for Scientific and Industrial Research
CSR	Corporate Social Responsibility
CSRD	Corporate Sustainability Reporting Directive
CTD	Committee on Trade and Development
CTEO	Chief Trade Enforcement Officer
CUTS	Consumer Unity & Trust Society
CWiPP	Centre for Wellbeing in Public Policy
CYELP	Croatian Yearbook of European Law and Policy
DAC	Development Assistance Committee
DESA-UNSD	Department of Economic and Social Affairs-Statistic Division
DFI	Development Finance Institution
DFID	Department for International Development
DLDD	Desertification/Land Degradation and Drought
DMC	Domestic Material Consumption
DOALOS	Division for Ocean Affairs and the Law of the Sea
DP	Deputy Coroner
DPO	Disabled People's Organisation
DS	Dispute Settlement

List of Abbreviations

DSB	Dispute Settlement Body
DSU	Dispute Settlement Understanding
EBRD	European Bank for Reconstruction and Development
EC	European Community
ECESA	Executive Committee of Economic Social Affairs
ECFR	European Charter of Fundamental Rights
ECHR	European Convention on Human Rights
ECJ	European Court of Justice
ECOSOC	Economic and Social Council
ECOWAS	Economic Community of West African States
ECPA	Energy and Climate Partnership of the Americas
ECSC	European Coal and Steel Community
ECSR	European Committee of Social Rights
ECT	Energy Charter Treaty
ECtHR	European Court of Human Rights
EEA	European Environment Agency
EEC	European Economic Community
EEG	Renewable Energy Sources Act
EEZ	Exclusive Economic Zone
EFA	Education for All
EFSA	European Food Safety Authority
EGA	Environmental Goods Agreement
EIA	Environmental Impact Assessments
EIB	European Investment Bank
EIF	Enhanced Integrated Framework
EJIL	European Journal of International Law
EME	Emerging Market Economy
EMS	Environmental Management System
EOC	Equal Opportunities Commission
EPA	Environmental Protection Agency
EPO	European Patent Office
EPRS	European Parliamentary Research Services
ESCR	Economic, Social and Cultural Rights
ESD	Education for Sustainable Development
ESIL	European Society of International Law
ETD	Energy Taxation Directive
ETO	Extraterritorial Obligation
ETS	Emission Trading Scheme
EU	European Union

EU ETS	EU Emission Trading Scheme
eucrim	European Criminal Law Associations' Forum
EUIPO	European Union Intellectual Property Office
Euromed	Euro-Mediterranean Women's Foundation
EuZW	Europäische Zeitschrift für Wirtschaftsrecht
EYIEL	European Yearbook of International Economic Law
FAO	Food and Agriculture Organization of the UN
FCC	Federal Constitutional Court
FCN	Friendship, Commerce and Navigation Treaties
FDI	Foreign Direct Investment
FEANTSA	European Federation of National Organisations Working with the Homeless
FEMM	European Parliament Committee on Women's Rights and Gender Equality
FET	Fair and Equitable Treatment
FHC	Free Health Care
FIDIC	Fédération Internationale des Ingénieurs Conseils [International Federation of Consulting Engineers]
FIES	Food Insecurity Experience Scale
FLEGT	Forest Law Enforcement Governance and Trade
FRA	European Union Agency for Fundamental Rights
FS	Food System
FTA	Free Trade Agreement
G20	Group of Twenty
GAATW	Global Alliance Against Trafficking in Women
GANHRI	Global Alliance of National Human Rights Institutions
GAP	Global Action Programme
GATS	General Agreement on Trade in Services
GATT	General Agreement on Tariffs and Trade
GAVI	Global Alliance for Vaccines and Immunization
GC	General Court
GCED	Global Citizenship Education
GCM	Global Compact for Migration
GCSI	Global Commons Stewardship Index
GDP	Gross Domestic Product
GDPR	General Data Protection Regulation
GEF	Global Environment Facility
GEM	Global Education Meeting
GEMR	Global Education Monitoring Report
GERD	Grand Ethiopian Renaissance Dam

List of Abbreviations

GFP	Global Focal Point for the Rule of Law
GG	Grundgesetz [German Basic Law]
GHG	Greenhouse Gas
GICA	Global Infrastructure Connectivity Alliance
GIF	Global Indicator Framework
GLAAS	Global Analysis and Assessment of Sanitation and Drinking-Water
GNH	Gross National Happiness
GPG	Gender Pay Gap
GPP	Green Public Procurement
GREVIO	Group of Experts on Action against Violence against Women and Domestic Violence
GRI	Global Reporting Initiative
GSF	Global Strategic Framework for Food Security
GSML	Global Mean Sea Level
GSP	Generalised Scheme of Preferences
GSP+	Generalized System of Preferences with references to sustainable development and good governance
GSTP	Global System of Trade Preferences
HESI	Higher Education Sustainability Initiative
HILJ	Harvard International Law Journal
HJIL	Heidelberg Journal of International Law
HLDE	High-Level Dialogue on Energy
HLPF	High-Level Political Forum
HR	Human Rights
HRB	Human Rights Brief
HRBA	Human Rights Based Approach
HRC	Human Rights Council
HRE	Human Rights Education
HRQ	Human Rights Quarterly
IAA	International Arbitral Awards
IAAE	International Association Autism-Europe
IACommHR	Inter-American Commission on Human Rights
IACtHR	Inter-American Court of Human Rights
IAEA	International Atomic Energy Agency
IAEG-SDGs	Inter-Agency and Expert Group on SDG Indicators
IAS	Invasive Alien Species
IATT	Inter-Agency Task Team
ICAO	International Civil Aviation Organization
ICC	International Criminal Court
ICCPR	International Covenant on Civil and Political Rights

ICEP	Index of Coastal Eutrophication
ICERD	International Convention on the Elimination of All Forms of Racial Discrimination
ICESCR	International Covenant on Economic, Social and Cultural Rights
ICJ	International Court of Justice
ICJL	International Journal of Law in Context
ICLEI	International Council for Local Environmental Initiatives
ICLQ	International & Comparative Law Quarterly
ICLS	International Conference of Labour Statisticians
ICMW	International Convention on the Protection of the Rights of All Migrant Workers and Members of their Families
ICRC	International Committee of the Red Cross
ICS	Improved Biomass Cookstove
ICSFT	International Convention for the Suppression of the Financing of Terrorism
ICSID	International Centre for Settlement of Investment Disputes
ICT	Information and Communication Technology
ICWE	International Conference on Water and Environment
IDA	International Development Association
IDB, IADB	Inter-American Development Bank Group
IDFC	Infrastructure Development Finance Company
IDI	Institut de Droit International [Institute of International Law]
IDL	International Development Law
IDLO	International Law Development Organization
IDS	International Development Strategy
IEA	International Energy Agency
IEAG	Independent Expert Advisory Group on a Data Revolution for Sustainable Development
IFAD	International Fund for Agricultural Development
IFC	International Finance Corporation
IFF	Illicit Financial Flow
IFI	International Financial Institution
IG-UTP	International Guidelines on Urban and Territorial Planning
IIA	International Institute of Agriculture
IIED	International Institute for Environment and Development
IISD	International Institute for Sustainable Development
IJDEE	International Journal of Developing and Emerging Economies
IL	International Law
ILA	International Law Association
ILC	International Law Commission

List of Abbreviations

ILDC	International Law in Domestic Courts
ILO	International Labour Organisation
ILOSTAT	International Labour Organization Department of Statistics
ILUC	Indirect Land-use Change
IMF	International Monetary Fund
IMO	International Martitime Organization
INMUJERES	National Institute of Women of Mexico
INTERIGHTS	International Centre for the Legal Protection of Human Rights
IO	International Organization
IOM	International Organization for Migration
IOSR-JHSS	International Organization of Science Research Journal of Humanities and Social Science
IPCC	Intergovernmental Panel on Climate Change
IPMG	Indigenous Peoples' Major Group for Sustainable Development
IRC	International Reference Center
IRENA	International Renewable Energy Agency
IRES	International Recommendations for Energy Statistics
IRIS	International Recommendations for Industrial Statistics
ISA	International Seabed Authority
ISARM	Internationally Shared Aquifer Resources Management
IsDB	Islamic Development Bank
ISDL	International Sustainable Development Law
ISDS	Investor-State Dispute Settlement
ISIC	International Standard Industrial Classification of All Economic Activities
ISPRS	International Society for Photogrammetry and Remote Sensing
ITC	International Trade Centre
ITF	International Transport Forum
ITLOS	International Tribunal on the Law of the Sea
ITPGRFA	International Treaty on Plant Genetic Resources for Food and Agriculture
ITTU	International Tropical Timber Agreement
ITU	International Telecommunications Union
IUCN	International Union for Conservation of Nature
IUU	Illegal, Unregulated and Unreported
IWGIA	International Work Group for Indigenous Affairs
IWRM	Integrated Water Resources Management
IWT	Illegal Wildlife Trade
JCMS	Journal of Common Market Studies
JCULP	Global Studies in Japanese Cultures Program

JEFTA	Japan-EU Free Trade Agreement
JEP	Journal of Economic Perspectives
JHEC	Yearbook of the International Society for History Didactics
JICA	Japan International Cooperation Agency
JICJ	Journal of International Criminal Justice
JIEL	Journal of International Economic Law
JMCC	Commercial Court division of the Jamaica Supreme Court of Judicature
JMP	Joint Monitoring Programme
JPOI	Johannesburg Plan of Implementation
JRPS	Justice, Rights and Public Security unit of the World Bank
JWELB	Journal of World Energy Law & Business
KBA	Key Biodiversity Area
LCA	Life Cycle Assessment
LCT	Life Cycle Thinking
LDC	Least Developed Country
LDN	Land Degradation Neutrality
LGBTQ	Lesbian, Gay, Bisexual, Transgender, Queer/Questioning
LIBE	Committee on Civil Liberties, Justice and Home Affairs
LLDC	Landlocked Developing Country
LLIC	Low-Lying Islands and Coasts
LPG	Liquefied Petroleum Gas
MARPOL	International Convention for the Prevention of Pollution from Ships
MDAC	Mental Disability Advocacy Center
MDG(s)	Millennium Development Goal(s)
MESECVI	Follow-up Mechanism to the Bélem do Pará Convention
MF	Material Footprint
MFN	Most favoured nation
MGCI	Mountain Green Cover Index
MGoS	Major Groups and other Stakeholders
MIGA	Multilateral Investment Guarantee Agency
MIT	Massachusetts Institute of Technology
MJIL	Michigan Journal of International Law
MJSDL	McGill Journal of Sustainable Development Law
MoI	Means of Implementation
MPA	Marine Protected Area
MPI	Multi-purpose Indicator
MRS	Materials Research Society
MSME	Micro, Small and Medium-sized Enterprises
MSY	Maximum Sustainable Yield

List of Abbreviations

MTA	Material Transfer Agreement
MTO	Money Transfer Operator
NAALC	North American Agreement on Labour Co-operation
NACE	Nomenclature statistique des activités économiques dans la Communauté européenne [Nomenclature of Economic Activities in the European Community]
NAFTA	North American Free Trade Agreement
NATO	Nord Atlantic Treaty Organization
NDC	Nationally Determined Contributions
NEC	New European Census
NEPAD	New Partnership for Africa's Development
NFRD	Non-Financial Reporting Directive
NGO	Non-Governmental Organisation
NHRI	National Human Rights Institution
NIEO	New International Economic Order
NIPFP	National Institute of Public Finance and Policy
NJCL	Nordic Journal of Commercial Law
NOAA	National Oceanic and Atmospheric Administration
NQHR	Netherlands Quarterly oh Human Rights
NUA	New Urban Agenda
OAS	Organization of American States
OAS-DSD	Department of Sustainable Development of the Organization of American States
OAU	Organization of African Unity
OCB	Organizational Citizenship Behaviour
ODA	Official Development Assistance
OECD	Organisation for Economic Cooperation and Development
OEF	Organisational Environmental Footprint
OETS	Oceans Economy and Trade Strategies
OHCHR	Office of the High Commissioner for Human Rights
OPAC	Optional Protocol to the Convention on involvement of children in armed conflict
OPSC	Optional Protocol to the Convention on sale of children, child prostitution and child pornography
OTLA	Office of Trade and Labor Affairs
OWG	Open Working Group
PA	Paris Agreement
PASEC	Programme d'analyse des systèmes éducatifs des la confemen
PCA	Permanent Court of Arbitration
PCA (EU)	Partnership and Cooperation Agreement

PCIJ	Permanent Court on International Justice
PDCA	Political Dialogue and Cooperation Agreement
PEEREA	Protocol on Energy Efficiency and Related Environmental Aspects
PEF	Product Environmental Footprint
PIACC	Programme for the International Assessment of Adult Competencies
PIL	Public Interest Litigation
PIRLS	Progress in International Reading Literacy Study
PISA	Programme for International Student Assessment
PM10	Particulate Matter with aerodynamic diameters $\leq$ 10 μm
PM2.5	Particulate Matter with aerodynamic diameters $\leq$ 2.5 μm
PMTCT	Prevention of Mother-to-Child Transmission of HIV
PNAS	Proceedings of the National Academy of Sciences of the United States of America
POP	Persistent Organic Pollutants
PoU	Prevalence of undernutrition
PPM	Process and Production Method
PPP	Polluter-pays principle
PPP	Public Private Partnership
PRS	Poverty Reduction Strategy
PSMA	Agreement on Port State Measures
PSONR	Permanent Sovereignty Over Natural Resources
PTA	Preferential Trade Agreement
QIL	Questions of International Law; Questions de Droit International; Questioni di Diritto Internazionale
R&D	Research and Development
RASFF	Rapid Alert System for Food and Feed
RBC	Responsible Business Conduct
RBO	International River Basin Organization
RCP	Representative Concentration Pathway
REACH	Registration, Evaluation, Authorisation and Restriction of Chemicals
RECIEL	Review of European, Comparative & International Law
RES	Resolution
RPS	Renewable Portfolio Standards
RTA	Regional Trade Agreement
RTD	Right to Development
SACMEQ	Southern and Eastern Africa Consortium for Monitoring Educational Quality
SALT	Society for Alternative Learning and Transformation
SAMOA	Small Island Development States Accelerated Modalities of Action
SARS	Severe acute respiratory syndrome

List of Abbreviations

SARS-CoV-2	Severe acute respiratory syndrome coronavirus 2
SBSTTA	Subsidiary Body on Scientific, Technical and Technological Advice
SCC	Supreme Court of Canada
SCI	Supreme Court of India
SCM	Agreement on Subsidies and Countervailing Measures
SCN	Supreme Court of the Netherlands
SCP	Sustainable Consumption and Production
SCSL	Special Court for Sierra Leone
SD	Sustainable Development
SDBS	Structural and Demographic Business Statistics
SDG(s)	Sustainable Development Goal(s)
SDSN	Sustainable Development Solutions Network
SE4ALL	Sustainable Energy for All
SERAC	Social and Economic Rights Action Center
SFM	Sustainable Forest Management
SFS	Sustainable Food System
SIA	Sustainable Impact Assessment
SIDS	Small Island Developing States
SLoCaT	Partnership on Sustainable, Low Carbon Transport
SME	Small and Medium-sized Enterprises
SNA	System of National Accounts
SOE	State-owned Enterprises
SPS	Agreement on Sanitary and Phytosanitary Measures
SRFC	Sub-Regional Fisheries Commission
SRH	Sexual and Reproductive Health
SSNR	Small-scale Nuclear Reactor
SSRN	Social Science Research Network
STI	Science, Technology and Innovation
SuRe	Standard for Sustainable and Resilient Infrastructure
TBT	Agreement on Technical Barriers to Trade
TECA	Technologies and Practices for Small Agricultural Producers
TECDOC	Technical Document
TEL	Transnational Environmental Law
TERCE	Terces Estudio Regional Comparativo y Explicativo [Third Regional Comparative and Explanatory Study]
TEU	Treaty on European Union
TFA	Trade Facilitation Agreement
TFEU	Treaty on the Functioning of the European Union
TFFD	Transboundary Freshwater Dispute Database
TFM	Technology Facilitation Mechanism (UN)

TIMSS	Trends in International Mathematics and Science Study
TNC	Transnational Company
TRIMS	Agreement on Trade Related Investment Measures
TRIPS	Agreement on Trade-Related Aspects of Intellectual Property Rights
TSD	Trade and Sustainability Chapter
TST	Technical Support Team of the United Nations
US	United States
UDHR	Universal Declaration of Human Rights
UHC	Universal Health Coverage
UK	United Kingdom
UN	United Nations
UN DPO	UN Department of Peace Operations
UN ESCWA	UN Economic and Social Commission for Western Asia
UN GC	UN Global Compact
UN OROLSI	UN Office of Rule of Law and Security Institutions
UN WOMEN	UN Entity for Gender Equality and the Empowerment of Women
UNAIDS	UN Programme of HIV/AIDS
UNCAC	UN Convention against Corruption
UNCCD	UN Convention to Combat Desertification in those Countries Experiencing Serious Drought and/or Desertification, Particularly in Africa
UNCED	UN Conference on Environment and Development
UNCIO	UN Conference on International Organization
UNCITRAL	UN Commission on International Trade Law
UNCLOS	UN Commission on the Law of the Sea
UNCSD	UN Conference on Sustainable Development
UNCTAD	UN Commission on Trade and Development
UNCTAD STIP	UN Conference on Trade and Development Science, Technology and Innovation Policy Reviews
UNCTAD TRAINS	UN Conference on Trade and Development – Trade Analysis Information System
UNDESA	UN Department of Economic and Social Affairs
UNDP	UN Development Programme
UNDRIP	UN Declaration on the Rights of Indigenous People
UNDROP	United Nations Declaration on the Rights of Peasants and Other People Working in Rural Areas
UNDRR/UNISDR	UN Office for Disaster Risk Reduction
UNECE	UN Economic Commission for Europe
UNECLAC	UN Economic Commission for Latin America and the Caribbean
UNEP	UN Environment Programme

List of Abbreviations

UNEP-CTCN	UN Environmental Programme-Climate Technology Centre and Network
UNEP-WCMC	UN Environment
UNESCO	UN Educational, Scientific and Cultural Organization
UNESCO-UIS	UNESCO Institute for Statistics
UNFCCC	UN Framework Convention on Climate Change
UNFPA	UN Population Fund
UNFSA	UN Fish Stock Agreement
UNGA	UN General Assembly
UNGP	UN Guiding Principles for Business and Human Rights
UN-Habitat	UN Human Settlements Programme
UNHCR	UN High Commissioner for Refugees
UNICEF	UN Children's Fund
UNODC	UN Office on Drugs and Crime
UN-OHRLLS	UN Office of the High Representative for the Least Developed Countries, Landlocked Developing Countries and Small Island Developing States
UNPRI	UN Principles for Responsible Investment
UNSC	UN Security Council
UNSCN	UN System Standing Committee on Nutrition
UNSD	UN Statistic Division
UNSG	UN Secretary General
UNSTATS	United Nations Statistical Division
UNTS	UN Treaty Series
UNWC	UN Watercourse Convention
UNWTO	UN World Tourism Organization
USA	United States of America
USAID	United States Agency for International Development
USMCA	United States-Mexico-Canada Trade Agreement
VCLT	Vienna Convention on the Law of Treaties
VCLTIO	Vienna Convention on the Law of Treaties between States and International Organizations or between International Organizations
VG-FSP	Voluntary Guidelines for Flag State Performance
VNR	Voluntary National Review
WASH	Water, Sanitation and Hygiene
WAVE	Women against Violence Europe
WCED	World Commission on Environment and Development
WCL	Washington College of Law
WCS	World Conservation Strategy
WDPA	World Database on Protected Areas

WDR	World Development Report
WEF	World Economic Forum
WEOG	Western European and Others Group
WFP	United Nations World Food Programme
WHO	World Health Organization
WHO FCTC	World Health Organization Framework Convention on Tobacco Control
WIPO	World Intellectual Property Organization
WIR	World Investment Report
WJP	World Justice Project
WMO	World Meteorological Organization
WSQ	Women's Studies Quarterly
WSSD	World Summit on Sustainable Development
WTO	World Trade Organization
WTO IDB	World Trade Organization Integrated Database
WWF	World Wide Fund For Nature
YIEL	Yearbook of International Environmental Law
ZaöRV	Zeitschrift für ausländisches öffentliches Recht und Völkerrecht
ZEuS	Zeitschrift für Europarechtliche Studien

Table of Cases

International Courts and Tribunals

Table of Cases

Table of Cases

Table of Cases

Table of Cases

Table of Cases

Table of Cases

Table of Cases

Table of Cases

Table of Cases

Judicial Committee of the Privy Council

Permanent Court of International Justice (Predecessor of ICJ, PCIJ)

Table of Cases

Arbitrational Tribunals

Table of Cases

Table of Cases

Table of Cases

Table of Cases

Table of Cases

Table of Cases

Table of Cases

Table of Cases

Introduction

Select Bibliography: Matthew D. Adler and Marc Fleurbaey (eds), *The Oxford Handbook of Well-Being and Public Policy* (Oxford University Press, Oxford 2016); Helen Ahrens et al. (eds), *Equal Access to Justice for All and Goal 16 of the Sustainable Development Agenda: Challenges for Latin America and Europe* (LIT Verlag, Zurich 2019); Shawkat Alam and Sumudu Ataputtu and Carmen G. Gonzalez and Jona Razzaque (eds) *International Environmental Law and the Global South* (Cambridge University Press, New York 2015); Shawkat Alam and Jahid Hossain Bhuiyan and Jona Razzaque (eds), *International Natural Resources Law, Investment and Sustainability* (Routledge, UK/USA 2019); Bård-Anders Andreassen and Hans-Otto Sano and Siobhán Mclnerney-Lankford (eds), *Research Methods in Human Rights: A Handbook* (Edward Elgar Publishing, UK/USA 2017); Jean D'Aspremont, 'Wording in International Law' 25(3) *Leiden Journal of International Law*, 575-602; Sumudu A. Ataputtu and Carmen G. Gonzalez and Sara L. Seck (eds), *The Cambridge Handbook of Environmental Justice and Sustainable Development* (Cambridge University Press, UK/USA/Australia/India/Singapore 2021); Helmut P. Aust and Janne E. Nijman (eds), *Research Handbook on International Law and Cities* (Edward Elgar Publishing, UK/USA 2021); Susan Averett and Laura M. [VNV] Argys and Saul D. Hoffman (eds), *The Oxford Handbook of Women and the Economy* (Oxford University Press, Oxford 2018); Virginie Barral, 'Sustainable Development in International Law: Nature and Operation of an Evolutive Legal Norm' (2012) 23(2) *European Journal of International Law*, 377-400; Daniel Bodansky and Jutta Brunnée and Lavanya Rajamani, *International Climate Change Law* (Oxford University Press, New York 2017); Michael Bowman and Peter G. G. Davies and Edward J. Goodwin (eds), *Research Handbook on Biodiversity and Law* (Edward Elgar Publishing, UK/USA 2016); Alan Boyle and David Freestone (eds), *International Law and Sustainable Development: Past Achievements and Future Challenges* (Oxford University Press, Oxford 1999); Thom Brooks (ed), *The Oxford Handbook of Global Justice* (Oxford University Press, Oxford 2020); Roger Brownsword and Eloise Scotford and Karen Yeung (eds), *The Oxford Handbook of Law, Regulation and Technology* (Oxford University Press, Oxford 2017); Gian Luca Burci and Brigit C. A. Toebes (eds), *Research Handbook on Global Health Law* Edward Elgar Publishing, UK/USA (2018); Elisabeth Bürgi Bonanomi, *Sustainable Development in International Law Making and Trade* (Edward Elgar Publishing, UK/USA 2015), 9-52; Sabino Cassese (ed), *Research Handbook on Global Administrative Law* (Edward Elgar Publishing, UK/USA 2016); Cinnamon P. Carlarne and Kevin R. Gray and Richard Tarasofsky (eds), *The Oxford Handbook of International Climate Change Law* (Oxford University Press, Oxford 2016); Jason Chuah (ed), *Research Handbook on Maritime Law and Regulation* (Edward Elgar Publishing, UK/USA 2019); Caroline S. Clauss-Ehlers and Aradhana Bela Sood and Mark D. Weist (eds), *Social Justice for Children and Young People: International Perspectives* (Cambridge University Press, UK/USA/Australia/India/Singapore 2020); Marie-Claire Cordonier Segger and Christopher Gregory Weeramantry (eds), *Sustainable Development Principles in the Decisions of International Courts and Tribunals, 1992-2012* (Routledge, UK/USA 2017); Yossi Dahan and Hanna Lerner and Faina Milman-Sivan (eds), *Global Justice and International Labour Rights* (Cambridge University Press, UK/USA/Australia/India/Singapore 2016); Petra Dannecker, 'The Sustainable Development Goals: A New Space for Action?' in Cenan Al-Ekabi and Stefano Ferretti (eds), *Yearbook on Space Policy 2016* (Springer, Cham 2018), 175; Susan David and Ilona Boniwell and Amanda Conley Ayers (eds), *The Oxford Handbook of Happiness* (Oxford University Press, Oxford 2013); Sara E. Davies and Jacqui True (eds), *The Oxford Handbook of Women, Peace, and Security* (Oxford University Press, Oxford 2019); John C. Dernbach and Federico Cheever, 'Sustainable Development and Its Discontents' (2015) 4(2) *Transnational Environmental Law*, 247-287; Surya Deva and David Birchall (eds), *Research Handbook on Human Rights and Business* (Edward Elgar Publishing, UK/USA 2020); David Dodds and Felix Donoghue and Jimena Leiva Roesch, *Negotiating the Sustainable Development Goals: A Transformational Agenda for an Insecure World* (Routledge, UK/USA 2017); Mark A. Drumbl and Jastine C. Barrett (eds), *Research Handbook on Child Soldiers* (Edward Elgar Publishing, UK/USA 2019);Pierre-Marie Dupuy and Jorge E. Viñuales (eds), *International Environmental Law* (2nd ed., Cambridge University Press, Cambridge 2018); James G. Dwyer (ed), *The Oxford Handbook of Children and the Law* (Oxford University Press, Oxford 2020); Mark Elder and Magnus Bengtsson and Lewis Akenji, 'An Optimistic Analysis of the Means of Implementation for Sustainable Development Goals: Thinking about Goals as Means' (2016) 8 *Sustainability*, 962; Sally Engle Merry and Kevin E. Davis and Benedict Kingsbury (eds), *The Quiet Power of Indicators, Measuring Governance, Corruption, and the Rule of Law* (Cambridge University Press, New York 2015); Koen De Feyter and Gamze Erdem Türkelli and Stéphanie de Moerloose (eds), *Encyclopedia of Law and Development* (Edward Elgar Publishing, UK/USA 2021); Duncan French, *Global Justice and Sustainable Development* (Martinus Nijhoff Publishers, Leiden 2010); Duncan French and Louis J. Kotzé (eds), *Research Handbook on Law, Governance and Planetary Boundaries* (Edward Elgar Publishing, UK/USA 2021); Duncan French and Louis J. Kotzé (eds), *Sustainable Development Goals – Law, Theory and Implementation* (Edward Elgar Publishing, UK/USA 2018); Markus Gehring and Marie-Claire Cordonier Segger, *Sustainable Development in World Trade Law* (Kluwer Law International, The Hague 2005); Alexander Gillespie, *Long Road to Sustainability: The Past, Present, and Future of International Environmental Law and Policy* (Oxford

Introduction

University Press, Oxford 2018); Lawrence O. Gostin and Benjamin Mason Meier (eds), *Foundations of Global Health & Human Rights* (Oxford University Press, New York 2020); Winfried Huck, 'Horizontale und vertikale Wirkungen der Nachhaltigkeitsziele der Vereinten Nationen im System des Rechts' in Achim Michalke and Martin Rambke and Stefan Zeranski (eds), *Vernetztes Risiko- und Nachhaltigkeitsmanagement, Erfolgreiche Navigation durch die Komplexität und Dynamik des Risikos* (Springer-Gabler, Wiesbaden 2018), 67; Winfried Huck, 'The UN Sustainable Development Goals and Global Public Goods, The Quest for Legitimacy' in Massimo Iovane and Fulvio M. Palombino and Daniele Amoroso and Giovanni Zarra (eds), *The Protection of General Interests in Contemporary International Law: A Theoretical and Empirical Inquiry* (Oxford University Press, Oxford 2021); Winfried Huck et al., 'The Right to Breathe Clean Air and Access to Justice – Legal State of Play in International, European and National Law' (2021) 13(10) *International Environmental Law (eJournal)*; Winfried Huck and Jennifer Maaß, 'Gaining a foot in the door: Giving Access to Justice with SDG 16.3?' (2021) 2021-5 *C-EENRG Working Paper*; Svatava Janoušková and Tomas Hák and Bedřich Moldan, 'Global SDGs Assessments: Helping or Confusing Indicators?'(2018) 10(5) *Sustainability*, 1-14; Philip N. Jefferson (ed), *The Oxford Handbook of the Economics of Poverty* (Oxford University Press, Oxford 2012); Markus Kaltenborn and Markus Krajewski and Heike Kuhn (eds), *Sustainable Development Goals and Human Rights* (SpringerOpen, Cham 2020); Markus Kaltenborn and Markus Krajewski and Heike Kuhn (eds), *Sustainable Development Goals and Human Rights* (SpringerOpen, Cham 2020); Judith E. Koons, 'What Is Earth Jurisprudence? Key Principles to Transform Law for the Health of the Planet' (2009) 18 *PENN ST. ENVTL. L. REV*, 47-69; Carol Lancaster and Nicolas Van de Walle (eds), *The Oxford Handbook of the Politics of Development* (Oxford University Press, Oxford 2018); Walter Leal Filho et al. (eds.), *Peace, Justice and Strong Institutions* (Springer, Cham 2021); Emma Lees and Jorge E. Viñuales, *The Oxford Handbook of Comparative Environmental Law* (Oxford University Press, Oxford 2019); Jennifer A. Leitch, 'Having a say: 'access to justice' as democratic participation' (2015) 4 *UCL Journal of Law and Jurisprudence*, 76-108; Carlos R. Fernández Liesa and Castor M. Díaz Barrado and Paloma Durán y Lalaguna (eds), *International Society and Sustainable Development Goals* (Aranzadi by Thomson Reuters, Spain 2016); Vito De Lucia, 'Towards an Ecological Philosophy of Law: A Comparative Discussion' (2013) 4(2) *Journal of Human Rights and the Environment*, 167-190; Mukul Majumdar et al. (eds), *Fundamental Economics – Encyclopedia of Life Support Systems – Vol. II* (UNESCO-EOLSS Publishers, Abu Dhabi 2010); James R. May and Erin Daly, 'The Role of Human Dignity in Achieving the UN Sustainable Development Goals' in Tuula Honkonen and Seita Romppanen (eds), *International Environmental Law-making and Diplomacy Review* 2019 (University of Eastern Finland, Joensuu 2020), 15; Ralph Michaels, Verónica Ruiz Abou-Nigm and Hans van Loon (eds), *The Private Side of Transforming our World – UN Sustainable Development Goals 2030 and the Role of Private International Law* (Intersentia, Cambridge/Antwerp/Chicago 2021); Kate Miles (ed), *Research Handbook on Environment and Investment Law* (Edward Elgar Publishing, UK/USA 2019); Massimiliano Montini, 'Designing law for sustainability' in Volker Mauerhofer and Daniela Rupo and Lara Tarquinio (eds), *Sustainability and Law* (Springer, Cham 2020), 33-48; A.C. Onuora-Oguno, W.O. Egbewole and T.E. Kleven (eds), *Education Law, Strategic Policy and Sustainable Development in Africa – Agenda 2063* (Palgrave Mcmillan/Springer Nature, Cham 2018); Anne Orford and Florian Hoffmann and Martin Clark (eds), *The Oxford Handbook of the Theory of International Law* (Oxford University Press, Oxford 2016); Ursula Oswald Spring et al. (eds), *Peace Studies, Public Policy And Global Security – Encyclopedia of Life Support Systems – Vol. VI* (UNESCO-EOLSS Publishers, Abu Dhabi 2010); Ann Petermans and Rebecca Cain (eds), *Design for Wellbeing – An Applied Approach* (Routledge, UK/USA 2019); Christopher Fleming and Matthew Manning (eds), *Routledge Handbook of Indigenous Wellbeing* (Routledge, UK/USA 2019); Ernst Ulrich Petersmann, *Multilevel Constitutionalism for Multilevel Governance of Public Goods* (Hart Publishing, UK/USA 2017); Benoit Frydman, 'From accuracy to accountability: Subjecting global indicators to the rule of law' (2017) 13(4) *International Journal of Law in Context*, 450-64; Andreas Philippopoulos-Mihalopoulos and Victoria Brooks (eds), *Research Methods in Environmental Law: A Handbook* (Edward Elgar Publishing, UK/USA 2017); Donald Rothwell and Alex G. Oude Elferink and Karen Nadine Scott (eds), *The Oxford Handbook of the Law of the Sea* (Oxford University Press, Oxford 2015); Phillipe Sands, 'International Law in the Field of Sustainable Development' (1994) 65(1) *British Yearbook of International Law*, 303-8; U. Sarangi, 'International Trade and Sustainable Development Goals (SDGs) of Economies: A Way Forward' (2017) 8 *J. Int. Econ.*, 77-101; Nico J. Schrijver and Friedl Weiss and Bruno Simma and Kamal Hossain, *International Law and Sustainable Development, Principles and Practice* (Martinus Nijhoff Publishers, Leiden 2004); Nico J. Schrijver, *The Evolution of Sustainable Development in International Law: Inception, Meaning and Status* (Martinus Nijhoff Publishers, Leiden 2008); Noha Shawki (ed), *International Norms, Normative Change, and the UN Sustainable Development Goals* (Lexington Books, London 2016); Satvinder Singh Juss (ed), *Research Handbook on International Refugee Law* (Edward Elgar Publishing, UK/USA 2019); Mike Slade and Lindsay Oades and Aaron Jarden (eds), *Wellbeing, Recovery and Mental Health* (Cambridge University Press, UK/USA/Australia/India/Singapore 2017); William Talbott, *Human Rights and Human Well-Being* (Oxford University Press, New York 2010); Erika Techera and Jade Lindley and Karen N. Scott (eds), *Routledge Handbook of International Environ-*

mental Law (Routledge, UK/USA 2020); Peter Meijes Tiersma and Lawrence Solan (eds), *The Oxford Handbook of Language and Law* (Oxford University Press, Oxford 2012); Luke Tomlinson, *Procedural Justice in the United Nations Framework Convention on Climate Change – Negotiating Fairness* (Springer International Publishing, Cham/Heidelberg/New York/Dordrecht/London 2015); Wouter Vandenhole and Ellen Desmet and Didier Reynaert (eds), *Routledge International Handbook of Children's Rights Studies* (Routledge, UK/USA 2015); Jorge E. Viñuales (ed), *The Rio Declaration on Environment and Development, A Commentary* (Oxford University Press, Oxford 2015);Emily Webster and Laura Mai (eds), *Transnational Environmental Law in the Anthropocene: Reflections on the Role of Law in Times of Planetary Change* (Routledge, UK/USA 2021); Inga Winkler and Carmel Williams (eds), *The Sustainable Development Goals and Human Rights: A Critical Early Review* (Routledge, UK/USA 2018); Rüdiger Wolfrum, *The Max Planck Encyclopedia of Public International Law – Volume I* (Oxford University Press, Oxford 2013).

I. Introduction

1   The 17 Sustainable Development Goals (SDGs) and their related 169 targets were adopted at the United Nation's (UN) 70th birthday by a resolution of the UN General Assembly (GA) on 25 September 2015 titled 'Transforming our world: the 2030 Agenda for Sustainable Development' (Global Agenda 2030).[1] The SDGs came into effect on 1 January 2016 and they are supposed to stimulate action for 15 years until 2030.[2]

2   The Global Agenda 2030 consists of six interrelated sections:

1. Preamble
2. Declaration,
3. 17 SDGs,
4. Further guidance on the means of implementation and the Global Partnership

---

[1] A/RES/70/1, *Resolution adopted by the General Assembly on 25 September 2015, Transforming our world: the 2030 Agenda for Sustainable Development.*

[2] A/RES/70/1, para. 21.

5. Further guidance on follow-up and review
6. Instruments mentioned in the section entitled 'Sustainable Development Goals and targets'[3]

A 'solid foundation' of the Global Agenda 2030 and the SDGs are, in particular, **3** 'all major United Nations conferences' as well as the twice-cited Rio Declaration on Environment and Development (1992), each of which also serves to interpret the Global Agenda 2030.[4]

One of the most comprehensive websites providing detailed information to the Glob- **4** al Agenda 2030 is:

– https://sdgs.un.org/goals

Other contributory websites are: **5**

– https://sdg-pathfinder.org/
– https://sdg-tracker.org/
– https://sdgcompass.org/
– https://www.unsdsn.org/
– https://www.un.org/sustainabledevelopment/progress-report/

ILA Guidelines for legal interpretation: **6**

– 2002 New Delhi Declaration of Principles of International Law Relating to Sustainable Development
– 2012 Sofia Guiding Statements on the Judicial Elaboration of the 2002 New Delhi Declaration of Principles of International Law Relating to Sustainable Development
– 2014 ILA Declaration of Legal Principles Relating to Climate Change, Committee on Legal Principles Relating to Climate Change (Resolution 2/2014)
– 2020 ILA Guidelines on the Role of International Law in Sustainable Natural Resources Management for Development

Attempts have been made since the 1980s to bridge the divide between developed **7** and less developed countries by way of promoting sustainable development in international law.[5] The term 'sustainable development', being the raison d'être of the Global Agenda 2030, is the most frequently stated word in the whole agenda.

The SDGs are not international law in a classical sense, but their basic elements, their **8** building blocks belong to international law and are reflected and utilised in interregional law (such as in the EU, the Americas or in ASEAN) as well as in national public and private law.[6]

The SDGs were adopted with a non-binding resolution and can be classified as a **9** typical expression of soft law. However, it can be observed that they invade the matrix of different vertical and horizontal legal orders and become entrenched, e.g. in free trade agreements (FTA), investment and other agreements within and outside the EU, and are discussed in a variety of different legal fields, including private law.

---

[3] Dupuy and Viñuales, *International Environmental Law* (2nd edn, 2018), 21.
[4] A/RES/70/1, paras. 11 f.; Dupuy and Viñuales, *International Environmental Law* (2nd edn, 2018), 21.
[5] Cordonier Segger, 'Commitments to Sustainable Development Through International Law and Policy' in Cordonier Segger and H. E. Judge Weeramantry, *Sustainable Development Principles in the Decisions of International Courts and Tribunals, 1992 – 2012* (2017), 29, 34.
[6] Michaels and Ruiz Abou-Nigm and van Loon (eds), *The Private Side of Transforming our World – UN Sustainable Development Goals 2030 and the Role of Private International Law* (2021); Huck, 'The EU and the Global Agenda 2030: Reflection, Strategy and Legal Implementation' (2020) 2020-1 *C-EENRG Working Papers*, 1-26.

10   They rather entered the legal stage as part of interpretations, guidelines or even blueprints, to later become a regulation with a normative core.

11   The SDGs and the Global Agenda 2030 draw their language from international treaties, resolutions, and conferences from the realm of the UN the language of which points to legal obligations between states. The origin of sustainable development can be traced to the idea of intergenerational development and the mitigation or prevention of environmental damage and potential risks of damage. The history and tradition of environmental law seems to overshadow the development of other areas, such as economic and social issues.

12   The frequently used lens of environmental law reflects a type of a focused 'silo-thinking' approach within the roots and traditions of environmental law itself, which the Global Agenda 2030 just vowed to avoid.

13   The challenge seems to be to remain an unbiased neutral observer, not trying to integrate a purely ecological mindset, but also keeping an eye on economic growth and science, technology and innovation (STI). With that being said, these perspectives are certainly not opposed to each other, but should be brought together to achieve an equilibrium through proportionality. Economic growth understood in a smart way that does not come at the expense of the environment and human rights, but is strongly supported with STI, remains the driving force for participation, good governance, and an income allowing living on a decent basis in the future. Without economic growth, inequalities are likely to persist and permeate the societies in line with the coming population growth carrying the seed of instability.

14   Economic growth is still recognised today as one of the forces that contribute to unleashing a destructive effect immanent to it and endangering or damaging the planetary boundaries of biophysical systems with unregulated and unrestrained growth. Therefore, new forms of a circular economy, a green and a blue economy are approaches that may succeed in generating growth while respecting planetary boundaries. Much will depend on the technology, which must succeed in satisfying the growing needs of humanity, needs that are elementary and relate to healthy food, access to safe drinking water, health, housing and still more. A growing world population will probably only be able to meet basic needs with new technologies, which is why education for everybody is so essential.

15   The outreach to the civil society in every country from an UN perspective is not self-explanatory. The SDGs are constructed with elements from the legal sphere to demonstrate their incapability of enforcement in a scenery of a non-binding value based setting.

16   It is quite a paradox that an approach emphasising the non-binding nature is even more successful in an evolutionary sense over the timeline and its impact in the legal matrix with the specific degree of adaptation to the different legal cultures in comparison to a stricter setting with binding effects.

17   Yet, states are integrating at least parts and concepts of the SDGs in their national policies and programmes and even in their legislation. International organisations (IOs) and interregional organisations have integrated them in their programmes and outcome. The simultaneous acceptance and behaviour of such a large number of actors (including IOs and interregional organisations) reflects not only a singular and isolated event, but a partially coordinated and sometimes simultaneous, albeit uncoordinated, but nevertheless positive reactive behaviour of many actors in the legal matrix.

However, even confronted with this enthusiastic estimation, the Global Agenda 2030 is still a resolution that poses many challenges and difficulties. One of the difficulties lies in the lack of funding for the overt educational efforts and to stem all the other efforts, which are to be targeted through 169 sub-targets to achieve the SDGs. Other difficulties lie in the vast amount of targets, (sometimes) not coherent indicators, lack of willingness and readiness, and the different meta-theories and hermeneutics of interpretation, to name but a few. Whether the SDGs and their intentions are on the rise or in the status of decline remains an open question. However, there is no concept in sight that would build on such a broad consensus in the UN and would reach as many organisations in the legal matrix on a global scale.

II. Outline

To understand how the key features of the SDGs reach their optimum without inter- **18** fering with each other, their historical origins and starting point are first shown. Then the methods are explained to give every reader a transparent view of the normativity of the SDGs. After setting out the methods, the principles enshrined in the Global Agenda 2030 and those of the SDGs, as well as their inherent principles of normativity are discussed.

It should be clear that based on a systematic approach, it is worthwhile to analyse **19** the internal and external systematic interconnections to give a perspective on how the SDGs are integrated and applied on a horizontal level in the matrix of international law referring to the UN and IOs.

The internal level refers to certain principles set out in the Global Agenda 2030 and **20** the SDGs, whose meaning and function are essential for their interpretation and which need to be emphasised. Secondly, the vertical impact in the legal matrix is scrutinised, which means that the interregional level and the national level as well as the recipients of integration of the SDGs are recognised. These vertical levels encompass various degrees, legal views form from a supra-regional perspective are included and as well development of a normative level.

Although the *Normative Kraft des Faktischen* is coined by Jellinek, the point here is to observe and acknowledge a development of certain facts that are capable of successively condensing into a level of normativity.

The vertical level first grade means the interregional level which refers to solid rela- **21** tions of an interstate character, such as those of EU, ASEAN, USMCA, or CARICOM.

The vertical level second grade encompasses the national level, and besides, the **22** vertical level third grade embracing the transnational standards like standards and recommendation of private NGOs and private institutions influencing in particular the applicable private law connected to the SDGs.[7]

The introduction to this commentary describes the basics of the general issues and **23** structures that generally apply to all 17 goals and their 169 targets and associated indicators, and supports understanding of the complex and intricate foundation from which the Global Agenda 2030 has emerged. The second and disproportionately larger part of this commentary relates to the interpretation of the SDGs which, as the more specified section, builds upon and is nourished by the principles presented in the introduction. In-depth insights into each of the SDGs will be given, thereby considering those aspects deemed most gravitational by the author.

The vast majority of chapters in the second section of this commentary assess the **24** systemic jurisprudential relevance of each SDG and further its normative core and impact. The task is to find out what actually is legally contained in the SDGs and how

---

[7] Michaels and Ruiz Abou-Nigm and van Loon (eds), *The Private Side of Transforming our World – UN Sustainable Development Goals 2030 and the Role of Private International Law* (2021).

this containment can be implemented in a legal sense. What is their meaning as a text and a notion? How can we use them, for instance, in a court or judicial hearing as arguments in any other legal environment?

25 This approach attempts to formulate a response based on possible guidance to the application of the normativity of the SDGs in a legal realm of any kind in practice. The main purpose is to furnish the legal dimension of the SDGs with arguments from the legal landscape in their very respective field and to try to integrate the normative arguments related to the SDGs (and their predecessors) so that specific arguments can be derived that enrich legal reasoning. Ideally, this will result in an array of arguments that come to bear as a modern and globally shared understanding and response to salient issues in matters to be legally assessed.

26 In order to understand the approach interpretation in the second section, it is necessary to clarify the working method. Thus, the essential document, the Global Agenda 2030, of which the SDGs are an inherent part, must be analysed with a systematic approach that will deliver additional content for any target of the SDG.

27 The regular scheme of the table of contents of the individual SDGs is based on the following structure:

A. Background and Origin
B. Scope and Dimensions
C. Interdependences
D. Jurisprudential Significance
E. Conclusion

III. Evolutionary Aspects of Sustainable Development

1. Overview

28 The Global Agenda 2030 summarises the concept of sustainable development that has been developed together with member states, international organisations and in global partnerships for about 50 years. The concept of sustainable development is extensively described and explained.[8]

29 It is recognised to 'be more than a mere concept, but as a principle with normative value' which is likely to play a key role in determining important environmental disputes of the future.[9]

---

[8] Sands, 'International Law in the Field of Sustainable Development' (1994) 65(1) *British Yearbook of International Law*, 303-8; Boyle and Freestone, *International Law and Sustainable Development: Past Achievements and Future Challenges* (1999); Schrijver and Weiss and Simma and Hossain, *International Law and Sustainable Development, Principles and Practice* (2004); Gehring and Cordonier Segger, *Sustainable Development in World Trade Law* (2005); Schrijver, *The Evolution of Sustainable Development in International Law: Inception, Meaning and Status* (2008); French, *Global Justice and Sustainable Development* (2010); Barral, 'Sustainable Development in International Law: Nature and Operation of an Evolutive Legal Norm' (2012) 23(2) *European Journal of International Law*, 377-400; Bonanomi, *Sustainable Development in International Law Making and Trade* (2015), 9-52; Cordonier Segger with H. E. Judge Weeramantry, Sustainable Development Principles in the Decisions of International Courts and Tribunals, 1992-2012 (2017); Alam and Bhuiyan and Razzaque, International Natural Resources Law, Investment and Sustainability (2019); Montini, 'Designing law for sustainability' in Mauerhofer et al., *Sustainability and Law* (2020), 34; Ataputtu and Gonzalez and Seck, *The Cambridge Handbook of Environmental Justice and Sustainable Development* (2021).

[9] ICJ, *Gabčíkovo-Nagymaros Project (Hungary/Slovakia)*, Separate Opinion of Vice-President Weeramantry in Gabcykovo Nagymaros, 25 September 1997, 85.

Blatant inequality was already known in the roman antique period. The health condi-   30
tion of the small percentage of the wealthy class, which was only 3 per cent, superseded
the average population. The growth of income remained static while the wealth of the
top 1 per cent rose by factor 40 over the period of five generations. To maintain peace
in Rome and elsewhere, Rome developed over time a first systematic welfare, in which
subsidised food was brought to the needy poor.[10] The Cloaca Maxima in Rome and the
great achievement of the Romans of managing fresh water and wastewater in Rome,
which was for a long time unmatched, point to early concepts of water and sanitation
disposal (SDG 6).[11]

The roots of this concept can be traced back in the professional terminology of   31
forestry, when in Germany, inspired by the English author John Evelyn and the French
statesman Jean-Baptiste Colbert, rich families began to plan their dynasties' woodlands
'nachhaltig' – in order to hand them along undiminished to future generations. The
term itself was then coined in 1713 by Hans Carl von Carlowitz, head of the Royal Mining Office in the Kingdom of Saxony, to address the challenge of a predicted shortage of
timber, the key resource of that time.[12]

'The merit to have introduced the term 'sustainable' into political language, however,   32
belongs to the Club of Rome. In March 1972, this globally operating think-tank published the epoch-making report on the 'Limits to Growth', written by a group of scientists, led by Dennis and Donella Meadows of the 'Massachusetts Institute of Technology'
(MIT)'.[13]

In 1987 the United Nations World Commission on Environment and Development   33
released the report 'Our Common Future', the so-called Brundtland Report which entails
the influential definition of sustainable development, and emphasises intergenerational
linkages and even the time bound evolution of technology and a new era for economic
growth:

> Humanity has the ability to make development sustainable to ensure that it meets the needs of the
> present without compromising the ability of future generations to meet their own needs. The concept
> of sustainable development does imply limits – not absolute limits but limitations imposed by the
> present state of technology and social organization on environmental resources and by the ability of
> the biosphere to absorb the effects of human activities. But technology and social organization can be
> both managed and improved to make way for a new era of economic growth.[14]

It should be noted that the definition of sustainable development was not considered   34
a closed and static definition, but rather an open definition that comprises open and
different frameworks and impacts where a democratic choice must be made to get it
right:

> Yet in the end, sustainable development is not a fixed state of harmony, but rather a process of change
> in which the exploitation of resources, the direction of investments, the orientation of technological
> development, and institutional change are made consistent with future as well as present needs.[15]

---

[10] Gillespie, *The long road to sustainability* (2017), 9.

[11] De Kleijn, *The Water Supply of Ancient Rome* (2001); Hansen, 'Water And Waste Water In Imperial
Rome' (1983) 19.2 *JAWRA Journal of the American Water Resources Association*, 263-9; Bradley and Stow,
Rome, pollution and propriety: dirt, disease and hygiene in the eternal city from antiquity to modernity
(2012).

[12] Grober, *Deep roots-a conceptual history of 'sustainable development' (Nachhaltigkeit)* (2007), 6; Montini, 'Designing law for sustainability' in Mauerhofer et al., *Sustainability and Law* (2020), 34.

[13] Blewitt, *Understanding sustainable development* (2012), 15.

[14] A/42/427, *Report of the World Commission on Environment and Development: Our Common Future*,
10 March 1987 (Brundtland Report), para. 27.

[15] A/42/427, Brundtland Report (1987), para. 30.

2. The Contemporary Understanding of the SDGs

35   The concept of sustainable development as such encompasses the economic and social spheres (of development) and the ecological sphere in an equilibrated mode. They are tied together and none of these notions should be inferior to one another. The term reflects balanced scales and figuratively refers to the concept of justice as an equilibrium between different, most often conflicting interests.

36   Until the resolution could be adopted in its entire form and impact, a process of international negotiations lasting several years preceded it. The basis for all 17 goals lies in the concept of sustainable development itself. In the history of the UN, a broad definition of sustainable development has been introduced in the late 1980 s. As one of the first official documents describing sustainable development as such, the report of the World Commission on Environment and Development called 'Our Common Future' does provide an already far-reaching definition. Sustainable development is referred to as 'development which meets the needs of the present without compromising the ability of future generations to meet their own needs'.[16]

37   The report has already pointed out the complexity of sustainable development. 'Our Common Future' recognises the state of a thriving economy, long considered the backbone of overall development,[17] and the resulting focus on economic growth as insufficient for sustainable development. Important factors such as technological progress, a fair distribution of resources, ecological aspects and political stability have been acknowledged as inseparable components of sustainable development.[18] Poverty is distinctly identified as one of the core components to be tackled within the whole process of sustainable development.[19] Remarkably, the report builds on the assumption that economic growth is achievable 'within the limits of environmental integrity'[20] and thus laid the foundation for unified international operations in subsequent years.[21]

38   In June 1992, the UN held one of the most significant conferences towards a mutual approach on sustainable development. The United Nations Conference on Environment and Development (UNCED), also referred to as 'Earth Summit', was a landmark meeting of representatives of 178 states to foster and concretise the universal goal of sustainable development.[22] The outstanding impact of the conference is reflected in its numerous outcomes, such as the Rio Declaration on Environment and Development and the so-called Agenda 21. Recognising the principles of the 1987 WCED report, the Rio Declaration, within the framework of its 27 principles, aimed to establish an international network of mutual cooperation between states and society in the field of sustainable development while protecting the integrity of the environment and eradicating poverty worldwide.[23] In this respect, the world community was called upon to comply with the given principles by fundamentally respecting human rights and environmental protective measures. Agenda 21 is a direct continuation of the principles of the Rio Declaration. It presents active steps for the implementation of strategies for sustainable

---

[16] Drexhage and Murphy, *Sustainable Development: From Brundtland to Rio 2012*, 6; A/42/427 (1987) Brundtland Report, 54.

[17] Dannecker, *The Sustainable Development Goals: A New Space for Action?* in Al-Ekabi and Ferretti, *Yearbook on Space Policy 2016, Space for Sustainable Development* (2018), 176.

[18] Report of the WCED 'Our Common Future' (1987), paras. 27-30.

[19] Report of the WCED 'Our Common Future' (1987), para. 27: 'A world in which poverty is endemic will always be prone to ecological and other catastrophes.'

[20] Palmer, The Earth Summit: What Went Wrong at Rio? (1992) 70(4) *Wash. U. L. Q.* 1005 (1011).

[21] Palmer, The Earth Summit: What Went Wrong at Rio? (1992) 70(4) *Wash. U. L. Q.* 1005 (1011).

[22] https://sustainabledevelopment.un.org/sdgs.

[23] United Nations Conference on Environment and Development – Report by the Director-General (1992), 3 f.

development and, despite its legally non-binding nature, represents a meaningful set of instruments. This was the first time that a highly comprehensive global plan for the implementation of sustainable development in the 21st century was adopted on more than 270 pages in 39 chapters at the global level.[24] Thus, the special feature of Agenda 21 was its in-depth approach on sustainable development which already addressed intertwined core areas ranging from the promotion and protection of human health over the conservation of biological diversity to women's rights.[25] In the pursuit of more effective implementation of sustainable development, Agenda 21 paved the way for resolution 47/191 in December 1992 which established the United Nations Commission on Sustainable Development (UNCSD).[26] UNCSD focused on evaluating the transformation of Agenda 21's objectives into active steps and fostering collaboration between states and governments for achieving the outcomes of UNCED.[27]

Meanwhile, concerns on human rights and lasting solutions for eradicating extreme poverty in the world increased.[28] The increasing efforts of a multitude of nations to achieve better global development in the light of more frequent UN conferences in the 1990 s gave leeway for broad goals that were to set new standards and momentum at the turn of the millennium. The then UN Secretary General Kofi Annan therefore initiated the inauguration of so-called 'Millennium Development Goals' (MDGs).[29] In this context, on 8 September 2000, the UNGA adopted the United Nations Millennium Declaration by resolution 55/2 which, notably, was unanimously endorsed by all (then) 189 UN member states. The MDGs published within the framework of the Millennium Declaration represented an important instrument for the entire world to achieve universal development goals to which all states had committed to.[30] **39**

The total of eight MDGs were to be achieved within a time frame of 15 years until 2015 and included the following subjects: **40**

1. Eradicate extreme poverty and hunger
2. Achieve universal primary education
3. Promote gender equality and empower women
4. Reduce child mortality
5. Improve maternal health
6. Combat HIV/AIDS, malaria and other diseases
7. Ensure environmental sustainability
8. Develop a global partnership for development[31]

In 2007, the MDG Achievement Fund was created as a financial framework to support implementation of the MDGs.[32] After 15 years, the effectiveness of the MDGs **41**

---

[24] The Stakeholder Forum for a Sustainable Future, Review of implementation of Agenda 21 and the Rio Principles, 1; see Agenda 21 – A blueprint for action for global sustainable development into the 21st century.

[25] See Agenda 21 – A blueprint for action for global sustainable development into the 21st century.

[26] Kamau, Chasek and O'Connor, *Transforming Multilateral Diplomacy: The Inside Story of the Sustainable Development Goals* (2018), 3.

[27] A/RES/47/191, *Institutional arrangements to follow up the United Nations Conference on Environment and Development*, 2.

[28] Hulme, *The Millennium Development Goals (MDGs): A Short History of the World's Biggest Promise* (2009), 10.

[29] Durán y Lalaguna and Burelli, *The Transition from MDGs to SDGs* (2019), 24.

[30] https://www.sdgfund.org/mdgs-sdgs.

[31] ICLEI briefing sheet, From MDGs to SDGs: What are the Sustainable Development Goals? (2015), 2.

[32] Durán y Lalaguna and Burelli, The transition from MDGs to SDGs, 29.

as such is still controversial.[33] A major criticism is that the targets should not apply universally to all countries equally. Goals 1 to 7 were intended exclusively for developing countries and thus in no way addressed any similar concerns in emerging and industrialised countries.[34]

42   Prior to the expiry of the MDGs, the UN began working on a new plan and the setting of new targets for the post-2015 era. The UN Conference on Sustainable Development Rio+20 in Rio de Janeiro in June 2012 significantly contributed to the drafting of new goals for sustainable development. 20 years after the United Nations Conference on Environment and Development with its fundamental Agenda 21, the 'Rio+20' outcome document 'The future we want'[35] was published, which formed the basis for the SDGs introduced three years later.[36] For this purpose, the MDGs were considered as a benchmark and the SDGs were intended to extend the dimension of MDGs.[37] 'The future we want' outlined the basic substance and the essence of the SDGs. According to this document, the SDGs should, unlike the MDGs, be universally valid for all, and should also be actively implementable and easy to understand for each state and stakeholder.[38] International cooperation in this respect should be intensified and an Open Working Group (OWG)[39] should be set up to identify the respective individual goals.[40] Furthermore, the importance of an uninterrupted flow of information was reaffirmed and the impetus for financial plans was given.[41]

43   In 2013, the Open Working Group consisting of representatives from 70 countries wishing to take part in the working process of the OWG inaugurated the negotiations on the establishment of the SDGs. Besides, stakeholders from 'governments, civil society, academia, the private sector, and of course the UN System'[42] participated as well in the discourses of the OWG. In addition to the key aspect of determining the number of SDGs to be established, the concrete contents of each individual goal and their sub-targets were discussed and established on the basis of scientific findings in the final instance.[43] In 2014, the so-called SDG Fund was found 'to act as a bridge in the transition from MDGs to SDGs'.[44] In this context, the Addis Ababa Action Agenda (AAAA) as the outcome document of the Third International Conference on Financing for the Development was published in July 2015 addressing the financing of the post-2015 era regarding the Sustainable Development Goals.[45]

---

[33] See Guibou, Critical analysis of the Millennium Development Goals (MDGs), 2 ff.; Dannecker, The Sustainable Development Goals: A New Space for Action? in Al-Ekabi and Ferretti, *Yearbook on Space Policy 2016, Space for Sustainable Development* (2018), 179; Dasandi and Hudson and Pegram, Post-2015 Development Agenda Setting in Focus Governance and Institutions, 3 ff.

[34] Dannecker, The Sustainable Development Goals: A New Space for Action? in Al-Ekabi and Ferretti, *Yearbook on Space Policy 2016, Space for Sustainable Development* (2018), 178.

[35] Adopted by UNGA in A/RES/66/288.

[36] Stevens and Kanie, 'The transformative potential of the Sustainable Development Goals (SDGs)' (2016) 16 *Int Environ Agreements*, 393 (394).

[37] https://sustainabledevelopment.un.org/sdgs.

[38] A/RES/66/288*, *The future we want*, para. 247.

[39] See A/67/L.48.

[40] A/67/L.48, para. 248.

[41] A/67/L.48, para. 251.

[42] Seth, 'The negotiation process of the 2030 Agenda' in Durán y Lalaguna and Díaz Barrado and Burelli (eds), *SDGs, Main Contributions and Challenges* (2019), 15.

[43] Seth, *The negotiation process of the 2030 Agenda* in Durán y Lalaguna and Díaz Barrado and Burelli (eds), *SDGs, Main Contributions and Challenges* (2019), 17 ff.

[44] Durán y Lalaguna and Burelli, 'The transition from MDGs to SDGs' in Durán y Lalaguna and Díaz Barrado and Burelli (eds), *SDGs, Main Contributions and Challenges* (2019), 30.

[45] See A/RES/69/313, *Addis Ababa Action Agenda*.

After a 16-month lasting period of negotiations under the auspices of the OWG, a 44
first draft of defined Sustainable Development Goals emerged.[46] The results of the OWG
by then served as basis for the still continuing negotiations for the Global Agenda 2030
which found an end in August 2015.[47]

Finally, during the 70th anniversary of the main session of the UN General Assembly 45
on 25 September 2015, the new '2030 Agenda for Sustainable Development'[48] beheld the
light of day to achieve a universal sustainable development in its economic, social and
environmental aspects.[49] In the spirit of Art. 3 of the Universal Declaration of Human
Rights (UDHR), the SDGs shall guarantee the well-being of every human being on the
planet while ensuring economic progress and environmental protection.[50]

The growing world population of approximately 11 billion people in 2100 will need 46
to try to maintain their livelihoods such as housing, food and drinking water, based on
what should be a sustainable economic model in the face of climate change, but probably
not every country will accept this new approach.

IV. Preparation for a New Approach:
The Main Character of the New Approach

The UN describes the SDGs as integrated and indivisible, and they should balance 47
the three dimensions of sustainable development: the economic, social and environmental, a key concept that was already taken up in 'The future we want' from 11 September
2012.[51] Balancing in this regard means achieving proportionality to bring the frequently
conflicting interests of all three sectors into equilibrium. The SDGs are referring to the
MDGs[52] and revitalising a global partnership[53] (SDG 17),[54] bringing together Governments, the private sector, civil society[55], the UN system and other actors. It is national
governments, that therefore have the primary responsibility for follow-up and review in
order to reflect at the national, regional and global levels, concerning the progress made
in implementing the Goals and targets over the coming 15 years.[56] While the SDGs are

---

[46] Le Blanc, 'Towards integration at last? The Sustainable Development Goals as network of targets'
(2015) No. 141 *DESA Working Paper*, 1 (3); see also: A/68/970, *Report of the Open Working Group of the
General Assembly on Sustainable Development Goals*.

[47] Seth, 'The negotiation process of the 2030 Agenda' in Durán y Lalaguna and Díaz Barrado and Burelli (eds), *SDGs, Main Contributions and Challenges* (2019), 19 ff.

[48] With the official title being: A/RES/70/1, 'Transforming Our World – the 2030 Agenda for Sustainable
Development'.

[49] Huck, 'Horizontale und vertikale Wirkungen der Nachhaltigkeitsziele der Vereinten Nationen im
System des Rechts' in Michalke and Rambke and Zeranski (eds), *Vernetztes Risiko- und Nachhaltigkeitsmanagement, Erfolgreiche Navigation durch die Komplexität und Dynamik des Risikos* (2018), 67.

[50] Leal Filho, *Die Nachhaltigkeitsziele der UN: eine Chance zur Vermittlung eines besseren Verständnisses
von Nachhaltigkeitsherausforderungen* (2019), 2.

[51] A/RES/66/288, *The future we want*, para. 1.

[52] The Millennium Declaration, endorsed by 189 countries, committed nations to a new global partnership to reduce extreme poverty and it set out a series of targets to be reached by 2015. These have
become known as the Millennium Development Goals (MDGs); A/RES/55/2, *United Nations Millennium
Declaration*.

[53] A/RES/70/1, para. 39, the scientific and academic community is mentioned in para. 52.

[54] Cooper and French, 'SDG 17: partnership for Goals – cooperation within the context of a voluntarist
framework' in French and Kotzé *Sustainable Development Goals, Law Theory and Implementation* (2018),
271 et seqq.; Dupuy and Viñuales, *International Environmental Law* (2nd edn, 2018), 20.

[55] Mentioned ten times in A/RES 70/1, paras. 6, 39, 41, 52, 17.17, 60, 70, 79 and 84; a definition of the
term 'civil society', instead, is lacking.

[56] A/RES/70/1, para. 47.

mainly aspirational,[57] they can also be seen as part of an explicit global preparation for norm setting.

48   The distinct aspects and the multifaceted character of this wide-ranging, unique approach erect some hurdle to direct cognition on the means and effects in a legal environment. Fresh thinking is required to move beyond the (transitory) response offered and demanded by the broad concept of sustainable development.

49   A transformation will only succeed in every respective state if their societies are ready for this kind of profound transformation. If laws are passed in which the SDG's sub-targets are democratically incorporated into the societies, necessary legal instruments must be available for this purpose. The laws passed in this way must be legally reviewable by those affected before the competent courts to determine their effectiveness and depth of regulation. Without legal protection, the SDGs are a toothless tiger.

50   In particular, a reactivation of a global partnership requires, out of the spirit of equal responsibility, that people in this global partnership are considered in transparent, participatory processes. They must also be given the right to demand accountability. The results must be adopted in democratic processes, which must eventually be judicially reviewable (system of norm control). Assemblies that are general, lack impact and then fail to generate accountability are weak and will not be accepted in the long run. The SDGs only make sense if they are translated into legal formats.[58]

V. Normative Dimensions of the SDGs

51   Despite being expressed as political goals, Art. 13(1) UN Charter,[59] member states, interregional organisations such as the EU,[60] ASEAN,[61] or CARICOM,[62] and international organisations[63] are stimulated to integrate the SDGs and their concepts and notions on a legal basis in a horizontal and vertical system by laws, regulations, decisions or agreements,[64] examples of which can be widely observed.[65] An inter-agency coordination

---

[57] A/RES/70/1, para. 247.

[58] Dupuy and Viñuales, *International Environmental Law* (2nd edn, 2018), 23, 24.

[59] Huck and Kurkin, 'The UN Sustainable Development Goals (SDGs) in the Transnational Multilevel System' (2018) 2 *HJIL (ZaöRV)*, 375 (383).

[60] Huck and Kurkin, 'The UN Sustainable Development Goals (SDGs) in the Transnational Multilevel System' (2018) 2 *HJIL (ZaöRV)*, 375 (394).

[61] Huck, 'ASEAN und EU: Vertrauen, Konsultation und Konsens statt "immer engerer Union"' (2018) *EuZW*, 886-91.

[62] The Caribbean Community (CARICOM) is an international organization of fifteen Caribbean nations and dependencies, whose main objective is to promote economic integration and cooperation among its members, to ensure that the benefits of integration are equitably shared, and to coordinate foreign policy. The organisation was established in 1973; see Seatzu, 'The Caribbean Community (CARICCM)' in Odello and Seatzu (eds), *Latin American and Caribbean International Institutional Law* (2015), 219 et seqq.; SDGs are mentioned widely here: ACP Group, ACP Negotiating mandate for a post-Cotonou Partnership Agreement with the EU [Mandate], Adopted on 30 May 2018 by the 107th Session of the ACP Council of Ministers, held in Lomé, Togo, ACP/00/011/18 FINAL.

[63] The Executive Committee of Economic and Social Affairs Plus (ECESA Plus) brings together 50 plus UN entities (including Funds and Programmes, Regional Commissions, Convention Secretariats, Specialized Agencies, International Financial Institutions, the WTO and ILO), as well as UN research institutes. It is convened and supported by the Department of Economic and Social Affairs (UN-DESA), building on ECESA, see https://sustainabledevelopment.un.org/unsystem (accessed 16.11.2021).

[64] Huck and Kurkin, 'The UN Sustainable Development Goals (SDGs) in the Transnational Multilevel System' (2018) 2 *HJIL (ZaöRV)*, 375 (398).

[65] Such as the EU Green Deal or the ASEAN Community Vision 2025; see for an overview Huck and Kurkin, 'The UN Sustainable Development Goals (SDGs) in the Transnational Multilevel System' (2018) 2 *HJIL (ZaöRV)*, 375 (392 et seqq.).

mechanism called the Executive Committee of Economic and Social Affairs Plus (ECESA Plus) brings together on horizontal level 50 plus UN entities.[66] It is quite amazing that all of these IOs try to integrate the SDGs in their specific realm of competence.

Towards a vertical approach, examples for an integration of the SDGs in different **52** kinds of agreements between the EU and other states like the Japan-EU Free Trade Agreement (JEFTA)[67] or the Comprehensive Economic and Trade Agreement (CETA) and even the Political Dialogue and Cooperation Agreement (PDCA) between Cuba and the EU demonstrate direct effects of the SDGs.[68] Therefore, the SDGs could be qualified as an expression of a materially uncodified value system causing indirect effects located in the context of global governance.[69]

VI. Dignity and the Sustainable Development Goals

As an agenda striving for development, the Global Agenda 2030 with its inherent **53** SDGs touch on the root causes of inequality between people and between states, thereby striving to 'ensure that all human beings can fulfil their potential in dignity'.[70]

The Global Agenda 2030 sets a framework encompassing many of the relevant po- **54** litical and socio-economic factors which are associated with the enabling of human beings to participate dignified in life. The aspired state of societies described in the Global Agenda 2030 is shaped by its origin in and the respect for all human rights, including the right to development with the means of gender equality, women's and girl's empowerment and the promotion of peace and inclusivity within all societies.[71] The condition to be achieved is even further shaped by the agenda's inherent instruments. These suggest the creation of a condition that allows opportunities for all people. In realising human rights respectively in the context of each SDG in relation to peoples or states' realities or state of development 'an equitable global economic system [is established] in which no country or person is left behind, enabling decent work and productive livelihoods for all, while preserving the planet for our children and future generations'.[72] These condition forms as a means in itself 'the ally of people's demands for a quality of life that their equal human dignity requires'.[73]

---

[66] For a detailed list see EC-ESA Plus Members: https://sustainabledevelopment.un.org/unsystem/ecesaplus; Huck and Kurkin, 'The UN Sustainable Development Goals (SDGs) in the Transnational Multilevel System' (2018) 2 *HJIL (ZaöRV)*, 375 (375).

[67] Huck and Kurkin, 'The UN Sustainable Development Goals (SDGs) in the Transnational Multilevel System' (2018) 2 *HJIL (ZaöRV)*, 375 (402).

[68] EU Commission, EU-Cuba: new landmark agreement entering into force on 1 November 2017, IP/17/4301, 31.10.2017; Huck, 'EU und Kuba: Wirtschafts- und Nachhaltigkeitsdimensionen im ersten Political Dialogue and Cooperation Agreement' (2017) *EuZW*, 249 et seqq.

[69] Petersmann, *Multilevel Constitutionalism for Multilevel Governance of Public Goods* (2017), 190; Frydman, 'From accuracy to accountability: Subjecting global indicators to the rule of law' (2017) *International Journal of Law in Context*, 450-64.

[70] A/RES/70/1, preamble.

[71] A/RES/69/313, *Addis Ababa Action Agenda of the Third International Conference on Financing for Development* (Addis Ababa Action Agenda – AAAA), 17 August 2015, para. 2.

[72] A/RES/69/313, *Addis Ababa Action Agenda of the Third International Conference on Financing for Development* (Addis Ababa Action Agenda – AAAA), 17 August 2015, para. 2.

[73] In transferring the thoughts of the capability approach of A. Sen and M. Nussbaum to the question as *what* the SDGs can be understood as, yet notwithstanding the critiques on these both theories and the many other approaches which might be useful when classifying the SDGs philosophically; Sen, *Development as Freedom* (1999); Nussbaum, *Creating Capabilities, The Human Development Approach* (2011), 186.

55   In contemporary interpretation, human dignity comprises six elements: (1) Every human being has value; (2) Every human is of equal worth; (3) Dignity is inherent in human beings, independent of space and time (and thus independent of any legal acknowledgement); (4) Dignity is universally immutable (and thus bears features of intergenerational equity); (5) Dignity instantiates rights (namely those that protect the continuance of dignity); and (6) Dignity carries the standard of living to which every human being is entitled by virtue of being human (and which is articulated by many of the SDGs).[74]

56   Although the targets of the SDGs might not address all groups of people equally, it is to be understood that the fulfilment of the SDGs yield a condition that achieves a balanced form of equality between people (and between states) by melting away the most glaring inequalities, and thus protects human dignity. Where inequalities prevail or increase, however, this means in following a thought coined by Stiglitz, the 'flipside of shrinking opportunity'[75]: Human dignity can only exist unimpaired when opportunities are created and provided for all.

57   This development towards a society with equally shared opportunities, which avoids and reduces inequality, was one of the main ideas that shaped the creation of the Global Agenda 2030.[76] It is this idea, too, that bears the understanding of how human dignity is to be respected and upheld following this very agenda.

58   Notions on dignity can be found in the Global Agenda 2030 exactly five times at prominent places with quite far-reaching connotations: as a main pillar within the preamble[77]; as a fundamental and irrevocable characteristic of every human being[78]; as a basic prerequisite for the implementation of the Agenda's vision[79]; as a description of what today's societies are lacking[80]; and as a part of the description of the aspired condition of all societies.[81] Achieving the SDGs, which implement the vision of the Global Agenda 2030, thus represents the unfettered form of dignity for all human beings.

59   By tracing the origins of human dignity in the evolution of sustainable development shaped by the UN's fundamental ideas[82] and universal human rights instruments[83], its close and inseparable linkage not only to the respect for human rights, but also for 'the *rule of law*, justice, equality and non-discrimination; [and] of respect for race, ethnicity and cultural diversity' discloses.[84]

60   The SDGs' predecessors, the MDGs drew on a "humanistic' and social justice [...] that put people at the centre of development'. The MDGs were nourished by Sen's capability approach, which understands development to be a freedom of choice where

---

[74] May and Daly, 'The Role of Human Dignity in Achieving the UN Sustainable Development Goals' in Honkonen and Romppanen (eds), *International Environmental Law-making and Diplomacy Review 2019* (2020), 15 (22 f.).

[75] Dodds and Donoghue and Leiva Roesch (eds), *Negotiating the Sustainable Development Goals, a transformational agenda for an insecure world* (2017), 13.

[76] Dodds and Donoghue and Leiva Roesch (eds), *Negotiating the Sustainable Development Goals, a transformational agenda for an insecure world* (2017), 13.

[77] A/RES/70/1, preamble.

[78] A/RES/70/1, para. 4.

[79] A/RES/70/1, para. 8.

[80] A/RES/70/1, para. 14.

[81] A/RES/70/1, para. 50.

[82] Amongst others: Outcome document of the Stockholm Conference (1972); Rio Declaration; the Agenda 21; Johannesburg Declaration on Sustainable Development; Millennium Development Goals.

[83] Amongst others: UN Charter; Universal Declaration of Human Rights; International Covenant on Civil and Political Rights; International Covenant on Economic, Social and Cultural Rights.

[84] A/RES/70/1, para. 8.

each capability constitutes a valuable 'being or doing' (to be chosen by people).[85] This anthropocentric understanding of putting people into the centre of concern was reaffirmed during the nascence of the MDG's when former Secretary General Kofi Annan stated in his report that 'the dignity and worth of the human person, respect for human rights and the equal rights of men and women, and a commitment to social progress as measured by better standards of life, in freedom from want and fear alike' would form the ground of existence of the UN.[86]

Some authors argue that dignity in the sense of sustainable development might   61
include the dignity of nature and the greater environment.[87] This might at first glance constitute a logically (and perhaps necessarily) derived expansion of the fundamental concept of sustainable development as *the* parental thought of the Global Agenda 2030 and the SDGs. However, a closer look at the Global Agenda 2030 reveals its emergence and vision borne in the Anthropocene, which manifests human beings as central point of concern. The SDGs, even the environmentally coined ones (SDGs 13, 14, 15), reveal, at least in the means of implementation, that this agenda mostly strives for *human* development and dignity.[88]

Whether anthropocentrism may be interpreted negatively or positively, or is shaped   62
by the many different (legal-)philosophical considerations,[89] it is not to be forgotten that in the genesis of the SDGs, human beings were given central place.[90] Yet, environmental concerns were seen as a systemic[91] and life-supporting necessity,[92] thereby enabling for the dignified shaping of human lives. The jurisprudential interpretation, too, to a considerable extent does not indicate another view so far.

The fundamental connection of all SDGs to human rights is obvious. Human dignity   63
is upheld through the respect and realisation of these rights, and instrumentally also through the realisation of environmental rights.

VII. Theoretical Approach

A fresh start towards a theory must clearly take into account the different historical   64
stratified situations and resist the attempt to understand sustainable development pri-

---

[85] Sen, *Development as Freedom* (1999); see also: United Nations General Assembly Open Working Group on Sustainable Development Goals, *Compendium of TST Issues Briefs October 2014*, 84.

[86] Annan, *We, the Peoples, the Role of the United Nations in the 21st Century* (2000), 6 [found in: May and Daly, 'The Role of Human Dignity in Achieving the UN Sustainable Development Goals' in Honkonen and Romppanen (eds), *International Environmental Law-making and Diplomacy Review 2019* (2020)].

[87] See e.g. Bosselmann, *The principle of Sustainability: Transforming Law and Governance* (2008), 135; De Lucia, 'Towards an Ecological Philosophy of Law: A Comparative Discussion' (2013) 4(2) *Journal of Human Rights and the Environment*, 167-90.

[88] See e.g. SDG 13.b, SDG 14.b, SDG 14.c (which point to the declaration 'The future we want' where the conservation and sustainable use of the oceans and sea contributes to 'poverty eradication, sustained economic growth, food security and creation of sustainable livelihoods and decent work'), SDG 15.a and SDG 15.b (which are to be measured on official development assistance).

[89] For an overview of the manifold philosophical ground see Adelman, 'The Sustainable Development Goals, anthropocentrism and neoliberalism' in French and Kotzé, *Sustainable Development Goals, Law Theory and Implementation* (2018), 15-40.

[90] See Dodds and Donoghue and Leiva Roesch (eds), *Negotiating the Sustainable Development Goals, a transformational agenda for an insecure world* (2017), 128-35, 149-64.

[91] See for a further distinction of sustainable development and environmentalism: Voigt, *Sustainable Development as a Principle of International Law, Resolving Conflicts between Climate Measures and WTO Law* (2009), 48 f.

[92] United Nations General Assembly Open Working Group on Sustainable Development Goals, *Compendium of TST Issues Briefs October 2014*, 207.

marily as an issue of environmental law or to reduce the SDGs to necessary measures against climate change. Of course, the multilateral fight against human-induced climate change is an essential task. However, it does not stand-alone. Nor can there be a temporal decoupling from other SDGs. Preceding the theoretical grasp of the concept, the individual building blocks that currently make up the SDGs in their current expression are dissected. This is not about the author's assessments and views, but about a sober inventory of existing building blocks and content of the Global Agenda 2030. The first question to be asked is which content shapes the Global Agenda 2030 and what relationship exists between this content and the SDGs. If information can be provided here based on a comprehensive analysis, the further, subsequent question is: Are the SDGs as targets amenable to legal interpretation according to the classical method, in which hermeneutics, language and theoretical premises play a role? What are the essential contents covered by the SDGs and their targets? Are generally applicable, legally relevant definitions available for this? Are the SDGs and their targets consistent with the measurement points? Are the indicators consistent with the goals? Next, the scope of application of the respective SDGs must be determined, taking into account their historical development. Drawing on this, the connections with the Global Agenda 2030 will be presented.

65   Subsequently, it will be determined whether and to what extent decisions of international, interregional and, rather rarely, national jurisdiction exist that can be understood as an independent reflection on central concerns of the SDGs and their contents. In addition, where meaningful material is available, the decisions of, for example, WTO dispute settlement bodies and other arbitration tribunals are included insofar as they can provide a concrete reference.. The *Normative Kraft des Faktischen* will also be included. It is meant here as a factual development, that has the potential, in a sense of a tendency, to possibly expose a detectable normativity. It could not be excluded possible that the first traces of a emergence of customary law is to be witnessed, what must not be the case necessarily. The necessity to draw attention on the factual during an interpretation can be underlined with the famous WTO Appellate Body Report, *Canada – Autos*[93], where Article I:1 GATT was interpreted to include legal and de facto discrimination.

Without going into greater detail on Jellineks normative power of the factual in the theoretical discourse, Jellinek looked at the emergence of law and recognised the factual as the basis. Customary law, he thought, does not arise from the popular spirit and not from the general conviction that something is law, but it arises out of the general mental quality which regards the ever-repeating factual as the normative.[94]

Against this background, an assessment of the respective section on the SDGs can then take place, where an appropriate classification can be made.

66   Of course, the relationship between the various building blocks must be examined in the sense of an internal and external system, which will have to be differentiated, since one or rather more SDGs also have interdependencies. Only then is it possible to put the facets together to form a whole. Due to the abundance of different building blocks of the SDGs, it is necessary to identify which building blocks are related to each other and how. The determination of the relationship results from the text of the resolution and from

---

[93] WT/DS139/AB/R, WT/DS142/AB/R, *Canada – Certain Measures Affecting The Automotive Industry*, AB-2000-2, 31 May 2000, para. 84.

[94] Jellinek, *Allgemeine Staatslehre* (3rd edn, processed by Walter Jellinek), 339; see Bersier Ladavac and Bezemek and Schauer (eds), *The Normative Force of the Factual* (2019); and there especially Bezemek, 'The 'Normative Force of the Factual': A Positivist's Panegyric' in Bersier Ladavac and Bezemek and Schauer (eds), *The Normative Force of the Factual* (2019), 65-77.

the number and frequency with which certain words are mentioned in the resolution, as well as from the analysis of scientific and shadow reports.

The accumulation of words can be regarded at least as an indication that a certain 67 emphasis within the text is intended, which also points to a legal gravitas. Such a deepening of a meaning does not hold true in an absolute sense, it is rather refutable above all by later resolutions and agreements by which a term can be given a different dimension or a different weighting in a different context. In practice, however, this should be the exception rather than the rule and the word count should be a reliable indication of, firstly, a stronger or lesser significance and, secondly, also an indication of a differentiated assessment of the weighting of various terms in a context, e.g. a resolution. And it should be noted, that *cum grano salis* one additional word has the power to alter the meaning of all the others, regardless of how frequently they have been used in the text.

The focus is on the question of a deeper justice, which is revealed, for example, in 68 different current points of reference. Here, the special basic elements, which I name in this way, and which precede the concept in the version of the Global Agenda 2030, are to be mentioned. In this respect, justice refers to elementary foundations that call for peace, but also for planetary stability and respect for biophysical limits. The elimination of inequalities plays a major role since inequalities add to the bitter taste of injustice. In this respect, attention must be paid to how injustice can be avoided, mitigated or neutralised. In this regard, it must be remembered that the most diverse goals of the Global Agenda 2030 have not defined goals and parameters that invite silo thinking for those who exquisitely understand 'their' SDG and silo and have precisely measured the boundaries and content of the respective thematic area. The deeper meaning and expression of the Global Agenda 2030 is precisely to bring complementary and other interests into balance with each other in the sense of an inner equilibrium to justice. This rather shows the disadvantage of a Global Agenda 2030 á la carte.

It fits this framework that the issue of justice is emphasised by the Global Agenda 69 2030 in different places. Closely linked to equity is the endeavour to resolve inequalities and, above all, to open up access to those who have hitherto stood before closed doors. The capability approach developed by Sen and Nussbaum provides the decisive basic ideas here and endorses the role of dignity across the agenda. Access thus appears as a postulate based on equality, granting everyone an equal chance to realise a concrete opportunity in life and thus enabling them to enter into a fair competition of ideas, thoughts and the realisation of goals, and thus at least advocates equality on the level of opportunity.

Inequality, which is incidentally seen as a deeper reason for serious research on the 70 question of happiness in economy and society, is another concept and basic building block that has a supporting function in the structure of the Global Agenda 2030. In this respect, the research on happiness in the economy and the development of indicators to measure it are an important further argument that can underpin the rationale here. It is obvious that the subjective feeling of happiness is linked to certain factors that enter into a more or less strong correlation with the SDGs. However, most of the SDGs are also elements that serve to justify well-being and happiness.

The last argument that could be useful for the development of a legally workable 71 theory concerns the question of whether and to what extent modern FTAs provide individuals or groups with access to courts or proceedings in which their concerns can be heard, appreciated and taken into account.

Introduction

VIII. Methodology

72   It is quite a challenging task to unveil the internal and external systematic principles that bring forth a salient expression of the normative core of the SDGs (→ Intro mn. 27 ff.). The first answer is thus connected to the question of what the focus is and what methodology is used to determine the normative impact and the jurisprudential significance of each of the 17 specific goals with 169 targets and 231 unique indicators.[95] The SDGs are complex, manifold in depth and width, rooted in historical background, wrapped in resolutions and binding treaties, converged with the AAAA, challenging to grasp as one single piece or to even explain in one or two sentences in any regard. They are often recognisable with a legal conceptual history anchored in decisions and principles, as they are present in the state of legal, academic and practical thought and their future is foreseeable at least (to a certain degree) until 2030.

73   Thus, firstly, we have to look at the object (the SDGs) of our analyses and secondly, we have to brace upon the methodological approach.

74   The attempt is to unveil a quantum of normativity, even if it is not a real 'core', and its jurisprudential relevance ensues from systematic analyses. The background for this question is related to at least three open questions left by French and Kotzé.[96] They pointed to three main questions that are currently unanswered and for whose systematic application in practice a holistic view of the interconnectedness of national, interregional, international and transnational law is needed.

75   Firstly, an absence of the status of the goals in law, which could approach a lawyer in understanding, critiquing, and giving effect to the SDGs are lacking. Secondly, the SDGs raise questions concerning outdated notions of rights and responsibilities, culminating in the ambivalent role of civil society, which rarely be of influence in states and the global political process. Thirdly, the process of implementing the SDGs is interdisciplinary and comprises different methods and sciences, but lawyers should bring structure, clarity of language and a focus of implementation.

76   It is therefore essential to start with an analytical, systematic approach, which involves first deconstructing the Global Agenda 2030 covering much more than the SDGs. The pure reflection of the SDGs would be to turn a blind eye on the engulfing normative and legal aspects of the content of the entire resolution text.

77   The Global Agenda 2030 consists of a preamble, a declaration, and the SDGs framed by it. However, the systemic concept of the Global Agenda 2030 is not limited to these components. Preferably, it contains segments with distinct roles and effects at different levels. The means of implementation and the follow-up cannot be overlooked.

78   Equally, if not more critical is the measurement of the outcome of all SDGs. The quality of the implementation of the SDGs in practice is measured according to the follow-up process with indicators. Indicators can be recognised as a governance tool to measure reality within a given reference frame and to present politics a closer view if there is any need for decisive action or, at last, a justified omission.

79   A holistic methodological perspective thus involves embracing the comprehensive context of the Global Agenda 2030 and its interconnected elements as a prism of consid-

---

[95] The total number of indicators listed in the global indicator framework A/RES/71/313 (E/CN.3/2021/2, Annex) of SDG indicators is 247. However, these twelve indicators repeat under several targets: 7.b.1/12.a.1; 8.4.1/12.2.1; 8.4.2/12.2.2; 10.3.1/16.b.1; 10.6.1/16.8.1; 13.2.1/13.b.1 (with a slight amendment); 15.7.1/15.c.1; 15.a.1/15.b.1; 1.5.1/11.5.1/13.1.1; 1.5.3/11.b.1/13.1.2; 1.5.4/11.b.2/13.1.3; 4.7.1/12.8.1/13.3.1; https://unstats.un.org/sdgs/indicators/indicators-list/.

[96] French and Kotzé, 'Introduction' in French and Kotzé (eds), *Sustainable Development Goals, Law, Theory and Implementation* (2018), 11 f.

20

eration of the vertical and horizontal legal matrix. The question remains how to crack down the iridescent and, at the same time, precious multifaceted targets, indicators, and principles of every SDG.

Many of these principles and main concepts derive from the Rio Declaration on Envi-   80 ronment and Development, were reformulated, and time-bound articulated incrementally over the timeline of concluded resolutions and conventions by the UNGA (→ Intro mn. 28 f., 39 ff., 254, 265 ff.). The SDGs, frequently displayed as coloured boxes with highly praised content, look-alike gifts of a birthday party, which in fact, they are, should unveil and set free their enshrined normative content, which is placed as a nucleus to every goal, target, and its specific accompanying indicator. The task is literally to 'look afresh'[97] into those cute, coloured boxes, to see what is in there, what could give weight for an argument needed in a case. Once the SDGs have been deconstructed into their specific systematic interconnections, it becomes visible whether there is at least any normative impact yielding from the SDGs and their indicators.

Since the SDGs and the SDG framework can be seen as a consequent evolution of the   81 attempt to give leeway to the concept of normative development, an in-depth assessment of the principles shaping the SDG framework cannot be unfolded. Most of them are already analysed and well introduced in the practice of courts and academic writing.

The core normativity of each SDG in its own wrapped presence should be revealed   82 as much as possible to allow them to be operationalised as an additional legal argument in any kind of legal practice. It must be taken into account that many of the principles and main narratives have their predecessor's encapsulate in international law. They do not occur unexpectedly, metaphorically speaking out of the blue, on the international stage of law but do have some evident roots in the past, and sometimes their underlying meaning remained entirely unchanged with some adjustment to the present.

We have further accepted an interpretation-grid for the outcome of the SDGs. Why is   83 that? In reality, the success of achievement by the SDGs is based on indicators, defined to measure the outcome of the efforts to an SDG orientated achievement. Observing them properly, one will find out directly that the terms of the targets will pave the way to extensive interpretations. Mostly the indicators are narrowing and then shaping the SDGs, giving space for highflying spirits. But the indicators are the instruments that measure the facts against the aspirational targets. At least the observations through indicators and the revealed success or failure depend prominently on the measurement with the indicators and not on the goals.

1. Operationalising the SDGs in a Theoretical Way

To oversee one SDG, a target, one noun, or one indicator in a legal way, one should   84 analyse on the subsequent levels following a logical order of a legal hierarchy.

First: The meaning of the specifically used noun in one of the authentic UN-lan-   85 guages – if there are different meanings – should be interpreted in a way that the maximum of the content could be put in place. To unfold the normative core of a noun one should interpret in a way we have described.

Second: The systematic environment of one noun, principle and so on needs to be   86 scrutinised, so that one builds links to other similar goals, targets and / or indicators in the same field on the same hierarchical level.

Third: The external indicators or external targets surrounding or building conjunc-   87 tion with the specific question put first are identified.

---

[97] *Case Concerning the Gabčíkovo-Nagymaros Project (Hungary v Slovakia)*, Judgment, 25 September 1997, para. 140.

88   Fourth: Principles are detected that provide information about how the targets or indicators are legally surrounded in a direct relationship These principles are erected as some kind of architecture to enshrine a goal, target, indicator, and will shape their specific legal or normative attribute. One can discover those principles

    a)   at the same level enshrined at the indicator or the target or the goal
    b)   at the level of the explanation of the SDGs
    c)   at the preamble and the declaration to the political section of the resolution (Global Agenda 2030)
    d)   in 'integrated' internal treatises and other resolutions and legal instruments or legal concepts Addis Ababa Action Agenda (AAAA), WTO, Charter of the UN, Rio Declaration etc.

89   Fifth: Further external treatises, resolutions and international law (according to Art. 38 ICJ Statute) should be considered.

90   Sixth: Additionally, it should be observed in which trajectory the SDGs were received in the legal matrix of horizontal and vertical structures of national, interregional and international law. Is there any influence possible of neighbouring legal acts?

91   The analysis shows how a certain target or indicator is integrated and legally (internationally) anchored and how they work, how they are interrelated in the legal matrix, what the language or cultural and technological background means. What do legal decisions based on a specific normative core and indirectly or directly linked to a specific SDG, target or indicator mean? The following analyses refer to interregional forms of cooperation such as the EU, which is entitled to set law in different types of forms.

92   In the following section, the principles serve as the foundation of examination as well as a legal manifestation of primary expressions to shape the SDGs. A much more detailed analysis is provided in the following chapters.

2. Operationalising the SDGs in a Practical Sense

93   As sustainable development has grown in prominence, its critics have become more numerous and more vocal. Three major lines of criticism are that the term is 'too boring' to command public attention, 'too vague' to provide guidance, and 'too late' to address the world's problems.[98]

94   The policy space created by the concept of sustainable development is being filled by a wide variety of laws, policies, and activities. The understanding of sustainability underlying these laws and activities is the shared creation of millions of practitioners all over the world. Their constant and repeated interactions and experiences refine and improve both understanding and outcomes. Each community can be expected to work out the specific meaning of sustainability based on its own history, natural resources, economic situation and other conditions.[99]

95   Sustainable development provides an essential normative framework setting out basic criteria for making those evaluations. It does not answer all questions and there are frequently several reasonable answers to the same question, but starting in the right place makes better decisions and better laws more likely.[100]

---

[98] Dernbach and Cheever, 'Sustainable Development and Its Discontents' (2015) 4(2) *Transnational Environmental Law*, 247 (247).

[99] Dernbach and Cheever, 'Sustainable Development and Its Discontents' (2015) 4(2) *Transnational Environmental Law*, 247 (286).

[100] Dernbach and Cheever, 'Sustainable Development and Its Discontents' (2015) 4(2) *Transnational Environmental Law*, 247 (287).

And indeed it is not difficult to identify a wide and presumably not coherent under- **96** standing of sustainable development.

The Global Agenda 2030 with the inherent SDGs and review process have an imme- **97** diate impact in the following steps, where the principles and concepts and normative impact enshrined in the SDGs are applied. That means that the framework of this agenda and its impact on the level of decision-making is increasing. Decision-making can be divided in the field of programs, action agendas and other non-legal-application driven by political framework. Another area includes decisions arising from laws, regulations, even in the area of judicial decisions, where the impact of certain SDGs or aspects of some of the SDGs can be easily identified. Legal reasoning and the applicability of laws, regulation leads to interpretational leeway in the following situations:

1. Interpretation during the applicability of the Goals, their target itself (in the vertical and horizontal matrix)
2. Interpretation of the scope, space and interlinkages to further principles and quoted concepts in the text leading to a new approach in order to solve or to contribute to questions in the legal realm of the vertical and horizontal matrix
3. Consideration of the building of appropriate indicators to answer to which reality / occurrence has an indicator to point, on what occurrence in the society to retrieve a sound answer
4. Reflecting and interpreting the outcome of the measurement of SDGs by indicators during the review process for political omissions and action in the vertical and horizontal political and legal matrix
5. Preparing measures and instruments to establish legal acts on international, interregional, national and local levels
6. Interpretation and filling the discretionary space with the concepts and the weight of the 'wrapped' SDGs by applying legal instruments through administrative entities or any other judicial institution
7. Considering the Global Agenda 2030 and the SDGs at a court hearing or decision about cases concerning the laws encompassing direct or indirect references to the principles of the Global Agenda 2030 and the SDGs
8. Considering the Global Agenda 2030 and the SDGs at a hearing, or any other form of participation on any form of an administrative level prior to a relevant administrative decision covering questions of planning, licensing or similar questions
9. Filling the voids in private law and standards in a transnational sense based on private contracts regarding construction, investment, shipping, company law, digitalisation, labor law and many other form of private consensus based contracts and standards deriving from powerful private organised companies and groups
10. Interpretation of discretionary powers and bases with local authorities, states, interregional institutions and international organisations
11. Interpretation of discretionary powers to pave the way towards to a Partnerships with private entities in order to achieve SDG 17
12. Interpretation and discretion and applicability of proportionality in terms of concluding an investment agreement, a public private partnership agreement with states or transnational companies in order to gain economic targets while reacting in a sustainable and equitable manner
13. Formulation of new politics, like plans, programs, guidelines etc. which will lead over the time to new legal measures reiterating the new approach
14. Formulation of new transnational, domestic, interregional and international law regardless of whether private or public law based on the Global Agenda and the SDGs

15. Treaties and rules of customary international law should be interpreted in the light of principles of sustainable development; interpretations which might seem to undermine the goal of sustainable development should only take precedence where to do otherwise would undermine fundamental aspects of the global legal order, infringe the express wording of a treaty or breach a rule of *jus cogens*.[101]

98   The Global Agenda 2030 and the SDGs clearly illustrate the broad foundation on which they are built. Their inherent principles can be found on innumerable horizontal and vertical levels of the matrix of law. Depending on their temporal origin, these principles can either be attributed to the nascence of the SDGs as an influencing factor or as a measure initiated by them. Due to the holistic concept, which aims to be implemented at all achievable levels,[102] further manifestations can be found on political, legal and civil tiers including different stakeholders and justify different levels of resilience.

99   The systematic approach of the Global Agenda 2030 and the SDGs influence the following analysis of the main internal and external principles of the Global Agenda 2030 bearing in mind, that the approach of universal applicability in practice relies on the integrated and indivisible character[103] of the SDGs and at the same time balancing the 3 dimensions of the SDGs. This makes the applicability on certain topics quite cumbersome. It is therefore useful to deconstruct the Global Agenda 2030 and its architecture in order to identify the main common principles that are necessary to work at different scales as described.

100   Having this in mind, it is time to turn to the Global Agenda 2030 and describe the internal and external principles which permeate the resolution as such.

101   The systematic separation of the Global Agenda's internal principles and its external participatory principles incorporated by reference underscores the complex overall architecture of the Global Agenda 2030 internally and externally. This particular architecture points to the resolution not only as a politically important instrument for achieving ambitious goals, but also for integrating and situating the Global Agenda 2030 in the broad concert of a multilateral order based on international law. Can these principles be at least reduced to a common nucleus that unites them in their diversity? Is there a space of a construction of a new approach already sketched in the resolution itself? Can different principles and / or a different nucleus be identified for the Global Agenda 2030 and the 17 SDGs themselves? To analyse those questions we will take a close look on the principles of the Global Agenda 2030 and differentiate between principles, which are internally viable, and those which are externally of the Global Agenda and where is a reference set either directly or indirectly.

102   To identify these fundamental principles and the building blocks of the SDGs, my proposal is to distinguish between internal and external principles, each of which stabilises and underpins the core of the Global Agenda 2030: the SDGs.

3. Systematic Word Count

103   Systematic word counting is a simple tool to measure the number of words used in a given text and to infer the gravity rate of the terms and their hierarchy from the result.

---

[101] ILA, Resolution No. 7/2012, 2012 Sofia Guiding Statements on the Judicial Elaboration of the 2002 New Delhi Declaration of Principles of International Law Relating to Sustainable Development, Guiding Statement No. 2.

[102] See A/RES/70/1, para 39: 'global engagement [...] bringing together Governments, the private sector, civil society, the U55N system and other actors and mobilizing all available resources.'

[103] A/RES/70/1, para 55.

Word count is known in many disciplines to seek for an unbiased and objective outcome.[104] This tool provides clarity through a quantitative analysis of the different words and their use in a text. **104**

Although, the observation seems to be logical that not everything that counts can be counted and not everything that can be counted counts,[105] the approach of a word count provides nonetheless objective and systematic support to understand a text not primarily from interpretation or a meta-theoretical or ontological point of view, but from the pure and positive text itself, without hindrance and from any approach that clouds the sheer view and interpretation of that specific text. **105**

Even if the absence of empirical objectivism is to be lamented, terms (and their notions) are nevertheless the tools with which reality is observed and constructed.[106] **106**

Yet, it should be noted that at least any additional word *cum grano salis* can immediately change the meaning of the text and nullify even the highest count of certain words in a legal sense. But as a simple approach to a non-legal text that tends to be a source of other normative concepts and a guide to legal plans, schemes, laws and regulations in the global multi-level system of laws, it can be useful to start with. **107**

The word count in A/RES/70/1 reveals the following score: **108**

1.	Development	205	16.	Rights	23
2.	Sustainable (including Sustainability)	227	17.	Climate Change	20
3.	2030	75	18.	Equality	18
				Peace	18
4.	Goals	64		Law	18
5.	Economic	61	19.	Growth	17
6.	Technology (including technological)	53	20.	Girls	15
			21.	Private	16
7.	Human (including Humanity)	44	22.	Equitable	13
8.	Inclusive	40		Planet	13
9.	Social	39		Empower	13
	Equality (including equal and inequality)	39	23.	Ocean	11
10.	Environment	35	24.	Addis Ababa Action Agenda	9
11.	Women	32		International law	9
12.	Science (including scientific)	30		Inequality	9
13.	Poverty	28	25.	Natural resources	8
	Water	28		Hunger	8
14.	Innovation (including innovative)	27		Business	8
			26.	Indicator(s)	7
15.	Climate	26		World Trade Organization	7

---

[104] 'The object of this paper is to introduce a simple technique which is of value in the study of Roman law. This is the use of word counts and word frequencies', Honoré, 'Word Frequencies and the Study of Roman Law' (1972) 30.2 *The Cambridge Law Journal*, 280-93; 'A controversial area of forensic linguistics is 'Stylometry'. This technique involves word counts of various types, and the measurement, Gibbons, 'Language and the law' (1999) 19 *Annual Review of Applied Linguistics*, 156-73; Al-Mosaiwi, and Johnstone, 'In an absolute state: Elevated use of absolutist words is a marker specific to anxiety, depression, and suicidal ideation' (2018) 6.4 *Clinical Psychological Science*, 529-42; Stirman and Pennebaker, 'Word use in the poetry of suicidal and nonsuicidal poets' (2001) 63.4 *Psychosomatic medicine*, 517-22.

[105] So the title by Khalil, 'Not everything that counts can be counted and not everything that can be counted counts' (2014) 38(2) *The Psychiatric Bulletin*, 86.

[106] D'Aspremont, 'Wording in International Law' 25(3) *Leiden Journal of International Law*, 575-602.

Introduction

109   Following the hierarchy of words counted up to the most ten used words in the resolution, the following sentence could be formulated only using the hierarchy of words:

110   Resolution 70/1 stresses that development (1) in a sustainable manner (2) should be achieved by 2030 (3) with the goals (4) by integrating the economy (5), serving the ideal of humanity (6) and by not ignoring the inclusive (7) approach of fundamental social (8) and environmental (9) aspects as well as the equality of women (10).

111   If one were to rely solely on the quantitative consideration of the word count, the analysis of the least mentioned terms which are mentioned only one time to a maximum of four times (see no. 27-31) would lead to the problematic conclusion that injustice (31), corruption (30), transformation (30), multilateralism (29), the *rule of law* (29) and dignity (29) firstly reflect a much lower level of attention in the resolution and secondly, as a consequence, show a lower need to pay attention to and address these issues in the multi-level system of law. The low representation of these terms in the resolution also demonstrate that only the gap between the terms mentioned many times (no. 1-10) and the terms mentioned least is reasonably high. It could be concluded that the low representation of terms such as *rule of law* indicates that the associated legal mechanisms are not seen as primary solutions in this context. The same applies to the issue of corruption, the fight against which could make a central contribution to sustainability, but is clearly not one of the primary goals and main topics driving the Global Agenda 2030.

112   It could lead to the disturbing question, what if in the future sustainable development supersedes the deeper meaning of the *rule of law*? Would the immense battle against climate change justify weakening the *rule of law*? Certainly that would not be called legally an acceptable idea, but it points to the perspective that to achieve the goals an acceptance of 'weaker' concepts and provisions like corruption and the lack of the rule of law could justify an earlier win of certain goals.

113   Word count could serve as an internal hierarchy of used terms to indicate, in an objective sense, whether a high or low level of attention could be diplomatically prevailed upon.

IX. The Internal and External Systematic Approach

114   This chapter discusses the principles and main concepts that run through the Global Agenda 2030. Those principles serve as a kind of a layer which are linked to every SDG connecting the specific goal with the different settings, concepts and arguments found in conferences as well as to the legal principles of international law. Some of them are highlighted in the resolution as particularly important in the chapter 'Our shared principles and commitments', while others stand out in other parts of the resolution, signalling a more limited and selective scope. It is therefore necessary to define the tasks, the scope and the hierarchy of the principles used, while explaining their respective areas of application.

Some of the principles and the most influential ideas, which shape the Global Agenda **115**
2030 and the SDGs including their application, are clearly mentioned in the text of the
resolution at the preamble or declaration and are therefore referred to as 'principles'
in the declaration.[107] However, some principles where not addressed as a general term
but were referred to in the context of a specific goal[108] or even explicitly quoted in the
section of the 'Means of implementation and the Global Partnership'.[109] Other principles
and guiding concepts are equally mentioned and quoted in the 'Follow-up and review'
process[110] of the implementation of the SDGs[111] or in the in explanation of the 'New
Agenda'[112] or in the introduction to the SDGs[113] underlining the proposals the Open
Working Group (OWG) on SDGs[114] and the character of the SDGs and targets as
'integrated and indivisible'.[115]

The relationship and the impact of the principles is hard to separate. It is thus evident **116**
that the World Health Organisation's Framework Convention on Tobacco Control, cited
in SDG 3,[116] which relates to health, has limited scope in the Global Agenda 2030, despite its general importance, and will not directly influence many other goals. Sometimes
explicitly named principles within the SDGs are mentioned and their specific space of
applicability extends across one SDG, although they are not directly mentioned in the
general principles. Those principles serve as general block to extract further guiding
advice when the applicability of the SDGs get ambiguous. All principles, concepts and
guidance are intended to give birth to a new agenda when the SDGs and their inherent
process amalgamate with the underlying principles to form a new approach.

The Global Agenda 2030 and the SDGs can be attributed to a large number of **117**
internationally recognised principles of international law and the international law as
such,[117] either directly or through the interpretation of the individual objectives.

Some of the main principles and Treaties of the Global Agenda 2030 and the SDGs **118**
are specified and are explicitly quoted[118]:

- Charter of the United Nations, including full respect for international law,
- Universal Declaration of Human Rights,
- International Human Rights Treaties,
- Millennium Declaration,
- All principles of the Rio Declaration on Environment and Development, including the
  principle of common but differentiated responsibilities, as set out in Principle 7
- 2005 World Summit Outcome[119]

---

[107] A/RES/70/1, paras. 10-3.
[108] A/RES/70/1, SDG 14, 14.a; see Intergovernmental Oceanographic Commission Criteria and Guidelines on the Transfer of Marine Tech Paralogy.
[109] A/RES/70/1, paras. 28, 42: Istanbul Declaration and Programme of Action or the African Union's
Agenda 2063, 47, 60-71.   .
[110] A/RES/70/1, paras. 72-91.
[111] A/RES/70/1, para. 75: Framework of the Inter-Agency and Expert Group on Sustainable Development Goal Indicators. Resolution A/RES/71/313. adopted by the General Assembly on Work of the
Statistical Commission pertaining to the 2030 Agenda for Sustainable Development on 6 July 2017.
[112] A/RES/70/1, para. 24: the Rome Declaration on Nutrition and the Framework for Action; para 28:
10-Year Framework of Programmes on Sustainable Consumption and Production Patterns; A/RES/70/1,
para 31: United Nations Framework Convention on Climate Change (UNFCC).
[113] A/RES/70/1, paras. 54-9.
[114] A/RES/70/1, para. 54.
[115] A/RES/70/1, paras. 5, 18, 55 and 71.
[116] A/RES/70/1, SDG 3, 3.a.
[117] A/RES/70/1, paras. 10, 18, 19, 23, 30, 35, 14.5, 14.c.
[118] A/RES/70/1, Introduction, para. 12.
[119] A/RES/70/1, Introduction, para. 10.

Introduction

119   A foundation for sustainable development was already laid through various declarations, conferences and academic writing, judicial decisions in international, interregional, e.g. European and national law, crystallizing a clear consciousness about content and reach of the term sustainable development which influenced the Global Agenda 2030 and the SDGs. Those declarations and conferences are explicitly quoted in the text of the resolution to underline the different historical layers on which the concept of sustainable development has been built. The text of the principles and commitments of the resolution quotes the following historically formative elements of influence:

- Rio Declaration on Environment and Development
- World Summit on Sustainable Development
- World Summit for Social Development
- Programme of Action of the International Conference on Population and Development
- Beijing Platform for Action
- United Nations Conference on Sustainable Development
- Fourth United Nations Conference on the Least Developed Countries
- Second United Nations Conference on Landlocked Developing Countries
- Third International Conference on Small Island Developing States
- Third United Nations World Conference on Disaster Risk Reduction[120]
- (once again) the Rio Declaration on Environment and Development, including, inter alia, the principle of common but differentiated responsibilities, as set out in principle 7 thereof[121]
- Commitment to international law[122]
- (indirect) commitment to Multilateralism by stating that 'States are strongly urged to refrain from promulgating and applying any unilateral economic, financial or trade measures not in accordance with international law and the Charter of the United Nations'[123]
- Concept of sustainable development with three dimensions: economic, social and environmental[124]
- Principle of integrated, indivisible and balanced SDGs,[125] global in nature and universally applicable[126]
- Matrix of a vertical local, national (including governments[127] and national parliaments[128]), regional, international and horizontal level including the UN System and other international institutions extended to the private sector[129], business[130] the civil

---

[120] All so far named conferences and Declaration are quoted at A/RES/70/1, para. 11.

[121] A/RES/70/1, para. 12.

[122] A/RES/70/1, paras. 18, 19, 23, 30, 35, 14.5, 14.c.

[123] A/RES/70/1, para. 30 and regarding trade: 17.10, 68, multilateral institutions: 74(i) and multilateral environmental agreements: 67.

[124] A/RES/70/1, para. 2.

[125] A/RES/70/1, paras. 5, 18, 58.

[126] A/RES/70/1, paras. 5, 18, and in particular para. 58.

[127] A/RES/70/1, para. 52.

[128] A/RES/70/1, para. 79.

[129] A/RES/70/1, para. 41: 'the role of the diverse private sector, ranging from micro-enterprises to cooperatives to multinationals'.

[130] A/RES/70/1 para. 52.

society[131], the indigenous peoples[132], philanthropic organisations[133], public private partnerships[134] and the scientific and academic community[135]

– Empowerment of the most vulnerable: all children, youth, persons with disabilities (of whom more than 80 per cent live in poverty), people living with HIV/AIDS, older persons, indigenous peoples, refugees and internally displaced persons and migrants.[136]

– A new approach is needed regarding the interrelated commitments of conferences and summits[137]

The SDGs are thus more than a global agenda. Rather, their impact gives birth to **120** something new that originally came from the scenery of environmentalism and has now evolved into a broader and complex current of a real or desired legal narrative of a somehow normative conceptual movement, aiming at the sphere where the theory of law ends and informal law begins, fulfilling the unanswered 'new approach' of the resolution itself.[138] Following the systematic approach of this commentary, one cannot ignore the principles, treatises, concepts and ideas building an architecture for the SDGs, shaping and influencing them at the same time formulated later and match perfectly into those fundaments. The principles in the declaration and in further parts of the agenda as a political agenda 'of unprecedented scope and significance'[139], recurring to principles already developed by conferences, resolutions and reiterated often the existence of principles, which are now not encompassed directly by every SDGS but are wrapped around them and building a kind of a normative and legal cocoon or layers. The resolution is embedded in a way that the mere core as such remain a non-binding resolution but with much different kind of layers achieving a gravity in the space of the evolution of concepts, normativity they start to enter the realm of law itself.

X. The Internal Principles of the SDGs

The resolution, as a political agenda 'of unprecedented scope and significance'[140] has **121** found its way into various political and legal levels of the international community through a wide range of measures, processes and instruments. However, there is not only evidence that the SDGS have influenced the legal level of international law but furthermore influence the interregional and national level as well. In the vertical and horizontal matrix of law and its different expressions the Global Agenda 2030 including the SDGs were subsequently integrated mostly politically but incrementally legally as well. The Global Agenda 2030 and the entailed SDGs demonstrates that their unique and striking concept of a political, ecological, social and planetary change or adjustment is unanimously accepted and therefore integrated into different levels of the realm of law in the following spheres: international, transnational, interregional, national and also in private law and standards. Therefore the SDGs are the core part but endorsed by the Global Agenda 2030, thus clearly separate but at the same time connected. The

---

131 A/RES/70/1, para. 39: 'the private sector, civil society', 41.
132 A/RES/70/1, paras. 23, 25, 52, 79.
133 A/RES/70/1, para. 41.
134 A/RES/70/1, para. 17.
135 A/RES/70/1, para. 52.
136 A/RES/70/1, para 23.
137 A/RES/70/1, para. 13: 'a new approach is needed'.
138 A/RES/70/1, para. 13.
139 A/RES/70/1, para. 6.
140 A/RES/70/1, para. 6.

overwhelming evolution and their rootedness in international law and human rights provides a notion of closer and more distant layers bearing their own weight in the respective legal field. Therefore the internal principles catch a more decisive attention. They are interwoven in a direct sense, mostly taken from another and refined for the direct understanding. Sometimes the distinction is problematic, e.g. the AAAA is considered an integral part of the Global Agenda 2030, but was adopted at a separate conference with its own name and history. In this respect, the AAAA remains independent, even if it is referred to and integrated into the Global Agenda.

1. The '5 P'-Principle

122   The internal Principles comprise and guide the content of the resolution and the SDGs.

123   The overarching principles of the Global Agenda 2030 can easily be extracted from its preambular paragraphs, serving as an overarching inscription to the gate of the Global Agenda 2030. The mentioned levels 'People, Planet, Prosperity, Peace and Partnership'[141] describe the scope and the ambition of the Global Agenda 2030 on the highest level of a systematic internal hierarchy.

124   The preamble of the Global Agenda 2030 notably is similar in content with the Rio Declaration (1992), where the Rio topics were translated into the '5 Ps' from cooperation into 'peace' and 'partnership', social development into 'People' environmental protection into 'planet' and economic growth and development into 'prosperity'.[142]

125   The overarching objectives in the Global Agenda 2030 now state five key messages, abbreviated as '5 P':

–   Focus on human dignity (People)
–   Protect the planet (Planet)
–   Promote prosperity for all (Prosperity)
–   Promoting peace (Peace)
–   Establishing global partnerships: (Partnership)

126   These five major columns illustrate the linkage of the agenda with the anthropocentric approach of the SDGs. Although the protection of 'Mother Earth' has been included in these five basic principles, it emerges that it also serves to 'support the needs of the present and future generations.'[143] By picking up this core principle of sustainable development and quoting indirectly *Gro Harlem Brundtland's* famous definition, the intergenerationally grounded agenda included the biological systems that are the provision for any kind of life on this particular planet. Therefore, it is an agenda, which originates and is strictly linked to human needs, which cannot be separated from this principle, thus promoting the planet as a compulsory prerequisite provision.

127   A consideration that would focus solely on a right of nature of whatever kind and would thus lose the interconnectedness with people would no longer be congruent with the Global Agenda 2030 and the SDGs. As demonstrated above, the SDGs are indivisible and place people at the centre of consideration, who are, however, bound in their own interest to respect nature within its limits and not to harm it without harming themselves. In the end, trade-offs have to be made in individual cases and conflicting interests have to be weighed against each other in the sense of proportionality.

---

[141] A/RES/70/1, preamble, 2.
[142] A/CONF.151/26 (Vol. I); Dupuy and Viñuales, *International Environmental Law* (2nd edn, 2018), 21.
[143] A/RES/70/1, preamble, 2.

a) Ratio and Correlation to Sustainability

The '5 Ps' do not refer directly to sustainable development as the basic narrative of all   **128**
agendas and outcomes of so many resolutions, but interestingly sustainable development
is accompanied by the key word 'Peace' as the fourth pillar and people and planet are
explained with further content of the key content of the term sustainable development.
By looking at them as a completely figurative and modern 'new approach' could clarify
that the 5 Ps are built on sustainable development as their very own basis but serve as a
foundation and not as a new expression of the content of A/RES/70/1.

b) New Approach of Extended Sustainable Development

The 5 Ps do not alter the definition of sustainable development, which is also referred   **129**
to in the text of the resolution itself as having its three dimensions unchanged.[144] Yet,
an extension is created which goes further than the previous related term of sustainable
development. Sustainable Development will now be taken as a basis for building five
overarching *leitmotifs* and in their foundations the defining power of sustainability is
added textually for stabilisation. This new figuration could be a 'new approach' that
serves as a *leitmotif* and is linked to the essential contents of the definition of sustainable
development. Consequently, it is a new, broader figuration of the concept of sustainable
development, which in this respect also includes the issues of the planetary boundaries
of the earth and security aspects. Consequently, sustainability today no longer has only
a social, economic and human dimension, but is complemented by the security and
planetary dimensions.[145]

c) Relationship and Interpretational Guide of the 5 Ps

According to the guiding principle that the SDGs and the embracing agenda are   **130**
indivisible and follow an integrative nature, the interpretation is that all of the 5 Ps
are standing for themselves. Each and all of them demonstrating the core aspects of
an extended meaning of the term sustainable development. Sustainable development
and its different contents of different science approaches is here confronted with a set
of memorabilia, short terms covering the main pillars of the modern version of an
extended sustainability. These five terms, the '5 Ps' consist of five short descriptions, so
that their content is filled as a box with a specific meaning in a specific scenery for
the transformation triggered. None of the principles may neutralise another principle or
cast a shadow to favour one principle over another. Those 5 Ps are interconnected and
have a maximal space as possible without being overshadowed or minimised by another
principle.[146]

d) SDGs 'wrapped' by Layers of Principles rooted in International Law

The Global Agenda 2030 contains numerous references and principles are made, cre-   **131**
ated by historically grounded internal and external resolutions, treatises and standards
as well. The reiteration and the reference of and to other instruments does not directly
impact on the SDGs, but indirectly affect them in wrapping them with a lot of different
binding and non-binding instruments which determine their meaning. **There should be**

---

[144] A/RES/70/1, preamble.

[145] See ILA Draft Resolution No 4/2020, *The Role of International Law in Sustainable Natural Resources
Management for Development*, 79th Kyoto Conference of the International Law Association held in Kyoto,
Japan, 29th November to 13th December 2020.

[146] A/RES/70/1, preamble, 1 and 2; the same applies to the SDGs, see paras. 5, 18, 55.

made a difference between principles and the setting of a reference. The mere setting of a reference means that within an SDG, a target or an indicator can be a can provide a link to expand and reflect on the legal environment, although the SDGs as a resolution are not directly part of a surrounding treaty. A clear and transparent analysis could shed light into the different principles and indirect and direct layers of the global agenda. With this in mind, we start to examine the '5 Ps' a little more closely.

i. People (P1)

132 The core of the headline 'People' is directly explained and does mean 'all human beings' included in the following text: 'End up poverty and hunger, in all their forms and dimensions, and to ensure that all human beings can fulfil their potential in dignity, which does mean warranty of the state obligations and equality and in a healthy environment'.[147]

133 People as one of the *leitmotifs* are not coincidentally at the first place to be mentioned. The Global Agenda 2030 is called 'an Agenda of the people, by the people and for the people'.[148] The SDGs consist of a wide understanding of a 'people-centred' set of goals, targets and indicators[149] which applies to all nations, all people and all segments of societies[150] and therefore including and highlighting explicitly indigenous peoples.[151] The scope of people is clearly defined and entails all people without any exclusion but shed a spotlight on vulnerable people, in particular all children, youth, persons with disabilities, people living with HIV/AIDS, older persons, indigenous peoples, refugees and internally displaced persons and migrants.[152]

134 This means that LGBTQ people are included and any attempt to exclude them would fail. LGBT stands for Lesbian, gay, bisexual and transgender. The Q can stand for 'questioning' (as in still exploring one's sexuality) or 'queer', or sometimes both.[153]

135 With people as its main target the Global Agenda 2030 is drawing a direct line from the Stockholm conference in 1972[154] to the Rio Declaration, the Agenda 21, the MDGS and to the SDGs providing the Global Agenda 2030 with the essence of what is at the core of the outcomes from the many conferences and concepts shaped between 1972 and 2015. The anthropocentric approach reaches further than to the Stockholm Conference in 1972, namely to the founding of the UN Charter (Preamble: 'reaffirm faith in fundamental human rights', 'reaffirm faith in the dignity and worth of the human person'). This approach is repeated in the famous Brundtland report, which formulates the most recognised definitions of sustainable development, putting people at the centre as a part of generations:

> Sustainable development is development that meets the needs of the present without compromising the ability of future generations to meet their own needs. It contains at least the following key concepts: "The concept of 'needs', in particular, the essential needs of the world's poor, to which

---

147 A/RES/70/1, preamble, 2.
148 A/RES/70/1, para. 52.
149 A/RES/70/1, para 2.
150 A/RES/70/1, para. 4.
151 A/RES/70/1, paras. 23, 25, 79: '[Government] reviews should draw on contributions from indigenous peoples'.
152 A/RES/70/1, para. 23.
53 Jones et al., 'Lesbian, Gay, Bisexual, Transgender, and Queer Youth and Social Justice' in Clauss-Ehlers et al. (eds), *Social Justice for Children and Young People: International Perspectives* (2020), 123-37.
154 Schrijver, *The Evolution of Sustainable Development in International Law: Inception, Meaning and Status* (2008), 43, referring to the Club of Rome report 'The Limits to Growth' (1972), motivating the Conference.

overriding priority should be given; and the idea of limitations imposed by the state of technology and social organization on the environment's ability to meet present and future needs.

In Principle 5 of the Rio Declaration, the major goal of the Global Agenda 2030 was already included and formulated very clearly: **136**

> [h]uman beings are at the centre of concerns for sustainable development. They are entitled to a healthy and productive life in harmony with nature. Principle 1 of the Rio Declaration takes a clearly anthropocentric stance structuring efforts towards sustainable development around human beings:[155] All States and all people shall cooperate in the essential task of eradicating poverty as an indispensable requirement for sustainable development.

Moreover, Art. 1 of the UDHR states that all human beings are born free and equal in dignity and rights. In addition, dignity related to economic and social rights, Art. 22 UDHR and Art. 23(3) UDHR explain that everyone who works has the right to just and favourable remuneration ensuring for himself and his family an existence worthy of human dignity, and supplemented, if necessary, by other means of social protection. People are further on related to the right to health and the right to related services, so that everyone has the right to a standard of living adequate for the health and well-being of himself and of his family, including food, clothing, housing and medical care and necessary social services, and the right to security in the event of unemployment, sickness, disability, widowhood, old age or other lack of livelihood in circumstances beyond her or his control, Art. 25 No 1 UDHR. **137**

According to the UN Special Rapporteur on human rights, the right to food is the right to have regular, permanent and unrestricted access, either directly or by means of financial purchases, to quantitatively and qualitatively adequate and sufficient food corresponding to the cultural traditions of the people to which the consumer belongs, and which ensures a physical and mental, individual and collective, fulfilling and dignified life free of fear. This definition is in line with the core elements of the right to food as defined by General Comment No. 12 of the United Nations Committee on Economic, Social and Cultural Rights (the body in charge of monitoring the implementation of the International Covenant on Economic, Social and Cultural Rights in those states which are party to it). The Committee declared that 'the right to adequate food is realized when every man, woman and child, alone or in community with others, has physical and economic access at all times to adequate food or means for its procurement'.[156] **138**

The normative impact of P1 reaches from the Charter of the UN, the UDHR to the ICESCR and many treatises covering the vast areas of the lives of human beings. **139**

ii. Planet (P2)

While the planet is arrayed alongside humans, it is the causality of human actions or omissions such as pollution or degradation of the planet's ecological systems that is required and can hardly be denied to enable the application of the Global Agenda 2030. Therefore and through the harm of humankind to the planet, P2 states: 'to protect the planet from degradation, including through sustainable consumption and production, sustainably managing its natural resources and taking urgent action on climate change, so that it can support the needs of the present and future generations'. The importance and singularity of the planet is highlighted already in the first sentence of the agenda stating: 'This Agenda is a plan of action for people, planet and prosperity'.[157] **140**

---

[155] Viñuales, 'The Principles enshrined in the Rio Declaration' in Viñuales (ed.), *The Rio Declaration on Environment and Development, A Commentary* (2015), 22.

[156] https://www.ohchr.org/EN/Issues/Food/Pages/FoodIndex.aspx.

[157] A/RES/70/1, preamble, 1.

Introduction

141   Since more than ten years, the GA is considering perspectives on the topic of Earth jurisprudence, with a focus on ecological economics and Earth-centred law, rooted in non-anthropocentric teachings.[158] The planet has not become a legal person but the notable approach of the UN for harmony with nature, which not only includes biodiversity, suggests that certain features of nature are increasingly being legally protected or even given unique rights that are being recognised in court or in administrative planning. 'Over the past decade, an array of Earth-centred law, also known as Earth jurisprudence, has been gaining ground in an increasing number of Member States.'[159]

142   For the past decade, the UN's Harmony with Nature programme has documented and analysed legislation and policies on the rights of Nature in 35 countries, which have either already been adopted or are currently being worked on.[160] It has also documented and analysed collaboration among non-governmental organisations (NGOs), civil society organisations, legislators and legislative bodies working together to draft, adopt and implement laws or policies recognising nature as a subject of rights and / or a legal 'person', protected by law.[161]

143   Thus P 2 is dedicated to the planet and its biological support system being at risk[162] which is a principle of its own, interwoven with the rest of the principles to amplify mutually and equally in a most connected way the outcome of the SDGs themselves.

144   Earth jurisprudence is a philosophy of law to promote a greater respect for nature that is based on the idea that humans are only one part of a wider community of beings and that the welfare of each member of that community is dependent on the welfare of the Earth as a whole.[163] This idea creates more and more attention.[164]

145   However, it should be noted that the first concepts of Earth Jurisprudence were elaborated much earlier. The UN took a first step towards recognising the rights of nature in June 2012 with the outcome document of the Rio + conference 'The future we want' , acknowledging that the Earth and its ecosystems are our home and that some countries recognise the rights of nature in the context of the promotion of sustainable development. They also agreed that, in order to achieve a just balance among the needs of present and future generations, it is necessary to promote harmony with nature.[165] The human rights of the 'people' as the first and most important dedication of the

---

[158] A/RES/75/266, para. 11: 'The breakthroughs made and actions taken in the second half of 2019 and the first half of 2020 provide a glimpse of a larger picture that is still unfolding. A special supplement to the present report, compiling over 170 examples of activities implementing the Harmony with Nature programme is available online: http://files.harmonywithnatureun.org/uploads/upload1019.pdf.

[159] A/75/266, para. 36 (quote 28): Information on legislation and policies featured in section V is available on the Harmony with Nature website at http://harmonywithnatureun.org/rightsOfNature/ and www.harmonywithnatureun.org/rightsOfNaturePolicies/.

[160] A/RES/75/266, para. 53 (fn. 35): 'Argentina, Australia, Bangladesh, Belize, Belgium, Bolivia (Plurinational State of), Brazil, Canada, Colombia, Chile, Costa Rica, Denmark, Ecuador, El Salvador, France, Guatemala, Hungary, India, Ireland, Italy, Mexico, Netherlands, New Zealand, Nigeria, Philippines, Portugal, Romania, Spain, South Africa, Sweden, Switzerland, Uganda, United Kingdom of Great Britain and Northern Ireland, United States of America and Holy See'.

[161] A/75/266, paras. 36, 53.

[162] A/RES/70/1, preamble, para. 14.

[163] http://www.harmonywithnatureun.org/ejInputs/.

[164] Kotzé and Kim, 'New Dimensions of the Earth System Law' *Environmental Policy and Law Preprint*, 1-14; Burdon, 'Ecological law in the Anthropocene'(2020) 11.1-2 *Transnational Legal Theory*, 33-46; Webster and Mai *Transnational Environmental Law in the Anthropocene: Reflections on the Role of Law in Times of Planetary Change* (2021).

[165] A/RES/66/288, para 39.

Global Agenda 2030 provide an essential pathway to motivate governments to address climate change and other biophysically processes that impact on people.[166]

Nevertheless, the planet – without legally rights of its own[167] – both stands separated **146** from and interlinked with humanity at the same time.[168] The planet is not recognised as a legal entity. Griggs argues on the background of population growth that 'the stable functioning of Earth systems — including the atmosphere, oceans, forests, waterways, biodiversity and biogeochemical cycles are a prerequisite for a thriving global society. With the human population set to rise to [approximately] 9 billion by 2050, definitions of sustainable development must be revised to include the security of people and the planet.'[169]

One of the first impressions that the ecological systems are in danger can be retrieved **147** in the UN Stockholm Conference 1972 where the status is described:

> We see around us growing evidence of man-made harm in many regions of the earth: dangerous levels of pollution in water, air, earth and living beings; major and undesirable disturbances to the ecological balance of the biosphere; destruction and depletion of irreplaceable resources and gross deficiencies, harmful to the physical, mental and social health of man, in the man-made environment, particularly in the living and working environment.[170]

At the same conference, the concept of 'Earthwatch' was launched and defined for **148** conducting assessments of the global environment.[171]

Dating back to the 60 s, in the initial letter from 20 May 1968 Sweden considered a **149** conference to the Secretary General of the UN, explaining the need for such a conference with 'problems such as air and water pollution, depletion of soil and the disturbance of ecological balance'.[172]

Adopted more than 48 years apart, this resolution and the later Rio Declaration **150** highlighted the rise of international environmental law and at that time the adoption of the 'World Charter for Nature'[173], which enshrines some of the lines of today's SDGs, such as: 'All areas of the earth, both land and sea, shall be subject to these principles of conservation'[174] and the UN being aware that '[c]ivilization is rooted in nature, which has shaped human culture and influenced all artistic and scientific achievement, and living in harmony with nature, gives man the best opportunities for the development of his creativity, and for the rest and recreation'.[175]

And it is remarkable that as early as 1972, at the Stockholm conference, the UN **151** developed an Action Plan containing 'the global environmental assessment programme (Earthwatch)'[176] and it is interesting how the action plan was embedded in a sophistic

---

[166] Phelan, 'The Environment, a Changing Climate, and Planetary Health in Gostin and Mason Meier (eds), Foundations of Global Health & Human Rights'(2020), 429.

[167] Timmon, 'Earth Jurisprudence and Lockean Theory: Rethinking the American Perception of Private Property' (2011) 1 *Earth Jurisprudence and Environmental Justice Journal*, 1, 103-16;; Koons, 'What Is Earth Jurisprudence? Key Principles to Transform Law for the Health of the Planet' (2009) 18 *PENN ST. ENVTL. L. REV*, 47.

[168] A/RES/70/1, preamble, para. 1: 'The Goals [...] in areas of critical importance for humanity and the planet', para. 51: 'an Agenda [...] a charter for people and planet in the twenty-first century'.

[169] Griggs et al., 'Sustainable development goals for people and planet' (2013) 495 *Nature*, 305.

[170] A/CONF.48/14/Ref.1, *Report of the United Nations Conference on the Human Environment*, Stockholm, 5-16 June 1972, para. 3.

[171] UN Systems – Wide Earthwatch, Origins 1972-1979.

[172] E/4466/Add.1, Letter dated 20 May 1968 from the Permanent Representative of Sweden addressed to the Secretary-General of the United Nations, 2.

[173] A/RES/37/7, adopted 29 October 1982 in the annex of this resolution.

[174] A/RES/37/7, para. 3.

[175] A/RES/37/7, preamble.

[176] A/CONF.48/14/Rev.1, Part One, II. C. The Action Plan.

arrangement of different steps: The Environmental Assessment (Earthwatch) includes different kind of functions all interconnected with the recommendations of the outcome of the conference such as Evaluation and Review Research, Monitoring and Information Exchange. The Earthwatch assessment programme was accompanied by two other categories. First, the environmental management, which was designed to facilitate comprehensive planning that takes into account the side effects of man's activities and thereby to protect and enhance the human environment for present and future generations. The intergenerational aspect which is significant for the Global Agenda 2030 can easily be detected in the Stockholm conference. Second, supporting measures had been designed, which is quite typical for such a programme and quite similar to the policies and principles enshrined into the Global Agenda 2030 and the SDGs. Both were related to measures required for the activities in the other two categories (environmental assessment and environmental management) and covered among others significant steps such as education, training and public information, organisational arrangements, financial and other forms of assistance.[177]

152 Principle 7 of the Rio Declaration on Environment and Development which is precisely, interlinked with the Global Agenda 2030 states in the first sentence: 'States shall cooperate in a spirit of global partnership to conserve, protect and restore the health and integrity of the Earth's ecosystem'. Therefore, one can debate whether there is a difference between the Earth's ecosystem and the planet as such. Does the Earth's ecosystem exclude something like that or not?

153 Only in the preamble of the Rio Declaration it states '[r]ecognizing the integral and interdependent nature of the Earth' which raises awareness that the integral and interdependent nature of the Earth is something that does not overlap with the Earth's ecosystems mentioned in Principle 7. Ideally, both expressions encompass all and complete all systems that are interdependent and integral for sustaining any life on Earth.[178]

154 This clause, deviating from the interconnection to the anthropocentric approach of Rio (and Stockholm), was integrated on the initiative of the United States of America (USA), which was, according to Francioni, followed by the presentation of a civil society group.[179]

155 With Principle 2 of the Rio Declaration, the natural resources of the Earth, including the air, water, land, flora and fauna, and especially representative samples of natural ecosystems must be safeguarded for the benefit of present and future generations through careful planning or management, as appropriate.[180] The idea of preventing degradation can also be traced back to Principles 3 and 5 dealing with vital renewable resources and '[t]hat the non-renewable resources of the earth must be employed in such a way as to guard against the danger of their future exhaustion'.[181]

156 The working group in a draft declaration expressed its concern about the state of the Earth with such (prophetic) words: 'We see around us growing evidence of man-made harm in many regions of the earth: dangerous levels of pollution in water, air, earth

[177] A/CONF.48/14/Rev., paras. 1, 6, 27 f.

[178] A/CONF.151/26 (Vol. I), *Report of the United Nations Conference on Environment and Development**, Rio de Janeiro, 3-14 June 1992.

[179] Francioni, 'The Preamble of the Rio Declaration' in Viñuales, *The Rio Declaration on Environment and Development, A Commentary* (2015), 91 (fn. 35).

[180] A/CONF/48/14/Ref.1, *Report of the United Nations Conference on the Human Environment*, Stockholm, 5-16 June 1972.

[181] A/CONF/48/14/Ref.1, *Report of the United Nations Conference on the Human Environment*, Stockholm, 5-16 June 1972, para. 5.

and living beings; major and undesirable disturbances to the ecological balance of the biosphere [...]'.[182]

Whether the promise may be considered a failure,[183] given the unique changes tak- **157**
ing place on the planet, only the future will tell. A too pessimistic, even apocalyptic perspective does not help anyone. Taking into account the importance and the unique position of the planet is the right thing to do. To recognise the existing ecosystems and nature as a whole – of which we are part of – is recognised as the basis, which humans should not disturb and adversely alter, but on the contrary should preserve the (mostly) existing balance on Earth now and for the future is consequential, and this includes the intergenerational equity.[184]

iii. Prosperity (P3)

The third P states '[w]e are determined to ensure that all human beings can enjoy **158**
prosperous and fulfilling lives and that economic, social and technological progress occurs in harmony with nature'.[185]

P 3 is thus dedicated to prosperity which is hardly a linear goal, but depends on dif- **159**
ferent prerequisites combined together. Prosperity is implicitly understood with a view to the future as the sum of economic, social and technological progress. Here too, harmony with nature must be maintained and serve as a prerequisite for prosperity. The outside world, commonly named as nature, is indivisibly linked with the ecosystems, which can largely be described as nature, although a distinction can be made between animate and inanimate nature. The desire to achieve the goal of prosperity is not explicitly found in the Stockholm conferences and the Rio documentation. However, sustained, inclusive and sustainable economic growth seems to be essential for prosperity.[186] Prosperity is therefore a part of a meta-proportionality in this kind of sense to achieve. But different point of views are related to the question how to measure growth and then prosperity. Ecological economics have been emerged linking planetary health and human well-being. Alternatives to gross domestic product (GDP) as a measure of well-being are entering policy arenas at various levels of government, and advances in the field of ecological economics are being made in various countries.[187] The GA points, among others, to the Canadian Index of Well-Being, which is inspired by the genuine progress indicator and by the Gross National Happiness Index of Bhutan (→ Intro mn. 13 f., 32 ff.).

iv. Peace (P4)

The fundamental purpose and necessity of peace as a basic prerequisite for the **160**
realisation of the Global Agenda 2030 are clearly formulated in the resolution itself: 'We

---

[182] A/CONF/48/14/Ref.1, *Report of the United Nations Conference on the Human Environment*, Stockholm, 5-16 June 1972, Appendix 'Draft Declaration on the Human Environment', para. 3 (of the draft declaration).

[183] See Francioni, 'The Preamble of the Rio Declaration' in Viñuales, *The Rio Declaration on Environment and Development, A Commentary* (2015).

[184] Brown Weiss, 'Intergenerational Equity' in Wolfrum (ed), *Max Planck Encyclopedia of Public International Law* (2013); https://www.sciencedirect.com/science/article/pii/S2589811619300023#bbib62; http://www.earthsystemgovernance.org/research/taskforce-on-earth-system-law/; http://www.earthsystemgovernance.org/publications/esg-journal/; https://www.cambridge.org/core/books/architectures-of-earth-system-governance/architectures-of-earth-system-governance/705CED457997498023FA02F7425F7E2A.

[185] A/RES/70/1, preamble, 1.

[186] A/RES/70/1, para. 27.

[187] A/RES/70/1, para. 19.

are determined to foster peaceful, just and inclusive societies which are free from fear and violence. There can be no sustainable development without peace and no peace without sustainable development.'[188]

161 The fourth pillar, which is responsible for the 5 P concept, is based on peace and security. Principle 25 of the Rio Declaration already stipulated that peace, development and environmental protection are interdependent and indivisible. Sustainable development has a *conditio sine qua non* that is peace. Without peace internally and externally, sustainable development as a complex concept, as set out in the Global Agenda 2030, is hardly conceivable. Guarantors in the legal system are, for example, the UN Security Council, NATO and the serious efforts towards disarmament, the *rule of law* principle and many other contributors to the SDGs. As far as it can be observed, the Security Council has not yet had to decide whether sustainable development is threatened by measures to which the Security Council would have to respond.[189]

162 Sustainable development cannot be realised without peace and security; and peace and security will be at risk without sustainable development. The new Agenda recognises the need to build peaceful, just and inclusive societies that provide equal access to justice and that are based on respect for human rights (including the right to development), on effective rule of law and good governance at all levels and on transparent, effective and accountable institutions that women have a role in peacebuilding and State-building.[190]

163 The importance of the principle of peace is reflected in SDG 5, SDG 10 and SDG 16 (but not only there), where it is addressed in greater depth (→ Intro mn. 181, 234).

v. Partnership (P5)

164 The principle of partnership is defined as follows:

> We are determined to mobilize the means required to implement this Agenda through a revitalized Global Partnership for Sustainable Development, based on a spirit of strengthened global solidarity, focused in particular on the needs of the poorest and most vulnerable and with the participation of all countries, all stakeholders and all people.[191]

165 As a basic prerequisite for the adoption of the Global Agenda 2030 in the form of the United Nations General Assembly resolution, this principle points to the need for the global community to work together. It is through partnerships that the SDGs can be operationalised. Partnership means creating peaceful connections that are expressed at the state level at least in bilateralism, and in the sense of the Global Agenda 2030 in multilateralism. However, this principle includes not only states, but all other stakeholders and all people as well, which makes this creation of a means of implementation so special. Going beyond all existing UN mandates, it leads to far-reaching legal and non-legally assessable links and also lays the foundation for the far-reaching financing needed to implement this agenda.

166 With the stand-alone goal 17 and its own section within the Global Agenda 2030, it has been given an independent and far-reaching interpretative space. In addition,

---

[188] A/RES/70/1, preamble, para. 1.

[189] See further Viñuales, 'The Rio Declaration on Environment and Development: Preliminary Study' in Viñuales, *The Rio Declaration on Environment and Development, A Commentary* (2015), 54.

[190] A/RES/70/1, para. 35; see also para. 42: We recognize the major challenge to the achievement of durable peace and sustainable development in countries in conflict and post-conflict situations; SDG 4.7: '[...] culture of peace and non-violence; and SDG 16: [p]romote Peaceful societies.

[191] A/RES/70/1, preamble, 1.

its discussion can be found in all SDGs as well as in the other internal and external principles (→ Intro mn. 181, 234).

vi. Conclusion to the 5 Ps

Within the means of implementation and the Global Partnership the principle of **167** national ownership, labour rights as well as environmental and health standards in accordance with relevant international standards and agreements and other ongoing initiatives in this regard such as the Guiding Principles on Business and Human Rights (UNGP, Ruggie Principles) and the labour standards of the International Labour Organization (ILO), the Convention on the Rights of the Child and key multilateral environmental agreements, for parties to those agreements, are acknowledged.[192] The requirements of the follow-up and review processes manifest the ILA principle 'of integration and interrelationship, in particular in relation to human rights and social, economic and environmental objectives.'[193]

This complex and convoluted presentation of the background to the Global Agenda **168** 2030 is based on the holistic approach it pursues. The resolution attempts to fully incorporate the foundations that exist today, which have grown over decades, and to develop them further under the aspect of sustainable development. Such a comprehensive consideration is necessary due to the interrelated challenges and commitments recognised at these conferences. Therefore, integrated solutions are indispensable.[194]

2. Multilateralism and the Inherent Care for Cooperation

Furthermore, the agenda follows a systematic approach of effective multilateralism[195] **169** urging states to refrain from any unilateral economic, financial or trade measures not in accordance with international law.[196]

Multilateralism includes mutual political agreements (not only) under the direction **170** of the UN as well as multilaterally organised financial and trading sectors also comprising trade liberalisation. The UN currently renewed their commitment to multilateralism 'to find new ways of working together'.[197]

A definition of multilateralism could be described along with the fact that it refers to **171** relations among three or more states in accordance with certain principles coming up from the ground where multilateralism is rooted. Bilateralism and unilateral behaviour are the counterpart and not able to be part of the definition of multilateralism.[198] The commitment for multilateralism can be illustrated further in the call that states are strongly urged to refrain from promulgating and applying any **unilateral** measures not in accordance with international law and the Charter of the United Nations that impede the full achievement of economic and social development, particularly in developing countries.[199] In particular the urgent demand for taking action against climate change depends on the willingness to cooperate with states and international organisations in

---

[192] A/RES/70/1, para 67.
[193] A/RES/70/1, paras. 72 ff.
[194] A/RES/70/1, para. 13.
[195] A/RES/55/2, Millennium Declaration, paras. 6, 13, 30; A/RES/60/1, *2005 World Summit Outcome*, paras. 6, 16, 27, 36, 38, 78.
[196] A/RES/70/1, para 30.
[197] A/RES/74/4, para. 27(g); see in an EU context: Art. 21(1) TEU; Art. 45(1) no 1(c) TEU.
[198] Ruggie, 'Multilateralism: the anatomy of an institution' (1992) 46(3) *International Organization*, 568.
[199] A/RES/70/1, para. 30.

good faith to accept and enhance the scientific knowledge on climate change and its effects.[200]

172   States, in cooperation with relevant international organisations, shall ensure that the consideration of climate change mitigation and adaptation is integrated into their laws, policies and actions at all relevant levels, in accordance with draft Article 3(3) of the 2014 ILA Legal Principles Relating to Climate Change. According to draft Article 8, States shall cooperate with each other to implement the interrelationship principle in all areas of international law, whenever necessary, as illustrated in the following areas: Climate Change and International Trade and Investment, Climate Change and International Human Rights Law and Climate Change and Law of the Sea.

173   In sum, the term 'multilateral' is an adjective that modifies the noun 'institution'. What distinguishes the multilateral form from other forms is that it coordinates behaviour among three or more states on the basis of generalised principles of conduct.[201] The principle of multilateralism underlines as one core principle the Global Agenda 2030, the SDGs, and the follow-up and review system as well.[202] Cooperation as one of the provisions of multilateralism furthermore underlines the different partnerships and forms of cooperation between states, people and businesses. The term 'multilateralism' appears four times in the resolution to describe (among others) 'a [...] multilateral trading system under the World Trade Organization'.[203] Whether this trading system is now – at the time of writing these lines – to be cited as a striking example, can probably only be answered in the future. However, multilateralism as an elaborate tool is demonstrated through a different kind of action, notably the mainstreaming of the three dimensions of sustainable development. The UN has documented their experience that leads to the conclusion that different levels of national, interregional and international coordination and work is a process of applying the SDGs in a joint, collaborative and multilateral work.[204]

174   The task of the UN to develop a coherent system-wide strategy for the coordinated and synergistic implementation strategy bears an inherent approach of multilateralism.[205] Cooperation assists to avoid duplication among agencies, ensures synergies, and ultimately enhances the support of the United Nations system to developing countries. An inter-agency coordination mechanism in this regard is the Executive Committee of Economic and Social Affairs Plus (ECESA Plus), which brings together 50 plus UN entities in- and outside the UN System. Joint follow-up action by the UN system on specific thematic issues is also conducted through collaborative mechanisms, such as UN-Water, UN-Oceans, UN-Energy, and the High Level Task Force on Global Food and Nutrition Security.[206]

175   Cooperation also runs through the institutional measures aimed at the inherent review process. Inputs to the High-level Political Forum (HLPF) on Sustainable Development are documented on an online review platform to compile voluntary inputs from different actors such as countries participating in the voluntary national reviews

---

[200] ILA, Washington Conference (2014): *Legal Principles Relating to Climate Change*, Art. 8 (International cooperation', 8.1. and 8.4; Rajamani et al., *International Law Association – Washington Conference (2014): Legal Principles Relating to Climate Change (July 2, 2014). Report of the International Law Association's Committee on Legal Principles Relating to Climate Change* (Washington, 2014).

[201] Ruggie, 'Multilateralism: the anatomy of an institution' 46(3) *International Organization*, 574.

[202] A/RES/70/684, Summary, para 1.

[203] A/RES/70/1, SDG 17.10, and para. 68.

[204] A/RES/A/74/72 E/2019/13, para 57.

[205] A/RES/A/74/72 E/2019/13, para 58.

[206] See https://sustainabledevelopment.un.org/unsystem.

(VNR),[207] inputs from ECOSOC functional commissions, intergovernmental bodies and forums, inputs from major groups and other stakeholders, as well as contributions from multi-stakeholder partnerships and voluntary commitments. Critical milestones for the follow-up and review process must complement and support national and regional reviews and be guided by the principles as defined in the Global Agenda 2030.[208] The review architecture is centred around the HLPF which provides political guidance and recommendations and is supported by functional commissions of ECOSOC and other intergovernmental bodies and forums.[209] The whole framework represents a unique form of global participation and cooperation not only between members of the UN, countries and intergovernmental entities, but also external stakeholders of various kinds who may submit proposals.

3. Equity Principle

Even though, equity is not specifically recognised as a principle under Article 38(2) of **176** the ICJ statute, it is widely recognised as a general principle of international law[210] and is understood to mean 'fairness, impartiality and equality of treatment'.[211]

In international law, situations often arise where states have competing, or conflicting **177** interests and legal conventions cannot adequately address those, in particular in cases under environmental law where the interests of states may not be aligned due to the differences in their technological capabilities, economic development and priorities. This is also the case for the interests of different generations, as present generations may not care or know about the interests of future generations and thus, exploit the environment to the detriment of those who will live after them. The principle of 'inter-generational equity' has therefore gained high significance in international environmental law. In this regard, the principle of 'equity' has been applied in international environmental law as a way to provide standards for resource sharing and also of caring for it.[212]

The principle of equity is central to the attainment of sustainable development. It **178** refers to both inter-generational equity (the right of future generations to enjoy a fair level of the common patrimony) and intra-generational equity (the right of all peoples within the current generation of fair access to the current generation's entitlement to the Earth's natural resources).[213]

When matters of sustainable development are raised in judicial and quasi-judicial **179** decision-making, the principle of equity (incorporating notions of intergenerational equity, intragenerational equity and substantive equality) and the goal of the eradication of poverty should, at minimum, be contextualised.[214]

Several international environmental law treaties and conventions contain an explicit **180** reference to the principle of equity. For instance, UNCLOS in the preamble states the

---

[207] A/RES/70/1, para. 79.

[208] A/RES/70/684, paras. 8, 74.

[209] A/RES/70/1, para. 85; A/RES/70/684, paras. 10, 11.

[210] Henkin and Pugh and O Shachter, *International Law* (3rd ed. 1993), 114.

[211] Lapidoth, 'Equity in International Law in Equity in international law, Is there a role for equity in international law?' (1987) 81 *Am. Soc'y Int'l L. Proc.*, 126, 138.

[212] Brown Weiss, 'Intergenerational Equity', in Max Planck Encyclopedia of Public International Law (2013).

[213] ILA New Delhi Declaration of principles of international law relating to sustainable development, adopted by the International Law Association (ILA) at its 70th Conference held in New Delhi from 2 to 6 April 2002, published as UN/A/57/329.

[214] ILA, Resolution No. 7/2012, 2012 Sofia Guiding Statements on the Judicial Elaboration of the 2002 New Delhi Declaration of Principles of International Law Relating to Sustainable Development, Guiding Statement No. 4.

promotion of 'the equitable and efficient utilization' of the ocean's resources as one of its objectives, and the Convention on Biological Diversity states that 'the conservation of biological diversity, the sustainable use of its components and the fair and equitable sharing of the benefits arising out of the utilization of genetic resources'.[215]

181   The principle of equity is one of the core tenets of sustainable development and specifically the principle of inter-generational equity forms the basis of sustainable development which can already be read from the definition adopted by the Brundtland Commission.[216]

182   In the context of sustainable development goals, the principle of equity finds place in SDG 15.6 which aims to '[p]romote fair and equitable sharing of the benefits arising from the utilization of genetic resources and promote appropriate access to such resources, as internationally agreed' whereas the international principle of the *rule of law* can be directly applied to SDG 16.3. Further, sustainable development cannot be envisaged without ensuring equitable access to quality education at all levels and to health care and social protection, and this has rightly formed part of the vision of the SDGs.[217]

183   In the Global Agenda 2030, traces of equity are to be found in:

–   A world with equitable and universal access to quality education at all levels, to health care and social protection [...] (para. 7)
–   A just, equitable, tolerant, open and socially inclusive world in which the needs of the most vulnerable are met [...] (para. 8)
–   We commit to providing inclusive and equitable quality education at all levels [...] (para. 25); and
–   Promote a universal, rules-based, open, non-discriminatory and equitable multilateral trading system under the World Trade Organization (SDG 17.10)

4. Principle of Access to Justice

184   The principle of *access to justice* constitutes a fundamental cornerstone in the implementation of the Global Agenda 2030.[218] The 'equal access to justice' is realised not only as 'a basic principle of the *rule of law*'[219], but serves as an essential prerequisite for peaceful, just and inclusive societies.[220] *Access to justice* has a significant impact on the conditions of people's lives in all spheres and can be considered a central component of sustainable development in all areas of the Global Agenda 2030.[221] According to the UN, *access to justice* is defined as

> a core element of the rule of law. It is a fundamental right in itself and an essential prerequisite for the protection and promotion of all other human rights. Access to justice encompasses the right to a fair trial, including equal access to and equality before the courts, and seeking and obtaining just and

---

[215] Article 1, Convention on Biological Diversity, 1992; see further Francioni, 'Equity in International Law' in Wolfrum, *Max Planck Encyclopedia of Public International Law* (2013).

[216] A/42/427 (1987) Brundtland Report,: 'development that meets the needs of the present without compromising the ability of future generations to meet their own needs'.

[217] A/RES/70/1, para 7.

[218] Huck and Maaß, 'Gaining a Foot in the Door: Giving Access to Justice with SDG 16.3?' (2021) 2021-5 *C-EENRG Working Papers*, 7 f.

[219] Lima and Gomez, 'Access to Justice: Promoting the Legal System as a Human Right' in Leal Filho et al. (eds.), *Peace, Justice and Strong Institutions* (2021), 1 (1).

[220] A/RES/70/1, paras. 8, 35, SDG 16.3.

[221] Altmann Borbón, 'Strengthening Sustainable Development and Access to Justice: Democratising Democracy' in Ahrens et al. (eds), *Equal Access to Justice for All and Goal 16 of the Sustainable Development Agenda: Challenges for Latin America and Europe* (2019), 207 (207 ff).

timely remedies for rights violations. Guaranteeing access to justice is indispensable to democratic governance and the rule of law as well as to combat social and economic marginalization.[222]

In this context, access to justice represents the   **185**

ability to obtain a just and timely remedy for violations of rights as put forth in national and international norms and standards [...]. It applies to civil, administrative and criminal spheres of national jurisdictions, including customary and religious justice mechanisms, international jurisdictions, as well as alternative and restorative dispute resolution mechanisms [...].[223]

This definition underpins the extensive scope of this principle. Notably, *access to jus-* **186**
tice is of a hybrid character, which means that on the one hand, it represents a fundamental right itself but on the other hand further consists of numerous individual (human) rights, such as the right to a fair trial, the right to equality before the courts and before law (Art. 7 UDHR), the right to equal access to courts, the right to effective remedy (Art. 8 UDHR), the right to timely resolution and the right to non-discrimination (Art. 7 UDHR) in conjunction with the independence of the judiciary.[224] Thereby, it enables 'the realisation of a range of other civil, cultural, economic, political and social rights and is an invaluable tool for empowering the most vulnerable groups [...]'.[225] Thus, *access to justice* 'is the right of all individuals to use the legal tools and mechanisms to protect their other rights. There is no access to justice when, for economic, social, or political reasons, people are discriminated against by law and justice systems'.[226] Parties of criminal proceedings are granted the right to legal aid.[227] Moreover, access to justice is an expression of and fosters active participation in democratic governance.[228]

Remarkably, 'failure of justice systems to meet justice needs compounds inequality **187**
[and] erodes trust in institutions' (→ Goal 10 mn. 33, Goal 16 mn. 9 ff.) which thereby endangers the applicability of the *rule of law* as a whole.[229] In international law, *access to justice* is reflected several times in its various forms. Next to the UDHR, the two other major sources of human rights law, the ICCPR and the ICESCR, as well as the CEDAW,

---

[222] A/HRC/37/25, *Right to access to justice under article 13 of the Convention on the Rights of Persons with Disabilities – Report of the Office of the United Nations High Commissioner for Human Rights*, (2017), para. 3.

[223] A/HRC/25/35, *Access to justice for children – Report of the United Nations High Commissioner for Human Rights*, (2013), para. 4.

[224] Ahrens, 'SDG 16.3 Promote the rule of law at the national and international levels, and ensure equal access to justice for all: Its impact on Latin America in the light of the American Convention on Human Rights' in Ahrens et al. (eds), *Equal Access to Justice for All and Goal 16 of the Sustainable Development Agenda: Challenges for Latin America and Europe* (2019), 3 (11); Basic Principles on the Independence of the Judiciary, Adopted by the Seventh United Nations Congress on the Prevention of Crime and the Treatment of Offenders held at Milan from 26 August to 6 September 1985 and endorsed by General Assembly resolutions 40/32 of 29 November 1985 and 40/146 of 13 December 1985; The 2012 adopted UN declaration on the rule of law requires the state level to take 'all necessary steps to provide fair, transparent, effective, non-discriminatory and accountable services that promote access to justice for all, including legal aid', A/RES/67/1 (2012), para. 14.

[225] Beqiraj and McNamara, *International Access to Justice: Legal Aid for the Accused and Redress for Victims of Violence – A Report by the Bingham Centre for the Rule of Law* (2015), 8.

[226] Lima and Gomez, 'Access to Justice: Promoting the Legal System as a Human Right' in Leal Filho et al. (eds), *Peace, Justice and Strong Institutions* (2021), 1 (1).

[227] The term of legal aid encompasses 'legal advice, assistance and representation for persons detained, arrested or imprisoned, suspected or accused of, or charged with a criminal offence and for victims and witnesses in the criminal justice process that is provided at no cost for those without sufficient means or when the interests of justice so require', UN Principles and Guidelines on Access to Legal Aid in Criminal Justice Systems ('UN Principles on Legal Aid'), Resolution A/RES/67/187 (2012), para. 8.

[228] Leitch, 'Having a say: 'access to justice' as democratic participation' (2015) 4 *UCL Journal of Law and Jurisprudence*, 76 (95 ff).

[229] World Justice Project, *Realizing Justice for All – World Justice Report 2019* (2019), 5.

the CERD, the ICMW, the CRC and the CRDP contain legal expressions of the principle of *access to justice*.[230] At the European level, the European Convention on Human Rights (ECHR) and the Charter of Fundamental Rights of the EU and the Aarhus Convention of the UNECE provide provisions concerning *access to justice*.[231] For an effective *access to justice* for all, first, major barriers and obstacles have to be removed such as the often high costs of court proceedings, their complex nature, which is difficult for many people to understand and a generally fragile legal system with tenuous law enforcement.[232] Only after removing these obstacles, it can be ensured that people are given a genuine 'chance of accessing justice', which is what makes *access to justice* effective.[233]

188   The principle of *access to justice* is most visibly enshrined in SDG 16, namely in SDG 16.3 where the *rule of law* is aimed to be promoted by concomitantly ensuring equal *access to justice* for all, thus emphasising the significance of equality in *access to justice*.[234]

189   In the overall context of the Agenda 2030, effective *access to justice* positively impacts inclusive (economic) growth (→ Goal 8 mn. 4 ff, 10), social justice, the functioning of the principle of equity (→ Intro mn. 176 ff.), the well-being of the people (→ Intro mn. 216 ff., Goal 3 mn. 3, 14, 19) and the overall equality within the society (→ Goal 10 mn. 16 ff.).[235]

190   Often linked to *access to justice* is the principle of participation in the context of good governance. Following the ILA and their observation the 'principle of good governance has remained largely outside the jurisprudence of the International Court of Justice (ICJ), elements of the principle can be seen in the existence and activities of judicial and quasi-judicial bodies. This principle should be endorsed more broadly'.[236]

191   Participation is seen as a *conditio sine qua non* for responsive, transparent and accountable governments as well as a condition for the active engagement of equally responsive, transparent and accountable civil society. The need of individual participation is recognised particularly as a tool for empowerment for women (SDG 5.5).[237]

5. Principle of Integrated Nature of the Sustainable Development Goals

192   The 17 SDGs along with the 169 associated targets together aim to advance global development while securing inter-generational equity. These goals and targets are interlinked, integrated and indivisible, and thus, together form a global policy framework for sustainable development.[238] This is one of the outstanding core messages of the Global Agenda 2030; it is to be understood as a whole and not as a random collection of isolated goals that can be picked up and instrumentalised individually. As different goals may

---

[230] Arts. 7 and 8 UDHR, Arts. 2, 9, 14 and 26 ICCPR, Art. 2 ICESCR, Art. 15 CEDAW, Art. 5 (a) CERD, Art. 18 ICMW, Arts. 37 (d) and 40 CRC, Art. 13 CRDP.

[231] Arts. 6 and 13 ECHR, Art. 47 CFR, Art. 9 Aarhus Convention.

[232] UNDP, *Access to Justice – Practice Note* (2004), 4.

[233] Lima and Gomez, 'Access to Justice: Promoting the Legal System as a Human Right' in Leal Filho et al. (eds.), *Peace, Justice and Strong Institutions* (2021), 1 (1).

[234] Huck and Maaß, 'Gaining a foot in the door: Giving Access to Justice with SDG 16.3?' (2021) 2021-5 C-EENRG Working Paper.

[235] https://www.oecd.org/fr/gov/access-to-justice.htm; Manuel and Manuel, 'Achieving equal access to justice for all by 2030 – Lessons from global funds' (2018) 537 *ODI Working Paper*, 1 (8).

[236] 2012 Sofia Guiding Statements on the Judicial Elaboration of the 2002 New Delhi Declaration of Principles of International Law Relating to Sustainable Development, Resolution No. 7/2012, No. 8.

[237] A/RES/70/1, para. 20; see also ILA New Delhi Declaration of principles of international law relating to sustainable development (2002), No 5.1 'The principle of public participation and access to information and justice', published as A/57/329; Sofia Guiding Statements on the Judicial Elaboration of the 2002 New Delhi Declaration of Principles of International Law Relating to Sustainable Development, Resolution No. 7/2012, Committee on International Law on Sustainable Development, No. 7.

[238] A/RES/70/1, paras. 17 f.

impact the attainment of other goals, a systematic assessment of the trade-offs involved is necessary while implementing policies in pursuance of the SDGs. For the SDGs to be successful an integrated approach is necessary even in their implementation by every level of governance – global, regional, national, sub-national and local and all sectors of society and they must be dealt as one system.[239]

Coordination mechanisms must be set up between organisations and agencies work-   **193** ing on different goals at the national, regional and international level to ensure coherence and holistic impact of efforts as there are several interlinkages between the SDGs. These interlinkages between the SDGs have been mapped in second, interpretative part of this book.

6. Principle of the Three Dimensions of Sustainable Development

The Global Agenda 2030 adopted as a declaration committing to achieve sustainable   **194** development in three dimensions – 'economic, social and environmental – in a balanced and integrated manner'.[240] However, this commitment was made in conjunction with a commitment to international law' and consistent with 'the rights and obligations of States under international law'.[241] Balancing the three pillars of sustainable development remains one of the biggest challenges to achieving the SDGs and thus realise the vision of the Global Agenda 2030. These three pillars often conflict with one another, and pursue (focal) policies that mostly advance merely one dimension of sustainable development, must be carefully weighed against the trade-offs involved in relation to the impact of the policy on another dimension. Additionally the planet and peace must be enshrined as mentioned above (→ Intro mn. 140 ff., 160 ff.).

Sustainable development requires the balanced integration of economic, social and   **195** environmental dimensions.

Integration of these three dimensions is an urgent shift in policy approach because of   **196** the widening income and other gaps in society and the breach of planetary boundaries, which places humanity increasingly at risk.

While the precise origins of these three pillars of sustainable development as funda-   **197** mental to its conceptual formulation remain unclear, broadly, their roots are traced back to Agenda 21[242], the Brundtland Report[243] and the 2002 World Summit on Sustainable Development.[244] These three pillars are embedded in the scheme of the SDGs and their targets and scope which is discussed in greater detail in the commentary part of this book.

7. Principle of Sustainable, Inclusive and Sustained Economic Growth

The scope of the SDGs must be understood in the context of the principles of interna-   **198** tional law. 'Shared prosperity' of all states is arguably the ultimate driver of international cooperation which is reflected in several of the SDGs such as SDG 1.b, SDG 2.a, SDG 4.c, SDG 6.a, SDG 7.a, SDG 16.a. The recital to the Marrakesh Agreement Establishing

---

[239] ILA New Delhi Declaration of principles of international law relating to sustainable development (2002), No 7.1 -7.3: 'The principle of integration and interrelationship, in particular in relation to human rights and social, economic and environmental objective', published as UN/A/57/329.

[240] A/RES/70/1, para. 2.

[241] A/RES/70/1, para. 18.

[242] A/CONF.151/26/Rev.l (Vol. l) (1992) Agenda 21, para. 8.4.

[243] A/42/427 (1987) Brundtland Report.

[244] A/CONF.199/20* (2002) Report of the World Summit on Sustainable Development, Johannesburg, South Africa, 26 August–4 September 2002; Moldan, Janouskova and Hak., 'How to understand and measure environmental sustainability: indicators and targets' (2012) 17 *Ecological Indicators*, 4-13.

the World Trade Organization[245] recognises that the trade and economic relations of the parties must be conducted to raise living standards, ensure employment and sustained economic growth, and expand trade in goods and services but in a manner that is in conformity with the principles and objective of sustainable development and is consistent with the needs and concerns of varying levels of economic development. This could be understood to be between different member states but also within each state.

199   The preamble of the WTO Agreement lists various objectives, including 'raising standards of living', 'seeking both to protect and preserve the environment' and 'expanding the production of and trade in goods and services, while allowing for the optimal use of the world's resources in accordance with the objective of sustainable development'.[246] The preamble concludes with the resolution 'to develop an integrated, more viable and durable multilateral trading system'. Based on this language, we understand the WTO Agreement, as a whole, to reflect the balance struck by WTO members between trade and non-trade-related concerns. However, none of the objectives listed above, nor the balance struck between them, provides specific guidance on the question of whether Article XX of the GATT 1994 is applicable to paragraph 11.3 of China's Accession Protocol.[247]

200   The internal approach of the Global Agenda 2030 directs the application, scope and the interpretation of the SDGs and while also guiding the search for and definition of indicators, the process of measurement and the interpretation of results.

201   The UN formulated that *a new approach* is needed to address all the commitments of these major conferences and summits in an integrated way.[248]

202   At least the political will-forming process thus usually translates the guiding ideas into laws. The emergence of a normative order can thus be recognised through a systematic approach. The resolution harbours to legally binding instruments and non-legally binding instruments such as resolutions and conferences, which are also integrated into the agenda and steer the multi-faceted process of the 'new approach' of the Global Agenda 2030 in traditional international law, but also in a revitalised global partnership, which is quite a new instrument and creates an expansion of space in the dogmatic scenery of the state-state relationship.

8. The Matrix of Outcome Orientation

203   Realising the SDGs, requires the coordination of activities at different levels of policy-making – at international, national, local levels as well as across levels of governance.[249] In this context, a division can be made between vertical and horizontal policy integration. Vertical policy integration deals with the coordination of different levels of government. Coordination with local governments plays a crucial role, as many SDGs and the Global Agenda 2030 have a clear local dimension.[250] As a result, responsibilities for certain SDGs and targets lies with local governments, leaving them to make the relevant

---

[245] WTO Agreement: Marrakesh Agreement Establishing the World Trade Organization, Apr. 15, 1994, 1867 U.N.T.S. 154.

[246] WTO Agreement: Marrakesh Agreement Establishing the World Trade Organization, Apr. 15, 1994, 1867 U.N.T.S. 154, preamble.

[247] WT/DS431/AB/R, WT/DS432/AB/R, WT/DS433/AB/R, *China – Raw Materials*, Appellate Body Reports, para. 306.

[248] A/RES/70/1, paras. 11, 12, 13.

[249] UN, *Working Together: Integration, institutions and the Sustainable Development Goals, World Public Sector Report 2018* (2018), 3.

[250] A/RES/70/1, paras. 34, 45, 52, SDGs 6.b, 8.9, 12.b, 13.b, 15.9, 15.c; UN, *Working Together: Integration, institutions and the Sustainable Development Goals, World Public Sector Report 2018* (2018), 36.

policy on a national scale.[251] Moreover, in various countries many areas covered by the SDGs are the responsibility of local governments.[252] Because of their proximity to the people, they can formulate policies that are more effective.[253] This process of decentralization and devolution began in 1992 with Agenda 21 which recognised the important role of vertical integration and full involvement of local governments in sustainable development.[254] A strong normative pathway within vertical policy integration is to require governments at all levels to adopt policies consistent with the SDGS through the enactment of laws or regulations.[255] In contrast to vertical policy integration, horizontal policy integration addresses coordination across levels of governments and sectors.[256] As the SDGs are cross-sectoral, individual departments and their ministers need to work together in order to meet the SDGs.[257] Another important aspect is policy coherence. When policies are made at different levels as well as across levels of government, policy coherence is essential to avoid tensions and inconsistencies.[258] Furthermore, effective vertical and horizontal integration is crucial for the implementation as well as for the follow-up and review of the SDGs.[259] In particular, SDG 16 calls to build 'effective, accountable institution at all levels'.

9. A Revitalized Global Partnership

Stipulated in the stand-alone SDG 17, the principle of a Revitalized Global Partnership for Sustainable Development,[260] as a means of implementation, forms a core condition for the implementation of the Global Agenda 2030 (→ Intro mn. 208). The origins of global partnership in the development context go back to the report 'Our Common Future', in which the first reflections on partners were made,[261] as well as in Agenda 21 and the Rio Declaration, in which the parties affirmed their will to strengthen global partnership.[262] The concept of a global partnership for development received further concrete emphasis at the UN Millennium Summit in 2000 and specified 'in the Monterrey Consensus and the Johannesburg Plan of Implementation'.[263] It was decided 'to create an environment – at the national and global levels alike – which is conducive to development and to the elimination of poverty'.[264] In addition, MDG 8 included the pursuit of a

204

---

[251] UN, *Working Together: Integration, institutions and the Sustainable Development Goals, World Public Sector Report 2018* (2018), 36.

[252] UN, *Working Together: Integration, institutions and the Sustainable Development Goals, World Public Sector Report 2018* (2018), 36.

[253] OECD, *Better Policies for Sustainable Development 2016: A Framework for Policy Coherence* (2016), 74.

[254] UN, *Working Together: Integration, institutions and the Sustainable Development Goals, World Public Sector Report 2018* (2018), 36.

[255] UN, *Working Together: Integration, institutions and the Sustainable Development Goals, World Public Sector Report 2018* (2018), 43.

[256] UN, *Working Together: Integration, institutions and the Sustainable Development Goals, World Public Sector Report 2018* (2018), 16.

[257] UN, *Working Together: Integration, institutions and the Sustainable Development Goals, World Public Sector Report 2018* (2018), 16.

[258] OECD, *Better Policies for Sustainable Development 2016: A Framework for Policy Coherence* (2016), 73.

[259] UN, *Working Together: Integration, institutions and the Sustainable Development Goals, World Public Sector Report 2018* (2018), 24, 36.

[260] A/RES/70/1, preamble, paras. 39 f., 60, 62.

[261] A/42/427 (1987) Brundtland Report, paras. 2, 43, 46, 58.

[262] A/CONF.151/26/Rev.l (Vol. l) (1992) Agenda 21, para. 3; Tokuç, *Rio Declaration on Environment and Development (UN)* (2013), 2087; A/CONF.151/26 (Vol. I), Report of the United Nations Conference on Environment and Development (1992), preamble and principles 7 and 21.

[263] United Nations System, *A renewed global partnership for development* (2013), 3.

[264] A/RES/55/2, *United Nations Millennium Declaration*, 8 September 2000, para. 12.

global partnership for development.[265] The concept of global partnership has been continued in the 'Future we want' outcome document[266] of the Rio+20 Conference in 2012 and finally comprehensively provided for in SDG 17 (→ Goal 17 mn. 5 ff.).

205   A partnership in the sense of the Global Agenda 2030 should bring developing countries on a par with developed countries.[267] The slight but significant difference between partnerships lies in the two respective responsibilities of states: On the one hand, as duty bearer, especially with regard to human rights, and central provider of public goods and services, and on the other hand, as facilitator and mediator of actions of various public and private 'stakeholders'.[268]

206   In this context, however, it also becomes apparent that global partnership should by no means only take place between states. Important stakeholders from the global economy, politics (such as NGOs) and civil society must be included in the global partnership system in order to effectively implement and achieve the SDGs. This is particularly reflected in SDG 17.16, which provides for multi-stakeholder partnerships, and in SDG 17.17, which refers to effective public, public-private and civil society partnerships.[269] Global partnerships are to be implemented through a wide-ranging set of specific means that provide far-reaching support, especially in developing countries (→ Intro mn. 208 ff.).

207   In this context, the AAAA[270] constitutes the core document for enhanced partnership between the public and the private sector which, with a focus on the financial implementation of the SDGs, provides a framework for partnerships between the diverse stakeholders (→ Intro mn. 288 ff.). Martens summarises these aspirations as follows: 'The trend towards partnerships with the private sector is based on a simple assumption: global problems are too big and the public sector is too weak to solve them alone'.[271]

10. Means of Implementation and the Revitalized Global Partnership

208   The preamble of the Global Agenda 2030 mentions the Revitalized Global Partnership as *the* driving force to implement the agenda through such a partnership based on a spirit of global solidarity and with the participation of all countries, all stakeholders and all people.[272]

209   The concept of the demanded partnership as understood in the Rio Declaration refers to a cooperation between states and people 'in good faith and in a spirit of partnership in the fulfilment of the principles embodied in this Declaration and in the further development of international law in the field of sustainable development.'[273]

210   Apart from the history of the genesis and evolution of Principle 27, significant outcomes can be identified such as 'public-private partnership' programmes and projects

---

[265] https://www.un.org/millenniumgoals/global.shtml.

[266] A/RES/66/288, *The future we want*, with reference to 'global partnership' in paras. 34 and 55, with reference to 'new partnerships' in paras. 71 and 253.

[267] https://www.oecd.org/dev/development-posts-sdg-global-partnership.htm.

[268] Martens, 'The Role of Public and Private Actors and Means in Implementing the SDGs: Reclaiming the Public Policy Space for Sustainable Development and Human Rights' in Kaltenborn and Krajewski and Kuhn (eds), *Sustainable Development Goals and Human Rights* (2020), 207 (208).

[269] UNGA Open Working Group on Sustainable Development Goals, *TST Issues Brief: Means of Implementation – Global Partnership for achieving sustainable development* (2014), 1.

[270] A/RES/69/313, Addis Ababa Action Agenda, paras. 10, 42, 46, 48, 49, 76, 77, 115, 117, 120 and 123.

[271] Martens, 'The Role of Public and Private Actors and Means in Implementing the SDGs: Reclaiming the Public Policy Space for Sustainable Development and Human Rights' in Kaltenborn and Krajewski and Kuhn (eds), *Sustainable Development Goals and Human Rights* (2020), 207 (209).

[272] A/RES/70/1, preamble (Partnership).

[273] A/CONF.151/26 (Vol. I), Principle 27.

developed after Rio between governments, NGOs and business groups, initially under the auspices of the UN Commission on Sustainable Development (CSD), streamlined since 2000 by the UN Global Compact programme (with a focus on business stakeholders). Following the dissolution of the CSD in the wake of the Rio+20 Conference, coordination of the programme continues under the aegis of the new HLPF on Sustainable Development.[274]

The UN sought early on to provide a forum to include stakeholder input. Major **211** Groups and other Stakeholders (MGoS) were accepted as an integral part to the development, acceptance and adoption of the 2030 Agenda for Sustainable Development. Since the adoption of the agenda, those MGoS worked with Governments on implementation through projects, initiatives, advocacy, knowledge-sharing, and monitoring of the Global Agenda 2030. This work, as it is beneficiary, is to be distinguished from the specific competence of the UN. These groups, which provide content in the area of practical development, are outsourced from the UN system and are therefore self-coordinated and independent of the UN Secretariat.[275]

The input of MGoS and the engagement in the Voluntary National Review (VNR) **212** Sessions follows provisions limiting the statements within two minutes and the written statement is strongly recommended to be kept within 300 words.[276] The involvement of civil society in the programme of the main groups was launched with the aim of bringing the views of these sectors of society into the intergovernmental processes.[277] Several groups recognised as focal points for UNDESA, ECOSOC are acknowledged and have their own website sections as e.g. Business and Industry, Children and Youth, Farmers, Indigenous People, NGOs, Scientific and Technological Community, Women, Workers and Trade Unions, Persons with Disabilities, Volunteers, Ageing, Education and Academia.[278]

The CSD, established by the UNGA in December 1992 to ensure the follow-up **213** to the Earth Summit, provided access to Major Groups and was at the forefront of experimentation in this domain.[279]

> The involvement of MGoS in the HLPF has been formalised through parameters to promote transparency, enable consultation and at the same time emphasise the intergovernmental nature, namely that they are accredited to:
>
> (a) Attend all official meetings of the forum;
> (b) Have access to all official information and documents;
> (c) Intervene in official meetings;
> (d) Submit documents and present written and oral contributions;
> (e) Make recommendations;
> (f) Organize side events and round tables, in cooperation with Member States and the Secretariat.[280]

While it sounds very tempting to engage with the UN on the SDGs, it is important **214** to realise that under the premises of the UN Charter, the UN operates in the realm

---

[274] Sand, 'Principle 27, Cooperation in a Spirit of Global Partnership' in Viñuales (ed), *The Rio Declaration on Environment and Development, A Commentary*, 622.

[275] https://sustainabledevelopment.un.org/mgos.

[276] UN, HLPF, Process for Major Groups and other Stakeholders (MGoS) Engagement in the Voluntary National Review (VNR) Sessions, 2 May 2019.

[277] https://sustainabledevelopment.un.org/mgos.

[278] See https://sustainabledevelopment.un.org/mgos.

[279] See all major Documents of the CSD here: https://sustainabledevelopment.un.org/intergovernmental/csd.

[280] See A/RES/67/290, paras. 14 f.

of international law to which individuals rarely have access or are accepted on a legal basis. Representatives of the MGoS are by no means representatives or staff of the UN. They remain part of the civil society. If a group or an initiative wishes to make contact, previous registration is needed.[281]

215   The SDGs consists of 'Outcome' targets and 'Means of Implementation' (MoI) targets.[282] These MoI can be found in each of the SDGs and as a stand-alone goal in SDG 17.[283] The relevant sections are finance, technology, capacity building, trade, policy and institutional coherence, multi-stakeholder partnerships and data, monitoring and accountability.[284] According to the UN, MoI are 'the interdependent mix of financial resources, technology development and transfer, capacity-building, inclusive and equitable globalization and trade, regional integration, as well as the creation of a national enabling environment required to implement the new sustainable development agenda, particularly in developing countries'.[285] The MoI targets were introduced late in the SDG negotiation process and provided an opportunity to address some of the concerns of member states about how the SDGs should be achieved.[286] While developed countries, in particular the Group of Western European and Other States (WEOG) preferred to include MOI in each SDG, complementary to a stand-alone SDG addressing MOI, developing countries (G 77) favoured the limitation to a single stand-alone SDG.[287] They expressed concern that MoIs as sub-targets would be overly influenced by the interests of the WEOG. In this context, the issue of financing was of particular attention.[288] While the G 77 favoured specific additional external financing, the WEOG wanted to emphasise domestic financing and avoid specific commitments.[289] As a result, three separate global meetings were held devoted exclusively to financing (→ Intro mn. 43).[290]

11. Principle of Well-Being

216   The principle of well-being constitutes a multi-layered concept that extends through all areas of the Global Agenda 2030. There is no universally accepted, comprehensive definition of well-being since various scientific disciplines enlighten well-being from different angles. Thus, the whole concept of well-being is rather to be described by its numerous dimensions which give a clearer overview of the role and impact of the

---

[281] See https://sustainabledevelopment.un.org/partnerships/about#criteria.

[282] Bartram et al., 'Policy review of the means of implementation targets and indicators for the sustainable development goal for water and sanitation' (2018) 1(3) *npj Clean Water*, 1 (1).

[283] Elder and Bengtsson and Akenji, 'An Optimistic Analysis of the Means of Implementation for Sustainable Development Goals: Thinking about Goals as Means' (2016) 8 *Sustainability*, 962 (966).

[284] Elder, Bengtsson and Akenji, 'An Optimistic Analysis of the Means of Implementation for Sustainable Development Goals: Thinking about Goals as Means' (2016) 8 *Sustainability*, 962 (964).

[285] UNGA Open Working Group on Sustainable Development Goals, *Compendium of TST Issues Briefs* (2014), 107-21.

[286] Bartram et al., 'Policy review of the means of implementation targets and indicators for the sustainable development goal for water and sanitation' (2018) 1 (3) *npj Clean Water*, 1 (1).

[287] Dodds and Donoghue and Leiva Roesch, *Negotiating the Sustainable Development Goals, A transformational agenda for an insecure world* (2017), 85; Elder and Bengtsson and Akenji, 'An Optimistic Analysis of the Means of Implementation for Sustainable Development Goals: Thinking about Goals as Means' (2016) 8 *Sustainability*, 962 (962).

[288] Elder and Bengtsson and Akenji, 'An Optimistic Analysis of the Means of Implementation for Sustainable Development Goals: Thinking about Goals as Means' (2016) 8 *Sustainability*, 962 (962).

[289] Elder and Bengtsson and Akenji, 'An Optimistic Analysis of the Means of Implementation for Sustainable Development Goals: Thinking about Goals as Means' (2016) 8 *Sustainability*, 962 (962).

[290] Elder and Bengtsson and Akenji, 'An Optimistic Analysis of the Means of Implementation for Sustainable Development Goals: Thinking about Goals as Means' (2016) 8 *Sustainability*, 962 (967).

principle within the Global Agenda 2030.[291] These angles include, inter alia, the layers of social, economic, environmental, physical, emotional and cultural well-being.[292] Human well-being is regarded as the 'state of individuals' life situation'.[293] It 'incorporates both subjective and objective elements that are context and population-specific'.[294] Subjective well-being refers to a person's intrinsic, personal assessment 'of their lives as a whole' encompassing multiple factors such as 'life satisfaction, […] emotional wellbeing, and […] psychological wellbeing'.[295] A core component of[296] or even interchangeably used with subjective well-being is happiness which can be defined as 'the pursuit of positive emotion, seeking maximum pleasure and a pleasant life overall with instant gratification'.[297]

However, there are indications that well-being should be assessed more comprehensively than solely through the human-centred approach. By referring to the protection of planetary boundaries[298] and the harmony with nature approach,[299] the Global Agenda 2030 sets clear signs for the well-being of the environment (→ Goal 12 mn. 44, 56 f., 88, 95). This is illustrated by the interchangeable meanings of environmental well-being with concepts of ecological and environmental integrity as the 'wholeness of […] ecosystem structure and function' and with approaches such as 'healthy ecosystems' and 'the planet as patient'. The well-being of the environment is inextricably linked with the well-being of all humans, not only because the environment provides our vital habitat and essential natural resources such as air and water, but also because the improvement of human well-being clearly depends on the consumption and exploitation of other natural resources in order to achieve economic growth, for example (→ Goal 8, Goal 12).[300] This in turn improves the well-being of the group and of each individual. But 'if these resources are exploited at a non-sustainable rate, well-being and standard of living for future generations will be compromised'.[301] Social well-being encompasses aspects such as 'social integration, social contribution, social coherence, social actualization, and so-

217

---

[291] Stevens et al., 'Wellbeing, happiness and flourishing – Different views on a common goal' in Petermans and Cain (eds), *Design for Wellbeing – An Applied Approach* (2019), 13 (14 ff.).

[292] Manning and Fleming, 'Understanding wellbeing' in Fleming and Manning (eds), *Routledge Handbook of Indigenous Wellbeing* (2019), 3 (6 f.).

[293] McGillivray, 'Human Well-being: Issues, Concepts and Measures' in McGillivray et al. (eds), *Human Well-Being – Studies in Development Economics and Policy* (2007), 1 (3).

[294] Manning and Fleming, 'Understanding wellbeing' in Fleming and Manning (eds), *Routledge Handbook of Indigenous Wellbeing* (2019), 3 (5).

[295] Petermans and Cain, 'Setting the scene for design for subjective wellbeing' in Petermans and Cain (eds), *Design for Wellbeing – An Applied Approach* (2019), 3 (6).

[296] Adler and Fleurbaey, 'Introduction' in Adler and Fleurbaey (eds), *The Oxford Handbook of Well-Being and Public Policy* (2016), 1 (1).

[297] David and Boniwell and Conley Ayers, 'Introduction' in David and Boniwell and Conley Ayers (eds), *The Oxford Handbook of Happiness* (2013), 1 (4).

[298] A/RES/70/1, preamble ('Planet') and paras. 3, 13, 33, 59.

[299] A/RES/70/1, preamble ('Prosperity'), para. 9 and SDG 12.8.

[300] 'Economic well-being is defined as having present and future financial security. Present financial security includes the ability of individuals, families, and communities to consistently meet their basic needs (including food, housing, utilities, health care, transportation, education, childcare, clothing, and paid taxes), and have control over their day-to-day finances. It also includes the ability to make economic choices and feel a sense of security, satisfaction, and personal fulfillment with one's personal finances and employment pursuits. Future financial security includes the ability to absorb financial shocks, meet financial goals, build financial assets, and maintain adequate income throughout the life-span', Council on Social Work Education, https://www.cswe.org/Centers-Initiatives/Initiatives/Clearinghouse-for-Economic-Well-Being/Working-Definition-of-Economic-Well-Being.

[301] Neller and Neller, 'Environment well-being and human well-being' in Oswald Spring et al. (eds), *Peace Studies, Public Policy And Global Security – Encyclopedia of Life Support Systems – Vol. VI* (2010), 80 (80 ff.).

cial acceptance',[302] with the concept of social justice central role in human well-being.[303] Further general factors which heavily influence the well-being of groups and individuals range from the just and sustainable distribution of resources, access to resources, equality and inequality (of opportunities), the principle of equity and respective (human) rights (→ Goal 10).[304]

218 SDG 3 represents a special expression of human well-being by combining human health with physical and mental well-being (→ Goal 3 mn. 19).

12. Principle of International Trade

219 International trade is characterised by distinct features and 'refers to the transfer of goods and services which include capital goods from one country to another [...] [and] without international trade, nations would be limited to the goods and services produced within their own borders'.[305] The particularity of international trade is that it incurs significantly more costs and can be more difficult to conduct than trade within a country, not least due to key factors such as trade barriers like customs duties or other barriers such as different 'language, legal system or culture' between the countries.[306]

220 Early attempts of connection between trade and sustainable development were made in the outcome document of the Earth Summit in Rio de Janeiro in 1992, namely in the Agenda 21 (Chapter 2) and later in the Johannesburg Plan of Implementation (Chapters V and X). Agenda 21 provided significant impetus for a so-called 'supportive international economic environment'.[307] Such an environment is to be supported by an 'open, equitable, secure, non-discriminatory and predictable multilateral trading system'[308] in order to 'improve [all countries'] economic structures and improve the standard of living of their populations through sustained economic development'[309], '[e]conomic integration processes'[310] especially to integrate developing countries into the global trade system as well as enhanced trade liberalisation.[311] The 'Future We Want'[312] Report of the Rio+20 conference emphasises the inextricable link between international trade, the environment and development by referring to the Convention on International Trade in Endangered Species of Wild Fauna and Flora (CITES).[313]

221 In its current form, the principle of international trade has a core position within the Global Agenda 2030. This becomes evident by the agenda's open acknowledgement that

---

[302] Oades and Mossman, 'The Science of Wellbeing and Positive Psychology' in Slade and Oades and Jarden (eds), *Wellbeing, Recovery and Mental Health* (2017), 7 (9).

[303] Austin, 'Well-being and Social Justice: In Defence of the Capabilities Approach' (2016), 8 *CWiPP Working Paper*, 1 (2).

[304] Adler and Fleurbaey, 'Introduction' in Adler and Fleurbaey (eds), *The Oxford Handbook of Well-Being and Public Policy* (2016), 1 (1 ff); Talbott, *Human Rights and Human Well-Being* (2010).

[305] Hassan and Aboki and Anyesha Audu, 'International Trade: A Mechanism for Emerging Market Economies (2014) 2 *IJDEE*, 24 (26).

[306] Hassan and Aboki and Anyesha Audu, 'International Trade: A Mechanism for Emerging Market Economies (2014) 2 *IJDEE*, 24 (26).

[307] https://sustainabledevelopment.un.org/topics/trade.

[308] A/CONF.151/26/Rev.l (Vol. l), Report of the United Nations Conference on Environment and Development, Rio de Janeiro, 3–14 June 1992, Vol. I, Resolutions Adopted by the Conference (Agenda 21), para. 2.5.

[309] A/CONF.151/26/Rev.l (Vol. l) (1992) Agenda 21, para. 2.9 a.

[310] A/CONF.151/26/Rev.l (Vol. l) (1992) Agenda 21, para. 2.8.

[311] A/CONF.151/26/Rev.l (Vol. l) (1992) Agenda 21, paras. 2.7, 2.8.

[312] A/RES/66/288, *The future we want*, para. 203.

[313] CITES is an international agreement between governments which aim is to ensure that international trade in specimens of wild animals and plants does not threaten the survival of the species. The convention entered into force on 1 July 1975.

'international trade is an engine for inclusive economic growth and poverty reduction, and contributes to the promotion of sustainable development'.[314] Thus, international trade is regarded as an important 'means of implementation for the achievement of the SDGs'.[315] Similar to the Agenda 21, Agenda 2030[316] clearly underlines the core role of a 'universal, rules-based, open, transparent, predictable, inclusive, non-discriminatory and equitable multilateral trading system'[317] and trade liberalisation by openly committing to the WTO. Within the latter's framework, member states shall 'redouble their efforts to promptly conclude the negotiations on the Doha Development Agenda'.[318]

International trade is considered a catalyst for growth and sustainable development in general. Due to its possible contribution to economic growth of a country and the concomitant growth in income of the people, international trade may serve to reduce global, regional and societal inequalities ($\rightarrow$ Intro mn. 225 ff.).[319] The instruments of economic integration and trade liberalisation through the channels of the WTO intend to reduce inequalities between states which is usually measured by an increasing GDP.[320] Though, it has to be pointed out that trade can equally have a negative impact on developing countries and sustainable development.[321] Moreover, the purpose of the indicator of GDP to measure economic and sustainable growth is highly controversial ($\rightarrow$ Intro mn 225 ff.). Therefore, to make trade an all-encompassing positive instrument for achieving the SDGs, trade must become more inclusive and beneficial to all, and create wealth and decent jobs, especially for the poor. Governments should work together to resist inward-looking and protectionist pressures, and to ensure that the benefits of trade are spread more widely and more equitably. International institutions should work with governments to address any distributional effects of international trade and trade agreements and promote world trade growth that is consistent with the SDGs. National Governments should work towards improving market access conditions for the exports of Least Developed Countries (LDCs), Landlocked Developing Countries (LLDCs) and Small Island Developing States (SIDS) by reducing the trade costs facing them and simplifying and harmonising preferential rules of origin. Governments should reduce the potential for regulatory measures in the areas of food, health, environment, and labour policies to inadvertently function as non-tariff barriers to exports from developing countries.[322]

Accordingly, the Global Agenda 2030 highlights the provision of trade-related capacity-building for developing countries, including African countries, least developed countries, landlocked developing countries, SIDS and middle-income countries, including for the promotion of regional economic integration and interconnectivity.[323]

222

223

---

[314] A/RES/70/1, para. 68.

[315] https://sustainabledevelopment.un.org/topics/trade.

[316] See SDG 2.b, SDG 3.b, SDG 8.a, SDG 10.a, SDG 14.6, SDGs 17.10 to 17.12.

[317] A/RES/70/1 para. 68.

[318] A/RES/70/1, para. 68.

[319] Sarangi, 'International Trade and Sustainable Development Goals (SDGs) of Economies: A Way Forward' (2017) 8 *J. Int. Econ.*, 77 (81); Hoekman, 'Trade and the Post-2015 Development Agenda' in Helble and Shepherd (eds), *WIN–WIN – How International Trade Can Help Meet the Sustainable Development Goals* (2017), 32 (35); Urata and Narjoko, 'Trade and Inequality' in Helble and Shepherd (eds), *WIN–WIN – How International Trade Can Help Meet the Sustainable Development Goals* (2017), 175 (175 ff.).

[320] Urata and Narjoko, 'Trade and Inequality' in Helble and Shepherd (eds), *WIN–WIN – How International Trade Can Help Meet the Sustainable Development Goals* (2017), 175 (178 ff.).

[321] https://sustainabledevelopment.un.org/topics/trade.

[322] Sarangi, 'International Trade and Sustainable Development Goals (SDGs) of Economies: A Way Forward' (2017) 8 *J. Int. Econ.*, 77 (81 f.).

[323] A/RES/70/1, para. 68.

224   Next to the WTO, UNCTAD and the International Trade Center (ITC) exert influence on international trade.[324]

13. Strong Economic Foundations – Essence of Sustained, Inclusive and Sustainable Economic Growth Prosperity

225   The concept of economic growth refers to 'the increase in wealth over time and is usually measured in terms of variation in Gross Domestic Product (GDP), which comprises the entire value-added produced within national boundaries in a given timeframe'. The effects of economic growth can be recognised by multiple factors such as 'progresses in science and medicine, education and public health, trade and globalization, and stable and capable governments and institutions'.[325] Gross Domestic Product (GDP) is the principal measurement of national output, representing the total value of all final goods and services within the System of National Accounts (SNA) production boundary produced in a particular economy (that is, the dollar value of all goods and services within the SNA production boundary produced within a country's borders in a given year).[326]

226   Respectively, sustained economic growth can be defined as the event that per capita income in a society exhibits a secular or long-run tendency to expand over time, though the process may be marked by intermittent periods of stagnation and decay such as those caused by business cycles.[327]

227   Inclusive and sustainable economic growth includes social and environmental aspects so that the overall growth of the economy also leads to social development, social justice and prosperity with respect for and protection of human rights, equitable distribution of resources within society and the consequent reduction of inequalities.[328] Sustainable economic growth must take place within such a framework that resources and profits are generated, obtained and consumed without detriment to future generations since sustainable economic growth represents 'a process of growth where the welfare of society does not steadily decline over time due to excessive use of limited environmental resources or environmental damage caused by production and consumption activities'.[329] This clearly includes the sustainable and responsible management of the balance of nature and its resources[330] and is endorsed unequivocally by the provision and sustainable consumption of sustainable energy for sustainable economic growth.[331]

---

[324] https://sustainabledevelopment.un.org/topics/trade.

[325] Chiappero-Martinetti and von Jacobi and Signorelli, 'Human Development and Economic Growth' in Hölscher and Tomann (eds), *Palgrave Dictionary of Emerging Markets and Transition Economics* (2015), 224.

[326] https://unstats.un.org/sdgs/metadata/files/Metadata-08-02-01.pdf.

[327] Roy, 'Sustainable Growth' in Majumdar et al. (eds), *Fundamental Economics – Encyclopedia of Life Support Systems – Vol. II* (2010), 35 (36).

[328] Ketschau, 'Social sustainable development or sustainable social development – two sides of the same coin? The structure of social justice as a normative basis for the social dimension of sustainability' (2017) 12 *Int. J. of Design & Nature and Ecodynamics*, 338 (341); Dahan, Lerner and Milman-Sivan, 'Global labor rights as duties of justice' in Dahan, Lerner and Milman-Sivan (eds), *Global Justice and International Labour Rights* (2016), 53 (63).

[329] Roy, 'Sustainable Growth' in Majumdar et al. (eds), *Fundamental Economics – Encyclopedia of Life Support Systems – Vol. II* (2010), 35 (35).

[330] Brad et al., 'Environmentally Sustainable Economic Growth' (2016) 18 *Amfiteatru Economic*, 446 (446 ff.).

[331] Armeanu and Vintilă and Gherghina, 'Does Renewable Energy Drive Sustainable Economic Growth? Multivariate Panel Data Evidence for EU-28 Countries' (2017) 10 *Energies*, 381 (381 ff).

Economic growth is generally associated with reducing poverty and inequalities, creating jobs, promoting human and social development (e.g. in the areas of education and health) and consequently the positive transformation of a society.[332]   **228**

However, the concept of continuous economic growth, which should generate exclu-   **229** sively positive effects for society, is also criticised and called into question. Particularly with regard to the measurement of economic growth by the sole indicator of GDP, the 'Beyond GDP' approach promises for a more comprehensive assessment of people's well-being with various indicators that 'reflect the distribution of well-being in society and its sustainability across its social, economic and environmental dimensions' (→ Intro mn. 216 f.).[333] The GDP receives competition, inter alia, from the Bhutan Gross National Happiness (GNH) Index and the World Happiness Index which consciously include happiness as a significant manifestation of well-being in the assessment of the quality of life that increases through (economic) growth.[334] Furthermore, the so-called degrowth[335] movement actively confronts and criticises the paradigm of growth inspired since the Club of Rome report in 1972.[336] Mostly the limits of the Earth's ecosystem are stressed to justify that the idea of growth will do harm to the ecosystem and stands against a sustainable and a more equitable world. In this concept, the economic productivity stands against the sustainable development.[337] In this context, it is criticised that growth and trade are not aligned with the term Anthropocene which should be understood to be more than merely a scientific term for a geological epoch. This term is connected with planetary boundaries of the Earth system understandable as biophysical boundaries. From the point of view of the Anthropocene, humankind must respect those biophysical boundaries that otherwise could cause severe environmental damages. SDGs 8 and 12 are seen as fully dependent on marine and terrestrial resources (→ Goal 8 and Goal 12). Earth system governance should therefore be a guiding principle that connects the disparate SDGs in a systematic sense. It is recognised that the formation of inclusive societies is indispensable, although the outcome that the SDGs can achieve is fully dependent on the underlying Earth system and its planetary boundaries. The mere perpetuation and continuation of socio-economic growth thinking as it can be retrieved

---

[332] Department for International Development (UK), *Growth – Building jobs and prosperity in developing countries* (2008), 1 ff.

[333] Stiglitz and Fitoussi and Durand, *Beyond GDP: Measuring What Counts for Economic and Social Performance* (2018); Costanza et al, 'Beyond GDP: The Need for New Measures of Progress' (2009) 4 *The Pardee Papers*, 1 (1 ff.).

[334] https://ophi.org.uk/policy/gross-national-happiness-index/; Helliwell and Layard and Sachs and De Neve, *World Happiness Report 2021* (Sustainable Development Solutions Network, New York 2021).

[335] 'Degrowth is an idea that critiques the global capitalist system which pursues growth at all costs, causing human exploitation and environmental destruction. The degrowth movement of activists and researchers advocates for societies that prioritize social and ecological well-being instead of corporate profits, over-production and excess consumption. This requires radical redistribution, reduction in the material size of the global economy, and a shift in common values towards care, solidarity and autonomy. Degrowth means transforming societies to ensure environmental justice and a good life for all within planetary boundaries', further information: https://www.degrowth.info/en/degrowth-definition/.

[336] Meadows et al., *The Limits to Growth: A Report for the Club of Rome's Project on the Predicament of Mankind* (1972); see further: Andreucci and Engel-Di Mauro, 'Capitalism, socialism and the challenge of degrowth: introduction to the symposium' (2019) 30 *Capitalism Nature Socialism*, 176 (176 ff.); Asara et al., 'Socially sustainable degrowth as a social-ecological transformation: repoliticizing sustainability' (2015) 10 *Sustainability Science*, 375 (375 ff.); D'Alisa and Demaria and Kallis, *Degrowth: a vocabulary for a new era* (2014).

[337] Guercio, *Brief for GSDR 2015 Sustainability and economic de-growth* (2015), 1 (1 ff.).

in the SDGs as an interwoven texture conveys a missed opportunity, but not a straight-forward thinking in the face of global challenges.[338]

230   Although the critique is well formulated and deeply grounded in science, the SDGs are reflecting the sustainability of growth without neglecting it. In particular, SDG 8.4 emphasises that improving global resource efficiency in consumption and production and seeking to decouple economic growth from environmental degradation must be in line with the 10-year Framework for Sustainable Consumption and Production (10YFP) with developed countries taking the lead.

231   The 10-year planning document adopted at the Rio+20 Conference contains an initial, non-exhaustive list of five programme areas: consumer information; sustainable lifestyles and education; sustainable public procurement; sustainable buildings and con-struction; and sustainable tourism, including ecotourism.[339]

232   The 5 Ps and other principles are directing to the question of inclusive green and blue growth, which is hard to ignore (→ Intro mn. 122 ff.). An equally important role play the concepts of Material Footprint (MF) which 'is the attribution of global material ex-traction to domestic final demand of a country while the total MF is the sum of the ma-terial footprint for biomass, fossil fuels, metal ores and non-metal ores'[340] as well as Do-mestic Material Consumption (DMC).[341]

14. Conclusion

233   The internal principles enshrine a body of different legal principle shedding light on the different role the concept of sustainable development plays today in the framework of international law and in the matrix of law as such. As the ILA has pointed out in their resolutions the sustainable development as it has been evolved in the last years has been impacted by environmental law but has to be acknowledged on the basis of the text of the global agenda as a principle with a set of multiple principles applicable in range of international, interregional and national law as well. The function of the internal building blocks are serving as legal fundaments for the applicability in the overall legal framework. Science and growth do not have a legal content, but sustainability does not mean to rule against the economy and the growth but to listen and insert the outcome of science in the specific realm of creating or applying law.

XI. External Principles

234   Discussed below are those external principles, concepts and notions that are referred to in the Global Agenda 2030 resolution, either through a direct or indirect reference to an external principle or an outcome of a conference which is relevant. For example,

---

[338] Kotzé, 'The Sustainable Development Goals: an existential critique' in French and Kotzé (eds), *Sustainable Development Goals – Law, Theory and Implementation* (2018), 51 ff.

[339] High-Level Political Forum on Sustainable Development, *The 10 Year Framework of Programmes on Sustainable Consumption and Production Patterns (10YFP)* (2012), 3; https://sustainabledevelopment.un.org/index.php?page=view&type=400&nr=1444&menu=35.

[340] https://wesr.unep.org/indicator/index/8_4_1.

[341] 'Domestic Material Consumption (DMC) and MF need to be looked at in combination as they cover the two aspects of the economy, production and consumption. The DMC reports the actual amount of material in an economy, MF the virtual amount required across the whole supply chain to service final demand. A country can, for instance have a very high DMC because it has a large primary production sector for export or a very low DMC because it has outsourced most of the material intensive industrial process to other countries. The material footprint corrects for both phenomena', UNStats, *SDG indicator metadata, SDG 8.4.1*, Last updated: 4 February 2021.

the Global Agenda 2030 states that, 'The new Agenda is guided by the purposes and principles of the Charter of the United Nations [...] is grounded in the Universal Declaration of Human Rights, international human rights treaties [...] is informed by other instruments such as the Declaration on the Right to Development.'[342] The Global Agenda 2030 also 'reaffirms the outcomes of all major United Nations conferences and summits'.[343] The main questions that arise in this context concern the implications of these references and the formulation of a normative core of the Global Agenda 2030 precipitated by their inclusion. While the Global Agenda 2030 recognises that the 'challenges and commitments identified at these major conferences and summits are interrelated and call for integrated solutions' and also that in order to address these challenges effectively, there is a need for a 'new approach', it is not apparent whether this new approach has any standard of normativity at its core. Indeed, it could be argued that the concept of sustainability has some degree of normativity intrinsically tied to it. However, whether the Global Agenda 2030 envisions the setting of normative standards to achieve the SDGs is not obvious.

Another important question that arises is to what extent the references have an **235** impact on the interpretation of the targets of specific SDGs and on the indicators that are supposed to measure the outcome of the targets.

1. Charter of the United Nations

The Global Agenda 2030 as such and the SDGs are guided by the purposes and **236** principles of the Charter of the UN and by international law.[344] The Global Agenda 2030 contains a reference to Chapter I of the UN Charter which lays out the purposes and principles of the UN.[345] These principles include, among others, the equality and self-determination of nations, respect of human rights, fundamental freedoms and the obligation to cooperate with the UN Security Council in resolving conflicts. These 'purposes and principles' reflect a premise that the effectiveness of the UN would be enhanced with broad guidelines to guide the actions of its organisations and member states.[346] There are several principles of the UN that fundamentally guide both the UN and member states in achieving the Global Agenda 2030. These include:

- Sovereign equality of member states
- Fulfilment in good faith of obligations under the Charter
- Peaceful settlement of international disputes
- Respect for the territorial integrity or political independence of each state
- Assistance to the UN in its actions in accordance with the Charter
- Acting in accordance with the Charter to maintain international peace and security
- Non-interference by the UN in state affairs[347]

2. Universal Declaration of Human Rights

Without any exaggeration, the Universal Declaration of Human Rights (UDHR), **237** composed as a non-legal binding declaration, is widely acknowledged as a milestone

---

[342] A/RES/70/1, para. 10.

[343] A/RES/70/1, para. 11.

[344] A/RES/70/1, para. 10.

[345] See also McIntyre, 'International water law and SDG 6: mutually reinforcing paradigms' in French and Kotzé (eds), *Sustainable Development Goals, Law, Theory and Implementation* (2018), 175.

[346] Rensmann, 'Reform' in Wolfrum and Simma (eds), *The Charter of the United Nations, A Commentary* (2012), 29.

[347] Art. 2 UN Charter.

document in the history of human rights. The UDHR was drafted by representatives with different legal and cultural backgrounds from all regions of the world and proclaimed by the UNGA in Paris on 10 December 1948.[348] The UDHR sets out fundamental human rights to be universally protected and was translated into over 525 languages.[349] The instructive legislative history reveals the following statements: Although not considering the Declaration to have legal authority as an interpretation of the relevant provisions of the Charter,

> the representative of the United Kingdom stated that the "moral authority of the document that would be adopted" by the General Assembly, nevertheless, "would serve as a guide to Governments in their efforts to guarantee human rights by legislation and through their administrative and legal practice.[350]

The representative of Mexico

> remarked that the draft Declaration was of the greatest importance. It would not involve legal obligations, but that would not diminish the value of the document. He said that it would define the human rights, which States undertook to recognize and would serve as a criterion to guide and stimulate them. At the moment, he contended, it would be difficult to go further.[351]

238   The implication for each step considered, from their perspective of interpretation, means that the UDHR must be a guide and a legal instrument to steer the considerations and the trajectory of the applicable SDGs or indicators, or even the outcome of those indicators, which could mean that the outcome could lead to any political and legal decision whether it is any kind of omission or any kind of action.

239   One further fundamental principle of the Global Agenda 2030 and the SDGs is grounded in the UDHR[352] which follows the fundamental principles of human dignity, fairness, equality, mutual respect and independence (→ Intro mn. 53 ff.).[353]

3. International Human Rights Treaties

240   Beyond being grounded in the UDHR, the Global Agenda 2030 pays full attention to international human rights treaties.[354] There are nine core conventions of the UN pertaining to human rights. Some of the treaties are supplemented by optional protocols dealing with specific concerns. Each of these instruments has established a committee of experts to monitor implementation of the treaty provisions by its State parties.

241   Both the Millennium Declaration and the World Summit Outcome refer to the UN Charter,[355] to the principles of justice and international law[356] and all (internationally recognised) human rights.[357]

242   There are nine (9) core international human rights instruments including the optional protocols listed below[358]:

---

[348] UN General Assembly, Universal Declaration of Human Rights, 1948, 217 A (III).

[349] https://www.ohchr.org/en/udhr/pages/introduction.aspx.

[350] UN, *Yearbook of the United Nations 1948 – 49* (1950), 527.

[351] UN, *Yearbook of the United Nations 1948 – 49* (1950), 527.

[352] A/RES/70/1, para. 10.

[353] Universal Declaration of Human Rights, 1948, 217 A (III), Art. 29, para. 2.

[354] A/RES/70/1, para. 10.

[355] A/RES/55/2, *United Nations Millennium Declaration*, paras. 1, 3, 4, 9; A/RES/60/1, *2005 World Summit Outcome*, paras., *inter alia*, 2, 5, 70, 71, 72, 73, 139, 146.

[356] A/RES/55/2, *United Nations Millennium Declaration*, paras. 4, 30; A/RES/60/1, *2005 World Summit Outcome*, paras. 5, 77.

[357] A/RES/55/2, *United Nations Millennium Declaration*, paras. 4, 9, 24, 25; A/RES/60/1, *2005 World Summit Outcome*, paras. 4, 9, 12, 119, 120, 121.

[358] https://www.ohchr.org/en/professionalinterest/pages/coreinstruments.aspx.

1. International Convention on the Elimination of All Forms of Racial Discrimination, 1965
2. International Covenant on Civil and Political Rights, 1966
3. International Covenant on Economic, Social and Cultural Rights, 1966
4. Convention on the Elimination of All Forms of Discrimination against Women, 1979
5. Convention against Torture and Other Cruel, Inhuman or Degrading Treatment or Punishment, 1984
6. Convention on the Rights of the Child, 1989
7. International Convention on the Protection of the Rights of All Migrant Workers and Members of Their Families, 1990
8. International Convention for the Protection of All Persons from Enforced Disappearance, 2006
9. Convention on the Rights of Persons with Disabilities, 2006
10. Optional Protocol to the Covenant on Economic, Social and Cultural Rights, 2008
11. Optional Protocol to the International Covenant on Civil and Political Rights, 1966
12. Second Optional Protocol to the International Covenant on Civil and Political Rights, aiming at the abolition of the death penalty, 1989
13. Optional Protocol to the Convention on the Elimination of Discrimination against Women, 1999
14. Optional protocol to the Convention on the Rights of the Child on the involvement of children in armed conflict, 2000
15. Optional protocol to the Convention on the Rights of the Child on the sale of children, child prostitution and child pornography, 2000
16. Optional Protocol to the Convention on the Rights of the Child on a communications procedure, 2014
17. Optional Protocol to the Convention against Torture and Other Cruel, Inhuman or Degrading Treatment or Punishment, 2002
18. Optional Protocol to the Convention on the Rights of Persons with Disabilities, 2006

4. Committee on World Food Security, 1974

The Committee on World Food Security (CFS) was founded in 1974. Faced with **243** a food and financial crisis as well as the problem of rising hunger coupled with an ineffective CFS, the Committee agreed to reform in 2009.[359] According to its reform, CFS is an international and intergovernmental platform following the aim to eliminate hunger, ensure food security and nutrition for all as well as the realisation of the right to adequate food in the light of national food security.[360]

The Global Agenda 2030 [r]eaffirms the important role and inclusive nature of the **244** Committee on World Food Security and welcome the Rome Declaration on Nutrition and the Framework for Action.[361]

Its work is supported by the FAO, IFAD and WFP.[362] The Committee developed **245** Voluntary Guidelines on the Responsible Governance of Tenure of Land, Fisheries and Forests in the Context of National Food Security (CFS-VGGT), Principles for Responsible Investment in Agriculture and Food Systems (CFS-RAI) and Framework for Action

---

[359] CFS:2009/2 Rev.2, paras. 1 f.
[360] CFS:2009/2 Rev.2, para. 11; CFS:2009/2 Rev.2, para. 4.
[361] A/RES/70/1, paras. 17, 24, SDG 2.
[362] CFS 2016/43/6, para 2.

for Food Security and Nutrition in Protracted Crisis (CFS-FFA), all of which were published together in the Global Strategic Framework for Food Security and Nutrition (GSF) in 2017.[363] In addition, in 2019 the CFS adopted a multi-year Programme of Work 2020-2023 with the overall objective to 'eliminat[e] hunger and malnutrition through improved policy convergence/coherence at global level', following three strategic objectives.[364] With regard to the Global Agenda 2030, the Committee supports its implementation, in particular SDG 2.[365]

5. Declaration on the Right to Development, 1986

246   The Declaration on the Right to Development (RTD) was adopted by the UNGA in 1986 with the objective to recognise an inalienable right to development and to refocus the goal of development to improve the well-being of the people. It also recognised that 'all peoples are entitled to participate in, contribute to, and enjoy economic, social, cultural and political development, in which all human rights and fundamental freedoms can be fully realized.'[366] Without ending the violation and abuse of basic human rights, e.g. through racism, racial discrimination, and the situations that enable such abuse, including occupation, foreign interference or dominance, 'development' cannot be envisaged, which is emphasised by this declaration.[367] The consensus-building regarding the scope of the RTD has been an ongoing process.[368] The first time the right was described as an 'integral part of fundamental human rights' was in the Vienna World Conference on Human Rights which reaffirmed the right to development as established in the Declaration on the Right to Development.[369] The RTD is now reflected in several documents of the UN[370] and is also reaffirmed in the Global Agenda 2030,[371] although a normative core is missing furnishing it as a legal norm.

6. United Nations Framework Convention on Climate Change, 1992

247   The United Nations Framework Convention on Climate Change (UNFCCC) is a universal international agreement that considers climate change as 'the common concern of humankind' and aims to promote 'international cooperation on climate change'.[372]

248   Furthermore, it shall determine 'the parameters for global discourse and [providing] an essential forum for dialogue and decision-making on climate change matters'.[373] It was adopted on 9 May 1992 at the UNGA in New York, subsequently ratified at the UNCED (Earth Summit) and entered into force in 1994. The UNFCCC emerged alongside the other outcome documents of the Earth Summit, namely the CBD, the

---

[363] CFS, *Global Strategic Framework for Food Security and Nutrition (GSF)* (2017), 12 ff.

[364] CFS 2019/46/7, paras. 2, 4, 14, 52.

[365] CFS 2016/43/6, para. 4.

[366] A/RES/41/28, *Declaration on the Right to Development*, Art. 1.

[367] 41/28, *Declaration on the Right to Development*, Arts. 5, 6.

[368] On the US opposition to the RTD see Marks, 'The Human Right to Development: Between Rhetoric and Reality' (2004) 17 *Harvard Human Rights Journal*, 137, 141 ff.

[369] A/CONF.157/23, *Vienna Declaration on Programme of Action*, para. 10.

[370] A/RES/55/2, *United Nations Millennium Declaration*, para. 11.

[371] A/RES/70/1, para. 10.

[372] Tomlinson, *Procedural Justice in the United Nations Framework Convention on Climate Change – Negotiating Fairness* (2015), 4.

[373] Carlarne and Gray and Tarasofsky, 'International Climate Change Law: Mapping the Field' in Carlarne and Gray and Tarasofsky (eds), *The Oxford Handbook of International Climate Change Law* (2016), 4.

Agenda 21, the Rio Declaration and the Forest Principles.[374] In 2021, the UNFCCC has 197 Parties, making its membership almost universal.[375]

The substantive scope of the UNFCCC encompasses the basic definitions, the objective and principles of the Convention (Arts. 1-3), respective commitments on mitigating and globally adapting to climate change and on financing and technology transfer (Arts. 4-6), as well as the specific mechanisms for implementing the Convention (Arts. 7-14).[376] In this context, as stated in Art. 2, the overall 'ultimate' objective of the UNFCCC is to 'achieve [...] stabilization of greenhouse gas concentrations in the atmosphere at a level that would prevent dangerous anthropogenic interference with the climate system' which is to be assessed as a declarative 'non-binding aim, rather than as a legal commitment'.[377] This level is to be reached as slow or fast as the ecosystems are able to adapt naturally to climate change, that the food production is not threatened and that sustainable economic development is possible.[378] Thus, the UNFCCC clearly combines international efforts against climate change with the environmental, social and economic levels of sustainable development, with outstanding connections to SDG 13, SDG 2 and SDG 8 (→ Goal 13, Goal 2, Goal 8).[379] However, combating the consequences of climate change requires funding from the developed countries. **249**

SDG 13.a therefore calls for the implementation of **250**

> the commitment undertaken by developed-country parties to the United Nations Framework Convention on Climate Change to a goal of mobilizing jointly $100 billion annually by 2020 from all sources to address the needs of developing countries in the context of meaningful mitigation actions and transparency on implementation and fully operationalize the Green Climate Fund through its capitalization as soon as possible.

Moreover, as a 'focal point for the development of the norms and principles of international climate change law', the UNFCCC is based upon several principles such as the principle of intergenerational equity,[380] the principle of common but differentiated responsibilities and respective capabilities (CBDR),[381] the principle of precaution and **251**

---

[374] For this reason, the UNFCCC is also referred to as one of the three Rio Conventions, together with the further Rio Conventions of the UN Convention on Biological Diversity and the UN Convention to Combat Desertification, which was adopted three years later, Freestone, 'The United Nations Framework Convention on Climate Change—The Basis for the Climate Change Regime' in Carlarne and Gray and Tarasofsky (eds), *The Oxford Handbook of International Climate Change Law* (2016), 99 f.

[375] https://knowledge4policy.ec.europa.eu/organisation/unfccc-united-nations-framework-convention -climate-change_en.

[376] Bodansky and Brunnée and Rajamani, *International Climate Change Law* (2017), 118.

[377] Bodansky and Brunnée and Rajamani, *International Climate Change Law* (2017), 120 ff.

[378] Art. 2 UNFCCC.

[379] Bodansky and Brunnée and Rajamani, *International Climate Change Law* (2017), 125.

[380] Art. 3.1 UNFCCC.

[381] The CBDR principle has become an important principle in international climate change law and originates in Principle 7 of the Rio Declaration. Carlarne, Gray and Tarasofsky describe the CBDR principle in the following way:

[...] the international community shares a common responsibility for protecting the global atmosphere, but that the responsibility for addressing global climate change should be differentiated among States (arguably) based on historical contribution to the problem as well as present capacity to respond [...].

Respectively, parties to the Convention are classified in three annexes, depending on, among other things, whether they are developed states or not. In this vein, developed countries are the main responsible in achieving the goal of the UNFCCC, however, the notion of 'respective capabilities' imposes obligations on each party of the UNFCCC, regardless of being developed or developing, Carlarne and Gray and Tarasofsky, 'International Climate Change Law: Mapping the Field' in Carlarne and Gray and Tarasofsky (eds), *The Oxford Handbook of International Climate Change Law* (2016), 14 f.; see also ILA, *New Delhi Declaration of Principles of International Law Relating to Sustainable Development* (2002).

cost-effectiveness[382] as well as the principle of sustainable development.[383] Special attention is given to the priorities of developing countries' related to 'economic and social development and poverty eradication' which are to be fully taken into account by developed countries in their commitments (→ Goal 8, Goal 1).[384] One of the commitments of the parties to the UNFCCC is to publish regular reports on their greenhouse gas emissions and the respective developments.[385]

252   The UNFCCC as a framework convention is decisively complemented by so-called Conferences of the Parties (COP) which regularly take place and whose outcome documents concretise the Parties' commitments under the UNFCCC. The most known COPs of the past and future are the COP3 in Kyoto 1997 (Kyoto Protocol), COP7 in Marrakesh 2001 (Marrakesh Agreement), COP15 in Copenhagen 2009 (Copenhagen Accord), COP16 in Cancún 2010 (Cancún Agreement), COP21 in Paris 2015 (Paris Agreement) and COP26 in Glasgow 2021.

253   It is criticised that the UNFCCC is weak in meeting its objectives not least because the UNFCCC is more of a negotiating platform and therefore depends to a large extent 'on the ability of the Parties to reach an agreement under an appropriate timescale'.[386] Moreover, despite the supplementary outcome documents to the UNFCCC calling for a reduction in greenhouse gas emissions, there is still no concrete greenhouse gas 'concentration level that the regime should seek to achieve, pursuant to Article 2'.[387]

7. Rio Declaration on Environment and Development, 'Earth Summit', 1992

254   The Rio Declaration on Environment and Development (Rio Declaration) is a key reference document on sustainable development that was produced in the United Nations Conference on Environment and Development (UNCED) which was held in Rio de Janeiro, Brazil, from 3-14 June 1992, also known as the Earth Summit. It sets out 27 principles which, although not binding, have become the basis for defining moral obligations of states in relation to the environment. The Rio Declaration cannot be understood without its historical context, and its focus on balancing the conflicting interests of environment protection and economic and social development of developing countries.[388] This is reflected in the principle of CBDR which allocates responsibilities relating to environmental protection according to the environmental burdens of states and the technologies and financial resources at their disposal.[389] The differentiated responsibility of industrialised and developing countries was one of the most debated issues in the genesis of the Rio Declaration, as it led to conflicts regarding the distribu-

---

[382] Art. 3.3 UNFCCC.

[383] See also Principle 2 of the Rio Declaration; within the preamble, reference is further made to Principle 21 of the Stockholm Declaration. Besides, developing countries express further concerns to be considered, especially by developed countries, such as the respect for the principle of sovereignty, respect for the 'priority needs of developing countries for the achievement of sustained economic growth and the eradication of poverty' (SDG 8 and SDG 1) and access to resources to meet the growing energy consumption of developing countries (SDG 7), preamble of the UNFCCC.

[384] Art. 4.7 UNFCCC.

[385] Art. 4.1 (a) UNFCCC.

[386] Boyle and Singh Ghaleigh, 'Climate Change and International Law beyond the UNFCCC' in Carlarne and Gray and Tarasofsky (eds), *The Oxford Handbook of International Climate Change Law* (2016), 29.

[387] See Huck et al., 'The Right to Breathe Clean Air and Access to Justice – Legal State of Play in International, European and National Law' (2021) 13(10) *International Environmental Law (eJournal)*; Bodansky and Brunnée and Rajamani, *International Climate Change Law* (2017), 126.

[388] Viñuales, *Rio Declaration on Environment and Development, A Commentary* (2015), 3.

[389] A/CONF.151/26/Rev.1 (Vol. I), *Report of the United Nations Conference on Environment and Development*, Principle 7.

tion of blame between states for the current state of the environment and its legal status is still disputed today.[390] This debate also shines light on the difficulties of concluding agreements between states and the importance of cooperation. The Global Agenda 2030 has reaffirmed all the principles of the Rio Declaration on Environment and Development.[391]

8. Conference of the Parties to the Convention on Biological Diversity, 1993

The Convention on Biological Diversity (CBD) was adopted at the United Nations   255
Conference on Environment and Development (UNCED) in 1992, entering into force in 1993.

In this regard, the Global Agenda 2030 states:

> [t]o promote sustainable tourism, to tackle water scarcity and water pollution, to strengthen cooperation on desertification, dust storms, land degradation and drought and to promote resilience and disaster risk reduction. Therefore [w]e look forward to the thirteenth meeting of the Conference of the Parties to the Convention on Biological Diversity to be held in Mexico.[392]

The CBD received a great response, which led to many countries signing the Convention already during the conference.[393] The outcome document was the result of North-South compromises reached in a complex negotiation process.[394] Developing countries were in a strong negotiating position as their countries contain the largest amount of biodiversity in the world.[395] They were willing to make concessions because the CBD gave them greater control over access to their biological resources.[396] The Convention recognises the far-reaching importance of biodiversity and thus the need to conserve it not only for present but also for future generations.[397] The three main objectives of the Convention are 'conservation of biodiversity, sustainable use of its components and the fair and equitable sharing of the benefits arising out of the utilization of genetic resources'.[398] In order to realise the same benefits for all the Convention aims at granting access to genetic resources and the transfer of relevant technologies.[399] Thus, the Convention goes beyond the aspect of conservation (including in-situ and ex-situ conservation) and preservation of the environment and its biodiversity.[400] It also addresses the aspects of sustainable use of biological resources, the regulation of access to genetic resources, and the sharing of benefits arising from the use of these resources.[401] Considering sovereignty rights[402], the CBD follows the principle that states

---

[390] See Cullet, 'Principle 7: Common but Differentiated Responsibilities' in Viñuales, *The Rio Declaration on Environment and Development, A Commentary* (2015), 236.

[391] A/RES/70/1, para 11.

[392] A/RES/70/1, para. 33.

[393] McGraw, 'The CBD – Key Characteristics and Implications for Implementation' (2002), 11 (1) *RECIEL*, 17 (17).

[394] McGraw, 'The CBD – Key Characteristics and Implications for Implementation' (2002), 11 (1) *RECIEL*, 17 (27).

[395] McGraw, 'The CBD – Key Characteristics and Implications for Implementation' (2002), 11 (1) *RECIEL*, 17 (17).

[396] McGraw, 'The CBD – Key Characteristics and Implications for Implementation' (2002), 11 (1) *RECIEL*, 17 (17).

[397] Convention on Biological Diversity, preamble.

[398] Convention on Biological Diversity, Art. 1.

[399] Convention on Biological Diversity, Art. 1.

[400] McGraw, 'The CBD – Key Characteristics and Implications for Implementation' (2002), 11 (1) *RECIEL*, 17 (23.

[401] McGraw, 'The CBD – Key Characteristics and Implications for Implementation' (2002), 11 (1) *RECIEL*, 17 (23).

[402] Convention on Biological Diversity, Art. 1.

have 'the sovereign right to exploit their own resources pursuant to their own environmental policies, and the responsibility to ensure that activities within their jurisdiction or control do not cause damage to the environment of other States or of areas beyond the limits of national jurisdiction.'[403]

9. Programme of Action of the International Conference on Population and Development, 1994

257   The shaping of a population is inextricably linked with development and realisation of environmental goals. As the pressure on basic resources increases with a constantly growing population, leading to scarcity and often their complete depletion, not only the environment but the population that heavily depends on such resources as well as economic development suffers. It was in the background of this realisation that there is a need for 'increased international cooperation in regard to population in the context of sustainable development' that the 'International Conference on Population and Development' was held in Cairo, Egypt in 1994.[404] The conference adopted a Programme of Action which built on the 'international consensus that has developed since the World Population Conference at Bucharest in 1974 and the International Conference on Population at Mexico City in 1984, to consider the broad issues of and interrelationships between population, sustained economic growth and sustainable development, and advances in the education, economic status and empowerment of women'.[405] In particular the provision of sexuality education and sexual and reproductive health (SRH) services belongs to current challenges.[406]

258   In this context, the Programme of Action set out interdependent qualitative and quantitative goals that were to be realised within 20 years[407] (extended for further action[408]) that advance population and development objectives.[409] The Programme of Action conceptualised 'sustainable development' as 'a means to ensure human well-being, equitably shared by all people today and in the future' and stressed that the 'interrelationships between population, resources, the environment and development should be fully recognised, properly managed and brought into harmonious, dynamic balance.'[410]

259   While the Programme of Action did not set any definite population related goals, it emphasised the need to internalise population concerns in planning and actions for achieving sustainable development.[411] With the Global Agenda 2030, all principles of the

---

[403] Convention on Biological Diversity, Art. 3.

[404] A/CONF.171/13/Rev.1, *Report of the International Conference on Population and Development*, Chapter I, Annex, preamble, para. 1.2.

[405] A/CONF.171/13/Rev.1, *Report of the International Conference on Population and Development*, Chapter I, Annex, preamble, para.1.5.

[406] Chandra-Mouli et al., 'Twenty years after International Conference on Population and Development: where are we with adolescent sexual and reproductive health and rights?' (2015) 56.1 *Journal of Adolescent Health*, S1 (S2).

[407] A/CONF.171/13/Rev.1, *Report of the International Conference on Population and Development*, Chapter I, Annex, preamble, para. 1.4.

[408] A/RES/65/234, *Follow-up to the International Conference on Population and Development beyond 2014*.

[409] A/CONF.171/13/Rev.1, *Report of the International Conference on Population and Development*, Chapter I, Annex, preamble, para. 1.12.

[410] A/CONF.171/13/Rev.1, *Report of the International Conference on Population and Development*, Chapter I, Annex, preamble, Chapter II, Principle 6.

[411] United Nations Population Fund (UNFPA), *Programme of Action of the International Conference on Population Development, Twentieth Anniversary Edition* (2014), 214.

Programme of Action of the International Conference on Population and Development have been reaffirmed.[412]

10. World Summit for Social Development, 1995

The World Summit for Social Development was held in Copenhagen in March **260** 1995. The summit ended with the adoption of the Copenhagen Declaration on Social Development,[413] and the Programme of Action of the World Summit for Social Development.[414] The Copenhagen Declaration on Social Development adopted ten commitments that were to promote the goals of

(1) enabling people to achieve social development by taking several measures at national and international level;
(2) eradicating poverty;
(3) full employment;
(4) social integration and non-discrimination;
(5) equality and equity between men and women;
(6) universal and equitable access to quality education;
(7) economic, social and human resource development of Africa and lease developed countries;
(8) ensuring that structural development goals include social development goals;
(9) efficient utilisation of resources for social development;
(10) improving and strengthening cooperation and partnerships at the international, regional and sub-regional level.

These commitments serve to 'guide national, regional and internationally agreed **261** policies, rights and obligations'.[415] The main objective of the summit was to put people and social integration at the centre of the development goals.[416] The issues highlighted at the summit were of particular relevance to the work of the International Labour Organization (ILO) and to this extent the summit successfully placed issues of poverty reduction, employment and social integration on the table for discussion at a global level and linked it to the development agenda.[417]

11. Beijing Platform for Action, 1995

Hailed as 'most comprehensive global policy framework and blueprint for action',[418]   **262** the Beijing Declaration[419] and Platform for Action for Equality, Development and Peace[420] was the outcome document of the fourth world conference on women held in Beijing in 1995 (**Beijing Conference**). Even though the first world conference on women

---

[412] A/RES/70/1, *Transforming our world: the 2030 Agenda for Sustainable Development*, para. 11.

[413] A/CONF.166/9, *Report of the World Summit for Social Development*, Chapter I, Resolution 1, Annex I.

[414] A/CONF.166/9, *Report of the World Summit for Social Development*, Chapter I, Resolution 1, Annex II.

[415] Department of Social and Economic Affairs, *The Social Summit Ten Years Later* (2005), 5.

[416] A/CONF.199/20, *Report of the World Summit on Sustainable Development*, Chapter I, Resolution 1, Annex I, para. 8.

[417] Hunt and Jacob and Gallagher, 'Progress, Problems, and Prospects: R2P 15 Years after the World Summit' (2020) 12.4 *Global Responsibility to Protect*, 359-62.

[418] UN Women, *Beijing Declaration and Platform for Action: Beijing+5 Political Declaration and Outcome* (2014).

[419] A/CONF.177/20/Rev.1, *Report of the Fourth World Conference on Women*, Chap. I, Resolution 1, Annex II.

[420] A/CONF.177/20/Rev.1, *Report of the Fourth World Conference on Women*, Chap. I, Resolution 1, Annex II.

was held as long ago as 1975 in Mexico City,[421] which was followed by the second the third conference in Copenhagen in 1980[422] and in Nairobi in 1985,[423] the Beijing conference achieved remarkable feat as it produced a framework that covered broad-spanning areas concerning women's rights and freedoms. These include environment, decision-making, girl children, economy, poverty, violence,[424] human rights, education and training, institutional mechanisms, health, media and armed conflict.

263   To date, the Beijing Declaration and the Platform for Action provide guidance for countries to take definitive steps towards women's rights and freedoms and realising gender equality in all spheres of life. Twenty years after the adoption of the Beijing Declaration and Platform for Action, it has been noted that the change towards gender equality has been very slow.[425]

264   Moreover, climate change has not been a political priority[426] and that with the current pace of progress, it would take us 75 years to reach a stage where women can get equal pay for equal work as men.[427] Gender equality remains a critical priority in the post-2015 agenda and finds focus in SDG 5. Realising equal treatment and human rights of women and girls is fundamental to achieving sustainable development. Lessons from implementation of the Platform of Action shed light on five areas that must be prioritized to accelerate the achievement of the goal of gender equality:

> transforming discriminatory social norms and gender stereotypes; transforming the economy to achieve gender equality and sustainable development; ensuring the full and equal participation of women in decision-making at all levels; significantly increasing investments in gender equality; and strengthening accountability for gender equality and the realization of the human rights of women and girls.[428]

12. Millennium Declaration, 2000

265   On 8 September 2000, the UNGA adopted goals regarding peace, development, environment, human rights, the vulnerable, hungry, and poor, Africa, and the UN named the Millennium Declaration.[429] The adoption of the Millennium Declaration was the major outcome of the Millennium Summit and led to the adoption of the Millennium Development Goals (MDGs), comprising eight international development goals which were to be achieved by 2015.

266   The SDGs are the successors to the MDGs and the new agenda is largely built on the Millennium Declaration.[430] The 2015 MDG Report identifies unresolved issues, with

---

[421] E/CONF.66/34, *Report of the World Conference of the International Women's Year.*

[422] A/CONF.94/35, *Report of the World Conference of the United Nations Decade For Women: Equality, Development and Peace.*

[423] A/CONF.116/28/Rev.1, *Report of the World Conference to Review and Appraise the Achievements of the United Nations Decade for Women: Equality, Development and Peace.*

[424] Pietrobelli et al., 'Violence against women in Italy after Beijing 1995: the relationship between women's movement(s), feminist practices and state policies.' (2020) 28.2 *Gender & Development*, 377-92; Rudolf, 'Freedom from Violence, Full Access to Resources, Equal Participation, and Empowerment: The Relevance of CEDAW for the Implementation of the SDGs' in Kaltenborn and Krajewski and Kuhn, *Sustainable Development Goals and Human Rights*, 73, 75 ff.

[425] UN Women, *The Beijing Declaration and Platform For Action Turns 20* (2015), 9.

[426] Allotey and Pascale and Denton, 'Challenges and priorities for delivering on the Beijing Declaration and Platform for Action 25 years on'(2020) 396.10257 *The Lancet*, 1053-5.

[427] International Labour Organization (ILO), *Report of the Director General: A New Era of Social Justice, One-hundredth Session, International Labour Conference* (2011).

[428] UN Women, *The Beijing Declaration and Platform For Action Turns 20* (2015),5.

[429] A/RES/55/2, *United Nations Millennium Declaration.*

[430] A/RES/70/1, para. 10.

the result that the Global Agenda 2030[431] explicitly draws on 'the achievements of the Millennium Development Goals and seeks to address their unfinished business'.[432] The review of the MDG Agenda concluded structural and systematic strengths and a number of weaknesses of the contributions.[433]

13. World Summit on Sustainable Development (WSSD), Johannesburg Summit, 2002

The World Summit on Sustainable Development (WSSD) held in Johannesburg in **267** 2002 was convened to review the progress on the sustainable development agenda since the Earth Summit in 1992. The key outcome documents of the WSSD comprise the Johannesburg Plan of Implementation[434] and the Johannesburg Declaration on Sustainable Development.[435] In contrast to the Rio Declaration, which was instrumental in shifting the focus of the global community towards sustainable development, the WSSD contributed more to the implementation of the resolutions taken at the Rio conference by focusing on strengthening multilateral cooperation between governments and institutions. The WSSD was also called the 'Summit of Implementation'.[436] The implementation plan comprises 11 chapters, including one chapter that deals specifically with Africa (others include poverty eradication, changing unsustainable patterns of consumption and production, health, means of implementation, small island developing states, among others).[437] An interesting aspect of the WSSD outcomes were the 'partnerships' which were 'understood as policy networks or multi-sectoral alliances that are designed specifically to implement legal and political agreements in the area of sustainable development'.[438] While these partnerships open the doors for multi-level cooperation between governmental and non-governmental organisations, they are voluntary in nature and their role in the environmental governance framework is not clearly defined.

The success of the WSSD was questioned, even though it reaffirmed the goals set out **268** in the Rio Declaration and, in the absence of new commitments, set eager timetables for meeting specific targets towards sustainable development.[439] The Global Agenda 2030 has reaffirmed all the principles of the WSSD.[440]

---

[431] UN, *The Millennium Development Goals Report 2015* (2015).

[432] A/RES/70/1, para. 2.

[433] See in particular: UN System Task Team on the Post-2015 UN Development Agenda, Review of the contributions of the MDG Agenda to foster development: Lessons for the post-2015 UN development agenda (Discussion Note), March 2012, 6, 8.

[434] A/CONF.199/20, *Report of the World Summit on Sustainable Development, Chapter I*, Resolution 2.

[435] A/CONF.199/20, *Report of the World Summit on Sustainable Development, Chapter I*, Resolution 1.

[436] Streck, 'The World Summit on Sustainable Development: Partnerships as New Tools in Environmental Governance' (2002) 13(1) *Yearbook of International Environmental Law*, 63 (64).

[437] A/CONF.199/20, *Report of the World Summit on Sustainable Development, Chapter I*, Resolution 2; See on public participation, access to information and justice: Cordonier Segger and Khalfan and Gehring and Toering, 'Prospects for Principles of International Sustainable Development Law after the WSSD: Common but Differentiated Responsibilities, Precaution and Participation'(2003) 12(1) *Review of European, Comparative & International Environmental Law*, 64.

[438] Streck, 'The World Summit on Sustainable Development: Partnerships as New Tools in Environmental Governance' (2002) 13(1) *Yearbook of International Environmental Law*, 63 (70).

[439] Vina and Hoff and DeRose, 'The Outcomes of Johannesburg: Assessing the World Summit on Sustainable Development' (2003) 23 *Sais Review*, 53 (8).

[440] A/RES/70/1, para. 11.

Introduction

14. New Partnership for Africa's Development (NEPAD), 2002

269   At the beginning of the 21st century, the Heads of State or Government of the then Organization of African Unity (OAU) initiated the Africa's first political framework to strategically address the socio-economic development of the continent, the New Partnership for Africa's Development (NEPAD), which was ultimately adopted by the new African Union (AU) in 2002.[441] The new framework which is 'based [...] on a commitment to the Millennium Development Goals (MDGs)'[442] grew out of the conviction of African states and peoples to free themselves from the effects of the colonial past and to shape the future in a self-determined way. NEPAD thereby represents a strategic framework that is actively led by Africa itself underpinning Africa's strive for independent engagement to solve pan-African challenges to exploit its potential for positive, sustainable change.[443] The programme of the New Partnership for Africa's Development[444] are combined with the African Union's Agenda 2063 of importance and stated to be explicitly integral to the Global Agenda 2030.[445]

270   In this context, NEPAD strives to achieve the following far-reaching and overall objectives: the eradication of poverty, the impetus for and achievement of sustainable growth and development and the full integration of Africa in the global economic system (Africa as an active partner in the world economy).[446] Equally in focus stands the empowerment of women[447] and the general halting of 'the [...] marginalisation of Africa in the globalisation process and the social exclusion of the vast majority of its peoples'.[448] To effectively achieve these objectives, several principles are set out in the NEPAD. Restoring peace and security, enhancing democracy and establishing good governance on the political, economic and corporate level are thereby regarded as preconditions for sustainable development. Furthermore, fostering regional and global economic integration, building 'more productive partnerships with bilateral and multilateral partners'[449] and 'private sector development partners'[450] as well as 'domestic ownership and leadership' belong to NEPAD's principles.[451] Moreover, NEPAD encompasses a set of sectoral priorities to 'bridge existing gaps between Africa and the developed countries', e.g. in the fields of infrastructure, energy, health, education and water and sanitation.[452] Thus, NEPAD shall help Africa to renew its international position and relation with developed countries 'while improving the standard of living of the African people'.[453] Since 2018, the former NEPAD Planning and Coordinating Agency (NEPAD Agency)

---

[441] https://au.int/en/organs/nepad; https://www.un.org/development/desa/socialperspectiveondevelopment/issues/new-partnership-for-africas-development-nepad.html.

[442] Funke and Nsouli, 'The New Partnership for Africa's Development (NEPAD): Opportunities and Challenges' (2003) WP/03/69 *IMF Working Paper*, 1 (4).

[443] Hope, 'From crisis to renewal: Towards a successful implementation of the New Partnership for Africa's Development' (2002) 101 *African Affairs*, 387 (389).

[444] A/57/304, Annex.

[445] Reaffirming the importance and supportive function: A/RES/70/1, paras. 42, 64.

[446] A/57/304, para. 1.

[447] A/57/304, para. 67.

[448] A/57/304, para. 2.

[449] Hope, 'From crisis to renewal: Towards a successful implementation of the New Partnership for Africa's Development' (2002) 101 *African Affairs*, 387 (395).

[450] Funke and Nsouli, 'The New Partnership for Africa's Development (NEPAD): Opportunities and Challenges' (2003) *IMF Working Paper WP/03/69*, 1 (3).

[451] Hope, 'From crisis to renewal: Towards a successful implementation of the New Partnership for Africa's Development' (2002) 101 *African Affairs*, 387 (390 ff).

[452] A/57/304, paras. 98 ff.

[453] Hope, 'From crisis to renewal: Towards a successful implementation of the New Partnership for Africa's Development' (2002) 101 *African Affairs*, 387 (389).

was transformed into African Union Development Agency-NEPAD (AUDA-NEPAD). This new entity is now serving not only the purposes of the NEPAD but focuses on the AU's overall development project's implementation, including the Agenda 2063.[454] A profound partnership with the Council for Scientific and Industrial Research (CSIR) shall 'accelerate technology development in Africa'.[455]

Despite its intention to make Africa more financially independent, NEPAD is criti-   271
cised for still being largely dependent on foreign financial support for its full implementation.[456] Besides, the goals are defined in a highly broad manner meaning that they need to be broken down into sub-goals to successfully implement them at regional and local level.[457]

15. World Summit Outcome, 2005

On 24 October 2005, the UNGA adopted the World Summit Outcome which was the   272
resulting agenda of the 2005 World Summit convened as a follow-up to the Millennium Summit held in 2000. The World Summit Outcome focussed on development, human rights, security issues and strengthening of the UN.[458] The outcome document adopted at the World Summit further reaffirmed the commitment of all member states to achieving the MDGs.[459]

16. Istanbul Declaration and Programme of Action, 2011

The Istanbul Declaration and Programme of Action were adopted during the Fourth   273
United Nations Conference on the Least Developed Countries in Turkey in 2011 (→ Intro mn. 274 ff.).

17. Fourth United Nations Conference on the Least Developed Countries, 2011

The UNGA began emphasising the importance of identifying least developed coun-   274
tries[460] subsequent to the request of the United Nations Conference on Trade and Development (UNCTAD) in 1968 which called for special measures to benefit least developed countries by international bodies that were generally responsible for assisting developing countries.[461] At present, the list of least developed countries consists of 46 countries and is reviewed every three years by the United Nations Economic and Social Council (ECOSOC).[462] A three-fold criteria is used by ECOSOC to identify least developed countries which is (1) gross national income per capita, (2) development of human assets and (3) economic and environment vulnerability.[463] The UN recognises least

---

[454] AUDA-NEPAD, https://www.nepad.org/microsite/who-we-are-0#about_us.

[455] AUDA-NEPAD, https://www.nepad.org/news/press-release-auda-nepad-and-csir-partnership-accelerate-africas-transformation-agenda.

[456] https://www.cigionline.org/articles/will-nepad-become-another-failed-african-initiative/.

[457] Funke and Nsouli, 'The New Partnership for Africa's Development (NEPAD): Opportunities and Challenges' (2003) WP/03/69 *IMF Working Paper*, 1 (22).

[458] A/RES/60/1, *2005 World Summit Outcome*, para. 16.

[459] A/RES/60/1, *2005 World Summit Outcome*, para. 17.

[460] A/RES/2724(XXV), *Identification of the Least Developed Among the Developing Countries*.

[461] Proceedings of the United Nations Conference on Trade and Development, Second Session, Vol. I and Corr.1 and 3 and Add.1 and 2, Report and Annexes (United Nations Publication, Sales No.: E.68.II.D.14), 54.

[462] https://unctad.org/topic/least-developed-countries/recognition.

[463] UN Committee for Development Policy and UN Department of Economic and Social Affairs, *Handbook on the Least Developed Country Category: Inclusion, Graduation and Special Support Measures* (2018), 7 f.

developed countries 'low-income countries confronting severe structural impediments to sustainable development. They are highly vulnerable to economic and environmental shocks and have low levels of human assets'.[464]

275   The First United Nations Conference on the Least Developed Countries (UNCLDC) was held in 1981 in Paris to respond to the special needs of the least developed countries and their challenges.[465] The second UNCLDC was held in 1990 in Paris,[466] and the third in Belgium in 2001.[467] The most recent and fourth UNCLDC was decided to be held in Turkey in 2011.[468] The objective of the conference was to undertake a comprehensive appraisal of the action plan that was adopted at the third UNCLDC that was held in 2001 in Brussels, Belgium, as well as to formulate policies in the light of the appraisal and new challenges in the next decade.[469] The conference adopted the Istanbul Declaration and the Programme of Action for the Least Developed Countries for the decade 2011-2020. The Istanbul Declaration recognised that least developed countries (LDC) require special attention and targeted support to address their developmental needs. The Istanbul Declaration acknowledged the importance of Official Developmental Assistance (ODA) from developed countries to least developed countries (LDC) in this context. Some of the emerging challenges to which the LDC are particularly exposed, such as economic shocks, climate change, increasing natural hazards and disasters, as well as actions by the least developed countries and their developing counterparts to increase the resilience of and mitigate the impact on the LDC, were also outlined at the conference.[470] A report published in 2020 on the implementation of the Programme of Action adopted in the Fourth UNCLDC notes that three countries have graduated from the category of LDC since 2011 and five more will graduate by 2024.[471] However, the report also notes that LDC will be negatively affected by the current SARS-CoV-2 pandemic[472] which has severely impacted them and exacerbated their struggles. This global crisis is expected to drive an additional 32 million people in least developed countries into absolute poverty.[473] The fifth UNCLDC, to be held in Doha, Qatar in January 2022 will be critical to assess the suffering and enable and accelerate the recovery of LDC from the pandemic.

18. United Nations Conference on Sustainable Development, 2012

276   The UN Conference on Sustainable Development was held in Rio de Janeiro, Brazil in 2012,[474] twenty years after the UN Conference on Environment and Development

---

[464] https://www.ohchr.org/EN/Issues/Development/Pages/LeastDevelopedCountries.aspx.

[465] A/RES/34/203, *United Nations Conference on Least Developing Countries.*

[466] A/RES/42/177, *Second United Nations Conference on the Least Developed Countries.*

[467] A/RES/52/187, *Implementation of the Programme of Action for the Least Developed Countries for the 1990s.*

[468] A/RES/63/227, *Implementation of the Brussels Programme of Action for the Least Developed Countries for the Decade 2001–2010*; A/RES/64/213, *Fourth United Nations Conference on the Least Developed Countries.*

[469] A/CONF.219/7, *Report of the Fourth United Nations Conference on the Least Developed Countries.*

[470] A/CONF.219/7, *Report of the Fourth United Nations Conference on the Least Developed Countries,* 37-41.

[471] A/75/72–E/2020/14, *Implementation of the Programme of Action for the Least Developed Countries for the Decade 2011–2020,* 2.

[472] A/75/72–E/2020/14, *Implementation of the Programme of Action for the Least Developed Countries for the Decade 2011–2020,* 4.

[473] UNCTAD/LDC/2020, *The Least Developed Countries Report 2020 – Productive capacities for the new decade,* 13.

[474] A/RES/64/236, *Implementation of Agenda 21, the Programme for the Further Implementation of Agenda 21 and the outcomes of the World Summit on Sustainable Development*; A/66/287, *Implementation*

in 1992 and was also held in Rio (Rio+20 conference). The outcome document of the conference 'The future we want' resolved to accelerate progress towards sustainable development by deciding to adopt a set of goals for sustainable development which should incorporate all three dimensions of sustainable development and their interlinkages.[475] By doing so, the conference set out the vision for post-2015 agenda for sustainable development. 'The future we want' recognised that the MDGs were a useful tool to focus on specific development goals within the broader agenda of sustainable development and it was decided that goals for sustainable development would be developed without taking away the focus from achieving the MDGs.[476] The conference also stressed the importance of a green economy for achieving sustainable development. While the adoption of green economy policies was left to individual governments according to their national policies,[477] the outcome document sets out guidelines for such policies in the context of sustainable development and poverty eradication, defining the contours within which they should be developed.[478] Another significant outcome of the conference was the decision to establish a high-level political forum 'building on the strengths, experiences, resources and inclusive participation modalities of the Commission on Sustainable Development, and subsequently replacing the Commission'.[479] The objectives of the HLPF included, *inter alia*, providing leadership and recommendations for sustainable development, delivering a platform for dialogue, reviewing progress on sustainable development commitments, facilitating the sharing of best practice, strengthening the use of evidence in policy making and improving data collection and analysis.[480]

19. 10-Year Framework of Programmes on Sustainable Consumption and Production Patterns, 2012

The 10 Year Framework of Programmes on Sustainable Consumption and Production Patterns (10YFP) was adopted as a voluntary programme during the United Nations Conference on Sustainable Development (Rio+20) in Brazil in 2012 and addresses the aspect, that 'fundamental changes in the way societies produce and consume are indispensable for achieving global sustainable development'.[481] **277**

This concept was echoed in the Global Agenda 2030, which stipulates that states, stakeholders and individuals should move 'towards more sustainable patterns of consumption and production' and that the 10YFP should be implemented to fundamentally change the way our societies produce and consume goods and services.[482] Sustainable consumption and production is the core of SDG 12 while SDG 12.1 and SDG 8.4 directly call for the implementation of the 10YFP. **278**

These programmes should be designed to support the achievement of the goals and objectives defined in chapter 3 'Changing unsustainable patterns of consumption and production' of the Johannesburg Plan of Implementation covering a time period from 2012 to 2022 while being built on Agenda 21, the Rio Declaration on Environment **279**

---

of Agenda 21, the Programme for the Further Implementation of Agenda 21 and the outcomes of the World Summit on Sustainable Development; A/RES/66/197, Implementation of Agenda 21, the Programme for the Further Implementation of Agenda 21 and the outcomes of the World Summit on Sustainable Development.
[475] A/RES/66/288, *The future we want*, para. 246.
[476] A/RES/66/288, *The future we want*, para. 246.
[477] A/RES/66/288, *The future we want*, para. 59.
[478] A/RES/66/288, *The future we want*, para. 58.
[479] A/RES/66/288, *The future we want*, para. 84.
[480] A/RES/66/288, *The future we want*, para. 85.
[481] A/RES/66/288, para. 226; A/CONF.216/5, para. 1.
[482] A/RES/70/1, para. 28.

and Development as well as the Johannesburg Plan of Implementation.[483] It consists of six programmes: (1) Consumer information, (2) Sustainable lifestyles and education, (3) Sustainable public procurement, (4) Sustainable buildings and construction, (5) Sustainable Tourism and (6) Sustainable Food System.[484] While the first five programmes were already part of the adopted 10YFP at Rio+20, the programme on Sustainable Food Systems was added in 2014 after a proposal from FAO and UNEP.[485] The 10YFP includes a common vision, common values, function, organisational structure and means of implementation. The programme aims to improve international cooperation and achieve a shift towards sustainable consumption and production. Moreover, it intends to 'develop[...], replicat[e] and scal[e] up [sustainable consumption and production] and resource efficiency initiatives, at national and regional levels, decoupling environmental degradation and resource use from economic growth, and thus increasing the net contribution of economic activities to resource efficiency and productivity, poverty eradication, social development and environmental sustainability'.[486]

20. African Union's Agenda 2063 and the Agenda 2063 – The Africa We Want, 2013

280   The 'Agenda 2063 – The Africa We Want'[487] is a comprehensive and ambitious 'master plan'[488] to fundamentally transform 'the African continent for the next fifty years commencing in 2013'.[489] The desire for such an agenda was initially expressed at the ceremony of the 50th anniversary of the African Union (AU) at the Organization of African Unity in 2013 together with the jointly declared Solemn Declaration and ultimately 'adopted at the 24th Ordinary Session of the African Heads of State and Government in 2015 in Addis Ababa'.[490] As a 'normative and strategic framework'[491] for all African countries with far-reaching goals and aspirations, it 'aims to achieve socio-economic and political transformation through the optimum use of natural resources'.[492] Emanating from and guided by the African Union's overall vision of 'an integrated, prosperous and peaceful Africa, driven by its own citizens, representing a dynamic force in the international arena' the Agenda 2063 builds upon the will and the driving power of the African people and thus stakeholders from diverse areas of society, politics and business, such as 'civil society, women and youth, the private sector [and] [...] cultural organisations' were involved in the negotiation process.[493] In alignment with the Solemn Declaration which emphasises the right to self-determination of the

---

[483] A/CONF.216/5, para. 1.

[484] A/CONF.216/5, para. 8; UNDESA, *The 10 Year Framework of Programmes on Sustainable Consumption and Production Patterns (10YFP)* (2014), 4.

[485] UNDESA, *The 10 Year Framework of Programmes on Sustainable Consumption and Production Patterns (10YFP)* (2014), 4.

[486] UNDESA, *The 10 Year Framework of Programmes on Sustainable Consumption and Production Patterns (10YFP)* (2014), 1.

[487] Mentioned to be supported in A/RES/70/1, paras. 42, 64.

[488] https://au.int/en/agenda2063/overview.

[489] African Peer Review Mechanism, *Agenda 2063 and SDGs – Implementation in Africa* (2020), 32.

[490] Tella, 'Agenda 2063 and Its Implications for Africa's Soft Power' (2018) 49 *Journal of Black Studies*, 714 (715).

[491] Tella, 'Agenda 2063 and Its Implications for Africa's Soft Power' (2018) 49 *Journal of Black Studies*, 714 (716).

[492] Mhangara et al., 'Towards the Development of Agenda 2063 Geo-Portal to Support Sustainable Development in Africa' (2019) 8 *ISPRS Int. J. Geo-Inf.*, 1 (4).

[493] Addaney, 'The African Union's Agenda 2063: Education and Its realization' in Onuora-Oguno, Egbewole and Kleven (eds), *Education Law, Strategic Policy and Sustainable Development in Africa – Agenda 2063* (2018), 181 (185).

African continent in the post-colonial era,[494] Agenda 2063 directs its action towards seven particular aspirations that should guide the strategic implementation of the entire agenda, namely in the fields of (1) inclusive growth and sustainable development, (2) political integration of the African continent, (3) good governance, democracy, respect for human rights, justice, and the *rule of law*, (4) peace and security in Africa, (5) cultural identity, values, heritage and ethics, (6) development which is driven by people (particularly women and youth) and (7) Africa as a strong, united, and influential global player and partner.[495] Respectively, the Agenda 2063 seeks for an all-encompassing, multifaceted transformation of the African continent in numerous action areas ranging from education, health, agriculture, the environment, gender equality, infrastructure to finance.[496] However, there is criticism that Agenda 2063 lacks the necessary means for comprehensive practical implementation and a firm commitment by states and the AU.[497]

Agenda 2063 had a significant influence on the framing of the Global Agenda 2030 **281** and its SDGs. Four key African institutions, the New Partnership for Africa's Development (NEPAD) Agency, the UNDP Regional Bureau for Africa, the UN Economic Commission for Africa and the African Development Bank designed a Common African Position (CAP) to represent the African voice in the Agenda 2030's negotiation process. Remarkably, the CAP was 'the only continental contribution towards' the Global Agenda 2030 in so that the CAP's proposals are clearly and to a large extent reflected in the Global Agenda 2030. Consequently, there is about 90 per cent congruence between the Agenda 2063 and the Global Agenda 2030.[498] The African Union's Agenda 2063 is recognised as important and is explicitly considered inherent to the global 2030 Agenda.[499]

21. Rome Declaration on Nutrition and the Framework for Action, 2014

The Rome Declaration on Nutrition together with a Framework for Action was **282** adopted in Rome in 2014 during the Second International Conference on Nutrition hosted by the FAO and WHO. The Rome declaration is highlighted as welcome in the Global Agenda.[500]

It was noted that since the last International Conference on Nutrition in 1992, **283** improvement had been made globally in reducing hunger and malnutrition.[501] Nevertheless, progress has been unequal and not made fast enough.[502] Therefore, the Rome Declaration aims to 'eradicate hunger and prevent all forms of malnutrition worldwide [...]; as well as reverse the rising trends in overweight and obesity and reduce the burden of diet-related noncommunicable diseases in all age groups'.[503] It reaffirms 'the right of everyone to have access to safe, sufficient, and nutritious food, consistent with the right to adequate food and the fundamental right of everyone to be free from

---

[494] African Union Commission, *Agenda 2063 – The Africa We Want – First Ten Year Implementation Plan 2013-2023* (2015), 11.

[495] African Union, *Agenda 2063 – The Africa We Want* (2015), para. 8.

[496] https://au.int/agenda2063/goals.

[497] Addaney, 'The African Union's Agenda 2063: Education and Its realization' in Onuora-Oguno, Egbewole and Kleven (eds), *Education Law, Strategic Policy and Sustainable Development in Africa – Agenda 2063* (2018), 181 (182).

[498] African Peer Review Mechanism, *Agenda 2063 and SDGs – Implementation in Africa* (2020), 35.

[499] A/RES/70/1, paras. 42, 64: 'reaffirm the importance of supporting'.

[500] A/RES/70/1, para. 24.

[501] ICN2 2014/3 Corr.1, para. 1.

[502] ICN2 2014/3 Corr.1, para. 1.

[503] ICN2 2014/2 para. 15(a).

hunger'.[504] The accompanying Framework for Action, as a guide for implementation, is voluntary.[505] It recommends 60 policy options and strategies 'to create an enabling environment and to improve nutrition in all sectors', which may be incorporated into national nutrition, health, agriculture, development and investment plans.[506] The recommendations address the following issues: enabling environment, sustainable food system, international trade and investment, nutrition education and information, social protection, health system, breastfeeding, wasting, stunting, childhood overweight and obesity, anemia in women of reproductive age, health service, water, sanitation, hygiene, food safety, antimicrobial resistance and accountability.[507] The Rome Declaration on Nutrition and the Framework for Action are linked to SDG 2, 3, 5, 6, 16.

22. Second United Nations Conference on Landlocked Developing Countries, 2014

284   Landlocked developing countries, as the name suggests, are those that lack territorial access to the sea. The challenges faced by landlocked developing countries pertain to their geographical disadvantage of not having territorial access to sea which restricts them from the use of direct water transport for international or global trade, directly increasing the costs of transport and trade. At present, there are 32 landlocked developing countries.[508] The Second United Nations Conference on Landlocked Developing Countries was held in Vienna, Austria in 2014 and adopted the Vienna Programme of Action for Landlocked Developing Countries for the Decade 2014-2024.[509] The conference sought to review the Almaty Programme of Action which was adopted at the International Ministerial Conference of Landlocked and Transit Developing Countries and Donor Countries and International Financial and Development Institutions on Transit Transport Cooperation in 2003 in Almaty, Kazakhstan, as well as to identify evolving needs and challenges of landlocked countries. Since the Almaty Programme of Action, several polices have been initiated by landlocked countries and transit countries to address 'physical and non-physical aspects of transit transport'[510] in particular the inability to secure their access to seaports.

285   Landlocked countries are under strain with the lack of access to seaports. The priorities for action for the Second United Nations Conference on Landlocked Developing Countries include: Fundamental transit policy issues; Infrastructure development and maintenance: (a) Transport infrastructure, (b) Energy and information and communications technology infrastructure; International trade and trade facilitation: (a) International trade, (b) Trade facilitation; Regional integration and cooperation; Structural economic transformation; Means of implementation.[511]

---

[504] ICN2 2014/2 para. 3.
[505] ICN2 2014/3 Corr.1, para. 2.
[506] ICN2 2014/3 Corr.1, paras. 2, 4.
[507] ICN2 2014/3 Corr.1, para. 4.
[508] https://www.un.org/ohrlls/content/list-lldcs.
[509] A/CONF.225/7, *Report of the second United Nations Conference on Landlocked Developing Countries*.
[510] A/RES/69/15, SIDS Accelerated Modalities of Action (SAMOA) Pathway, para. 7; Faye et al., 'The challenges facing landlocked developing countries' (2004) 5.1 *Journal of Human Development*, 31-68.; Transport, in particular transit through corridors are analysed here: Arvis and Smith and Carruthers, *Connecting landlocked developing countries to markets: Trade corridors in the 21st century* (2011).
[511] A/RES/69/15, SIDS Accelerated Modalities of Action (SAMOA) Pathway, paras. 23-72.

23. Third International Conference on Small Island Developing States (SIDS), 2014

Small Island Developing States (SIDS) were recognised in Agenda 21 as a distinct **286** group of countries which are ecologically fragile and vulnerable. It was noted that 'their small size, limited resources, geographic dispersion and isolation from markets, place them at a disadvantage economically and prevent economies of scale.'[512] SIDS have a large share of global biodiversity owing to their geographic isolation.[513] The use of science is acknowledged to strengthen the political discourse and decision making[514] in the challenges faced by SIDS are akin to those faced by island states but with further constraints of small land size, SIDS are particularly vulnerable to the impacts of climate change.[515] At present, SIDS comprises 38 member states and 20 non-member states or associate members of the Regional Commission.[516] The Third International Conference on Small Island Developing States was held in Samoa in 2014 with the theme 'The sustainable development of small island developing States through genuine and durable partnerships'.[517] This conference culminated in the SIDS Accelerated Modalities of Action (SAMOA) Pathway, which recognises the particular vulnerability of SIDS to the adverse impacts of climate change and sea level rise, and impedes their efforts to achieve sustainable development.[518] With the inevitable further exacerbation of the effects of climate change on SIDS, their very existence is under threat. The high cost of adaptation and mitigation requires international cooperation.[519] The SAMOA Pathway pledges efforts towards implementation of the Barbados Programme of Action for the Sustainable Development of Small Island Developing States (BPOA)[520] adopted at the UN Global Conference on the Sustainable Development of SIDS in 1994 along with the Barbados Declaration[521] and the Mauritius Strategy of Implementation for the further implementation of the BPOA adopted at the high level Mauritius International Meeting held in Mauritius in 2005 to review the BPOA.[522] The SAMOA Pathway also expanded the scope of the UN Office of the High Representative for the Least Developed Countries, Landlocked Developing Countries and Small Island Developing States (UN-OHRLLS) established in 2001 with functions recommended by the Secretary General relating to least developed countries, landlocked developing countries and SIDS to

---

[512] A/CONF.151/26 (Vol. II), *Report of the United Nations Conference on Environment and Development*, para. 17.123.

[513] A/CONF.151/26 (Vol. II), *Report of the United Nations Conference on Environment and Development*, para. 17.124.

[514] Thompson, 'Science diplomacy within sustainable development: A SIDS perspective'(2018) 9 *Global Policy*, 46.

[515] A/CONF.151/26 (Vol. II), *Report of the United Nations Conference on Environment and Development*, para. 17.125; Scobie, 'Sustainable development and climate change adaptation: Goal interlinkages and the case of SIDS' in Klöck and Fink (eds), *Dealing with climate change on, small islands: Towards effective and sustainable adaptation?* (2019), 101.

[516] https://www.un.org/ohrlls/content/about-small-island-developing-states.

[517] A/RES/67/207, *Follow-up to and implementation of the Mauritius Strategy for the Further Implementation of the Programme of Action for the Sustainable Development of Small Island Developing States*; A/RES/66/288, *The future we want*.

[518] A/RES/69/15, *SIDS Accelerated Modalities of Action (SAMOA) Pathway*, para. 31.

[519] Office of the High Representative for the Least Developed Countries, Landlocked Developing Countries and Small Island Developing States.

[520] A/RES/69/15, *SIDS Accelerated Modalities of Action (SAMOA) Pathway*, para. 22.

[521] A/CONF.167/9, *Report of the Global Conference on the Sustainable Development of Small Island Developing States*.

[522] United Nations General Assembly Resolution (A/RES/65/2), Outcome document of the High-level Review Meeting on the Implementation of the Mauritius Strategy for the Further Implementation of the Programme of Action for the Sustainable Development of Small Island Developing States.

ensure the mainstreaming of the Samoa Pathway and issues related to small island developing States in the work of the United Nations system and enhance the coherence of the issues of those States in United Nations processes, including at the national, regional and global levels, and continue to mobilize international support and resources to support the implementation of the Samoa Pathway by small island developing States.[523]

24. Third United Nations World Conference on Disaster Risk Reduction, 2015

287   The Sendai Framework for Disaster Risk Reduction 2015-2030 is a voluntary, non-binding agreement adopted at the third UN World Conference on Disaster Risk Reduction in Sendai in 2015. The adoption of the Sendai Framework was received with particular interest by the Asia-Pacific Region.[524] The adoption was preceded by an intensive and difficult drafting process and took place at a time when the impact of disaster was increasing.[525] As a result, disasters hampered the achievement of sustainable development.[526] The Sendai Framework is the successor to the Hyogo Framework for Action 2005-2015, so the Sendai Framework was built on the lessons learned from its predecessor.[527] It aims to protect life, health, livelihoods, ecosystems, cultural heritage and critical infrastructure from natural and man-made hazards to create a safer world for the present and the future generation.[528] To achieve this goal, seven targets and four priorities for action have been included in the Framework along with 13 guiding principles for implementation.[529] The four priority areas are: (1) 'Understanding disaster risk', (2) 'Strengthening disaster risk governance to manage disaster risk', (3) 'Investing in disaster risk reduction for resilience' and (4) 'Enhancing disaster preparedness for effective response and to "Build Back Better" in recovery, rehabilitation and reconstruction'.[530] A major innovation of the Sendai Framework is the increased emphasis on disaster risk management instead of the previous emphasis on disaster management, which puts a direct focus on the drivers of disaster risks.[531] Thus, in addition to reducing disaster risks, the focus is on preventing new risks as well as reducing existing risks and building resilience.[532] Furthermore, the scope of disaster risk reduction has been expanded to include man-made hazards and associated risks.[533]

---

[523] A/RES/69/15, *SIDS Accelerated Modalities of Action (SAMOA) Pathway*, para. 120; The priorities related to SIDS is also reflected in SDG 3.c; SDG 4.b and SDG 4.c; SDG 7.b; SDG 9.a; SDG 10.b; SDG 13.b and SDG 14.7 and SDG 14.a; SDG 17.18; Allen et al., 'Modelling National Transformations to Achieve the SDGs within Planetary Boundaries in Small Island Developing States' (2021) 4 *Global Sustainability*, E15.

[524] Wahlström, 'New Sendai Framework Strengthens Focus on Reducing Disaster Risk' (2015), 6 *Int J Disaster Risk Sci*, 200 (200).

[525] Kelman and Glantz, 'Analyzing the Sendai Framework for Disaster Risk Reduction' (2015), 6 *Int J Disaster Risk Sci*, 105 (105).

[526] A/RES/69/283, para. 10.

[527] A/RES/69/283, para. 16.

[528] A/RES/69/283, paras. 3, 15, 16; Wahlström, 'New Sendai Framework Strengthens Focus on Reducing Disaster Risk' (2015), 6 *Int J Disaster Risk Sci*, 200 (200).

[529] In detail see: A/RES/69/283, paras. 18-20.

[530] A/RES/69/283, para. 20.

[531] A/RES/69/283, para. 6.

[532] Wahlström, 'New Sendai Framework Strengthens Focus on Reducing Disaster Risk' (2015), 6 *Int J Disaster Risk Sci*, 200 (200).

[533] A/RES/69/283, para. 15.

25. Addis Ababa Action Agenda, 2015

The Global Agenda 2030 and specifically the SDGS are related to the AAAA which is **288** the financing agenda to the Global Agenda 2030 and has been qualified an integral part of it.[534]

In 2015, after the content and extent of all 17 SDGs was presented by the Open **289** Working Group for SDGs in 2013.[535] 174 UN member states adopted the outcome document of the UN Third International Conference on Financing for Development in Addis Ababa.[536]

The aim of the AAAA is to support, complement and help to contextualise the **290** Global Agenda's means of implementation objectives which is related to domestic public resources, domestic and international private business and finance, international development cooperation, international trade as an engine for development, debt and debt sustainability, addressing systemic issues and science, technology, innovation (STI) and capacity-building, as well as data, monitoring and follow-up.[537]

Establishing a framework for the financing of the 15 years lasting implementation pe- **291** riod of the SDGs, the AAAA delineates the direction of joint action for the SDGs' for states as well as stakeholders of civil society, the business sector and international organisations (→ Goal 17 mn. 10).[538] In this context, consideration is given to resource flows on the international and national level with special focus on domestic resource mobilisation.[539] The AAAA as outcome document is part of the Financing for Development initiative (FfD initiative) and builds on the previous conferences of Monterrey and Doha.[540] Within FfD, the UN were ought to be more involved in 'international economic affairs', not least in accordance with Art. 1, 5 and 55 UN Charter.[541] The AAAA serves to finance the entire 2030 Agenda and highlights seven 'cross-cutting areas' that promote synergies between the SDGs: social protection (Art. 12), hunger and malnutrition (Art. 13), infrastructure (Art. 14), inclusive and sustainable industrialisation (Art. 15), employment, decent work and enterprises (Art. 16), ecosystems (Art. 17) and peaceful and inclusive societies (Art. 18).[542]

By enhancing the participation of public and private resources within the goal of **292** financially supporting the implementation of the UN SDGs, interconnected fields such as technology development and trade shall be strengthened in their outreach.[543] The AAAA consists of seven action areas which are enumerated by letters (A-G): A. Domestic public resources, B. Domestic and international private business and finance, C. International development cooperation, D. International trade as an engine for de-

---

[534] A/RES/70/1 paras. 40, 62.

[535] https://sustainabledevelopment.un.org/content/documents/4518SDGs_FINAL_Proposal%20of%20 OWG_19%20July%20at%201320hrsver3.pdf.

[536] Bolton, 'Comparing the Paris Agenda with the 2030 and Addis Ababa Action Agenda' (2020) 886 *K4D Helpdesk Report*, 1 (4); A/RES/69/313 of 27 July 2015.

[537] A/RES/70/1, para. 62.

[538] http://www.fao.org/sustainable-development-goals/overview/means-of-implementation-and-the-th ird-international-conference-on-financing-for-development/ffd3/en/.

[539] Chhibber, 'Assessing and Evaluating the Addis Ababa Action Agenda (AAAA)' (2016) 166 *NIPFP Working Series*, 3 (5).

[540] Airey, 'Financing for Development' in De Feyter and Erdem Türkelli and de Moerloose (eds), *Encyclopedia of Law and Development* (2021), 87 (88).

[541] Airey, 'Financing for Development' in De Feyter and Erdem Türkelli and de Moerloose (eds), *Encyclopedia of Law and Development* (2021), 87 (89).

[542] Michel, *Beyond Aid – The Integration of Sustainable Development in a Coherent International Agenda* (2016), 40.

[543] Ministry for Foreign Affairs Sweden, *Report on the implementation of the Addis Ababa Action Agenda on financing for development*, 7.

velopment, E. Debt and debt sustainability, F. Addressing systemic issues, G. Science, technology, innovation and capacity building.

293   Critics, however, complain that the AAAA does not provide significant new sources of funding for its goals and that it maintains the supremacy of developed countries in the global economic power structure by concentrating AAAA actions in established global organisations such as the IMF, World Bank, IMFC and OECD, where developed countries predominate, to the detriment of developing countries' capacities in policy making.[544]

26. Technology Facilitation Mechanism (TFM), 2015

294   The UN Technology Facilitation Mechanism (TFM) was created by the AAAA to support the implementation of the SDGs and was launched with the 2030 Agenda on Sustainable Development in September 2015.[545] From the outset, the Division for Sustainable Development Goals DSDG/DESA has been serving as Secretariat for the 'Interagency Task Team on Science, Technology and Innovation for the SDGs' (IATT) and for the Secretary General's appointed 'Group of high-level representatives of scientific community, private sector and civil society' (10-Member Advisory Group) to support the TFM.[546] The TFM is referenced in SDG 17.6 in order to enhance North-South, South-South and triangular regional and international cooperation on and access to science, technology and innovation and enhance knowledge sharing on mutually agreed terms through the TFM.

295   The TFM comprises four components: the IATT; the 10-Member Group of representatives from civil society, the private sector and the scientific community; the annual Multistakeholder Forum on Science, Technology and Innovation for the SDGs (STI Forum); and the TFM online platform as a gateway for information on existing STI initiatives, mechanisms, and programs. The gateway serves as a 'one-stop-shop' for information on science, technology and innovation that can contribute to achieving the SDGs, building partnerships and matchmaking.[547] In particular, Artificial Intelligence (AI) is one of the emerging technologies that is of high importance in this section to avoid a digital divide.[548]

27. United Nations Conference on Housing and Sustainable Urban Development, 2016

296   The New Urban Agenda (NUA) was adopted without reservations at the United Nations Conference on Housing and Sustainable Urban Development (Habitat III) in Quito in 2016.[549]

297   The conference was already planned during the GA at the conclusion of the Global Agenda 2030. Therefore, the Global Agenda 2030 states that '[w]e look forward to the upcoming United Nations Conference on Housing and Sustainable Urban Development

---

[544] Montes, 'Five Points on the Addis Ababa Action Agenda' (2016) 24 *South Centre Policy Brief*, 1 (1 ff.).

[545] A/RES/70/1, para 70; see also Walsh and Murphy and David Horan, 'The role of science, technology and innovation in the UN 2030 agenda' (2020) 154 *Technological Forecasting and Social Change*, 119957.

[546] https://sdgs.un.org/tfm.

[547] https://www.unep.org/explore-topics/technology/what-we-do/technology-facilitation-mechanism.

[548] UN, *Resource Guide on Artificial Intelligence (AI) Strategies* (2021): The Resource Guide on Artificial Intelligence (AI) Strategies is a UN publication laying out existing resources on artificial intelligence ethics, policies and strategies on national regional and international level, 4 f.

[549] UN, *New Urban Agenda* (2017), iv.

to be held in Quito before the scenery of the impact of cities on the global climate system urban, the population trends and the development strategies and policies.'[550]

Both the conference and the development of the agenda were characterised by a par-   **298** ticipatory approach, involving governments, parliamentarians, civil society, local communities, the private sector, professionals as well as the academic community.[551] Despite Habitat I in 1976 and Habitat II in 1996, some important obstacles and challenges to improve the life quality for urban residents have still not been adequately addressed.[552] Therefore, the agenda contains a 'shared vision for a better and sustainable future' by promoting and striving for sustainable urban development.[553] It envisages 'cities for all', which includes the 'equal use and enjoyment of cities' without any discrimination and the creation of 'just, safe, healthy, accessible, affordable, resilient and sustainable cities'.[554] In addition, the agenda incorporates human rights by striving for the design of cities where all people have access to equal rights and fundamental freedoms.[555] To achieve this vision, the agenda follows three principles: (1) 'leaving no one behind', (2) 'ensure sustainable and inclusive urban economies' and (3) 'ensure environmental sustainability'.[556] The focus of the agenda is on urban prosperity, urban resilience and inclusion.[557] It emphasises the link between sustainable urbanisation and the creation of jobs, livelihood opportunities and improved quality of life, and also focuses on the inclusion of all these aspects in urban planning.[558] Thus, the agenda contains a paradigm shift based on the science of cities by setting standards and principles for planning, building, development management and improvement of urban areas.[559] Furthermore, the New Urban Agenda is linked to the 2030 Agenda, in particular through SDG 11.[560]

28. Instruments mentioned in the Section entitled 'Sustainable Development Goals and targets'

The World Health Organization Framework Convention on Tobacco Control (WHO   **299** FCTC) represents the first treaty negotiated under the auspices of the WHO entering into force in 2005.[561] The convention reaffirmed 'the right of all people to the highest standard of health', while representing 'a paradigm shift in developing a regulatory strategy to address addictive substances'.[562] The WHO FCTC is linked explicitly to SDG 3.a.

The Sendai Framework for Disaster Risk Reduction 2015-2030 was adopted at the   **300** third UN World Conference on Disaster Risk Reduction in Sendai in 2015 and is linked explicitly to SDG 11.b (→ Intro mn. 287 ff.).

The United Nations Convention on the Law of the Sea (UNCLOS) was adopted in   **301** 1982 in Jamaica. It establishes a 'comprehensive regime of law and order in the world's

---

[550] A/RES/70/1, para. 34.
[551] A/RES/71/256, para. 1; UN-Habitat, *The New Urban Agenda* (2020), x; UN, *New Urban Agenda* (2017), v.
[552] A/RES/71/256, paras. 3 f.
[553] UN-Habitat, *The New Urban Agenda* (2020), x; A/RES/71/256, para 22.
[554] A/RES/71/256, para. 11.
[555] A/RES/71/256, para. 12.
[556] A/RES/71/256, para. 14.
[557] A/RES/71/256, paras. 11, 14, 18.
[558] UN-Habitat, *The New Urban Agenda* (2020), x.
[559] UN, *New Urban Agenda* (2017), iv; A/RES/71/256, para. 15.
[560] A/RES/71/256, para. 9.
[561] WHO-FCTC, *WHO Framework Convention on Tobacco Control* (2005), 3 f.
[562] WHO-FCTC, *WHO Framework Convention on Tobacco Control* (2005), 3.

oceans and seas establishing rules governing all uses of the oceans and their resources'[563] (→ Goal 14 mn. 16 ff.).

302   The outcome document 'The future we want'[564] includes far-reaching sustainability goals related to 'poverty eradication, food security and sustainable agriculture, energy, sustainable transport, sustainable cities, health and population and promoting full and productive employment'.[565] SDG 14.c highlights paragraph 158 of 'The future we want', which intends to enhance the conservation and sustainable use of oceans according to international law of the United Nations Convention on the Law of the Sea.

29. Conclusion

303   According to the text of the Global Agenda 2030, all major UN conferences, summits and their outcomes have laid a solid foundation for sustainable development and have helped to shape the new Agenda.[566] These include at least the conferences presented, whose aims and outcomes should lead to a more equilibrated world as the decades go by.

304   The external principles, treaties, etc. are like layers wrapped around the core of the SDGs and their internal principles in relation to a specific SDG or as principles in a general sense. Furthermore, the external principles as outcome of conferences refer to specific demands and needs, informing governments, individuals, organisations assisting them to create a just answer in the preparation and applicability of treatises, bilateral agreements or contracts, laws and regulations. The conferences contextualise the specific SDGs and demonstrate through their outcomes a willingness to move forward at least to the point where the 'new approach' begins. Moving forward means accepting the inherent methods of interpretation in a particular state or at interregional or international level, but requires for implementation informed and guided by external principles that metaphorically function as guardrails.

XII. Systematic Follow-up and Review of the Global Agenda 2030

305   The systematic follow-up and review process in the legal matrix is guided by the specific principles outlined in the Global Agenda 2030.[567]

306   The High-Level Political Forum on Sustainable Development (HLPF) is the responsible forum conducting the review-process under the auspices of the Economic and Social Council. Reviews are voluntary, while encouraging reporting, and include developed and developing countries as well as relevant UN entities and other stakeholders, including civil society and the private sector. The HLPF supports the participation of key groups and other relevant stakeholders in the follow-up and review processes based on Resolution 67/290.[568] The SDGs are subject to a track progress of implementation,[569] with an open, inclusive, participatory and transparent approach for all people.[570]

307   The entire process is voluntary and is controlled by the countries. Different political margins and priorities of the countries are to be accommodated.[571]

---

[563] https://www.un.org/depts/los/convention_agreements/convention_overview_convention.htm.
[564] A/RES/66/288, preamble.
[565] https://www.eea.europa.eu/policy-documents/the-future-we-want-2013declaration.
[566] A/RES/70/1, para. 11.
[567] A/RES/70/1, para. 72.
[568] A/RES/67/290, *Format and organizational aspects of the high-level political forum on sustainable development*, 23 August 2013.
[569] A/RES/70/1, para. 74(b).
[570] A/RES/70/1, para. 74(d).
[571] A/RES/70/1, para. 74(a).

The expectation articulated by the Global 2030 Agenda includes in the follow-up process that monitoring on the applicable SDGs is 'rigorous and based on evidence, informed by country-led evaluations and data which is high-quality, accessible, timely, reliable and disaggregated by income, sex, age, race, ethnicity, migration status, disability and geographic location and other characteristics relevant in national contexts.[572]   **308**

Tracking focuses on the goals and targets, which are reviewed using a set of global indicators. These are complemented by indicators at the regional and national levels.[573] The national level, the interregional level and the global level are addressed differently. Whereas national review should be conducted in a country-led and country-driven manner that uses regular and inclusive reviews from national parliaments or similar institutions,[574] the focus at the regional level is on peer learning through voluntary reviews, sharing of best practices and a constant and benevolent cooperation between commissions and organisations.[575] At the global level, the HLPF spans their network and provides 'political leadership, guidance and recommendations' and thus promotes 'system-wide coherence and coordination of sustainable development policies'.[576]   **309**

1. High-Level Political Forum on Sustainable Development

The HLPF is intended to serve as the universal intergovernmental platform of the UN for the follow-up and review of the Global Agenda 2030 and the inherent 17 SDGs.[577] The HLPF convened its first plenary session on 24 September 2013.[578] While originating in the UNCSD (Rio+20),[579] the HLPF has become the successor of the CSD,[580] now convening at the level of Heads of State and Government.[581]   **310**

The HLPF is expected to take a holistic view of the implementation of the SDGs. Its mandate includes assessing the progress, achievements and challenges of developed and developing countries in achieving the SDGs and ensuring that the Global Agenda 2030 remains relevant and ambitious.[582] The current thematic focus of the HLPF 2021 and ECOSOC is dedicated to sustainable and resilient recovery from the SARS-CoV-2 pandemic.[583]   **311**

The main tasks of the HLPF are to provide: **312**

–   Political leadership
–   Guidance and recommendations for sustainable development

---

[572] A/RES/70/1, para. 74(g).

[573] A/RES/70/1, para. 75.

[574] A/RES/70/1, paras. 78 f.

[575] A/RES/70/1, paras. 80 f.

[576] A/RES/70/1, para. 82.

[577] A/RES/70/1, para. 82; A/RES/70/299, Follow-up and review of the 2030 Agenda for Sustainable Development at the global level, 29.7.2016; Abbott and Bernstein, 'The high-level political forum on sustainable development: Orchestration by default and design'(2015) 6.3 *Global Policy*, 222-33; Nilsson, *Important interactions among the sustainable development goals under review at the high-level political forum 2017* (2017).

[578] https://sustainabledevelopment.un.org/hlpf.

[579] A/RES/66/288, Annex, para. 84.

[580] A/RES/67/290, *Format and organizational aspects of the high-level political forum on sustainable development*, 9 July 2013, preamble.

[581] A/RES/67/290, para. 6(a).

[582] A/RES/70/684, paras. 18, 20.

[583] A/RES/74/298, *Review of the implementation of General Assembly resolution 67/290 on the high-level political forum on sustainable development, resolution 70/299 on the follow-up and review of the 2030 Agenda for Sustainable Development at the global level and resolution 72/305 on the strengthening of the Economic and Social Council*, 12.8.2020, para. 3.

- Follow-up and review progress in the implementation of sustainable development commitments
- the integration of the three dimensions of sustainable development in a holistic and cross-sectoral manner at all levels
- Have a focused, dynamic action-oriented agenda, ensuring the appropriate consideration of new and emerging sustainable development challenges[584]

313 The HLPF political declaration[585] issued a call for accelerated action to meet the SDGs of the Global Agenda 2030. In particular, the commitment to take more and faster action was made on the following aspects:

- Mobilise adequate and well-directed financing
- Enhance national implementation
- Strengthen institutions for more integrated solutions
- Bolstering local action to accelerate implementation
- Harnessing STI with a greater focus on digital transformation for sustainable development
- Investing in data and statistics for the SDGs, to strengthen national statistical capacities to address the gaps in data on the SDGs in order to allow countries to provide high – quality, timely, reliable, disaggregated data and statistics and to fully integrate the Sustainable Development Goals in our monitoring and reporting systems[586]

314 According to the vertical level of the Global Agenda 2030 in the framework of the follow-up and review mechanisms, member states should 'conduct regular and inclusive reviews of progress at the national and sub-national levels, which are country-led and country-driven.'[587] The national reviews are voluntary and should be based on a certain method. It should be noted that major groups other relevant stakeholders should participate on the voluntary national Reviews (VNR).[588]

2. Voluntary National Reviews

315 According to the vertical level the Global Agenda 2030 encourages member states to 'conduct regular and inclusive reviews of progress at the national and sub-national levels. As stipulated in paragraph 84 of the agenda, regular reviews by the HLPF are to be voluntary, country-led, conducted by both developed and developing countries, and provide a platform for partnerships, including through the participation of major groups and other relevant stakeholders.

---

[584] A/RES/67/290, para. 2.

[585] A/RES/74/4, *Political declaration of the high-level political forum on sustainable development convened under the auspices of the General Assembly*, 15 September 2019.

[586] https://sustainabledevelopment.un.org/vnrs/.

[587] A/RES/70/1, para. 79; Jönsson and Bexell, 'Localizing the sustainable development goals: the case of Tanzania' (2021) 39.2 *Development Policy Review*, 181-96; Forestier and Kim, 'Cherry-picking the Sustainable Development Goals: Goal prioritization by national governments and implications for global governance' (2020) 28.5 *Sustainable Development*, 1269-78; to case studies from Botswana's journey towards the Global Agenda 2030 see Keitumetse and Osireditse and Norris, *Sustainability in Developing Countries* (2020).

[588] A/RES/70/1, para. 84.

These Voluntary National Reviews (VNRs)[589] are intended to be a cornerstone of the framework for follow-up and review of the implementation of the Global Agenda 2030 at the HLPF.[590]   316

With a reporting guide,[591] the UN clarifies the need for a structured and comparable outcome. Countries are encouraged to structure the report along guidelines that provide an overview of the follow-up to the 2030 Agenda and promote consistency and comparability between different countries' reports. At best, their review should outline how stakeholders, national and local governments, legislative bodies, national regulatory/audit, human rights or other institutions, the public, civil society and the private sector have been involved in the implementation and review of the Global Agenda 2030, including the SDGs. The review shall demonstrate how the integration of the goals into the country's legislation, policies, plans, budgets and programmes, including the sustainable development strategy, if any, has contributed to the successful implementation of the SDGs and targets.   317

The UN's view that the survival of many societies and the planet's biological support system is at risk[592] sounds dramatic and is a description of an increasingly widespread perception that leads to political action. Even though it seems to be common knowledge that global cooperation in the sense of SDG 17 is the appropriate choice to tackle global challenges where only one or two states would most likely fail, multilateralism is under pressure and seems to lose its (so far) uncontested persuasive power. In the flowing current of unbridled globalisation, the world is being pushed to its very limits, with climate change being the most significant challenge of all among many issues.[593] Globally and multilaterally agreed responses and powerful global action are not yet in sight. Thus, the SDGs remain not the only, but a highly potent response by all member states of the UN, additionally relying on the support of a global partnership between public and private entities. This turns the Global Agenda 2030 into a unique and important resolution that has the power to motivate action in the multi-level system.   318

3. Measurement by Indicators

The current Global Indicator Framework[594] (GIF) has been developed by the Inter-Agency and Expert Group on SDG Indicators (IAEG-SDGs). The GIF is refined annually and reviewed comprehensively by the UN Statistical Commission. Indicators at the regional and national levels developed by UN member states complement the GIF.[595]   319

---

[589] See Kindornay, *Progressing national SDGs implementation: An independent assessment of the voluntary national review reports submitted to the United Nations High-level Political Forum on Sustainable Development in 2017* (2018).

[590] UN, *Updated Voluntary common reporting guidelines for voluntary national reviews at the high-level political forum for sustainable development* (HLPF) (2021).

[591] UN, *Updated Voluntary common reporting guidelines for voluntary national reviews at the high-level political forum for sustainable development (HLPF)* (2021).

[592] A/RES/70/1, para. 14.

[593] A/RES/70/1, para. 14: 'Climate change is one of the greatest challenges of our time'; Dupuy and Viñuales, *International Environmental Law* (2nd edn, 2018), 171 ff.

[594] The original global indicator framework was adopted by the General Assembly on 6 July 2017 and is incorporated into A/RES/71/313, adopted by the General Assembly on Work of the Statistical Commission pertaining to the 2030 Agenda for Sustainable Development, Annex; see for a current overview: https://unstats.un.org/sdgs/indicators/indicators-list.

[595] The list includes 232 indicators on which general agreement has been reached. The total number of indicators listed in the global SDG indicator framework is 247, but as 12 indicators are repeated under two or three different goals, the actual total number of individual indicators in the list is 231; further information: https://unstats.un.org/sdgs/indicators/indicators-list/; https://unstats.un.org/wiki/display/SDGeHandbook/Home.

Introduction

320　Although standards and indicators[596] have attracted a high level of academic interest for years,[597] a general conclusion in practice can only be drawn when some requirements concerning data are highly developed, generally operational and between states interlinked and consistent regarding methods, quality and accessibility. A frequent criticism is that global indicators usually reflect only the internal and ethnocentric biases of their designers,[598] so that the designers, for example, from the Global North, are biased against the South.[599] The simplification function of the indicators regarding complex institutions and processes is ultimately thwarted overcome by the difficulty of evaluating the data.[600]

321　In addition, there is a need for better understanding between the development of indicators and their use.[601] Other critics highlight the lack of interdependencies of the SDGs not reflected in the indicators.[602] The UN Office on Drugs and Crime (UNODC) recommends that a good performance indicator should be 'SMART' which means specific (precise and unambiguous), measurable (amenable to independent validation), achievable (realistic with the resources available), relevant (contributes to expected result within Organisation's mandate), and time-bound (achievable within a specific time frame).[603] If this framework of agreed global indicators is used inconsistently, e.g. if only arbitrarily selected indicators or additional indicators are used, results will be correspondingly inconsistent, incomprehensible or doubtful.[604] In particular, reliable disaggregated data will be needed to conduct the process of measurement.[605] Disaggregated data concerning the SDGs should differ between income, sex, age, race, ethnicity, migratory status, disability and geographic location, or other characteristics.[606] Critics states among others those different and inconsistent results published publicly may cause severe misunderstanding or doubts on the capability to assess SDGs implementation.[607] Further the use of disaggregated data reveal tensions between the right to privacy and

---

[596] Davis and Kingsbury and Merry, 'Introduction: Global Governance by Indicators' in Davis et al. (eds), *Governance by Indicators. Global Power through Quantification and Rankings* (2012),1 ff.; https://unstats.un.org/sdgs/indicators/database/.

[597] Botero and Nelson and Pratt, 'Indices and Indicators of Justice, Governance and the Rule of Law: An Overview' (2011) 3 *Hague J Rule Law* (2011), 15; Cassese and Casini, 'Taming Honey Birds? The Regulation of Global Indicators' (2012) *SSRN eJournal*.

[598] Infantino, 'Global indicators' in Cassese (ed), *Research Handbook on Global Administrative Law* (2016), 348.

[599] Infantino, 'Global indicators' in Cassese (ed), *Research Handbook on Global Administrative Law* (2016), 361.

[600] Nelson Espelan and Sauder, 'The Dynamism of Indicators' in Davies et al., *Governance by Indicators, Global Power through Quantification and Rankings* (2012), 87.

[601] Morse, 'Analysing the Use of Sustainability Indicators' in Malito and Bhuta and Umbach (eds), *The Palgrave Handbook of Indicators in Global Governance* (2018), 446, 509; Forestier and Kim, 'Cherry-picking the Sustainable Development Goals: Goal prioritization by national governments and implications for global governance'(2020) 28.5 *Sustainable Development*, 1269-78.

[602] Huck, 'The UN Sustainable Development Goals and the Governance of Global Public Goods, The Quest for Legitimacy' (2021) in Iovane et al. (eds), *The Protection of General Interests in Contemporary International Law: A Theoretical and Empirical Inquiry* (2021), 361-82; Nash et al., 'To achieve a sustainable blue future, progress assessments must include interdependencies between the sustainable development goals' (2020) 2.2 *One Earth* 2.2, 161-73.

[603] UNODC, *Results-based Management and the 2030 Agenda for Sustainable Development* (2018), 30.

[604] Janoušková and Hák and Moldan, 'Global SDGs Assessments: Helping or Confusing Indicators?'(2018) 10(5) *Sustainability*, 1-14.

[605] A/RES 70/1, para. 48.

[606] A/RES/71/313, *Global indicator framework for the Sustainable Development Goals and targets of the 2030 Agenda for Sustainable Development*; A/RES/68/261, *Fundamental Principles of Official Statistics*.

[607] Janoušková and Hák and Moldan, 'Global SDGs Assessments: Helping or Confusing Indicators?'(2018) 10(5) *Sustainability*, 1-14.

the efforts to promote equality through the collection of such data.[608] Data and related to data applied indicators play a crucial role in the process of measurement that can be understood to an extent a *conditio sine qua non* for political outcome-based decision making.[609] And decision can be taken through positive action or (legal relevant) omission on every vertical and horizontal level. In a *rule of law*[610] framed political environment. the process of decision making of each state could be more or less informal or based on formal instruments of action grounded in the respective realm of constitutional and administrative principles (→ Goal 16 mn. 22 ff). It seems quite apparent that complete process of collecting data, the creation and application of indicators and the specific outcome of measurement is as a prerequisite to make appropriate and lawful political decisions.

4. The Importance of Indicators

The Global Agenda 2030 envisages 'a world in which [...] democracy, good gover- **322** nance and the rule of law [...] are essential for sustainable development [...]'.[611] Within the Sustainable Development Strategy, a set of global indicators[612] is being utilised to monitor and evaluate the progress made towards achieving the overall goals and specific objectives.[613] Unfortunately, no agreement or any other legal basis exists as to the definition of scope and content of a global indicator, as this usually depends upon the sector in which they are used.[614] Siems and Nelken have presented a list of different types of indicators mainly in the international context.[615] The description of an indicator given by Davis, Kingsbury and Merry, as below, seems to be very appropriate, although definitions also come from the OECD[616] and the UN.[617]

> An indicator is a named collection of ranked-ordered data that purports to represent the past or projected performance of different units. The data are generated through a process that simplifies raw data about a complex social phenomenon. The data, in this simplified and processed form, are capable of being used to compare particular units of analysis (such as countries or institutions or corporations), synchronically or over time, and to evaluate their performance by reference to one or

---

[608] Winkler and Satterthwaite, 'Leaving no one behind? Persistent inequalities in the SDGs' in Winkler and Williams (eds),*The Sustainable Development Goals and Human Rights, A critical early review* (2018), 64.

[609] A/RES 70/1, para. 48.

[610] To the two features of the global and the national *rule of law*, see Macchia, 'The rule of law and transparency in the global space' in Cassese (ed), *Research Handbook on Global Administrative Law* (2016), 262 et seqq.; see to the questions on how to measure the *rule of law* see Macchia, 273 et seqq.; see for an interpretation of the rule of law in the context of the Global Agenda 2030 and SDGs Huck and Maaß, 'Gaining a foot in the door: Giving Access to Justice with SDG 16.3?' (2021) 2021-5 *C-EENRG Working Paper*.

[611] A/RES/70/1, paras. 4, 9, 35.

[612] On the nine factors and 47 indicators of the World Justice Project and the connection to the SDGs see Dougherty and Gryskiewicz and Ponce, *Measuring the Rule of Law: The World Justice Project's Rule of Law Index* in Malito and Bhuta and Umbach (eds), *The Palgrave Handbook of Indicators in Global Governance* (2018), 255 et seqq.

[613] Rickels et al., 'Indicators for Monitoring Sustainable Development Goals: An Application to Oceanic Development in the EU, Kiel Institute for the World Economy' (2015) 2019 *Working Paper*.

[614] Infantino, 'Global indicators' in Cassese (ed), *Research Handbook on Global Administrative Law* (2017), 348.

[615] Siems and Nelken, *Global social indicators and the concept of legitimacy. International Journal of Law in Context* (2017), 436-49.

[616] OECD, *Handbook on Constructing Composite Indicators* (2013).

[617] UN, *The United Nations Rule of Law Indicators Implementation Guide and Project Tools* (2011).

more standards. (…) Indicators often take the form of, or can readily be transformed into, numerical data.[618]

323   Moreover, data gaps for the usability of global indicators are not only evident in developing countries[619] but also in industrialised countries, and filling these gaps requires financial resources as well as knowledge sharing and investment in human capital.[620] To illustrate the situation, reference can be made to the UN Economic and Social Commission for Asia and the Pacific (UNESCAP) 2017 Statistical Yearbook[621] which points to the large number of data gaps in critical areas such as poverty, climate change, environment, gender, inequality, and governance.[622] Therefore, from a higher level it is currently very likely that the outcome of measurement will only provide a blurred view of the global approach to 'transform our world' and precise results are at least missing. The 2018 UN Women report 'Turning Promises into Action: Gender equality in the 2030 Agenda for Sustainable Development' points out that less than a third of the data needed for monitoring the gender-specific indicators are currently available.[623] Whether new adjustments even in the EU may result in a better outcome remains to be seen in the future.[624]

324   The UN has reported on experiences in collecting data from different states in Africa.[625] Further challenges lie in need for disaggregated data and indicators, which is described as extremely burdensome, is sometimes not possible for some indicators and is forbidden for some aspects in some countries (race and ethnicity).[626] The work also needs to respond to the demands of policymakers, in particular where disaggregation has an impact on public, social, and private policies. An example from UNEP is their work on gender and environment, which was as a direct request by policy-makers.[627]

5. Legal Implication of the Use of Indicators

325   Since the 1990 s, the use of indicators as a technology of governance[628] has become a global trend[629] and the UN quite often uses them as well as international, regional, and national organisations, and international NGOs.[630] As a rule, indicators are produced in a much less formal process than is the case in an open, political, transparent, and demo-

---

[618] Davis and Kingsbury and Merry, 'Introduction: Global Governance by Indicators' in Davis et al. (eds), *Governance by Indicators. Global Power through Quantification and Rankings* (2012), 3, 6.

[619] Williams and Hunt, 'Neglecting human rights: accountability, data and Sustainable Development Goal 3', in Winkler and Williams (eds), *The Sustainable Development Goals and Human Rights, A critical early review* (2018), 115.

[620] Eurostat, *Sustainable development in the European Union – Monitoring report on progress towards the SDGs in an EU context — 2018 edition*, 18 September 2018, 18.

[621] UN, *Statistical Yearbook for Asia and the Pacific 2017, Measuring SDG progress in Asia and the Pacific: Is there enough data?* (2017), ii.

[622] Adams and Judd, 'The Ups and Downs of Tiers: Measuring SDG Progress' (2018) 22 *Global Policy Watch*.

[623] UN Women, *Turning Promises into Action* (2018), 16, 49, 59, 254 et seqq.

[624] EU Commission (Eurostat), *EU SDG Indicator set 2019, Result of the review in preparation of the 2019 edition of the EU SDG monitoring report*, Final version, 08 January 2019.

[625] See further for Indicators in Africa, Edouard and Bernstein, 'Challenges for Measuring Progress towards the Sustainable Development Goals'(2016) 20(3) *African Journal of Reproductive Health*, 49.

[626] UN, *IAEG-SDG Workstream on Data Disaggregation*, 5.-8.11.2018.

[627] UN DESA, Statistic Division, STA/441/2/165A/3, 7 December 2018.

[628] Goodwin, 'The poverty of numbers: reflections on the legitimacy of global development indicators' (2017) *International Journal of Law in Context*, 487.

[629] Infantino, 'Global indicators' in Cassese (ed), *Research Handbook on Global Administrative Law* (2017), 349.

[630] Kelley and Simmons, 'Introduction: The Power of Global Performance Indicators' (2019), 19-06 *Public Law Research Paper (Faculty Scholarship at Penn Law)*, 2042.

cratic discourse. The method of production and its impact merits attention, especially since interconnections between indicators and the law become apparent when legal norms refer to indicators and so contribute to satisfying legal objectives.[631] The consistency is also reflected in the method: when an indicator is applied to a data set by which an objective is or is not achieved, this essentially comes down to a compilation of facts and events. This collection of specific data is correlated with the indicator – similar to subsumption in the original sense of the word – in order to obtain a judicial result.

The power of indicators has become more important in policy formation and polit-   **326** ical decision making. How does the use of global indicators change the nature of decision-making? In addition to providing a knowledge base, they also impact government policy decisions, which is comparable to lawmaking but softly and quietly. Based on the measurable values, the politics of a country are often steered in a certain direction, triggered by the evaluation of the indicators.[632] The scholarly interest focused on the production and aggregation of qualitative datasets has increased.[633] In particular, the question of quality of data reflects a specific normative space that refers to certain indicators. This topic enshrines the question of the legitimacy of (global social) indicators, which is and will remain relevant.[634] As long as those indicators can be deconstructed and reveal the explicit and mostly normative related content, then those ideas can be combined with the (democratic) aspects of legitimacy.[635] Thus, the SDGs become a precious tool to align global governments action and may be the starting point for global standard-setting in the long(er)-term.

6. Conclusion

Against the background of the normative concept of the SDGs with its specific   **327** impact on different levels in international, European, national and transnational law and on the revitalised global partnership at least indicators may be characterised as functional equivalent to legal norms creating an impact on the fundaments for active decision or omissions in a legal framework of governance. Indicators have specific different roles and are instruments of government, but sometimes they tend to influence the outcome of political action framed by principle of the respective national legal framework.[636] In practice, it can be evaluated that it is quite difficult to steer a process of data collection with disaggregated data at a sufficient level with a minimum standard of privacy and data protection. The question of legitimacy calls for a closer look at the complete process

---

[631] Davis and Kingsbury and Merry, 'Introduction: Global Governance by Indicators' in Davis et al. (eds), *Governance by Indicators. Global Power through Quantification and Rankings* (2012), 20; Koch and Krellenberg, 'How to contextualize SDG 11? Looking at indicators for sustainable urban development in Germany'(2018) 7.12 *ISPRS International Journal of Geo-Information*, 464.

[632] Merry and Davis and Kingsbury, 'Introduction: The Local-Global Life of Indicators: Law, Power, and Resistance' in Merry and Davis and Kingsbury (eds), *The Quiet Power of Indicators, Measuring Governance, Corruption, and the Rule of Law* (2015), 1.

[633] See the special issue: Global Social Indicators: Constructing Transnational Legitimacy (2017) 13(4) *International Journal of Law* which includes a selection of papers first presented at the workshop convened by David Nelken and Mathias Siems on the Legitimacy of Global Social Indicators, held at the Dickson Poon School of Law, King's College, London, on 14–15 March 2016; Nelken, 'Introductory note' (2017) *International Journal of Law in Context*, 433.

[634] Nelken and Siems, 'Introduction: Global social indicators: Constructing transnational legitimacy' (2017) *International Journal of Law in Context*, 434 f.

[635] Huck, 'The UN Sustainable Development Goals and Global Public Goods, The Quest for Legitimacy', Iovane and Palombino and Amoroso and Zarra, *The Protection of General Interests in Contemporary International Law: A Theoretical and Empirical Inquiry* (2021), 358.

[636] Malito and Bhuta and Umbach, 'Conclusions: Knowing and Governing' in Malito and Bhuta and Umbach (eds), *The Palgrave Handbook of Indicators in Global Governance* (2018), 509.

Introduction

of collecting data, the measurement and the winning of a specific outcome to justify legal actions as described above. The phenomenon of rampant corruption and the impact on reliable data, applying indicators and the outcome related to the question of legitimacy and moreover to the overarching principle of the *rule of law* with its different approaches in the international and national arena, puts the question of legitimacy in the centre of interest. Corruption with its disintegrating power can significantly change the measurement process and the outcome. The multifaceted expression of globalisation is characterised not only by a change of level but also by a change in the forms of regulation. Indicators are therefore one of the most potent emerging forms of global regulation, and they can be seen metaphorically as a parallel universe to the law.

Goal 1
End poverty in all its forms everywhere

1.1 By 2030, eradicate extreme poverty for all people everywhere, currently measured as people living on less than $1.25 a day

1.2 By 2030, reduce at least by half the proportion of men, women and children of all ages living in poverty in all its dimensions according to national definitions

1.3 Implement nationally appropriate social protection systems and measures for all, including floors, and by 2030 achieve substantial coverage of the poor and the vulnerable

1.4 By 2030, ensure that all men and women, in particular the poor and the vulnerable, have equal rights to economic resources, as well as access to basic services, ownership and control over land and other forms of property, inheritance, natural resources, appropriate new technology and financial services, including microfinance

1.5 By 2030, build the resilience of the poor and those in vulnerable situations and reduce their exposure and vulnerability to climate-related extreme events and other economic, social and environmental shocks and disasters

1.a Ensure significant mobilization of resources from a variety of sources, including through enhanced development cooperation, in order to provide adequate and predictable means for developing countries, in particular least developed countries, to implement programmes and policies to end poverty in all its dimensions

1.b Create sound policy frameworks at the national, regional and international levels, based on pro-poor and gender-sensitive development strategies, to support accelerated investment in poverty eradication actions

Word Count related to 'Poverty'
A/RES/70/1 - Transforming our world: the 2030 Agenda for Sustainable Development: 28
Instruments mentioned in A/RES7/0/1 in the section entitled: 'Sustainable Development Goals and targets':
A/RES/69/313 - Addis Ababa Action Agenda of the Third International Conference on Financing for Development adopted on 27 July 2015: 14
A/RES/66/288 - The future we want (Rio +20 Declaration) adopted on 27 July 2012: 65
A/RES/55/2 - United Nations Millennium Declaration adopted on 8 September 2000: 10

Select Bibliography: Jason Beckett, 'Creating Poverty' in Anne Orford and Florian Hoffmann (eds), *The Oxford Handbook of the Theory of International Law* (Oxford University Press, Oxford 2016), 985; Christina Binder, Jane A. Hofbauer, Flávia Piovesan and Amaya Úbeda de Torres (eds), *Research Handbook on International Law and Social Rights* (Edward Elgar Publishing, UK/USA 2020), 1; Meghan Campbell, *Women, Poverty, Equality – The Role of CEDAW* (Hart Publishing, UK/USA 2018), 5; Katarzyna Cichos and Amanda Lange Salvia, *SDG 1 – No Poverty – Making the Dream a Reality* (Emerald Publishing, UK 2019), 1; Fons Coomans, 'Application of the International Covenant on Economic, Social and Cultural Rights in the Framework of International Organisations' in Armin von Bogdandy and Rüdiger Wolfrum (eds), *Max Planck Yearbook of United Nations Law* (Martinus Nijhoff Publishers, Leiden 2007), 359; Olivier De Schutter, 'L'interdépendance des droits et l'interaction des systèmes de protection: les scénarios du système européen de protection des droits fondamentaux' (2000), *Droit en Quart-Monde*, 5; Bas De Gaay Fortman, 'Poverty as a failure of entitlement: do rights-based approaches make sense?' in Lucie Williams (ed), International poverty law – An emerging discourse (ZedBooks, London/New York 2006), 34; Marsha A. Freeman, Christine Chinkin and Beate Rudolf, *The UN Convention on the Elimination of All Forms of Discrimination Against Women: A Commentary* (Oxford University Press, New York 2012), 351; Beth Goldblatt, 'Gender, poverty and the development of the right to social security' (2014) 10 (4) *International Journal of Law in Context*, 460; Stephane Hallegatte, Marianne Fay and Edward B. Barbier, 'Poverty and climate change: introduction' (2018) 23 *Environ Dev Econ*, 217; Winfried Huck and Claudia Kurkin, 'The UN Sustainable Development Goals (SDGs) in the Transnational Multilevel System' (2018) 2 *Heidelberg Journal of International Law (HJIL)/ Zeitschrift für ausländisches öffentliches Recht und Völkerrecht (ZaöRV)*, 375; Philipp N. Jefferson, 'Global poverty – Trends, measures and antidotes' in Bent Greve (ed), *Routledge International Handbook of Poverty* (Routledge, UK/US 2020), 119; Sarah Joseph, 'Trade Law and Investment Law', in Dinah Shelton (ed), *The Oxford Handbook of International Human Rights Law* (Oxford University Press, New York 2013), 846; Takhmina Karimova and Christophe Golay, 'Principle 5 – Poverty Eradication' in Jorge E. Viñuales (ed), *The Rio Declaration on Environment and Development: A Commentary* (Oxford University Press, Oxford 2015), 181; Daniel Landau, Rosalind Dixon and Amartya Sen, 'Constitutional Non-Transformation?: Socioeconomic Rights beyond the Poor' in Katharine G Young (ed), The Future of Economic and Social Rights (Cambridge University Press 2019); Kathleen Lawlor, Erin Sills, Stibniati Atmadja, Liwei Lin and Karnjana Songwathana, ' SDG 1: No Poverty – Impacts of Social Protection, Tenure Security and Building Resilience on Forests' in Pia Katila, Carol J. Pierce Colfer, Wil de Jong, Glenn Galloway, Pablo Pacheco and Georg Winkel (eds), *Sustainable Development Goals: Their Impacts on Forests and People* (2019); Stephen P. Marks, and Alice Han, 'Health and Human Rights through Development – The Right to Development, Rights-Based Approach to Development, and Sustainable Development Goals' in Lawrence O Gostin and Benjamin Mason Meier, *Foundations of Global Health & Human Rights* (Oxford University Press, Oxford 2020), 329; Fiona McKay, 'What Outcomes for Victims?' in Dinah Shelton (ed), *The Oxford Handbook of International Human Rights Law* (2013), 921-54; Katrin Merhof, 'Building a bridge between reality and the constitution: The establishment and development of the Colombian Constitutional Court' (2015) in 13(3) *I•CON*, 714–732; Krista Nadakavukaren Schefer, 'Human Rights', in Thomas Cottier and Krista Nadakavukaren Schefer (eds), *Elgar Encyclopedia of International Economic Law* (2017), 248; Aoife Nolan, 'Art. 27 The Right to a Standard of Living Adequate for the Child's Development' in John Tobin, *The UN Convention on the Rights of the Child: A Commentary* (2019), 1021-34; Ernst-Ulrich Petersmann, 'Human Rights in International Investment Law and Adjudication: Legal Methodology Questions' in Julien Chaisse, Leïla Choukroune and Sufian Jusoh (eds), *Handbook of International Investment Law and Policy* (Springer 2020); Thomas Pogge, 'Fighting global poverty' (2017) 13(4) *International Journal of Law in Context*, 512; Margot E. Salomon, 'Why should it matter that others have more? Poverty, inequality, and the potential of international human rights law' (2011) 37 *Rev. Int. Stud.*, 2152; Hans-Otto Sano, 'How Can a Human Rights-Based Approach Contribute to Poverty Reduction? The Relevance of Human Rights to Sustainable Development Goal One' in Markus Kaltenborn, Markus Krajewski and Heike Kuhn, *SDGs and Human Rights* (Springer Nature Switzerland AG, Cham 2019); Joseph E. Stiglitz, Jean-Paul Fitoussi and Martine Durand, *Beyond GDP, Measuring What Counts For Economic And Social Performance* (OECD, Paris 2018).

A. Background and Origin of SDG 1

According to the SDG Report of 2021, it is visible that the SARS-CoV-2 pandemic is **1**
having the worst economic fallout globally since the Great Depression and will continue
to push tens of millions of people back into poverty.[1] Whereas poverty had steadily
declined till 2015, it was even before the pandemic, that projections estimated still 6 per
cent of the world's population will be living in poverty in 2030.[2] The number of people
who will additionally live in poverty due to the pandemic is estimated at 71 million
worldwide,[3] most of them in South Asia and the sub-Saharan region.[4] According to the
Report, the pandemic will have immediate as well as long-term economic consequences
for the people around the world, which can lead them to poverty.[5] Mostly affected are
the least developed countries. The unemployment was not covered by social benefits of
the countries.[6] While in Europe 44 per cent received unemployment payments, only 3
per cent of the unemployed got paid in sub-Saharan Africa.[7]

In 2021, the majority of the world still lives in poverty. SDG 1.1 defines that people **2**
live in poverty when living on less than 1.25$.[8] According to the World Data Bank,
two-thirds of the population in this world live on less than 10$-int per day and every
tenth person is living with less than 1.90$-int per day.[9] To tackle poverty, SDG 1 with
seven targets, yet only 5 indicators has been set at the forefront of the SDG agenda.[10] Its
predecessor, MDG 1, focused on extreme poverty and hunger[11] and was nourished in
2013, when the World Bank set a new goal to end extreme poverty in a generation, the
target is to not have more than three per cent of the people in the world living on just
1.90$-int a day.[12]

And poverty will rise in the future. According to the World Bank and the HRC, the **3**
effects of climate change will aggravate the situation, e. g. at 2°C of warming, 100–400
million more people could be at risk of hunger and 1–2 billion more people may no
longer have adequate water.[13] The HRC points out that, 'climate change will exacerbate
existing poverty and inequality. It will have the most severe impact in poor countries and
regions, and the places where poor people live and work. Developing countries will bear
an estimated 75–80 per cent of the cost of climate change.'[14]

---

[1] UN, *The Sustainable Development Goals Report 2021* (2021), 26.
[2] UN, *The Sustainable Development Goals Report 2020* (2020), 24.
[3] UN, *The Sustainable Development Goals Report 2020* (2020), 24.
[4] UN, *The Sustainable Development Goals Report 2021* (2021), 26.
[5] UN, *The Sustainable Development Goals Report 2021* (2021), 26.
[6] UN, *The Sustainable Development Goals Report 2020* (2020), 26.
[7] UN, *The Sustainable Development Goals Report 2020* (2020), 26.
[8] https://unstats.un.org/sdgs/metadata/.
[9] Roser and Ortiz-Ospina, 'Global Extreme Poverty' (2013) *OurWorldInData.org*.
[10] https://unstats.un.org/wiki/display/SDGeHandbook/Goal+1.
[11] https://www.un.org/millenniumgoals/poverty.shtml.
[12] https://www.un.org/en/sections/issues-depth/poverty/.
[13] A/HRC/41/39, *Climate change and poverty Report of the Special Rapporteur on extreme poverty and human rights*, 17 July 2019, para. 8; referring to World Bank, *World Development Report 2010: Development and Climate Change* (2010), 5.
[14] A/HRC/41/39, *Climate change and poverty Report of the Special Rapporteur on extreme poverty and human rights*, 17 July 2019, para. 11.

I. History of Poverty Alleviation by the UN

4   SDG 1 is aligned with MDG 1 but is broader in scope. MDG 1 had three targets which included to 'halve the proportion of people whose daily income is less than 1.25$', to 'achieve full and productive employment, as well as decent work for all, including young people and women', and to 'halve proportion of individuals suffering from hunger in the period between 1190 and 2015'.[15] SDG 1.1 imbibes an outdated definition of extreme poverty with only income below the threshold of 1.25$ falling within its ambit, whereas the threshold income for classifying extreme poverty today is less than 1.90$.[16]

5   In June 1972, the UN Conference on the Human Environment – first of many conferences on international environmental issues – was held in Stockholm.[17] The conference adopted the Stockholm Declaration, which dealt with several subjects including poverty reduction. The conference was pushing a 'new liberation movement which was supposed to free men from the threat of their thraldom to environmental perils of their own making'.[18] Elimination of mass poverty, racial prejudice and economic injustices was seen imperative for the success of the movement.[19] Following up on this ideal, in 1992, the General Assembly declared the 17 October as the International Day of eradication of poverty.[20]

6   At the UN Conference on Environment and Development in 1992, the Rio Declaration on Environment and Development was adopted. The declaration consists of 27 principles with one of the key principles (Principle 5) concerns the eradication of poverty[21] as it has always been considered the prime purpose of development.[22] Principle 5 of the Rio Declaration was preceded by Principle 1[23] and 8[24] of Stockholm Declaration.

7   The UN Conference on Environment and Development was followed by the World Summit for Social Development in March 1995, which was the largest gathering of world leaders at the time where the Governments reached a new consensus on the need to put people at the centre of development.[25] The summit ended with the adoption of the Copenhagen Declaration with chapter 2 of the declaration entirely devoted to eradication of poverty.[26]

---

[15] https://www.mdgmonitor.org/mdg-1-eradicate-poverty-hunger/.

[16] https://www.mdgmonitor.org/mdg-1-eradicate-poverty-hunger/.

[17] A/CONF. 48/14 Rev. 1, *Report of the United Nations on the Human Environment*, 5-16 June 1972.

[18] A/CONF. 48/14 Rev. 1, *Report of the United Nations on the Human Environment*, 5-16 June 1972, para. 34.

[19] A/CONF. 48/14 Rev. 1, *Report of the United Nations on the Human Environment*, 5-16 June 1972, para. 34.

[20] A/RES/47/196, *Observance of an International Day for the Eradication of Poverty*, 31 March 1993.

[21] A/CONF.151/26, *Report of the United Nations Conference on Environment and Development (Vol. I)*, 3-14 June 1992.

[22] Karimova and Golay, 'Principle 5 – Poverty Eradication' in Viñuales (ed), *The Rio Declaration on Environment and Development: A Commentary* (2015), 9, 181.

[23] A/CONF. 48/14 Rev. 1, *Report of the United Nations on the Human Environment*, 5-16 June 1972, Principle 1: Man has the fundamental right to freedom, equality and adequate conditions of life, in an environment of a quality that permits a life of dignity and well-being, and he bears a solemn responsibility to protect and improve the environment for present and future generations. In this respect, policies promoting or perpetuating apartheid, racial segregation, discrimination, colonial and other forms of oppression and foreign domination stand condemned and must be eliminated.

[24] A/CONF. 48/14 Rev. 1, *Report of the United Nations on the Human Environment*, 5-16 June 1972, Principle 4: 'Economic and social development is essential for ensuring a favorable living and working environment for man and for creating conditions on earth that are necessary for the improvement of the quality of life.'

[25] https://sustainabledevelopment.un.org/topics/povertyeradication.

[26] https://sustainabledevelopment.un.org/topics/povertyeradication.

The end of 1995 saw the declaration of the First United Nations Decade for Eradica- 8
tion of Poverty for the period 1997-2006 by the UN General Assembly.[27] In 2007, the
Secretary General published a report on the implementation of the First United Nations
Decade for the Eradication of Poverty (1997-2006), calling upon governments to 'focus
their efforts and policies on addressing the root causes of poverty'.[28] With 'The future
we want',[29] the vision to free humanity from poverty and hunger was set-out as a matter
of urgency.[30] It was stressed that eradicating poverty is fundamental to developing
sustainably:

> We recognize that poverty eradication, changing unsustainable and promoting sustainable patterns
> of consumption and production and protecting and managing the natural resource base of economic
> and social development are the overarching objectives of and essential requirements for sustainable
> development.[31]

Poverty reduction being an indispensable prerequisite for sustainable development 9
was also affirmed by the Open Working Group on Sustainable Development in 2014.[32]
Another pressing issue in recent years has been that of climate change inducing poverty,
which is also addressed in the 2015 Paris Agreement (PA).[33] The General Assembly
declared the Second United Nations Decade for the Eradication of Poverty (2008-2017)
in December 2007[34] with the theme 'Full Employment and Decent Work for All', and the
Third United Nations Decade for the Eradication of Poverty (2018-2027) in December
2017 with the theme 'Accelerating Global Actions for a World Without Poverty'[35]. The
FAO also includes in one of its three global goals the goal to end poverty and has
committed to support the achievement of SDG 1.1 by 2030.[36] Besides the FAO, several
further supranational organisations such as the World Bank and the Global Fund have
also shown a firm commitment to join the battle against poverty.[37]

II. Causes of Poverty

It is not only difficult but almost impossible to pin down the cause of poverty to 10
any one factor or even to a few factors. While low or no income may seem an obvious
cause of poverty,[38] the cause(s) can be as varied as their impact on human suffering
and include hunger and malnutrition, limited access to education and access to water,
clean sanitation and hygiene.[39] Another cause is discrimination, be it social, religious,

---

[27] A/RES/50/107, *Observance of the International Year for the Eradication of Poverty and proclamation of the first United Nations Decade for the Eradication of Poverty*, 26 January 1996.

[28] A/62/267, *Implementation of the first United Nations Decade for the Eradication of Poverty (1997-2006) Report of the Secretary-General*, 17 August 2007.

[29] A/RES/66/288, *The future we want*, 27 July 2012.

[30] A/RES/66/288, *The future we want*, 27 July 2012.

[31] A/RES/66/288, *The future we want*, 27 July 2012, Annex, para 4.

[32] A/68/970, *Report of the Open Working Group of the General Assembly on Sustainable Development Goals*, 12 August 2014, 6.

[33] UN, *Paris Agreement* (2015).

[34] A/RES/62/205, *Second United Nations Decade for the Eradication of Poverty (2008-2017)*, 10 March 2008.

[35] A/RES/72/233, *Implementation of the Second United Nations Decade for the Eradication of Poverty (2008-2017)*, 30 January 2018.

[36] FAO, *FAO framework on rural extreme poverty: Towards reaching Target 1.1 of the SDG* (2019), 1.

[37] Pogge, 'Fighting global poverty' (2017) 13(4) *International Journal of Law in Context*, 2.

[38] https://www.un.org/development/desa/socialperspectiveondevelopment/issues/poverty-eradication.html.

[39] https://www.un.org/development/desa/socialperspectiveondevelopment/issues/poverty-eradication.html.

gender based or any other kind, which marginalises certain sections of society leaving them without a voice or access to justice, creating inequality.[40] Violent conflicts also adds to the worsening of poverty for when conflict erupts, it hits poor people the hardest.[41] Crises and challenges of the 21st century – climate change or epidemics such as the SARS-CoV-2 pandemic – also directly compound poverty in the world.[42]

III. Relation to Human Rights

11   An examination of the causes and impact of poverty necessitates the simultaneous consideration of human rights.[43] Extreme poverty is caused by lack of income, a lack of access to basic services and social exclusion,[44] which is illuminated by the Multidimensional Poverty Index of the United Nations Development Program (UNDP).[45] The obvious link between extreme poverty and human rights stems from the fact that people living in extreme poverty lack access to human rights. In particular, the lack of access to education, health services, clean drinking water and basic sanitation plays an important role in tackling (extreme) poverty which will be discussed under the respective SDGs in the following chapters. The apparent mutual relationship between poverty and human rights violations is well illustrated by the example of children being deprived of the opportunity to get educated which not only makes it difficult for them to escape poverty but also significantly increases the likelihood that their children too will live in poverty. Conversely, poverty can also be a cause of human rights violations, as can be seen in many cases globally when poor people are forced to work in unsafe and unhealthy environments due to not having other alternatives.[46] To recapitulate the words of Nelson Mandela, '[o]vercoming poverty is not a gesture of charity. It is an act of justice. It is the protection of a fundamental human right, the right to dignity and a decent life. While poverty persists, there is no true freedom.'[47]

IV. Definitions

1. Poverty

12   Several definitions of poverty exist. The 1998 UN definition of poverty states:

> Fundamentally, poverty is a denial of choices and opportunities, a violation of human dignity. It means lack of basic capacity to participate effectively in society. It means not having enough to feed and cloth[e] a family, not having a school or clinic to go to, not having the land on which to grow one's food or a job to earn one's living, not having access to credit. It means insecurity, powerlessness and exclusion of individuals, households and communities. It means susceptibility to

---

[40] https://www.concernusa.org/story/causes-of-poverty/.
[41] Fünfgeld, *Poverty and conflict: an analytical framework* (2005), 1; Marks, *Poverty and Conflict* (2016), 1.
[42] https://www.oxfam.org/en/press-releases/half-billion-people-could-be-pushed-poverty-coronavirus-warns-oxfam.
[43] https://www.ohchr.org/EN/Issues/Poverty/Pages/About.aspx.
[44] A/HRC/7/15, *Report of the independent expert on the question of human rights and extreme poverty, Arjun Sengupta**, 28 February 2008, para. 13.
[45] UNDP, *Global Multidimensional Poverty Index 2020: Charting Pathways Out Of Multidimensional Poverty: Achieving the SDGs* (2020), 4; UNDP, *Global Multidimensional Poverty Index 2019, Illuminating Inequalities* (2019).
[46] https://www.coe.int/en/web/compass/poverty.
[47] UN Press Release (SG/SM/19138-OBV/1806), *Quoting Nelson Mandela on His Centenary, Secretary-General Says Overcoming Poverty 'Is Not an Act of Charity, It Is an Act of Justice'* (2018).

violence, and it often implies living on marginal or fragile environments, without access to clean water or sanitation.[48]

The OHCHR explained in 2004 that the 'that the defining feature of a poor person is 13 that she has very restricted opportunities to pursue her well-being' which equals 'as low levels of capability' in the sense of Sen's capability approach.[49]

2. Extreme Poverty

The meaning of extreme poverty was defined in 1995 by the UN in the report of the 14 World Summit for Social Development in Copenhagen as 'a condition characterized by severe deprivation of basic human needs, including food, safe drinking water, sanitation facilities, health, shelter, education and information. It depends not only on income but also on access to services.'[50] The term extreme poverty also refers to those people living on less than 1.90$-int a day.[51]

The United States Agency for International Development defines extreme poverty as: 15

> The inability to meet basic consumption needs on a sustainable basis. People who live in extreme poverty lack both income and assets and typically suffer from interrelated, chronic deprivations, including hunger and malnutrition, poor health, limited education, and marginalization or exclusion.[52]

B. Scope and Dimensions of SDG 1

Being the first SDG, SDG 1 can be seen as the gateway to the Agenda 2030. The 16 topics of poverty and its eradication cover a wide range of legal issues, economic interrelationships and global cooperation concepts. The wording of the first target already reflects the overarching goal of SDG 1 in its all-encompassing scope: Extreme poverty is to be eradicated for everyone everywhere in the world (SDG 1.1). In addition, the number of people in all forms of poverty is to be halved by 2030 (SDG 1.2).

Poverty is universally present, and the ambitious nature of SDG 1 emphasises the ur- 17 gency of tackling this issue globally. In this context, the role of law permeates all social, economic and political areas of poverty and its causes.[53] The causes and consequences of poverty directly affect many other SDGs. As one of the greatest challenges currently facing humankind, not least exacerbated by the global SARS-CoV-2 pandemic, poverty frequently is an intrinsic factor for deficits in areas of the other SDGs.[54]

I. Legal Foundations

According to the UN the proportion of population below the international poverty 18 line is defined as people '[l]iving in households below the international poverty line

---

[48] https://www.un.org/press/en/1998/19980520.eco5759.html; further reading: Sen, *Poverty and Famines* (1981).

[49] OHCHR, *Human Rights and Poverty Reduction, A Conceptual* Framework (2004), 7; further reading: Sen, *Development as Freedom* (1999).

[50] UN, *Report of the World Summit for Social Development*, 6-12 March 1995.

[51] https://ourworldindata.org/extreme-poverty.

[52] https://www.usaid.gov/ending-extreme-poverty.

[53] Beckett, 'Creating Poverty' in Orford and Hoffmann (eds), *The Oxford Handbook of the Theory of International Law* (2016), 985 (989 ff.).

[54] Cichos and Lange Salvia, *SDG 1 – No Poverty – Making the Dream a Reality* (2019), 1 ff.; De Schutter, *Tackling extreme poverty in times of crisis: Key challenges facing the fight against poverty and thematic priorities for the Special Rapporteur on extreme poverty and human rights*, 1 May 2020.

where the average daily consumption (or income) per person is less than $1.90 a day measured at 2011 international prices adjusted for purchasing power parity (PPP)'.[55]

19   The legal classification of poverty and poverty reduction is complex and requires a multi-layered and comprehensive analysis of various sources and statutes of international law. The interdependencies between poverty and numerous factors of a legal and non-legal nature demonstrate not least the interwoven position of the topic of poverty in the overall structure of SDGs. The international importance of poverty is envisaged by the efforts of the General Assembly to implement the third United Nations Decade for the Eradication of Poverty lasting from 2018 to 2027 to support the realisation of the SDGs.[56]

1. Human Rights and Economic, Social and Cultural Rights

20   Art. 25 of the Universal Declaration on Human Rights (UDHR) provides a core legal basis for the elimination of poverty. The right to an adequate standard of living may be considered as the basis for the eradication of poverty aimed for in SDG 1. Moreover, it is essential that SDG 1.1 'should be read as a continuation of the concerns stated in Article 25, the standard of living provision'.[57] Art. 25 UDHR also contains other significant rights that include aspects such as

> food, clothing, housing and medical care and necessary social services, and the right to security in the event of unemployment, sickness, disability, widowhood, old age or other lack of livelihood in circumstances beyond his control.

21   Almost identical in wording is Art. 11 of the International Convention on Economic, Social and Cultural Rights (ICESCR).[58] This is no coincidence, since in 1966 the rights enshrined in the UDHR were included almost identically in two subsequent treaties: in the International Covenant on Civil and Political Rights (ICCPR) and the International Covenant on Economic, Social and Cultural Rights (ICESCR).[59] The importance of the ICESCR in the context of poverty is illustrated by the fact that

> [p]overty is created by socio-economic processes, and those processes are in turn effected through, and regulated by, international law; thus poverty is a 'legal regime'. […] The intention is to create and concentrate wealth, but the production of poverty is a necessary and known by-product of the creation and consolidation of wealth. The consolidation of extreme wealth entails the creation of extreme poverty; the latter is deliberate in the sense of being a known consequence of the pursuit

[55] https://unstats.un.org/wiki/display/SDGeHandbook/Indicator+1.1.1.

[56] A/RES/72/233, *Implementation of the Second United Nations Decade for the Eradication of Poverty (2008–2017)*, 20 December 2017; A/73/298, *Implementation of the Third United Nations Decade for the Eradication of Poverty (2018–2027), Report of the Secretary-General*, 6 August 2018.

[57] Brown, *The Universal Declaration of Human Rights in the 21st Century – A Living Document in a Changing World – A report by the Global Citizenship Commission* (2016), 54.

[58] Karimova and Golay, 'Principle 5 – Poverty Eradication' in Viñuales (ed), *The Rio Declaration on Environment and Development: A Commentary* (2015), 181 (193 f.): 'More than 160 countries have ratified the ICESCR, which makes it a major source of protection of ESCR [Economic, Social and Cultural Rights] at the international level.'; see further on the ICESCR: Saul, Kinley and Mowbray, *The International Covenant on Economic, Social and Cultural Rights: Commentary, Cases, and Materials* (2014), 1 (1 ff.); Binder et al., *Research Handbook on International Law and Social Rights* (2020).

[59] World Health Organization, *Health and human rights – International Covenant on Economic, Social and Cultural Rights* 16 December 1966, 1; see also: https://www.escr-net.org/resources/section-5-background-information-icescr; Coomans, 'Application of the International Covenant on Economic, Social and Cultural Rights in the Framework of International Organisations' in von Bogdandy and Wolfrum (eds), *Max Planck Yearbook of United Nations Law* (2007), 359 (359 ff.).

of the former. [...] The processes of wealth creation and concentration are managed through law; consequently, the corollary processes of poverty creation are also creatures of law.[60]

Therefore, international law and legal regimes fulfil an essential role and task in the fight against global poverty. The international chain of economic relations, production, trade and cooperation between already poor states and the industrialised countries is thus at the centre of global poverty creation and will therefore be examined in greater detail in the following. As regards Art. 11 of the ICESCR,[61] poverty related aspects cover fields such as the improvement of living conditions, the requirement to equitably distribute goods for the coverage of everyone's needs as well as a functioning framework of international cooperation.[62] **22**

Emphasis is again placed on the fact that poverty eradication requires the implementation of a number of fundamental rights directly linked to the objectives of other SDGs. In its Guiding Principles on Extreme Poverty and Human Rights (UNGP), the Office of the United Nations High Commissioner for Human Rights (OHCHR) outlined the interdependencies between various human rights and the fight against extreme poverty. The UNGP are intended to help states and governments to guarantee the rights of people in extreme poverty and to direct national policies towards protecting these rights and supporting the implementation of strategies against poverty.[63] **23**

Rights which are directly linked to the eradication of poverty hereby are: **24**

- Right to life and physical integrity
- Rights to liberty and security of the person
- Right to equal protection before the law, access to justice and effective remedies (→ Goal 16 mn. 9, 24)
- Right to recognition as a person before the law (→ Goal 16 mn. 31 f.)
- Right to privacy and to protection for home and family
- Right to an adequate standard of living (Art. 11 ICESCR)
- Right to adequate food and nutrition (Art. 11 ICESCR) (→ Goal 2 mn. 31 f., 33)
- Rights to water and sanitation (Art. 11 ICESCR) (→ Goal 6 mn. 30 ff.)

---

[60] Beckett, 'Creating Poverty' in Orford and Hoffmann (eds), *The Oxford Handbook of the Theory of International Law* (2016), 985 (989).

[61] ICESCR, Art. 11:

1. The States Parties to the present Covenant recognize the right of everyone to an adequate standard of living for himself and his family, including adequate food, clothing and housing, and to the continuous improvement of living conditions. The States Parties will take appropriate steps to ensure the realization of this right, recognizing to this effect the essential importance of international co-operation based on free consent.

2. The States Parties to the present Covenant, recognizing the fundamental right of everyone to be free from hunger, shall take, individually and through international co-operation, the measures, including specific programmes, which are needed:

(a) To improve methods of production, conservation and distribution of food by making full use of technical and scientific knowledge, by disseminating knowledge of the principles of nutrition and by developing or reforming agrarian systems in such a way as to achieve the most efficient development and utilization of natural resources;

(b) Taking into account the problems of both food-importing and food-exporting countries, to ensure an equitable distribution of world food supplies in relation to need.

[62] Karimova and Golay, 'Principle 5 – Poverty Eradication' in Viñuales (ed), *The Rio Declaration on Environment and Development: A Commentary* (2015), 181 (194).

[63] UN Human Rights Office of the High Commissioner, *Guiding Principles on Extreme Poverty and Human Rights* (2012); A/HRC/21/39, *Final draft of the guiding principles on extreme poverty and human rights, submitted by the Special Rapporteur on extreme poverty and human rights, Magdalena Sepúlveda Carmona*, 18 July 2012.

- Right to adequate housing, security of tenure and prohibition of forced eviction (Art. 11 ICESCR)
- Right to the highest attainable standard of physical and mental health (Art. 12 ICE-SCR) (→ Goal 3 mn. 2, 15)
- Right to work and rights at work (→ Goal 8 mn. 58 f., 61)
- Right to social security (Art. 9 ICESCR)
- Right to education (Art. 13 ICESCR) (→ Goal 4 mn. 14 ff., 28 ff.)
- Rights to take part in cultural life and to enjoy the benefits of scientific progress and its applications[64]

25   In the legal processing of poverty, it is essential to distinguish between the causes and effects of poverty. A special analysis of various factors in the context of poverty is required. Beckett assigns to poverty a special status consisting of 'the myriad and messy entanglements between human rights, economics, development, and international law: their relations of domination and subjugation; of complicity and compromise'.[65]

26   Within the Guiding Principles on Extreme Poverty and Human Rights, poverty is further depicted as an issue going beyond the field of economy, being 'rather a multidimensional phenomenon that encompasses a lack of both income and the basic capabilities to live in dignity'.[66]

27   The numerous definitions of poverty in the literature give a good indication of the extent to which the topic is treated in science. However, the core of poverty is not always so obvious. Within the 'Statement on Poverty and the International Covenant on Economic, Social and Cultural Rights' of the United Nations Economic and Social Council, poverty is described as

> a human condition characterized by the sustained or chronic deprivation of the resources, capabilities, choices, security and power necessary for the enjoyment of an adequate standard of living and other civil, cultural, economic, political and social rights.[67]

28   The wording 'deprivation of the resources, capabilities, choices, security and power' clearly represents the core of poverty and its economic, social, legal and ecological dimensions: At its core, poverty is always about access to resources, rights, services, etc. As soon as access to one or more of these factors is denied to one or more persons due to discrimination, economic hardship or other causes, the risk of poverty is high.[68]

29   Particular attention should be paid to the forward-looking interpretation of the rights under the ICESCR.

30   The right to an adequate standard of living (Art. 11 ICESCR) implies the guarantee of continuous improvement of the living conditions underlying this right and constitutes

---

[64] A/HRC/21/39, *Final draft of the guiding principles on extreme poverty and human rights, submitted by the Special Rapporteur on extreme poverty and human rights, Magdalena Sepúlveda Carmona*, 18 July 2012.

[65] Beckett, 'Creating Poverty' in Orford and Hoffmann (eds), *The Oxford Handbook of the Theory of International Law* (2016), 985 (999).

[66] A/HRC/21/39, *Final draft of the guiding principles on extreme poverty and human rights, submitted by the Special Rapporteur on extreme poverty and human rights, Magdalena Sepúlveda Carmona*, 18 July 2012, para. 2; Karimova and Golay, 'Principle 5 – Poverty Eradication' in Viñuales (ed), *The Rio Declaration on Environment and Development: A Commentary* (2015), 181 (191).

[67] E/C.12/2001/10, *Substantive issues arising in the implementation of the International Covenant on Economic, Social and Cultural Rights: Poverty and the International Covenant on Economic, Social and Cultural Rights*, 10 May 2001, para. 8; Karimova and Golay, 'Principle 5 – Poverty Eradication' in Viñuales (ed), *The Rio Declaration on Environment and Development: A Commentary* (2015), 181 (191).

[68] Jefferson, 'Global poverty – Trends, measures and antidotes' in Greve (ed), *Routledge International Handbook of Poverty* (2020), 119 (126 ff.).

the core right concerning poverty eradication.[69] The multidimensional nature of poverty and the clear and in-depth independencies between SDG 1 and the following SDGs make all rights and provisions of the ICESCR highly important concerning the eradication of global poverty.[70]

2. The Role of States

States have a special responsibility in the fight against poverty. Not least because   **31**
states must protect the rights to which their citizens are entitled and enable their implementation. In this context, Art. 2 (1) of the ICESCR is to be regarded as the underlying norm regarding state obligations.[71] The obligations under Art. 2 (1) ICESCR concern all social, economic and cultural rights contained in the ICESCR and therefore also apply to all ICESCR rights mentioned in this Commentary. The UN Commission on Economic, Social and Cultural Rights entitles the state's duty to act by emphasising that a 'minimum core obligation to ensure the satisfaction of, at the very least, minimum essential levels of each of the rights is incumbent upon every State party'.[72] Karimova and Golay divide the overall nature of states' obligations in Art. 2 (1) into three essential obligations:

1. the obligation to take steps through all appropriate means, including and especially legislative measures
2. the obligation to take steps with a view to progressively achieving the full realisation of ICESCR
3. the obligation to take steps, to the maximum of all available resources, both those within a country and those available from the international community and assistance.[73]

---

[69] Saul, Kinley and Mowbray, *The International Covenant on Economic, Social and Cultural Rights: Commentary, Cases, and Materials* (2014), 862; Salomon, 'Why should it matter that others have more? Poverty, inequality, and the potential of international human rights law' (2011) 37 *Rev. Int. Stud.*, 2137 (2152); Karimova and Golay, 'Principle 5 – Poverty Eradication' in Viñuales (ed), *The Rio Declaration on Environment and Development: A Commentary* (2015), 181 (193).

[70] The rights of the ICESCR are the following: 'the right to self-determination of all peoples (article 1); the right to non-discrimination based on race, colour, sex, language, religion, political or other opinion, national or social origin, property, birth or other status (article 2); the equal right of men and women to enjoy the rights in the ICESCR (article 3); the right to work (articles 6–7); the right to form and join trade unions (article 8); the right to social security (article 9); protection and assistance to the family (article 10); the right to an adequate standard of living (article 11); the right to health (article 12); the right to education (articles 13–14); and the right to cultural freedoms (article 15)', World Health Organization, *Health and human rights – International Covenant on Economic, Social and Cultural Rights* (2006).

[71] Art. 2(1) ICESCR:
1. Each State Party to the present Covenant undertakes to take steps, individually and through international assistance and co-operation, especially economic and technical, to the maximum of its available resources, with a view to achieving progressively the full realization of the rights recognized in the present Covenant by all appropriate means, including particularly the adoption of legislative measures.
2. The States Parties to the present Covenant undertake to guarantee that the rights enunciated in the present Covenant will be exercised without discrimination of any kind as to race, colour, sex, language, religion, political or other opinion, national or social origin, property, birth or other status.
3. Developing countries, with due regard to human rights and their national economy, may determine to what extent they would guarantee the economic rights recognized in the present Covenant to non-nationals.

[72] General Comment No. 3: The nature of States parties' obligations (Art. 2(1) of the Covenant) (1990), para. 10; Salomon, 'Why should it matter that others have more? Poverty, inequality, and the potential of international human rights law' (2011) 37 *Rev. Int. Stud.*, 2137 (2140).

[73] Karimova and Golay, 'Principle 5 – Poverty Eradication' in Viñuales (ed), *The Rio Declaration on Environment and Development: A Commentary* (2015), 181 (195).

32   The scope of steps states are obliged to take in order to comply with the ICESCR does not only cover one single aspect of governmental purposes. Rather, the scope covers a wide range of different areas such as 'legislative, administrative, judicial, economic, social and educational measures'.[74] States must therefore take a holistic approach to ensuring profound and comprehensive implementation of ICESCR. This includes in particular the factor of access to resources for all people. Considering the root causes of poverty, lack of access is a fundamental problem in almost all areas[75] and will be examined further throughout this commentary.

33   Since legislative measures form a prerequisite for the effective realisation of rights, their sound design is of particular relevance to combat discrimination and other forms of inequality.[76]

34   For the ICESCR to be implemented globally and uniformly in all states, this also requires that states that do not have the necessary resources are willing to accept support from other states (Art. 2(3) ICESCR).[77] Here, this form of international cooperation serves the following purpose:

> facilitating the full realization' of the Covenant's rights, and points to the provisions in various Articles that allude to states parties' collective responsibilities to cooperate regarding equitable food distribution (Article 11), the conservation, development and diffusion of scientific and cultural benefits (Article 15), and, alongside UN bodies and specialized agencies, the rendering of technical assistance that promotes implementation of the Covenant (Articles 22 and 23).[78]

35   Specifically, states have to tackle poverty at a multidimensional level and respond with targeted, effective measures against the background of the 'duties to progressively realize rights to an adequate standard of living, including food and housing, to the highest attainable standards of health and to social security'.[79] Under the roof of enabling access to fundamental needs for everyone, states' measures to eradicate poverty encompass inter alia the fields of

> increasing responsible and pro-poor investment, developing rural infrastructure, promoting technology transfer and capacity development, diversifying rural employment, ensuring the responsible governance of tenure, improving access to health, education, water and sanitation services; promoting gender equality and decent work; and improving access to social protection programmes.[80]

36   States are thus obliged to protect each individual person in their economic, social and cultural rights and to ensure that the ICECSR are implemented, especially when people are increasingly dependent on state assistance due to illness, age or accident. As SDG 1.2 indicates, nationally appropriate social protection systems and measures for all should be guaranteed. In this context, Art. 9 ICESCR[81] forms the legal basis of SDG 1.2. General Comment No. 19 then describes the Right to Social Security as

---

[74] Karimova and Golay, 'Principle 5 – Poverty Eradication' in Viñuales (ed), *The Rio Declaration on Environment and Development: A Commentary* (2015), 181 (196).

[75] De Gaay Fortman, 'Poverty as a failure of entitlement: do rights-based approaches make sense?' in Williams (ed), *International poverty law – An emerging discourse* (2006), 34 (34 ff.).

[76] See Saul and Kinley and Mowbray, *The International Covenant on Economic, Social and Cultural Rights: Commentary, Cases, and Materials* (2014), 137.

[77] Karimova and Golay, 'Principle 5 – Poverty Eradication' in Viñuales (ed), *The Rio Declaration on Environment and Development: A Commentary* (2015), 181 (196).

[78] Saul, Kinley and Mowbray, *The International Covenant on Economic, Social and Cultural Rights: Commentary, Cases, and Materials* (2014), 139.

[79] FAO, *Legal measures to eradicate rural poverty* (2019), 2.

[80] FAO, *Legal measures to eradicate rural poverty* (2019), 2.

[81] Art. 9 ICESCR: 'The States Parties to the present Covenant recognize the right of everyone to social security, including social insurance'.

the right to access and maintain benefits, whether in cash or in kind, without discrimination in order to secure protection, inter alia, from (a) lack of work-related income caused by sickness, disability, maternity, employment injury, unemployment, old age, or death of a family member; (b) unaffordable access to health care; (c) insufficient family support, particularly for children and adult dependents.[82]

This definition follows the 1952 ILO's Social Security (Minimum Standards) Convention (No. 102) by linking income support to work interruptions based on nine contingencies.[83] In addition to general disadvantage experienced by women on the basis of gender, certain groups of women face greater inequality by other forms of discrimination based on factors such as race, disability, age, religion, ethnic and indigenous status, or geographical location. This discrimination often translates into economic disadvantage, affecting access to resources, especially for vulnerable groups of women, resulting in greater poverty.[84] 37

The main objective of establishing and safeguarding a social security system is to protect the human dignity of each individual, particularly in situations where the individual is unable to defend his or her rights himself or herself because of illness, disability, and unemployment, an accident at work or old age. Participation in social life should be guaranteed and social exclusion prevented.[85] It is therefore up to states to implement and safeguard the right to social security including social insurance for everyone without any form of discrimination.[86] 38

This apparently includes the duty of states to eliminate discrimination against women, people with disabilities, children and indigenous people.[87] Especially regarding the vulnerable situation of children, states are called upon to take the following measures: 39

the taking of targeted measures protecting children from the harmful impact of poverty on their development, health, and education; ensuring access to clean water, adequate sanitation, food, and shelter, as well as education, social, and health services; the allocation of adequate human, technical, and financial resources to provide support to families; the provision and strengthening of infrastructure and/or multi-sectoral coordination; the establishment of a social protection framework or social security system; the elimination of regional disparities in terms of child poverty and rights enjoyment; and the collection of data and monitoring of trends in poverty. [...] States have also been asked [...] to implement legislation focused on social protection, social welfare, and ending child poverty.[88]

International support and development aid is characterised by the right to development. Based on the Declaration on the Right to Development[89] 'states should cooperate with each other in ensuring development and eliminating obstacles to development'.[90] 40

---

[82] E/C.12/GC/19, *General Comment No. 19 The right to social security (art. 9)*, 4 February 2008, para. 2.

[83] Goldblatt, 'Gender, poverty and the development of the right to social security' (2014) 10(4) *International Journal of Law in Context*, 460 (463).

[84] Goldblatt, 'Gender, poverty and the development of the right to social security' (2014) 10(4) *International Journal of Law in Context*, 460 (466).

[85] E/C.12/GC/19, *General Comment No. 19 The right to social security (art. 9)*, 4 February 2008, paras. 1, 3.

[86] E/C.12/GC/19, *General Comment No. 19 The right to social security (art. 9)*, 4 February 2008, para. 4.

[87] Art. 13 Convention on the Elimination of All Forms of Discrimination against Women (1979), Art. 4 Convention on the Rights of Persons with Disabilities (2002); Art. 4 Convention on the Rights of the Child (1989), Art. 15 United Nations Declaration on the Rights of Indigenous Peoples (2007).

[88] Nolan, 'Art. 27 The Right to a Standard of Living Adequate for the Child's Development' in Tobin (ed), *The UN Convention on the Rights of the Child: A Commentary* (2019), 1021 (1034).

[89] A/RES/41/128, *Declaration on the right to Development*, 4 December 1986; see also: Ngang and Kamga and Gumede, *Perspectives on the right to development* (2018).

[90] Cichos and Lange Salvia, *SDG 1 – No Poverty – Making the Dream a Reality* (2019), 21; General Comment No. 3: The nature of States parties' obligations (Art. 2, para. 1 of the Covenant) (1990), para. 14; Kamga and Ngang, *Insights Into Policies and Practices on the Right to Development* (2020).

Those obstacles might be of economic, political, legal and sociocultural nature and are commonly hindering the development of states and regions. Conversely, impeded development hinders progress in eradicating poverty.[91] The development aspect focuses on the equitable distribution and redistribution of resources worldwide to improve the economic situation of people. Furthermore, the physical and mental health of people plays a vital role in the fight against poverty ($\rightarrow$ Goal 3 mn. 14, 19).[92] The duty of states to engage in international development cooperation between industrialised and developing countries is reflected in SDG 1.5, which also points to the broad issue of resource allocation of resources as the umbrella of international development cooperation.

41   In the context of international assistance and cooperation between states, two key areas stand out: inequalities and discrimination. Particularly in view of the dynamic interdependencies of the SDGs, these two areas need to be constantly addressed as a belt layer.

II. Inequalities, Poverty and Law

42   Inequalities represent the main cause of poverty and law plays a crucial role in the reallocation of resources since 'legal rules are deeply implicated in maintaining and strengthening status quo power and wealth inequalities, resulting in substantial poverty worldwide'.[93] Inequalities are deeply examined in the framework of SDG 10 but as inequalities reinforce the effects of poverty and vice-versa they have to be mentioned in this section as well. Inequalities exist between states as well as between individuals within societies. Both have in common the lack of adequate access to necessary resources. At the individual level, this includes the access to education, to sanitary and health services, to judiciary participation and social inclusion. Since this area corresponds with the issue of discrimination, it is explained in more detail below in section 3 ($\rightarrow$ Goal 1 mn. 50 ff.).

43   Inequalities between states and the issue of poverty are closely interlinked with trade and global trade systems. While it was long assumed that trade exclusively promoted the welfare of states, the view has changed today. The economic development of a country is of great importance as trade enhances growth and growth helps to reduce poverty.[94] Trade liberalisation helps developing countries to gain access to world markets. However, as with any other political measure, trade liberalisation 'will create both winners and losers'.[95]

44   Legal frameworks have a profound effect on international allocation of income, resources and power.[96] This also applies to trade. International law and its enforcement play a crucial role in establishing a fair and adequate trade liberalisation without depriving the poor from their already limited resources. The liberalisation of international

---

[91] Rabie, *A Theory of Sustainable Sociocultural and Economic Development* (2016), 127 ff.; Karimova and Golay, 'Principle 5 – Poverty Eradication' in Viñuales (ed), *The Rio Declaration on Environment and Development: A Commentary* (2015), 181 (195 ff.).

[92] Marks and Han, 'Health and Human Rights through Development – The Right to Development, Rights-Based Approach to Development, and Sustainable Development Goals' in Gostin and Meier (eds), *Foundations of Global Health & Human Rights* (2020), 329 (329).

[93] Williams, 'Towards an emerging international poverty law' in Williams (ed), *International poverty law – An emerging discourse* (2006), 1 (1).

[94] Mitra, 'Trade, Poverty and Inequality' in Bhagwati, Krishna and Panagariya (eds), *The World Trade System – Trends and Challenges* (2016), 55 (55 f.).

[95] Mitra, 'Trade, Poverty and Inequality' in Bhagwati, Krishna and Panagariya (eds), *The World Trade System – Trends and Challenges* (2016), 55 (56).

[96] Williams, 'Towards an emerging international poverty law' in Williams (ed), *International poverty law – An emerging discourse* (2006), 1 (1).

trade has to be implemented within the framework of international law standards in order to prevent a shift of power towards multinational companies.[97] With the aim of reducing poverty, economic openness and assistance to particularly developing countries is a core concern that must be addressed by international legal statutes.[98]

The WTO pledges for a trade-centred approach to poverty reduction by stating that **45** 'access to international markets may deliver higher average incomes to farmers who specialise in producing export crops, but may bring greater competition that reduces the demand for poor workers in import competing sectors'.[99]

A main obstacle of economic development are the historic roots of colonialism with **46** continuing effects on the economic and governmental structures in many developing countries.[100] Additionally, international investment law and the instrument of foreign direct investment (FDI) may support the reduction of poverty in specific regions.[101]

SDG 1.5 focuses on the resilience of poor and vulnerable people towards climate-re- **47** lated catastrophes and other economic, social and environmental disasters. Thereby, it is noticeable that inequalities may not only arise from economic systems but also from climate change, climate-related extreme events and other disasters. Natural disasters and other dangerous events caused by climate change as a catalyst worsen the situation of people, hitting vulnerable and already poor groups of people the hardest. Moreover, natural disasters are also a major cause of global poverty. Approximately 26 million people fall into poverty due to natural disasters every year, particularly due to floods and drought.[102]

Consequently, the Special Rapporteur on extreme poverty and human rights pledges **48** for various measures concerning climate action and law. Here, the focus is on economic transformation towards a climate-friendly economy and on strengthening the social, economic and cultural rights of every individual, realised in harmony with the climate. Furthermore, the Special Rapporteur urges the international community to transform the current international human rights regime by mentioning the threats of climate change to democracy and civil and political rights and to almost every human right.[103]

Art. 2 of the Paris Agreement on Climate Change contains the overall aims of the **49** agreement by indicating the overall context of climate change, sustainable development and the eradication of poverty making thus the international community aware of the inseparable connections between climate change and poverty.

III. Vulnerable Groups and Discrimination

Vulnerable groups in the context of poverty need special protection and special atten- **50** tion in international policy and legal analysis. Women, children, people with disabilities, indigenous groups and beyond suffer to significantly from discrimination in their soci-

---

[97] See for instance OECD, *OECD Guidelines for Multinational Enterprises* (2011).

[98] Prieto-Acosta, 'Biodiversity versus biotechnology: an economic and environmental struggle for life' in Williams (ed), *International poverty law – An emerging discourse* (2006), 49 (71).

[99] World Trade Organization and World Bank Group, *Trade and Poverty Reduction – New Evidence of Impact in Developing Countries* (2018), 6; see also: Joseph, *Blame it on the WTO? – A Human Rights Critique* (2011).

[100] Rabie, *A Theory of Sustainable Sociocultural and Economic Development* (2016), 127 (127 f.).

[101] Subedi, *International Investment Law – Reconciling Policy and Principle* (2020), 7 (7 f.).

[102] Hallegatte, Fay and Barbier, 'Poverty and climate change: introduction' (2018) 23 *Environ Dev Econ*, 217 (223).

[103] A/HRC/41/39, *Climate change and poverty Report of the Special Rapporteur on extreme poverty and human rights*, 17 July 2019.

eties or even from discriminatory policies of their home states (→ Goal 5 mn. 21, 32, Goal 10 mn. 23 ff.).[104]

51   These discriminatory inequalities regarding poverty in societies consist of several spheres of which both economic and social access to fundamental resources are of core importance. Concerning social issues of access, it is striking that poverty in this respect is described 'as a set of social roles, low status and social dishonour – the idea of the 'underclass' is an extreme example'. This ultimately leads to 'the problem of exclusion, where people are denied access to essential resources because they are left out, shut out or pushed out' due to discriminatory attitudes. Moreover, there is 'a lack of entitlement, in the sense that poor people do not have the rights to access and use resources that others can'.[105] The SDGs aim to follow an inclusive approach in their implementation strategies.[106] The social inclusion of these and other discriminated groups must be at the centre of legal efforts to successfully eliminate the underlying roots of persistent poverty. This is the effective method to sustainably transform societies towards inclusive, respective and equitable ones.[107]

52   Women still make up a large proportion of the world's poor population, not least because of various forms of social exclusion which is linked to profound inequalities in terms of social, cultural, political and economic aspects. It is more than likely that the pandemic will have a more intensive impact to the vulnerable groups than as to other and will expose the members of vulnerable groups to a greater extent to the margins of poverty.[108] 'The gender dimensions of poverty are causally related to women's unequal position in all realms of society'.[109] Rooted in preserved labour division women are frequently denied of their rights to work and to freely choose a preferred job. This disadvantage in the labour market leads to a pre-determined larger poverty of women. Once women belong to other vulnerable, discriminated minority groups, the discrimination and exclusion of women and thus the violation of their fundamental rights are dramatically intensified. Women are generally made more difficult to own land and property in general, both at the social level and through legal obstacles.[110] As a result, women are denied substantively justiciable rights and access to legal bodies.[111] The rights to land ownership and other productive resources of women are enshrined in

---

[104] Dornan, 'Children, Poverty and the Sustainable Development Goals' (2017) 31 *Children & Society*, 157 (157 ff.); Goldblatt, 'Gender, poverty and the development of the right to social security' (2014) 10 *ICJL*, 460 (460 ff.); Convention on the Elimination of All Forms of Discrimination against Women (1979); Convention on the Rights of the Child (1989), Convention on the Rights of Persons with Disabilities (2002); United Nations Declaration on the Rights of Indigenous Peoples (2007); ILO Convention No. 169 Convention Concerning Indigenous and Tribal Peoples in Independent Countries (1989).

[105] Spicker, 'Social exclusion and the relational elements of poverty' in Koehler et al. (eds), *The Politics of Social Inclusion – Bridging Knowledge and Policies Towards Social Change* (2020), 81 (82).

[106] A/RES/70/1, *Transforming our world: the 2030 agenda for sustainable development*, 21 October 2015, para. 3: '[…] just and inclusive societies'; para. 8: '[…] socially inclusive world'; para. 9: '[…] inclusive and sustainable economic growth'.

[107] Spicker, 'Social exclusion and the relational elements of poverty' in Koehler et al. (eds), *The Politics of Social Inclusion – Bridging Knowledge and Policies Towards Social Change* (2020), 81 (94 ff.).

[108] UN Women, Press release 02.09.2020; OHCHR, Press release, 11.09.2020: 176 million people could fall into poverty when using a poverty baseline of 3.20 USD/day. This is equivalent to an increase in the poverty rate of 2.3 percentage points compared to a no-COVID-19 scenario.'; UN Press release 17.09.2020: 'Globally, the number of children living in poverty soared to nearly 1.2 billion – a 15 per cent increase since the pandemic hit earlier this year, according to a technical note on impact of COVID-19 on child poverty, issued on Thursday by the UN Children's Fund (UNICEF) and the NGO Save the Children.'

[109] Goldblatt, 'Gender, poverty and the development of the right to social security' (2014) 10 *ICJL*, 460 (466).

[110] Goldblatt, 'Gender, poverty and the development of the right to social security' (2014) 10 *ICJL*, 460 (466).

[111] https://www.un.org/press/en/2018/wom2143.doc.htm.

and legally protected through various international covenants and frameworks on which many states have given their consensus.[112]

> Even where women do own resources or bring in income they may not be able to fully access or control these in patriarchal settings where men are designated household heads [...]. Women also face exclusion from political representation, decision-making and full participation in many parts of the world, which has an impact on their life chances and material position.[113]

The abolition of unjust and discriminatory situations of women suffering from pover-   **53** ty worldwide and especially the empowerment of women through international action are therefore 'an essential precondition for the eradication of global poverty'.[114]

This is not least due to the fact that women play a central role in the care and raising   **54** of children. Considering this in light of the fact that family income often remains in the hands of men and little is spent on the everyday needs of children and women, women have an even more important role to play in the fight against poverty. Furthermore, women's equal right to bank loans, mortgages, and other forms of financial credit as being entitled in Art. 13 (b) of the Convention on the Elimination of All Forms of Discrimination against Women 'serves to ensure women's economic autonomy'.[115]

> In many States parties, women encounter difficulties in obtaining bank loans and public subsidies and have less access to finance for business purposes. Typical obstacles are conditions that women frequently cannot meet because of past discrimination: the requirement of a certain amount of prior experience, of an uninterrupted employment history, or of individually owned assets.[116]

Child poverty and poverty among women are thus inextricably linked and frequently   **55** share the same causes.[117] Empowering women in their existing but fundamentally violated rights is one of the core targets within SDG 1, namely SDG 1.4 and SDG 1.a, and must be achieved by all legal means.

Girls in particular must be strengthened in their right to an adequate education and   **56** access to schooling and must be supported by the state. In many cases, compulsory schooling already exists, but it is not sufficiently implemented and protected. Girls must be protected from the consequences of poverty, which often keeps them away from education, either because there is not enough money or because boys are preferred over them for school education (→ Goal 4, Goal 5).[118]

The existing legal conventions and frameworks serve a solid base for global action,   **57** however, especially concerning the Convention on the Elimination of All Forms of Dis-

---

[112] UN Women and OHCHR, *Realizing women's rights to land and other productive resources* (2013), 5 ff.; Universal Declaration of Human Rights (1948), Art. 2; International Covenant on Civil and Political Rights (1966), Art. 3; Convention on the Elimination of All Forms of Discrimination against Women (1979); Convention on the Rights of the Child (1989); Convention on the Rights of Persons with Disabilities (2002); United Nations Declaration on the Rights of Indigenous Peoples (2007); The International Convention on the Elimination of All Forms of Racial Discrimination (1965); International Convention on the Protection of the Rights of All Migrant Workers and Members of Their Families (1990).
[113] Goldblatt, 'Gender, poverty and the development of the right to social security' (2014) 10 ICJL, 460 (466).
[114] E/C.12/2001/10, *Substantive issues arising in the implementation of the International Covenant on Economic, Social and Cultural Rights: Poverty and the International Covenant on Economic, Social and Cultural Rights*, 10 May 2001, para. 5.
[115] Freeman, Chinkin and Rudolf, *The UN Convention on the Elimination of All Forms of Discrimination Against Women: A Commentary* (2012), 351.
[116] Freeman, Chinkin and Rudolf, *The UN Convention on the Elimination of All Forms of Discrimination Against Women: A Commentary* (2012), 351.
[117] Bradshaw, Chant and Linneker, 'Gender and poverty: what we know, don't know and need to know for agenda 2030' (2017) 24 *Gend. Place Cult.*, 1667 (1667 ff.).
[118] Goonesekere, 'Civil and Political Rights and Poverty Eradication' in Van Bueren (ed), *Freedom from Poverty as a Human Right – Law's Duty to the Poor* (2010), 51 (57 ff.).

crimination against Women (CEDAW) it is striking that no concrete provision dealing with women in poverty exists. Nevertheless, the interrelated and extensive rights of women in the Convention are of considerable importance and address the multidimensional scope of the issue of poverty and women in a differentiated manner.[119]

58   SDG 1.2 focuses on the poverty reduction of men, women and children emphasising thus the outstanding and vulnerable position of children regarding the eradication of poverty. Children make up a significant part of the world's poor population. Their protection and support is essential for sustainable, equitable and inclusive new generations and thus build the ground for sustainable development. Poverty has severe effects on children during their growth concerning physical, mental and social aspects which impedes their future opportunities as adults and thus intervenes in their human and social, economic and cultural rights. Children are especially seen as vulnerable as they are not or less able to defend and follow their rights.[120] There are three reasons why children's special position is to be considered and protected as regards their socio-economic rights:

> First, poor children face very specific challenges with regard to their socioeconomic rights due to both the biological and socially constructed characteristics of childhood. Second, children are particularly vulnerable to violations of their socioeconomic rights owing to their more limited ability vis-à-vis other groups to protect themselves from such violations and/or to take advantage of protections that are available. Finally, it is crucial that there be a move away from the traditional – and false – presumptions that (a) children's socioeconomic rights-related interests are identical to those of their parents, family unit or carers, and (b) children's socioeconomic rights-related needs will necessarily be met by their family/carers.[121]

59   To combat child poverty and to make aware of its severe impact on a new generation, it is of upmost importance to ensure 'that reducing child poverty is an explicit national policy'.[122] For this purpose, international and regional legal conventions need to be implemented fully and with great urgency in a manner that all children profit from their legal rights.[123]

C. Interdependences of SDG 1

60   According to the preamble of the Global Agenda 2030, 'eradicating poverty in all its forms and dimensions, including extreme poverty is the greatest global challenge and an indispensable requirement for sustainable development.' This being a multidimensional task,[124] progress of SDG 1 is closely linked to the progress of all other goals.[125]

61   The preamble of the Global Agenda 2030 reveals the strong connection with SDG 2.[126] Poverty and hunger build a mutually reinforcing connection. Poverty tends to

---

[119] Campbell, *Women, Poverty, Equality – The Role of CEDAW* (2018), 5 f.

[120] Nolan, 'Rising to the Challenge of Child Poverty: The Role of the Courts' in Van Bueren (ed), *Freedom from Poverty as a Human Right – Law's Duty to the Poor* (2010), 231 (231 ff.); Nolan, 'Art. 27 The Right to a Standard of Living Adequate for the Child's Development' in Tobin (ed), *The UN Convention on the Rights of the Child: A Commentary* (2019), 1021 (1033).

[121] Nolan, 'Rising to the Challenge of Child Poverty: The Role of the Courts' in Van Bueren (ed), *Freedom from Poverty as a Human Right – Law's Duty to the Poor* (2010), 231 (237).

[122] End Child Poverty Global Coalition, *Putting children first – A policy agenda to end child poverty* (2016), 6.

[123] Example for regional convention: African Charter on the Rights and Welfare of the Child (1990).

[124] See FAO, *Legal measures to eradicate rural poverty*, (2019).

[125] Open Working Group on Sustainable Development Goals, Annex 1 (1).

[126] A/RES/70/1, preamble: 'We are determined to end **poverty and hunger**, in all their forms and dimensions, and to ensure that all human beings can fulfil their potential in dignity and equality and in a healthy environment.'

coincide with hunger. Yet with people suffering from constant malnutrition, lifting themselves out of poverty is almost impossible. Thus, improving nutrition and food security (SDG 2.1, SDG 2.2) supports the realisation of human potential and can help break the intergenerational cycle of poverty (SDG 1.1, SDG 1.2).[127]

Since the majority of the poor live in rural areas,[128] increasing agricultural produc-   62
tivity and income of small-scale food producers would also contribute to poverty re-
duction.[129] An increase of agricultural production, productivity and income requires supportive policies that benefit poor communities in rural areas and reduce their vulnerability to negative environmental impacts.[130]

Lacking food and nutrition (SDG 2.2) negatively impacts on the status of health   63
and well-being (SDG 3).[131] A healthy population also creates the basic conditions for economic growth, which in turn leads to a reduction of poverty.[132] Poverty reduction has a greater impact on health in the presence of poverty-related diseases such as AIDS, tuberculosis and malaria, but also neglected tropical diseases, diarrhoeal and respiratory diseases and the consequences of malnutrition (SDG 3.3).

Moreover, poverty reduction is highly dependent on inclusive and equitable educa-   64
tion and the promotion of life-long learning opportunities (SDG 4.1, SDG 4.5) which can be deemed a basic prerequisite.[133] Gaining access to education is even more difficult in countries that are severely affected by poverty with frequently no access to free education.[134]

Since women and girls are all too often hold insecure jobs, earn less and thus are   65
merely able to save less, and living close to poverty they are affected by poverty to a greater extent (SDG 5).[135] However, women significantly contribute to feeding and caring for the family.[136] Mitigating poverty can counteract a shortage of resources within families (SDG 1.b) and can prevent inequality being exacerbated (SDG 10.2, SDG 10.3).

Since poverty can also be understood as the absence of an adequate standard of   66
living,[137] there are also important links to SDG 7.[138] Supplying the population with affordable, reliable and sustainable energy (SDG 7.1) can contribute significantly to poverty reduction (SDG 1.4).[139] However, decarbonisation of energy (SDG 7.2) can lead to rising energy prices, so that poor sections of the population are in turn cut off from energy supplies.[140]

The interlinkage between SDG 8 and SDG 1 is striking. Through sustainable eco-   67
nomic growth and work for all as well as a resilient infrastructure and sustainable industrialization (SDG 9), the foundations are laid for all sections of the population to

---

[127] Griggs et al., *A Guide to SDG Interactions: From Science to Implementation* (2017), 45.

[128] FAO, *Legal measures to eradicate rural poverty* (2019).

[129] Griggs et al., *A Guide to SDG Interactions: From Science to Implementation* (2017), 45.

[130] Griggs et al., *A Guide to SDG Interactions: From Science to Implementation* (2017), 10.

[131] Van Soest et al., 'Analysing interactions among Sustainable Development Goals with Integrated Assessment Models' (2019) 1 *Global Transitions,* 214 (214); Griggs et al., *A Guide to SDG Interactions: From Science to Implementation* (2017), 85.

[132] Griggs et al., *A Guide to SDG Interactions: From Science to Implementation* (2017), 85.

[133] Lawlor et al., 'SDG 1: No Poverty – Impacts of Social Protection, Tenure Security and Building Resilience on Forests' in Katila et al. (eds), *Sustainable Development Goals: Their Impacts on Forests and People* (2019), 17; see also FAO, *Legal measures to eradicate rural poverty* (2019).

[134] HLPF, *Discussion on SDG 4 – Quality education* (2019).

[135] UN, *Policy Brief: The Impact of COVID-19* (2020).

[136] UN Women, *Women and Sustainable Development Goals,* (5).

[137] FAO, *Legal measures to eradicate rural poverty,* (2019).

[138] Independent Group of Scientists appointed by the Secretary-General, *Global Sustainable Development Report 2019: The Future is Now – Science for Achieving Sustainable Development,* (2019), 6.

[139] Griggs et al., *A Guide to SDG Interactions: From Science to Implementation* (2017), 138.

[140] Griggs et al., *A Guide to SDG Interactions: From Science to Implementation* (2017), 138.

have access to income and thus escape monetary poverty. This could also be achieved by reducing inequality within and among countries (SDG 10). Furthermore, income can help achieve an adequate standard of living and prevent exclusion from society,[141] thus affecting all dimensions of poverty reduction.

68   Due to an increasing population density in cities, poverty is becoming an increasingly urban phenomenon[142] where slums represent one of the greatest social exclusions and a significant factor of poverty.[143] By creating safe and affordable housing or at least upgrading slums (SDG 11.1), poverty can thus be combated. As more and more people live in cities due to a strong global urbanisation, poverty is also increasingly urban.

69   People living in poverty are more likely to be affected by climate change (SDG 1.5), as they are mostly dependent on agriculture which is a significant factor in climate change.[144] The poor most often have little or no protection against extreme weather conditions or long-term climate change[145] (SDG 13.1, SDG 13.b).

70   Small Island Developing States and Least Developed Countries are particularly economically dependent on sustainable oceans and fisheries and other sea-related sectors which are strongly influenced by the health of the ocean.[146] By protecting and strengthening oceans (SDG 14), poverty in sea-dependent countries can be reduced.[147]

71   Desertification (SDG 15.3) poses the particular threat of deprived livelihoods, which often depend on agriculture, especially in drylands to poor people.[148] Counteracting desertification (SDG 15) and maintaining sustainable ecosystems (SDG 15.1, SDG 15.2) thus diminishes poverty and enables people to realise their potential.

D. Jurisprudential Significance of SDG 1

72   Global poverty, which, albeit off track, had been declining until 2019, has now increased exorbitantly due to the SARS-CoV-2 pandemic. The global lock-downs, accompanying rise in unemployment, distressed social security systems and the worsening inequality have led to a reversal of the previously recorded downward trend.[149] For the first time in ten years, the proportion of the world population living in poverty has risen.[150] With the poorest people in vulnerable situations most affected by the SARS-CoV-2 pandemic, exacerbated by the effects of climate change,[151] the fight against poverty becomes even more urgent. It is noticeable that people living in or near poverty bear the greatest burden with concomitant loss of 'the full enjoyment of a wide range of

---

[141] FAO, *Legal measures to eradicate rural poverty* (2019).

[142] UN, *Tracking Progress Towards Inclusive, Safe, Resilient and Sustainable Cities and Human Settlements,* (2018), 11.

[143] Arimah, *Slums as Expressions of social exclusion: Explaining the relevance of slums in African countries* (2001), 2.

[144] Griggs et al., *A Guide to SDG Interactions: From Science to Implementation* (2017), 40.

[145] A/HRC/RES/32/33, *Human rights and climate change,* 18 July 2016, 2.

[146] Griggs et al., *A Guide to SDG Interactions: From Science to Implementation* (2017), 178.

[147] Griggs et al., *A Guide to SDG Interactions: From Science to Implementation* (2017), 178.

[148] Millennium Ecosystem Assessment, *Ecosystems and Human Well-being: Synthesis* (2005), 13.

[149] UN, *The Sustainable Development Goals Report 2020 (2020),* 24.

[150] ECOSOC, E/2020/L.20–E/HLPF/2020/L.1, *Ministerial declaration of the high level segment of the 2020 session of the Economic and Social Council and the 2020 high level political forum on sustainable development, convened under the auspices of the Council, on the theme 'Accelerated action and transformative pathways: realizing the decade of action and delivery for sustainable development',* paras. 2, 4, 12.

[151] A/HRC/41/39, *Climate change and poverty Report of the Special Rapporteur on extreme poverty and human rights,* 17 July 2017, paras. 9-12, 88: identifying the greatest risks as being food insecurity, forced migration, disease and death.

rights'.[152] Another serious phenomenon which so far mainly affected high- and middle-income countries leads to an increase in poverty, manifesting greater societal inequality. In the digital age, States transform towards a 'digital welfare state', the development of which, while natural and necessary, excludes people which are lacking legal identity and thus neglects their ability to participate, e.g. in social services or elections.[153] Since '[e]radicating poverty by 2030 is the overarching objective of the sustainable development agenda'[154] and was also before in the SDGs' predecessors, the MDGs,[155] it can be concluded from the SDGs' multidimensional approach[156] that poverty is directly linked to the absence or insufficiency of 'health, education and standard of living'.[157] As only one factor of many, the 'robust and stable economic growth – measured by the increase in GDP per capita'[158] helps reduce poverty. Another factor directly affecting the poverty of an individual or society is the states' adherence to human rights. These 'are closely linked and mutually reinforcing' sustainable development objectives,[159] and are therefore adversely affected by poverty as a 'cause and a consequence of human rights violations'.[160]

It follows from the tripartite typology[161] of the underlying human rights that are   **73**
interlaced with the Global Agenda 2030 and the SDGs that states not only have to respect and protect these rights, but to implement them effectively. Therefore, 'the State cannot remain indifferent to the circumstances of life that separate the guarantee of the

---

[152] A/HRC/41/39, *Climate change and poverty Report of the Special Rapporteur on extreme poverty and human rights*, 17 July 2017, paras. 1, 9; A/HRC/31/52, *Report of the Special Rapporteur on the issue of human rights obligations relating to the enjoyment of a safe, clean, healthy and sustainable environment*, 1 February 2016, paras. 23-32.

[153] A/74/493, *Extreme poverty and human rights, Note by the Secretary-General*, 11 October 2019, paras. 8 f., 11-14.

[154] A/69/700, *The road to dignity by 2030: ending poverty, transforming all lives and protecting the planet Synthesis report of the Secretary General on the post 2015 sustainable development agenda*, para. 67; Lawlor et al., 'SDG 1: No Poverty – Impacts of Social Protection, Tenure Security and Building Resilience on Forests' in Katila et al. (eds), *Sustainable Development Goals: Their Impacts on Forests and People* (2019), 18.

[155] UN General Assembly Open Working Group on Sustainable Development Goals, *Compendium of TST Issues Briefs* (2014), 1; and was acknowledged by the UN even before, amongst others, in A/RES/50/107, *Observance of the International Year for the Eradication of Poverty and proclamation of the first, United Nations Decade for the Eradication of Poverty*, 26 January 1996, preamble.

[156] HLPF, *2017 HLPF Thematic Review of SDG 1: End Poverty in All its Forms Everywhere*, 3.

[157] Lawlor et al., 'SDG 1: No Poverty – Impacts of Social Protection, Tenure Security and Building Resilience on Forests' in Katila et al. (eds), *Sustainable Development Goals: Their Impacts on Forests and People* (2019), 17.

[158] UN General Assembly Open Working Group on Sustainable Development Goals, *Compendium of TST Issues Briefs* (2014), 9.

[159] UN General Assembly Open Working Group on Sustainable Development Goals, *Compendium of TST Issues Briefs* (2014), 139.

[160] https://www.ohchr.org/EN/Issues/Poverty/Pages/About.aspx.

[161] This typology refers to the three obligations of States to respect human rights (not to interfere with the exercise of a right guaranteed); to protect human rights (not to accept abuses); and to fulfil human rights (to provide the means for an effective exercise of human rights); A/RES/70/1, paras. 10, 19; Similar obligations apply to Transnational Corporations and other Business Enterprises: A/RES/70/1, para. 67(fn); further reading on this issue: A/HRC/17/31, Annex: *Report of the Special Representative of the Secretary General on the Issue of Human Rights and Transnational Corporations and Other Business Enterprises*; Ruggie, *Guiding Principles on Business and Human Rights: Implementing the United Nations "Protect, Respect and Remedy"*; OHCR, *The Business and Human Rights Dimension of Sustainable Development: Embedding "Protect, Respect and Remedy" in SDGs implementation* Geneva, 30.6.2017; Schönherr and Findler Martinuzzi, 'Exploring the Interface of CSR and the Sustainable Development Goals' (2017) 24(3) *Transnational Corporations* (UNCTAD), 33 ff.; see also: Huck and Kurkin, 'The UN Sustainable Development Goals (SDGs) in the Transnational Multilevel System' (2018) 2 *HJIL*, 375.

individual's freedoms from her or his effective capacity to enjoy these freedoms.[162] This equally applies to economic, social and cultural rights and civil and political rights.

74   Beyond its impact on most vulnerable groups, the particular danger of the multidimensionality of poverty lies in its frequent passing on to future generations, which creates and endures 'intergenerational cycles of poverty.'[163] As one of the largest groups, it is children that live in poverty, followed by a disproportionately high number of women 'owing to the multifaceted and cumulative forms of discrimination that they endure.'[164] If further factors such as conflicts, natural disasters and economic downturns are added, this development exacerbates and a downward spiral is created, which primarily affects the already poor and whose dismantling (for a national economy) is hardly quantifiable in costs. 'People living in extreme poverty are often neglected or overlooked by politicians, service providers and policy-makers due to their lack of political voice, financial and social capital and their chronic social exclusion' and exposes them disproportionately to human rights violations.[165]

75   SDG 1 opposes this severe situation on the monetary dimension (SDG 1.1) as well as on all other dimensions (SDG 1.2). Diverse discussions orbit the targets of SDG 1, in particular about universal basic income and even normative approaches such as moral and ethical obligations to eradicate poverty or considering the human rights-based bottom-up approaches[166] on the one hand and about neoliberal economic policies with the instruments of 'deregulation, privatization and [...] market reform against the dominance of the welfare state'[167] on the other. In this context, the focus is on the identification of global and local interactions and a distribution of resources and commodities controlled by market prices. However, irrespective of the focus, the eradication of poverty leads to the realisation of equality.[168]

76   Against this background, the UN has repeatedly discussed the issue of 'alleviation of poverty' as a means of facilitating development. A substantive right to development entangling all economic, social and cultural human rights, and thereby giving dignity was not firstly stressed as necessary[169] with the First UN Decade for the Eradication

---

[162] De Schutter, 'L'interdépendance des droits et l'interaction des systèmes de protection : les scénarios du système européen de protection des droits fondamentaux' (2000), *Droit en Quart-Monde*, 5, found in: Tulkens, Françoise, 'The contribution of the European Convention on Human Rights to the poverty issue in times of crisis' (2015), *Seminar on Human Rights for European Judicial Trainers*, 9.

[163] HLPF, *2017 HLPF Thematic Review of SDG 1: End Poverty in All its Forms Everywhere*, 1; A/HRC/21/11, *Guiding Principles on Extreme Poverty and Human Rights* (2012), para. 32.

[164] A/HRC/21/11, *Guiding Principles on Extreme Poverty and Human Rights* (2012), para. 23.

[165] A/HRC/21/11, *Guiding Principles on Extreme Poverty and Human Rights* (2012), preface.

[166] Sano, 'How Can a Human Rights-Based Approach Contribute to Poverty Reduction? The Relevance of Human Rights to Sustainable Development Goal One', in Kaltenborn et al., *SDGs and Human Rights* (2019), 13; see also: Karimova and Golay, 'Principle 5, Poverty Eradication', in Viñuales, *The Rio Declaration on Environment and Development* (2015), 187.

[167] Sano, 'How Can a Human Rights-Based Approach Contribute to Poverty Reduction? The Relevance of Human Rights to Sustainable Development Goal One', in Kaltenborn et al., *SDGs and Human Rights* (2019), 13 f.; Stiglitz and Fitoussi and Durand, *Beyond GDP, Measuring What Counts For Economic And Social Performance* (2018).

[168] https://www.eesc.europa.eu/sites/default/files/resources/docs/mg-compilation-doc-owg-10.pdf (Cluster 1).

[169] A/RES/41/128, *Declaration on the Right to Development, Adopted by General Assembly*, 4 December 1986: development is an inalienable human right by virtue of which every human person and all peoples are entitled to participate in, contribute to, and enjoy economic, social, cultural and political development, in which all human rights and fundamental freedoms can be fully realized; A/RES/50/107, *Observance of the International Year for the Eradication of Poverty and proclamation of the first, United Nations Decade for the Eradication of Poverty*, 26 January 1996, paras. 4(c), (d), 20-2.

of Poverty[170] but can already be extrapolated from the language of the UDHR.[171] In context, this means to ensure that 'persons living in poverty must be enabled to effectively use resources and capabilities in so that they can enjoy the whole spectrum of human rights'.[172] The 'alleviation of poverty' is regarded as the *leitmotif* and reveals both the basic framework and 'necessary condition for sustainable human development': the New International Economic Order (NIEO).[173] Although not binding in nature, it enflanks the stipulations of International Development Law (IDL) to realign the structures of the North-South disparity that has existed since decolonisation at the latest and to ensure greater socio-economic justice and equality. Internal and external factors, ranging from (humanitarian) conflict situations and economic or financial crises to climate change and (now) global health crises, have always influenced the intended restructuring of societies and have repeatedly allowed poverty, hunger and inequality to germinate. While changes in the structure of states and overall progress indeed have been recorded, it remains with the immutability of neo-liberalism, that continually strives for (economic) growth, in large parts of our world. Moreover, the foreign trade and development instruments used, cooperation or technology transfers that govern economic activities lead to further disputes and manifest existing structures in their complexity and compatibility with development, especially in the least developed countries. This very classical understanding of IDL could come into contrast with the basic idea of sustainable development. For example, the EU tries to translate the SDGs in different concepts, like the New European Consensus (NEC)[174], which now strives to harmonise ecological, economic and social levels in a more individual-centred[175] system with the purpose of creating capabilities for the development of each individual, and also of states. This means a consolidation of (new) accompanying principles such as good governance, democracy and respect for human rights, and tightening the conditionality for the world's poorest and most vulnerable states, as they tend to face the most change in order to remain connected to development programmes or to benefit from further opportunities. The more susceptible to internal and external levers, the more unequal appears the highly politicised restructuring that seems (still) possible at all.[176]

Against the backdrop of this fragile system, SDG 1 conveys a right to development in the form of exclusion from poverty. Consequently, the presence of poverty, in the sense of the SDGs, means the absence of access to development, at least to a large extent. The first step for tackling poverty requires an access to the different aspects of development. The second step entails the provision of financial assistance that sustainable development enriches to unfold. As a result, only these opportunities allow for an increase in the more or less achievable equality of the different social classes. In the sense of SDG 1, the focus should therefore be on poor population groups, in particular with regard to gender equality and the highly vulnerable group of children and other vulnerable

77

---

[170] A/RES/50/107, *Observance of the International Year for the Eradication of Poverty and proclamation of the first, United Nations Decade for the Eradication of Poverty*, 26 January 1996.

[171] Sarkar, *International Development Law, Rule of Law, Human Rights and Global Finance* (2020), 124.

[172] Tulkens, 'The contribution of the European Convention on Human Rights to the poverty issue in times of crisis' (2015), *Seminar on Human Rights for European Judicial Trainers*, 9.

[173] Further reading: Jouannet, 'How to Depart from the Existing Dire Condition of Development', in Cassesse, *Realizing Utopia, The Future of International Law* (2012).

[174] Huck, 'Die EU und die Globale Agenda 2030 der Vereinten Nationen: Reflexion, Strategie und rechtliche Umsetzung' (2019) 14 *EuZW*, 581 (583).

[175] Yusuf, 'The Role That Equal Rights and Self-Determination of Peoples can Play in the Current World Community' in Cassese, *Realizing Utopia, The Future of International Law* (2012), 388 f.

[176] See Jouannet, 'How to Depart from the Existing Dire Condition of Development' in Cassesse, *Realizing Utopia, The Future of International Law* (2012), 392-401.

groups. Since national definitions of poverty are used as a basis (SDG 1.2), a dimension of 'development out of poverty' is thus stipulated with a very broad scope. The approach of SDG 1, to eradicate poverty primarily through financial means, illustrates two things in particular: (a) This SDG is not intended to achieve an actual redistribution (of assets, values and resources) but a one-sided increase; and (b) it pursues a vision primarily characterised by political and moral responsibilities.

78   The solution offered by SDG 1 is therefore to create a just and inclusive policy-making and governance framework that leads to more productive work under conditions of freedom, dignity and equality and to provide not just access, but quality access.[177] However, despite being political in nature or a policy guideline,[178] 'ending poverty in all its forms everywhere' can be found in jurisprudence and is also reflected to a large extent in jurisprudential reality. This goal, which is strongly supported by the idea of governance, therefore influences the development and intertwining of law at various levels.

I. Jurisdiction on Vision and Objectives

79   The inability to access legal and justice services can be both a result and a cause of disadvantage, poverty, and inequality in income and employment opportunities, educational attainment and health conditions. Therefore, people-centred legal and justice services go beyond a fair and effective justice system to greater objectives such as inclusive growth, equality, poverty-reduction, social justice and social inclusion. The core of access to justice is equality and social inclusion in the light of the 'leave no one behind' imperative of the Global Agenda 2030.[179] Since in particular the economic, social and cultural human rights overlap with the imperative of the Global Agenda 2030 and SDG 1, interpretative jurisdiction can be found at all levels examined. SDG 1 represents the cross-section and thus surrounds and permeates the (human) rights assignable in other SDGs and the related jurisprudence. SDG 1, whether of political nature or not, therefore functions like a chalice that embraces the right to development, thus referring to other rights, such as the right to food,[180] the right to water or the right to education,[181] regardless of their respective legal status (→ Goal 1 mn. 20 ff., 40). The juridical consideration is thus closely interwoven with the further considerations within all other SDGs,[182] and can therefore by no means stand alone (→ Intro mn. 192 f.).

1. International Jurisdiction

80   A recent case of the International Court of Justice (ICJ) particularly illustrates the multidimensionality of poverty. In the turmoil of the case of *The Gambia v. Myanmar*,

---

[177] UN General Assembly Open Working Group on Sustainable Development Goals, *Compendium of TST Issues Briefs* (2014), 139.

[178] See Karimova and Golay, 'Principle 5, Poverty Eradication' in Viñuales, *The Rio Declaration on Environment and Development* (2015), 186.

[179] OECD, *Governance as an SDG Accelerator, Country Experiences and Tools* (2019).

[180] Further reading: Sen, *Famines and Poverty* (1981).

[181] This list could be continued with the right to an adequate standard of living (see Art. 25 UDHR; Art. 11 ICESCR; Art. 27 CRC), right to social security (Art. 22 UDHR; Art. 9 ICESCR; Art. 28 CRPD; Art. 26 CRC), equal rights of women in economic life (Arts. 11, 13, 14(2)(g), 15(2), 16(1) CEDAW) or access to employment, housing, culture, health care and many more.

[182] Since all of them are characterised by economic, social and cultural and, to some degree, political and civil (human) rights.

which involves a large number of human rights violations[183] against a minority population as a protected group under the Genocide Convention, multiple human rights concerns are addressed.[184] Although this case is likely to take some time to come to terms
with, the manifold efforts to reduce poverty and create stability for sustainable peace are
already visible. The violation of human rights obligations affects to a large extent the
most vulnerable and poorest parts of a population, whether these are recognised or not,
and poverty in itself creates a vulnerable starting point for human rights violations.[185]
The rights widely affected show the intensity of the repercussions at various levels,
while at the same time highlighting the legal areas that need to be applied. However,
the particular gravity and urgency of the situation can already be seen in the fact that
the court has granted a part of the provisional measures requested by The Gambia.
These include, for example, the immediate prevention of all acts of 'destruction of lands
and livestock, deprivation of food and other necessities of life, or any other deliberate
infliction of conditions of life calculated to bring about the physical destruction of the
Rohingya group in whole or in part'[186] to be carried out.[187]

Three cases from the IACtHR show the cross-cutting issues covered by SDG 1. In　**81**
Sawhoyamaxa v. Paraguay and *Yakhye Axa Indigenous Community*, ancestral lands had
to be restituted after the indigenous communities had been forcibly displaced. The
failure to provide life-sustaining conditions and denial of a life in dignity also led to the
deaths of many members of this population group, most of them children. Referring
to the American Convention of Human Rights (ACHR), the IACtHR found a violation
of the right to life, along with the right to food and water, and the collective right to
private property. The State was obliged to provide and give access to basic goods and
services for the communities. This positive action to be taken by the State urgently, was
stated to be necessary to fulfil the 'dignified life standard'[188] of people. The IACtHR
characterised extreme poverty as 'poor health conditions and [poor] medical care, the
working conditions of exploitation to which they were subjected, and the restrictions
imposed on them to own crops and cattle and to exercise freely their traditional
subsistence activities.'[189] Although the land was legitimately owned by the indigenous
population, the state failed for many years to return the ancestral lands, or even to
grant them access and use at all. The resulting psychological and moral burden on the
indigenous population and the sensed lack of protection was also considered a violation
of the right to humane treatment, which in each case resulted in land restitution, land
titling, and disposing alternative land[190] as well as monetary compensation, damages,

---

[183] See A/HRC/39/CRP.2, *Report of the detailed findings of the Independent International Fact-Finding Mission on Myanmar*, 17.09.2018, para. 238-40, 429 ff.

[184] *Application of the Convention on the Prevention and Punishment of the Crime of Genocide (The Gambia v. Myanmar)*, Provisional Measures, Order, 23. January 2020, ICJ Reports (2020), 3.

[185] See A/HRC/39/CRP.2, *Report of the detailed findings of the Independent International Fact-Finding Mission on Myanmar*, 17.09.2018, para. 405.

[186] *Application of the Convention on the Prevention and Punishment of the Crime of Genocide (The Gambia v. Myanmar)*, Provisional Measures, Order, 23 January 2020, ICJ Reports (2020), para. 12.

[187] *Application of the Convention on the Prevention and Punishment of the Crime of Genocide (The Gambia v. Myanmar)*, Provisional Measures, Order, 23 January 2020, ICJ Reports (2020), paras. 59, 61.

[188] *Indigenous Community Sawhoyamaxa v Paraguay*, Judgment, 29 March 2006, IACtHR; *Yakye Axa Indigenous Community*, Judgment, Merits, Reparations and Costs, 17 June 2005, IACtHR, paras. 161 f., 176; see also *Case Of The Xákmok Kásek Indigenous Community v. Paraguay (Xákmok Kásek case)*, Judgment, Merits, Reparations, and Costs, 24 August 2010, IACtHR.

[189] *Indigenous Community Sawhoyamaxa v Paraguay*, Judgment, 29 March 2006, IACtHR, para. 73 (61).

[190] These consequences were set in previous decisions of the IACtHR, see e.g. *Mayagna (Sumo) Awas Tingni Community v. Nicaragua*, Judgment, 31 August 2001, IACtHR.

and development funds and moreover leading to employment, food, healthcare, and other sources of livelihood.[191]

82   In addition to the significance for indigenous populations, similar case law can be found with a focus on women, persons with disabilities, children, racial and ethnic minorities and migrants, frequently in an accumulative manner.[192]

83   Based on the principle that the 'Convention, indeed, is a living instrument to be interpreted in the light of present-day conditions',[193] the ECtHR developed a significant jurisprudence which illustrates the added value of the European Convention on Human Rights (ECHR) in the field of poverty. This is demonstrated, for example, by the protection it provides for the most vulnerable in access to justice (→ Intro mn. 184-91 and Goal 16 mn. 9 ff.) In this respect, the ECtHR, on the basis of Art. 6 ECHR

> on a case-by-case basis, acted as a bar to disproportionate financial obstacles preventing economically vulnerable individuals from gaining access to justice, whether on account of excessive court fees, either laid down in advance or adjusted depending on the amount of the claim, or on account of the refusal to admit ordinary appeals or appeals on point of law to the detriment of persons whose lack of resources made it impossible for them even to begin to pay the amount ordered by the judgment in question.[194]

84   A particularly grievous example of the ECtHR's bottom line is a case in which 15 disabled children died of starving in a state home due to state inactivity in supply assistance. The ECtHR found a clear violation of the right to life.[195] In contrast to a similar case of an asylum-seeking family whose disabled child died on the street after a period of four weeks without any state support, the ECtHR did not find a violation of the right to life, but assumed degrading treatment in breach of Article 3 of the ECHR.

85   Elsewhere, however, the special protection of the family is prioritised before the ECtHR and strengthens in particular the rights of women and children to enable and maintain a family life even in extreme poverty. The court decided that families living in poverty which are mostly led by women 'cannot be punished for their deprivation and their children should not be 'rescued' from them. Instead, and because children are not the exclusive responsibility of parents, states must fulfil their supportive role and provide material and other forms of assistance to make family life possible.'[196]

86   That this idea of state duties is by no means the determining factor can be seen from further applications to the ECtHR which were declared inadmissible, when (social) state spending was cut in times of economic crises to not jeopardise overall systemic structures, while at the same time further promoting inequalities which is in stark

---

[191] See also Additional Protocol to the American Convention on Human Rights in the Area of Economic, Social and Cultural Rights (1988).

[192] See e.g. *Street Children (Villagrán Morales et al.) v. Guatemala*, Judgment, 26 May 2001, IACtHR, paras. 144, 191; *Yakye Axa Indigenous Community*, Judgment, 17 June 2005, IACtHR, paras. 161 f., 176; *Indigenous Community Members of the Lhaka Honhat (Our Land) Association v. Argentina*, Judgment, 6 February 2020, IACtHR.

[193] Tulkens, 'The contribution of the European Convention on Human Rights to the poverty issue in times of crisis' (2015) *Seminar on Human Rights for European Judicial Trainers*, 8.

[194] ECtHR, *Bakan v. Turkey*, Judgment of 12 June 2007, paras. 66 et seq. 37; ECtHR, *Mehmet and Suna Yiğit v. Turkey*, Judgment of 17 July 2007; ECtHR, *Stankov v. Bulgaria*, Judgment of 12 July 2007; ECtHR, *Cour v. France*, Judgment of 3 October 2006; all found in: Tulkens, 'The contribution of the European Convention on Human Rights to the poverty issue in times of crisis' (2015) *Seminar on Human Rights for European Judicial Trainers*, 12.

[195] ECtHR, *Nencheva and Others v. Bulgaria*, no. 48609/06, Judgment of 18 June 2013, para. 154.

[196] ECtHR, *Soares de Melo v. Portugal*, application No.72850/14; further reading: David, Valeska, 'ECtHR condemns the punishment of women living in poverty and the 'rescuing' of their children' (2016) in *Strasbourg Observers*.

contrast to individual targets of SDG 1 (e.g. SDG 1.3, 1.4, 1.5).[197] The reduction of the applicants salary or pension were not assumed to place a too excessive burden on the applicants 'to expose them to subsistence difficulties incompatible with Article 1 of Protocol No. 1'.[198] The state was deemed to have acted within its margin of appreciation, which illustrates the application of the principle of proportionality in another light, allowing further exacerbating poverty of individuals as long as it is in fair balance to public interest. The Court has frequently declared its inaccessibility in similar cases, most recently even using the concept of sustainability,[199] to preserve 'the sustainability of the social security system for future generations'.[200]

Development can also be observed in the African Commission on Human and **87** Peoples' Rights.[201] While in the *Ogoni case*[202] in 2001 the Commission did not make a connection to a right to development in the improvement of the environment, health, land and natural resources of the Ogoni population, the court applied such a connection explicitly in a case in 2010 for the first time[203] directly to and, moreover, determined the right to development to be equitable, non-discriminatory, participatory, accountable, and transparent, [equipped] with equity and choice (→ Goal 2 mn. 68).[204] This development is all the more astonishing when considering that the right to development played an important role in African history in particular, as it was already embedded in the NIEO and CERDS, the foundations of the ACP-EEC Lomé II Conventions.[205]

2. European Jurisdiction

As with the Global Agenda 2030 and the SDGs, the EU, as part of its fully endorsed **88** policy programme, insists on the implementation of relevant sustainability targets to reduce poverty and related negative effects overall. In the European New Green Deal, but also with reference to Rio+20,[206] the EU recognises a 'green economy in the context of sustainable development and poverty eradication as one of the important tools available for achieving sustainable development'.[207] The EU uses various instruments to implement SDG 1 to create an inclusive economy, such as cohesion policy and financing[208] and showed a decrease in the share of persons at risk of poverty or social exclusion in

---

[197] *Koufaki and Adedy v. Greece (dec.)*, application nos. 57665/12 and 57657/12, Information Note on the Court's case-law No. 163.

[198] ECtHR, *Austerity measures, Protection of property (Article 1 of Protocol No. 1)* (2018).

[199] ECtHR, *Da Conceição Mateus v. Portugal and Santos Januário v. Portugal*, application no. 62235/12 and no. 57725/12; ECtHR, *da Silva Carvalho Rico v. Portugal*, application no. 13341/14; ECtHR, *Mamatas and Others v. Greece*, application nos. 63066/14, 64297/14 and 66106/14; ECtHR, *Mockienė v. Lithuania*, application no. 75916/13; ECtHR, *Aielli and Others and Arboit and Others v. Italy*, applications no. 27166/18 and 27167/18.

[200] ECtHR, *Aielli and Others and Arboit and Others v. Italy*, applications no. 27166/18 and 27167/18; ECHR 268 (2018) 19.07.2018.

[201] See also African Charter on Human and Peoples' Rights (1981).

[202] ACmHPR, *SERAC and CESR v. Nigeria (Ogoni case)*, paras. 53-5.

[203] Schrijver, Nicolaas, 'Self-determination of peoples and sovereignty over natural wealth and resources' in UN, *Realizing the Right to Development, Essays in Commemoration of 25 Years of the United Nations Declaration on the Right to Development* (2013), 125.

[204] ACmHPR, *Centre for Minority Rights Development (Kenya) and Minority Rights Group International on behalf of Endorois Welfare Council v. Kenya*, para. 277.

[205] Sarkar, *International Development Law, Rule of Law, Human Rights and Global Finance* (2020), 125.

[206] A/RES/66/288, *The Future we want (Rio +20 Declaration)*, adopted on 27 July 2012.

[207] A/RES/66/288, *The Future we want (Rio +20 Declaration)*, adopted on 27 July 2012, paras. 12, 56 ff.

[208] An overview of the instruments used is available here: https://ec.europa.eu/sustainable-development /goal1_en.

the EU before the SARS-CoV-2 outbreak.[209] In addition to this economic development and transition to sustainable societies, which leaves no one behind, European case law is particularly reiterating the handling and application of social benefits to avoid poverty and inhumane treatment (→ Goal 8 mn. 11 ff.).

89   Since 2015, the European Court of Justice (ECJ) has increasingly decided in cases relevant to refugee law. In the preliminary decision proceedings of *Ahmad Shah Ayubi v. Bezirkshauptmannschaft Linz-Land*,[210] the ECJ based its decisions on the principle of equal treatment between nationals and 'refugees who temporarily reside in the EU'. They 'must be entitled to the same level of social assistance as that provided to nationals of the Member States which granted them refugee status'.[211] On the basis of the principles of non-discrimination[212] already prevalent in the EU and the primacy of EU law over the national law of the Member States,[213] the ECJ thus met the requirements of the human rights definition of the 'adequate standard of living'. Equal treatment must be applied irrespective of whether the beneficiary of subsidiary protection status is a refugee or a national. The Austrian court applying this decision further clarified that the applicant 'could claim only the minimum subsistence benefits under Austrian law'. This demonstrates a further EU principle that, although the living conditions of third-country nationals may not be undercut either, relative deprivation or poverty is taken as a basis for determining this poverty line.[214] This is determined on the basis of the ascertainable difference between a person's disposable income and resources in relation to the adequate or socially acceptable conditions within their living environment, as well as their ability to participate in economic, social and cultural activities and the possible exercise of their (European) fundamental rights.[215] Interestingly, the ECJ also explained that social security for adequate housing cannot be guaranteed exclusively by financial payments, but also, for example, by accommodation in hostels or similar accommodation. Although this may have corresponded to the tense situation of the Austrian housing market at the time, it can already be deduced how far an adequate standard of living may be determined in this context.

90   In a preliminary ruling of the ECJ, the focus was on the quantification of poverty in pension, which must not be disproportionate.[216] The ECJ with reference to Art. 8 of the Insolvency Directive (2008/94) concluded that if pension funds were reduced due to the employer's insolvency, the reduction would be manifestly disproportionate if it resulted in a serious impairment of the employee's ability to meet her or his needs. The court based its assessment on the at-risk-of-poverty threshold set by Eurostat for the Member

---

[209] Eurostat, 'Downward trend in the share of persons at risk of poverty or social exclusion in the EU' (2019), 158/2019 *News Release*, 1.

[210] ECJ, Case C-713/17, 21.11.2018, *Ahmad Shah Ayubi v. Bezirkshauptmannschaft Linz-Land*, ECLI: EU:C:2018:929, paras. 21, 24 f., therein referring to ECJ, Case C-443/14 and C-444/14, 01.03.2016, *Alo and Osso*, EU:C:2016:127, paras. 48, 50 f.

[211] ECJ, Case C-713/17, 21.11.2018, *Ahmad Shah Ayubi v. Bezirkshauptmannschaft Linz-Land*, ECLI:EU: C:2018:929, para. 29.

[212] ECJ on prohibition of discrimination: judgments of 4.5.1999, *Sürül*, C-262/96, EU:C:1999:228, paras. 63, 74; of 22.12.2010, *Gavieiro and Iglesias Torres*, C-444/09 and C-456/09, EU:C:2010:819, para. 78; and of 6.3.2014, *Napoli*, C-595/12, EU:C:2014:128, paras. 48, 50.

[213] ECJ, Case C-103/88, 1989 *Costanzo*, ECR 1839, para. 33; ECJ, Case C-208/05, 2007, *ITC Innovative Technology Center GmbH v Bundesagentur für Arbeit*, ECR I-181, paras. 68 f.; ECJ, Case C-429/09, 25.11.2010, *Fuß*, EU:C:2010:717, para. 40.

[214] In Germany for instance the threshold of relative poverty is 60 per cent of the average income; https://www.bpb.de/nachschlagen/zahlen-und-fakten/globalisierung/52680/armut.

[215] https://www.coe.int/en/web/compass/poverty.

[216] ECJ, Case C-168/18, *Pensions-Sicherungs-Verein VVaG (PSV) v Günther Bauer*, 19.12.2019, ECLI:EU: C:2019:1128.

State concerned. In accordance with the idea of proportionality, which is strongly pronounced in European Union law, a quite distinct threshold to extreme poverty has thus been established in the EU that deviates from SDG 1 on the one hand but also emphasises that if this threshold is not infringed, there is no state obligation to actively intervene on the other.

In the so-called *Jawo case*[217], a similar decision was ruled by the ECJ when evaluating　　91 the possibility to transfer asylum applicants under the Dublin III Regulation.[218] The court denied their transfer to a Member State 'if the living conditions would expose them to a situation of extreme material poverty amounting to inhuman or degrading treatment within the meaning of Article 4 European Charter of Human Rights (ECHR)'. In this regard, the Court held that the threshold was only met where such deficiencies, in light of all the circumstances of the individual case, attained a particularly high level of severity beyond a high degree of insecurity or a significant degradation of living conditions. The latter finding is also supported by the jurisprudence of the ECtHR. Correspondingly, national courts had the obligation to examine on the basis of information that is objective, reliable, specific and properly updated and having regard to the standard of protection of fundamental rights guaranteed by EU law, whether there was a real risk for the applicant to find himself in such situation of extreme material poverty.[219] While this does not provide a clear definition of 'great poverty' itself, it declares on how it is to be determined.

3. Arbitration Proceedings

Arbitration proceedings touch the areas covered by SDG 1 in multiple ways, primari-　　92 ly relating to a human rights context in economic and natural resources proceedings, and in particular with respect to the right to water, land rights and expropriation. These rights, amongst others, are the basis for stability, prosperity and health and thus for poverty reduction.[220] In Investor-state dispute settlement (ISDS), a formula for the consideration of human rights in general was developed early on.[221] According to this formula, the 'required "relation" between the human rights at stake, the investment, and on what kind of rights the tribunal deems to be covered by the investment definition and the applicable law clause' applies.[222] Although investment agreements refer to the consideration of international law[223] and in some cases allow the application of the domestic law of the host state with its own recognised human rights law, obligations manifested

---

[217] ECJ, Case C-163/17, *Abubacarr Jawo v Bundesrepublik Deutschland*, 19.03.2019, ECLI:EU:C: 2019:218.

[218] Regulation (EU) No 604/2013 of the European Parliament and of the Council of 26 June 2013.

[219] https://www.asylumlawdatabase.eu/en/content/cjeu-judgment-case-c-16317-jawo; https://www.dw .com/en/hungary-illegally-held-asylum-seekers-ecj-rules/a-53431848; https://easo.europa.eu/asylum-rep ort-2020/27-jurisprudence-court-justice-eu-cjeu; further reading: Galea, 'The Jawo case: The limits of the principle of mutual trust' (2019) *European Law Blog*.

[220] See Seif, 'Business and Human Rights in International Investment Law: Empirical Evidence' in Chaisse and Choukroune and Jusoh (eds), *Handbook of International Investment Law and Policy* (2020), 15.

[221] *Biloune and Marine Drive Complex Ltd v. Ghana Investments Centre and the Government of Ghana*, Award Jurisdiction and Liability, 27 October 1989, 95 ILR 18417; *Chevron Corporation (USA) and Texaco Petroleum Corporation (USA) v. Ecuador*, UNCITRAL, Partial Awards on the Merits, 30 March 2010, para. 166.

[222] Petersmann, 'Human Rights in International Investment Law and Adjudication: Legal Methodology Questions' in Chaisse and Choukroune and Jusoh (eds), *Handbook of International Investment Law and Policy* (2020), 13.

[223] Therefore taking into account other international treaties, customary international law, and general principles of law.

in the area of stabilising states through development and poverty reduction must be fulfilled. The above-mentioned consideration of whether fair and equitable treatment of the disputed agreement is actually taken into account under the agreement in question represents the bottleneck that must be overcome for the purposes of implementation and enforcement. Human rights law is frequently declared not applicable to the specific case.[224]

93   This general difficulty prevents to some extent the enforcement and resilience of human rights by not taking them into account, thus reducing access to justice (→ Goal 16 mn. 55, 67).[225] With the *Phoenix case* of the ICSID, a bottom line was found in this regard, in that that the tribunal held that

> no ICSID protection should be granted to investments made in violation of the most fundamental rules of protection of human rights, like investments made in pursuance of torture or genocide or in support of slavery or trafficking of human organs.[226]

94   This boundary was extended in *Hamester v Ghana*, where the Tribunal stated that 'investment will not be protected if it has been created in violation of national or international principles of good faith; [...] It will also not be protected if it is made in violation of the host State's law'.[227] As a so-called 'clean hands doctrine', it prevents at least considerable violations, which, although not in their origin, include human rights violations to the extent that they are recognised in the host state itself. However, this is still exclusively a matter of establishing proportionality, which is independently announced by the respective tribunal, usually with little control and transparency. Enforcement through this remains fraught with further difficulties (→ Goal 1 mn. 102 ff.) As a further restriction of this limit, its application is usually only evident at the beginning of an investment (establishment phase), but not beyond that in the further course.[228]

4. Domestic Jurisdiction

95   Domestic jurisdiction reflects international and European jurisdiction to a certain extent. As far-reaching as the 'chalice' of SDG 1 is interwoven with human rights law, so too – at least in some places – is national jurisdiction. Here too, the interplay between social benefits and different human or fundamental rights is particularly evident.

96   In a case before the Columbia Constitutional Court, for example, a public litigation procedure was used to determine and manifest the structural poverty within the country 'the positive steps the State must take to compensate for material inequality between groups, rather than limiting itself to a definition of equality before the law premised on state abstention'.[229] In particular, children and youths who are informal waste pickers were identified as protected vulnerable and marginalised groups. The court referred to

---

[224] *Pezold and others v. Republic of Zimbabwe*, ICSID Case No. ARB/10/15, Procedural Order No. 2 (26 June 2012), para. 57; see also Petersmann, 'Human Rights in International Investment Law and Adjudication: Legal Methodology Questions' in Chaisse and Choukroune and Jusoh (eds), *Handbook of International Investment Law and Policy* (2020), 18-20.

[225] *Urbaser v. Argentina*, ICSID Case No. ARB/07/26, Award (2016), paras. 1144, 1188-92, 1200.

[226] *Phoenix Action, Ltd. v. The Czech Republic*, ICSID Case No. ARB/06/5, Award (15 April 2009), para. 78; found in: Petersmann, 'Human Rights in International Investment Law and Adjudication: Legal Methodology Questions' in Chaisse and Choukroune and Jusoh (eds), *Handbook of International Investment Law and Policy* (2020), 25.

[227] *Gustav F W Hamester GmbH & Co KG v. Republic of Ghana*, ICSID Case No. ARB/07/24, Award (18 June 2010), paras. 123 f.

[228] Further reading: Seif, 'Business and Human Rights in International Investment Law: Empirical Evidence' in Chaisse and Choukroune and Jusoh (eds), *Handbook of International Investment Law and Policy* (2020).

[229] Colombia Constitutional Court, T-291/09 (T-2043683), Judgment, 23.04.2009.

the constitution as a public contract that must be interpreted not economically but in terms of human rights, even in the case of privatisation (here the waste management of the city of Cali). In a very similar case in Bogotá, the entire waste collection policy had to be reformed, unfortunately with little external impact. In Colombia, on the other hand, the petitioners' requests for monitoring as well as to reports and requests submitted by CIVISOL, the involved NGO, as defender and implementation overseer were not answered at all.[230]

In a case before the German Federal Constitutional Court (FCC),[231] the subsistence minimum for a dignified life was defined on a meta-level by addressing the essential constitutional requirements for the design of basic welfare benefits (Hartz IV) from the German Basic Law (Art. 1(1) in conjunction with Art. 20(1) of the Basic Law). The FCC stated that 'a coherent guarantee of both a person's physical and sociocultural existence' and human dignity 'is afforded every person [and] cannot be lost even on grounds of supposedly "undignified" behaviour'.[232] However, the court also noted that certain types of benefit sanctions may well be applicable. These sanctions are subject to strict proportionality requirements and a limited federal states' (Bundesländer) margin of appreciation which must allow sanctioned persons to avert these sanctions through their own conduct. This means the German Basic law's guarantee of human dignity can certainly be curtailed.   **97**

Another type of declining people's human rights can be seen in the more recent *SyRI*   **98**
case (Nederlanden). In this case before the District Court of the Hague, the question on how states obligations are neglected when welfare state authorities using digital innovations *de facto* deny access to information and justice, particularly for the poorest of the population. The used registration system in the Netherlands for, amongst others, social benefits, SyRI, was determined as threatening the right to social security, discriminating and thus fuelling inequalities. The court with recourse to the UN Special Rapporteur on extreme poverty and human rights[233] stated that 'the use of SyRI [was] insufficiently transparent and verifiable' and thus violating the right to respect for private and family life, home and correspondence under Art. 8(2) ECHR.[234] In particular, the court assessed the added value of the new technology used as disproportionate to the infringement of the right to respect for private life, which includes the rights to personal development and self-determination.[235] A similar case can also be seen in India in 2018, when due to lacking legal identity in the form of an Aadhaar ID number, a biometrics identification system, social benefits were stopped which had the effect of people dying.[236]

II. The Enforcement of No Poverty

The general problem of enforcement of rights originating in human rights law is   **99**
mostly a lack of enforcement mechanisms[237] due to the limited powers or competences

---

[230] https://www.escr-net.org/caselaw/2013/colombia-constitutional-court-t-29109.

[231] FCC (BVerfG), 05.11.2019 – 1 BvL 7/16 –.

[232] FCC (BVerfG), 05.11.2019 – 1 BvL 7/16 –, paras. 205-9.

[233] A/74/493, *Extreme poverty and human rights, Note by the Secretary-General*, 11 October 2019.

[234] *SyRI case*, ECLI:NL:RBDHA:2020:1878.

[235] *SyRI case*, ECLI:NL:RBDHA:2020:1878, 6.23 f.

[236] Supreme Court of India, *Justice K.S. Puttaswamy and Another v. Union of India and Others*, Writ Petition (Civil) No. 494 of 2012, Judgment of 26.09.2018; further reading: https://privacyinternational.org/long-read/2299/initial-analysis-indian-supreme-court-decision-aadhaar, https://www.hrw.org/news/2018/01/13/india-identification-project-threatens-rights.

[237] Further reading: McKay, 'What Outcomes for Victims?' in Shelton, *The Oxford Handbook of International Human Rights Law* (2013), 921-54.

of most of the human rights courts or commissions. Even in the more specialised field of investor-state dispute settlement, it appears to be more of a limited application of rights[238] that prevents effective enforcement. At the international level, there may be some compliance mechanisms, but these translate at best in reports on the violations found and do not request any redress. There may be exceptions in some regional human rights courts, but ample room for improvement still remains.[239]

100   As could be read from international jurisdiction of the IACtHR, the enforcement of judicially determined claims also manifests in quite direct communication by the courts to the defeated states and their monitoring during implementation (→ Goal 1 mn. 81 f.). However, amongst others in the *Sawhoyamaxa case*, it was not until 2014 that the state of Paraguay formally transferred the land back to the Sawhoyamaxa tribe.[240] A reconditioning of the land and the fulfilment of further obligations have not yet been fulfilled. Until 2018 the enforcement of the established rights remains constrained. This phenomenon of lengthy and overdue periods of implementation is recurrent in many jurisdictions and prevents effective legal protection. All three decisions indicated above have become notable as strategic litigation[241] due to the intended 'broader social change beyond the claimant communities' and have also received much international attention and support from various NGOs. Nevertheless, the enforcement of human rights still involves considerable effort, not only in these cases but in general, and not least with an utmost long-term perspective.

101   One factor that not only limits the enforcement of a right to development or, according to the vision of SDG 1, not to be poor, is not only states but also transnational corporations and other businesses operating within states. On the one hand, these support the development of states, especially in least developed or developing countries, increase its GDP and reduce the unemployment rate, and are thus beneficial to overall prosperity and the reduction of poverty. At the same time, however, it is precisely those companies that frequently and repeatedly violate human rights.[242] Their financial and political weight and influence regularly prevent or delay the perception of remedies or in private claims 'fail to proceed a judgment' at all or do not proceed them in an adequate manner which even more exacerbates in cross-border cases.[243] The UNGP[244] could provide a comprehensive response to this issue and, among other things, ensure that rights holders are at the heart of remedies. It is noticeable, however, that tensions in this area persist.

---

[238] For instance, property protection is to be considered as an obligation of a host state and therefore it is sometimes mentioned as a human right.

[239] Nadakavukaren Schefer, 'Human Rights', in Cottier and Nadakavukaren Schefer, *Elgar Encyclopedia of International Economic Law* (2017), 248.

[240] After having been evicted from their traditional lands in the 1990 s, the first petition in this case was submitted to the IACtHR in 2001 which pronounced its judgement in favour for the Sawhoyamaxa tribe in 2006.

[241] Further reading: Strategic Litigation Impacts, https://www.justiceinitiative.org/uploads/8c45f0be-d3be-40d6-aae8-a0b046bf6511/slip-land-rights-20170620.pdf.

[242] See A/72/162, *Report of the Working Group on the issue of human rights and transnational corporations and other business enterprises*, 18.7.2017.

[243] A/HRC/32/19, *Improving accountability and access to remedy for victims of business-related human rights abuse Report of the United Nations High Commissioner for Human Rights*, 10.05.2016, para. 2.

[244] Ruggie, *Guiding Principles on Business and Human Rights: Implementing the United Nations "Protect, Respect and Remedy" Framework* (2011).

III. De Facto Influences on Jurisdiction

Since their establishment, the Bretton Woods Institutions, namely the International **102** Monetary Fund (IMF) and the World Bank, have exerted influence on policies and the interpretation of law and rights. With their worldwide support for development projects, mainly financial, with the primary goal of eradicating global poverty, but also through their numerous analyses, reports, evaluation systems and recommendations, they perform an immense guidance and capacity function.[245]

As an overarching factor, these institutions, particularly WTO law and international **103** economic law (IEL) strongly influence the jurisdiction of poorer states, since market asymmetries between states are possible under their aegis and corresponding (preferential) free trade agreements are concluded.[246] Whether and to what extent these are conducive or obstructive to the development of a state or individual can hardly be adequately explained within this commentary. In any case, these instruments allow for a wide variety of dispute settlement mechanisms and the application of a wide variety of laws. However, access to justice and transparency are often lacking (→ Intro mn. 184-91, Goal 16 mn. 9 f.).

But it is not always about providing access to justice to uplift the poor and vulnerable **104** and, in this sense, creating a more equal society. A holistic view requires taking into account structural, social and economic factors. The causes of this limited access to justice are the lack of expression, education and access to decision-making and also political disempowerment as a result of a lack of accountability (→ Goal 16 mn. 73, 78).[247]

More recent influencing factors include the advancing digitalisation, especially of **105** the welfare state. The non-recognition of individuals, e.g. due to lacking legal identity in the form of a passport or a national insurance number, leads to their exclusion and participation in social benefits or the right to vote.[248] This development, if not counteracted immediately, is likely to increase in the future, further aggravating the risk of poverty for the most vulnerable groups.

E. Conclusion on SDG 1

The successful fight against poverty seems to be a quite Herculean task that demands **106** a great deal from institutions, governments, and societies with a specific engagement in multilateralism. Pandemics such as SARS-CoV-2 have the power reducing the likelihood of ending poverty by 2030. The ambitious objectives of the Addis Ababa Action Agenda (AAAA) to generate sophisticated funding will be even more difficult to achieve. The causes and the sheer existence of poverty accompanied with deprivation depends obviously not on the judgment of courts and awards of alternative dispute settlement as such. As it has been indicated by a short glimpse of existing jurisprudence, poverty

---

[245] See e.g. World Bank Environmental and Social Framework, 4.8.2016; Bandow and Vasquez, *Perpetuating poverty: the World Bank, the IMF and the developing world* (1994).

[246] Joseph, 'Trade Law and Investment Law', in Shelton, *The Oxford Handbook of International Human Rights Law* (2013), 846; see also UNCTAD, *The Least Developed Countries Report 2019* (2019); UNCTAD, *Trade And Development Report 2019, Financing A Global Green New Deal* (2019).

[247] De Schutter, *Closing Speech: The contribution of access to justice to the post-2015 agenda, How access to justice can help reduce poverty*, 22 May 2013.

[248] Nyamori, 'No healthcare, voting without Huduma Namba, bill proposes' (2019) *Standard Digital*; Mahlaka, 'Post office set to take over cash payments from CPS' (2018) *The Citizen* [both found in: A/74/493, *Extreme poverty and human rights, Note by the Secretary-General*, 11.10.2019].

as such creates a status of segregation and stigmatisation and excludes people from access to food, water, housing, education, well-being and decent jobs. Holding people prisoned in poverty from a fair access to human development paves the way to human rights violations. The question of the proportionality of living conditions, which can be (re-)balanced through the access to at least fair education, health, housing and justice as cornerstones of an overall framework to combat poverty, remains open and unsolved as long as the willingness of adjustment throughout the member states is underdeveloped domestically and internationally.

107   However, there are those who argue that a little more money and smarter aid is needed to help people in extreme poverty, as '[if] we could magically transfer money into the bank accounts of the world's poor'.[249]

108   The fight against poverty must take into account all aspects of social reality, as reflected in numerous SDGs, and also recognise the link of being victimised due to poverty or being a victim kept in poverty for criminal purposes. A trafficker's actions can create or exacerbate a victim's vulnerability (extremely poor wages causing poverty, restricted movement causing isolation or seizure of identity documents causing fear of deportation).[250]

109   However, poverty-stricken countries must be involved in those projects that serve to reduce poverty. The World Bank and the IMF initiated the development of Poverty Reduction Strategy Papers (PRSP) in 1999, creating an interesting far reaching approach,[251] which could be revitalised and optimised for the future.

110   Country driven processes are foreseen and are drawn up by the governments of the countries affected by poverty. Both local reference groups and external partner organisations are involved in the participatory development process encompassing the poor and vulnerable groups and representatives as well.[252] The broadness of the participatory approach seems to be the right way to alleviate poverty. Therefore, it was just to describe the poverty reduction strategy (PRS) process as '[a]n iterative process of participation, planning, implementation, assessment of set targets and indicators, and feedback'.[253]

111   Regular participation has always been qualified as key in continuously improving poverty reduction strategies. Public Participation is qualified as essential to foster sustainable development and good governance – free of corruption, thereby upholding an effective protection of human rights which is complemented by an effective accessible judicial or administrative procedure, ensuring impartial and just investigations, even in transboundary cases.[254] (→ Goal 16 mn. 11 f.

112   However, a uniform picture can hardly be established. But two levels recur consistently: the idea of proportionality and human dignity, the consideration of which provides

---

[249] Deaton, *The Great Escape* (2013), 268.

[250] Jovanovic, 'The Essence of Slavery: Exploitation in Human Rights Law' (2020) 00 *Human Rights Law Review*, 1 (23 f.).

[251] IMF, Poverty Reduction Strategy Papers (PRSP), 28.12.2016 including country documents and staff assessments, https://www.imf.org/external/np/prsp/prsp.aspx.

[252] Klugman, *A Sourcebook for Poverty Reduction Strategies, Volume 1: Core Techniques and Cross-Cutting Issues* (2002), 239.

[253] Klugman, *A Sourcebook for Poverty Reduction Strategies, Volume 1: Core Techniques and Cross-Cutting Issues* (2002), 239.

[254] ILA, *New Delhi Declaration of Principles of International Law Relating to Sustainable Development*, 2002, para. 5.1; see: ILA New Delhi Declaration of Principles of International Law Relating to Sustainable Development (2002) 2 *International Environmental Agreements: Politics, Law and Economics*, 209-16; Schrijver, 'Advancements in the principle of international law on sustainable development' in Cordonier Segger and C. G. Weeramantry (eds), *Sustainable Development Principles in the decisions of International Courts and Tribunals* (2017), 107; see also: Schrijver, *The Evolution of Sustainable Development in International Law: Inception, Meaning and Status* (2008), 257.

(peaceful) stability and, at the same time, for the alleviation of poverty (→ Intro mn. 13, 47, 53 ff.).

In that vein, the Special Rapporteur on extreme poverty and human rights Oliver **113** De Schutter identified three key challenges after being appointed in 2020. Firstly, the concept of 'Making Social Protection Floors Universal' still awaits the implementation of the International Labour Conference about Social Protection Floors Recommendation as an 'unfinished task'. Secondly, he finds striking arguments to search for '[a] new and more inclusive development pathway requires that we transform the current shape of globalization -- a form of globalization in which transnational corporations locate the most labor-intensive segments of global production chains'. The call for a change can be heard in economics and other disciplines (→ Intro mn. 129).[255] And thirdly, he qualified the 'Adequate Participation of People in Poverty' as an essential prerequisite according to SDG 1 for the eradication of extreme poverty, transmitted from generation to generation.[256]

Poverty goes hand in hand with other inequalities. In many countries of the world, **114** women are overrepresented among the poor that serve to exclude them from full and equal participation in society. There is not only one just response to tackle the gendered variation of poverty but '[s]tructural economic reforms at the global and domestic level alongside political, social and cultural transformations are named as one convincing tool for the future'.[257]

Achieving social security as set as a central feature in SDG 1.3 appears in numerous **115** human rights conventions, human rights instruments of many regional bodies and in the constitutions and legislation of many States.

Sen has revealed the nexus about poverty as a capability deprivation[258] meaning that **116** even relative deprivation in terms of income can yield in absolute deprivation in terms of capabilities, which could be the case in '[b]eing relatively poor in a rich country'.[259] Sen also argues that the use of family income could be and is used disproportionately in the sense that boys are often preferred against girls leading to sex bias perceived in many countries in North Africa and in Asia. The deprivation of girls results in greater mortality, medical neglect, undernourishment and even poverty is likely.[260]

The capability approach is underlying SDG 1.4 to ensure in particular the poor and **117** the vulnerable, to be equipped with equal rights to economic resources as well as access to basic services.

As noted in the discussion of the international law above, equality and non-discrimi- **118** nation against women are central human rights, closely related to the realisation of other rights, including the right to social security. Equality, understood substantively, offers a valuable means of developing the right to social security from a gender perspective.

---

[255] De Schutter, *Tackling extreme poverty in times of crisis: Key challenges facing the fight against poverty and thematic priorities for the Special Rapporteur on extreme poverty and human rights*, 1.5.2020; A/HRC/WG.2/19/CRP.1 *The international dimensions of the right to development: a fresh start towards improving accountability*, Olivier De Schutter, 22.01.2018.

[256] De Schutter, *Tackling extreme poverty in times of crisis: Key challenges facing the fight against poverty and thematic priorities for the Special Rapporteur on extreme poverty and human rights*, 1.5.2020.

[257] Goldblatt, 'Gender, poverty and the development of the right to social security'(2014) 10(4) *International Journal of Law in Context*, 460 (462).

[258] Sen, *Development as Freedom* (1999), 85.

[259] Sen, *Development as Freedom* (1999), 89.

[260] Sen, *Development as Freedom* (1999), 88 f.

Substantive equality can be used in a transformative manner to address structural inequalities and achieve far-reaching social change.[261]

119   The strict application of *locus standi* rule is widespread and well known to avoid a claim before the court that is not rooted in the sphere of rights of the claimant but much more based on a general interest, e.g. in Germany where popular claims are systematically and generally have been excluded in most legal areas [Ausschluss der Popularklage].[262]

120   An interesting instrument here is 'Public Interest Litigation (PIL)' in India. PIL, as practised in India and supported by the Indian Supreme Court, has been described as 'following a doctrine of procedural relaxation in cases of human rights violations' to facilitate both 'access to justice and furnishing of proof.'[263]

121   A further instrument to simplify the enforcement of law, particularly of constitutional rights (of individuals) was created with the tutela as a form of constitutional injunction. As an informal and less expensive instrument aiming at facilitating access to rapid constitutional justice, it has been used in Colombia since 1991. This far-reaching instrument can, under certain conditions, even oppose awards from arbitration proceedings and lead to their annulment (admissibility of constitutional injunctions against arbitral awards).[264] However, despite its intention to simplify legal procedures, only a small percentage of these tutelas are heard at all in the Constitutional Court, admittedly after time-consuming review. This system, which is frequently used and facilitates access to justice and due process could also be adapted in other legal families, but only after the necessary processes have been optimised.[265] Both PIL and tutela are also frequently used in a wider context of strategic litigation.[266]

122   Finally, the fight against poverty, the strong emphasis on multilateralism facing climate change, the lack of funding, and the unfolding of a pandemic could weaken the willingness to finance it, thus jeopardising one of the key objectives of the Global Agenda 2030.

---

[261] Goldblatt, 'Gender, poverty and the development of the right to social security'(2014) 10(4) *International Journal of Law in Context*, 460 (471).

[262] Brems and Adekoya, 'Human Rights Enforcement by People Living in Poverty: Access to Justice in Nigeria' (2010) 54(2) *Journal of African Law*, 258 (266).

[263] Brems and Adekoya, 'Human Rights Enforcement by People Living in Poverty: Access to Justice in Nigeria' (2010) 54(2) *Journal of African Law*, 258 (274 f.).

[264] Sentencia SU033/18, Expediente T-4.273.880, *Acción de Tutela instaurada por Gestión Energética S.A. E.S.P. -GENSA- contra el Tribunal de Arbitramento conformado para dirimir las controversias surgidas entre la Compañía Eléctrica de Sochagota S.A. E.S.P. -CES- y las sociedades Gestión Energética S.A. E.S.P. –GENSA- y la Empresa de Energía de Boyacá S.A. E.S.P. –EBSA-*; further reading: Rincón, 'Colombia's Constitutional Court declares that constitutional injunctions (tutela) proceed against awards in international arbitration' (2019) *Transnational Notes*.

[265] Further reading: Landau, Dixon and Sen, 'Constitutional Non-Transformation?: Socioeconomic Rights beyond the Poor' in Young (ed), *The Future of Economic and Social Rights* (2019); Merhof, 'Building a bridge between reality and the constitution: The establishment and development of the Colombian Constitutional Court' (2015) in 13(3) *I•CON*, 714-32.

[266] https://www.justiceinitiative.org/uploads/8c45f0be-d3be-40d6-aae8-a0b046bf6511/slip-land-rights-20170620.pdf.

Goal 2
End hunger, achieve food security and improved nutrition and promote sustainable agriculture

2.1 By 2030, end hunger and ensure access by all people, in particular the poor and people in vulnerable situations, including infants, to safe, nutritious and sufficient food all year round

2.2 By 2030, end all forms of malnutrition, including achieving, by 2025, the internationally agreed targets on stunting and wasting in children under 5 years of age, and address the nutritional needs of adolescent girls, pregnant and lactating women and older persons

2.3 By 2030, double the agricultural productivity and incomes of small-scale food producers, in particular women, indigenous peoples, family farmers, pastoralists and fishers, including through secure and equal access to land, other productive resources and inputs, knowledge, financial services, markets and opportunities for value addition and non-farm employment

2.4 By 2030, ensure sustainable food production systems and implement resilient agricultural practices that increase productivity and production, that help maintain ecosystems, that strengthen capacity for adaptation to climate change, extreme weather, drought, flooding and other disasters and that progressively improve land and soil quality

2.5 By 2020, maintain the genetic diversity of seeds, cultivated plants and farmed and domesticated animals and their related wild species, including through soundly managed and diversified seed and plant banks at the national, regional and international levels, and promote access to and fair and equitable sharing of benefits arising from the utilization of genetic resources and associated traditional knowledge, as internationally agreed

2.a Increase investment, including through enhanced international cooperation, in rural infrastructure, agricultural research and extension services, technology development and plant and livestock gene banks in order to enhance agricultural productive capacity in developing countries, in particular least developed countries

2.b Correct and prevent trade restrictions and distortions in world agricultural markets, including through the parallel elimination of all forms of agricultural export subsidies and all export measures with equivalent effect, in accordance with the mandate of the Doha Development Round

2.c Adopt measures to ensure the proper functioning of food commodity markets and their derivatives and facilitate timely access to market information, including on food reserves, in order to help limit extreme food price volatility

Word Count related to 'Hunger' and 'Nutrition'
A/RES/70/1 – Transforming our world: the 2030 Agenda for Sustainable Development: 'Hunger': 8 'Nutrition': 7
Instruments mentioned in A/RES/70/1 in the section entitled: 'Sustainable Development Goals and targets':
A/RES/69/313 - Addis Ababa Action Agenda of the Third International Conference on Financing for Development adopted on 27 July 2015: 'Hunger': 3 'Nutrition': 7
A/RES/66/288 - The future we want (Rio +20 Declaration) adopted on 27 July 2012: 'Hunger': 8 'Nutrition': 7
A/RES/55/2 - United Nations Millennium Declaration adopted on 8 September 2000: 'Hunger': 3 'Learning': 0

Select Bibliography: Bina Agarwal, 'Food Security, Productivity and Gender Inequality' in Ronald J. Herring (ed), *The Oxford Handbook of Food Politics and Society* (Oxford University Press, Oxford 2015), 273; Chantelle Bazerghi, Fiona H. McKay and Matthew Dunn, 'The Role of Food Banks in Addressing Food Insecurity: A Systematic Review' (2016) 41 *J Community Health*, 732; Juliana Dias Bernardes Gil, Pytrik Reidsma, Ken Giller, Lindsay Todman, Andrew Whitmore, Martin van Ittersum, 'Sustainable development goal 2: Improved targets and indicators for agriculture and food security' (2019) 48 *Ambio*, 685; Priscilla Claeys and Nadia C.S. Lambek, 'Introduction: In Search of Better Options: Food Sovereignty, the Right to Food and Legal Tools for Transforming Food Systems' in Nadia C. S. Lambek et al. (eds), *Rethinking Food Systems – Structural Challenges, New Strategies and the Law* (Springer Dordrecht, Heidelberg, New York, London 2014), 7; Jennifer Clapp, *Food security and international trade – Unpacking disputed narratives* (FAO, Rome 2015), 10; Ian G. Díaz, and Andrea Nuila H, Global Network for the Right to Food and Nutrition, *Right to Food and Nutrition Watch, Women's Power in Food Struggles* (2019); FAO, IFAD, UNICEF, WFP and WHO, *The State of Food Security and Nutrition in the World 2020, Transforming food systems for affordable healthy diets* (FAO, Rome 2020); Food and Agriculture Organization of the United Nations, *Sustainable food systems – Concept and framework* (FAO, Rome 2018), 1; Food and Agriculture Organization of the United Nations, *Climate change and food security: risks and responses* (FAO, Rome 2016), 31; Beatrice Garske, Katharine Heyl, Felix Ekardt, Lea Moana Weber and Wiktoria Gradzka, 'Challenges of Food Waste Governance: An Assessment of European Legislation on Food Waste and Recommendations for Improvement by Economic Instruments' (2020), 9 *Land* 2020, 231; Mark Gibson, *The Feeding of Nations – Redefining Food Security for the 21st Century* (CRC Press by Taylor & Francis Group, USA 2012), 236; Simone Hutter, 'Starvation in Armed Conflicts: An Analysis Based on the Right to Food' (2019), 17(4) *Journal of International Criminal Justice*, 723; International Development Law Organization (IDLO), *Realizing The Right To Food, Legal Strategies And Approaches* (2019), 55; Lidija Knuth and Margret Vidar, *Constitutional and Legal Protection of the Right to Food Around the World – FAO Right to Food Studies* (Rome 2011); Pascal Lamy, 'Trading towards global food security' in Pascal Lamy, *The Geneva Consensus – Making Trade for All* (Cambridge University Press, Cambridge 2013), 68; Matias E. Margulis, 'The World Trade Organization and Food Security after the Global Food Crises' in Drache and Jacobs (eds), *Linking Global Trade and Human Rights – New Policy Space in Hard Economic Times* (Cambridge University Press, Cambridge 2014), 236; B. O'Connor, 'Right to adequate food' in Thomas Cottier and Krista Nadakavukaren Schefer, *Elgar Encyclopedia of international Economic Law* (2017), 652; Anne Saab, 'Genetically Modified Organisms' in Emma Lees, Jorge E. Viñuales (eds), *The Oxford Handbook of Comparative Environmental Law* (Oxford University Press, Oxford 2019); Anne

Saab, 'An International Law Approach to Food Regime Theory' (2018) 31 *Leiden Journal of International Law*, 251; Ben Saul and David Kinley and Jacqueline Mowbray, 'Article 11: The Right to an Adequate Standard of Living' in Ben Saul and David Kinley and Jacqueline Mowbray, *The International Covenant on Economic, Social and Cultural Rights: Commentary, Cases, and Materials* (2014), 866 Charlotte Streck and Darragh Convay, 'Forestry and Agriculture under the UNFCCC – A jigsaw waiting to be assembled? in Cinnamon P. Carlarne, Kevin R. Gray and Richard Tarasofsky, *The Oxford Handbook of International Climate Change Law* (Oxford University Press, Oxford 2016), 564; Girmay Teklu, 'Analysis on Legal Status of The Right to Food' (2019) 7 *J Pol Sci Pub Aff*, 1; Bernd M.J van der Meulen, 'The Structure of European Food Law' (2013) 2 *Laws*, 69; Andreas J. Wiesand, 'Food (Right to, and Cultural Dimensions of, F.)', in Andreas J. Wiesand, Kalliopi Chainoglou and Anna Sledzinska-Simon in collaboration with: Yvonne Donders, Culture and Human Rights: *The Wroclaw Commentaries*, De Gruyter 2017, 167; World Food Programme and Food and Agriculture Organization of the United Nations, *The State of Food Insecurity in the World – Addressing food insecurity in protracted crises* (FAO, Rome 2010), 8; Shyam S. Yadav, V. S. Hegde, Abdul Basir Habibi, Mahendra Dia and Suman Verma, 'Climate Change, Agriculture and Food Security' in Shyam Singh Yadav, Robert J. Redden, Jerry L. Hatfield, Andreas W. Ebert and Danny Hunter (eds), *Food Security and Climate Change* (John Wiley & Sons Ltd., USA/UK 2019), 1.

A. Background and Origin of SDG 2

According to the World Health Organization (WHO) enough food is produced **1** to feed everyone.[1] Nevertheless, one in nine people worldwide suffer from acute or chronic hunger, starvation, famine conditions or insecure food.[2] This number worsened significantly due to the global SARS-CoV-2 pandemic, pushing back the achievements of recent years which had, amongst others, been made with the means of SDG 2.[3] In seeking to end hunger and malnutrition, achieve food security, improve nutrition and promote sustainable agriculture, SDG 2 is confronted with a death toll of 9 million people dying every year of hunger and hunger-related diseases.[4]

In 2020, the Food and Agriculture Organization (FAO), amongst other international **2** organisations (IOs) noted that the targets contained in SDG 2 are no longer achievable by 2030.[5] The overall negative trend in the expansion of hunger and its pervasive impacts is on the rise for the third consecutive year, leading to a deterioration in progress towards SDG 2.[6]

SDG 2 comprises eight targets and 15 indicators with the first five targets focusing **3** on food security and agricultural sustainability, whereas the last three targets point to market-related issues aiming at increasing agricultural investments and reducing market restriction, distortions and volatility.[7]

---

[1] https://www.who.int/news-room/detail/15-07-2019-world-hunger-is-still-not-going-down-after-three-years-and-obesity-is-still-growing-un-report.

[2] FSIN and Global Network against food crises, *2021 Global Report On Food Crises, Joint Analysis For Better Decisions* (2021), 14; https://www.wfp.org/publications/2019-hunger-map.

[3] FSIN and Global Network against food crises, *2021 Global Report On Food Crises, Joint Analysis For Better Decisions* (2021), 10.

[4] https://www.theworldcounts.com/challenges/people-and-poverty/hunger-and-obesity/how-many-people-die-from-hunger-each-year.

[5] FAO, IFAD, UNICEF, WFP and WHO, *The State of Food Security and Nutrition in the World 2020. Transforming food systems for affordable healthy diets. Rome* (2020).

[6] E/2019/68, *Special edition: progress towards the Sustainable Development Goals, Report of the Secretary-General*, 8 May 2019, para. 8; E/2020/L.20–E/HLPF/2020/L.1, *Draft ministerial declaration of the high-level segment of the 2020 session of the Economic and Social Council and the high-level political forum on sustainable development, convened under the auspices of the Council, submitted by the President of the Council, Mona Juul (Norway)*, 17 July 2020, para. 7.

[7] Dias Bernardes Gil et al., 'Sustainable development goal 2: Improved targets and indicators for agriculture and food security', 48 *Ambio*, 685 (686).

I. UN History of Eradicating Global Hunger

4   The first UN Conference on Food and Agriculture was held from 18 May to 3 June 1943 in Hot Springs with the participation of 44 governments. As a result, the 'Conference decided on the establishment of a permanent organization in the field of food and agriculture'.[8] In 1945, the predecessor of the FAO, the International Institute of Agriculture (IIA)[9] became a special agency of the UN.[10] On 16 November 1974, for the first time, hunger and malnutrition were mentioned as a global issue during the World Food Conference.[11] The adopted Universal Declaration on the Eradication of Hunger and Malnutrition[12] included that every man, woman and child 'has the inalienable right to be free from hunger and malnutrition in order to develop fully and maintain their physical and mental faculties'.[13] Moreover, one of the fundamental responsibilities of governments (and states in general) is to work together to get to a higher food production and more equitable and efficient distribution of food between the countries.[14]

5   In 1992, the FAO and WHO convened for the International Conference on Nutrition in Rome, where the World Declaration and Plan of Action for Nutrition was submitted to the Conference.[15] The plan included nine priority themes such as improving household food security, promoting breast-feeding, protecting consumers through improved food quality and safety and many more.[16] With the UN Millennium Declaration in 2000, the goal of eradicating extreme hunger was included in MDG 1, next to poverty.[17]

6   In the same year, the Commission on Human Rights decided to appoint a special rapporteur on the right to food.[18] Under the roof of the United Nations Human Rights Office of the High Commissioner, the Special Rapporteur on the Right to Food 'is an independent expert appointed by the Human Rights Council to examine and report back on a country situation' with focus on the implementation of the right to food.[19] The first report by the Special Rapporteur on the right to food, Mr. Jean Ziegler, was

---

[8] https://research.un.org/en/foodsecurity/un-milestones.

[9] The International Institute of Agriculture (IIA) was founded in 1905 in Rome by King Vittorio Emanuele III upon the initiative of David Lubin, see on the history of the FAO: https://digitallibrary.un.or g/record/1467413?ln=en#:~:text=It%20starts%20with%20the%20International,the%20initiative%20of%20 David%20Lubin.

[10] http://www.fao.org/3/x5584E/x5584e01.htm#i.%20letter%20to%20governments%20transmitting %20t.

[11] E/CONf.65/20, *Report of the World Food Conference*, 5-16 November 1974.

[12] Universal Declaration on the Eradication of Hunger and Malnutrition, Adopted on 16 November 1974 by the World Food Conference convened under General Assembly resolution 3180 (XXVIII) of 17 December 1973; and endorsed by General Assembly resolution 3348 (XXIX) of 17 December 1974.

[13] Universal Declaration on the Eradication of Hunger and Malnutrition, Adopted on 16 November 1974 by the World Food Conference convened under General Assembly resolution 3180 (XXVIII) of 17 December 1973; and endorsed by General Assembly resolution 3348 (XXIX) of 17 December 1974, para. 1.

[14] Universal Declaration on the Eradication of Hunger and Malnutrition, Adopted on 16 November 1974 by the World Food Conference convened under General Assembly resolution 3180 (XXVIII) of 17 December 1973; and endorsed by General Assembly resolution 3348 (XXIX) of 17 December 1974, paras. 2, 4.

[15] FAO, *International Conference on Nutrition* (1992), ICN/92/2.

[16] FAO, *Food, Nutrition and Agriculture* (2002).

[17] MDG 1.3 very precisely read to 'halve the proportion of individuals suffering from hunger in the period between 1990 and 2015', A/RES/55/2, *United Nations Millennium Declaration*, 18 September 2000.

[18] A/RES/2000/10, *The Right to Food*, 17 April 2000.

[19] https://www.ohchr.org/en/issues/food/pages/foodindex.aspx.

submitted on 7 February 2001 in accordance with the Commission on Human Rights resolution 2000/10[20] and the right to food was defined as follows:

> The right to food is the right to have regular, permanent and free access, either directly or by means of financial purchases, to quantitatively and qualitatively adequate and sufficient food corresponding to the cultural traditions of the people to which the consumer belongs, and which ensures a physical and mental, individual and collective, fulfilling and dignified life free of fear.[21]

Furthermore, on 1 April 2016, the UN declared the 'United Nations Decade of Action   7
on Nutrition'[22] lasting from 2016 to 2025. Based on the outcomes and conclusions of the Second International Conference on Nutrition (Outcome Document: Framework for Action[23]) and the 2030 Agenda for Sustainable Development. 'The UN Decade of Action on Nutrition will provide an umbrella for a wide group of actors to work together to address these and other pressing nutrition issues in order to achieve the goals set out in the 2030 Agenda'.[24] Respective current developments are regularly reflected in Reports by the Secretary-General.[25]

One of the clearly expressed determinations of the right to food is contained in   8
Art. 11 of the International Covenant on Economic, Social and Cultural Rights (ICE-SCR) which outlines the right to an adequate standard of living, including food, and the fundamental right of every person to be free from hunger (→ Goal 2 mn. 16 ff.).[26]

Several economic obstacles prevent or stop the realisation of the right to food which   9
are as follows:

(a) Problems related to developments in world trade, particularly the agricultural policies of developed countries, as sanctioned by the World Trade Organization (WTO), which perpetuate malnutrition and hunger in the South;
(b) External-debt servicing and its impact on food security, including the structural adjustment programmes of the International Monetary Fund (IMF), which consistently aggravate undernourishment and malnutrition in debtor countries;
(c) Developments in biotechnology, including genetically modified plants, ownership of international patents by agribusinesses from the North and worldwide protection of those patents, hampering access to food and the availability of food;
(d) Wars and their destructive impact on food security;
(e) Corruption;
(f) Access to land and credit;

---

[20] E/CN.4/2001/53, *The right to food, Report by the Special Rapporteur on the right to food, Mr. Jean Ziegler, submitted in accordance with Commission on Human Rights resolution 2000/10*, 7 February 2001.

[21] E/CN.4/2001/53, *The right to food, Report by the Special Rapporteur on the right to food, Mr. Jean Ziegler, submitted in accordance with Commission on Human Rights resolution 2000/10*, 7 February 2001.

[22] A/RES/70/259, *Resolution adopted by the General Assembly on 1 April 2016, 70/259. United Nations Decade of Action on Nutrition (2016–2025)*, 15 April 2016; see also: https://www.who.int/nutrition/decade -of-action/en/.

[23] http://www.fao.org/3/a-mm215 e.pdf; see also: http://www.fao.org/policy-support/tools-and-publicat ions/resources-details/en/c/422096.

[24] https://www.unscn.org/en/topics/un-decade-of-action-on-nutrition.

[25] A/74/794, *Implementation of the United Nations Decade of Action on Nutrition (2016–2025), Report of the Secretary-General*, 13 April 2020; A/72/829, *Implementation of the United Nations Decade of Action on Nutrition (2016–2025), Report of the Secretary-General*, 11 April 2018; A/RES/72/306, *Resolution adopted by the General Assembly on 24 July 2018, 72/306. Implementation of the United Nations Decade of Action on Nutrition (2016–2025)*, 25 July 2018.

[26] A/RES/2200A (XXI), *International Covenant on Economic, Social and Cultural Rights, Adopted and opened for signature, ratification and accession by General Assembly resolution 2200A (XXI) of 16 December 1966, entry into force 3 January 1976, in accordance with article 27*, 16 December 1966; see for an overview of the International Standards on the Right to Food: https://www.ohchr.org/EN/Issues/Food/Pages/Stand ards.aspx.

(g) Discrimination against women and its impact on the realisation of the right to food.[27]

10   Although the term 'hunger' was not expressed in the outcome document of the 1972 Stockholm Conference, the condition of suffering from inadequate food supply, however, was. Despite the focus being mainly on environmental protection, the concepts of 'malnutrition' and 'food' were also discussed during the conference, with the aim to enable people to a dignified life by establishing adequate conditions of life through achieving food security and supply with adequate food.[28] It was stated, that '[i]n the developing countries most of the environmental problems are caused by underdevelopment. Millions continue to live far below the minimum levels required for a decent human existence, deprived of adequate food and clothing, shelter and education, health and sanitation.'[29]

11   The largest population share who cannot afford healthy diets live in Asia (1.9 billion) and Africa (965 million). Many others live in Latin America and the Caribbean (104.2 million), with the fewest share living in Northern America and Europe (18 million).[30] The costs of ensuring a healthy diet are significantly higher than the international poverty line, established at USD 1.90-int[31] purchasing power parity (PPP) per day. This puts healthy diets beyond the reach of those living in poverty or just above the poverty line.[32] According to the FAO, the number of people affected by hunger still continues to increase. This trend which already began in 2014 shows a sharp increase triggered by the global SARS-CoV-2 pandemic. Against the additional backdrops of the many conflicts worldwide which lead to the displacement of people or the destruction of livelihoods and cultivable land, and accompanied by the serious threats and consequences of climate change such as droughts, floods, rising temperatures, further reducing the fertile ground for combating hunger, it is unlikely that this trend will be successfully interrupted.[33] Compared to 2014, nearly 60 million more undernourished people are living now on this planet than in 2014. It is expected that in 2050 a total of 20 percent of the global population will suffer from hunger and malnutrition.[34]

---

[27] E/CN.4/2001/53, *The right to food, Report by the Special Rapporteur on the right to food, Mr. Jean Ziegler, submitted in accordance with Commission on Human Rights resolution 2000/10*, 7 February 2001.

[28] A/Conf.48/14 / Rev.1, *Report of the United Nations Conference on the Human Environment, Stockholm, Sweden*, 5-16 June 1972, Principle 1, *1 (ex. 1)*, the term 'food' is stated 65 times in the report.

[29] A/Conf.48/14 / Rev.1, *Report of the United Nations Conference on the Human Environment, Stockholm, Sweden*, 5-16 June 1972, para. 4.

[30] FAO, IFAD, UNICEF, WFP and WHO, *The State of Food Security and Nutrition in the World 2020, Transforming food systems for affordable healthy diets* (2020), 65 f.

[31] An analysis of UN Women and UNDP showed that 'by 2021 approx. 435 million women and girls will be living on less than USD 1.90 a day, including 47 million pushed into poverty as a result of COVID-19', FSIN and Global Network against food crises, *2021 Global Report On Food Crises, Joint Analysis For Better Decisions* (2021), 23.

[32] FAO, IFAD, UNICEF, WFP and WHO, *The State of Food Security and Nutrition in the World 2020, Transforming food systems for affordable healthy diets* (2020), 65 f.

[33] A/HRC/43/44, *Critical perspective on food systems, food crises and the future of the right to food Report of the Special Rapporteur on the right to food**, 21 January 2020, paras. 44-57.

[34] FAO, *The state of Food security and Nutrition in the World 2020* (2020), Executive Summary.

II. Agriculture and Hunger

SDG 2.4. encompasses the developing of sustainable agricultural systems.[35] On 7   **12**
June 1905, the International Institute of Agriculture was founded in Rome which was
primarily intended as clearinghouse for the collection of agricultural statistics.[36] After
World War II, it was handed over to the FAO and the UN.[37] The advancing globalisation
has led, among other things, to investors operating in foreign countries, such as food
companies, landlords and mining or forestry industries, sometimes with the support of
the respective host states, practising 'land grabbing' and thus threatening in particular
the existence of indigenous and tribal people. These often suffer from the 'lost access to
traditional (forest) livelihoods and food resources'[38] due to their (forced) displacement.
But also 'small-scale farmers, landless peasants, nomad sand peasants practising shifting
cultivation or other rural people especially from ethnic and cultural communities practising traditional forms of agriculture, hunting or fishing are explicitly threatened.[39]

Agriculture plays a crucial role in achieving the goal of zero hunger. It provides   **13**
livelihoods for more than 2.5 billion people, mostly poor farmers and has a significant
impact on the goals to end poverty and inequality. In this context, organic agriculture
is more sustainable than conventional farming. The growing demand comes from the
customers nowadays who are concerned about the negative implications of the conventional agriculture.[40]

B. Scope and Dimensions of SDG 2

SDG 2 covers the broad and urgent field of global hunger, combined with food   **14**
security, improved nutrition and sustainable agriculture. The legal framework for the
understanding and the implementation of each target is thus equally broad and multifaceted. In this respect, the legal scope and dimensions of SDG 2 range from human
rights, international food systems and trade, the protection of vulnerable people, climate
related policies, sustainable agriculture, population growth, the role of IOs to the current
and heavy consequences of a global pandemic.

---

[35] See e.g. FAO, Revised World Soil Charter (2015); FAO, Voluntary Guidelines for Sustainable Soil
Management (2017); FAO and Committee on World Food Security, Voluntary Guidelines on the Responsible Governance of Tenure of Land, Fisheries and Forests in the Context of National Food Security
(2012); FAO, Voluntary Guidelines for Flag State Performance (2015); FAO, Voluntary Guidelines for
Securing Sustainable Small-Scale Fisheries in the Context of Food Security and Poverty Eradication
(2018).

[36] Rutherford, 'The International Institute of Agriculture. By Asher Hobson' (1932) 26(5), *American
Political Science Review*, 950-1.

[37] http://www.fao.org/3/x5584e/x5584e00.htm.

[38] Opportunities for these people are neglected, for instance, through huge fish trawlers or development
projects such as dams, power plants, coal or sand mines or mineral industries; see amongst many others:
E/CN.4/2006/44/Add.2, *Economic, Social And Cultural Rights, The right to food, Report of the Special
Rapporteur on the Right to Food*, Mr. Jean Ziegler, 20 March 2006.

[39] Wiesand, 'Food (Right to, and Cultural Dimensions of, F.)', in Wiesand and Chainoglou and Sledzinska-Simon in collaboration with Donders, *Culture and Human Rights: The Wroclaw Commentaries* (2016),
167; A/HRC/RES/39/12, *United Nations Declaration on the Rights of Peasants and Other People Working in
Rural Areas*, 8 October 2018, preamble, Art. 2.2; see further A/RES/73/165, *United Nations Declaration on
the Rights of Peasants and Other People Working in Rural Areas*, 21 January 2019, Arts. 2, 10, 13, 14, 17, 18
and 19.

[40] Open Working Group (OWG), *3rd Open Working Group Challenged to Adopt Food Sovereignty
Campaign for People's Goals for Sustainable Development*.

15   The scope of SDG 2 is constituted by several crucial keywords such as hunger, malnutrition, food and food systems (→which against the background also determines the legal framework.

I. Elementary Definitions

1. Malnutrition

16   According to the WHO Malnutrition refers 'deficiencies, excesses, or imbalances in a person's intake of energy and / or nutrients.'[41] Different forms of malnutrition such as undernutrition include wasting and underweight, micronutrient-related malnutrition, which includes micronutrient deficiencies and overweight and diet-related non-communicable diseases.[42]

2. Hunger

17   According to the FAO, '[h]unger is an unpleasant or painful physical sensation caused by insufficient intake of food energy. It becomes chronic when the person does not regularly consume a sufficient number of calories (food energy) to lead a normal, active and healthy life.'[43] The FAO uses the Prevalence of Undernourishment (PoU) indicator to estimate the extent of hunger in the world, so 'hunger' may also be referred to as undernourishment.

18   The world's progress towards achieving SDG 2 is measured by the prevalence of undernutrition (PoU) and the prevalence of moderate or severe food insecurity within a population, based on the Food Insecurity Experience Scale (FIES).[44]

19   However, it is to be noted that no universal definition of hunger exists but most frequently is determined by the amount of dietary energy deficiency calculated based on average daily calorie intake.[45]

3. Undernourishment

20   According to the UN Statistics SDG Handbook on indicators,

> [t]he prevalence of undernourishment (PoU) is the proportion of the population whose habitual food consumption is insufficient to provide the dietary energy levels that are required to maintain a normal active and healthy life. It is expressed as a percentage.
>
> Undernourishment is defined as chronic hunger, a condition where a person has inadequate access to food amounts necessary to provide the energy required for conducting a normal, health and active life, given their individual dietary energy requirements over a period of at least one year. The concept encompasses three aspects: availability of food, inequality in access to that food, and minimum dietary energy requirements compatible with long term good health.[46]

21   The FAO complements this definition with undernourishment being a condition where a person is not able to acquire enough food to meet the minimum energy

---

[41] https://www.who.int/news-room/fact-sheets/detail/malnutrition.
[42] https://www.who.int/news-room/fact-sheets/detail/malnutrition.
[43] http://www.fao.org/hunger/en/.
[44] http://www.fao.org/sustainable-development-goals/indicators/2.1.2/en/.
[45] Yigzaw, 'Hunger And The Law: Freedom From Hunger As A Freestanding Right' (2014) 36(3) *Houston Journal of International Law*, 655 (657-71).
[46] https://unstats.un.org/wiki/display/SDGeHandbook/Indicator+2.1.1.

requirements.[47] The FAO does not distinguish between the term 'undernourishment' and 'hunger'.[48] The dietary energy terms are denoted

> in kilo-calories and divided by the total population and the number of days in the year to come up with the average daily per capita dietary energy available for human consumption. This dietary energy value is used as a proxy for the habitual dietary energy consumption per capita per day. To smooth annual fluctuations, a three-year average is calculated.[49]

4. Food Security

The 1996 World Food Summit adopted the following definition on food security: **22**

> Food security, at the individual, household, national, regional and global levels [is achieved] when all people, at all times, have physical and economic access to sufficient, safe and nutritious food to meet their dietary needs and food preferences for an active and healthy life'.[50] Food security exists when all people at all times to have access 'sufficient, safe and nutritious food which meets their dietary needs and food preferences for an active and healthy life' and insecurity exists when people do not have adequate access to food.[51]

According to the Committee on World Food Security of the FAO, Food and nutrition   **23** security exists when

> all people, at all times, have physical, social and economic access to food, which is safe and consumed in sufficient quantity and quality to meet their dietary needs and food preferences; and is supported by an environment of adequate sanitation, health services and care, allowing for a healthy and active life.[52]

An important aspect of food security is the level of dietary energy adequacy in a pop-   **24** ulation. The measured (in)adequacy indicates the capacity to sustain development and resultingly the efforts needed to reduce poverty, including finding solutions to hunger and malnutrition through improving food availability and access by the population. The monitoring allows conclusions to be drawn about 'changes in the overall availability of food, in households' ability to access it, and in socio-economic, geographic location and demographic characteristics of the population [...] differences across countries and global regions in any given moment in time'. Food insecurity may lead to reduced food intake which contributes to severe forms of undernutrition, including hunger.[53]

5. Food Systems

In particular, in the international context (but not alone) of the eradication of hunger,   **25** food systems play a central role. The FAO defines food systems as follows:

> Food systems (FS) encompass the entire range of actors and their interlinked value-adding activities involved in the production, aggregation, processing, distribution, consumption and disposal of food

---

[47] http://www.fao.org/sustainable-development-goals/indicators/211/en/; see for the determination of minimum energy requirements: FAO, *Human energy requirements, Report of a Joint FAO/WHO/UNU Expert Consultation*, 17-24 October 2001.

[48] http://www.fao.org/hunger/en/.

[49] https://unstats.un.org/wiki/display/SDGeHandbook/Indicator+2.1.1.

[50] FAO, *Rome Declaration on World Food Security and World Food Summit Plan of Action, World Food Summit*, 13-17 November 1996, para. 1.

[51] FAO, *Voluntary Guidelines to support the progressive realization of the right to adequate food in the context of national food security*, Adopted by the 127th Session of the FAO Council November 2004 (2005), paras. 15 f.

[52] CFS 2012/39, *Thirty-ninth Session, Rome, Italy, Final Report*,15-20 October 2012; FAO, *The state of Food security and Nutrition in the World 2020* (2020), Executive Summary.

[53] https://unstats.un.org/wiki/display/SDGeHandbook/Indicator+2.1.2.

products that originate from agriculture, forestry or fisheries, and parts of the broader economic, societal and natural environments in which they are embedded.

The food system is composed of sub-systems (e.g. farming system, waste management system, input supply system, etc.) and interacts with other key systems (e.g. energy system, trade system, health system, etc.). Therefore, a structural change in the food system might originate from a change in another system; for example, a policy promoting more biofuel in the energy system will have a significant impact on the food system.[54]

26 As a matter of concern in combating world hunger, food systems equally need to be sustainable, not least in order to fully achieve SDG 2. Therefore, the FAO also delivers the definition for sustainable food systems:

A sustainable food system (SFS) is a food system that delivers food security and nutrition for all in such a way that the economic, social and environmental bases to generate food security and nutrition for future generations are not compromised. This means that:

- It is profitable throughout (economic sustainability);
- It has broad-based benefits for society (social sustainability); and
- It has a positive or neutral impact on the natural environment (environmental sustainability)[55]

II. Legal Foundations

1. The Right to Food

27 Just as the topic is very multifaceted, the legal classification of hunger, food security, nutrition and agriculture in international law is equally wide-ranging. One of the well-known legal achievements is the right to food. Already confirmed in the Universal Declaration of Human Rights (UDHR) as a universal human right in Art. 25, being incorporated in the right to an adequate standard of living,[56] the right to food, in more concrete terms, is internationally recognised in General Comment No. 12 of the Committee on Economic, Social and Cultural Rights (CESCR). It states:

The right to adequate food is realized when every man, woman and child, alone or in community with others, has physical and economic access at all times to adequate food or means for its procurement.[57]

28 The legal foundation of the right to food consists of the essential factors availability, accessibility and adequacy. All these factors serve the successful implementation of the right to food. Availability is intended to ensure that (1) a person can feed and provide for her/himself through self-cultivation and natural resources, or (2) that the supply and

---

[54] FAO, *Sustainable food systems – Concept and framework* (2018), 1.

[55] FAO, *Sustainable food systems – Concept and framework* (2018), 1; see also: Bricas, 'Urbanization Issues Affecting Food System Sustainability' in Brand et al. (eds), *Designing Urban Food Policies – Concepts and Approaches* (2017), 1 (3): The food system represents a set of interrelated activities regarding the production, dissemination, processing and use of food, waste and the required resources [whereby] the food system concept is [...] encompassing production and all that precedes and succeeds it. [...] Waste as output of food production can also be seen as a food system component with the aim of minimizing waste quantities and recycling the intractable part, thus promoting sustainability.

[56] UDHR (1948), Art. 25: Everyone has the right to a standard of living adequate for the health and well-being of himself and of his family, including food, clothing, housing and medical care and necessary social services, and the right to security in the event of unemployment, sickness, disability, widowhood, old age or other lack of livelihood in circumstances beyond his control.

[57] E/C.12/1999/5, *Substantive Issues Arising In The Implementation Of The International Covenant On Economic, Social And Cultural Rights: General Comment 12 The right to adequate food (art. 11)*, 12 May 1999, para. 6.

distribution of sufficient food through efficient market systems from the manufacturing site to the places of demand functions.[58]

Accessibility is divided into economic accessibility and physical accessibility. 29

> Economic accessibility implies that personal or household financial costs associated with the acquisition of food for an adequate diet should be at a level such that the attainment and satisfaction of other basic needs are not threatened or compromised.[59]

Furthermore, physical accessibility means that food is always physically available for everyone. Both concepts of availability and accessibility place emphasis on the special role of vulnerable people such as women, children, indigenous people, elderly people and physically disabled people.[60] 30

Adequacy means that food and nutrition must be of a certain quality and must comply with further conditions such as cultural values, age, sex and living conditions.[61] 31

The effective implementation of the right to food is supported by the Food and Agriculture Organization's Voluntary Guidelines adopted by the General Council of the FAO in 2004.[62] These serve as indications of successful integration of the right to food into the national food security. Concretely, the guidelines may assist states and stakeholders to implement the right to food 'in the context of national food security, in order to achieve the goals of the Plan of Action of the World Food Summit'.[63] Given the particular need to protect vulnerable people, the right to food is to be considered also on the basis of the *Convention of the Rights of the Child*[64], the *Convention on the Elimination of All Forms of Discrimination Against Women*[65], the *Convention on the Rights of Persons with Disabilities*[66] as well as the four *Geneva Conventions*[67] on humanitarian treatment in war. 32

---

[58] E/C.12/1999/5, *Substantive Issues Arising In The Implementation Of The International Covenant On Economic, Social And Cultural Rights: General Comment 12 The right to adequate food (art. 11)*, 12 May 1999, para. 12.

[59] E/C.12/1999/5, *Substantive Issues Arising In The Implementation Of The International Covenant On Economic, Social And Cultural Rights: General Comment 12 The right to adequate food (art. 11)*, 12 May 1999, para. 13.

[60] E/C.12/1999/5, *Substantive Issues Arising In The Implementation Of The International Covenant On Economic, Social And Cultural Rights: General Comment 12 The right to adequate food (art. 11)*, 12 May 1999.

[61] Claeys and Lambek, 'Introduction: In Search of Better Options: Food Sovereignty, the Right to Food and Legal Tools for Transforming Food Systems' in Lambek et al. (eds), *Rethinking Food Systems – Structural Challenges, New Strategies and the Law* (2014), 1 (7); Office of the United Nations High Commissioner for Human Rights, *The Right to Adequate Food – Factsheet 34* (2010), 3.

[62] FAO, *Voluntary Guidelines to support the progressive realization of the right to adequate food in the context of national food security*, Adopted by the 127th Session of the FAO Council November 2004, The voluntary guidelines include a wide range of proposals and implementation guidelines for states and stakeholders. The topics covered range from democracy, good governance and the rule of law to economic development policy, market systems, institutions, international food aid, up to consumer protection and protection of vulnerable people.

[63] FAO, *Voluntary Guidelines to support the progressive realization of the right to adequate food in the context of national food security*, Adopted by the 127th Session of the FAO Council November 2004 (2005); see also: WFS 96/REP, *United Nations World Food Summit*, 13–17 November 1996.

[64] A/RES/44/25, Convention on the Rights of the Child of 20 November 1989.

[65] A/RES/34/180, Convention on the Elimination of All Forms of Discrimination Against Women *of* 18 December 197.

[66] A/RES/61/106, Convention on the Rights of Persons with Disabilities of 24 January 2007.

[67] A/HRC/9/9, Protection of the human rights of civilians in armed conflict (Geneva Conventions of 1864, 1906, 1929 and 1949 and in the Additional Protocols of 1977).

2. The Role of States

33   The international situation of hunger crisis and local food shortages puts states at the centre of attention. Regarding international law, governments hold the core responsibility to guarantee the implementation of human rights.[68] Art. 2 of the ICESCR indicates that states have the duty to progressively achieve 'the full realization of the rights recognized in the present Covenant by all appropriate means, including particularly the adoption of legislative measures'.[69] Thus, the law and legal approaches to the field of hunger and malnutrition serve as significant points of reference for broad analyses.[70] Based on the obligation under Art. 2 ICESCR, General Comment No. 12 in para. 14 sets a bottom line for the state's duty to act, whereby states must guarantee access to a minimum basic supply of essential food. Under the jurisdiction of a state, this basic supply for everyone must be 'sufficient, nutritionally adequate and safe, to ensure their freedom from hunger'.[71] In this context, the choice of words 'freedom from hunger' can be misinterpreted. The FAO clarifies that the obligation of states to guarantee 'freedom from hunger' does not mean that states are obliged to distribute free food to every human being. It is further stated that 'the right to adequate food is primarily the right to feed oneself in dignity'.[72]

> States' obligations mean that the elimination or alleviation of hunger cannot be considered a matter of charity but a question of legal entitlement, where actions move from discretionary acts among governments, donors, non-governmental organizations.[73]

34   More specifically, under Art. 11(2) of the ICESCR, a certain number of states' obligations are set out. It should be pointed out that obligations of a state to realise the right to food are not limited to the states' own possibilities, but includes international cooperation and commitment by other states as well. Here, the focus is laid on the use of scientific and technical knowledge 'to improve methods of production, conservation and distribution of food'.[74] Particular attention is drawn to the agrarian systems which shall be developed and reformed 'in such a way as to achieve the most efficient development and utilization of natural resources'.[75]

35   On the basis of General Comment No. 12, states are bound by specific fundamental obligations. The right to food can only be effectively implemented when states fulfil these obligations which entail the obligations:

–   to respect existing access to adequate food
–   to protect individuals from being deprived of their right to food by enterprises or individuals

---

[68] Teklu, 'Analysis on Legal Status of The Right to Food' (2019) 7 *J Pol Sci Pub Aff*, 1 (5).

[69] International Covenant on Economic, Social and Cultural Rights, Article 2.

[70] Claeys and Lambek, 'Introduction: In Search of Better Options: Food Sovereignty, the Right to Food and Legal Tools for Transforming Food Systems' in Lambek et al. (eds), *Rethinking Food Systems – Structural Challenges, New Strategies and the Law* (2014), 1 (5).

[71] E/C.12/1999/5, *Substantive Issues Arising In The Implementation Of The International Covenant On Economic, Social And Cultural Rights: General Comment 12 The right to adequate food (art. 11)*, 12 May 1999, para. 14; Teklu, 'Analysis on Legal Status of The Right to Food' (2019) 7 *J Pol Sci Pub Aff* 1 (5).

[72] FAO, *Guidance Note: Integrating the right to adequate food into food and nutrition security programmes* (2013), 8; see on human dignity in the context of the right to food also: A/75/219, *The right to food in the context of international trade law and policy, Note by the Secretary-General*, 22 July 2020, paras. 33 ff.

[73] FAO, *Guidance Note: Integrating the right to adequate food into food and nutrition security programmes* (2013), 8.

[74] International Covenant on Economic, Social and Cultural Rights, Art. 11.(2).

[75] International Covenant on Economic, Social and Cultural Rights, Art. 11(2).

– to fulfill the right to food by engaging 'in activities intended to strengthen people's access to and utilisation of resources and means to ensure their livelihood, including food security' as well as by directly realising the right to food for people who unable 'to enjoy the right to adequate food by the means at their disposal'[76]

III. International Food Systems, Food Security and the Right to Food

One of the core terms of SDG 2 is food security. As laid down before, **36**

> food security, at the individual, household, national, regional and global levels [is achieved] when all people, at all times, have physical and economic access to sufficient, safe and nutritious food to meet their dietary needs and food preferences for an active and healthy life.

This definition reveals the clear link to market-driven food production and market- **37** regulated food distribution. It can thus be assumed that this approach to food security is based on a neoliberal view of development. According to the World Food Programme and the FAO, 'food insecurity exists when people do not have adequate physical, social or economic access to food'.[77] Based on the neoliberal approach of food security, there is a deeper definition for food insecurity stating that 'food insecurity exists because 'food production and its distribution do not meet the needs of the world's population'.[78]

Food Security is not an empty concept. The food people eat defines their health. And **38** new observations reveal that '[h]ealthy diets are unaffordable to many people, especially the poor, in every region of the world. The most conservative estimates suggest that they are unaffordable for more than 3 billion people in the world. Healthy diets (SDG 3) are estimated to be, on average, five times more expensive than diets that meet only dietary energy needs through a starchy staple.' It has been stated that '[t]he cost of a healthy diet exceeds the international poverty line (established at USD 1.90 purchasing power parity (PPP) per person per day), making it unaffordable for the poor.'[206]

All diets have hidden costs, which must be understood to identify trade-offs and **39** synergies in relation to other SDGs. Two hidden, yet most critical costs relate to the health (SDG 3) and climate-related (SDG 13) consequences of our dietary choices and the food systems that support these. However, not all healthy diets are sustainable and not all diets designed for sustainability are always healthy. This important nuance is not well understood and is missing from ongoing discussions and debates on the potential contribution of healthy diets to environmental sustainability.

The cost also exceeds average food expenditures in most countries in the Global **40** South. Around 57 per cent or more of the population cannot afford a healthy diet throughout Sub-Saharan Africa and Southern Asia.

Under current food consumption patterns, diet-related health costs linked to mortal- **41** ity and non-communicable diseases are projected to exceed USD 1.3 trillion per year by 2030. On the other hand, the diet-related social cost of greenhouse gas emissions

---

[76] E/C.12/1999/5, *Substantive Issues Arising In The Implementation Of The International Covenant On Economic, Social And Cultural Rights: General Comment 12 The right to adequate food (art. 11)*, 12 May 1999, para. 14; see also: https://www.ohchr.org/en/issues/food/pages/foodindex.aspx.

[77] World Food Programme and FAO, *The State of Food Insecurity in the World – Addressing food insecurity in protracted crises* (2010), 8; see also: Bazerghi and McKay and Dunn, 'The Role of Food Banks in Addressing Food Insecurity: A Systematic Review' (2016) 41 *J Community Health*, 732 (732): 'Food insecurity occurs whenever the availability of nutritionally adequate and safe foods, or the ability to acquire acceptable food in a socially acceptable way, is limited or is uncertain.'

[78] Webster and Zumbansen, 'Introduction: Transnational Food (In)Security' (2018) 9 *Transnatl. Leg. Theory*, 175 (178).

associated with current dietary patterns is estimated to be more than USD 1.7 trillion per year by 2030.

42   However, not all healthy diets are sustainable and not all diets designed for sustainability are always healthy. This important nuance is not well understood and is missing from ongoing discussions and debates on the potential contribution of healthy diets to environmental sustainability.

43   To increase the affordability of healthy diets, the cost of nutritious foods must come down. The cost drivers of these diets are seen throughout the food supply chain, within the food environment, and in the political economy that shapes trade, public expenditure and investment policies. Tackling these cost drivers will require large transformations in food systems with no one-size-fits-all solution and different trade-offs and synergies for countries.[207]

44   Increasing availability of and access to nutritious foods that make up healthy diets must be a key component of stronger efforts to achieve the targets set in the Global Agenda 2030. The availability of dietary energy per person has increased globally over the past two decades. However, this has not translated into an increase in the availability of nutritious foods that contribute to healthy diets. There are large discrepancies in the per capita availability of foods from different food groups across countries of different income levels. Low-income countries rely more on staple foods and less on fruits and vegetables and animal source foods than high-income countries.

45   The quality of people's diets worsens with increasing constraints on their access to food, putting them at higher risk of undernutrition as well as overweight and obesity. Among other factors, cost is a key determinant of access to food. These trends in hunger, food insecurity and malnutrition must be reversed. SARS-CoV-2 is expected to exacerbate these trends, rendering vulnerable people even more vulnerable. Urgent action is needed in order to meet the 2030 targets, even as the world prepares for the impact of the pandemic.[208]

46   While considerable difficulties in accessing food persist, access to healthy diets is even more challenging. One of the biggest challenges is the current cost and unaffordability of healthy food.

47   To ensure the proper implementation of the right to food for everyone, several major factors within the framework of food security have a significant role to play (→ Goal 2 mn. 26).

1. Inequalities

48   The main causal factor for hunger is seen in the far-reaching and in-depth area of inequalities. The broad scope of different types of inequalities represent the basis that needs to be fundamentally addressed.[79] These inequalities range from 'inequality in access to land and other productive resources, lack of income to purchase food on the market, and lack of employment opportunities'.[80] Moreover, inequalities occur between states, people, genders and minority groups (→ Goal 10, Goal 5). Thus, further factors for the occurrence of food insecurity such as climate change, conflicts, rapid

---

[79] See Sen, *Poverty and Famines – An Essay on Entitlement and Deprivation* (1981); Gonzales, 'International Economic Law and the Right to Food' in Lambek et al. (eds), *Rethinking Food Systems – Structural Challenges, New Strategies and the Law* (2014), 165 (184): '[…] the underlying causes of world hunger are poverty and inequality.'

[80] Gonzales, 'International Economic Law and the Right to Food' in Lambek et al. (eds), *Rethinking Food Systems – Structural Challenges, New Strategies and the Law* (2014), 165 (184).

population growth as well as uneven and slow economic growth always build on the general causality of existing inequalities.[81]

2. Climate Change, Population Growth and Food Security

Climate change as one of the currently most urgent global threats has a particularly   49
strong impact on food security, agriculture and therefore also on food systems (→ Goal 13 mn. 47 f., Goal 10 mn. 48, 53, Goal 15 mn. 22, 26 f.) The ever-growing world population consequently requires an ever-increasing amount of adequate food with an estimated increase in global food production of 70-100 per cent by 2050. The steadily obvious climate distortions affect the agricultural sector in particular, which is very susceptible to extreme drought, flooding and other climatic disasters.[82]

3. Inequalities between States and international Trade for Food

There are significant inequalities regarding the economic status of countries around   50
the world. These inequalities are intensified by unbalanced trade conditions (→ Goal 10 mn. 51 ff.) The ICESCR General Comment No. 12 specifies the extraterritorial demands towards states in international trade.[83] In this respect, states must guarantee 'that these agreements do not violate the right to food of vulnerable populations in other nations'.[84] Trade as such may serve both as facilitator and threat for ensuring food security. Properly applied trade can help disadvantaged countries in the world to stay connected to world markets and thus to global resources for food. With targeted trade measures, developed countries can promote both the delivery of food and the development of local economic power.[85]

Given the ongoing urbanisation from about 50 percent in 2015 to 70 percent in 2050   51
with a population growth of about one billion people by 2030, the increased need for food security and ongoing globalisation is expressed with scaled-up international trade and foreign direct investment (FDI) in the food and water sectors. In addition to the increased demand for resources, rising energy and water consumption is also becoming a significant factor that is likely to lead to supply insecurities and conflicts in the future (→ Goal 6 mn. 25, 89 ff.).[86]

---

[81] FAO, *Climate change and food security: risks and responses* (2016), 31; Hepburn, *Food and Nutrition Security, Income Inequality, and Trade: Recent Trends and Considerations for Inequality and Sustainability – Background paper to the IISD workshop Geneva, Switzerland, September 13, 2019* (2019), 3 ff.

[82] Further reading: Yadav et al., 'Climate Change, Agriculture and Food Security' in Yadav et al. (eds), *Food Security and Climate Change* (2019), 1 (3); Streck and Convay, 'Forestry and Agriculture under the UNFCCC – A jigsaw waiting to be assembled?' in Carlarne and Gray and Tarasofsky (eds), *The Oxford Handbook of International Climate Change Law* (2016), 564 (567); Mbow et al., 'Food Security' in Shukla et al., *Climate Change and Land: an IPCC special report on climate change, desertification, land degradation, sustainable land management, food security, and greenhouse gas fluxes in terrestrial ecosystems* (2019), 439.

[83] E/C.12/1999/5, *Substantive Issues Arising In The Implementation Of The International Covenant On Economic, Social And Cultural Rights: General Comment 12 The right to adequate food (art. 11)*, 12 May 1999, para. 36.

[84] Gonzales, 'International Economic Law and the Right to Food' in Lambek et al. (eds), *Rethinking Food Systems – Structural Challenges, New Strategies and the Law* (2014), 165 (169).

[85] Clapp, *Food security and international trade – Unpacking disputed narratives* (2015), 10; see also: Lamy, 'Trading towards global food security' in Lamy (ed), *The Geneva Consensus – Making Trade for All* (2013), 68 ff.; Margulis, 'The World Trade Organization and Food Security after the Global Food Crises' in Drache and Jacobs (eds), *Linking Global Trade and Human Rights – New Policy Space in Hard Economic Times* (2014), 236 ff.

[86] Dodds and Donoghue and Roesch, *Negotiating the Sustainable Development Goals – A transformational agenda for an insecure world*, (2017) 150-2; Mbow et al., 'Food Security' in Shukla et al., *Climate*

4. Women, Children and other Vulnerable Groups

52   Despite their crucial role in improving food systems, women around the world still suffer from discriminatory inequality in terms of rights in relation to the production and management of food and resources (→ Goal 5 mn. 16, 37 ff., Goal 10 mn. 71 f., 83 ff.). Women make up 70 per cent of the worlds hungry. The Special Rapporteur on the right to food emphasises the significance of women's empowerment in the tackling of global hunger within the annual Report:

> While achieving gender equality is the direct focus of Goal 5, the concept is reflected in 36 targets and 45 indicators throughout the Goals. […] The Sustainable Development Goals promote more equitable access to land and productive resources for women and girls as a critical component of gender equality (target 5.a) and a precondition to achieving zero hunger and malnutrition (target 2.3). If granted the same resource access as men, women could increase yields on their farms by 20–30 per cent, which could raise total agricultural output in developing countries by 2.5–4 per cent per annum and reduce the number of hungry people in the world by 12–17 per cent. To realize this potential, however, States need to remove restrictive and discriminatory laws and customs that perpetuate inequality between men and women.[87]

53   Including women in food systems and giving them the power to decide over their proper lands not only enhances the development towards more sustainable food systems. Furthermore, strengthening and fostering women's rights ensures the sustainable development for the coming generations as well:

> Mothers who are well nourished during pregnancy and lactation enhance the life chances and growth abilities of their children. […] Moreover, women owning land face significantly lower risk of domestic violence, which in turn, would reduce their own and their children's health and nutrition risks linked with such violence.[88]

IV. International Organisations related to Food and Nutrition

54   The following is a list of international organisations with relation to food and nutrition.

- Food and Agriculture Organization of the United Nations (FAO)
- United Nations World Food Programme (WFP)
- United Nations System Standing Committee on Nutrition (UNSCN)
- World Health Organisation (WHO)
- United Nations Children's Fund (UNICEF)
- United Nations Entity for Gender Equality and the Empowerment of Women (UN WOMEN)
- Office of the United Nations High Commissioner for Human Rights (OHCHR)
- World Trade Organization (WTO)
- International Fund for Agricultural Development (IFAD)
- Committee on World Food Security (CFS)
- Organisation for Economic Cooperation and Development (OECD)

Change and Land: an IPCC special report on climate change, desertification, land degradation, sustainable land management, food security, and greenhouse gas fluxes in terrestrial ecosystems (2019), 447.

[87] A/74/164, *Interim report of the Special Rapporteur on the right to food*, 15 July 2019, paras. 22 ff.

[88] Agarwal, 'Food Security, Productivity and Gender Inequality' in Herring (ed), *The Oxford Handbook of Food Politics and Society* (2015), 273 (287).

- Office of the High Representative for the Least Developed Countries, Landlocked Developing Countries and Small Island Developing States
- World Bank

C. Interdependences of SDG 2

Ending poverty and hunger in all their forms and dimensions is one of the most **55** salient goals of the Global Agenda 2030.[89] This multidimensional SDG can be subclassified into three dimensions: A social dimension (ending hunger and malnutrition, SDG 2.1, SDG 2.2), an economic dimension (increasing agricultural productivity and incomes, SDG 2.3, SDG 2.a) and an environment dimension (ensuring sustainable food production systems, SDG 2.4, SDG 2.5).[90] This is why SDG 2 is interconnected with an overwhelming majority of the other SDGs and their subgoals.[91]

The connection between hunger (SDG 2.1, SDG 2.2.) and poverty (SDG 1) stands **56** out in particular since poverty is accompanied by hunger and malnutrition and cannot be defeated under constant malnutrition. Hunger deteriorates the status of health and well-being (SDG 3).[92] SDG 2 enables and reinforces SDG 1 through food security.[93] Since the majority of the poor live in rural areas, increasing agricultural productivity and income of small-scale food producers (SDG 2.4) also contribute to poverty reduction.[94]

The absence of hunger and malnutrition and an increase of sustainable and produc- **57** tive agriculture have a direct impact on a variety of social factors. Suffering from malnutrition affects the quality of education people are able to perceive as well as their intellectual capacity (SDG 4.1, SDG 4.a), the equal rights of women and girls who have a key role in the production of food (SDG 5.4, SDG 5.5), the availability of water as a key resource for agriculture (SDG 6.1, SDG 6.2), the access to affordable and sustainable energy as a product of biofuel and biogas (SDG 7.1), decent work for all (SDG 8.5)

Since hunger mainly affects poor people living in politically unstable or conflict-rid- **58** den countries, they are deprived of equal opportunities (SDG 10.3) and have no or fewer opportunities to claim their rights and participate effectively in society (SDG 16.3, SDG 16.7, SDG 16.10).[95]

Extreme weather conditions have a major impact on agricultural productivity which **59** may threaten the food supply of people. A sustainable use and management of resources in agriculture (SDG 15.1, SDG 15.2) contributes to tackling climate change (SDG 13.1) and helps maintain and stabilise food and nutrient supply.[96]

Fishing can play a more important role in the fight against malnutrition. By in- **60** creasing productivity, hunger can thus be actively combated. However, overfishing can

---

[89] A/RES/70/1, *2030 Agenda for Sustainable Development*, 21 October 2015, preamble: 'We are determined to end poverty and hunger, in all their forms and dimensions, and to ensure that all human beings can fulfil their potential in dignity and equality and in a healthy environment'.

[90] Griggs et al., *A Guide to SDG Interactions: From Science to Implementation* (2017), 34.

[91] Independent Group of Scientists appointed by the Secretary-General, *Global Sustainable Development Report 2019: The Future is Now – Science for Achieving Sustainable Development*, (2019), 28.

[92] Van Soest et al., 'Analysing interactions among Sustainable Development Goals with Integrated Assessment Models' (2019) 1 *Global Transitions*, 210 (214).

[93] Griggs et al., *A Guide to SDG Interactions: From Science to Implementation* (2017), 45.

[94] Griggs et al., *A Guide to SDG Interactions: From Science to Implementation* (2017), 45.

[95] Griggs et al., *A Guide to SDG Interactions: From Science to Implementation* (2017), 35-42.

[96] Griggs et al., *A Guide to SDG Interactions: From Science to Implementation* (2017), 40.

endanger oceans, seas and marine resources (SDG 14.2) in the long term and thus also jeopardise food security (SDG 2.1, SDG 2.4).[97]

D. Jurisprudential Significance of SDG 2

61   Ending hunger and all forms of malnutrition is considered a priority issue[98] since the overall level remains between 800 and 1,000 million people starving[99] and has partially even worsened, albeit the world already producing 'enough food to feed the world population'.[100] This ascertainable backward trend was already evident before the outbreak of the SARS-CoV-2 pandemic and is now even more reinforced. Girls and women in particular are and have been deprived of the right to (adequate) food. It can be seen that 'girls are twice as likely to die from malnutrition and preventable childhood diseases than boys, and it is estimated that almost twice as many women suffer from malnutrition than men.'[101] Yet women are key to food security. They play vital roles in the production and preparation of food, in agriculture and in earning incomes to feed their families, as well as mediators of nutrition education within the family, if they themselves are educated.[102]

62   Inequalities and hunger are even more reinforced by the SARS-CoV-2 pandemic since global value and supply chains are heavily disrupted leading to higher unemployment rates. In times of writing this book, due to the global lock-downs, an innumerable amount of children and youth are being kept out of schools and have no access to humanitarian or social structures and institutions, which diminishes their possibility to receive regular and adequate nutrition and moreover reduces the overall food security.

I. Jurisdiction on Vision and Objectives

63   The Global Agenda 2030 aiming to end hunger in 'all [...] forms and dimensions' everywhere puts people at the centre so that all life can thrive.[103] To be fulfilled, SDG 2 needs an enabling environment. The closely related goals found at all levels thus represent the conditions within which SDG 2 can be achieved. SDG 2 seeks to end hunger, improve nutrition and implement sustainable agriculture that does justice to the current human population (but also to the expected population growth) and provide secure sources of food and supplies. This objective is linked to a wide range of international and national economic law and human rights issues that repeatedly arise at different levels of jurisdiction.

---

[97] Nilsson et al., 'Mapping interactions between the sustainable development goals: lessons learned and ways forward' (2018) 13 *Sustainability Science*, 1489 (1494).

[98] E/2020/L.20–E/HLPF/2020/L.1, *Draft ministerial declaration of the high-level segment of the 2020 session of the Economic and Social Council and the high-level political forum on sustainable development, convened under the auspices of the Council, submitted by the President of the Council, Mona Juul (Norway),* 17 July 2020, para. 17.

[99] 1996 World Food Summit, found in: O'Connor, 'Right to adequate food' in Cottier and Schefer, *Elgar Encyclopedia of international Economic Law* (2017), 653.

[100] Ziegler et al., *The Fight for the Right to Food: Lessons Learned* (2011), 3.

[101] See Ziegler et al., 'The Right to Food of the Most Vulnerable People' (2011), in *The Fight for the Right to Food,* 23; Although hardly provable in its entirety due to a lack of global statistics on malnutrition or undernourishment.

[102] Díaz and Nuila, Global Network for the Right to Food and Nutrition, *Right to Food and Nutrition Watch, Women's Power in Food Struggles* (2019).

[103] A/RES/70/1, *2030 Agenda for Sustainable Development,* 21 October 2015, paras. 3, 7.

1. International Jurisdiction

Two judicial decisions illustrate the widespread issue of land grabbing evoking the **64** status of malnutrition and lack of food:

The extent to which the right to food is linked with SDG 2.4 is demonstrated by the **65** decision of the UN Human Rights Committee in 2016,[104] in which the Committee found that the right to life had been violated due to the states failure to enforce its environmental obligations, resulting in the death of the smallholder *Portillo Cáceres*, a member of a Paraguayan indigenous group. The unauthorised use of prohibited agrotoxins and the contamination of drinking water within the community, argued by the State of Paraguay as a purely environmental concern without reference to the right to life or any related human rights. The decision was based on General Comment No. 36 which was adopted merely a few months before[105] and held that as a violation of the State's obligation, a life that has to 'be free from acts or omissions that would cause [one's] unnatural or premature death'.[106] The ailments caused by the use of agrotoxins in several farmers of the group were considered sufficiently harmful and threatening to their livelihoods to qualify as a violation of the broadly interpreted right to life (*culpa in vigilando*). This jurisdiction directly links environmental concerns with human rights obligations[107] and obliges the state obligation to 'all appropriate measures to address the general conditions in society that may give rise to threats to the right to life'.[108]

This landmark decision was recently reaffirmed with the so-called *Nuestra Tierra* **66** *case*.[109] The court clarified and elaborated in more detail on the states' obligations of the management of natural resources in connection to land and use rights. After decades of denying proper access to justice, the IACtHR, referring inter alia to Art. 26 ECHR, ruled that the state of Argentina was violating the related rights of indigenous people by denying the indigenous communities their right to communal property, a healthy environment, adequate food, water, cultural identity, and, moreover, failed to fulfil its judicial responsibility and protective function. With the participation of eight different *amicus curiae* urging in particular the maintenance of natural cycles and the sustainable use of natural resources, the IACtHR decided that the 'State must take positive steps to ensure [the indigenous peoples'] rights'. Affected indigenous communities must be enabled to effectively participate with regard to every activity that may affect the integrity of land and natural resources, which includes, in any relevant circumstances, the conduct of adequate, free and informed prior consultations.[110] Since the distinct right to food of indigenous people 'often depends closely on their access to and control over their lands

---

[104] Human Rights Committee, 20.09.2019, - CCPR/C/126/D/2751/2016 - Communication 2751/2016.

[105] General Comment No. 36 was adopted on 30 October 2018 by the UN Human Rights Committee.

[106] CCPR/C/GC/36, *General comment No. 36, Article 6: right to life*, 03 September 2019, para. 3.

[107] This link has already been judicially identified at various levels: *Advisory opinion OC-23/17 of 15 November 2017 on the environment and human rights*, 15 November 2017, IACtHR series A, No. 23, paras. 47, 108 ff.; and *Kawas-Fernández v. Honduras*, merits, reparations and costs, 3 April 2009, IACtHR series C, No. 196, para. 148; African Commission on Human and Peoples' Rights, *Social and Economic Rights Action Center & the Center for Economic and Social Rights v. Nigeria*, communication No. 155/96, 27 October 2001, and general comment No. 36, para. 3; *Özel and Others v. Turkey*, Judgment of 17 November 2015, ECtHR, paras. 170-1, 200; *Budayeva and Others v. Russia*, Judgment of 20 March 2008, ECtHR, paras. 128-30, 133, 159; *Öneryildiz v. Turkey*, Judgment of 30 November 2004, ECtHR, paras. 71, 89-90, 118.

[108] https://www.escr-net.org/caselaw/2020/portillo-caceres-and-others-v-paraguay-ccprc126d27512016 -communication-27512016.

[109] *Case of Indigenous Communities Members of the Association Lhaka Honhat (Nuestra Tierra) vs. Argentina*, Judgment of 6.2.2020, paras. 203 and fn. 193 therein, 243.

[110] *Case of Indigenous Communities Members of the Association Lhaka Honhat (Nuestra Tierra) vs. Argentina*, Judgment of 6.2.2020, paras. 194 ff.; see also *Case of Indigenous Communities Members of the Asso-*

and other natural resources in their territories, the right 'should not be understood in a restrictive sense' since otherwise it is not adequately fulfilled.[111]

67   The IACtHR did not only focus on the concepts of the right to food on adequacy, food security and access, but in particular on sustainability as a further concept. Additionally, the rights of indigenous people were assessed not as exclusive rights, but rather as complementary to existing rights, such as environmental rights, taking into account Principle 22 of the Rio Declaration (Agenda 21). Yet, the court did not merely reiterate the historical development of sustainability at UN level, but also within the independent American declarations that pursue the goals of the Global Agenda 2030 which makes it a landmark decision and a means for the SDGs. Moreover, in the expert opinion 23/17 sustainability was determined under interpretation of indigenous rights and clarification of the sustainable design and use of environment to promote the dignity and well-being of human beings.[112]

68   The issue of 'land grabbing' and land being a source of livelihood has been affirmed in more cases of the IACtHR with respect to indigenous people that were not taken into consideration during negotiations of host states and investors[113] and therefore violating the states' obligation to guarantee the community's territorial rights. The African Commission decided similarly in the *Ogoni case* and stated that Nigeria violated the right of the Ogoni people to freely dispose of its natural wealth and resources by issuing oil concessions on Ogoni lands without having involved the Ogoni communities.[114]

2. European Jurisdiction

69   Due to the economic origin of the EU, the EU legislation on food and the according obligations for the individual member states mirror the fundamental freedoms anchored in the EU besides a human rights context that is to be evaluated controversially in the EU. Despite the Treaty of Lisbon which anchored the promotion of a 'respect for human rights' (now set in Art. 2 TEU), human rights are deemed to be of high importance externally since the EU understands itself as a bearer of values, but are of a merely peripheral interest when searching for effects within the EU.[115] Nevertheless, the EU legislation relating to a right to food was expanded in the frame of the Common Commercial Policy (CCP) after the 'mad cow disease' (BSE) breakout in 2001. To strengthen the food economy against such risks, the EU General Food Law (Regulation (EC) No. 178/2002) was adopted, and the European Food Safety Authority (EFSA) was established to protect consumers from health risks and fraud in the European food market. Despite the intention to facilitate access to information and traceability throughout the food chain, to strengthen the precautionary principle (characteristic of the EU) and the right of action

---

ciation *Lhaka Honhat (Nuestra Tierra) vs. Argentina*, Interpretation of the Judgment on the Merits, Reparations and Costs, 24.11.2020, para. 28.

[111] *Case of Indigenous Communities Members of the Association Lhaka Honhat (Nuestra Tierra) vs. Argentina*, Judgment of 6.2.2020, para. 254.

[112] *Case of Indigenous Communities Members of the Association Lhaka Honhat (Nuestra Tierra) vs. Argentina*, Judgment of 6.2.2020, paras. 203 and fn. 193 therein, 243.

[113] *Case of the Indigenous Community Yakye Axa v Paraguay*, 17 June 2005, IACtHR (Ser. C) No. 125, Judgment, paras. 158(a), (e), 241(6), 211-7, 221, 241(7); *Case of the Indigenous Community Xákmok Kásek v. Paraguay*, IACtHR, Judgment, Merits, Reparations, and Costs, 24 August 2010.

[114] Social and Economic Rights Action Center *(SERAC) and the Center for Economic and Social Rights v Nigeria*, Communication No. 155/96, (2001) AHRLR 60, 27 October 2001, African Commission on Human and Peoples' Rights, paras. 2-4, 7-9, 64-6.

[115] See Williams, 'Human Rights in the EU' (2015) in Arnull and Chalmers (eds), *The Oxford Handbook of European Union Law*, 250; see also Van der Meulen, 'The Structure of European Food Law' (2013) 2 *Laws*, 69 (97).

against companies and authorities, as well as to stop harmful practices such as misleading labelling, there have been several food scandals[116] since then, the reappraisal of
which clearly shows that consumer rights can only be pursued and enforced to a limited
extent. Moreover, the EU created the Rapid Alert System for Food and Feed (RASFF) to
tackle crises in order to provide the Member States' food and control authorities with
information about serious risks of food safety. Article 50 of General Food Law establishes the rapid alert system for food and feed as a network involving the Member States and
as well Suisse, Norway and Liechtenstein.[117]

Despite being operationalised through trade agreements, the right to food within   **70**
the EU is complemented by trade instruments which (shall) enhance or maintain the
price stability in food markets, whereby this is more of economic efficiency and mainly
serves for the security of supply at all. However, the jurisdiction of the European Court
of Justice (ECJ) is of conservative nature when evaluating human rights obligations in
whole[118] and with respect to the right to food specifically.

Despite this reluctance to actively develop human rights in judicial terms, ECJ case   **71**
law in relation to the food security required by SDG 2 and the right of access to
information linked to the human right to food does in any case reveal the limits of the
generally rather economic process of finding justice. In two recent *Glyphosate cases*, the
ECJ stated that the European Food Safety Agency (EFSA) could not be prevented from
providing information and thus enabling access to information if health risks existed
or seemed possible. Referring to the Aarhus Convention, the ECJ clarified that in order
to ensure this duty, information must not be merely an end in itself, but other risks,
existing or hypothetical, must also be made available to applicants.[119] These cases are of
particular importance in that on the same day, the ECJ also annulled the authorisation
granted by the Commission to market lead chromates deemed to be carcinogenic.

It remains to be seen whether the recently developed Farm to Fork Strategy,[120] an   **72**
initiative of the New European Green Deal, will bring about the required holistic change
to food chains, food production and consumption behaviour towards sustainability
on the one hand, and new legal avenues of interpretation to promote sustainability
and thus strengthen the right to food as defined in SDG 2 for all on the other. The
strategy lacks for instance peasants and other small-scale food producers who provide
concrete proposals to foster food sovereignty[121] but contains, however, a huge amount of
investment strategic approaches with a focus on international cooperation.

3. Arbitration Proceedings

The WTO also develops validity and application for the subject area of SDG 2, since   **73**
the WTO is mandated to steer free trade multilaterally and eliminate distortive measures

---

[116] Such as the Horsemeat scandal in 2013, Lactalis scandal of 2017/18, Fipronil scandal in 2017 or the
'rotten-meat' scandals of 2006/2007, 2009 and 2019.

[117] EU, *RASFF — The Rapid Alert System for Food and Feed — Annual Report 2019* (2020), 6.

[118] Since the ECJ is considering the necessity and proportionality and therefore weighing out fundamental freedoms against commercial interest but is not seizing the worth of human rights such as the
human right to life, see amongst others: ECJ, Case C-36/02, 18.03.2004, *Omega v Bonn*, ECLI:EU:C:
2004:162; ECJ, Case C-112/00, 12.06.2003, *Schmidberger v Austria*, ECLI:EU:C:2003:333.

[119] Judgment of the General Court (Eighth Chamber) of 7 March 2019, *Antony C. Tweedale v European
Food Safety Authority*, T-716/14, ECLI:EU:T:2019:141; Judgment of the General Court of 7 March 2019,
Hautala and Others v EFSA T-329/17, ECLI:EU:T:2019:142.

[120] *Farm to Fork Strategy, For a fair, healthy and environmentally-friendly food system*, adopted under the
new presidency of Ursula von der Leyen on 20 May 2020.

[121] More information on this topic: Saab, 'An International Law Approach to Food Regime Theory'
(2018) 31 *Leiden Journal of International Law*, 251 (255).

as far as possible. The WTO Agreement on Agriculture (AoA) was drafted to discipline food production rather than to guarantee the right to food.[122] Yet, like WTO rules relating to sanitary and phytosanitary measures or technical barriers to trade, it applies in particular to the area of food safety and a state's hygiene policy. Beyond, the Agreement on Trade-Related Aspects of Intellectual Property (TRIPS), an annex to the agreement establishing the WTO, has been instrumental in privatising and commodifying food or even practice patenting which bears the risk of putting the diversity of livestock and plants at risk. In this respect, jurisdiction seizes the deemed risk that 'farmers could be forced into a relationship of dependence by such patents and be subjugated to the market power of a handful of seed corporations and their patent status.'[123] To a certain extent, this is also reflected in jurisdiction. WTO dispute settlements are primarily dealing with distortions of competition, patent protection and risk assessment regarding the food safety of a product,[124] which under WTO law must be based on (majority) scientific evidence and international food safety regulations.[125] Above all, transparency obligations must be observed, for example by publishing the relevant regulations[126] on food safety and applying them to the marketable goods (→ Goal 2 mn. 22 f.).[127]

74   With a closer look at investment agreements, the concessions on access to markets, fair and equitable treatment (FET), compensation for expropriation ('land grabbing' (→ Goal 2 mn. 12, 64 ff.)) or the ban on performance requirements (for the investors[128]) have a considerable influence on safe food and nutrition. Although a growing number of investment treaties refer to human rights relevant topics such as human life and health, the due process of law or the protection of the environment and public welfare, treaty standards are most often interpreted quite broadly, therefore expanding the investors' protection[129] within these already cost-intensive proceedings.

75   Another issue can be found in *Pacific Rim Mining Corp. vs. El Salvador*,[130] where water has been polluted with high levels of cyanide due to mining activities. The mining corporation, after having been subjected to several regulations of the host state, merged with another corporation to make use of their exploitation permits. In El Salvador, which is densely populated and has limited water resources, environmental impact assessments as well as feasibility studies are required to obtain exploratory permission. In order to choose an arbitration forum, the mining corporation relied on their Nevada office instead of acting under its original nationality to utilise CAFTA's investment rules which it assumed to be more advantageous. The case was ruled in favour of El Salvador but burdened the state over many years with high preliminary expenses thereby

---

[122] O'Connor, 'Right to adequate food' in Cottier and Schefer, *Elgar Encyclopedia of international Economic Law* (2017), 653; Saab, 'An International Law Approach to Food Regime Theory' (2018) 31 *Leiden Journal of International Law*, 251 (255).

[123] https://www.naturland.de/en/1838-no-patents-on-life.html.

[124] *Japan – Measures Affecting Agricultural Products*, WT/DS76/R, Report of the Panel (27 October 1998) and WT/DS76/AB/R, Report of the Appellate Body (22 February 1999); *Japan – Measures Affecting Agricultural Products*, WT/DS76/AB/R, Report of the Appellate Body (22 February 1999), para. 93.

[125] See e.g. *EC – Hormones dispute*, WT/DS26/R/USA and WT/DS48/R/CAN, 18 August 1997, WT/DS26/AB/R, WT/DS48/AB/R, 16 January 1998; *EC – Trade Description of Sardines*, WT/DS231/AB.

[126] See e.g. FAO/WTO, Trade and Food Standards, https://www.wto.org/english/res_e/booksp_e/tradefoodfao17_e.pdf.

[127] *Japan – Measures Affecting Agricultural Products II*, Appellate Body Report, WT/DS76/AB/R, 19 March 1999, para. 105.

[128] Requirements could be local employment quotas, local material quotas and further linkages to the domestic economy.

[129] *Occidental Petroleum Corporation and Occidental Exploration and Production Company v Republic of Ecuador*, ICSID Case No. ARB/06/11.

[130] *Pac Rim Cayman LLC v. Republic of El Salvador*, ICSID Case No. ARB/09/12.

jeopardising the enforcement of 'existing legal requirements aimed at protecting the country's resources'. In any case, the pollution of water accompanied with the restriction of state law enforcement significantly affects food security and thus impedes the right to food.[131]

It is striking that instruments that would contribute to a right to food or to the **76** contents of SDG 2 already exist. Their application, however, seems to take account of the neoliberalism of the global food economy. Hunger and food insecurity are interpreted abstractly as problems of production methods, which are addressed through present technological innovations, private sector engagement, and economic market-based mechanisms.[132] The same approach appears to endanger or even circumvent the application of rights in host states, especially in investment law. Moreover, the control of markets, which is hardly possible multilaterally at this point in time, leads to a detrimental influence on the implementation of SDG 2.

4. Domestic Jurisdiction

At present, no more than 23 states have constitutionally anchored an independent **77** right to food.[133] Nevertheless, it is gaining importance through increasing judicial interpretation on national levels, either by implicitly deriving it from other rights or by linking it to civil and political rights at the national (or regional) level.

This can be found, most notably in India, with regard to the vulnerable group of **78** lactating women who have been denied access to food rations and prenatal as well as children health benefits which they were entitled to under several national benefit programs. For example, the women living in poverty in a Delhi slum had not been issued a food ration card, like 55 per cent of the population of Delhi at that time, due to a governmental cap. With reference to Article 21 of the Constitution (right to life), the court assessed the curtailment of the right to food as a significant impairment of the right to life.[134] This case shows the vital link between the right to food, adequate nutrition and reproductive health services to enable a safe motherhood. It also 'use[d] constitutional litigation to secure rights and services for poor women and children'[135] and thus forms part of already existing Indian case law,[136] which emphasise three aspects in particular: the right to food was recognised as a fundamental right which is inherent to the right to life; the entitlements pertaining to the right to food were specified and enforced; and the implementation of the court's decision was continuously monitored and reported on.

---

[131] https://www.iisd.org/itn/2017/03/13/all-claims-dismissed-oceanagold-to-pay-usd-8-million-in-cost s-pac-rim-cayman-llc-v-el-salvador-icsid-case-no-arb-09-12/#:~:text=Pac%20Rim%20Cayman%20LLC% 20 v,El%20Salvador%2C%20ICSID%20Case%20No.&text=The%20tribunal%20ordered%20the%20minin g,towards%20El%20Salvador's%20legal%20costs.

[132] Saab, 'An International Law Approach to Food Regime Theory' (2018) 31 *Leiden Journal of International Law*, 251 (257).

[133] Knuth and Vidar, *Constitutional and Legal Protection of the Right to Food Around the World* (2011), found in: IDLO, International Development Law Organization (IDLO), *Realizing The Right To Food, Legal Strategies And Approaches* (2019), 23.

[134] *Premlata w/o Ram Sagar & Ors. v. Govt. of NCT Delhi*, High Court of New Delhi, W.P.C. 7687 of 2010, para 10.

[135] https://www.escr-net.org/caselaw/2015/premlata-wo-ram-sagar-ors-v-govt-nct-delhi-wpc-7687 -2010.

[136] *People's Union for Civil Liberties v. Union of India & Ors*, Supreme Court of India, Civil Original Jurisdiction, Writ Petition (Civil) No.196 of 2001; *Francis Coralie Mullin v Administrator*, Union Territory of Delhi (1981) 2 SCR 516 and also to be found in Bangladesh: *Dr Mohiuddin Farooque v Bangladesh and Others* (1998) 50 DLR, 84; more information on these cases: Birchfield and Corsi, 'The Right to Life Is the Right to Food: People's Union for Civil Liberties v. Union of India & Others' (2009) *WCL*, 15-8.

79   The starting point of this development, which illustrates the impact of social rights and social rights litigation on the distribution of food and resources, may be found in *People's Union for Civil Liberties v. Union of India & Ors.* The Supreme Court of India (SCC) had to decide on petitions concerning the enforcement of the right to food (especially food schemes and the application of the Famine Code) after starvation deaths occurred in a part of India, even though the state had excess grain that was 'kept for official times of famine, and various schemes throughout India for food distribution'[137] (which were also not functioning). The court agreed with the petitions to a high degree and derived the right to food from the right to life.[138] Since then the Court accompanies the implementation of the ruling with annual hearings as a mechanism for the continuous monitoring and reporting of the implementation of the Court's decisions.[139]

80   In 2012, the German Federal Constitutional Court (FCC) decided that cash benefits for asylum seekers provided by the Asylum Seekers Benefit Act were compatible with its Constitution and held on former decisions to affirm that the state has the obligation to ensure a 'dignified minimum existence', which is to be defined as a 'comprehensive fundamental rights guarantee'. Therefore, states have to assure the supply with access to food, clothing, household items, housing, heating, hygiene health and social assistance to persons in need. The benefits awarded to the asylum seekers under the law in question were deemed insufficient to guarantee a dignified minimum existence and the court emphasised that a humane minimum subsistence level must be determined on the basis of 'real and actual needs' to build upon a realistic measurement which must not generalise in its concrete form.[140]

II. The Enforcement of a 'Right to Zero Hunger'?

81   An effort could indicate the future enforcement of a right to food. Readable from *Premlata w/o Ram Sagar & Ors. v. Govt. of NCT Delhi* is that the existing constitutional jurisdiction was used to strategically secure human rights (→ Goal 2, mn. 78). As part of a larger movement in India to use constitutional litigation to secure rights and services for poor women and children, the affected community members were actively involved with both the case and the implementation of the interim order. This provides a progressive vision for advocacy which combines the power of grassroots strategic litigation with the construction of community-based networks to increase accountability. Apart from this type of involvement in the enforcement process, it is noticeable that enforcement

---

[137] https://www.escr-net.org/caselaw/2006/peoples-union-civil-liberties-v-union-india-ors-supreme-court-india-civil-original.

[138] Already traceable to *Franic Caralie v Union of Territory of Delhi* (1981) 1 SCC, 608:
We [the Court] think that the right of life includes the right to live with human dignity and all that goes along with it, namely, the bare necessaries of life such as adequate nutrition, clothing and shelter over the head and facilities for reading, writing and expressing oneself in diverse forms, freely moving about and mixing and comingling with fellow human beings; and in: *Court in Chameli Singh v. State of U. P.*, 1996 (2) SCC 549:
The Right to Live that is guaranteed in any civilised society implies the right to food, water, shelter, education, medical care, and a decent environment. These are basic rights known to any civilised society. The civil political and cultural rights enshrined in the Universal Declaration of Human Rights and convention or under the Constitution of India cannot be exercised without these basic human rights.

[139] https://www.escr-net.org/caselaw/2006/peoples-union-civil-liberties-v-union-india-ors-supreme-court-india-civil-original.

[140] Federal Constitutional Court of Germany, Judgment of the First Senate of 18.7.2012, 1 BvL 10/10, ECLI:DE:BVerfG:2012:ls20120718.1bvl001010, paras. 64-6; Courtis, *Courts and the Legal Enforcement Economic, Social and Cultural Rights. Comparative Experiences of Justiciability (2008) Human Rights and Rule of Law Series No 2.* (2008).

depends heavily on the political and economic conditions, and that progress can be slow and diminishes even further with the complexity of the remedies. Some courts may issue additional remedies to ensure compliance with the judgement or orders or be granted supervisory jurisdiction.[141] It is crucial to integrate enforcement and implementation of measures into a broader advocacy strategy, being supported by 'social mobilization, community organization, awareness and media campaigns'.[142]

III. De Facto Influences on Jurisdiction

SDG 2 is particularly influenced by the effects of climate change.[143] The environ-   **82**
mental and accompanying structural changes are currently being exacerbated by the SARS-CoV-2 pandemic (→ Goal 13 mn. 92). Besides, humanitarian crises and conflicts are detrimental to human societies at all and to SDG 2 in particular. The lack of stability and enabling structures, as can also be found in SDG 1,[144] limit the right to (adequate) food to a considerably since these are major causes of famine or conflict-induced food insecurity which is due to displacement, destruction and disruption (of food stocks and markets) or starvation (of civilians) as a method of warfare (→ Goal 1 mn. 80, 92, 112).[145] Accordingly, humanitarian law and the *ius ad bellum* in afflicted areas constitute an influence that should not be underestimated. These areas of law become particularly relevant with the cooperation of various NGOs and IO's as humanitarian, development and peacebuilding actors, stabilising these interlocking conflictive situations and ensuring, among other things, the development of infrastructure and the availability, access, and safety of food.[146] Further organisations are globally networked and able to influence economic developments through intensive cooperation.

As could be read from the international jurisdiction, investment and industry are   **83**
main factors of development which heavily influence developing or less-developed countries (as host states) and possibly lead to development-induced displacement is an increasingly widespread phenomenon with devastating impact (→ Goal 2 mn. 64 ff.). An estimated 15 million people each year are forced to relocate and resettle as a result of interventions of economic actors.[147] This specifically puts pressure on vulnerable groups

---

[141] International Development Law Organization (IDLO), *Realizing The Right To Food, Legal Strategies And Approaches* (2019), 54.

[142] International Development Law Organization (IDLO), *Realizing The Right To Food, Legal Strategies And Approaches* (2019), 55.

[143] Mbow et al., 'Food Security' in Shukla et al., *Climate Change and Land: an IPCC special report on climate change, desertification, land degradation, sustainable land management, food security, and greenhouse gas fluxes in terrestrial ecosystems* (2019).

[144] For more information on this issue, see: https://www.escr-net.org/news/2018/gaza-blockade-posing-serious-threats-economic-social-and-cultural-rights; https://www.escr-net.org/news/2017/yemeni-civil-society-leaders-condemn-worsening-worlds-largest-humanitarian-crisis; https://www.escr-net.org/news/2017/new-videos-showing-programs-displaced-and-conflict-affected-people-myanmar.

[145] S/RES/2417 (2018), Adopted by the Security Council at its 8267th meeting, on 24 May 2018, paras. 1, 2, 5; However, this international humanitarian law resolution is equally deemed to not be sufficiently prohibitive against causing starvation of civilian population which is partly seen as 'justifiable collateral damage' and to not being respected in practice; more information on this issue: Zappalà, 'Conflict Related Hunger, 'Starvation Crimes' and UN Security Council Resolution 2417 (2018)' (2019) 17 *JICJ*, 881 (899 f.); Lander and Richards, 'Addressing Hunger and Starvation in Situations of Armed Conflict – Laying the Foundations for Peace' (2019), 17(4) *Journal of International Criminal Justice*, 675-98; Hunter, 'Starvation in Armed Conflicts: An Analysis Based on the Right to Food' (2019), 17(4) *Journal of International Criminal Justice*, 723-52.

[146] See e.g. S/RES/2417 (2018), Adopted by the Security Council at its 8267th meeting, on 24 May 2018.

[147] https://documents-dds-ny.un.org/doc/UNDOC/GEN/G15/003/04/PDF/G1500304.pdf?OpenElement, para. 39 f.

such as indigenous people or people living in municipal areas. Due to their financial size and relevance for the development of host states, TNC's are able to exert considerable influence on political and judicial processes.[148] The impact of forced displacement on the Global Agenda 2030 and particularly on SDG 2 can hardly be predicted.[149]

84   The WTO also defines a not negligible framework since SDG 2.b refers directly to the Doha Development Round in order to prevent and eliminate all forms of agricultural export subsidies and export measures, but moreover its main purpose lies in stimulating free trade. The still idle discussion and multilateral disagreement thus represent a considerable restriction in the implementation of SDG 2 and the framed right to food. Since trade law under the guise of the WTO covers agricultural subsidies and tariffs applied to agricultural products, the availability, access and prices of food are also touched upon.[150]

85   Derived from the human rights-based right to food and its aspirations to international economic law, the contents of SDG 2 do not merely represent a minimum limit that must not be undercut. Rather, it shows and is judicially acknowledged at all levels that adequate food (supply) must be guaranteed by states. This applies equally to a sufficiently nutritious supply and a food supply that is not detrimental to health, which leads to health problems such as obesity and diabetes, for example.[151] What the term adequacy of food actually means, however, can only be determined in a scattered manner and is likely to be a source of further controversy in the future. Particularly against the background of a sustainable transformation of food security and sustainable food production, this could lead to investment-related distortions that need to be carefully managed. It is clear that the existing policy and jurisdiction is complemented by a variety of soft law instruments and economic control organizations. However, de facto consideration and implementation seems to be more than weak in many places. It has yet to be established how sustainability actually needs to be shaped in order to adequately protect the most vulnerable groups of children and women as well as indigenous people.

E. Conclusion on SDG 2

86   Today, the relevant institutions agree that there is no shortage of food, but that there is nevertheless a significant increase in hunger, malnutrition and disease-related phenomena such as obesity. The findings paint a very strange picture, in which hunger is widespread despite abundant food, and food may also have a disease-causing effect. Unforeseeable events, such as SARS-CoV-2, also exert considerable pressure on vulnerable groups in so that current forecasts are rather gloomy. The objectives of SDG 2 seem to be achievable in 2030 – at least if the forecasts for 2021 are met.

87   Food production is closely linked to the changes caused by climate change (SDG 13). Food and the distribution of food are also closely linked to infrastructure (SDG 9), global food supply chains (SDG 12), demand and electricity for refrigeration and storage of protein-containing food, such as easily perishable dairy, meat and fish products (SDG 7). Where there are no roads, it is difficult to distribute food. Soil change due to increasing climate-induced drought, increase in pests of all kinds, water shortages, legal

---

[148] https://documents-dds-ny.un.org/doc/UNDOC/GEN/G15/003/04/PDF/G1500304.pdf?OpenEleme nt, para. 44.

[149] FAO, *Fifteen years implementing the Right to Food Guidelines, Reviewing progress to achieve the 2030 Agenda* (2019), 31.

[150] Saab, 'An International Law Approach to Food Regime Theory' (2018) 31 *Leiden Journal of International Law*, 251 (253 ff.).

[151] See also O'Connor, 'Right to adequate food' in Cottier and Nadakavukaren Schefer, *Elgar Encyclopedia of international Economic Law* (2017), 652.

and illegal overfishing of the oceans (SDG 14), to name but a few, is reaching a dynamic that can generate a change in food supply, especially when demand increases, due to the continuous growth of the population. Combating hunger is and has always been an integral part of the concept of sustainable development.

Although there are many obstacles to overcome, SDG 2 is reaching out to achieve **88** Zero Hunger by 2030. But as FAO, IFAD, UNICEF and further custodian agencies of the UN have analysed 'the number of people affected by hunger would surpass 840 million by 2030. A preliminary assessment suggests that the SARS-CoV-2 pandemic may add between 83 and 132 million people to the total number of undernourished in the world in 2020 depending on the economic growth scenario.'[152]

Unfortunately, all efforts made so far are not sufficient to underline a positive outlook **89** on 2030 as the FAO, IFAD, UNICEF, amongst others, have found out and put it quite frankly in the words that '[t]he world is not on track' to achieve SDG 2. 'Food insecurity can worsen diet quality and consequently increase the risk of various forms of malnutrition, potentially leading to undernutrition as well as overweight and obesity'[153] (SDG 3). The estimation of people suffering from hunger are currently (2020) about 690 million, or 8.9 percent of the world population and according to FAO analysis the number will increase by 10 million people in one year and by nearly 60 million in five years.[154]

Since having been introduced by the FAO in 2014, the Food Insecurity Experience **90** Scale (FIES) has rapidly become a global reference for measuring food insecurity based on household and / or individual data. Many institutions responsible for food security assessments, including statistical offices and other governmental agencies, have adopted it as a standard tool for food security.[155]

The FAO and further custodian agencies of the UN are observing and this is unfortu- **91** nately not surprising, that women are much more exposed to hunger than men and that hunger has a clear indication to gender inequalities (SDG 5).

It has been unveiled that malnutrition and food insecurity has shown a clear gender **92** interconnection as to the '[g]lobal level, the prevalence of food insecurity is higher among women than men. The gender gap in accessing food increased from 2018 to 2019.'[156]

The FAO has analysed very clearly that until 2030, the world will not reach the SDG 2 **93** targets for hunger and malnutrition. They observed that '[a]fter decades of long decline, the number of people suffering from hunger has been slowly increasing since 2014.' And they see that the '[p]rojections for 2030, even without considering the potential impact of SARS-CoV-2, serve as a warning that the current level of effort is not enough to reach Zero Hunger ten years from now.'[157]

Following the FAO, the current food systems have been successful at producing **94** low-cost calories, but healthy diets remain costly and unaffordable for billions of people

---

[152] FAO, IFAD, UNICEF, WFP and WHO, *The State of Food Security and Nutrition in the World 2020, Transforming food systems for affordable healthy diets* (2020), xvi.

[153] FAO, IFAD, UNICEF, WFP and WHO, *The State of Food Security and Nutrition in the World 2020, Transforming food systems for affordable healthy diets* (2020), 3.

[154] FAO, IFAD, UNICEF, WFP and WHO, *The State of Food Security and Nutrition in the World 2020, Transforming food systems for affordable healthy diets* (2020), 3.

[155] FAO, IFAD, UNICEF, WFP and WHO, *The State of Food Security and Nutrition in the World 2020, Transforming food systems for affordable healthy diets* (2020), 16.

[156] FAO, IFAD, UNICEF, WFP and WHO, *The State of Food Security and Nutrition in the World 2020, Transforming food systems for affordable healthy diets* (2020), 3.

[157] FAO, IFAD, UNICEF, WFP and WHO, *The State of Food Security and Nutrition in the World 2020, Transforming food systems for affordable healthy diets* (2020), 60.

in the world. However, considering only the cost and affordability of different diets fails to account for the hidden costs associated with food production and consumption.

95   Two hidden costs of our dietary patterns and of the food systems supporting them relate to the health-related costs for many people (SDG 3) and the climate-related costs that the world as a whole incurs (SDG 13).[158]

96   According to FAO the current most likely ongoing food consumption patterns demonstrate the first hidden cost as diet-related health costs linked to non-communicable diseases andmortality are projected to exceed USD 1.3 trillion per year by 2030. A shift of the consumer behaviours to healthy diets would lead to an estimated reduction of up to 97 per cent in direct and indirect health costs, thus creating significant savings that could be invested to lower the cost of nutritious foods.

97   The second hidden costs are linked to diet-related social cost of greenhouse gas (GHG) emissions associated with current dietary patterns, which are projected to exceed USD 1.7 trillion per year by 2030. The adoption of healthy diets that include sustainability considerations would reduce the social cost of GHG emissions by an estimated 41 to 74 percent in 2030.[159]

98   The consequences should be to reduce the different cost of nutritious foods and try to ensure access and the affordability of healthy diets. This sounds at first glance easy what is not. It would mean, a transformation of existing food systems and make them more resilient against shock wavers caused by pandemic such as SARS-CoV-2. Much more than actions related to the private sector the politics should take the lead and focus on suitable actions across the food supply chains to tackle the costs of nutritious foods. Such actions which normally would be enacted after parliamentary debates by laws and regulations should '[e]nhance efficiencies in food storage, processing, packaging, distribution and marketing, while also reducing food losses.'[160]

---

[158] FAO, IFAD, UNICEF, WFP and WHO, *The State of Food Security and Nutrition in the World 2020, Transforming food systems for affordable healthy diets* (2020), 93.

[159] FAO, IFAD, UNICEF, WFP and WHO, *The State of Food Security and Nutrition in the World 2020, Transforming food systems for affordable healthy diets* (2020), 93.

[160] FAO, IFAD, UNICEF, WFP and WHO, *The State of Food Security and Nutrition in the World 2020, Transforming food systems for affordable healthy diets* (2020), 138.

Goal 3
Ensure healthy lives and promote well-being for all at all ages

3.1 By 2030, reduce the global maternal mortality ratio to less than 70 per 100,000 live births

3.2 By 2030, end preventable deaths of newborns and children under 5 years of age, with all countries aiming to reduce neonatal mortality to at least as low as 12 per 1,000 live births and under-5 mortality to at least as low as 25 per 1,000 live births

3.3 By 2030, end the epidemics of AIDS, tuberculosis, malaria and neglected tropical diseases and combat hepatitis, water-borne diseases and other communicable diseases

3.4 By 2030, reduce by one third premature mortality from non-communicable diseases through prevention and treatment and promote mental health and wellbeing

3.5 Strengthen the prevention and treatment of substance abuse, including narcotic drug abuse and harmful use of alcohol

3.6 By 2020, halve the number of global deaths and injuries from road traffic accidents

3.7 By 2030, ensure universal access to sexual and reproductive health-care services, including for family planning, information and education, and the integration of reproductive health into national strategies and programmes

3.8 Achieve universal health coverage, including financial risk protection, access to quality essential health-care services and access to safe, effective, quality and affordable essential medicines and vaccines for all

3.9 By 2030, substantially reduce the number of deaths and illnesses from hazardous chemicals and air, water and soil pollution and contamination

3.a Strengthen the implementation of the World Health Organization Framework Convention on Tobacco Control in all countries, as appropriate

3.b Support the research and development of vaccines and medicines for the communicable and non-communicable diseases that primarily affect developing countries, provide access to affordable essential medicines and vaccines, in accordance with the Doha Declaration on the TRIPS Agreement and Public Health, which affirms the right of developing countries to use to the full the provisions in the Agreement on Trade-Related Aspects of Intellectual Property Rights regarding flexibilities to protect public health, and, in particular, provide access to medicines for all

3.c Substantially increase health financing and the recruitment, development, training and retention of the health workforce in developing countries, especially in least developed countries and small island developing States

3.d Strengthen the capacity of all countries, in particular developing countries, for early warning, risk reduction and management of national and global health risks

Word Count related to 'Health': 33

A/RES/70/1 – Transforming our world: the 2030 Agenda for Sustainable Development: 33

Instruments mentioned in A/RES/70/1 in the section entitled: 'Sustainable Development Goals and targets':

World Health Organization Framework Convention on Tobacco Control (United Nations, Treaty Series, vol. 2302, No. 41032)

Declaration on the TRIPS agreement and public health (Doha WTO Ministerial 2001: TRIPS WT/MIN(01)/DEC/2, 20 November 2001, adopted on 14 November 2001)

Agreement on Trade-Related Aspects of Intellectual Property Rights

A/RES/69/313 – Addis Ababa Action Agenda of the Third International Conference on Financing for Development adopted on 27 July 2015: 20

A/RES/66/288 – The future we want (Rio +20 Declaration) adopted on 27 July 2012: 53

A/RES/55/2 – United Nations Millennium Declaration adopted on 8 September 2000: 0

Select Bibliography: Frederick M. Abbott, The Doha Declaration on the TRIPS Agreement and Public Health: Lighting a Dark Corner at the WTO' (2002) 5 *JIEL*, 469 (505); Jeffery Atik, 'Trade and Health' in Daniel Bethlehem, Donald McRae, Rodney Neufeld, Isabelle Van Damme (eds.), *The Oxford Handbook of International Trade Law* (Oxford University Press, Oxford 2009), 597; Gian Luca Burci, Andrew Cassels, 'Health' in Jacob Katz Cogan, Ian Hurd, Ian Johnstone, *The Oxford Handbook of International Organizations* (Oxford University Press, Oxford 2016), 447; Helen Keller and Corina Heri, 'The Committees on Human Rights and Economic, Social and Cultural Rights' in Simon Chesterman, David M Malone and Santiago Villalpando (eds), *The Oxford Handbook of United Nations Treaties* (Oxford University Press, New York 2019), 422; Angus Deaton, *The Great Escape, Health, Wealth and the Origins of Inequality* (Princeton University Press, Princeton 2013); Elizabeth Eckermann, 'SDG 3: a Missed Opportunity to Transform Understandings and Monitoring of Health, Well-Being and Development?' in *Applied Research Quality Life*, 261; Anne-Maree Farrell, John Devereux, Isabel Karpin, and Penelope Weller, *Health law: frameworks and context* (Cambridge University Press, Cambridge 2017); David P Fidler, 'Global Health Jurisprudence: A Time of Reckoning' (2008) 96 (2) *Geo LJ*, 393; Christopher Fleming and Matthew Manning, *Routledge Handbook of Indigenous Wellbeing* (Routledge, London 2019); Eilionóir Flynn, 'Art. 13 Access to Justice', in Ilias Bantekas, Michael Ashley Stein, Dimitris Anastasiou, *The UN Convention on the Rights of Persons with Disabilities: A Commentary* (Oxford University Press, Oxford 2018), 383; Lawrence O. Gostin, *Global Health Law* (Harvard University Press, Cambridge 2014); Sunil S. Gu, Plain Tobacco Packaging's Impact on International Trade and the Family Smoking Prevention and Tobacco Control Act in the U.S. and Drafting Suggestions (2017) 16 *Wash. U. Global Stud. L. Rev.*, 197; Winfried Huck, Jennifer Maaß, Saparya Sood, Tahar Benmaghnia, Alexander Schulte, Sarah Heß and Marc-Anthony Walter, 'The Right to Breathe Clean Air and Access to Justice – Legal State of Play in International, European and National Law' (2021) 13(10) *International Environmental Law (eJournal)*; Walter Kälin and Jörg Künzli, *The Law of International Human Rights Protection* (Oxford University Press, Oxford/New York 2019); Markus Kaltenborn, Markus Krajewski and Heike Kuhn, *Sustainable Development Goals and Human Rights Volume 5*, (SpringerOpen, Cham 2020); Pranee Liamputtong, *Public Health: Local and Global perspectives* (Cambridge University Press, Cambridge 2016); Roger Magnusson, *Advancing the Right to Health: The Vital Role of Law* (World Health Organization 2017); Mathauer I., Mathivet B., Kutzin J.; *Free health care policies: opportunities and risks for moving towards UHC* (World Health Organization, Geneva 2017); Rosemary A. McFarlane, John Barry, Guéladio Cissé, Maya Gislason, Marta Gruca, Higgs Kerryn, Pierre Horwitz, Giang Huu Nguyen, Jane O'Sullivan, Subashis Sahu and Colin D. Butler, 'SDG 3: Good Health and Well-Being – Framing Targets to Maximise Co-Benefits for Forests and People' in Pia Katila, Carol J. Pierce Colfer, Wil De Jong, Glenn Galloway, Pablo Pacheco and Georg Winkel (eds), *Sustainable Development Goals: Their Impacts on*

Forests and People (Cambridge University Press, Cambridge 2019), 72; Mark McGillivray, 'Human Well-being: Issues, Concepts and Measures' in McGillivray et al. (eds), *Human Well-Being. Studies in Development Economics and Policy* (Palgrave Macmillan UK, London 2007), 1; Stefania Negri, ' Human Health and Human Rights, 13 Healthy Oceans for Healthy Lives: The Contribution of the World Health Organization to Global Ocean Governance' in David Joseph Attard, Malgosia Fitzmaurice and Alexandros Ntovas (eds), The IMLI Treatise On Global Ocean Governance, Volume II: UN Specialized Agencies and Global Ocean Governance (Oxford University Press, Oxford 2018 OUP), 262; John Tobin, The Right to Health in International Law, (Oxford University Press, Oxford 2012); Brigit Toebes, 'International health law: an emerging field of public international law' (2015), 55(3) *Indian Journal of International Law*, 299; Brigit Toebes, Rhonda Ferguson, Milan M. Markovic and Obiajulu Nnamuchi (eds), *The Right to Health: A Multi-Country Study of Law, Policy and Practice* (T. M. C. Asser Press, Springer, Berlin, Heidelberg 2014); UNAIDS, *Inter-Agency Task Team (IATT) on HIV and Young People, Global Guidance Briefs, HIV Interventions for Young People* (2008); Y. S. Wong, P. Allotey and D. D. Reidpath, 'Sustainable development goals, universal health coverage and equity in health systems: the Orang Asli commons approach' (2016) 1:e12 *Glob Health Epidemiol Genom*, 1; World Health Organization, *Advancing the right to health through the universal periodic review* (WHO, Geneva 2019).

A. Background and Origin of SDG 3

The health of people is a matter of daily life. Regardless of age, gender, socio-econo-   1
mic or ethnic background, health is the important, essential and fundamental asset a
human being may hold.[1] Health as a legal and political substantive matter to be defined
can be traced back to the International Sanitary Conferences which lasted from 1851
to 1938.[2] The conferences were initiated by the grievous impact of cholera that entered
Europe through the Ottoman Empire.[3] After World War First, the League of Nations
designated health as a governmental concern in Article 23(f) of the Covenant of the
League of Nations where member states vowed to 'endeavour to take steps in matters
of international concern for the prevention and control of disease'.[4] This development
led to two independent health organisations co-existing in Europe: (1) the International
Office of Public Hygiene (Office international d'Hygène publique – OIHP) in Paris;
and (2) the Health Organization of the League of Nations. During the United Nations
Conference on International Organization (UNCIO, 1945), the organisation which later
should be called the World Health Organization (WHO) was established.[5] The newly
formed WHO in 1948 introduced for the first time the idea of the most reachable
standard of health in international law.[6] This manifested in the WHO's constitution
which acknowledged the right to health as one of the founding principles of the WHO.[7]
The WHO defined human health in the preamble of its constitution as 'a state of   2
complete physical, mental and social well-being, being more than the mere absence of
disease or infirmity.[8] The right to health has since been accepted as a basic human right
in different official documents of the UN.[9] The state of human health connects the legal
affiliation to the right to health as a human right which is explained by the UN High

---

[1] OHCHR, *The Right To Health* (2008), 1.
[2] https://search.archives.un.org/united-nations-conference-on-international-organization-uncio-1945; WHO, *First Ten years* (1958), 3.
[3] Howard-Jones, *The scientific background of the International Sanitary Conference 1851 – 1938* (1975), 11.
[4] Borowy, *Coming to Terms with World Health: The League of Nations Health Organization 1921-1946* (2009), 30.
[5] WHO, *First Ten years* (1958), 38.
[6] Tobin, *The Right to Health in International Law* (2012), 27.
[7] Browne, *Sustainable Development Goals and UN Goal setting* (2017), 50.
[8] A/RES/131, *Constitution of the World Health Organization*, 19 November 1947.
[9] https://www.who.int/en/news-room/fact-sheets/detail/human-rights-and-health; Kaltenborn and Krajewski and Kuhn, *Sustainable Development Goals and Human Rights* (2020), 54.

Commissioner for Human Rights (OHCHR) as a right to have access to health care and building of hospitals.[10] The Committee on Economic, Social and Cultural Rights (CESCR), the body responsible for monitoring the International Covenant on Economic, Social and Cultural Rights (ICESCR), defines health as 'a fundamental human right indispensable for the exercise of other human rights'.[11] The CESCR connects the right to health with factors including safe drinking water, safe food, healthy working and environmental conditions and gender equality.[12] The ICESCR gives both mental and physical health equal consideration and recognises that '[e]very human being is entitled to the enjoyment of the highest attainable standard of health conducive to living a life in dignity'.[13] The Millennium Development Goals (MDGs) included special sessions based on health such as on HIV/AIDS and to fight actively epidemics.[14] The MDGs did not mention health explicitly but were related to health with MDG 4 (reduce child mortality), MDG 5 (promote maternal health) and MDG 6 (fight malaria, HIV/AIDS, and other diseases).[15] The SDGs are grounded in the Universal Declaration of Human Rights (UDHR), fully respecting international law[16] and thus are inherently bound to its human rights background and to its predecessors.[17] Health is central to the three dimensions of sustainable development and both benefits from and contributes to development.[18] Health as understood in SDG 3 against its background indicates how people-centred, rights-based, inclusive and equitable development is to be realised.

3   SDG 3 is associated with 13 targets and 28 indicators.[19] It 'takes into account widening economic and social inequalities, rapid urbanisation, threats to the climate and the environment, the continuing burden of HIV and other infectious diseases, and emerging challenges such as non-communicable diseases'.[20] During the SDG negotiating process it was examined that '[t]he SDGs are an attempt to help deliver healthy lives and health security for all people'.[21] This is also supported by the fact that the SDGs were declared as 'decision-making framework' for maintaining and achieving human well-being.[22] Moreover, the increasing health challenges demand for an interlinked approach to meet

---

[10] https://www.ohchr.org/EN/Issues/ESCR/Pages/Health.aspx.

[11] E/C.12/2000/4, *Substantive Issues Arising In The Implementation Of The International Covenant On Economic, Social And Cultural Rights General Comment No. 14 (2000): The right to the highest attainable standard of health (article 12 of the International Covenant on Economic, Social and Cultural Rights)*, 11 August 2000.

[12] OHCHR, *The Right To Health* (2008), 3.

[13] OHCHR, *The Right To Health* (2008), 9; WHO, *Health in 2015 from MDGs to SDGs* (2015), 4.

[14] A/RES/70/1, *Transforming our world: the 2030 agenda for sustainable development* (2015).

[15] A/RES/55/2, *United Nations Millennium Declaration* (2000).

[16] A/RES/70/1, *Transforming our world: the 2030 agenda for sustainable development* (2015), para. 10.

[17] A/HRC/38/37, *Contributions of the right to health framework to the effective implementation and achievement of the health-related Sustainable Development Goals Report of the United Nations High Commissioner for Human Rights*, 10 April 2018, para. 13; A/RES/66/288, *The future we want*, 11 September 2012.

[18] A/HRC/38/37, *Contributions of the right to health framework to the effective implementation and achievement of the health-related Sustainable Development Goals Report of the United Nations High Commissioner for Human Rights*, 10 April 2018, para. 13.

[19] A/RES/71/313 (E/CN.3/2021/2), Global indicator framework for the Sustainable Development Goals and targets of the 2030 Agenda for Sustainable Development, SDG 3. Chon and Roffe and Abdel-Latif, *The Cambridge Handbook of Public-Private Partnerships, Intellectual Property Governance, and Sustainable Development* (2018), 48.

[20] https://www1.undp.org/content/brussels/en/home/sustainable-development-goals/goal-3-good-health-and-well-being.html.

[21] Dodds and Donoghue and Leiva Roesch, *Negotiating the Sustainable Development Goals, A transformational agenda for an insecure world* (2017), 156.

[22] Dernbach and Cheever, 'Sustainable Development and Its Discontents' (2015) 4(2) *Transnational Environmental Law*, 247-87.

the Goals effectively. Most of the other 16 SDGs have a direct impact on human health and / or well-being. Within the SDG network, the interlinkages to SDG 2 'Zero Hunger' and SDG 6 'Clean Water and Sanitation' protrude clearly since these directly affect the health of human beings. In the specific context of well-being, it is clearly linked to SDG 9.1 which seeks to provide 'quality, reliable, sustainable, and resilient infrastructure' and thus, comprises a significant external influencing factor of well-being. In some cases, poor starting conditions in other SDG areas increase the risk of contracting diseases by twice or prevent the possibility of recovery.[23] According to the Independent Group of Scientists, health is one of many critical dimensions of well-being and 'measuring and directly tackling inequalities and deprivations are requirements for advancing well-being.'[24] Thus, well-being embraces different levels of an idea. It incorporates both substantive aspects such as access and availability to nutrient food as well as immaterial aspects such as health, education and capabilities.

Major progress has been made in improving the health of millions of people, increas- **4** ing life expectancy, reducing maternal and child mortality and combating the leading communicable diseases. Still, progress is not happening fast enough with regard to addressing HIV/AIDS,[25] major diseases, such as malaria or tuberculosis. At least half of the global population does not have access to essential health services or suffer undue financial issues. More and concrete efforts are needed to achieve universal health coverage and sustainable financing for health.[26]

The adverse effects of climate change on physical and mental health are well-docu- **5** mented or increasingly recognisable, with the effects of climate change even promoting a large number of diseases.[27] The United Nations Framework Convention on Climate Change (UNFCCC) builds the regulatory framework for the matter of climate change. The natural impact of climate and weather on human health are amplified by climate change, which is now an increasingly important determinant of public health.[28] Health can be affected by immediate and direct risks such as heatwaves, extreme weather events and altered air quality.[29] Climate change thus can affect the survival, distribution and behaviour of mosquitos and ticks that carry diseases, but also can have an effect on the quality of food and water, mental health and well-being. An indirect risk arises from changes and disruptions in ecological systems such as food yields, bacterial growth rates and water quality. Reduced food yields lead to health impairment such as hunger, under-nutrition, child stunting and premature death.[30] The air we breathe is becoming increasingly unhealthy due, among other things, to the burning of fossil fuels, which

---

[23] Dodds and Donoghue and Leiva Roesch, *Negotiating the Sustainable Development Goals, A transformational agenda for an insecure world* (2017), 157.

[24] Independent Group of Scientists appointed by the Secretary-General, *Global Sustainable Development Report 2019: The Future is Now – Science for Achieving Sustainable Development*, (2019), 38.

[25] Further reading UNAIDS, *End Inequalities. End Aids. Global Aids Strategy 2021-2026* (2021).

[26] UN ECOSOC, *Special edition: progress towards the Sustainable Development Goals* (2016).

[27] A/HRC/44/48, *Right of everyone to the enjoyment of the highest attainable standard of physical and mental health Report of the Special Rapporteur on the right of everyone to the enjoyment of the highest attainable standard of physical and mental health*, 15 April 2020, paras. 71-5; see also A/75/163, *Right of everyone to the enjoyment of the highest attainable standard of physical and mental health, Note by the Secretary-General*, 16 July 2020, paras. 43, 47.

[28] Balbus et al., 'Introduction: Climate Change and Human Health', in Crimmins et al., *The Impacts of Climate Change on Human Health in the United States: A Scientific Assessment* (2016), 24.

[29] McMichael and Costello, 'Health risks, present and future, from global climate change' (2012) *BMJ*, 1 (2).

[30] Balbus et al., 'Introduction: Climate Change and Human Health', in Crimmins et al., *The Impacts of Climate Change on Human Health in the United States: A Scientific Assessment* (2016), 24.

release carbon dioxide (CO_2), a greenhouse gas (GHG) that contributes to the rise in global temperatures ($\rightarrow$ Goal 13 mn. 49, 88).[31]

6   Higher temperatures lead, amongst others, to higher allergens and harmful air pollutants. Heatwaves increasingly result in wildfires, which deteriorate the air quality due to immense CO_2 emissions and affect people's health in various ways,[32] thereby depriving them from participating in a decent and dignified life ($\rightarrow$ Goal 13 mn. 3, 48 ff.).[33]

7   To achieve SDG 3 means ending AIDS, tuberculosis, malaria, neglected tropical diseases (NTDs), and preventing global health issues such as the dire SARS-CoV-2 pandemic that we are experiencing at the time of writing this book. To this end, respecting human rights and building transparency and trust[34] which is backed up by adequate financing of health and well-being services as well as health education are essential.[35] To effectively raise revenues, a diversifying of sources of funding through taxes or compulsory national insurance is needed, while pooling and sharing the cost of healthcare across the population.[36] The Addis Ababa Action Agenda of the Third International Conference on Financing Development (AAAA) recognises that taxes on tobacco 'can be an effective and important means to reduce tobacco consumption and health-care costs, and represent a revenue stream for financing for development in many countries.'[37] Acknowledged solutions for financing SDG 3 include crowdfunding, impact investment, environmental trust funds and taxes, e.g. on fuel.[38] However, the least developed countries will continue to rely on international financial assistance to achieve the SDGs.

8   SDG 3.5 is to prevent substance abuse such as narcotic drugs and harmful use of alcohol. The outcome document of the 2016 UNGA Special session on the World Drug Problem includes the prevention and treatment of drug abuse as well as other health related issues. The International Standards on Drug Use Prevention and the UNODC-WHO International Standards for the Treatment of the Drug Use Disorders, the UNODC, aims to prevent drug use and promote the healthy and safe development of children and youth, as well as providing them services for the treatment, and rehabilitation of drug use disorders.[39]

B. Scope and Dimensions of SDG 3

9   Good health and well-being is of considerable significance in the structure of the SDGs not only because of the wide range of the subject matter it covers. The legal

---

[31] For a legal state of view see: Huck et al., 'The Right to Breathe Clean Air and Access to Justice – Legal State of Play in International, European and National Law' (2021) in 13(10) *International Environmental Law (eJournal)*; UNECE, Convention on Long-Range Transboundary Air Pollution (1979) and its Protocol to the 1979 Convention on Long-Range Transboundary Air Pollution on Further Reduction of Sulphur Emissions (1998).

[32] https://www1.apha.org/-/media/files/pdf/factsheets/climate/air_quality.ashx.

[33] Huck et al., 'The Right to Breathe Clean Air and Access to Justice – Legal State of Play in International, European and National Law' (2021) in 13(10) *International Environmental Law (eJournal)*, 7.

[34] DIHR, *SARS-COV-2 Response and Recovery Must Build on Human Rights and SDGs* (2020), 4.

[35] Walker and Pekmezovic and Walker, G., *Sustainable Development Goals: Harnessing business to achieve SDGs through finance, Technology and Law reform* (2019), 304.

[36] https://www1.undp.org/content/brussels/en/home/sustainable-development-goals/goal-3-good-healt h-and-well-being.html.

[37] A/RES/69/313, *Addis Ababa Action Agenda of the Third International Conference on Financing for Development (Addis Ababa Action Agenda)*, 17 August 2015, para. 32.

[38] https://www1.undp.org/content/brussels/en/home/sustainable-development-goals/goal-3-good-healt h-and-well-being.html.

[39] https://www.unodc.org/unodc/en/Human-rights/health.html.

spectrum of SDG 3 encompasses universal concepts of implementation as well as highly-sensitive political spheres which requires a holistic view of current global conditions in medicine, infrastructure, economy and politics.

Within the complex and diversified system of SDG 3, it divides into five core topics[40] **10** which cover maternal and childhood health (SDG 3.1 and SDG 3.2); communicable and non-communicable major diseases (SDG 3.3 and SDG 3.4); the avoidance of external risks (SDG 3.5 'alcohol abuse' and SDG 3.6 'drug abuse'); the cautionary principle, the precautionary principle and risk minimization (SDGs 3.7 to 3.9) which reflects in particular the Rio principles 14, 15 and 16; and the principle of common but differentiated responsibilities (CBDR) (SDG 3.9) which are to be accompanied by financial frameworks for health and the establishment of governmental structures to strengthen the reduction of health risks in all countries[41] (SDGs 3.a to 3.d). SDG 3 addresses the non-deniable linkage of the natural environment and human health.[42] Overall, SDG 3 can be assigned to the New Delhi Principle 4 'Precautionary approach to human health, natural resources and ecosystems'.[43]

A whole range of legal issues are addressed by SDG 3.3 which aims to end communi- **11** cable diseases and epidemics worldwide and has thus achieved daily relevance.[44] SDG 3.4 covers two broad areas: (1) reducing premature deaths from non-communicable diseases, and (2) the general objective of supporting mental health and well-being which brings forth a wide range of legal issues. The right to universal access to reproductive health care services is likewise illuminated in the context of national policies (SDG 3.7). As an essential element of the right to health, universal health coverage including the access to medicines and vaccines is also examined (SDG 3.8). In this context, Research and Development (R&D) and the suitable financing framework play a crucial role in implementation (SDG 3.b and SDG 3.c). Furthermore, diseases caused by chemicals, water pollution and air pollution are addressed in the light of legal analyses (SDG 3.9).[45] Finally, the strive for the implementation of the WHO Framework Convention on Tobacco Control as well as the establishment of a system of early warning, risk reduction and management of national and global health risks are enlightened (SDG 3.a and SDG 3.d). The areas of maternal and child mortality (SDG 3.1 and SDG 3.2), deaths from road traffic accidents (SDG 3.6) and drug and alcohol abuse (SDG 3.5) are less legally ascertainable and play a minor role in the examinations.[46]

---

[40] A different classification (7-part) was made by the WHO in 2018, see: *World Health Statistics 2018: Monitoring health for the SDGs* (2018), (Chapter 2) 4.

[41] UN ECOSOC, *Special edition: progress towards the Sustainable Development Goals* (2016), para. 20.

[42] A/HRC/44/48, *Right of everyone to the enjoyment of the highest attainable standard of physical and mental health Report of the Special Rapporteur on the right of everyone to the enjoyment of the highest attainable standard of physical and mental health*, 15 April 2020, para. 73.

[43] A/Conf.199/8, *New Delhi Declaration of principles of international law relating to sustainable development*, 9 August 2002, 5.

[44] See A/HRC/38/37, *Contributions of the right to health framework to the effective implementation and achievement of the health-related Sustainable Development Goals Report of the United Nations High Commissioner for Human Rights*, 10 April 2018, para. 16.

[45] See e.g. Stockholm Convention on Persistent Organic Pollutants (2001); FAO, Voluntary Guidelines for Sustainable Soil Management (2017); FAO and Committee on World Food Security, Voluntary Guidelines on the Responsible Governance of Tenure of Land, Fisheries and Forests in the Context of National Food Security (2012); FAO, Revised World Soil Charter (2015).

[46] The language of SDG 3 thus reflects the human rights background of the right to health, see A/HRC/34/25, *Question of the realization in all countries of economic, social and cultural rights Report of the Secretary-General*, 14 December 2016, paras. 8, 10.

I. Elementary Definitions

12   In order to be able to fundamentally grasp the far-reaching effect of SDG 3, it is necessary to describe the most important terms in the context of their significance under international law. Beginning with the caption 'Good health and well-being', the first attention is given to the concept of 'good health'. Various definitions in conventions of international law, the WHO as well as in science illustrate the volatility of the term. The WHO defines health as 'state of complete physical, mental and social well-being and not merely the absence of disease or infirmity'[47] and includes the important aspect that it is not enough for a body to be free of diseases and complaints to be classified as 'healthy'. Rather, the WHO extends the spectrum of the concept of health within its scope to include mental and social components. However, the definition is controversial among many scientists due to its limited and incomplete nature. Since health as a complex construct is exposed to volatile environmental influences, the concept of health encompasses much more than just objective criteria such as life expectancy and infant mortality.[48] The health of each individual is indivisibly linked to the health of the community.[49] The Ottawa Charter of 1986 provides a related delineation stating that 'health is, therefore, seen as a resource for everyday life, not the objective of living'.[50]

13   Moreover, SDG 3, unlike the WHO definition, takes into account the significant component of ecological and environmental influences on health in its spectrum.[51] This proves to be more than necessary, as environmental influences on health and the promotion of health were already identified as being significant in the WHO Ottawa Charter of 1986. In the Charter, a list of prerequisites and factors for maintaining health stands out in particular. The list contains the fundamental conditions and resources for health as 'peace, shelter, education, food, income, a stable ecosystem, sustainable resources, social justice and equity'.[52] Thus, it is obvious that health and the achievement of general health for all is by no means based on physical and mental integrity alone. Rather, the listed social and environmental indicators play a vital role in the implementation of SDG 3 and underline the far-reaching interdependencies of SDG 3 with all other SDGs (→ Goal 3 mn. 46 ff.).[53] This forms the basis for a global view of health and expands the meaning of the term 'well-being' as well.

14   Well-being in literature is characterised quite differently. The WHO does not define this term independently, but refers to it as part of the definition of health. The definition of McGillivray goes much further, describing well-being as the 'state of individuals' life situation'.[54] This is directly or indirectly connected with aspects such as 'quality of life, living standards, [...] human development, [...] social welfare, [...] life satisfaction, prosperity, needs fulfilment, [...] empowerment, [...] poverty, human poverty and, more

---

[47] A/RES/131, *Constitution of the World Health Organization*, 19 November 1947.

[48] Yach, 'Health and illness: the definition of the World Health Organization' (1998) 10 *Ethik Med*, 7.

[49] Mintser, Ermakova and Lyabakh, 'Individual and Social Health: definitions and approaches to evaluation' (1992) 28 *Cybern Syst Anal*, 953.

[50] WHO, *Ottawa Charter* (1986).

[51] McFarlane et al., 'SDG 3: Good Health and Well-Being – Framing Targets to Maximise Co-Benefits for Forests and People' in Katila et al. (eds), *Sustainable Development Goals: Their Impacts on Forests and People* (2019), 72 (74).

[52] WHO, *Ottawa Charter* (1986).

[53] McFarlane et al., 'SDG 3: Good Health and Well-Being – Framing Targets to Maximise Co-Benefits for Forests and People' in Katila et al. (eds), *Sustainable Development Goals: Their Impacts on Forests and People* (2019), 72 (74).

[54] McGillivray, 'Human Well-being: Issues, Concepts and Measures' in McGillivray et al. (eds), *Human Well-Being. Studies in Development Economics and Policy* (2007), 1 (3).

recently, happiness'.[55] Another approach is the definition of the Millennium Ecosystem Assessment conceptual framework which 'considers health as one of five components of well-being, along with material sufficiency, security, good human relations, and freedom and choice'.[56] Generally speaking, five categories can be derived to better classify well-being as such: physical, social and emotional, economic, cultural and spiritual as well as subjective (perceived) well-being.[57] Yet, it has to be considered that the whole socio-economic view in the holistic approach of well-being is not covered by SDG 3. The targets in SDG 3 solely refer to physical and mental health[58] which leads to the question how the nature of well-being could be legally classified at all.

II. Legal Foundations

The initial reference point for the legal classification of health is the human right to   15
health. Listed in Art. 12 of the ICESCR, it comprises 'the right of everyone to the enjoyment of the highest attainable standard of physical and mental health'.[59] The wording clarifies that this is not the right to (permanent) health. Rather, it is intended to establish the right to a healthy life with access to adequate medical resources in case of illness.[60] In the context of human rights including economic, social and cultural rights, the right to health can be considered from the following perspectives:

1. Right to Health

The right to health is not covered by the mere definition of health. The UDHR al-   16
ready recognises in Art. 25 a right to a life of health with other factors such as the provision of food, clothing, housing and appropriate medicine. These 'socio-economic factors that promote conditions in which people can lead a healthy life', show the far-reaching dimension of the right to health and the associated interference with other SDGs.[61] Fundamental references to the right to work, Art. 6 ICESCR, the right to security at work, in Art. 7, the right to social security, Art. 9 and the right to adequate living, Art. 11 ICESCR reflect the far-reaching connections to other SDGs.[62] Therefore, the right to health goes hand in hand with the right to each of the socio-economic factors.[63] A comprehensive description of the scope of the right to health is provided in General Comment No. 14. Accordingly, the core elements of the right to health include both freedoms, such as the

---

[55] McGillivray, 'Human Well-being: Issues, Concepts and Measures' in McGillivray et al. (eds), *Human Well-Being. Studies in Development Economics and Policy* (2007), 1 (3).

[56] McFarlane et al., 'SDG 3: Good Health and Well-Being – Framing Targets to Maximise Co-Benefits for Forests and People' in Katila et al. (eds), *Sustainable Development Goals: Their Impacts on Forests and People* (2019), 72 (74).

[57] Fleming and Manning, *Routledge Handbook of Indigenous Wellbeing* (2019), 6 f.

[58] Eckermann, 'SDG 3: a Missed Opportunity to Transform Understandings and Monitoring of Health, Well-Being and Development?' *Applied Research Quality Life*, 261.

[59] UN, *International Covenant on Economic, Social and Cultural Rights, adopted and opened for signature, ratification and accession by General Assembly resolution 2200A (XXI) of 16.12.1966, entry into force 03.01.1976, in accordance with article 27*, Article 12.

[60] Kälin and Künzli, *The Law of International Human Rights Protection* (2019), 303.

[61] Saul and Kinley and Mowbrey, *The International Covenant on Economic, Social and Cultural Rights: Commentary, Cases, and Materials* (2014), 984.

[62] Farrell et al., *Health law: frameworks and context* (2017), 51.

[63] E/C.12/2000/4, *Substantive Issues Arising In The Implementation Of The International Covenant On Economic, Social And Cultural Rights General Comment No. 14 (2000): The right to the highest attainable standard of health (article 12 of the International Covenant on Economic, Social and Cultural Rights)*, 11 August 2000, para. 11; A/RES/73/165, *United Nations Declaration on the Rights of Peasants and Other People Working in Rural Areas*, Art. 23.

freedom of self-control over the body and health, e.g. the freedom to reproduce as well as entitlements. The latter consist of the right to a health protection system that guarantees equal opportunities for all.[64] The so-called AAAQ principles represent an integral part of the implementation of the right to health and serve as a guideline for the public authorities and thus primarily for states. States are obliged to ensure the availability, accessibility, acceptability and quality of health and health-care facilities.[65] In the analysis of the individual targets, the AAAQ principles serve as a framework for implementation scoping.

17 Moreover, the right to health, like all human rights, imposes three types or levels of obligations on States parties: the obligations to respect, protect and fulfil. In turn, the obligation to fulfil contains obligations to facilitate, provide and promote. It is internationally agreed that States parties have a core obligation to ensure the satisfaction of, at the very least, minimum essential levels of each of the rights enunciated in the Covenant, including essential primary health care.[66] Moreover, the right to health includes certain components, which are legally enforceable. Any person or group victim of a violation of the right to health should have access to effective judicial or other appropriate remedies at both national and international levels.[67] As mentioned before the right to health imposes various obligations on States parties that are of immediate effect, albeit some of them may be realised progressively.[68]

18 In General Comment No. 3, the Committee confirms that the following core conditions should not fall short:

(a) To ensure the right of access to health facilities, goods and services on a non-discriminatory basis, especially for vulnerable or marginalised groups;

(b) To ensure access to the minimum essential food which is nutritionally adequate and safe, to ensure freedom from hunger to everyone;

(c) To ensure access to basic shelter, housing and sanitation, and an adequate supply of safe and potable water;[69]

(d) To provide essential drugs, as from time to time defined under the WHO Action Programme on Essential Drugs;

(e) To ensure equitable distribution of all health facilities, goods and services[70]

---

[64] E/C.12/2000/4, *Substantive Issues Arising In The Implementation Of The International Covenant On Economic, Social And Cultural Rights General Comment No. 14 (2000): The right to the highest attainable standard of health (article 12 of the International Covenant on Economic, Social and Cultural Rights)*, 11 August 2000, para. 8.

[65] Toebes, 'International health law: an emerging field of public international law' (2015), 55(3) *Indian Journal of International Law*, 299.

[66] See E/C.12/2000/4, *Substantive Issues Arising In The Implementation Of The International Covenant On Economic, Social And Cultural Rights General Comment No. 14 (2000): The right to the highest attainable standard of health (article 12 of the International Covenant on Economic, Social and Cultural Rights)*, 11 August 2000, para. 43.

[67] E/C.12/2000/4, *Substantive Issues Arising In The Implementation Of The International Covenant On Economic, Social And Cultural Rights General Comment No. 14 (2000): The right to the highest attainable standard of health (article 12 of the International Covenant on Economic, Social and Cultural Rights)*, 11 August 2000, para. 59.

[68] E/C.12/2000/4, *Substantive Issues Arising In The Implementation Of The International Covenant On Economic, Social And Cultural Rights General Comment No. 14 (2000): The right to the highest attainable standard of health (article 12 of the International Covenant on Economic, Social and Cultural Rights)*, 11 August 2000, paras. 30 f.

[69] Gray, *Drinking Water Quality: Problems and Solutions* (2008), 37 ff.

[70] E/C.12/2000/4, *Substantive Issues Arising In The Implementation Of The International Covenant On Economic, Social And Cultural Rights General Comment No. 14 (2000): The right to the highest attainable standard of health (article 12 of the International Covenant on Economic, Social and Cultural Rights)*, 11 August 2000, para. 43.

2. Well-Being

As described above, the multifaceted picture of well-being is not congruently covered   19
by SDG 3. However, there are several steps taken by the UN to approach well-being in
terms of its socio-economic characteristics. Happiness is increasingly perceived as an
important component of well-being. The political basis for the international pursuit of
the recognition of happiness is resolution 65/309 which emphasises the relevance of happiness within human life and describes it as 'a fundamental human goal' and a 'universal
aspiration'.[71] In the same turn, the international day of happiness was proclaimed recognising the equal importance of 'sustainable development, poverty eradication, happiness
and the well-being of all people'.[72] Despite these diplomatic efforts to conceptualise the
term of happiness there is no evident reference to happiness in any target of SDG 3.

III. International Organisations Related to Health and Well-Being

The following is a list of international organisations (IO) with relevance to health and   20
well-being:

- World Health Organization (WHO)
- United Nations Children's Fund (UNICEF)
- United Nations Entity for Gender Equality and the Empowerment of Women
  (UN WOMEN)
- Office of the United Nations High Commissioner for Human Rights (OHCHR)
- United Nations Office on Drugs and Crime (UNODC)
- UN Water
- World Trade Organization (WTO)[73]
- United Nations World Food Programme (WFP)
- Food and Agriculture Organization of the United Nations (FAO)
- Office of the High Representative for the Least Developed Countries, Landlocked
  Developing Countries and Small Island Developing States
- World Bank

IV. Public Health and Global Health: Framing the Scope of SDG 3

The terminology of 'Global Health' and 'Public Health' indicates the international   21
dimensions of health-relevant topics in the context of the targets of SDG 3. In this
respect, the term global health refers to 'collaborative trans-national research and action
for promoting health for all' all over the world, no matter where or how people live.[74]
Further, global health shall 'reduce health threats that traverse national borders, such
as emerging infectious diseases' as well as 'reduce the enduring and unconscionable
burdens of endemic disease and early death among the world's poor'.[75] While public
health has different definitional approaches, the purpose of public health is common
to all definitions. Besides health professions, the health care system and health services,
the term also covers the health of the public (population). The overall objective is to

---

[71] A/RES/65/309, *Happiness: towards a holistic approach to development*, 25 August 2011.
[72] A/RES/66/281, *International Day of Happiness*, 12 July 2012.
[73] See also World Trade Organization Agreement on Sanitary and Phytosanitary Measures (1994).
[74] Stratton, *Health in the Context of Global Health* (2015), 545.
[75] Dagron and Gostin, *Global Health Law* (2014), 951.

improve and maintain the health of all and to prevent disease and premature death.[76] This global contextualisation of the scope of health topics in SDG 3 can be used to frame the legal spheres of the targets.

V. SDG 3 and the State – Public Health Responsibilities

22   Ensuring the health of all is therefore a global challenge. It is not only because of the transregional dimensions of public health that states and their policies play a significant role in achieving this goal. States have the crucial responsibility of providing health care to the population. This means that they must provide and continuously guarantee access, availability and quality of adequate health care equitably available to everyone.[77] These State responsibilities are also reflected in the right to health.[78] Saul, Kinley and Mowbray summarise the duties of the State as the

> special obligation to provide those who do not have sufficient means with the necessary health insurance and health-care facilities, and to prevent any discrimination on internationally prohibited grounds in the provision of health care and health services, especially with respect to the core obligations of the right to health.[79]

23   The right to health moreover comprises a comprehensive understanding of the right to health that emerges from the interferences between the individual right to health and the health of the public.[80]

1. Legal Context of the Targets

24   The main objective of global and public health is to ensure access to health care resources for all people through equity. Global and public health can only be achieved on the basis of equity and the applied rule of law. All SDG 3 targets are interlinked by the equity imperative and require global governance and states to implement this requirement in full. Upon this, the AAAQ principles clarify the nature of the targets and their interdependencies (→ Goal 3 mn. 16 ff.). Accessibility is the core aspect and focus of all target implementation. In this context, accessibility means that medical resources, goods and services to maintain health must be accessible to everyone, regardless of cultural, gender or generational background. This includes in particular older people and minority groups, such as indigenous groups.[81] Special attention is paid to the rights of women and children, which must be particularly promoted and protected in order to achieve the equity principle.[82] Within this context, SDG 3.7 and SDG 3.8 play a prominent role. The

---

[76] Liamputtong, *Public Health: Local and Global Perspectives* (2019), 3.

[77] Liamputtong, *Public Health: Local and Global Perspectives* (2019), 162 f.

[78] E/C.12/2000/4, *Substantive Issues Arising In The Implementation Of The International Covenant On Economic, Social And Cultural Rights General Comment No. 14 (2000): The right to the highest attainable standard of health (article 12 of the International Covenant on Economic, Social and Cultural Rights)*, 11 August 2000, para. 12.

[79] Saul and Kinley and Mowbrey, *The International Covenant on Economic, Social and Cultural Rights: Commentary, Cases, and Materials* (2014), 987.

[80] Magnusson, *Advancing the Right to Health: The Vital Role of Law* (2017), 1.

[81] E/C.12/2000/4, *Substantive Issues Arising In The Implementation Of The International Covenant On Economic, Social And Cultural Rights General Comment No. 14 (2000): The right to the highest attainable standard of health (article 12 of the International Covenant on Economic, Social and Cultural Rights)*, 11 August 2000, para. 12(b); A/RES/61/295, United Nations Declaration on the Rights of Indigenous Peoples (2 October 2007), Arts. 17, 21, 23, and 24; ILO Convention No. 169 Convention Concerning Indigenous and Tribal Peoples in Independent Countries (1989); African Commission on Human and Peoples' Rights, ACHPR/Res.372(LX)2017, Resolution on the Protection of Sacred Natural Sites and Territories (2017).

[82] Liamputtong, *Public Health: Local and Global perspectives* (2019), 14.

far-reaching objective in SDG 3.8 to create universal health coverage 'has the means to link equitable social and economic development' by ensuring that 'all people obtain the health services they need' by combining 'financial risk protection with equitable access to essential services'.[83] This comprehensive task of providing universal health coverage is the responsibility of states and governments.[84] The principles of availability and quality are inseparably linked to this. SDG 3.8 explicitly demands the provision of access to high quality healthcare services and quality and affordable medicines and vaccines for all. This expression is to be based on the principle of equity, which shall ensure that all can afford these (health) services regardless of their economic background and must be deemed a precondition to providing access to these resources.[85] As a further condition for adequate access, health care facilities, goods and services must be available in sufficient quantities.[86]

SDG 3.7 is directly linked to the concept of universal health coverage and strives for   **25** universal access to sexual and reproductive health care services, including the necessary information. SDG 3.9 is directly linked to the sanitary determinants of health. Indeed, it is essential to ensure attainable access to clean and safe water and sanitation to prevent diseases based on water pollution.[87]

SDG 3.4 covers all aspects of non-communicable diseases (NDC) as well as the   **26** maintenance of mental health and well-being. 'NDC are those diseases that are chronic and cannot be transmitted from person to person'[88] such as cancer, diabetes or cardiovascular diseases. Reference is made here to SDG 3.5 (alcohol and drug use), SDG 3.a (WHO Framework Convention on Tobacco Control) and SDG 3.b (research and development). The concept of well-being described above is mentioned in SDG 3.4 with regard to mental health. Nevertheless, mental health (the ability to cope with everyday life even under stressful and challenging conditions) is inseparably linked to physical health.[89]

2. SDG 3.3: End Epidemics and Combat Communicable Diseases

Particular attention has been given to SDG 3.3. The interdependencies between the   **27** State and the law, as well as the obligations of States to maintain public health, can be well outlined with reference to infectious diseases and pandemics. The global SARS-CoV-2 pandemic underscores the importance of global health systems and challenges all states to prevent such pandemics in a more rigorous and coordinated manner. While

---

[83] Wong et al., *Sustainable development goals, universal health coverage and equity in health systems: the Orang Asli commons approach* (2016), 1.

[84] Farrell et al., *Health Law: frameworks and context* (2017), 335.

[85] E/C.12/2000/4, *Substantive Issues Arising In The Implementation Of The International Covenant On Economic, Social And Cultural Rights General Comment No. 14 (2000): The right to the highest attainable standard of health (article 12 of the International Covenant on Economic, Social and Cultural Rights)*, 11 August 2000, para. 12(b).

[86] E/C.12/2000/4, *Substantive Issues Arising In The Implementation Of The International Covenant On Economic, Social And Cultural Rights General Comment No. 14 (2000): The right to the highest attainable standard of health (article 12 of the International Covenant on Economic, Social and Cultural Rights)*, 11 August 2000, para.12(a).

[87] E/C.12/2000/4, *Substantive Issues Arising In The Implementation Of The International Covenant On Economic, Social And Cultural Rights General Comment No. 14 (2000): The right to the highest attainable standard of health (article 12 of the International Covenant on Economic, Social and Cultural Rights)*, 11 August 2000, para. 12(b).

[88] Farrell et al., *Health law: frameworks and context* (2017), 358.

[89] Procter et al., *Mental Health* (2017), 5.

recent years brought progress in the fight against known diseases such as AIDS and malaria,[90] severe new challenges from new diseases emerge suddenly.

28   The SARS-CoV-2 pandemic has called into question methods of combating diseases that were long considered effective. Global risk assessment systems to effectively combat disease outbreaks have gained in political relevance and legal impact.[91] Infectious diseases pose new and major challenges to global health governance. SDG 3.b, SDG 3.c and SDG 3.d, which form the basis for effective international action, receive increasing focus.

VI. Universal Health Coverage and Free Health Care

29   One of the main concerns during the HLPF 2017 was how to achieve equity in the health sector. Health equity means that everyone has a fair opportunity to live a long healthy life and should not be disadvantaged because of their income, age, gender, sexual orientation or other factors. Implementation of SDG 3 requires the acceptance of differences and seek to mitigate the risks of inequality through prioritisation of equity, inclusivity and social justice. Universal health coverage (UHC) is another key element for achieving equity in health and in particular access to health services.[92] In this context, it is worth noting that the Oceans Conference and the review of SDG 14 at the 2017 HLPF recognise the importance of oceans for health – particularly in light of the threats that undermining the world's ocean systems (through pollution, overfishing, climate change, etc.) poses to human health and nutrition.[93] The 'One Health' perspective, which deals with health determinants integrating human, animal and ecosystems health, with a special focus on emerging and re-emerging infectious diseases. In the same vein, the justice sector plays a vital role in delivering health, particularly with greater recognition of the frequency and health implications of violence, including gender-based violence and elder violence, and the need for stronger systems to address it.[94]

30   Free health care policies – or politiques de gratuité – are about removing formal user fees. The removal of fees may apply to all health services, to the primary care level, to selected population groups, to selected services for everyone, or to selected services for specific population groups characterised by medical or economic vulnerability. Evidence about the impact of FHC policies in terms of financial protection and health service utilisation is mixed. If well-designed and implemented, FHC policies can expand coverage in countries with few resources and can therefore be part of a strategy and a catalyst to move towards universal health coverage (UHC).[95]

---

[90] https://www.un.org/sustainabledevelopment/health/.

[91] World Health Organization, *SARS-COV-2 Strategy Update* (2020); see also: DIHR, *SARS-COV-2 Response and Recovery Must Build on Human Rights and SDGs* (2020), 5.

[92] See Expert Group Meeting on Integrated Approaches to Implementing Sustainable Development Goal 3 in preparation for the 2017 HLPF, 16 June 2017; https://sustainabledevelopment.un.org/content/do cuments/16156SDG_3_EGM_outcome_REV_5_July.pdf.

[93] Due to the ongoing challenges of the SARS-CoV-2 pandemic, the subsequent UN Oceans Conference has already been postponed twice and is now expected to take place in mid-2022, the outcome document of which will provide further guidance on this nexus of human health; see Expert Group Meeting on Integrated Approaches to Implementing Sustainable Development Goal 3 in preparation for the 2017 HLPF, 16 June 2017.

[94] See Expert Group Meeting on Integrated Approaches to Implementing Sustainable Development Goal 3 in preparation for the 2017 HLPF, 16 June 2017.

[95] See https://www.who.int/news-room/fact-sheets/detail/free-health-care-policies.

VII. A Specific Look on the Indicators of SDG 3

The indicators, developed by the Inter-Agency and Expert Group on SDG Indicators 31
(IAEG-SDGs) and published in the Global Indicator Framework (GIF),[96] generally
indicate that success is measured based on simple numbers, which are set in relation to
a larger number that frequently is used to reflect the population. Thus, the indicators
of SDG 3.3 are based almost exclusively on the relative numbers of people suffering
from diseases such as AIDS, tuberculosis, malaria and Hepatitis B measured against
either 1,000 or 100,000 people in the (uninfected) population. Indicator 3.3.5 alone
refers to the general number of people requiring interventions against neglected tropical
diseases without being put in relation to the population. It is to be criticised that the
broad field of communicable diseases, which goes far beyond the diseases mentioned,
does not provide any indicators for measurement. Especially the outbreak of the SARS-
CoV-2 pandemic shows that a greater differentiation of indicators is needed in order to
adequately measure and assess the extent of SDG 3.3 of communicable diseases.

Similarly, indicators 3.4.1 and 3.4.2 do not cover the entire spectrum of non-commu- 32
nicable diseases and mental health, as only mortality rates for cardiovascular diseases,
cancer, diabetes and chronic respiratory disease are measured. Measuring mental health
solely on the basis of the suicide rate does not in any way reflect the various forms
and developments of mental illness.[97] Indicator 3.8 provides a detailed enumeration of
factors for measuring universal health coverage with reference to the group of most
disadvantaged people which indicates that special attention should be paid to minority
groups. However, no conclusive list of which group belongs to these 'most disadvantaged' people is mentioned.

It can be criticised that minorities and groups requiring special protection, such 33
as indigenous people, children and especially the group of women, who are to be
empowered,[98] are not consistently taken into account within the indicators. In order to
adequately reflect the principle of equity as a core element of SDG 3, a stronger focus
on these groups of people, aspects of intergovernmental cooperation and governmental
policies and structures as well as socio-economic determinants of health should be
appreciated in the indicators.

VIII. Systematic Interpretation of SDG3

This theme is to be seen in the longstanding development of sustainable development 34
and the promise of health, which was reflected early on in the Principle 1 of the Rio
Declaration, stating that '[h]uman beings are at the centre of concerns for sustainable
development. They are entitled to a healthy and productive life in harmony with nature.'

The entitlement of a Health in harmony with nature reflects a continuous stream 35
of concepts and ideas leading to Harmony with Nature. Here, the Secretary General of
the UN presents descriptions and trends in the implementation of Earth jurisprudence
through legislation, policy, education and public engagement worldwide.[99]

---

[96] A/RES/71/313, *Work of the Statistical Commission pertaining to the 2030 Agenda for Sustainable Development*, 10 July 2017.

[97] Procter et al., *Mental Health* (2017), 5 ff.

[98] Saul and Kinley and Mowbrey, *The International Covenant on Economic, Social and Cultural Rights: Commentary, Cases, and Materials* (2014), 987.

[99] A/RES/75/220, *Harmony with Nature*, 30 December 2020, paras. 8, 14; see also A/RES/73/221, *Harmony with Nature, Report of the Secretary-General*, 23 July 2018, para. 14.

36   The experts stressed that an ecological approach to law was required that includes instruments for restorative justice, enforcement of the rights of nature, complex natural resource governance and cross-fertilisation with human rights and the rights of future generations of all species. They shared examples of local governments that had merged laws on the rights of nature with existing legal doctrines recognised by the courts, as well as cases where rights of nature have been implemented through citizen education without the need for enforcement through the judicial system. The importance of raising awareness among judges and lawyers of the concept of legal standing for nature was also underlined.

37   Over the last decade, Earth jurisprudence[100] can be seen as one of the fastest growing legal movement of the twenty-first century. The most significant consequence of acknowledging human interconnectedness and inextricability from the rest of the world has been casting the non-human world as a legal subject with a number of jurisdictions adopting constitutional provisions, legislative initiatives and / or judicial decisions recognising Earth's inherent rights.[101]

1. WTO, TRIPS and Health

38   The legal obligation creating a state and international system of health care could be confronted with the international legal system of Trade[102] and specifically intellectual property rights covering medicine, devise and pharmaceuticals as well as R&D.

39   Therefore, one can only touch shortly the potential tensions between the rights base approach of the wider content of the SDGs covering all the treatises and standards, which is reflected in Appendix 2 Declaration on the TRIPS Agreement and Public Health WT/MIN(01)/DEC/2, Adopted on 14 November 2001.[103]

40   The WTO is not the primary international institution responsible for addressing the public health needs of developing countries as this task falls within the remit of the WHO.[104]

41   The WTO became a central focus in global public health affairs because it took on the role of developing and regulating patent policy, but neglected to exercise this mandate with attention to its broader implications.[105]

42   Thus, the TRIPS Agreement, as one pillar of the WTO, can deny individuals and even states access to what is necessary to build an equitable system that guarantees, or seeks to guarantee access to health care, and if possible, even health coverage.

43   Whether the WTO TRIPS Agreement, with its comprehensive protection of trade aspects, predominantly protects the need of individuals and groups for affordable access to medicines and treatments or, rather, commercial property and thus overrides the right

---

[100] Further information on UN Harmony with Nature http://www.harmonywithnatureun.org/unDocs/.

[101] A/RES/75/220, *Harmony with Nature*, 30 December 2020; A/74/236, *Harmony with Nature, Report of the Secretary-General*, 26 July 2019, para. 129; see also https://2d350104-a104-42f3-9376-3197e7089409.fil esusr.com/ugd/23bc2d_ee924cccc4f6469cace7222a707d77fa.pdf; for a current overview http://www.harm onywithnatureun.org/unDocs/.

[102] Atik, 'Trade and Health' in Bethlehem, McRae, Neufeld, Van Damme (eds), *The Oxford Handbook of International Trade Law* (2009), 597.

[103] Correa, *Trade Related Aspects of Intellectual Property Rights: A Commentary on the TRIPS Agreement* (2007), 563.

[104] Abbott, 'The Doha Declaration on the TRIPS Agreement and Public Health: Lighting a Dark Corner at the WTO' (2002) 5 *Journal of International Economic Law*, 469 (505).

[105] Abbott, 'The Doha Declaration on the TRIPS Agreement and Public Health: Lighting a Dark Corner at the WTO' (2002) 5 *Journal of International Economic Law*, 469 (505).

to health in its manifold expressions, cannot be discussed in detail here.[106] However, many attempts have been made within the context of the WTO, but efforts towards a new global R&D treaty have been derailed by northern states, so probably in the future a south-south co-operation could pave the way for a model which could be more attuned to the demands of people outside the northern hemisphere.[107]

2. Ocean and Health

New research areas have been developed on interrelationships that have since been 44 obvious: Oceans and human health, which is now a new interdisciplinary area of research, to study the closely linked connections between the marine environment and public health.[108] Many of the basic needs such as food and water depend on the oceans. Worldwide, fish is an important resource for food security and nutrition. Mariculture in particular has the potential to supply a significant part of the ever-increasing global demand.[109] The oceans are also a possible source of water for human consumption. Desalination of seawater, which is energy-intensive and still too expensive to replace the use of local freshwater, could be the viable future alternative to alleviate regional scarcity and growing water conflicts. Worldwide, some 700 million people do not have access to enough clean water and by 2025 the number is expected to swell to 1.8 billion.

The capacity of developing countries for early warnings, risk reduction and the 45 engagement of global health risks, needs a systematic approach organised and financed on an international level.[110] Also, the stringent implementation of the WHO Framework Convention on Tobacco Control is related to an equipped state who is in charge to follow the framework and strengthen its constitutional basis.

C. Interdependences of SDG 3

Advancing human well-being – including material well-being, health, education, 46 participation, access to a clean and safe environment and resilience – is deemed a cornerstone for the further transformation towards sustainable development[111] and indispensable for the demanded sustainable transformation.[112] SDG 3 counts as one of the agendas main goals and is historically rooted in the global task to end poverty and hunger (SDG 1.1, SDG 2.1, SDG 2.2).[113]

---

[106] Further information: Wills, *Contesting World Order?: Socioeconomic Rights and Global Justice Movements* (2017), 153 ff.

[107] Wills, *Contesting World Order?: Socioeconomic Rights and Global Justice Movements* (2017), 194.

[108] Negri, 'Human Health and Human Rights, 13 Healthy Oceans for Healthy Lives: The Contribution of the World Health Organization to Global Ocean Governance' in Attard and Fitzmaurice and Ntovas (eds), *The IMLI Treatise On Global Ocean Governance, Volume II: UN Specialized Agencies and Global Ocean Governance* (2018), 261.

[109] Negri, 'Human Health and Human Rights, 13 Healthy Oceans for Healthy Lives: The Contribution of the World Health Organization to Global Ocean Governance' in Attard and Fitzmaurice and Ntovas (eds), *The IMLI Treatise On Global Ocean Governance, Volume II: UN Specialized Agencies and Global Ocean Governance* (2018), 262.

[110] A/RES/69/313, *Addis Ababa Action Agenda of the Third International Conference on Financing for Development (Addis Ababa Action Agenda)*, 17 August 2015, para. 77.

[111] See A/RES/70/1, para. 14.

[112] Independent Group of Scientists appointed by the Secretary-General, *Global Sustainable Development Report 2019: The Future is Now – Science for Achieving Sustainable Development* (2019), xxii.

[113] Independent Group of Scientists appointed by the Secretary-General, *Global Sustainable Development Report 2019: The Future is Now – Science for Achieving Sustainable Development*, (2019), 38.

47   Being intertwined with almost every SDG,[114] a poor health condition hinders people to fulfil their potential and being a major prerequisite for development thus also confines economic growth.[115]

48   Achieving well-being and good health enhances social factors such as the ability to learn, school attendance and educational achievement (SDG 4.4),[116] income and housing (SDG 8.1, SDG 8.3) and is recognised within other SDGs.[117] Health adequate services and resources, including infrastructure (SDG 9.1), food security and agricultural production (SDG 2.1, SDG 2.2), decent work (SDG 8), sustainable consumption (SDG 12.4, SDG 12.8), provision of water and sanitation (SDG 6.2, SDG 6.3), access to energy (SDG 7.1), and resilient and inclusive cities that provide universal access to housing and transport (SDG 11.1, SDG 11.3, SDG 11.6, SDG 11.7).[118]

49   Fostering gender equality (SDG 5.1, SDG 5.2) improves better health. Women's health issues are deemed under-prioritised (SDG 3.1). Whereas mothers take most of the health decisions for their children, the empowerment of girls and women can lead to easy health gains (SDG 3.2). In consequence, their views and knowledge about how to achieve a healthy state of mind and body lead to improved child and family member's health outcomes (SDG 3.7, SDG 5.6). Increasing participation of women in the paid work force (SDG 5.4, SDG 5.5, SDG 5.a) can lead to overall economic gains and thus improved health.[119]

50   Ensuring access to water of an adequate quality, sufficient supply and sanitation (SDG 6.1, SDG 6.2), significantly reduces the risk of health diseases (SDG 3.2, SDG 3.3, SDG 3.9).[120]

D. Jurisprudential Significance of SDG 3

51   While no unequivocal reference to SDG 3 as a basis for judicial decisions has been made in case law so far, its contents are repeatedly examined from different points of view in a wide variety of contexts and to varying degrees, in some cases in great detail. In the jurisdiction of international and national courts, tribunals and, beyond that, in dispute settlement proceedings, recurring reflections are made and its contents are expressed mostly in an economic, social and cultural rights context by reference to the relevant human rights instruments.[121] In this context, slightly different tendencies in the discussion and evaluation of substantive concerns can be identified in international jurisdiction. A jurisprudential contemplation of SDG 3 thus appears admissible, at least to some of its levels and judicial contexts.

---

[114] See from a holistic and detailed analytical perspective in particular the interdependences with nearly every of the 17 goals, Griggs et al., *A Guide to SDG Interactions: From Science to Implementation* (2017), 91; see also A/71/304, *Right of everyone to the enjoyment of the highest attainable standard of physical and mental health, Note by the Secretary-General*, 5 August 2016, paras. 7, 19.

[115] Griggs et al., *A Guide to SDG Interactions: From Science to Implementation* (2017), 85.

[116] Griggs et al., *A Guide to SDG Interactions: From Science to Implementation* (2017), 86, 91.

[117] SDG 5.6, SDG 12.4, SDG 14.2, SDG 14.a.

[118] Griggs et al., *A Guide to SDG Interactions: From Science to Implementation* (2017), 84.

[119] Griggs et al., *A Guide to SDG Interactions: From Science to Implementation* (2017), 86, 91.

[120] Atapattu and Gonzalez and Seck, *Intersections of Environmental Justice and Sustainable Development: Framing the Issues* (2021), 2; Martens and Ellmers (eds), *Agenda 2030: Wo steht die Welt?, 5 Jahre SDGs – eine Zwischenbilanz* (2020), 94.

[121] ILA, *Conference Report Sydney, Role Of International Law In Sustainable Natural Resource Management For Development* (2018), 31.

I. Jurisdiction on Vision and Objectives

When considering the general objective of SDG 3 on a broader level, a distinction is first made between the 'right to health' and a 'right to well-being',[122] both of which are linked to the condition of a peaceful life in a safe and environmentally sound environment (→ Goal 3 mn. 15 ff., → Goal 16 mn. 67). **52**

1. International Jurisdiction of Human Rights Courts

The fundamental assumption that the standard of living is linked with the health of humans and their environment, even detached from a temporal level, was made by the International Court of Justice (ICJ) in its Advisory Opinion *Legality of the Threat or Use of Nuclear Weapons*.[123] In this decision, the ICJ referred to the Rio Declaration,[124] which serves as one of the parental foundations of the SDGs.[125] The conditions of a peaceful life are closely linked to the economic, social and cultural rights (ESCR) as being set up in the ICESCR[126] and the ICCPR[127] which are broadly acknowledged as prerequisite for human development.[128] In its case law, the IACtHR has repeatedly ruled that the 'right to life' being one of these ESCR is closely linked to personal integrity and humane treatment and dignity which are based, amongst others, on human health care.[129] The IACtHR also defines the nucleus of the 'right to health' to consist of 'its interdependence with the right to life and the right to personal integrity'.[130] In *Sawhoyamaxa v Paraguay*, the court assessed the violation of personal integrity in the context of the removal of indigenous people, as particularly vulnerable group, as well as several deaths within this **53**

---

[122] See E/C.12/2000/4, *Substantive Issues Arising In The Implementation Of The International Covenant On Economic, Social And Cultural Rights General Comment No. 14 (2000): The right to the highest attainable standard of health (article 12 of the International Covenant on Economic, Social and Cultural Rights)*, 11 August 2000.

[123] *Legality Of The Threat Or Use Of Nuclear Weapons*, Advisory Opinion, 8 July 1996, Reports of Judgements, Advisory Opinions And Orders (1996), para. 29; see also *Pulp Mills on the River Uruguay (Argentina v. Uruguay)*, Advisory Opinion, 20 April 2010, paras. 160 f., and Separate Opinion of Judge Cançado Trindade.

[124] *Legality Of The Threat Or Use Of Nuclear Weapons*, Advisory Opinion, 8 July 1996, Reports of Judgements, Advisory Opinions And Orders (1996), para. 30.

[125] A/RES/70/1, *Transforming our world: the 2030 agenda for sustainable development* (2015), 21 October 2015, para. 11.

[126] UN, *International Covenant on Economic, Social and Cultural Rights, Adopted and opened for signature, ratification and accession by General Assembly resolution 2200A (XXI) of 16.12.1966, entry into force 03.01.1976, in accordance with article 27*.

[127] International Covenant on Civil and Political Rights, adopted by UNGA Resolution 2200A (XXI) on 16.12.1966, and in force from 23.03.1976 in accordance with Article 49 of the covenant.

[128] Principle 1 of the Stockholm Declaration of 1972: 'Man has the fundamental right to freedom, equality and adequate conditions of life, in an environment of a quality that permits a life of dignity and well-being'; RES/45/94, *Need to ensure a healthy environment for the well-being of individuals*, 14 December 1990: 'everyone has the right to an adequate standard of living for his or her own health and wellbeing and that of his or her family and to the continuous improvement of living conditions'; Principle 1 of the Rio Declaration: 'human beings are [...] entitled to a healthy [...] life'; and further regional human rights instruments, amongst others, Art. 10 of the San Salvador Protocol to the American Convention on Human Rights; Art. 26 of the American Convention (Pact of San José); Additional Protocol to the American Convention on Human Rights in the Area of Economic, Social and Cultural Rights, ratified by Ecuador on March 25, 1993.

[129] *Albán Cornejo v Ecuador*, IACtHR Judgement, 22 November 2007, paras. 117, 176 and further judgements referred to therein.

[130] *Suárez Peralta v Ecuador*, IACtHR Judgement, 21 May 2013, para. 101; and is also reflected in domestic jurisdiction, see e.g. *RJSA, widow of R (on behalf of GRS in the capacity of official guardian) v Peruvian Superior Court*, Appeal to the Constitutional Court, No 3081-2007-PS/TC, ILDC 969 (PE 2007), 9 November 2007, para. 23.

group as a breach of a states' obligation to guarantee socio-economic conditions and safeguard the right to life.[131] This decision represents an advancement as it departs from its previous ruling made in *Yakhye Axa v Paraguay*[132] where the state was not found to be responsible for individual deaths. However, the IACtHR declared the right to life being the starting point for all other rights and that states are obliged to create 'living conditions that are compatible with the dignity of the human person' and shall overcome 'conditions that impede or obstruct access to a decent existence.'[133] In its further statements, it linked the right to health, the right to food and the right to water as indispensable elements of a decent life.[134] In another case of the IAA, *Eritrea – Ethiopia*[135], such state obligations are described as 'natural resources', which are expressed, among other things, in the provision of health care by a state[136] which complies with the covenant obligations of the ICESCR.[137] The importance of this classification has been emphasised once again by the IACtHR, as that the court stated that 'direct' justiciability is a prerequisite to fully realise the right to health. In this respect, it emphasised that as a court, in order to effectively guarantee an appropriate jurisprudence for the right to health and access to jurisdiction, it must itself fulfil certain obligations. The court then referred in particular to its competence under the Pact of San José, 'to move in this direction of social justice.'[138] This also complies with the obligations of the ICESCR since States are committed 'to take the necessary steps to the maximum of its available resources' (→ Goal 3 mn. 15 ff.).

2. European Jurisdiction

54   Elements of a decent life are also determined in European case law. In *Dubetska v Ukraine*, for instance, the ECtHR did not presuppose *per se* an injury to individual health or the quality of life. Rather, it is determined by all circumstances, in particular by the intensity and duration of the environmental hazard.[139] However, in so far access to information about the characteristics of goods is concerned, the ECJ in *Neptune Distribution* assumed a close connection with the protection of human health, which is of 'general interest' and therefore 'may justify limitations on the freedom of expression and information of a person carrying on a business or his freedom to conduct a business'. Irrespective of an actual identified risk to human health, a risk assessment must be

---

[131] *Case of the Sawhoyamaxa Indigenous Community v. Paraguay*, IACtHR Judgement, Merits, Reparations and Costs, 29 March 2006, paras. 150-3, 191; see also *The Social and Economic Rights Action Center and the Center for Economic and Social Rights v. Nigeria*, African Commission on Human and Peoples' Rights (AfCHPR), Comm. No. 155/96 (2001), Merits, 27 October 2001, paras. 44-8 (although not being a party to the ICESCR at that time); further information on this case: Coomans, 'The Case Ogoni case before the African Commission on Human and People's Rights' (2003) *52 ICLQ*, 749 (753).

[132] *Case of the Yakye Axa Indigenous Community v. Paraguay*, IACtHR Judgment, Merits, Reparations and Costs, 17 June 2005.

[133] *Case of the Yakye Axa Indigenous Community v. Paraguay*, IACtHR Judgment, Merits, Reparations and Costs, 17 June 2005, paras. 161 f.

[134] *Case of the Yakye Axa Indigenous Community v. Paraguay*, IACtHR Judgment, Merits, Reparations and Costs, 17 June 2005, paras. 167, 169; see also, *Case of the 'Street Children' (Villagran-Morales et al.) v. Guatemala*, IACtHR Judgment, Merits, 19 November 1999, para. 144.

[135] *Eritrea-Ethiopia Claims Commission*, Reports of International Arbitral Awards, Final Award, Ethiopia's Damages Claims, 17 August 2009, Vol. XXVI.

[136] *Eritrea-Ethiopia Claims Commission*, Reports of International Arbitral Awards, Final Award, Ethiopia's Damages Claims, 17 August 2009, Vol. XXVI, para. 21.

[137] Since States are obliged by the ICESCR 'to take the necessary steps to the maximum of its available resources', Art. 2 (1) ICESCR.

[138] *Suárez Peralta v Ecuador*, IACtHR Judgement, 21 May 2013, para. 10.

[139] *Dubetska and others v Ukraine*, ECtHR Judgement, 05 March 2011, Application no. 30499/03, paras. 105 f.

consistent with the purpose of protection against the background of the precautionary principle.[140] Insofar a threat to public health within the European Union is deemed of a potential nature, an adoption of restrictive measures is permissible.[141] In its decision *Dextro Energy v EC*, the ECJ stated that human health concerns are a high good, and that the (European) Union legislator must be given a wide discretion to protect them, in order to be able to reduce risks adequately and being able to make proportionate decisions taking into account scientific facts as well as political, economic and social issues.[142] With this and further decisions, the court placed the generally accepted nutritional and health principles above deviating scientific studies in order to remain consistent with an overarching principle of health maintenance given in the EU. The ECJ made a further fundamental finding in the case *TestBioTech v Commission*, referring to the Aarhus Convention and the Treaty on the Functioning of the European Union (TFEU). Environmental law in European consideration shall deem 'a broad meaning, not limited to matters relating to the protection of the natural environment in the strict sense'.[143] The court added that health, and other related issues, such as the management or availability of water resources and land use or energy supply and town and country planning as well as fiscal provisions are inseparable issues of environmental law in European legislation and must be interpreted very broadly.[144]

3. Arbitration Proceedings

Aspects of good health and well-being are also assessed in arbitration proceedings.   55
In *EC – Asbestos* the WTO Appellate Body (AB) fundamentally stated that the 'preservation of human life and health [is] a value that is both vital and important in the highest degree'.[145] In several decisions, the AB gave context to what this preservation includes and dealt in particular with the risk assessment of products. The determination of the 'likeness', the substitute property of a product, is thus significantly influenced by the health risks it poses.[146]

II. Jurisdiction on SDG 3 Targets

Both the jurisdiction examined and additional jurisdiction can be assigned to some   56
extent explicitly to the individual targets of SDG 3. Regarding SDG 3.7 and SDG 3.8 specifically the term 'access' against the background of health and well-being has to be accompanied by services of general interest. In this respect, the state has to guarantee access to health systems.[147] In addition, Judge Cançado Trindade, in a separate opinion, noted that there exists a particular obligation for states but also 'beyond the strictly

---

[140] ECJ, Case C-157/14, 17.12.2015, *Neptune Distribution*, ECLI:EU:C:2015:823, paras. 74-84; and the jurisdiction referred to therein: *Hertel v Switzerland*, 25.08.1998, ECtHR Reports of Judgments and Decisions 1998-VI, § 47; *Bergens Tidende and Others v Norway*, ECtHR no. 26132/95, ECHR 2000-IV, § 51.

[141] ECJ, Case C-157/14, 17.12.2015, *Neptune Distribution*, ECLI:EU:C:2015:823, para. 82.

[142] ECJ, Case C-296/16 P, 08.06.2017, *Dextro Energy v EC*, ECLI:EU:C:2017:437, paras. 49 ff.

[143] ECJ, Case T-33/16, 14.03.2018, *TestBioTech v Commission*, ECLI:EU:T:2018:135, para. 44.

[144] ECJ, Case T-33/16, 14.03.2018, *TestBioTech v Commission*, ECLI:EU:T:2018:135, para. 45.

[145] *EC – Measures Affecting Asbestos and Asbestos-Containing Products (EC – Asbestos)*, WT/DS135/AB/R, Appellate Body Report (5 April 2001), para. 172.

[146] *EC – Measures Affecting Asbestos and Asbestos-Containing Products (EC – Asbestos)*, WT/DS135/AB/R, Appellate Body Report (5 April 2001), para. 119; *US – Measures Affecting the Production and Sale of Clove Cigarettes (Clove Cigarettes)*, WT/DS406/AB/R, Appellate Body Report (24 April 2012), paras. 156-75.

[147] *Case of the Sawhoyamaxa Indigenous Community v. Paraguay*, IACtHR Judgment, Merits, Reparations and Costs, 29 March 2006, paras. 155, 166.

inter-State dimension' to ensure access to 'notify and share information with the affected populations' in case that 'human health and the well-being of peoples were seriously at risk.'[148] This opinion marked the foundations for an extension and transfer of such corresponding obligations to non-state actors.

57   In context of SDG 3.8, a clear development emerges, particularly with regard to access to safe medicines and vaccines for all in the European judicial area. The ECtHR has rejected a number of applications in which compulsory vaccination of children was presumed to be an impermissible restriction of human life and self-determination on the basis of various human rights protected by the European Charter of Human Rights (ECHR). By refusing access to the courts judicial path, the ECtHR made it clear that the good of public health must be regarded as superior to an individuals' right to respect for private and family life, the freedom of conscience, the right to education and the associated respect for parents' philosophical conviction.[149]

58   In 2013, a nine-year old girl died from an asthma attack after preceding serious respiratory illness which was, according to the coroner, due to the exposure to levels of nitrogen dioxide and particulate matter in the air of London, severely exceeding the WHO guidelines. On 16 December 2020, the Deputy Coroner (DC) ruled that there was a 'recognised failure to reduce the level of nitrogen dioxide to within the limits set by EU and domestic law, which possibly contributed to her death'.[150] Moreover, the relevant institutions did not provide sufficient 'information about the health risks of air pollution and its potential to exacerbate asthma'. The legal basis for the inquest is constituted by the Coroners and Justice Act (CJA) 2009 which in § 5(1) (b) sets out 'how' and 'in what circumstances' someone died, and in § 5(2) sets out the further purpose of determining whether there has been a violation of a right under the European Convention on Human Rights. With the DC's official finding that the death was caused by 1 a) acute respiratory failure; 1 b) severe asthma; 1 c) air pollution exposure, the DP consequently concluded the violation of the right to life guaranteed in Art. 2 of the ECHR. Thus, a precedent (at least in the common law family of the UK) has been set which may hold the responsible authorities accountable and demand action.

59   This *Ella Adoo-Kissi-Debrah case* is presumably the first case worldwide to directly establish air pollution as a cause of death. Until now, air pollution has well been linked to premature deaths, but not in an official investigation that led to legal consequences. In fact, this did not even occur in the so-called *Dieselgate Cases* which involved the manipulation of car software that led to an excessive amount of particulate matter being released during fuel combustion.[151] It is likely that this landmark decision will be used as a basis for legal reasoning in public interest litigation (PIL) in the future.

60   SDG 3.a und SDG 3.b are reflected in various decisions relating to *Tobacco* in which public health is deemed a societal interest under Arts. 8.1, 20 TRIPS.[152] The importance

---

[148] *Pulp Mills on the River Uruguay (Argentina v. Uruguay)*, Advisory Opinion, 20 April 2010, paras. 156, 161 f., Separate Opinion of Judge Cançado Trindade.

[149] ECHR, *Vavřička v. Czech Republic*, Application no. 47621/13, *Novotná v. Czech Republic*, Application no. 3867/14, *Hornych v. Czech Republic*, Application no. 73094/14, *Brožík v. Czech Republic*, Application no. 19306/15, *Dubský v. Czech Republic*, Application no. 19298/15, *Roleček v. Czech Republic*, Application no. 43883/15.

[150] London Inner South Coroner's Court, Inquest touching the death of Ella Roberta Adoo Kissi-Debrah, Inquest opened on 17 December 2019, https://www.innersouthlondoncoroner.org.uk/news/2020/nov/inquest-touching-the-death-of-ella-roberta-adoo-kissi-debrah.

[151] Overview of the cases: https://www.cleanenergywire.org/factsheets/dieselgate-timeline-car-emissions-fraud-scandal-germany.

[152] *Australia – Certain Measures Concerning Trademarks, Geographical Indications And Other Plain Packaging Requirements Applicable To Tobacco Products And Packaging*, WT/DS435/R, WT/DS441/R WT/DS458/R, WT/DS467/R, Reports Of The Panels (28 May 2018), para. 7.2588; *British American Tobacco*,

of this classification is also reflected in investor-state dispute settlement such as *Philip Morris v Uruguay*[153] and *Philip Morris v Australia*.[154] The tribunal held that states are not obliged to proof a direct causal link of a measure on public health outcomes if these measures are to be assumed a 'reasonable attempt to address a public health concern and are taken in good faith'.[155] In its more recent decisions, the Permanent Court of Arbitration (PCA) continues to consider this approach.[156] Additionally, it opened the path of litigation for so-called counter claims insofar host states adopt 'measures to protect human, animal, or plant life or health' the breach of which means a violation of domestic and international law which in turn inevitably leads to investor liability.[157] SDG 3.b explicitly refers to the WTO Agreement on Trade-Related Aspects of Intellectual Property Rights (TRIPS). In a human rights context, TRIPS is globally opposed since it is deemed to be counteractive to the right to life and health due to it reducing access (to medicines) and patenting life.[158]

Relating to risk reductions and risk management (SDG 3.d), for instance, the EU legislation is allowed 'a broad discretion [...] which entails political, economic and social choices on its part, and in which it is called upon to undertake complex assessments'.[159] In the broader scope of international law, the right to health contains the duty to report infectious disease outbreaks which is part of states' obligations. A violation of this obligation leads to international responsibility by reference to the ICESCR. Recent developments, such as the SARS-CoV-2 pandemic, are likely to be reflected in the legal system in the near future. How this will affect the jurisdiction of international law or that of the legal families affected will have to be monitored further.

61

C-491/01, para. 123; further reading: Frankel and Gervais, 'Plain Packaging and the Interpretation of the TRIPS Agreement' (2013) in *46 Vanderbilt Journal of Transnational Law*, 1149 (1149); Gu, 'Plain Tobacco Packaging's Impact on International Trade and the Family Smoking Prevention and Tobacco Control Act in the U.S. and Drafting Suggestions' (2017) *16 Wash. U. Global Stud. L. Rev.*, 197 (197).

[153] *Philip Morris Brands Sàrl, Philip Morris Products S.A. and Abal Hermanos S.A. v. Oriental Republic of Uruguay (Philip Morris v Uruguay)*, ICSID Case No. ARB/10/7; and gives further impetus to this arbitral award when in its further jurisdiction, Philip Morris' claim was found to be inadmissible due to an abuse of rights pertaining to a corporate restructuring in face of the upcoming dispute, see *Philip Morris v Australia*.

[154] *Philip Morris Asia Limited v The Commonwealth of Australia (Philip Morris v Australia)*, UNCITRAL, PCA Case No. 2012-12.

[155] Bernasconi-Osterwalder and Brauch (eds) and Schacherer, *International Investment Law and Sustainable Development: Key cases from the 2010s* (2018), 43.

[156] See e.g. *Arbitration under Chapter Ten of the Dr-Cafta and the UNCITRAL Arbitration Rules (2010) between David Aven et al. and The Republic Of Costa Rica (Aven v Costa Rica)*, ICSID Case No. UNCT/15/3, Final Award (18 September 2018), paras. 236 f.

[157] *Arbitration under Chapter Ten of the Dr-Cafta and the UNCITRAL Arbitration Rules (2010) between David Aven et al. and The Republic Of Costa Rica (Aven v Costa Rica)*, ICSID Case No. UNCT/15/3, Final Award, (18 September 2018), paras. 734, 737-8.

[158] Lester and Mercurio and Davies, *World Trade Law, Text, Materials and Commentary* (2018) 865; Asia Pacific Research Network, *Re-thinking TRIPS in the WTO: NGOs Demand Review and Reform of TRIPS at Doha Ministerial Conference* (2003).

[159] CJEU, C-491/01, *British American Tobacco*, ECLI:EU:C:2002:741, para. 123; CJEU, C-269/13 P, *Acino v Commission*, ECLI:EU:C:2014:255, paras. 57 f.; see also CJEU, C-491/01, *British American Tobacco (Investments) and Imperial Tobacco*, ECLI:EU:C:2002:741, para. 123; CJEU, C-154/04, C-155/04, *Alliance for Natural health and Others*, ECLI:EU:C:2005:449, para. 52.

III. The Transfer of International Jurisdiction into National Jurisprudence

62   International jurisdiction is frequently assumed not to be enforceable since it is not States which create judicial orders but international courts or bodies which therefore depend on a States' good will to adopt their opinion on specific cases.[160] But here too, developments can be observed in international judicial practice. A poignant example from 2010 gives a clear indication that principles of international law and in particular the right to health are indeed recognised in domestic jurisdiction. In *Laxmi Mandal*[161] the right to health, including the right to nutrition and medical care, was justified after one woman had given birth in full public view and another woman had died postpartum caused by the denial of maternal healthcare. The decision was grounded on various international human rights instruments, including the ICESCR, and made 'enforceable in courts of law by using the device of a 'continuing mandamus'.[162]

63   And it is not only States' social obligations in the wake of the right to health that are reflected in domestic jurisdiction but also ecologic obligations which have a distinct impact on human health and well-being. In the *Urgenda case* the Supreme Court of the Netherlands established a positive obligation to take measures for the prevention of climate change in that it ordered the Netherlands to reduce its greenhouse gas (GHG) emissions with at least 25 per cent by the end of 2020, compared to 1990 levels. Following a decision at first instance still based on Dutch law by reference to the doctrine of hazardous negligence, the arguments in the cross-appeal were based on the protection of the right to life and to private and family life with reference to Arts. 2 and 8 ECHR.[163] In addition, the Court took into account in its reasoning the UNFCCC, the 2015 Paris Agreement, the obligation to exercise due diligence in preventing significant transboundary harm, and the precautionary principle[164] which are inherent in the Global Agenda 2030 and the SDGs (→ Intro mn. 140 ff., 229). The Supreme Court confirmed this view and rejected in full the State's requests to deviate, and emphasised that the responsibility of individual states can be determined even dissociated from a joint responsibility, in this case of climate change, of several states.[165] Despite being controversial, this decision subsequently gave rise to a number of lawsuits[166] which amongst other things unambiguously refer to the contents of SDG 3, assuming intergenerational justice

---

[160] See Schiff Berman, 'Jurisdictional Pluralism' in Allen et al. (eds), *The Oxford Handbook of Jurisdiction in International Law* (2019), 141.

[161] High Court of Delhi, 4 June 2010, WP(C) Nos 8853 of 2008, *Laxmi Mandal v Deen Dayal Harinagar Hospital & Ors.*

[162] Constantinides, 'Economic and Social Rights' in Nollkaemper et al. (eds), *International Law in Domestic Courts: A Casebook* (2018), 682.

[163] Dutch Supreme Court, *The State of the Netherlands v Stichting Urgenda*, 20.12.2019, ECLI:NL:HR: 2019:2006, paras. 5.6.2 and Summary of the judgement, conclusion.

[164] Dutch Supreme Court, *The State of the Netherlands v Stichting Urgenda*, 20.12.2019, ECLI:NL:HR: 2019:2006, paras. 31(c), (d), 4.7, 5.3.2, 5.6.2.

[165] Dutch Supreme Court, *The State of the Netherlands v Stichting Urgenda*, 20.12.2019, ECLI:NL:HR: 2019:2006, paras. 5.7.1-5.8; see for further information on this case: Noellkaemper and Burgers, 'A New Classic in Climate Change Litigation: The Dutch Supreme Court Decision in the Urgenda Case' (2020) *EJIL Talk*; 'State of the Netherlands v. Urgenda, Foundation Hague Court of Appeal Requires Dutch Government to Meet Greenhouse Gas Emissions Reductions By 2020' (2019), *132 Harv. L. Rev.*, 2090.

[166] See e.g. Colombia Supreme Court, *Future Generations v. Ministry of the Environment and Others*, Judgment, 05.04.2018, Reg. No 11001-22-03-000-2018-00319-00; Lahore High Court, *Maria Khan et al. v. Federation of Pakistan et al.*, 15.02.2019, Writ Petition No.8960 of 2019; also by calling on the IACtHR: Republic of Colombia, Request for an Advisory Opinion from the Inter-American Court of Human Rights Concerning the Interpretation of Article 1 (1), 4 (1) and 5 (1) of the American Convention on Human Rights, and Advisory Opinion OC-23/17, 15 November 2017.

as an indispensable prerequisite for the right to life, which thus becomes a right to health and future.

IV. De Facto Influences on Jurisdiction

As a phenomenon of globalisation, a growing number of non-state actors influence   **64**
the shaping and creating of health-related law, regulation and jurisprudence. They take up the cause of SDG 3 such as the *Bill and Melinda Gates Foundation*, the *Bloomberg Foundation*, the *International Red Cross and Red Crescent Movement* or *Physicians for Human Rights*.[167] These actors, NGOs, mostly formed as welfare organisations, charitable or humanitarian institutions and associations, are a 'defining characteristic'[168] of public health globalisation. They frequently cooperate in transnational networks and equally influence states legislation[169] and jurisdiction,[170] in some cases to a considerable extent. Due to their (financial) size, domestic NGOs are able to evade states and to exert severe pressure on them as well as on businesses or investors. They also use the possibility of third party funding[171] and thus are capable of financing international and national proceedings of interest. By this means, NGOs and other non-state actors can exert a significant influence on the development of jurisdiction with regard to (public) health even beyond their ability to act as *amicus curiae* in (international) proceedings.

UNAIDS works with many different partners at a global, regional and country level   **65**
to make a progress for children and mothers affected by HIV/AIDS. UNAIDS is the lead organisation for following Inter-Agency Task Teams (IATT):

- Prevention of Mother-to-Child Transmission of HIV (PMTCT)
- Care and Support for Children affected by AIDS
- Young People and HIV/AIDS
- Education[172]

The Prevention of Mother-to-Child Transmission of HIV (PMTCT) is a group of   **66**
28 multilateral, government and non-governmental organisations that are committed to strengthening partnerships and programs that address the survival of pregnant woman, mothers and children living with HIV.[173] This team was built to protect the people and to end the AIDS epidemic due to HIV.

---

[167] Further relevant NGOs in the area of 'good health and well-being' include Global Fund to Fight AIDS, Tuberculosis, and Malaria, the International Finance Facility for Immunization, UNITAID, Amnesty International, Doctors without Borders, Talitha Kum.

[168] Fidler, 'Global Health Jurisprudence: A Time of Reckoning' (2004) 96(2) *Georgetown Law Journal*, 393 (409).

[169] One such example is the *US Conflict minerals transparency Act*, which was based on the increased efforts of NGOs and the resulting pressure to enable consumers to make informed choices. Further examples include the *Revision of the International Health Regulations* (IHR 2005), WHA Doc. 58.3 (May 23, 2005), or the *Pandemic and All-Hazards Preparedness Act*, Pub. L. No. 109-417, 120 Stat. 2831 (codified as amended in scattered sections of 6, 21, 38, and 42 U.S.C.).

[170] See instead of many *United States — Import Prohibition of Certain Shrimp and Shrimp Products (US – Shrimp)*, WT/DS58/23 (26 January 2001).

[171] See e.g. Dhotan, 'Luring NGOs to International Courts: A Comment on CLR v. Romania' (2015) in *75 ZaöRV*, 635-69.

[172] See UNAIDS, *Inter-Agency Task Team (IATT) on HIV and Young People, Global Guidance Briefs, HIV Interventions for Young People* (2008).

[173] E.g. UNODC, *Prevention of Mother-to-Child Transmission of HIV in Prisons: A Technical Guide* (2019).

67   The IATT on Children affected by AIDS protects and promotes the rights of children affected by HIV and AIDS through providing a forum for supporting a coordinated and expanded evidence-based response.[174]

68   UNAIDS provides the strategic direction and technical support needed to catalyse and connect leadership from governments, the private sector and communities to deliver life-saving AIDS services.[175]

E. Conclusion on SDG 3

69   The short form of SDG 3 seems to be somehow misleading. As it points to 'Good Health and Well-Being', the used expressions give space for high spirits in a vast area. However, the high hopes created with the short form is not directly covered with SDG 3 and the indicators, as a corresponding instrument, are not targeting this vast area in an absolute sense. The complexity of an examination of SDGs 3 is thus potentially very large and the areas indirectly linked to health have been referred to as the 'right to health plus' approach.[176] Therefore, it should be stressed that SDG 3 does not aim for every individual to be in good health, but rather to '[e]nsure healthy lives and promote well-being for all at all ages', based on a global working basis of equality, which makes a significant difference for further interpretation.

70   The content of SDG 3 is wrapped in different layers of international law and a changing institutional landscape,[177] analysed, commented and theorised from brilliant scholars. And it does not surprise that health was already at the heart of the MDGs and remains a key element of the Global Agenda 2030.[178] But the progress of the MDGs has been recognised as uneven, particularly in Africa, least developed countries, landlocked developing countries and Small Island developing States and some of the MDGs remained off track until their expiry, in particular those related to maternal, new-born and child health and to reproductive health.[179]

71   The content of SDG 3 in a legal field continues to be essential for gaining a people-centred understanding of development.[180] Health in the understanding of the WHO and the right to health have a different background and substance and therefore must be defined to lead to a different scope of understanding and applicability.

72   In accordance with Art. 12(1) of the ICESCR, the States parties recognise 'the right of everyone to the enjoyment of the highest attainable standard of physical and mental health', while Art. 12(2) enumerates, by way of illustration, a number of 'steps to be taken by the States parties [...] to achieve the full realization of this right'.[181] Because health is

---

[174] UNAIDS, *Inter-Agency Task Team (IATT) on HIV and Young People, Global Guidance Briefs, HIV Interventions for Young People* (2008).

[175] https://www.unaids.org/en/whoweare/about.

[176] Farrell and Devereux and Karpin and Weller, *Health Law: Frameworks and Context* (2017), 49.

[177] Burci and Cassels, 'Health' in Katz Cogan and Hurd and Johnstone (eds), *The Oxford Handbook of International Organizations* (2016), 450 ff.

[178] Negri, 'Healthy Oceans for Healthy Lives: The Contribution of the World Health Organization to Global Ocean Governance' in Attard, Fitzmaurice and Ntovas (eds.), *The IMLI Treatise On Global Ocean Governance, Volume II: UN Specialized Agencies and Global Ocean Governance* (2018), 281; See Negri, 'Sustainable Development and Global Health: Positioning Health in the Post-2015 Development Agenda' in Fitzmaurice and Maljean-Dubois and Negri (eds), *Environmental Protection and Sustainable Development from Rio to Rio+20* (2014), 264-85.

[179] A/RES/70/1, *Transforming our world: the 2030 agenda for sustainable development* (2015), 21 October 2015, para. 16.

[180] See Chapter 1 of the Rio Declaration.

[181] E/C.12/2000/4, *Substantive Issues Arising In The Implementation Of The International Covenant On Economic, Social And Cultural Rights General Comment No. 14 (2000): The right to the highest attainable*

so evidently a precondition for life, the right to health is connected with the UDHR, in which the rights to health and an adequate standard of living are conjoined in Art. 25.[182] To describe health legally, the General Comment No 14 (2000) under para. 1 describes that '[h]ealth is a fundamental human right indispensable for the exercise of other human rights'. This does not constitute a definition but at least explains the fundamental legal gravity of this specific topic, embedded in the history of the UN and horizontally in treaties, conventions, declarations and vertically in interregional and national laws and regulations as well.

The subject of health as it is defined in the ICESCR unveils among others an exten- **73** sive socio-economic background. It is not surprising that the right to health as a nebulous concept[183] and at the same time existential condition has gained weight, importance, recognition and reflection in international law as it is separately embedded in many other treaties and conventions. The normativity of those treaties is accepted and it is necessary to mention at least the following: Art. 24 of the UN Convention on the Rights of the Child; Art. 16 of the African Charter on Human and Peoples' Rights or Art. 25[184] of the UN Convention on the Rights of Persons with Disabilities accompanied by the right to effective access to justice for persons with disabilities on an equal basis with others according to Art. 13 of this UN Convention.[185]

The right to health with somehow not in any case transparent contents is recognised **74** as an essential provision of human life and livelihood and it is expanded in the present to different fields such as Global Justice, Universal Health Coverage (UHC), environment, gender and Earth jurisprudence and includes new diseases and pandemics. A large number of international legal and policy regimes by traditional as well as new international organisations and a range of other actors are focussed on that broad topic.[186] Today health as an SDG[187] is related to major topics such as health inequity, health and environment,[188] health and gender, and for instance health and corruption (SDG 16). In particular, health inequity can be perceived as one of the main challenges at present, which is hard to achieve. Health and health services are closely related to SDG 3, SDG 5, SDG 16 and SDG 17.[189] From the perspective of the WHO, many people are prevented from enjoying a good quality of life and well-being because of barriers to fair and equal opportunities for health.[190]

The scope of the right to health enshrines further the functioning of public health **75** and health care facilities and services[191] and in particular the accessibility depends on four overlapping dimensions: non-discrimination, physical accessibility, economic

---

standard of health (article 12 of the International Covenant on Economic, Social and Cultural Rights), 11 August 2000, para. 2.

[182] Saul and Kinley and Mowbray, *The International Covenant on Economic, Social and Cultural Rights: Commentary, Cases, and Materials* (2014), 977.

[183] Tobin, *The Right to Health in International Law* (2012).

[184] See Weller, 'Art. 25 Health' in Bantekas and Stein and Anastasiou (eds), *The UN Convention on the Rights of Persons with Disabilities: A Commentary*, (2018), 705 ff.; Burci and Cassels, 'Health' in Katz Cogan and Hurd and Johnstone (eds), *The Oxford Handbook of International Organizations* (2016), 447 ff.

[185] See Flynn, 'Art. 13 Access to Justice', in Bantekas and Stein and Anastasiou, *The UN Convention on the Rights of Persons with Disabilities: A Commentary* (2018), 383.

[186] Burci and Cassels, 'Health' in Katz Cogan and Hurd and Johnstone (eds), *The Oxford Handbook of International Organizations* (2016), 447 ff.

[187] https://www.who.int/data/gho/data/themes/sustainable-development-goals/GHO/sustainable-development-goals.

[188] World Health Organization, *Guidelines for drinking-water quality* (2011).

[189] WHO, *Environmental health inequalities in Europe. Second assessment report* (2019), 5.

[190] WHO, *Environmental health inequalities in Europe. Second assessment report* (2019) 1.

[191] E/C.12/2000/4, *Substantive Issues Arising In The Implementation Of The International Covenant On Economic, Social And Cultural Rights General Comment No. 14 (2000): The right to the highest attainable*

accessibility (affordability), information accessibility. The equality of access to health care and health services has to be emphasised.[192] Beneath the task of the WHO in realising the right to health at the international, regional and country levels, the function of UNICEF in relation to the right to health of children is of particular importance.[193] Other important international organisations in- and outside the UN also play an active role for health such as UNDP, World Bank, ILO, IMF, OECD and WTO. This list must be extended to national interregional agencies and ministries in a wider sense and NGOs like the Red Cross and many others.[194]

76   Since '[g]lobal health jurisprudence helps us understand how law relates to the protection of public health nationally and globally',[195] the section of jurisdiction considered points unequivocally to the embedding and dependency of good health and well-being both in social systems and in ecological systems. Claims show that not exclusively individuals but also groups such as indigenous people pursue the right to health in manifold contexts against a state. Frequently, these lead to compensation and further measures which are intended to bring about balance. The jurisdiction reflects not solely a human-centric approach but also that its dependence on a cross-border status of ecological health and well-being. This contains sharing (of burdens, duties and benefits) and conserving of natural resources or at least doing no irrevocable harm to a humans' environment on the behalf of the well-being for humanity, also detached from a precise temporal frame, but rather with permanent validity.[196]

77   Contents and development of the jurisdiction correlate with various aspects of SDG 3 and provide some clear references to the concept of sustainable development but to date, including the more recent decisions, have not yet considered the SDGs in whole or SDG 3 as supporting pillars for judicial reasoning. In some cases, the concept of sustainability is weighed against the overarching goal of SDG 3. This could, however, be applied equally to the efficiency and proportionality principles of law as to a concrete development initiated by the SDGs. It is apparent, though, that the relationship of humans to their environment is gaining importance, specifically in international jurisdiction, which must be attributed to the right to health and other related rights, albeit to varying degrees. Yet there are distinct developments that consider evident principles of the SDGs and are likely to point the way forward in future health jurisdiction. In addition, this SDG is interconnected throughout the text of the SDGS with the aim for universal access to sexual and reproductive health[197] (SDG 5.6) connected to the Programme of Action of

---

standard of health (article 12 of the International Covenant on Economic, Social and Cultural Rights), 11 August 2000, 12 (a).

[192] E/C.12/2000/4, *Substantive Issues Arising In The Implementation Of The International Covenant On Economic, Social And Cultural Rights General Comment No. 14 (2000): The right to the highest attainable standard of health (article 12 of the International Covenant on Economic, Social and Cultural Rights),* 11 August 2000, 12(b).

[193] General Comment No. 63. (2000) CESCR, Committee On Economic, Social And Cultural Rights, Twenty-second session, Geneva, 25 April-12 May 2000.

[194] Burci and Cassels, 'Health' in Katz Cogan and Hurd and Johnstone (eds), *The Oxford Handbook of International Organizations* (2016), 450 f.

[195] Fidler, 'Global Health Jurisprudence: A Time of Reckoning' (2004) 96(2) *Georgetown LJ*, 393 (411).

[196] See also ILA, *Conference Report Sydney, Role Of International Law In Sustainable Natural Resource Management For Development* (2018), 31.

[197] A/RES/70/1, *Transforming our world: the 2030 agenda for sustainable development* (2015), 21 October 2015, SDG 5.6.

the International Conference on Population and Development and the Beijing Platform for Action and the outcome documents of their review conferences.[198]

Since SDG 3 can be acknowledged as one of the 'major' SDGs, the complexity **78** and interconnectedness to other SDGs makes it difficult to trace the core of its own specific normativity. First, SDG 3 is not addressing primarily an individual right to health or the (not existing because not grantable) right to be healthy[199] but much more the corresponding systemic counterpart of an existing, capable and throughout well-functioning health system, which is eligible to respond to the different targets. The systemic approach does not mean that the right to health is neglected, but as a right, it must meet with international state obligations where those individual rights can be satisfied by various instruments of the health system provided, maintained and offered on an acknowledged quality level on the basis of equity by the state.

In the light of the pandemic and its deteriorating impacts, it must be organised **79** to provide access to affordable essential medicines and vaccines, following the Doha Declaration on the TRIPS Agreement and Public Health (SDG 3.b), which affirms the right of developing countries to provide access to medicines for all.[200]

---

[198] See International Conference on Population and Development Programme of Action, https://www.unfpa.org/; *Beijing Declaration and Platform for Action*, The Fourth World Conference on Women, 4 to 15 September 1995; further information: The Beijing Platform for Action, https://beijing20.unwomen.org/en/.

[199] Bantekas and Oette, *International Human Rights Law and Practise* (2016), 428; E/C.12/2000/4, *Substantive Issues Arising In The Implementation Of The International Covenant On Economic, Social And Cultural Rights General Comment No. 14 (2000): The right to the highest attainable standard of health (article 12 of the International Covenant on Economic, Social and Cultural Rights)*, 11 August 2000, paras. 8 f.

[200] Sachs et al., *The Sustainable Development Goals and COVID-19. Sustainable Development Report 2020* (2020), 4 f.; Safitri et al., 'COVID-19 Impact on SDGs and the Fiscal Measures: Case of Indonesia' (2021) 18(6) *Int. J. Environ. Res. Public Health*, 2911; Shulla et al. 'Effects of COVID-19 on the Sustainable Development Goals (SDGs)' (2021) 2 *Discov Sustain*, 15; UN, *Shared Responsibility, Global Solidarity: Responding to the socio-economic impacts of COVID-19* (2020); UN, *The Sustainable Development Goals Report 2020* (2020); UN Women, *Will the Pandemic Derail Hard-Won Progress on Gender Equality?* (2020).

Goal 4
Ensure inclusive and equitable quality education and promote lifelong learning opportunities for all

4.1 By 2030, ensure that all girls and boys complete free, equitable and quality primary and secondary education leading to relevant and effective learning outcomes

4.2 By 2030, ensure that all girls and boys have access to quality early childhood development, care and pre-primary education so that they are ready for primary education

4.3 By 2030, ensure equal access for all women and men to affordable and quality technical, vocational and tertiary education, including university

4.4 By 2030, substantially increase the number of youth and adults who have relevant skills, including technical and vocational skills, for employment, decent jobs and entrepreneurship

4.5 By 2030, eliminate gender disparities in education and ensure equal access to all levels of education and vocational training for the vulnerable, including persons with disabilities, indigenous peoples and children in vulnerable situations

4.6 By 2030, ensure that all youth and a substantial proportion of adults, both men and women, achieve literacy and numeracy

4.7 By 2030, ensure that all learners acquire the knowledge and skills needed to promote sustainable development, including, among others, through education for sustainable development and sustainable lifestyles, human rights, gender equality, promotion of a culture of peace and non-violence, global citizenship and appreciation of cultural diversity and of culture's contribution to sustainable development

4.a Build and upgrade education facilities that are child, disability and gender sensitive and provide safe, non-violent, inclusive and effective learning environments for all

4.b By 2020, substantially expand globally the number of scholarships available to developing countries, in particular least developed countries, small island developing States and African countries, for enrolment in higher education, including vocational training and information and communications technology, technical, engineering and scientific programmes, in developed countries and other developing countries

4.c By 2030, substantially increase the supply of qualified teachers, including through international cooperation for teacher training in developing countries, especially least developed countries and small island developing States

Word Count related to 'Education' and 'Learning'
A/RES/70/1 - Transforming our world: the 2030 Agenda for Sustainable Development: 'Education': 22 'Learning': 7
Instruments mentioned in A/RES/70/1 in the section entitled: 'Sustainable Development Goals and targets':
A/RES/69/313 - Addis Ababa Action Agenda of the Third International Conference on Financing for Development adopted on 27 July 2015: 'Education': 12 'Learning': 3
A/RES/66/288 - The future we want (Rio +20 Declaration) adopted on 27 July 2012: 'Education': 33 'Learning': 6
A/RES/55/2 - United Nations Millennium Declaration adopted on 8 September 2000: 'Education': 1 and 'Learning': 0

Select Bibliography: Margaret F. Bello (ed), *Women Education and Development: A Continuous Revolution* (Society Publishing, Oakville 2019); Ellen Boeren, 'Understanding Sustainable Development Goal (SDG) 4 on "quality education" from micro, meso and macro perspectives' (2019) 65(2) *International Review of Education,* 277; Armin von Bogdandy and Matthias Goldmann, 'The Exercise of International Public Authority through National Policy Assessment – The OECD's PISA Policy as a Paradigm for a New International Standard Instrument' (2009) in *IILJ* (Working Paper 2009/2); Laurence Burgorgue-Larsen, 'Economic and Social Rights' in Laurence Burgorgue-Larsen and Amaya Úbeda de Torres (eds), *The Inter-American Court of Human Rights: Case Law and Commentary* (2012), 619; Marc Anthony Camilleri and Adriana Camilleri, 'The Sustainable Development Goal on Quality Education' (2020) in Samuel O. Idowu, René Schmidpeter and Liangrong Zu (eds), *The Future of the UN Sustainable Development Goals, CSR, Sustainability, Ethics & Governance* (Springer, Cham 2020), 1; Brendan Cantwell and Hamish Coate and Roger King (eds), *Handbook on the Politics of Higher Education* (Edward Elgar Publishing, Cheltenham/ Northampton 2018); CESCR, *General Comment No. 13: The Right to Education* (Art. 13) Adopted at the Twenty-first Session of the Committee on Economic, Social and Cultural Rights, on 8 December 1999, UN Doc. E/C.12/1999/10, para. 6(a), 7; Marie Claire Cordonier Segger and Alexandra Harrington, 'Environment and Sustainable Development', in Simon Chesterman, David M. Malone and Santiago Villalpando, *The Oxford Handbook of United Nations Treaties* (OUP, Oxford 2019), 226; Council of Europe/European Court of Human Rights, *Guide on Article 2 of Protocol No. 1 to the European Convention on Human Rights: Right to education* (2020); Timothy A. O. Endicott, 'Law and Language' in Jules Coleman and Scott Shapiro, *The Oxford Handbook on Jurisprudence & Philosophy of Law* (OUP, Oxford 2017), 935; Marselha Gonçalves Margerin, 'The Right to Education: A Multi-Faceted Strategy for Litigating before the Inter-American Commission on Human Rights' (2010), 17(4) *HRB*, 19; Leon Gordenker and Christer Jönsson, 'Evolution in Knowledge and Norms', in Thomas G. Weiss and Sam Daws, *The Oxford Handbook on the United Nations* (OUP, Oxford 2018), 113; Gerald Grace, 'Education: Commodity or public good?' (1989), 37(3) *British Journal of Educational Studies*; Stephen P. Heyneman and Bommi Lee, 'International organizations and the future of education assistance' (2016), 48 *International Journal of Educational Development*, 9-22; High Level Political Forum (HLPF) on Sustainable Development, Discussion on SDG 4 – Quality education, Background Note (HLPF, 2019); High Level Political Forum (HLPF), *Review of SDG implementation and interrelations among goals Discussion on SDG 4 – Quality education, Background Note* (UN, New York 2019); Incheon Declaration and Framework for Action for the Implementation of SDG 4, Ensure inclusive and equitable quality education and promote lifelong learning opportunities for all; Incheon Declaration, Towards inclusive and equitable quality education and lifelong learning for all, preamble; Independent Group of Scientists appointed by the Secretary-General, *Global Sustainable Development Report 2019: The Future is Now – Science for Achieving Sustainable Development* (United Nations, New York, 2019); Sarah Joseph and Melissa Castan (eds), *The International Covenant on Civil and Political Rights: Cases, Materials, and Commentary* (3rd ed, OUP, Oxford 2013); Helen Keller and Corina Heri, 'The Committees on Human Rights and economic, social and cultural rights' in Simon Chesterman and David

M. Malone and Santiago Villalpando (eds), *The Oxford Handbook of United Nations Treaties* (OUP, Oxford 2019), 423; David Landau and Rosalind Dixon, 'Constitutional Non-Transformation? Socioeconomic Rights beyond the Poor' in Katharine G. Young (ed), *The future of economic and social rights* (CUP, Cambridge 2019), 110; Krista Nadakavukaren Schefer (ed), *Poverty and the International Economic Legal System: Duties to the World's Poor* (CUP, Cambridge 2013); Martha C. Nussbaum (ed), *Creating Capabilities, The Human Development Approach* (The Belknap Press of Harvard University Press, Cambridge/Massachusetts/London 2011); M. J. Peterson, 'General Assembly' in Thomas G. Weiss and Sam Daws (eds), *The Oxford Handbook on the United Nations* (OUP, Oxford 2018), 127; Michael A. Rebell, 'The Right to Education in the American State Courts' in Katharine G. Young (ed), *The future of economic and social rights* (CUP, Cambridge 2019), 138; Judith Resnik, 'Courts and Economic and Social Rights/Courts as Economic and Social Rights' in Katharine G. Young (ed), *The future of economic and social rights* (CUP, Cambridge 2019), 260; Evan Rosevear and Ran Hirschl and Courtney Jung, 'Justiciable and Aspirational Economic and Social Rights in National Constitutions' (2019) in Katharine G. Young (ed), *The future of economic and social rights* (Cambridge University Press, Cambridge 2019), 64; Madoka Saito, 'Amartya Sen's Capability Approach to Education: a Critical Exploration' (2003), 37(1) *Journal of Philosophy of Education*, 17; William A. Schabas (ed), *The European Convention on Human Rights: A Commentary* (Oxford University Press, Oxford 2015), 995; Paul Schiff Berman, 'Jurisdictional Pluralism' in Stephen Allen, Daniel Costelloe, Malgosia Fitzmaurice, Paul Gragl and Edward Guntrip (eds), *The Oxford Handbook of Jurisdiction in International Law* (Oxford University Press, Oxford 2019), 121; Amartya Sen, 'Capability and Well-Being' in Martha C. Nussbaum and Amartya Sen (eds), *The Quality of Life* (Clarendon Press, Oxford 1993), 30; Amartya Sen (ed), *The Idea of Justice* (The Belknap Press of Harvard University Press, Cambridge/Massachusetts 2009); Cristina Sin, Orlanda Tavares, Sónia Cardoso and Maria João Rosa (eds), *European Higher Education and the Internal Market, Tensions Between European Policy and National Sovereignty* (Palgrave Macmillan, 2018); L. P. Tikly, 'The Future of Education for All as a Global Regime of Educational Governance' (2017), 61(1) *Comparative Education Review*, 1; UNESCO, *Right to Education, Handbook 2019* (UN, New York 2019); UNESCO, *Shaping the Future we want, UN Decade Of Education For Sustainable Development (2005-2014), Final Report* (UNESCO, Paris 2014); UNESCO, *Unpacking SDG 4 – Fragen und Antworten zur Bildungsagenda 2030* (UNESCO, Bonn 2017), 14; UNESCO, A. Leicht, J. Heiss and W. J. Byun (eds), *Issues and trends in Education for Sustainable Development* (UNESCO, Paris 2018); Elaine Unterhalter, 'The Many Meanings of Quality Education: Politics of Targets and Indicators in SDG4' (2019) 10 *Global Policy*, 40; Antoni Verger and S. L. Robertson, 'The GATS game changer: international trade regulation and the constitution of a global education marketplace', in, S. L. Robertson, K. Mundy, A. Verger and F. Menashy, *Public Private Partnerships in Education: New Actors and Modes of Governance in a Globalizing World* (Edward Elgar Publishing, Cheltenham 2012), 104; Antoni Verger and Xavier Bonal, 'Educational Services' in Thomas Cottier and Krista Nadakavukaren Schefer, *Elgar Encyclopedia of International Economic Law* (Edward Elgar Publishing, Cheltenham/Northampton 2017), 445; Johanna Weselek, Bildung für nachhaltige Entwicklung als Basis für die Sustainable Development Goals?' in Walter Leal Filho (eds), *Aktuelle Ansätze zur Umsetzung der UN-Nachhaltigkeitsziele* (Springer Spektrum, Berlin 2019), 135; Gareth Williams, 'Higher education: Public good or private commodity?' (2016), 14(1) *London Review of Education.*

A. Background and Origin of SDG 4

1   Seen as one of the entry points for transformation, quality education is a 'means of achieving key aspects of the global development agenda.'[1] Considering just a few facts on education in these days, it becomes apparent that children, particularly girls and multiple disadvantaged groups such as indigenous or displaced people are suffering most from missing or insufficient education. Millions of children and adults remain deprived of educational opportunities, many as a result of social, cultural and economic factors.[2] Over the last 65 years the global literacy rate increased by 4 percent every 5 years from 42 percent in 1960 to 86 percent in 2019 with the poorest countries in the world

---

[1] Independent Group of Scientists appointed by the Secretary-General, *Global Sustainable Development Report 2019: The Future is Now – Science for Achieving Sustainable Development* (2019), xxii.

[2] A/RES/69/313, *Addis Ababa Action Agenda of the Third International Conference on Financing for Development*, 17 August 2015, paras. 78, 111; UNESCO, *Shaping the Future we want, UN Decade Of Education For Sustainable Development (2005-2014), Final Report* (2014); https://www.un.org/sustainabledevelopment/education/.

still having large segments of illiterate population.[3] The average literacy rate affects the societal development, amongst others, relating to GDP and labour productivity growth in the long term as well as affecting social inequalities. The children and youth out of school amounted to 260 million worldwide in 2018. Due to the SARS-CoV-2 pandemic, these number increased to 1.6 billion children and youth and it is not foreseeable how long this situation will persist. At the same time, nearly 369 million children rely on school meals and now need to look for other sources for daily nutrition.[4] Despite all progress made, the world is currently not on track to meet 2030 education targets.[5]

Individual targets of SDG 4 already deviate significantly from the objectives defined,   **2** which could lead to an equally significant intensification of global, regional and national relations if this important lever for sustainable development were to be eliminated.[6]

Those data indicates that the question of a right to quality education, which is   **3** entailed by SDG 4, emerges equally as questions of non-discrimination, of equality of opportunities and universal access thereto. These build the basic prerequisites for safeguarding the enjoyment of a right to education. A 'full enjoyment of the right to education' is deemed 'as fundamental to achieving sustainable development'.[7] Since the right to education is grounded in the concept of human dignity[8] and was classified as an economic right, a social right and a cultural right, and in some instances also a civil and political right. It epitomises the 'indivisibility and interdependence of all human rights'[9] with a special focus on minorities and the particularly vulnerable group of girls and women.

I. History of the Right to Education

The realisation of a fundamental right to education is deeply rooted in Art. 26 Uni-   **4** versal Declaration of Human Rights (UDHR) which stipulates a free, at least elementary and fundamental education, to be available to all people for two purposes: the 'full development of the human personality and to the strengthening of respect for human rights'. In addition, education shall contribute to the empowerment of individuals, and thus to societal and most of all social cohesion as well as to the maintenance of peace. These aims are to be achieved to promote understanding, tolerance and friendship among all nations, racial or religious groups. The wording of this human right has been reproduced fully in Art. 13 of the ICESCR and has been further specified in the CESCR's largest General Comment No. 11 which reiterates the objectives of safeguarding and addressing the 'sense of dignity', giving opportunity to 'all persons to participate effectively in a free society' and in promoting mutual understanding with respect to ethnic, religious or national diversity. Above all, education should serve the purpose of enabling people to fully develop their personality which finds expression in setting up capabilities

---

[3] Roser and Ortiz-Ospina, 'Literacy' (2016), *OurWorldInData.org*.

[4] https://www.un.org/sustainabledevelopment/education/.

[5] UN, *The Sustainable Development Goals Report 2020* (2020), 32.

[6] For example, a projected 5-10 per cent or >10 per cent deviation for targets 4.2. Early childhood development; 4.1 Enrolment in secondary education; 4.3 Enrolment in tertiary education; 4.6 Literacy among youth and adults; See Independent Group of Scientists appointed by the Secretary-General, *Global Sustainable Development Report 2019: The Future is Now – Science for Achieving Sustainable Development* (2019), 10.

[7] https://en.unesco.org/themes/right-to-education.

[8] UNESCO, *Right to Education, Handbook 2019* (2019), 44.

[9] E/1992/23, *CESCR General Comment No. 11: Plans of Action for Primary Education (Art. 14)*, 10 May 1999, para. 2; A/CONF.157/23, *Vienna Declaration and Programme of Action*, 12 July 1993, para. 5.

for any individual to participate in (quality) education.[10] According to the General Comment No. 13, the ICESCR must be interpreted in particular against the background of non-discrimination[11] and equality[12] and thus, consequently encompasses the right to education.

The right to education has been included in numerous human rights instruments, such as the Convention on the Rights of the Child (CRC), the Convention on the Elimination of All Forms of Discrimination against Women (CEDAW), the Convention on the Rights of Persons with Disabilities (CRPD) as well as in the UN Declaration on the Rights of Indigenous People[13] (UNDRIP) (→ Goal 4 mn. 28 ff.).

5   As with any other human right, states have the obligation to respect, protect and fulfil the right to education. Referring to the ICESCR, this means to avoid measures that hamper the enjoyment of the right to education and prevent third parties from interfering, and to actively enable and assist individuals and communities to enjoy the right to education. The right to education thus imposes both negative and positive obligations which a state is obliged to implement at different velocities. In this context the so-called 4 A's, as an instrument to address inequality, have established which must be taken into account within the states' obligation to fulfil.

II. The 4 A's

6   *Availability* means to provide 'functioning educational institutions and programmes [...] in sufficient quantity within the jurisdiction of the State party.' The specific form to be taken depends on the individual context,[14] e.g. the degree of development of the state. In any case, these include the provision of 'buildings or other protection from the elements, sanitation facilities for both sexes, safe drinking water, trained teachers receiving domestically competitive salaries, teaching materials' (→ Goal 4 mn. 46 ff.).[15] Therefore, granting availability emphasises the right to education at first being a states' financial investment as well as being an indispensable means of realising other human rights. Moreover, an entanglement to the function of SDG 4 in the overall network of the SDGs becomes apparent (→ Goal 4 mn. 41 ff.).

---

[10] See for more information on the concept of creating equal capabilities: Sen, *The Idea of Justice* (2010); Sen, 'Capability and Well-Being' in Nussbaum and Sen (eds), *The Quality of Life* (1993); Nussbaum, *Creating Capabilities, The Human Development Approach* (2011); Aristotle, *Politics* (Book 3); Saito, 'Amartya Sen's Capability Approach to Education: a Critical Exploration' (2003), 37(1) *Journal of Philosophy of Education*.

[11] Art. 2(2) ICESCR: 'will be exercised without discrimination of any kind'.

[12] The CESCR mentions specifically the UNESCO Convention against Discrimination in Education, the relevant provisions of the Convention on the Elimination of All Forms of Discrimination against Women, the International Convention on the Elimination of All Forms of Racial Discrimination, the Convention on the Rights of the Child and the ILO Indigenous and Tribal Peoples Convention, 1989 (Convention No. 169), UNESCO Convention against Discrimination in Education.

See E/C.12/1999/10, *Implementation Of The International Covenant On Economic, Social And Cultural Rights General Comment No. 13 (Twenty-first session, 1999) The right to education (article 13 of the Covenant)*, 8 December 1999, paras. 31-4.

[13] Despite being partly controversially discussed, a connection can be drawn at least via ILO Convention 169, Concerning Indigenous and Tribal Peoples in Independent Countries.

[14] See for more information on building and using the context principle: Endicott, 'Law and Language' in Coleman and Shapiro, *The Oxford Handbook on Jurisprudence & Philosophy of Law* (2004), 935-86.

[15] E/C.12/1999/10, *Implementation Of The International Covenant On Economic, Social And Cultural Rights General Comment No. 13 (Twenty-first session, 1999) The right to education (article 13 of the Covenant)*, 8 December 1999, paras. 6(a), 7.

Accessibility means that education in its diverse forms of institutions and programmes   7
shall be (a) physically and (b) economically accessible to everyone in a (c) non-discriminatory manner within the 'jurisdiction of a State party' which demands for integrated
legal and regulatory frameworks.[16] As a consequence, all, in particular the most vulnerable groups, in law and fact, must be enabled to receive education which is in the best
interests of the student

> within safe physical reach, either by attendance at some reasonably convenient geographic location
> (e.g. a neighbourhood school) or via modern technology (e.g. access to a "distance learning" pro-
> gramme); [...] affordable to all [...] whereas primary education shall be available "free to all", States
> parties are required to progressively introduce free secondary and higher education;[17]

Acceptability expresses in a minimum educational standard that must be followed. It   8
includes the acceptable form to be relevant relating to the substance of education, the
curricula and the teaching methods, in a culturally appropriate manner and of good
quality. This is valid for students and in specific cases for parents or legal guardians ($\rightarrow$
Goal 4 mn. 54).

Adaptability requires to provide an adaptive education respecting new and emerging   9
needs which societies or communities have to face due to their internal development
and condition or to external factors to being able to respond adequately 'to the needs of
students within their diverse social and cultural settings.'[18]

III. UN History of Quality Education

In addition to its human rights embedding, the emergence of (quality) education   10
as an entitlement of every human being is rooted as an ever growing basis of values
and normative foundation of sustainable development within the UN. The provision
of basic learning needs,[19] the necessity and complexity of education was anchored as a
cross-referential theme in Agenda 21. The Agenda focused on reorienting education towards sustainable development, increasing public awareness, and promoting training.[20]
Subsequently, education was addressed in the Dakar Framework for Action with a
greater focus on the welfare role of the state in creating transparent and accountable[21]
education systems that are supplemented and supported by bold and comprehensive

---

[16] A/HRC/44/39, *Right to education: impact of the SARS-COV-2 crisis on the right to education; concerns,
challenges and opportunities, Report of the Special Rapporteur on the right to education*, 15 June 2020, para.
17(e).

[17] E/C.12/1999/10, *Implementation Of The International Covenant On Economic, Social And Cultural
Rights General Comment No. 13 (Twenty-first session, 1999) The right to education (article 13 of the
Covenant)*, 8 December 1999, para. 6(b).

[18] E/C.12/1999/10, *Implementation Of The International Covenant On Economic, Social And Cultural
Rights General Comment No. 13 (Twenty-first session, 1999) The right to education (article 13 of the
Covenant)*, 8 December 1999, para. 6(d); see also: Abidjan Principles, overarching principle 1, para. 14(d).

[19] *World Declaration on Education for All*, 5- 9 March 1990, Art. 1.

[20] A/CONF.151/26/Rev.1 (Vol. I and Vol. I/Corr.1, Vol. II, Vol. III and Vol. III/Corr.1), UN Conference
on Environment & Development Rio de Janeiro, *Agenda 21*, 3-14 June 1992, Ch. 36.

[21] According to *Dakar Framework for Action Education for All: Meeting our Collective Commitments*,
26-28 April 2000, Expanded Commentary, paras. 9, 55 f., this meant to:

> develop or strengthen existing national plans of action [...] be integrated into a wider poverty reduc-
> tion and development framework, [...] developed through more transparent and democratic processes,
> involving stakeholders, especially peoples' representatives, community leaders, parents, learners, non-gov-
> ernmental organizations (NGOs) and civil society. [...] buttressed by a management information system
> that benefits from both new technologies and community participation.

educational partnerships at all levels of society.[22] Education was already incorporated in Millennium Development Goal (MDG) 2. Children everywhere, boys and girls alike, should be empowered to complete a full course of primary schooling. This goal was measured against three indicators: 2.1 Net enrolment ratio in primary education; 2.2 Proportion of pupils starting grade 1 who reach last grade of primary; and 2.3 Literacy rate of 15-24 year-olds, women and men. Against the more comprehensive, stakeholder-oriented approach of SDG 4 with its seven targets, three means of implementation and twelve indicators, these illustrate that MDG 2 was much more limited in scope, not only due to its focus on developing countries and LDCs. Quality education received further consideration when the Johannesburg Plan of Implementation (JPOI) in 2002 was adopted during the World Summit on Sustainable Development (WSSD). With the JPOI, MDG 2 and overarching goals on the framing of education were reaffirmed: to achieve universal primary education by 2015; to eliminate gender disparity in primary and secondary education by 2005 and at all levels of education by 2015 as goal of the Dakar Framework for Action on Education for All. Therefore, it was intended to establish 'a wide range of formal and non-formal continuing educational opportunities, including volunteer community service programmes to end illiteracy and emphasize the importance of lifelong learning.'[23]

11   Through further efforts of the UN, such as the UNESCO's launch of the Decade of Education for Sustainable Development (ESD) from 2005 to 2014, the inclusion and reinforcement as key to shaping values that are supportive of sustainable development, and in consolidating sustainable societies in 'The future we want',[24] the Global Action Programme (GAP) on ESD was proclaimed in 2014 and followed by the World Conference on Education for Sustainable Development and the Muscat Agreement. The latter was adopted at the Global Education For All Meeting (GEM) in 2014. The draft of the SDGs embraced ESD in the proposed targets for the post-2015 agenda.[25] In the wake of the UN Conference on Sustainable Development (Rio+20), the Higher Education Sustainability Initiative (HESI) was created as a partnership of several sponsor UN entities[26] aiming at galvanising commitments from higher education institutions to teach and encourage research on sustainable development, greening campuses and support local sustainability efforts.[27] An additional focus has been placed by the Incheon Declaration on the elimination of discrimination in access to education. The Declaration adopted the exact wording of SDG 4 while its own endeavours were focused on 'access, equity and inclusion, quality and learning outcomes, within a lifelong learning approach.'[28]

12   SDG 4 emerged from extensive consultations between 2012 and 2015, in which the vision of quality education that is free, inclusive and focused on equality in particular conflicted with a narrower vision that pleaded for a focus on well-defined learning outcomes for young people. While the proponents of the discourse on rights and inclusion prevailed relating to the text of the goal and its targets, they had less access to the process of developing indicators. On the one hand this was due to the institutional history asso-

---

[22] *Dakar Framework for Action Education for All: Meeting our Collective Commitments,* 26-28 April 2000, Expanded Commentary, para. 12.

[23] UN, *Plan of Implementation of the World Summit on Sustainable Development* (2002), Sect. X, paras. 123 f.

[24] United Nations Decade of Education for Sustainable Development; A/RES/66/288, *The future we want,* 11 September 2012, paras. 229-35.

[25] https://sustainabledevelopment.un.org/topics/education.

[26] UNESCO, UN-DESA, UNEP, Global Compact, and UNU.

[27] https://sustainabledevelopment.un.org/topics/education.

[28] *Education 2030, Incheon Declaration, Towards inclusive and equitable quality education and lifelong learning for all* (2015), preamble, para. 5.

ciated with the development of education metrics, and on the other hand a result of the global movement Education for All (EFA) that had engaged in securing the 'text on the targets, but did not maintain this for the debate on indicators.'[29] As can be read from the SDGs examined before, SDG 4 thus holds high tensions and contradictions between its original vision and the outcome in the targets and indicators which mainly refer to differing economic, socio-cultural and political perspectives of stakeholders during its negotiating process.[30] And while the negotiations relating to its specific targets were mainly driven by the EFA which intended to stimulate the adoption of a broad and comprehensive SDG in education, the negotiations relating to indicators were not. In addition, disputes arose regarding the different values of the negotiating state representatives, organisations and other stakeholders, as well as discourses around equity and inclusion.[31] The later negotiation process was mainly driven between the EFA, its steering committee, the Open Working Group (OWG) and the Sustainable Development Solutions Network (SDSN), each of which had different ideas about dimension and scope of an education goal for the SDGs (→ Goal 4 mn. 14 ff.).[32] The different currents were first united during the World Education Forum in May 2015, and were concluded in November 2015 when the Incheon Framework for Action for the Incheon Declaration was adopted. This development not only enabled inclusion and equalities to be the key features of SDG 4 but also to actively promote a focus on the narrower view on learning outcomes which now can be read from the indicators that measure SDG 4.[33]

B. Scope and Dimensions of SDG 4

SDG 4 encompasses seven targets, three means of implementation and twelve indi-   **13**
cators.[34] Against its background and origin, the more exact meaning and scope of SDG 4 unfolds by considering legally relevant definitions and further legally significant references.

I. Legal Characteristics

Politically referred to as 'public good',[35] education is a fundamental human right[36]   **14**
which is connected to several (state) responsibilities with different degrees. Providing

---

[29] Unterhalter, 'The Many Meanings of Quality Education: Politics of Targets and Indicators in SDG4' (2019) 10 *Global Policy*, 40.

[30] See for a deeper analysis: Tikly, 'The Future of Education for All as a Global Regime of Educational Governance' (2017) 61(1) *Comparative Education Review*, 1-36.

[31] Unterhalter, 'The Many Meanings of Quality Education: Politics of Targets and Indicators in SDG4' (2019) 10 *Global Policy*, 40.

[32] Unterhalter, 'The Many Meanings of Quality Education: Politics of Targets and Indicators in SDG4' (2019) 10 *Global Policy*, 41.

[33] Unterhalter, 'The Many Meanings of Quality Education: Politics of Targets and Indicators in SDG4' (2019) 10 *Global Policy*, 42.

[34] A/RES/71/313, *Work of the Statistical Commission pertaining to the 2030 Agenda for Sustainable Development*, 10 July 2017, Annex: *Global indicator framework for the Sustainable Development Goals and targets of the 2030 Agenda for Sustainable Development*; see for a current overview: https://unstats.un.org/s dgs/indicators/indicators-list/.

[35] SDG-Education 2030 Steering Committee, *2017 HLPF submission* (2017), 2; see for more information: Williams, 'Higher education: Public good or private commodity?' (2016) 14(1) *London Review of Education*; Grace, 'Education: Commodity or public good?' (1989) 37(3) *British Journal of Educational Studies*.

[36] SDG-Education 2030 Steering Committee, *2017 HLPF submission* (2017), 2.

quality education in a sustainable sense is key for sustainable development and decisive for the implementation of the Global Agenda 2030.[37] SDG 4 focuses on lifelong learning in every stage of an individuals' life and covers early childhood development (SDG 4.2), primary and secondary (SDG 4.1) or technical, vocational, tertiary education and access to higher education (SDG 4.3) which is characterised by an inclusive approach. Since quality education shall be made accessible to everyone, SDG 4 enshrines a non-discriminatory approach with a specific focus on children, gender equality and the protection of minorities[38] since these are the groups most affected if the right to education is curtailed.[39]

15   Its origin and close connection to the human right to education underlines the importance of SDG 4 within the SDG agenda. As a so-called standard social right that can be found in almost 82 per cent of global constitutions,[40] it can be classified on the social level of the concept of sustainable development which serves the purpose to improve an individuals' decent life by supporting autonomy and well-being.[41] It is therefore seen as an accomplishment of humankind and, as fundamental, albeit limited human right[42] in international law.[43]

16   Since education is the source for any further development of a human being, the right to education is closely related to the question of 'equality, equity, but also efficiency'.[44] Thus, education for all shall be reached by granting access to education and to respective institutions, and also through the equal empowerment of men and women and boys and girls.[45] It constitutes an entitlement for every human being but should not be a privilege or a subject to politics. Albeit in fact it often is, SDG 4 includes a non-discriminatory approach of education for children, young people, adults and older people of either gender (→ Goal 4 mn. 36 ff.).[46]

17   It is noteworthy that the right to education can be derived both as a self-standing right and as an accessory right. Though this right is primarily linked to the learner as the bearer of this right, it is the contextualisation within its legal basis that is decisive. In similar circumstances, different bearers of rights can be identified, if, besides the original right to education, another right such as the right to religious self-determination, is also applied and shows an educationally relevant connection. As a result, different partici-

---

[37] https://www.undp.org/content/undp/en/home/sustainable-development-goals/goal-4-quality-education.html.

[38] This refers to indigenous people, children and youth in (armed) conflict, refugees, migrants, people suffering from forced displacement and people with disabilities including multiple deprived groups such as females within one or more of these groups and could foreseeably be extended in its significance to people affected by climate change.

[39] A/HRC/44/39, *Right to education: impact of the SARS-COV-2 crisis on the right to education; concerns, challenges and opportunities, Report of the Special Rapporteur on the right to education*, 15 June 2020, para. 13.

[40] Rosevear and Hirschl and Jung, 'Justiciable and Aspirational Economic and Social Rights in National Constitutions' in Young (ed), *The future of economic and social rights* (2019), 64.

[41] Resnik, 'Courts and Economic and Social Rights/Courts as Economic and Social Rights' in Young (ed), *The future of economic and social rights* (2019), 260.

[42] Art. 26 Universal Declaration on Human Rights; Art. 13 International Covenant on Economic, Social and Cultural Rights.

[43] UNESCO, *Unpacking Sustainable Development Goal 4 – Education 2030* (2016), 8.

[44] A/HRC/44/39, *Right to education: impact of the SARS-COV-2 crisis on the right to education; concerns, challenges and opportunities, Report of the Special Rapporteur on the right to education*, 15 June 2020, para. 15.

[45] UNESCO, *Unpacking Sustainable Development Goal 4 – Education 2030* (2016), 8.

[46] A/RES/70/1, *Transforming our world: the 2030 Agenda for Sustainable Development*, 21 October 2015, SDG 4.1 – SDG 4.7 'girls and boys, women and men, youth and adults, all learners, persons with disabilities, indigenous peoples and children in vulnerable situations'; see also UNESCO, *Right to Education Handbook* (2019), 28.

pants can each be bearer of the right, for example, both parents and their children ($\rightarrow$ Goal 4 mn. 53 ff.). Additionally, different levels of exercising the right to education could result insofar as different participants are obliged to exert this right such as states, public or private educational institutions or further private and economic actors.[47] This represents a difficult and confusing legal situation that is hardly comprehensible and must be evaluated in contextual points of reference.

It basically entails various obligations, such as the provision or supply of educational facilities, teaching materials, qualified teaching staff and methods, scholarships as well as various channels for accessing them.[48] These lead to a variety of other stakeholders who are connected to the right to education by means of other human rights[49] and thus extend it in their spheres of reference. **18**

II. Elementary Definitions

1. Education

Education is understood as a 'process of facilitating learning or the acquisition of knowledge, skills, values, beliefs and habits. Quality education specifically entails issues such as appropriate skills development, gender parity, provision of relevant school infrastructure, equipment, educational materials and resources, scholarships or teaching force.'[50] **19**

Education must be measured against the aims of education set up with General Comment No. 1 on Art. 29 CRC[51]: **20**

– the holistic development of the full potential of the child (29(1) (a)),
– including development of respect for human rights (29(1) (b)),
– an enhanced sense of identity and affiliation (29(1) (c)),
– and his or her socialization and interaction with others (29(1) (d))
– and with the environment (29(1) (e))

As a qualitative dimension, Comment No. 1 stresses the inherent dignity of a child to be recognised and that education must 'be child-centred, child-friendly and empowering'. Education should foster 'life skills, to strengthen the child's capacity to enjoy the full range of human rights and to promote a culture which is infused by appropriate human rights values to be and act with self-esteem and self-confidence. In this context, education has to be understood as a provision of life experiences and learning processes which enable 'to develop their personalities, talents and abilities and to live a full and satisfying life within society' which is confirmed by the 2015 Incheon Declaration and extended. Skills, values and attitudes should be developed that 'enable citizens to lead healthy and fulfilled lives, make informed decisions, and respond to local and global challenges.'[52] Education thus works as a catalyst for development and health intervention in its own right. **21**

---

[47] Nadakavukaren Schefer, *Poverty and the International Economic Legal System: Duties to the World's Poor* (2013), 384.

[48] Face-to-face education, remote learning and further.

[49] For example, through the staff of the various educational institutions, such as teachers, lecturers, administrative staff, maintenance staff, cafeteria staff, and socially and psychologically trained personnel could establish a link with the right to decent work.

[50] https://en.unesco.org/themes/education/sdgs/material/04.

[51] CRC/GC/2001/1, Convention on the Rights of the Child Annex IX General Comment No. 1 (2001) Article 29 (1): The Aims Of Education, 17 April 2001.

[52] https://en.unesco.org/themes/education-health-and-well-being.

22   In addition, ESD is explicitly recognised in the SDGs as part of SDG 4.7, together with Global Citizenship Education (GCED), which UNESCO promotes as a complementary approach. ESD enables all individuals to contribute to achieving the SDGs by equipping them with the knowledge and competencies they need to understand the SDGs and to engage as informed citizens in bringing about the necessary transformation.[53]

2. Equitable Education

23   SDG 4.1 and SDG 4.5 call for the elimination of disparities to ensure equal access to all levels of education for all children and vulnerable. This means that indicators across all education targets should be disaggregated by sex, location, wealth and disability status (as well as other personal and household characteristics, where relevant) in order to identify and address the barriers that so many groups continue to face.[54]

3. Inclusive Education

24   Inclusive education refers to securing and guaranteeing the right of all children to access, presence, participation and success in their local regular school. Inclusive education calls upon neighbourhood schools to build their capacity to eliminate barriers to access, presence, participation, and achievement for all learners to be able to provide excellent educational experiences and outcomes for all children and young people.[55] Inclusive education is secured through principles and actions of fairness, justice and equity which are to be understood in a comprehensible manner to promote understanding, tolerance and friendship among all nations, racial or religious groups (→ Goal 4 mn. 4). It is a political aspiration and an educational methodology[56] which applies to all children and youths, including those with disabilities[57] or of indigenous background.[58]

4. Literacy, Numeracy and Skills

25   Literacy means 'understanding, evaluating, using and engaging with written texts to participate in society, to achieve one's goals and to develop one's knowledge and potential.' According to the Programme for the International Assessment of Adult Competencies (PIACC) framework, which, as a programme for evaluating adult skills, 'measures the key cognitive and workplace skills needed for individuals to participate in society and for economies to prosper'.[59] Three cognitive strategies show if a full understanding of a text is achieved: (1) Access and identify tasks require the reader to locate information in a text; (2) Integrate and interpret tasks require the reader to understand the relationship between parts of the text; (3) Evaluate and reflect tasks call on the reader to draw on information, understandings, and knowledge that is external to the text.[60]

---

[53] UNESCO, *Education for Sustainable Development Goals* (2017), 8.

[54] UNESCO Institute for Statistics (UIS), *Sustainable Development Data Digest, Laying The Foundation To Measure Sustainable Development Goal 4* (2016), 56.

[55] UNESCO/GEMR, *Defining the scope of inclusive education* (2018), 8.

[56] UNESCO/GEMR, *Defining the scope of inclusive education* (2018), 2.

[57] A/RES/61/106, *Convention on the Rights of Persons with Disabilities* (CRPD), 24 January 2007, Art. 24.

[58] A/RES/61/295, *United Nations Declaration on the Rights of Indigenous Peoples* (UNDRIP), 2 October 2007, Art. 14, 15, 17, 21; UNESCO/GEMR, *Defining the scope of inclusive education* (2018), 9.

[59] https://www.oecd.org/skills/piaac/.

[60] UNESCO, *Functional literacy and numeracy* (2017), 11, 16; for deeper insights, see: OECD, *PIAAC Literacy: A Conceptual Framework* (2009), 7 ff., OECD's PIAAC assessment is by far the world's most visi-

Numeracy means 'the ability to access, use, interpret, and communicate mathematical **26** information and ideas, in order to engage in and manage the mathematical demands of a range of situations in adult life. Numerate behavior involves managing a situation or solving a problem in a real context, by responding to mathematical content/information/ideas represented in multiple ways.'[61] Numeracy highly correlates with the rate of literacy of an individual.[62]

Skills of learners mean work-specific skills and developing high-level cognitive and **27** non-cognitive, transferable skills such as problem solving, critical thinking, creativity, teamwork, communication skills and conflict resolution, which can be used across a range of occupational fields.[63]

III. Legal Foundations of the Right to Education

The legal foundations that determine the scope of SDG 4 reflect to a large extent the **28** fundamental human rights treaties and conventions already mentioned and, in more detail, the respective comments on them (→ Goal 4 mn. 4 f.). An entry point can be assumed to lie in Article 26 UDHR,[64] which directly establishes the right to education and already implies an inclusive and equitable approach.

1. Universal Declaration of Human Rights (UDHR)

Article 26:

1. Everyone has the right to education. Education shall be free, at least in the elementary and fundamental stages. Elementary education shall be compulsory. Technical and professional education shall be made generally available and higher education shall be equally accessible to all on the basis of merit.
2. Education shall be directed to the full development of the human personality and to the strengthening of respect for human rights and fundamental freedoms. It shall promote understanding, tolerance and friendship among all nations, racial or religious groups, and shall further the activities of the United Nations for the maintenance of peace.
3. Parents have a prior right to choose the kind of education that shall be given to their children.

Access to education is regarded as a basic human right for all children and young **29** people. This is strengthened through other human rights instruments such as the Convention on the Rights of the Child (CRC).[65] Like the Covenant, the Convention on the Rights of the Child does not contain a derogation clause. The Committee on the Rights of the Child has made clear that restrictions imposed on children's rights in order to protect public health 'must be imposed only when necessary, be proportionate and kept to an absolute minimum'. Additionally, any such restrictions should reflect the principle of the best interests of the child set out in Art. 3(1) CRC which includes restrictions on the child's right to education enshrined in Art. 28 CRC.[66]

---

ble international assessment of adult skills, one that yields demonstrably valid, reliable and comparable estimates of literacy and numeracy skill and for the key outcome and determinants co-variates needed by policy makers.

[61] UNESCO, *Functional literacy and numeracy* (2017), 23; further reading: OECD, *PIAAC Numeracy: A Conceptual Framework* (2009), 21.

[62] UNESCO, *Functional literacy and numeracy* (2017), 24.

[63] UNESCO, *Unpacking Sustainable Development Goal 4 – Education 2030* (2016), 12.

[64] A/RES/217A, *Universal Declaration of Human Rights,* 10 December 1948, Art. 26.

[65] A/RES/44/25, *Convention on the Rights of the Child,* 20 November 1989, Art. 28 f.

[66] A/HRC/44/39, *Right to education: impact of the SARS-COV-2 crisis on the right to education; concerns, challenges and opportunities, Report of the Special Rapporteur on the right to education,* 15 June 2020, para. 13; Committee on the Rights of the Child, *SARS-CoV-2 Statement* (7 April 2020).

2. Human Rights Instruments

30   Other instruments have been struck to protect this basic human right of access to and participation in quality and inclusive education for vulnerable population groups: the Convention against Discrimination in Education – CADE (Treaty Series, vol. 429, No. I-6193, 1960)[67]; International Convention on the Elimination of All Forms of Racial Discrimination – CERD (General Assembly Resolution 2106 (XX), Art. 5e(v), 1965); the International Covenant on Economic, Social and Cultural Rights – ICESCR (General Assembly Resolution 2200A (XXI), Art. 13, 1966)[68]; the Convention on the Elimination of All Forms of Discrimination against Women – CEDAW (General Assembly Resolution 34/180, Art. 10, 1979)[69]; the Convention on the Rights of the Child – CRC (Article 28 (right to education) and Art. 29(1) (aims for education in relation to children), 1989)[70]; the International Convention on the Protection of the Rights of All Migrant Workers and Members of their Families – CMW (General Assembly Resolution 45/158, Art. 30, 1990); and the Convention on the Rights of Persons with Disabilities – CRPD (General Assembly Resolution 61/106, Art. 24, 2006).

31   These international agreements are respectively monitored through UN committees[71] which audit various structural, process and outcome indicators and identify legislation, public policies, budgets and infringements that are relevant to the covered (economic, social and cultural) rights.[72] States' anti-discrimination legislation and regulations also act to protect the right of all children and young people to an inclusive and quality education. Non-Governmental Organisations (NGOs), Disabled People's Organisations (DPOs) and communities actively support these internationally agreed rights at the grass roots.[73]

32   The more recent Incheon Declaration and Framework for Action for the implementation of SDG 4 emphasises the meaning of SDG 4 to follow a 'humanistic vision of education and development based on human rights and dignity; social justice; inclusion; protection; cultural, linguistic and ethnic diversity; and shared responsibility and accountability' (→ Goal 4 mn. 11 f.). This declaration, which is to be evaluated merely in political terms, refers to education as a public good, a fundamental human right and a basis for realising other rights. It bears duties to the civil society, teachers and educators, the private sector, communities, families, youth and children and specifically to the state as a standard and norm setting organ.[74]

---

[67] *UNESCO Convention against Discrimination in Education* (adopted 14 December 1960, entered into force 14 December 1960) 429 UNTS 93 (CADE).

[68] *International Covenant on Economic, Social and Cultural Rights* (adopted 16 December 1966, entered into force 3 January 1976) 993 UNTS 3 (ICESCR).

[69] *Convention on the Elimination of All Forms of Discrimination Against Women* (adopted 18 December 1979, entered into force 3 September 1981) 1249 UNTS 13 (CEDAW).

[70] *Convention on the Rights of the Child* (adopted 20 November 1989, entered into force 2 September 1990) 1577 UNTS 3 (CRC); related: CRC/GC/2001/1, Convention on the Rights of the Child Annex IX General Comment No. 1 (2001) Article 29 (1): The Aims Of Education, 17 April 2001.

[71] For example: The *Committee on the Rights of the Child*, a body of 18 independent experts monitor the implementation of the CRC by its State parties, and of two Optional Protocols to the Convention, on involvement of children in armed conflict (OPAC) and on sale of children, child prostitution and child pornography (OPSC); https://www.ohchr.org/en/hrbodies/crc/pages/crcintro.aspx; The *Committee on the Rights* The UNESCO Executive Board monitors the implementation of CADE.

[72] UNOHCHR, *Human Rights Indicators, A Guide to Measurement and Implementation* (2012); UNOHCHR, *Manual on Human Rights Monitoring, Monitoring economic, social and cultural rights* (2011).

[73] UNESCO/GEMR, *Defining the scope of inclusive education* (2018), 9.

[74] *Incheon Declaration and Framework for Action for the Implementation of SDG 4* (2015), 28.

On the regional level of the EU, the right to education which inextricably forms the   33
European understanding of SDG 4[75] can be read from the Treaty on the Functioning of
the European Union (TFEU):

Art. 165

The Union shall contribute to the development of quality education by encouraging cooperation between Member States and, if necessary, by supporting and supplementing their action, while fully respecting the responsibility of the Member States for the content of teaching and the organisation of education systems and their cultural and linguistic diversity […].

The Charter of Fundamental Rights of the European Union also manifests this right: 34

Art. 14 Right to education

1. Everyone has the right to education and to have access to vocational and continuing training.
2. This right includes the possibility to receive free compulsory education.
3. The freedom to found educational establishments with due respect for democratic principles and the right of parents to ensure the education and teaching of their children in conformity with their religious, philosophical and pedagogical convictions shall be respected, in accordance with the national laws governing the exercise of such freedom and right.

It must be noticed that the competence for education, its design and provision of ac-   35
cess does not belong to the EU but to its Member States respectively, albeit this strict
delimitation has been partially blurred by European case law (→ Goal 4 mn. 60 ff.).

IV. Non-Discrimination, Equality and Equity

SDG 4 covers formal, non-formal and informal education and is of crucial impor-   36
tance for social development (→ Goal 4 mn. 19 ff.). The right to education formulated in
the ICESCR is almost mirrored in SDG 4 and unlike their predecessors, the MDGs,
which focused on universal primary school enrollment, it intends to make education a
catalyst for a broader societal change toward sustainable development. Similarly, primary and secondary as well as vocational education should be made accessible to all without discrimination. A right to higher education, on the other hand, is either reserved for
the capacities of the individual or is to be stimulated and encouraged primarily in 'least
developed countries, small island developing States and African countries'. Since education is the source for any further development of a human being, SDG 4 and the right to
education are closely related to the question of equality. The equivalence of education is
thus, a significant factor in the abolition of inequalities and 'a central component of social cohesion'. Moreover, lacking education can result in social exclusion and diminish
citizen and social life participation and as a result impede social cohesion within societies (→ Goal 1 mn. 10 f., 14 f., Goal 2 mn. 61).[76]

According to its anchoring in human rights, education empowers people to lift them-   37
selves out of poverty and participate fully in society[77] through the means of lifelong

---

[75] The Global Agenda 2030 and the SDGs are fully acknowledged within the EU and build a key driver for all European policy frameworks and for their internal and external actions.

[76] Copeland and Daly, 'Varieties of poverty reduction: Inserting the poverty and social exclusion target into Europe 2020' (2012) 22 *Journal of European Social Policy,* 273–287; Resnik, 'Courts and Economic and Social Rights/Courts as Economic and Social Rights' in Young (ed), *The future of economic and social rights* (2019), 282; Camilleri and Camilleri, 'The Sustainable Development Goal on Quality Education' in Idowu and Schmidpeter and Zu (eds) *The Future of the UN Sustainable Development Goals, CSR, Sustainability, Ethics & Governance* (2020), 3.

[77] E/C.12/1999/10, *Implementation Of The International Covenant On Economic, Social And Cultural Rights General Comment No. 13 (Twenty-first session, 1999) The right to education (article 13 of the Covenant),* 8 December 1999, para. 1.

learning and universality[78] inclusiveness and (gender) equality and shall be reached by granting access to education and to respective institutions and through the equal empowerment of women and men, girls and boys (→ Goal 1 mn. 60 ff., Goal 2 mn. 55 ff., → Goal 5 mn. 46).[79] Although it is conceptualised as a ubiquitous approach, it mainly links its outcomes with 'individuals' in the form of a bottom-up developed approach. The well-educated individuals are 'carriers' which spread the SDGs values and measures and consequently implement a sustainable and non-discriminating life. The emerging opportunities shall mitigate socio-economic inequalities between individuals and subsequently between states and result in socio-economic self-determination which illustrates a link to international development law (IDL).

38   Inequality and the access to education is triggered adversely by the global societal issues of increasing global migration and forced displacement. SDG 4 in itself is deemed an agenda for empowerment giving social orientation and accelerating the well-being of peoples which in turn also works as a key driver in an economic sense.[80] Vulnerable groups such as children and youth refugees,[81] internally displaced children, stateless children and children whose right to education has been depleted by war and insecurity in many cases 'suffer from multiple deprivations'.[82] The alignment with SDG 5 'Gender Equality' and SDG 10 'Reduced Inequalities' makes it necessary to consider their human rights backgrounds as well when evaluating the meaning of SDG 4[83] even though the human right to education is a limited one.[84]

V. International Organisations related to education

39   Various agencies of the UN work on contributing to quality education in manifold contexts. UN Agencies currently responsible are as follows:

– UN Educational, Scientific and Cultural Organization
– UN Children's Fund
– UN Development Programme
– Global Education First Initiative
– UN Population Fund: Comprehensive sexuality education
– UN Office of the Secretary General's Envoy on Youth
– UNSDGF
– the UNESCO-convened SDG Education 2030 Steering Committee
– UNICEF
– UNFPA

---

[78] 'understood as a universality of principles (human rights), universality of reach (focus on equity and inclusion), and universality of country coverage', UNESCO, UNESCO, *Unpacking Sustainable Development Goal 4 – Education 2030* (2016), 10.

[79] UNESCO, *Unpacking Sustainable Development Goal 4 – Education 2030* (2016), 8.

[80] HLPF on Sustainable Development, Discussion on SDG 4 – Quality education, Background Note, 3, https://sustainabledevelopment.un.org/content/documents/23669BN_SDG4.pdf; Camilleri and Camilleri, 'The Sustainable Development Goal on Quality Education' in Idowu and Schmidpeter and Zu (eds), *The Future of the UN Sustainable Development Goals. CSR, Sustainability, Ethics & Governance* (2020), 3 f.

[81] A/RES/69/313, *Addis Ababa Action Agenda of the Third International Conference on Financing for Development*, 27 July 2015, para. 78; A/73/262, *Report of the Special Rapporteur on the right to education*, Note by the Secretary-General, 27 July 2018.

[82] HLPF, *Review of SDG implementation and interrelations among goals Discussion on SDG 4 – Quality education, Background Note*, 2.

[83] *Incheon Declaration and Framework for Action for the Implementation of SDG 4* (2015), 13.

[84] Further information on the issue of inequality pertaining to education: Milanovic, *Global Inequality, A new Approach for the Age of Globalization* (2016).

– UN Woman
– EFA (Education for All)
– UN-sub-organisations like the Special Rapporteur on the right to education

Further agencies that support education globally outside the UN are the OECD, **40** the ILO and the financiers on an international level such as the World Bank, African Development Bank, Asia Development Bank, as well as donators on the national level which are, amongst others, USAID, JICA (Japan), DFID (UK), CIDA (Canada).[85]

C. Interdependences of SDG 4

The SARS-CoV-2 pandemic has led to school, kindergarten and day-care closures **41** worldwide and therefore tightened social and economic consequences and inequalities (SDG 10.2, SDG 10.3) far beyond their educational role and period of the closures (→ Goal 10 mn. 67 ff.).[86] School and other learning and care institutions highly contribute to the safety, health, service (SDG 3.7, SDG 3.8) and nutrition (SDG 2.1, SDG 2.2) of children and youth.[87]

Since education contributes to the governance and security of the individual,[88] SDG 4 **42** is connected to every other SDG, but shares its strongest interconnection to SDG 5, SDG 8, SDG 10, SDG 12 and SDG 13.

Inequalities in education remain a big challenge which most often occur among girls **43** who live in rural and poor communities (SDG 1.2, SDG 1.4). They frequently face multiple disadvantages through gender discrimination and violence, sexual and reproductive health issues, including teenage pregnancy and poverty, which bar them from enrolling in learning institutions.[89] Ensuring that all girls have access to free, equitable and quality education (SDG 4.1, SDG 4.2, SDG 4.3) helps to end all forms of discrimination and harmful practices against girls and women everywhere (SDG 5.1, SDG 5.3).

Education and learning empowers women (SDG 4.1, SDG 4.3) and girls to participate **44** effectively in society and in decision-making in political, economic and public life and promotes equal opportunities and the realisation of their potential (SDG 5.5, SDG 16.9, SDG 16.b).[90]

Rural and indigenous people, children living in conflict, orphans, migrants, nomads, **45** children with disabilities, persons living with HIV/AIDS and other linguistic and cultural minorities are frequently excluded from educational systems (SDG 4.1, SDG 4.2, SDG 4.6) which diminishes their ability to obtain decent jobs (SDG 8.5).

---

[85] Heyneman and Lee, 'International organizations and the future of education assistance' (2016) 48 *International Journal of Educational Development*, 9-22.

[86] https://en.unseco.org/covid19/educationresponse/consequences.

[87] See Martens and Ellmers and Pokorny on behalf of Global Policy Watch, *COVID-19 and the SDGs, The impact of the coronavirus pandemic on the global sustainability agenda* (2020), 3; https://www.wfp.org/news/futures-370-million-children-jeopardy-school-closures-deprive-them-school-meals-unicef-and-wfp.

[88] UNGA Open Working Group on Sustainable Development Goals, *Compendium of TST Issues Briefs* (2014), 58.

[89] UNGA Open Working Group on Sustainable Development Goals, *Compendium of TST Issues Briefs* (2014), 59.

[90] UNGA Open Working Group on Sustainable Development Goals, *Compendium of TST Issues Briefs* (2014), 59.

D. Jurisprudential Significance of SDG 4

46   Access to education, with its many facets, contributes to social development. Consequently, '[q]uality, pertinent, and culturally sensitive education' is essential for the maintenance and security of societies. Minorities such as indigenous people, displaced persons and refugees, disabled people and to a great extent girls and women are particularly affected by restrictions on access to education or to its discriminatory exertion.[91] These groups are particularly often subject to structural discrimination 'inherited from the legacies of colonization, slavery, and inequality; language and cultural barriers; and geographic isolation'.[92] However, stereotyped (gender) roles and other harmful practices[93] also significantly restrict this right. And in times of writing this book, SARS-CoV-2 interrupted the traditional way of learning by governmental measures of quarantine and others taken to prevent further outbreaks. Without further evidence, it is likely that the accumulation of knowledge in the ongoing steam of education is being disrupted, affecting many young people, in particular those in dire need of education in the vague prospect of a better life, such as migrants, women and young girls. Presumably, the SARS-CoV-2 pandemic will exacerbate more deeply rooted societal inequalities and partially counteract opportunities for a decent life, well-being, good health through education, and as a consequence, decent work and income.

47   The right to education can be found to some extent 'in 81 percent of constitutions being justiciable in 59 percent'.[94] However, the 'extent to which individuals can claim legal protection of their right to education depends upon which treaties their State government has ratified, resulting in a legal obligation to respect, protect, and fulfil the rights contained in those treaties. This includes obligations to be fulfilled immediately, as well as those to be progressively realised through States 'taking steps toward' fully realising the right to education, and thereby using the maximum of available resources.[95]

I. Jurisdiction on Vision and Objectives

48   The origin of SDG 4 illustrates the vision and objective for SDG 4 that deviates from the targets and indicators (→ Goal 4 mn. 48 ff.). This is evident at various levels, including the jurisdiction, which in different ways does justice to the right or even restricts its implementation.

---

[91] UNESCO, *Right to Education, Handbook 2019* (2019), 81-103.

[92] Gonçalves Margerin, *The Right to Education: A Multi-Faceted Strategy for Litigating before the Inter-American Commission on Human Rights* (2010) 17(4) *HRB*, 19 (20).

[93] Further detrimental factors undermining girls' and women's capabilities exist such as harmful gender stereotypes and wrongful gender stereotyping, child marriage, lack of inclusive and quality learning environments and inadequate and unsafe education infrastructure, including sanitation, poverty and gender-based violence against women and girls; More information on this issue: UNESCO, *Right to Education, Handbook 2019* (2019); Tembon and Fort, *Girls' Education in the 21st Century Gender Equality, Empowerment, and Economic Growth* (2008); Bello, *Women Education and Development: A Continuous Revolution* (2019).

[94] Rosevear et al., 'Judicial and Aspirational Rights' in Young (ed.). *The future of economic and social rights* (2019), 51.

[95] To be interpreted in the light of CESCR General Comment No. 3: *The Nature of States Parties' Obligations (Art. 2, Para. 1, of the Covenant)*, Contained in E/1991/23, *Committee on Economic, Social and Cultural Rights : report on the 5th session*, 26 November-14 December 1990, which sets the effective action a state is obliged to take to realise economic, social and cultural right to be a matter of priority; see also https://ijrcenter.org/thematic-research-guides/education/.

1. International Jurisdiction

Different Human Rights Courts addressed the right to education in varying contexts 49 with a high yield, allowing indications of a first current to be derived, helping identify the essence of SDG 4.

The IACtHR decided in several cases that the provision of education is included with- 50 in the measures of protection that every child has, according to Art. 19 of the American Convention on Human Rights (ACHR) which can emanate positive obligations which originate from the human right to life. The IACtHR considered specific state obligations in particular in cases regarding children and multiple deprived groups such as children in custody, indigenous children, and migrant children. The right to life is interpreted to be linked not only to the preservation of dignified living conditions, but also to the creation of circumstances that allow access to benefit such a life. Thus, it interprets the right to life more broadly as a right to a dignified existence.[96] In *Villagrán Morales et al. v Guatemala*[97], the IACtHR held that the non-renewal of a pregnant girl's school enrolment was not permissible and that states have the obligation to guarantee 'conditions of life with dignity, of segurity *(sic!)* and integrity of the human person.' The court also stated that '[t]he project of life is ineluctably linked to freedom, as the right of each person to choose her own destiny'.[98]

Thus, the IACtHR considers this state obligation to be part of customary internation- 51 al law, which was further clarified in *Juvenile Reeducation Institute v Paraguay*.[99] Education, vocational training programmes and other alternatives to institutional care were declared as being part of human well-being which must be offered proportionally to the circumstances.[100] An infringement should lead to a duty of full restitution (*restitutio in integrum*),[101] albeit realising this is not possible in many cases. For this reason, the IACtHR ordered fair pecuniary and non-pecuniary compensation which consisted of the states' obligation to vocational assistance and a special education program for former inmates. In clarifying that it assumes the right to education to be part of the right to life,[102] this judicial evaluation reveals an obvious link to SDG 3. With reference to the ILO Convention No. 169, the Court declared economic, social, and cultural rights as being inseparable to a dignified life a part of which is to maintain and develop one's spiritual and cultural life. Notably, the IACtHR states this to be valid for the multiple

---

[96] The IACtHR, on the basis inter alia of the IACHR, assesses socio-economic rights much more broadly than the right to education as enshrined in the Additional Protocol to the American Convention on Human Rights in the Area of Economic, Social and Cultural Rights (Protocol of San Salvador) of 1988 (entered into force in 1999); see Heyns and Killander, 'Universality and the Growth of Regional Systems' in Shelton (eds), *The Oxford Handbook of International Human Rights Law*, 678.

[97] *Villagrán Morales et al. v. Guatemala*, Merits, Judgment, 19 November 1999, IACtHR, (ser. C) No. 63, 78.

[98] *Villagrán Morales et al. v. Guatemala*, Merits, Judgment, 19 November 1999, IACtHR, (ser C) No. 63, 78, paras. 8, 144; see also: IACtHR, Report No. 33/02 (Friendly Settlement), *Mónica Carabantes Galleguillos*, Petition 12, 046, Chile, 12 March 2002.

[99] *Juvenile Reeducation Institute v. Paraguay*, Preliminary Objections, Merits, Reparations, and Costs, Judgment, 2 September 2004, Inter-Am Ct. H.R. (ser. C) No. 112, 134.3–134.4, para. 258.

[100] *Juvenile Reeducation Institute v. Paraguay*, Preliminary Objections, Merits, Reparations, and Costs, Judgment, 2 September 2004, Inter-Am Ct. H.R. (ser. C) No. 112, 134.3–134.4, para. 230.

[101] *Juvenile Reeducation Institute v. Paraguay*, Preliminary Objections, Merits, Reparations, and Costs, Judgment, 2 September 2004, Inter-Am Ct. H.R. (ser. C) No. 112, 134.3–134.4, para. 259; see also Case of the *Gómez Paquiyauri Brothers*, para. 187; *Case of the 19 Tradesmen*, para. 219; *Case of Molina Theissen*, para. 39; *Case of Bulacio*, para. 72; *Case of Juan Humberto Sánchez*, para. 149; *Case of Las Palmeras*, Reparations, para. 38.

[102] *Yakye Axa Indigenous Community v. Paraguay*, Merits, Reparations and Costs, Judgment, 17 June 2005, IACtHR (ser. C) No. 125, 50.1, 50.10; *Sawhoyamaxa Indigenous Community v. Paraguay*, Merits, Reparations and Costs, Judgment, 29 March 2006, IACtHR (ser. C) No. 146, 73(1), paras. e), h).

deprived group of children without having been registered and therefore lacking legitimisation to being granted access to school.[103]

52   It is remarkable that the IACtHR interprets the right to life very broadly and in accordance with the UDHR and the UNDRIP as a 'right to life with dignity' specifically when children or indigenous communities are involved. Drawing on various human rights instruments, but mostly not on the San Salvador Protocol, which includes the right to education,[104] it consolidates matters relating to health, education, housing, food, and access to drinking water in comprehensive assessments and sheds light on the interdependencies between SDG 4 and the SDG 1, SDG 2, SDG SDG 6 (→ Goal 4 mn. 41 ff.). In doing so, it corresponds to the intention of the SDGs and the Global Agenda 2030 as interwoven, holistic approaches.[105]

53   The ECtHR acknowledges the ECHR as the 'constitutional instrument of European public order'[106] in the field of human rights. Since the right to education is included in the first Protocol to the ECHR, the ECtHR is competent to receive 'applications from any person, non-governmental organisation or group of individuals claiming to be the victim of a violation', Art. 34 ECHR, by any of the 47 States parties, insofar a state has ratified both the ECHR and this Protocol. A number of cases were given due comment by the ECtHR to aspects such as discrimination, school fees, language of instruction, and educational freedom. The right to education according to the ECHR includes both the individual right of each person to non-discriminatory[107] access to adequate education and, as a complementary addition, the right of parents to influence (to some extent) the education of their children.[108] However, the ECHR does not include a positive obligation to create opportunities for education. Rather, it obliges each signatory state to refrain from any detrimental effect on this right[109] and thus emphasises the duty of non-interference.

54   It is notable that the ECtHR places minorities in particular under special protection. In *DH and others v Czech Republic*,[110] the Court ruled that exclusion or segregation of children of the same ethnic background from regular school life and their enrolment in special schools hamper the exchange and ability to participate in a diversified daily life, and thus must be considered discriminatory. While a strong emphasis on the protection

---

[103] *Girls Yean and Bosico v. Dominican Republic*, Preliminary Objections, Merits, Reparations, and Costs, Judgment, 8 September 2005, IACtHR (ser. C) No. 130, 85(a)(1), 25, para. 115; Further reading on Education for migrants, refugees and other displaced people: UNESCO, *Global Education Monitoring Report* (2018), Background paper prepared for the 2019 Global Education Monitoring Report, Migration, displacement and education: Building bridges, not walls, The status of the right to education of migrants: International legal framework, remaining barriers at national level and good examples of states' implementation.

[104] To date the Protocol has been ratified by only fifteen of the twenty-three States which have ratified the American Convention and recognized the jurisdiction of the Court; Burgorgue-Larsen, 'Economic and Social Rights' in Burgorgue-Larsen and Úbeda de Torres (eds), *The Inter-American Court of Human Rights: Case Law and Commentary* (2012), 613 (619).

[105] Burgorgue-Larsen, 'Economic and Social Rights' in Burgorgue-Larsen and Úbeda de Torres (eds), *The Inter-American Court of Human Rights: Case Law and Commentary* (2012), 613 (621).

[106] *Bosphorus Hava Yolları Turizm ve Ticaret Anonim Şirketi v. Ireland* [GC], Judgment, 30 June 2005, ECHR 45036/98, para.156.

[107] *Case of Leyla Şahin v. Turkey*, Judgment, 10 November 2005, ECtHR 44774/98.

[108] In particular with regard to religious and philosophical convictions and is moreover considered *lex specialis* to Art. 9 of the Convention (Freedom of thought, conscience and religion); Council of Europe/European Court of Human Rights, *Guide on Article 2 of Protocol No. 1, Right to education* (2020), 5.

[109] Schabas, *The European Convention on Human Rights: A Commentary* (2015), 995.

[110] *DH and others v Czech Republic* (2008) 47 EHRR 3; see also PCIJ, *Minority Schools in Albania*, Advisory Opinion (1935), Ser. A/B, No. 64.

of minorities exists, this does not occur mandatorily. In 2017, the ECtHR ruled[111] that Swiss authorities acted in line with the ECHR when it prevented two Muslim parents from removing their daughters from mixed swimming classes as mandated by the school curriculum. It was stressed that inclusive schooling played a special role in the process of social integration, especially where children of foreign origin were concerned, and took precedence over the parents' religious or philosophical convictions.[112] It corresponded to its previous case law and also places the State's duty of non-interference under the principle of proportionality.[113] With reference to the First Protocol to the European Convention, the ECtHR also applied this principle to the added right of parents to influence their child's education where the state refused to grant a possibility to exempt from a compulsory class on Christianity.[114] A violation of the added parental right[115] was assumed by the Court due to only allowing partial-exemptions which placed too high burden on parents to expose personal beliefs and to remain informed of each lesson's topic to determine if it contradicts their beliefs.[116] The jurisdiction considered and by taking into account the principle of proportionality shows that the right to education in the context of the ECHR is not an absolute right, but is rather subject to implied limitations. However, it is interpreted much more broadly than its wording for without it would not fulfil its purpose and aim[117] and, in the opinion of the ECtHR, also includes secondary and tertiary education, which was extended in individual cases to courses for professional accreditation.[118] The ECtHR also indicated that university education is deemed a human right.[119]

A categorical exclusion of national provisions allowing for corporal punishment in schools was decided in in *Campbell and Cosans v UK* where the ECtHR held that the state had failed to respect parents' philosophical convictions.[120] Similarly, the Committee on the Rights of the Child has since required States parties to take measures toward prohibiting and eliminating corporal punishment and other cruel or degrading forms of punishment of children.[121]

55

---

[111] *Osmanoğlu and Kocabaş v Switzerland*, 10 January 2017, ECtHR 29086/12.

[112] UNESCO, *Right to Education, Handbook 2019* (2019), 273; Council of Europe, *Guide on Article 2 of Protocol No. 1 to the European Convention on Human Rights: Right to education* (2018).

[113] The principle of proportionality, an established custom within the EU, is respected by the ECtHR and means that limitations to a right are permissible if these are foreseeable ('provided by law'), pursue a legitimate purpose and bear a reasonable link of proportionality between the means applied and the aim to be achieved; see e.g. *Case of Leyla Şahin v. Turkey*, Judgment, 10 November 2005, ECtHR 44774/98.

[114] *Case of Folgerø and Others v. Norway*, Judgment, 29 June 2007, ECtHR 15472/02, para. 53.

[115] The right to education can partly to be understood as an accessory right on different levels of application, the classification of which is to be derived from the relevant legal basis, e.g. if it is applied on the basis of a non-discrimination or equality clause; see Nadakavukaren Schefer, *Poverty and the International Economic Legal System: Duties to the World's Poor* (2013), 384.

[116] *Case of Folgerø and Others v. Norway*, Judgment, 29 June 2007, ECtHR 15472/02, para. 85-102.

[117] *Timishev v. Russia*, Judgment, 13 December 2005, ECHR No. 55762/00 and 55974/00, para. 64; see Schabas, *The European Convention on Human Rights: A Commentary* (2015), 995.

[118] *Ponomaryovi v. Bulgaria*, Judgment, 21 June 2011, ECHR No. 5335/05, para. 49; *Case of Leyla Şahin v. Turkey*, Judgment, 10 November 2005, ECtHR 44774/98, paras. 134-42; *Mürsel Eren v. Turkey*, Judgment, 7 February 2006, ECtHR 60856/00, paras. 40 f.; *Tarantino and Others v. Italy*, Judgment, 2 April 2013, ECHR 25851/09, 29284/09 and 64090/09, para. 43; *Altinay v. Turkey*, Judgment, 9 July 2013, ECHR 37222/04; *Kök v. Turkey*, 19 October 2006, ECtHR 1855/02, paras. 56-60.

[119] *Tarantino and Others v. Italy*, 2 April 2013, ECHR 25851/09, 29284/09, and 64090/09, Partly Dissenting Opinion of Judge Pinto de Albuquerque.

[120] *Campbell and Cosans v. The United Kingdom*, Judgment, 25 February 1982, ECtHR, Series A no. 48, 25, 4 EHRR 293, paras. 39-41.

[121] See CRC, CRC/C/GC/8, *General Comment No. 8, The Right of the Child to Protection from Corporal Punishment and other Cruel or Degrading Forms of Punishment*, 2 March 2007, para. 2.

56   Emphasis is also placed on non-discriminatory access to education. Unequal treatment of different groups is permissible, insofar unequal treatment is *de facto* eliminated.[122] This can be read in a case where French-speaking parents wanted their children to be educated in French while attending school in multilingual Belgium. The ECtHR did not find a positive obligation for school institutions to follow language instructions or preferences of parents in primary and secondary education when an official national language is provided.[123]

57   The European Committee of Social Rights (ECSR) put emphasis on legislation or policies alone not to be sufficient to fulfil the requirements of availability, accessibility, acceptability and adaptability to realise the economic, social and cultural right of education (→ Goal 4 mn. 6 ff.).[124] Within a reasonable timeframe, the State must show measurable progress and ensure financing consistent with the maximum use of its available resources. The Committee also highlighted that financial constraints cannot be used to justify a denial of access to education for children with intellectual disabilities. Access in this specific context also encompasses inclusion within the mainstream educational system[125] and complements the concept of inclusive schooling (→ Goal 4 mn. 24).

58   The right to education in extensive contexts has been related to peace (→ Intro mn. 212). The African Commission on Human Rights (ACHR), which stresses the universality and indivisibility of all human rights by treating economic, social and cultural rights in the same way as civil and political rights, raised complaints in crisis-ridden Zaïre (now DR Congo). After several years of the states' inaction and disregard (1989-1995) for the complaints made to governments about numerous human rights violations, the Commission ruled that, among other serious human rights violations, the closure of universities and secondary schools violated the right to education[126] included in Art. 17 of the African Convention.

59   Also before the ACHR, the *Case of the Talibés children*, one of merely three decisions of the Commission to date, gained importance when this decision clarified that state responsibility does not only include the creation of a legally relevant framework, but that the circumstances must also be created that lead to the protection of fundamental rights, i.e. that these can be enforced effectively and resiliently (→ Goal 4 mn. 28 ff.).[127] In this case, which concerned more than 100,000 children, the African Commission examined the practice of juvenile offenders which is deeply embedded in Senegalese culture.[128] The children and youths forced to beg several hours a day on a daily basis by teaching personnel of private Qur'an schools under the threat of corporal punishment are deprived of their right to education, among other identified human rights violations. Moreover, the responsibility of the state was extended to private schools and thus to

---

[122] *Case Of Oršuš and Others v. Croatia*, Judgement, 16 March 2010 ECtHR 15766/03: Access to education for Roma children, para. 148; *Case "relating to certain aspects of the laws on the use of languages in education in Belgium"* (merits), 23 July 1968, 30-32, paras. 3-5, Series A no. 6, para. 10; *Thlimmenos v. Greece* [GC], Judgement, 6 April 2000, ECHR 34369/97, para. 44; and *Stec and Others v. the United Kingdom* [GC], 12 April 2006, ECHR 65731/01, para 51.

[123] *Case relating to certain aspects of the laws on the use of languages in education in Belgium' by Belgium*, Judgment, 23 July 1968, ECtHR, Series A no. 6, paras. 6-7 (I. B. 3).

[124] *International Association Autism-Europe (IAAE) v. France*, ESCR No. 13/2002.

[125] *Mental Disability Advocacy Center (MDAC) v. Bulgaria*, ESCR No. 41/2007; *International Centre for the Legal Protection of Human Rights (INTERIGHTS) v. Croatia*, ESCR No. 45/2007.

[126] African Commission, Free Legal Assistance Group, Lawyers' Committee for Human Rights, Union Interafricaine des Droits de l'Homme, *Les Témoins de Jehovah v Zaïre* 25/89-47/90-56/91-100/93, para. 48.

[127] African Commission, *Talibés children*, Decision No 003/Com/001/2012.

[128] https://www.escr-net.org/caselaw/2015/centre-human-rights-university-pretoria-and-rencontre-afri caine-pour-defense-droits, more information on this case: Perdigao, 'Begging for a better life': the plight of Talibés in Senegal' (2010) 9 *Comments on Africa*.

third parties (such as individuals and institutions). Even though Senegal had created suitable legal frameworks beforehand, their enforceability in fact was noted as insufficient but being mandatory to fulfil the right to education.

2. European Union Jurisdiction

In the EU, very few cases concerning the quality of education are brought before its **60** judicial review mechanisms. Existing jurisdiction revealing the right to education within the EU, however, does not inevitably indicate that specific contents of SDG 4 or the concept of sustainable development are taken into account which is due to the fact that competence in educational matters almost entirely belongs to the individual member states of the EU.[129] The EU in this context is confined to a supportive role, at best a coordinating or capacity-building one, Art. 6(e) TFEU. Nevertheless, high-quality education in the EU is covered by policy frameworks[130] and supported by cooperation and funding.[131] The respective policy approaches are to be measured against the EU's sustainability commitments, and given its acknowledgement,[132] against the SDGs themselves. European aspirations and political guidelines on education clearly reflect the structure of SDG 4.[133]

Within the relevant jurisdiction, the EU is primarily concerned with the question **61** of equal treatment in a European sense, and thus mainly deals with the accessibility to (quality) education.[134] In the request for the preliminary ruling *Bragança Linares Verruga*, financial aid for higher education studies had been declared to concede to a student son over 18 years of age of a self-employed man not having the Belgian nationality. The ECJ declared a linkage to residing conditions to be of inappropriate and indirect discriminating nature, since it is mainly foreign nationals being non-residents and has repeatedly confirmed this in its case law.[135]

---

[129] As an exception, however, the EU enjoys full competence to legislate in the sensitive area of education/diploma recognition for regulated and liberal professions, such as medicine, law and architecture, Art. 53 TFEU, but is not competent to legislate in the academic recognition of all other higher education.

[130] Planned or already implemented EU policies on sustainable education, amongst many others: *Resolution on further developing the European Education Area to support future-oriented education and training systems*, 24.10.2019, draft doc. 13298/19; *Proposal for a COUNCIL RECOMMENDATION on High Quality Early Childhood Education and Care Systems*, 24.4.2019, 9246/18 + ADD 1 -COM(2018) 271 final; *Proposal for a Council Recommendation on a comprehensive approach to the teaching and learning of languages*, 17.4.2019, draft doc. 9229/18 + ADD 1; *Communication from the Commission to the European Parliament, the European Council, the Council, the European Economic and Social Committee and the Committee of the Regions, A New European Agenda for Culture*, 22.5.2018COM(2018) 267final; *Communication From The Commission To The European Parliament, The European Council, The Council, The European Economic And Social Committee And The Committee Of The Regions, Engaging, Connecting and Empowering young people: a new EU Youth Strategy*, 22.5.2018, COM(2018) 269final; Council conclusions on moving towards a vision of a European Education Area, 23.5.2018, doc. 9012/18.

[131] See e.g. ET 2020 framework, Education and Training monitor or funding instruments such as the Erasmus+ programme and the European Structural and Investment Funds.

[132] See instead of many: European Commission, COM(2016) 739 final.

[133] See e.g. *Proposal for a Council Recommendation on High Quality Early Childhood Education and Care Systems*, 24.4.2019, 9246/18 + ADD 1 -COM(2018) 271 final, para 1.

[134] ECJ, C-238/15, 14.12.2016, *Bragança Linares Verruga and Others*, EU:C:2016:949.

[135] ECJ, C-238/15, 14.12.2016, *Bragança Linares Verruga and Others*, EU:C:2016:949, para. 43; see also: ECJ, Joined Cases C-401/15 to C-403/15, 15.12.2016, *Noémie Depesme and Others v Ministre de l'Enseignement supérieur et de la Recherche*, ECLI:EU:C:2016:955; ECJ, C-20/12, 20.06.2013, *Giersch and Others*, EU:C:2013:411, paras. 44, 53, 56, 68; ECJ, C-542/09, 14.06.2012, *Commission v Netherlands*, EU:C:2012:346, para. 38; and ECJ, C-40/05, 11.01.2007, *Kaj Lyyski v Umeå universitet*, ECLI:EU:C:2007:10, paras. 35 f., 38.

62   Under the auspices of the European Area of Higher Education and the provoking Bologna Process,[136] the ECJ has established a far-reaching jurisdiction pertaining to several educational rights such as diploma recognition, the equal-to-nationals schooling of workers and their children, teacher mobility, and the ability of having equal access to studying in another member state than one's own. Although the EU having mostly been excluded during the Bologna Process, the fulminant decisions of the ECJ on these issues are deemed a single European Higher Education System *mutatis mutandis* as an indisputable part of the EU single market and its fundamental freedoms. The ECJ in its decisions found close ties between higher education, the labour market and the fundamental freedom of free movement of people[137] and mainly decided in favour of promoting the circulation of students and their access to higher education.[138]

63   This far-reaching evaluation became apparent, for example, in the landmark decision *Donato Casagrande v. City of Munich*, in which the ECJ found a connection to transfer powers to the (at that time) Community in the area of educational and training policy although 'it is not as such included in the spheres which the Treaty has entrusted to the Community institutions'.[139] This was only limited by the identification of the legal basis for the adoption of the Erasmus programme. Merely reference to Art. 167 (at that time Art. 128 EC) under the title 'Preservation and Promotion of Culture' did not constitute a legally sufficient basis, so that, in addition, the EU competences in this area were opened up by referring to the competence supplement clause Art. 352 TFEU (at that time Art. 235 EC).[140] The distinct influence of the EJC judgments in the domestic educational sector can also be seen in *Commission v. Austria*. This decision confirmed once again that the EU has competence in the area of vocational training and thus also for higher and university education, which constitutes a part of it.[141] The ECJ moreover underlined the principle of equal treatment, which 'prohibits not only overt discrimination based on nationality but also all covert forms of discrimination which, by applying other distinguishing criteria, lead in fact to the same result' with the result that Member States of the EU were obliged to acknowledge diplomas of any EU citizen as equivalent to fully enable students to enjoy their fundamental freedom of free movement.

---

[136] This process aimed to reform the structures of higher education systems in a convergent way and thus increase the global competitiveness of the European system of higher education. It evolved in the Bologna Declaration of 1999 (pledged by 29 countries) the content of which substantially overlapped with well-established Community policy fields at that time such as student mobility and diploma recognition. Fundamental principles had already been acknowledged before in the Bologna Magna Charta Universitatum of 1988. The Bologna Process was critically reflected upon as regarding education almost exclusively as an economic commodity; see Confederation of EU Rectors' Conferences and the Association of European Universities (CRE), *The Bologna Declaration on the European space for higher education: an explanation*, 1-10; *Joint declaration of the European Ministers of Education Convened in Bologna on the 19th of June 1999*; further information: Garben, 'The Bologna Process and the Lisbon Strategy: Commercialisation of Higher Education through the Back Door?' (2010) 6(6) *CYELP*, 209.

[137] ECJ, Case C-76/05, 11.09.2007, *Schwarz v. Finanzamt Bergisch Gladbach*, ECLI:EU:C:2007:492, paras. 86-90 and the case-law cited therein.

[138] Sin et al. (eds), *European Higher Education and the Internal Market, Tensions Between European Policy and National Sovereignty* (2018), 5.

[139] ECJ, Case-9/74, 3.7.1974, *Donato Casagrande v. Landeshauptstadt München*, ECLI:EU:C:1974:74, ECR 773, para. 12.

[140] ECJ, Case-242/87, 30.5.1989, *Commission v. Council (Erasmus)*, ECLI:EU:C:1989:217.

[141] ECJ, Case C-147/03, 7.7.2005, *Commission v. Austria* [2005] ECR I-5969, ECLI:EU:C:2005:427, para. 32 f. and the case-law cited therein.

3. Arbitration Proceedings

In international arbitration proceedings the subject of education can hardly be 64
found. In some cases, education received by individuals is used as a reference point
for analysing the centre of a person's family, social, and political life in conducting
nationality tests[142] or the creation of education facilities is considered to be an 'active'
contribution of an existing contract.[143] But there is no focus or definition yet of what
constitutes sustainable or qualitative education. However, since education and education
services move away from a mainly local offer to an almost ubiquitous service, it is
conceivable that trade or investment arbitration proceedings will in future deal with
(quality) educational matters[144] or with individual targets of SDG 4, insofar as education
is perceived as a marketable commodity or investment good. This seems plausible e.g.
(to some extent) in private schools and universities linking new non-governmental
funding streams or dealing with its market liberalisation or commercialising and privatising[145] and developing new (electronic) education services markets.[146] Examples of
such procedures are particularly conceivable when trade and investment agreements
deal with (qualified) education and thus exceed competences that would otherwise
be the responsibility of individual states.[147] The importance of education, however, is
recognised by the WTO, since it is seen as a key driver of innovation and decent work.[148]

4. Domestic Jurisdiction

'At national level, judicial mechanisms and access to justice play a crucial role in 65
enforcing the right to education and ensuring legal accountability.'[149] In addition, it is
obvious that strong influencing factors of (quality) education is bound to and mainly affects the most vulnerable groups of girls and women and indigenous people. Specifically
detrimental are gender induced discrimination and the constrained access to education,
e.g. due to lacking legal identity which reduces the overall mobility of people and their
access to basic government social services such as health, education and employment.
Moreover, language barriers and conflict-related displacement prevent females and indigenous people from participating in educational services.[150]

---

[142] PCA Case No 2016-17, In the Matter of an Arbitration under the Dominican Republic-Central
America-United States Free Trade Agreement, Signed On August 5, 2004 (The "Dr-Cafta") and the
UNCITRAL Arbitration Rules (as adopted in 2013), *Michael Ballantine and Lisa Ballantine and the
Dominican Republic*, 3.9.2019 Final Award; PCA Case No 2018-56, In the matter of an arbitration under
the UNCITRAL arbitration rules (2013) *Carrizosa Gelzis v The Republic of Colombia*, para. 444.

[143] PCA Case No 2016-39/Aa641, Arbitration under the Rules of Arbitration of the United Nations
Commission on International Trade Law, *Glencore Finance (Bermuda) Ltd. v Plurinational State Of Bolivia*.

[144] See Cantwell and Coate and, *Handbook on the Politics of Higher Education* (2018), 193 f.

[145] Further information on this issue: WTO, *Symposium on issues confronting the world trading system,
Summary reports by the moderators*, 6 and 7 July, World Trade Organization, Geneva, Switzerland.

[146] Education is one of the 12 services sectors administered in the context of the General Agreement of
Trade and Services and thus can be included and applied in trade and investment agreements; Verger and
Bonal, 'Educational Services' in Cottier and Schefer (eds), *Elgar Encyclopedia of International Economic
Law* (2017), 445.

[147] Verger and Robertson, 'The GATS game changer: international trade regulation and the constitution
of a global education marketplace', in Robertson et al. (eds), *Public Private Partnerships in Education: New
Actors and Modes of Governance in a Globalizing World* (2012).

[148] Further information on this issue: Meeting of the Council for Trade-Related Aspects Of Intellectual
Property Rights, Held on 1 March 2016, *Item 11: Intellectual Property And Innovation: Education And
Diffusion*, Extract from Document IP/C/M/81/ADD.

[149] UNESCO, *Right to Education, Handbook 2019* (2019), 275.

[150] https://www.indigenouspeoples-sdg.org/index.php/english/all-resources/ipmg-position-papers-and
-publications/ipmg-reports/global-reports/124-inclusion-equality-and-empowerment-to-achieve-sustain
able-development-realities-of-indigenous-peoples/file.

66   The first case of the Equal Opportunities Commission (EOC) of Hong Kong established an important finding on the creation of equal opportunities for women and men by reference to the standards in interpreting sex discrimination established by CEDAW. This decision is characterised by two particular reasons: (1) the standards for assessing a discriminatory situation were derived and declared valid for both women and men. (2) Hong Kong had recognised CEDAW only a few years earlier in 1996. Thus, this case gave significant impetus for the integration of CEDAW into the domestic legal system.[151]

67   In a more recent case the High Court of Uganda[152] has ruled that the financing discrepancy affected the quality of education in the Public-Private-Partnership schools, and the ability of students to receive an education equal to the education being given at government grant-aided and public schools. Citing national and international law,[153] the court reasoned the State's obligation not to infringe the right to education as well as to prevent private companies from violating this and other human rights.

II. The Impact of International Jurisprudence on National Law

68   International judicial control mechanisms such as regional Human Rights Commissions or even the Courts of Human Rights are not capable of enforcing their opinions and judgments in national legal systems directly. The same applies, for instance, to the ECtHR which is not competent to repeal national law or judgments. The responsibility of enforcing its judgements is carried by the Committee of Ministers of the Council of Europe. Human Rights Committees are also dependent of the acknowledgment and joint work with the states' governments affected since these are mostly capable of recommending approaches or procedures to adjust the addressed issues.

69   The case law of the IACtHR shows that the aim is rather to sensitise the parties involved with regard to the consideration and application of human rights and to oblige states to provide human rights education.

70   Independent of these regulated minor possibilities of assertion, there are few other possibilities of transfer to national appreciation. In *Talibés children*, for instance, a collaborative approach[154] was chosen to transform the 'normative promise of socio-economic rights into tangible reality' found before the African Commission. This decision and the subsequent cooperation between the Government and the Commission underlined that state responsibility does not only imply acting along with formal legal protection, but also with the creation of opportunities for its effective implementation as sustainable solutions.[155] The Commission's findings were transferred into the Senegalese National Strategies on Social Protection and on Economic and Social Development in 2013. Both address issues concerning the protection of children. Another national policy adopted focuses on childhood protection and includes sections focusing on the eradication of forced child begging. Although this policy has generated several initiatives, which

---

[151] *Equal Opportunities Commission v. Director of Education*, 22.01.2001, High Court of Hong Kong No. 1555 of 2000.

[152] *Initiative for Social and Economic Rights v. Attorney General*, High Court of Uganda at Kampala, Civil Suit No. 353 of 2016.

[153] Art. 21, 30, 34(2) of the Ugandan Constitution, the ICESCR and the CRC, CRC General Comment No. 16, which states that 'States must take all necessary, appropriate and reasonable measures to prevent business enterprises from causing or contributing to abuses of children's rights', *Initiative for Social and Economic Rights v. Attorney General*, High Court of Uganda at Kampala, Civil Suit No. 353 of 2016, paras. 11-8.

[154] https://www.escr-net.org/node/366331.

[155] African Commission, *Talibés children*, Decision No 003/Com/001/2012.

include the mapping and shut down of all illegal private Qu'ranic Schools (daaras) as well as sensitisation programs on child begging, no satisfactory secure conditions or 'meaningful results in ameliorating the situation of the *Talibés children* could be established to date[156] and much remains to be done.[157]

An overall increase in the inclusion of economic and social rights in constitutions   71 worldwide can be observed which have become changed from so-called aspirational rights to judicial rights, particularly in the years 2000 to 2016.[158] Despite this development with a significant increase in the justiciability of the right to education, the actual enforcement of this right is not satisfactorily achievable at every level since it is particularly dependent on the conditions within the individual state on the one hand,[159] and of the importance attached to that right in the relevant jurisdiction on the other.[160]

III. De Facto Influences on Jurisdiction

The evaluation of the right to education before the courts, specifically with reference   72 to human rights, has so far shown that this right is of little independent significance. Rather, it is considered in conjunction with other human rights and contextualised in its formulation. This is related to the fact that this right had to be implemented primarily progressively by states which gave them considerable leeway in implementation but did not include the obligation to establish a right to 'to an effectice remedy'. Judicial accountability for this right was established in 2008 with General Comment No. 3[161] which defined the implementation of economic, social and cultural rights as an obligation for states as a 'matter of priority'.[162] In this way, a division into obligations for states to be implemented immediately and those to be implemented progressively was created and consequently a justiciable state responsibility had been established, partly extraterritorially and extended to private actors. Thus, this right has only recently gained access to jurisprudential significance. However, since states must continue to recognise the protocol containing the right to education, its enforceability still depends on the willingness of states to cooperate.

---

[156] https://www.escr-net.org/caselaw/2015/centre-human-rights-university-pretoria-and-rencontre-afri caine-pour-defense-droits.

[157] https://www.unodc.org/westandcentralafrica/en/2020-04-27-talibes-covid.html; https://www.hrw.or g/news/2019/12/16/senegal-failure-end-abuses-quranic-schools.

[158] Rosevear and Hirschl and Jung, 'Justiciable and Aspirational Economic and Social Rights in National Constitutions' (2019) in Young (ed), *The future of economic and social rights*, 64.

[159] See Schiff Berman, 'Jurisdictional Pluralism' in Allen et al. (eds), *The Oxford Handbook of Jurisdiction in International Law*, 141.

[160] Different currents can be identified where economic and social rights are evaluated very differently in the courts. In Brazil, Hungary, Indonesia or Nigeria, for example, pro-middle class decisions are taken more frequently than in Colombia, India or South Africa, where decisions are more likely to be pro-poor; more information on this issue: Landau and Dixon, 'Constitutional Non-Transformation? Socioeconomic Rights beyond the Poor' (2019) in Young (ed), *The future of economic and social rights* (2019), 115, 131.

[161] General Comment No. 3: *The Nature of States Parties' Obligations (Art. 2, para. 1 of the Covenant)*, Contained in E/1991/23, *Committee on Economic, Social and Cultural Rights : report on the 5th session*, 26 November-14 December 1990.

[162] Keller and Heri, 'The Committees on Human Rights and economic, social and cultural rights' in Chesterman and Malone and Villalpando (eds), *The Oxford Handbook of United Nations Treaties* (2019), 423; for further information on this issue see: Young, 'Waiting for Rights: Progressive Realization and Lost Time' in Young and Sen (eds), *The Future of Economic and Social Rights* (2019), 654.

73   A number of campaigns have been launched in support of the right to education.[163] With regard to jurisdiction, however, there is so far little evidence of a significant influence of this public or social work.

74   The structure of the different education systems within States is also likely to have a further influence. Often as an issue of (federal) state concern, educational institutions are financed from tax revenues that are also collected within the federal state. In some cases, these are assessed at municipal level and receive corresponding financial support. This can, for example, lead to increasing inequality if poor areas receive a lower overall tax return, from which in turn fewer financial resources can be made available to provide quality education. It can be seen, for example, in *Rodriguez v San Antonio Independent School District*[164] that the jurisdiction excluding a constitutional right to education subsequently led to courts in various states finding such a right inherent in their respective state constitutions. They also drew a very precise picture of the shaping of the right to education as a justiciable right the infringement of which entails a remedy.[165]

E. Conclusion on SDG 4

75   The SARS-CoV-2 pandemic shows that there is an urgent need to strengthen health systems in many of the most vulnerable countries. Without universal access to treatments and vaccines, achieving high-quality treatments will be made much more difficult ($\rightarrow$ Goal 3).[166]

76   SDG 4 is aiming at quality education interconnected in its normative dimension to the dignity of any individual, to equality to support people, including the most vulnerable in their rights to education. Thus, this specific SDG covers a vast realm in different perspectives inside its scope, its external systematic outreach to educations related goals and to the main principles as well. Moreover, several aspects of the SDGs and constitutional provisions of each state are intertwined and can hardly be separated from each other.[167]

77   The content of SDG 4 refers to preparing and delivering equality through government efforts and investment in the educational sector aimed at achieving quality education or skills and at a minimum literacy and numeracy, accessible to all, including persons with disabilities, indigenous peoples and children in vulnerable situations.

78   SDG 4 is orchestrated with treatises, declarations, resolutions, programmes and other international outcomes of different actors at the international level. The Incheon Decla-

---

[163] E.g. 'indigenous women in the Mbororo pastoralist communities in Cameroon started a campaign on promoting equal access to education which offered scholarships to girls, carried sensitization campaigns and encouraged pastoralists to stay put so that their children can access education. Other organizations joined the fight against inequality in the education sector by encouraging families to give equal opportunities to their children, sensitization on gender-based violence, and working on ending early and forced marriages in the Mbororo community. Today many Mbororo girls are educated, some work in various sectors while others are in universities. Illiteracy among Mbororo women and girls of the Northwest region has gone down.'.

[164] *San Antonio Independent School District v. Rodriguez*, 411 U.S. 1 (1973).

[165] More information on this issue: Rebell, 'The Right to Education in the American State Courts' (2019) in Young (ed), *The future of economic and social rights* (2019), 138.

[166] UN, *The Sustainable Development Goals Report 2020* (2020), 2.

[167] UNESCO, *Global Education Monitoring Summary Report* (2016), 8 sheds light that all of the 16 SDGs are interconnected with SDG 4.

ration[168] has committed support to SDG 4 and the Global Agenda 2030. The term SDG 4-Education 2030 encompasses both SDG 4 as well as education-related targets across the other SDGs[169] and stresses the interrelated and interconnected SDGs that are interdependent. Since 2005, the World Programme for Human Rights Education (WPHRE) exists, and it has just entered the fourth phase (2020 – 2024)[170] to promote education-alienated with the SDGs. Human rights education (HRE) is going back to the adoption of the resolution from 7 December 1965 on the Declaration on the Promotion among Youth of the Ideals of peace, mutual respect and understanding between peoples[171] that was explicitly included in SDG 4.7 and measured with one indicator developed in 2020 to held States accountable for their HRE implementation.[172] Human rights education, in general, can be considered as a fundamental pillar and useful tool to tackle global mostly interconnected challenges, such as violent extremism and conflicts.[173]

The primary address as a duty-bearer of SDG 4 is the respective state, which has **79** obligations for reviewing the current status of the education system and, e.g. assist to modernise school facilities and – where necessary – creating new ones to offer a prerequisite of rooms, buildings, washing and sanitation facilities, to allow at least a minimum of quality education.

However, in practice, it is the indicators that determine what exactly is measured, by **80** whom and by which method. If results are available based on such measurements, they form the basis for political, executive and legal decisions. Sometimes, however, there is a lack of convergence between goals and indicators such as SDG 4.1 providing for free and equitable education which is measured e.g. by the '[p]roportion of children and young people (a) in grades 2/3 [...]'.

The first expression of education in modern international law can be recognised in **81** the UDHR, that grants everyone a right to education and providing free access to the elementary stages (Art. 26(1) UDHR). Parents are included as well and have a prior right to choose the kind of education for their children (Art. 26(3) UDHR). Higher education shall be made equally accessible to all, but limited by capacity (Art. 13(2) (c) of the International Covenant on Economic, Social and Cultural Rights (ICESCR). Individuals and groups are entitled according to an Optional Protocol to the ICESCR to submit complaints related to the ICESCR. Further definitions and rights regarding educations are enshrined in a wide variety of declarations and legally binding instruments (→ Goal 4 mn. 28 ff.) Access to Justice based on the SDGs is still lacking and needs further theoretical justifications[174] despite being enshrined in a wide variety of declarations and legally binding instruments (→ Goal 4 mn. 28 ff., → Goal 16).[175]

The targets of SDG 4 have incorporated, extended and intensified this specific back- **82** ground of the described Human Rights. Education is to be acknowledged as one of the essential SDGs to achieve human rights, dignity and sustainability and make all people

---

[168] UNESCO, *Education 2030: Incheon Declaration and Framework for Action for the implementation of Sustainable Development Goal 4* (2015).

[169] UNESCO, *Right to Education handbook* (2019), 159.

[170] OHCHR, A/HRC/42/23, *Draft plan of action for the fourth phase (2020–2024) of the World Programme for Human Rights Education*, 26 July 2019.

[171] A/RES/20/2037, *Declaration on the Promotion Among Youth of the Ideals of Peace, Mutual Respect and Understanding Between Peoples*, 7 December 1965.

[172] https://www.humanrights.dk/business/tools/sdg-47-human-rights-education-monitoring-tool.

[173] A/HRC/35/6, *Panel discussion on the implementation of the United Nations Declaration on Human Rights Education and Training: good practices and challenges*, 27 March 2017, para. 48.

[174] Huck and Maaß, 'Gaining a foot in the door: Giving Access to Justice with SDG 16.3?' (2021) *C-EENRG Working Paper Series*.

[175] A/HRC/42/23, *Draft plan of action for the fourth phase (2020–2024) of the World Programme for Human Rights Education*, 26 July 2019, see paras. 2-8.

capable of achieving prosperity and of accomplishing the different columns on which the 5 Ps are built ($\rightarrow$ Intro mn. 122 ff.).

83   The complete task of the state is to delineate and to specify the minimum level for quality education which should not be undercut in education (SDG 4.1). Thus, the minimum proficiency level for the measurement of the outcome of those targets and measured with indicators corresponds to the minimum set of skills or knowledge required for reading or mathematics.[176]

84   To measure the outcome properly with statistical measures on different levels (national, European and international), it needs some prerequisites regarding the quality of disaggregated data. Various regional and international assessments do assist in measuring the outcome such as the Programme d'analyse des systèmes éducatifs de la CONFE-MEN (PASEC),[177] the Progress in International Reading Literacy Study (PIRLS)[178], the Programme for International Student Assessment (PISA)[179], the Southern and Eastern Africa Consortium for Monitoring Educational Quality (SACMEQ),[180] the Tercer Estudio Regional Comparativo y Explicativo (TERCE)[181] and the Trends in International Mathematics and Science Study (TIMSS).[182]

85   Most of the SDGs call upon the respective responsible state to invest in educational institutions and materials that serve the goal of education. To measure SDG 4.2 '[p]roportion of children aged 24–59 months who are developmentally on track in health, learning and psychosocial well-being, by sex' and 'the percentage of children [...] who participate in one or more organized learning programs, including programs that offer a combination of education and care'.[183] An organised learning programme is defined as 'a coherent set or sequence of educational activities designed with the intention of achieving pre-determined learning outcomes or the accomplishment of a specific set of educational tasks'. Examples of organised learning programmes are early childhood and primary education programmes.[184] Typical for early childhood education is a holistic approach to support children's early cognitive, physical, social and emotional development and to introduce young children to organized instruction outside the family context.[185] In order to ensure equality for women and girls at all levels from primary to tertiary education and vocational training (SDG 4.3) and for those in need of protection, including people with disabilities, indigenous peoples and children in vulnerable situations (SDG 4.5), certain preconditions must be created to ensure access. Safe transport routes, free from criminal behaviour or violence, must be organised by the state. School transport must be available to all at low cost, yet it is not.

---

[176] https://unstats.un.org/wiki/display/SDGeHandbook/Indicator+4.1.1.

[177] PASEC, *Programme d'analyse des systemes educatifs de la confemen*, http://www.pasec.confemen.org/.

[178] IEA, *Progress in International Reading Literacy Study (PIRLS)*, http://www.iea.nl/pirls.

[179] OECD, Programme for International Student Assessment (PISA), https://www.oecd.org/pisa/aboutpisa/.

[180] The Southern and Eastern Africa Consortium for Monitoring Educational Quality (SACMEQ), http://www.sacmeq.org/?q=sacmeq-projects/sacmeq-iv.

[181] UNESCO, Tercer Estudio Regional Comparativo y Explicativo (TERCE), http://www.unesco.org/new/es/santiago/education/education-assessment-llece/terce/.

[182] IEA, Trends in International Mathematics and Science Study (TIMSS), http://www.iea.nl/timss_2015.html.

[183] A/RES/71/313, E/CN.3/2021/2, *Global indicator framework for the Sustainable Development Goals and targets of the 2030 Agenda for Sustainable Development*; see for a current overview: https://unstats.un.org/sdgs/indicators/indicators-list/.

[184] Early childhood and primary education are defined in the 2011 revision of the International Standard Classification of Education (ISCED 2011); https://unstats.un.org/wiki/display/SDGeHandbook/Indicator+4.1.1.

[185] https://unstats.un.org/wiki/display/SDGeHandbook/Indicator+4.2.2.

As a more general aspiration, the goals are targeting to increase the skills of young   **86**
adults with relevant skills (SDG 4.4). However, what are the skills in this context? What
should be measured and what is relevant, and on the opposite what can be judged as
irrelevant due to the educational background for different learning targets and environments? The measurement of relevant skills by indicators is defined as the percentage of
youth (aged 15-24 years) and adults (aged 15 years and above) that have undertaken
certain computer-related activities in a given time period (e.g. last three months). The
underlying concept of measurement thus reveals more of the term 'relevant skills' that
are here (only) 'computer-related activities' which include:

–   Copying or moving a file or folder
–   Using copy and paste tools to duplicate or move information within a document
–   Sending e-mails with attached files (e.g. document, picture, and video)
–   Using basic arithmetic formulae in a spreadsheet
–   Connecting and installing new devices (e.g. modem, camera, printer)
–   Finding, downloading, installing and configuring software
–   Creating electronic presentations with presentation software (including text, images,
    sound, video or charts)
–   Transferring files between a computer and other devices[186]
–   Writing a computer program using a specialised programming language

In that context, no other skills will be measured as those related to information and   **87**
communication Technology (ICT).[187] Further youth and a substantial part of adults
should achieve literacy and numeracy (SDG 4.6). The *fixed level of proficiency* is the
benchmark of basic knowledge in a domain (literacy or numeracy) measured through
learning assessments. Currently, there are no universal standards to determine the fixed
level of proficiency that have been validated by the international community or countries.

The concepts of *functional literacy and numeracy* are based on the UNESCO defini-   **88**
tion. Therefore, a person is *functionally literate* who can engage in all those activities in
which literacy is required for the effective functioning of their group and community
and also for enabling them to continue to use reading, writing and calculation for
their own and the community's development. The assessment of functional literacy and
numeracy cover various proficiency levels ranging from a low level to the mastery of the
requisite domain.[188]

The fulfilment of SDGs needs thorough and stable financing, which seems to be chal-   **89**
lenging to achieve. Nevertheless, to ensure that all learners acquire sufficient knowledge
and skills needed to promote sustainable development (SDG 4.7) could even get costly.
The measurement by the indicator is concrete and is at least a demand for financing
the level of education. The measurement by indicators looks at (a) electricity; (b) the
Internet for pedagogical purposes; (c) computers for pedagogical purposes; (d) adapted
infrastructure and materials for students with disabilities; (e) basic drinking water;
(f) single-sex basic sanitation facilities; and (g) basic handwashing facilities (as per
the WASH indicator definitions). Whether there is a non-violent or a violent learning

---

[186] A computer refers to a desktop computer, a laptop (portable) computer or a tablet (or similar
handheld computer). It does not include equipment with some embedded computing abilities, such as
smart TV sets or cell phones, see https://unstats.un.org/wiki/display/SDGeHandbook/; https://unstats.un.
org/wiki/display/SDGeHandbook/Indicator+4.4.1.
[187] https://unstats.un.org/wiki/display/SDGeHandbook/Indicator+4.4.1.
[188] https://unstats.un.org/wiki/display/SDGeHandbook/Indicator+4.6.1.

environment, is not entailed by the indicator, and thus there will be no outcome of measurement related to this question.

90   In particular, SDG 4.7 reveals a significant deficit of basic handwashing facilities in many schools around the world affecting teachers and students at the same time. The UN observed that in areas where schools are closed because of the pandemic, this also means that schools will be unable to practice essential hygiene measures when children go back to school.[189]

91   For millions of children, a school is more than an educative facility, rather it is a safe place, where they are protected against violence and where they receive free meals, health and nutrition services such as vaccinations, deworming and iron supplements. During the current pandemic, many schools were closed and school meals were cancelled. Furthermore, the UN observes that the SARS-CoV-2 pandemic has been accompanied by an increase in violence against children.[190]

92   According to the UNESCO, 55 per cent of Member States of the UN have a justiciable right to education, where only 27 percent of UN Member states dispose of directive principles or aspirational rights to education and 18 percent do not have a state constitutional right to education.[191] This variety of constitutional frameworks regarding the right to education shed light on the burdensome process to claim this right before a court. Nonetheless, legal measures play a vital role for the legal enforcement of the right to education including the right to be heard by judges, which is not everywhere the case (→ Goal 16).

93   This, in turn, requires states to put in place the necessary legal arrangements to make the right to education justiciable. A recognition of the right to education to guarantee access in the domestic legal order is the first step.[192] A justiciable right to education means that when this right is violated, the right-holder can take her or his claim before an independent and impartial body, and if the claim is upheld, be granted a remedy, which can then be enforced.[193]

94   A closer look at the jurisdiction related to quality education or to specific contents of SDG 4 presents a heterogeneous picture. The importance of the (human) right to education is emphasised frequently while at the same time hardly any independent legal meaning can be derived. The independent judicial evaluation of the right to education without recourse to other human rights associated are merely to be found in very specific contexts. In view of the importance of education as an instrument of empowerment, being an enabler for most other SDGs and for attaining a life in dignity, the right to education has not yet been adequately reflected upon, particularly not insofar it is gauged against the substance of SDG 4. Moreover, no clear, uniform line leading to reliable implementation could be found. And yet it is noticeable that the different jurisdictions, although not directly named, deal with the vision and targets of SDG 4 and shed light on its meaning against a human rights background. The concept of sustainable development is implicitly met when rights are interpreted in a unified way and even expanded.

95   Finally, it should be reiterated that legality and normativity serve as the best fundament for a success of education in the scope of the Global Agenda 2030 providing girls, women and the most vulnerable with an unfettered access to education managed on the basis of equality (→ Goal 16).

---

[189] UN, *The Sustainable Development Goals Report* (2020), 33.
[190] UN, *The Sustainable Development Goals Report* (2020), 33.
[191] UNESCO, *Right to Education handbook* (2019), 243.
[192] UNESCO, *Right to Education handbook* (2019), 183.
[193] UNESCO, *Right to Education handbook* (2019), 242.

Goal 5
Achieve gender equality and empower all women and girls

5.1 End all forms of discrimination against all women and girls everywhere

5.2 Eliminate all forms of violence against all women and girls in the public and private spheres, including trafficking and sexual and other types of exploitation

5.3 Eliminate all harmful practices, such as child, early and forced marriage and female genital mutilation

5.4 Recognize and value unpaid care and domestic work through the provision of public services, infrastructure and social protection policies and the promotion of shared responsibility within the household and the family as nationally appropriate

5.5 Ensure women's full and effective participation and equal opportunities for leadership at all levels of decision-making in political, economic and public life

5.6 Ensure universal access to sexual and reproductive health and reproductive rights as agreed in accordance with the Programme of Action of the International Conference on Population and Development and the Beijing Platform for Action and the outcome documents of their review conferences

5.a Undertake reforms to give women equal rights to economic resources, as well as access to ownership and control over land and other forms of property, financial services, inheritance and natural resources, in accordance with national laws

5.b Enhance the use of enabling technology, in particular information and communications technology, to promote the empowerment of women

5.c Adopt and strengthen sound policies and enforceable legislation for the promotion of gender equality and the empowerment of all women and girls at all levels

Word Count related to 'Gender' and 'Women' and 'Girls'
A/RES/70/1 – Transforming our world: the 2030 Agenda for Sustainable Development: 'Gender': 17 and 'Women': 32 and 'Girls': 16
Instruments mentioned in A/RES/70/1 in the section entitled: 'Sustainable Development Goals and targets':
A/RES/69/313 – Addis Ababa Action Agenda of the Third International Conference on Financing for Development adopted on 27 July 2015: 'Gender': 14 and 'Women': 29 and 'Girls': 6
A/RES/66/288 – The future we want (Rio +20 Declaration) adopted on 27 July 2012: 'Gender': 26 and 'Women': 59 and 'Girls': 2
A/RES/55/2 – United Nations Millennium Declaration adopted on 8 September 2000: 'Gender': 2 and 'Women': 6 and 'Girls': 2

Select Bibliography: Caroline Bettinger-Lopez, 'Violence Against Women: Normative Developments in the Inter-American Human Rights System' in Rashida Manjoo and Jackie Jones (eds), *The Legal Protection Of Women From Violence: Normative Gaps In International Law* (Routledge Press, 2018); Ruiz Blanca Rodríguez and Ruth Rubio-Marin, 'The Gender of Representation: On Democracy, Equality and Parity' (2008) 6 *INT'L J. CONST. L.* 287; Meghan Campbell, *Women, Poverty, Equality – The Role of CEDAW* (Hart Publishing, UK/USA 2018); Hilary Charlesworth, 'Women' in Simon Chesterman, David M. Malone and Santiago Villalpando (eds), *The Oxford Handbook of United Nations Treaties* (Oxford University Press, Oxford 2019), 249; Barnali Choudhoury, 'Rights of Women' in Thomas Cottier and Krista Nadakavukaren Schefer (eds), *Elgar Encyclopedia of International Economic Law* (Edward Elgar Publishing, Cheltenham/Northampton 2017), 653; Sofia Ciuffoletti, '"Regardless of their sex" or "biological differences", An analysis of the European Court of Human Rights' case law on women in prison' (2020) 11(2) *Rev. Direito Práx*; Marie-Claire Cordonier Segger and Alexandra Harrington, 'Environment and Sustainable Development' in Simon Chesterman and David M. Malone, *The Oxford Handbook of United Nations Treaties*, 226; Council of Europe, *Gender Equality Strategy 2018-2023* (Council of Europe 2018), 13; Simone Cusack and Lisa Pusay, 'CEDAW and the rights to non-discrimination and equality' (2013) 14 *Melb. J. Int'l L.*, 1; Simone Cusack, 'The CEDAW as a legal framework for transnational discourses on gender stereotyping' in Anne Hellum and Henriette Sinding Aasen (eds), *Women's Human Rights – CEDAW in International, Regional and National Law* (Cambridge University Press, UK/USA 2013), 124; Felix Dodds, David Donoghue and Jimena Leiva Roesch, *Negotiating the Sustainable Development Goals, A transformational agenda for an insecure world* (Routledge, UK/USA 2017); Bernard Duhaime, 'Women's Rights In Recent Inter-American Human Rights Jurisprudence' (2017) *ASIL Proceedings*, 257 (258); European Commission, *2019 Report on equality between women and men in the EU* (EU, Luxembourg 2019); European Parliament, *Discriminatory Laws Undermining Women's Rights*, PE603.489 (EU, Brussels 2019); Alda Facio and Martha I. Morgan, 'Equity or Equality for Women? Understanding CEDAW's Equality Principles' (2009) 60 *Ala. L. Rev.*, 1133; Brian Farrell, *Habeas Corpus in International Law* (Cambridge University Press, Cambridge 2017); Therese Ferguson et al, *SDG 4 – Quality Education – Inclusivity, Equity and Lifelong Learning for All* (Emerald Publishing Limited, UK 2019); Arvonne S. Fraser, 'Becoming Human: The Origins and Development of Women's Human Rights' in Stephanie Farrior (ed), *Equality and Non-Discrimination under International Law: Volume II* (Routledge, UK/USA 2016), 215; Sandra Fredman, 'Engendering socio-economic rights' in Anne Hellum and Henriette Sinding Aasen (eds), *Women's Human Rights – CEDAW in International, Regional and National Law* (Cambridge University Press, UK/USA 2013), 217; Marsha A. Freeman, Christine Chinkin and Beate Rudolf, *The UN Convention on the Elimination of All Forms of Discrimination Against Women: A Commentary* (Oxford University Press, Oxford 2012); Anne T. Gallagher, 'The International Legal Definition of "Trafficking in Persons": Scope and Application' in Prabha Kotiswaran (ed), *Revisiting the Law and Governance of Trafficking, Forced Labor and Modern Slavery* (Cambridge University Press, UK/USA/Australia/India/Singapore 2017), 83; Judith Gardam and Michelle Jarvis, 'Women and Armed Conflict: The International Response to the Beijing Platform for Action' (2000) 32 *Colum. Hum. Rts. L. Rev.*, 1; Aisha K. Gill, 'Introduction – Violence Against Women and the Need for International Law' in Rashida Manjoo and Jackie Jones (eds), *The Legal Protection of Women From Violence – Normative Gaps in International Law* (Routledge, UK/USA 2018), 1; Aysel Gunindi Ersoz, 'The Role of university education in the determination of gender perception: The case of the Gazi University' (2012) 47 *Procedia Soc Behav Sci*, 401; Hurst Hannum, Dinah L. Shelton, S. James Anaya and Rosa Celorio (eds), *International Human Rights – Problems of Law, Policy and Practice* (6th edition, Wolters Kluwer, New York 2018); HLPF, *2017 HLPF Thematic review of SDG 5: Achieve gender equality and empower all women and girls* (HLPF 2017); Rikki Holtmaat, 'The CEDAW: a holistic approach to women's equality and freedom' in Anne Hellum and Henriette Sinding Aasen (eds), *Women's Human Rights – CEDAW in International, Regional and National Law* (Cambridge University Press, UK/USA 2013), 95; International Trade Centre, *Mainstreaming Gender in Free Trade Agreements* (ITC, Geneva 2020); Jackie Jones, 'The Importance of International Law and Institutions' in Rashida Manjoo and Jackie Jones (eds), *The Legal Protection of Women From Violence – Normative Gaps in International Law* (Routledge, UK/USA 2018), 9; Liezelle Kumalo and Romi Sigsworth, 'Women, peace and security-implementing the Maputo Protocol in Africa' (2016) 295 *Institute for Security Studies Papers*, 1-24; Fleur van Leeuwen, 'Women's rights are human rights!': the practice of the United Nations Human Rights Committee and the Committee on Economic, Social and Cultural Rights' in Anne Hellum and Henriette Sinding Aasen (eds), *Women's Human Rights – CEDAW in International, Regional and National*

Law (Cambridge University Press, UK/USA 2013), 242; Claire Mahon, 'The Role of Women' in Jorge E. Viñuales, *The Rio Declaration on Environment and Development, A Commentary* (OUP, Oxford 2015), 509; Jens Martens, Bodo Ellmers and Vera Pokorny, *COVID-19 and the SDGs The impact of the coronavirus pandemic on the global sustainability agenda* (Social Watch/Global Policy Watch/Global Policy Forum, Uruguay/USA/Germany 2020; José-Antonio Monteiro, 'Gender-Related Provisions In Regional Trade Agreements' (2018), Staff Working Paper ERSD-2018-15 *World Trade Organization Economic Research and Statistics Division*; Karen Morrow, 'Gender and the Sustainable Development Goals' in Duncan French and Louis J. Kotzé, *Sustainable Development Goals, Law – Theory and Implementation*, (Edward Elgar Publishing, Cheltenham/Northampton 2018), 151; Angelica-Nicoleta Neculăesei, 'Culture and Genderrole Differences' (2015) 17 *Int. J. Cross Cult. Manag.*, 31; Johanna Niemi, Lourdes Peroni and Vladislava Stoyanova (eds), *International law and violence against women – Europe and the Istanbul Convention* (Routledge, UK/USA 2020); Umesh Chandra Pandey and Chhabi Kumar, *SDG 5 – Gender equality and empowerment of women and girls* (Emerald Publishing Limited, UK 2020); Gayatri H. Patel, *Women and International Human Rights Law – Universal Periodic Review in Practice* (Routledge, UK/USA 2020); David L. Richards and Jilienne Haglund, *Violence Against Women and the Law* (Routledge, UK/USA 2016); Beate Rudolf, 'Freedom from Violence, Full Access to Resources, Equal Participation, and Empowerment: The Relevance of CEDAW for the Implementation of the SDGs' in Markus Kaltenborn, Markus Krajewski and Heike Kuhn (eds), *Sustainable Development Goals and Human Rights* (Springer Nature Switzerland AG, Switzerland 2020), 73; Ben Saul, David Kinley and Jaqueline Mowbrey, *The International Covenant on Economic, Social and Cultural Rights: Commentary, Cases, and Materials* (Oxford University Press, Oxford 2014); Rhona K.M. Smith, *Texts and Materials on International Human Rights* (4th edition, Routledge, UK/USA 2020); Paul M. Taylor, *A Commentary on the International Covenant on Civil and Political Rights – The UN Human Rights Committee's Monitoring of ICCPR Rights* (Cambridge University Press, UK/USA/Australia/India/Singapore 2020); UN Women, *Gender Equality, Women´s rights in review 25 Years after Beijing* (UN Women, USA 2020).

A. Background and Origin of SDG 5

Conceived as a 'holistic and all-encompassing'[1] stand-alone goal of the 'social level' of   1 the concept of sustainable development, SDG 5 is intended to prevent gender-based inequality as one of the 'most pervasive forms of inequality found in all societies and impacts the largest proportion of the world's population compared to all other forms of inequality.'[2] Moreover, this form of inequality is incisive because it is not only discriminatory, but also relates to one of the most vulnerable parts of society. The linkage of the perceived discrimination to several factors, and in particular to sex, is thus reinforced which, by other terms, would equal a doubling of discrimination.[3] As a matter of fact, gender inequality frequently is not recognised as an issue because people are 'accustomed to the prevalence of inequality in society.'[4] SDG 5 embodies the efforts to achieve 'the Convention on the Elimination of All Forms of Discrimination Against Women (CEDAW), the Convention on the Rights of the Child (CRC), and the ICESCR and also environmental accords [...]'.[5] However, not only do these fundamental conventions already differ in their definitions of the term 'discrimination',[6] but certain states

---

[1] See Meesters and Hellema, 'Are the SDGs Doomed to Fail? The Cost of Inaction on Gender Equality' (2018) 4 *Forum-Asia Working Paper series*, 45.

[2] Tesfaye and Wyant, 'Achieving Gender Equality and Empowering all Women and Girls', in: Shawki (ed), *International Norms, Normative Change, and the Sustainable Development Goals* (2016), 136.

[3] Meant is a 'Multiple discrimination of especially vulnerable groups'; Rudolf and Beate, 'Freedom from Violence, Full Access to Resources, Equal Participation, and Empowerment: The Relevance of CEDAW for the Implementation of the SDGs' in Kaltenborn, Krajewski and Kuhn (eds), *Sustainable Development Goals and Human Rights* (2020), 77.

[4] https://www.unocha.org/story/"gender-equality-not-only-women's-issue-it-everyone's-issue".

[5] Cordonier Segger and Harrington, 'Environment and Sustainable Development' in Chesterman and Malone (eds), *The Oxford Handbook of United Nations Treaties* (2019), 226; see also Charlesworth, 'Women', in Chesterman and Malone and Villalpando, *The Oxford Handbook of United Nations Treaties* (2019), 256 (Historical derivation of these human rights conventions as basic principles).

[6] CEDAW goes beyond those of the ICERD in this respect.

expressed reservations to CEDAW in particular. It is thus unclear how this distinction, taking into account the various reservations, is also reflected in the recognition of the SDGs of these states. This illustrates and serves as an example for the varying degrees of gravity and complexity of the SDGs within the recognising states of the UN community.[7]

2   Although SDG 5 does not refer to other types of gender than women and girls and are also not mentioned directly at the European level,[8] they, nevertheless, include all other forms of gender such as LGBTI, which stands for lesbian, gay, bisexual, transgender and intersex.[9]

3   These are considered as 'gender identity' and are therefore subordinated to the term 'gender'[10] the differentiation of which is crucial since '[t]he gender categorization of each person—their registration in, usually, the male or female gender—is a central element in determining any individual's legal position in relation to other individuals and the state. Gender status is arguably crucial to pursue and achieve gender-related public interests and fundamental rights.'[11]

4   Since 'gender equality remains a matter of profound disagreement between states',[12] the Global Agenda 2030 presents 'an enormous opportunity' to achieve not just gender equality, but to end poverty and hunger, combat inequalities within and among countries, build peace, just and inclusive societies, protect and promote human rights and ensure lasting protection of the planet and its natural resources.[13] Gender equality, as it is deeply connected with international human rights, 'also has a multiplier effect across all other development areas.'[14] Every aspect of gender equality, for example, greatly impacts SDG 3 'Good Health and Well-Being' since women without empowerment or lacking services, education or further aspects of well-being may negatively affect their families in whole.[15] Against the background of its interconnectedness to international human rights, it is remarkable that SDG 5 does not relate to actual 'rights' but refers to terms such as 'empower' or 'strengthen'. The ambiguous language used in SDG 5 leads to ongoing, controversial discussions, which argue, amongst other things, for a 'devaluation of gender issues by dissociating them from the recognised realm of human rights, diluting coverage by distancing or even divorcing gender from the established

---

[7] Charlesworth, 'Women', in Chesterman and Malone and Villalpando (eds), *The Oxford Handbook of United Nations Treaties* (2019), 258 f.

[8] EC, Goal 5, *Achieve gender equality and empower all women and girls*; https://ec.europa.eu/sustainable -development/goal5_en.

[9] OHCHR, *Born Free and Equal* (2019), vii; OHCHR, *Joint UN statement on Ending violence and discrimination against lesbian, gay, bisexual, transgender and intersex people* (2015).

[10] Tesfaye and Wyant, 'Achieving Gender Equality and Empowering all Women and Girls', in Shawki (ed), *International Norms, Normative Change, and the Sustainable Development Goals* (2016), 135; dissenting view: Meesters and Hellema, 'Are the SDGs Doomed to Fail? The Cost of Inaction on Gender Equality' (2018) 4 *Forum-Asia Working Paper series*, 49 ('no reflection on gender diversity').

[11] Osella, '"De-gendering" the civil status? A public law problem' (2020) 18(2) *International Journal of Constitutional Law*, 471-75.

[12] Morrow, 'Gender and the Sustainable Development Goals' in French and Kotzé (eds), *Sustainable Development Goals, Law, Theory and Implementation* (2018), 151; see also: Charlesworth, 'Women', in Chesterman and Malone and Villalpando (eds), *The Oxford Handbook of United Nations Treaties* (2019), 253 (she highlights the differing views of feminist movements between the Global North and the Global South, which give different weight to various women's rights).

[13] SDG Knowledge Hub, Wahlén, Policy Brief, *Achieving Gender Equality to Deliver the SDGs* (2017).

[14] https://www.sdgfund.org/goal-5-gender-equality; see also A/68/202, *A Life of Dignity for all: Accelerating Progress Towards the Millennium Development Goals and Advancing the United Nations Development Agenda Beyond 2015, Report of the Secretary-General*, 26 July 2013.

[15] Tesfaye and Wyant, 'Achieving Gender Equality and Empowering all Women and Girls', in Shawki (ed), *International Norms, Normative Change, and the Sustainable Development Goals* (2016), 138; see also: Meesters and Hellema, 'Are the SDGs Doomed to Fail? The Cost of Inaction on Gender Equality' (2018) 4 *Forum-Asia Working Paper series*, 43.

'anti-discrimination' and 'equality rights-based' agendas, [...]'.[16] The language used is also discussed controversially on other points. In this context, religious and ethical aspects are of particular importance in this SDG. The different perspectives within the international community, for instance on 'women's reproductive health and reproductive rights' or on what actually represents a 'harmful practice', led to strong opposition even during the development of this SDG.[17]

The importance of empowering women and girls is underlined firstly by the structure 5 of the SDGs itself since SDG 5 unfolds its radiance into nine other SDGs: SDG 1.4, 1.b; SDG 2.3; SDG 4.1, 4.2, 4.3, 4.5, 4.6, 4.7, 4.a; SDG 6.2; SDG 8.5; SDG 10.2, 10.3; SDG 11.2, (11.5), 11.7; (SDG 13.b); (SDG 16.b)[18]; SDG 17.18 (→ Goal 5 mn. 65 ff.). The empowerment reached through anchoring gender equality and interlinked issues in such a broad and cross-cutting[19] manner is assumed to 'make a crucial contribution to progress across all the Goals and targets'.[20] Secondly, the history of sustainable development gives insight on the crucial importance: Already with the so-called Brundtland report[21], the status and position of women was assessed to be a cultural value and thus touches upon the basic human right of self-determination which plays a pivotal role and is significantly influencing every form of social development such as health, housing or food production.

In the UN document 'The future we want', gender equality and women's empower- 6 ment was clearly defined and frequently highlighted throughout. The General Assembly concluded '[t]he vital role of women and the need for their full and equal participation and leadership in all areas of sustainable development, and decide to accelerate the implementation of our respective commitments in this regard as contained in the Convention on the Elimination of All Forms of Discrimination against Women,[22] as well as Agenda 21, the Beijing Declaration and Platform for Action and the United Nations Millennium Declaration.'[23]

It was recognised that gender equality and women's empowerment are important for 7 sustainable development, that women have a vital role to play in achieving sustainable development and for the common future.[24]

This document marks a further step into the right direction, when at the World 8 Conference on Environment and Development in 1987 the role of women had been

---

[16] Morrow, 'Gender and the Sustainable Development Goals' in French and Kotzé (eds), *Sustainable Development Goals, Law, Theory and Implementation* (2018), 170 (fn. 119); (draft) declaration UN ECOSOC, E/2017/L.29–E/HLPF/2017/L.2; so too: Dodds and Donoghue and Leiva Roesch (eds), 'Negotiating the Sustainable Development Goals, A transformational agenda for an insecure world' (2017), 66, and 94 (mainly pressed by the EU and Argentina (see Tesfaye and Wyant (fn. 15), 137), whereas the African group rejected this, as they felt that a clearer focus on human rights could be detrimental to economic development).

[17] Charlesworth, 'Women', in Chesterman and Malone and Villalpando (eds), *The Oxford Handbook of United Nations Treaties* (2019), 259; Dodds and Donoghue and Leiva Roesch (eds), *Negotiating the Sustainable Development Goals, A transformational agenda for an insecure world* (2017), 38; for example, the definition of the term 'child' was intensively discussed due to the distinctly different definitions.

[18] SDG 16 only refers implicitly to women and girls since it uses the term 'all'.

[19] Morrow, 'Gender and the Sustainable Development Goals' in French and Kotzé (eds), *Sustainable Development Goals, Law, Theory and Implementation* (2018), 157.

[20] A/RES/70/1, *Transforming our world: the 2030 Agenda for Sustainable Development*, 21 October 2015, para. 20.

[21] World Commission on Environment and Development, *Report of the World Commission on Environment and Development, Our Common Future* (1987).

[22] UN, Treaty Series, vol. 1249, No. 20378, *Convention on the Elimination of All Forms of Discrimination against Women*, 8 December 1979.

[23] A/RES/66/288, *The future we want*, 11 September 2012, paras. 236-44.

[24] A/RES/66/288, *The future we want*, 11 September 2012, paras. 31, 45.

recognised as '[p]opulation policies' and 'birth rates and family planning'[25] as not concealing the right to self-determination.

9   The new approach to environment and development was linked to the observation that the position of women in society in particular needs improvement in terms of social development, especially in local participation in decision making.[26]

10   Further impetus was given when Principle 20 of the Rio Declaration in the explicit context of environmental management and development was anchored as 'a broad statement of recognition' thereby referring to the inherent legal value of the ICCPR as well as the CEDAW.[27] Since then the empowerment of girls and women has starkly been included in joint UN declarations[28] with slightly different connotations but at any rate as a necessity for (successful) human societal coexistence.

11   However, the underlying (structural, legislative and economic) norms or reforms that would support the demanded empowerment are often proclaimed rhetorically, but are not institutionally processed. Unless a shift in power and an adequate redistribution of resources is reached, the development initiated with SDG 5 will not serve to eradicate inequality.[29]

12   The diverse backgrounds and fundamental principles underlying SDG 5 raise awareness of the necessity that gender equality (a) is not a uniform, homogeneous entity that can be applied equally to all women. Rather, it is, as is with most other SDGs, highly context-dependent; (b) requires a sensitive structure that eradicates differences in treatment, but at the same time allows for special treatment where necessary. This structure leads to tensions which may not be easily resolved; and in consequence, (c) must not refer exclusively to women and girls, but, in contrast to the direct wording of this SDG, must also include and address men and boys (as well as all other genders besides the binary categorisation). Otherwise gender equality remains an issue in the sphere of women and girls and thus inequality could not be resolved.

B. Scope and Dimensions of SDG 5

13   SDG 5 might be seen as one of the most far-reaching and significant goals of the Global Agenda 2030 covering the wide range of women's and girl's fundamental human rights, gender equality as well as the empowerment of women and girls within family, society and the global legal and political framework. At least half of world's human population is made of women and girls, thus enforcing their fundamental human rights and ensuring gender equality is a task of humankind.[30] The indicators of SDG 5 provide a supporting function for the implementation of SDG 5 and serve as a benchmark for

---

[25] A/RES/66/288, *The future we want*, 11 September 2012, paras. 43, 51.

[26] A/RES/66/288, *The future we want*, 11 September 2012, para. 43.

[27] Mahon, 'The Role of Women' in Viñuales, *The Rio Declaration on Environment and Development, A Commentary* (2015), 513.

[28] A/Conf.171/13, *Programme of Action, Report of the International Conference on Population of Development* (1994); *UN Millennium Declaration* (2000); *Plan of Implementation of the World Summit on Sustainable Development* (2002) (Johannesburg Plan of Implementation).

[29] Tesfaye and Wyant, 'Achieving Gender Equality and Empowering all Women and Girls', in Shawki (ed), *International Norms, Normative Change, and the Sustainable Development Goals* (2016), 137, 146; Meesters and Hellema, 'Are the SDGs Doomed to Fail? The Cost of Inaction on Gender Equality' (2018) 4 *Forum-Asia Working Paper series*, 47.

[30] https://www.ohchr.org/en/professionalinterest/pages/cedaw.aspx.

continuous and selective monitoring of progress.[31] Moreover, the Global Agenda 2030 highlights in paragraph 20[32] the strategic approach of gender mainstreaming in the overall implementation of every single SDG, including continuous gender-sensitivity in the review processes.[33]

I. Elementary Definitions

Even if it may appear at first glance that SDG 5 is self-evident in itself, fundamental definitions are not as obvious as they might seem. For this reason, it is indispensable to situate core definitions related to women's and girl's empowerment and gender quality in the overall structure of SDG 5. **14**

It is essential to consider the definition of women and girls against the background of SDG 5 and its corresponding international legal instruments such as CEDAW. Although CEDAW does not hold a legal definition itself, it is strongly assumed that girls are also covered by the wording of women (by being women under the age of 18). In this context, there are obviously far-reaching cultural differences in view of the social recognition of the transition from girl to woman. Society's expectations towards girls in some places frequently lead to forced marriage or childbirth even before they are physically or psychologically ready for it, which constitutes detrimental discrimination. Therefore, promoting special attention to girls and their rights is of utmost importance.[34] **15**

Based on the approach of SDG 5 to promote gender equality, the term of 'gender' and 'gender equality' stand out. Gender is seen as **16**

> a social and cultural construct, which distinguishes differences in the attributes of men and women, girls and boys, and accordingly refers to the roles and responsibilities of men and women. Gender-based roles and other attributes, therefore, change over time and vary with different cultural contexts. The concept of gender includes the expectations held about the characteristics, aptitudes and likely behaviours of both women and men (femininity and masculinity).[35]

> In most societies there are differences and inequalities between women and men in responsibilities assigned, activities undertaken, access to and control over resources, as well as decision-making opportunities. Gender is part of the broader socio-cultural context. Other important criteria for socio-cultural analysis include class, race, poverty level, ethnic group and age.[36]

Gender is to be understood as the socially developed image of and role expectations towards men and women. Here, the cultural[37] aspect should not be underestimated as **17**

---

[31] However, there are also points of criticism regarding the complete coverage of all relevant aspects of each target by the indicators, see UNSTATS, *Goal 5 – Achieve gender equality and empower all women and girls* (2016).

[32] A/RES/70/1, *Transforming our world: the 2030 Agenda for Sustainable Development*, 21 October 2015, para. 20.

[33] Rudolf, 'Freedom from Violence, Full Access to Resources, Equal Participation, and Empowerment: The Relevance of CEDAW for the Implementation of the SDGs' in Kaltenborn and Krajewski and Kuhn (eds), *Sustainable Development Goals and Human Rights* (2020), 73 (76 f.).

[34] Freeman and Chinkin and Rudolf, *The UN Convention on the Elimination of All Forms of Discrimination Against Women: A Commentary* (2012), 14 f.

[35] United Nations Children's Fund – UNICEF Regional Office for South Asia, *Gender Equality – Glossary of Terms and Concepts* (2017), 2.

[36] https://www.un.org/womenwatch/osagi/conceptsandefinitions.htm.

[37] Culture […] is […] the whole complex of distinctive spiritual, material, intellectual and emotional features that characterize a society or a social group. It includes not only arts and letters, but also modes of life, the fundamental rights of the human being, value systems, traditions and beliefs; Definition of culture in UNESCO, *Mexico City Declaration on Cultural Policies, World Conference on Cultural Policies Mexico City, 26 July – 6 August 1982* (1982).

culture is one of the most influential factors on the societal perception of gender,[38] alongside with (scientific) education[39] and political ideologies.[40] Long-established and misconceived beliefs and attitudes about the cultural value of men and women that place women in an inferior position are a major obstacle to the strengthening, establishment and dissemination of women's rights and ultimate gender equality. Legal change and the successful and sustainable implementation of universal human rights, especially women's rights, laid down in numerous international human rights treaties such as CEDAW, Beijing Action Platform, ICESCR, ICCPR are difficult to manifest socially when faced with such cultural connotations.[41]

18   Contrary to gender, sex is defined as the biological and physiological 'differences between women and men'.[42] This differentiation between gender and sex is of utmost importance, since CEDAW as one of the core legal treaties in the field of women's rights,[43] is based on the belief that

> discrimination against women is not based on sex—i.e. biological differences between women and men—but on gender—i.e. social constructions of what makes a woman and what makes a man. Its focus on gendered societal power relations is also the reason why CEDAW expressly obligates states to work towards overcoming gender stereotypes.[44]

19   Looking at the title of SDG 5, the overarching concept of gender equality holds a particular position within the targets. Based on the above-mentioned perception of gender, the term gender equality[45]

> refers to the equal rights, responsibilities and opportunities of women and men and girls and boys. Equality does not mean that women and men will become the same but that women's and men's rights, responsibilities and opportunities will not depend on whether they are born male or female. Gender equality implies that the interests, needs and priorities of both women and men are taken into consideration, recognizing the diversity of different groups of women and men. Gender equality is not a women's issue but should concern and fully engage men as well as women. Equality between women and men is seen both as a human rights issue and as a precondition for, and indicator of, sustainable people-centered development.[46]

---

[38] Neculăesei, 'Culture and Gender Role Differences' (2015) 17 *Int. J. Cross Cult. Manag.*, 31 (32 f.).

[39] Gunindi Ersoz, 'The Role of university education in the determination of gender perception: The case of the Gazi University' (2012) 47 *Procedia Soc Behav Sci*, 401 (403 ff.).

[40] Neculăesei, 'Culture and Gender Role Differences' (2015) 17 *Int. J. Cross Cult. Manag.*, 31 (33); see further: Pandey and Kumar, *SDG 5 – Gender equality and empowerment of women and girls* (2020), 4; Fraser, 'Becoming Human: The Origins and Development of Women's Human Rights' in Farrior (ed), *Equality and Non-Discrimination under International Law: Volume II* (2016), 215 (215 ff.).

[41] Organisation for Economic Co-operation and Development, *Questions about culture, gender equality and development cooperation* (2000).

[42] Gunindi Ersoz, 'The Role of university education In the determination of gender perception: The case of the Gazi University' (2012) 47 *Procedia Soc Behav Sci*, 401 (403); United Nations Children's Fund – UNICEF Regional Office for South Asia, *Gender Equality – Glossary of Terms and Concepts* (2017), 7.

[43] Rudolf, 'Freedom from Violence, Full Access to Resources, Equal Participation, and Empowerment: The Relevance of CEDAW for the Implementation of the SDGs' in Kaltenborn and Krajewski and Kuhn (eds), *Sustainable Development Goals and Human Rights* (2020), 73 (75 ff.).

[44] Rudolf, 'Freedom from Violence, Full Access to Resources, Equal Participation, and Empowerment: The Relevance of CEDAW for the Implementation of the SDGs' in Kaltenborn and Krajewski and Kuhn (eds), *Sustainable Development Goals and Human Rights* (2020), 73 (79); see for gender stereotypes in particular: Sotonye-Franck, 'Harmful gender-stereotyping under Article 10(c) CEDAW and school exclusion of adolescent pregnant girls in Kenya and Tanzania' in Smyth and Lang and Thompson (eds), *Contemporary Challenges to Human Rights Law* (2020), 171 (171 ff., 175).

[45] See A/RES/34/180, *Convention on the Elimination of All Forms of Discrimination Against Women* (1979), Art. 3.

[46] https://www.un.org/womenwatch/osagi/conceptsanddefinitions.htm; see also UNICEF's definition of gender equality:

Thus, gender equality pursues the recognition of equal valuing of women and men   **20**
within societies, so that hierarchical ways of thinking and structures which attach a lower value to women are dissolved and their substance removed.[47] With SDG 5.1, gender
equality directly corresponds with the theoretical structures that underlie SDG 10 ($\rightarrow$
Goal 10 mn. 16 ff.). Therefore, the concept of equity in relation to gender is also relevant.
Based on the general definition of equity tackling 'the political and moral questions that
can lead to lasting solutions'[48] alongside with the empowerment of respective groups
with social, economic, political and civil rights,[49] gender equity refers to 'the fair and just
treatment of both sexes that takes into account the different needs of the men and wom-
en, cultural barriers and (past) discrimination of the specific group' ($\rightarrow$ Goal 10 mn. 22,
26).[50]

In this context, the definition of discrimination against women follows the concept of   **21**
gender and is defined in CEDAW as follows:

> Any distinction, exclusion or restriction made on the basis of sex which has the effect or purpose
> of impairing or nullifying the recognition, enjoyment or exercise by women, irrespective of their
> marital status, on the basis of equality of men and women, of human rights and fundamental
> freedoms in the political, economic, social, cultural, civil or any other field.[51]

In this respect, CEDAW addresses the distinction between *de jure* and *de facto* dis-   **22**
crimination, emphasising the existing multilayered forms of discrimination throughout
the law, society and policies.[52]

A severe form of women's human rights violations are indisputably all forms of   **23**
violence against women and girls (SDG 5.2). The United Nations Declaration on the

---

The concept that women and men, girls and boys have equal conditions, treatment and opportunities
for realizing their full potential, human rights and dignity, and for contributing to (and benefitting from)
economic, social, cultural and political development. Gender equality is, therefore, the equal valuing by
society of the similarities and the differences of men and women, and the roles they play. It is based
on women and men being full partners in the home, community and society. Equality does not mean
that women and men will become the same but that women's and men's rights, responsibilities and
opportunities will not depend on whether they are born male or female. Gender equality implies that the
interests, needs and priorities of both women and men and girls and boys are taken into consideration,
recognizing the diversity of different groups and that all human beings are free to develop their personal
abilities and make choices without the limitations set by stereotypes and prejudices about gender roles.
Gender equality is a matter of human rights and is considered a precondition for, and indicator of,
sustainable people-centred development;
United Nations Children's Fund – UNICEF Regional Office for South Asia, *Gender Equality – Glossary
of Terms and Concepts* (2017), 2.

[47] United Nations Children's Fund – UNICEF Regional Office for South Asia, *Gender Equality –
Glossary of Terms and Concepts* (2017), 2; United Nations Development Programme, *Humanity Divided:
Confronting Inequality in Developing Countries* (2013), 162.

[48] Oestreich, 'SDG 10: Reduce inequality in and among countries' (2018) 37 *Social Alternatives*, 34 (34).

[49] International Covenant on Economic, Social and Cultural Rights (1966) and International Covenant
on Civil and Political Rights (1966); see also Oestreich, 'SDG 10: Reduce inequality in and among
countries' (2018) 37 *Social Alternatives*, 34 (34).

[50] Gender equity further includes the equality of outcomes and results and it ensures that women and
men and girls and boys have an equal chance, not only at the starting point, but also when reaching the
finishing line, United Nations Children's Fund – UNICEF Regional Office for South Asia, *Gender Equality
– Glossary of Terms and Concepts* (2017), 3; see also: Choudhoury, 'Rights of Women' in Cottier and
Nadakavukaren Schefer (eds), *Elgar Encyclopedia of International Economic Law* (2017), 653.

[51] A/RES/34/180, *Convention on the Elimination of All Forms of Discrimination Against Women* (1979),
Art. 1.

[52] Example for *de jure* discrimination: 'In some countries, a woman is not allowed to leave the country
or hold a job without the consent of her husband', example for *de facto* discrimination: 'A man and woman
may hold the same job position and perform the same duties, but their benefits may differ', United Nations
Children's Fund – UNICEF Regional Office for South Asia, *Gender Equality – Glossary of Terms and
Concepts* (2017), 1.

Elimination of Violence Against Women (1993) provides a clear definition embracing numerous forms of violence (but not being limited to those).[53]

24   Violence against women includes

> any act of gender-based violence that results in, or is likely to result in, physical, sexual, or psychological harm or suffering to women, including threats of such acts, coercion or arbitrary deprivation of liberty, whether occurring in public or private life [...][54], [encompassing] physical, sexual and psychological violence occurring in the family, including battering, sexual of female children in the household, dowry related violence, marital rape, female genital mutilation and other traditional practices harmful to women, non-spousal violence and violence related to exploitation; physical, sexual and psychological violence occurring within the general community, including rape, sexual abuse, sexual harassment and intimidation at work, in educational institutions and elsewhere; trafficking in women and forced prostitution; and physical, sexual and psychological violence perpetrated or condoned by the state, wherever it occurs.[55]

25   Comparable to the nature of discrimination against women, all forms of violence against women[56] are deeply rooted in 'patriarchy and women's subordination' interlinked with 'historically unequal power relations between women and men' having 'led to men dominating and discriminating against women and preventing their full advancement'.[57]

26   Another important term within the scope of SDG 5 is 'gender mainstreaming'. It provides a strategic approach of the UN and is meant to be the process to be applied in order to achieve gender equality. The intended purpose of gender mainstreaming is the assessment of

> implications for girls and boys and men and women of any planned action, including legislation, policies and programmes. It is a strategy for making girls' and women's, as well as boy's and men's, concerns and experiences an integral dimension of the design, implementation, monitoring and evaluation of policies and programmes so that girls and boys and women and men benefit equality, and inequality is not perpetuated.[58]

27   As an immense form of violence against women, trafficking in humans, especially in women and girls is particularly stressed, as can also be seen in SDG 5.2. Internationally, there are several definitions of trafficking in humans followed by a persistent discussion on the legal dimensions and delimitation of various forms of trafficking.[59] However, there is a broadly 'internationally accepted definition for "human trafficking" since the

---

[53] A/RES/48/104, *Declaration on the Elimination of Violence against Women* (1993), Art. 2.

[54] A/RES/48/104, *Declaration on the Elimination of Violence against Women* (1993), Arts. 1, 2.

[55] A/RES/48/104, *Declaration on the Elimination of Violence against Women* (1993), Art. 2.

[56] See further on violence against women: Niemi and Peroni and Stoyanova, *International law and violence against women – Europe and the Istanbul Convention* (2020); Richards and Haglund, *Violence Against Women and the Law* (2016); Patel, *Women and International Human Rights Law – Universal Periodic Review in Practice* (2020), 179 ff.; Committee on the Elimination of Discrimination against Women, General recommendation No. 19: Violence against women (1992); Committee on the Elimination of Discrimination against Women; CEDAW/C/GC/35, *General recommendation No. 35 on gender-based violence against women, updating general recommendation No. 19*, 14 July 2017; see for the work of the Special Rapporteur on violence against women, its causes and consequences, https://www.ohchr.org/EN/Issues/Women/SRWomen/Pages/SRWomenIndex.aspx.

[57] A/RES/48/104, *Declaration on the Elimination of Violence against* Women (1993), Preamble; Gill, 'Introduction – Violence Against Women and the Need for International Law' in Manjoo and Jones (eds), *The Legal Protection of Women From Violence – Normative Gaps in International Law* (2018), 1 (3).

[58] United Nations Children's Fund – UNICEF Regional Office for South Asia, *Gender Equality – Glossary of Terms and Concepts* (2017), 5.

[59] Gallagher, 'The International Legal Definition of "Trafficking in Persons": Scope and Application' in Kotiswaran (ed), *Revisiting the Law and Governance of Trafficking, Forced Labor and Modern Slavery* (2017), 83 (83 ff.); Office of the United Nations High Commissioner for Human Rights, *First decade of the mandate of the Special Rapporteur on trafficking in persons, especially women and children* (2014), 23 f.

year 2000'.[60] Art. 3 of the Protocol to Prevent, Suppress and Punish Trafficking in Persons Especially Women and Children, supplementing the United Nations Convention against Transnational Organized Crime (2000) includes both definitions of human trafficking as well as of exploitation in that respect.

> (a) "Trafficking in persons" shall mean the recruitment, transportation, transfer, harbouring or receipt of persons, by means of the threat or use of force or other forms of coercion, of abduction, of fraud, of deception, of the abuse of power or of a position of vulnerability or of the giving or receiving of payments or benefits to achieve the consent of a person having control over another person, for the purpose of exploitation. Exploitation shall include, at a minimum, the exploitation of the prostitution of others or other forms of sexual exploitation, forced labour or services, slavery or practices similar to slavery, servitude or the removal of organs; (b) The consent of a victim of trafficking in persons to the intended exploitation set forth in subparagraph (a) of this article shall be irrelevant where any of the means set forth in subparagraph (a) have been used; (c) The recruitment, transportation, transfer, harbouring or receipt of a child for the purpose of exploitation shall be considered "trafficking in persons" even if this does not involve any of the means set forth in subparagraph (a) of this article; (d) "Child" shall mean any person under eighteen years of age.[61]

Furthermore, the special form of trafficking in women and girls has drawn more **28**
attention on the international scene leading to a respective special definition, specifying
trafficking in women as

> all acts involved in the recruitment and/or transportation of a woman within and across national borders for work or services by means of violence, or threat of violence, abuse of authority or dominate position, debt bondage, deception, or other forms of coercion.[62]

This definition was published by the Global Alliance Against Trafficking in Wom- **29**
en (GAATW) simultaneously with the definition of forced-labor and slavery-like
practices.[63] In this context, trafficking in persons not only exists between countries, but
also within a country, and hence has both an international and a domestic outreach.[54]

Nevertheless, it is particularly striking that '[n]either 'exploitation of the prostitution **30**
of others' nor 'sexual exploitation' is defined in international law and it is clear that

---

[60] JHEC Editorial Board, 'The Nexus between Human Trafficking, Enslavement and Conflict-Related Sexual Violence is Obvious': Views of the Editorial Board' (2020) 1 *JHEC*, 5 (11).

[61] A/RES/55/25, *United Nations Convention against Transnational Organized Crime*, 8 January 2001, Protocol to Prevent, Suppress and Punish Trafficking in Persons Especially Women and Children, supplementing the United Nations Convention against Transnational Organized Crime, Art. 3.

[62] Chew, 'Global Trafficking in Women: Some Issues and Strategies' (1999) 27 *WSQ*, 11 (14).

[63] Chew, 'Global Trafficking in Women: Some Issues and Strategies' (1999) 27 *WSQ*, 11 (13 f.), definition of forced-labor and slavery-like practices: 'The extraction of work or services from any woman or the appropriation of the legal identity and/or physical person of any women by means of violence or threat of violence, abuse of authority or dominate position, debt bondage, deception or other forms of coercion'; League of Nations, *Slavery Convention* 1926; United Nations Economic and Social Council, E/RES/ 608(XXI), *Supplementary Convention on the Abolition of Slavery, the Slave Trade, and Institutions and Practices Similar to Slavery*, 7 September 1956; International Labour Organization, Abolition of Forced Labour Convention, 1957 (No. 105); see further: Global Alliance Against Traffic in Women, *Annual Report 2019* (2019); Wijers and Lap-Chew, *Trafficking in Women – Forced Labour and Slavery-like Practices in Marriage, Domestic Labour and Prostitution* (1999).

[64] United Nations Human Rights Office of the High Commissioner, *Human Rights and Human Trafficking – Fact Sheet No. 36* (2014), 3.

the drafters of the Protocol[65] deliberately avoided attaching any definitions to these stipulated purposes'.[66]

31   In the most recent report of the situation of women and girls in several Arab states, the situation reveals setbacks and disturbing evidence for the lack of enjoyment of rights for women in many societies.

32   CEDAW is the international instrument of greatest importance to gender justice in the Arab States region. It provides a comprehensive framework for the development of laws and policies to address gender justice. As of 2019, the only states in the region yet to ratify CEDAW are Somalia and Sudan. Most other Arab States maintain reservations to Art. 2 (non-discriminatory policy measures), Art. 9(2) (nationality rights), Art. 15 (equality before the law) and Art. 16 (equality in marriage and family life) of CEDAW, as well as Art. 29 (mechanism for States to resolve interstate disputes). Except for Art. 29, these reservations generally relate to concerns that national laws and policies remain consistent with Sharia principles.[67]

33   "Femicide' refers to the killing of women and girls because of their gender – it is an extreme form of gender-based violence. So-called 'honour' crimes occur when the perpetrator seeks to justify or excuse an act of violence based on their belief that the victim has brought dishonour upon the family or clan. This perceived 'dishonour' is often the result of engaging in or being suspected of engaging in adultery or *zina*, failure to enter or maintain an arranged marriage, choosing to marry by own choice, adopting a dress code unacceptable to the family, or engaging in sexual relations with a person of the same sex'.[68]

34   In some Arab States, the perpetrators of femicide receive more lenient sentences than people convicted of other murders due to judicial discretion and laws that prescribe special leniency or mitigation for murders committed in the so-called 'heat of passion'.[69]

II. Legal Foundations

35   The wording and objectives of SDG 5 are based on existing universal legal frameworks. Remarkably, the far-reaching dimension of gender equality and the empowerment of women and girls alongside with their fundamental human rights is reflected in several international legal sources binding each signatory state upon the respective commitments. The following description shows how international law and SDG 5 correlate and which rights and international obligations arise from this or already exist.

36   Throughout this commentary, law and legal instruments are reflected within the framework of the Global Agenda 2030. Likewise, the law with regard to SDG 5 and the protection and empowerment of women fulfils an extraordinarily crucial role, which was even emphasised at the level of the Human Rights Council.

---

[65] 'Protocol' here refers to United Nations, A/RES/55/25, *United Nations Convention against Transnational Organized Crime*, 8 January 2001, Protocol to Prevent, Suppress and Punish Trafficking in Persons Especially Women and Children, supplementing the United Nations Convention against Transnational Organized Crime.

[66] United Nations Office on Drugs and Crime, Issue Paper, *The Concept of 'Exploitation' in the Trafficking in Persons Protocol* (2015), 9.

[67] UN ESCWA, UNFPA, UN Women, UNDP, *Gender Justice & Equality before the law* (2019), 25.

[68] UN ESCWA, UNFPA, UN Women, UNDP, *Gender Justice & Equality before the law* (2019), 49.

[69] UN ESCWA, UNFPA, UN Women, UNDP, *Gender Justice & Equality before the law* (2019), 49; '[S]uch provisions have their origins in the Ottoman Penal Code of 1858 (Art. 188), which was based on the French Penal Code of 1810'.

The law is an essential mechanism for women's enjoyment of human rights. Law is both informed by and the creator of norms in society. Laws determine the values and operating principles by which actions and behaviours are deemed acceptable, or criminalized and stigmatized, and can have an enabling or chilling effect on women's human rights.[70]

1. Human Rights and Women: Universal Declaration of Human Rights, ICESCR and ICCPR

With regard to the legal character of SDG 5, both the framework of universal human   37
rights and its associated legal sources clearly stand out. Almost each SDG pursues its objective in the light of one or more specific human rights which is straightly illuminated throughout this commentary. Considering that human rights belong to all people,[71] women are equally addressed as men. Therefore, each international human rights framework directly covers the needs and rights of all women, making each human right relevant and essential to the empowerment of women and girls.[72] The special position of women is highlighted by particular references in several provisions explicitly stating the term of 'women'.[73] The concepts of equality and dignity as substantive values of human rights 'mean that not subjugation but participation, not dependency but autonomy, not slavery but freedom are the key notions in this human rights value orientation'.[74] In addition to the UDHR encompassing the scope of fundamental human rights, the ICESCR[75] alongside with the ICCPR[76] specify particular rights within the respective frameworks (either economic, social and cultural or civil and political) in a 'legally enforceable manner' (→ Goal 1, Goal 2, Goal 3, Goal 4, Goal 6, Goal 7, Goal 8, Goal 10, Goal 13, Goal 16).[77] All human rights in these and other human rights treaties under international law are indispensable in their full extent for the successful implementation of gender equality and the empowerment of women and girls. In the

---

[70] A/HRC/35/29, *Report of the Working Group on the issue of discrimination against women in law and in practice*, 19 April 2017, para. 17; Jones, 'The Importance of International Law and Institutions' in Manjoo and Jones (eds), *The Legal Protection of Women From Violence – Normative Gaps in International Law* (2018), 9 (9).

[71] 'All human beings are born free and equal in dignity and rights', United Nations Universal Declaration of Human Rights (1948), Art. 1.

[72] Holtmaat, 'The CEDAW: a holistic approach to women's equality and freedom' in Hellum and Aasen (eds), *Women's Human Rights – CEDAW in International, Regional and National Law* (2013), 95 (97 ff.).

[73] E.g. Universal Declaration of Human Rights (1948), Art. 16 (1): 'Men and women of full age, without any limitation due to race, nationality or religion, have the right to marry and to found a family. They are entitled to equal rights as to marriage, during marriage and at its dissolution'; International Covenant on Economic, Social and Cultural Rights (1966), Art. 7(a) (i): 'Fair wages and equal remuneration for work of equal value without distinction of any kind, in particular women being guaranteed conditions of work not inferior to those enjoyed by men, with equal pay for equal work'; International Covenant on Civil and Political Rights (1966), Article 3: 'The States Parties to the present Covenant undertake to ensure the equal right of men and women to the enjoyment of all civil and political rights set forth in the present Covenant'.

[74] Holtmaat, 'The CEDAW: a holistic approach to women's equality and freedom' in Hellum and Aasen (eds), *Women's Human Rights – CEDAW in International, Regional and National Law* (2013), 95 (98).

[75] See further: Smith, *International Human Rights Law* (2018), 44 ff.; Saul and Kinley and Mowbray, *The International Covenant on Economic, Social and Cultural Rights: Commentary, Cases, and Materials* (2014); Ssenyonjo, *Economic, Social and Cultural Rights in International Law* (2016); McBeth, Nolan and Rice, *The International Law of Human Rights* (2017), 119 (119 ff.).

[76] See further: Smith, *International Human Rights Law* (2018), 44 ff., 48 ff.; Taylor, *A Commentary on the International Covenant on Civil and Political Rights – The UN Human Rights Committee's Monitoring of ICCPR Rights* (2020); Hannum et al. (eds), *International Human Rights – Problems of Law, Policy and Practice* (2018), 78 ff.; Farrell, *Habeas Corpus in International Law* (2017), 48 ff.; Kälin and Künzli, *The Law of International Human Rights Protection* (2019), 37 ff.; McBeth and Nolan and Rice, *The International Law of Human Rights* (2017), 72 ff.

[77] Smith, *International Human Rights Law* (2018), 31; see further for ICESCR and ICCPR: Smith, *International Human Rights Law* (2018), 44 ff.

subsequent review of the targets of SDG 5, the relevance of universal human rights in the context of each individual target will be examined. For this purpose, all relevant human rights within the UDHR, the ICESCR and the ICCPR help to illustrate a draft scope and dimensions of a selection of already existing universal women's rights in the international human rights framework (non-exhaustive):

- Right to life and physical integrity (Art. 6 ICCPR, Art. 3 UDHR)
- Rights to liberty and security of the person (Art. 9 ICCPR, Art. 3 UDHR)
- Right to equal protection before the law, access to justice and effective remedies (Art. 14 ICCPR, Art. 8 UDHR, Art. 11 UDHR) (→ Goal 16)
- Right to recognition as a person before the law (Art. 16 ICCPR, Art. 6 UDHR) (→ Goal 16)
- Right not to be submitted to slavery, servitude, forced labour or bonded labour (Article 4 UDHR)
- Right to privacy and to protection for home and family (Art. 12 UDHR)
- Equal right of men and women to the enjoyment of all economic, social and cultural rights (Art. 3 ICESCR)
- Right to an adequate standard of living (Art. 11 ICESCR)
- Right to adequate food and nutrition (Art. 11 ICESCR) (→ Goal 2))
- Rights to water and sanitation (Art. 11 ICESCR (→ Goal 16))
- Right to adequate housing, security of tenure and prohibition of forced eviction (Art. 11 ICESCR)
- Right to the highest attainable standard of physical and mental health (Art. 12 ICESCR, Art. 25 UDHR (→ Goal 3))
- Right to work and rights at work (Art. 6 and 7 ICESCR, Art. 23 UDHR, Art. 24 UDHR (→ Goal 8))
- Right to social security (Art. 9 ICESCR, Art. 22 UDHR, Art. 25 UDHR)
- Right to education (Art. 13 ICESCR, Art. 26 UDHR (→ Goal 4))
- Right to freedom of thought, conscience and religion (Art. 18 ICCPR, Art. 18 UDHR)
- Right to freedom of expression (Art. 19 ICCPR, Art. 19 UDHR)
- Prohibition of discrimination on the basis of race, colour, sex, language, religion, political or other opinion, national or social origin, property, birth, or other status (Art. 2 ICESCR, Art. 26 ICCPR)
- Right not to be subjected to torture and/or cruel, inhuman, degrading treatment or punishment (Art. 7 ICCPR)
- Right to be free from gendered violence
- Right to freedom of association (Art. 22 ICCPR, Art. 20 UDHR)
- Right to freedom of movement (Art. 12 ICCPR, Art. 13 UDHR)
- Right to vote and be elected and to public services (Art. 25 ICCPR, Art. 21 UDHR)
- Right of children to special protection (Art. 24 ICCPR, Convention on the Protection of the Child)
- Right of self-determination (Art. 1 ICESCR)
- Right of ethnic, religious or linguistic minorities to enjoy their own culture, to profess and practise their own religion, or to use their own language (Art. 27 ICCPR)
- Right of all peoples to enjoy and utilize fully and freely their natural wealth and resources (Art. 25 ICESCR)
- Right to take part in cultural life and to enjoy the benefits of scientific progress (Art. 15 ICESCR, Art. 27 UDHR)
- Right to seek and to enjoy asylum (Art. 14 UDHR)

- Right to nationality (Art. 15 UDHR)
- Right to marry and to found a family (Art. 16 UDHR)
- Right to own property (Art. 17 UDHR)

Given this picture, it might appear that women's rights are already comprehensively **38** covered by international law. However, there is still a substantial need for the enforcement of particularly women's rights, emphasising their still frequently disadvantaged position worldwide.[78] Specific provisions relate to 'the equal right of men and women' to the enjoyment of all rights within the respective Covenant (Art. 3 ICESCR; Art. 3 IC-CPR). Moreover, both the ICESCR and ICCPR include the obligation of states to respect and to ensure all rights within the corresponding Covenant 'without distinction of any kind, such as [...] sex' (Art. 2(2) ICESCR; Art. 2(1) ICCPR).[79] Special rights are granted to families, mothers and children within Art. 10 ICESCR, including the frequently mentioned rights to non-discrimination and equality.[80] Thus, Art. 10 ICESCR underlines the particular role of women when being mothers and the role of girls ('all children and young children', Art. 10(3) ICESCR). Against the background of Art. 10 ICESCR, General Comment No. 16 on Art. 3 ICESCR refers to violence against women by committing states 'to provide victims of domestic violence, who are primarily female, with access to safe housing, remedies and redress for physical, mental and emotional damage' as well as to 'take appropriate measures to eliminate violence against men and women and act with due diligence to prevent, investigate, mediate, punish and redress acts of violence against them by private actors'.[81] Moreover, General Comment No. 16 obliges states to safeguard rights to work,[82] to own, control or use housing, land, property to 'access to or control means of food production'.[83]

In the context of ICESCR and ICCPR, General Comment No. 16 on Article 3 ICE- **39** SCR,[84] General Comment No. 20 on Article 2.2 ICESCR,[85] General Comment No. 28 on

---

[78] Van Leeuwen, "Women's rights are human rights!': the practice of the United Nations Human Rights Committee and the Committee on Economic, Social and Cultural Rights' in Hellum and Aasen (eds), *Women's Human Rights – CEDAW in International, Regional and National Law* (2013), 242 (245 ff.).

[79] Charlesworth, 'Women' in Chesterman and Malone and Villalpando (eds), *The Oxford Handbook of United Nations Treaties* (2019), 249 (256).

[80] Saul and Kinley and Mowbray, *The International Covenant on Economic, Social and Cultural Rights: Commentary, Cases, and Materials* (2014), 723.

[81] E/C.12/2005/4, General Comment No. 16 (2005), *The equal right of men and women to the enjoyment of all economic, social and cultural rights (art. 3 of the International Covenant on Economic, Social and Cultural Rights),* 11 August 2005, para. 27; Saul and Kinley and Mowbray, *The International Covenant on Economic, Social and Cultural Rights: Commentary, Cases, and Materials* (2014), 231 f.

[82] E/C.12/2005/4, General Comment No. 16 (2005), *The equal right of men and women to the enjoyment of all economic, social and cultural rights (art. 3 of the International Covenant on Economic, Social and Cultural Rights),* 11 August 2005, para. 23 ff; see also Art. 11, Convention on the Elimination of All Forms of Discrimination against Women; Freeman and Chinkin and Rudolf, *The UN Convention on the Elimination of All Forms of Discrimination Against Women – A Commentary* (2012), 279 ff.

[83] E/C.12/2005/4, General Comment No. 16 (2005), *The equal right of men and women to the enjoyment of all economic, social and cultural rights (art. 3 of the International Covenant on Economic, Social and Cultural Rights),* 11 August 2005, para. 28.

[84] E/C.12/2005/4, General Comment No. 16 (2005), *The equal right of men and women to the enjoyment of all economic, social and cultural rights (art. 3 of the International Covenant on Economic, Social and Cultural Rights),* 11 August 2005.

[85] E/C.12/GC/20, General comment No. 20 (2009), *Non-discrimination in economic, social and cultural rights (art. 2, para. 2 of the International Covenant on Economic, Social and Cultural Rights),* 2 July 2009.

Article 3 ICCPR[86] and General Comment No. 18 on Art. 2 ICCPR[87] envisage the states' duties to ensure equality between men and women as well as to guarantee the fulfilment of the non-discrimination principle.[88]

2. Human Rights and Women: CEDAW

40   Universal human rights, which prohibit discrimination on the basis of gender in all respects as outlined above, were soon considered insufficient to effectively address the realities of the persistent and high levels of discrimination against women and girls worldwide.[89] This immanent 'gender-neutral symmetrical approach'[90] was extended and specified through the introduction of CEDAW which explicitly prohibits discrimination against women reflecting the 'categorical difference'[91] between discrimination against women and against men.[92] CEDAW is to be seen as the core international treaty in the area of women's human rights, constituting 'an international bill of rights for women'[93] and seeking for 'commitment to eliminate discrimination against women and achieve gender equality'.[94] CEDAW recognises the UDHR's values of dignity and equality[95] of every human being and, based on this, stresses that 'discrimination against women violates the principles of equality of rights and respect for human dignity'.[96] Besides, the preamble indicates in paragraph 7 that any discrimination against women impedes them from fully participating 'in the political, social, economic and cultural life of their countries'[97] leading to women's prevention 'from bringing their potentialities to the service of their countries and humanity'.[98] CEDAW stands out in its nature as a treaty with a special focus on combating the root causes of discrimination against women. The wording of Art. 5[99] plays a special role here, since it establishes the fundamental principle of

---

[86] Office of the High Commissioner for Human Rights, CCPR/C/21/Rev.1/Add.10, CCPR General Comment No. 28 (2000), *The Equality of Rights Between Men and Women (Art. 3 of the International Covenant on Civil and Political Rights)*.

[87] Office of the High Commissioner for Human Rights, *CCPR General Comment No. 18: Non-discrimination*, 10 November 1989 (Art. 2(1) of the International Covenant on Civil and Political Rights).

[88] States' duties include inter alia the obligation to respect, to protect and to fulfil, see further: Saul and Kinley and Mowbray, *The International Covenant on Economic, Social and Cultural Rights: Commentary, Cases, and Materials* (2014), 223 ff.

[89] Hellum and Aasen, 'Introduction' in Hellum and Aasen (eds), *Women's Human Rights – CEDAW in International, Regional and National Law* (2013), 1 (2).

[90] Hellum and Aasen, 'Introduction' in Hellum and Aasen (eds), *Women's Human Rights – CEDAW in International, Regional and National Law* (2013), 1 (2).

[91] Rudolf, 'Freedom from Violence, Full Access to Resources, Equal Participation, and Empowerment: The Relevance of CEDAW for the Implementation of the SDGs' in Kaltenborn, Krajewski and Kuhn (eds), *Sustainable Development Goals and Human Rights* (2020), 73 (79).

[92] Rudolf, 'Freedom from Violence, Full Access to Resources, Equal Participation, and Empowerment: The Relevance of CEDAW for the Implementation of the SDGs' in Kaltenborn and Krajewski and Kuhn (eds), *Sustainable Development Goals and Human Rights* (2020), 73 (79).

[93] Freeman and Chinkin and Rudolf, *The UN Convention on the Elimination of All Forms of Discrimination Against Women: A Commentary* (2012), 2.

[94] Campbell, *Women, Poverty, Equality – The Role of CEDAW* (2018), 5.

[95] See further on CEDAW's equality principles: Facio and Morgan, 'Equity or Equality for Women? Understanding CEDAW's Equality Principles' (2009) 60 *Ala. L. Rev.*, 1133 (1133 ff.); see for the distinction between formal and substantive equality: Fredman, 'Engendering socio-economic rights' in Hellum and Aasen (eds), *Women's Human Rights – CEDAW in International, Regional and National Law* (2013), 217 (223 ff.).

[96] CEDAW (1979), preamble, paras. 1, 7.

[97] CEDAW (1979), preamble, para. 7.

[98] Rudolf, 'Freedom from Violence, Full Access to Resources, Equal Participation, and Empowerment: The Relevance of CEDAW for the Implementation of the SDGs' in Kaltenborn and Krajewski and Kuhn (eds), *Sustainable Development Goals and Human Rights* (2020), 73 (75).

[99] CEDAW, Art. 5:

CEDAW to draw attention to gender differences. As defined, sex is based on biological differences between men and women, while gender reflects the social constructs of and expectations towards women and men within society embedded in gendered power relations. 'These power relations are upheld by gender stereotypes[100] [...] [and] ensure a hierarchy between men and women [...]' (see SDG 5.1) (→ Intro mn. 263).[101] This is particularly significant as women are still highly discriminated against 'through a great variety of discriminatory laws and practices, beliefs, customs and traditions all over the world, which are based on gender stereotypes and fixed parental gender roles'.[102]

However, CEDAW is an essential source of law worldwide not only in its role as   **41** an important convention to combat discrimination against women. Moreover, the objectives of CEDAW are identical to those of the SDGs and thus to SDG 5. From this perspective, CEDAW can be regarded as the legal framework and instrument for the implementation of SDG 5 worldwide.[103]

International recognition of the relevance of women's human rights was fostered   **42** in treaties following the CEDAW. In 1993, representatives of 171 States adopted by consensus the Vienna Declaration and Programme of Action of the World Conference on Human Rights,[104] and in 1995, 189 states (the entire community of states at that time) agreed to the so-called Beijing Declaration and Platform for Action, thus creating the historically 'most progressive blueprint ever for advancing women's rights' (→ Intro mn. 263).[105] Particular attention is to be drawn to the profound interlinkages of CEDAW with various other legal frameworks, such as family law. These interlinkages and their observance in the implementation process of SDG 5 are crucial for a holistic, compre-

---

States Parties shall take all appropriate measures: (a) To modify the social and cultural patterns of conduct of men and women, with a view to achieving the elimination of prejudices and customary and all other practices which are based on the idea of the inferiority or the superiority of either of the sexes or on stereotyped roles for men and women; (b) To ensure that family education includes a proper understanding of maternity as a social function and the recognition of the common responsibility of men and women in the upbringing and development of their children, it being understood that the interest of the children is the primordial consideration in all cases.

[100] see Freeman and Chinkin and Rudolf, *The UN Convention on the Elimination of All Forms of Discrimination Against Women: A Commentary* (2012), 246 f.; Saul and Kinley and Mowbray, *The International Covenant on Economic, Social and Cultural Rights: Commentary, Cases, and Materials* (2014), 230.

[101] Rudolf, 'Freedom from Violence, Full Access to Resources, Equal Participation, and Empowerment: The Relevance of CEDAW for the Implementation of the SDGs' in Kaltenborn and Krajewski and Kuhn (eds), *Sustainable Development Goals and Human Rights* (2020), 73 (79).

[102] Holtmaat, 'The CEDAW: a holistic approach to women's equality and freedom' in Hellum and Aasen (eds), *Women's Human Rights – CEDAW in International, Regional and National Law* (2013), 95 (98).

[103] Rudolf, 'Freedom from Violence, Full Access to Resources, Equal Participation, and Empowerment: The Relevance of CEDAW for the Implementation of the SDGs' in Kaltenborn and Krajewski and Kuhn (eds), *Sustainable Development Goals and Human Rights* (2020), 73 (82).

[104] https://www.un.org/en/development/devagenda/humanrights.shtml; Vienna World Conference on Human Rights, A/CONF.157/23, *Vienna Declaration and Programme of Action* (1993), see para. 18: 'The human rights of women and of the girl-child are an inalienable, integral and indivisible part of universal human rights'.

[105] https://beijing20.unwomen.org/en/about; Rudolf, 'Freedom from Violence, Full Access to Resources, Equal Participation, and Empowerment: The Relevance of CEDAW for the Implementation of the SDGs' in Kaltenborn and Krajewski and Kuhn (eds), *Sustainable Development Goals and Human Rights* (2020), 73 (78 f); A/CONF./177/20/Rev.1, *Fourth World Conference on Women* (1995), see para. 9: 'Ensure the full implementation of the human rights of women and of the girl child as an inalienable, integral and indivisible part of all human rights and fundamental freedoms'; see further: Smith, *Texts and Materials on International Human Rights* (2020), 514 ff., 521 ff.

hensive and effective establishment of gender equality and the empowerment of women and girls.[106]

43 CEDAW's objectives, for gender equality and empowerment of women and girls, being identical with the SDGs,[107] serve as a meaningful starting point for a rights-based empowerment of women and girls worldwide.

44 SDG 5.1 includes a comprehensive and urgent call for the elimination of all forms of discrimination against women around the world. This imperative is found as a defining approach to discrimination in Art. 1 of CEDAW and continues to exist throughout the subsequent articles. CEDAW's first mentioned obligation for states concerns the anchoring of the principle of equality between men and women in the states' respective constitutions as well as the general adoption and implementation of legal measures and policies aimed at eliminating discrimination against women.[108] Particular emphasis is laid to Arts. 2(c), 2(e) and 2(f) of which the former includes the establishment of legal protection of women's rights on an equal basis as men's rights before judiciary.[109] Art. 2(e) points out the significant requirement 'to address discrimination against women by private or non-State actors'.[110] In the light of Art. 2's general obligation to adopt legal measures, Art. 2(f) imposes on the key aspect of modifying existent laws and legal measures discriminating against women. This reformatory obligation of states shall, in the light of Art. 5(a), lead to a transformation in the area of social and cultural consideration of patterns of conduct of men and women, ultimately eliminating hierarchical gender perceptions and structures as well as customary practices and prejudices 'based on the idea of the inferiority or the superiority of either of the sexes or on stereotyped roles for men and women'.[111] Besides, Art. 2 basically illustrates and legally embodies SDG 5.c focusing on the adoption and strengthening of sound policies and enforceable legislation. The considerable significance of the fight against stereotypes and thus the fight against one of the core causes of discrimination against women is made clear by Arts. 2(f), 5(a) as well as Art. 10(c) on the elimination of stereotypes in education. In their scope, Art. 2(f) and 5(a) serve as a wide-ranging umbrella within CEDAW, whereby the fight against stereotypes applies in particular to the objectives in Arts. 6 to 16.[112]

45 Arts. 6 to 16 list the further obligations of the states, which in their scope come into contact with numerous other human rights as well as other women's rights in various fields. Therefore, within the systematics of SDG 5, SDG 5.1 (eliminating all forms of discrimination against women everywhere) forms an umbrella for the other targets and should always serve as a reference when assessing SDG 5.2 to 5.c.[113]

---

[106] Rudolf, 'Freedom from Violence, Full Access to Resources, Equal Participation, and Empowerment: The Relevance of CEDAW for the Implementation of the SDGs' in Kaltenborn, Krajewski and Kuhn (eds), *Sustainable Development Goals and Human Rights* (2020), 73 (82 f.).

[107] See Rudolf, 'Freedom from Violence, Full Access to Resources, Equal Participation, and Empowerment: The Relevance of CEDAW for the Implementation of the SDGs' in Kaltenborn and Krajewski and Kuhn (eds), *Sustainable Development Goals and Human Rights* (2020), 73 (82).

[108] CEDAW, Art. 2.

[109] CEDAW, Art. 2(a).

[110] Freeman and Chinkin and Rudolf, *The UN Convention on the Elimination of All Forms of Discrimination Against Women: A Commentary* (2012), 87.

[111] Freeman and Chinkin and Rudolf, *The UN Convention on the Elimination of All Forms of Discrimination Against Women – A Commentary* (2012), 90; Art. 5(a), Convention on the Elimination of All Forms of Discrimination against Women.

[112] Cusack, 'The CEDAW as a legal framework for transnational discourses on gender stereotyping' in Hellum and Aasen (eds), *Women's Human Rights – CEDAW in International, Regional and National Law* (2013), 124 (132 f.).

[113] see Freeman, Chinkin and Rudolf, *The UN Convention on the Elimination of All Forms of Discrimination Against Women – A Commentary* (2012), 52; Rudolf, 'Freedom from Violence, Full Access to Resources, Equal Participation, and Empowerment: The Relevance of CEDAW for the Implementation

Although not explicitly addressed in SDG 5, the fundamental right to education, es- **46** pecially with regard to underage girls, holds an outstanding position. It is indispensable to guarantee the right of girls (and also adult women) to education from the state side with full effectiveness ($\rightarrow$ Goal 4 mn. 38). Notwithstanding the fact that education is not mentioned directly in SDG 5, SDG 4 clearly refers to the universal right of girls to education. It is important to emphasise this inalienable right in SDG 4, as education is the ultimate key to a sustainable generation and society that is changing in line with the SDGs.[114] Similarly, education is crucial for the elimination of stereotypes within society, ultimately paving the way for women's opportunities to participate actively and without limits in political, economic and social life (SDG 5.5).[115]

SDG 5.5 is legally reflected inter alia in Art. 7 CEDAW and aims at ensuring 'women's **47** full and effective participation and equal opportunities for leadership at all levels of decision-making in political, economic and public life'. Art. 7 obliges states to 'eliminate discrimination against women in the political and public life'.[116] This intention is substantiated by concrete rights to be granted to women on an equal basis with men.[117] Women's representation and active presence in all public, political and economic fields of a country's societal life shall thus be enhanced alongside with the lasting goal of providing women with the opportunity to effectively and sustainably contribute at all levels of decision-making.[118] The legal sphere of women's effective participation and opportunities for leadership positions also extends to the international representation of states. By Art. 8, states are obliged to ensure that women have the same opportunities as men to represent their governments at the international level and to participate in the work of international organisations.[119]

Especially with regard to the rights of women in rural areas, the right to ownership **48** and control over land and other forms of property, financial services, inheritance and natural resources in SDG 5.a is of extraordinary importance. In this context, Art. 14[120] is the only provision in CEDAW concerning the rights of rural women, but all the rights set out in CEDAW also apply to rural women.[121] The empowerment of women in relation to gain access to ownership and control over land and other forms of property, financial services, inheritance and natural resources (SDG 5.a) represents an indispens-

---

of the SDGs' in Kaltenborn and Krajewski and Kuhn (eds), *Sustainable Development Goals and Human Rights* (2020), 73 (82).

[114] UNESCO, *Beyond commitments – How countries implement SDG 4* (2019), 9 f.

[115] Freeman, Chinkin and Rudolf, *The UN Convention on the Elimination of All Forms of Discrimination Against Women – A Commentary* (2012), 263 f.

[116] CEDAW, Art. 7.

[117] Convention on the Elimination of All Forms of Discrimination against Women, Art. 7: the right to vote in all elections and public referenda and to be eligible for election to all publicly elected bodies, the right to participate in the formulation of government policy and the implementation thereof and to hold public office and perform all public functions at all levels of government as well as the right to participate in non-governmental organizations and associations concerned with the public and political life of the country.

[118] Freeman, Chinkin and Rudolf, *The UN Convention on the Elimination of All Forms of Discrimination Against Women – A Commentary* (2012), 198 f.

[119] Freeman, Chinkin and Rudolf, *The UN Convention on the Elimination of All Forms of Discrimination Against Women – A Commentary* (2012), 221 f.

[120] Freeman, Chinkin and Rudolf, *The UN Convention on the Elimination of All Forms of Discrimination Against Women – A Commentary* (2012), 357 ff.

[121] Committee on the Elimination of Discrimination against Women, CEDAW/C/GC/34, *General recommendation No. 34 on the rights of rural women*, 7 March 2016, para. 2.

able instrument for the sustainable and effective inclusion of all women into the society and enables women to become more independent.[122]

49 The aspiration to ensure women's access to sexual and reproductive health and reproductive rights[123] within SDG 5.6 is legally envisaged in Art. 12 CEDAW. Hereby, CEDAW obliges states to especially grant access to family planning by implementing 'appropriate measures [...] to ensure women's access to services 'in the areas of family planning, pregnancy, confinement and during the post-natal period,' and to sexual and reproductive health services'.[124] Furthermore, the general right to health is to be related to SDG 5.6 and Art. 12 CEDAW serves as a catalyst for the enforcement of women's right to health in particular (→ Goal 3 mn. 24).[125]

III. International Conventions and Declarations

50 Several declarations and international agreements support the fight for women empowerment and their equal rights.

1. The Beijing Platform for Action

51 The Beijing Platform for Action (Beijing Declaration) and its follow-up documents stand for an important guideline for women's empowerment and equality policy. It is recognised as one building block for a condition for people-centred sustainable development. The Beijing Declaration was signed by 189 countries at the Fourth United Nations World Conference on Women in Beijing in 1995, and set in forth a comprehensive programme for equality between women and men (→ Intro mn. 262 f.).[126]

52 The document, which is in full conformity with the purposes and principles of the Charter of the United Nations and international law, comprises 12 critical areas of concern.[127]

53 In each of these critical areas, the specific problem is diagnosed and strategic objectives are proposed with concrete actions to be taken by various actors in order to achieve those objectives. The critical areas of concern are as follows:

- Women and the environment
- Women in power and decision-making
- The girl child
- Women and the economy
- Women and poverty
- Violence against women

---

[122] The Global Initiative for Economic, Cultural and Social Rights, *Using CEDAW to Secure Women's Land and Property Rights – A Practical Guide*, 5 f.

[123] See further: Turshen, *Women's Health Movements – A Global Force for Change* (2020), 191 ff.; Freeman, Chinkin and Rudolf, *The UN Convention on the Elimination of All Forms of Discrimination Against Women – A Commentary* (2012), 311 ff.; De Vido, *Violence against women's health in international law* (2020); Patel, *Women and International Human Rights Law – Universal Periodic Review in Practice* (2020), 79 ff.; Iyioha, *Women's Health and the Limit of Law – Domestic and International Perspectives* (2020).

[124] Freeman, Chinkin and Rudolf, *The UN Convention on the Elimination of All Forms of Discrimination Against Women – A Commentary* (2012), 320.

[125] Committee on the Elimination of Discrimination against Women, *CEDAW General Recommendation No. 24: Article 12 of the Convention (Women and Health)* (1999), para. 2.

[126] Beijing Declaration and Platform for Action, adopted at the 16th plenary meeting, on 15 September 1995; UN Women, The United Nations, Fourth World Conference on Women, Beijing, China – September 1995, Action for Equality, Development and Peace, Platform for Action, Mission statement.

[127] https://www.un.org/womenwatch/daw/beijing/platform/plat1.htm#statement.

- Human rights of women
- Education and training of women
- Institutional mechanisms for the advancement of women
- Women and health
- Women and the media
- Women and armed conflict[128]

Most of the goals have not been achieved in late 2021. Despite the efforts of govern- **54** ments and non-governmental organisations around the world, obstacles to women's participation persist. Vast political, economic and ecological crises continue in many parts of the world. These include wars of aggression, armed conflicts, colonial or other forms of alien domination or foreign occupation, civil wars and terrorism and most recently SARS-CoV-2 putting down achievements, where they have been identified under severe pressure.[129]

The following international conventions should be mentioned as well to obtain a **55** more complete picture of SDG 5, since these contribute to its implementation. Yet differences remain in comparison to the unification to an effective mechanism and the existing agreements have a complementary effect to CEDAW.[130]

2. Convention of Belém do Pará

The Inter-American Convention on the Prevention, Punishment, and Eradication of **56** Violence against Women, known as the Convention of Belém do Pará (where it was adopted in 1994), defines violence against women, establishes that women have the right to live a life free of violence and that violence against women constitutes a violation of human rights and fundamental freedoms.[131]

Several targets of SDG 5 fall within the scope of the Convention of Belém do Pará **57** such as SDG 5.1 (Art. 6(a)), SDG 5.2 (Art. 3, 6) and SDG 5.3 (Art. 4(h), 4(c), 6(b)).

The National Institute of Women of Mexico (INMUJERES) has supported the trans- **58** lation of the Convention to 13 indigenous languages.[132] The text of the Convention has also been translated into some languages that are commonly used in the Americas, including Aymara, Dutch, Guarani, (Haitian) Creole, Quechua (Bolivia) and Quechua (Peru).[133]

---

[128] Waldron, 'From the Margins to the Mainstream: The Beijing Declaration and Platform for Action' (1996) 33 *Canadian Yearbook of International Law/Annuaire Canadien De Droit International*, 123-48; Gardam and Jarvis, 'Women and Armed Conflict: The International Response to the Beijing Platform for Action' (2000) 32 *Colum. Hum. Rts. L. Rev.*, 1; CEPAL, NU, 'Regional report on the review of the Beijing Declaration and Platform for Action in Latin American and Caribbean countries, 25 years on.' (2019); Pietrobelli et al., 'Violence against women in Italy after Beijing 1995: the relationship between women's movement (s), feminist practices and state policies' (2020) 28.2 *Gender & Development*, 377-92.

[129] UN Women, Global Framework No 9, https://www.un.org/womenwatch/daw/beijing/platform/plat1.htm#statement.

[130] Bernard, 'The Synergy of "Rights" Conventions: The Convention on the Elimination of All Forms of Discrimination Against Women (CEDAW), the Convention on the Rights of the Child (CRC), the Inter-American Convention on the Prevention, Punishment and Eradication of Violence Against Women (The Convention of Belem do Para)', Paper presented at the Caribbean Conference on the Rights of the Child: Meeting the Post Ratification Challenge (Belize 1996).

[131] Bettinger-Lopez, 'Violence Against Women: Normative Developments in the Inter-American Human Rights System' in Manjoo and Jones (eds), *The Legal Protection Of Women From Violence: Normative Gaps In International Law* (2018); Kamminga, 'Due Diligence: A Useful Tool to Combat Violence against Women?' in Westendorp (ed), *The Women's Convention Turned 40* (2020).

[132] https://www.oas.org/en/MESECVI/convention.asp.

[133] https://www.oas.org/en/MESECVI/convention.asp.

59   Arts. 3 to 6 of the Convention are subject to a specific follow-up control mechanism. Due to the need to an effective implementation of the Convention the so-called and abbreviated MESECVI Process was created. MESECVI is a systematic and permanent multilateral evaluation methodology based on exchange and technical cooperation between the States Party to the Convention and a Committee of Experts.

60   It is recognised as the first legally binding international treaty that criminalises all forms of violence against women, particularly sexual violence.[134]

3. The Maputo Protocol

61   Another international human rights instrument established by the African Union is the Protocol to the African Charter on Human and Peoples' Rights on the Rights of Women in Africa, better known as the Maputo Protocol. The Protocol recognises that gender inequality undermines social, economic and political participation, concomitantly affecting human security. On 25 November 2005, the Protocol has been ratified by the required 15 member nations of the African Union and thus entered into force.[135]

4. The Istanbul Convention

62   The Convention on Preventing and Combating Violence against Women and Domestic Violence (Istanbul Convention) was adopted by the Committee of Ministers of the Council of Europe on 7 April 2011. It is the first instrument in Europe to set legally binding standards specifically to prevent gender-based violence, protect victims of violence and punish perpetrators.[136]

63   The Convention covers a broad range of measures, including obligations ranging from awareness-raising and data collection to legal measures on criminalising different forms of violence. To ensure an implementation of the Convention, a two-pillar monitoring mechanism, consisting of an independent expert body (GREVIO), and a Committee of the Parties (which follows up on GREVIO reports and makes recommendations to the parties concerned) was created.

64   The EU Parliament adopted an interim resolution in 2017, based on a report prepared jointly by the Civil Liberties (LIBE) and Women's Rights (FEMM) Committees. Subsequently, in a resolution of 4 April 2019, the EU Parliament asked the European Court of Justice to issue an opinion to resolve the legal uncertainty on the compatibility of the accession proposals and procedure with the Treaties.[137] As of March 2021, the

---

[134] https://www.oas.org/en/mesecvi/about.asp.

[135] Overview of countries which have signed, ratified / acceded to the Protocol to the African Charter on Human and Peoples Rights on the Rights of Women in Africa: https://au.int/sites/default/files/treaties/37077-sl-PROTOCOL%20TO%20THE%20AFRICAN%20CHARTER%20ON%20HUMAN%20AND%20PEOPLE%27S%20RIGHTS%20ON%20THE%20RIGHTS%20OF%20WOMEN%20IN%20AFRICA.pdf; further reading: Addadzi-Koom, 'Of the Women's Rights Jurisprudence of the ECOWAS Court: The Role of the Maputo Protocol and the Due Diligence Standard' (2020) 28 *Fem Leg Stud*, 155-78; Ngozi and Iyioha and Tope Durojaye, 'The Violence Against Persons Prohibition Act, the Maputo Protocol and the Rights of Women in Nigeria' (2018), 39(3) *Statute Law Review*, 337-47; Ayeni, 'The impact of the African Charter and the Maputo Protocol in selected African states' (2016); Kumalo and Sigsworth, 'Women, peace and security-implementing the Maputo Protocol in Africa' (2016) 295 *Institute for Security Studies Papers*, 1-24.

[136] Chart of signatures and ratifications of the treaty: https://www.coe.int/en/web/conventions/full-list/-/conventions/treaty/210/signatures; further reading: McQuigg, *The Istanbul Convention, Domestic Violence and Human Rights* (2017); Grans, 'The Istanbul Convention and the Positive Obligation to Prevent Violence' (2018) 18(1) *Human Rights Law Review*, 133-55.

[137] European Parliament, *The Istanbul Convention: A tool to tackle violence against women and girls* (2020); ECJ, Advocate General's Opinion in Avis 1/19, Press Release No 37/21, 11.03.2021.

'Istanbul Convention' has been signed by all EU Member States, and ratified by 21.[138] However, on 20 March 2021 Turkey withdrew from the Convention and already in July 2020, the Polish government announced its intention to withdraw. Since the Convention also provides for EU accession to the extent of its competences, this would require the European Parliament's consent.[139]

C. Interdependences of SDG 5

Promoting gender equality, eradicating poverty (SDG 1.2, SDG 1.4, SDG 1.4), and reducing other forms of inequality (SDG 10.2, SDG 10.3) are closely interlinked.[140] Since their objectives reinforce each other,[141] these can be seen as the main axis to address the multidimensional and overlapping nature of poverty[142] the elimination of which is a main aim of the SDGs.   65

Particularly women, as a multiply deprived vulnerable group, suffer from poverty. Inequalities in income, wealth and gender perception frequently translate into inequalities of opportunity (SDG 10.2) through unequal access to childhood nutrition (SDG 1.2), education (SDG 4.1, SDG 4.2)[143], health care and services (SDG 3.7, SDG 3.8, SDG 5.6) or social discrimination (SDG 5.2, SDG 5.3) which exacerbates fundamental needs such as food (SDG 2.1, SDG 2.2) and the opportunity to participate in society (SDG 5.5, SDG 16.9)[144] and which inhibits them to break out from the cycles of intergenerational poverty and deprivation.[145]   66

Since girls and women form two thirds of all illiterates worldwide,[146] gender equality (SDG 5.1) is key to mitigate inequalities in access to education (SDG 4.5).[147] In some parts of the world, girls are denied schooling, often combined with a low age at marriage, where they predominantly perform household chores from early on, leaving no capacity for education.[148] This is further exacerbated through discriminatory marriage and school laws which prohibit girls from attending school during pregnancy.[149] To   67

---

[138] Austria, Belgium, Croatia, Cyprus, Denmark, Estonia, Finland, France, Germany, Greece, Ireland, Italy, Luxembourg, Malta, Netherlands, Poland, Portugal, Romania, Slovenia, Spain and Sweden.

[139] https://www.europarl.europa.eu/legislative-train/theme-area-of-justice-and-fundamental-rights/file -eu-accession-to-the-istanbul-convention.

[140] Van Soest et al., 'Analysing interactions among Sustainable Development Goals with Integrated Assessment Models' (2019) 1 *Global Transitions,* 210 (213).

[141] United Nations Entity for Gender Equality and the Empowerment of Women, *Women and Sustainable Development Goals* (2018), 20.

[142] Independent Group of Scientists appointed by the Secretary-General, Global Sustainable Development Report 2019: The Future is Now – Science for Achieving Sustainable Development, (2019), xxiii.

[143] The link between SDG 4 and SDG 5 is particularly strong and bi-directional. Gender aspects are noted in SDG 4.1: 'all girls and boys'; SDG 4.2: 'all girls and boys'; SDG 4.3: 'all women and men'; SDG 4.5: 'eliminate gender disparities'; SDG 4.6: 'both men and women'; United Nations Entity for Gender Equality and the Empowerment of Women, *Women and Sustainable Development Goals* (2018), 10; United Nations Entity for Gender Equality and the Empowerment of Women, *Women and Sustainable Development Goals* (2018), 10; Van Soest et al., 'Analysing interactions among Sustainable Development Goals with Integrated Assessment Models' (2019) 1, *Global Transitions,* 210 (213).

[144] United Nations Entity for Gender Equality and the Empowerment of Women, *Women and Sustainable Development Goals* (2018), 5.

[145] Independent Group of Scientists appointed by the Secretary-General, Global Sustainable Development Report 2019: The Future is Now – Science for Achieving Sustainable Development, (2019), 43.

[146] UNESCO, *Promise of Gender Equality Key Actions 2018-2019* (2020), 11.

[147] United Nations Entity for Gender Equality and the Empowerment of Women, *Women and Sustainable Development Goals* (2018), 10.

[148] European Parliament, PE603.489, *Discriminatory Laws Undermining Women's Rights* (2020).

[149] European Parliament, PE603.489, *Discriminatory Laws Undermining Women's Rights* (2020).

successfully combat poverty (SDG 1.2, SDG 1.5), quality education in which all genders can participate is indispensable (SDG 4.3).[150]

68   Approximately 70 per cent of the health workforce is occupied by female employees.[151] Thus, women represent the largest share of workers who work in a traditionally low-paid profession (SDG 8.8) where they are more exposed to SARS-CoV-2 than men[152] (→ Goal 1 mn. 31 ff., 50 ff.). Additionally, women are much more likely to perform unpaid work such as caring for children, elderly, sick and other needy people (SDG 5.4).[153] In times of conflict or crisis such as the current pandemic, where global health systems focus on fighting SARS-CoV-2, reproductive and sexual health services are neglected (SDG 3.7).[154] This threatens to increase the already high maternal mortality rate[155] even further and to compromise women's health (SDG 3.1, SDG 3.8).

69   Although indications points that more men than women die from the effects of SARS-CoV-2,[156] the impact of the (short and longer term) socio-economic effects of the pandemic fall disproportionately on women.

70   To ensure the effective participation of women and girls in society and to protect against gender discriminatory acts, a functioning and fair legal system is needed (SDG 16). However, only 20 per cent of all parliamentarians worldwide are female,[157] leaving women with a very weak voice in shaping, establishing and implementing fair legal systems. Through women's empowerment, the presumably evolving higher proportion of female parliamentarians is also likely to result in a more consistent pursuit of the SDGs, as women are more inclined to invest in human development and environmental sustainability.[158] SDG 16 and specifically the *rule of law* (SDG 16.3) thus play a fundamental role in achieving gender equality.[159]

D. Jurisprudential Significance of SDG 5

71   The jurisprudential relevance of SDG 5 is hardly estimable, since almost half of the world's population is directly affected by gender equality norms and standards, and that the entire world population is shaped by the scope such norms and standards touch upon. The complexity of (legal) relationships girls and women as well as boys and

---

[150] United Nations Entity for Gender Equality and the Empowerment of Women, *Women and Sustainable Development Goals* (2018), 5.

[151] Boniol et al., *Gender equity in the health workforce: Analysis of 104 countries, Health Workforce Working* (2019), 1.

[152] Griffith et al., 'Men and COVID-19: A Biopsychosocial Approach to Understanding Sex Differences in Mortality and Recommendations for Practice and Policy Interventions' (2020) 17(200247) *Prev Chronic Dis*.

[153] Martens et al., *COVID-19 and the SDGs The impact of the coronavirus pandemic on the global sustainability agenda* (2020), 3.

[154] Martens et al., *COVID-19 and the SDGs The impact of the coronavirus pandemic on the global sustainability agenda* (2020), 3.

[155] United Nations General Assembly Open Working Group on Sustainable Development Goals, *Compendium of TST Issues Briefs October 2014*, 216.

[156] Griffith et al., 'Men and COVID-19: A Biopsychosocial Approach to Understanding Sex Differences in Mortality and Recommendations for Practice and Policy Interventions' (2020) 17(200247) *Prev Chronic Dis*.

[157] United Nations General Assembly Open Working Group on Sustainable Development Goals, *Compendium of TST Issues Briefs October 2014*, 217.

[158] United Nations General Assembly Open Working Group on Sustainable Development Goals, *Compendium of TST Issues Briefs October 2014*, 218.

[159] United Nations Entity for Gender Equality and the Empowerment of Women, *Women and Sustainable Development Goals* (2018), 29; Van Soest et al., 'Analysing interactions among Sustainable Development Goals with Integrated Assessment Models' (2019) 1 *Global Transitions*, 210 (213).

men are engaging in can at least be measured by their crucial economic impact.[160] In many places, however, the abstract, all-encompassing law with its evolving norms and standards is not sufficiently gender-responsive to actually ensure the protection of girls and women.[161] Laws and institutions demonstrably have a different effect on girls and women than on men, often to a disproportionately amount.[162] Efforts to abolish this discriminatory (male) universalism exist, but are not to be found in the wider field.[163]

Discriminatory family and civil status laws, including inheritance law, exist in reality 　72 and are difficult to reform as such. Although gender mainstreaming and gender equality is a basic requirement in many policies, the development, education and economic opportunities for girls and women in particular are severely hampered, for example by discriminatory marriage and labour laws. The still widespread social norms, according to which men are regarded as the (most important) economic provider of the family and women being allowed to work in the informal sector at best, largely without protection under labour law against harassment or discriminatory practices, place an additional drawback on them.[164]

I. Jurisdiction on Vision and Objectives

The jurisdiction in the areas covered by SDG 5 is notably progressive and rapidly 　73 developing, although slightly different trends can be identified. It is striking, however, that the transfer and application of the respective jurisdiction is fraught with distinct obstacles or is not sufficiently systematically structured.

The inability to access legal and justice services can be both a result and a cause 　74 of disadvantage, poverty, and inequality in income and employment opportunities, educational attainment and health conditions. People-centred legal and justice services go beyond a fair and effective justice system to greater objectives such as inclusive growth, equality, poverty-reduction, social justice and social inclusion. The core of access to justice is equality and social inclusion in the light of the 'leave no one behind' imperative of the Global Agenda 2030.[165]

1. International Jurisdiction

The jurisdiction of the IACtHR in particular is not only clear in terms of protecting 　75 the particularly vulnerable group of girls and women, but is also very progressive. In accordance with, or beyond, the strong legislative framework of child, women and

---

[160] McKinsey Global Institute, *How advancing women's equality can add $12 trillion to global growth, Report* (2015).

[161] Undurraga, 'Engendering a constitutional moment: The quest for parity in the Chilean Constitutional Convention' (2020) 18(2) *International Journal of Constitutional Law*, 466 (470).

[162] Undurraga, 'Engendering a constitutional moment: The quest for parity in the Chilean Constitutional Convention' (2020) 18(2) *International Journal of Constitutional Law*, 466-70; Rodríguez Ruiz and Rubio-Marin, 'The Gender of Representation: On Democracy, Equality and Parity' (2008) 6 *INT'L J. CONST. L.*, 287 (303); see also Choudhoury, 'Rights of Women' in Cottier and Nadakavukaren Schefer (eds), *Elagr Encyclopedia of International Economic Law* (2017), 653 f.

[163] For instance, in Latin America the *principle of parity* (Chile) is applied which means that (normative) universalism is liberated from 'the illusions of abstraction (which made it a male universalism) and making it a reality'; see Undurraga, 'Engendering a constitutional moment: The quest for parity in the Chilean Constitutional Convention' (2020) 18(2) *International Journal of Constitutional Law*, 466-70.

[164] European Parliament, *Discriminatory Laws Undermining Women's Rights* (2019), 7.

[165] OECD, *Governance as an SDG Accelerator: Country Experiences and Tools* (2019), XX.

gender-specific protection,[166] various principles have been elevated by verdict into the status of internationally established (customary) law.

76   One clear interpretation of SDG 5.2 is 'the first international adjudicative decision to qualify rape as torture under international law',[167] which has since been repeatedly classified in this way by the IACtHR and the Inter-American Commission on Human Rights.[168] In addition to this basic classification, quite broad definitions of rape and sexual violence have been drawn up and are now established as such:

> [S]exual violence consists of actions with a sexual nature committed with a person without their consent, which besides including the physical invasion of the human body, may include acts that do not imply penetration or even any physical contact whatsoever,[169]

77   considering it also a violation of the right to human treatment and to private life and dignity.[170]

78   In *López Soto et al. v. Venezuela*, 'the Court interpreted that sexual slavery, as a violation of human rights, was covered by the prohibition contained in Art. 6 of the [American] Convention,[171] regardless of the existence of a specific context.' In the court's view, two aspects must be verified to classify a situation as sexual slavery: (a) the exercise of attributes of the right to property over a person, and (b) the existence of acts of a sexual nature that restricted or annulled the sexual autonomy of that person.[172]

---

[166] In addition to international instruments of protection such as the Convention on the Rights of the Child and CEDAW, the Inter-American Convention on the Prevention, Punishment, and Eradication of Violence Against Women, June 9, 1994, 33 ILM 1534 (1994) and the Belém do Pará Convention are regularly being considered.

[167] *Raquel Martín de Mejía v. Peru*, Case 10.970, Inter-Am. Comm'n H.R, Report No. 5/96, OEA/Ser.L/V/II.91 Doc. 7, found in: Duhaime, Bernard, 'Women's Rights In Recent Inter-American Human Rights Jurisprudence' (2017) *ASIL Proceedings*, 257 (258).

[168] E.g. under consideration of the Belém do Pará Convention on the Prevention, Punishment, and Eradication of Violence Against Women: *Ana and Gonzalez Perez v. Mexico*, Case 11.565, Inter-Am. Comm'n H.R., Report No. 53/01, OEA/Ser., L/V/II.111 Doc. 20 (2000); *Miguel Castro-Castro Prison v. Peru*, Merits, Reparations and Costs, Judgment, IACtHR, InterAm. Ct. H.R. (ser. C) No. 160 (Nov. 25, 2006); *González et al. (Cotton Field) v. Mexico*, Preliminary Objection, Merits, Reparations, and Costs, Judgment, IACtHR, (ser. C) No. 205 (Nov. 16, 2009); *Fernández Ortega v. Mexico*, IACtHR, (ser. C) No. 215 (May 7, 2009).

[169] Definition to be found in: e.g. *Castro-Castro*, supra note 12, para. 306 ff.; amongst others referred to in: *Rosendo Cantú et al. v. Mexico*, Preliminary Objections, Merits, Reparations and Costs, IACtHR, (ser. C) No. 216, 31 August 2010, para. 118; *Fernández Ortega v. Mexico*, IACtHR, (ser. C) No. 215 (May 7, 2009), para. 1229.

[170] E.g. *Rosendo Cantú et al. v. Mexico*, Preliminary Objections, Merits, Reparations and Costs, IACtHR. (ser. C) No. 216, 31 August 2010, para. 118; *Fernández Ortega v. Mexico*, IACtHR, (ser. C) No. 215 (May 7, 2009), para. 1229.

[171] Freedom from Slavery of the American Convention On Human Rights (1969), Art. 6:

1. No one shall be subject to slavery or to involuntary servitude, which are prohibited in all their forms, as are the slave trade and traffic in women.

2. No one shall be required to perform forced or compulsory labor. This provision shall not be interpreted to mean that, in those countries in which the penalty established for certain crimes is deprivation of liberty at forced labor, the carrying out of such a sentence imposed by a competent court is prohibited. Forced labor shall not adversely affect the dignity or the physical or intellectual capacity of the prisoner.

3. For the purposes of this article, the following do not constitute forced or compulsory labor:

work or service normally required of a person imprisoned in execution of a sentence or formal decision passed by the competent judicial authority. Such work or service shall be carried out under the supervision and control of public authorities, and any persons performing such work or service shall not be placed at the disposal of any private party, company, or juridical person; military service and, in countries in which conscientious objectors are recognized, national service that the law may provide for in lieu of military service; service exacted in time of danger or calamity that threatens the existence or the well-being of the community; or work or service that forms part of normal civic obligations.

[172] *López Soto et al. v. Venezuela*, Judgement, 26 September 2018, IACtHR, paras. 176-78, Summary of judgement: http://www.corteidh.or.cr/docs/casos/articulos/resumen_362_esp.pdf; Interpretation of the

The IACtHR underlined that 'sexual slavery was a particular form of slavery[173] in   **79**
which sexualised violence is primarily committed in the exercise of the attributes of
the right to property over a person. For this reason, in such cases, factors related to constraints to the activity and sexual autonomy of the victim constituted strong indicators
of the exercise of dominance of a perpetrator. Sexual slavery differed from other similar
practices of slavery that were not of a sexual nature. Additionally, the element of slavery
was determinant in distinguishing such acts from other forms of sexual violence. By
identifying such conducts as a form of slavery, all the obligations associated with the
nature *jus cogens* of its prohibition – in other words, its absolute and peremptory nature
– became applicable.'[174]

In a case before IACommHR,[175] however, no disproportionate impact on women   **80**
from an employment relationship which was exclusively occupied by women was found.
The applicant, who was employed in a children's home, had to work almost 24 hours in
consecutive periods, while the nature of her employment relationship demanded a maternal care role, without fulfilling any duties and obligations towards her under labour
law. Although judicial access was granted to her, the Commission did not conclude that
she was being 'exploited' in the sense of an overriding applicable standard that would
apply to private-law employment contracts or could even constitute a breach of state
obligations:

> [T]here exist international standards on such issues and a system for their international supervision,
> particularly in the framework of the International Labour Organization. Nevertheless, such issues
> are beyond the scope of Article 5 of the Convention, which is not intended to govern ordinary
> labor relations or to impose specific standards on States with respect to employment conditions and
> working hours in the framework of labor contracts, whether in the public or the private sector.[176]

This case may show the limit in the otherwise very progressive inter-American legal   **81**
system which maintains a high standard of protection. The Commission shows a more
precise boundary in particular when it states that 'specific, extreme working conditions
that harm a person's physical, psychological, or moral integrity are coupled with circumstances that make the employment relationship a form of, or analogous to, involuntary
servitude'.[177] When comparing the possible SDG 5.1 and SDG 5.2, it is also noticeable
that this form of exploitation cannot be assigned. On the one hand, indicator 5.1.1 solely
refers to the existence of adequate protective frameworks, but not to their actual performance or the way they are applied. The second indicator, 5.2.1, which deviates from
SDG 5.2 formulation 'Eliminate all forms of violence [...] in the public and private
sphere [...] and other types of exploitation', is measured exclusively on the exercise of violence and exploitation of a current or former intimate partner. Moreover, the indicator
5.2.2, which does not have this limitation, only refers to forms of sexual violence and not
to other types of exploitation. It is all the more interesting that care and domestic work
are generally included in SDG 5.4, provided that they are unpaid and thus belong to the

---

Judgment on the Merits, Reparations and Costs: http://www.corteidh.or.cr/docs/casos/articulos/seriec_37
9_esp.pdf.

[173] See for the IACtHR's definition of slavery: *López Soto et al. v. Venezuela*, Judgement, 26 September
2018, IACtHR, paras. 174-5.

[174] Inter-American Court of Human Rights, *Annual Report 2018* (2019), 116; See for the IACtHR's
definition of slavery: *López Soto et al. v. Venezuela*, Judgement, IACtHR, 26 September 2018, paras. 176-8.

[175] *Tellez Blanco v. Costa Rica*, IACommHR, Petition 712-03, Report No. 29/07, OEA/Ser.L/V/II.130,
doc. 22 rev. 1 (2007).

[176] *Tellez Blanco v. Costa Rica*, Petition 712-03, IACommHR, Report No. 29/07, OEA/Ser.L/V/II.130,
doc. 22 rev. 1 (2007), 12-5.

[177] *Tellez Blanco v. Costa Rica*, Petition 712-03, IACommHR, Report No. 29/07, OEA/Ser.L/V/II.130,
doc. 22 rev. 1 (2007), 15.

private sphere. If, however, these are carried out in an exploitative framework that originates from a labour-law basis or so-called *modern day slavery*, the scope of SDG 5 does not unfold and also cannot be located in SDG 8 (→ Goal 8 mn. 33 ff., 63 ff.).

82   In *Atala Riffo and Daughters v. Chile*, for example, the IACtHR for the first time assessed that sexual orientation and gender identity are protected categories under the American Convention on Human Rights and that the same sex couples are to be handled legally as a heterosexual couple alike. According to this, this includes 'state obligations concerning change of name, gender identity, and rights derived from a relationship between same-sex couples'.[178] However, whether the vulnerable group of LGBTI / LGBTQ can be read into SDG 5 seems rather questionable. If one interprets SDG 5 in terms of its indicators, this group does not seem to be explicitly included. The case described would then acquire its significance because of the illustration of the multiple discrimination of women. The Global Agenda 2030 should take this group into account, and SDG 10 should certainly be applied more clearly to avert any such looming inequalities (→ Goal 10 mn. 86).

83   In addition to the strategy for the implementation of gender equality of the European Council, there are three international legal instruments for the protection of human dignity in the European area with explicit reference to the significance of SDGs as a framework: Council of Europe Convention on Preventing and Combating Violence against Women and Domestic Violence (Istanbul Convention)[179]; Council of Europe Convention on Action against Trafficking in Human Beings; Council of Europe Convention on the Protection of Children against Sexual Exploitation and Sexual Abuse (Lanzarote Convention).[180] These specifically include the fundamental safeguards against stalking, forced marriage, female genital mutilation, forced abortion, forced sterilisation and sexual harassment. Together with the strategy and the general prohibition of discrimination enshrined in the ECHR,[181] they constitute the main framework within which the ECtHR carries out its judicial assessments.

84   The ECtHR bases its jurisdiction on gender equality fundamentally on the principle of 'gender equality as one of the main objectives in the Member States of the Council of Europe'.[182] In particular, the ECtHR interprets Art. 14 (prohibition of discrimination) verbatim, according to which 'sex' is explicitly included among the prohibited grounds of discrimination. Since the ECHR also contains the formula 'or other status', the Court is now beginning to discuss the concept of 'gender equality', for example in the case of *Leyla Şahin v Turkey*,[183] when it states, '[g]ender equality – [is] recognised by the European Court of Justice as one of the key principles of the Convention and as an objective to be attained by the Member States of the Council of Europe'. Albeit this case proved to be highly controversial, the use of both terms and the given broad understanding of

---

[178] *Atala Riffo and Daughters v. Chile*, Advisory Opinion OC-24/17, IACtHR, (ser. A) No. 24 (Nov. 24, 2017), amongst other, paras. 201-5.

[179] Further reading: Policy Department for Citizens' Rights and Constitutional Affairs, *Tackling violence against women and domestic violence in Europe. The added value of the Istanbul Convention and remaining challenges*, Study requested by the European Parliament's Committee on Women's Rights and Gender Equality (FEMM) (2020).

[180] Council of Europe, *Gender Equality Strategy 2018-2023* (2018), 13.

[181] European Convention on Human Rights, entered into force on 1 June 2010, Art. 14.

[182] Council of the European Union, *Council conclusions on the European Pact for gender equality for the period 2011 – 2020, 3073rd Employment, Social Policy, Health and Consumer Affairs Council* (2011):
THE COUNCIL OF THE EUROPEAN UNION acknowledges that equality between women and men is a fundamental value of the European Union and that gender equality policies are vital to economic growth, prosperity and competitiveness.

[183] *Leyla Şahin v. Turkey*, 10 November 2005, ECtHR [GC] no. 44774/98.

equality before the law (for women and men)[184] by the ECtHR can be interpreted quite progressively. More recently, it can be understood that the ECtHR indicates an evolving but all the more broad tendency of understanding gender equality,[185] which overall supports the substance of SDG 5.

In a case before the CESCR, 'a strong articulation of the rights to social security and **85** to substantive gender equality' was acknowledged for the first time and recognised as an issue of global relevance.[186] When the state 'failed to provide [the claimant] with timely and adequate retirement plan eligibility information and denied her pension based on disproportionate and discriminatory grounds', the Committee found that the rights to social security, Art. 9 ICESCR, to non-discrimination, Art. 2(2) ICESCR and to gender equality, Art. 3 ICESCR was violated. With the participation of a large number of NGOs and human rights activists, in this case a direct link was found between social security and its sustainable design which must not be denied in ensuring retirement pension systems.

A landmark decision, was taken in 2019 by the ECOWAS Community Court of **86** Justice (ECOWAS CCJ).[187] This claim was preceded by a strict exclusion of pregnant schoolgirls from participation in school lessons and only partial replacement in special institutions exclusively for them. The pregnancy rate in Sierra Leone had risen sharply during a nine-month lockdown due to the Ebola pandemic 2014/15. In this case, the court reiterated the admissibility of *actio popularis*,[188] the accompanying legal action by WAVES and the involvement of NGOs such as Amnesty International. Referring to numerous human rights instruments,[189] the court ruled 'that an unlawful ban on pregnant adolescent girls from attending school' had occurred and that the use of separate schools is discriminatory and a violation of the right to (equal) education.[190] In its reasoning the court also referred to similar incidents concerning the ethnic group of Roma and the derivation of a discriminatory act before the ECtHR, albeit a dissenting opinion in that case did not support this conclusion.[191] In other pending cases, the far-reaching decision of the ECOWAS CCJ is used, also against the background that the overturned ban pronounced is *de facto* still in effect. At least as a pillar for the

---

[184] *Leyla Şahin v. Turkey*, 10 November 2005, ECtHR [GC] no. 44774/98, paras. 115 f.

[185] *Opuz v. Turkey*, 9 June 2009, ECtHR Application No. 33401/02; *Talpis v. Italy*, 2 March 2017, ECtHR Application No. 41237/14; See also the landmark case: *Konstantin Markin v. Russia*, Judgment, 22 March 2012, ECtHR Application No. 30078/06, para. 142 stating: 'the difference in treatment cannot be justified by reference to traditions prevailing in a certain country. The Court has already found that States may not impose traditional gender roles and gender stereotypes'; further reading on this issue: Ciuffoletti, '"Regardless of their sex" or "biological differences", An analysis of the European Court of Human Rights' case law on women in prison' (2020) 11(2) *Rev. Direito Práx.*

[186] CESCR, *Marcia Cecilia Trujillo Calero v. Ecuador*, Communication 10/2015, UN Doc. E/C.12/63/D/10/2015 (26 March 2018).

[187] *Women Against Violence and Exploitation in Society (WAVES) v. The Republic of Sierra Leone*, Judgment, 12 December 2019, ECOWAS CCJ, ECW/CCJ/JUD/37/19.

[188] See e.g. *Rev. Father Solomon MFN v. FRN*, ECOWAS CCJ, ECW(CCJ/JUD/06/19; *SERAP v. FRN*, CCJELR, paras. 32, 34.

[189] Amongst others: African Charter on Human and Peoples' Rights; the African Charter on the Rights and Welfare of the Child; the Protocol to the African Charter on the Rights of Women in Africa; the United Nations Educational, Scientific and Cultural Organization Convention against Discrimination in Education; the Convention on the Rights of the Child; the Convention on the Elimination of Discrimination against Women; the International Covenant on Economic, Social and Cultural Rights; and the Universal Declaration on Human Rights.

[190] *Women Against Violence and Exploitation in Society (WAVES) v. The Republic of Sierra Leone*, Judgment, 12 December 2019, ECOWAS CCJ, ECW/CCJ/JUD/37/19, 29.

[191] *Case of Oršuš and Others v. Croatia*, Judgment, 16 March 2010, ECtHR Application no. 15766/03, paras. 156 f., 178-85.

interpretation and application of SDG 5, this case can support public interest litigation and related campaigns.

2. European Jurisdiction

87   'The very first gender-related article was found in the 1957 Treaty of Rome establishing the European Economic Community (EEC) requiring each member state to guarantee the application of the principle of equal pay for women and men.'[192] Among the most important cases of European jurisdiction for the further development of the then economic community (EC) is the *Defrenne case*.[193] The claimant was awarded a lower wage than her male colleagues for equal work. The ECJ clearly found a less favourable treatment on the ground of sex (sex discrimination). In this ruling, the court emphasised the importance of the 'economic and social dimension of the Union', the achievement of which is assisted by non-discrimination. Since then, gender equality in the development of the EU has been starkened in many areas and its understanding is highly influenced by the SDGs today.[194]

88   Although equality and non-discrimination are enshrined as fundamental values in the EU Treaties in Art. 2 and are interwoven as a horizontal clause with the EU's policy objectives, requiring positive action from Member States respectively, it is anti-/non-discrimination that is most prominent in legally enforceable obligations. Moreover, gender equality *de facto* mostly remains in the sphere of non-legal measures,[195] although the EU committed in its objectives to promoting gender equality, Art. 3(3) TEU. Since the EU has shared competences in pursuing gender equality, 'the EU gender directives include a limited exception in EU anti-discrimination law for positive action measures' in so that positive action is possible, even though there is no need to pursue it. However, in accordance with the principle of subsidiarity, it is mostly up to the Member States to take positive action, most of which are voluntary (self-regulation and standard-setting).[196]

89   A main issue relating to gender equality in the EU is 'gender-based positive action in employment'. The considerable varying significance and connotation of positive action between Member States is one of the main reasons for this, and is complemented by the absence of a *de facto* monitoring of the effectiveness and enforcement of adopted positive action measures while at the same time the EU's influence on its Member States is comparatively insignificant.[197]

90   However, the principal ECJ cases concerning special measures have arisen in the context of gender equality; namely the *Kalanke case*, the *Marschall case* and the *Abrahamsson case* which together 'defined the limits on how far special measures can be

---

[192] Monteiro, 'Gender-Related Provisions In Regional Trade Agreements' (2018), Staff Working Paper ERSD-2018-15 *World Trade Organization Economic Research and Statistics Division*, 4.

[193] ECJ, C-43/75, 08.04.1976, *Gabrielle Defrenne v. Société anonyme belge de navigation aérienne Sabena (Defrenne)*, ECLI:EU:C:1976:56.

[194] https://ec.europa.eu/info/policies/justice-and-fundamental-rights/gender-equality/gender-equality-strategy_en; European Commission, Crowley and Sansonetti, *New Visions For Gender Equality 2019* (2019); see also Council of the European Union, A comprehensive approach to accelerate the implementation of the UN 2030 Agenda for sustainable development – Building back better from the COVID-19 crisis, Council conclusions (9850/21), 22 June 2021.

[195] McCrudden, 'Resurrecting positive action' (2020) 18(2) *Int. J. Const. Law*, 429-33.

[196] McCrudden, 'Resurrecting positive action' (2020) 18(2) *Int. J. Const. Law*, 429-33; see also European Commission, *2019 Report on equality between women and men in the EU* (2019).

[197] McCrudden, 'Resurrecting positive action' (2020) 18(2) *Int. J. Const. Law*, 429-33.

taken to compensate for the previous disadvantages suffered by, in these particular cases, female workers over the years.'[198]

With its further case law, the ECJ has established that discrimination on the grounds　**91** of a person's gender reassignment is covered by the prohibition of discrimination on grounds of sex,[199] which was subsequently manifested in recital 3 of Recast Directive 2006/54.[200] In ECJ jurisdiction, other genders are also considered, whereas the EU itself in its policies, and in particular in the EU Gender Action Plan (GAP) II only includes the binary sexes male and female.[201] The GAP III, which is currently being developed, does not contain any further categorisation either,[202] although this is more widely understood, particularly before the CEDAW Committee, the ECtHR and also at UN level.[203] The ECJ, here too, appears to be more committed and dynamic in carrying out its mandate, as this is politically substantiated and should promote the advancement of European law in this respect. This is despite the fact that the inclusion of other genders and the inclusion of LGBTI/Q rights was excluded from the SDGs negotiation process as highly controversial issue between the UN Member States.[204]

It is all the more noticeable that the ECJ conducts a comprehensive proportionali-　**92** ty-based assessment in its jurisdiction, and follows the 'EU's own broadly Aristotelian understanding of equality [where] positive action is an aspect of equality rather than an exception to it.'[205] That means that differential treatment can be justified if the measure is proportionate to the intended objective. This sometimes leads to legal reasoning which do not initially seem to be in line with the European legal framework.

To shed some light on the content of SDG 5.4: The ECJ recently held in a preliminary　**93** ruling[206] that a pension supplement granted to women with two or more children to compensate for pension rights not acquired due to maternity leave and childcare, unlawfully infringed equality between men and women. In so doing, the court decided on the basis of the equal suitability of men and women to care for children. The supplement which had only been given to women, however, constituted unjustifiable direct discrimination in this respect, even if women in fact (for a variety of reasons) usually have these cuts in their professional careers.[207] The ECJ also stated that in this case Art. 157(4)

---

[198] ECJ, C-450/93, 17.10.1995, *Eckhard Kalanke v. Freie Hansestadt Bremen*, ECLI:EU:C:1995:322; ECJ, C-409/95, 11.11.1997, *Hellmut Marschall v. Land Nordrhein-Westfalen*, ECLI:EU:C:1997:533; ECJ, C-407/98, 06.07.2000, *Katarina Abrahamsson and Leif Anderson v. Elisabet Fogelqvist*, ECLI:EU:C:2000:367.

[199] ECJ, C-13/94, 30.04.1996, *P v. S and Cornwall County Council*, ECLI:EU:C:1996:170.

[200] Directive 2006/54/EC of the European Parliament and of the Council of 5 July 2006 on the implementation of the principle of equal opportunities and equal treatment of men and women in matters of employment and occupation (recast), OJ L 204, 26.7.2006, 23-36.

[201] European Parliament, *Discrimnatory Laws Undermining Women's Rights* (2019), 9.

[202] See *EU Action Plan of Gender equality and women's empowerment in external relations for 2021-2025*, Roadmap, Ref. Ares(2020)1416496 – 06/03/2020.

[203] European Parliament, *Discrimnatory Laws Undermining Women's Rights* (2019), 9.

[204] Dodds and Donoghue and Leiva Roesch, *Negotiating the Sustainable Development Goals, A transformational agenda for an insecure world* (2017), 103, 106.

[205] McCrudden, *Gender-based positive action in employment in Europe, A comparative analysis of legal and policy approaches in the EU and EEA, A special report* (2019), 213.

[206] ECJ, C-450/18, 12.12.2019, *WA v Instituto Nacional de la Seguridad Social (INSS)*, Request for a preliminary ruling, ECLI:EU:C:2019:1075.

[207] See e.g. https://www.oecd.org/dev/development-gender/Unpaid_care_work.pdf, 'Around the world, women spend two to ten times more time on unpaid care work than men. This disproportionate burden of unpaid care work borne by women contributes to a worldwide pensions gender gap'; ILO, http://www w.ilo.org/wcmsp5/groups/public/---dgreports/---dcomm/---publ/documents/publication/wcms_4573 17.pdf, Nearly 65 per cent of people above retirement age without any regular pension are women. [...] the way in which inequalities in the labour market and in employment translate into the sphere of social protection often turns on the extent to which there are mechanisms in existence that can compensate for

TFEU was inapplicable, which specifically allows this type of compensatory measure.[208] However, it was precisely the assessment that a rule applies indiscriminately to male and female workers that led to the opposite result in a similar case.[209]

94   Another important issue concerns 'the provision made in national law for a shift of the burden of proof in sex discrimination cases.' Due to the difficulties associated with proving discrimination, the ECJ developed an approach that allows for a shift in the burden of proof,[210] which was later enshrined in legislative acts.[211] This applies equally to the area of goods and services, but not to criminal proceedings, which means that the respondent of an alleged victim of discrimination must prove that there was no violation of the principle of equal treatment.[212]

3. Arbitration Proceedings

95   As it is the case at all levels with legal authority, the existing influence either of women or on women has a particular effect on the noticeable, sometimes considerable, differential treatment at a more systemic level. Three aspects in particular can be identified: (1) the most-often abstract and gender-blind norms of trade liberalisation policies do not consider specific needs of different genders at all. (2) The (partial) absence or under-representation of women in the processes of the emergence of international trade norms leads to norms in application that respond little or not at all to different gender-specific needs. And (3) especially review mechanisms themselves still accommodate mainly men as judges, experts or party representatives with the consequence that the application and interpretation of norms is still mainly male-dominated and inherently subject to this gender bias or partiality.[213]

96   The large number of different bilateral, regional and multilateral agreements accessible to the various review mechanisms of arbitration or dispute resolution contains both explicit and implicit references to gender, e.g. in the area of human rights.[214] The provisions 'address various issues and remain highly heterogeneous'.[215] It appears therefore to be more a matter of equal representation in the dispute settlement or other arbitrational proceedings that needs to be addressed when it comes to the influence and impact of gender issues within dispute settlement.

---

gender inequality in employment, such as the recognition of periods spent caring for children or older persons in the pension system.

[208] ECJ, C-450/18, 12.12.2019, *WA v Instituto Nacional de la Seguridad Social (INSS)*, Request for a preliminary ruling, ECLI:EU:C:2019:1075, paras. 52 f., 64 f.

[209] ECJ, C-366/18, 18.09.2019, *José Manuel Ortiz Mesonero v UTE Luz Madrid Centro*, ECLI:EU:C: 2019:757, paras. 23-5, 36-8.

[210] ECJ, C-109/88, 17.10.1989, *Handels- og Kontorfunktionærernes Forbund I Danmark v Dansk Arbejdsgiverforening, acting on behalf of Danfoss*, ECLI:EU:C:1989:383; ECJ, C-104/10, 21.07.2011, *Patrick Kelly v National University of Ireland (University College, Dublin)*, ECLI:EU:C:2011:506; ECJ, C-415/10, 19.04.2012, *Galina Meister v Speech Design Carrier Systems GmbH*, ECLI:EU:C:2012:217.

[211] See Art. 19 of Recast Directive 2006/54/EC and Article 9 of Directive 2004/113/EC.

[212] European Commission, *Gender equality law in Europe, How are EU rules transposed into national law in 2016?* (2016), 73.

[213] Tobalagba and Jos, *Arbitrating Business And Human Rights: What's In It For Women?* (2020).

[214] See e.g. International Trade Centre, *Mainstreaming Gender in Free Trade Agreements* (2020), foreword; Monteiro, 'Gender-Related Provisions In Regional Trade Agreements' (2018), Staff Working Paper ERSD-2018-15 *World Trade Organization Economic Research and Statistics Division*, 2 ff.

[215] Monteiro, 'Gender-Related Provisions In Regional Trade Agreements' (2018), Staff Working Paper ERSD-2018-15 *World Trade Organization Economic Research and Statistics Division*, 4.

A particular problem is the limited accountability, as arbitration proceedings are **97**
regularly only accessible to the public if the negotiating parties explicitly permit this. In
publicly accessible awards, it is noticeable that gender certainly influences outcomes.[216]

It is also noticeable that the different legal consequences allow a clear assessment **98**
of the gravity of the applicable norms. Thus, for example, after a violation of the
most-favoured nation clause, the losing state is subject to considerable reprisals, whereas
after a non-fulfilment of human rights obligations, which derive, for example, from
CEDAW, there is no direct legal consequence[217] and even within the various arbitration
proceedings they play only a subordinate role. Although, international law and its
principles, and therefore also relevant standards for the protection of girls and women
must be taken into account in these proceedings. Yet, international economic law as
a legal regime itself most often does not connect with non-economic issues which
leads to women's rights being disregarded or even excluded.[218] As a result, arbitration
proceedings do not regularly lead to a satisfactory resolution of the proceedings or to
direct obligations for the infringing party.

Insofar as gender mainstreaming clauses can be traced back to so-called trade and **99**
sustainable development chapters (TSD), as in the case of the EU, these clauses are subject to their own dispute settlement mechanism, which in form and effect is much more
flexible than the regular review mechanisms within the various trade and investment
instruments. However, these mechanisms have not been activated to date and thus do
not allow any conclusions to be drawn about the success of their application in the
implementation and follow-up of gender-specific standards.

This means that the gender aspects covered by SDG 5 are not yet of independent **100**
legal significance. Rather, what matters first is the gender-responsive or gender-sensitive
design of the instruments[219] accessible to arbitration and the underlying systematics as a
whole. Subsequently, a meticulous analysis must be made of the extent to which SDG 5
can actually provide a comprehensive framework and exert influence within the various
methods of review.

4. Domestic Jurisdiction

The pandemic caused by the spread of SARS-CoV-2 has exacerbated the already **101**
blatant forms of violence and oppression against women and girls. Consequently, states
should prioritise the prevention of and response to violence against women and girls in
national plans for SARS-CoV-2 response and recovery.[220]

Progressive case law of the Supreme Court of India (SCC) dealt with the question of **102**
the classification of sexual harassment and very concisely illustrates the contents of SDG
5.2. In *Vishaka v. State of Rajasthan*[221], the SCC stated that sexual harassment at the
workplace includes more than a harassing behaviour. Rather, it all the more 'covers situa-

---

[216] See e.g. Lipsky and Lamare and Gupta, 'The effect of gender on awards in employment arbitration
cases: The experience in the securities industry' (2011) [Electronic version]; paper presented at the
Sixty-Third Annual Meeting of the Labor and Employment Relations Association, Denver, Colorado.

[217] See 'Women's Rights, the World Trade Organization and International Trade Policy' (2002) 4 *Wom-
en's Rights and Economic Change*, 3 f.

[218] Choudhoury, 'Rights of Women' in Cottier and Nadakavukaren Schefer (eds), *Elgar Encyclopedia of
International Economic Law* (2017), 653.

[219] A proposal for an arrangement can be found here: International Trade Centre, *Mainstreaming Gender in Free Trade Agreements* (2020), 13 ff.

[220] WHO, OHCHR, UNESCO et al, *Eliminating female genital mutilation, An interagency statement*
(2008); A/75/274, *Intensification of efforts to eliminate all forms of violence against women and girls*, Report
of the Secretary-General, 30 July 2020, para. 46.

[221] *Nisha Priya Bhatia v. Union of India*, SCC India, 2020 SCC OnLine SC 394.

tions wherein the woman employee is subjected to prejudice, hostility, discriminatory attitude and humiliation in day to day functioning at the workplace' the occurrence of which constitutes a violation or harm of dignity. With this decision, the SCC filled a *lacuna* in the existing legislation pertaining to the protection of women at the workplace due to gender-induced harmful behaviour. The court specifically held a 'violation of her fundamental rights to life and dignity as a result of the improper handling of her complaint of sexual harassment.'[222] *Vishaka* resulted from a public interest litigation filed by NGOs engaged in the sphere of gender equality and women's empowerment (→ Goal 1 mn. 120 f., Goal 10 mn. 105 ff.). The court acknowledged the violation of the right to gender equality and the dignity of working women and explicitly seized this case as an opportunity to promote gender equality and, therefore, characterised sexual harassment as a violation of the fundamental right to exercise a profession, gender equality, freedom of life and dignity.[223]

103   Another landmark decision by the SCC of India,[224] which strengthened 'women's property rights and gender equality', provides an insight into the assessment of SDG 5.a. In this case, the two daughters of a deceased person were equally entitled to a share of commonly owned property alongside their brothers, albeit 'in light of the reality that daughters until [the 2005 amendment to the Hindu Succession Act] did not have an equal claim on ancestral property in India.'[225] This case lessens the scope of misinterpretation of the relevant legal provisions by lower courts and could have the potential to break up the previously cemented non-participation of women in property, land and other resources and related legal positions and gradually lift them out of their impoverishment.

104   Before the German Constitutional Court, a woman from Mauretania, however, elucidated her life reality, ubiquitous in many places, that poses a serious threat to women and girls. In the statement of claim of 18 June 2019, she claimed that, as a member of a 'slave tribe' and as a woman without the protection of her family, she would not be able to secure her subsistence level in the event of a return to Mauritania. Referring to valid observations, she pointed out that women in Mauritania were legally and extra-legally discriminated against because of the far-reaching application of Sharia law and religion, tradition and the corresponding attitude of the State bodies that Mauritania was one of the poorest countries in Africa and was characterised by great social and economic inequality between two classes.[226]

II. The Enforcement of a 'Right to Gender Equality'

105   As could be seen in the several cases mentioned, it is everything but clear to what extent gender equality is implemented in a progressive way. Yet, it is striking that the legal framework already exists in many areas of gender equality and is receiving further impetus.

---

[222] *Nisha Priya Bhatia v. Union of India*, SCC India, 2020 SCC OnLine SC 394, para. 112 (iv).

[223] Sanjay and Mishra, 'Scandalizing the judiciary: An analysis of the uneven response of the Supreme Court of India to sexual harassment allegations against judges' (2020) 18(2) *International Journal of Constitutional Law*, 563-90.

[224] *Danamma Suman Surpur & Another v Amar & Others*, SCC of India, Civil Appeal Nos. 188-189 of 2018.

[225] Overview of the case: https://www.escr-net.org/caselaw/2018/danamma-suman-surpur-another-v-a mar-others-civil-appeal-nos-188-189-2018.

[226] German Federal Constitutional Court (FCC), 2 BvR 854/20, Order of the First Chamber of the Second Senate of 25 September 2020, ECLI:DE:BVerfG:2020:rk20200925.2bvr085420, mn. 1-45.

The implementation of SDGs is supported almost universally at the state level, e.g.   **106** through the establishment of inter-ministerial committees, national sustainable development strategies, capacity assessment and expansion in both statistical and financial terms.[227] Making gender mainstreaming and gender equality a priority issue while improving (protective) legislation in an attempt to fill data gaps for measuring progress might initially be expected to seamlessly realise the enforcement of a right to gender equality as well. However, the aspired effects on enforcement depend on the remedies and sanctions national laws provide for.

Moreover, even the most progressive legal practice makes it clear that enforcement   **107** often fails because of two obstacles: (a) unofficial structures prevent the application of a judgment in whole or in part[228] and (b) the transition of international judgments into national judicial decisions lags behind substantive matter.

III. De Facto Influences on the Jurisdiction

The effects of globalisation and the accompanying liberalisation of trade, including   **108** in services, often lead to deregulation and the opening of service sectors to private participation, for example in the critical areas of health and education. The notion of maximum private investment combined with the 'introduction of user fees, and poor quality or even a complete lack of provision to the poorest communities' directly affects girls and women, as they are more likely to be employed in the informal sectors worldwide.[229]

Concomitant with this form of privatisation, the privatising of conflict-solving in   **109** case of human-rights breaches remains a major challenge. Transnational Companies (TNCs) often solve the human rights violations by paying money (private damages) rather than through arbitration. Or, and this is the more severe constraint, financially (omni-)potent TNCs threaten states that insist on respecting human rights obligations with cost-intensive litigation which understandably could not be pursued by developing or least-developed states to not jeopardise their state systems.

Besides institutional issues such as lacking female staff or adequately trained staff, it is   **110** noticeable that female victims often do not take legal action at all, either because they are unaware of their existing rights, e.g. due to a lack of education, or because girls and women often have limited access to the family's financial resources and are therefore unable to pay for fees or expenses for legal assistance. These and other restrictions on the implementation of the *rule of law* lead to reduced access to justice,[230] especially for women and girls, and are directly detrimental to the implementation and judicial interpretation of SDG 5 (→ Goal 16 mn. 9 ff., 22 ff.).

On a third, yet not legally binding level, the development of jurisdiction is influ-   **111** enced by soft law instruments. The Guiding Principles on Business and Human Rights

---

[227] HLPF, *2017 HLPF Thematic review of SDG 5: Achieve gender equality and empower all women and girls* (2017), 5 f.

[228] To name but a few: corruption, delays, social / societal caveats.

[229] See Save the Children, *An Unnecessary Evil?, User fees for healthcare in low-income countries* (2005); Khun and Manderson, 'Poverty, user fees and ability to pay for health care for children with suspected dengue in rural Cambodia' (2008) 7(10) *Int J Equity Health*, 7 ff.

[230] Huck and Maaß, 'Gaining a foot in the door: Giving Access to Justice with SDG 16.3?' (2021) *C-EENRG Working Papers*; UNDP/UN Women/UNFPA/ESCWA, *Gender Justice & Equality before the law, Analysis of Progress and Challenges in the Arab States Region* (2019), 17 ff.; see also United Nations General Assembly Open Working Group on Sustainable Development Goals, *Compendium of TST Issues Briefs October 2014*, 230.

(UNGP)[231] refer to the application and interpretation of various human rights instruments and serve as a framework for corporate action. The unanimous approval of the UNGP by the UN Human Rights Council is now considered a milestone that also stimulated the discussion on women's rights and, at least in a reflective way, continues to influence the further development of law in the area covered by SDG 5.

E. Conclusion on SDG 5

112   The empowerment of girls and women is one of the outstanding goals set by the Global Agenda 2030, rightly emphasising that this is one of its outstanding tasks. Empowerment presupposes that international legally binding agreements are transposed into national binding and enforceable law, where they are accepted above all by those societies whose cultural, traditional or religious beliefs have made it difficult or impossible for women to access society and have directly or indirectly supported sexualised violence or honour killings.[232]

113   The increase in femicides, the deepening of disenfranchisement and the increase in violence against women during the SARS-CoV-2 pandemic bear an eloquent witness to the circumstances to which women are exposed. Girls and women need attention, protection and the chance of a fair access to economic and political participation which will enable them to seize fair opportunities which societies must not deny them. Of particular relevance is the economic and legal environment in which women and girls live.[233]

114   Since 2015, states have intensified the reform of laws, policies and programmes to promote gender equality. Overall, the main priorities of the last five years according to the UN include:

- Elimination of violence against women and girls
- Access to health care, including sexual and reproductive health care
- Political participation and representation
- Quality education, training and lifelong learning for women and girls[234]

115   The complex and more detailed demands to address SDG 5 issues interdependent with other SDGs are difficult to achieve and could derail depending on the pandemic situation that will affect the world in 2020 and for an unpredictable time beyond.[235]

116   The spectrum of rights denied to women and girls is alarmingly long and in stark contrast to the long lists constituting women rights.

117   Contrary to CEDAW, the reality is a different one. Not only is the gender-based denial of equal opportunities for women and girls in accessing the respective societies problematic and often unacceptable in political and economic terms, but it also remains

---

[231] Guiding Principles on Business and Human Rights, Implementing the United Nations "Protect, Respect and Remedy" Framework (2011).

[232] A/RES/70/1, *Transforming our world: the 2030 Agenda for Sustainable Development*, 21 October 2015, preamble: '[T]hey seek to realize the human rights of all and to achieve gender equality and the empowerment of all women and girls', and paras. 3, 20: '[R]ealizing gender equality and the empowerment of women and girls will make a crucial contribution to progress across all the Goals and targets'.

[233] A/RES/70/1, *Transforming our world: the 2030 Agenda for Sustainable Development*, 21 October 2015, para. 27.

[234] E/CN.6/2020/3, *Review and appraisal of the implementation of the Beijing Declaration and Platform for Action and the outcomes of the twenty-third special session of the General Assembly Report of the Secretary-General*, 13 December 2019, para. 4.

[235] https://www.unwomen.org/en/what-we-do/2030-agenda-for-sustainable-development.

one of the shocking obstacles when the lives and health of girls and women throughout the world are seriously threatened or even violated.[236]

Despite many efforts of states to enforce laws on violence against women, the review   118
of the UN indicated that significant barriers to the effective implementation and enforcement of laws remain in place, including a lack of adequate resources, very low reporting rates, institutional barriers and the existence of patriarchal systems and gender stereotypes prevalent within security, police and justice institutions.[237]

Femicide, female genital mutilation, trafficking in girls and women and other serious   119
crimes against women, remain a blatant reality in many societies forming a violation of promises and concessions made at diplomatic conferences or even in legally binding treaties.

The widely practised forms of 'stay-at-home' and 'shelter-in-place' orders during the   120
pandemic had shown dramatic effects for many women and girls which increasingly experienced worldwide domestic violence. Therefore, the UN recommended that

> [p]olice and justice services are urged to ensure that incidents of violence against women and girls are accorded high priority, ensuring women access to protection orders and holding perpetrators to account. States should introduce specific measures to address backlogs and enable women to have access to courts, including specialized courts, for example, through videoconferencing, and telephone and mobile courts. [...][238]

Another recommendation of the UN is that '[s]tates should, without delay, ratify   121
the ILO Violence and Harassment Convention, 2019 (No. 190). They should prioritize actions that create culture change in order to eliminate sexual harassment in the world of work'.[239]

Trafficking in women and girls has its roots in the systemic and structural inequal-   122
ity and discrimination between the sexes, which is reflected in many of the SDGs: high poverty (SDG 1), lack of access to education (SDG 4), gender inequality and various forms of violence against women (SDG 5) and the concentration of women in precarious and informal employment (SDG 8). On a broader level, inequality within and between countries (SDG 10), conflict situations and humanitarian crises (SDG 16) also make women and girls more vulnerable to deception, coercion and exploitation. Human trafficking still exists because the impunity of the perpetrators makes it a high reward, low risk crime. While traffickers are able to make substantial financial gains, it is the survivors of trafficking who pay the price because they suffer devastating and irreparable consequences throughout their lives, including the violation of their fundamental human rights, the deprivation of their dignity and long-term health and economic damage.[240]

The experience of previous health crises has demonstrated that women and girls,   123
including migrant and refugee women and girls, were at heightened risk of gender based violence, intimate partner violence and sexual exploitation, abuse and trafficking, and the same is expected to remain true for SARS-CoV-2.[241]

---

[236] https://www.unwomen.org/en/what-we-do/ending-violence-against-women/facts-and-figures.

[237] A/75/274, *Intensification of efforts to eliminate all forms of violence against women and girls, Report of the Secretary-General*, 30 July 2020, para. 2.

[238] A/75/274, *Intensification of efforts to eliminate all forms of violence against women and girls, Report of the Secretary-General*, 30 July 2020, para. 49.

[239] https://www.ilo.org/dyn/normlex/en/f?p=NORMLEXPUB:12100:0::NO::P12100_ILO_CODE:C190 ; A/75/274, *Intensification of efforts to eliminate all forms of violence against women and girls, Report of the Secretary-General*, 30 July 2020, para. 55.

[240] A/75/289, *Trafficking in women and girls, Report of the Secretary-General*, 7 August 2020, paras. 3, 5.

[241] A/75/289, *Trafficking in women and girls, Report of the Secretary-General*, 7 August 2020, para. 20; UN Women, *Addressing the impacts of the COVID-19 pandemic on women migrant workers* (2020).

124   Besides trafficking, the open question of equality needs to be stressed. Equal rights within marriage exists not everywhere. Currently, many women are required by law to obey their husbands (in 19 countries), and marital rape is often not explicitly criminalized (in 111 countries).[242] Laws on marriage, divorce, custody, inheritance, nationality and employment are qualified as a key to equal citizenship rights because they share in determining legal autonomy for women.[243]

125   Women and girls in the world's poorest and most marginalized communities have contributed the least to the climate emergency but are suffering the brunt of its catastrophic effects. Women's access to land, which is already restricted, is being further undermined by environmental degradation and land grabbing. Food and water shortages, polluted air and increasingly severe climate-related disasters such as droughts, floods or wildfires are taking a disproportionate toll on their health and rights.[244]

126   Fundamental to the success of SDG 5 is the creation of legal foundations that enable all women to access justice in a functioning legal system. The fact that this is also a demand by the courts in Germany underlines the great importance of the close connection between SDG 16 and SDG 5.

127   Many of the SDGs will be unattainable without formal legal equality. This includes the gender equality targets of SDG 5, as well as the targets relating to poverty, health, education, decent work, economic growth, and peace and justice.

128   Gender justice requires States to ensure that the internationally accepted concept of the *rule of law* is understood and respected (SDG 16).

129   The SDGs are based on a deeper foundation of the *rule of law*, on equality, by which is meant the mitigation of inequalities to the greatest extent possible, and equality between men and women as a deep awareness of the equality of all human beings, derived from an array of legally binding treaties, norms, declarations, among others (→ Goal 10 mn. 4 ff.).

130   The scope and content of the rights and freedoms required for the comprehensive empowerment of girls and women are at all times a litmus test of humanity and freedom in a society for all people. Without a strong *rule of law* which is implemented at national level in accordance with CEDAW implications and guarantees women and girls comprehensive rights and access to independent courts, it will remain quite difficult to achieve SDG 5.

---

[242] UN Women, *Gender Equality, Women's rights in review 25 Years after Beijing* (2020), 22.
[243] UN ESCWA, UNFPA, UN Women, UNDP, *Gender Justice & Equality before the law* (2019), 12.
[244] UN Women, *Gender Equality, Women´s rights in review 25 Years after Beijing* (2020), 20.

Goal 6
Ensure availability and sustainable management of water and sanitation for all

6.1 By 2030, achieve universal and equitable access to safe and affordable drinking water for all

6.2 By 2030, achieve access to adequate and equitable sanitation and hygiene for all and end open defecation, paying special attention to the needs of women and girls and those in vulnerable situations

6.3 By 2030, improve water quality by reducing pollution, eliminating dumping and minimizing release of hazardous chemicals and materials, halving the proportion of untreated wastewater and substantially increasing recycling and safe reuse globally

6.4 By 2030, substantially increase water-use efficiency across all sectors and ensure sustainable withdrawals and supply of freshwater to address water scarcity and substantially reduce the number of people suffering from water scarcity

6.5 By 2030, implement integrated water resources management at all levels, including through transboundary cooperation as appropriate

6.6 By 2020, protect and restore water-related ecosystems, including mountains, forests, wetlands, rivers, aquifers and lakes6.a By 2030, expand international cooperation and capacity-building support to developing countries in water- and sanitation-related activities and programmes, including water harvesting, desalination, water efficiency, wastewater treatment, recycling and reuse technologies

6.b Support and strengthen the participation of local communities in improving water and sanitation management

Word Count related to 'Water' and 'Sanitation'

A/RES/70/1 - Transforming our world: the 2030 Agenda for Sustainable Development: 'Water': 22 'Sanitation': 6

Instruments mentioned in A/RES/70/1 in the section entitled: 'Sustainable Development Goals and targets':

A/RES/69/313 - Addis Ababa Action Agenda of the Third International Conference on Financing for Development adopted on 27 July 2015: 'Water': 5 'Sanitation': 5

A/RES/66/288 - The future we want (Rio +20 Declaration) adopted on 27 July 2012: 'Water': 32 'Sanitation': 7

A/RES/55/2 - United Nations Millennium Declaration adopted on 8 September 2000: 'Water': 3 'Sanitation': 0

A/CONF.151/26 (Vol. I) - Rio Declaration On Environment And Development, 12.09.1992: 'Water': 626 'Sanitation': 51

Select Bibliography: Catarina de Albuquerque, *Realizing the Human Rights to Water and Sanitation, A Handbook by the UN Special Rapporteur Catarina de Albuquerque, Volumes 1–9: Introduction, Frameworks, Financing, Services, Monitoring, Justice, Principles, Checklists and Sources* (UN, Geneva 2014); Catarina De Albuquerque, *On The Right Track: Good Practices In Realising The Rights To Water And Sanitation* (UN, Lisbon 2012); Lady Justice Arden, 'Water for All? Developing a Human Right to Water in National and International Law' (2016) 65 *ICLQ*, 771; Robert Bos (ed) *Manual of the Human Rights to Safe Drinking Water and Sanitation for Practitioners* (IWA Publishing, London 2016); Slavko Bogdanović, *The International Law Association Helsinki Rules: Contribution to International Water Law* (Koninklijke Brill NV, Leiden/Boston 2018); Laurence Boisson de Chazournes, *Fresh Water in International Law* (Oxford University Press, Oxford 2013); Laurence Boisson de Chazournes, Makane Moïse Mbengue, Mara Tignino, Komlan Sangbana and Jason Rudall (eds), *The UN Convention on the Law of the Non-Navigational Uses of International Watercourses: A Commentary* (Oxford University Press, Oxford 2018); Laurence Boisson de Chazournes, *International Law and Freshwater: The Multiple Challenges,* (Publishing International, 2013); Laurence Boisson de Chazournes and Christina Leb, 'Benefit-sharing in international water law: a multidisciplinary undertaking' in Mara Tignino and Christian Béthault (eds), *Research Handbook on Freshwater Law and International Relations* (Edward Elgar Publishing Limited, UK/USA 2018), 391; Catherine Brölmann, '*Sustainable Development Goal 6 as a Game Changer for International Water Law*' (2018) 7 *ESIL Reflections*, 1; Elisabeth Bürgi Bonanomi, *Sustainable Development in International Law Making and Trade* (Edward Elgar, Cheltenham/Northampton 2015); Rutgerd Boelens and Tom Perreault and Jeroen Vos (eds), *Water Justice* (Cambridge University Press, Cambridge 2018); Enamul Choudhury and Shafiqul Islam (eds), *Complexity of Transboundary Water Conflicts: Enabling Conditions for Negotiating Contingent Resolutions* (Anthem Press, London/New York 2018); Aristoteles Constantinides, 'Economic and Social Rights' in André Nollkaemper, August Reinisch, Ralph Janik and Florentina Simlinger (eds), *International Law in Domestic Courts: A Casebook* (Oxford University Press, Oxford 2018); Mariel Dimsey, 'Right to Water' in Thomas Cottier and Krista Nadakavukaren Schefer (eds), *Elgar Encyclopedia of International Economic Law* (Edward Elgar Publishing, Cheltenham/Northampton 2017), 642; Pierre-Marie Dupuy and Jorge E. Viñuales, *International Environmental Law* (4 Ed., Cambridge University Press, Cambridge 2018); Gabriel Eckstein, Ariella D'Andrea, Virginia Marshall, Erin O'Donnell, Julia Talbot-Jones, Deborah Curran and Katie O'Bryan, 'Conferring Legal Personality on the World's Rivers: A Brief Intellectual Assessment' (2019) in *Water International* (Texas A&M University School of Law Legal Studies Research Paper No. 19-30); Bree Farrugia, 'The human right to water: defences to investment treaty violations' (2015), 31 *Arbitration International*, 261; Stephen M Gardiner and Allen Thompson, *The Oxford Handbook of Environmental Ethics* (Oxford Univeristy Press, Oxford, 2017); Anurag Garg, 'Water Pollution from Pulp and Paper Mills' 20 *Advances in Environmental Research* (2012); Markus Gehring, Freedom-Kai Phillips and Emma Lees, 'The European Union' in Emma Lees and Jorge E. Viñuales, *The Oxford Handbook of Comparative Environmental Law* (Oxford University Press, Oxford 2019), 165; N. F. Gray, *Drinking Water Quality: Problems and Solutions* (2nd edn, Cambridge University Press, Cambridge 2008); Claude Henry and Laurence Tubiana, *Earth at Risk, Natural Capital and the Quest for Sustainability* (Columbia University Press, New York, 2018); Ellen Hey, 'Distributive Justice and Procedural Fairness in Global Water Law' in Jonas Ebbesson and Phoebe Okowa (eds), *Environmental Law and Justice in Context* (Cambridge University Press 2009); Shafiqul Islam and Kaveh Madani (eds), *Water Diplomacy in Action: Contingent Approaches to Managing Complex Water Problems* (Anthem Press, London/New York 2017); Anoop Jain and Jay Graham, 'The human right to sanitation' in Janine M.H. Selendy (ed), *Water and Sanitation-Related Diseases and the Changing Environment: Challenges, Interventions and Preventive Measures* (2nd edn, Wiley Blackwell, USA/UK 2019); Michael Kidd and Loretta Feris, 'Introduction: water and the law: towards sustainability' in Michael Kidd et al. (eds), *Water and the Law: Towards Sustainability* (Edward Elgar Publishing, UK/USA 2014); Eva Kremere, Edward Morgan and Pedi Obani, *SDG 6 – Clean Water and Sanitation: Balancing the Water Cycle for Sustainable Life on Earth* (Emerald Publishing, United Kingdom 2020); Itzchak E. Kornfeld, *Transboundary Water Disputes: State Conflict and the Assessment of Their Adjudication* (Cambridge University Press, Cambridge 2019); Malcolm Langford and Anna F.S. Russell, 'Introduction: The Right to Water in Context' in Malcolm Langford and Anna F.S. Russell (eds), *The Human Right to Water: Theory, Practice and Prospects* (Cambridge University Press, Cambridge

2017); Christina Leb, *Cooperation in the Law of Transboundary Water Resources* (Cambridge University Press, Cambridge 2013); Stephen C. McCaffrey, Christina Leb and Riley T. Denoon (eds), *Research Handbook on International Water Law* (Edward Elgar Publishing Limited, UK/USA 2019); Elizabeth Jane Macpherson (eds.), *Indigenous Water Rights in Law and Regulation: Lessons from Comparative Experience* (Cambridge University Press, Cambridge 2019); Stephen C. McCaffrey. *The Law of International Watercourses*, (3rd edn, Oxford University Press, Oxford 2019); Owen McIntyre, 'International water law and SDG 6' in Duncan French and Louis J. Kotzé (eds), *Sustainable Development Goals, Law, Theory and Implementation* (Edward Elgar Publishing, Cheltenham/Northampton 2018), 173; Anu Mittal, 'Right to Clean Water' in Neerja Gurnani (ed), *Constitutional & Administrative Law* (2015); Mike Muller and Christophe Bellmann, *Trade and Water: How Might Trade Policy Contribute to Sustainable Water Management?* (International Centre for Trade and Sustainable Development (ICTSD), Geneva 2016); Jimena Murillho Chavarro, *The Human Right to Water: A Legal Comparative Perspective at the International, Regional and Domestic Level* (Intersentia Ltd, Cambridge 2015); Pedi Obani and Joyeeta Gupta, 'The Human Right to Water and Sanitation: Reflections on Making the System Effective' in Anik Bhaduri et al. (eds), *The Global Water System in the Anthropocene: Challenges for Science and Governance* (Springer International Publishing, Switzerland, 2014); Arundhati A. Satkalmi, Research Guide on Transboundary Freshwater Treaties and Other Resources (2017), NYU Law, https://www.nyulawglobal.org/globalex/Transboundary_Freshwater_Treaties1.html#_Major_Global_and (last accessed 28.10.2021, 15:45); Ken Weinthal Conca and Erika, 'The Political Dimensions of Water' in Ken Conca and Erika Weinthal (eds), *The Oxford Handbook of Water Politics and Policy* (Oxford University Press, Oxford 2018); Zeray Yihdego, *The Fairness 'Dilemma' in Sharing the Nile Waters: What Lessons from the Grand Ethiopian Renaissance Dam for International Law?* (Koninklijke Brill NV, Leiden/Boston 2017); Soheila Zareie, Omid Bozorg-Haddad and Hugo A. Loáiciga, 'A state-of-the-art review of water diplomacy' (2020) 22 *Environ Dev Sustain*, 7; Mark Zeitoun, Naho Mirumachi and Jeroen Warner, *Water Conflicts: Analysis for Transformation* (Oxford University Press, Oxford 2020)

A. Background and Origin of SDG 6

Water, as one of the planets (most precious) natural resources,[1] follows physics as an   1
element and thus the different states of aggregation liquid, vapor or ice. Water occurs in and on the earth and even above as clouds and other weather phenomena. Besides, water is detectable in the solar system and even outside of it.[2] But fresh water is and ever has been a precious and limited element. During the Roman empire, fresh water was a valuable resource. Romans used it for a variety of productive activities like irrigation and milling, but were also interested in water for financial (e.g. tax revenue derived from agriculture) and ideological reasons.[3] In the Republican literature, water was connected to the assumption that it should be free and open to all.[4]

Water is and has been a *conditio sine qua non* for the existence of humankind, most   2
plants and animals, the protection of which has been acknowledged since the dawn of time.[5] Also from a human rights perspective, safe drinking water and sanitation are considered essential elements for the preservation of health and life.[6]

Between 2000 and 2017, the proportion of the global population using safely man-   3
aged drinking water, increased from 61 per cent to 71 per cent. And despite the fact that 90 per cent of the world's population at least had basic drinking water services,

---

[1] A/RES/70/1, *Transforming our world: the 2030 Agenda for Sustainable Development*, 21 October 2015, para. 33.

[2] NASA, *Jet Propulsion Laboratory, Mars Ice Deposit Holds as Much Water as Lake Superior*, (2016); PHYSOrg, *Water-worlds are common: Exoplanets may contain vast amounts of water* (2018); https://www.nasa.gov/jpl/the-solar-system-and-beyond-is-awash-in-water.

[3] Bannon, 'Fresh Water in Roman Law: Rights and Policy' (2017) 107 *Journal of Roman Studies*, 60 (60).

[4] Bannon, 'Fresh Water in Roman Law: Rights and Policy' (2017) 107 *Journal of Roman Studies*, 60 (61).

[5] See *Case concerning the Gabčíkovo-Nagymaros Project (Hungary/Slovakia)*, 25 September 1997, Dissenting Opinion of H. E. Judge Christopher Gregory Weeramantry, 98 ff.

[6] UNESCO, *The United Nations World Water Development Report 2019: Leaving No One Behind* (2019), 1.

still 785 million people still lacked these.[7] The number of the global population using safely managed sanitation services increased from 28 per cent in 2000 to 45 percent in 2017, but besides those gains, an estimated 2 billion people still don't have access to basic sanitation.[8] To achieve universal access to basic sanitation services by 2030, a doubling of the current annual rate of progress is required.[9] The recent interim guidance – water, sanitation, hygiene, and waste management during the SARS-CoV-2 pandemic – by the WHO provides details of WASH services. According to that guidance two out of five people as well as half of all schools worldwide do not have a handwashing facility with soap and premises.[10]

4   As a part of the global environmental commons[11] and manifestation of an irrevocable human right, the right to water is now considered to belong to the first category of rights as set out in the Universal Declaration of Human Rights (UDHR) of 1948[12] as part of good health and well-being.[13] During the UN Water Conference of 1977, the right to water was initially recognised and ever since has been developed and evolved into the human right of water and sanitation that it is today,[14] even though the first reference to water had already been included in the Convention on the Elimination of All Discrimination against women 1979.[15] In the following years, the right to water was increasingly mentioned in international conferences, for example in January 1992 at the International Conference on Water and Environment (ICWE) in Dublin.[16] At the ICWE, the Dublin Statement on Water and Sustainable Development was created also known as the Dublin Principles which focus on the increasing scarcity of water as a result from overuse of water.[17] The Dublin Principles consist of four principles focusing on water. Principle 4 states that '[...] it is vital to recognize first the basic right of all human beings to have access to clean water and sanitation at an affordable price'.[18] The United Nations International Conference on Population and Development affirmed in 1994 that all individuals '[h]ave the right to an adequate standard of living for themselves and their families, including food [...] water and sanitation'.[19]

---

[7] UN, *Sustainable Development Goals Report 2019* (2019), 34.

[8] UN, *Sustainable Development Goals Report 2020* (2020), 36.

[9] UN, *Sustainable Development Goals Report 2019* (2019), 35.

[10] https://washdata.org/sites/default/files/documents/reports/2020-05/JMP-2020-COVID-global-hygiene-snapshot.pdf.

[11] Independent Group of Scientists, *The Future Is Now, Science For Achieving Sustainable Development, Global Sustainable Development Report 2019* (2019): the term 'water' is spread throughout the report 260 times with the most diverse reference points.

[12] A/RES/217(III), *Universal Declaration of Human Rights*, 10 December 1948.

[13] Dimsey, 'Right To Water' in Cottier and Schefer (eds.) *Elgar Encyclopedia of International Economic Law* (2017), 641-43.

[14] UN, *Report of the United Nations Water Conference* (1977).

[15] OHCR, *Convention on the Elimination of All Forms of Discrimination against Women*, (CEDAW), Art. 14(2) h).

[16] http://www.wmo.int/pages/prog/hwrp/documents/english/icwedece.html.

[17] https://www.gwp.org/contentassets/05190d0c938f47d1b254d6606ec6bb04/dublin-rio-principles.pdf.

[18] http://www.wmo.int/pages/prog/hwrp/documents/english/icwedece.html.

[19] A/CONF.171/13/Rev.1, *Report of the International Conference on Population and Development*, 5-13 September 1994.

The first authoritative definition of the right to water[20] in international law is ex-   5
pressed in the General Comment No 15.[21] The right to water in 2002[22] can in turn be
derived from the ICESCR[23]:

> The human right to water entitles everyone to sufficient, safe, acceptable, physically accessible and
> affordable water for personal and domestic uses. An adequate amount of safe water is necessary
> to prevent death from dehydration, to reduce the risk of water-related disease and to provide for
> consumption, cooking, personal and domestic hygienic requirements.

According to the UN, approximately over 30 UN agencies organise water and san-   6
itation programmes. In 1977, the UN's Inter-Secretariat Group for Water Resources
started to coordinate UN activities in the field of water. Subsequently, in 2003, the
UN Administrative Coordination Committee's Subcommittee on Water Resources was
transformed into UN-Water and was endorsed by the UN System Chief Executives
Board for Coordination. UN-Water nowadays plays a coordinating role within the UN,
to ensure that the UN family 'delivers as one' in response to water-related challenges.[24]

After establishing UN-Water, the UN General Assembly adopted a historical mile-   7
stone resolution which recognises 'the right to safe and clean drinking water and sanitation as a human right that is essential for the full enjoyment of life and all human
rights'.[25] The right to safe drinking water and the right to sanitation have been recognised as closely related but distinct human rights since 2015 by the General Assembly.[26]
And even the predecessors of the SDGs, the MDGs which were adopted by the United
Nations Millennium Declaration, included the access to water in MDG 7.C:

> Halve, by 2015, the proportion of the population without sustainable access to safe drinking water
> and basic sanitation;

> – The world has met the target of halving the proportion of people without access to improved
>   sources of water, five years ahead of schedule.
> – Between 1990 and 2015, 2.6 billion people gained access to improved drinking water sources.
> – Worldwide 2.1 billion people have gained access to improved sanitation. Despite progress, 2.4
>   billion are still using unimproved sanitation facilities, including 946 million people who are still
>   practicing open defecation.

B. Scope and Dimensions of SDG 6

SDG 6 addresses the broad field of water supply and sanitation. Hereby, the essential   8
element of water is attributed to an entire SDG. Besides its biological importance as the
fundamental resource for the maintenance and improvement of life, water has gained
more and more political relevance and plays a decisive role in international politics
and, to an increasing extent, in international law. The spectrum of SDG 6 ranges from
non-discriminatory access for states and individuals to clean and affordable water to
adequate water quality, efficient water use, ecosystems, access to sanitation and the
international cooperation accompanying its implementation (→ Goal 17).

---

[20] Thor, 'The Human Right to Water in the United States: Why So Dangerous?' (2013) in 26 *Global Business & Development Law Journal*, 315-41.

[21] E/C.12/2002/11 (UN CESCR), *General Comment No. 15 (2002), The right to water (Arts. 11 and 12 of the International Covenant on Economic, Social and Cultural Rights)*, 20 January 2003.

[22] E/C.12/2002/11 (UN CESCR), *General Comment No. 15 (2002), The right to water (Arts. 11 and 12 of the International Covenant on Economic, Social and Cultural Rights)*, 20 January 2003, para. 2.

[23] Bürgi Bonanomi, *Sustainable Development in International Law Making and Trade* (2015), 258, 271.

[24] IISD, '32nd UN-Water Meeting' (2020) 82(40) *UN-Water Bulletin*.

[25] A/64/L.63/REV.1, *The human right to water and sanitation*, 26 July 2010.

[26] A/HRC/RES/33/10, *The Human Rights to Safe Drinking Water and Sanitation*, 5 October 2016.

9   According to the WHO, a minimum of 7.5 (up to 15) litres per capita each day will meet the requirements of most people under most conditions.[27] The amount of water required to support life and health in an emergency varies with climate, the general state of health of the people affected and their level of physical fitness. Other suggestions point out that the full realisation of the right to water requires at least 50-100 litres per person per day.[28] Equal access to sufficient safe and affordable water and adequate and equitable sanitation and hygiene can mean the difference between prosperity and poverty, well-being and ill-health, and even living and dying.[29]

I. Elementary Definitions

10   SDG 6 considers the term 'water' as the central issue, which despite its well-known characteristics requires a definitional approach. 'Water is the most abundant inorganic liquid in the world. [...] The unique substance is odorless, colorless and tasteless [and] covers 71 % of the earth completely.'[30] General Comment No. 15 on the Right to Water describes water as 'a limited natural resource and a public good fundamental for life and health.'[31] Despite the apparent abundance of water on our planet, the definition of the General Comment reflects with great clarity the fundamental problem to which SDG 6 is dedicated. The majority of the water on Earth is salt water that cannot be consumed by humans. Only a small portion is fresh water, which is indispensable as life resource for every single human being, as there can be no life without water.[32] Desalination plants gain increasing significance with regard to alternative sources of water supply. It is to be observed to what extent the economic affordability of such desalination plants is developing and thus could play a central role for developing countries with coasts, for instance. The legal framework for the use of the oceans for freshwater extraction will continue to be the focus of attention in the future.[33]

11   The small amount of clear, clean and usable water available for an ever-increasing population is therefore one of the greatest challenges humankind is facing and one that must be solved in a sustainable manner. There are warnings, meanwhile, that global crises regarding access to water and its equitable distribution are on the increase.[34] The global dimension of water that becomes apparent from this also illustrates the interdependencies of SDG 6 with various other SDGs (→ Goal 6 mn. 60 ff.). The concept of water also includes important components such as access to water, adequate water quality, equitable distribution and environmentally relevant aspects. Of particular importance is the area of international relations and international cooperation, which must prevent potential global conflicts over water in the light of SDG 16 (→ Goal 16 mn. 4).[35]

---

[27] See https://www.who.int/water_sanitation_health/emergencies/qa/emergencies_qa5/en/.

[28] Bos, *Manual of the Human Rights to Safe Drinking Water and Sanitation for Practitioners* (2016), 96.

[29] UN, *Integrated Approaches for Sustainable Development Goals Planning: The case of Goal 6 on Water and Sanitation* (2017), 816.

[30] Spellman, *The Science of Water: Concepts and Applications* (2015), 1.

[31] E/C.12/2002/11 (UN CESCR), *General Comment No. 15 (2002), The right to water (Arts. 11 and 12 of the International Covenant on Economic, Social and Cultural Rights)*, 20 January 2003, para. 1.

[32] Conca and Weinthal, 'The Political Dimensions of Water' in Conca and Weinthal (eds), *The Oxford Handbook of Water Politics and Policy* (2018), 3 (3).

[33] Schwabach, 'Desalination and International Watercourse Law' (2013) 2013 *Utah L Rev.*, 297 (297 ff.); Boisson de Chazournes, *Fresh Water in International Law* (2013), 1.

[34] Kidd and Feris, 'Introduction: water and the law: towards sustainability' in Kidd et al (eds), *Water and the Law: Towards Sustainability* (2014), 1 (1); see also: Dupuy and Viñuales, *International Environmental Law* (2018).

[35] Zeitoun et al., *Water Conflicts: Analysis for Transformation* (2020), 1 f.

Another elementary concept is that of sanitation which includes 'the provision of fa-   12
cilities and services for the safe disposal of human urine and faeces [and] the maintenance of hygienic conditions, through services such as garbage collection and wastewater disposal'.[36] Thus, water and sanitary facilities are directly connected as a matter of
every persons' daily necessity to use sanitary facilities. Access to clean and equally accessible sanitation facilities is fundamental to achieving and maintaining hygiene standards.
This in turn is of great relevance for the maintenance of public health as many diseases
are transmitted via human faeces ($\rightarrow$ Goal 3 mn. 46 ff.).[37] Like water, sanitation is seen
as a public good, which means that 'the use of these services by one should not diminish
the use by others and no one should be excluded from their use'.[38] SDG 6.1 and SDG 6.2
illustrate this special position as a public good by repeatedly mentioning the words 'equitable' and 'for all'. However, the term of public goods is not yet clearly defined in law
and should therefore be treated with caution in legal analysis.[39] As with SDG 3, the implementation of SDG 6 across society, based on equality, is therefore of central significance.

SDG 6 is designed to 'ensure the availability and sustainable management of water   13
and sanitation for all'. MDG 7.C is continued by the successor SDG 6.1 and SDG 6.2
which focus on achieving universal access to water and sanitation.[40] The definitions in
this context are to be highlighted.

1. Availability

General Comment No. 15 defines availability as '[t]he water supply for each person   14
[that] must be sufficient and continuous for personal and domestic uses, including
drinking, personal sanitation, washing clothes, food preparation, and personal and
household hygiene'.[41]

2. Accessibility

Accessibility to water means that water supply and sanitation infrastructure must be   15
built and located in an area that is easily accessible for anyone and giving consideration
to elderly people, children, people with disabilities and the chronically ill. Factors affecting actual accessibility include: the design of the facilities, the time and distance to get
to the water or reach a sanitation facility, and the physical security.[42] The WHO and
UNICEF define access to water as 'drinking water from an improved water source that

---

[36] Emeziem, 'The human right to clean water and sanitation – a perspective from Nigeria' in Chaisse
(ed), *Charting the Water Regulatory Future: Issues, Challenges and Directions* (2017), 195 (203).

[37] Jain and Graham, 'The human right to sanitation' in Selendy (ed), *Water and Sanitation-Related
Diseases and the Changing Environment: Challenges, Interventions and Preventive Measures* (2019), 17 (17).

[38] Obani and Gupta, 'The Human Right to Water and Sanitation: Reflections on Making the System
Effective' in Bhaduri et al (eds), *The Global Water System in the Anthropocene: Challenges for Science and
Governance* (2014), 385 (386).

[39] Huck, 'The UN Sustainable Development Goals and the Governance of Global Public Goods: The
Quest for Legitimacy' in Iovane et al., *The Protection of General Interests in Contemporary International
Law: A Theoretical and Empirical Inquiry* (2021).

[40] pS-Eau, *WASH Services in the Sustainable Development Goals* (2016), 14.

[41] E/C.12/2002/11, *General Comment No. 15 (2002), The right to water (arts. 11 and 12 of the International Covenant on Economic, Social and Cultural Rights)*, 20 January 2003, para.12(a); see also FAO,
Revised World Soil Charter (2015), principle 5.

[42] UN-Water, *The United Nations World Water Development Report 2019: Leaving no one behind* (2019).

is located on premises, available when needed and free from faecal and priority chemical contamination".[43]

3. Affordability

16   The term affordability implies that everyone must be able to afford water and sanitation services in a way that does not limit their capacity to achieve other basic goods and services such as food, health and education, which are fundamental to human rights.[44] People must be able to pay for their water and sanitation services, which means 'that the price paid to meet all these must not limit the peoples capacity to buy other goods and services'.[45]

4. Non-Discrimination

17   Discrimination in international human rights law is defined as 'any distinction, exclusion, or restriction which has the purpose or the effect of impairing or nullifying the recognition, enjoyment or exercise, on an equal basis with others, of human rights and fundamental freedoms in the political, economic, social, cultural, civil or any other field.[46]

18   Non-discrimination is a main principle in human rights, which demands that states prioritise the needs of people who are discriminated against and marginalised groups of population.[47] 'The right to water and sanitation require an explicit focus on the most disadvantaged and marginalized, as well as an emphasis on participation, empowerment and transparency'.[48] For states to overcome the existing discrimination, they must develop specific strategies to correct the situation of those who face discrimination. Regarding the terms of access to water and sanitation, groups and individuals who have been identified as potentially marginalised include women, children inhabitants living in poverty, nomadic, persons living with disabilities and people living in water-scarce regions.[49]

II. Legal Foundations

1. Water in International Law

19   In international law, fundamental rules on water law have only existed for a few decades. These are enshrined in the Helsinki Rules of 1966, which were drafted and published by the International Law Association (ILA).[50] The ILA holds a 'consultative status, as an international non-governmental organisation, with a number of the UN's specialised agencies and is dedicated to 'the study, clarification and development of international law'.[51] In this respect, the Helsinki Rules evolved into a core legal framework for international water related cases. Bogdanović describes the Helsinki rules as follows:

---

[43] WHO/UNICEF, *Progress on drinking water, sanitation and hygiene: 2017 update and SDG baseline* (2017).

[44] UN-Water, *The United Nations World Water Development Report 2019: Leaving no one behind* (2019).

[45] De Albuquerque, *Realising the Human Rights to water and Sanitation* (2014), 35.

[46] Art. 1(1) Convention on the Elimination of All Forms of Discrimination against Women (CEDAW).

[47] Boisson, *International Law and Freshwater: The Multiple Challenges* (2013), 62.

[48] Boisson, *International Law and Freshwater: The Multiple Challenges* (2013), 62.

[49] Boisson, *International Law and Freshwater: The Multiple Challenges* (2013).

[50] Bogdanović, *The International Law Association Helsinki Rules: Contribution to International Water Law* (2018), 1.

[51] https://www.ila-hq.org/index.php/about-us.

The Helsinki Rules on the Uses of the Waters of International Rivers, known under the abbreviated title Helsinki Rules, soon became widely known and accepted by the international community as a source of general rules of international law on the use and protection of the waters of shared drainage basins, applicable in case of absence of a treaty or binding custom. In the following years, the Helsinki Rules became an inspiration for building up relations between states sharing the same freshwaters either through the signing of water treaties, or as a basis for resolution of water disputes.[52]

International law thus recognises rules for the transboundary management of inter- **20** national river basins and offers states a legal basis for solving problems relating to water abstraction by rivers. For this purpose, an international river and an international lake are considered as those that lie 'between the territories of two or more than two States'.[53]

While SDG 6.4 and SDG 6.5 stand out markedly, with SDG 6.4 the concept of water **21** use-efficiency gains attention. In international law, the efficient use of water is important insofar as states must adhere to 'reasonable and equitable share in the beneficial uses of the waters of an international drainage basin'.[54] Reasonable and equitable utilisation of water constitutes one of the principles of international water law that is closely linked with the duty of states to cooperate,[55] which is explored in more detail under SDG 6.5. Regarding the meaning of 'responsible' and 'equitable' use of water, there are different views in the literature.[56] Boisson de Chazournes and Leb apply the term of benefit sharing to approach the water use among watercourse states. They provide the following definition:

> Benefit sharing on transboundary water systems is the process of allocating the benefits derived from water uses and non-uses rather than allocating the water itself. It offers opportunities for the redistribution of costs and benefits to achieve fairness. [...] Benefit sharing involves the sharing of directly and indirectly derived benefits, beyond simply sharing the quantity of water.[57]

The ILA Commentary on the Helsinki Rules emphasises that developed countries **22** should invest more in efficient water use technologies than developing countries (SDG 6.A). The obligation for efficiency should therefore be linked to the financial situation of the states. In view of the individual situation of each state, certain governmental steps to avoid waste of water as well as maximum efficiency in its use can then be expected from the states.[58]

SDG 6.5 is directly linked to SDG 6.4 and regulates water resource management **23** including the necessary transboundary cooperation between states. Being major sources

---

[52] Bogdanović, *The International Law Association Helsinki Rules: Contribution to International Water Law* (2018), 2.

[53] Bogdanović, *The International Law Association Helsinki Rules: Contribution to International Water Law* (2018), 68.

[54] International Law Association, *The Helsinki Rules on the Uses of the Waters of International Rivers*, Helsinki, August 1966 from Report of the Fifty-Second Conference, Helsinki, 14-20 August 1966, (London, 1967), Art. IV.

[55] Boisson de Chazournes and Leb, 'Benefit-sharing in international water law: a multi-disciplinary undertaking' in Tignino and Béthault (eds), *Research Handbook on Freshwater Law and International Relations* (2018), 391 (391).

[56] See e.g. McIntyre, 'International water law and SDG 6: mutually reinforcing paradigms' in French and Kotzé (eds), *Sustainable Development Goals: Law, Theory and Implementation* (2018), 173 (192 ff.); Rieu-Clarke, *International Law and Sustainable Development: Lessons from the Law of International Watercourses* (2005), 103 ff.; Bogdanović, *The International Law Association Helsinki Rules: Contribution to International Water Law* (2018), 70; Leb, *Cooperation in the Law of Transboundary Water Resources* (2013), 88.

[57] Boisson de Chazournes and Leb, 'Benefit-sharing in international water law: a multi-disciplinary undertaking' in Tignino and Béthault (eds), *Research Handbook on Freshwater Law and International Relations* (2018), 391 (391).

[58] *The Helsinki Rules Comment*, Art. IV, https://www.internationalwaterlaw.org/documents/intldocs/ILA/Helsinki_Rules-original_with_comments.pdf.

of water, international river basins are a significant factor in the cross-border water supply of states. Especially in areas with water scarcity, the use of these river basins has developed into a conflict-ridden international issue, not only in recent decades.[59] Due to the mutual dependencies between the states bordering these waters, many states feel compelled to cooperate with each other. However, factors such as national security, conflict-torn relations with bordering states, and self-interested profit-seeking also play a considerable role in the reality of cross-border cooperation.[60] Cooperation as such is the convergence of states and is embodied by international agreements or treaties through which the states pursue 'a common purpose that produces mutual benefits'.[61]

24   In this context, the UN Watercourse Convention (UNWC) of 1997 provides the foundations of the 'duty of states to cooperate' in international water law.[62] As one of the core principles the 'duty to cooperate', Art. 8 of the UNWC states that:

> Watercourse States shall cooperate on the basis of sovereign equality, territorial integrity, mutual benefit and good faith in order to attain optimal utilization and adequate protection of an international watercourse.[63]

25   The legal dimension of this provision is not yet fully specified, though it can be said that it implies obligations on states such as 'the duty to exchange information [...] [and] duties to consult and negotiate with [...] States in a good faith effort to address their concerns'.[64] Current policy is increasingly focusing on crises and conflicts caused by failed cooperation. The efforts of states bordering on riverbeds based on the concept of water diplomacy tend to fail.[65] This 'diplomatic fallout [...] result[s] from interstate water arrangements that are neither equitable nor sustainable'.[66]

26   An arrangement for water cooperation is a bilateral or multilateral treaty, convention, agreement or any other formal arrangement between riparian countries that provides a framework for cooperation on transboundary water management. UNECE and the International Hydrological Programme of UNESCO are the custodian agencies of indicator 6.5.2, and they have developed this methodology in a consultative process that included countries, international agencies and other experts.

27   Not least because these frequently failed arrangements on watercourses[67] affect mostly vulnerable groups of society (e.g. through loss of access to water due to dried-out

---

[59] Zeitoun et al., *Water Conflicts: Analysis for Transformation* (2020), 1 f.

[60] Leb, *Cooperation in the Law of Transboundary Water Resources* (2013), 20.

[61] Leb, 'Implementation of the General Duty to Cooperate' in: McCaffrey et al (eds), *Research Handbook on International Water Law* (2019), 95 (96).

[62] United Nations Convention on the Law of the Non-navigational Uses of International Watercourses (1997); see also UNECE Convention on the protection and use of transboundary watercourses and international lakes (1992).

[63] United Nations Convention on the Law of the Non-navigational Uses of International Watercourses, Art. 8; further reading: Boisson de Chazournes et al., *The UN Convention on the Law of the Non-Navigational Uses of International Watercourses: A Commentary* (2018), 123 ff.

[64] McIntyre, 'International water law and SDG 6: mutually reinforcing paradigms' in French and Kotzé (eds), *Sustainable Development Goals: Law, Theory and Implementation* (2018), 173 (195); United Nations Convention on the Law of the Non-navigational Uses of International Watercourses, Art. 9; further reading: Boisson de Chazournes et al., *The UN Convention on the Law of the Non-Navigational Uses of International Watercourses: A Commentary* (2018), 123 ff.

[65] See Yihdego, *The Fairness 'Dilemma' in Sharing the Nile Waters: What Lessons from the Grand Ethiopian Renaissance Dam for International Law?* (2017); Salman and Uprety, *Shared Watercourses and Water Security in South Asia: Challenges of Negotiating and Enforcing Treaties* (2018).

[66] Zeitoun et al., *Water conflicts: Analysis for transformation* (2020), 2.

[67] See the Nile river basin in Zeitoun et al., *Water conflicts: Analysis for transformation* (2020), 3 ff.; Zareie et al., 'A state-of-the-art review of water diplomacy' (2020) 22 *Environ Dev Sustain*, 7; see further Southern African Development Community (SADC) Revised Protocol on Shared Watercourses in the Southern African Development Community (2000); Water Charters of the Senegal and Niger Rivers and

riverbeds), there is a great need to take effective steps to make these arrangements sustainable in the international context.[68] Water diplomacy is increasing significantly in relevance in international law and thus poses a major challenge for SDG 6.5.[69]

Furthermore, there are clear references to the state's duty to cooperate to respect   **28** social and human needs in order to realise the human right to water.[70] States have the responsibility to use their special position and power, especially in the area of transboundary cooperation in watercourses, to safeguard and implement the right to water.[71] Against this background, the high interdependence between SDG 6 and SDG 16 is worth noting.[72]

In view of the manifold uses of water in everyday life and the resulting legal aspects,   **29** various other spheres are affected by SDG 6. Water pollution from industrial waste but also improper disposal of sanitary waste remains a fundamental obstacle to obtaining an appropriate water quality.[73] SDG 6.3 is dedicated to ensuring healthy and potable water by reducing pollution, dumping and chemicals in water. The aim is to enable used water to be reused through recycling. This environment related target is closely interlinked with the preservation and maintenance of ecosystems embodied in SDG 6.6.[74] In international water law, Arts. 20 and 21 of the UNWC reflect an example of codification in the field of environmental and ecosystems protection concerning water.[75]

---

the Lake Chad Water Basin (2000); Statute of the River Uruguay (1975) between Uruguay and Argentina; The Guaraní Aquifer Agreement (2010); A/RES/63/124, *The law of transboundary aquifers*, 15 January 2009; Agreement on the Cooperation for the Sustainable Development of the Mekong River Basin (1995); Agreement Between the Government of the People's Republic of China and the Government of the Russian Federation Concerning Reasonable Use and Protection of Transboundary Waters (2008).

[68] Zeitoun et al., *Water conflicts: Analysis for transformation* (2020), 2 f.

[69] See Durgeshree, 'Damming and Infrastructural Development of the Indus River Basin: Strengthening the Provisions of the Indus Waters Treaty' (2018) 8 *AsianJIL*, 372; Nagheeby and Piri D. and Faure, 'The Legitimacy of Dam Development in International Watercourses: A Case Study of the Harirud River Basin' (2019) 8 *TEL*, 247 (247 ff.); Suykens, *The Law of the River: Transboundary River Basin Management and Multi-Level Approaches to Water Quantity Management* (2018); Boelens and Perreault and Vos, *Water Justice* (2018); Kornfeld, *Transboundary Water Disputes: State Conflict and the Assessment of Their Adjudication* (2019); Choudhury and Islam, *Complexity of Transboundary Water Conflicts: Enabling Conditions for Negotiating Contingent Resolutions* (2018); Islam and Madani, *Water Diplomacy in Action: Contingent Approaches to Managing Complex Water Problems* (2017).

[70] McIntyre, 'International water law and SDG 6: mutually reinforcing paradigms' in French and Kotzé (eds), *Sustainable Development Goals: Law, Theory and Implementation* (2018), 173, 195 ff.

[71] See E/C.12/2002/11 (UN CESCR), *General Comment No. 15 (2002), The right to water (Arts. 11 and 12 of the International Covenant on Economic, Social and Cultural Rights)*, 20 January 2003, para. 35:
States parties should ensure that the right to water is given due attention in international agreements and, to that end, should consider the development of further legal instruments. With regard to the conclusion and implementation of other international and regional agreements, States parties should take steps to ensure that these instruments do not adversely impact upon the right to water.

[72] See Amezaga et al., 'SDG 6: Clean Water and Sanitation – Forest-Related Targets and Their Impacts on Forests and People' in Katila et al. (eds), *Sustainable Development Goals: Their Impacts on Forests and People* (2019), 197:
Second, the success of SDG 6 depends on the existence of national and global institutions able and willing to implement the goal. While the WASH sector has spent nearly 20 years trying to achieve global targets, the level of institutional readiness for the new water resources targets is frequently low or non-existent at the country level.

[73] See Gray, *Drinking Water Quality: Problems and Solutions* (2008).

[74] See, amongst others: Ramsar Convention on Wetlands of International Importance Especially as Waterfowl Habitat (1971); Protocol for the Implementation of the 1991 Alpine Convention in the field of Soil Protection (1998), Arts. 3, 8, 9 and 11; Revised African Convention on the Conservation of Nature and Natural Resources (2003), Article VII.

[75] McIntyre, 'International water law and SDG 6: mutually reinforcing paradigms' in French and Kotzé (eds), *Sustainable Development Goals: Law, Theory and Implementation* (2018), 185 ff.; Martin-Ortega et al. (eds), *Water Ecosystem Services: A Global Perspective* (2015).

With regard to international watercourses, these regulations require states to jointly protect the surrounding ecosystems and to prevent, reduce and combat any pollution of the respective watercourse.[76] Furthermore, the supply of adequate and clean water to cities with their steadily growing populations is an equally considerable challenge and must be tackled not least in the context of SDG 11.[77]

2. Right to Water and Sanitation

30   The right to water is linked to the highest attainable standard of health (Art. 12(1) ICESCR) and the rights to adequate housing and adequate food (Art. 11(1) ICESCR).[78]

31   The freedoms include the right to maintain access to existing water supplies necessary for the right to water, and the right to be free from interference, such as the right to be free from arbitrary disconnections or contamination of water supplies. By contrast, the entitlements include the right to a system of water supply and management that provides equality of opportunity for people to enjoy the right to water.[79]

32   Water and water facilities, sanitation and services must be accessible without discrimination, within the jurisdiction of a State Party to all people, including children, women, rural and deprived people, indigenous people, nomadic and traveller communities, refugees, asylum-seekers, prisoners and detainees.[80] Accessibility has four overlapping dimensions relying on the non-discrimination principle and enshrining physical accessibility, economic accessibility and information accessibility as well as the application of the prohibition of discrimination, including *de facto* discrimination.[81]

33   The right to water is defined and described in its form and scope in General Comment No. 15 which states '[t]he human right to water entitles everyone to sufficient, safe, acceptable, physically accessible and affordable water for personal and domestic uses'. In this context, it is emphasised that water is absolutely necessary for life and therefore too little of water is lethal.[82] Furthermore, the right to water 'falls within the category of guarantees essential to secure an adequate standard of living' according to Art. 11 ICESCR.[83] A vital step of the UN to promote efforts towards a human right to water and sanitation was made on 28 July 2010 with Resolution 64/292.[84]

> [T]he United Nations General Assembly explicitly recognized the human right to water and sanitation [through Resolution 64/292] and acknowledged that clean drinking water and sanitation are

---

[76] United Nations Convention on the Law of the Non-navigational Uses of International Watercourses, Arts. 20 and 21; further reading: Boisson de Chazournes et al. (eds), *The UN Convention on the Law of the Non-Navigational Uses of International Watercourses: A Commentary* (2018), 193 ff.

[77] Ho, *Thirsty Cities: Social Contracts and Public Goods Provision in China and India* (2019).

[78] E/C.12/2002/11 (UN CESCR), *General Comment No. 15 (2002), The right to water (Arts. 11 and 12 of the International Covenant on Economic, Social and Cultural Rights)*, 20 January 2003, para. 3.

[79] E/C.12/2002/11 (UN CESCR), *General Comment No. 15 (2002), The right to water (Arts. 11 and 12 of the International Covenant on Economic, Social and Cultural Rights)*, 20 January 2003, para. 10.

[80] E/C.12/2002/11 (UN CESCR), *General Comment No. 15 (2002), The right to water (Arts. 11 and 12 of the International Covenant on Economic, Social and Cultural Rights)*, 20 January 2003, para. 16.

[81] E/C.12/2002/11 (UN CESCR), *General Comment No. 15 (2002), The right to water (arts. 11 and 12 of the International Covenant on Economic, Social and Cultural Rights)*, 20 January 2003, paras. 12, 14.

[82] E/C.12/2002/11 (UN CESCR), *General Comment No. 15 (2002), The right to water (arts. 11 and 12 of the International Covenant on Economic, Social and Cultural Rights)*, 20 January 2003, para. 2.

[83] Langford and Russell, 'Introduction: The Right to Water in Context' in Langford and Russell (eds), *The Human Right to Water: Theory, Practice and Prospects* (2017), 1 (7).

[84] See also A/HRC/RES/18/1, *The human right to safe drinking water and sanitation*, 12 October 2001; A/HRC/RES/24/18, *The human right to safe drinking water and sanitation*, 8 October 2013; A/HRC/RES/27/7, *The human right to safe drinking water and sanitation*, 2 October 2014; UN RES 68/157, *The human right to safe drinking water and sanitation*, 12 February 2014; UN RES 70/169, *The human rights to safe drinking water and sanitation*, 22 February 2016.

essential to the realisation of all human rights. The Resolution calls upon States and international organisations to provide financial resources, help capacity-building and technology transfer to help countries, in particular developing countries, to provide safe, clean, accessible and affordable drinking water and sanitation for all.[85]

The right to water entails a number of obligations on the part of states towards each individual and places particular emphasis on support for developing states in this context. SDG 6.a pushes this approach and aims to increase international cooperation (SDG 6.5) to support water and sanitation-related projects.[86]   **34**

Similar to the right to health, core elements of the right to water are the factors availability, accessibility and quality, and these can be used as benchmarks for implementing the right to water. Availability means the existence of sufficient and continuous water for personal and domestic use.[87] According to the WHO, the availability is sufficient once everyone has at least 7.5 (up to 15) litres of water available per day. An optimum would be 100 - 200 litres per day and person.[88] Accessibility comprises the physical, economic and non-discriminatory accessibility of water.[89] Furthermore, the factor of accessibility implies the right to information on water-related issues.[90] Thus, 'access to water must be safe, indiscriminate, and affordable'[91] which leads to the overarching concept of equity. The United Nations Human Rights Office of the High Commissioner established '[t]he mandate of the Special Rapporteur on the human rights to safe drinking water and sanitation [...] to examine [...] crucial issues and provide recommendations to Governments, to the United Nations and other stakeholders'.[92] Furthermore, the United Nations General Assembly introduced the International Water Action Decade called 'Water for Sustainable Development' for the period of 2018 - 2028, 'to further improve cooperation, partnership and capacity development in response to the ambitious 2030 Agenda. Commencing on World Water Day, 22 March 2018, and concluding on World Water Day 2028, the Decade builds on the achievements of the previous "Water for Life" Decade, 2005-2015'.[93]   **35**

This concept of access to clean water, which was already the cornerstone of General Comment No. 15, is comprehensively taken up by SDG 6.1. Everyone should have universal and equal access to safe and affordable drinking water by 2030. In view of the international conflicts, the right to water should guarantee that such conflicts are resolved on the basis of and with a focus on the human rights of every human being by simultaneously ensuring clean water and fair water management.[94]   **36**

---

[85] https://www.un.org/waterforlifedecade/human_right_to_water.shtml.

[86] See Murillho Chavarro, *The Human Right to Water: A Legal Comparative Perspective at the International, Regional and Domestic Level* (2015).

[87] E/C.12/2002/11 (UN CESCR), *General Comment No. 15 (2002), The right to water (arts. 11 and 12 of the International Covenant on Economic, Social and Cultural Rights)*, 20 January 2003, para. 12(a).

[88] Weber, *Grundwasser im Völkerrecht* (2018), 72 f.; World Health Organization, *Guidelines for Drinking-Water Quality* (2017).

[89] E/C.12/2002/11 (UN CESCR), *General Comment No. 15 (2002), The right to water (arts. 11 and 12 of the International Covenant on Economic, Social and Cultural Rights)*, 20 January 2003, para. 12(c).

[90] E/C.12/2002/11 (UN CESCR), *General Comment No. 15 (2002), The right to water (arts. 11 and 12 of the International Covenant on Economic, Social and Cultural Rights)*, 20 January 2003, para. 12(c).

[91] Boisson de Chazournes, *Fresh Water in International Law* (2013), 155.

[92] https://www.ohchr.org/EN/Issues/WaterAndSanitation/SRWater/Pages/SRWaterIndex.aspx.

[93] https://sustainabledevelopment.un.org/wateractiondecade.

[94] Arden, 'Water for all? Developing a human right to water in national and international law' (2016) 65 *ICLQ*, 771 (789); Hey, 'Distributive Justice and Procedural Fairness in Global Water Law' in Ebbesson and Okowa (eds), *Environmental Law and Justice in Context* (2009); see also A/RES/73/165, *United Nations Declaration on the Rights of Peasants and Other People Working in Rural Areas*, Art. 21.

37   Indigenous peoples are a vulnerable group in the international context of water and water law. As in other SDGs, they have a distinct position in international law and require particular consideration ($\rightarrow$ Goal 3 mn. 11, 25, 44).[95] For centuries, indigenous people have experienced an increased repression in their influence on the use of water. In order to protect and strengthen the special rights of these peoples, also with regard to their cultural values and ideas, it is not least necessary to include the peoples in processes of law-making and to ensure their participation in water resource management.[96]

38   SDG 6.2 embodies a special element of SDG 6 by combining the fields of water, sanitation and hygiene. This target shows the inseparable interaction of sanitation, water and hygienic living conditions; thus, the literature summarises the combination as the acronym 'WASH'.[97] The right to water and sanitation must be approached from the perspective of the right to sanitation.

> Inadequate sanitation leads to contamination of the environment, of public spaces, and of water bodies through feces and wastewater. Therefore, contamination has a negative impact on public health and the life and wellbeing of everyone in the community, affecting their human rights to health, life, food, and a healthy environment.[98]

39   The indispensable safeguarding of health, the environment and equal rights through access to adequate sanitation illustrates the considerable social significance of the right to sanitation in the overall functioning of the SDGs and also of human rights. Water in its natural sources can only be protected from pollution by a functioning sanitation system with access and use for all, thus ensuring a closed cycle of water use.[99]

40   In view of the globally recognisable consequences of a lack of sanitation, the need for a human right to sanitation is clear. The relevance of a right to sanitation is particularly evident in the immense impact on health and water pollution. The fact that children are ultimately prevented from attending school and workers are unable to perform their work productively must also be considered ($\rightarrow$ Goal 4 mn. 6, $\rightarrow$ Goal 8 mn. 61). Despite all this, the legal status of the right to sanitation has not yet been completely defined.[100] Though, considerable steps towards the international recognition of the right to sanitation were taken by the UN through various resolutions.[101]

41   General Comment No. 15 has already identified non-discrimination in access to and supply of water as one of the obligations of the state.[102] It is striking that a special focus on women and girls and other persons in vulnerable situations is only explicitly

---

[95] See for instance ILO Convention No. 169 Convention Concerning Indigenous and Tribal Peoples in Independent Countries (1989), Arts. 25, 26 and 31; A/RES/61/295, *United Nations Declaration on the Rights of Indigenous Peoples*, 2 October 2007, Arts. 25 and 32.

[96] Mcpherson, *Indigenous Water Rights in Law and Regulation: Lessons from Comparative Experience* (2019), 1 f.; see also: Langford and Russell, 'Introduction: The Right to Water in Context' in Langford and Russell (eds), *The Human Right to Water: Theory, Practice and Prospects* (2017), 84 ff.; Misiedjan, *Towards a Sustainable Human Right to Water: Supporting Vulnerable People and Protecting Water Resources*, (2019).

[97] Kremere et al., *SDG 6 – Clean Water and Sanitation: Balancing the Water Cycle for Sustainable Life on Earth* (2020), 9.

[98] Winkler, 'The Human Right to Sanitation' (2016) 37 *U. Pa. J. Int'l L.*, 1331 (1331 f.).

[99] Winkler, 'The Human Right to Sanitation' (2016) 37 *U. Pa. J. Int'l L.*, 1331 (1338).

[100] Langford and Russell, 'Introduction: The Right to Water in Context' in Langford and Russell (eds), *The Human Right to Water: Theory, Practice and Prospects* (2017), 345 (345 ff.).

[101] A/RES/68/157, *The human right to safe drinking water and sanitation*, 12 February 2014; A/RES/70/1, *Transforming Our World: The 2030 Agenda For Sustainable Development*, 21 October 2015; UN RES 70/169, *The human rights to safe drinking water and sanitation*, 22 February 2016; A/HRC/RES/24/18, *The human right to safe drinking water and sanitation*, 8 October 2013; A/HRC/RES/27/7, *The human right to safe drinking water and sanitation*, 2 October 2014.

[102] E/C.12/2002/11 (UN CESCR), *General Comment No. 15 (2002), The right to water (Arts. 11 and 12 of the International Covenant on Economic, Social and Cultural Rights)*, 20 January 2003, paras. 13 ff.

mentioned in SDG 6.2.[103] Clearly, women and girls need special protection in the field of sanitation and hygiene, which includes feminine hygiene (→ Goal 5 mn. 125).[104]

Through the right to sanitation and the right to water, the human being stands **42** directly in focus regarding the implementation of the further targets of SDG 6, i.e. it is not possible to provide water for all for intake as well as for sanitation purposes if the water ecosystems in nature do not function properly (SDG 6.6).[105]

III. Specific Look at the Indicators

Valid and reliable aggregated data are provided by WHO/UNICEF Joint Monitoring **43** Programme for Water Supply, Sanitation and Hygiene (JMP)[106] which are an essential for accountability, transparency and participation. The e-handbook on Sustainable Development Goals Indicators addresses in general and in particular the growing need for well-prepared information targeted towards national statisticians to collect, calculate, and monitor the SDGs. It serves the national statistician with critical aspects such as concepts, definition, sources, calculations that are essential to measuring indicators.[107] Sometimes indicators are not yet developed, and the user is informed that United Nations Statistics Division (UNSD) worked in consultation with each indicators' custodian agency(ies) to prepare these chapters.[108]

Those data enables transparently monitored progress, and, on this basis, governments **44** and responsible agencies and entities can be held accountable. However, many countries lack the financial, technical, institutional and human resources to acquire and analyse data. The UN has published that only less than half of Member States have comparable data available on progress towards meeting each of the global SDG 6 targets.[109] Almost 60 per cent of countries do not have data available for more than four global indicators of SDG 6, and only 6 per cent reported on more than eight global indicators, which reveals a significant knowledge gap.[110]

SDG 6 with eight targets is to be measured through 11 indicators, the current status **45** of which is readable from the UN-Water SDG 6 Data Portal as follows:

71 per cent of the world's population use a safely managed drinking water (indicator **46** 6.1.1), 45 per cent use a safely managed sanitation service (indicator 6.2.1 a) and 60 per cent of the world's population have access to a basic handwashing facility (indicator 6.2.1 b).[111]

SDG 6.1 pursues to achieve access for all to safe drinking water.[112] The related **47** indicator 6.1.1 tracks the proportion of population having access at least to an improved

---

[103] SDG 6.2: 'By 2030, achieve access to adequate and equitable sanitation and hygiene for all and end open defecation, paying special attention to the needs of women and girls and those in vulnerable situations'.

[104] Winkler, 'The Human Right to Sanitation' (2016) 37 *U. Pa. J. Int'l L.*, 1331 (1384).

[105] Boisson de Chazournes, *Fresh Water in International Law* (2013), 160.

[106] See https://washdata.org/how-we-work and to inequalities: https://washdata.org/monitoring/inequalities.

[107] See UN Statistics Wiki, *E-Handbook on Sustainable Development Goals Indicators* https://unstats.un.org/wiki/display/SDGeHandbook/Home.

[108] See UN Statistics, https://unstats.un.org/wiki/display/SDGeHandbook/Goal+6 (15.04.2021).

[109] UN, *Integrated Approaches for Sustainable Development Goals Planning: The case of Goal 6 on Water and Sanitation*, (2017), 17.

[110] UN, *Integrated Approaches for Sustainable Development Goals Planning: The case of Goal 6 on Water and Sanitation*, (2017), 11.

[111] https://sdg6data.org.

[112] A/RES/70/1, *Transforming Our World: The 2030 Agenda For Sustainable Development*, 21 October 2015, para. 35.

drinking water source that is available on the premises whenever needed and free from faecal and chemical contamination.[113] The definition of 'improved' drinking water includes 'piped water into dwelling, yard or plot; public taps or standpipes; boreholes and tube wells; protected spring and delivered water and rainwater'.[114] The drinking water from an improved source that does not fulfil the mentioned criteria is called a 'basic' service if the collection time of the water is not more than 30 minutes. Sources of water further away are categorised as 'limited'.[115]

48   SDG 6.2 aims at achieving access for all to sanitation and hygiene.[116] This target has one indicator which can be differentiated into indicator 6.2.1 a and indicator 6.2.1 b. Indicator 6.2.1 a captures the proportion of population that is using an improved sanitation facility, which is not shared with other households. This facility includes a system that 'safely separates excreta from human contact throughout the sanitation chain, either through safe containment and disposal in situ, or through safe transport and treatment/reuse off premises'.[117] The improved sanitation includes flush/pour latrines and composting toilets or pit latrines with slabs.[118] Indicator 6.2.1 b focuses on hygiene tracks by measuring the proportion of population with handwashing facility with a soap and water on premises.

49   SDG 6.3 calls for improving water quality by halving the proportion of untreated wastewater and challenges countries to increase wastewater collection and treatment, so that sewage consistently meets national standards. Indicator 6.3.1 ('Proportion of wastewater safely treated') defines water that is of no further immediate value for the purpose for which it had been used or produced because of the quality and quantity of occurrence.[119]

50   The next target focuses on water use and scarcity (SDG 6.4).[120] This target encompasses indicator 6.4.1 (change in water-use efficiency over time) and indicator 6.4.2 (level of water stress). Indicator 6.4.1 is about using less water to carry the communities' economic activities and measures the financial value produced by an economy (i.e. gross domestic product – GDP) relative to the volume of water that is used. It also includes water use in agriculture, industry and mining.[121] Water-efficient economies are recognised to achieve a high GDP per unit freshwater withdrawal.[122] Water scarcity or stress included in indicator 6.4.2 defines as the total quantity of freshwater withdrawals as a share of internal resources.[123]

51   The result of the dependency of many sectors on water is that the water resources are limited and naturally confined to water basins.[124] Most of the world's freshwater resources are transboundary, and coordination and cooperation across national borders

---

[113] Ortigara and Kay and Uhlenbrook, *A Review of the SDG 6 Synthesis Report 2018 from an Education, Training and Research Perspective* (2018), 8.

[114] https://unstats.un.org/sdgs/metadata/files/Metadata-06-01-01.pdf.

[115] https://www.sdg6monitoring.org/indicator-611/, Indicator 6.1.1.

[116] A/RES/70/1, *Transforming Our World: The 2030 Agenda For Sustainable Development*, 21 October 2015, para. 35.

[117] UN Water, *Integrated Monitoring Guide for SDG 6* (2016), 6.

[118] https://www.sdg6monitoring.org/indicator-621/, Indicator 6.2.1.

[119] WHO, *Progress on safe treatment and use of wastewater: piloting the monitoring methodology and initial findings for SDG indicator 6.3.1* (2018),11.

[120] A/RES/70/1, *Transforming Our World: The 2030 Agenda For Sustainable* Development, 21 October 2015, para. 35.

[121] Ortigara and Kay and Uhlenbrook, *A Review of the SDG 6 Synthesis Report 2018 from an Education, Training and Research Perspective* (2018), 9.

[122] https://sdg-tracker.org/water-and-sanitation, SDG 6.4.

[123] https://sdg-tracker.org/water-and-sanitation, Indicator 6.4.2.

[124] https://www.sdg6monitoring.org/indicators/target-65/, SDG 6.5.

can be challenging. Indicator 6.5.1 tracks the degree of integrated water resources management (IWRM) implementation[125], by assessing the four key components of institutions, policies, management tools and financing. IWRM takes into account the different users and uses of water with the aim of promoting positive social, economic and environmental impacts at all levels, including at the cross-border level.[126] Indicator 6.5.2 (Proportion of transboundary basin area with an operational arrangement for water cooperation) measures and monitors the proportion of a cross-border area within a country that is covered by an 'operational arrangement' defined as a treaty, agreement, convention or other formal arrangement.[127]

An arrangement for water cooperation is a bilateral or multilateral treaty, convention, 52 agreement or any other formal arrangement between riparian countries that provides a framework for cooperation on transboundary water management. UNECE and the International Hydrological Programme of UNESCO are the custodian agencies of indicator 6.5.2, and they have developed this methodology in a consultative process that included countries, international agencies and other experts.[128] References to the indicator 6.5.2 comprises among other documents the main conventions and other international acknowledged documents.[129]

More attention needs to be paid to transboundary cooperation here, as purely trans- 53 boundary cooperation is essential for natural resource management.[130] The aspect of bi- and multilateral cooperation respectively its implementation[131] lies in the focus of indicator 6.5.2 dealing with the '[p]roportion of [a] transboundary basin area with an operational arrangement for water cooperation'. The indicator 6.5.2 is related to SDG 6.5: By 2030, implement integrated water resources management at all levels, including through transboundary cooperation as appropriate. Transboundary basins include river and lake basins and aquifers shared between two or more sovereign states. For the

---

[125] https://www.sdg6monitoring.org/indicator-651/, Indicator 6.5.1.

[126] UN Water, *Integrated Monitoring Guide for SDG 6* (2016), 17.

[127] Ortigara and Kay and Uhlenbrook, *A Review of the SDG 6 Synthesis Report 2018 from an Education, Training and Research Perspective* (2018), 10.

[128] See https://unstats.un.org/wiki/display/SDGeHandbook/Indicator+6.5.2.

[129] Official SDG Metadata URL, https://unstats.un.org/sdgs/metadata/files/Additional-SDG-indicator-metadata-JUL2017.zip; Internationally agreed methodology and guideline URL, http://www.unwater.org/publications/step-step-methodology-monitoring-transboundary-cooperation-6-5-2/; UN, *Convention on the Law of the Non-Navigational Uses of International Watercourses* (1997); UNECE, *Convention on the Protection and Use of Transboundary Watercourses and International Lakes* (1992); UN, *Draft Articles on the Law of Transboundary Aquifers*, UNGA, 63rd Session, Supplement No. 10 (A/63/10); UNECE, *Convention on the Protection and Use of Transboundary Watercourses and International Lakes: A Globalizing Framework* (2013); https://www.unece.org/fileadmin/DAM/env/water/meetings/Water_Convention/2016/10Oct_From_Practitioner_to_Practitioner/Presentations/6.3.Presentation_reporting_TtT.pdf; UNECE and UNESCO, *Progress on Transboundary Water Cooperation – Global baseline for SDG indicator 6.5.2.* (2018); UN-Water, *Integrated Monitoring of Water and Sanitation related SDG Targets: Indicator 6.5.2 – Transboundary cooperation* (2018); GEF, *Transboundary Waters Assessment Programme*, http://www.geftwap.org/; Oregon State University, *Transboundary Freshwater Dispute Database (TFDD)*, http://www.transboundarywaters.orst.edu/publications/atlas/index.html; Oregon State University, *International River Basin Organization (RBO) Database*, http://www.transboundarywaters.orst.edu/research/RBO/index.html; UNECE, *Second Assessment of Transboundary Rivers, Lakes and Groundwaters* (2011); ISARM, *Regional Inventories of Transboundary Groundwaters*, http://www.isarm.org/.

[130] Ortigara and Kay and Uhlenbrook, *A Review of the SDG 6 Synthesis Report 2018 from an Education, Training and Research Perspective* (2018), 10.

[131] United Nations Economic Commission for Europe (UNECE), *Progress on transboundary water cooperation under the water convention, Report on Implementation of the Convention on the Protection and Use of Transboundary Watercourses and International Lakes* (2018).

purposes of this indicator, the extent of the basin is the catchment area for river and lake basins, and the surface area of transboundary aquifer systems.[132]

54   The Convention on the Protection and Use of Transboundary Watercourses and International Lakes, Art. 1(2), stipulates that 'effects on the environment include effects on human health and safety, flora, fauna, soil, air, water, climate, landscape and historical monuments or other physical structures or the interaction among these factors; they also include effects on the cultural heritage or socio-economic conditions resulting from alterations to those factors'.[133]

55   According to the International Law Commission (ILC), the obligation not to cause significant harm to the environment of other States has an established status in a transboundary context. It has been particularly relevant concerning shared natural resources, such as sea areas, international watercourses and transboundary aquifers. This principle has also been confirmed and clarified in international and regional jurisprudence.[134] The obligation to share information and to cooperate in this context is reflected in the Convention on the Law of the Non-navigational Uses of International Watercourses.[135]

56   There are further connections to SDGs:

–   SDG 6.5 By 2030, implement integrated water resources management at all levels, including through transboundary cooperation as appropriate
–   SDG 6.6 By 2020, protect and restore water-related ecosystems, including mountains, forests, wetlands, rivers, aquifers and lakes
–   SDG 11.5 By 2030, significantly reduce the number of deaths and the number of people affected and substantially decrease the direct economic losses relative to global gross domestic product caused by disasters, including water-related disasters, with a focus on protecting the poor and people in vulnerable situations

IV. UN Water as a Core Unit for Water

57   UN-Water helped shaping SDG 6.[136] Their role is to coordinate all the UN organisations that focus on water to deliver the same response to water related challenges and to gather stakeholders' proposals to facilitate synergies and joint efforts[137] in three ways: (1) Inform Policies; (2) Monitor and Report; and (3) Inspire Action.[138]

58   The UN-Water Global Analysis and Assessment of Sanitation and Drinking-Water (GLAAS) is a systematic of the UN that provides 'policy- and decision-makers at all levels with an analysis of the investments and enabling environment to make informed decisions for sanitation, drinking-water and hygiene.'[139]

59   There are various NGOs that focus on WASH services such as the WASH Alliance which is a multi-national consortium of over a hundred partners worldwide, cooperating with local NGOs, governments and businesses to make sure everybody in the world

---

[132] See https://unstats.un.org/wiki/display/SDGeHandbook/Indicator+6.5.2, Indicator 6.5.2.

[133] UNECE, *Convention on the Protection and Use of Transboundary Watercourses and International Lakes*, 17 March 1992, 269.

[134] ILC, *Report of the International Law Commission, Seventy-first session (29 April–7 June and 8 July–9 August 2019)*, United Nations A/74/10, 279.

[135] ILC, *Report of the International Law Commission, Seventy-first session (29 April–7 June and 8 July–9 August 2019)*, United Nations A/74/10, 287; Boisson de Chazournes et al., *The UN Convention on the Law of the Non-Navigational Uses of International Watercourses: A Commentary* (2018).

[136] https://www.unwater.org/about-unwater/.

[137] pS-Eau, *WASH Services in the Sustainable Development Goals* (2016), 10.

[138] https://www.unwater.org/about-unwater/.

[139] https://www.unwater.org/publication_categories/glaas/.

has access to water and sanitation. One of the biggest WASH NGOs that is supported by the EU, WHO, UNICEF and many more is the International Red Cross (IRC).[140] The World Water Council is an international multi-stakeholder platform organisation whose mission is to prepare activity basic water issues at all levels, including the highest decision-making level, by engaging people in debate challenging conventional thinking. The task they have is to promote awareness, build political commitment and trigger action on water issues.[141]

C. Interdependences of SDG 6

Water means life, it is of vital importance,[142] and is a fundamental building block for **60** sustainable, economic and ecological development.[143] SDG 6 expresses this finding[144] and its objectives form the basis for achieving many of the objectives contained in the other SDGs[145] such as eradicating poverty through securing access to water supply, wastewater treatment and sanitation (SDG 1.4, SDG 1.5),[146] safeguarding food supply (SDG 2.1, SDG 2.4), health (SDG 3.2, SDG 3.3) or energy supply (SDG 7.1, SDG 7.2, SDG 7.a) (→ Intro mn. 14, 46, 146).[147]

Clean water and sanitation for all lead to poverty reduction (SDG 1.4), indicating a **61** linkage between these SDGs. Yet, the development of poverty alleviation infrastructure could have a negative impact on water quality.[148]

Improving access to water supply and sanitation reduces the risk of disease (e.g. **62** diarrhoea due to contaminated water) (SDG 3.2, SDG 3.3, SDG 6.2, SDG 6.3) since the most frequent cause of death among children under 5 years of age is due to a lack of water or its contamination[149] and mitigates the likelihood of malnutrition (SDG 2.1, SDG 2.4).[150]

---

[140] IRC comes from International Reference Centre for Community Water Supply, which was earlier the name in 1968 (founded by the WHO and Dutch government) to mid-1980 s, when it changed into IRC International Water and Sanitation Centre; https://www.ircwash.org/faq.

[141] WWC, *What we do,* https://www.worldwatercouncil.org/en/about-us.

[142] Henry and Tubiana, *Earth at Risk, Natural Capital and the Quest for Sustainability* (2018), 35.

[143] A/RES/66/288, *The Future we want* (2012), para. 119; Henry and Tubiana, *Earth at Risk, Natural Capital and the Quest for Sustainability* (2018), 35; A/74/72–E/2019/13, *Mainstreaming of the three dimensions of sustainable development throughout the United Nations system* (2019), para. 24.

[144] UN-Secretary General, *Mainstreaming of the three dimensions of sustainable development throughout the United Nations system,* 7.

[145] UN-Water, *Water and Sanitation Interlinkages across the 2030 Agenda for Sustainable Development* (2016), 6 and see in detail Annex 1: Summary of interlinkages between targets related to Sustainable Development Goal 6, 42-44; see also A/74/72–E/2019/13, *Mainstreaming of the three dimensions of sustainable development throughout the United Nations system* (2019), para. 25.

[146] UN-Water, *Water and Sanitation Interlinkages across the 2030 Agenda for Sustainable Development* (2016), 16.

[147] UN, General Assembly Economic and Social Council, *Mainstreaming of the three dimensions of sustainable development throughout the United Nations system,* 7 (no. 24); UN, *Integrated Approaches for Sustainable Development Goals Planning: The case of Goal 6 on water and sanitation* (2017), 16; A/RES/66/288, *The Future we want* (2012), para. 119.

[148] UN-Water, *Water and Sanitation Interlinkages across the 2030 Agenda for Sustainable Development* (2016), 15.

[149] UN-Water, *Water and Sanitation Interlinkages across the 2030 Agenda for Sustainable Development* (2016), 17; http://www.who.int/mediacentre/factsheets/fs178/en/.

[150] A/74/72–E/2019/13, *Mainstreaming of the three dimensions of sustainable development throughout the United Nations system,* para. 25; UN-Water: *Water and Sanitation Interlinkages across the 2030 Agenda for Sustainable Development* (2016), 17.

63   According to a study in Ghana, achieving access to water for all makes it possible for girls not to spend time on fetching water, allowing them to take advantage of educational opportunities instead (SDG 4.5, SDG 4.6) which reveals that achieving water and sanitation for all also reduces inequalities including those related to gender (SDG 5.1, SDG 5.a, SDG 10.2).[151]

64   Agricultural and industrial production highly depend on (clean) water supply, which is underlined by the fact that 80 per cent of global jobs are to some extent dependent on water or wastewater (SDG 8.4, SDG 8.9).[152] Moreover, access to drinking water improves the health of workers which may positively affect their productivity (SDG 8.2, SDG 8.8).[153]

65   Wastewater in particular is often contaminated by chemical substances or bacteria that enter water bodies or seas (SDG 6.3, SDG 6.6, SDG 6.a), which affects water quality, ecosystems and wildlife (SDG 14.3, SDG 15.4, SDG 15.8).[154] SDG 6 thus links water consumption (SDG 12.1, SDG 12.2, SDG 14.c, SDG 15.1, SDG 15.3), processing and particularly its cleanliness (SDG 12.4, SDG 14.1, SDG 14.2, SDG 14.3) to the achievement of all environmental SDGs.[155]

D. Jurisprudential Significance of SDG 6

66   '[T]he protection and improvement of the human environment is a major issue which affects the well-being of peoples and economic environment throughout the world.'[156] This statement takes on a deeper meaning in context of SDG 6 'Clean Water and Sanitation' considering the fact that only 3 percent of all water on Earth is fresh water that can be purified into drinking water. At the same time, this resource is shared by an ever-increasing mass of the world's population leading to a correlating stressful scarcity. According to the UN, the world's population will increase by 2 billion people to an expected 9.7 billion by 2050.[157] Population growth will mostly concentrate in the currently poorest of the least developed or developing countries.[158] This development is accompanied by water scarcity due to heat, pollution and climate change, desertification and land degradation.

67   In 2010, with a resolution on the human right to water and sanitation, the UN recognised the human right to safe drinking water and sanitation as 'essential to the

---

[151] UN-Water, *Water and Sanitation Interlinkages across the 2030 Agenda for Sustainable Development* (2016), 17 f.; see also UNESCO World Water Assessment Programme, *2015: The United Nations World Water Development Report 2015: Water for a Sustainable World* (2015).

[152] UN-Water, *Water and Sanitation Interlinkages across the 2030 Agenda for Sustainable Development* (2016), 22 f.

[153] UN-Water, *Water and Sanitation Interlinkages across the 2030 Agenda for Sustainable Development* (2016), 23.

[154] UN-Water, *Water and Sanitation Interlinkages across the 2030 Agenda for Sustainable Development* (2016), 28 ff.

[155] See overview of all linked destinations in UN-Water, *Water and Sanitation Interlinkages across the 2030 Agenda for Sustainable Development* (2016), 32 and considering synergies and possible conflicts between SDG 6 and other SDGs, Annex 1, 42.

[156] A/CONF.48/14/Rev.1, *Report of the UN Conference on the Human Environment*, 16 June 1972, preamble.

[157] UN DESA, *Population Division, World Population Prospects 2019: Highlights (2019)*, (ST/ESA/SER.A/423), 37.

[158] India, Nigeria, Pakistan, the Democratic Republic of the Congo, Ethiopia, the United Republic of Tanzania, Indonesia, Egypt but also in the United States of America (in descending order of the expected increase), https://www.un.org/development/desa/publications/world-population-prospects-2019-highlights.html.

full enjoyment of life and all human rights'[159] and derived it from the right to an adequate standard of living,[160] which is inextricably linked to the right to the enjoyment of the highest attainable standard of physical and mental health and the right to life and human dignity. This recognition as a basic understanding for SDG 6 underlines its importance and relevance towards a plenty of other SDGs. This resolution, now recognised by 122 states, was supported by two further resolutions in 2011, which emphasised good practices in the implementation of the right to water and sanitation and should ensure its financial implementation. Prior to this specification of the right to water and sanitation, the UN Commission on Human Rights (UNHCR) already noted in 2007 that the 'access to safe drinking water' should be considered 'as a human right' defined to be 'the right to equal and non-discriminatory access to a sufficient amount of safe drinking water for personal and domestic uses – drinking, personal sanitation, washing of clothes, food preparation and personal and household hygiene – to sustain life and health'.[161] Other human rights treaties and other instruments such as instruments and standards have also recognised a human right to water.[162]

However, the treatment, protection and access to water have not yet been able to **68** establish a global right to water[163] or the state of a 'global public good'[164] whereas, on the other hand, it is seen as a 'source of economic benefit'. The actual (resilient) state of a right to water to date remains unclear.[165] A correspondingly large number of legal disputes have arisen both internationally and domestically, in particular in the context of

---

[159] A/RES/64/292, *The human right to water and sanitation*, 3 August 2010, para. 1.

[160] The UN already derived this to be inherent in Art. 11(1) ICESCR in 2002, see General Comment No. 15 (2002), *The right to water (arts. 11 and 12 of the International Covenant on Economic, Social and Cultural Rights)* (E/C.12/2002/11), para. 3.

[161] A/HRC/6/3, *Report of the UNHCR on the scope and content of the relevant human rights obligations related to equitable access to safe drinking water and sanitation under international human rights instruments*, 16 August 2007, para. 66.

[162] See amongst others: Convention on the Elimination of All Forms of Discrimination Against Women (CEDAW), Art. 14, para. 2(h); Convention on the Rights of the Child (CRC), art. 24, para. 2(c); Geneva Convention relative to the Treatment of Prisoners of War (1949), Arts. 20, 26, 29, 46; Geneva Convention relative to the Treatment of Civilian Persons in Time of War (1949), Arts. 85, 89, 127; respectively the Additional Protocol I (1977), Arts. 54, 55 and the Additional Protocol II (1977), Arts. 5, 14; Mar Del Plata Action Plan of the UN Water Conference, preamble; A/CONF.151/26/Rev.1 (Vol. I and Vol. I/Corr.1, Vol. II, Vol. III and Vol. III/Corr.1), United Nations Conference on Environment & Development, *Agenda 21*, 3-14 June 1992, para. 18.47; A/CONF.151/PC/112, The Dublin Statement on Water and Sustainable Development, International Conference on Water and the Environment, Principle No. 3; Programme of Action, *Report of the UN International Conference on Population and Development*, 5-13 September 1994, Principle No. 2; Recommendation (2001) 14 of the Committee of Ministers to Member States on the European Charter on Water Resources; Resolution 2002/6 of the UN Sub-Commission on the Promotion and Protection of Human Rights on the promotion of the realization of the right to drinking water; see also the report on the relationship between the enjoyment of economic, social and cultural rights and the promotion of the realization of the right to drinking water supply and sanitation (E/CN.4/Sub.2/2002/10).

[163] Although it was already proposed by the CESCR (E/C.12/2002/11), General Comment No 15 to ICESCR, stating that '[w]ater is a limited natural resource and a public good fundamental for life and health', and that '[w]ater should be treated as a social and cultural good, and not primarily as an economic good' (2002).

[164] Boisson de Chazournes, *Fresh Water in International Law* (2013), 82; Few other currents assume water to a 'common heritage' or 'public good', see European Charter of Water Resources adopted by the Committee of Ministers of the Council of Europe on 17 October 2001; see Lake Geneva Region Water Charter, adopted by concerned States (Geneva, 27 October 2005); see E/C.12/2002/11 (UN CESCR), *General Comment No. 15 (2002), The right to water (Arts. 11 and 12 of the International Covenant on Economic, Social and Cultural Rights)*, 20 January 2003.

[165] Boisson de Chazournes, *Fresh Water in International Law* (2013), 54; Barral, 'Towards Judicial Coordination For Good Water Governance?' (2018) 67 *ICLQ*, 931 (931); see also Farrugia, 'The human right to water: defences to investment treaty violations' (2015) 31(2) *Arbitration International*, 261 (266 f.).

investment arbitrations.[166] The severity and magnitude of such proceedings are likely to increase in the future.

I. Jurisdiction on Vision and Principles

69   As a resource given economic, social, and political characteristics,[167] clean water is a resource which is critical to the implementation and ignition of the SDGs in their entirety. States must respect, protect, and fulfil carious obligations in order to ensure that water is available, accessible, and affordable (substantive dimension) (→ Goal 6 mn. 14 ff.). Availability, in this context, is assessed in jurisdiction specifically by the term 'accessibility' which is of crucial importance. Moreover, the affordability of water and related services is reflected in various cases as well as 'principles of transparency, information, participation and justice' (procedural dimension)[168] which are recognised in different judicial contexts so that a legal consideration on single terms seems possible. To the extent possible, the legal enforcement and specifically the judicial weighing and evaluation of a right to water and sanitation will be highlighted to grasp an understanding of what it means to apply this (human) right or SDG 6 in a non-discriminatory manner.

1. International Jurisdiction

70   SDG 6 seeks to ensure the availability of water and sanitation for all which should also be managed sustainably. Two aspects can be derived from this: Since the SDGs represent an all-encompassing agenda, the basic supply applies to all people as individuals, regardless of their status, but also to all other stakeholders, such as states and economic actors. SDG 6 thus pursues the same direction as is reflected in case law.

71   Regarding access to water and sanitation, the IACtHR decided in *López Álvarez v Honduras* that a state is obliged to maintain a minimum standard of sanitation regardless of an individuals' status, even if convicted and imprisoned. The meaning of 'minimum standard' must be comparable to the international standards on the subject in order to ensure a decent life in dignity.[169] The IACtHR thus directly endorsed the judgment of the ECtHR of the *Kudla v Poland* case in which it was ruled that the availability of sufficient water and sanitation, as an essential part of health and well-being, for the highly vulnerable group of detainees must be adequately ensured as part of their

---

[166] Dimsey, 'Right to Water' in Cottier and Schefer (eds), *Elgar Encyclopedia of International Economic Law* (2017), 641 (642).

[167] United Nations Conference on Environment & Development, *Agenda 21*, 3-14 June 1992, para 18.8; E/C.12/2002/11, *General Comment No. 15 (2002)*, stating that '[w]ater is a limited natural resource and a public good fundamental for life and health', and that '[w]ater should be treated as a social and cultural good, and not primarily as an economic good'. UN Committee on Economic, Social and Cultural Rights, General Comment No 15 to the International Covenant on Economic, Social and Cultural Rights, (2002).

[168] For more information on dividing the right to water into substantive and procedural dimensions, see: Barral, 'Towards Judicial Coordination For Good Water Governance?' (2018) 67 *ICLQ*, 931 (931); Viñuales, 'A Human Rights Approach to Extraterritorial Environmental Protection? An Assessment' in Bhuta (ed), *The Frontiers of Human Rights* (2016), 205.

[169] *López Álvarez v Honduras*, Judgment, 1 February 2006, IACtHR, paras. 54(51), 105, 209; and in the same sense: *Raxcacó-Reyes*, Judgment, 15 September 2005, IACtHR, paras. 99, 134, also referring to the United Nations Standard Minimum Rules for the Treatment of Prisoners, 'in order to interpret the content of the right of prisoners to decent and humane treatment [which] prescribe the basic rules for a prisoner's accommodation, hygiene, medical care and exercise'; *Fermín Ramírez*, Judgment, 20 June 2005, IACtHR, para. 130(f); *Caesar*, Judgment, 11 March 2005, Series C 123, para. 134; see also: UN, *Standard Minimum Rules for the Treatment of Prisoners, adopted by the First United Nations Congress on the Prevention of Crime and Treatment of Offenders*, held in Geneva in 1995, and adopted by the Economic and Social Council in its resolutions 663C (XXIV) of July 31, 1957, and 2076 (LXVII) of May 13, 1977.

basic rights to a decent and dignified life and must not be curtailed.[170] In a number of cases, the IACtHR also linked human dignity (as a prerequisite for decent life or decent existence) with the provision of water and sanitation to a sufficient extent.[171] The court declared this a state obligation albeit that an 'impossible or disproportionate burden is not imposed upon the authorities'.[172] To this end, the IACtHR derived a 'right to water' from the right of humane treatment.[173] Referring to the CESCR and relevant WHO data, the IACtHR defined the minimum quantity of water as 'according to international standards, [as] a minimum of 7.5 litres per day per person to meet all their basic needs, including food and hygiene'.[174]

The second aspect is concerned with the requirement of a sustainable management   **72** of water and sanitation, which is broadly reflected in international jurisdiction as a protective concept of international environmental law, which, among other things, imposes unanimous obligations on states. Against the background of the joint use of resources and the assessment of risks in dealing with and processing resources, the 'preservation of the ecological balance as a central role in the overall system of protection'[175] and the duty to avoid transboundary harm as 'a foundational principle of customary international environmental law'[176] are central issues (→ Goal 6 mn. 85).

The ECtHR, similar to the IACtHR and the ICJ, considered a minimum standard for   **73** water supply and sanitation to be determined by the most vulnerable groups. In *Iacov Stanciu v Romania*, the ECtHR referred in addition to relevant domestic requirements, to the standard minimum rules issued by the UN and the CESCR as relevant international standards[177] and classified a deviation from them to be inhumane or degrading treatment which violates the right to physical well-being guaranteed under Art. 3 ECHR. The ECtHR not only recognised existing minimum standards, but also extended the notion of state liability within the scope of the ECHR to private sector actions if a state fails to adequately regulate the private actor in question.[178]

---

[170] *López Álvarez v Honduras*, Judgment, 1 February 2006, IACtHr, paras. 106, 209, and therein referring to *Kudla v Poland*, Judgment, 26 October 2000, ECtHR, No. 30210/96, para. 94.

[171] *Vélez Loor v Panama*, Judgment, 23 November 2010, IACtHR, paras. 196 ff.; *Case Of The Xákmok Kásek Indigenous Community v Paraguay (Xákmok Kásek case)*, Judgment, Merits, Reparations, and Costs, 24 August 2010, IACtHR, para. 195 f.; *Indigenous Community Sawhoyamaxa v Paraguay*, Judgment, 29 March 2006, IACtHR, paras. 152-4 and the huge amount of jurisdiction cited therein.

[172] *Indigenous Community Sawhoyamaxa v Paraguay*, Judgment, 29 March 2006, IACtHR, para. 155.

[173] Murillo Chávarro, 'The Right to Water in the Case-Law of the Inter-American Court of Human Rights' (2014) 7(1) *ACDI*, 39 (52), see also: *Institute for Human Rights and Development in Africa v Angola*, African Commission (7-22 May 2008), Communication 292/04, paras. 51-2, but based on the right to food and sanitation (FN7).

[174] E/C.12/2002/11 (UN CESCR), *General Comment No. 15 (2002), The right to water (Arts. 11 and 12 of the International Covenant on Economic, Social and Cultural Rights)*, 20 January 2003, U.N. Doc. HRI/GEN/1/Rev.7, 106, para. 12 and Bartram and Howard, *Domestic water quantity, service level and health* (WHO 2003), WHO/SDE/WSH/03.02, 9: The estimation is based on requirements of lactating women who engage in moderate physical activity in above-average temperatures.

[175] *Case Concerning Pulp Mills On The River Uruguay (Argentina v Uruguay)*, Judgment, 20 April 201, ICJ Reports 2010, paras. 175, 177.

[176] *Trail smelter case (United States, Canada)*, Reports Of International Arbitral Awards, 16 April 1938 and 11 March 1941, 1905-1982, para. 1978 (VI); *Costa Rica v Nicaragua Construction of a road in Costa Rica along the river San Juan; Certain Activities Carried out by Nicaragua in the Border Area (Costa Rica v Nicaragua)*, Provisional Measures, Order, 13 December 2013, ICJ Reports 398 (19).

[177] *Iacov Stanciu v Romania*, Judgment, 24 July 2012, ECtHR App. No 35972/05, paras. 120, 179.

[178] See e.g. *López Ostra v Spain*, 9 December 1994, ECtHR App No 16798/90; for further information see Arden, 'Water for All? Developing a Human Right to Water in National and International Law' (2016) 65 *ICLQ*, 771-89; see for further information: Hey, 'Distributive Justice and Procedural Fairness in Global Water Law' in Ebbesson and Okowa (eds), *Environmental Law and Justice in Context* (2009); Murillo Chávarro, 'Extraterritorial Application of the Human Right to Water in a Transboundary Watercourse

2. European Jurisdiction

74   Since the ECJ is *'the* leading voice in the practical enforcement and operation of environmental law across Europe',[179] this court plays an important role as an interpretive indicator for the creation of future policies and legislation within the EU. Under two main instruments of water protection within the EU, namely the Water Framework Directive[180] according to river basins (but not to political or administrative boundaries) and the Aarhus Convention which guarantees access to (environmental) information and justice,[181] the information and public participation through Environmental Impact Assessments are enabled. Specifically, the right to public participation became new impetus in the ECJ's decision in *Protect Natur-, Arten- und Landschaftsschutz Umweltorganisation v Bezirkshauptmannschaft Gmünd*. In this case, an environmental NGO sought to obtain access to jurisdiction. With reference to both the Water Directive and the Aarhus Convention, the ECJ decided that environmental NGOs must have access to justice in water law proceedings and that they should be granted party status. Only in this way could the right to an effective remedy before a court be fulfilled and therefore meet the principle of proportionality.[182]

75   Apart from its autonomous instruments and specifications for the protection of water, elements of international law form an integral part of its own legal system, such as the UN Convention of the Law of the Sea.[183] Despite the fact that the EU's courts, as interpreters of international norms, in part continue to restrict their application in favour of the EU's own principles and standards, the European hierarchy of norms at least suggests that relevant instruments of EU secondary law[184] must be compliant with international agreements adopted by the EU.[185]

3. Arbitration Proceedings

76   Considering the overarching vision of SDG 6, it is mainly against the background of the utilisation of water, often by private companies under the guise of investment agreements, that it is deemed as being influenceable. Since water itself is a marketable commodity, it is subject to the application of the WTO General Agreement on Tariffs and Trade (GATT) and / or the General Agreement on Tariffs and Services (GATS)

Context' in Murillo Chávarro (ed), *The Human Right to Water: A Legal Comparative Perspective at the International, Regional and Domestic Level* (2015).

[179] Gehring and Phillips and Lees, 'The European Union' in Lees and Viñuales, *The Oxford Handbook of Comparative Environmental Law* (2019), 149 (165).

[180] Directive 2000/60/EC Of The European Parliament And Of The Council of 23 October 2000 establishing a framework for Community action in the field of water policy, OJ L 327, 22.12.2000 including amendments.

[181] Convention On Access To Information, Public Participation In Decision-Making And Access To Justice In Environmental Matters, done at Aarhus, Denmark, on 25 June 1998; in conjunction with EU Reg 1367/2006 as well as Directives 2003/4/EC and 2003/35/EC.

[182] ECJ, Case C-164/15, 20.12.2017, *Protect Natur-, Arten- und Landschaftsschutz Umweltorganisation v Bezirkshauptmannschaft Gmünd*, ECLI:EU:C:2017:987, paras. 34, 90 f., 102; see referring to proportionality also: ECJ, Case C-73/16, 27.09.2017, *Puškár*, C-73/16, EU:C:2017:725, paras. 59-65 and the case-law cited.

[183] See ECJ, Case C-308/06, 03.06.2008, *The Queen on the application of International Association of Independent Tanker Owners (Intertanko) and Others v Secretary of State for Transport*, ECLI:EU:C: 2008:312, paras. 42-5 and the jurisdiction cited therein.

[184] Instead of many: Directive 2005/35/EC of the European Parliament and of the Council of 7 September 2005 on ship-source pollution and on the introduction of penalties for infringements.

[185] ECJ, Case C-61/94, 10.09.1996, *Commission v Germany*, ECLI:EU:C:1996:313, para. 52; Case C-341/95, 14.07.1998, *Gianni Bettati v Safety Hi-Tech Srl*, ECLI:EU:C:1998:353, para. 20.

insofar it is subject to services such as capturing, purifying or distribution.[186] The trade and investment agreements covered by these provisions, on the one hand, affect the physical access to water and its affordability, which in consequence creates tensions between the putative right to water and opposing investor rights.[187] Additionally, the relations between states and private actors are under scrutiny, in particular with regard to the liberalisation of drinking water and sewage sectors, associated obligations and liability issues in the light of the widely acknowledged precautionary principle. On the other hand, investments by other industries that either engage in water-intensive production or pollute water-related ecosystems such as rivers, lakes, forests, wetlands or aquifers with industrial waste, sewage or emissions are particularly controversial.[188] Arbitration proceedings and investment tribunals in this regard 'become increasingly utilised as a basis for establishing rights and obligations'.[189] It is apparent that a right to water has already been recognised in such proceedings.[190] An accompanying valid legislative framework going beyond this, however, is clearly limited to date.[191]

The Appellate Body (AB) in particular expressed its views on whether certain mea-   **77** sures as an expression of interference with the fundamental principles of the WTO are permissible (under Art. XX(g) GATT) insofar as they are necessary to protect 'common interests' and 'shared values'.[192] The AB accepted, in particular, measures to protect and ensure access to high quality water as being appropriate measures,[193] thus confirming its finding in *US – Shrimp* that natural resources can be significantly and adversely affected by human economic activities, irrespective of their classification as living, non-living or mineral,[194] and that they are subject to the application of Art. XX(g) GATT. In consequence, water, in its various aggregate and storage states, can be classified under these provisions.[195]

Further arbitration proceedings also take up this idea of a state worthy of protection   **78** and understand it as a 'right to be free from (environmental) harm' which is to a very high degree inherent to sustainability, a principle that – as already described above – is also applied by the ICJ and is accompanied by a duty to prevent, or at least mitigate this significant harm to the environment.[196]

---

[186] Boisson de Chazournes, *Fresh Water in International Law* (2013), 86.

[187] See Farrugia, 'The human right to water: defences to investment treaty violations' (2015) 31(2) *Arbitration International*, 261 (268).

[188] For example, pulp and paper mills are considered one of the most polluting industries worldwide since their producing processes depend on 'large amounts of fresh water and produce enormous quantities of wastewater' and are the 'major sources of highly polluted water' which cannot be purified anymore due to the high chemical contamination, Garg, 'Water Pollution from Pulp and Paper Mills' 20 *AER*, 245 (245); see also Kriebaum, 'The Right to Water Before Investment Tribunals' (2018) 16-36 *Brill Open Law 1*, 16 (17).

[189] Boisson de Chazournes, *Fresh Water in International Law* (2013), 78.

[190] Kriebaum, 'The Right to Water Before Investment Tribunals' (2018) *Brill Open Law 1*, 16 (36).

[191] One such example could lie in the United Nations Conference on Trade and Development (UNCTAD), *Investment Policy Framework for Sustainable Development* of 2012.

[192] *Korea—Measures Affecting Imports of Fresh, Chilled and Frozen Beef*, WT/DS161/AB/R, WT/DS169/AB/R, AB-2000-8 Report (11 December 2000), para. 162.

[193] See e.g. *EC—Measures Affecting Asbestos and Asbestos-Containing Products*, AB-2000-11, Report of the Appellate Body (12 March 2001); *United States—Restrictions on Imports of Tuna*, DS21/R—39S/155, Report of the Panel, (3 September 1991); *United States—Standards for Reformulated and Conventional Gasoline*, WT/DS2/R, Report of the Appellate Body (20 May 1996).

[194] Be it accessible or taken from a source or not.

[195] Further information on Trade and Water: Muller and Bellman, *Trade and Water: How Might Trade Policy Contribute to Sustainable Water Management?* (2016).

[196] PCA, *Iron Rhine Railway (Belgium v Netherlands)*, Award in the Arbitration regarding the Iron Rhine ('Ijzeren Rijn') Railway between the Kingdom of Belgium and the Kingdom of the Netherlands (24 May 2005), ICGJ 373, para. 59.

79   The assumption of a right to water will receive further impetus at the latest with the so-called *Water Wars cases* of the ICSID which showed the issue of implementing a resilient right to water if it is assumed to include availability, safety and accessibility ($\rightarrow$ Goal 6 mn. 14 ff., 83)[197] In *AdT v Bolivia*, a concession claim, 'the Tribunal held that international human rights condition the treatment that an investor is entitled to receive from a state and that human rights impose obligations on the investor itself. The Tribunal's explicit recognition of these dual consequences of international human rights law breaks new ground. International investment tribunals have not yet found that human rights obligations have an impact on investor protection, let alone that international human rights law could establish separate obligations for investors.'[198] Within this award, the BIT's relation to international law and human rights is explicitly examined and balanced, noting that '[t]he BIT has to be construed in harmony with other rules of international law of which it forms part, including those relating to human rights.'[199] In its reasoning, and that is ground-breaking, the WTO tribunal acknowledged 'the right to water' as a human right and balanced the international law principle *pacta sunt servanda* against the human right of access to water.[200] An equally far-reaching ruling by the Tribunal in the *Vivendi case* in 2007 showed that in the interest of safeguarding public health and a populations' well-being 'by referring to access to clean water as 'a fundamental human need', the way was paved for the right to water as being part of an essential public policy which could be used as tool of defence to claims of non-compliance with treaty provisions for a host state.[201]

80   In addition, the trade in bulk water as well as in virtual water and product standards represent further relevant points of reference for potential future disputes triggered by a worsening global situation. It is not yet clarified to what extent these issues are covered by WTO provisions. However, it is conceivable that in the future 'free resources' such as atmospheric water, groundwater and rainwater, but also water used or polluted in the production of goods will be subject to international disputes. The latter examples in particular could be linked to the process and production methods (PPMs) which could possibly be a decisive factor in determining whether these are considered 'like products'. This assessment, which is already being carried out in WTO disputes, could result in a different tax or regulation of products, i.e. a different treatment based on the sustainability of the product or its production process, which could thus be able to circumvent the most-favoured-nation principle, the national treatment principle or justify technical barriers to trade (TBT), and therefore allow discrimination based on sustainability.[202] This could have a considerable steering effect and strengthen the progress of the global sustainability transformation.

---

[197] *Aguas del Tunari v Bolivia (Water Wars/Cochabamba)*, ICSID Case No ARB/02/3 and related thereto *Urbaser S.A. and Corsorcio de Aguas Bilbao Bizkaia, Bilbao Bizkaia Ur Partzuergoa v The Argentine Republic*, ICSID Case No ARB/07/26 (8 December 2016); further discussion on this issue: Murthy, 'The Human Right(s) to Water and Sanitation: History, Meaning, and the Controversy Over Privatization' (2013) 31(1) *BJIL*, 89 (97).

[198] Attanasio and Sainati, *Urbaser S.A. and Consorcio de Aguas Bilbao Bizkaia, Bilbao Biskaia Ur Partzuergoa v. The Argentine Republic ICSID*, Extract in AJIL, Vol. 111 (3), July 2017, 744-50.

[199] *Urbaser S.A. and Consorcio de Aguas Bilbao Bizkaia, Bilbao Biskaia Ur Partzuergoa v. The Argentine Republic*, ICSID, Case No ARB/07/26 (8 December 2016), para. 1200.

[200] *Urbaser S.A. and Consorcio de Aguas Bilbao Bizkaia, Bilbao Biskaia Ur Partzuergoa v. The Argentine Republic*, ICSID, Case No ARB/07/26 (8 December 2016), para. 1205-10.

[201] See Farrugia, 'The human right to water: defences to investment treaty violations' (2015) 31(2) *Arbitration International*, 261 (269).

[202] See for further information: Temmerman, 'Trade in Virtual Water and Product Standards' in Cottier and Schefer (eds), *Elgar Encyclopedia of International Economic Law* (2017), 645-7; Boisson de Chazournes, *Fresh Water in International Law* (2013), 79 ff.

4. Domestic Jurisdiction

The preceding principles also find expression in domestic jurisdiction and can be   **81**
applied in some cases quite obviously to single targets of SDG 6. In *Spraytech Société
d'arrosage* the Supreme Court of Canada (SCC) emphasised the relevance of the precautionary principle and dismissed the claimants' appeal which sought to declare a
pesticide-restricting by-law as inapplicable. In its reasoning the SCC also referred to
the interconnectedness of ecosystems, which must necessarily be taken into account
when determining the harm of pesticides on human health.[203] In addition, it considered
discrimination induced by the by-law to be unavoidable and lawful.

A more distinct development in which reference to the contents of SDG 6 is made can   **82**
be identified in Indian jurisdiction. Early on, India applied principles of sustainability
in its jurisdiction in order to protect the environment and especially its water resources.
In *Vellore Citizens Welfare Forum v Union of India*, it weighed out the precautionary
principle and the polluter pays principle related to pollution control of tanneries.[204]
Although no explicit right to water is acknowledged in India, it is still implicitly attached
to the right to life protected by constitution and is integrated into the concept of a
healthy environment. The right to life thereby encompasses the entitlement of citizens
to receive safe drinking water (potable water).[205] The Supreme Court of India (SCI)
has ruled in a number of cases that the right to life, among other things, is granted
a right to pollution-free drinking water [...] for full enjoyment of life, which gives an
individual right of claim.[206] Moreover, the SCI stated that the obligation of the state
exceeds beyond water supply regulation and also includes a duty to prevent health
hazards. In addition, the SCI ruled out inventory protection for environment-affecting
industries.[207] In several cases an actual right to water or this being a part of the right to
life was recognised.[208] These claims were mostly brought in the form of public interest
litigations (PIL).[209] Despite the fact that this 'implied right' has received considerable
support and strong emphasis through the progressive jurisprudence that recognises the
importance of this resource, the actual pollution of water such as in the Ganges and the,
in some places, poor sanitation conditions suggest that the essence of life has neither
been given sufficient availability nor sustainable management.

A remarkably far-reaching decision was made by the High Court of Kenya. In *Peter K*   **83**
Waweru v Republic, the court acknowledged water and a clean environment to be granted by nature[210] the access to which should not be restricted by anyone and that all future
development must be sustainable.[211] A similarly far-reaching decision was made by the
court of appeal (Lobatse) in Botswana in 2011 concerning the use of boreholes in the

---

[203] *114957 Canada Ltée (Spraytech Société d'arrosage) v Hudson (Town)*, Judgment (28 June 2001), 2001
2 SCR 241, paras. 31 f., 55.

[204] *Vellore Citizens' Welfare Forum and State of Tamil Nadu (joining) v Union of India and ors*, Original
public interest writ petition, 1996 5 SCC/SCR 647/241, paras. 12–133.

[205] Mittal, 'Right to Clean Water' in Gurnani, *Constitutional & Administrative Law*, http://www.lawctop
us.com/academike/right-to-clean-water/.

[206] *Subhash Kumar v State of Bihar*, Supreme Court of India (1991).

[207] *A.P. Pollution Control Board II v. Prof. M.V. Nayudu* (2000), *M.C. Mehta v Kamalnath*, Supreme
Court of India (1997).

[208] *Narmada Bachao Andolan v Union of India*, Supreme Court of India (2000); *State of Karnataka v
State of Andhra Pradesh*, Supreme Court of India (2000); for further information see Arden, 'Water for
All? Developing a Human Right to Water in National and International Law' (2016) 65 *ICLQ*, 771–789.

[209] Mittal, 'Right to Clean Water' in Gurnani, *Constitutional & Administrative Law*, http://www.lawctop
us.com/academike/right-to-clean-water/.

[210] The decision at this paragraph refers to the 'Creator'.

[211] *Peter K. Waweru v. Republic*, Misc. Civ. Appli. 118 of 2004 (2 March 2006), The High Court of Kenya
at Nairobi, Judgment, para. 4.

Central Kalahari Game Reserve (CKGR) to ensure the supply of water to the Basarwa community. Notably, the court invoked a 'right to water' based on both the ICESCR and the General Comment No. 15,[212] solely a few months after its adoption. With this decision, it fostered the establishment of socio-economic rights in the legal development and domestic jurisprudence of Botswana, which had previously not formally recognised these rights constitutionally. However, it did not decide more broadly on states' obligations to provide basic services or to protect the particularly vulnerable group of indigenous people, as there was no corresponding application by the claimants.[213] Again in Africa before the High Court of South Gauteng (Johannesburg), a decision was made in favour of the residents of Phiri, who invoked their constitutionally enshrined right to water and a sufficient supply of it. The court decided on a minimum quantity of water per person[214] and defined 'availability' on the basis of the CESCR and WHO guidelines to be sufficient and continuous. Moreover, the court defined 'accessibility' to be 'physical and economically accessible on a non-discriminatory basis'.[215] However, this far-reaching decision was overturned by the Constitutional Court of South Africa which declared the previous assessment of the case to be irrational and discriminatory and not covered by the Constitution. This utmost conservative and restrictive decision is seen as 'reflective of the increasingly deferential and conservative approach adopted by the Court in the context of socio-economic rights cases'[216] and could therefore stand in the way of a transformation in the sense of SDG 6.

II. Jurisdiction on Targets and Indicators

84   Referring to the improvement of water quality (SDG 6.3) and the protection and restoring of water-related ecosystems (SDG 6.6), fundamental decisions of international courts show an intricate picture when referring to groundwater. In *Gabčíkovo-Nagymaros*, the ICJ stated very clearly that environmental protection is to be subordinated to other purposes if a risk cannot be determined as being imminent. By giving greater weight to the principle of *pacta sunt servanda* than to Hungary's reasoning, at that time, to protect its groundwater, the contamination of which Hungary considered to be an excessively high risk, the ICJ emphasised that no deviation from the principles of international law may be made for the purpose of environmental protection.[217] Thereby, the intrinsic value of international watercourses has been recognised in international law.[218]

85   Besides the access to water, as discussed above, transboundary impacts on water systems play a particular role in the targets of SDG 6. Even though it does not address

---

[212] *Mosetlhanyane and others v. Attorney General of Botswana (Access to Water on Ancestral Lands)*, Civil Appeal No. CACLB-074-10, Judgement (27 January 2011), para. 15.

[213] Though, there was certainly the court's indication that 'the government is under no obligation to provide any essential service to them', *Mosetlhanyane and others v. Attorney General of Botswana (Access to Water on Ancestral Lands)*, Civil Appeal No. CACLB-074-10, Judgment (27 January 2011), paras. 45, 73.

[214] *Mazibuko and others v City of Johannesburg*, High Court of South Gauteng, Case No 06/13865, Judgment, 30 April 2008, paras. 46 f., 126, 181.

[215] *Mazibuko and others v City of Johannesburg*, High Court of South Gauteng, Case No 06/13865, Judgment, 30 April 2008, para. 36.

[216] https://www.escr-net.org/caselaw/2009/lindiwe-mazibuko-others-v-city-johannesburg-others-case-cct-3909-2009-zacc-28.

[217] *Case Concerning the Gabčíkovo-Nagymaros Project (Hungary v Slovakia)*, Judgment, 25 September 1997, paras. 140-2; see also McCaffrey, *The Law of International Watercourses* (2019), 209.

[218] *Certain Activities Carried Out by Nicaragua in the Border Area (Costa Rica v. Nicaragua)*, Compensation Owed by the Republic of Nicaragua to the Republic of Costa Rica, Judgment, 2 February 2018.

holistic ecological interrelationships,[219] such as the connection of water systems to marine ecosystems, but rather focuses on national borders, it nevertheless covers trans-boundary issues (→ Goal 14 mn. 65).[220] To a fundamental extent, the system of mutual cooperation between riparian states and equitable and reasonable sharing of resources, as well as joint obligations, such as the inter-state notification of upcoming measures, routine information exchange,[221] establishment of Environmental Impact Assessments (EIA) or compensation for pollution and other harmful activities, are reflected in the case law.[222] Developments in this regard can also be seen in domestic jurisdictions. The access to private remedies for transboundary harm through domestic courts which has been granted to individuals by the 1997 UN Convention found expression, for instance, in the *Pakoota litigation* before the US Supreme Court that, after a multi-decade dispute, involved the contamination of groundwater and sediment by hazardous substances released at the site and thus, on the one hand, gave voice to affected individuals and, on the other hand, justified the liability of a private actor (for dumping industrial waste into the Columbia River) by reference to the Comprehensive Environmental Response, Compensation, and Liability Act (CERCLA).[223]

In particular, the terms 'transboundary cooperation' and 'international cooperation **86** and capacity-building' (SDG 6.5 and SDG 6.a) have already been fundamentally illumi-nated in the above-mentioned jurisdiction and have been assessed as established by customary international law and characterised by mutuality. The ICJ in *Pulp Mills*, by drawing on further jurisprudence, has emphasised that the principle of prevention is based on the due diligence of states to prevent 'significant damage to the environment of another state' by all available means, be it caused by their own activities or by the actors authorised on their territory.[224] The concept of affirmative cooperation, which was coined by the ILC, is thus reflected to a considerable extent.[225] However, it is evident that an EIA must be carried out in advance of a project, 'where there is a risk that the proposed industrial activity may have a significant adverse impact in a transboundary context, in particular, on a shared resource.' The content of these EIA, however, must

---

[219] Even SDG 6.6, which relates to the protection and restoration of water-related ecosystems, is measured by using one single indicator, focusing on the change in the extent of water-related ecosystems over time (SDG 6.6.1), without going into relevant factors in greater detail.

[220] See, amongst others: UNEP/GPA/IGR.3/5, Manila Declaration on Furthering the Implementation of the Global Programme of Action for the Protection of the Marine Environment from Land-based Activities (2011); Kuwait Regional Convention for Co-operation on the Protection of the Marine Environ-ment from Pollution (1978) and its Protocol concerning Marine Pollution resulting from Exploration and Exploitation of the Continental Shelf (1989); International Maritime Organization, International Convention for the Prevention of Pollution from Ships (MARPOL) (1973) and its Protocol of 1978; International Maritime Organization, Convention on the Prevention of Marine Pollution by Dumping of Wastes and Other Matter (London Convention) (1972) and its Protocol of 1996.

[221] McIntyre, 'International water law and SDG 6' in French and Kotzé (eds), *Sustainable Development Goals* (2018), 173 (199).

[222] *Case relating to the Territorial Jurisdiction of the International Commission of the River Oder,* Judg-ment, 10 September 1929, PCIJ Seventeenth (Ordinary) Session; *Case Concerning the Gabčíkovo-Nagy-maros Project (Hungary v Slovakia)*, Judgment, 25 September 1997, ICJ Reports 1997; *Case Concerning Pulp Mills On The River Uruguay (Argentina v Uruguay)*, Judgment, 20 April 201, ICJ Reports 2010.

[223] *Pakootas v. Teck Cominco Metals, Ltd. (Pakoota litigation)*, No. 16-35742 (9th Cir. 2018).

[224] *Case Concerning Pulp Mills On The River Uruguay (Argentina v Uruguay)*, Judgment, 20 April 201, ICJ Reports 2010, para. 101, citing therein: *Corfu Channel (United Kingdom v. Albania)*, Merits, Judgment, ICJ Reports 1949, 22 and *Legality of the Threat or Use of Nuclear Weapons*, Advisory Opinion, ICJ Reports 1996 (I), 242 (para. 29).

[225] See Art. 5(2) Convention on the Law of the Non-navigational Uses of International Watercourses 1997, UNGA RES/51/229, annex.

be determined on a case-by-case basis.[226] The meaning of 'significant harm' remains unclear.[227] Beyond that, a number of important terms for the contextual definition and identification of SDG 6, such as 'integrated water resource management', have little legally definable content yet.[228]

III. The Enforcement of a 'Right to Water'?

87   The enforcement of a right to water derived from SDG 6 is, besides all uncertainties already existing in International Water Law alone,[229] mostly dependent of good governance and international cooperation. If the private sector is allowed to impact on the availability, safety or accessibility to water, parties concerned such as states, individuals or other groups of interest must be protected through a strong regulatory frame.[230] This comprehensive and coherent framework does not satisfactorily exist yet, including in international water law. The fact that in other contexts, such as in *Nestlé bottled water*, legal recourse and remedies are still not being opened up to protect consumers (as human rights holders) indicates that a right to water is not acknowledged uniformly and thus is not enforceable to a satisfactory extent.[231]

88   Instruments and measures of policy regulation to open up the legal enforcement of a 'right to water' may be water pricing or water rights trading which are assumed to promote a sustainable and efficient water use. Initial developments in this regard can be seen, for example, in the efforts to revise the water law in China.[232] The same applies to water extraction rights and wastewater discharge fees which are to be managed by national water agencies.[233] It remains to be seen which incentives will be transferred into policy objectives in the future and how coherence will be ensured. There are certainly risks if access to and redistribution of water would simply be made more costly and thus placed in the hands of a few.

---

[226] *Case Concerning Pulp Mills On The River Uruguay (Argentina v Uruguay)*, Judgment, 20 April 201, ICJ Reports 2010, paras. 204 f.

[227] McCaffrey, *The Law of International Watercourses* (2019), Part 4, Ch. 11, 507-23.

[228] McIntyre, 'International water law and SDG 6' in French and Kotzé (eds), *Sustainable Development Goals* (2018), 173 (195).

[229] International Water Law does not acknowledge a long-term temporal scope such as the concept of sustainable development demands it. It also lacks an overall normative framework which connects its various areas and thus allows a global redistribution and legal management beyond territorial boundaries, see: Brölmann, 'Sustainable Development Goal 6 as a Game Changer for International Water Law' (2018) 7(5) *ESIL Reflections*, 1 (3).

[230] Dimsey, 'Right to Water' in Cottier and Schefer (eds), *Elgar Encyclopedia of International Economic Law* (2017), 641 (643).

[231] *Cindy Baker v Nestle S.A. et al.*, US District Court, Central District Of California, Order Granting Defendant's Motion to Dismiss (Doc. No. 15), 3 January 2019; see also https://www.courthousenews.com/l awsuit-over-microplastics-in-nestle-water-thrown-out/.

[232] Attempts to protect and manage water sustainably aligned to SDG 6 through political instruments can also be seen, amongst others, in the European Green Deal (COM(2019) 640 final) and the associated EU Farm to Fork Strategy (COM(2020) 381 final) or the EU Biodiversity Strategy for 2030 (COM(2020) 380 final), which also include measures for sustainable water resource management. In this context, previously identified factors, such as the absence of the necessary complexity of governance frameworks and a lack of financial resources, were identified as factors preventing success.

[233] See e.g. World Bank, *The Danube Water Program*.

IV. De Facto Influences on Jurisdiction

With the rapidly growing global population and the unequal population density   **89** in urban areas, which are not necessarily located in the same geographical area as consumable or usable water resources, the inequitable distribution of water and related services is also increasing. As former UN Secretary-General Kofi Annan, as well as many other international officials, warned that '[f]ierce competition for fresh water may well become a source of conflict and wars in the future'.[234] This might be accompanied by a corresponding development that is moving away from civil jurisdiction and arbitration proceedings or considering them as merely subordinate procedural steps. It is probable to assume that in the future this area will increasingly be addressed within the *ius contra bellum*, which is intended to prevent conflicts; *ius in bello*, which gives a legal framework during military interventions; and *ius post bellum* which seeks to re-establish peaceful order in the post-military conflict period.[235]

A further development can be found, inter alia, in the *Basarwa Community* decision   **90** mentioned above (→ Goal 6 mn. 83). With regard to granting protection and / or supply rights to particularly vulnerable groups residing in land areas designated as game preserves, it has been observed that private property owners focus on environmental protection issues in order to undermine the rights of these groups.[236] If this indicates a future development, this might undermine just decisions under the guise of considering environmental concerns as conflicting rights. The triad of the concept of sustainable development could provide a remedy to this. However, it would have to be given greater consideration in the process of legal decision-making and balancing of interests. For this purpose, intensive training of the judiciary would be necessary. The Bangalore Principles of Judicial Conduct[237] could already contain a first guideline for a commensurate response, as they take up values and guidelines relevant to sustainability. However, their clarity and conciseness will probably be far from being sufficient yet.

The World Bank, as one of the largest multilateral funders of water projects world-   **91** wide, under the auspices of SDG 6 and SDG 14, acts as an initiator and funder for sustainable water investments, and particularly water supply and sanitation projects. Through its diverse functions, such as Executive Committee Member of the Green Bond Principles and its constant development of strategic partnerships, the World Bank has a considerable steering function and thus could benefit SDG 6. These activities represent both opportunities and risks with regard to future jurisdiction. It is conceivable that litigation will decrease overall, either because of the actual sustainable orientation or

---

[234] McCaffrey, *The Law of International Watercourses* (2019), 12, 24 f.; further information on the issue of water scarcity due to distributive justice see also: Hey, 'Distributive justice and procedural fairness in global water law', in Ebbeson and Okowa (eds), *Environmental Law And Justice In Context* (2009), 351; see for further information: UNESCO, UN-Water, *United Nations World Water Development Report 2020: Water and Climate Change* (2020).

[235] Vitzthum and Proelß, *Völkerrecht* (2019), 596.

[236] See *Xákmok Kásek Indigenous Community v Paraguay*, IACtHR (2010): 'the Court noted its concern that the wildlife refuge could be a new and sophisticated method adopted by the owners of private property to "block the original peoples' claim on the territory [...] under the cover of the law and even invoking purposes as pure as the conservation of the environment."'; see also https://www.escr-net.org/cas elaw/2011/mosetlhanyane-and-others-v-attorney-general-botswana-civil-appeal-no-caclb-074-10.

[237] UN ECOSOC, *The Bangalore Principles of Judicial Conduct (The Bangalore Draft Code of Judicial Conduct 2001 adopted by the Judicial Group on Strengthening Judicial Integrity, as revised at the Round Table Meeting of Chief Justices held at the Peace Palace, The Hague, November 25-26, 2002)*; further attempts are emerging, for example, when judicial colloquiums are being held that focus on SDGs: https:// www.iucn.org/news/world-commission-environmental-law/201904/judicial-colloquium-geneva-focuses -sdgs-and-promoting-environmental-rule-law-pan-european-region.

because of the World Bank being the funder of a conflicted project.[238] Thus, it exerts considerable influence on water governance. It is evident, and this is a contentious issue, that the World Bank is continuing to promote the privatisation of the water sector under the guise of the SDGs and could prevent a manifestation of a human right to water.[239]

92   The Global Compact Project 'CEO Water Mandate' which commits businesses world-wide to sustainable water management, could also exert a nascent influence.[240]

93   The European Citizens' Initiative on the 'Right2Water' is also to be noted to be influencing, at least on a regional level. This initiative was supported by 1.8 million people and called for water to be recognised as a human right. At least ostensibly, this initiative has a considerable influence on European policy.[241]

94   Moreover, territorial sovereignty and the narrow framing which interlinks water law and water rights with state boundaries but not with ecosystems' boundaries could be a stumbling stone in future jurisdiction. This fundamental basic assumption about (riparian) states influences most of the jurisdiction in that it covers state solutions, duties, obligations or liabilities, but no further aspects to do justice to the vision and targets of SDG 6. This, in turn, could prevent from indicating a future way, e.g. for the creation of integrated (regulatory) frameworks since the identification, interpretation and elucidation are in the very own nature of courts and other judicial organs.[242]

E. Conclusion on SDG 6

95   The existence and the applicability of the right to safe drinking water and sanita-tion[243] reflected in a broader sense in the targets and indicators of SDG 6 becomes a necessity interconnected with the need for legal enforcement of the right to water and the right to sanitation deserving the attention from a legal perspective. Even under Roman law, the access to water was known, and over the times, many scholars have weighed and highlighted stellar arguments in favour to advocate from a legal point of view. Yet, an unambiguous, precise set of norms or the recognition of this sector as international customary law, including indigenous people and their ecosystems,[244] is still missing.

---

[238] Further information: Mumssen and Saltiel and Kingdom, *Aligning Institutions and Incentives for Sustainable Water Supply and Sanitation Services, Report of the Water Supply and Sanitation Global Solutions Group, Water Global Practice* (2018) and *Regulation of Water Supply and Sanitation in Bank Client Countries, A Fresh Look* (2018).

[239] See e.g. the global water justice movement in response to the private sector: https://www.tni.org/en/Art./global-water-justice-movement-challenges-world-banks-attempt-to-promote-privatization-of; https://www.epsu.org/Art./global-water-justice-movement-denounces-world-bank's-strategy-promote-privatization-water; Brölmann, 'Sustainable Development Goal 6 as a Game Changer for International Water Law' (2018) 7(5) *ESIL Reflections*, 1 (3); Murthy, 'The Human Right(s) to Water and Sanitation: History, Meaning, and the Controversy Over Privatization' (2013) 31(1) *BJIL*, 89 (91 ff., 127).

[240] Further information: https://ceowatermandate.org/resilience/launch- .

[241] Further information: https://www.right2water.eu/; https://ec.europa.eu/environment/water/water-drink/information_en.html.

[242] Brölmann, 'Sustainable Development Goal 6 as a Game Changer for International Water Law' (2018) 7(5) *ESIL Reflections*, 1 (3).

[243] A/RES/70/1, Transforming Our World: The 2030 Agenda For Sustainable Development, 21 October 2015, para. 7.

[244] Macpherson, 'Justifying Indigenous Water Rights: Jurisdiction and Distribution' in Macpherson, *Indigenous Water Rights in Law and Regulation: Lessons from Comparative Experience*, (2019), 17; Eckstein et al., 'Conferring Legal Personality on the World's Rivers: A Brief Intellectual Assessment' (2019) in *Water International* (Texas A&M University School of Law Legal Studies Research Paper No. 19-30); Schromen-Wawrin, 'Representing Ecosystems in Court: An Introduction for Practitioners' (2018) in 31(2) *Tulane Environmental Law Journal*, 279 ff.

The observation that the SDGs incorporate the concept of sustainability as outlined   96
earlier in this book has permeated the multi-level system of law, which also reflects the
application and normativity of the SDGs, thereby creating a global consensus on the application of targets measured by indicators (→ Intro mn. 35 ff., 61, 129). Those actions
are discharged under a new and integrated approach[245] of systematically thinking for integrated solutions in a sense that the principles of the Global Agenda 2030 and the SDGs
are interdependent. Therefore, it should be acknowledged that with the growing recognition of the fair distribution of water, the right to water and sanitation will become even
more recognised in international law.[246] This process is speeding up and is fuelled by
sometimes dynamic occurrences such as population (growth and density), water scarcity, droughts, agriculture, that is essential for a growing population[247] and multiple effects
to water and health caused by climate change.

The emanation of those rights is accompanied by facts that put the accessibility, the   97
fair distribution of water and sanitation under severe pressure. According to the UN,
humankind will have to face and (hopefully) avert a global water crisis with 40 per
cent shortfall in freshwater resources by 2030 coupled with a strongly growing world
population.[248] A shortfall of water and at the same time growth of population are
ingredients for a non-healthy mixture leading presumably to tensions and most probably
to migration as well.

Looking at the intricate deploy of water in its different states of aggregation, the   98
accessibility to freshwater and sanitation often remains unfair. While water resources
are embedded in all forms of development (e.g. food security, health promotion and
poverty reduction) in sustaining economic growth in agriculture, industry and energy
generation, and in maintaining healthy ecosystems,[249] freshwater, in sufficient quantity
and quality, remains essential for all aspects of life. To demystify the right to water,
it does not mean that water supply services must be available free, but it must be
affordable even for those with little or no income.[250]

The pressure on the accessibility to freshwater amazingly results from agriculture.   99
Agriculture (including irrigation, livestock and aquaculture) is recognised by far the
largest water consumer, accounting for 69 percent of annual water withdrawals globally.
Industry (including power generation) accounts for 19 per cent and households for 12
per cent. All these water uses can pollute freshwater resources. Population growth, agricultural intensification, urbanisation, industrial production and pollution, are beginning

---

[245] A/RES/71/1, New York Declaration for Refugees and Migrants, 3 October 2016, paras. 13, 17.

[246] Arden, 'Water for all? Developing a human right to water in national and international law' (2016)
65 *ICLQ*, 771 (789).

[247] See OWG – Session 'Water Supply and Sanitation' (May 23, 2013): To grasp the difficulties on
managing the topic of water, one should bear in mind that the accessibility of water is linked to external
effects. One of an array of occurrences is population: 'In 1950, just 60 years ago, there were only 2.5 billion
people in the world, 10 years ago there were 6 billion people on the planet. By 2020 there are expected to
be 7.5 billion of us. And, current growth rates, we are projected to reach over 9 billion beyond 2030.' The
incremental growth of people creates an urgent demand for water for health and sanitation, agribusiness
and many others.

[248] See UN Water Action Decade, https://www.un.org/sustainabledevelopment/water-action-decad
e/; in UNGA 71/222, the General Assembly proclaims the period from 2018 to 2028 the International
Decade for Action, 'Water for Sustainable Development' to further improve cooperation, partnership and
capacity development in response to the ambitious 2030 Agenda. In December 2016, the UNGA unanimously adopted the resolution 'International Decade (2018–2028) for Action – Water for Sustainable
Development'.

[249] UN, *Sustainable Development Goal 6 Synthesis Report 2018 on Water and Sanitation* (2018), 10.

[250] Bos, *Manual of the Human Rights to Safe Drinking Water and Sanitation for Practitioners* (2016), 5.

to overwhelm[251] traditional consumption and agricultural patterns are to be questioned, especially in view of the impact of climate change.

100   Climate change affects the terrestrial water cycle through many different processes. According to the IPCC, a limit to global warming to 1.5 °C is expected to reduce the probability of extreme drought, precipitation deficits, and risks associated with water availability (i.e. water stress) in some regions.[252] The FAO works on such matter as 'Drought Risk Management, Coping with water scarcity in agriculture or Water for the rural poor'.[253] The consequences of human-caused actions of pollution puts much more weight on the already existing pressure on freshwater and proper sanitation.[254] The hydrological changes induced by climate change exacerbate the sustainable management of water resources, which adds severe pressure. Migration is most likely to increase, although the causality of temperature change, water stress and migration is still not clearly understood.[255] Although water as such is not mentioned explicitly in the Paris Agreement, it is an essential component of almost all strategies to combat climate change.[256] However, even when a mechanism linking SDG 13 to the goals of the Paris Agreement is lacking, it does not undermine the interdependency of SDG 13 and SDG 6.[257] The SDGs are integrated and indivisible and balance the three dimensions of sustainable development.[258] In a systematic and holistic[259] theoretical perspective, almost every goal and target of the SDGs are interlinked,[260] and some of them are building clusters, gravity centres (or patterns) which are significant, like water, climate change, hunger and health. Those SDGs are an example of the interlinkages and the integrated nature of the SDGs. None of the SDGs should be displaced or taken over by another SDG but stand next to each other to the same extent and serve as a topic-related focus in a cluster as extensive as possible.

---

[251] UN, *Sustainable Development Goal 6 Synthesis Report 2018 on Water and Sanitation* (2018), 10.

[252] IPCC, *Global Warming of 1.5 °CP* (2018), Special Report, 178.

[253] See FAO, http://www.fao.org/land-water/en/.

[254] UNESCO, UN-Water, *2020: United Nations World Water Development Report 2020: Water and Climate Change* (2020).

[255] Wrathall et al., on behold of the Food and Agriculture Organization of the United Nations, *Water stress and human migration: a global, georeferenced review of empirical research* (2018), ix.

[256] UNESCO, UN-Water, *2020: United Nations World Water Development Report 2020: Water and Climate Change* (2020), 2.

[257] A/RES/70/1, *Transforming Our World: The 2030 Agenda For Sustainable Development*, 21 October 2015, para. 31: 'We acknowledge that the United Nations Framework Convention on Climate Change (UNFCCC) is the primary international, intergovernmental forum for negotiating the global response to climate change'. The Paris Agreement was adopted on 12 December 2015 at the twenty-first session of the Conference of the Parties to the UNFCCC held in Paris from 30 November to 13 December 2015, see UN Treaty Collection: https://treaties.un.org/pages/ViewDetails.aspx?src=TREATY&mtdsg_no=XXVII-7-d& chapter=27&clang=_en;

The Paris Agreements' long-term temperature goal is to keep the increase in global average temperature to well below 2 °C above pre-industrial levels; and to pursue efforts to limit the increase to 1.5 °C. In A/RES/70/1, *Transforming Our World: The 2030 Agenda For Sustainable Development*, 21 October 2015, para. 31 states:

We note with grave concern the significant gap between the aggregate effect of parties' mitigation pledges in terms of global annual emissions of greenhouse gases by 2020 and aggregate emission pathways consistent with having a likely chance of holding the increase in global average temperature below 2 degrees Celsius, or 1.5 degrees Celsius above pre-industrial levels.

[258] A/RES/70/1, *Transforming Our World: The 2030 Agenda For Sustainable Development*, 21 October 2015, preamble (subpara. 3), paras. 2, 5, 74(b).

[259] See De Albuquerque, *On The Right Track: Good Practices In Realising The Rights To Water And Sanitation* (2012), 36.

[260] A/RES/74/419, *Resolution adopted by the General Assembly on 15 October 2019, political declaration of the high-level political forum on sustainable development convened under the auspices of the General Assembly*, para. 19.

The normative content of SDG 6 and the right to water sanitation is reflected in the   101
General Comment No. 15 (2002), where the right to water includes both freedoms and
entitlements.[261] Although the right to water is not explicitly mentioned in the ICESCR,
water as a limited natural resource falls within the category of guarantees essential in
Art. 11 of ICESCR, and has been recognised as a human right.[262]

The different contents of the right to water addressing not only the individual but   102
also corresponding obligations and duties of the state to respect, protect and fulfil which
includes the obligations to facilitate, promote and provide[263] and the obligation of states
provide the basis of violations of the right to water.[264] Several violations through actions
or omissions of the right to water and the right to sanitation occur[265] and deprive
the entitled individual or group of their right to access to water. The enforcement of
the right to water and sanitation must be legally guaranteed. Individuals and groups
should have access to effective judicial or other appropriate remedies at both national
and international levels,[266] against states with respect to environmental issues ensuring
the provision of 'effective access to judicial and administrative proceedings, including
remedy and redress'. All victims of violations of the right to water should be entitled
to adequate reparation, including restitution, compensation, satisfaction or guarantees
of non-repetition. National ombudsmen, human rights commissions, and similar institutions should be permitted to address violations of the right.[267]

Jurisdiction that falls within the scope of SDG 6 does not show a consistent line and   103
weighting, neither internationally nor domestically. However, at international level, the
ICJ emphasises access to and protection of water and the associated responsibility of
states to protect the environment of neighbouring states or areas and thus considers a
transboundary level to be inevitable. At a regional level, the EU, despite its unambiguous
instruments of water protection, is diverse on environmental law perspectives which
underscores the EU's environmental regulation. While the ECJ seeks to 'enduringly
revitalize the ties of shared environmental objectives and imperatives',[268] the exact
formulation and meaning of the terms covered by SDG 6 are legally unsatisfactorily
definable. The legal meaning of single targets of SDG 6 such as the term 'sustainable
management' or more precise definitions such as the 'increase of water-use efficiency',
has not yet been ascertained in jurisdiction, or only in scattered cases which highly rely
on their specific context. Therefore, they are unlikely to be of conclusive value.[269] The
depiction of a coherent overall concept or uniform legal knowledge is reserved for the

---

[261] E/C.12/2002/11 (UN CESCR), *General Comment No. 15 (2002), The right to water (arts. 11 and 12 of the International Covenant on Economic, Social and Cultural Rights)*, 20 January 2003, para. 10.

[262] E/C.12/2002/11 (UN CESCR), *General Comment No. 15 (2002), The right to water (arts. 11 and 12 of the International Covenant on Economic, Social and Cultural Rights)*, 20 January 2003, para. 1.

[263] E/C.12/2002/11 (UN CESCR), *General Comment No. 15 (2002), The right to water (arts. 11 and 12 of the International Covenant on Economic, Social and Cultural Rights)*, 20 January 2003, paras. 25-9.

[264] E/C.12/2002/11 (UN CESCR), *General Comment No. 15 (2002), The right to water (arts. 11 and 12 of the International Covenant on Economic, Social and Cultural Rights)*, 20 January 2003, para. 39.

[265] E/C.12/2002/11 (UN CESCR), *General Comment No. 15 (2002), The right to water (arts. 11 and 12 of the International Covenant on Economic, Social and Cultural Rights)*, 20 January 2003, paras. 42 ff.

[266] See General Comment No. 9 (1998), para. 4, and Principle 10 of the Rio Declaration on Environment and Development.

[267] E/C.12/2002/11 (UN CESCR), *General Comment No. 15 (2002), The right to water (Arts. 11 and 12 of the International Covenant on Economic, Social and Cultural Rights)*, 20 January 2003, paras. 55 f.

[268] Gehring and Phillips and Lees, 'The European Union' in Lees and Viñuales, *The Oxford Handbook of Comparative Environmental Law* (2019), 149 (169).

[269] For further discussion on this issue: De Albuquerque, *On The Right Track: Good Practices In Realising The Rights To Water And Sanitation* (2012), 27; Murthy, 'The Human Right(s) to Water and Sanitation: History, Meaning, and the Controversy Over Privatization' (2013) 31(1) *BJIL*, 89 (113).

further development in legal processes, but under the most diverse influencing factors, which are likely to become even more precarious in the exacerbating struggle for water.

104   From a legal perspective, the demand for 'good governance' and access to justice must be transformed into the applicability and legal enforcement of the principles of human rights concerning the right to water and sanitation (→ Goal 16 mn. 3 ff., 9). Adopting a human rights-based approach to development could improve to achieve climate justice concerning water.[270] As a pillar for implementing SDG 6, the inclusion of good water governance is essential. Governance structures frequently tend to be weak and fragmented with room for improvement in many countries and interregional organisations. Good water governance means to create rules and regulations in a systematic way which are acknowledged, applied, monitored and comply with the rule of law in politics and throughout society. Essential parts of policy processes in that realm are participation and multi-stakeholder engagement. Having a transparent and neutral platform for government and citizen groups in place supports the local government.[271] Participation is seen among others as a critical governance function where planning, coordination, regulation, and licensing must be added.[272] In this light, the Paris Agreement and the Human Rights Council also refer to equity and human rights[273] which are profoundly linked with SDG 6.[274] As a result, the pathway leading to equity also paves the way for climate justice.[275] Citizen participation as an environmental issue is encapsulated in Principle 10 of the Rio Declaration on Environment and Development, underlining citizen participation in environmental issues. This principle sets out three fundamental rights: access to information, access to public participation and access to justice, as key pillars of sound environmental governance.[276] Putting the arguments together, it appears quite impossible to perceive the content of the SDGs outside the sphere of normativity.

---

[270] UNESCO, *UN-Water, 2020: United Nations World Water Development Report 2020: Water and Climate Change* (2020), 159.

[271] UN, *Integrated Approaches for Sustainable Development Goals Planning: The case of Goal 6 on Water and Sanitation* (2017), 15.

[272] UNESCO, *UN-Water, 2020: United Nations World Water Development Report 2020: Water and Climate Change* (2020), 6.

[273] UNESCO, *UN-Water, 2020: United Nations World Water Development Report 2020: Water and Climate Change* (2020), 35.

[274] See A/HRC/RES/41/21 of 23 July 2019, stressing the access of persons with disabilities in particular to [...] safe drinking water and sanitation, further 'noted the importance for some of the concept of "climate justice" when taking action to address climate change'.

[275] Beck, 'Inside the System, Outside the Box: Palau's Pursuit of Climate Justice and Security at the United Nations) (2014) 3(1) *Transnational Environmental Law*, 17-29: 'Palau announced, in 2011, that it would take the issue of climate change to the ICJ', 24; Caney, 'Cosmopolitan Justice, Responsibility, and Global Climate Change' (2005) 18(4) *Leiden Journal of International Law*, 747-75; see further https://www.ohchr.org/EN/Issues/HRAndClimateChange/Pages/HRClimateChangeIndex.aspx; see also Strauss, 'Climate Change Litigation: Opening the Door to the International Court of Justice' (2009) 3 *School of Law Faculty Publications*; Strauss, 'The Legal Option: Suing the United States in International Forums for Global Warming Emissions' (2003) 33 *ELR 10185.*

[276] UNESCO, *UN-Water, 2020: United Nations World Water Development Report 2020: Water and Climate Change* (2020), 155.

Goal 7
Ensure access to affordable, reliable, sustainable and modern energy for all

7.1 By 2030, ensure universal access to affordable, reliable and modern energy services

7.2 By 2030, increase substantially the share of renewable energy in the global energy mix

7.3 By 2030, double the global rate of improvement in energy efficiency

7.a By 2030, enhance international cooperation to facilitate access to clean energy research and technology, including renewable energy, energy efficiency and advanced and cleaner fossil-fuel technology, and promote investment in energy infrastructure and clean energy technology

7.b By 2030, expand infrastructure and upgrade technology for supplying modern and sustainable energy services for all in developing countries, in particular least developed countries, small island developing States and landlocked developing countries, in accordance with their respective programmes of support

Word Count related to 'Energy'
A/RES/70/1 - Transforming our world: the 2030 Agenda for Sustainable Development: 16
Instruments mentioned in A/RES/70/1 in the section entitled: 'Sustainable Development Goals and targets':
A/RES/69/313 - Addis Ababa Action Agenda of the Third International Conference on Financing for Development adopted on 27 July 2015: 15
A/RES/66/288 - The future we want (Rio +20 Declaration) adopted on 27 July 2012: 30
A/RES/55/2 - United Nations Millennium Declaration adopted on 8 September 2000: 0

Select Bibliography: Alam Shawkat, Jahid Hossain Bhuiyan and Jona Razzaque (eds), *International Natural Resources Law, Investment and Sustainability* (Routledge, UK/USA 2019); James Bacchus, *The Willing World – Shaping and Sharing a Sustainable Global Prosperity* (Cambridge University Press, UK/USA/Australia/India/Singapore 2018); Barry Barton et al (eds), *Energy Security – Managing Risk in a Dynamic Legal and Regulatory Environment* (Oxford University Press, Oxford 2004); Neil Simcock et al (eds), *Energy Poverty and Vulnerability – A Global Perspective* (Routledge, UK/USA 2017); Adrian J. Bradbook and Judith Gail Gardam, 'Placing Access to Energy Services within a Human Rights Framework' (2006) 28 *HRQ*, 389; Adrian J. Bradbook and Ralph D. Wahnshafft, 'International Law and Global Sustainable Energy Production and Consumption' in in Adrian J. Bradbook et al (eds), *The Law of Energy for Sustainable Development* (Cambridge University Press, Cambridge 2005), 181; Gavin Bridge et al., *Energy and Society*

– *A Critical Perspective* (Routledge, UK/US 2018); Stuart Bruce and Sean Stephenson, 'SDG 7 on Sustainable Energy for All – Contributions of International Law, Policy and Governance' (2016) *UNEP/CISDL Issue Brief* (UNEP/CISDL, Montreal 2016); Stuart Bruce, 'Climate Change Mitigation through Energy Efficiency Laws – from International Obligations to Domestic Regulation' (2013) 31 *J. Energy Nat. Resour. Law*, 327; Stuart Bruce, 'International Law and Renewable Energy – Facilitating Sustainable Energy for All?' (2013) 14 *Melb. J. Int'l L.*, 34; Brugger Christian, 'Reflections on the moral foundations of a right to energy' in Lakshman Guruswamy, *International Energy and Poverty – The emerging contours* (Routledge, UK/USA 2015), 68; Karl-Michael Brunner, Sylvia Mandl and Harriet Thomson, 'Energy Poverty, Energy Equity in a World of High Demand and Low Supply' in Debra J. Davidson and Matthias Gross (eds), *The Oxford Handbook of Energy and Society* (Oxford University Press, USA 2018), 297; Robin Burgess, Michael Greenstone, Nicholas Ryan and Anant Sudarshan, 'The Consequences of Treating Electricity as a Right' (2020) 34 *JEP*, 145; Peter D. Cameron, *International Energy Investment Law –The Pursuit of Stability* (Oxford University Press, Oxford 2010); Kristen A. Carpenter and Jacquelyn Amour Jampolsky, 'Indigenous peoples – from energy poverty to energy empowerment' in Lakshman Guruswamy, *International Energy and Poverty – The emerging contours* (Routledge, UK/USA 2015), 39; Aleh Cherp and Jessica Jewell, 'The concept of energy security: Beyond the four As' (2014) 75 *Energy Policy*, 415; CISDL, Marie-Claire Cordonier Segger and Alexandra Harrington (eds), *SDG 7 on Sustainable Energy for All, A Toolkit of Legal & Institutional Practices* (CISDL, Montreal 2019); Penelope Crossley, *Renewable Energy Law – An International Assessment* (Cambridge University Press, UK/USA/Australia/India/Singapore 2019); Hugh Dyer and Maria Julia Trombetta (eds), *International Handbook of Energy Security* (Edward Elgar Publishing, UK/USA 2013); European Commission, *Clean energy for all Europeans* (EU, Brussels 2019), 8 f; Katrin Großmann and Antje Kahlheber, 'Energy poverty in an intersectional perspective – On multiple deprivation, discriminatory systems, and the effects of policies' in Neil Simcock, Harriet Thomson, Saska Petrova and Stefan Bouzarovski (eds), *Energy Poverty and Vulnerability – A Global Perspective* (Routledge, UK/USA 2017), 12; Iñigo de Guayo, Lee Godden, Donald D. Zillman, Milton Fernando Montoya, and José Juan González (eds), *Energy Justice and Energy Law* (Oxford University Press, Oxford 2020), 3; Karolis Gudas, 'Right to Electricity' in Thomas Cottier and Krista Nadakavukaren Schefer, *Elgar Encyclopedia of International Economic Law* (2017), 647 f.; Wang Guoyu, Jianing Guan and Lei Li, 'Energy Justice and Construction of Community with a Shared Future of Mankind' in Gunter Bombaerts, Kirsten Jenkins, Yekeen A. Sanusi and Wang Guoyu (eds), *Energy Justice Across Borders* (Springer Nature Switzerland, Switzerland 2020), 217; Heffron Raphael J. and Kim Talus, 'The Evolution of Energy Law and Energy Jurisprudence – Insights for Energy Analysts and Researchers' (2016) 19 *Energy Res. Soc. Sci.*, 1; Herman Lior, 'Energy as an Instrument in Global Politics' in Kathleen J. Hancook and Juliann Emmons Allison (eds), *The Oxford Handbook of Energy Politics* (Oxford University Press, Oxford 2021), 293; Anna Herranz-Surrallés, 'Energy diplomacy under scrutiny: parliamentary control of intergovernmental agreements with third-country suppliers' (2017) 40 *West Eur. Polit.*; David F. von Hippel, Tatsujiro Suzuki, James H. Williams, Timothy Savage and Peter Hayes, 'Evaluating The Energy Security Impacts Of Energy Policies' in Benjamin K. Sovacool (ed), *The Routledge Handbook of Energy Security* (2011), 74; Winfried Huck and Claudia Kurkin, 'The UN Sustainable Development Goals (SDGs) in the Transnational Multilevel System' (2018) 2 *HJIL/ ZaöRV*, 375; Pamela Jagger, Robert Bailis, Ahmad Dermawan, Noah Kittner and Ryan McCord, 'SDG: Affordable and Clean Energy – How Access to Affordable and Clean Energy Affects Forests and Forest-Based Livelihoods' in Pia Katila, Carol J. Pierce Colfer, Wil De Jong, Glenn Galloway, Pablo Pacheco and Georg Winkel (eds), *Sustainable Development Goals: Their Impacts on Forests and People* (Cambridge University Press 2019), 206; Thoko Kaime and Robert L. Glicksmann, 'An International Legal Framework for SE4All – Human Rights and Sustainable Development Law Imperatives' (2015) 38 *Fordham Int. Law J.*, 1405; Markus Krajewski, 'The impact of international investment agreements on energy regulation' in Christoph Herrmann and Jörg Philipp Terhechte, *European Yearbook of International Economic Law* (Springer, Berlin/Heidelberg 2013), 343; Murodbek Laldjebaev, Benjamin K. Sovacool and Karim-Aly S. Kassam, 'Energy security, poverty, and sovereignty – Complex interlinkages and compelling implications' in Lakshman Guruswamy (ed), *International Energy and Poverty – The emerging contours* (Routledge, UK/USA 2015), 97; Leal-Arcas Rafael (ed), *Commentary on the Energy Charter Treaty* (Edward Elgar Publishing, UK/USA 2018); Fatima McKague, Rob Lawson, Michelle Scott and Ben Wooliscroft, 'Understanding energy poverty through the energy cultures framework' in Neil Simcock, Harriet Thomson, Saska Petrova and Stefan Bouzarovski (eds), *Energy Poverty and Vulnerability – A Global Perspective* (Routledge, UK/USA 2017), 33; Kate Miles (ed), *Research Handbook on Environment and Investment Law* (Edward Elgar Publishing, UK/USA 2019); Godwell Nhamo, Charles Nhemachena, Senia Nhamo, Vuyo Mjimba and Ivana Savić, *SDG 7 – Ensure Access to Affordable, Reliable, Sustainable, and Modern Energy* (Emerald Publishing Limited 2020); Benjamin K. Sovacool and Michael H. Dworkin, *Global Energy Justice – Problems, Principles and Practices* (Cambridge Univeristy Press, Cambridge 2014); Kim Talus (ed), *Research Handbook on International Energy Law* (Edward Elgar Publishing, UK/USA 2014); United Nations and High-Level Dialogue on Energy (HLDE), *Theme Report on Energy, Access towards the Achievement Of SDG 7 and Net-Zero Emissions* (UN, New York 2021); Martijn Wilder and Lauren Drake, 'International Law and the Renewable Energy Sector' in Carlarne, Gray and Tarasofsky (eds), *The Oxford Handbook of International Climate Change Law* (Oxford University Press, Oxford 2016), 357; Jeffrey D. Wilson, 'Energy Interdependence' in Kathleen J. Hancook and Juliann Emmons Allison (eds), *The Oxford Handbook of Energy Politics* (Oxford University Press, Oxford 2021), 151; World Health Organization (WHO), *Access to Modern Energy Services for Health Facilities in Resource-Constrained Settings - A Review of Status, Significance, Challenges and Measurement* (WHO/World Bank, Geneva/Washington, 2014).

A. Background and Origin of SDG 7

Before the outbreak of the SARS-CoV-2 pandemic, the overall access to electricity   1
in the poorest countries had begun to accelerate. At the same time, energy efficiency, the use of renewable energy supply as well as the number of people covered by a mobile network increased. The biggest issues then had been 800 million people more being without any access to electricity and the lack of clean fuels and technologies used specifically in private households, including for cooking, transportation and heating.[1] Since 2020, due to the global pandemic, all progress made is stagnating or had even reversed. The challenges related to the provision of clean and sustainable energy are likely to become more challenging in the future.

According to the UN, 'human survival and development depend on access to energy   2
for heating homes, manufacturing goods and connecting across distances.'[2] Being a key factor in the first industrial revolution, energy has since been leading to a steady increase in prosperity.[3] SDG 7 forms a key enabling factor to sustainable development that promotes social and economic progress.[4] However, 13 per cent of the world's population still does not have access to electricity.[5] In addition, 3 billion people worldwide rely on burning biomass or waste for heating and cooking.[6] The resulting gases are responsible for an estimated 3.8 million deaths per year.[7] With more than 95 per cent, Sub-Saharan Africa and Asia represent the overwhelming majority of all people without access to electricity.[8] Women and children still suffer the most from 'the main negative impacts of fuel collection and transport, indoor air pollution, and time-consuming and unsafe cooking technologies.'[9] The availability of energy is essential for a multitude of daily tasks and is hardly dispensable for human life.

In 1972, with the Stockholm Declaration, the connection of clean, sustainable energy   3
to 'most effective development of the world's energy resources, with due regard to the

---

[1] E/2019/68, *Special edition: progress towards the Sustainable Development Goals, Report of the Secretary-General*, 08 May 2019, para. 28.

[2] Independent Group of Scientists appointed by the Secretary-General, *Global Sustainable Development Report 2019: The Future is Now – Science for Achieving Sustainable Development*, (2019), 76.

[3] Griggs et al., *A Guide to SDG Interactions: From Science to Implementation* (2017), 130.

[4] United Nations General Assembly Open Working Group on Sustainable Development Goals, *Compendium of TST Issues Briefs October 2014* (2014), 99.

[5] https://www.un.org/sustainabledevelopment/energy/.

[6] Independent Group of Scientists appointed by the Secretary-General, *Global Sustainable Development Report 2019: The Future is Now – Science for Achieving Sustainable Development* (2019), 76; United Nations General Assembly Open Working Group on Sustainable Development Goals, *Compendium of TST Issues Briefs October 2014* (2014), 99; https://www.un.org/sustainabledevelopment/energy/.

[7] IEA, IRENA, UNSD, World Bank Group and WHO, *2020 Tracking SDG 7, The Energy Progress Report* (2020), 73; Independent Group of Scientists appointed by the Secretary-General, *Global Sustainable Development Report 2019: The Future is Now – Science for Achieving Sustainable Development* (2019), 76.

[8] IEA, IRENA, UNSD, World Bank Group and WHO, *2010 Tracking SDG 7, The Energy Progress Report* (2020), 4, 63; United Nations General Assembly Open Working Group on Sustainable Development Goals, *Compendium of TST Issues Briefs October 2014* (2014), 100.

[9] SE4ALL, *Global Tracking Framework* (2013), 80.

environmental effects of energy production and use'[10] was identified a crucial factor to address climate change. While the emphasis then had been on the pollution of radioactive waste or nuclear emissions, its siting of the ultimate storage areas and transporting,[11] the focus worldwide shifted to CO_2-neutrality of the form and supply of energy and its supporting function in combatting climate change.

4   With the 1987 Brundtland Report, the World Commission on Environment and Development (WCED) reaffirmed the necessity of energy for daily survival and beyond that '[f]uture development crucially depends on its long-term availability in increasing quantities from sources that are dependable, safe, and environmentally sound. At present, no single source or mix of sources is at hand to meet this future need.'[12] Moreover, the WCED stated that 'every effort should be made to develop the potential for renewable energy, which should form the foundation of the global energy structure during the 21st Century.'[13] Sustainable energy must be seen in the context of the Brundtland Report's definition of sustainable development[14] as 'development that meets the needs of the present without compromising the ability of future generations to meet their own needs.'[15] In the report, concerns have already been expressed about climate change[16] and nuclear energy. Nuclear energy in particular was discussed controversially against the background of low CO_2 emissions and despite all the existing risks.[17] Overall, energy has been described as 'a mix upon which the welfare of individuals, the sustainable development of nations, and the life-supporting capabilities of the global ecosystem depend.'[18] In this way, a first approach for a definition of sustainable energy was created.

5   However, the acknowledgement of the connection between sustainable development and energy is not constant. Energy is not explicitly mentioned in the Rio Declaration,[19] nor did the MDGs contain an explicit target relating to energy.[20] Nevertheless, energy has been crucial for the realisation of the MDGs which formed 'a key prerequisite'.[21]

6   In 2011, the UN Secretary General launched the Sustainable Energy for All (SE4ALL) initiative.[22] The initiative aimed to provide access to modern energy services and to double both the share of renewable energy and the global rate of improvement in

---

[10] *Stockholm Declaration* (1972), Recommendation 59.

[11] This critical assessment of nuclear energy and its usage still can be found today, for example, in the Federal Republic of Germany or in the Republic of Austria, see e. g. ECJ, Case C-594/18P, 22.09.2020, *Austria v Commission* (Hinkley Point C), ECLI:EU:C:2020:742.

[12] WCED, *Report of the World Commission on Environment and Development: Our Common Future* (1987), Part I, Chapter 7, para. 1.

[13] WCED, *Report of the World Commission on Environment and Development: Our Common Future* (1987), Part I, Chapter 7, para. 88.

[14] IAEA, *Energy And Sustainable Development* (Bulletin 54-1 2013).

[15] WCED, *Report of the World Commission on Environment and Development: Our Common Future* (1987), Chapter 12, para. 1; A/RES/70/1, paras. 7, 27.

[16] WCED, *Report of the World Commission on Environment and Development: Our Common Future* (1987), Chapter 1, paras. 28, 32, Chapter 6, para. 4; Chapter 7, paras. 11, 19 ff.

[17] WCED, *Report of the World Commission on Environment and Development: Our Common Future* (1987), Part I, Chapter 7, paras. 47-53; IAEA, *Energy And Sustainable Development* (Bulletin 54-1 2013).

[18] WCED, *Report of the World Commission on Environment and Development: Our Common Future* (1987), Part I, Chapter 7, para. 116.

[19] A/CONF.151/26, *Report of the United Nations Conference on Environment and Development, Rio de Janeiro*, 3-14 June 1992, Rio Declaration on Environment and Development (Vol. I).

[20] https://sustainabledevelopment.un.org/majorgroups/post2015.

[21] United Nations General Assembly Open Working Group on Sustainable Development Goals, *Compendium of TST Issues Briefs October 2014* (2014), 99.

[22] https://www.seforall.org/sites/default/files/SG_Sustainable_Energy_for_All_vision.pdf.

energy efficiency[23] with the means of catalysing 'major new investments'[24] 2012 then was declared as 'International Year of Sustainable Energy for All'.[25] The endeavours were reaffirmed with the declaration of the UN Decade of Sustainable Energy for All (2014 – 2024).[26] In the outcome document of the United Nations Conference on Sustainable Development (Rio+20), 'the critical role that energy plays in the development process, as access to sustainable modern energy services contributes to poverty eradication, saves lives, improves health and helps to provide for basic human needs'[27] was recognised and stressed that 'these services are essential to social inclusion and gender equality, and that energy is also a key input to production.'[28] Additionally, the importance of global partnerships to achieve a universal supply of sustainable energy was emphasised[29] which today is included in SDG 7.a that addresses this aspect by enhancing 'international cooperation to facilitate access to clean energy research and technology' and promoting 'investment in energy infrastructure and clean energy technology'.

The attention based on previous resolutions has made the integration of energy into   7
SDGs inevitable. However, different approaches were discussed to accommodate this. It was discussed whether energy should be a stand-alone goal or whether it should be combined with related goals in a cluster. The Sustainable Development Solutions Network (SDSN) proposed a goal including '[c]urb Human-Induced Climate Change and Ensure Clean Energy for All'[30] which, however, has not been successful. Instead, energy was given a stand-alone goal. Among various initiatives, the SE4All initiative of the Secretary-General[31] has prevailed.

The preparatory work on SDG 7 shows the clear awareness of climate change which   8
is a main driver of the UN's action.[32] Three major thematic debates have been held, which are not separate but interlinked: partnerships, water and sanitation, and energy.[33] The participants in the bottom-up process have made clear that sustainable development set out in the MDGs had to be expanded, with targets on inequalities, economic growth, decent jobs, cities and human settlements, industrialisation, energy, climate change,

---

[23] Dodds and Donoghue and Leiva Roesch, *Negotiating the Sustainable Development Goals, A transformational agenda for an insecure world* (2017), 58.

[24] Investment in energy (transition) is assumed to deliver on manifold interconnected areas at the same time, and thus enhancing the sustainable transition significantly: United Nations General Assembly Open Working Group on Sustainable Development Goals, *Compendium of TST Issues Briefs October 2014* (2014), 99; A/69/700, *The road to dignity by 2030: ending poverty, transforming all lives and protecting the planet, Synthesis report of the Secretary-General on the post-2015 sustainable development agenda*, 4 December 2014, para. 94.

[25] A/RES/65/151, *International Year of Sustainable Energy for All*, 16 February 2011, para. 1.

[26] A/RES/67/215, *Promotion of new and renewable sources of energy*, 20 March 2013, para. 2.

[27] A/RES/66/288, *The future we want*, 11 September 2012, para.125.

[28] A/RES/66/288, *The future we want*, 11 September 2012, para.125.

[29] United Nations General Assembly Open Working Group on Sustainable Development Goals, *Compendium of TST Issues Briefs October 2014* (2014), 99.

[30] Sustainable Development Solutions Network, *An Action Agenda for Sustainable Development* (2013), 19.

[31] United Nations General Assembly Open Working Group on Sustainable Development Goals, *Compendium of TST Issues Briefs October 2014* (2014), 103; Dodds and Donoghue and Leiva Roesch, *Negotiating the Sustainable Development Goals, A transformational agenda for an insecure world* (2017), 58.

[32] Dodds and Donoghue and Leiva Roesch, *Negotiating the Sustainable Development Goals, A transformational agenda for an insecure world* (2017), 136 f.

[33] A/69/700, *The road to dignity by 2030: ending poverty, transforming all lives and protecting the planet, Synthesis report of the Secretary-General on the post-2015 sustainable development agenda*, 4 December 2014, para. 42.

sustainable consumption and production, peace, justice and institutions.[34] To achieve the aspired transformation and gain prosperity[35] for all and to grow a strong, inclusive and transformative economy, it demands participation in an inclusive, more sustainable sense. 'People want energy and industry, among other things, which creates both: good decent jobs, social security, food security and, at the same time, forms of energy that help combat climate change.'[36]

9   The debate on the sustainability of nuclear energy, which already prevailed at the time of the Brundtland Report, is still relevant today. Existing nuclear power plants contribute significantly to saving carbon dioxide (CO_2).[37] However, a significant increase in the share of nuclear energy in the global energy mix would require undiscovered uranium resources, thereby leading to high CO_2-emissions during the extraction and dismantling cycles, in so that the overall savings would be rather moderate.[38] In addition, the discussion turns to the question if the new generation of small-scale nuclear reactors (SSNR), which are starting to be developed around the world will be a more safe and a cheaper alternative to renewables.[39] Due to the renewed interest in the member states of the International Atomic Energy Agency (IAEA) in the development and operation of this new type, the IAEA is also providing information on environmental impact assessments.[40] In the EU, Estonia is the member state which plans to build Europe's first SSNR.[41]

10   Recent IAEA annual projections show that nuclear power will continue to play a key role in the world's low-carbon energy mix, with global nuclear electrical capacity seen nearly doubling by 2050 which is further ignited by the climate change mitigation efforts as a key potential driver for maintaining and expanding the use of nuclear power.[42] Commitments made under the Paris Agreement and other initiatives could support nuclear power development, provided the necessary energy policies and market designs are established to facilitate investments in dispatchable, low carbon technologies.[43] Nuclear power could provide solutions for electricity consumption growth, air quality concerns, the security of energy supply and price volatility of other fuels and make a major contribution to affordable and reliable energy.[44] Yet, the sustainability of this form of energy is not conclusively discussed worldwide.[45] According to the IEA, solar PV, wind

---

[34] A/69/700, *The road to dignity by 2030: ending poverty, transforming all lives and protecting the planet, Synthesis report of the Secretary-General on the post-2015 sustainable development agenda*, 4 December 2014, para. 45.

[35] A/69/700, *The road to dignity by 2030: ending poverty, transforming all lives and protecting the planet, Synthesis report of the Secretary-General on the post-2015 sustainable development agenda*, 4 December 2014, para. 74.

[36] A/69/700, *The road to dignity by 2030: ending poverty, transforming all lives and protecting the planet, Synthesis report of the Secretary-General on the post-2015 sustainable development agenda*, 4 December 2014, para. 54.

[37] IAEA, Nuclear Power for Sustainable Development (2017), 2.

[38] Englert et al., 'Is nuclear fission a sustainable source of energy?' (2012) 4 *MRS Bulletin*, 417 (423).

[39] Parshley, 'The countries building miniature nuclear reactors' (2020) *Future Planet (March, 9, 2020)*.

[40] IAEA, *Considerations for Environmental Impact Assessment for Small Modular Reactors*, IAEA-TEC-DOC-1915 (2020).

[41] https://www.euractiv.com/section/politics/short_news/estonia-plans-to-build-europes-first-small-sc ale-nuclear-reactor/.

[42] According to the International Energy Agency [6], the use of nuclear power has avoided more than 60 gigatons of CO_2 emissions over the past 50 years; https://www.iaea.org/newscenter/pressreleases/iaea-r eport-nuclear-power-to-continue-to-play-key-role-in-low-carbon-electricity-production.

[43] IAEA, *Energy, Electricity and Nuclear Power Estimates for the Period up to 2050* (2020), 3.

[44] https://sustainabledevelopment.un.org/content/documents/19913IAEA_Brochure_NP_for_Sustaina ble_Development.pdf, 2.

[45] ECJ, Case C-594/18P, 22.09.2020, *Austria v Commission* (Hinkley Point C), ECLI:EU:C:2020:742.

and hydropower are currently seen as the most important types of renewable energy.[46] Today, nuclear energy contributes to 10 per cent of the global electricity production.[47] Nevertheless, risks posed by nuclear waste and possible accidents as well as significant environmental impact resulting from them must be taken into account.

By 2050, global final energy consumption is projected to increase by approximately   11 30 per cent and electricity production is expected to double according to the estimated growth of world population. Worldwide, fossil fuels remain the dominant energy source for electricity production at about 63 per cent in 2019, with their share having changed little since 1980.

B. Scope and Dimensions of SDG 7

I. Elementary Definitions

SDG 7 contains a number of significant terms that need to be highlighted and delin-   12 eated. These terms initially appear to be unambiguous but profoundly diverge against the background of international law. In international law, there is a fundamentally consistent absence of universally acknowledged definitions of terms mentioned in SDG 7. This might constitute an obstacle for an effective legal implementation of SDG 7.[48]

It appears to offer a basically straightforward concept of what energy services should   13 look like to be modern, but this is deceptive. Due to the lack of a legal definition, modern energy is again defined by common use of the World Bank and the International Energy Agency (IEA) which classify modern energy by stating a 'threshold of 500 kWh per year per urban household [–] and just half this rate for rural households. This means an international definition of modern energy access at 50-100 kWh per person per year'.[49] This opens up room for interpretation of 'modern energy'[50] in the sense of SDG 7.1, which is framed more precisely by its two indicators.

SDG 7.1 pledges for universal access to affordable, reliable, and modern energy   14 services for all. The International Energy Agency provides an approach for a definition of energy access in accordance with SDG 7.1. It is emphasised that there is no common, globally adopted definition of energy access and the following definition is therefore based on shared criteria of various definitional approaches.[51] Therefore, known definitions are based on the wide use by international organisations,[52] but are not grounded

---

[46] https://www.iea.org/reports/renewables-2020/renewable-electricity-2#abstract.

[47] IAEA, *Energy, Electricity and Nuclear Power Estimates for the Period up to 2050* (2020), 2.

[48] Bruce and Stephenson, 'SDG 7 on Sustainable Energy for All – Contributions of International Law, Policy and Governance' (2016) *UNEP/CISDL Issue Brief*, 7.

[49] Moss (Center for Global Development), *SDG Seven: Update the 'Modern' in Universal Modern Energy Access* (2015).

[50] At least it can be connoted with 'increased electrification of all end uses, combined with a decarbonized power sector'; IEA, IRENA, UNSD, World Bank Group and WHO, *2020 Tracking SDG 7, The Energy Progress Report* (2020), 85.

[51] International Energy Agency, *Defining energy access, 2020 methodology* (2020); see a more detailed overview: UN and HLDE, *Theme Report on Energy, Access towards the Achievement Of SDG 7 and Net-Zero Emissions* (2021), 16 f.; further interpretation in context of just transitioning: UN and HLDE, *Theme Report on enabling SDGs through Inclusive, Just Energy Transitions towards the Achievement Of SDG 7 and Net-Zero Emissions* (2021).

[52] E.g. apart from the International Energy Agency: World Bank, United Nations Sustainable Energy for All initiative (SE4ALL).

in the framework of international law.[53] Thus, modern energy access is described as a household having reliable and affordable access to both clean cooking facilities[54] and electricity, which is enough to supply a basic bundle of energy services initially, and then an increasing level of electricity over time to reach the regional average.[55]

15   This definition of access to energy primarily covers the access of population (households) to electricity (indicator 7.1.1) and thus excludes other entities such as economic entities (companies, factories) and public institutions (schools, hospitals) from the definition. However, certainly, these entities also require fundamental and modern access to energy and are indispensable for an overall sustainable economic and social development of societies.[56] Moreover, the second area measures the number of people using clean fuels and technologies for domestic cooking, heating and lighting divided by total population reporting any cooking, heating or lighting (indicator 7.1.2).[57]

16   The wording of SDG 7.1 refers to modern energy, inter alia, drawing attention to the definitional extent of the term 'modern energy'. The appropriate indicator 7.1.2, however, does not point to equivocal 'modern energy' but to 'clean fuels and technologies' building the concept of a definition. Therefore, clean fuel and technologies are defined by the emission rate targets and specific fuel recommendations that are contained in the 'WHO Guidelines for Indoor Air Quality: Household Fuel Combustion'.[58]

17   Within the definitions set of modern, clean and renewable energy, the scope of energy services can already be seen. Energy services are divided into access to electricity and access to clean cooking facilities. Electricity access entails a household having initial access to sufficient electricity to power a basic bundle of energy services – at a minimum, several lightbulbs, phone charging, a radio and potentially a fan or television – with the level of service capable of growing over time. [...] Access to clean cooking facilities means access to (and primary use of) modern fuels and technologies, including natural gas, liquefied petroleum gas (LPG), electricity and biogas, or improved biomass cookstoves (ICS) that have considerably lower emissions and higher efficiencies than traditional three-stone fires for cooking.[59] Furthermore, the access to clean cooking facilities shall ensure clean in-house air quality by avoiding the use of 'traditional biomass in the form of wood, charcoal, and dung in open fires or inefficient stoves for cooking and heating'.[60]

---

[53] Bruce and Stephenson, 'SDG 7 on Sustainable Energy for All – Contributions of International Law, Policy and Governance' (2016) *UNEP/CISDL Issue Brief*, 7.

[54] Further specified as: 'household access to safer and more sustainable (i.e. minimum harmful effects on health and the environment as possible) cooking and heating fuels and stoves', International Energy Agency, *Defining energy access, 2020 methodology* (2020).

[55] International Energy Agency, *Defining energy access, 2020 methodology* (2020).

[56] With special focus on the following components: 'access to modern energy that enables productive economic activity, e.g. mechanical power for agriculture, textile and other industries [and] access to modern energy for public services, e.g. electricity for health facilities, schools and street lighting', International Energy Agency, Defining energy access, 2020 methodology (2020).

[57] https://unstats.un.org/wiki/display/SDGeHandbook/Indicator+7.1.2.

[58] https://www.who.int/airpollution/guidelines/household-fuel-combustion/en/; https://unstats.un.org/wiki/display/SDGeHandbook/Indicator+7.1.2; see also UN and HLDE, *Theme Report on Energy, Access towards the Achievement Of SDG 7 and Net-Zero Emissions* (2021).

[59] International Energy Agency (IEA), *Defining energy access, 2020 methodology* (2020); the IEA defines parameters for 'enough electricity' access as
electricity to power four lightbulbs operating at five hours per day, one refrigerator, a fan operating 6 hours per day, a mobile phone charger and a television operating 4 hours per day, which equates to an annual electricity consumption of 1 250 kWh per household with standard appliances, and 420 kWh with efficient appliances.

[60] https://www.unescap.org/our-work/energy/clean-cooking.

It does not follow clearly from the wording of SDG 7 whether nuclear energy is **18** also covered. It could be covered by the term 'modern technology' (SDG 7.1) and at the same time not be a *clean* technology in the sense of the definition of indicator 7.1.2. However, with the definitions set in the indicators 7.1.1 and 7.1.2, the meaning of the term 'modern energy' as well as the general communication of the UN indicate that nuclear energy plays a decisive role in the achievement of SDG 7 and many other SDGs. Despite being discussed controversially and some countries have decided not to 'retain the nuclear energy technology going forward in their future energy mix, most countries remain committed to it, or even plan to expand it [...] to meet their clean development needs' and to decarbonise their energy system.[61] Nevertheless, the exact form of implementation of the SDGs is up to the respective states that recognise them. Thus, it lies within their responsibility to decide whether nuclear energy will become or remain relevant for them.

Within the scope of energy access, the affordability aspect is to be highlighted. **19** Regarding SDG 7.1, access to energy such as electricity is affordable when it is economically accessible. This is in accordance with the nature of electricity which 'is considered to be both a commodity and service'.[62]

Moreover, the concepts of energy poverty[63], energy security[64] and energy sovereignty **20** play a significant role and were highlighted already in the preparatory work of the SDGs.

Energy poverty in relation to energy access is defined as the '[l]ack of household **21** access to electricity and energy services and dependence on solid biomass fuels for cooking'.[65] This is directly related to the inability to pay for existing energy services, thus severely affecting the affordability factor.[66] Besides, '[e]nergy poverty, or the inability to access or afford energy, impacts on the capability of households to attain the level of energy services necessary to participate in society'.[67] In combination with energy poverty,

---

[61] UNECE, *Application of the United Nations Framework Classification for Resources and the United Nations Resource Management System: The Role of Nuclear Energy in Sustainable Development - Entry Pathways* (Draft), EGRM-11/2020/INF.5 (2020), 23; see also: https://sdg.iisd.org/news/nuclear-power-co nference-discusses-atoms4climate/; further reading: UNECE, *Integrated life cycle management of nuclear fuel resources for sustainable energy: A concept note*, ECE/ENERGY/GE.3/2020/6 (2020).

[62] Nhamo et al., *SDG 7 – Ensure Access to Affordable, Reliable, Sustainable, and Modern Energy* (2020), 70.

[63] See further: Bridge et al., *Energy and Society – A Critical Perspective* (2018), 129 ff.; Del Guayo, 'Energy Poverty and Energy Access – A Legal Analysis' in del Guayo et al. (eds), *Energy Justice and Energy Law* (2020), 31 (31 ff.); Brunner and Mandl and Thomson, 'Energy Poverty, Energy Equity in a World of High Demand and Low Supply' in Davidson and Gross (eds), *The Oxford Handbook of Energy and Society* (2018), 297 (297 ff.); Simcock et al., *Energy Poverty and Vulnerability – A Global Perspective* (2017); Guruswamy, *International Energy and Poverty – The emerging contours* (2015); Sovacool and Dworkin, *Global Energy Justice – Problems, Principles and Practices* (2014), 223 ff.

[64] See further: Bridge et al., *Energy and Society – A Critical Perspective* (2018), 200 ff.; Dyer and Trombetta, *International Handbook of Energy Security* (2013); Sovacool, *The Routledge Handbook of Energy Security* (2011); Goldthau and Sovacool, 'The uniqueness of the energy security, justice, and governance problem' (2012) 41 *Energy Policy*, 232 (232 ff.); Laldjebaev, Sovacool and Kassam, 'Energy security, poverty, and sovereignty – Complex interlinkages and compelling implications' in Guruswamy (ed), *International Energy and Poverty – The emerging contours* (2015), 97 (97 ff.); Urban, *Energy and Development* (2020), 30 ff.; Barton et al., *Energy Security – Managing Risk in a Dynamic Legal and Regulatory Environment* (2004).

[65] Laldjebaev and Sovacool and Kassam, 'Energy security, poverty, and sovereignty – Complex interlinkages and compelling implications' in Guruswamy (ed), *International Energy and Poverty – The emerging contours* (2015), 97 (98).

[66] Großmann and Kahlheber, 'Energy poverty in an intersectional perspective – On multiple deprivation, discriminatory systems, and the effects of policies' in Simcock et al. (eds), *Energy Poverty and Vulnerability – A Global Perspective* (2017), 12 (29).

[67] McKague et al., 'Understanding energy poverty through the energy cultures framework' in Simcock et al. (eds), *Energy Poverty and Vulnerability – A Global Perspective* (2017), 33 (33); Großmann and

the concept of energy vulnerability emphasises the distinction between energy poverty as a descriptor of a state at a given point in time, on the one hand, and vulnerability as a set of conditions that characterise the emergence and persistence of deprivation, on the other. Energy poverty also leads to significant health problems caused by emissions from open fires in poor households.

22   The vulnerability approach hinges upon the notion that energy poverty itself is a fluid state, which a household may enter or exit after an externally- or internally-induced change in housing, social, political or economic circumstances. As a result, the energy vulnerability demographic will always be larger than that of people who are energy poor. In essence, energy vulnerability thinking operates with risks and probabilities, because they express the likelihood of becoming energy poor. When combined with approaches that focus on the entire 'energy chain' via which utility services get delivered to consumers, the vulnerability paradigm destabilises the 'affordability-access binary to encompass the nature and structure of the built environment of the home, as well as the articulation of social practices and energy needs.'[68]

23   The aspect of reliability concerning energy services is of utmost importance within SDG 7. It refers to the permanent and largely disruption-free supply of modern (climate-friendly and renewable) energy. This can be impaired by several factors, such as poor or old infrastructure as well as external influences such as climatic distortions and the weather, thus making it difficult or impossible for people to access modern energy.[69] The importance of reliability arises from the overarching concept of energy security. The latter reflects the broad purpose of SDG 7.1 referring to reliable, adequate and affordable energy.[70] There are more than 40 different definitions for the concept of energy security so that the scope of energy security is not uniformly delineated which may even lead to incoherence and ambiguities regarding energy security.[71] The following definitions serve as a general overview.

24   The IEA defines energy security as 'the uninterrupted availability of energy sources at an affordable price'[72] which is similar to the definition of the European Commission.[73] Furthermore, energy security is described as 'a condition in which a nation and all, or most, of its citizens and businesses have access to sufficient energy resources at

---

Kahlheber, 'Energy poverty in an intersectional perspective – On multiple deprivation, discriminatory systems, and the effects of policies' in Simcock et al (eds), *Energy Poverty and Vulnerability – A Global Perspective* (2017), 12 (29).

[68] Bouzarovski et al., 'Introduction' in Simcock et al. (eds), *Energy Poverty and Vulnerability – A Global Perspective* (2017), 1 (3).

[69] Nhamo et al., *SDG 7 – Ensure Access to Affordable, Reliable, Sustainable, and Modern Energy* (2020), 68 ff.

[70] Crossley, *Renewable Energy Law – An International Assessment* (2019), 112.

[71] Von Hippel et al., 'Evaluating The Energy Security Impacts Of Energy Policies' in Sovacool (ed), *The Routledge Handbook of Energy Security* (2011), 74; Sovacool, 'Introduction – Defining, measuring and exploring energy security' in Sovacool (ed), *The Routledge Handbook of Energy Security* (2011), 3 ff.

[72] https://www.iea.org/topics/energy-security, the IEA states:
Energy security has many aspects: long-term energy security mainly deals with timely investments to supply energy in line with economic developments and environmental needs. On the other hand, short-term energy security focuses on the ability of the energy system to react promptly to sudden changes in the supply-demand balance.

[73] To be understood as '[u]ninterrupted physical availability of energy products on the market at a price which is affordable for all consumers (private and industrial)': European Commission, *Green Paper – Towards a European strategy for the security of energy supply* (29 November 2000) COM (2000) 769 final; see more recently https://ec.europa.eu/info/news/focus-energy-security-eu-2020-avr-27_en; European Commission, *Clean energy for all Europeans* (2019), 8 f.

reasonable prices for the foreseeable future free from serious risk of major disruption of service'.[74]

Energy sovereignty encompasses the ability of 'local people [to determine] their ener- 25
gy systems in ways that are culturally relevant and ecologically sustainable'[75] Besides, energy sovereignty is a framework that recognises the individual, community, or nation's rights, and strengthens their abilities to exercise choice within all components of energy systems, including sources, means of harnessing, and uses, in order to satisfy their needs for energy[76] with particular reference to the rights of indigenous people.[77]

With regard to SDG 7.2, there is a focus on renewable sources of energy,[78] con- 26
stituting one of the two strands of energy fuel source classification, alongside of fossil fuels.[79] 'Renewable energy includes all forms of energy produced from renewable sources in a sustainable manner, including bioenergy, geothermal energy, hydropower, ocean energy (including tidal, wave, and ocean thermal energy), solar energy, and wind energy'.[80] However, it should be noted that no universal legal definition of renewable energy exists to date. From the legal perspective, there is disagreement in 'whether certain types of energy should be deemed renewable and thus benefit from the programmes designed to accelerate their adoption, or whether they should be excluded on other

---

[74] Barton et al., 'Introduction' in Barton et al. (eds), *Energy Security – Managing Risk in a Dynamic Legal and Regulatory Environment* (2004), 1 (5); Crossley, *Renewable Energy Law – An International Assessment* (2019), 112; Sovacool, 'Introduction – Defining, measuring and exploring energy security' in Sovacool (ed), *The Routledge Handbook of Energy Security* (2011), 3.

[75] Laldjebaev and Sovacool and Kassam, 'Energy security, poverty, and sovereignty – Complex inter-linkages and compelling implications' in Guruswamy (ed), *International Energy and Poverty – The emerging contours* (2015), 97 (98).

[76] Laldjebaev and Sovacool and Kassam, 'Energy security, poverty, and sovereignty – Complex inter-linkages and compelling implications' in Guruswamy (ed), *International Energy and Poverty – The emerging contours* (2015), 97 (103).

[77] Laldjebaev and Sovacool and Kassam, 'Energy security, poverty, and sovereignty – Complex inter-linkages and compelling implications' in Guruswamy (ed), *International Energy and Poverty – The emerging contours* (2015), 97 (102).

[78] See further on renewable energy: Jelley, *Renewable Energy – A Very Short Introduction* (2020); Peake, *Renewable Energy – Power for a Sustainable Future* (2017); Everett et al., *Energy Systems and Sustainability – Power for a Sustainable Future* (2011).

[79] Crossley, *Renewable Energy Law – An International Assessment* (2019), 19; see also Wawryk, 'International Energy Law: An Emerging Academic Discipline' in Babie and Leadbeter (eds), *Law as Change – Engaging with the Life and Scholarship of Adrian Bradbrook* (2014), 223 (226): 'Energy sources may be renewable (an energy source that can be easily replenished) or nonrenewable (an energy source that is used up and cannot be recreated). Non-renewable energy sources include the fossil fuels — oil, natural gas, and coal — and uranium (used to make nuclear energy)'.

[80] See Statute of IRENA (162 Member States), Art. III:
In this Statute the term "renewable energy" means all forms of energy produced from renewable sources in a sustainable manner, which include, inter alia:
1. bioenergy;
2. geothermal energy;
3. hydropower;
4. ocean energy, including inter alia tidal, wave and ocean thermal energy;
5. solar energy; and
6. wind energy;
See also Wilder and Drake, 'International Law and the Renewable Energy Sector' in Carlarne and Gray and Tarasofsky (eds), *The Oxford Handbook of International Climate Change Law* (2016), 357 (361); IRENA/FC/Statute, *Statute of the International Renewable Energy Agency*, 26 January 2009, Article 3; Wawryk additionally mentions the following renewable energy sources:
hot dry rock, energy crops, wood waste, agricultural waste, waste from processing of agricultural products, food waste, food processing waste, bagasse, black liquor, biomass-based components of municipal solid waste, landfill gas, sewage gas and biomass-based components of sewage, Wawryk, 'International Energy Law – An Emerging Academic Discipline' in Babie and Leadbeter (eds), *Law as Change – Engaging with the Life and Scholarship of Adrian Bradbrook* (2014), 223 (226).

environmental and policy grounds'.[81] Certain energy sources, such as peat energy, are controversial due to their environmental impacts and are thus labelled as unsustainable, excluding these sources from the definition of 'renewable energy'. Nevertheless, from the legislative perspective, there are endorsements for a wider interpretation of 'renewable energy'. Some energy sources, such as nuclear energy, are not renewable *per se*. Yet, it is advocated that nuclear energy, for example, should nonetheless be included among the renewable energies 'if the purpose of the legislation is to encourage the accelerated deployment of low carbon electricity generation'.[82]

27 Since SDG 7 impacts all three dimensions of sustainable development, '[r]enewable energy technologies represent a major element in strategies for greening economies everywhere in the world and for tackling the critical global problem of climate change'.[83] The diverse definitions of renewable energy unite in that their consumption does not deplete their future availability. These include, albeit not conclusively, solar, wind, ocean, hydropower, geothermal resources, and bioenergy (in the case of bioenergy, which can be depleted, sources of bioenergy can be replaced within a short to medium-term frame). Readable from SDG indicator 7.2.1 is the focus

> on the amount of renewable energy actually consumed rather than the capacity for renewable energy production, which cannot always be fully utilized. By focusing on consumption by the end user, it avoids the distortions caused by the fact that conventional energy sources are subject to significant energy losses along the production chain.[84]

28 SDG 7.3 strives for the improvement in energy efficiency which has gained global awareness,[85] despite the fact that SDG 7.1 and SDG 7.2. have 'typically been prioritized compared to energy efficiency'.[86] Its comprehensive role within SDG 7 and the other SDGs becomes more clear with its definition. Energy efficiency aims at the reduction of energy consumption while delivering the same level of service.[87] Energy efficiency can act as an incentive for investments in clean energy and research into new energy concepts, as it offers benefits to both society and the economy, notably through cost savings from energy efficiency.[88] In this context, a specific type of energy source arises, alongside with fossil sources and renewable sources, when considering that 'energy conservation, which encompasses measures to reduce consumer demand for energy,

---

[81] Crossley, *Renewable Energy Law – An International Assessment* (2019), 19.

[82] Crossley, *Renewable Energy Law – An International Assessment* (2019), 19:
It is important to note that 'no form of energy is free from monetary and environmental costs', thus the final determination of what constitutes renewable energy is often the result of a politically mediated debate. This means that other factors such as the impact on local employment prospects and protecting indigenous energy sources for energy security reasons also tend to figure in debates about whether to include a particular energy source as 'renewable'.

[83] https://unstats.un.org/wiki/display/SDGeHandbook/Indicator+7.2.1.

[84] https://unstats.un.org/wiki/display/SDGeHandbook/Indicator+7.2.1; information on the international standard to develop energy statistics: UNDESA, *International Recommendations for Energy Statistics (IRES)* (2018).

[85] See e.g. UN and HLDE, *Theme Report on Energy, Access towards the Achievement Of SDG 7 and Net-Zero Emissions* (2021); UN and HLDE, *Theme Report on Energy Transition, Towards the Achievement of SDG 7 and Net-Zero Emissions* (2021), 45 ff.

[86] Monkelbaan, *Governance for the Sustainable Development Goals – Exploring an Integrative Framework of Theories, Tools and Competencies* (2019), 89.

[87] Monkelbaan, *Governance for the Sustainable Development Goals – Exploring an Integrative Framework of Theories, Tools and Competencies* (2019), 89.

[88] Monkelbaan, *Governance for the Sustainable Development Goals – Exploring an Integrative Framework of Theories, Tools and Competencies* (2019), 89.

including through improved energy efficiency, [and] may also be seen as an energy resource because of its potential role in satisfying society's demand for energy'.[89]

II. Legal Foundations

In determining the legal scope of SDG 7, it is important to note that there is no single   **29** international legal source on which the regulatory framework of all targets of SDG 7 is clearly and fully based. Nevertheless, there are certain particular but relevant sets of rules in the form of international, regional[90] and bilateral treaties,[91] as well as in the form of special international energy law.[92] In addition, rights and legal requirements also exist in the social sphere, particularly with regard to human rights.[93] The multifaceted aspects of SDG 7, ranging from access to affordable and modern energy, renewable energy sources and their delimitation and evaluation, to global energy efficiency and the necessary technologies and infrastructure, provide an introductory overview of the associated fragmented legal landscape. These various sources of legal provisions providing a guiding network for the SDG 7 implementation[94] are presented in terms of their essential significance and their position within the structure of SDG 7.

At the international stage, there are several treaties with the aim 'to facilitate de-   **30** centralised sustainable energy policy choices and investment' by balancing 'incentives and disincentives' in the energy sector.[95] States as well as non-state actors are hereby encouraged to implement a transition towards new, sustainable energy systems.[96] Due to their distinct nature of the particular area of regulation, those treaties are illuminated respectively within the following chapters.

There are various attempts and approaches to identify and delimitate the existence   **31** and scope of international energy law. There is no single international entity to be responsible for setting universal rules in the energy sector[97] but rather some organisations that are leading in specific energy regimes such as the IAEA in the nuclear law regime. It follows that a clear identification of an all-encompassing energy law in the international

---

[89] Wawryk, 'International Energy Law: An Emerging Academic Discipline' in Babie and Leadbeter (eds), *Law as Change – Engaging with the Life and Scholarship of Adrian Bradbrook* (2014), 223 (226); https://unstats.un.org/wiki/display/SDGeHandbook/Indicator+7.3.1.

[90] See e.g. Protocol for the implementation of the Alpine Convention of 1991 in the field of energy (1998).

[91] Bruce and Stephenson, 'SDG 7 on Sustainable Energy for All – Contributions of International Law, Policy and Governance' (2016) *UNEP/CISDL Issue Brief*.

[92] Nordtveit, 'International energy law in perspective – The relationship between national and international energy law' in Hunter et al. (eds), *The Routledge Handbook of Energy Law* (2020), 42 (42 ff.).

[93] Bruce and Stephenson, 'SDG 7 on Sustainable Energy for All – Contributions of International Law, Policy and Governance' (2016) *UNEP/CISDL Issue Brief*.

[94] Bruce and Stephenson, 'SDG 7 on Sustainable Energy for All – Contributions of International Law, Policy and Governance' (2016) *UNEP/CISDL Issue Brief*.

[95] Bruce and Stephenson, 'SDG 7 on Sustainable Energy for All – Contributions of International Law, Policy and Governance' (2016) *UNEP/CISDL Issue Brief*.

[96] Bruce and Stephenson, 'SDG 7 on Sustainable Energy for All – Contributions of International Law, Policy and Governance' (2016) *UNEP/CISDL Issue Brief*.

[97] Nordtveit, 'International energy law in perspective – The relationship between national and international energy law' in Hunter et al (eds), *The Routledge Handbook of Energy Law* (2020), 42 (47).

scene requires a progressive approach which then will help to understand the dynamic legal backgrounds[98] underlying SDG 7.[99]

32   For this purpose, the classification of energy law as such is to be addressed as the reference to international spheres of energy law can thus be made. Energy law depicts 'the rules and regulations that are relevant for energy activity or energy services throughout the whole life span of energy activity, from the division of energy resources, the production, transport, distribution and finally marketing of energy'.[100] Thus, energy law regulates 'the energy-related rights and duties of various stakeholders over the energy resources over the energy life-cycle'.[101] This is a highly valuable and significant approach, as all aspects of every type of energy activity is taken into account.[102] Stakeholders are not limited to being only states or only individuals. The diverse and dynamic field of energy activity throughout the globe includes multilateral financial institutions, private investors, international organisations, the energy industry, energy consumers as well as governments of developed and developing countries.[103] Nevertheless, energy law considers state actions to be within its sphere of influence and also takes into account and regulates interstate issues concerning the use of different energy sources.[104]

33   As mentioned above, international treaties on energy serve as a core source of international energy regulations,[105] alongside with other sources of international law such as customary law being established by international stakeholders in the energy sector.[106] The sources of international law mentioned in Art. 38 of Statute of the International Court of Justice[107] must therefore also be considered in case of the emergence and development of international energy law. Following these principles, 'customary international

---

[98] In addition to the existing forms of energy that we use on our planet, forms of energy generated in outer space, for example, are becoming increasingly important for the future energy design: IDEST, Craspart and Marescaux, *Legal Aspects of Solar Power Satellites, Final Report* (2020); Heffron, 'Thinking Globally: An Accelerated Just Transition to a Low-Carbon Economy' (2020) 1(1) *Global Energy Law and Sustainability*, ix-xiii.

[99] Nordtveit, 'International energy law in perspective – The relationship between national and international energy law' in Hunter et al (eds), *The Routledge Handbook of Energy Law* (2020), 42 (42).

[100] Nordtveit, 'International energy law in perspective – The relationship between national and international energy law' in Hunter et al (eds), *The Routledge Handbook of Energy Law* (2020), 42 (42).

[101] Heffron and Talus, 'The Evolution of Energy Law and Energy Jurisprudence – Insights for Energy Analysts and Researchers' (2016) 19 *Energy Res. Soc. Sci.*, 1 (2).

[102] '[…] all areas of the energy lifecycle from extraction to production to operation to consumption and waste management for all energy sources', Heffron and Talus, 'The Evolution of Energy Law and Energy Jurisprudence – Insights for Energy Analysts and Researchers' (2016) 19 *Energy Res. Soc. Sci.* 1 (2).

[103] Vedavalli, *Energy for Development – Twenty-First Century Challenges of Reform and Liberalization in Developing Countries* (2007), XX f., 437.

[104] Talus, 'Internationalization of energy law' in Talus (ed), *Research Handbook on International Energy Law* (2014), 3 (3 f.).

[105] Bruce and Stephenson, 'SDG 7 on Sustainable Energy for All – Contributions of International Law, Policy and Governance' (2016) *UNEP/CISDL Issue Brief.*

[106] Wawryk, 'International Energy Law – An Emerging Academic Discipline' in Babie and Leadbeter (eds), *Law as Change – Engaging with the Life and Scholarship of Adrian Bradbrook* (2014), 223 (227).

[107] Article 38 ICJ Statute:

1. The Court, whose function is to decide in accordance with international law such disputes as are submitted to it, shall apply:

a. international conventions, whether general or particular, establishing rules expressly recognized by the contesting states;

b. international custom, as evidence of a general practice accepted as law;

c. the general principles of law recognized by civilized nations;

d. subject to the provisions of Article 59, judicial decisions and the teachings of the most highly qualified publicists of the various nations, as subsidiary means for the determination of rules of law.

law [basically] applies to all states' whereas treaties and conventions generally only commit states being party to the respective treaty or convention.[108]

Moreover, national energy laws and national energy principles constitute an impor-   **34** tant benchmark and starting point for global energy principles and international legal guidelines.[109] The role of national energy laws and existing 'regulatory principles'[110] has increased for the international energy law framework as various factors contributed to the internationalisation of national legal principles and instruments. These factors are, for instance, the transboundary interstate dependence on certain energy sources encouraged states to create harmonised and efficient cooperation as well as the strive of states 'to attract international investment in energy projects'[111] which requires national laws aligned to the needs of foreign investors.[112]

Besides, soft law, such as 'treaties expressed in non-mandatory language, and also   **35** the non-binding codes, guidelines, resolutions, directives, standards or model codes of international bodies, including intergovernmental organisations', forms a source of international energy law.[113] The SDGS enshrined in the Global Agenda 2030 in the form of a UNGA resolution also belong to the category of soft law,[114] which means that they can influence international law to a certain extent and may guide it in a certain direction. Combining these three types of sources, international energy law[115] can be described as a conglomeration of rules of custom, treaties, national and regional laws, and principles of intergovernmental and non-governmental international institutions,

---

[108] Nordtveit, 'International energy law in perspective – The relationship between national and international energy law' in Hunter et al (eds), *The Routledge Handbook of Energy Law* (2020), 42 (47).

[109] '[…] such as licensing contracts and production sharing contracts in the petroleum industry, systems for the trading of natural gas or electricity, access to transport facilities […]', Nordtveit, 'International energy law in perspective – The relationship between national and international energy law' in Hunter et al (eds), *The Routledge Handbook of Energy Law* (2020), 42 (43); Wawryk, 'International Energy Law – An Emerging Academic Discipline' in Babie and Leadbeter (eds), *Law as Change – Engaging with the Life and Scholarship of Adrian Bradbrook* (2014), 223 (227).

[110] […] regulatory principles relevant to energy law […] [for example] common principles of energy law applied across countries, even though there is no treaty binding the Parties to apply these principles of law. An example is the global spread of principles of national laws for deregulating national electricity and gas industries; Wawryk, 'International Energy Law – An Emerging Academic Discipline' in Babie and Leadbeter (eds), *Law as Change – Engaging with the Life and Scholarship of Adrian Bradbrook* (2014), 223 (227).

[111] Nordtveit, 'International energy law in perspective – The relationship between national and international energy law' in Hunter et al (eds), *The Routledge Handbook of Energy Law* (2020), 42 (46).

[112] Nordtveit, 'International energy law in perspective – The relationship between national and international energy law' in Hunter et al (eds), *The Routledge Handbook of Energy Law* (2020), 42 (44 ff.), see for a detailed depiction of national energy law's internationalisation: Wawryk, 'International Energy Law – An Emerging Academic Discipline' in Babie and Leadbeter (eds), *Law as Change – Engaging with the Life and Scholarship of Adrian Bradbrook* (2014), 223 (228 ff.).

[113] Wawryk, 'International Energy Law – An Emerging Academic Discipline' in Babie and Leadbeter (eds), *Law as Change – Engaging with the Life and Scholarship of Adrian Bradbrook* (2014), 223 (227).

[114] On the question of the extent to which Agenda 2030 and the SDGs have legal force: Huck and Kurkin, 'The UN Sustainable Development Goals (SDGs) in the Transnational Multilevel System' (2018) 2 *HJIL/ZaöRV*, 375 (391 f.); Huck, 'SDGs im transnationalen Recht – bindend oder nicht bindend, das sei hier die Frage!' in Huck (ed), *Direct Effects of UN Sustainable Development Goals (SDGs) – Umsetzung und Anwendung der SDGs in der Praxis – Sachstand und Perspektive* (2019), 4 (4 ff.); see on the role of soft law in international law making: Boyle, 'Soft-law in international law making' in Evans (ed), *International Law* (2014), 118 (118 ff.); Thirlway, *The Sources of International Law* (2019), 186 ff.

[115] See further on international energy law: Hunter et al. (eds), *The Routledge Handbook of Energy Law* (2020); Naseem, *International Energy Law* (2017); Zedalis, *International Energy Law – Rules Governing Future Exploration, Exploitation and Use of Renewable Resources* (2016); Talus, *Research Handbook on International Energy Law* (2014); Park, *International Law for Energy and the Environment* (2013); Lyster and Bradbrook, *Energy Law and the Environment* (2006), 34 ff.

which together regulate the various facets of energy production, supply, consumption and trade.[116]

36   Consequently, international energy law[117] may be regarded as one of many international law disciplines, alongside with e.g. international human rights law, international environmental law and the law of the sea.[118] Furthermore, international energy law is, to a large extent, supplemented by specific legal regulations of individual energy sources, such as wind energy, oil and gas energy, nuclear energy, hydropower energy, solar energy or fossil fuels.[119]

37   The wide-ranging content of international energy law thus covers areas at multiple levels of the law, which can be roughly divided into the following categories in the context of the present analysis of SDG 7: (a) States' roles in energy related issues (all targets) and (b) social rights such as human rights (special focus on SDG 7.1 with an overall importance for all targets of SDG 7). All these areas contain subsections, which are examined in more detail below.

III. States' Roles in Energy related Issues

38   Energy is indispensably important for a states' proper functioning and its striving for economic growth and prosperity.[120] Therefore, it is the aspiration of states to seek new energy sources and systems to meet national energy needs,[121] giving states an increasingly significant role in the global energy scene.[122] This is not least due to the fact that 'energy resources are unevenly distributed around the world, making some countries energy exporters and other importers'.[123] These highly dynamic conditions lead to a considerable degree of interdependence between states concerning global energy networks. This inevitably results in different interests between energy-exporting countries and countries that rely on energy imports.[124] International regulations are of major relevance and legal principles such as the sovereignty of states over their own

---

[116] Wawryk, 'International Energy Law – An Emerging Academic Discipline' in Babie and Leadbeter (eds), *Law as Change – Engaging with the Life and Scholarship of Adrian Bradbrook* (2014), 223 (228).

[117] Lyster and Bradbook, *Energy Law and the Environment* (2006), 34 ff.

[118] Nordtveit, 'International energy law in perspective – The relationship between national and international energy law' in Hunter et al. (eds), *The Routledge Handbook of Energy Law* (2020), 42 (43).

[119] Wawryk, 'International Energy Law – An Emerging Academic Discipline' in Babie and Leadbeter (eds), *Law as Change – Engaging with the Life and Scholarship of Adrian Bradbrook* (2014), 223 (236 ff.).

[120] A/69/700, *The road to dignity by 2030: ending poverty, transforming all lives and protecting the planet, Synthesis report of the Secretary-General on the post-2015 sustainable development agenda*, 4 December 2014, para. 74.

[121] Wilson, 'Energy Interdependence' in Hancook and Allison (eds), *The Oxford Handbook of Energy Politics* (2021), 151 (151).

[122] See Sovacool and Florini, 'Examining the Complications of Global Energy Governance' (2012) 30 *J. Energy Nat. Resour. Law*, 235 (235 ff.).

[123] Nordtveit, 'International energy law in perspective – The relationship between national and international energy law' in Hunter et al (eds), *The Routledge Handbook of Energy Law* (2020), 42 (45); see also: Wilson, 'Energy Interdependence' in Hancook and Allison (eds), *The Oxford Handbook of Energy Politics* (2021), 151 (151): 'Energy-rich producers need to gain access to important markets for capital and exports, while energy-poor consumers need to access affordable energy inputs from abroad.'

[124] Wilson, 'Energy Interdependence' in Hancook and Allison (eds), *The Oxford Handbook of Energy Politics* (2021), 151 (151): 'Producers [of energy exporting countries] favor high prices that maximize returns, consumers [energy importing countries] prefer low prices that improve energy security, and both sides seek to set international rules that vest them with control over these important markets. Energy interdependence is therefore a coordination game, in which the benefits of intergovernmental cooperation are overlaid by distributional tensions over how to share joint gains.'

resources or their access to energy resources provide an important contribution to regulation.[125]

Nevertheless, it is of main importance to holistically consider the different regimes of 39 energy law on the one hand, and States' distinct roles on the other. As the International Law Association (ILA) indicates that there is

> a need to address the interconnectedness between sustainable energy and the management of food and water resources through a nexus governance approach. There is also a need to consider activities in relation to ocean resources such as methane hydrates. States should ensure that there is transparency and oversight in the regulation and management of sustainable and renewable energy as a sector.[126]

Therefore, States 'should adapt their legal and regulatory systems for energy [to] 40 promote and incentivize the generation and use of sustainable and renewable energy across all sectors and the economy as a whole, and support energy citizenship'.[127]

1. The Principle of National Resource Sovereignty

States hold a fundamental right to control their natural resources within their own 41 territory based on the principle of permanent sovereignty over natural resources, being 'closely connected with energy resources'.[128] This directly includes the states' right to independently use and benefit[129] from their own natural resources as well as establish the legal rules for the use. Besides, national sovereignty over natural resources encompasses 'the right to decide if the resources shall be exploited and how and when in such a case this shall take place'.[130]

Particularly due to the aspirations of post-colonial states, the scope of this principle is 42 laid on several United Nations resolutions and declarations shaping the national leeway over national resources.[131] The 1962 United Nations General Assembly (UNGA) Resolution 1803 constitutes the permanent sovereignty over natural resources with added emphasis on the term 'permanent'.[132] The principle of national sovereignty was further established in 1974 UNGA Resolution 3281 (XXIX)[133] and in international declarations

---

[125] Nordtveit, 'International energy law in perspective – The relationship between national and international energy law' in Hunter et al (eds), *The Routledge Handbook of Energy Law* (2020), 42 (45, 49).

[126] ILA, Resolution 1/2020, *Committee on the Procedure of International Courts and Tribunals, The 79th Kyoto Conference of the International Law Association*, 29 November-13 December 2020, 17.

[127] ILA, Resolution 1/2020, *Committee on the Procedure of International Courts and Tribunals, The 79th Kyoto Conference of the International Law Association*, 29 November-13 December 2020, 17.

[128] Heffron et al., 'A treatise for energy law' (2018) 11 *JWELB*, 34 (39).

[129] Including the right to guide the search for and the specific use of energy sources by making use of the profits of the natural resources.

[130] Nordtveit, 'International energy law in perspective – The relationship between national and international energy law' in Hunter et al (eds), *The Routledge Handbook of Energy Law* (2020), 42 (49).

[131] Heffron et al., 'A treatise for energy law' (2018) 11 *JWELB*, 34 (40).

[132] A/RES/1803(XVII), *Permanent sovereignty over natural resources*, 14 December 1962, stating in the preamble: 'the inalienable right of all States freely to dispose of their natural wealth and resources in accordance with their national interests, and on respect for the economic independence of States'; see also Revised African Convention on the Conservation of Nature and Natural Resources (2003).

[133] A/RES/3281(XXIX), *Charter of Economic Rights and Duties of States*, 12 December 1974, Art. 2(1): Every State has and shall freely exercise full permanent sovereignty, including possession, use and disposal, over all its wealth, natural resources and economic activities; and Art. 3: In the exploitation of natural resources shared by two or more countries, each State must co-operate on the basis of a system of information and prior consultations in order to achieve optimum use of such resources without causing damage to the legitimate interest of others.

such as the Stockholm Declaration of 1972[134] and the Rio Declaration of 1992.[135] Although the principle of permanent national sovereignty over natural resources is recognised in international law,[136] there are far-reaching pressures on this principle from several other legal tendencies such as human rights aspects in the energy sector, environmental concerns in the use of energy and diplomatic requirements that affect a nations' total sovereignty.[137] In this context, the term of energy sovereignty largely coincides with that of national sovereignty over natural resources, although energy sovereignty additionally focuses on the rights of individuals and groups within a state in relation with energy (→ Goal 7 mn. 25) In particular, the position of indigenous peoples under energy sovereignty against the background of human rights are to be mentioned. Energy sovereignty is going beyond the nation level and further encompasses the household and community level within states.[138]

43   Within the principle of national sovereignty, the sovereignty over offshore energy resources particularly stands out in connection with the 1982 United Nations Conventions on the Law of the Sea (UNCLOS). The increasing application and use of offshore wind turbines or any other marine energy source entails legal questions concerning states' coastal sovereignty over the territorial areas in the sea.[139] For this purpose, UNCLOS provides a suitable framework for the establishment of binding rights and duties for states facilitating the regulation for the construction and use of marine renewable energy sources within the exclusive economic zone[140] and the continental shelf[141] of coastal states.[142] These clear regulations, with special focus on Arts. 56(1) (a) and 77(1) UNC-

---

[134] A/RES/2994 (XXVII), *Declaration of the UN Conference on the Human Environment* (1972), Principle 21:

States have, in accordance with the Charter of the United Nations and the principles of international law, the sovereign right to exploit their own resources pursuant to their own environmental policies, and the responsibility to ensure that activities within their jurisdiction or control do not cause damage to the environment of other States or of areas beyond the limits of national jurisdiction.

[135] A_CONF.151_26_Vol.I, *Declaration of the UN Conference on the Environment and Development* (1992), Principle 21.

[136] Heffron et al., 'A treatise for energy law' (2018) 11 *JWELB*, 34 (40): the framework for the exercise of national sovereignty is provided by national jurisprudence.

[137] Nordtveit, 'International energy law in perspective – The relationship between national and international energy law' in Hunter et al. (eds), *The Routledge Handbook of Energy Law* (2020), 42 (50).

[138] Laldjebaev and Sovacool and Kassam, 'Energy security, poverty, and sovereignty – Complex interlinkages and compelling implications' in Guruswamy (ed), *International Energy and Poverty – The emerging contours* (2015), 97 (102 ff.); see also Carpenter and Jampolsky, 'Indigenous peoples – from energy poverty to energy empowerment' in Guruswamy (ed), *International Energy and Poverty – The emerging contours* (2015), 39 (39 ff.).

[139] Bruce and Stephenson, 'SDG 7 on Sustainable Energy for All – Contributions of International Law, Policy and Governance' (2016) *UNEP/CISDL Issue Brief*, 4.

[140] Definition of exclusive economic zone in Art. 55 UNCLOS:

The exclusive economic zone is an area beyond and adjacent to the territorial sea, subject to the specific legal regime established in this Part, under which the rights and jurisdiction of the coastal State and the rights and freedoms of other States are governed by the relevant provisions of this Convention.

[141] *United Nations Convention on the Law of the Sea*, 10 December 1982, Art. 77(1): 'The coastal State exercises over the continental shelf sovereign rights for the purpose of exploring it and exploiting its natural resources'; definition of continental shelf: Art. 76(1) UNCLOS:

The continental shelf of a coastal State comprises the seabed and subsoil of the submarine areas that extend beyond its territorial sea throughout the natural prolongation of its land territory to the outer edge of the continental margin, or to a distance of 200 nautical miles from the baselines from which the breadth of the territorial sea is measured where the outer edge of the continental margin does not extend up to that distance.

[142] Nordtveit, 'International energy law in perspective – The relationship between national and international energy law' in Hunter et al (eds), *The Routledge Handbook of Energy Law* (2020), 42 (51):

LOS help to foster and enhance the objectives of SDG 7.2, SDG 7.a and SDG 7.b[143] since states are legally entitled and enabled to explore and exploit the coastal zone for energy generation through 'water, currents and wind'.[144] Specific commitments to cooperation between states, e.g. to promote and transfer marine-related technologies and science[145] and to support developing countries in the field of maritime technology[146] 'may further assist attainment of SDG 7'.[147]

2. Energy Diplomacy and Energy Security

The interdependence of states on the energy market leads to strategic action of a **44** state with regard to others to fulfil its own energy needs and to enhance economic growth. Therefore, states must gain access to the energy sources they need through contracts with energy providing states, e.g. by setting up geopolitical energy policies or global energy governance policies. In this regard, states seek cooperative approaches with other states[148] but moreover seek to work jointly with private actors or associations on standards to ensure a reliable energy supply.[149]

One example is the ASEAN Centre for Energy (ACE), ASEAN Plan of Action for **45** Energy Cooperation (APAEC) 2016-2025, PHASE II: 2021 – 2025, 2020, Jakarta. The APAEC Phase II: 2021-2025 builds on the outcome of the APAEC Phase I: 2016 – 2020 and sets out ambitious targets and initiatives to enhance energy security and sustainability and thus also supports SDG 7. Another example is the decision to intensify cooperation between the EU and the ADEA which includes energy.[150]

Compared to the energy sector, there are similar cooperation attempts in the field of **46** international watercourses, summarised under term of water diplomacy, going beyond the strict interpretation of territorial sovereignty in matters of cooperative water sharing (→ Goal 6 mn. 21, 85).[151] Related to this, another possible instrument for states to meet their energy needs is establishing diplomatic relations in the energy sector called

---

The sovereignty over the EEZ [exclusive economic zone] and the continental shelf is still not as total as overland territory and the territorial waters. The jurisdiction over the EEZ and continental shelf is limited to what is needed for exploration of the natural resources under coast state jurisdiction;
see also Art. 56(1) (a) UNCLOS.

[143] Bruce and Stephenson, 'SDG 7 on Sustainable Energy for All – Contributions of International Law, Policy and Governance' (2016) *UNEP/CISDL Issue Brief*, 4.

[144] *United Nations Convention on the Law of the Sea*, 10 December 1982, Article 56(1) (a):
In the exclusive economic zone, the coastal State has: (a) sovereign rights for the purpose of exploring and exploiting, conserving and managing the natural resources, whether living or non-living, of the waters superjacent to the seabed and of the seabed and its subsoil, and with regard to other activities for the economic exploitation and exploration of the zone, such as the production of energy from the water, currents and winds.

[145] Art. 266(1) UNCLOS.

[146] Art. 266(2), Art. 269(1) UNCLOS.

[147] Bruce and Stephenson, 'SDG 7 on Sustainable Energy for All – Contributions of International Law, Policy and Governance' (2016) *UNEP/CISDL Issue Brief*.

[148] Wilson, 'Energy Interdependence' in Hancook and Allison (eds), *The Oxford Handbook of Energy Politics* (2021), 151 (152).

[149] Huck, 'Informal International Law-Making in the ASEAN: Consensus, Informality, and Accountability' (2020) 80(1) *ZaöRV/HJIL*, 101 (132).

[150] Federal Government (FRG), *Guidelines on the Indo-Pacific* (2020), 15, 31 [CLIENT II], renewables 33; Master Plan on ASEAN Connectivity 2025 (2016), 54; further reading Barra and Svec, 'Reinforcing Energy Governance under the EU Energy Diplomacy: A Proposal for Strengthening Energy Frameworks in Africa' (2018) 9(2) *European Journal of Risk Regulation*, 245-67.

[151] Nordtveit, 'International energy law in perspective – The relationship between national and international energy law' in Hunter et al. (eds), *The Routledge Handbook of Energy Law* (2020), 42 (50).

'energy diplomacy'.[152] The comparison to water diplomacy is highly accurate as energy diplomacy can also be divided into two purposes: (1) to meet the national energy demands and (2) to prevent conflicts.[153] Taking into account the example of transboundary watercourse diplomacy, there is an apparent energy related aspect when it comes to dam building matters. Here, a clear reference to the concept of water diplomacy in SDG 6 can be made.

47   In the case of the Nile Basin, Ethiopia is seeking to harness hydropower through the construction of the Grand Ethiopian Renaissance Dam (GERD), which would directly impact the river water flow in the neighbouring countries such as Egypt and Sudan.[154] This example illustrates the conflict-preventing function of energy diplomacy, as riparian countries strive to find a cooperative solution to avoid a possible armed conflict.[155]

48   To meet national energy demands, energy-importing states may also enter into diplomatic relations with energy exporting states. For those importing states, access to energy can be qualified 'as a national priority and thus a vulnerability'.[156] Energy vulnerability in this sense is directly connected to a country's productive and economic power and ability to provide enough economic capacity and growth for employment as well as to a country's social stability and the supply of sufficient energy to its population.[157] On the other side, the energy exporting countries see themselves in a strengthened position towards importing countries and this might have unjust impacts on the global energy market.[158]

49   Here, legal rules transfer obligations to states when it comes to transborder energy supplies and cooperative approaches. The obligation to cooperate is found, for example, in the framework of marine energy resources, namely in Arts. 74(3) and 83(3) of UNCLOS. Furthermore, the principle of cooperation laid down the United Nations Charter Arts. 1 and 2 provide a basis for the obligation to cooperate.[159]

50   Moreover, energy diplomacy includes the concept of energy security in combination with the objective of SDG 7.1 to ensure universal access to affordable, reliable and modern energy which holds a significant function. SDG 7.1 not only covers the social aspect of an individual's access to energy (→ Goal 7 mn. 14 f., 56). States are obliged to ensure reliable, modern and affordable energy supplies from energy exporting countries once there is not enough energy in their own territory. Thus, states seek to guarantee energy

---

[152] Herman, 'Energy as an Instrument in Global Politics' in Hancook and Allison (eds), *The Oxford Handbook of Energy Politics* (2021), 293 (296).

[153] Zeitoun, Mirumachi and Warner, *Water Conflicts – Analysis for Transformation* (2020), 5 ff., 109; Herranz-Surrallés, 'Energy diplomacy under scrutiny: parliamentary control of intergovernmental agreements with third-country suppliers' (2017) 40 *West Eur. Polit.*, 183 (191 f); Herman, 'Energy as an Instrument in Global Politics' in Hancook and Allison (eds), *The Oxford Handbook of Energy Politics* (2021), 293 (294, 296).

[154] Kimenyi and Mbaku, *Governing the Nile River Basin – The Search for a New Legal Regime* (2015), 105 ff.; see further Yihdego, *The Fairness 'Dilemma' in Sharing the Nile Waters: What Lessons from the Grand Ethiopian Renaissance Dam for International Law?* (2017).

[155] Berndtsson et al., 'The Grand Ethiopian Renaissance Dam – Conflict and Water Diplomacy in the Nile Bassin' in Islam and Madani (eds), *Water Diplomacy in Action – Contingent Approaches to Managing Complex Water Problems* (2017), 253 (253 ff.).

[156] Herman, 'Energy as an Instrument in Global Politics' in Hancook and Allison (eds), *The Oxford Handbook of Energy Politics* (2021), 293 (296).

[157] Herman, 'Energy as an Instrument in Global Politics' in Hancook and Allison (eds), *The Oxford Handbook of Energy Politics* (2021), 293 (296).

[158] Herman, 'Energy as an Instrument in Global Politics' in Hancook and Allison (eds), *The Oxford Handbook of Energy Politics* (2021), 293 (296).

[159] Nordtveit, 'International energy law in perspective – The relationship between national and international energy law' in Hunter et al (eds), *The Routledge Handbook of Energy Law* (2020), 42 (52).

security for a reliable and constant access to energy resources, may it be of internal or external source. Energy security encompasses the assurance of

> the physical availability of oil and gas imports, notwithstanding the rising prominence of electricity in the global supply mix [...] [ranging to] geopolitical relations associated with the international energy trade, particularly with respect to the need to manage oil markets.[160]

Hereby, energy conservation may serve as a suitable instrument for the maintenance   **51** of energy security.[161] The principle of affordability of energy is one of four principles within the concept of energy security, alongside with availability, accessibility and acceptability of energy.[162]

Energy security is threatened by poor energy infrastructure.[163] Energy security can be   **52** supported by increased energy efficiency, revealing a clear link between SDG 7.1, SDG 7.2 and especially SDG 7.3. The IEA indicates that

> [b]y reducing overall energy demand, efficiency can reduce reliance on imports of oil, gas and coal. Energy efficiency can therefore play a crucial role in ensuring both long- and short-term energy security in a cost-effective manner. Energy efficiency also reduces the likelihood of supply interruptions; the only energy source that cannot be interrupted is the energy that is not used. Also, in the event of a disruption, efficiency measures can work with emergency conservation measures to reduce demand.[164]

Treaties of legal significance for the energy sector contain the 1994 Energy Charter   **53** Treaty (ECT),[165] including its Protocol on Energy Efficiency and Related Environmental Aspects, also called Energy Efficiency Protocol (SDG 7.3, SDG 7.a) which provides principles and guidance for the promotion and development of energy efficient and cooperative policies that are consistent with sustainable development and fuller reflect environmental costs and benefits, Art. 1 (2) (a) – (c). The ECT as a multilateral framework for energy cooperation is 'designed to promote energy security through more open and competitive energy markets, respecting the principles of sustainable development and sovereignty over energy resources, based on the principles in the Energy Charter.'[166] The ECT concerns the effective implementation of SDG 7 with 'a broad range of obligations in support of SDG 7, including free trade in energy materials and products, freedom of energy transit through pipelines and grids, investment protection and dispute resolution'[167] as well as prioritising the promotion of renewable energy and cleaner fuels. The ECT serves important incentives for 'facilitating cooperation and knowledge ex-

---

[160] Bridge et al., *Energy and Society – A Critical Perspective* (2018), 204.

[161] Bridge et al., *Energy and Society – A Critical Perspective* (2018), 205.

[162] Bridge et al., *Energy and Society – A Critical Perspective* (2018), 207, affordability and acceptability include moral and ethical questions regarding energy and sustainable development.

[163] Cherp and Jewell, 'The concept of energy security: Beyond the four As' (2014) 75 *Energy Policy*, 415 (419).

[164] https://www.iea.org/reports/multiple-benefits-of-energy-efficiency/energy-security.

[165] *Energy Charter Treaty*, opened for signature 17 December 1994 (entered into force 16 April 1998); further reading Hobér, *Energy Charter Treaty – A Commentary* (2020); Leal-Arcas, *Commentary on the Energy Charter Treaty* (2018); concerning investment dispute settlement under the ECT: Roe and Happold, *Settlement of Investment Disputes under the Energy Charter Treaty* (2011).

[166] https://eur-lex.europa.eu/legal-content/EN/TXT/HTML/?uri=LEGISSUM:l27028&from=EN.

[167] CISDL, Cordonier Segger and Harrington, *SDG 7 on Sustainable Energy for All, A Toolkit of Legal & Institutional Practices* (2019), 24; Bruce and Stephenson, 'SDG 7 on Sustainable Energy for All – Contributions of International Law, Policy and Governance' (2016) *UNEP/CISDL Issue Brief*, 5 f.

change'[168] in particular by supporting energy legislation development in developing countries (SDG 7.a and SDG 7.b).[169]

54   The Statute of the International Renewable Energy Agency (IRENA Statute)[170] forms another important legal component with a focus on renewable energies.[171] Comparable to the ECT, the IRENA Statute regulates information exchange and knowledge transfer and promotes international cooperation in the scope of SDG 7.2, SDG 7.a and SDG 7.b.[172] The United Nations Framework Convention on Climate Change (UNFCCC) including its Kyoto Protocol and Paris Agreement lay legal foundations for the states to actively combat climate change with close linkages to energy and energy transformations.[173]

55   On the global trade scene, the WTO sets relevant trade instruments and within trade, investment[174] in the energy sector is a core factor for achieving SDG 7 to set up infrastructure and clean energy technology (SDG 7.a).[175]

3. The Social Scope of Energy

56   SDG 7.1 strives for the universal access to affordable, reliable and modern energy services which includes the access of every single household to these energy services.

---

[168] Bruce and Stephenson, 'SDG 7 on Sustainable Energy for All – Contributions of International Law, Policy and Governance' (2016) *UNEP/CISDL Issue Brief*, 6.

[169] Bruce and Stephenson, 'SDG 7 on Sustainable Energy for All – Contributions of International Law, Policy and Governance' (2016) *UNEP/CISDL Issue Brief*, 6.

[170] IRENA/FC/Statute, *Statute of the International Renewable Energy Agency*, 26 January 2009; Wilder and Drake, 'International Law and the Renewable Energy Sector' in Carlarne and Gray and Tarasofsky (eds), *The Oxford Handbook of International Climate Change Law* (2016), 357 (363 ff.); see also Pan-Arab Renewable Energy Strategy 2030 of the League of Arab States (2013).

[171] See Bruce, 'International Law and Renewable Energy – Facilitating Sustainable Energy for All?' (2013) 14 *Melb. J. Int'l L.*, 34 (34 ff.); Bruce, 'Climate Change Mitigation through Energy Efficiency Laws – from International Obligations to Domestic Regulation' (2013) 31 *J. Energy Nat. Resour. Law*, 327 (327 f.).

[172] IRENA Statute, Art. 4:

As a centre of excellence for renewable energy technology and acting as a facilitator and catalyst, providing experience for practical applications and policies, offering support on all matters relating to renewable energy and helping countries to benefit from the efficient development and transfer of knowledge and technology [...];

Bruce and Stephenson, 'SDG 7 on Sustainable Energy for All – Contributions of International Law, Policy and Governance' (2016) *UNEP/CISDL Issue Brief*, 2.

[173] Bruce and Stephenson, 'SDG 7 on Sustainable Energy for All – Contributions of International Law, Policy and Governance' (2016) *UNEP/CISDL Issue Brief*, 3; United Nations Framework Convention on Climate Change, 9 May 1992, preamble, para. 22:

Recognizing that all countries, especially developing countries, need access to resources required to achieve sustainable social and economic development and that, in order for developing countries to progress towards that goal, their energy consumption will need to grow taking into account the possibilities for achieving greater energy efficiency and for controlling greenhouse gas emissions in general, including through the application of new technologies on terms which make such an application economically and socially beneficial [...].

[174] See Cameron, *International Energy Investment Law –The Pursuit of Stability* (2010); Nadakavukaren Schefer, *International Investment Law –Text, Cases and Materials* (2020); Alam and Bhuiyan and Razzaque, *International Natural Resources Law, Investment and Sustainability* (2019); Miles, *Research Handbook on Environment and Investment Law* (2019).

[175] Bruce and Stephenson, 'SDG 7 on Sustainable Energy for All – Contributions of International Law, Policy and Governance' (2016) *UNEP/CISDL Issue Brief*, 4; Bacchus, *The Willing World – Shaping and Sharing a Sustainable Global Prosperity* (2018), 246 ff.; Cottier et al., 'Energy in WTO law and policy' in Cottier and Delimatsis (eds), *The Prospects of International Trade Regulation – From Fragmentation to Coherence* (2011), 211 (211 ff.); Ottinger, 'Legal Frameworks for Energy for Sustainable Development' in Bradbook et al. (eds), *The Law of Energy for Sustainable Development* (2005), 103 (103 ff.); Bradbook and Wahnshafft, 'International Law and Global Sustainable Energy Production and Consumption' in Bradbook et al. (eds), *The Law of Energy for Sustainable Development* (2005), 181 (181 ff.).

Thus, SDG 7 is more than only a state-related goal. It puts important aspirations for the individual's energy supply. In this context, the key concepts are energy poverty, energy justice, energy vulnerability of certain groups as well as human rights based approaches.

Energy justice is a newly emerged concept being envisaged throughout the other concepts of energy poverty, human rights and also international law.[176] Energy justice covers concerns regarding the accessibility of energy as well as 'the whole chain of energy utilization, all participants on the benefit and harm of justice in a more systematic view that concerns justice problems in energy use'.[177]   **57**

Energy poverty is of certain concern as it deprives people of a full participation in society, especially affecting society's most vulnerable groups, such as women, children and indigenous peoples.[178]   **58**

Within the human rights framework, the question of whether a human right to energy exists, even in an indirect manner, attracts increased attention.[179]   **59**

C. Interdependences of SDG 7

Following the background and origin of SDG 7, ensuring access to energy constitutes an important enabler for most other SDGs. With the Stockholm Declaration, the connection of clean, sustainable energy to 'most effective development of the world's energy resources, with due regard to the environmental effects of energy production and use'[180] is identified as a key factor to address climate change, with the then particular emphasis on the pollution of radioactive waste or nuclear emissions, the siting of the ultimate storage areas and transporting. This assessment of nuclear energy can still be found today, for example, in the Federal Republic of Germany or Austria, while worldwide the focus shifted to CO_2-neutrality of this form of energy and thus its supporting function in the combating of climate change.   **60**

But moreover, with the 2012 The future we want declaration it was recognised that   **61**

> access to sustainable modern energy services contributes to poverty eradication, saves lives, improves health and helps to provide for basic human needs. We stress that these services are essential to social inclusion and gender equality, and that energy is also a key input to production.[181]

---

[176] Del Guayo et al., *Energy Justice and Energy Law* (2020), 5.

[177] Guoyu and Guan and Li, 'Energy Justice and Construction of Community with a Shared Future of Mankind' in Bombaerts et al. (eds), *Energy Justice Across Borders* (2020), 217 (219).

[178] McKague et al., 'Understanding energy poverty through the energy cultures framework' in Simcock et al. (eds), *Energy Poverty and Vulnerability* (2017), 33 (33 ff.); Großmann and Kahlheber, 'Energy poverty in an intersectional perspective – On multiple deprivation, discriminatory systems, and the effects of policies' in Simcock et al. (eds), *Energy Poverty and Vulnerability – A Global Perspective* (2017), 12 (12 ff.); Carpenter and Jampolsky, 'Indigenous peoples – from energy poverty to energy empowerment' in Guruswamy (ed), *International Energy and Poverty – The emerging contours* (2015), 39 (39 ff.); Wickramasinghe, 'Energy for rural women – beyond energy access' in Guruswamy (ed), *International Energy and Poverty – The emerging contours* (2015), 231 (231 ff.); Bridge et al., *Energy and Society – A Critical Perspective* (2018), 129 ff.

[179] Brugger, 'Reflections on the moral foundations of a right to energy' in Guruswamy (ed), *International Energy and Poverty – The emerging contours* (2015), 68 (68 ff.); Bradbook and Gardam, 'Placing Access to Energy Services within a Human Rights Framework' (2006) 28 *HRQ*, 389 (389 ff.); Burgess et al., 'The Consequences of Treating Electricity as a Right' (2020) 34 *JEP*, 145 (145 ff.); Löfquist, 'Is there a universal human right to electricity?' (2020) 24 *Int J Hum Right*, 711 (711 ff.); Kaime and Glicksmann, 'An International Legal Framework for SE4All – Human Rights and Sustainable Development Law Imperatives' (2015) 38 *Fordham Int. Law J.*, 1405 (1405 ff.).

[180] *Stockholm Declaration* (1972), Recommendation 59.

[181] A/RES/66/288, *The future we want*, 11 September 2012, para.125.

62   Giving the world's poorest people access to energy means giving them the opportunity to participate in the modern world. Although energy does not autonomously lift people out of poverty, energy works as an accelerator through supporting providing and processing food (SDG 2.1, SDG 2.2), foster people's health and well-being (SDG 3.4, SDG 3.9), mitigating gender-related inequalities (SDG 5.a, SDG 5.b) (→ Goal mn. 65 ff.). Beyond, providing energy helps create decent and modern jobs and thus stimulates economic resilience and growth (SDG 8.2, SDG 8.4) and fosters innovation, modern infrastructure and industries (SDG 9.1, SDG 9.4, SDG 9.5, SDG 9.a, SDG 9.b, SDG 9.c) and moreover, accelerates access to education (SDG 4.a).

63   Through energy (supply) innovation and investment in sustainable energy (SDG 7.b), shared value, shared prosperity, long-term decarbonisation and sustainable management of natural resources (which counteracts climate change) can be achieved (SDG 12.6, SDG 12.8, SDG 12.a).[182] In this regard, energy used to empower agricultural machines, such as water pumps, water purification systems and other mechanised farming equipment enhances agricultural production (SDG 15.3) leads to more reliable food sources and / or production (e.g. during drought periods).

64   With access to affordable and clean energy, people's health is less likely to be affected by air pollution or polluted water, including in rural areas (SDG 3.9, SDG 6.3, SDG 6.a). In 2018, 2.6 billion people still lacked access to efficient and clean cooking systems,[183] leaving people exposed to air pollution from the use of fossil fuels such as kerosene. The resulting diseases cause about 4 million premature deaths each year.[184] Additionally, renewable energy can be a reliable power source for hospitals, as one out of four hospitals in Sub-Saharan countries are not electrified.[185] Water purification structures with an installed solar-powered water-purification system can turn water with high salt content into potable water.

65   Access to renewable and reliable energy also accelerates the industrialisation and urbanisation process (SDG 9), as energy is the main contributor to economy, infrastructure, the sustainable design of cities and communities (SDG 11) and the creation of new higher-paying jobs (although some businesses will need to reinvent themselves and / or need to re-train some workers) for many countries.[186] Therefore, giving access to renewable and energy-efficient technologies to the poorer populations, can spur innovation processes and reinforce local, regional and national industrial, infrastructure and employment objectives.[187]

66   An immediate upscaling of renewable energy and energy-efficient processes is strongly linked to keep the global warming to well below 2°C above and limit the increase to 1.5°C, as demanded by Art. 2 of the Paris Agreement (SDG 13.1) and helps

---

[182] A/69/700, *The road to dignity by 2030: ending poverty, transforming all lives and protecting the planet, Synthesis report of the Secretary-General on the post-2015 sustainable development agenda*, 4 December 2014, paras. 73 f., 94.

[183] UN and HLDE, *Theme Report on Energy, Access towards the Achievement Of SDG 7 and Net-Zero Emissions* (2021), 21; E/2020/57, *Report of the progress towards the Sustainable Development Goals*, 28 April 2020, para. 69.

[184] Due to heart disease, stroke, cancer, and other non-communicable diseases, as well as childhood pneumonia; UN and HLDE, *Theme Report on Energy, Access towards the Achievement Of SDG 7 and Net-Zero Emissions* (2021), 17; see on the right to clean air: Huck et al., 'The Right to Breathe Clean Air and Access to Justice - Legal State of Play in International, European and National Law' (2021) 13(10) *International Environmental Law (eJournal)*.

[185] WHO, *Access to Modern Energy Services for Health Facilities in Resource-Constrained Settings* (2014), 3-7.

[186] Griggs et al., *A Guide to SDG Interactions: From Science to Implementation* (2017), 155.

[187] Griggs et al., *A Guide to SDG Interactions: From Science to Implementation* (2017), 133.

limit the harmful impact on ecosystems and biodiversity (SDG 15.2, SDG 15.5).[188] By achieving the goals of SDG 7, the world can be on track to reduce greenhouse gas emissions sustainably and permanently and helps prevent impacts, which are caused, amongst others, by fuel and gas transport activities (e.g. oil tanker accidents) and facilities, which extract oil on the sea (e.g. Deep Water Horizon Oil Spill).[189]

Although renewable and clean energy are deemed more sustainable than fossil-fuel   **67** generated energy, the question of what happens, when things fall apart is often neglected. According to a survey of solar users in nine counties in Kenya, nearly one-fifth of all solar products stop working within 18 months of purchase, and 65 per cent of these solar products are kept or left behind when they stop working.[190] This exceedingly short product life cycle, which is not yet technologically extendable, is juxtaposed with a rather high manufacturing process that is fraught with many human rights and environmental rights issues, and the irreversible loss of natural resources.[191] Moreover, building facilities to produce renewable energy may also run counter the sub-goals of SDG 14 and SDG 15, as e.g. building dams could lead to a loss of biodiversity (in the sea and on land).

D. Jurisprudential Significance of SDG 7

In considering SDG 7, it is first noticeable that affordable and clean energy do not   **68** necessarily coincide in their essence.[192] Mobilising adequate and well-directed financing of (energy) infrastructure is indispensable for becoming a sustainable society.[193] Since the energy sector in its diversity is covered by environmental and sustainability policies in many places or is subject to environmental or sustainability requirements and assessments within the scope of trade and investment agreements, it can be read that a sustainable, modern energy supply fulfils various fundamental tasks within a population.[194]

All forms of human usable energy exert some degree of influence on environmental   **69** and social conditions,[195] yet the energy sector contributes to about two thirds of all

---

[188] FCCC/CP/1997/L.7/Add.1, *Kyoto Protocol To The United Nations Framework Convention On Climate Change*, 10 December 1997; Griggs et al., *A Guide to SDG Interactions: From Science to Implementation* (2017), 135.

[189] See in more detail of SDG 7 and SDG 13: UN and HLDE, *Theme Report on Energy Transition, Towards the Achievement of SDG 7 and Net-Zero Emissions* (2021), 45 ff.

[190] Cross and Murray, 'The afterlives of solar power: Waste and repair off the grid in Kenya' (2018) 44 *Energy Research & Social Science*, 100-9.

[191] See on this issue in general: Smith and Scott, 'Energy without Injustice, Indigenous Participation in Renewable Energy Generation' in Ataputtu and Gonzalez and Seck, *The Cambridge Handbook of Environmental Justice and Sustainable Development* (2021); Dhillion, 'Benefit sharing for project risk-conflict reduction and fostering sustainable development: Current understanding and mechanisms' in Almered Olsson and Gooch, *Natural Resource Conflicts and Sustainable Development* (2019), 147-65.

[192] E/2019/68, *Special edition: progress towards the Sustainable Development Goals, Report of the Secretary-General*, 08 May 2019, para. 42: 'The Asia-Pacific region has made notable headway on poverty, quality education and affordable and clean energy, but has also gone backwards on clean water and sanitation, decent work and economic growth and responsible consumption and production.'

[193] E/2019/68, *Special edition: progress towards the Sustainable Development Goals, Report of the Secretary-General*, 08 May 2019, para. 80; Bruce and Stephenson, 'SDG 7 on Sustainable Energy for All – Contributions of International Law, Policy and Governance' (2016) *UNEP/CISDL Issue Brief*, 1; further reading: Marhold, *Energy in International Trade Law Concepts, Regulation and Changing Markets* (2021).

[194] A/RES/66/288, *The future we want*, 11 September 2012, para. 125.

[195] Further reading: Halff and Sovacool and Rozhon, *Energy poverty: global challenges and local solutions* (2014).

greenhouse gas emissions.[196] Energy in its very nature is subject to different legal regimes and is thus also subject to judicial review mechanisms. The essential aspect of '[d]ecarbonizing and increasing the efficiency of existing and new energy infrastructures' is crucial for a sustainable shift in energy supply and usage as well as adaptation to climatic changes which was already demanded with the UNFCCC[197] as well as during the creation process of the SDGs.[198]

70   The partially diametric approach of individual goals on energy access of SDG 7 and the goals of SDG 13, which are to combat climate change, e.g. through the massive use of fossil fuels, is not well founded.[199] This interplay can be seen in various factual contexts, including in jurisdiction, where the (harmful) influence of companies in the energy sector is a particular issue, (→ Goal 7 mn. 91 ff.).[200]

71   Worldwide, coal and fossil fuel industries still play a significant role and are in some cases subsidised or promoted in other ways, partly because of national or regional efforts to protect competition and occupational safety, and they are particularly detrimental to 'effective measures against climate change and the transformation towards sustainable energy systems'.[201]

72   Energy transition cases are of particular importance and illustrate the relevance for sustainable development.[202] On the one hand, there are measures supporting competition, such as 'feed-in tariffs, quotas such as renewable portfolio standards (RPSs), and preferential tax treatment or other subsidies'[203] which are subject to judicial review in a large part of the established case law (and in particular in arbitration proceedings). On the other hand, it is often the tension between foreign direct investments, investment protection and the desire of a state to condition investments to existing or tightened environmental regulations that leads to dispute settlement or arbitration procedures.

---

[196] Payosova, 'Climate Change Mitigation and Renewable Energy' in Cottier and Nadakavukaren Schefer (eds), *Elgar Encyclopedia of International Economic Law* (2017), 625.

[197] FCCC/CP/1997/L.7/Add.1, *Kyoto Protocol To The United Nations Framework Convention On Climate Change*, 10 December 1997, Art. 2: Each Party included in Annex 1 […] shall:

(a) Implement […] policies and measures […], such as:

(i) Enhancement of energy efficiency in relevant sectors of the national economy; […]

(iv) Research on, and promotion, development and increased use of, new and renewable forms of energy

(viii) Limitation and/or reduction of methane through recovery and use in waste management, as well as in the production, transport and distribution of energy;

see also Cordonier Segger, 'Commitments to Sustainable Development' in Cordonier Segger and Weeramantry (eds), *Sustainable Development Principles in the Decisions of International Courts and Tribunals, 1992-2012* (2017), 77.

[198] UNGA Open Working Group on Sustainable Development Goals, *Compendium of TST Issues Briefs*, 102.

[199] Kaltenborn et al., *SGDs and Human Rights* (2020), 114.

[200] Further reading: Leal-Arcas et al., 'The Contribution of Free Trade Agreements and Bilateral Investment Treaties to a Sustainable Future' (2019) 23(1) ZEuS, 3-76; Krajewski, 'The impact of international investment agreements on energy regulation' in Herrmann and Terhechte (eds), *European Yearbook of International Economic Law* (2012), 343-71.

[201] Kaltenborn et al., *SGDs and Human Rights* (2020), 212.

[202] Schacherer and Hoffmann, 'International investment law and sustainable development' in Krajewski and Hoffmann (eds), *Research Handbook on Foreign Direct Investment* (2019), 582.

[203] Gundlach, 'Climate Change and Energy Transition' in Lees and Viñuales (eds), *The Oxford Handbook on Comparative Environmental Law* (2019), 561.

I. Jurisdiction on Vision and Objectives

The vision of SDG 7 to ensure affordable, reliable, sustainable and modern energy   **73**
leads to the idea that this could be condensed into a right to energy/electricity ($\rightarrow$ Goal
7 mn. 17, 59). While such a right, which would in principle mean a socio-economic
right, can be found in some states, and international human rights instruments also refer
explicitly and implicitly to the possibility of a right to electricity. However, this at best
regional recognition is not reflected globally. Presuming that a right to electricity would
not be an independent right, but a derived right, a logical link would be the right to
life.[204] In any case, this link cannot be found in the jurisdiction either and is therefore
likely to remain in the theoretical sphere. Yet, even if a connection were possible, no
right to access to *sustainable*, *affordable* or *clean* energy could be derived.

1. International Jurisdiction

The fact that the content of SDG 7 leads to conflicting objectives with other SDGs   **74**
on the agenda can be clearly seen from international case law. The supply and clean,
sustainable design of energy supply is sometimes in direct contradiction with other goals
of the agenda, not only insofar these goals are characterised by social justice, but also
when environmental goals are equally pursued.

Both are exemplified in *Lubicon Lake Band v Canada*[205]. The Ominayak and Lubicon   **75**
indigenous groups, having exhausted all domestic authorities, called the Human Rights
Council (HRC) after the federal government had sold part of their traditional land to
various energy producing companies (e.g. leases for oil and gas exploration). The investments were mainly intended to support the city's competitiveness, but also to ensure a
modern energy supply in the region. In addition to the *de facto* expropriation of the indigenous population, the operation of the various investment projects led to considerable, partly irreversible environmental damage. The blatant violations of many of the
SDGs highlight the significant potential for conflict that SDG 7 may bring. Interestingly,
the Human Rights Council declined to consider an alleged violation of the Canadian indigenous tribes' right to self-determination, as protected by Art. 1 ICCPR, through the
exploitation of energy resources on their traditional lands. Instead, it considered the
tribe's claims under Art. 27 ICCPR, concerning the right to culture.[206]

Similar issues with relevance to SDG 7 can also be found at the regional level. In   **76**
several cases, the ECtHR examined the relationship between energy supply and property
rights. More specifically, the cases concerned the assessment of whether renewable energy measures took precedence over private property and the extent to which this could

---

[204] Indoor air pollution from the use of combustible fuels for household energy caused 4.3 million
deaths in 2012, with women and girls accounting for 6 out of 10 of these deaths, https://www.un.org/susta
inabledevelopment/energy/; see Gudas, 'Right to Electricity' in Cottier and Nadakavukaren Schefer (eds),
Elgar Encyclopedia of International Economic Law (2017), 647; see in context of the right to clean air: Huck
et al., 'The Right to Breathe Clean Air and Access to Justice - Legal State of Play in International, European
and National Law' (2021) 13(10) *International Environmental Law (eJournal)*.

[205] Human Rights Committee (UNHRC), *Lubicon Lake Band v. Canada*, Communication No. 167/1984
(26 March 1990), U.N. Doc. Supp. No. 40 (A/45/40) at 1 (1990).

[206] UNHRC, *Ominayak (Lubicon Lake Band) v. Canada*, Communication No. 167/1984 (26 March
1990), U.N. Doc. Supp. No. 40 (A/45/40) at 1 (1990), paras. 32.2, 33; see also Safdi and Jodoin, 'The
principles of sustainable development in the practice of UN human rights bodies' in Cordonier Segger and
Weeramantry, *Sustainable Development Principles in the Decisions of International Courts and Tribunals,
1992-2012* (2017), 462.

be justified. These cases are some of those in which the Court found that environmental concerns took precedence over private property rights.[207]

77   In the *Fägerskiöld v Sweden case*,[208] the Court weighed two environmental levels, the supply of 'green energy for the purpose of a sustainable country and noise pollution to the applicants'.[209] In its negative opinion in the case, it made direct reference to sustainable development and recognised that

> there is no doubt that the operating of the wind turbine is in the general interest as it is an environmentally friendly source of energy which contributes to the sustainable development of natural resources. It observes that the wind turbine at issue in the present case is capable of producing enough energy to heat between 40 and 50 private households over a one-year period, which is beneficial both for the environment and for society.

2. European Jurisdiction

78   The Energy Union Framework[210] comprises the contents of the SDGs for the EU Member States in the same substance, or at least substantially follows from these. The specific inclusion of the European energy policy in Art. 194 TFEU as an objective 'in a spirit of solidarity between Member States [...] and taking into account the need to preserve and improve the environment' is supplemented by the inclusion of Art. 191(1) TFEU as being of cross-cutting relevance in the field of environmental protection, and serves in particular climate protection.[211] In addition, the contents of SDG 7 are clearly and comprehensively pronounced in political terms at the further EU (special) legislative level.[212]

---

[207] Gouritin, 'Sustainable development principles in the European Court of Human Rights' in Cordonier Segger and Weeramantry (eds), *Sustainable Development Principles in the Decisions of International Courts and Tribunals, 1992-2012* (2017), 523.

[208] *Fägerskiöld v Sweden* [2008] ECtHR 37664/04 under 'the law', pt. 1 [found in: Gouritin, 'Sustainable development principles in the European Court of Human Rights' in Cordonier Segger and Weeramantry (eds), *Sustainable Development Principles in the Decisions of International Courts and Tribunals, 1992-2012* (2017), 520].

[209] Gouritin, 'Sustainable development principles in the European Court of Human Rights' in Cordonier Segger and Weeramantry (eds), *Sustainable Development Principles in the Decisions of International Courts and Tribunals, 1992-2012* (2017), 524.

[210] European Commission, COM(2015) 80 final, Energy Union Package Communication from the Commission the European Parliament, the Council, the European Economic and Social Committee, the Committee of the Regions and the European Investment Bank, *A Framework Strategy for a Resilient Energy Union with a Forward-Looking Climate, Change Policy*, 25.02.2015; see for an overview of the progress made: https://ec.europa.eu/info/news/clean-energy-all-europeans-package-completed-good-consumers-good-growth-and-jobs-and-good-planet-2019-may-22_en; and an overview on renewable energy in the EU based on the Directive (EU) 2018/2001 on the promotion of the use of energy from renewable sources, which establishes a common system to promote energy from renewable sources and has to become law in EU countries by 30 June 2021: https://eur-lex.europa.eu/legal-content/EN/TXT/?uri=LEGISSUM:4372645&qid=1607009315141.

[211] See amongst many https://ec.europa.eu/commission/news/energy-union-vision-reality-2019-apr-09-0_en.

[212] The main regulatory frameworks related to energy and energy transition are currently: Directive (EU) 2018/2001 of the European Parliament and of the Council of 11 December 2018 on the promotion of the use of energy from renewable sources (recast) (Renewable Energy Directive); the Directive 2012/27/EU of the European Parliament and of the Council of 25 October 2012 on energy efficiency, amending Directives 2009/125/EC and 2010/30/EU and repealing Directives 2004/8/EC and 2006/32/EC (Energy Efficiency Directive); the Directive on Energy Performance of Buildings; and the (to be revised) Council Directive 2003/96/EC of 27 October 2003 restructuring the Community framework for the taxation of energy products and electricity (Energy Taxation Directive); further reading: Hancher and Talus and Wüstenberg, 'Retrospective application of legal rules in the European Union: recent practice in the energy sector' (2020) *Journal of Energy & Natural Resources Law*; Hesselman and Varo and Laakso, 'The Right to Energy in the European Union' (2019), ENGAGER European Energy Poverty, Policy Brief

Other areas of particular jurisprudential relevance are primarily concerned with   79

–   GSP+ Schemes which 'remove import duties from products coming into the EU market from vulnerable developing countries',[213] if a beneficiary country ratifies and effectively 'implements core international human and, labour rights, environment and good governance conventions'[214];
–   Preferential Trade agreements, if asymmetric market access into the EU is also granted if the (third country) contracting party fulfils sustainability conditions under the relevant treaty;
–   Carbon pricing to shift energy systems 'cap & trade' – EU Emission Trading Scheme (EU ETS)[215];
–   Carbon Border Adjustment Mechanism (CBAM)[216] to be applied from 2021 on;
–   further specific cases dealing with the interpretation of measures referring to the Energy Tax Directive[217]

Jurisdiction dealing with aspects of energy can primarily be found in cases concern-   80
ing measures affecting trade and is judicially assessed in particular with regard to the EU-wide prohibition of restrictions on the free movement of goods, Art. 34 TFEU (former Art. 30 EC). This most often concerns the weighting of the sustainability of measures and the pricing in the energy supply sector, i.e. the protection of (intra-)European competition. In the *PreussenElectra case*[218], a preliminary ruling procedure, the ECJ established in 2001 that the German controversial 'Stromeinspeisungsgesetz' (Electricity Feed Act - EFA) was compatible with the free movement of goods. This EFA had provided for the obligatory purchase and payment of sustainable energy for electricity supply companies within the (geographical) area of supply.[219] In the applicants' view, this basic obligation as a green energy surcharge was of discriminatory nature,[220] since it distorted prices and gave preferential treatment to German companies or electricity producers. The ECJ, however, emphasised the European obligation to comply with its international

---

No. 2, 49/2019 *University of Groningen Faculty of Law Research Paper*; on current concerns in EU energy law see generally https://europeanlawblog.eu/category/energy-law/.

[213] https://ec.europa.eu/trade/policy/countries-and-regions/development/generalised-scheme-of-prefer ences.

[214] European Commission, The EU's Generalised Scheme of Preferences (GSP), Regulation (EU) No 978/2012 Of The European Parliament And Of The Council of 25 October 2012 applying a scheme of generalised tariff preferences and repealing Council Regulation (EC Treaty) in conjunction with Commission Delegated Regulation (EU) 2020/129 of 26 November 2019 amending the vulnerability threshold set out in point 1(b) of Annex VII to Regulation (EU) No 978/2012 of the European Parliament and the Council applying a scheme of generalised tariff preferences No 732/2008.

[215] European Commission, *The EU Emissions Trading System (EU ETS)*, https://ec.europa.eu/clima/sites /clima/files/factsheet_ets_en.pdf; see also https://ec.europa.eu/clima/policies/ets_en.

[216] European Commission, *State of the Union Address 2020*, Speech of Ursula von der Leyen of 16 September 2020, 10, 19; Remeur on behalf of European Parliamentary Research Services (EPRS), *Carbon emissions pricing, Some points of reference* (2020), 1-11.

[217] *Council Directive 2003/96/EC of 27 October 2003 restructuring the Community framework for the taxation of energy products and electricity* (Energy taxation directive – ETD), OJ EU L 283/51; as part of the European Green Deal, the directive will be revised in June 2021 to align it with climate objectives.

[218] ECJ, Case C-379/98, 13.03.2001, *PreussenElektra AG v Schleswag AG, in the presence of Windpark Reußenköge III GmbH and Land Schleswig-Holstein*, ECLI:EU:C:2001:160.

[219] Under the Electricity Feed Act: hydraulic energy, wind energy, solar energy, gas from waste dumps and sewage treatment plants, or products or residues and biological waste from agriculture and forestry work.

[220] The (legal) basis for the basic eligibility (including financial eligibility) for support for the development of new and renewable energy sources, as provided for in Directive 2009/28/EC of 23 April 2009 on the promotion of the use of energy from renewable sources, is already set out in Art. 194(1) (c) TFEU; see Bings, 'Art. 194 TFEU' in Streinz (ed), *EUV/AEUV* (2018), mn. 28.

obligations under the Kyoto Protocol[221], which moreover, had been transposed into the EU's own renewable energy resources programmes. Referring to the principle of European integration, it emphasised that in principle 'policy is also designed to protect the health and life of humans, animals and plants' and that, against the background of international commitments to avert climate change, 'the development of the use of renewable energy sources is therefore one of the priority objectives'. The market design of using renewable energy (supply), which may distort competition, does not in any case constitute a breach of Article 34 TFEU.[222] The ECJ had thus laid the foundation for significantly promoting the use of renewable energies. Following the replacement of the EFA by the Renewable Energy Sources Act (EEG) in 2012, *PreussenElektra* is still considered a leading decision, but was further specified[223] in the subsequent jurisdiction.[224] Also in cases involving other Member States on EU energy law, the judicial review of the admissibility of measures to increase the share of renewable energy in the global energy mix (SDG 7.2) at European level is primarily based on the assessment of state aid or granting of further financial subsidies.[225]

81   Notably, the ECJ has stated elsewhere that the need for protection of the EU environmental objective is significantly lower. Following a 'solar energy boom', the governments of Spain, the Czech Republic and Romania faced increasing cost pressures caused by incentive programmes that significantly exceeded the intended increase in value.

82   In its decision on the joined cases C-180/18, C-86/18 and C-287/18[226], the ECJ referred to the renewable energy directive (2009/28/EC) and confirmed the previous practice of member states reducing the amount of support already granted to renewable energy projects as being in conformity with EU legislation. It also stated that such a reduction was consistent with the principles of legal certainty and reliability, as market participants must, as a matter of principle, expect incentives to be decreased, phased out or removed.[227] The generally strongly anchored goal of environmental protection seems to have been overtaken by economic objectives.

83   With reference to nuclear energy, the ECJ opened an at least theoretical possibility for the EU bodies to intervene in the choice and design of the energy mix of the member states, which regularly lies in the competences of the member states themselves. The ECJ stated that while the EU cannot determine the energy mix for energy policy considerations, this is possible for environmental or sustainability policy considerations in applying Art. 192(2) (c) TFEU. However, a large number of EU member states would not sup-

---

[221] *Kyoto Protocol to the United Nations Framework Convention on Climate Change*, 11 December 1997, UN Treaty Series, vol. 2303, 162.

[222] ECJ, Case C-379/98, 13.03.2001, *PreussenElektra AG v Schleswag AG, in the presence of Windpark Reußenköge III GmbH and Land Schleswig-Holstein*, ECLI:EU:C:2001:160, paras. 74 f.

[223] In most cases, the mandatory EEG levy (EEG-Umlage-Erhebung), according to which 'grid operators are "entitled and obliged" to impose the EEG levy on end consumers, which makes the clear determination of unjustified state aid in the respective context quite different, cf. sections 60(1) sentence 1, 60 a sentence 1, 61(1), 61i(1) sentence 1 EEG 2017.

[224] Amongst more: ECJ, Case C-405/16, 28.03.2019, *Germany v Commission*, ECLI:EU:C:2019:268; General Court (GC), Case T-479/11 – Case T-157/12, appeal of Case C-438/16 P, 19.09.2018, *Commission v France and IFP Énergies Nouvelles*, ECLI:EU:C:2018:737; GC, Case C-594/18 P, 22.09.2020, *Austria v European Commission*, ECLI:EU:C:2020:742.

[225] Further reading: Catherine Banet on behalf of Centre on Regulation in Europe (CERRE), *State Aid Guidelines for Environmental Protection and Energy (EEAG)* (2020), https://cerre.eu/wp-content/uploads/2 020/09/CERRE_State-Aid-Guidelines-for-Environmental-Protection-and-Energy-EEAG_September-202 0.pdf.

[226] ECJ, joined Cases C-180/18, C-286/18 and C-287/18, 11.07.2019, *Agrenergy Srl and Fusignano Due Srl v Ministero dello Sviluppo Economico*, ECLI:EU:C:2019:605.

[227] ECJ, joined Cases C-180/18, C-286/18 and C-287/18, 11.07.2019, *Agrenergy Srl and Fusignano Due Srl v Ministero dello Sviluppo Economico*, ECLI:EU:C:2019:605, paras. 44, 46.

port a nuclear phase-out, and corresponding legislative projects at EU level would therefore probably not be successful.[228] However, it can be read from the EU SDG indicator set that the forms of energy used for transition are still not clearly addressed whereas the HLEG Draft Climate Mitigation Taxonomy proposal to the EU continues to list nuclear power plants as energy distributors, although it already refers to its critical consideration.[229] Equally ambiguous remains the first delegated act on sustainable activities for climate change adaptation and mitigation objectives of the EU.

3. Arbitration Proceedings

Since energy in its merchantable forms is subject to different disciplines of trade in goods or services, the WTO framework, amongst others, is applicable to the scope of SDG 7. The dispute settlement mechanism of the WTO has not yet been frequently used to settle disputes within the energy regime. The few comprehensible dispute settlement procedures dealt exclusively with *Certain measures relating to Renewable Energy*.   84

For example, Argentina demanded consultations with the EU in 2013 in a subsidies case[230] and claimed that the sustainability targets set by the EU and the linking of various excise duty rate reductions (financial support schemes) cannot be achieved by non-EU producers, which would violate the principle of national treatment. A decision has not yet been made in a comprehensible manner; consultations are still ongoing.[231]   85

Most recently, a decision was made in a panel proceeding initiated by India concerning various US tax incentives, tax credits and tax refunds in the field of renewable energies.[232] The panel in favour of India found that the measures constitute less favourable treatment within the meaning of Article 4:III GATT which must be remedied. The decision is subject to review by the Dispute Settlement Body. Similarly, China initiated (still ongoing) consultations with the US, most recently joined by the EU.[233] And there have also been consultations with Canada, prompted by Japan, on feed-in-tariffs, which the US and the EU have joined. In the procedure, neither the Panel nor the Appellate Body could find a violation of the national treatment principle. Since Canada provided   86

---

[228] ECJ, C-594/18P, 22.09.2020, *Österreich v Commission* (Hinkley Point C), ECLI:EU:C:2020:742; EC, EU SDG Indicator set 2021, *Result of the review in preparation of the 2021 edition of the EU SDG monitoring report*, Final version of 15/01/2021, 17.

[229] HLEG Proposal to the European Commission, Informal Supplementary Document On Sustainable Taxonomy, 7; EC, C(2021) 2800/3, Commission Delegated Regulation (EU) (provisional version) supplementing Regulation (EU) 2020/852 of the European Parliament and of the Council by establishing the technical screening criteria for determining the conditions under which an economic activity qualifies as contributing substantially to climate change mitigation or climate change adaptation and for determining whether that economic activity causes no significant harm to any of the other environmental objectives, published on 21 April 2021.

[230] *EU and Certain Member States – Certain Measures on the Importation and Marketing of Biodiesel and Measures supporting the Biodiesel Industry Request for Consultations by Argentina*, WT/DS459/1, 23 May 2013, legal bases invoked: Art. XXIII GATT 1994, Art. 4.1, Art. 7.1 and Art. 30 of the Agreement on Subsidies and Countervailing Measures (SCM Agreement), Art. 8 of the Agreement on Trade-Related Investment Measures (TRIMs Agreement) and Article 14 Agreement on Technical Barriers to Trade (TBT Agreement).

[231] https://docs.wto.org/dol2fe/Pages/SS/directdoc.aspx?filename=q:/WT/DS/459-1.pdf&Open=True; https://www.wto.org/english/tratop_e/dispu_e/cases_e/ds459_e.htm.

[232] DS510, *United States — Certain Measures Relating to the Renewable Energy Sector*, https://www.wto.org/english/tratop_e/dispu_e/cases_e/ds510_e.htm.

[233] DS563, *United States — Certain Measures Related to Renewable Energy*, Request for Consultation of 14 August 2018, https://www.wto.org/english/tratop_e/dispu_e/cases_e/ds563_e.htm.

feed-in-tariffs for electricity, but Japan imported electricity generation equipment, no 'likeness of products' and thus no competitive relationship could be established.[234]

87   In addition to dispute settlement proceedings, which are concerned with the fair and equitable organisation of trade, the energy-producing and distributing sectors are becoming increasingly important, particularly in the context of investment protection. For example, it can be observed that in the interaction between investments and the environmental regulations affecting them, legal requirements are not complied with and / or are not enforced.

88   In the 2007 case *Vattenfall v Germany I*[235] before the ISDS Tribunal, a 'Swedish energy corporation was granted a provisional permit to build a coal-fired power plant near the city of Hamburg. In an effort to protect the Elbe river from the waste waters dumped from the plant, environmental restrictions were added before the final approval of its construction.'[236] The investor initiated a dispute, arguing the environmental rules would amount to an expropriation and therefore constitute a violation of Germany's obligation to afford foreign investors 'fair and equitable treatment'. The case was ultimately settled in 2011, when the city of Hamburg agreed to lower the demanded environmental standards (Energy Charter Treaty – ECT invoked).[237] This case was followed by the case *Vattenfall v Germany II*[238] in 2012, which most recently was concluded to discontinue with the agreement of the parties not being publicly available.[239] Both cases and those of other large energy companies in Germany must also be assessed in the light of Germany's planned nuclear energy phase-out, which repeatedly came to a standstill due to a tightening of German environmental law, inter alia as a result of these proceedings. These and other proceedings[240] are particularly controversial because the negotiations, which are usually not publicly comprehensible, result in arbitral awards that will not be subject to appeal or revision and are suitable for preventing relevant adjustments to environmental and energy law, which are also necessary for sustainability transformation. Beyond that, it is difficult to see any clear direction in these cases, as decisions have been made in favour of both states and investors.[241]

89   More recently, the ICSID delivered a decision over a claim brought under the Energy Charter Treaty (ECT).[242] A group of investors from the Spanish solar energy sector has notified the Spanish government of its intention to initiate arbitration proceedings under the investment protection provisions of the ECT. The investors most recently

---

[234] DS412, *Canada — Certain Measures Affecting the Renewable Energy Generation Sector*, https://www.wto.org/english/tratop_e/dispu_e/cases_e/ds412_e.htm.

[235] *Vattenfall AB and others v. Federal Republic of Germany I*, ICSID Case No. ARB/09/6.

[236] https://isds.bilaterals.org/?-key-cases-.

[237] http://isds.bilaterals.org/?case-study-vattenfall-v-germany-i&lang=en; see also The Protocol on Energy Efficiency and Related Environmental Aspects (PEEREA) to the Energy Charter Treaty (1994); European Energy Charter (1991).

[238] *Vattenfall AB and others v. Federal Republic of Germany (II)*, ICSID Case No. ARB/12/12.

[239] *Vattenfall AB and others v. Federal Republic of Germany (II)*, ICSID Case No. ARB/12/12, Order Of the Tribunal taking Note of the Discontinuance of the Proceeding, 9 November 2021, A first preliminary hearing took place on 19.11.2020 after Germany's application for a dismissal of the tribunal had been denied a few months before. However, by letters of 2 November 2021 the Tribunal took note of the Parties' agreement to discontinue the proceeding.

[240] *Jean-Pierre Lecorcier and Michael Stein v Italian Republic*, ICSID Case No. ARB/14/3; *Charanne v Spain*, SCC case no. V 062/2012; *Isolux v Spain* SCC Case V2013/153; *Eiser v Spain* ICSID Case No. ARB/13/36; *Antin v Spain* ICSID Case No. ARB/13/31.

[241] Schacherer and Hoffmann, 'International investment law and sustainable development' in Krajewski and Hoffmann (eds), *Research Handbook on Foreign Direct Investment* (2019), 583.

[242] *Case of Landesbank Baden-Württemberg (LBBW) and others v. Kingdom of Spain*, ICSID Case No. ARB/15/45; see also *BayWa r.e. renewable energy GmbH and BayWa r.e. Asset Holding GmbH v. Kingdom of Spain*, ICSID Case No. ARB/15/16.

challenged the government's decision to retroactively change laws that allow solar energy producers to charge higher tariffs. Initially, these laws were introduced to encourage investment in renewable energy projects.[243] These complement the series of previous decisions taken under the ECT in the wake of the ECJ's *Achmea case*.[244] The ICSID's decision sheds light on the European Commission's currently increasing efforts to reform the ECT on a wide scale and underlines the existing trend of arbitral tribunals constituted under the ECT to reject intra-EU jurisdictional objections (despite contrary views expressed by most EU member states).[245]

It remains to be seen how intra-EU investor-state arbitration will develop in the future against the most recent background of the termination of all intra-EU BITs and which focus it might be subject to. In any case, solutions will certainly be found in the course of its implementation which in one way or another will affect and influence the implementation of SDG 7. **90**

4. Domestic Jurisdiction

Within energy (transition) policy, two approaches can be identified worldwide: (1) 'energy transition policy through comprehensive legislation or regulation'; and (2) approaches 'in a more piecemeal fashion'.[246] These are observable approaches 'whose components serve the competing priorities of energy security, economic growth, and climate change mitigation' and do not aim at expressly decarbonising, which is not the case in climate change policies, for example.[247] **91**

Following the political approaches, domestic jurisdiction in the scope of SDG 7 can most often be found in the area of reviewing, updating or transitioning of energy efficiency standards.[248] Recent cases do also determine the possibilities to establish liability on the part of private actors (see below *Lliuya*). However, neither the wider human rights background nor a human right to energy or electricity[249] are discernibly claimed very often before domestic courts. One case from 2020, however, exemplifies this obvious connection through alleging violations of human rights, including the right to a healthy environment and the right to access electricity from renewable sources. The **92**

---

[243] Crockett, 'The integration principle in ICSID awards' in Cordonier Segger and Weeramantry (eds), *Sustainable Development Principles in the Decisions of International Courts and Tribunals, 1992-2012* (2017), 552.

[244] ECJ, Case C-284/16, 06.03.2018, *Slovak Republic v. Achmea B.V. (Achmea case)*, ECLI:EU:C:2018:158; The ECJ decided that the arbitration clause contained in Article 8 of the 1991 Dutch-Slovak BIT adversely affects the autonomy of EU law and is therefore incompatible with EU law. The judgment builds on a dispute between the Dutch insurer Achmea B.V. (formerly known as Eureko B.V.) and Slovakia; further reading Fouchard (Smith) and Krestin, 'The Judgment of the ECJ in Slovak Republic v. Achmea – A Loud Clap of Thunder on the Intra-EU BIT Sky!' (2018) *Kluwer Arbitration Blog*.

[245] Further reading: Stefan, 'Intra-EU Disputes under the Energy Charter Treaty: Quo Vadis?' (2019) *Kluwer Arbitration Blog*, for a EU review of the Achmea case see: United States District Court For The District Of Columbia, *Eiser Infrastructure Limited And Energia Solar Luxembourg S.A R.L. V. The Kingdom Of Spain*, Respondent.Civil Action No. 1:18-Cv-1686, Proposed Brief of the European Commission on Behalf of the European Union as *Amicus Curiae* in Support of the Kingdom of Spain, 15 ff., available at https://ec.europa.eu/competition/court/eiser_en.pdf.

[246] Gundlach, 'Climate Change and Energy Transition' in Lees and Viñuales (eds), *The Oxford Handbook on Comparative Environmental Law* (2019), 533.

[247] Gundlach, 'Climate Change and Energy Transition' in Lees and Viñuales (eds), *The Oxford Handbook on Comparative Environmental Law* (2019), 554.

[248] See e. g. *New York v. Brouillette*, No. 20-cv-9362 (S.D.N.Y., filed Nov. 9, 2020); *Natural Resources Defense Council v. Brouillette*, No. 20-cv-9127 (S.D.N.Y., filed Oct. 30, 2020); *BP p.l.c. v. Mayor & City Council of Baltimore*, No. 19-1189 (U.S.).

[249] Gudas, 'Right to Electricity' in Cottier and Nadakavukaren Schefer (eds), *Elgar Encyclopedia of International Economic Law* (2017), 647 f.

programme provided for the use of fossil fuels at the expense of investment in renewable energy, which is instrumental in reducing greenhouse gas emissions and promoting adaptation to climate change. Greenpeace Mexico filed a complaint[250] with the Mexico City District Court against Mexico's new energy sector programme 2020-2024, after the programme had been adopted a few months before. The NGO complained the policy to be unconstitutional, thereby violating 'the rights to a healthy environment and sustainable development and for obstructing Mexico's compliance with its international commitments to tackle climate change.'[251] The court decided that the public policies were unlawfully modifying the rules of the energy market, and were violating the right to a healthy environment of Mexicans. The case is now under appeal.

93   In 2016, a German court dismissed a case brought by a Peruvian farmer against the unsustainable action of the German energy provider RWE on the basis that the company had not fulfilled its duty to protect Peruvians from flooding caused by climate change which was triggered by the companies' behaviour (in energy production). However, the court of appeal declared the case to be admissible. This is the first time that a court has ruled that a private company can in principle be held liable for its share in causing climate change-related damage to private property (→ Goal 13, mn. 52 ff.). If the German courts rule in favour of the plaintiff, the scope of liability for large greenhouse gas (GHG) emitters will have to be redefined on a large scale.[252] Moreover, the way a company, i.e. an energy provider, generates its commodity would have to be measured against the entire value chain, which would have a considerable influence on its design and would directly contribute to SDG 7 and climate change mitigation (SDG 13). The Philippines Commission on Human Rights is currently investigating whether foreign fossil fuel companies have violated the human rights of Filipinos who have endured climate-related disasters.[253]

94   Referring to nuclear power and nuclear waste, a new development can be identified in India which seeks to increase the size of its nuclear fleet. India is also developing reprocessing capacity and capacity to enrich its domestic stockpile of thorium, a fissile fuel that is less volatile than conventionally enriched uranium and not capable of being used for nuclear weapons.[254] Due to India's exceptionally progressive and large-scale approach, it is to be expected that legal disputes concerning compensation claims or investment protection will develop in the future. While this development could lead to an impetus for SDG 7, it might also involve further legal uncertainties.

---

[250] *Greenpeace Mexico v. Ministry of Energy and Others* (on the National Electric System policies), Juicio de amparo indirecto 104/2020, 17 November 2020.

[251] *Greenpeace Mexico v. Ministry of Energy and Others* (on the National Electric System policies), Juicio de amparo indirecto 104/2020, 17 November 2020, 169 f.; see for an English case summary http://climatec asechart.com/climate-change-litigation/non-us-case/greenpeace-mexico-v-ministry-of-energy-and-other s-on-the-national-electric-system-policies/.

[252] https://business-humanrights.org/en/rwe-lawsuit-re-climate-change.

[253] https://www.amnesty.org/en/latest/news/2019/12/landmark-decision-by-philippines-human-rights -commission-paves-way-for-climate-litigation/; https://www.amnesty.org/en/latest/news/2018/12/landm ark-human-rights-and-climate-change-investigation-could-help-millions-worldwide/.

[254] Gundlach, 'Climate Change and Energy transition', in Lees and Viñuales (eds), *The Oxford Handbook of Comparative Environmental Law* (2019), 570; see also World Nuclear Association, Nuclear Power in India (updated July 2020), https://www.world-nuclear.org/information-library/country-profiles/countries -g-n/india.aspx.

II. De Facto Influences on the Jurisdiction

In the case law shown, but also beyond, there are indications that the legal regime **95** of climate protection[255] in particular will have a strong influence on the interpretability, judicial evaluation and jurisprudential relevance of a right to sustainable (affordable and clean) energy. Already now, indications can be seen in climate change litigation, which will naturally exert influence due to the strong thematic overlap of the legal fields.

Private actors, in particular the so-called carbon majors, exert considerable influence **96** on the future visibility of the contents of SDG 7 and a right to energy in a broader sense since these are supposed to provide the highest share of renewable energy investments.[256] The numerous links with climate protection efforts are obvious and bring the institutions and organisations that finance them into focus. For example, the Asian Infrastructure Investment Bank, the Global Infrastructure Hub, the New Development Bank, the Asia Pacific Project Preparation Facility, the World Bank Group's Global Infrastructure Facility and the Africa50 Infrastructure Fund, as well as the increase in the capital of the Inter-American Investment Corporation,[257] with their own financing policies, have a weighty position in shaping the energy markets and can exert an immense steering effect with regard to the sustainable design of energy provision.

International organisations such as the Sustainable Energy for All initiative, Power **97** Africa, the NEPAD Africa Power Vision and the Global Renewable Energy Islands Network of the IRENA are likely to have further influence in the future, as they promote the provision of energy on a large scale and also play a decisive role in determining how energy provision will be valued in the future. Judicial disputes and jurisprudential considerations will in turn have to be aligned with these transnational standards in the future.

Overall, the multilateral and national development banks,[258] the various UN agencies **98** and national institutions, development partners and the private sector form a complex interplay that has not yet been adequately addressed by the judiciary in many places.

E. Conclusion on SDG 7

Law that is of direct relevance to the contents of SDG 7 still must be deemed **99** underdeveloped. A resilient right to energy, especially to clean and sustainable energy, is not yet to be found or not to a sufficient extent for legal application. Upon closer examination, it is noticeable that the issues attributable to SDG 7 in their entirety in the judicial assessment provide at best an indirect indication of a right to energy. If the effects that can be ascertained at all are measured using the indicators of SDG 7, it is hardly possible to present any intersection. The narrow scope of the indicators, which

---

[255] See in the context of energy supply and deforestation: Lees and Viñuales, *The Oxford Handbook of Comparative Environmental Law* (2019), 551; Jagger et al., 'SDG: Affordable and Clean Energy – How Access to Affordable and Clean Energy Affects Forests and Forest-Based Livelihoods' in Katila et al. (eds), *Sustainable Development Goals: Their Impacts on Forests and People* (2019), 206-36.

[256] Assab, 'Scaling up Renewable Energy Investment for Sustainable Development', in Yang (ed), *Cases on Green Energy and Sustainable Development* (2020), 96; UN and HLDE, *Theme Report on Finance and Investment towards the Achievement of SDG 7 and Net-Zero Emissions* (2021).

[257] A/RES/69/313, *Addis Ababa Action Agenda of the Third International Conference on Financing for Development*, adopted on 27 July 2015, para. 14.

[258] Which already supported and influenced the SDG negotiation process as 'a group of friends' of Sustainable Energy for All; Dodds and Donoghue and Leiva Roesch, *Negotiating the Sustainable Development Goals, A transformational agenda for an insecure world* (2017), 58 f.

have not been expanded in the recent revision[259] and thus continue to focus primarily on developing and least developed countries, basically exclude various court decisions and therefore also an evolving foundation of legal interpretation. At most, a teleological interpretation, which is inherent in the SDGs and the Global Agenda 2030 as a holistic approach, opens up the possibility of considering those spheres of energy policy and law which cannot be located in developing countries. However, these areas, which are not the focus of SDG 7, can only serve as a moderate basis for argumentation if SDG 7 is attempted to be given legal significance. Why developed countries are explicitly excluded from the aims of SDG 7 and are only addressed in the context of knowledge and technology transfer, facilitation and investment can hardly be explained by the fact that they are the main emitters and users of non-clean and non-renewable energies. While a debate on this subject cannot be conducted within the scope of this commentary, a fundamental reconsideration or reassessment, however, seems worthwhile, especially against the background of noticeable developments in the closely interwoven field of climate protection (→ Goal 13).

---

[259] Global Indicator Framework, Annual Refinements from the 52nd session in March 2021 (Annex) contained in E/CN.3/2021/2; https://unstats.un.org/sdgs/indicators/indicators-list/.

Goal 8
Promote sustained, inclusive and sustainable economic growth, full and productive employment and decent work for all

8.1 Sustain per capita economic growth in accordance with national circumstances and, in particular, at least 7 per cent gross domestic product growth per annum in the least developed countries

8.2 Achieve higher levels of economic productivity through diversification, technological upgrading and innovation, including through a focus on high-value added and labour-intensive sectors

8.3 Promote development-oriented policies that support productive activities, decent job creation, entrepreneurship, creativity and innovation, and encourage the formalization and growth of micro-, small- and medium-sized enterprises, including through access to financial services

8.4 Improve progressively, through 2030, global resource efficiency in consumption and production and endeavour to decouple economic growth from environmental degradation, in accordance with the 10-Year Framework of Programmes on Sustainable Consumption and Production, with developed countries taking the lead

8.5 By 2030, achieve full and productive employment and decent work for all women and men, including for young people and persons with disabilities, and equal pay for work of equal value

8.6 By 2020, substantially reduce the proportion of youth not in employment, education or training

8.7 Take immediate and effective measures to eradicate forced labour, end modern slavery and human trafficking and secure the prohibition and elimination of the worst forms of child labour, including recruitment and use of child soldiers, and by 2025 end child labour in all its forms

8.8 Protect labour rights and promote safe and secure working environments for all workers, including migrant workers, in particular women migrants, and those in precarious employment

8.9 By 2030, devise and implement policies to promote sustainable tourism that creates jobs and promotes local culture and products

8.10 Strengthen the capacity of domestic financial institutions to encourage and expand access to banking, insurance and financial services for all

8.a Increase Aid for Trade support for developing countries, in particular least developed countries, including through the Enhanced Integrated Framework for Trade-related Technical Assistance to Least Developed Countries

8.b By 2020, develop and operationalize a global strategy for youth employment and implement the Global Jobs Pact of the International Labour Organization

Word Count related to 'growth' 'employment' 'decent work'
A/RES/70/1 - Transforming our world: the 2030 Agenda for Sustainable Development: 'growth': 17 'employment': 15 'decent work': 6
Instruments mentioned in A/RES/70/1 in the section entitled: 'Sustainable Development Goals and targets':
A/RES/66/288 - The future we want (Rio +20 Declaration) adopted on 27 July 2012: 'growth': 25 'employment': 15 'decent work': 12
A/RES/69/313 - Addis Ababa Action Agenda of the Third International Conference on Financing for Development adopted on 27 July 2015: 'growth': 23 'employment': 6 'decent work': 7
A/RES/55/2 - United Nations Millennium Declaration adopted on 8 September 2000: 'growth': 0 'employment': 0 'decent work': 1

Goal 8 *Promote sustained, inclusive and sustainable economic growth, employment and work*

Select Bibliography: Juan Pablo Bohoslavsky, 'Guiding Principles to Assess the Human Rights of Economic Reforms? Yes' in Ilias Bantekas and Cephas Lumina (eds), *Sovereign Debt and Human Rights* (Oxford University Press, Oxford 2018), 411; Hendrik Van den Berg, *Economic Growth and Development* (3rd ed, World Scientific Publishing, Singapore 2017), 65; Enrica Chiappero-Martinetti, Nadia von Jacobi and Marcello Signorelli, 'Human Development and Economic Growth' in Jens Hölscher and Horst Tomann (eds), *Palgrave Dictionary of Emerging Markets and Transition Economics* (Palgrave Macmillan, London 2015), 224; Abhishek Choudhary, 'Global Justice' in Ali Farazmand (ed), *Global Encyclopedia of Public Administration, Public Policy, and Governance* (Springer International Publishing, Switzerland 2018); Marie-Claire Cordonier Segger, 'Sustainability, Global Justice, and the Law: Contributions of the Hon. Justice Charles Doherty Gonthier' (2010) 55 *McGill L.J.*, 337; Gary Craig et al, 'Editorial introduction: the modern slavery agenda: policy, politics and practice' in Gary Craig et al (eds), *The modern slavery agenda – policy, politics and practice in the UK* (Policy Press, UK/USA 2019), 10; Yossi Dahan, Hanna Lerner and Faina Milman-Sivan, 'Global labor rights as duties of justice' in Yossi Dahan, Hanna Lerner and Faina Milman-Sivan (eds), *Global Justice and International Labour Rights* (Cambridge University Press, Cambridge 2016), 63; John S. Dryzek and Jonathan Pickering, *The Politics of the Anthropocene* (Oxford University Press, Oxford 2019); Karen Dynan and Louise Sheiner, 'GDP as a Measure of Economic Well-being' (2018) *Hutchins Center Working Paper N° 43*, 1; Valentina Grado, 'Decent Work in Global Supply Chains: Mapping the Work of the International Labour Organization' in Marc Bungenberg, Markus Krajewski, Christian J. Tams, Jörg Philipp Terhechte and Adreas R. Ziegler (eds), 2019 European Yearbook of International Economic Law (Springer Nature, Cham 2020); Diane Bulan Hampton, 'Modern Slavery in Global Supply Chains: Can National Action Plans on Business and Human Rights Close the Governance Gap?' (2019) 4 *Business and Human Rights Journal*, 239; James Harrison, Mirela Barbu, Liam Campling, Ben Richardson and Adrian Smith, 'Governing Labour Standards through Free Trade Agreements: Limits of the European Union's Trade and Sustainable Development Chapters' (2019) 57(2) *Journal of Common Market Studies (JCMS)*, 260; Lynn Moore Healy and Rebecca Leela Thomas, *International Social Work – Professional Action in an Interdependent World* (3rd edition, Oxford University Press, Oxford 2021); John F. Helliwell, Richard Layard, Jeffrey Sachs, and Jan-Emmanuel De Neve, *World Happiness Report 2021* (Sustainable Development Solutions Network, New York 2021); Peter N. Hess., *Economic Growth and Sustainable Development* (Routledge, UK/USA 2016); Humbert Franziska, *The Challenge of Child Labour in International Law* (Cambridge University Press, UK/USA/Australia/Spain/South Africa/Singapore/Brazil/India 2009); ILO, OECD, IOM, UNICEF – Alliance 8.7, *Ending child labour, forced labour and human trafficking in global supply chains – Executive Summary*, (ILO, OECD, IOM, UNICEF, Geneva 2019); International Labour Organization, *Time to Act for SDG 8: Integrating Decent Work, Sustained Growth and Environmental Integrity* (International Labour Office, Geneva 2019); S. Nazrul Islam, *Rivers and Sustainable Development: Alternative Approaches and Their Implications* (Oxford University Press, Oxford 2020); Thilo J. Ketschau, 'Social sustainable development or sustainable social development - two sides of the same coin? The structure of social justice as a normative basis for the social dimension of sustainability' (2017) 12 *Int. J. of Design & Nature and Ecodynamics*, 341; Sigrid Alexandra Koob, Stinne Skriver Jørgensen and Hans-Otto Sano, 'Human rights and economic growth – an econometric analysis of the rights to education and health' (2018) 4 *Matters of Concern Human Rights' Research Papers*, 8 (The Danish Institute for Human Rights); Louis J. Kotzé, 'The Sustainable Development Goals: an existential critique' in Duncan French and Louis J. Kotzé (eds), *Sustainable Development Goals, Law, Theory and Implementation* (2017), 41; Brian Langille, 'The narrative of global justice and the grammar of law' in Yossi Dahan, Hanna Lerner and Faina Milman-Sivan (eds), *Global Justice and International Labour Rights* (Cambridge University Press, Cambridge 2016), 188; Brian Langille, 'What is International Labor Law For?' (2009) 3 *Law Ethics Hum. Rights*, 63; Axel Marx, Franz Ebert, Nicolas Hachez, 'Dispute Settlement for Labour Provisions in EU Free Trade Agreements: Rethinking Current Approaches, Politics and Governance' (2017) 5(4) *Politics and Governance*, 49-59; Gillian MacNaughton and Diane F. Frey, 'Decent Work, Human Rights and the Sustainable Development Goals' (2016) 47 *Georgetown Journal of International Law*, 607 (620); Gillian MacNaughton and Diane F. Frey, 'Decent Work for All: A Holistic Human Rights Approach' (2011) 26 *Am. U. Int'l L. Rev.*, 462; Tonia Novitz, 'Engagement with sustainability at the International Labour Organization and wider implications for collective worker voice' (2020) 159 *International Labour Review*, 466; George P. Politakis, 'The ILO's Standard-Setting' in Simon Chesterman, David M. Malone and Santiago Villalpando (eds), *The Oxford Handbook of United Nations Treaties* (Oxford University Press, Oxford 2019), 229; Santanu Roy, 'Sustainable Growth' in Mukul Majumdar, Ian Wills, Pasquale Michael Sgro and John M. Gowdy (eds), *Fundamental Economics – Encyclopedia of Life Support Systems – Vol. II* (UNESCO-EOLSS Publishers, Abu Dhabi 2010), 35; Christoph Scherrer, 'Superfluous Workers: Why SDG 8 Will Remain Elusive' in Markus Kaltenborn and Markus Krajewski and Heike Kuhn (eds), *Sustainable Development Goals and Human Rights* (Springer, Cham 2020), 133; UN Stats, *SDG 8.7.1 indicator metadata* (last updated: February 2021), https://unstats.un.org/sdgs/m etadata/files/Metadata-08-07-01.pdf (last accessed 27.06.2021, 19:45); Wolfgang Weiß and Cornelia Furculita, 'The EU in Search for Stronger Enforcement Rules: Assessing the Proposed Amendments to Trade Enforcement Regulation 654/2014' (2020) 23(4) *JIEL*, 865-84; Liangrong Zu, 'Decent Work' in Samuel O. Idowu, Nicholas Capaldi, Liangrong Zu and Ananda Das Gupta (eds) *Encyclopedia of Corporate Social Responsibility* (Springer-Verlag, Berlin/Heidelberg 2013).

A. Background and Origin of SDG 8

Economic growth can lead to increased economic activity and thus represents a key   1
factor for sustainable development in the long term through the creation of new jobs.[1]
According to the UN,

> Sustainable development recognizes that eradicating poverty in all its forms and dimensions, com-
> bating inequality within and among countries, preserving the planet, creating sustained, inclusive
> and sustainable economic growth (emphasis added) and fostering social inclusion are linked to each
> other and are interdependent.[2]

Inclusive and sustainable economic growth and employment and decent work for all   2
form therefore a central lever for the implementation of other SDGs.[3] Job opportunities
are a central part of many people's concerns worldwide.[4] For young adults in particular,
jobs are one of the main stress factors.[5]

However, the quality and quantity of job prospects are in jeopardy worldwide. Vari-   3
ous crises have led to a massive loss of jobs in the recent past.[6] The SARS-CoV-2 crisis
in particular has led to a massive destruction of jobs worldwide in 2020 and continues

---

[1] https://sdgcompass.org/wp-content/uploads/2016/04/Goal_8.pdf.

[2] A/RES/70/1, Transforming our world: the 2030 Agenda for Sustainable Development, para. 5.

[3] For the positive interactions between growth/employment/work and health/well-being see Griggs et al., *A Guide to SDG Interactions: From Science to Implementation* (2017), 102.

[4] United Nations General Assembly Open Working Group on Sustainable Development Goals, *Compendium of TST Issues Briefs October 2014*, 44.

[5] Dooley et al., *My World Survey 2, The National Study of Youth Mental Health in Ireland* (2019)., 71.

[6] United Nations General Assembly Open Working Group on Sustainable Development Goals, *Compendium of TST Issues Briefs October 2014*, 44.

to change the job market since.[7] The resulting negative consequences particularly affect workers in the informal sector, especially young people[8] and women.[9]

4   The creation of decent jobs is one aspect of inclusive economic growth and defines as follows:

> Growth (increase in the inflation-adjusted value of the goods and services produced by an economy over a given period of time) that generates decent jobs, gives opportunities for all segments of society, especially socially excluded groups, and distributes the income and non-income gains from prosperity more equally across society.[10]

5   Initial approaches and demands for sustainable economic growth can already be seen in the Brundtland Report. In her foreword to the Brundtland report, Gro Harlem Brundtland postulated: 'What is needed now is a new era of economic growth – growth that is forceful and at the same time socially and environmentally sustainable.'[11] This demand for economic growth must be seen in the context of the definition of sustainability as 'development that meets the needs of the present without compromising the ability of future generations to meet their own needs.'[12] Overall, the call for economic growth is of great importance in the Brundtland report.[13]

6   A link between economic growth and sustainable development can also be found in subsequent declarations. The Rio Declaration called for an open international economic system that promotes both economic growth and sustainable development.[14] Moreover, Agenda 21 urged for economic growth being needed in developing countries. In this context, a link to sustainable development and growth has always been highlighted:

> Investment is critical to the ability of developing countries to achieve needed economic growth (emphasis added) to improve the welfare of their populations and to meet their basic needs in a sustainable manner, all without deteriorating (emphasis added) or depleting the resource base that underpins development.[15]

7   The Rio + 20 Conference 2012 maintained[16] and further developed the link between economic growth and sustainable development. Particular attention was paid to development and economic growth in developing countries.[17] Besides, a link has been established between economic growth and decent work, leading to formulations very similar to the current wording of SDG 8 that can already be found in the outcome document

---

[7] Global Policy Watch, *COVID-19 and the SDGs The impact of the coronavirus pandemic on the global sustainability agenda,* 5.

[8] United Nations General Assembly Open Working Group on Sustainable Development Goals, *Compendium of TST Issues Briefs October 2014,* 44.

[9] United Nations Entity for Gender Equality and the Empowerment of Women, *Women and Sustainable Development,* 17.

[10] United Nations General Assembly Open Working Group on Sustainable Development Goals, *Compendium of TST Issues Briefs October 2014,* 81.

[11] Report of the World Commission on Environment and Development: Our Common Future, Chairman's foreword.

[12] Report of the World Commission on Environment and Development: Our Common Future, Part I, Chapter 2 IV, para. 1.

[13] The word combination 'economic growth' alone can be found 40 times in the report.

[14] UN, Report on the United Nations Conference on Environment and Development, A/CONF.151/26 (Vol. I), Principle 12.

[15] Agenda 21, para. 2.23.

[16] A/RES/66/288, *The future we want,* 11 September 2012, para. 147: 'We recognize that poverty eradication, full and productive employment and decent work for all, and social integration and protection are interrelated and mutually reinforcing, and that enabling environments to promote them need to be created at all levels.'

[17] A/RES/66/288, *The future we want,* 11 September 2012, para. 106.

'The future we want'.[18] The jobs should better meet the needs of the people and promote a sustainable use of resources,[19] thus creating a link to the definition of sustainable development of the Brundtland report. The importance of decent work for young people and women was highlighted in particular.[20] Accordingly, decent work meets the needs of today's generation without compromising those of future generations.

During the development of the SDGs, various approaches sought to integrate sustain-   **8** able economic growth and decent jobs in the post-2015 agenda. Overall, an approach combining economic growth and decent jobs has prevailed, that had already been pursued in 'The future we want'.[21]

With SDG 8.7 and SDG 8.8, an approach was created to strengthen labour rights and   **9** prevent forced labour. In 2016, 40.3 million people (71 per cent women, 29 per cent men) were held in modern slavery.[22] In many cases, these people are also working in supply chains that, inter alia, supply the Global North with products of various kinds, despite the Forced Labour Convention[23] being one of the most ratified ILO conventions, with 178 out of 187 member states.[24]

B. Scope and Dimensions of SDG 8

SDG 8 particularly stands out in the Global Agenda 2030 in many respects. Covering,   **10** on the one hand, economic growth in alignment with respect for the environment, SDG 8 reflects the economic dimension of sustainable development.[25] Bearing in mind the profound interdependencies between the social, ecological and economic dimensions of sustainable development, SDG 8 strikingly likewise covers the social dimension of sustainable development by focusing on decent work as second broad aspect.[26] As indicated before, SDG 8 is composed of three main thematic strands which can be entitled as 'sustainable economic growth', 'inclusive economic growth' as well as 'sustainable economic

---

[18] A/RES/66/288, *The future we want*, 11 September 2012, para. 58(d): 'Promote sustained and inclusive economic growth, foster innovation and provide opportunities, benefits and empowerment for all and respect for all human rights.' and para. 62: 'We encourage each country to consider the implementation of green economy policies in the context of sustainable development and poverty eradication, in a manner that endeavours to drive sustained, inclusive and equitable economic growth and job creation, particularly for women, youth and the poor.'

[19] A/RES/66/288, *The future we want*, 11 September 2012, para. 30.

[20] A/RES/66/288, *The future we want*, 11 September 2012, para. 148.

[21] For further approaches to implementing economic growth and decent jobs see United Nations General Assembly Open Working Group on Sustainable Development Goals, *Compendium of TST Issues Briefs October 2014*, 47.

[22] The latest global estimates showed 152 million children being in child labour and 25 million adults and children being in forced labour, including in global supply chains, Ending child labour, forced labour and human trafficking in global supply chains; ILO, OECD, IOM, UNICEF, *Ending child labour, forced labour and human trafficking in global supply chains – Executive Summary* (2019).

[23] International Labour Organization (ILO), Convention Concerning Forced or Compulsory Labour, 28 June 1930, No. 29 (entry into force: 01 May 1932).

[24] Hampton, 'Modern Slavery in Global Supply Chains: Can National Action Plans on Business and Human Rights Close the Governance Gap?' (2019) 4 *Business and Human Rights Journal*, 239 (248); Grado, 'Decent Work in Global Supply Chains: Mapping the Work of the International Labour Organization' in Bungenberg et al. (eds), 2019 *EYIEL* (2020).

[25] Islam, *Rivers and Sustainable Development: Alternative Approaches and Their Implications* (2020), 5 ff.; Dryzek and Pickering, *The Politics of the Anthropocene* (2018), 82 ff; A/RES/70/1, *Transforming our world: the 2030 Agenda for Sustainable Development*, para. 2.

[26] Novitz, 'Engagement with sustainability at the International Labour Organization and wider implications for collective worker voice' (2020) 159 *International Labour Review*, 463 (466).

growth and environmental integrity' (→ mn. 1 ff.).[27] In this context, the first strand encompasses SDG 8.1 to 8.3 and SDG 8.10 and SDG 8.a which primarily focus on the enhancement of economic productivity leading to an overall economic growth in countries. The second strand is embodied by SDGs 8.5, 8.6, 8.7 and 8.8 deals with the significant field of decent work and labour rights of all working people whereby SDG 8.5 can be considered to be at the core of the entire SDG 8.[28] The third strand emphasises the interconnection of the economic and social dimensions with the environmental dimension of sustainable development with regard to economic growth and its detachment from environmental deterioration (SDG 8.4 and SDG 8.9).[29] Considering the multilayered content of SDG 8, a differentiated view of the legal framework proves to be useful.

I. Elementary Definitions

1. Economic Growth and Decent Work

11   From an economic point of view, the concept of economic growth refers to 'the increase in wealth over time and it is usually measured in terms of variation in gross domestic product (GDP), which comprises the entire value-added produced within national boundaries in a given time-frame'.

12   According to the OECD, the GDP is defined as 'the standard measure of the value added created through the production of goods and services in a country during a certain period. As such, it also measures the income earned from that production, or the total amount spent on final goods and services (less imports). The OECD acknowledges that the 'GDP is the single most important indicator to capture economic activity' but it does not provide 'a suitable measure of people's material well-being for which alternative indicators may be more appropriate.'[30]

13   In the view of the EU the 'Gross Domestic Product (GDP) is a powerful and widely accepted indicator for monitoring short to medium term fluctuations in economic activity [...]'. The GDP is recognised as the 'best single measure of how the market economy is performing', despite of all of its shortcomings.[31]

14   The definition of GDP and their content is contested regarding the limitations and exclusions in particular, and the question still remains, if other of the several indexes could capture the human and environmental issues of life more precisely and provide for a better answer.

15   GDP does not include goods and services that cannot be valued or have not been valued by statistical offices (non-market goods and services). These include, amongst others, household production, admission-free beach visits and wildlife watching. Consequently, GDP does not measure well-being beyond GDP metrics, which include environmental and social aspects of economic activities. Furthermore, GDP as the overall measure of economic welfare does not capture aspects of inequality. A comparison of,

---

[27] ILO, *Time to Act for SDG 8: Integrating Decent Work, Sustained Growth and Environmental Integrity* (2019), 5 ff.
[28] ILO, *Time to Act for SDG 8: Integrating Decent Work, Sustained Growth and Environmental Integrity* (2019), 14 f.
[29] ILO, *Time to Act for SDG 8: Integrating Decent Work, Sustained Growth and Environmental Integrity* (2019), 23 f.
[30] https://data.oecd.org/gdp/gross-domestic-product-gdp.htm; OECD, *OECD Economic Outlook, Volume 2021 Issue 1* (2021), 13.
[31] COM(2009) 433 final, *GDP and beyond Measuring progress in a changing world* (2009), 9.

for example, the consumption possibilities of the poor compared to those of the rich is therefore not possible at all (→ Goal 10)[32]

However, GDP misses the content related to the period of a longer term economic, 16 social progress and notably the ability of a society to tackle issues such as climate change, resource efficiency or social inclusion are not included in the measurement of the GDP. Therefore, GDP must be complemented with other indicators and statistics, covering happiness or other economic, social and environmental issues, on which people's well-being critically depends.'[33]

Alternative indicators are in particular those attempting to integrate major questions 17 of the sustainable development framework and from the authors' perspective, the most impressive are discussed by Stiglitz, Sen and Fitoussi (2009)[34], Stiglitz, Fitoussi and Durand (2018),[35] the UNDP Human Development Index and the Anthropocene[36] and the World Happiness Report 2021 (→ Intro mn. 225 ff.).[37]

In a more systematic way the examples of these alternative indicators are related to 18 the following groups:

- **Enlarged GDP indicators** start from GDP (or other figures from the System of National Accounts) but adjust for some of its shortcomings to deliver a more comprehensive overview of a country's wealth or well-being
- **Social indicators** give insights into a broad range of social issues, concerns and trends such as life expectancy, poverty rates, unemployment rates, disposable income, and education levels, etc. They are also used to give insights into broader notions of social progress
- **Environmental indicators** cast light over the state and development of issues such as natural resources, environmental pollution and waste, as well as related issues such as human health
- **Well-being indicators** are used to broadly illustrate people's general satisfaction with life, or give a more nuanced picture of quality of life in relation to their jobs, family life, health conditions, and standards of living[38]

Since 2007 the EU displays on the platform 'Beyond GDP' new perspectives on the 19 discussion about new indicators beyond GDP.[39]

In a broader sense, economic growth depends on the content of the specific indicator 20 and is thereby characterised by various factors ranging from 'innovation and technology [to] [...] financial and human capital'. Recognisable consequences of economic growth can be 'progresses in science and medicine, education and public health, trade and globalization, and stable and capable governments and institutions'.[40] Another approach defines economic growth as

---

[32] https://ec.europa.eu/environment/beyond_gdp/FAQ_en.html.

[33] COM(2009) 433 final, *GDP and beyond Measuring progress in a changing world* (2009), 9.

[34] Stiglitz and Sen and Fitoussi, *Report by the Commission on the Measurement of Economic Performance and Social Progress* (2019), https://ec.europa.eu/eurostat/documents/8131721/8131772/Stiglitz-Sen-Fitoussi-Commission-report.pdf.

[35] Stiglitz and Fitoussi and Durand, *Beyond GDP: Measuring What Counts for Economic and Social Performance* (2018), https://doi.org/10.1787/9789264307292-en.

[36] http://hdr.undp.org/en/dashboard-human-development-anthropocene; UNDP, *Human Development Report 2020, The next frontier, Human development and the Anthropocene* (2020).

[37] Helliwell and Layard and Sachs and De Neve, *World Happiness Report 2021* (2021).

[38] https://ec.europa.eu/environment/beyond_gdp/FAQ_en.html.

[39] COM(2009) 433 final, *GDP and beyond Measuring progress in a changing world* (2009), 9.

[40] Chiappero-Martinetti and von Jacobi and Signorelli, 'Human Development and Economic Growth' in Hölscher and Tomann (eds), *Palgrave Dictionary of Emerging Markets and Transition Economics* (2015), 223 (224).

the process by which a society expands its production and consumption opportunities over time. It involves increased output of commodities (goods as well as services) as well as creation of new commodities that are either directly consumed or enter as inputs in production of other commodities[41]

21   Thereby,

Gross domestic product (GDP) is the value of the goods and services produced by the nation's economy less the value of the goods and services used up in production. GDP is also equal to the sum of personal consumption expenditures, gross private domestic investment, net exports of goods and services, and government consumption expenditures and gross investment.[42]

22   Thus, economic growth serves not only for increases in economic productivity of a country but also contributes to its social and societal development. With regard to people living in extreme poverty, economic growth constitutes the fundamental catalyst for enhancing 'the material standard of living and tends to reduce absolute poverty'.[43] The concept of

[s]ustained economic growth can be defined as the event that per capita income in a society exhibits a secular or long-run tendency to expand over time, though the process may be marked by intermittent periods of stagnation and decay such as those caused by business cycles.[44]

23   The view that the paradigm of economic growth only has positive effects on people and development, on the other hand, has been criticised from many sides for years, at least according to the criticism of the Club of Rome in 1972.[45] Amongst others, the degrowth movement pleads 'for societies that prioritize social and ecological well-being instead of corporate profits, over-production and excess consumption' (→ Intro mn. 225 ff.).[46]

24   Criticism mostly refers to exceeding the limits of the Earth's ecosystem[47] to argue that the idea of growth harms the ecosystem and is contrary to a sustainable and more equitable world. However, the approach of the Global Agenda 2030 endeavours to unite the different concepts of economic productivity and sustainable development.[48]

25   However, the concept of economic growth is intrinsically linked to social development within a society. Thereby, social development denotes a process whereby 'various forms of redistribution of opportunities, income, assets and power' contribute to 'the welfare of the people'. Notably, for the implementation of social development, institutions set up specifically for this purpose are to 'create a capacity for meeting human

---

[41] Roy, 'Sustainable Growth' in Majumdar et al. (eds), *Fundamental Economics – Encyclopedia of Life Support Systems – Vol. II* (2010), 35 (36).

[42] Dynan and Sheiner, 'GDP as a Measure of Economic Well-being' (2018) 43 *Hutchins Center Working Paper*, 1 (3); see also the concept of gross national product (GNP): GNP 'measures the value of output produced by the citizens and domestically-owned factors of production, regardless of the country in which the production actually takes place', Van den Berg, *Economic Growth and Development* (2017), 65.

[43] Hess, *Economic Growth and Sustainable Development* (2016), 3.

[44] Roy, 'Sustainable Growth' in Majumdar et al. (eds), *Fundamental Economics – Encyclopedia of Life Support Systems – Vol. II* (2010), 35 (36).

[45] Meadows and Meadows and Randers and Behrens III, *The Limits to Growth; A Report for the Club of Rome's Project on the Predicament of Mankind* (1972).

[46] https://www.degrowth.info/en/degrowth-definition/.

[47] See on the concept of planetary boundaries (to be understood as biophysical boundaries) Kotzé, 'The Sustainable Development Goals: an existential critique' in French and Kotzé, *Sustainable Development Goals, Law, Theory and Implementation* (2017), 51 f., 64.

[48] Guercio, *Brief for GSDR 2015, Sustainability and economic de-growth* (2015), further reading Andreucci and Engel-Di Mauro, 'Capitalism, socialism and the challenge of degrowth: introduction to the symposium' (2019) 30.2 *Capitalism Nature Socialism*, 176-88; Asara et al., 'Socially sustainable degrowth as a social–ecological transformation: repoliticizing sustainability' (2015) 10.3 *Sustainability Science*, 375-84; D'Alisa and Demaria and Kallis, *Degrowth: a vocabulary for a new era* (2014).

needs at all levels'.[49] In this vein, social development shall ensure that overall benefits in economic productivity are to be justly and sustainably distributed among the people while ensuring access to necessary 'public services and utilities'. Moreover, people shall be entitled to viably participate in societal decision-making thus actively contributing to the shaping of their living conditions.[50]

Respectively, the ideal goal of social development is to ensure social justice which is   26
'the state of a society when the distribution of rights, opportunities and resources can be rated as just'[51], thus 'reducing social and economic inequalities' (→ Goal 10).[52] Another concept is that of global justice, which theoretically focuses on how and with which in-stitutions an 'just distribution of benefits and burdens across the world' can be achieved and safeguarded (→ Intro mn. 184 ff.).[53]

In this context, the overall concept of sustainable economic growth 'refers to a growth   27
process where the welfare of society does not steadily decline over time due to excessive use of limited environmental resources or environmental damage caused by production and consumption activities.[54]

Decent work 'is concerned with the availability of employment in conditions of   28
freedom, equity, security, and human dignity' encompassing the four core aspects of 'employment conditions, social security, rights at the workplace, and social dialog[ue]'.[55] As such, decent work

> involves opportunities for work that is productive and delivers a fair income, security in the workplace and social protection for families, better prospects for personal development and social integration, freedom for people to express their concerns, organize and participate in the decisions that affect their lives and equality of opportunity and treatment for all women and men.[56]

Thus, decent work is characterised by the concept of 'freedom of association and the   29
right to collective bargaining'.[57] Particularly, the 'economic indicator' of labour produc-tivity is integrally linked to decent work and economic growth as it represents the total volume of output (measured in terms of GDP) produced per unit of labour (measured in terms of the number of employed persons) during a given time reference period. The indicator allows data users to assess GDP-to-labour input levels and growth rates over time, thus providing general information about the efficiency and quality of human

---

[49] Healy and Thomas, *International Social Work – Professional Action in an Interdependent World* (2021), 62.

[50] Islam, *Rivers and Sustainable Development – Alternative Approaches and Their Implications* (2020), 5 ff.

[51] Ketschau, 'Social sustainable development or sustainable social development - two sides of the same coin? The structure of social justice as a normative basis for the social dimension of sustainability' (2017) 12 *Int. J. of Design & Nature and Ecodynamics*, 338 (341).

[52] The more general critics state that humankind is too attached to anthropocentric thoughts that is not aligned to Earth's systems and supply which may be naïve in light of the Interdependencies of marine and terrestrial resources; see e.g. Kotzé, 'The Sustainable Development Goals: an existential critique' in French and Kotzé, *Sustainable Development Goals, Law, Theory and Implementation* (2017), 51 f., 64; Dahan and Lerner and Milman-Sivan, 'Global labor rights as duties of justice' in Dahan and Lerner and Milman-Sivan (eds), *Global Justice and International Labour Rights* (2016), 53 (63).

[53] Choudhary, 'Global Justice' in Farazmand (ed), *Global Encyclopedia of Public Administration, Public Policy, and Governance* (2018); see in context of sustainable development Cordonier Segger, 'Sustainability, Global Justice, and the Law: Contributions of the Hon. Justice Charles Doherty Gonthier' (2010) 55 *McGill L.J.*, 337 (337 ff).

[54] Roy, 'Sustainable Growth' in Majumdar et al. (eds), *Fundamental Economics Vol. II – Encyclopedia of Life Support Systems* (2010), 35 (35).

[55] Zu, 'Decent Work' in Idowu et al. (eds) *Encyclopedia of Corporate Social Responsibility* (2013).

[56] https://www.ilo.org/global/topics/decent-work/lang--en/index.htm.

[57] Novitz, *The normative promise of sustainability for labour standards – and the limitations of the SDGs* (2020).

capital in the production process for a given economic and social context, including other complementary inputs and innovations used in production.[58]

30   Earth governance should therefore be a guiding principle that connects the mostly disconnected SDGs in a systematic sense. It is recognised that the formation of inclusive *societies* is crucial, although the outcome that the SDGs can achieve is fully dependent on the underlying Earth system and its planetary boundaries. The mere perpetuation and continuation of socio-economic growth thinking as it can be retrieved in the SDGs as an interwoven texture conveys a missed opportunity, but not a straightforward thinking in the face of global challenges.

31   SDG 8.4 specifically underlines the importance of improving global resource efficiency in consumption and production and endeavour to decouple economic growth from environmental degradation, in accordance with the 10-Year Framework of Programmes on Sustainable Consumption and Production (10YFP), with developed countries taking the lead and UNEP serving as the Secretariat (→ Goal 12 mn. 15 f.).[59]

32   The 5 P's and other principles (→ Intro mn. 122 ff.) also tie in the issue of inclusion and green and blue growth (SDG 8.4), which respectively focus on the Material Footprint (MF) as the mapping of global material extraction to a country's domestic final demand (virtual material quantity),[60] as well as Domestic Material Consumption (DMC) as the actual quantity of material consumed in an economy along a supply chain. DMC and MF need to be considered collectively in determining the sustainability status of economic growth, as they cover both production and consumption, and provide a realistic indication of the location of material-intensive industrial processes, and their relocation or removal, e.g. to developing countries or LDCs.[61]

2. Forced Labour, Modern Slavery, Human Trafficking and Child Labour

33   In SDG 8.7, forced labour, modern slavery, human trafficking and child labour are envisaged. In this regard, modern slavery constitutes the overarching term which includes the more specific forms of human trafficking, forced labour and child labour as well as 'forced and early marriage'.[62] At the international scene, no single concrete definition for modern slavery exists. A general attempt to define slavery can be found in the 1926 Slavery Convention[63], though, it reflects a rather obsolete picture of slavery by referring to 'ownership' which does not fully coincide with today's forms of modern slavery. Thus, Craig et al. determine three typical features of modern slavery, namely 'severe economic exploitation; an absence of human rights; and control through the threat or reality of violence or coercion'.[64]

---

[58] ILO, *ILO Manual – Decent Work Indicators – Guidelines for Producers and Users of Statistical and Legal Framework Indicators* (2013), 214.

[59] A/RES/66/288 of 27 July 2012, by which the UN General Assembly endorsed the outcome document of the United Nations Conference on Sustainable Development; further information: High-Level Political Forum On Sustainable Development, *The 10 Year Framework of Programmes on Sustainable Consumption and Production Patterns (10YFP)* (2012); https://sustainabledevelopment.un.org/index.php?page=view&type=400&nr=1444&menu=35.

[60] The total material footprint is the sum of the material footprints for biomass, fossil fuels, metal ores and non-metal ores.

[61] UN Stats, *SDG indicator metadata, SDG 8.4.1* (Last updated: 4 February 2021).

[62] https://www.antislavery.org/slavery-today/modern-slavery/.

[63] Art. 1(1) Slavery Convention: Slavery is the status or condition of a person over whom any or all of the powers attaching to the right of ownership are exercised.

[64] Craig et al., 'Editorial introduction: the modern slavery agenda: policy, politics and practice' in Craig et al. (eds), *The modern slavery agenda – policy, politics and practice in the UK* (2019), 1 (10).

Forced labour is defined in the ILO Forced Labour Convention of 1930, referring to **34**
'all work or service which is exacted from any person under the menace of any penalty
and for which the said person has not offered himself voluntarily'.[65] Notably,

> [f]orced labour can be imposed to adults and children, by State authorities, by private enterprises or
> by individuals. It is observed in all types of economic activity, such as domestic work, construction,
> agriculture, manufacturing, sexual exploitation, forced begging, etc. and in every country.[66]

The International Labour Organization (ILO) offers a set of 11 indicators which serve **35**
to further determine and identify cases of forced labour in real occasions: abuse of
vulnerability, deception, restriction of movement, isolation, physical and sexual violence,
intimidation and threats, retention of identity documents, withholding of wages, debt
bondage, abusive working and living conditions as well as excessive overtime.[67]

Forced labour is closely related to the term 'modern slavery' (SDG 8.7). However, no **36**
precise definition of modern slavery exists. One approach could be the following:

> Slavery is a social phenomenon existing on the far end of a continuum of oppression, where human
> beings completely dominate and exploit other human beings and this domination results in physical,
> psychological, and interpersonal trauma; financial and social instability and inequities; and dilution
> of the fundamental principles of democracy.[68]

The term 'human trafficking' is to be understood as **37**

> "Trafficking in persons" shall mean the recruitment, transportation, transfer, harbouring or receipt of
> persons, by means of the threat or use of force or other forms of coercion, of abduction, of fraud, of
> deception, of the abuse of power or of a position of vulnerability or of the giving or receiving of pay-
> ments or benefits to achieve the consent of a person having control over another person, for the pur-
> pose of exploitation. Exploitation shall include, at a minimum, the exploitation of the prostitution of
> others or other forms of sexual exploitation, forced labour or services, slavery or practices similar to
> slavery, servitude or the removal of organs.[69] ($\rightarrow$ Goal 5 mn. 27 ff.)

While the widespread problem of child labour receives international attention from **38**
'international organisations, non-governmental organisations, trade unions and other
interest groups',[70] comprehensive coverage of child labour is not easy to handle. Some
form of a commonly agreed definition on what constitutes child labour can be derived
from several human rights instruments[71] a nucleus of which has been expressed by the
ILO as follows:

> [W]ork that deprives children of their childhood, their potential and their dignity, and that is
> harmful to physical and mental development. It refers to work that: is mentally, physically, socially
> or morally dangerous and harmful to children; and/or interferes with their schooling by: depriving
> them of the opportunity to attend school; obliging them to leave school prematurely; or requiring
> them to attempt to combine school attendance with excessively long and heavy work.[72]

---

[65] Art. 2(1) Forced Labour Convention 1930 (No. 29).

[66] https://www.ilo.org/global/topics/forced-labour/definition/lang--en/index.htm.

[67] https://www.ilo.org/global/topics/forced-labour/publications/WCMS_ 203832/lang--en/index.htm.

[68] Nicholson et al., 'A Full Freedom: Contemporary Survivors' Definitions of Slavery' (2018) 18 *Human Rights Law Review*, 689 (702).

[69] A/RES/55/25, Protocol to Prevent, Suppress and Punish Trafficking in Persons, Especially Women and Children, Supplementing the U.N. Convention Against Transnational Organized Crime art. 3(a), Nov. 15, 2000, 2237 U.N.T.S. 319, Annex II, Art. 3.

[70] https://en.reset.org/knowledge/child-labour.

[71] ILO Minimum Age Convention, 1973 (No.138) (ratified by 173 countries in 2021), and the Worst Forms of Child Labour Convention, 1999 (No.182) (ratified by 187 countries in 2021), and by the United Nations Convention on the Rights of the Child (ratified by 196 countries in 2021, one country left).

[72] https://www.ilo.org/ipec/facts/lang--en/index.htm.

39   However, a major hindrance to applying such or other definitions lies in particular in the internationally different age-related classifications of what is to be considered a child. Whereas international conventions classify children 'as people aged 18 and under, individual governments – and different cultures – define "children" according to different ages or other criteria'.[73]

40   Beyond, child labour has to be regarded under the special aspects of childhood (culturally diverse perceptions) and definitory concepts of work and labour. In this context, the notion of labour is connoted with 'toil', 'exertion' and 'painful and strenuous effort'.[74] It is thus not equivalent with work in general which may further encompass different forms of work being 'beneficial, promoting or enhancing a child's physical, mental, spiritual, moral or social development without interfering with schooling, recreation and rest'. Thus, child labour holds 'intolerable' characteristics upon which child labour is identified.[75]

41   From a statistical point of view,

> [t]he number of children engaged in child labour corresponds to the number of children reported to be in child labour during the reference period (usually the week prior to the survey). The proportion of children in child labour is calculated as the number of children in child labour divided by the total number of children in the population. For the purposes of this indicator, children include all persons aged 5 to 17.[76]

42   The concept of child labour also includes hazardous work[77] and 'the worst forms of child labour other than hazardous work'.[78] Worst forms of child labour significantly comprise forced labour, human trafficking and modern slavery concerning children, namely:

> (a) all forms of slavery or practices similar to slavery, such as the sale and trafficking of children, debt bondage and serfdom, and forced or compulsory labour, including forced or compulsory recruitment of children for use in armed conflict; (b) the use, procuring or offering of a child for prostitution, for the production of pornography or for pornographic performances; (c) the use, procuring or offering of a child for illicit activities, in particular for the production and trafficking of drugs as defined in the relevant international treaties; and (d) work which, by its nature or the circumstances in which it is carried out, is likely to harm the health, safety, or morals of children.[79]

43   Hazardous child labour covers 'those [children] involved in any activity or occupation that, by its nature or the circumstances in which it is carried out, is likely to harm their health, safety, or morals'.[80]

---

[73] https://en.reset.org/knowledge/child-labour.
[74] Humbert, *The Challenge of Child Labour in International Law* (2009), 17.
[75] Humbert, *The Challenge of Child Labour in International Law* (2009), 18.
[76] UN Stats, SDG 8.7.1 indicator metadata (Last updated: February 2021).
[77] Art. 3(d) of ILO Convention No. 182 (1999); No. 3 of ILO Recommendation No. 190 (1999).
[78] Art. 3(a) – (c) of ILO Convention No. 182 (1999); Resolution concerning statistics of child labour, adopted by the 18th International Conference of Labour Statisticians (2008), para. 19.
[79] Art. 3(a) – (c) of ILO Convention No.182 (1999).
[80] Akhtar and Nyamutata, *International Child Law* (2020), 278; Art. 3(d) of ILO Convention No.182; According to No. 3 of ILO Convention No. 190 (1999), when determining hazardous work, consideration should be given, inter alia, to:
(a) work which exposes children to physical, psychological or sexual abuse, (b) work underground, under water, at dangerous heights or in confined spaces, (c) work with dangerous machinery, equipment and tools, or which involves the manual handling or transport of heavy loads, (d) work in an unhealthy environment which may, for example, expose children to hazardous substances, agents or processes, or to temperatures, noise levels, or vibrations damaging to their health, (e) work under particularly difficult conditions such as work for long hours or during the night or work where the child is unreasonably confined to the premises of the employer.

Within SDG 8.7, the recruitment and use of child soldiers represent a particular   44
concern within the framework of worst forms of child labour. Thus, the Paris Principles
on the Involvement of Children in Armed Conflict (2007) define child soldiers as
follows:

> A child associated with an armed force or armed group refers to any person below 18 years of age
> who is, or who has been, recruited or used by an armed force or armed group in any capacity,
> including but not limited to children, boys and girls, used as fighters, cooks, porters, spies or for
> sexual purposes.[81]

Recognised as one of the worst forms of child labour, the recruitment of child soldiers   45
is further classified as a war crime under the Rome Statute of the International Criminal
Court.[82]

The related indicator 8.7.1 covers the proportion and number of children aged 5-17   46
years engaged in child labour, by sex and age.[83]Three principal international legal instruments – ILO Convention No. 138 (Minimum Age) (C138), United Nations Convention
on the Rights of the Child (CRC), ILO Convention No. 182 (Worst Forms) (C182)
together set the legal boundaries for child labour, and provide the legal basis for national
and international actions against it.[84]

II. Legal foundations

The legal scope of SDG 8 is largely characterised by influences of the ILO. Looking at   47
the targets of SDG 8, a thorough and visible reference to labour and decent jobs is given.
Thus, the focus lays on international labour law and legal framework set by the ILO.

Economic growth, as one expression of the economic dimension of sustainable devel-   48
opment, is indispensable for the provision and expansion of decent work opportunities
within a country.[85] The international legal framework underpinning the sustained economic growth of countries is closely related to the legal aspects of inequalities, global
trade and the right to development (SDGs 8.1, 8.2, 8.3 and 8.10).[86] Moreover, economic
growth as such may serve as an endorsing driver for human rights.[87] Therefore, reference is made to SDG 10 which elaborates international inequalities between states and
those inequalities within countries, namely between the people (→ Goal 10).

---

[81] The Paris Principles – Principles and Guidelines on Children Associated with Armed Forces or
Armed Groups (2007), para. 2.1.

[82] Art. 8 No. 2 b xxvi and Article 8 No. 2(e) (vii), Rome Statute of the International Criminal Court, A/
CONF.183/9 of 17 July 1998; further reading: Kotiswaran, *Revisiting the Law and Governance of Trafficking, Forced Labor and Modern Slavery* (2017).

[83] UN Stats, SDG 8.7.1 indicator metadata (Last updated: February 2021).

[84] SDG 8.7.1 measures the proportion and number of children aged 5-17 years engaged in economic
activities at or above age-specific hourly thresholds (SNA production boundary basis):
Child labour for the 5 to 11 age range: children working at least 1 hour per week in economic activity;
Child labour for the 12 to 14 age range: children working for at least 14 hours per week in economic
activity; Child labour for the 15 to 17 age range: children working for more than 43 hours per week in
economic activity.

[85] https://www.ilo.org/global/topics/dw4sd/themes/employment-rich/lang--en/index.htm.

[86] See Alfarargi, *United Nations Special Rapporteur on the Right to Development – An introduction to the
mandate* (2017); Koob and Jørgensen and Sano, 'Human rights and economic growth – an econometric
analysis of the rights to education and health' (2018) 4 *Matters of Concern Human Rights' Research Papers*,
8 (8 ff.).

[87] Bohoslavsky, 'Guiding Principles to Assess the Human Rights of Economic Reforms? Yes' in Bantekas
and Lumina (eds), *Sovereign Debt and Human Rights* (2018), 402 (411).

1. Labour Law

49   The fundamental legal framework for the implementation of SDG 8 is highly shaped by international labour law, encompassing the rule-making and standard-setting by the ILO.

50   Before outlining the sources of international labour law, the general nature of labour law as such provides a useful insight into the dynamics of labour related regulations. Therefore, Langille describes labour law as

> that part of our law which structures the mobilization and deployment of human capital. Human capital is at the core of human freedom. Labour law is at its root no longer best conceived as law aimed at protecting employees against superior employer bargaining power in the negotiation of contracts of employment. That is now an empirically limited and normatively thin account of the discipline. Rather, we can say that labour law is now best conceived of as that part of our law which structures (and thus either constrains or liberates) human capital creation and deployment. Education ("Education is the key to all the human capabilities") and, especially, early childhood development strategies, are critical to human capital creation. But so is the set of policies which govern the lives of human beings when they enter the workforce–whether as employees, independent producers, or under any other legal rubric or economic arrangement or relation of production. Human capital must not only be created, it must be utilized, effectively deployed: that is, in the best sense of the word, exploited. The law which governs and structures these critical dimensions of our common life is labour law.[88]

51   In this vein, the law of labour is intrinsically linked with governance and societal aspects, thus making both national and international labour law a multi-layered construct whose interdisciplinary influences have always to be taken into account when scrutinising the legal regulatory framework of labour.[89]

2. International Labour Law

52   Initially founded in 1919, the ILO serves since 1946 as a specialised agency of the UN with its headquarters in Geneva, Switzerland. As such, its primary goals focus on the advancement of social justice and the promotion of decent work worldwide. In this context, the ILO strives for 'securing international peace' through social justice and for harmonising 'working conditions in countries competing for markets'.[90] Respectively,

> the ILO has a unique tripartite structure that brings together government, employer, and worker representatives from its 187 member states with a view to adopting international labor standards and elaborating policies and programs that ensure all parts of society prosperity and progress. Given an equal voice within the Organization's governance organs, the tripartite constituents exemplify the conditions necessary for the development of effective and universally applicable standards for labor and social protection.[91]

53   By virtue of its purpose and aspirations, the ILO provides the overall sources for international labour law by means of legal instruments. The most outstanding instruments are the international labour standards which can be adopted in form of both conventions and recommendations. Thereby, ILO conventions constitute international treaties having a binding legal effect for the ratifying member states, whereas ILO recommenda-

---

[88] Langille, 'The narrative of global justice and the grammar of law' in Dahan, Lerner and Milman-Sivan (eds), *Global Justice and International Labour Rights* (2016), 186 (195).

[89] Langille, 'The narrative of global justice and the grammar of law' in Dahan and Lerner and Milman-Sivan (eds), *Global Justice and International Labour Rights* (2016), 186 (188 ff.).

[90] Politakis, 'The ILO's Standard-Setting' in Chesterman and Malone and Villalpando (eds), *The Oxford Handbook of United Nations Treaties* (2019), 229 (229).

[91] Politakis, 'The ILO's Standard-Setting' in Chesterman and Malone and Villalpando (eds), *The Oxford Handbook of United Nations Treaties* (2019), 229 (229).

tions 'serve as non-binding guidelines'.[92] Accordingly, Conventions constitute the only legally 'enforceable' tool of the ILO when pursuing its goals internationally.[93] Moreover, the instruments of declarations and resolutions supplement the ILO's commitment in international legal standard-setting.[94]

3. ILO Conventions

Since its foundation, the ILO has developed numerous conventions that address   **54** specific rights and principles concerning work (SDG 8.8). Among these conventions, eight conventions are of outstanding importance and are therefore also referred to as 'the eight fundamental conventions'[95]:

1. Forced Labour Convention 1930 (No. 29)
   (as well as the concomitant 2014 Protocol)
2. Freedom of Association and Protection of the Right to Organise Convention 1948 (No. 87)
3. Right to Organise and Collective Bargaining Convention 1949 (No. 98)
4. Abolition of Forced Labour Convention 1957 (No. 105)
5. Discrimination (Employment and Occupation) Convention 1958 (No. 111)
6. Equal Remuneration Convention 1951 (No. 100)
7. Minimum Age Convention 1973 (No. 138)
8. Worst Forms of Child Labour Convention 1999 (No. 182)

These eight comprehensive conventions already cover a wide and profound range   **55** of workers' rights at the workplace. Notwithstanding this, the scope of international labour standards within the other conventions include other important aspects such as unemployment, maternity, protection against accidents, hours of work, wages and health.[96]

In addition, so-called Governance Conventions shall facilitate the 'functioning of the   **56** international labour standards system'.[97]

1. Labour Inspection Convention 1947 (No. 81)
2. Employment Policy Convention 1964 (No. 122)
3. Labour Inspection (Agriculture) Convention 1969 (No. 129)
4. Tripartite Consultation (International Labour Standards) Convention 1976 (No. 144)

---

[92] https://www.ilo.org/global/standards/introduction-to-international-labour-standards/conventions-and-recommendations/lang--en/index.htm.

[93] Langille, 'What is International Labor Law For?' (2009) 3 *Law Ethics Hum. Rights*, 47 (63).

[94] https://www.ilo.org/inform/online-information-resources/research-guides/labour-law/lang--en/index.htm.

[95] https://www.ilo.org/global/standards/introduction-to-international-labour-standards/conventions-and-recommendations/lang--en/index.htm.

[96] For instance: ILO Unemployment Convention No. 2 (1919), ILO Employment Promotion and Protection against Unemployment Convention No. 168 (1988), ILO Maternity Protection Convention No. 183 (2000), ILO Protection against Accidents (Dockers) Convention (Revised) No. 32 (1932), ILO Hours of Work (Industry) Convention No. 1 (1919), ILO Hours of Work (Commerce and Offices) Convention No. 30 (1930), ILO Protection of Wages Convention No. 95 (1949), ILO Occupational Safety and Health Convention No. 155 (1981).

[97] https://www.ilo.org/global/standards/introduction-to-international-labour-standards/conventions-and-recommendations/lang--en/index.htm.

4. ILO Declarations

57   Throughout the years, the ILO passed several Declarations on certain labour related issues. The purpose of such declarations, which are resolutions of the ILO, is to take a stand and deliver a 'formal and authoritative' pronouncement by reinforcing 'the importance which the constituents attach to certain principles and values', thus providing for 'symbolic and political undertakings of the member States'.[98]

58   Prominent ILO Declarations include the ILO Declaration on Social Justice for a Fair Globalization of 2008, the ILO Declaration on Fundamental Principles and Rights at Work of 1998, the Declaration on Gender Equality and the ILO Centenary Declaration for the Future of Work (2019)[99].

59   In this context, the ILO Declaration on Fundamental Principles and Rights at Work of 1998 stands out by its clear commitment to universal rights at work for all human beings, emphasising the holistic and significant connection 'between social progress and economic growth'.[100] Special focus is laid on vulnerable groups, such as migrants and unemployed people (SDG 8.6),[101] reiterating the four principles of the ILO:

1.   Freedom of association and the effective recognition of the right to collective bargaining;
2.   Elimination of all forms of forced or compulsory labour;
3.   Effective abolition of child labour; and
4.   Elimination of discrimination in respect of employment and occupation.[102]

60   The concerns of social justice and decent work are envisaged in the ILO Declaration on Social Justice for a Fair Globalization (SDG 8.5, SDG 8.6 and SDG 8.8). The incorporated Decent Work Agenda pursues 'four equally important strategic objectives of the ILO', namely 'promoting employment by creating a sustainable institutional and economic environment', 'developing and enhancing measures of social protection – social security and labour protection', 'promoting social dialogue and tripartism' as well as 'respecting, promoting and realizing the fundamental principles and rights at work'.[103]

5. Human Rights and Decent Work

61   The International Covenant on Economic, Social and Cultural Rights (ICESCR) contains various rights concerning workers (SDG 8.5, SDG 8.6 and SDG 8.8). In this context, work related rights are closely linked to other economic, social and cultural rights of the ICESCR, which depicts the interwoven nature of workers' rights in international human rights law as well. The most outstanding articles of the ICESCR in this regard are

---

[98] https://www.ilo.org/global/about-the-ilo/how-the-ilo-works/departments-and-offices/jur/legal-instr uments/WCMS_428589/lang--en/index.htm.

[99] International Labour Conference, *ILO Centenary Declaration for The Future of Work, adopted by the Conference at its One Hundred and Eighth Session*, Geneva, 21 June 2019.

[100] ILO Declaration on Fundamental Principles and Rights at Work and its Follow-up, adopted by the International Labour Conference at its Eighty-sixth Session, Geneva, 18 June 1998 (Annex revised 15 June 2010).

[101] A/RES/45/158, International Convention on the Protection of the Rights of All Migrant Workers and Members of Their Families, 18 December 1990.

[102] ILO Declaration on Fundamental Principles and Rights at Work and its Follow-up, adopted by the International Labour Conference at its Eighty-sixth Session, Geneva, 18 June 1998 (Annex revised 15 June 2010), para. 2.

[103] ILO Declaration on Social Justice for a Fair Globalization adopted by the International Labour Conference at its Ninety-seventh Session, Geneva, 10 June 2008, 9 ff.; further reading: MacNaughton and Frey, 'Decent Work, Human Rights and the Sustainable Development Goals' (2016) 47 *Georgetown Journal of International Law*, 607 (622).

Art. 6 (Right to Work), Art. 7 (Right to Just and Favorable Conditions of Work), Art. 8 (Union Rights), Art. 9 (Right to Social Security) and Art. 10 (Family Rights, especially in connection with the 'Right of working mothers to paid leave or leave with social security benefits' and the 'Right of children and young people to be protected from economic and social exploitation'). Furthermore, the general rights of Arts. 11-15 (Right to an Adequate Standard of Living, Right to Health, Right to Education, Cultural Rights) form a crucial basis for the comprehensive and all-encompassing implementation of workers' rights.[104]

Here, decent work (SDG 8.5) encompasses a variety of different rights covering the   62
'right to a decent income', the 'right of access to employment' as well as the 'right not to be unfairly deprived of employment'.[105]

6. Modern Slavery, Forced Labour, Child Labour and Human Trafficking

SDG 8.7 expressly concerns the eradication of all forms of forced labour, human   63
trafficking, child labour and ending modern slavery. International law provides several international agreements and conventions for achieving this goal. Those encompass agreements both of the ILO and other international bodies.

– ILO Forced Labour Convention 1930 (No. 29)
  (as well as the concomitant 2014 Protocol)
– ILO Abolition of Forced Labour Convention (Convention No. 105 of 1957).
– ILO Worst Forms of Child Labour Convention 1999 (No. 182)
– Slavery Convention (1926)
– Supplementary Convention on the Abolition of Slavery, the Slave Trade and Institutions and Practices Similar to Slavery
  (Supplementary Convention on Slavery, 1956).
– International Covenant on Civil and Political Rights (ICCPR, 1966).
– Convention on the Elimination of All Forms of Discrimination against Women 1979.
– Protocol to Prevent, Suppress and Punish Trafficking in Persons, Especially Women and Children, supplementing the United Nations Convention against Transnational Organized Crime (also referred to as 'Palermo Protocol', 2000)
– Convention on the Rights of the Child (1989), the Optional Protocol on the Sale of Children, Child Prostitution, and Child Pornography (2000)
– Convention relating to the Status of Refugees (1951) and its 1967 Protocol
– United Nations Convention against Transnational Organized Crime (Organized Crime Convention, 2000)
– Council of Europe Convention on Action against Trafficking in Human Beings (Anti-Trafficking Convention, 2005)

SDG 8 and its implementation is monitored by 16 indicators which, inter alia, serve   64
to 'identify areas of concern and inform policy formulation'.[106] Among the custodian

---

[104] McNaughton and Frey, 'Decent Work for All: A Holistic Human Rights Approach' (2011) 26 *Am. U. Int'l L. Rev.*, 441 (462 ff.).

[105] McNaughton and Frey, 'Decent Work for All: A Holistic Human Rights Approach' (2011) 26 *Am. U. Int'l L. Rev.*, 441 (465 f.); CESCR, General Comment No. 18, para. 34.

[106] ILO, *Decent Work and the Sustainable Development Goals – A Guidebook on SDG Labour Market Indicators* (2018), 4.

and partner agencies of the SDG 8 indicators are primarily the ILO, but also the World Bank, the OECD and UNICEF.[107]

65   In addition to the SDG 8 indicators, the ILO 'adopted a framework of Decent Work Indicators [within the so-called 'Framework on the Measurement of Decent Work'] that was presented to the 18th International Conference of Labour Statisticians in December 2008' and consists of 10 'substantive' and overarching elements[108] which serve as roof for the organisation of the concomitant statistical indicators and legal framework indicators.[109] Accordingly, statistical indicators represent indicators of quantitative nature which originate from official national data sources, whereas 'legal framework indicators are qualitative in nature primarily based on legal texts and other related textual information'.[110]

66   Comparing SDG 8.7 with its only related indicator 8.7.1, it is clearly noticeable that the latter only includes the aspect of child labour to measure the success of SDG 8.7, whereas SDG 8.7 also includes forced labour, human trafficking and modern slavery of people also of adult age groups.[111]

67   There are '[t]hree principal international legal instruments' which serve as a regulative framework concerning child labour. The first instrument is the ILO's Minimum Age Convention No. 138 (1973) regulating the minimum age at work and has been ratified by a considerable number of 173 member states of the ILO.[112]

68   The second important instrument is the ILO Convention on the Worst Forms of Child Labour No. 182 (1999) which gained particular significance by having ultimately been ratified by all ILO member states in 2020, achieving thus 'universal ratification'.[113]

69   The third instrument is the Convention on the Rights of the Child[114] which has been ratified by 196 states of the UN and thus, due to the absence of only the United States, represents an almost universally uniform basis not only for the fight against child labour, but also for the protection of all other rights of the child.[115] Furthermore,

> the resolutions adopted by the International Conference of Labour Statisticians (ICLS), the world's acknowledged standard-setting body in the area of labour statistics, provide the basis for translating the legal standards governing the concept of child labour into statistical terms for the purpose of child labour measurement. In accordance with the ICLS resolutions, child labour can be measured on the basis of the production boundary set by the United Nations System of National Accounts (SNA) or on the basis of the general production boundary.[116]

---

[107] ILO, *Decent Work and the Sustainable Development Goals – A Guidebook on SDG Labour Market Indicators* (2018), 5 f.

[108] The ten substantive elements are: employment opportunities; adequate earnings and productive work; decent working time; combining work, family and personal life; work that should be abolished; stability and security of work; equal opportunity and treatment in employment; safe work environment; social security; and social dialogue, employers' and workers' representation; ILO, *ILO Manual – Decent Work Indicators – Guidelines for Producers and Users of Statistical and Legal Framework Indicators* (2013), 12.

[109] ILO, *ILO Manual – Decent Work Indicators – Guidelines for Producers and Users of Statistical and Legal Framework Indicators* (2013), 12.

[110] ILO, *ILO Manual – Decent Work Indicators – Guidelines for Producers and Users of Statistical and Legal Framework Indicators* (2013), 12.

[111] Indicator 8.7.1: Proportion and number of children aged 5-17 years engaged in child labour, by sex and age.

[112] https://www.ilo.org/global/standards/subjects-covered-by-international-labour-standards/child-labour/WCMS_747376/lang--en/index.htm.

[113] https://www.ilo.org/global/about-the-ilo/newsroom/news/WCMS_749858/lang--en/index.htm.

[114] A/RES/44/25, *Convention on the Rights of the Child*, Art. 32.

[115] Convention on the Rights of the Child, 20 November 1989, Official Records of the General Assembly, Forty-fourth Session, Supplement No. 49 (A/44/49), 166.

[116] UN Stats, SDG 8.7.1 indicator metadata (Last updated: February 2021).

To effectively measure child labour with regard to the SDGs, factors such as age group   70
and working hours as well as night work[117] in the context of economic activity and / or
unpaid work in the household are taken into account.[118]

In 2019, the United Nations General Assembly (UNGA) unanimously adopted the   71
resolution 73/327 to mark the year 2021 as the 'International Year for the Elimination of
Child Labour' emphasising the commitment of the Member States

> to take immediate and effective measures to eradicate forced labour, end modern slavery and human
> trafficking and secure the prohibition and elimination of the worst forms of child labour, including
> recruitment and use of child soldiers, and by 2025 end child labour in all its forms.[119]

Furthermore, the resolution directly relates to the Global Agenda 2030 and stipulates   72
'the importance of revitalized global partnerships to ensure the implementation of the
2030 Agenda for Sustainable Development, including the implementation of the goals
and targets related to the elimination of child labour' ($\rightarrow$ Goal 17, $\rightarrow$ Intro mn. 164 ff.,
204 ff.).[120]

A practical expression of partnerships in the context of SDG 8.7 is the so-called   73
Alliance 8.7 which supports the achievement of SDG 8.7. More precisely, the alliance
seeks to accelerate action, conduct research, share knowledge and drive innovation. The
alliance consists of partners from various backgrounds such as 'countries, international
and regional organizations, workers' organizations, employer and business membership
organizations, civil society organizations, academic institutions and other relevant stakeholders and networks'.[121]

C. Interdependences of SDG 8

The ILO estimates that the SARS-CoV-2 pandemic, which has been rampant since   74
2020, will cause the sharpest increase in global unemployment since World War II,
setting back the emerging economy in particular and threatening workers' safety and
health, especially affecting those in the informal sectors.[122] Labour-intensive services
sectors are worst affected with workers losing their jobs or having their income and

---

[117] No. 3(e) of ILO Convention No. 190 (1999).

[118] SDG 8.7.1: Proportion and number of children aged 5-17 years engaged in economic activities at or
above age-specific hourly thresholds (SNA production boundary basis): Child labour for the 5 to 11 age
range: children working at least 1 hour per week in economic activity; Child labour for the 12 to 14 age
range: children working for at least 14 hours per week in economic activity; Child labour for the 15 to 17
age range: children working for more than 43 hours per week in economic activity.
SDG 8.7.2: Proportion and number of children aged 5-17 years engaged in economic activities and
household chores at or above age-specific hourly thresholds (general production boundary basis): Child
labour for the 5 to 11 age range: children working at least 1 hour per week in economic activity and/or
involved in unpaid household services for more than 21 hours per week; Child labour for the 12 to
14 age range: children working for at least 14 hours per week in economic activity and/or involved in
unpaid household services for more than 21 hours per week; Child labour for the 15 to 17 age range:
children working for more than 43 hours per week in economic activity, UN stats, SDG 8.7.1 indicator
metadata (Last updated: February 2021); see also Resolution concerning statistics of child labour, adopted
by the 18th International Conference of Labour Statisticians (2008), paras. 24, 28-30; ILO Night Work
Convention No. 171 (1990).

[119] A/RES/73/327, *International Year for the Elimination of Child Labour*, 2021.

[120] A/RES/73/327, *International Year for the Elimination of Child Labour*, 2021.

[121] https://www.alliance87.org/the-alliance/.

[122] Martens and Ellmers and Pokorny on behalf of Global Policy Watch, *COVID-19 and the SDGs, The
impact of the coronavirus pandemic on the global sustainability agenda*, 5.

working hours significantly reduced.[123] In contrast to previous crises, effects of the crisis hit different parts of the workforce unevenly, with young workers, women, self-employed, and low- and medium-skilled workers the hardest.[124] Moreover, child labour is likely to increase.[125]

75   Thus, the collapsed and only in few places slowly recovering economic growth exacerbates pre-existing inequalities (SDG 10.2, SDG 5.1 and SDG 5.2) in occupations and wages, and, through the unequal exposure to SARS-CoV-2 related risks and consequences, leads to an increase in poverty and social vulnerability.[126]

76   With economic growth, and full and productive and decent work for all, SDG 8 serves as an enabler for human development and poverty reduction and therefore is strongly linked to SDG 1. Since decent work and economic growth lifts people out of poverty directly, achieving SDG 8 is of particular importance for women (SDG 5) which represent the part of society that is most often, and sometimes multiply affected by poverty and (structural) inequalities. Implicit bias, social norms and the different distribution of work as well as the gendered impact of investments affect women to a far greater extent[127] which makes SDG 5 a key driver for achieving SDG 8.3, SDG 8.5, SDG 8.7 and SDG 8.8.[128]

77   An increased economic growth may enable governments to increase spending on healthcare including providing universal health coverage[129] which may be followed by increased health and well-being (SDG 3) and potentially enabling people to enter the workforce.[130] These interactions are bi-directional, with increased health and well-being enhancing productivity and income, allowing economic growth and higher employment to enable and reinforce health and well-being.[131]

78   Labour income may also support people in gaining (better) food (SDG 2), shelter (SDG 11), education (SDG 4), energy (SDG 7) and medical care (SDG 3).[132] The latter connection can also be found between SDG 8.8 (enhance safer working environments with avoiding exposure to hazardous chemicals and other hazardous substances) and SDG 3.8 which aims to reduce the number of deaths and illnesses from hazardous chemicals.

79   However, increasing economic growth may also imply, that employers and / or governments dispense with labour rights and standards.

80   Giving access to full and productive employment for all women and men, including young people and persons with disabilities (SDG 8.5), promoting to substantially reduce the proportion of youth not in employment, education or training (SDG 8.6), and to take immediate and effective measure to eradicate forced labour, end modern slavery and human trafficking and secure the prohibition and elimination the worst forms of child labour, including the recruitment and use of child soldiers (SDG 8.7), implies that

---

[123] See ILO, *ILO Monitor: COVID-19 and the world of work. Seventh edition,* 1 f.: A loss of 8.8 per cent of global working hours (equivalent to 255 million full-time jobs) were lost relative to the fourth quarter of 2019, and a loss of 3.0 per cent (equivalent to 90 million full-time jobs) for 2021 is expected.

[124] ILO, *ILO Monitor: COVID-19 and the world of work. Seventh edition,* 2.

[125] UN, *The Sustainable Development Goals Report 2020,* 40.

[126] UNDESA, *World Economic Situation And Prospects: June 2020 Briefing No. 138.*

[127] Further reading: Dwasi, 'Kenya: a Study in International Labor Standards and their Effect on Working Women in Developing Countries: the Case for Integration of Enforcement Issues in the World Bank's Policies' (1999) 17(2) *Wis. INT'L L.J.* 347-462.

[128] UN, *Financing for Development: Progress and Prospects, Report of the Inter-agency Task Force on Financing for Development 2017* (2017), 26.

[129] Griggs et al., *A Guide to SDG Interactions: From Science to Implementation* (2017), 102.

[130] Griggs et al., *A Guide to SDG Interactions: From Science to Implementation* (2017), 102.

[131] Griggs et al., *A Guide to SDG Interactions: From Science to Implementation* (2017), 102.

[132] Griggs et al., *A Guide to SDG Interactions: From Science to Implementation* (2017), 101.

those people may get the opportunity to attend and afford quality education (SDG 4.1, SDG 4.2 and SDG 4.3).

The sustainable use of oceans, seas and marine resources, and the conservation of   **81**
these resources may also support sustainable economic growth and fostering decent work, especially for island states, SIDS and coastal regions, as it enhances marine and maritime sectors such as fisheries, aquaculture and tourism (SDG 14).[133] But here, too, SDG 8 and SDG 14 are in a delicate interplay, the success of which depends on the sustainable design actually implemented. Taking measures to protect, restore and promote marine and coastal ecosystems might entail restrictions for economic activities and therefore limit its opportunities for economic growth and job creation (and vice versa).[134] It should be also mentioned, that tourism may provide a substantial (especially for island states) and important key driver for economic growth, but can also counteract SDG 14, as mass tourism or the expansion of tourism industry may lead to damages of the ecosystems of the sea and coastal areas.

D. Jurisprudential Significance of SDG 8

Apart from the related question of decent growth, the jurisprudential relevance of   **82**
SDGs 8 seems to be rather low. There is no specific jurisprudence on economic growth in line with national circumstances (SDG 8.1), on economic productivity through diversification, technological upgrading and innovation (SDG 8.2.) or on full employment (SDG 8.5 and SDG 8.6), although issues of inequality within work or the sustainable design of work should certainly hold developments in the future.

To date, only the following terms offer a spectrum of interpretation in legal terms: **83**
slavery (SDG 8.7), equal pay (SDG 8.5), protection of workers' rights and promotion of a safe working environment for all workers, including migrant workers, especially women migrants, and persons in precarious employment (SDG 8.8).[135]

The different approaches and targets of SDG 8 that point to the right to development   **84**
(RTD) combined with GDP makes it quite difficult to find the essence in the realm of jurisprudence.[136] The Addis Ababa Action Agenda (AAAA), the financial instrument of the Global Agenda 2030, for instance, elaborates the need for 'complementary actions' to accompany trade policy changes with a view to preparing a 'domestic enabling environment'.[137]

By covering forced labour, trafficking[138] and slavery,[139] SDG 8.7 also opens up juris-   **85**
diction and control by the International Criminal Court (ICC) since enslavement and

---

[133] Griggs et al., *A Guide to SDG Interactions: From Science to Implementation* (2017), 180.

[134] Griggs et al., *A Guide to SDG Interactions: From Science to Implementation* (2017), 192.

[135] See e.g. ICC, ICC-02/04-01/15, 10.01.2020, Motion for Immediate Ruling on the Request for Dismissal of the Charge of Enslavement; Zenz, *Coercive Labor and Forced Displacement in Xinjiang's Cross-Regional Labor Transfer Program, A Process-Oriented Evaluation* (2021).

[136] OHCHR, Realizing the Right to Development, Essays in Commemoration of 25 Years of the United Nations Declaration on the Right to Development (2013); OHCHR, *Frequently Asked Questions on the Right to Development, Fact Sheet No. 3* (2016); further reading: Schrijver, 'A new Convention on the human right to development: Putting the cart before the horse?' (2020) 38(2) *NQHR*, 84-93; Sengupta, 'Right to Development as a Human Right.' (2001) 36(27) *Economic and Political Weekly*, 2527-36.

[137] UNCTAD, *Trading into Sustainable Development: Trade, Market Access, and the Sustainable Development Goals, Developing Countries in International Trade Studies*, 10.

[138] A/RES/55/25, Protocol to Prevent, Suppress and Punish Trafficking in Persons, Especially Women and Children, Supplementing the U.N. Convention Against Transnational Organized Crime art. 3(a), Nov. 15, 2000, 2237 U.N.T.S. 319, Annex II, Art. 3.

[139] The following human rights conventions, among others, contain norms and definitions on slavery: 1977 Additional Protocols to the Geneva Conventions, 1989 Convention on the Rights of the Child

human trafficking including both labour and sex trafficking constitute crimes against humanity, and the recruitment and use of child soldiers constitute war crime.[140]

86   However, neither the ICC nor any other international tribunal has heard a case directly related to human trafficking, even though the particular vulnerability is recognised and at least the ICC is seeking investigations. Nevertheless, the ICC, as a criminal law tribunal, faces various problems in the run-up to officially initiated proceedings. So far only active in times of conflict, it is often difficult for the ICC to conduct (preliminary) investigations and evidence procedures, which is further complicated if the state in which the crime was committed does not cooperate.[141]

87   In addition, Rule 94 Slavery and Slave Trade is to be understood as a framework. State practice establishes this rule as a norm of customary international law applicable in both international and non-international armed conflicts.[142]

I. Jurisdiction on Vision and Objectives

1. International Jurisdiction

88   The political and legal structure of the Inter-Americas is built on numerous commitments of non-discrimination, both generally applicable and with a focus on vulnerable groups[143] such as children, women or indigenous people.[144] The obligation to create decent work follows from various human rights standards and policies, which are aligned with the Global Agenda 2030 and aim to combat poverty in particular.[145] It is noticeable that despite the existence of protective provisions under labour law, these are frequently either not followed or workers have *de facto* no access to these rights.[146] The close interconnection between decent work, inequality and discrimination and (especially structural) poverty is also reflected in the judicial assessment of the Inter-American Court of Human Rights (IACtHR). The IACtHR frequently deals with intersectional and structural discrimination, which has a particular impact on economic, social and cultural rights.[147] In the case of the *Hacienda Brazil Verde Workers v. Brazil*[148], the court elaborat-

---

(CRC), 1990 African Charter on the Rights and Welfare of the Child (regional instrument), 1999 International Labour Organization Convention, 2000 Optional Protocol to CRC (as global consensus that children should not be recruited and used by parties to conflict).

[140] Art. 7 of the Rome Statute of the International Criminal Court.

[141] Alhadi, 'Increasing Case Traffic: Expanding the International Criminal Court's Focus on Human Trafficking Cases' (2020) 41 *MICH. J. INT'L L.*, 541 (545).

[142] ICRC, Customary IHL Database, https://ihl-databases.icrc.org/customary-ihl/eng/docs/v1_rul_rule 94 (last accessed: 23.06.2021); see for an overview of practice related to the Rule 94: https://ihl-databases.icrc.org/customary-ihl/eng/docs/v2_rul_rule94.

[143] See Thornberry, *The International Convention on the Elimination of all Forms of Racial Discrimination, A Commentary* (2016), 364-8.

[144] Further reading: Swepston, 'Labour Rights, Article 17' in Hohmann and Weller, *The UN Declaration on the Rights of Indigenous People, A Commentary* (2018), 461-81.

[145] See Inter-American Commission On Human Rights, *Report on Poverty and Human Rights in the Americas, 27 July 2017*, 128-40.

[146] International Trade Union Confederation, *ITUC Global Rights Index 2018, The World's Worst Countries for Workers* (2018).

[147] Inter-American Commission On Human Rights, *Report on Poverty and Human Rights in the Americas, 27 July 2017*, 168; see also *Request for an Advisory Opinion submitted to the Inter-American Court of Human Rights, Scope of State Obligations under the Inter-American System with Regard to the Guarantee of Trade Union Freedom, its Relationship to Other Rights, and its Application from a Gender Perspective*, para. 2.

[148] IACtHR, *Case of the Hacienda Brazil Verde Workers v. Brazil*, Preliminary Objections, Merits, Reparations and Costs, Judgment of 20 October 2016, Series C No. 318, para. 343.

ed on the meaning of slavery, according to which 'through fraud, deception and false promises' people from the poorest areas of Brazil were lured to a fazenda and forced to work and live there under inhumane conditions and circumstances, in most cases without receiving any remuneration. Referring to large parts of the American Convention on Human Rights (ACHR), the IACtHR 'expanded on the content and scope of the concepts of slavery, servitude, slave trade and traffic in women, as well as forced labour' and established the absolute and universal prohibition of slavery under international law. The IACtHR declared Brazil responsible after the previous national jurisprudence had not established responsibility or sufficient investigations had not been carried out at all. It referred to a 'process of normalisation of the conditions to which people with certain characteristics were continually subjected in the poorer states of Brazil' (structural discrimination based on economic status) and, in addition to the violation of Arts. 6(1) (freedom from slavery) in relation to Arts. 1(1) (obligation to respect and ensure rights without discrimination), 3 (right to juridical personality), 5 (right to personal integrity), 7 (right to personal liberty), 11 (right to privacy) and 22 (freedom of movement and residence) of the ACHR, the court also found a violation of the right to access to justice,[149] which entailed not only restitution but also compensation (→ Goal 16 mn. 47 ff.). In its further jurisprudence, the IACtHR rules vehemently similar.[150]

In 2019, the ICC prosecuted and, in some cases, convicted several former leaders **89** of armed forces in the Democratic Republic of Congo (DRC) and the Central African Republic for various crimes against humanity, including rape, sexual slavery and the recruitment and conscription of children under the age of 15 into an armed group and their use to actively participate in hostilities, as well as further war crimes. The ICC's procedural activity and investigations in this grave issue, so far almost exclusively in conflict-affected areas, is of particular importance for the achievement of SDG 8.7 (→ mn. 115).[151]

The term 'conscription' is interpreted as **90**

> either the abduction of persons for specific use within an organisation or the forced military training of persons is independently sufficient to constitute conscription, as both practices amount to compelling a person to join an armed group.[152]

The ECtHR addressed the prohibition of slavery and forced labour on the basis of **91** Art. 4 of the ECHR, noting in particular the state obligations 'to put in place an appropriate legislative and administrative framework', to take operational measures and to investigate as positive obligations and elaborating on them.[153] In the case *S.M. v. Croat-*

---

[149] IACtHR, *Case of the Hacienda Brazil Verde Workers v. Brazil*, Preliminary Objections, Merits, Reparations and Costs, Judgment of 20 October 2016, Series C No. 318, paras. 339 f., 343; https://www.corteidh .or.cr/cf/Jurisprudencia2/overview.cfm?doc=1728&lang=en.

[150] IACtHR, *Juridical Condition and Rights of the Undocumented Migrants*, Advisory Opinion OC-18/03 of 17 September 2003, Series A No. 18.

[151] A/HRC/43/38, *Children and armed conflict, Report of the Special Representative of the Secretary-General for Children and Armed Conflict*, 24 December 2019, para. 50; see similar cases *Lubanga Case, The Prosecutor v. Thomas Lubanga Dyilo*, ICC-01/04-01/06; ICC, *The Prosecutor v. Joseph Kony, Vincent, Otti, Raska Lukwiya, Okot Odhiambo and Dominic Ongwen*; see also *Special Court for Sierra Leone* which was the first international tribunal to try and convict persons for the use of child soldiers; further reading Cohn, 'The Protection of Children and the Quest for Truth and Justice in Sierra Leone' (2001) 55(1) *Journal of International Affairs*, 1-34.

[152] SCSL, Trial Chamber, *Prosecutor v Sesay, Kallon and Gbao*, SCSL-04-15-T, Judgement (2 March 2009) (RUF Trial Judgment), para. 1695.

[153] ECtHR, *Guide on Article 4 of the European Convention on Human Rights, Prohibition of slavery and forced labour*, updated on 30 April 2021 (2021), 29; see e.g. ECtHR, *Rantsev v. Cyprus and Russia*, no. 25965/04, ECHR 2010 (extracts); ECtHR, *Chowdury and Others v. Greece*, no. 21884/15, 30 March 2017.

ia[154], the court clarified the inclusion of the concepts of 'trafficking in human beings' and 'exploitation of prostitution' within the material scope of Art. 4 ECHR and related these two concepts to each other. The ECtHR also underlined whether and how positive obligations, in particular procedural obligations, of states in the area of trafficking in human beings apply to cases of forced prostitution. This case is the first case before the ECtHR to consider the applicability of Art. 4 ECHR specifically to the trafficking and exploitation of women for the purposes of prostitution. What is striking is the court's assessment, which does not distinguish between 'slavery', 'servitude' or 'forced or compulsory labour',[155] that trafficking itself already opens the scope of application of Art. 4 ECHR. Following the principle of harmonious interpretation,[156] the ECtHR referred to the international instruments of the Anti-Trafficking Convention[157] and the Palermo Protocol[158], which provide a definition of human trafficking, to determine whether trafficking has occurred (→ Goal 5 mn. 27 ff.).[159] The court noted in particular that the

> notion of "forced or compulsory labour" under Article 4 of the Convention aims to protect against instances of serious exploitation, such as forced prostitution, irrespective of whether, in the particular circumstances of a case, they are related to the specific human-trafficking context. Moreover, any such conduct may have elements qualifying it as "servitude" or "slavery" under Article 4, or may raise an issue under another provision of the Convention […].[160]

92   In further defining the scope of Art. 4 ECHR, it referred in particular to the ILO 1930 Forced Labour Convention ('Convention No. 29') and the 1957 Abolition of Forced Labour Convention ('Convention No. 105') as well as Protocol to Convention No. 29 and Recommendation 203 on Supplementary Measures for the Effective Suppression of Forced Labour and other international instruments and elaborations of the ILO.[161] Trafficking degrades human beings, deprives them of their fundamental freedoms and cannot under any circumstances be reconciled with the basic understanding of a democratic society and the values of the ECHR.[162]

93   With regard to the protection of labour rights (SDG 8.8), the right to strike and freedom of association take on significance that cannot be realised everywhere in the world. In one case, the ECtHR directly and extensively referred to the application of ILO standards[163] after the dismissal of a railway driver who exercised his right to strike. In this

---

[154] ECtHR, *S.M. v. Croatia* [GC], no. 60561/14, 25 June 2020.

[155] In this respect, the court referred to the necessity of interpreting the ECHR according to 'present-day conditions' in order to fulfil its protective purpose and to ensure its effective application, rendering a distinction unnecessary; ECtHR, *Rantsev v. Cyprus and Russia*, no. 25965/04, ECHR 2010, para. 282.

[156] As a main principle, the ECtHR interprets the ECHR in the light of the rules of interpretation established with the Vienna Convention of 23 May 1969 on the Law of Treaties and therefore not only reads the ECHR itself in a consistent manner, but also considers instruments of international law in a manner that is consistent with each other, ECtHR, *Guide on Article 4 of the European Convention on Human Rights, Prohibition of slavery and forced labour*, updated on 30 April 2021 (2021), 5.

[157] Council of Europe Convention on Action against Trafficking in Human Beings.

[158] Protocol to Prevent, Suppress and Punish Trafficking in Persons Especially Women and Children, supplementing the United Nations Convention against Transnational Organized Crime.

[159] Three elements constitute human trafficking according to these instruments: actions, means and exploitative purpose (→ Goal 5 mn. 27 ff.).

[160] ECtHR, *S.M. v. Croatia* [GC], no. 60561/14, 25 June 2020, para. 300.

[161] ECtHR, *S.M. v. Croatia* [GC], no. 60561/14, 25 June 2020, paras. 140-6.

[162] ECtHR, *Rantsev v. Cyprus and Russia*, no. 25965/04, ECHR 2010, para. 282; as of February 2021 the ECtHR highlighted 33 cases relating to the violation of Art. 4 ECHR (prohibition of slavery and forced labour): https://www.echr.coe.int/Documents/FS_Forced_labour_ENG.pdf.

[163] ECtHR, *Ognevenko v Russia*, Appn no 44873/09, 20 November 2018; Although ILO standards are not always taken into account: ECtHR, *Association of Academics v Iceland*, Appn no 2451/16, 21 December 2015.

case, the ECtHR found a clear violation of Art. 11 of the ECHR (Freedom of assembly and association).

Another focus in labour rights protection proceedings is on differential treatment   94 and discrimination. The ECSR decided on a complaint where 'discrimination of medical practitioners workload, distribution of tasks, career opportunities and protection of health and safety' had been alleged to be discriminatory. 'The Committee confirmed that the non-objecting and objecting medical practitioners were in a comparable situation, because they had similar professional qualifications and worked in the same field of expertise. Consequently, the difference in treatment amounted to discrimination.'[164]

2. European Jurisdiction

The EU legislative framework, in particular the Green New Deal action plan and the   95 further legislative proposals and legislative strategies stemming from it, provides for a transformation of the European society aligned with the Global Agenda 2030, and in particular the competitive sustainability, cohesion and growth of the economy. The EU Green Deal, whose key component is the lasting ecological-economic decoupling, is particularly in line with SDG 8.4. The 2020 New Industrial Strategy[165] and the most recent update of this strategy[166] foresee a decoupling of economic growth from environmental degradation, which includes explicit provisions also for the design of the jobs foreseen in these industries (SDG 8.4).

In view of the current SARS-CoV-2 pandemic, the European Commission has drafted   96 a communication that provides for a 'European Skills Agenda for sustainable competitiveness, social fairness and resilience'. This agenda intends to counteract the negative economic effects of the pandemic and focuses on gaps in digital skills.[167] In addition, the political orientation is linked in particular to the action plan for the establishment and expansion of 'The European Pillar of Social Rights' as part of the Annual Sustainable Growth Strategy 2021[168], which is intended to anchor social and economic resilience and well-being and thus 'competitive sustainability' within the EU ('equal opportunities, inclusive education, fair working conditions and adequate social protection'[169]). The approach includes, among other things, restructuring the processes for acquiring skills

---

[164] ECSR, *Confederazione Generale Italiana del Lavoro (CGIL) v. Italy*, Complaint No. 91/2013, 12 October 2015, para. 48; see also relating to access to social security systems: ECSR, *Associazione Nazionale Giudici di Pace v. Italy*, Complaint No. 102/2013, 5 July 2016.

[165] COM(2020) 102 final, *Communication from the Commission to the European Parliament, the European Council, the Council, the European Economic and Social Committee and the Committee of the Regions, A New Industrial Strategy for Europe*, 10.3.2020.

[166] COM(2021) 350 final, *Communication from the Commission to the European Parliament, the Council, the European Economic and Social Committee and the Committee of the Regions, Updating the 2020 New Industrial Strategy: Building a stronger Single Market for Europe's recovery, {SWD(2021) 351 final} - {SWD(2021) 352 final} - {SWD(2021) 353 final}*, 5.5.2021.

[167] European Parliament Research Service (EPRS), *Digital automation and the future of work, Study, Panel for the Future of Science and Technology* (2021), 44; further instrument to mitigate the impact of the pandemic on the state of employment within the EU: Council Regulation (EU) 2020/672 on the establishment of a European instrument for temporary support to mitigate unemployment risks in an emergency (SURE) following the COVID-19 outbreak; and the Recovery and Resilience Facility.

[168] COM(2020) 575 final, *Communication From The Commission To The European Parliament, The European Council, The Council, The European Central Bank, The European Economic And Social Committee, The Committee Of The Regions And The European Investment Bank, Annual Sustainable Growth Strategy 2021*, 17.9.2020.

[169] COM(2020) 575 final, *Communication From The Commission To The European Parliament, The European Council, The Council, The European Central Bank, The European Economic And Social Committee, The Committee Of The Regions And The European Investment Bank, Annual Sustainable Growth Strategy 2021*, 17.9.2020, 8.

to make them more flexible and secure in future (flexicurity), in order to create the necessary employability and reintegration of workers[170] into the labour market in the face of securely changing technological and skill requirements. In 2020, the European Commission stated that the EU's external strategy with regard to the sustainable design of global supply and value chains, including the protection of labour rights, is to be implemented primarily through European trade and investment agreements. To ensure accountability, the EU will adapt the trade and investment policies currently under review, in particular with regard to the European General System of Preferences.[171]

97 The New Skills Agenda for Europe with the key initiative 'Blueprint for Sectoral Cooperation on Skills', the 'Digital Skills and Jobs Coalition' and the '2019 Pact for Skills' sets the wider programme[172] of the internal policies of the EU to contribute to SDG 8.1, SDG 8.2, SDG 8.3, SDG 8.5 and SDG 8.6 with the purpose of enhancing education and training for workers with lower and medium level skills who may be more susceptible to automation, enabling sector-specific partnerships, and allow for effective protection of labour rights in new business models that arise due to digitalisation such as minimum wage and hours of work regulation, social security, tax incentives or employment status (→ Goal 17).[173]

98 The legal framework of the EU with regard to the protection of labour rights is regulated in detail in the primary law of the EU and, in addition, in many cases in secondary law and was further developed by the ECJ. Within the framework of the fundamental freedoms used to realise the internal market, the free movement of people is protected in particular, which is filled out by the free movement of workers, Art. 45 TFEU, the freedom of establishment, Art. 49 TFEU, and the freedom to provide services, Art. 56 TFEU. These fundamental freedoms have in common that they prohibit, without exception, any form of open or direct discrimination. Only certain forms of unequal treatment (indirect discrimination) can be justified within a very narrowly interpreted framework, either for reasons of the protection of public order, security or health. Compelling reasons of public interest (public interest requirement) are also considered, which have been developed in unwritten legal principles by the ECJ in the course of the process of union integration. The concept of proportionality serves as one of the fundamental standards of assessment, which within the judicial evaluation provides for a two-step means-purpose relationship and then the assessment of any milder means to be used (appropriateness). The scope of protection for the different forms of work, service and establishment is set out in detail in secondary Union law.

---

[170] Accompanied by financing instruments such as the European Globalisation Adjustment Fund (EGF) or the European Social Fund Plus; further information: https://ec.europa.eu/social/main.jsp?catId= 326&l angId=en; https://ec.europa.eu/esf/main.jsp?catId=62&langId=en.

[171] EC, SWD(2020) 235 final, *Commission Staff Working Document, Promote Decent Work Worldwide, Responsible Global Value Chains for a Fair, Sustainable and Resilient Recovery from the Covid-19 Crisis,* 20.10.2020, 10; the Trade for Decent Work projects in cooperation with the ILO enhance employment as well as the protection of worker's rights further.

[172] In addition, there are other sector-specific (industrial) networks and political programmes such as the European Space Programme and European Defence Fund, Horizon 2020, Strategic Public Procurement, and many more.

[173] Notably, while the *Directive (EU) 2019/1152 of the European Parliament and of the Council of 20 June 2019 on transparent and predictable working conditions in the European Union* provides protection for workers in 'precarious contractual arrangements', it does not address ambiguities in employment status; see also: European Parliament Research Service (EPRS), *Digital automation and the future of work, Study, Panel for the Future of Science and Technology* (2021), 45-7.

The principle of non-discrimination can be exemplified by the preliminary ruling in 99
the *Feryn case*[174], in which the ECJ clarified, following a request from a Belgian court,
that the public announcement of a potential employer,

> that it will not recruit employees of a certain ethnic or racial origin constitutes direct discrimination
> in respect of recruitment within the meaning of Article 2(2)(a) of Council Directive 2000/43/EC of
> 29 June 2000 implementing the principle of equal treatment between persons irrespective of racial or
> ethnic origin.[175]

Such statements of an employer strongly dissuade certain candidates from accessing 100
the labour market at all and thus constitute a directly discriminatory recruitment policy
within the meaning of Art. 8(1) of Directive 2000/43 breaching the principle of equal
treatment which leads to a change of the burden of proof to the employer (modified burden of proof according to Art. 10 of Directive 2000/43).[176]

But also in less unambiguous cases, the ECJ has dealt with the question of whether 101
and to what extent a difference in treatment (or precisely no difference in treatment) can
be assessed as 'less favourable treatment'. The ECJ first of all focuses on the comparability of a situation or person by identifying 'a suitable comparator' and the difference of the
'protected grounds'.

The gender context (SDG 8.5) is of particular importance within the EU also with 102
regard to equal or comparable payment of salary to male and female employees (→
Goal 5 mn. 37, 87). The Gender Pay Gap (GPG) is defined as the difference between
the average gross hourly earnings of men and women expressed as a percentage of the
average gross hourly earnings of men (unadjusted gender pay gap) and exists in each
member state of the EU. The GPG almost remained stable throughout the last decade
and even deepened during the SARS-CoV-2 pandemic.[177]

'Under EU law, proving comparability in cases concerning equal pay involves estab- 103
lishing whether the work performed by a female worker is 'equal', or of 'equal value',
to work performed by a male worker, and whether there are differences in the salary
received by male and female workers. In this regard, the ECJ did not accept a comparison across companies. An apparent exception for finding a suitable 'comparator',
at least within the scope of employment, is where the discrimination suffered is due
to pregnancy. It is settled case law of the ECJ, that where the detriment suffered by
a woman is due to pregnancy, it constitutes direct discrimination based on sex, without
needing a comparator. The same applies in situations when discrimination is related to
maternity leave or undergoing in vitro fertilisation treatment.[178]

In this context, the ECJ also issues decisions that are closely aligned with the non- 104
discrimination requirements, but nevertheless allow *de facto* discriminatory treatment.
In the preliminary ruling *Nolte*, the question was to what extent a person had to be
considered as a member of the working population, if at the national (here: German)
level regulations did not provide for an attribution and thus access to social security
due to a too low number of working hours and consequently too low earnings. The

---

[174] ECJ, C-54/07, *Centrum voor gelijkheid van kansen en voor racismebestrijding v. Firma Feryn NV*, 10 July 2008.

[175] ECJ, C-54/07, *Centrum voor gelijkheid van kansen en voor racismebestrijding v. Firma Feryn NV*, 10 July 2008, para. 28.

[176] ECJ, C-54/07, *Centrum voor gelijkheid van kansen en voor racismebestrijding v. Firma Feryn NV*, 10 July 2008, ECLI:EU:C:2008:397, para. 34; see also ECJ, *Asociaţia Accept v. Consiliul Naţional pentru Combaterea Discriminării*, C-81/12, 25 April 2013, ECLI:EU:C:2013:275, para. 38.

[177] See European Parliamentary Research Service, *The coronavirus crisis: An emerging gender divide?* (2021).

[178] FRA and ECtHR and Council of Europe, *Handbook on European non-discrimination law, 2018 edition* (2018), 46.

ECJ made it clear that it was not a matter of '[t]he fact that a worker's earnings do not cover all his needs cannot prevent him from being a member of the working population' or that a certain number of hours are worked.[179] Rather, the *effet utile* ensures that, in order to implement the principle of equal treatment, the term worker or being a member of the working population applies for every person acting under a working contract. Nevertheless, the ECJ refrained from demanding an adjustment of the social contribution scheme in question. Referring to the member states' competence within social and employment policy, it ultimately denied the German legislation being indirectly discriminating due to the fact that the EU Directive does not exclude member states legislation and that it did not relate to any grounds of sex, even if it affects more women than men.[180]

3. Arbitration Proceedings

105   The WTO by its very nature has been established to facilitate trade worldwide with the purpose – albeit being only reflected in the preamble – of 'raising standards of living, ensuring full employment and a large and steadily growing volume of real income and effective demand'.[181] Originally, the Havana Charter, which was not approved by the congress of the US and never was set in forth, comprised labour provisions (Arts. 2 and 3) and was trade interrelated.[182]

106   With the 1996 Singapore Ministerial Declaration, the WTO renewed its 'commitment to the observance of internationally recognised core labour standards', while at the same time firmly rejecting the use of labour protection standards for protectionist reasons.[183] The WTO also made it clear that the competent body 'to set and deal with these standards' is the ILO, whose efforts the WTO seeks to support with the stimulation of 'economic growth and development fostered by increased trade and further trade liberalisation'. Nevertheless, the WTO reflected national sovereignty over labour law, which is also reflected in other WTO law when it is linked to product standards but does not regulate production processes in the sense of labour protection.[184] The WTO recognised the importance of its role as a driver of sustainability and job creator and pledged support within its mandate in its 2015 Nairobi Ministerial Declaration.[185]

107   The ILO core labour standards 'are mandatory as a matter of basic principles of law and perhaps of customary law'.[186] However, the ILO does not operate its own dispute settlement mechanism and is therefore dependent on existing fora for the enforcement of its standards, which, even if the ILO is involved in the procedure, are only taken into account in a very context-dependent manner.

108   The increased integration of sustainability requirements and, in particular, labour protection provisions and (domestic) labour standards in trade and investment agree-

---

[179] ECJ, C-317/93, *Inge Nolte v. Landesversicherungsanstalt Hannover*, 14 December 1995, para. 19 and the case law cited therein.

[180] ECJ, C-317/93, *Inge Nolte v. Landesversicherungsanstalt Hannover*, 14 December 1995.

[181] Agreement Establishing the World Trade Organization, preamble.

[182] Royer, *The Magna Carta of International Economic Life, The Havana Charter* (1949); https://www.wto.org/english/docs_e/legal_e/havana_e.pdf.

[183] WT/MIN(96)/DEC, *Singapore WTO Ministerial 1996: Ministerial Declaration*, 18 December 1996, para. 4.

[184] See Brown, 'Labour Protection' in Cottier and Nadakavukaren Schefer, *Elgar Encyclopedia of International Economic Law* (2017), 250.

[185] Nairobi Ministerial Declaration, Adopted On 19 December 2015, preamble.

[186] Art. XX(e) GATT is the only exception relating to labour (prison labour); see Cottier and Baumann, 'Minimum Standards' in Cottier and Nadakavukaren Schefer, *Elgar Encyclopedia of International Economic Law* (2017), 58-9.

ments worldwide can be observed, for example in recent regional trade agreements (RTAs)[187] such as NAFTA, which also obliges NAFTA parties to enforce their domestic labour rights with the North American Agreement on Labour Co-operation (NAALC).[188] These are either an original part of the agreement or trade and sustainable development chapters with specially created control mechanisms, often based on the 1998 ILO Declaration on Fundamental Principles and Rights at Work and its Follow-up, or to enforce and maintain domestic labour laws. The degree to which these provisions are binding and implemented varies considerably,[189] as do the possible legal consequences of non-compliance with social clauses within these agreements, but they often do not lead to trade sanctions because they are based on cooperation and capacity building ($\rightarrow$ Goal 17 mn. 22).

Within the complex web of trade and investment agreements under the guise of   109 WTO law, investment protection and the associated requirements for direct and indirect expropriation, it seems questionable to what extent an increase or amendment and enforcement of labour protection law is actually prompted by states. This is particularly evident in light of preferential trade agreements, which impact on states where deviations from labour protection and the unsustainable design of labour relations and development processes are most critical.[190] The ISDS procedures included in these agreements illustrate that, with few exceptions, the state's *right to regulate* has often had to succumb to the protection of foreign direct investment.[191]

In one case so far, the dispute settlement system of the CAFTA-DR[192] has been ap-   110 plied where Guatemala's failure to act 'conform to its obligations under Article 16.2.1(a) with respect to the effective enforcement of Guatemalan labor laws related to the right of association, the right to organize and bargain collectively, and acceptable conditions of work'. The United States sought to improve the Guatemalan labor law enforcement as a result of which a far-reaching Enforcement Plan between the parties had been signed in 2013. However, critical actions agreed to under the Enforcement Plan remained outstanding. The Panel in its 2018 Award gave deep insight on how to determine an exercise of labour rights are to be interpreted 'in a manner affecting trade', thereby infringing the CAFTA-DR.

Yet, the question also arises as to what extent the Aid for Trade[193] programme re-   111 quired under SDG 8.8 and the Enhanced Integrated Framework (EIF) for Trade-related Technical Assistance to Least Developed Countries (SDG 8.a) can be evaluated against the background of WTO law. The latter in particular, as the only multilateral partnership, is conducive to sustainable growth and reduction of poverty through appropriate national policies.[194] Labour rights, which are basically part of these policies, qualify in

---

[187] UNCTAD, *Trading into Sustainable Development: Trade, Market Access, and the Sustainable Development Goals, Developing Countries in International Trade Studies*, 5.

[188] Jarvis, 'Women's Rights and the Public Morals Exception of GATT Article 20' (2000) 22 *MICH.J. INT'LL.*, 219 (227).

[189] https://crsreports.congress.gov/product/pdf/IF/IF10046; https://crsreports.congress.gov/product/pdf/IF/IF10972; UNCTAD, *Trading into Sustainable Development: Trade, Market Access, and the Sustainable Development Goals, Developing Countries in International Trade Studies*, 5.

[190] See for a general critique on this issue: Gött, 'Linkages of Trade, Investment and Labour in Preferential Trade Agreements: Between Untapped Potential and Structural Insufficiencies' in Bungenberg et al. (eds), *2019 EYIEL*, 133-65.

[191] Brown, 'Labour Protection' in Cottier and Nadakavukaren Schefer, *Elgar Encyclopedia of International Economic Law* (2017), 250.

[192] *In the Matter of Guatemala – Issues Relating to the Obligations Under Article 16.2.1(a) of the CAFTA-DR*, Final Report Of The Panel, 14 June 2017.

[193] https://www.wto.org/english/tratop_e/devel_e/a4t_e/aid4trade_e.htm.

[194] https://www.wto.org/english/tratop_e/devel_e/teccop_e/if_e.htm.

certain respects as human rights and thus belong to the *acquis* of international law, the consideration of which was recognised in the *US-Gasoline* case, since WTO law 'is not to be read in clinical isolation from public international law'.[195] In this respect, these labour rights are in principle eligible for an exception as public morals[196] under Art. XX GATT, which stand up to the 'necessity test'. While some of the labour rights may qualify for this consideration, others may also be covered by the TBT Agreement and must therefore comply with the principle of non-discrimination.[197] This is particularly relevant when process and production methods are changed for the purpose of occupational health and safety or for the development of decent jobs, or when social labelling indicates a sustainable design of working methods and / or value chains.

4. Domestic Jurisdiction

112   A main threat to the fulfilment of SDG 8 concerns undignified work, which cannot be classified as the envisioned form of capabilities and, moreover, violates various human rights and / or fundamental rights. With regard to SDG 8.3, a recurring issue in jurisprudence is that in many developing countries, but not only there, most people do not have access to basic social protection. The often precarious and informal work lacks safety and health measures. Sometimes employment-related practices include bonded and exploitative labour without having the opportunity of access to justice at all.[198]

113   In 2015, the UK Modern Slavery Act which, according to the introduction, is an

> [a]ct to make provision about slavery, servitude and forced or compulsory labour and about human trafficking, including provision for the protection of victims; to make provision for an Independent Anti-slavery Commissioner; and for connected purposes,[199]

has been set forth. Similarly, Australia enacted the Modern Slavery Bill in 2018 which came into effect on 1 January 2019.[200] Both instruments contribute to SDG 8.7 and SDG 8.8 and may give rise to jurisdiction in the area of forced labour, modern slavery and human trafficking in the future.[201]

114   In *Nevsun Resources Ltd. v. Araya*[202], the Canadian Supreme Court stated that a private company may be held liable under Canadian law for violations of peremptory norms (*jus cogens*) of customary international law through corporate behaviour committed in other countries. Eritrean workers were subjected to various crimes against

---

[195] WT/DS2/AB/R, *United States – Standards for Reformulated and Conventional Gasoline*, AB-1996-1, 29 April 1996, 17.

[196] WTO ANALYTICAL INDEX, GATT 1994 – Article XX (Jurisprudence), paras. 59-64: 'The term 'public morals' denotes standards of right and wrong conduct maintained by or on behalf of a community or nation' [...] 'the content of these concepts for Members can vary in time and space, depending upon a range of factors, including prevailing social, cultural, ethical and religious values'; WT/DS285/AB/R, *United States – Measures Affecting the Cross-Border Supply of Gambling and Betting Services*, AB-2005-1, 7 April 2005, para. 296.

[197] Art. I GATT (most-favoured nation principle) and Art. III GATT (national treatment).

[198] See e.g. CEDAW/C/IND/CO/4-5, Concluding observations on the combined fourth and fifth periodic reports of India*, 24 July 2014, para. 28; CRPD/C/IND/CO/1, Committee on the Rights of Persons with Disabilities, Concluding observations on the initial report of India*, 25 September 2019, paras. 32(c), 56; CERD/C/IND/CO/19, *Consideration of Reports Submitted by States Parties under Article 9 Of The Convention, Concluding Observations of the Committee on the Elimination of Racial Discrimination*, para. 23.

[199] https://www.legislation.gov.uk/ukpga/2015/30/introduction.

[200] https://www.aph.gov.au/Parliamentary_Business/Bills_Legislation/Bills_Search_Results/Result?bId = r6148.

[201] See Sinclair and Nolan, 'Modern Slavery Laws in Australia: Steps in the Right Direction?' (2020) 5.1 *Business and Human Rights Journal*, 164-70.

[202] Supreme Court of Canada, 2020 SCC 5, *Nevsun Resources Ltd. v. Araya*, judgment, 28 February 2020.

humanity, including 'forced labour, slavery, cruel, inhuman or degrading treatment and [other] crimes against humanity [as well as] violations of domestic offences including conversion, assault, unlawful confinement, conspiracy and negligence' at an Eritrean mine majority-owned by the Canadian company Nevsun Resources. Crimes against humanity represent the least controversial examples of violations of *jus cogens* norms. Although the court did not take the case for decision, it declared the Eritrean workers affected to have legal standing in principle for action before the courts of British Columbia, where the company is based, and inferred at least potential liability for corporate conduct of private actors beyond the borders of their home state.[203] This case is of particular importance because, on the one hand, the Supreme Court excluded the validity of the *act of state doctrine*[204] for Canada and, on the other hand, 'opened a new front for transnational human rights claims: customary law claims based on customary international law'.[205] Thus, it appears possible that 'even if a norm has a strictly interstate character, it may be possible for the common law to "evolve so as to extend the scope of th[e] norm to bind corporations".[206] The decision reaffirms the obligation of domestic courts to actively engage in the development of international human rights norms to respond to the current challenges related to transnational corporations and their cross-border obligations. Against the backdrop of achieving SDG 8.7 in conjunction with SDG 8.8, this points to a legal development that, if upheld, would expose transnational corporations to liability through additional means and therefore should significantly strengthen not only SDG 8 but also SDG 16.3 (*access to justice*).[207]

Moreover, with relevance for SDG 8.7 (child), judicial authorities in the Democratic **115** Republic of the Congo (DRC), supported by the UN, applied the child protection law of 2009 (which stipulates that child recruitment is a crime punishable by up to 20 years of imprisonment). Several trials have been held or are still ongoing against leaders of armed forces (official and unofficial) in the DRC who, recruited and used children in (armed) conflicts or contributed to the sexual violence and abuse of children (that is still ongoing) and further war crimes and crimes against humanity. Sentences have been ruled from 15 years of imprisonment to life imprisonment.[208] Whether these developments are sufficient to safeguard children from exploitation and abuse in the sense of SDG 8.7 by 2025, given the many conflicts worldwide, seems more than doubtful. As important as this and further jurisdiction is, it is unfortunately not much more than a drop in the ocean. Too many investigations and prosecutions are lengthy and time-consuming, too often insufficient to dismantle the often widespread systematic

---

[203] https://www.scc-csc.ca/case-dossier/cb/2020/37919-eng.pdf; further reading: Walton, 'Nevsun Resources Ltd. v. Araya' (2021) 115(1) *AJIL*, 107-14.

[204] The *act of state doctrine* precludes domestic courts from assessing the sovereign acts of a foreign government.

[205] Walton, 'Nevsun Resources Ltd. v. Araya' (2021) 115(1) *AJIL*, 107 (107).

[206] Walton, 'Nevsun Resources Ltd. v. Araya' (2021) 115(1) *AJIL*, 107 (114).

[207] See for national case law the Customary IHL Database from the ICRC: https://ihl-databases.icrc.org/customary-ihl/eng/docs/src_vnaca.

[208] A/HRC/43/38, *Children and armed conflict, Report of the Special Representative of the Secretary-General for Children and Armed Conflict*, 24 December 2019, para. 47:
On 1 February 2019, Marcel Habarugira Rangira, a former officer of the Armed Forces of the Democratic Republic of the Congo who joined Nyatura as a commander, was sentenced to 15 years of imprisonment for child recruitment and use. In August 2019, the trial of Cobra Matata, former leader of the Force de résistance patriotique de l'Ituri, for war crimes and crimes against humanity, including child recruitment and use and sexual violence, began. The trial of Cheka, former commander of Nduma défense du Congo-Cheka, for war crimes, including child recruitment and use and sexual violence, is ongoing. Additionally, the sentencing in 2018 of Dominique Buyenge Birihanze, former commander of the Patriotes résistants congolais, to life imprisonment for child recruitment was confirmed on appeal in 2019.

structures and thus ensure effective child protection.[209] Moreover, however, condemning a few will not tackle the root of the problem and, more importantly, will not lead to children benefiting from sustainable reintegration or even recover physically and mentally.[210]

II. The Enforcement of a 'Right to Decent Work and Economic Growth'

116   Enforcing labour (protection) law and rights is difficult to realise. Although the right to work is enshrined in various human rights instruments, it can only be added to the right to work in a dignified manner in the overall context, as it is a social justice right that every state must progressively realise. The very nature of this right requires positive action on the part of the state in order to realise it.[211] However, it is evident in many places that this right and intertwined possibilities for human development are not accompanied by sufficient procedural rights to enforce it.

117   In the EU, the Commission has published three working papers on the issue of enforcement of labour protection and Trade and Sustainable Development chapters (TSD) in free trade agreements.[212] Complaints are received through the Single Entry point and the Commission states that there are different avenues available to trigger enforcement action with respect to trade and / or TSD and compliance with Generalised Scheme of Preferences (GSP) commitments. Some mechanisms exist already and new initiatives could complement them. With the appointment of a new Chief Trade enforcement Officer (CTEO) the Commission tries to drive forward and coordinate the enforcement activities, and created a new Enforcement Directorate with – inter alia – a new Single Entry Point ('SEP') for enforcement, market access and SMEs, and a new complaint system available to stakeholders.[213]

118   In the recent past, the EU for the first time resorted to dispute settlement procedures under its bilateral trade agreements, initiating a dispute (among others) over the right to workers under the EU-Korea Free Trade Agreement.[214]

119   The 2018 15-point Action Plan on Trade and Sustainable Development introduced cooperation with Member States as a key measure to revamp TSD implementation and enforcement. The plan includes cooperation at the level of capitals through the Commission's TSD Expert Group as well as through EU Delegations in partner countries. The same structure via the Commission's GSP Expert Group and the EU Delegations applies to the monitoring of compliance with the Generalised Scheme of Preferences (GSP).

---

[209] A/HRC/43/38, *Children and armed conflict, Report of the Special Representative of the Secretary-General for Children and Armed Conflict*, 24 December 2019, para. 17: 'difficulties to access and verify information'.

[210] A/HRC/43/38, *Children and armed conflict, Report of the Special Representative of the Secretary-General for Children and Armed Conflict*, 24 December 2019, para. 19.

[211] Hepple, 'Rights at Work' (2002) *ILO and International Institute for Labour Studies Geneva*, vii.

[212] European Commission, *Working approaches to the enforcement and implementation work of DG Trade*, 16 November 2020; see on EU sustainable policy-making: https://ec.europa.eu/trade/policy/policy-making/sustainable-development/.

[213] European Commission, *Working approaches to the enforcement and implementation work of DG Trade*, 16 November 2020, 5.

[214] European Commission, *Working approaches to the enforcement and implementation work of DG Trade*, 16 November 2020, 3 f.; further reading Weiß and Furculita, 'The EU in Search for Stronger Enforcement Rules: Assessing the Proposed Amendments to Trade Enforcement Regulation 654/2014' (2020) 23(4) *JIEL*, 865-84.

In 2021, the Commission will carry out a review of the 15-point action plan and a comparative study of third country practices.[215]

Closely linked to this right is the right to development, which is rejuvenated by SDG   120
8 to a right to economic growth, sometimes also referred to as right to welfare. This form of development is intended to act as a counter-narrative to poverty, which is in itself a 'deprivation of capabilities'.[216]

However, it is noticeable that the numerous complementary soft law standards,   121
recommendations or codes of conduct, such as those of the ILO, the Global Compact or the UNGP call for voluntary action and acknowledgement. Yet, these are not legally enforceable autonomously but accompany binding instruments as context of their legal interpretation.[217]

The gap between rulings or opinions issued by international courts and their imple-   122
mentation by domestic courts remains conspicuous. Further problems lie in the frequent absence of adequate remedial bodies or in the lack of access to justice at all.

III. De Facto Influences on Jurisdiction

With the recent development of the China – EU Investment Agreement (CAI) which   123
is planned to include labour law obligations, an innovative and modern shaping of decent work and economic growth could be created in the future. Although the negotiations on the CAI are currently suspended due to divergent expectations of human rights compliance, the CAI points to future opportunities and constraints in shaping international trade and investment agreements. The CAI presumably will set compromises on labour and environmental policies which shall remain with each party's right with the mere commitment to strive for high levels of protection and not constituting a material contractual ground falling under general dispute resolution procedures.[218] With simultaneously reduced emphasis on trade union rights and lacking commitment on labour rights, the structural and systematic features of both negotiating partners will presumably not align, neither economically, nor politically and thus hinder the achievement of, amongst others, SDG 8.3 and SDG 8.8.[219]

Whereas the inclusion and design of labour standards do not form part of the legal   124
acquis of the WTO,[220] EU Free Trade and Investment Agreements (FTAs) generally contain labour, environmental or sustainability standards in self-standing Trade and Sustainable Development Chapters (TSD) since the 2011 EU-Korea FTA.[221] However, such

---

[215] European Commission, *Working approaches to the enforcement and implementation work of DG Trade*, 16 November 2020, 5; see also European Commission, *Non paper of the Commission services*, *Feedback and way forward on improving the implementation and enforcement of Trade and Sustainable Development chapters in EU Free Trade Agreements*, 26 February 2018; Non-paper of the Commission services Trade and Sustainable Development (TSD) chapters in EU Free Trade Agreements (FTAs).

[216] Sen, *Development as Freedom* (1999), 87 ff.

[217] Hepple, 'Rights at Work' (2002) *ILO and International Institute for Labour Studies Geneva*, 18; further reading Kotiswaran, Prabha, *Revisiting the Law and Governance of Trafficking, Forced Labor and Modern Slavery* (2017).

[218] This form of design can also be found in previous EU agreements.

[219] Cotula, 'EU–China Comprehensive Agreement on Investment: An Appraisal of its Sustainable Development Section' (2021) *Business and Human Rights Journal*, 1-8.

[220] With the 1996 Singapore ministerial declaration, it was affirmed that the ILO constitutes 'the competent body to set and deal with these standards [core labour standards]' while also 'reject[ing] the use of labour standards for protectionist purposes'.

[221] Harrison et al., 'Governing Labour Standards through Free Trade Agreements: Limits of the European Union's Trade and Sustainable Development Chapters' (2019) 57(2) *JCMS*, 260 (261) but pointing to the EU CARIFORUM EPA in 2008 as a point of departure.

TSD do not form integral parts of the agreement which in case of non-compliance would constitute a breach of contract. By contrast, labour protection norms in US FTAs constitute genuine elements of the contract and unlike in EU agreements, these are also amenable to the regular dispute settlement mechanism and were first included in the North American Agreement on Labor Cooperation (NAALC), a side agreement to the 1994 North American Free Trade Agreement (NAFTA). U.S. labor provisions in FTAs developed since the 1980 s from side agreements being 'commitments not just to enforce a country's own domestic labor laws, but also to adopt and enforce core principles of the ILO', now constituting integral chapters in the FTA.[222]

125   In the US, the Office of Trade and Labor Affairs (OTLA), an agency of the US Department of Labors' Bureau of International Labor Affairs, is responsible for alleged violations of FTA labor commitments. OTLA reviews submissions of complaints if these qualify as issue 'relevant to the labor provisions in the NAALC or FTA and illustrate a country's failure to comply with its obligations', which may be followed by various procedures.[223] However, the U.S. 'has ratified only two of the core ILO conventions[224] [...] As a result, US FTAs do not include commitments to enforce the conventions themselves.'[225]

126   While U.S. trade agreements and programmes are tools to curb the import of goods from forced labour, a more effective global coordination of trade-related labour concerns presumably depends on the development of multilateral trade rules. However, given the exclusion of labour rights standards from WTO negotiations, it appears questionable as to how this can be achieved, given that the ILO cannot produce legally binding standards independently and coupled with economic growth which is also demanded for by SDG 8.[226]

127   Since 2019, a new global campaign has been launched under the title 'Act to protect children affected by armed conflict' which is driven by a conglomerate of several of the UN specialised agencies.[227]

However, despite all endeavours, it remains difficult to establish true

> 'responsibility of the Global North, for example restraining the exploitative behaviour of its transnational corporations, changing the rules of global trade and finance in favour of more policy space in the countries of the Global South, and, most important, moving to more sustainable production

---

[222] Further reading: Marx and Ebert and Hachez, 'Dispute Settlement for Labour Provisions in EU Free Trade Agreements: Rethinking Current Approaches, Politics and Governance' (2017) 5(4) *Politics and Governance*, 49-59; Marx et al., 'Dispute Settlement in the Trade and Sustainable Development Chapters of EU Trade Agreements' (2017) *Leuven Centre for Global Governance Studies*; CRS In Focus IF10046, Worker Rights Provisions in Free Trade Agreements (FTAs); CRS In Focus IF11308, USMCA: Labor Provisions; and CRS In Focus IF10645, Dispute Settlement in the WTO and U.S. Trade Agreements. CRS, Labor Enforcement Issues in U.S. FTAs, Updated December 18, 2020; https://crsreports.congress.gov/prod uct/pdf/IF/IF10972; https://crsreports.congress.gov/search/#/?termsToSearch=free%20trade%20otla&ord erBy=Relevance.

[223] Reviews, public reports, and recommendations for bilateral consultations or dispute settlement; search engine for CRS reports: https://crsreports.congress.gov; see for an overview of USMCA Labour Provisions: https://crsreports.congress.gov/product/pdf/IF/IF11308.

[224] ILO conventions No. 105 [Abolition of Forced Labour] and No. 182 [Worst Forms of Child Labour].

[225] MacNaughton and Frey, 'Decent Work, Human Rights and the Sustainable Development Goals' (2016) 47 *Georgetown Journal of International Law*, 607 (620); https://crsreports.congress.gov/ prod-uct/pdf/IF/IF10046.

[226] Congressional Research Service, *Section 307 and U.S. Imports of Products of Forced Labor: Overview and Issues for Congress*, R46631 (2021), 35.

[227] UNICEF, the Department of Peace Operations and the Department of Political and Peacebuilding Affairs, as well as civil society organizations and States Members of the United Nations. The United Nations Educational, Scientific and Cultural Organization (UNESCO) Special Envoy for Peace and Reconciliation, Forest Whitaker.

modes and lifestyles. All countries should strive to distribute work more evenly among the population'[228]

The issues addressed by SDG 8 are widespread and so are the *de facto* influences.   **128**
Since, by following the idea of SDG 8, developing countries, LDCs and conflict-struck countries should be supported foremost,[229] the main constraint in solving such issues lies in a financing gap not only of states but all the more of businesses themselves. This financial constraint particularly affects Micro-and-Small enterprises (MSEs) to a greater extent than other businesses. In order to close these gaps and effectively achieve SDG8 'innovative law reform' is needed.[230]

E. Conclusion on SDG 8

SDG 8 dwelling on '[p]romote sustained, inclusive and sustainable economic growth,   **129**
full and productive employment and decent work for all' calls for multiple ways for improvement. Most of the endeavoured ameliorations depend on political actions and the insertion of politics creating the provisions to achieve SDG 8. Most targets of SDG 8 are separated from a direct normative content, the normativity of the SDGs is clearly limited to some concepts enshrined in SDG 8.5.[231] It should not be overlooked that a government outside the public sector, has only little competencies and capabilities to break with interventions into the demands and offers of a specific markets, which is even more difficult, when this market is deemed to be a free one and following the rules of the WTO.

Decent work and equal pay are strongly linked to SDG 11 and SDG 5 and as an   **130**
urgent need related to the balance of power of the market. Chances for young people means the relentless offer of basic educational requirement in a thorough framework of education combining theoretical and practical lessons, in particular with a specific knowledge of the sphere of digitisation. The Doha Development Agenda of the WTO failed on the question on subsidies in agriculture, hampers the development of markets and the further scales of infrastructure, trade and services, something which hardly can't be compensated by preferential agreements like the GSP+ of the EU and the Everything-but-arms system (EBA) of the EU. In a country where getting a job is very tough, finding a job does not at the same time mean escaping poverty when minimum wages are sometimes less than 2 US dollars (if there is a minimum wage at all). Therefore, policies are needed that must stimulate and ensure job creation and business growth, fight poverty and hunger, and create fair prospects for education and on-the-job training for girls and boys alike (SDG 5, SDG 8.6).

A cornerstone for improving working conditions and opening up the market for girls,   **131**
women and men would be a comprehensive thoroughly and swift enforcement of all manifestations of modern slavery, human trafficking and child labour (SDG 8.7) and a consistent and clean application of the rule of law by state agencies and a well-trained and well-paid judiciary as well as the successful fight against corruption (SDG 16).

---

[228] Scherrer, 'Superfluous Workers: Why SDG 8 Will Remain Elusive' in Kaltenborn and Krajewski and Kuhn (eds), *Sustainable Development Goals and Human Rights* (2020), 133.

[229] See A/RES/70/1, SDG 8.7, SDG 8.a, SDG 8.b.

[230] See Pekmezovic and Alma and Walker, 'Achieving Sustainable Development Goal 8 in Small Island Developing States by Capital Raising Law Reform: Case Study of Fiji' in Butler and Lein and Salim, *Integration and International Dispute Resolution in Small States* (2018).

[231] By 2030 achieve full and productive employment and decent work for all women and men, including for young people and persons with disabilities, and equal pay for work of equal value.

Goal 9
Build resilient infrastructure, promote inclusive and sustainable industrialization and foster innovation

9.1 Develop quality, reliable, sustainable and resilient infrastructure, including regional and transborder infrastructure, to support economic development and human well-being, with a focus on affordable and equitable access for all

9.2 Promote inclusive and sustainable industrialization and, by 2030, significantly raise industry's share of employment and gross domestic product, in line with national circumstances, and double its share in least developed countries

9.3 Increase the access of small-scale industrial and other enterprises, in particular in developing countries, to financial services, including affordable credit, and their integration into value chains and markets

9.4 By 2030, upgrade infrastructure and retrofit industries to make them sustainable, with increased resource-use efficiency and greater adoption of clean and environmentally sound technologies and industrial processes, with all countries taking action in accordance with their respective capabilities

9.5 Enhance scientific research, upgrade the technological capabilities of industrial sectors in all countries, in particular developing countries, including, by 2030, encouraging innovation and substantially increasing the number of research and development workers per 1 million people and public and private research and development spending

9.a Facilitate sustainable and resilient infrastructure development in developing countries through enhanced financial, technological and technical support to African countries, least developed countries, landlocked developing countries and small island developing States

9.b Support domestic technology development, research and innovation in developing countries, including by ensuring a conducive policy environment for, inter alia, industrial diversification and value addition to commodities

9.c Significantly increase access to information and communications technology and strive to provide universal and affordable access to the Internet in least developed countries by 2020

Word Count related to 'infrastructure' 'industry/industrial/industrialization' 'innovation'
A/RES/70/1 - Transforming our world: the 2030 Agenda for Sustainable Development: 'infrastructure': 11 'industry/industrial/industrialization':11 'innovation': 25
Instruments mentioned in A/RES/70/1 in the section entitled: 'Sustainable Development Goals and targets:
A/RES/69/313 - Addis Ababa Action Agenda of the Third International Conference on Financing for Development adopted on 27 July 2015: 'infrastructure': 34 'industry/industrial/industrialization': 10 'innovation': 33
A/RES/66/288 - The future we want (Rio +20 Declaration) adopted on 27 July 2012: 'infrastructure': 10 'industry/industrial/industrialization': 8 'innovation/innovative': 19
A/RES/55/2 - United Nations Millennium Declaration adopted on 8 September 2000: 'infrastructure': 10 'industry/industrial/industrialization': 8 'innovation/innovative': 19

Select Bibliography: Carlos M Correa, 'Specific Concerns of Developing Countries in Intellectual Property Rights' in Cottier and Nadakavukaren Schefer, *Elgar Encyclopedia of International Economic Law* (2017), 531; European Commission 2003/361/EC, *Commission Recommendation Concerning the Definition of Micro, Small And Medium-Sized Enterprises* (6 May 2003); Eurostat, *Statistics on small and medium-sized enterprises* (2018); Steven Feldstein, 'Why Internet Access Is a Human Right, What We Can Do to Protect It' (2017), *Foreign Affairs*; Giovanny Vega-Barbosa and Lorraine Aboagye, 'Human Rights and the Protection of the Environment: The Advisory Opinion of the Inter-American Court of Human Rights' (2018) *EJIL:Talk!*; IISD, How Can Progress on Infrastructure, Industry and Innovation Contribute to Achieving the SDGs?, https://sdg.iisd.org/commentary/policy-briefs/how-can-progress-on-infrastructure-industry-and-innovation-contribute-to-achieving-the-sdgs/ (last accessed 27.06.2021, 20:17); International Law Commission, *Sixth Report on the Protection of Persons in the Event of Disasters*, by Mr. Eduardo Valencia-Ospina, Special Rapporteur (2013), UN Doc. A/CN.4/662, 9-16; IPCC, *Climate Change 2014, Impacts, Adaptions and Vulnerability, Working Group II Contribution to the Fifth Assessment Report of the Intergovernmental Panel on Climate Change* (Cambridge University Press, Cambridge 2014), 840; Sarah Joseph, 'Trade Law and Investment Law' in Dinah Shelton, *The Oxford Handbook of International Human Rights Law* (Oxford University Press, Oxford 2013), 846; Juliet Mian et al., *Critical Infrastructure Resilience – Understanding the landscape* (The Resilience Shift 2018); Sarah Murray (Martin Koehring, ed), *The Critical Role of Infrastructure for the Sustainable Development Goals* (The Economist Intelligence Unit Limited, 2019); Oreste Pollicino, 'Right to Internet Access: Quid Iuris?' in Andreas von Arnauld, Kerstin von der Decken and Mart Susi (eds), *The Cambridge Handbook on New Human Rights, Recognition, Novelty, Rhetoric* (Cambridge University Press, UK/USA/Australia/India/Singapore 2019), 263; Raniya Sobir, *Micro, Small and Medium-sized Enterprises (MSMEs) and their role in achieving the Sustainable Development Goals*, Department of Economic and Social Affairs (2020); The World Bank, *Small and Medium Enterprises (SMEs) Finance: Improving SMEs' Access to Finance and Finding Innovative Solutions to Unlock Sources of Capital*, https://www.worldbank.org/en/topic/smefinance (last accessed 27.06.2021, 19:06); J. Thompson, Kris Boschmans and Lora Pissareva, 'Alternative Financing Instruments for SMEs and Entrepreneurs: The case of capital market finance' (2018) 10 *OECD SME and Entrepreneurship Papers* (OECD Publishing, Paris 2018); Maria Fernanda Tomaselli, Joleen Timko, Robert Kozak, Justin Bull, Sean Kearney, Jack Saddler, Susan van Dyk, Guangyu Wang and Xinxin Zhu, 'SDG 9: Industry, Innovation and Infrastructure – Anticipating the Potential Impacts on Forests and Forest-Based Livelihoods' in Pia Katila, Carol J. Pierce Colfer, Wil De Jong, Glenn Galloway, Pablo Pacheco and Georg Winkel (eds.), *Sustainable Development Goals: Their Impacts on Forests and People* (Cambridge University Press, Cambridge 2019), 279; UNIDO, *Introduction to UNIDO: Inclusive and Sustainable Industrial Development* (UNIDO, Vienna 2015),; United Nations, *International Standard Industrial Classification of All Economic Activities (ISIC Revision 4)* (UN, New York 2008).

A. Background and Origin of SDG 9

SDG 9, which comprises eight targets and twelve indicators, is based on a total of **1** three pillars: industry, infrastructure and innovation.[1] These pillars primarily describe one of the key economic dimensions of the SDGs forming an economic dimension of SDG 9 which is closely linked to SDG 8 (labour and economic growth) (→ Intro mn. 123 ff., 198). Both SDGs assume that energy (SDG 7) is available and that people (SDG 5) have access to food (SDG 2), clean water and sanitation as basic needs. But with its

---

[1] Tomaselli et al., 'SDG 9: Industry, Innovation and Infrastructure – Anticipating the Potential Impacts on Forests and Forest-Based Livelihoods' Sustainable Development Goals: Their Impacts on Forests and People (2019), 279 (279); SDG Knowledge Hub, 'How Can Progress on Infrastructure, Industry and Innovation Contribute to Achieving the SDGs?' (2017).

approach to initiate and foster innovation, SDG 9 becomes a 'docking station' for all SDGs[2] and can be assessed the impetus for sustainable green and blue growth and prosperity

2   The UNIDO concluded the interrelations between industry, innovation and infrastructure as strong, since industry is an important source of technical innovation for achieving green objectives, such as increased resource- and energy-efficiency, low-carbon production, circular economies and climate action.[3]

3   Infrastructure has long been considered by the UN as a prerequisite for sustainable development.[4] Moreover, it can enable people to engage in economic activity[5] so that they in turn can act sustainably. The term 'infrastructure' covers a wide range of issues. This includes for example:

> Information and communication infrastructure, including broadband infrastructure – the information superhighways on which the global digital economy is being built; Energy and piped gas, piped water supply, sanitation and sewerage, and solid waste collection and disposal; Roads and major dam and canal works for irrigation and drainage; Other transport sectors-urban and interurban railways, bus rapid transit and other urban transport, ports and water ways, and air transport; Infrastructure for health care, education and skills development, etc.[6]

4   The SARS-CoV-2 pandemic underpins the importance of a functioning health infrastructure in particular. In the course of the division of labour in a globalised world, even rich countries with a functioning infrastructure were unable to meet their demand for medical supplies.[7] Overall, there is a globally unbalanced distribution of infrastructure, which particularly disadvantages rural and low-income urban areas,[8] some of which need cross-border connections (SDG 9.1). Achieving inclusive and sustainable growth and meeting environmental goals[9] requires long-term and large-scale investments.[10] Infrastructure planning is linked to public-law planning mechanisms that interact with and are steered by cities, and to a whole-of-society environment with a functioning legal framework applicable under the *rule of law* principle, ideally without corrosive effects of corruption (SDG 11, SDG 16).

---

[2] http://sdg.iisd.org/commentary/policy-briefs/how-can-progress-on-infrastructure-industry-and-innovation-contribute-to-achieving-the-sdgs/.

[3] https://www.unido.org/unido-sdgs; UNIDO, *UNIDO's medium-term programme framework 2018 – 2021*.

[4] UN, Agenda 21, para. 2.37.d: Promote and support the investment and **infrastructure required for sustainable economic growth** (emphasis added) and diversification on an environmentally sound and sustainable basis; UN, The future we want, mn. 149: We recognize the importance of job creation by investing in and developing sound, effective and efficient economic and **social infrastructure** (emphasis added) and productive capacities **for sustainable development** (emphasis added) and sustained, inclusive and equitable economic growth. We call upon countries to enhance **infrastructure investment for sustainable development** (emphasis added), and we agree to support United Nations funds, programs and agencies to help to assist and promote the efforts of developing countries, particularly the least developed countries, in this regard.

[5] The Economist, 'The critical role of infrastructure for the Sustainable Development Goals' (2019), 7.

[6] United Nations General Assembly Open Working Group on Sustainable Development Goals, *Compendium of TST Issues Briefs October 2014*, 83.

[7] Global Policy Watch, *COVID-19 and the SDGs The impact of the coronavirus pandemic on the global sustainability agenda*, 5.

[8] World Bank, 'The 2030 Sustainable Development Agenda and the World Bank Group: Closing the SDGs Financing Gap, 2019 Update', 71.

[9] United Nations General Assembly Open Working Group on Sustainable Development Goals, *Compendium of TST Issues Briefs October 2014*, 83; United Nations Environment Assembly of the United Nations Environment Programme, 'Sustainable infrastructure' UNEP/EA.4/L.6.

[10] UNCTAD, Investment Policy Framework For Sustainable Development, 6.

Industrialisation stimulates pull effects on other sectors and thus contribute to   5
sustainable economic development.[11] Moreover, industrialisation, aligned with the improvement of infrastructure, contributes to poverty eradication in the long term.[12]
According to UNIDO, the manufacturing sector and related service industries are highly
stimulating for the provision of jobs and income creation.[13]

The advocacy of modern industrialisation combined with infrastructure and inno-   6
vation seems easy to author but difficult to achieve in practice. The requirements to
succeed are numerous and lie not only in the lack of adequate funding, but also in a
competitive business environment, natural resources, engineering, administrative capacity, market institutions and adequate knowledge in the sector, as well as the need for
skilled and trained human resources.[14] The UNIDO Roadmap can be acknowledged as
one example of how to set a framework to conduct such a process and manifest modern
and sustainable partnerships of industrialisation (→ Goal 17).[15]

At the horizontal level, the UN Industrial Development Organization (UNIDO) are   7
involved to promote partnerships with the United Nations Conference on Trade and Development (UNCTAD), the Food and Agriculture Organization of the United Nations
(FAO), the International Labour Organization (ILO), the United Nations Environment
Programme (UNEP), the World Bank, the International Monetary Fund (IMF) and the
United Nations Development Programme (UNDP) to promote interdependencies to
foster industrialisation.

The industrialisation needed encompasses technology transfer, access to information   8
and communications technology, diversification, agribusiness value chain development,
trade, capacity-building, renewable energy and energy efficiency, industrial policy, special economic zones and industrial parks, action on climate change and human capital
development, while also strengthening public-private partnerships with a range of stakeholders, including those in the public and the private sectors, civil society organizations
and academia.[16]

However, an increasing degree of industrialisation also harbours risks. The United   9
Nations Conference on the Human Environment highlighted in 1972 already the importance of the interdependencies between environmental problems and industrialisation.[17]
Increasing industrialisation can lead to far-reaching changes in the environment.[18]
Therefore, the 1987 Brundtland Report referred to 'costs of [...] inappropriate industrialization'[19] and stressed the increasing need of energy for industrialization.[20] Subsequently, the dangers associated with industrialisation were further specified by the UN.[21]

---

[11] United Nations General Assembly Open Working Group on Sustainable Development Goals, *Compendium of TST Issues Briefs October 2014*, 82.

[12] UN Economic and Social Council, '2017 Special Meeting of ECOSOC on Innovations for Infrastructure Development and Promoting Sustainable Industrialization', 2.

[13] https://www.unido.org/unido-sdgs.

[14] https://www.unido.org/who-we-are/idda3.

[15] A/RES/70/293, *Third Industrial Development Decade for Africa (2016–2025)*; UNIDO, *ROADMAP Implementation of the Third Industrial Development Decade for Africa (2016–2025)* (2018).

[16] A/RES/70/293, Third Industrial Development Decade for Africa (2016–2025), para 8.

[17] UN, Report of the United Nations Conference on the Human Environment, Stockholm 1972, Chapter 1 Proclaim 5.

[18] Macioti, 'Industrial development and a sustainable environment' (1989) 16 *Science and Public Policy*, 262 (263).

[19] Report of the World Commission on Environment and Development: Our Common Future, Overview by the World Commission on Environment and Development, para. 68.

[20] Report of the World Commission on Environment and Development: Our Common Future, Overview by the World Commission on Environment and Development, para. 58.

[21] For example, Agenda 21 referred to 'severe strains on the water resources', Agenda 21, mn. 18.56.

In order to achieve an equitable distribution of newly created jobs in industry and to prevent resource exploitation and thus avoid inappropriate industrialisation, SDG 9 calls for inclusive and sustainable industrialisation.[22]

10   Together with science and technology, as acknowledged in the Global Agenda 2030 and the Addis Ababa Action Agenda (AAAA),[23] the development of innovation capacities 'has been proven to be an important prerequisite for the social and economic transformations that enable sustainable economic growth, human development and poverty eradication.'[24] Innovations relate in particular to science and technology[25] and can contribute significantly to inclusive growth.[26] However, with innovations to come, a loss or a change of jobs must also be considered.[27] Driving technologies that are currently being promoted are, amongst others, Artificial Intelligence (AI) and Robotics, Internet of Things (IoT), Big Data, Green Energy and biotechnology, block chain related services, digitisation, nanotechnologies.[28]

11   Different UN agencies are tasked to analyse and foster the results and effects of the development of Science, Technology and Innovation (STI) and facilitate fruitful cooperation and the Technology Facilitation Mechanism (TFM) (→ Goal 17).[29] For instance, the UNCTAD Science, Technology and Innovation Policy Reviews (STIP) reviews the status of member states and ongoing efforts in the area of national science, technology and innovation plans.[30] As part of the implementation of the TFM, the Global Pilot Programme on STI for SDGs Roadmaps was launched in 2019 with an initial group of five pilot countries (Ethiopia, Ghana, India, Kenya and Serbia, and since 2021 Ukraine). The programme based on a newly developed Guidebook for the Preparation of STI for SDGs Roadmaps[31] which has been jointly created by several UN Agencies such as UN-DESA, UNESCO, UNIDO, UNCTAD and the World Bank, together with other international partners such as the Government of Japan, the Joint Research Centre of the European Commission and the OECD. Valuable inputs were also provided by the Group of Twenty (G20) and the 10-Member Group, which is another component of the TFM.[32]

12   The TFM was established through the AAAA to support the implementation of the SDGs and was launched with the adoption of the Global Agenda 2030 in September 2015.

---

[22] United Nations General Assembly Open Working Group on Sustainable Development Goals, *Compendium of TST Issues Briefs October 2014*, 83; https://sdgs.un.org/topics/technology.

[23] A/RES/70/1, para. 70, SDG 17; A/RES/69/313, paras. 5, 33, 114 ff.

[24] United Nations General Assembly Open Working Group on Sustainable Development Goals, *Compendium of TST Issues Briefs October 2014*, 114; Report of the Secretary-General on 'Science, technology and innovation, and the potential of culture, for promoting sustainable development and achieving the Millennium Development Goals' for the 2013 Annual Ministerial Review, para. 29.

[25] Compare SDG 9.5 and 9.b.

[26] UN Economic and Social Council, '2017 Special Meeting of ECOSOC on Innovations for Infrastructure Development and Promoting Sustainable Industrialization', 2.

[27] IISD, Briefing Note on the STI Forum 2017, 2.

[28] UNCTAD, *Technology and Innovation Report 2021 - Catching technological waves: Innovation with equity* (2021), 109 ff.

[29] A/RES/70/1, para. 70; UNCTAD, *Technology and Innovation Report 2021 - Catching technological waves: Innovation with equity* (2021).

[30] See for an overview of Science, Technology and Innovation Policy Reviews: https://unctad.org/publications-search?f%5b0%5d=product%3A635.

[31] Two background papers supplement the Guidebook on available STI road mapping methodologies and on international partnerships; UN IATT, *Guidebook for the Preparation of Science, Technology and Innovation (STI) for SDGs Roadmaps* (2020); further information https://sdgs.un.org/topics/technology.

[32] Joint Research Centre (EC), Matusiak et al., *Background paper: Overview of the existing STI for SDGs roadmapping methodologies* (2021); https://ec.europa.eu/jrc/en/event/conference/un-sti-forum-2021; https://sdgs.un.org/tfm/ten-member-group; https://sdgs.un.org/tfm; https://sustainabledevelopment.un.org/partnership/?p=33852.

Further UN-related and non-UN agencies and organisation such as, amongst many   13
others, FAO, WTO, OECD support and facilitate the technology, know-how and innovation creation with their analyses, coordination and referral of partnerships, as well as capacity-building and education (→ Intro mn. 294 f.).[33]

It is essential to establish and expand communication and digitisation in order to   14
meet the existing challenges, which have become even greater due to the pandemic. The
numerous sectors of industry are setting the stage for delivering goods and services to
any place of the world with new technologies that are distributed everywhere and allow
access for everybody since infrastructure, industrial production, technology, and digital
economies are key drivers of growth and poverty eradication (→ Goal 17).[34]

The 1987 Brundtland Report contained the demand for increased capacities for   15
technological development,[35] which were taken up and elaborated in subsequent resolutions.[36] Key Challenges for capacity-building relate to internet access, inadequate
transport, Research and Development.[37]

To create a global sustainability effect through innovation, global cooperation is   16
needed (→ Goal 17).[38] Therefore, communication and availability of information is a
central component of SDG 9, which has been concretised in SDG 9.c.

It is obvious that these easily formulated tasksneed a significant amount of money to   17
transform societies and economies in such profound way. Moreover, the conditions for
specific growth and also the transformation of industry must be measured inherently
against the conditions of the environmental and social dimensions of sustainable development.

B. Scope and Dimensions of SDG 9

At first glance, SDG 9 is fairly straightforward in focussing on the broad themes of in-   18
frastructure, industrialisation and innovation, thereby reflecting their state of transition.

However, the true import of SDG 9 does not lie in these uncontroversial concepts but   19
in understanding the scope and breadth of the qualifiers used for these terms. Specifically, this SDG aims at development of, *sustainable, resilient* and *inclusive* infrastructure;
inclusive and *sustainable* industrialisation; and *innovation*. Thus, while the aims of SDG
9 are directed at progress on *infrastructure, industrialisation* and *innovation*, the scope

---

[33] See e.g. https://www.oecd.org/science/; https://www.oecd.org/science/emerging-tech/; WTO, *World Trade Report 2018: The future of world trade: How Digital Technologies are Transforming Global Commerce* (2018); http://www.fao.org/teca/en/about (Technologies and Practices for Small Agricultural Producers (TECA) serve as an online platform gathering successful agricultural technologies and practices on behalf of the FAO); UN, *Resource Guide on Artificial Intelligence (AI) Strategies* (2021), 4.

[34] http://sdg.iisd.org/commentary/policy-briefs/how-can-progress-on-infrastructure-industry-and-inn ovation-contribute-to-achieving-the-sdgs/.

[35] Report of the World Commission on Environment and Development: Our Common Future, Part I Chapter 2 III 6, para. 65: '[…] the capacity for technological innovation needs to be greatly enhanced in developing countries so that they can respond more effectively to the challenges of sustainable develop-ment.'

[36] E.g. UN, The future we want, mn. 72: We recognize the critical role of technology as well as the importance of promoting innovation, in particular in developing countries. We invite governments, as appropriate, to create enabling frameworks that foster environmentally sound technology, research and development, and innovation, including in support of green economy in the context of sustainable development and poverty eradication.

[37] http://sdg.iisd.org/commentary/policy-briefs/how-can-progress-on-infrastructure-industry-and-inn ovation -contribute-to-achieving-the-sdgs/.

[38] United Nations General Assembly Open Working Group on Sustainable Development Goals, *Compendium of TST Issues Briefs October 2014*, 115.

and true legal significance of this SDG can only be understood by analysing these qualifying expressions. In the case of innovation, the assessment of its scope must take place specifically in light of the absence of any qualifiers.

20   Examining the goal within this context makes it clear that while the reach and impact of this goal is unambiguous, many inherent challenges remain. Since this goal aims to promote economic prosperity as well as human rights and sustainability, this reveals often conflicting priorities necessary to achieve many of the targets of SDG 9. For instance, the expansion of small-scale industries, roads and transportation, or increasing access to information and communications technology may adversely impact forest ecosystems and forest-based livelihoods in case a balanced approach is not adopted towards attaining conflicting priorities.[39] In other words, the complexity of SDG 9 lies in the fact that it recognises that infrastructure, industrial growth, or innovation cannot come at any cost.

21   Given the all-encompassing nature of *infrastructure, industrialisation* and *innovation*, it is not far-fetched to say that SDG 9 is an aspirational goal with most targets serving as an enabler for achieving other SDGs. Consequently, the legal aspects of SDG 9 may, only be considered to a limited extent given the boundless nature of all areas addressed.

I. Infrastructure

22   Infrastructure is at the centre-stage of realising of all SDGs. A recent research has concluded that networked infrastructure (that provides and supports essential services such as energy, transportation, water, digital communication) influences on 72 per cent of all 17 SDG targets while non-networked infrastructure (comprising of a single asset type which facilitates the delivery of a service such as a school or a hospital) influences on 81 per cent of all SDGs and their sub-goals.[40] The role of infrastructure in everyday human activity is indispensable for drawing on one's opportunities.

23   The World Bank and other development banks have an important share of supporting infrastructure in many countries (Development finance institution, DFI). An international financial institution (IFI) is characterised by being established (or chartered) by more than one country and governed by international law. Well established IFIs that promote and support infrastructure with loans are, amongst others:

-   World Bank: MIGA, IFC, IDA
-   European Investment Bank (EIB)
-   Islamic Development Bank (IsDB)
-   Asian Development Bank (ADB)
-   Asian Infrastructure Investment Bank (AIIB)[41]
-   European Bank for Reconstruction and Development (EBRD)
-   Development Bank of Latin America (CAF)
-   Inter-American Development Bank Group (IDB, IADB)
-   African Development Bank (AfDB)

---

[39] Kozak et al., 'SDG 9: Industry, Innovation and Infrastructure – Anticipating the Potential Impacts on Forests and Forest-Based Livelihoods' in Katila et al. (eds), *Sustainable Development Goals: Their Impacts on Forests and People* (2019), 279 (284).

[40] UN Office for Project Services, *Infrastructure Underpinning Sustainable Development* (2018), 41.

[41] AIIB, *Transport Sector Strategy: Sustainable and Integrated Transport for Trade and Economic Growth in Asia*; https://www.aiib.org/en/policies-strategies/strategies/transport-strategy.html.

Infrastructure development, pivotal to economic growth, productive investment, job **24**
creation and poverty alleviation, is key to achieving the SDGs. Of particular priority
is financing the mammoth investment gaps in emerging market economies (EMEs)
(estimated at US \$1.3 trillion/year). This priority is repeatedly stressed by the explicitly
mandated G20, which historically, together with development and financing banks, have
been sovereign borrowers for most EMEs.[42]

A key facet of infrastructure that is accorded a high degree of priority under SDG **25**
9 is transportation. SDG 9.1 aims to 'develop quality, reliable, sustainable and resilient
infrastructure, including regional and trans-border infrastructure, to support economic
development and human well-being, with a focus on affordable and equitable access for
all'.

The transport sector strategy of the AIIB reveals the broad scope of the transporta- **26**
tion sector, defining in a short and precise definition the broad framework of transport,
which is

> a system of infrastructure and services that consists of various modes (e.g., road, rail, air, inland
> waterway and ocean shipping). Transport serve different passenger and freight transport markets:
> rural, urban, inter-city and international. Depending on the size and characteristics of the markets,
> these modes display highly varied economic and financial returns. In addition, the transport sector
> generates various environmental and social impacts.

According to that definition, transport regulation makes a clear distinction between **27**
the different modes of transport and relates to a legal matrix in international, interregional and national law and transnational law as well.[43] Additional distinctions have to
be made concerning, for example, the transport of dangerous goods.

While broad in its scope, the indicators to measure progress towards SDG 9.1 are **28**
narrowly formulated when measuring the 'proportion of the rural population who live
within 2 km of an all-season road'[44] and 'passenger and freight volumes, by mode of
transport'.[45] Thus seemingly, scope and breadth of SDG 9.1 is focused on transportation
or, at least, a great level of emphasis has been placed on it. The rationale for this metric
of assessment is that increase in passenger and freight volumes can be directly associated with improvements in infrastructure, and resulting socio-economic benefits.[46] At
the same time, it seems to ostensibly exclude other, yet essential, precisely innovative
concepts.[47]

While the Millennium Development Goals (MDGs) did not consider transportation **29**
as a specific goal, the importance of transportation in achieving the MDGs had soon
been realised. This can be seen as transportation related sub-goals are now linked
(directly and indirectly) with as many as eight SDGs: SDG 2 (zero hunger), SDG 3 (good

---

[42] https://www.worldbank.org/en/topic/financialsector/brief/infrastructure-finance.

[43] It would expand the dimension of this chapter to explain the many fields and sectors of the multilevel transport law in the horizontal and vertical matrix where it must be differentiated between private and public law on all levels; see for an overview the compilation of the most relevant documents: https://transp ortrecht.org/vorschriften/einfuehrung/ (in German); UNCTAD, Transport policy and legislation, https:// unctad.org/topic/transport-and-trade-logistics/policy-and-legislation; UNECE, https://unece.org/list-agre ements.

[44] A/RES/71/313, Indicator 9.1.1, Global indicator framework for the Sustainable Development Goals and targets of the 2030 Agenda for Sustainable Development.

[45] A/RES/71/313, Indicator 9.1.2, Global indicator framework for the Sustainable Development Goals and targets of the 2030 Agenda for Sustainable Development.

[46] https://unstats.un.org/wiki/display/SDGeHandbook/Indicator+9.1.2.

[47] Notwithstanding that roads as an antique concept are doubtless important, the modes of transportation needed for transition are much more diverse: Inland navigation, inland waterways, railway, sea
vessels, planes, flying drones, hyperloop and more to come.

health and well-being), SDG 6 (clean water and sanitation), SDG 7 (affordable and clean energy), SDG 9 (industry, innovation and infrastructure), SDG 11 (sustainable cities and communities), SDG 12 (responsible consumption and production), and SDG 13 (climate action).[48]

30   Throughout the formulation of the SDGs, transport has been deemed an enabler and seen as critical infrastructure to make basic needs accessible to all with convenience while ensuring safety and sustainability.[49] Thus, while in the context of transportation, the terms 'sustainable', 'resilient' and 'inclusive' have very far-reaching implications, these terms do not have a fixed meaning and are inherently contextual. This can be explained by the need to adopt the expanse of these terms as per the socio-economic context and geographical challenges of each nation. Land-locked countries may face entirely different transportation challenges than those relying on sea transport for their trade. What is certain, however, is that while the challenges may vary for each country, transportation infrastructure is a key priority for the achievement of most SDGs.

31   UNCTAD in discussing the key attributes of 'sustainable transport' emphasises the importance of environment (green transport), society (inclusive transport) and its economic dimension (efficient and competitive transport).[50] Freight transport systems are at the centre stage of the climate change debate. According to an OECD report, trade related international freight is expected to grow by a factor of 4.3 by 2050 which highlights the fact that CO_2 emissions from trade-related international freight are expected to increase by a factor of 3.9 between 2010 and 2050[51] and climate change goals cannot be met without making transport more energy efficient. Over the past few years, UNCTAD has consistently prioritised sustainability considerations in its work related to freight transport and has identified energy consumption and carbon emissions as a major challenge while balancing the twin goals of sustainability and of ensuring access and connectivity of supply chains to support trade at national, regional and global levels.[52] This is a typical example of the conflicting priorities set by the indicators measuring SDG 9.1. Sustainable infrastructure must consider all three dimensions of this SDG – societal, environmental and economic. In regard to transportation, this would mean weighing the contradicting priorities of more transportation with reducing fuel emissions against each other to ensure a trade-off that ensures that the benefit is greater than the cost of the priority foregone.

32   While the meaning of 'resilient' infrastructure naturally remains context-dependent, guidance may be taken from the sub-goals of SDG 9 and emergent standard-setting. Green infrastructure or blue-green infrastructure represent networks that address urban and climate challenges by building with nature. This approach combines, among others, stormwater management, climate adaptation, less heat stress, more biodiversity, food production, better air quality, sustainable energy production, clean water and healthy soils. Furthermore, they also integrate opportunities to enhance the quality of life through recreation, protection (e.g. from the sun) in and around cities.

33   The ecological framework for social, economic and environmental health of the environment to be generated in this way should produce infrastructure that is sustainable, low-carbon and resilient. Standards such as the Standard for Sustainable and Resilient

---

[48] UN-Habitat, UNEP, SloCaT, *Analysis of the Transport Relevance of Each of the 17 SDGs* (2015).

[49] UN-Habitat, UNEP, SloCaT, *Analysis of the Transport Relevance of Each of the 17 SDGs* (2015).

[50] UNCTAD D/B/C.I/MEM.7/11, *Sustainable freight transport systems: opportunities for developing countries, note by the UNCTAD secretariat* (2015).

[51] OECD/ITF (2015), *ITF Transport Outlook 2015*, OECD Publishing/ITF.

[52] UNCTAD TD/B/C.I/MEM.7/11, *Sustainable freight transport systems: Opportunities for developing countries (2015)*.

Infrastructure (SuRe)[53] accommodate this evolution and encourage e.g. renewable energy infrastructure and public transport systems.[54] The evolution of standards is supported by a wide variety of policy efforts, although it should be noted that these are still mostly nascent.[55]

SDG 9.4, which sets an ambitious goal of upgrading and retrofitting industries to   34
make them sustainable with all countries taking action as per their capabilities is a pre-requisite for the development of infrastructure, industrialisation and must guide all innovation. Thus, infrastructure should be evaluated for long-term outcomes and be future ready in so that it is resilient and will be able to withstand future shocks and stresses associated with environmental, economic, social and technological pressures (expected as well as unexpected) and ensure continued delivery of services to the most vulnerable sections of a society in a crisis.[56]

The relevance of sustainable infrastructure in the context of disaster-risk prevention   35
and mitigation must be specifically emphasised. To qualify as 'resilient', infrastructure must be geared to be resistant to disasters which is in line with several international conventions. The Tampere Convention on the Provision of Telecommunication Resources for Disaster Mitigation and Relief Operations that came into force in 2005 (Tampere Convention[57]), which recognises the importance of telecommunication in enabling a prompt and effective response in a disaster and aims to facilitate access to prompt telecommunication assistance in member states to mitigate its impact, is an example. At the international fora, there has been a great amount of focus on disaster risk-mitigation as well as impact-mitigation. Prevention (which includes both preparedness and mitigation) of disasters has been recognised as a principle of international law by the International Law Commission (ILC). While acknowledging this, the ILC also discussed that the prevention of disasters ties in directly with the duty to prevent human rights violations as well as the principle of prevention under international environmental law.[58] The duty to prevent disasters has also been endorsed in many international legal frameworks including the ILC's draft articles on the Protection of Persons in the Event of Disasters,[59] the Hyogo Framework for Action 2005-2015[60] and the Sendai Framework for Disaster Risk Reduction 2015-2030.[61] Additionally, the Convention on the Transboundary Effects of Industrial Accidents lays down the duties of member states to prevent transboundary

---

[53] https://sure-standard.org/.

[54] Ardoni, 'Routledge Handbook of Sustainable and Resilient Infrastructure (2018).

[55] See on green and blue policy efforts: Chirisa and Verna, 'Resilience and climate change in rural areas: a review of infrastructure policies across global regions' (2021) *Sustainable and Resilient Infrastructure*, 1-11; MacArthur et al., Canada's Green New Deal: Forging the socio-political foundations of climate resilient infrastructure?' (2020) 65 *Energy Research & Social Science*, 1-10; see on standard-setting: OECD, Kennedy and Corfee-Morlot, 'Mobilising Investment in Low Carbon, Climate Resilient Infrastructure' (2012) 46 *OECD Environment Working Papers*; European Bank of Development and Reconstruction (EBRD), *Sustainability Report 2020* (2021); EBRD, *Sustainability reporting disclosures in accordance with the GRI Standards* (2021).

[56] Murray, '*The Critical Role of Infrastructure for the Sustainable Development Goals*', The Economist Intelligence Unit Limited (2019), 9-10; see also Mian et al., '*Critical Infrastructure Resilience Understanding the landscape*', The Resilience Shift (2018).

[57] Tampere Convention on the Provision of Telecommunication Resources for Disaster Mitigation and Relief Operations (1998).

[58] International Law Commission, *Sixth Report on the Protection of Persons in the Event of Disasters*, by Mr. Eduardo Valencia-Ospina, Special Rapporteur (2013), UN Doc. A/CN.4/662, 9-16.

[59] International Law Commission, *Report of the International Law Commission on the Work of Sixty-fifth Session*, UN Doc. A/68/10 (2013), 73-7.

[60] Hyogo Framework for Action 2005-2015: Building the Resilience of Nations and Communities to Disasters.

[61] Sendai Framework for Disaster Risk Reduction 2015 – 2030.

effects of industrial disasters and in this regard states, *inter alia,* that parties to the convention must use appropriate technology in order to prevent industrial accidents and protect human beings and the environment that, moreover, must adopt legislative provisions and guidelines concerning safety measures and safety standards.[62] Building disaster-resilient infrastructure that enables a coordinated and timely response by states to prevent and mitigate the impact of disasters is central to meeting the objectives under these conventions. 'Sustainable' and 'resilient' infrastructure under SDG 9 must necessarily be understood against this background.

36   In regard to climate change, it is critical for infrastructure to not only be resilient to climate-change risks but also to support climate change goals and related SDGs. Thus, resilient infrastructure must be 'planned, designed, built and operated in a way that anticipates, prepares for, and adapts to changing climate conditions' and that can 'respond to, and recover rapidly from disruptions caused by these climate conditions'.[63] Adapting infrastructure to combine these attributes will require cooperation at national and regional level. The Tampere Convention on the Provision of Telecommunication Resources for Disaster Mitigation and Relief Operations[64], ILC draft articles on the Protection of Persons in the Event of Disasters,[65] along with other conventions such as the ASEAN Agreement on Disaster Risk Management and Emergency Response,[66] and the Convention on the Transboundary Effects of Industrial Accidents[67], all emphasise the importance of cooperation and coordination among states to prevent and manage response to disasters. The Global Infrastructure Connectivity Alliance (GICA) launched by the G20 aims to enable knowledge sharing regarding global infrastructure connectivity through transport, communications, energy and water networks.[68]

37   The Global Coalition for Disaster-Resilient Infrastructure (CDRI) led by India provides guidance to future pathways for cooperation between developed and developing nations to build disaster-resilient infrastructure.[69] The CDRI defines disaster-resilient infrastructure to be broader in scope than climate-resilient infrastructure, also including non-climate related disaster risks due to 'geophysical and geomorphological hazards such as earthquakes, landslides, tsunami and volcanic activity', or 'technological hazards like nuclear radiation, dam failures, chemical spills, explosions which are not directly linked to climate'.[70] This broad definition compels questioning whether climate change issues perhaps become too central in the 'sustainability' conversation and whether this happens at the cost of ignoring the social impact of disasters. Indeed, the present and future outcomes of technological advancements directed to mitigate the risks to infrastructure due to climate change or other factors, may in fact also help fight their impact on the society in many other adverse ways.

38   Despite the limited scope of the indicators for SDG 9, the scale and scope of the term 'infrastructure' as it emerges from the SDG itself is very large. For instance, 'sustainable' infrastructure aimed at supporting economic development and human well-being may

---

[62] Convention on the Transboundary Effects of Industrial Accidents (1992), Art. 6 r/w Annex IV.

[63] Organisation for Economic Co-operation and Development (OECD), *Climate-resilient Infrastructure,* Environment Policy Paper No. 14 (2018).

[64] Tampere Convention on the Provision of Telecommunication Resources for Disaster Mitigation and Relief Operations (1998).

[65] International Law Commission, *Report of the International Law Commission on the Work of Sixty-fifth Session,* UN Doc. A/68/10 (2013), 73-6.

[66] ASEAN Agreement on Disaster Management and Emergency Response 2005.

[67] Convention on the Transboundary Effects of Industrial Accidents (1992).

[68] https://www.gica.global/about-us/what-global-infrastructure-connectivity-alliance.

[69] SDG Knowledge Hub, *India Launches Global Coalition for Disaster-Resilient Infrastructure* (2019).

[70] https://cdri.world/coalition-for-disaster-resilient-infrastructure.php.

include not just infrastructure that enables mining of metals and minerals but also en-sures that human rights are respected in the process, thereby following the *rule of law* is followed.[71] Another example points to the investments required to make enable building resilient and sustainable infrastructure.[72] In this sense, 'sustainable' infrastructure also ties in with 'sustainable' and 'inclusive' industrialisation, and the scope of both terms must be understood more broadly than the narrowly interpretation that the indicators to the SDGs allow.

II. Industrialisation

To understand 'inclusive' and 'sustainable' industrialisation, guidance may be sought   **39** from the Lima Declaration adopted by the UN member states in 2013.[73] 'Inclusive' in this context means that 'industrial development must include all countries and all peo-ples, as well as the private sector, civil society organisations, multinational development institutions, all parts of the UN system, and offer equal opportunities and an equitable distribution of the benefits of industrialisation to all stakeholders.'[74] The term 'sustain-able' stresses on the 'need to decouple the prosperity generated from industrial activities from excessive natural resource use and negative environmental impacts.'

SDG 9.2 and SDG 9.3 focus on 'inclusive' and 'sustainable' industrialisation and   **40** increasing access of small-scale industries to financial services and markets.

While there may be many approaches, traditionally the size of the manufacturing   **41** sector has been an indicator of the level of industrialisation of a country. The indicators for SDG 9.2 assess the degree of compliance based on measures of employment in and proportion of contribution to GDP of the manufacturing sector. Employment is defined as all those of working age who, during a short reference period, were engaged in any activity to produce goods or provide services for pay or profit.[75]

In order to monitor labour markets and work patterns, the ILO recommends that   **42** states should adopt a national data collection strategy and reporting frequency. ILO-STAT contains statistics from national sources on employment. In this regard, the ILO recommends that

> [i]ndicators should be computed for the population as a whole and disaggregated by sex, specified age groups (including separate categories for youth), level of educational attainment, geographic region, urban and rural areas, and other relevant characteristics taking account of the statistical precision of the estimates.[76]

Indicators to assess SDG 9.3 provide metrics to measure the growth of small scale   **43** industries and ease of access to finance made available to them. Small-scale industrial enterprises, in the SDG framework also called 'small-scale industries', for the purpose of statistical data collection and compilation refer to 'statistical units, generally enterprises,

---

[71] UNDP (2019), *Users Guide - Assessing the Rule of Law in Public Administration: the Mining Sector* (2019).

[72] Murray, '*The Critical Role of Infrastructure for the Sustainable Development Goals*', The Economist Intelligence Unit Limited (2019), 11 f.

[73] United Nations Industrial Development Organization (UNIDO), *15th Session of UNIDO General Conference on Lima Declaration: Towards inclusive and sustainable industrial development* (2013).

[74] https://www.unido.org/inclusive-and-sustainable-industrial-development; see also UNIDO, *Introduction to UNIDO: Inclusive and Sustainable Industrial Development* (2015).

[75] ILO, *Resolution concerning statistics of work, employment and labour underutilization, adopted by the 19th International Conference of Labour Statisticians* (2013).

[76] ILO, *Resolution concerning statistics of work, employment and labour underutilization, adopted by the 19th International Conference of Labour Statisticians* (2013).

engaged in production of goods and services for market below a designated size class'.[77] Since states define the size class of these industries differently, it is difficult to compare data of different states. UNIDO proposes that all countries compile the data by a size class of 'small-scale industries' as with less than 20 persons employed. By contrast, in the EU, the category of micro, small and medium-sized enterprises (SMEs) is made up of enterprises which employ fewer than 250 persons.[78] Further, within the SME category, an enterprise which employs fewer than 50 persons is a small enterprise and one which employs fewer than 10 persons is a micro-enterprise.[79] Companies also have to meet an additional requirement of a maximum cap for annual turnover and / or annual balance sheet total to fall within each class.[80] Also in other areas around the world, these classifications exist under public law, mostly under commercial or tax law.

44   Small-scale industrial enterprises despite their small contribution to the total industrial output, have been seen as a game-changer in increasing employment especially in developing countries.[81] This is because they require limited capital investment and relatively unskilled labour and are capable of meeting local needs. SMEs comprise 99 per cent of businesses in the EU and employ two of every three employees.[82]

45   Globally, MSMEs represent more than 70 per cent of the global employment and 50 per cent of GDP.[83] According to the World Bank, there will be a need for 600 million jobs by 2030 to absorb the growing global workforce.[84] The development and growth of SMEs will play a critical role to create employment especially in emerging economies.[85] There is no doubt that creating adequate financing facilities for small-scale industrial enterprises should be a priority for states. The UNGA has declared June, 27th as MSME day to raise awareness regarding the contribution of MSMEs in the achievement of SDGs.[86] Small-scale industries have been worst hit during the pandemic and the priorities reflected in the indicators for SDG 9.3 are even more relevant in this context. In a survey conducted by ILO to, *inter alia,* assess the needs of different enterprises to cope with the impact of the pandemic, 65 per cent of MSMEs responded that access to short-term finance was their most important need.[87] Thus, providing small-scale industries with access to finance and affordable credit is important to achieve 'inclusive' industrialisation and many of the SDGs including SDG 1 (no poverty), SDG 8 (decent work and economic growth) and SDG 10 (reduced inequalities). Further, in consonance with SDG 9.4, small-scale industries must also be supported to grow sustainably.

---

[77] UNSTATS (2020), Indicator 9.3.1.

[78] European Commission 2003/361/EC, *Commission Recommendation Concerning the Definition of Micro, Small And Medium-Sized Enterprises* (6 May 2003).

[79] European Commission 2003/361/EC, *Commission Recommendation Concerning the Definition of Micro, Small And Medium-Sized Enterprises* (6 May 2003).

[80] European Commission 2003/361/EC, *Commission Recommendation Concerning the Definition of Micro, Small And Medium-Sized Enterprises* (6 May 2003).

[81] Sobir, '*Micro, Small and Medium-sized Enterprises (MSMEs) and their role in achieving the Sustainable Development Goals*', Department of Economic and Social Affairs (2020), 21-2.

[82] Eurostat, (2018) Statistics on small and medium-sized enterprises.

[83] ILO, *ILO SCORE Global COVID-19 Enterprise Survey* (2020).

[84] https://www.worldbank.org/en/topic/smefinance.

[85] https://www.worldbank.org/en/topic/smefinance.

[86] A/RES/71/279, *Micro-, Small and Medium-sized Enterprises Day.*

[87] ILO, *ILO SCORE Global COVID-19 Enterprise Survey* (2020).

III. Innovation

While SDG 9 may be viewed as an enabler to meet many other SDGs, SDG 9.5,   **46**
9.b and 9.c may be viewed as an enabler to meet the objectives of SDG 9 itself. Industrialisation and infrastructure when understood in the context of the scope of the terms
'resilient', 'inclusive' and 'sustainable' may not be realised without appropriate innovation
to develop and improve knowledge and technology.

In the absence of a qualifier for this section, and to assess the scope of 'innovation'   **47**
for the purposes of SDG 9, it multiple SDGs and their interlinkages must be taken into
account (→ Goal 9 mn. 58).

To this end, SDG 9.5 places emphasis on the importance of research and development   **48**
through its indicators which entail measurement of 'research and development expenditure as a proportion of GDP'[88] and 'researchers (in full time equivalent) per million
inhabitants'.[89] However, while these metrics give an overall view of the expenditure on
research and development and the number of people involved in full time research, they
do not aid in an understanding of whether the research has to be only in 'scientific'
disciplines as mentioned in SDG 9.5 and, if so, which scope of the term would be
embraced.

SDG 9.b which aims to 'support domestic technology development, research and   **49**
innovation in developing countries, including by ensuring a conducive policy environment for, inter alia, industrial diversification and value addition to commodities' is to be
assessed through the 'proportion of medium and high-tech industry value added in total
value added'.[90] While SDG 9.b and its indicator focus only on technology development,
SDGs 9.5 and SDG 9.b must be understood in the context of the other SDGs for the
realisation of SDG 9 to enhance sustainability-oriented research and innovation and focus on research related to energy efficient technology, focus on reduction of greenhouse
gases, to be climate resilient and future-ready. Technological progress and innovation
are instrumental for finding lasting solutions to both economic and environmental
challenges and it may be said that while these SDGs focus on research, technology
development and innovation in general, however, from a plain reading of these targets
and their indicators, the emphasis on sustainability in innovation is somewhat missing.

From innovation in credit financing to enabling sustainable freight transport, re-   **50**
search and development is a crucial enabler in reconciling conflicting environmental
and economic goals. Innovative financing instruments, lending and equity infrastructure
are necessary to enable access to affordable credit to small-scale industries.[91] There is a
need to boost such innovations in credit financing in developing countries.

However, a reasoned perspective regarding the scope and breadth of innovation un-   **51**
der SDG 9 may be that the road to innovation must be as broad as possible. Innovation
must not be constrained by the SDG or be subservient to it. Innovation reduction would
be a loss. Only if innovation is allowed to grow uninhibitedly and, in any direction,
can it lead to wondrous and game-changing outcomes that may actually help achieve
sustainability and resilience. One example is the innovation and progress in space

---

[88] A/RES/71/313, Global indicator framework for the Sustainable Development Goals and targets of the
2030 Agenda for Sustainable Development, Indicator 9.5.1.

[89] A/RES/71/313, Global indicator framework for the Sustainable Development Goals and targets of the
2030 Agenda for Sustainable Development, Indicator 9.5.2.

[90] A/RES/71/313, Global indicator framework for the Sustainable Development Goals and targets of the
2030 Agenda for Sustainable Development, Indicator 9.b.1.

[91] See Thompson and Boschmans and Pissareva, '*Alternative Financing Instruments for SMEs and
Entrepreneurs: The case of capital market finance*' (2018) 10 *OECD SME and Entrepreneurship Papers*.

technology, which plays a key role in maintaining and monitoring the performance of road infrastructure through the use of satellites, or in reducing the fuel consumption of driving through better planning using satellite maps. Chaining innovation and confining its scope within the realm of the SDGs may instead hinder and suppress innovation that could have helped in meeting the desired goals.

52   One of the most critical aspects of innovation and infrastructure is imbibed in SDG 9.c which aims at significantly increasing access to 'information and communications technology and strive to provide universal and affordable access to the Internet in least developed countries by 2020'. Internet is a powerful enabler of several human rights enshrined in international human rights conventions, such as the freedom to expression and opinion,[92] right to education,[93] freedom of association[94]. The pandemic has shown an entirely new perspective on the importance of access to internet, and the capabilities that access to internet can unleash. Drawing from lessons learnt so far from the SARS-CoV-2 pandemic, it can perhaps be argued that a 'right to internet' is also an essential enabler for the right to work.[95] While on one hand, the UN Human Rights Committee has recognised the importance of internet in serving as an enabler for innovation and development and called upon member states to adopt a human rights based approach in expanding access to internet.[96] Further, few countries have also recognised the right to access internet as a fundamental right by imbibing it in their constitution[97] and the ECtHR in its decisions also frequently favoured an interpretation of recognising access to internet to fall within the ambit of Art. 10 of the ECHR.[98] However, the right to access internet has not yet been accorded the status of a human right in international human rights conventions or treaties. Thus, the status of the right to access internet as a human right clearly remains undecided.[99]

53   The importance of access to internet and digital technology is acknowledged by the UN secretary general of in the following words:

> Digital technology is central to almost every aspect of the response to the pandemic, from vaccine research to online learning models, e-commerce and tools that are enabling hundreds of millions of people to work and study from home.
> But, the digital divide is now a matter of life and death for people who are unable to access essential health-care information. It is threatening to become the new face of inequality, reinforcing the social and economic disadvantages suffered by women and girls, people with disabilities and minorities of all kinds. In 2019, some 87 % of people in developed countries used the Internet, compared with just 19 per cent in the least developed countries.[100]

---

[92] Universal Declaration of Human Rights (UDHR) (1948), Art. 19; International Covenant on Economic, Social and Cultural Rights (ICESCR) (1966), Art. 19(2).

[93] UDHR (1948), Art. 26.

[94] UDHR (1948), Art. 20(1); ICESCR (1966), Art. 22(1).

[95] UDHR (1948), Art. 23.

[96] A/HRC/32/L.20, *The Promotion, Protection and Enjoyment of Human Rights on the Internet*, 27 June 2016; A/HRC/RES/38/7, *The Promotion, Protection and Enjoyment of Human Rights on the Internet*, 17 July 2018.

[97] See The Constitution of Greece, Art. 5A(2); The Constitution of Portugal, Art. 35; The Constitution of the Republic of Ecuador, Art. 16.

[98] See ECtHR, *Ahmet Yıldırım v. Turkey*, application no. 3111/10; ECtHR, *Kalda v. Estonia*, application no. 17429/10.

[99] See Pollicino, 'Right to Internet Access: Quid Iuris?' in Arnauld and Decken and Susi (eds), *The Cambridge Handbook on New Human Rights. Recognition, Novelty, Rhetoric* (2019); See also Feldstein, 'Why Internet Access Is a Human Right, What We Can Do to Protect It' (2017) *Foreign Affairs*.

[100] UN, *Digital Divide 'a Matter of Life and Death' amid COVID-19 Crisis, Secretary-General Warns Virtual Meeting, Stressing Universal Connectivity Key for Health, Development* (2020), Press Release SG/SM/20118.

As acknowledged by the UN Special Rapporteur Frank La Rue in the 'Report on the   54
promotion and protection of the right to freedom of opinion and expression',[101] access
to internet has two dimensions: access to online content, without any restrictions except
in a few limited cases permitted under international human rights law; and availability
of the necessary infrastructure and information communication technologies, such as
cables, modems, computers and software, to access the internet in the first place.

While the status of access to internet as a basic human right is still undecided, it is the   55
second dimension of access to internet that SDG 9.c aims to secure. The limited scope
of the indicator to SDG 9.c which measures the 'percentage of inhabitants living within
range of a mobile-cellular signal (2G, 3G, LTE or 5G to come), irrespective of whether
or not they are mobile phone subscribers or users'[102] is reflected in the fact that even
though by 2019, 'almost the entire world population (97 per cent) lived within reach
of a mobile cellular signal, and 93 per cent lived within reach of a mobile-broadband
signal', yet almost half the world's population does not use internet.[103] This is particularly
the case in least developed countries where only 19 per cent use the internet, compared
with 87 per cent in developed countries.[104] The need to expand the scope of SDG 9.c to
include assessment of internet users and enhance user capabilities is thus evident.

The potential of innovation will remain underemphasised without comprehending   56
the possibilities that artificial intelligence has opened up. The International Telecommu-
nications Union (ITU) is a specialised agency of the UN for information and communication technologies, and has become a 'key UN platform' for exploring the impact
of AI.[105] Recent reports submitted to the UNHRC highlight the potential impact of
AI technologies on human rights such as gender discrimination through algorithmic
discrimination and bias as well as its potential to improve women's health.[106] A recent
non-binding legal resolution adopted by the UN Economic Commission for Europe's
Global Forum on Road Traffic Safety to guide contracting parties to the 1949 and
1968 Vienna Conventions on Road Traffic in relation to the safe deployment of highly
and fully automated vehicles in road traffic also provide a glimpse into the potential
transformation possible because of AI.[107]

The potential of data for sustainable development and humanitarian action is also an   57
important facet of innovation under SDG 9. The UN Secretary-General's Independent
Expert Advisory Group on a Data Revolution for Sustainable Development (IEAG) has
made specific recommendations regarding the challenges posed by data, and called for
a UN-led effort to mobilise the data revolution for sustainable development[108] and is
complemented by UNCTAD's analysis and recommendation on STI.[109]

---

[101] A/HRC/17/27, *Report of the Special Rapporteur on the promotion and protection of the right to
freedom of opinion and expression*, 10 August 2011.

[102] A/RES/71/313, Global indicator framework for the Sustainable Development Goals and targets of
the 2030 Agenda for Sustainable Development, Indicator 9.c.1.

[103] UN, *The Sustainable Development Goals Report* (2020).

[104] UN, *The Sustainable Development Goals Report* (2020).

[105] https://futureoflife.org/ai-policy-united-nations/.

[106] Cullen, 'Why Artificial Intelligence Is Already a Human Rights Issue' (2018), *Oxford Human Rights
Hub*; A/HRC/35/9, UN Human Rights Council (UNHRC), *Report of the United Nations High Commissioner for Human Rights on promotion, protection and enjoyment of human rights on the Internet: ways to bridge
the gender digital divide from a human rights perspective* (May 5, 2017), para. 41.

[107] UNECE, *UNECE Adopts Resolution on the Deployment of Highly and Fully Automated Vehicles in
Road Traffic* (Oct. 9, 2018), Press Release.

[108] The United Nations Secretary-General's Independent Expert Advisory Group on a Data Revolution
for Sustainable Development (IEAG), *A World That Counts: Mobilising the Data Revolution for Sustainable
Development* (2014).

[109] UNCTAD, *Technology and Innovation Report 2021* (2021).

C. Interdependences of SDG 9

58   Sustaining economic growth, as advocated in SDG 8, implies providing sustainable industries, infrastructure projects and the promotion of innovation processes and research development for long-term economic development. Effects of the SARS-CoV-2-pandemic destabilise or halt projects and reverse progress done towards the goals of SDG 9. In case of the Aviation (especially the Air transport) sector, government's regulations to prevent the outbreak of SARS-CoV-2 have led to grounding of 90 per cent of all fleets.[110]

59   Since both, manufacturing and air transport are key drivers of overall economic growth, the pandemic had serious effects on the world's economy and research projects.[111] SDG 9 is strongly linked to SDG 2, SDG 3, SDG 4, SDG 7 and SDG 10.

60   In a globalised, industrialised and increasingly urbanised world, agribusiness und agri-food systems have been transforming rapidly into a highly industrialised sector, with significant medium- and large-scale investment and worldwide networks and global supply chains that deliver substantially transformed agricultural products to businesses and consumers in both distant and near economies and markets.[112] As demographic conditions and patterns of food demand are increasingly changing, the design and development of more efficient integrated systems of food production, processing, preservation and distribution as well as reliable transportation and logistics infrastructure with roads facilitations access to markets are needed.[113]

61   Integrating small-scale manufacturers into value chains and financial investment programs can be a huge contributor for of SDG 9, but if such infrastructure, research and financial services favours some producers over others, then achieving the sub-goals of SDG 9 might constrain achievements of SDG 2 and / or might even reduce equity in access to such infrastructure or sub-goals of other SDGs, e.g. building dams or wider asphalted roads would support water irrigation and / or lead to biodiversity losses, or even ignite other unsustainable practices.[114]

62   The significance of a fully developed infrastructure and an efficient research is vital to overcome a global health crisis such as the SARS-CoV-2 pandemic. The struggle of almost every country at the beginning of the pandemic to meet their demand of essential medical equipment and sanitation products, revealed that producing countries temporarily suspended exports our of national self-interest which hit poor countries the most as they were *de facto* excluded from access to such products due to price explosions that came with the increase in demand. This led many countries to reconsider which goods should be produced in a sovereign manner at the national level.[115] With the discovery and development of an efficient vaccine against SARS-CoV-2, nations are not only confronted with the question on how to obtain the vaccine, but also how to produce and distribute the vaccine all over the world. SDG 9.5 explicitly promotes to enhance scientific research and upgrade technological capabilities of all sectors in all countries (particularly developed countries), which could be a huge contributor for SDG

---

[110] in the first five months of the pandemic, passenger numbers plunged by 51.1 per cent compared with the same period in 2019), which will result in an estimated loss of $ 302 billion and 400 billion in gross operating revenues compared with 'business-as-usual' operations; ICAO, *Effects of Novel Coronavirus on Civil Aviation: Economic Impact Analysis* (2021).

[111] UN, *The Sustainable Development Goals Report 2020*, 42.

[112] FAO, *Territorial tools for agro-industry development: A Sourcebook* (2017).

[113] Griggs et al., *A Guide to SDG Interactions: From Science to Implementation* (2017), 38.

[114] Griggs et al., *A Guide to SDG Interactions: From Science to Implementation* (2017), 39.

[115] Martens and Ellmers and Pokorny on behalf of Global Policy Watch, *COVID-19 and the SDGs, The impact of the coronavirus pandemic on the global sustainability agenda* (2020), 9.

3. However, achieving targets of SDG 9 could impact on SDG 3 associated with land use, urbanisation, transport/mobility systems and residential development, e.g. motor-vehicle based infrastructural investment is a huge contributor for industrial achievements but also unintendedly produce health consequences, including air pollution from vehicle emissions, traffic accidents and the reduced physical activity from urban sprawl.[116]

SDG 9.c promotes to increase access to information and communications technology   **63** significantly and strives to provide universal and affordable access to the Internet in least development countries, which is strongly linked to the targets of SDG 4, as providing an affordable access to the Internet could help to make education accessible for everyone.

SDG 9.4 aims to upgrade infrastructure and retrofit industries to make them sus-   **64** tainable, with increased resource-use efficiency and greater adoption of clean and environmentally sound technologies and industrial processes, and thus SDG 9.4 is well-connected to SDG 7.

D. Jurisprudential Significance of SDG 9

The global and often interdependent interrelation of human societies not only leads   **65** to a changing environment of 'socio-political, technical and biological systems'. Rather, it is increasingly noticeable, particularly in these strenuous times of a global pandemic, that the human population as a 'super-organism', with the increasing complexity of its actions, is susceptible to the most diverse risks at all levels. This vulnerability to risk increasingly points to a systemic characteristic.[117] SDG 9 refers in its targets to the avoidance of precisely those risks that are likely to hinder industry, infrastructure and innovation.

In light of all UN member states affirming that adopting 'science, technology and   **66** innovation strategies as integral elements of [...] national sustainable development strategies [helps] to strengthen knowledge-sharing and collaboration',[118] this clarifies the areas of SDG 9 in which legally exploitable content can be found. With clear links to intellectual property claims, as well as to commercial and competition law, it is a cross-sectional goal that forms ties between innumerable areas, and in doing so, sets great reference e.g. to the energy or pharma sectors, transport, water and sanitation.[119] Beyond that, it is of highly political character, notably when it demands tax support, access to green financing (services) and (infrastructure) investments, environmental impact assessments, environmental investments, research and development as well as technological legacies that take into account the 'carbon constraint, energy security, and the need for climate adaptation'.[120] Every part mentioned covers huge areas in the legal field which themselves are widely and deeply anchored both in the public and private law sphere.

---

[116] Griggs et al., *A Guide to SDG Interactions: From Science to Implementation* (2017), 88.

[117] UNDRR, *Global Assessment Report on Disaster Risk Reduction* (United Nations Office for Disaster Risk Reduction (2019), iv.

[118] Addis Ababa Action Agenda (AAAA), para. 119: the AAAA as a financing instrument is inherent to the Global Agenda 2030, see A/RES/70/1, para. 40.

[119] AAAA, para.14.

[120] See United Nations General Assembly Open Working Group on Sustainable Development Goals, *Compendium of TST Issues Briefs October 2014*, 84.

67   Therefore, attaching legal significance to SDG 9 is indeed possible. At the same time, however, and specifically taking into account the restrictive and weak design of its associated indicators,[121] it also shows that this is feasible to a merely limited extent.

I. Jurisdiction on Vision and Objectives

68   Following the guiding principle of creating reliable and sustainable industries and infrastructures, it can be seen that the development of industries and infrastructures is, in principle, beneficial to the development of states and, in particular, contributes to the welfare of the society there. This principle was also recognised by the African Commission on Human and Peoples' Rights in the *Ogoni case*[122], for example, whereby the Commission made clear that the state does not have an exclusive right over its state territory or land when allowing to set up industrialisation. The Commission stressed in particular the positive and negative obligations of a state to fulfil and protect comprehensive human rights provisions towards its own population against violations of their rights by actions of private actors. Of particular note was the combination of various obligations (right to health, the right to dispose of wealth and natural resources, the right to a clean environment and family rights as well as the implied rights to food and housing/shelter) that places the conduct of private actors (of an oil spilling company) within the direct sphere of influence on the government of the state in which the harmful conduct is carried out.[123]

1. International Jurisdiction

69   The aspiration to build reliable and sustainable infrastructure, including in a regional and transboundary context (SDG 9.1) points to various aspects that need to be considered to ultimately meet this goal. A case before the ICJ, *Nicaragua v Costa Rica*[124], which concerned the construction of a road along a river course, illustrates the difficulties that can arise in the context of infrastructure development. In this case, the ICJ assessed not only the harmful interference with Nicaragua's ecosystems induced by transboundary canal construction works, but also issues relating to the 'right to sovereignty, to territorial integrity and to non-interference'[125] and the applicability of various international and regional rights, conventions, declarations and principles. With regard to the interference with ecosystems, the court followed 'the commentary to the International Law Commission's Draft Articles on Prevention of Transboundary Harm from Hazardous Activities,

---

[121] E.g. when quality, reliable, sustainable and resilient [regional and transborder] infrastructure (SDG 9.1) is demanded but is measured against the '[p]roportion of the rural population who live within 2 km of an all-season road' (9.1.1) or 'Passenger and freight volumes, by mode of transport' (9.1.2).

[122] African Commission on Human & Peoples Rights', *Social and Economic Rights Action Center (SER-AC) and Center for Economic and Social Rights (CESR) v. Nigeria* (Communication No. 155/96), Judgment of 27 May 2002.

[123] African Commission on Human & Peoples Rights', *Social and Economic Rights Action Center (SER-AC) and Center for Economic and Social Rights (CESR) v. Nigeria* (Communication No. 155/96), Judgment of 27 May 2002, 8-13.

[124] Joined cases of *Certain Activities Carried Out By Nicaragua in the Border Area* and *Construction of a Road in Costa Rica along the San Juan River (Nicaragua v. Costa Rica)*, Advisory Opinions and Orders, 16 December 2015.

[125] https://www.icj-cij.org/en/case/152.

that any detrimental impact of the construction of the road on the San Juan River need only to be susceptible of being measured to qualify as significant harm'.[126]

Similar, and in some cases even more far-reaching, questions are raised by other   70 infrastructure projects, some of which pose a considerable risk of conflict. For example, Ethiopia is pursuing 'economic development and power generation' for its population with the construction of the Grand Ethiopian Renaissance Dam (GERD). The dam under construction will change the future water supply through the Nile, which worries the riparian states Egypt and Sudan about their own future water supply and environmental changes and damage. By citing 'equitable and reasonable utilization without causing significant harm to neighbouring states', Ethiopia continues construction. Previous efforts to reach an out-of-court settlement have been unsuccessful. The situation continues to deteriorate and has already led to the involvement of the UN Security Council.

The linkage of infrastructure projects, especially in transboundary contexts, with   71 various environmental concerns, as well as in terms of affected sovereign rights and the emergence of conflicts, is likely to increase in the future given the impacts of climate change.

In the context of so-called 'landlocked states', the ICJ clarified that there would   72 neither be an international obligation to grant these states the right to sovereign access to the sea, nor could such a right arise from the fact that two disputing parties conduct protracted negotiations on such access. In this respect, no entitlement to infrastructure of a transboundary nature or such a form of enabling industrialisation for landlocked developing countries within the meaning of SDG 9.1 or SDG 9.a arises.[127] Although the ICJ clarified that its decision does not indicate any further negotiations between the parties to the dispute, Bolivia and Chile, the court also underlined the non-binding nature of resolutions, in this case the disputed resolution of the Organization of American States, which 'are not *per se* binding and cannot be the source of an international obligation'.[128] However, this decision was accompanied by three dissenting opinions and a declaration of President Yusuf which point to the different functions of law, the principle of good faith especially characterised as a means of preventing conflict, and, moreover, on the limits of the court which can only decide *ex aequo et bono* if the parties so request. President Yusuf concluded his declaration with the wise words of Hersh Lauterpacht that

> if a future relation is to be established on the basis of equity, then the existing legal position, which only in exceptional cases is entirely devoid of an element of equity and justice, must furnish one of the bases of the future settlement [...] It is incompatible with the dignity of the law that it should be disobeyed, but it is not incompatible with its dignity that it should be changed, once it has been ascertained, by the agreement of the parties.[129]

In *Advisory Opinion requested by Bolivia*, the IACtHR clarified the obligations of   73 the state intending to undertake an infrastructure project.[130] The court underlined that

---

[126] Further reading Cabrera Medaglia and Saldivia Olave, 'Sustainable development law principles in the Costa Rica v Nicaragua 1 territorial disputes' in Cordonier Segger and Weeramantry (eds), *Sustainable Development Principles in the Decisions of International Courts and Tribunals*, 1999-2012, 255-65.

[127] See e.g. African Commission on Human and Peoples' Rights, ACHPR/Res. 367 (LX) 2017, *Niamey Declaration on Ensuring the Upholding of the African Charter in the Extractive Industries Sector* (2017).

[128] ICJ, *Obligation to Negotiate Access to the Pacific Ocean (Bolivia v. Chile)*, Judgement of 1 October 2018, para. 171.

[129] ICJ, *Obligation to Negotiate Access to the Pacific Ocean (Bolivia v. Chile)*, Declaration of President Yusuf of 1 October 2018, para. 10.

[130] IACtHR, *Advisory Opinion OC-23/17 of November 15, 2017, Requested by the Republic of Colombia, the Environment and Human Rights*, para. 242.

not only pollution can cross borders, but also legal responsibility for state action.[131] In particular, it interpreted the application of Arts. 1(1), 4(1) and 5(1) of the American Convention on Human Rights (ACHR), the Cartagena Convention[132] and the Pact of San José

> when there is a danger that the construction and operation of major new infrastructure projects may have severe effects on the marine environment in the Wider Caribbean Region and, consequently, on the human habitat that is essential for the full enjoyment and exercise of the rights of the inhabitants of the coasts and / or islands of a State Party to the Pact, in light of the environmental standards recognized in international customary law and the treaties applicable among the respective States.[133]

74   The IACtHR also considered the relationship of the various legal instruments to each other[134] and emphasised that all instruments as a whole develop their meaning through those norms of human rights protection that serve the effective protection of these rights. Especially when individual instruments of environmental (protection) law are restricted in scope, it is the responsibility of the court to consider all instruments in question in its evaluation. The IACtHR thereby interpreted the jurisdiction in question very broadly and constructed a causal link between the state of origin and the impact outside this state territory and also extended this beyond individuals if

> an individual is under a State's jurisdiction, in respect of conduct undertaken outside the territory of the said State (extraterritorial conduct) or with effects outside its territory, if that State is exercising its authority over that person or when that person is under its effective control [...].[135]

75   The joint consideration of environmental rights and human rights against the background of the broad understanding of 'jurisdiction' not only strengthens the extraterritorial control capacity of state action for climate-related harms and thus also strengthens access to justice, but also points in particular to the form of operating mega-infrastructure projects in the Inter-Americas and the possibly emerging higher standard of expected regulation for states regulating activities of its enterprises abroad.[136]

76   In addition, the IACtHR has developed jurisprudence that allows the use, exploitation or geological transformation of indigenous lands, inter alia, for the construction of infrastructure or industries (SDG 9.1) 'as certain safeguards are observed' since Art. 21 ACHR is not of an absolute nature. For example, the indigenous population must be informed in advance and involved in the project, receive reasonable benefits or restitution and environmental and social impact assessments must be carried out.[137]

77   What is striking is the close interweaving of infrastructure projects with the protection of health in particular, which in various cases before the ECtHR has led to a duty on the part of the state to act in accordance with the principle of subsidiarity (→ Goal 3 mn. 54).

---

[131] Banda, 'Inter-American Court of Human Rights' Advisory Opinion on the Environment and Human Rights' (2018) 6(22) *ASIL Insights*.
[132] Convention for the Protection and Development of the Marine Environment of the Wider Caribbean Region.
[133] https://www.corteidh.or.cr/docs/opiniones/seriea_23_ing.pdf.
[134] Advisory Opinion OC-23/17 of November 15, 2017, Requested By The Republic of Colombia, The Environment and Human Rights, para. 32.
[135] Advisory Opinion OC-23/17 of November 15, 2017, Requested By The Republic of Colombia, The Environment And Human Rights, para. 81.
[136] Banda, 'Inter-American Court of Human Rights' Advisory Opinion on the Environment and Human Rights' (2018) 6(22) *ASIL Insights*; Vega-Barbosa and Aboagye, 'Human Rights and the Protection of the Environment: The Advisory Opinion of the Inter-American Court of Human Rights' (2018) *EJIL:Talks!*.
[137] See e.g. IACtHR, *Saramaka People v Suriname*, para. 129; IACtHR, *Claude-Reyes*, paras. 88-91.

The wording of SDG 9 suggests a wide scope for interpretation of what can constitute   **78**
infrastructure. The reference in SDG 9.1 to everything that supports 'economic development and human well-being' in conjunction with the universal validity of the sustainable
development concept opens the door to any inclusion of technologies that may arise in
the future. In this context, the ECtHR has considered the right of access to the internet
as essential to comply with the freedom of expression.[138] The court based its decisions in
all cases in particular on Art. 10 ECHR, thereby considering access to internet as a 'principal means of exercising the right to freedom of expression and information'.[139]

2. European Jurisdiction

At the European level, the already narrow scope and measurement of SDG 9 is   **79**
characterised by further restrictions in measurement. Only six indicators[140] provide
context for the significance of SDG9: (1) Gross domestic expenditure on Research and
Development (R&D); (2) R&D personnel; (3) Patent applications to the European Patent
Office (EPO); (4) Share of busses and trains in total passenger transport; (5) Share of
rail and inland waterways in total freight transport; and (6) Air emission intensity from
industry. This indicator relates to the 'Zero Pollution action plan' and will use PM2.5
emissions in NACE[141] sector C (manufacturing) divided by gross value added in the
same sector. In referring to sector C which includes a wide range of business branches,
this indicator, however, excludes other emission-releasing sectors such as Agriculture,
Forestry and Fishing (A), Mining and Quarrying (B), Electricity, Gas, Steam and Air
Conditioning Supply (D) or Water Supply; Sewerage, Waste Management and Remedi-
ation Activities (E) and Construction (F) which diminishes its reliability significantly.
SDG 9 is thus further narrowed down at European level to the abstract transport of
intellectual property and transport facilitation for industries. The two multi-purpose
indicators supplementing the indicator set show the average CO_2 emissions per km from
new passenger cars and tertiary educational attainment. With merely one link to climate
change-relevant industrial emissions, relevant climate change litigation determining the
substance in many fields of SDG 9 can therefore only be traced to a limited extent.

The underlying European policy framework for the identified priorities consists of   **80**
several legislative pillars. The Europe 2020 strategy has the purpose of 'improving the
conditions for innovation, research and development'.[142] The implementation is supported by separate funding instruments such as Horizon 2020 as the expiring EU Research
and Innovation programme[143] and the succeeding programme Horizon Europe[144] which

---

[138] ECtHR, *Vladimir Kharitonov v. Russia*, application no. 10795/14, Judgment of 20 July 2020; ECtHR, *Ahmet Yıldırım v. Turkey*, application no. 3111/10 [2012] ECHR 3003; ECtHR, *Kalda v. Estonia*, application no. 17429/10.

[139] ECtHR, Press Release, issued by the Registrar of the Court, ECHR 458 (2012), 18.12.2012, https://glo
balfreedomofexpression.columbia.edu/cases/ahmed-yildirim-v-turkey/.

[140] European Commission, *EU SDG Indicator set 2021, Result of the review in preparation of the 2021 edition of the EU SDG monitoring report, Final version of 15/01/2021*, 19.

[141] Nomenclature statistique des activités économiques dans la Communauté européenne [Nomencla-
ture of Economic Activities] (NACE) is a four-digit classification system for business branches or activity.

[142] This strategy pays special attention to 'increasing combined public and private investment in R&D
to 3% of GDP' by 2020 and thus establishes a special reference to SDG 9 and is complemented by further
industrial strategies and action plans such as the COM(2020) 98 final, *A new Circular Economy Action
Plan For a cleaner and more competitive Europe*, 11.3.2020.

[143] Horizon 2020 provides financial resources of approx. EUR 80 billion available over seven years
(2014 to 2020).

[144] With the financial support of Horizon Europe jobs that couple innovation and research shall be
created from 2021 to 2027.

'will continue to promote R&D at the intersection of disciplines, sectors and policies'[145] and also includes research on the mitigation of climate impact of transport. Further areas, in particular with relevance to the climate neutrality and circular economy to be developed, are covered by the EU New Green Deal[146], the Strategy on Shaping Europe's Digital Future[147], the New Industrial Strategy for Europe[148] and the legislative regulations and directives associated with these (→ Goal 13, Goal 14, Goal 15, Goal 6, Goal 3).

81   With the EU New Green Deal, the EU has created a policy framework that is closely aligned with the objectives of SDG 9. Almost identical in wording, the Green Deal calls for the development and expansion of smart infrastructure and transport, both in a cross-border and a regional context, in order to enhance human well-being[149] in a just and inclusive manner[150] and thus largely corresponds to SDG 9.1 and SDG 9.2. The restructuring of European industries is also called for in the form of 'upgrading to remain fit' (SDG 9.4) and, in particular, the EU's climate neutrality[151] is placed in the foreground, which is to be achieved with the help of carbon border adjustments, carbon adjustment pricing and trade mechanisms. This regulation in the area of CO_2 emission reduction[152] is accompanied by various taxation mechanisms[153] and shaped specifically by a variety of secondary legislation.[154] According to their wording and their basic understanding of the goals, the various EU strategies are thus aligned with SDG 9 which is primarily characterised by economic goals (SDG 7, SDG 8, SDG 9). It is to be expected that in the future the sustainability requirement, on the basis of the more detailed formulation of the secondary legislation, in connection with the general principle of coherence, Art. 7 TEU, the EU creates bases for claims for legal enforcement, which in detail are in fact strongly oriented towards the contents of SDG 9.

82   Whereas the scope of SDG 9.c primarily focuses on developing countries, the discussed 'right to internet' is regarded in the EU as belonging to the (digital) infrastructure (→ Goal 9 mn. 52).[155] Its significance and design is legally assessed by the ECJ, for instance, in the recent decision *Schrems II*.[156] In recognising the General Data Protection

---

[145] https://ec.europa.eu/eurostat/documents/3217494/11011074/KS-02-20-202-EN-N.pdf/334a8cfe-636a-bb8a-294a-73a052882f7 f.
[146] COM(2019) 640 final, EU New Green Deal.
[147] COM(2020) 67 final.
[148] COM(2020) 102 final.
[149] COM(2019) 640 final, EU New Green Deal, 6.
[150] COM(2019) 640 final, EU New Green Deal, 2, 20.
[151] COM(2019) 640 final, EU New Green Deal, 2, 4 ff., 18.
[152] COM(2019) 640 final, EU New Green Deal, 5 f.
[153] COM(2019) 640 final, EU New Green Deal, 5, 10, 17.
[154] EU New Green Deal, 5; Secondary legislation, e.g. Consolidated version of Directive 2003/87/EC of the European Parliament and of the Council establishing a scheme for greenhouse gas emission allowance trading within the Community amending Council Directive 96/61/EC; Regulation (EU) 2018/842 on binding annual greenhouse gas emission reductions by Member States from 2021 to 2030 contributing to climate action to meet commitments under the Paris Agreement and amending Regulation (EU) No 525/2013; Regulation (EU) 2018/841 on the inclusion of greenhouse gas emissions and removals from land use, land use change and forestry in the 2030 climate and energy framework, and amending Regulation (EU) No 525/2013 and Decision No 529/2013/EU; Directive 2014/94/EU on the deployment of alternative fuels infrastructure; TEN-T Regulation to accelerate the deployment of zero- and low-emission vehicles and vessels and the revised Council Directive 2003/96/EC restructuring the Community framework for the taxation of energy products and electricity.
[155] See COM(2019) 640 final, EU New Green Deal, 18; Digital infrastructure particularly includes supercomputers, clouds, ultra-fast network and artificial intelligence solutions.
[156] ECJ, *Data Protection Commissioner v Facebook Ireland Limited and Maximillian Schrems*, Request for a preliminary ruling from the High Court (Ireland), Judgment of the Court (Grand Chamber) of 16 July 2020, C-311/18, ECLI:EU:C:2020:559.

Regulation (GDPR) of the EU the ECJ stated that 'the protection of the data transferred that is required by EU law cannot be ensured by other means, where the data exporter established in the EU has not itself suspended or put an end to such a transfer.' It thus revised the *Schrems I* decision ('safe harbour decision') and provides precise information on how the provision of digital infrastructures and innovations must be organised at European level.

3. Arbitration Proceedings

Giving legal meaning to the term innovation, a task that is hardly possible to perform   83
in any case, can even less be achieved within the context provided by SDG 9. Since innovation ought to be achieved by increasing a countries' research capacity (SDG 9.5) and by creating conducive policies (SDG 9.b), SDG 9 reveals its governance character (→ Goal 9 mn. 46 ff.). As a consequence of the imprecise targets of SDG 9, the demanded measures are not of independent legal interest and cannot be used as a legal basis for the implementation of a specific innovation policy.

However, the external impact and protection of innovations in the field of intellectual   84
property is suitable and of considerable importance as an independent legal basis for litigation. Patents, design patents, and plant patents are the subject of various WTO agreements, such as the Agreement on Trade Related Aspects of Intellectual Property Rights (TRIPS[157]), the Paris Convention for the Protection of Industrial Property (patents, industrial designs, etc.), the Berne Convention for the Protection of Literary and Artistic Works (copyright) and other (free trade) agreements of the various legal families worldwide, which lay down additional obligations, e.g. to the TRIPS Agreement (TRIPS-plus). As can be found in the SDGs 9.a, SDG 9.b and SDG 9.c, asymmetries in the WTO frameworks are permissible for similar reasons, e.g. for Least Developed Countries (LDCs) that are WTO members.[158] TRIPS-plus allowed them to exempt from compliance with the TRIPS Agreement till 2021. For pharmaceutical products, this exception applies until 2033. Whether and to what extent the protection of intellectual property is conducive to innovation and thus to SDG 9 is viewed critically from an academic and economic perspective.[159] However, the denial of access to medical products, such as life-saving medicines affects the poorest populations most due to patent protection and the associated monopolisation and / or price increases of the products, which can threaten, for example, the right to health. In light of the SARS-CoV-2 pandemic, the ongoing debate about the need for protection (of exclusivity rights) to generate profits as an incentive for nascent and ongoing research and competition came to light once again. However, the lack of analysable cases to date prevents a legal evaluation on how to consider and shape law sustainably by the meaning of SDG 9 or the Global Agenda 2030.[160]

---

[157] 'The TRIPS Agreement plays a critical role in facilitating trade in knowledge and creativity, in resolving trade disputes over intellectual property, and in assuring WTO members the latitude to achieve their domestic objectives. The Agreement is legal recognition of the significance of links between intellectual property and trade', https://www.wto.org/english/thewto_e/whatis_e/tif_e/agrm7_e.htm.

[158] WTO rules at the same time allow for different forms of protection which might even more favour the interests of developed countries: Joseph, 'Trade Law and Investment Law' in Shelton, *The Oxford Handbook of International Human Rights Law* (2013), 846; Maljean-Dubois, 'Principle 9, Science and Technology' in Viñuales (ed), *The Rio Declaration on Environment and Development, A Commentary*, 280.

[159] Correa, 'Specific Concerns of Developing Countries in Intellectual Property Rights' in Cottier and Nadakavukaren Schefer, *Elgar Encyclopedia of International Economic Law* (2017), 531 f.

[160] To date, in WTO dispute settlement, merely two cases relate to pharmaceuticals (from 2010, in consultations) and 11 cases relate to patents, the most recent of is from 2001 (in consultations), https://www.wto.org/english/tratop_e/dispu_e/dispu_subjects_index_e.htm.

85   Nonetheless, dispute settlement procedures frequently focus on compliance with these rights, balancing the fundamental principles of the WTO, namely the most-favoured-nation principle and national treatment, with a particular focus on balanced protection and benefit sharing.

86   However, whether sustainable benefit sharing as demanded by the Global Agenda 2030 also applies to the area of industrial innovation addressed by SDG 9 appears doubtful against the background of the retrievable dispute settlement decisions (→ Goal 14 mn. 56, Goal 15 mn. 22 ff., 52).[161] WTO dispute settlement in the sustainable formulation of benefit sharing seems to be still in its infancy. In the understanding of the WTO dispute settlement, balanced protection, too, can at best be attributed to the preservation of disputed contracts, and thus to the legal principle of *pacta sunt servanda*, which might be remotely compatible with the concept of sustainability, and might be included in SDG 9 as a means of fulfilling its purpose, but not necessarily.

87   In three cases, the United States (US), the EU and Canada claimed against China for restricting trade in rare earths for a considerable period of time.[162] The raw materials in question, rare earths, tungsten and molybdenum, are strategic raw materials worldwide which are indispensable for the development of future industries and technologies. The restrictions imposed by China on these raw materials included 'restrictions [such as] export duties, export quotas, minimum export price requirements, export licensing requirements and additional requirements and procedures in connection with the administration of the quantitative restrictions'[163] Neither the Panel nor the Appellate Body could identify 'any cogent reason' in the 'conservation of its exhaustible natural resources, and necessary to reduce pollution caused by mining' argued by China[164] and rejected the applicability of Art. XX(g) GATT.

4. Domestic Jurisdiction

88   The design of sustainable infrastructures, industries and technologies is discussed in the majority of states worldwide and incorporated into a wide range of policy guidelines, resulting in legislative proposals and corresponding laws. The recent decision of the German Federal Constitutional Court (FCC) on a climate-relevant case demonstrates the judicial assessment of what constitutes sustainable infrastructures in alignment with the Paris Agreement and the reports of the IPCC, which define sustainable infrastructures as follows:

> These include, in particular, modifying existing infrastructure to better protect against heat, wind and flooding. In cyclone and flood-prone areas, the IPCC mentions low and aerodynamically designed buildings, sewage systems, dykes, flood embankments, filling of beaches, building rehabilitation, in cities sustainable infrastructure such as green roofs, parks and infiltration-capable traffic areas, and in agriculture efficient irrigation systems and the establishment of plants with high drought tolerance, but also resettlement.[165]

---

[161] Amongst other instruments, the Nagoya Protocol on Access to Genetic Resources and the Fair and Equitable Sharing of Benefits Arising from their Utilisation to the Convention on Biological Diversity includes specific regulation on benefit sharing in this context; see http://www.fao.org/sustainable-development-goals/news/detail-news/en/c/1045012/.

[162] DS431, DS432, DS433: *China — Measures Related to the Exportation of Rare Earths, Tungsten and Molybdenum*.

[163] https://www.wto.org/english/tratop_e/dispu_e/cases_e/ds431_e.htm.

[164] WT/DS431/AB/R, WT/DS432/AB/R, WT/DS433/AB/R, *China – Measures Related to the Exportation of Rare Earths, Tungsten and Molybdenum*, Reports of the Appellate Body, 7 August 2014 para. 5.6 (Panel Reports, para. 7.11).

[165] German Federal Constitutional Court, 1 BvR 2656/18, Order of the First Senate of 24 March 2021, para. 178; see IPCC, *Climate Change 2014, Impacts, Adaptions and Vulnerability* (2014), 840 ff., 844 ff.

However, the court strictly distinguishes between measures that are feasible domesti-   **89**
cally[166] and those that are feasible abroad which the German state could not carry out
on its own in any case. Nevertheless, this does not change its 'political responsibility or
responsibility under international law', which leads to 'the possibility of implementing
positive measures to protect people in the poorer and even harder-hit countries'.[167]

With reference to the necessary 'technical progress and other developments', the court   **90**
referred in particular to the extensive replacement or avoidance of CO_2-intensive processes and products. Although the comprehensive implementation of the necessary innovations 'in almost all economic processes and lifestyle practices' requires considerable
time and extensive socio-technical transformation, leading to longer transformation and
phase-out paths, the agreed protective purposes of internationally agreed instruments
may nevertheless lead to restrictions of freedom within the German state.[168]

II. De Facto Influences on Jurisdiction

Jurisdiction, especially stemming from the climate protection regime, affects, if indi-   **91**
rectly, the design of industrial processes and infrastructures, but also the development
of future innovations. Legislative amendments that are induced to comply with the
Paris Agreement and other instruments of environmental protection will, amongst others, confine or alter the scope of action with regard to CO_2 emissions and / or other
climate-impacting pollution by businesses and thus also tighten the subsequent judicial
reviews, in particular with regard to the extraterritorial applicability of asserted rights.[169]
Presumably, this will reflect the notion of intergenerational equity as set out in the
Global Agenda 2030.

Since SDG 9 is cross-sectional by its very nature, it is complemented by most different   **92**
standards according to the needs of the areas where it unfolds,[170] e.g. FAO Principles
for Responsible Investment in Agriculture and Food Systems or the International Fund
for Agricultural Development. These standards, although not assignable to the sphere
of legal positivism, serve the implementation of SDG 9 by requiring the simplification
and innovative development of industrial cooperation at its core and providing infrastructure.

Infrastructure gaps are to be closed with the means of international organisations of   **93**
the private sphere or within public-private partnerships. To form multilateral collabora-

---

[166] These include measures such as reducing the use of open spaces or deconstruction, unsealing,
renaturation and afforestation of suitable areas and the establishment of resistant plant varieties; German
Federal Constitutional Court, 1 BvR 2656/18, Order of the First Senate of 24 March 2021, para. 178.

[167] German Federal Constitutional Court, 1 BvR 2656/18, Order of the First Senate of 24 March 2021,
para. 179.

[168] German Federal Constitutional Court, 1 BvR 2656/18, Order of the First Senate of 24 March
2021, para. 179; a similar reasoning has been given by the Hoge Raad der Niederlande, Judgment of 20
December 2019, 19/00135, para. 7.4.3.

[169] See e.g. in the EU: the German Federal Constitutional Court, 1 BvR 2656/18, Order of the First Senate of 24 March 2021; Dutch Supreme Court, *The State of the Netherlands v Stichting Urgenda*, Judgment
of 20 December 2019, ECLI:NL:HR:2019:2007; Higher Regional Court Hamm (Germany), Case No. 2 O
285/15 (pending); However, creating a stricter legal situation judicially is bound to narrow specifications
and not in every case successful: see High Court of Ireland, *Friends of the Irish Environment v Ireland*, 2017
No. 793 JR, Judgment of 19 September 2019 (→ Goal 13 mn. 79).

[170] UN, *International Standard Industrial Classification of All Economic Activities (ISIC Revision 3.1)*
(2002); UN, *International Recommendations for Industrial Statistics 2008 (IRIS 2008)* (2011); OECD,
Structural and Demographic Business Statistics (SDBS) (2017); International Monetary Fund, *Public Sector
Debt Statistics: Guide for Compilers and Users* (2011); UN, *International Standard Industrial Classification
of All Economic Activities (ISIC Revision 4)* (2008).

tion mechanisms, multilateral development banks are of central importance in exerting influence on how financial capacity or capital is distributed worldwide. Essential actors in the field of infrastructure investment are, to name but a few:

- – Asian Infrastructure Investment Bank (AIIB)
- – European Investment Bank (EIB)
- – Global Infrastructure Hub
- – New Development Bank
- – Asia Pacific Project Preparation Facility
- – World Bank Group's Global Infrastructure Facility
- – Africa50 Infrastructure Fund
- – Infrastructure Development Finance Company (IDFC)
- – Inter-American Investment Corporation

94   These and other actors promote sustainable investment, including green finance governance and reform investment protection (ISDS). The interconnections among these actors, e.g. through joint participations in infrastructure projects, also illustrate the functionality of a global infrastructure forum, 'led by the multilateral development banks', which is also called for in the Global Agenda 2030 and its connected instruments.[171]

95   In addition, organisations of the UN system play a significant role in providing knowledge, capacity and partnership to bring the relevant actors in the direction of SDG 9. In particular, the UN Industrial Development Organization (UNIDO) focuses on advancing the linkages between infrastructure development, inclusive and sustainable industrialization and innovation.[172] The UN Conference on Trade and Development (UNCTAD) stimulates the fair and effective access to benefits thereby using 'trade, investment, finance, and technology as vehicles for inclusive and sustainable development' and triggering economic structural transformation.[173]

96   Further influence is exerted through the United Nations Commission on International Trade Law (UNCITRAL) which is specialised on commercial law reform worldwide to facilitate trade and investment, e.g. by giving access to financial services, credit and enhancing the integration of economic actors in the global value chains (SDG 9.3, also related to SDG 8.3 and 8.10), and providing infrastructure or helping understand privately funded infrastructure projects which are to be understood as international legal standards themselves. Thus, UNCITRAL helps understanding the standards and assists establishing a legal environment that is attractive to investors in infrastructure development (SDG 9.a).[174] Similar action is taken by the International Labor Organisation (ILO) which sets international labour standards and thus enhances social and economic justice (→ Goal 8).[175]

---

[171] AAAA, para. 14.

[172] AAAA, para. 15.

[173] TD/519/Add.2*, *From decision to action: Moving towards an inclusive and equitable global economic environment for trade and development, Fourteenth session Nairobi 17–22 July 2016*, paras. 56 ff.

[174] Exemplary are the *United Nations Convention on Contracts for the International Carriage of Goods Wholly or Partly by Sea* (New York, 2008) (Rotterdam Rules) of the UNCITRAL Working Group III, and the currently developed *Possible reform of investor-State dispute settlement (ISDS)*, A/CN.9/WG.III/WP.170, United Nations Commission on International Trade Law Working Group III (Investor-State Dispute Settlement Reform), Thirty-eighth session, Vienna, 14-18 October 2019.

[175] Exemplary are, to name but a few, the *ILO Centenary Declaration for the Future of Work* (2019), the *Tripartite declaration of principles concerning multinational enterprises and social policy (MNE Declaration)* (2017), the *ILO Declaration on Social Justice for a Fair Globalization* (2008); see also https://www.ilo.org/global/lang--en/index.htm.

E. Conclusion on SDG 9

SDG 9 emphasises a modern approach of green and blue and thus resilient industrial- **97** isation, covering transport on all modes, technologies and innovation. With its focus on industrial production, the promotion of development and trade, SDG 9 is clearly marked as an enabler for most of the other SDGs but requests a stimulating market and public legal environment. Besides this prerequisite, a strict *rule of law* concept is inevitable, enclosing transparent conduct against corruption.

Thus, SDG 9 unravels the necessity to jointly consider the processing and value **98** creation of raw materials as well as the establishment of structures and the associated encroachment on environmental and human rights concerns on the one hand, and the surrounding debates on intellectual property and the creation of access requirements on the other.

However, a clear distinction needs to be made between private law investment and **99** contract issues, frequently based on templates and model contracts commonly used in the construction industry (e.g. published by FIDIC and recommended by the World Bank for infrastructure projects), and public national law, which guides the seed stage from entrepreneurial start-ups to small and medium enterprises towards larger scale industry to clusters, reflecting a planning element at national and constitutional level.

Beyond that, SDG 9 can only be used to a limited extent to derive a legally relevant **100** frame of reference. Rather, it enriches other, legally more unambiguous SDGs with context in a supportive manner and points out needs that must be considered in the respective environments.

Indications exist that show, in conjunction with other corresponding SDGs, some de- **101** velopments are taking place that should be examined more closely in the future. For a distinct interpretation of the legal dimension of SDG 9, reference can be made here to the elaboration of the linked, relevant SDGs within this commentary ($\rightarrow$ Goal 9 mn. 58 ff.).

Transport and infrastructure, as the other two pillars of SDG 9, are intended to **102** increase the income of target countries. However, transport planning is a complex issue that depends on topography, climate and the environment and includes all accessible means of transport to other regions or countries. The World Bank and many other intergovernmental investment banks particularly support the complex infrastructure of transportation modes. The legal frameworks divided both in public and private laws and related to domestic, interregional and international laws, including standards and transnational (private law-based) regulations, have evolved to a highly specialised field and becomes even more sophisticated when a special mode of transport, such as sea shipping (another distinction between freight and passengers is to be made), air transport or shipping in rivers crossing several countries is at stake.

From a legal point of view, the current situation of innovation is framed by WTO **103** TRIPS, WIPO, UNCTAD, OECD, EUIPO and other specialised IO as well as by specialised agencies of the UN (IMO, ICAO, WMO). Frontier technologies are enabled to boost further innovations in their respective fields. UNCTAD counts 11 so-called 'frontier Technologies'[176] that foster innovation and reshape industrialisation. Innovation and technologies affect the legal framework and the question will be, as to how the applicability and the scope of this technology will impact different types of work and the methods we use traditionally to avoid or to solve juridical problems (Blockchain,

---

[176] UNCTAD (2021), 9: AI, IoT, Big Data, blockchain, 5G, 3D printing, robotics, drones, gene editing, nanotechnology and solar photovoltaic (Solar PV).

LegalTechs). The interrelated areas of the three pillars and new technologies create greater tensions in readiness and the possible usage of those innovative technologies. The observation that only a few countries deliver those technologies including the respective appropriate raw materials, but all countries are in need to be prepared or could lose their connectivity with industries, trade of goods and infrastructure.[177] This development points to an inherent inequality that could be mitigated by governments by laws, regulations or political based action keeping an eye on a classic aspect of inequality, gender inequality. In particular, girls and women need to be empowered in their skills to tackle the challenges of modern innovation, technologies, infrastructure and industrialisation.

---

[177] UNCTAD (2021), 10.

Goal 10
Reduce inequality within and among countries

10.1 By 2030, progressively achieve and sustain income growth of the bottom 40 per cent of the population at a rate higher than the national average

10.2 By 2030, empower and promote the social, economic and political inclusion of all, irrespective of age, sex, disability, race, ethnicity, origin, religion or economic or other status

10.3 Ensure equal opportunity and reduce inequalities of outcome, including by eliminating discriminatory laws, policies and practices and promoting appropriate legislation, policies and action in this regard

10.4 Adopt policies, especially fiscal, wage and social protection policies, and progressively achieve greater equality

10.5 Improve the regulation and monitoring of global financial markets and institutions and strengthen the implementation of such regulations

10.6 Ensure enhanced representation and voice for developing countries in decision-making in global international economic and financial institutions in order to deliver more effective, credible, accountable and legitimate institutions

10.7 Facilitate orderly, safe, regular and responsible migration and mobility of people, including through the implementation of planned and well-managed migration policies

10.a Implement the principle of special and differential treatment for developing countries, in particular least developed countries, in accordance with World Trade Organization agreements

10.b Encourage official development assistance and financial flows, including foreign direct investment, to States where the need is greatest, in particular least developed countries, African countries, small island developing States and landlocked developing countries, in accordance with their national plans and programmes

10.c By 2030, reduce to less than 3 per cent the transaction costs of migrant remittances and eliminate remittance corridors with costs higher than 5 per cent development

Word Count related to 'Inequality' and 'Equality'
A/RES/70/1 - Transforming our world: the 2030 Agenda for Sustainable Development: 'Inequality': 6 'Equality': 12
A/RES/69/313 - Addis Ababa Action Agenda of the Third International Conference on Financing for Development adopted on 27 July 2015: 'Inequality': 2 'Equality': 29
A/RES/66/288 - The future we want (Rio +20 Declaration) adopted on 27 July 2012: 'Inequality': 4 'Equality': 35
A/RES/55/2 - United Nations Millennium Declaration adopted on 8 September 2000: 'Inequality': 0 'Equality': 6

Select Bibliography: Holger Apel, 'Inequality in development: the 2030 Agenda, SDG 10 and the role of redistribution' (2020) 29 *Real-World Econ. Rev.*, 228; Karim Bahgat, Kendra Dupuy, Scott Gates, Håvard Mokleiv Nygård, Siri Aas Rustad, Håvard Strand, Henrik Urdal, Gudrun Østby, Gray Barrett and Solveig Hillesund, *Inequality and Armed Conflict: Evidence and Data* (PRIO – Peace Research Institute Oslo, Oslo 2017); Jean-Marie Baland, François Bourguignon, Jean-Philippe Platteau and Thierry Verdier (eds), *The Handbook of Economic Development and Institutions* (Princeton University Press, USA/UK 2020); Bimbika Sijapati Basnett, Rodd Myers and Marlène Elias, 'SDG 10: Reduced Inequalities – An Environmental Justice Perspective on Implications for Forests and People' in Pia Katila, Carol J. Pierce Colfer, Wil De Jong, Glenn Galloway, Pablo Pacheco and Georg Winkel(eds), Sustainable Development Goals: Their Impacts on Forests and People (Cambridge University Press, Cambridge 2019); Tanja Bastia, 'Migration and Inequality – An introduction' in Tanja Bastia (ed), *Migration and Inequality* (Routledge, UK/USA/Canada 2013), 1; Peter A.G. van Bergeijk and Rolph Van der Hoeven, 'The challenge to reduce income inequality (introduction and overview)' in Peter A.G. Van Bergeijk and Rolph Van der Hoeven (eds), *Sustainable Development Goals and Income Inequality* (Edward Elgar Publishing Limited, UK/USA 2017); Peter van den Bossche and Werner Zdouc, *The Law and Policy of the World Trade Organization* (4th edition, Cambridge University Press, UK/USA/Australia/India/Singapore 2017); Julien Chaisse and Tsai-yu Lin (eds), *International Economic Law and Governance – Essays in Honour of Mitsuo Matsushita* (Oxford University Press, Oxford 2016); Christian Olaf Christiansen and Steven L. B. Jensen, 'Histories of Global Inequality: Introduction' in Christian Olaf Christiansen and Steven L. B. Jensen (eds) *Histories of Global Inequality – New Perspectives* (Palgrave McMillan/Springer Nature Switzerland, Switzerland 2019), 1; Noah S. Diffenbaugh and Marshall Burke, 'Global warming has increased global economic inequality' (2019) 116 *PNAS*, 9808; Joan Maria Esteban, 'Inequality and Conflict' (2018) 27 *J. Income Distrib.*, 1; Sandra Fredman, 'Substantive equality revisited' (2016) 14 *Int. J. Const. Law* 712; James K. Galbraith, *Inequality and Instability, A Study of the World Economy Just Before the Great Crisis* (Oxford University Press, Oxford 2012); Hurst Hannum, Dinah L. Shelton, S. James Anaya and Rosa Celorio (eds), *International Human Rights – Problems of Law, Policy and Practice* (6th edition, Wolters Kluwer, New York 2018); S. Nazrul Islam and John Winkel, *Climate Change and Social Inequality* – DESA Working Paper No. 152 (United Nations – Department of Economic and Social Affairs, New York 2017); Sarah Joseph and Melissa Castan, *The International Covenant on Civil and Political Rights – Cases, Materials and Commentary* (3rd edition, Oxford University Press, Oxford 2013); Heike Kuhn, 'Reducing Inequality Within and Among Countries: Realizing SDG 10—A Developmental Perspective' in Markus Kaltenborn, Markus Krajewski and Heike Kuhn (eds), *Sustainable Development Goals and Human Rights* (Springer Nature Switzerland AG, Cham 2020); Donald Kate, 'Will inequality get left behind in the 2030 Agenda?' in Barbara Adams et al (eds), *Spotlight on Sustainable Development – Report by the Reflection Group on the 2030 Agenda for Sustainable Development* (Social Watch/ Third World Network/Global Policy Forum/Arab NGO Network for Development/Development Alternatives with Women for a New Era, Uruguay/Malaysia/Germany/Lebanon/Fiji 2016), 80; Todd A. Knoop, Understanding Economic Inequality – Bigger Pies and Just Deserts (Edward Elgar Publishing Limted, UK/USA 2020); Arnaud Lefranc, Nicolas Pistolesi and Alain Trannoy, 'Inequality of opportunities vs. inequality of outcomes: Are Western societies all alike?' (2008) 54 *Rev. Income Wealth*, 513; Gillian McNaughton, 'Vertical inequalities: are the SDGs and human rights up to the challenge?' (2017) 21 *Int. J. Hum. Right*, 1050; Branko Milanovic, *Global Inequality – A New Approach for the Age of Globalization* (The Belknap Press of Harvard University Press, USA/UK 2016); Sophia Moreau, *Faces of Inequality – A Theory of Wrongful Discrimination* (Oxford University Press, Oxford 2020); Tonia Novitz and Margherita Pieraccini, 'Agenda 2030 and the Sustainable Development Goals: 'Responsive, Inclusive, Pariticipatory and Representative Decision-Making?' in Margherita Pieraccini and Tonia Novitz (eds), *Legal Perspectives on Sustainability* (Bristol University Press, UK/USA 2020); Joel E. Oestreich, 'SDG 10: Reduce inequality in and among countries' (2018) 37 *Social Alternatives*, 34; Oxfam, An economy for the 1 % - Oxfam Briefing Paper (Oxfam GB, Oxford 2016); Umesh Chandra Pandey, Chhabi Kumar, Martin Ayanore and Hany R. Shalaby, *SDG 10 – Reduce Inequality Wihtin and Among Countries* (Emerald Publishing Limited, UK 2020); Thomas Piketty and Arthur Goldhammer, *The Economics of Inequality* (Harvard University Press,

Cambridge, Massachusetts, London 2015); Bernard Van Praag and Ada Ferrer-i-Carbonell, 'Inequalitiy and Happiness' in Brian Nolan, Wiemer Salverda, and Timothy M. Smeeding (eds), *The Oxford Handbook of Economic Inequality* (Oxford University Press, Oxford 2011); Amartya Sen, *Development as Freedom* (Oxford University Press, Oxford 1999); United Nations, *A UN framework for the immediate socio-econo-mic response to Covid-19* (United Nations, New York 2020); United Nations, *World Social Report 2020 – Inequality in a rapidly changing world* (United Nations publication, New York 2020).

A. Background and Origin of SDG 10

SDG 10 is predominantly concerned with the question of how and to what extent in-   1
equality within and among countries is to be reduced. With the SARS-CoV-2 pandemic, hurdles to achieve the targets of SDG 10 are posed which hit the most vulnerable groups the hardest.[1] Despite a slight tendency towards the decrease of inequality – such as lower income inequality in some countries and preferential trade status for lower-income countries – inequality in its various forms described in SDG 10 persists.[2]

However, the overall inequality, particularly with regard to the distribution of income   2
and wealth, worldwide endured, widened and showed negative long-term trends.[3] Over-coming inequality and leaving no one behind in the sense of SDG 10 means to enable the bottom 40 per cent of the population 'to benefit and participate in a country's broad-er economic growth' to reach shared prosperity without discrimination (SDG 10.3.) with the help of Official Development Assistance (ODA), orderly and safe migration policies, a stable growth of gross domestic product (GDP) and financial regulation.

Women and women with disabilities are particularly affected by inequality and   3
multiple discrimination, as well as intersectional discrimination based on religious, ethnic and gender prejudice (→ Goal 5). It is noticeable that workers, despite some considerable regional differences, 'are receiving a smaller share of the output they helped produce'.[4] Since inequality is considered an underlying cause of the 'problems the goals seek to address', the fight against inequality must be placed 'at the heart' of the SDGs in order not to be 'doomed to failure'.[5]

I. Inequality – Origin and Foundation of SDG 10

Human history shows that inequality constitutes a natural part of social coexistence.   4
In cases where inequality harshly manifested in poverty and thus in a reduction of capa-bilities and other forms of restriction of human well-being, this led to conflictual condi-tions, disturbances, turmoil and distortions which are entirely detrimental to human de-velopment.[6] A far-reaching framework has already been created at international level

---

[1] UN, *The Sustainable Development Goals Report 2020* (2020), 43; ECOSOC, E/2020/L.20–E/HLPF/2020/L.1, *Ministerial declaration of the high level segment of the 2020 session of the Economic and Social Council and the 2020 high level political forum on sustainable development, convened under the auspices of the Council, on the theme "Accelerated action and transformative pathways: realizing the decade of action and delivery for sustainable development"*, 17 July 2020, para. 8.

[2] UN, *The Sustainable Development Goals Report 2020* (2020); https://sdgs.un.org/goals/goal10.

[3] UN DESA, *TST Compendium Issues Brief* (2014), 209; Independent Group of Scientists, *The Future is Now: Science for Achieving Sustainable Development, Global Sustainable Development Report 2019* (2019), 10.

[4] UN, *The Sustainable Development Goals Report 2020* (2020), 44.

[5] Independent Group of Scientists, *The Future is Now: Science for Achieving Sustainable Development, Global Sustainable Development Report 2019* (2019), xvi.

[6] This did not exclude that turmoil and distortions occurred accompanying the demand for and imple-mentation of measures that create(d) equality; see for a comparative view on this issue: Oppenheimer,

with the UN Charter,[7] the Universal Declaration of Human Rights (UDHR),[8] the International Convention on the Elimination of All Forms of Racial Discrimination (ICERD),[9] the Convention on the Elimination of All Forms of Discrimination against Women (CEDAW)[10] (→ Goal 5 mn. 32, 40 ff.) and the Convention on the Rights of Persons with Disabilities (CRPD),[11] later extended by optional protocols,[12] each of which is also dedicated to the creation of equality in its own specific context. In particular, the creation and implementation of the earlier instruments in 1966/67 did not remain free of conflict, but contributed significantly to today's far-reaching recognition of the idea of equality and non-discrimination.[13] Anchoring equality as a means to an end on the Global (Development) Agenda is therefore essential to reduce differences between countries, as well as within countries, in order to achieve a long lasting peaceful coexistence.

5   In addition to natural phenomena such as the geographical location of states, their natural resources such as (fresh) water systems and economically exploitable natural resources, the level of development and, associated with it, the history of each state also affect the formation or manifestation of inequalities. Originating in colonialism (occupation), but also the process of decolonisation[14] and the continuous processing of its effects such as discrimination, racism, the erosion and / or suppression of political processes continue to maintain inequalities.[15] These issues have recently been supplemented by the importance of demographic development, the dynamics of which have a considerable influence on the development of countries.[16]

6   The endeavour to create as equal conditions as possible between states is supported by the principle of (state) sovereignty.[17] The UN Charter in Art. 1 declares the 'respect for the principle of equal rights and self-determination of peoples, and to take other appropriate measures to strengthen universal peace' with the means of international cooperation to jointly solve 'international problems of an economic, social, cultural, or humanitarian character' and promote 'respect for human rights and [...] fundamental freedoms for all without distinction as to race, sex, language, or religion'. This tenet can also be found in the foundations of Europe, e.g. in the expression of (international) solidarity

---

'The Ubiquity of Positive Measures for Addressing Systemic Discrimination and Inequality, A Comparative Global Perspective' (2019) 3.3–4 *Comparative Discrimination Law*, 1-114.

[7] Charter of the United Nations, 1945.

[8] A/RES/217(III), *Universal Declaration of Human Rights*, 10 December 1948.

[9] International Convention on the Elimination of All Forms of Racial Discrimination, 21 December 1965.

[10] A/RES/34/180, *Convention on the Elimination of All Forms of Discrimination against Women*, 18 December 1979.

[11] A/RES/61/106, *Convention on the Rights of Persons with Disabilities*, 24 January 2007.

[12] Amongst others: A/RES/54/4, *Optional Protocol to the Convention on the Elimination of All Forms of Discrimination against Women*, 15 October 1999; A/RES/54/263, Annex I, *Optional Protocol to the Convention on the Rights of the Child on the involvement of children in armed conflict*, 16 March 2001.

[13] For example through initiating the establishment of 'quota systems for disadvantaged groups [...] to reduce discrimination and promote diversity [and] voluntary inclusion programs'; see Oppenheimer, 'The Ubiquity of Positive Measures for Addressing Systemic Discrimination and Inequality, A Comparative Global Perspective' (2019) 3.3–4 *Comparative Discrimination Law*, 1 (7).

[14] Havercroft et al., 'Decolonising global constitutionalism' (2020) 9(1) *Global Constitutionalism*, 1-6.

[15] For far-reaching discussion on the causes of inequality see Guerriero, *The labour share of income around the world. Evidence from a panel dataset* (2012); Aristotle, *Politics* (350 BCE); Gosepath, 'Equality' in Zalta (ed), *The Stanford Encyclopedia of Philosophy* (2011); Sen, 'Equality of What?', in *The Tanner Lecture on Human Values* (1980), 197-220; Sen, *Inequality Reexamined* (1992).

[16] A/73/204, *Implementation of Agenda 21, the Programme for the Further Implementation of Agenda 21 and the outcomes of the World Summit on Sustainable Development and of the United Nations Conference on Sustainable Development Report of the Secretary-General*, 19 July 2018, para. 18.

[17] A/RES/70/1, *Transforming our world: the 2030 Agenda for Sustainable Development*, 21 October 2015, preamble and para. 39.

in the Treaty of Paris establishing the European Coal and Steal Community (ECSC) and repeatedly since the Treaties of Rome[18], even so in the agreements with their now former colonial states.[19] The Member States dedicated the EU to the principle of solidarity explicitly (Art. 2, 3, 21, 24, 31 TEU; Art. 67, 80, 122, 222 [solidarity clause] TFEU). At a global level, the MDGs included solidarity based on equity and social justice as one of the six fundamental values that were defined essential to international relations.[20]

Recent reports on solidarity state that, in addition to the pandemic situation, reactive 7 populism[21] as well as climate-change[22] are recognised as a main threat to the SDGs but, of course, to humankind at all.

The inherent inequality of different states due to different geographical locations was 8 taken into account, for example in the small island development States (SIDS) Accelerated Modalities of Action (SAMOA) Pathway[23] and the Vienna Programme of Action for Landlocked Developing Countries for the Decade 2014-2024,[24] which recognised the higher (financial) burden that these states face in mitigating climate change and already included it in the Global Agenda 2030 to counteract this form of inequality ($\rightarrow$ Intro mn. 284 ff., Goal 14 mn. 10, 47).

Further efforts to achieve 'inclusive, equitable development approaches to overcome 9 poverty and inequality' focus on the green economy,[25] which is expected to achieve a transformation through greater resource efficiency, sustainable consumption and production and through macroeconomic governance (green finance, technology and investments) by 2012.[26] The transformation process is still ongoing but with a stronger impetus. In the context of SIDS and coastal least developed countries, this orientation is supplemented by the blue economy,[27] which is characterised by low-carbon, efficient, and clean energy and is based on solidarity, in particular through sharing, circularity, collaboration, resilience, opportunity, and interdependence[28] including sustainable fisheries, ecosystem health and preventing pollution across borders and sectors[29] to sustainably lift people out of poverty.

In addition to inequalities between states, SDG 10 also covers inequalities within 10 states, including differences between households or individuals. The growing 'enormous

---

[18] Treaty Establishing the European Economic Community, 25 March 1957, preamble, Arts. 2, 3(k), 227(4).

[19] Kuhn, 'Reducing Inequality Within and Among Countries: Realizing SDG 10—A Developmental Perspective' in Kaltenborn and Krajewski and Kuhn (eds), *Sustainable Development Goals and Human Rights* (2020), 143.

[20] A/RES/55/2, *United Nations Millennium Declaration*, 8 September 2000, para. 6.

[21] A/RES/75/180, *Human rights and international solidarity*, 20 July 2020, para. 34.

[22] A/HRC/44/44, *International solidarity and climate change, Report of the Independent Expert on human rights and international solidarity*, 1 April 2020.

[23] A/RES/69/15, *SIDS Accelerated Modalities of Action (SAMOA) Pathway*, 15 December 2014.

[24] A/CONF.225/L.1*, *Vienna Programme of Action for Landlocked Developing Countries for the Decade 2014-2024*, 3 November 2014.

[25] See for a plain overview: UN DESA, *A guidebook to the Green Economy Issue 1: Green Economy, Green Growth, and Low-Carbon Development – history, definitions and a guide to recent publications* (2012).

[26] A/RES/66/288, *The future we want*, 11 September 2012, paras. 12, 56-74.

[27] See World Bank and United Nations Department of Economic and Social Affairs (UN DESA), *The Potential of the Blue Economy: Increasing Long-term Benefits of the Sustainable Use of Marine Resources for Small Island Developing States and Coastal Least Developed Countries* (2017).

[28] See World Bank and UN DESA, *The Potential of the Blue Economy: Increasing Long-term Benefits of the Sustainable Use of Marine Resources for Small Island Developing States and Coastal Least Developed Countries* (2017), 5.

[29] https://www.un.org/development/desa/en/news/sustainable/blue-economy.html; further reading in the context of SARS-CoV-2: Northrop et al., Secretariat of the High Level Panel for a Sustainable Ocean Economy, World Resources Institute, *A Sustainable and Equitable Blue Recovery to the COVID-19 Crisis* (2020).

disparities of opportunity, wealth and power' are striking, and are particularly noticeable in (youth) unemployment and gender inequality (→ Goal 5).[30]

II. Genesis of SDG 10

11   Even during the decolonisation processes, the idea of creating a level playing field was also taken into account in the field of sustainable development.[31]

12   In 1972, the so-called Stockholm Declaration declared in Principle 1 that freedom, equality and adequate living conditions are a fundamental right of humankind and that 'policies promoting or perpetuating apartheid, racial segregation, discrimination, colonial and other forms of oppression and foreign domination stand condemned and must be eliminated'.[32] Aware of the weight of the historical background, the Beyond 2015 Coalition, a global, civil alliance mainly consisting of NGOs, had been working since 2010 on the development of a participatory, inclusive process to anchor the issues of poverty and injustice from a human rights perspective as well as specific goals regarding gender and inequality, sustainable consumption and production, climate and peaceful and inclusive societies in the Global Agenda 2030.[33] At the international level, with the declaration 'The future we want' in 2012, representatives of states comprehensively recognised the abolition of inequality as a fundamental basis for sustainable development and as a pivotal point in the future development agenda yet to be established, also with reference to gender equality (→ Goal 5).[34] In January 2014, the Permanent Mission of Italy to the UN organised a roundtable to discuss 'The Threat of Growing Inequalities: Building More Just and Equitable Societies to Support Growth and Sustainable Development' when keynote speaker Joseph E. Stiglitz demanded the inclusion of a goal that counteracts extreme inequality.[35] A few months later, in August 2014, the basis for SDG 10 was developed and connoted in the Report of the Open Working Group (OWG) with the creation of equal access for all in different areas and with gender equality.

B. Scope and Dimensions of SDG 10

13   Inequalities are omnipresent both globally and within individual countries and encompass almost all areas of everyday life. Inequalities are at the heart of SDG 10 as it is deemed the cause of many human rights violations, a catalyst for the deterioration of the living conditions of numerous people and minority groups, as well as a consequence of policies and legal decisions. These thoughts were also carried by 'the heads of State and Government [which] pledged to reduce inequality within and among countries' when negotiating the Global Agenda 2030 and aiming 'to promote inclusion and leave no one behind'.[36]

---

[30] A/RES/70/1, *Transforming our world: the 2030 Agenda for Sustainable Development*, 21 October 2015, para. 14.

[31] Petrova, "Smoke and Mirrors': The Durban Review Conference and Human Rights Politics at the United Nations' (2010) 10(1) *Human Rights Law Review*, 129-50; Bennett, 'Decolonization, Environmentalism and Nationalism in Australia and South Africa' (2017) 41(1) *Itinerario*, 27-50.

[32] A/CONF. 48/14 Rev. 1, *Report of the UN Conference on the Human Environment Stockholm*, 5-6 June 1972 (Stockholm Declaration), Principle 1 (4).

[33] Dodds and Donoghue and Roesch, *Negotiating the Sustainable Development Goals, A transformational Agenda for an insecure world* (2017), 66.

[34] A/RES/66/288, *The future we want*, 11 September 2012, paras. 4, 37, 58, 107.

[35] Kaltenborn et al., *The SDGs and Human Rights* (2020), 142.

[36] United Nations, *World Social Report 2020 – Inequality in a rapidly changing world* (2020), 21.

The interdependencies with other SDGs are clearly visible, and the spheres that SDG   14
10 seeks to achieve with the aim of reducing inequalities between and within states are
multi-layered as they range from political relations at the intergovernmental level to the
strengthening of specific rights to social change (→ Goal 10 mn. 67 ff.). Within countries, inequalities addressed by SDG 10 concern the aspects of 'age, sex, disability, race,
ethnicity, origin [or] religion'.[37] As regards the inequalities between countries, SDG 10
addresses the fields of enhanced representation of developing countries on the international scene as well as orderly migration policies.[38] SDG 10 does not exclusively focus on
the worldwide economic redistribution of wealth and resources. 'It is more plausibly interpreted as a call for a reduction of inequities – those factors that prevent people and
states from having a fair shot at the achievement of prosperity and development'.[39] In the
overall structure of the Global Agenda 2030, inequalities can be seen as cause for numerous other global challenges, such as poverty (→ Goal 1), persistent unemployment
(→ Goal 8), environmental degradation (→ Goal 7, Goal 12, Goal 13, Goal 14, Goal 15),
political instability as well as violence and conflict (→ Goal 16).[40]

Moreover, climate change must be seen as one of the major drivers of increasing in-   15
equalities worldwide (→ Goal 7, Goal 13). Climate-related distortions lead not only, but
especially in developing countries, to a sharp increase in inequalities.[41] In this context,
the impact of climate change on poverty plays a central role as 'socially and economically disadvantaged and marginalised people are disproportionally affected by climate
change'[42] widening the gap (inequalities) between social groups of society (→ Goal 1,
Goal 2, Goal 4).[43] Apart from these inner-state distortions due to climate change,
the scope of climate change-related consequences also covers inequalities between the
countries.[44]

I. Elementary Definitions

To make the complexity of global inequalities tangible, the legal framework of inter-   16
national law provides a definition of inequality as 'the state of not being equal, especially
in status, rights, and opportunities'.[45] With this definition, legal dimensions become
discernible that encompass human and social, economic and cultural rights as well as
the aspect of access to fundamental resources such as access to education, water, clean
energy and more.[46]

---

[37] Basnett and Myers and Elias, 'SDG 10: Reduced Inequalities – An Environmental Justice Perspective
on Implications for Forests and People' in Katila et al. (eds), *Sustainable Development Goals: Their Impacts
on Forests and People* (2020), 315 (316).

[38] See SDG 10.6 and 10.7.

[39] Oestreich, 'SDG 10: Reduce inequality in and among countries' (2018) 37 *Social Alternatives*, 34 (34).

[40] Pandey et al., *SDG 10 – Reduce Inequality Within and Among Countries* (2020), 1 ff.

[41] Diffenbaugh and Burke, 'Global warming has increased global economic inequality' (2019) 116
PNAS, 9808 (9808 ff.).

[42] Islam and Winkel, *Climate Change and Social Inequality* – DESA Working Paper No. 152 (2017), 4.

[43] UN, *World Social Report 2020 – Inequality in a rapidly changing world* (2020), 93 ff.

[44] UN, *World Social Report 2020 – Inequality in a rapidly changing world* (2020), 88 ff.

[45] Basnett and Myers and Elias, 'SDG 10: Reduced Inequalities – An Environmental Justice Perspective
on Implications for Forests and People' in Katila et al. (eds), *Sustainable Development Goals: Their Impacts
on Forests and People (2020)*, 315 (316).

[46] Moreau, *Faces of Inequality – A Theory of Wrongful Discrimination* (2020), 121 ff.; Center for Economic and Social Rights (CESR), *From Disparity to Dignity – Tackling economic inequality through the Sustainable Development Goals* (2016), 11 f.

17   Kuhn divides the scope of SDG 10 into three layers, underlining the particular role of social, economic as well as ecological aspects affecting global inequalities.[47]

18   Concerning the inequalities among individuals within a state, the construction of equality and thus inequality is to be enlightened. Several types of inequality exist among individuals which are based on the interconnected links between the causes and consequences of inequalities. Alongside the inequality of outcome, an inequality of opportunity may also exist which needs to be defined separately and in a way that respects the multi-layered aspects and profound scope of global inequalities.[48] Inequality of outcome is respectively defined as the condition 'when individuals do not possess the same level of material wealth or overall living economic conditions'.[49]

19   Moreover, the relation between inequality of outcome and inequality of opportunity is determined as follows:

> Equal-opportunity theories differentiate between two fundamental sources of inequality among individuals: on the one hand, factors outside the realm of individual choice, usually referred to as circumstances; on the other hand, factors that individuals can be judged responsible for and that can be generically referred to as effort. One important principle emphasized by equal-opportunity theories is that differences in circumstances are not a morally acceptable source of inequality. On the contrary, inequality arising from differences in effort need not be corrected. As a consequence, any level of inequality of outcome can be compatible with equality of opportunity. However, when equality of opportunity prevails, no particular vector of circumstances should provide individuals with an advantage over any other vector.[50]

20   In the context of outcome inequalities, income inequality 'measures the distribution of income across households or individuals in an economy'.[51] It is therefore evident that inequalities are by no means based solely on economic indicators and economic situation. Rather, a distinction must be made between the existing economic circumstances and the social and societal conditions of individuals. Everyone should have the same opportunities for access to materials and resources and the same opportunities for participation and development within society. This means that 'all should enjoy equal access to opportunity – that one's chances to succeed in life should not be determined by circumstances beyond an individual's control'.[52]

21   Thus, inequality of outcomes comprises 'various material dimensions of human well-being, such as the level of income or level of educational attainment' and the dimension of inequality of opportunities involves inter alia aspects 'such as unequal access to employment or education' (→ Goal 4, Goal 8).[53]

22   When equality is to be achieved or inequalities reduced, the concept of equity is central. 'Equity, as opposed to equality, tackles the political and moral questions that can

---

[47] Kuhn, 'Reducing Inequality Within and Among Countries: Realizing SDG 10 – A Developmental Perspective' in Kaltenborn and Krajewski and Kuhn (eds), *Sustainable Development Goals and Human Rights* (2020), 137 (139 ff.).

[48] Therborn classifies the following types of inequality: 'resource inequality, vital inequality (inequality in health and in being biological organisms), and existential inequality (inequality in recognition)', see Christiansen and Jensen, 'Histories of Global Inequality: Introduction' in Christiansen and Jensen (eds) *Histories of Global Inequality – New Perspectives* (2019), 1 (3); Therborn, *The Killing Fields of Inequality* (2013), 48 ff.; see United Nations Development Programme (UNDP), *Humanity Divided: Confronting Inequality in Developing Countries* (2013), 19 ff.

[49] UN DESA, *Concepts of Inequality* (2015), 1; see for a distinction of types of (in)equality from a human rights perspective: Fredman, 'Substantive equality revisited' (2016) 14 *Int. J. Const. Law* 712 (720 f.).

[50] Lefranc and Pistolesi and Trannoy, 'Inequality of opportunities vs. inequality of outcomes: Are Western societies all alike?' (2008) 54 *Rev. Income Wealth*, 513 (515 f.).

[51] UNDP, *Humanity Divided: Confronting Inequality in Developing Countries* (2013), 20.

[52] UN, *World Social Report 2020 – Inequality in a rapidly changing world* (2020), 34.

[53] UNDP, *Humanity Divided: Confronting Inequality in Developing Countries* (2013), 16.

lead to lasting solutions. It means empowering the poor with a full spectrum of rights, both economic and social, and civil and political'.[54]

II. Legal Foundations

1. Inequality within Countries

SDG 10.1 to SDG 10.4 address inequalities within countries by tackling issues such **23** as increasing income growth (SDG 10.1),[55] inclusion of all by strengthening rights at the economic, social and political levels (SDG 10.2), establishing equal opportunities and combating discrimination at the institutional level (SDG 10.3), as well as fiscal, wage and social security policies[56] (SDG 10.4). These SDGs focus on the redistribution of wealth and benefits of economic growth within the national borders through various distributive policies, e.g. policies of social protection, fiscal policy of wealth distribution, health policies as well as education (→ Goal 3, Goal 4).[57] At national level, economic, social and cultural rights (ESCR) play a fundamental role. The wording of SDG 10.2 gives them a reasonably clear significance.[58]

Social inclusion and inequality is important for the rationale of the indicator and **24** measurement. The share of the population living below 50 per cent of median national income is a measure that is useful for monitoring the level and trends in social inclusion, relative poverty and inequality within a country. With these measurements, inequality is a demonstrable group and not just a narrative.

The share of people living below 50 per cent of the median is an indicator of relative **25** poverty and inequality of the income distribution within a country.[59]

The background of ESCR, enshrined in the International Covenant on Economic, **26** Social and Cultural Rights (1966) (ICESCR) is already envisaged under SDG 1 due to many interrelations between SDG 1 and SDG 10. Moreover, the role of ESCR is also illuminated in the context of SDG 2, SDG 3, SDG 4, SDG 5 as well as SDG 6.[60] Alongside the ICESCR covering the economic, social and cultural rights of individuals, the International Covenant on Civil and Political Rights (ICCPR)[61] forms one of the most

---

[54] Oestreich, 'SDG 10: Reduce inequality in and among countries' (2018) 37 *Social Alternatives*, 34 (34).

[55] See for a detailed analysis of SDG 10.1: McNaughton, 'Vertical inequalities: are the SDGs and human rights up to the challenge?' (2017) 21 *Int. J. Hum. Right*, 1050 (1058 ff.); UNDP, *Humanity Divided: Confronting Inequality in Developing Countries* (2013), 22 ff.; Van Bergeijk and Van der Hoeven, 'The challenge to reduce income inequality (introduction and overview)' in Van Bergeijk and Van der Hoeven (eds), *Sustainable Development Goals and Income Inequality* (2017), 1 ff.; Guerriero, *The labour share of income around the world. Evidence from a panel dataset* (2012).

[56] See for a detailed analysis of SDG 10.4, McNaughton, 'Vertical inequalities: are the SDGs and human rights up to the challenge?' (2017) 21 *Int. J. Hum. Right*, 1050 (1060).

[57] CESR, *From Disparity to Dignity – Tackling economic inequality through the Sustainable Development Goals* (2016), 20 ff.; UN, *World Social Report 2020 – Inequality in a rapidly changing world* (2020), 157 ff.

[58] SDG 10.2: 'By 2030, empower and promote the social, economic and political inclusion of all, irrespective of age, sex, disability, race, ethnicity, origin, religion or economic or other status'.

[59] UN Stats, https://unstats.un.org/sdgs/metadata/files/Metadata-10-02-01.pdf: indicator 10.2.1 is widely used for poverty measurement including Organization for Economic Cooperation and Development's (OECD) and Eurostat's indicators of risk of poverty or social exclusion as well.

[60] Fredman illuminates the legal status of the right to substantive equality within the framework of human rights law: Fredman, 'Substantive equality revisited' (2016) 14 *Int. J. Const. Law*, 712 (712 ff.).

[61] See Taylor, *A Commentary on the International Covenant on Civil and Political Rights – The UN Human Rights Committee's Monitoring of ICCPR Rights* (2020); Hannum et al., *International Human Rights – Problems of Law, Policy and Practice* (2018), 78 ff.; Smith, *International Human Rights Law* (2018), 48 ff.; Farrell, *Habeas Corpus in International Law* (2017), 48 ff.; Kälin and Künzli, *The Law of International Human Rights Protection* (2019), 37 ff.

important international human rights treaties consisting of multiple civil and political rights[62] applying to every human being regardless of gender, age or social affiliation.[63]

27   Numerous economists have analysed the question of inequality and paved the way for the perception that inequality within countries and between countries is persistent and much too high.

28   The SDG 10.3 related indicator 10.3.1 deals with the '[p]roportion of population reporting having personally felt discriminated against or harassed in the previous 12 months on the basis of a ground of discrimination prohibited under international human rights law'. International human rights law refers to the body of international legal instruments aiming to promote and protect human rights, including the UDHR and subsequent international human rights treaties adopted by the UN ($\rightarrow$ Intro mn. 137, 237 ff.). The term discrimination is defined as follows:

> Discrimination is any distinction, exclusion, restriction or preference or other differential treatment that is directly or indirectly based on prohibited grounds of discrimination, and which has the intention or effect of nullifying or impairing the recognition, enjoyment or exercise, on an equal footing, of human rights and fundamental freedoms in the political, economic, social, cultural or any other field of public life.[64]

29   The definition of harassment related to SDG 10.3 covers any form of discrimination when it is also based on prohibited grounds of discrimination and in particular may take the form of words, gestures or actions, which tend to annoy, alarm, abuse, demean, intimidate, belittle, humiliate or embarrass another or which create an intimidating, hostile or offensive environment. Although it is generally a pattern of behaviour, harassment can take the form of a single incident.[65]

30   The proposed survey module guided by the OHCHR recommends the use of the following list to measure the SDG 10.3

1. SEX: such as being a woman or a man
2. AGE: such as being perceived to be too young or too old
3. DISABILITY OR HEALTH STATUS: such as having difficulty in seeing, hearing, walking or moving, concentrating or communicating, having a disease or other health conditions and no reasonable accommodation provided for it
4. ETHNICITY, COLOUR OR LANGUAGE: such as skin colour or physical appearance, ethnic origin or way of dressing, culture, traditions, native language, indigenous status, or being of African descent
5. MIGRATION STATUS: such as nationality or national origin, country of birth, refugees, asylum seekers, migrant status, undocumented migrants or stateless persons

---

[62] For example, the right to life (Art. 6), right to liberty and security of person (Art. 9), right to freedom of thought, conscience and religion (Art. 18).

[63] Joseph and Castan, *The International Covenant on Civil and Political Rights – Cases, Materials and Commentary* (2013), 3 f.

[64] UN Stats, https://unstats.un.org/sdgs/metadata/files/Metadata-10-03-01.pdf; see Art. 1 of the International Convention on the Elimination of All Forms of Racial Discrimination (ICERD); Art. 1 of the Convention on the Elimination of All Forms of Discrimination against Women (CEDAW); Art. 2 of the Convention on the Rights of Persons with Disabilities (CRPD); General comment No. 18: Non-discrimination of the Human Rights Committee (paras. 6 and 7); and General Comment No. 20: Non-discrimination in economic, social and cultural rights (art. 2, para. 2, of the International Covenant on Economic, Social and Cultural Rights) (para. 7).

[65] UN Stats, https://unstats.un.org/sdgs/metadata/files/Metadata-10-03-01.pdf: which refers to General Comment No. 20 of the Committee on Economic, Social and Cultural Rights, and United Nations Secretary-General's bulletin (ST/SGB/2008/5) on Prohibition of discrimination, harassment, including sexual harassment, and abuse of authority.

6. SOCIO-ECONOMIC STATUS: such as wealth or education level, being perceived to be from a lower or different social or economic group or class, land or home ownership or not
7. GEOGRAPHIC LOCATION OR PLACE OF RESIDENCE: such as living in urban or rural areas, formal or informal settlements
8. RELIGION: such as having or not a religion or religious beliefs
9. MARITAL AND FAMILY STATUS: such as being single, married, divorced, widowed, pregnant, with or without children, orphan or born from unmarried parents
10. SEXUAL ORIENTATION OR GENDER IDENTITY: such as being attracted to person of the same sex, self-identifying differently from sex assigned at birth or as being either sexually, bodily and/or gender diverse
11. POLITICAL OPINION: such as expressing political views, defending the rights of others, being a member or not of a political party or trade union[66]

Against this background, it might be obvious that easily applicable and suitable **31** programmes are not at hand. It remains a question of the specific political realm and its context points to discriminatory laws and policies (SDG 10.3). The question of discriminatory laws are depending on the specific context of a country and its fundaments. The world is lacking a world government and even perfect rules should be criticised coming from such an institution which would apply those perfect rules in order equilibrate the question of inequality mirroring history, situation, chances, and brutal suppression.[67] Poverty is seen as capability deprivation as it diminishes political, social and economic choices of both individuals and societies (→ Goal 1).[68] The increase of the development of human happiness and social progress, however, would be likely to decrease the status of inequality (→ Goal 3).[69]

The relationship turns out to be of an inverse proportionality. SDG 10, as intended to **32** reduce inequalities both within and among countries, is further closely related to the concept of equity.[70] Equity as a broader concept, in the author's understanding, is based on the distributive justice by Aristoteles (→ Intro mn. 227 ff., Goal 5 mn. 11, Goal 16 mn. 9, 23). Inequalities within states must therefore be tackled on the basis of fundamental rights for each individual within the framework of equity. The focus here is on the empowerment of minority groups and vulnerable people, especially women, children, indigenous people[71] as well as disabled and older persons. The empowerment of these groups in their rights means that they have fair access to important resources of everyday life, both material resources and political and social resources, which are particularly anchored in the ICCPR. As a result, equity and equality of opportunities are achieved and fundamental social distortions, in other words inequalities, are lastingly reduced. Thus, the aim should be that everyone can make use of his or her economic, social, cultural as well as civil and political rights and enforce these rights in an equitable manner through institutions based on the *rule of law*, so that inner-state, social inequali-

---

[66] UN Stats, https://unstats.un.org/sdgs/metadata/files/Metadata-10-03-01.pdf.

[67] Havercroft et al., 'Decolonising global constitutionalism' (2020) 9(1) *Global Constitutionalism*, 1-6.

[68] Sen, *Development as Freedom* (1999), 87 f., 92 ff.

[69] Galbraith, *Inequality and Instability, A Study of the World Economy Just Before the Great Crisis* (2012), 13.

[70] Oestreich, 'SDG 10: Reduce inequality in and among countries' (2018) 37 *Social Alternatives*, 34 (36 ff.).

[71] UN, *World Social Report 2020 – Inequality in a rapidly changing world* (2020), 97 f.; see also ILO Convention No. 169 Convention Concerning Indigenous and Tribal Peoples in Independent Countries (1989); A/RES/61/295, *United Nations Declaration on the Rights of Indigenous Peoples* (2 October 2007).

ties and injustices are reduced (→ Goal 16 mn. 22 ff.).[72] At the heart of realising and strengthening political and civil rights lies the objective of reinforcing in particular the rights of citizens vis-à-vis the state. The achievement of equal opportunities for all and the subsequent equality in the outcome requires the fundamental granting of political and civil rights to each individual, especially in the event of misconduct by the state in this regard.

33   For a sustainable strengthening and establishment of equality, or rather to tackle inequality, it is in fact essential that not only the ESCR of each individual citizen are met by merely material satisfaction of their needs. The material provision of e.g. schools (right to education) or hospitals (right to health) is not necessarily sustainable in the long-term, as there is a risk that the general situation of citizens will deteriorate again if state governments make mistakes in this respect or if these substantive guarantees are poorly maintained.[73] Thus, accessibility to institutions, participation in the sense that people can influence political issues with their will, and accountability of institutions in the countries must be ensured. In addition, it is necessary to look at the conditions that are crucial for the existence and potential growth of happiness as a factor in combating inequality, such as income and a good environmental setting (→ Goal 3).[74]

34   Political and civil rights, especially vis-à-vis the state, sustainable equality in all its spheres may be reached andcitizens will be allowed to hold their governments accountable when their rights are being violated (e.g. right to education, right to an adequate standard of living, etc.) and to assert their rights before an independent judiciary.[75] SDG 10 and the objective of reduced inequalities between individuals within a state is therefore essential to ensure and maintain access to fair justice and legal systems (→ Goal 16 mn. 22 ff.).[76]

35   The obligations of states to ensure the implementation of each individual's economic, social and cultural rights enshrined in the ICESCR are profoundly enlightened within the chapters of SDG 1, SDG 2, SDG 3, SDG 4, SDG 5 and SDG 6.[77] In this context, it is crucial that the implementation of economic, social and cultural rights are pursued with equal importance and urgency as civil and political rights. SDG 10 can be seen as the binding link between ESCR and civil and political rights emphasising their equally essential role for the establishment of sustainable equality.[78] For the successful implementation and strengthening of these rights, it is essential to ensure and support the political representation of minorities and other vulnerable groups at the political level.[79]

36   The empowerment of rights of the most vulnerable is related to the issue of social exclusion or inclusion, which is examined in the context of poverty eradication in SDG 1.

---

[72] Oestreich, 'SDG 10: Reduce inequality in and among countries' (2018) 37 *Social Alternatives*, 34 (35 f.); CESR, *From Disparity to Dignity – Tackling economic inequality through the Sustainable Development Goals* (2016), 1 f.
[73] Oestreich, 'SDG 10: Reduce inequality in and among countries' (2018) 37 *Social Alternatives*, 34 (36 f.).
[74] Helliwell et al., *World Happiness Report 2020* (2020); Van Praag and Ferrer-i-Carbonell, 'Inequalitiy and Happiness' in Nolan and Salverda, and Smeeding (eds), *The Oxford Handbook of Economic Inequality* (2011), 364-83; Baland et al., *The Handbook of Economic Development and Institutions* (2020).
[75] Oestreich, 'SDG 10: Reduce inequality in and among countries' (2018) 37 *Social Alternatives*, 34 (37).
[76] CESR, *From Disparity to Dignity – Tackling economic inequality through the Sustainable Development Goals* (2016), 1.
[77] See here the FIAN International, *Maastricht Principles on Extraterritorial Obligations of States in the Area of Economic, Social and Cultural Rights* (2013).
[78] Oestreich, 'SDG 10: Reduce inequality in and among countries' (2018) 37 *Social Alternatives*, 34 (38).
[79] Pandey et al., *SDG 10 – Reduce Inequality Within and Among Countries* (2020), 38.

Particular attention must be paid to the existing social, economic and political in- **37**
equalities between women and girls and men and boys. As one of the largest vulnerable
groups affected by inequalities within countries and within societies, SDG 5 presents
and analyses in depth the inequality of women and girls in terms of gender equality and
the empowerment of women (SDG 10.2).[80]

In order to reduce inequalities between people, an environment should be created **38**
that provides equal opportunities and access for all people, especially children.[81]

Inequalities within states on a social, economic and political level between individu- **39**
als, but rather between different (ethnic and social)groups are often the cause of internal
conflicts and violent clashes.[82]

Apel classifies inequalities between various groups within the society as so-called hor- **40**
izontal inequalities, while inequalities between individuals are classified as vertical inequalities.[83] In this context, inequalities between different groups within society play a
far greater role in the emergence of inner-state conflicts and violent clashes. Factors that
drive these conflicts are among others the scope of inequalities between groups, ethnic
and social injustices and discrimination at the political level (→ Goal 16 mn. 36,
44 ff.).[84] 'The Gini coefficient, however, measures vertical inequality, i.e. income inequality between individuals, and thus fails to capture the conflict-inducing disparities between different societal groups' (→ Goal 8 mn. 15).[85]

Moreover, inequalities within cities raise the risk of violence and conflicts where large **41**
numbers of people live in a confined space.[86] Here, SDG 10 reveals strong connections
to SDG 11.

2. Inequalities between Countries

With estimates show[ing] that just eight men own the same wealth as the poorest **42**
half of the world,'[87] this indicates a severe economic asymmetry affecting all societies
worlwide.

Economic inequalities among countries in the world lead to fundamental distortions **43**
in the allocation of global resources and in the allocation of wealth and well-being, thus
affecting the well-being of whole societies at large.[88] As a result of inequalities, poverty is
one of the greatest sufferings of humankind nowadays.[89]

SDG 10 focuses on reduced inequality between countries based on SDG 10.5, SDG **44**
10.6 and SDG 10.7. The wording of 'reduced' indicates that no elimination of inequality

---

[80] https://www.unwomen.org/en/news/in-focus/women-and-the-sdgs/sdg-10-reduced-inequalities.

[81] UN, *World Social Report 2020 – Inequality in a rapidly changing world* (2020), 153 ff.; UNICEF, SDG
10: Addressing inequalities to leave no child behind, https://www.unicef.org/media/64366/file/sdg10_2pag
er_final.pdf.

[82] Bahgat et al., *Inequality and Armed Conflict: Evidence and Data* (2017), 1 ff.; Knowledge Platform –
Security & Rule of Law, https://www.kpsrl.org/blog/the-injustice-of-inequality-and-its-links-to-violence.

[83] Apel, 'Inequality in development: the 2030 Agenda, SDG 10 and the role of redistribution' (2020) 92
Real-World Econ. Rev, 228 (228 ff); see also Bahgat et al., *Inequality and Armed Conflict: Evidence and Data*
(2017), 1, 11; McNaughton, 'Vertical inequalities: are the SDGs and human rights up to the challenge?'
(2017) 21 *Int. J. Hum. Right,* 1050 (1050 ff.).

[84] Bahgat et al., *Inequality and Armed Conflict: Evidence and Data* (2017), 10 ff.; Bircan and Brück and
Vothknecht, *Violent Conflict and Inequality* (2010), 17 ff.; Esteban, 'Inequality and Conflict' (2018) 27 *J.
Income Distrib.,* 1 ff.

[85] Bircan and Brück and Vothknecht, *Violent Conflict and Inequality* (2010), 17 ff.

[86] https://www.weforum.org/agenda/2020/03/what-are-the-causes-of-urban-violence-inequality/.

[87] Oxfam, *An economy for the 99 % - Oxfam Briefing Paper* (2017), 1; see also Oxfam, *An economy for
the 1 %* (2016), 1: 'The richest 1% now have more wealth than the rest of the world combined'.

[88] UN, *World Social Report 2020 – Inequality in a rapidly changing world* (2020), 20.

[89] UN, *World Social Report 2020 – Inequality in a rapidly changing world* (2020), 21 ff.

is envisaged to realise. This also applies to economic inequality between countries where it is supposed to be 'that some inequality is inevitable'[90], meaning that SDG 10 does not pledge for an idealistic equal economic system.[91] Though, extreme economic inequality between countries 'is not inevitable' since '[i]t is created, perpetuated and exacerbated by laws, policies and practices of the sort that have dominated the global policy agenda of the last three decades'.[92] Thus, international law and current international regulations concerning the (re)distribution of goods and wealth (and hence the benefits of growth) lay in the focus of the objective to reduce inequalities between countries on the global scene.[93]

45   Even though 'there is no specific link to a right to development in SDG 10',[94] international law might be taken as one of the legal resources the tackling of inequality is based on.[95] The former Independent Expert on the right to development stated that 'equality is essential to any programme aimed at implementing human rights, such as the right to development'.[96]

a. SDG 10.5, SDG 10.6, SDG 10.7 and States' Obligations

46   To tackle economic inequalities between countries, it is noteworthy that '[d]evelopment or economic growth does not automatically reduce inequalities. The reduction of inequalities needs to be strategically implemented'.[97]

47   SDG 10.5 aims to 'improve the regulation and monitoring of global financial markets and institutions and strengthen the implementation of such regulations'.[98]

> According to the OECD financial deregulation and the corresponding expansions in bank credit and stock markets have been linked to a more unequal distribution of income,[99] via unequal bank lending, unequal distribution of stock market wealth and the high concentration of financial sector workers at the top end of the earnings distribution.[100]

48   States therefore have a special position in the regulation and control of financial markets, not least from a human rights perspective. The obligation of states to safeguard fundamental human rights also includes protection against abuse of the financial markets by third parties, as for example through 'predatory lending or financial speculation

---

[90] Oestreich, 'SDG 10: Reduce inequality in and among countries' (2018) 37 *Social Alternatives*, 34 (35).

[91] Oestreich, 'SDG 10: Reduce inequality in and among countries' (2018) 37 *Social Alternatives*, 34 (35).

[92] Donald, 'Will inequality get left behind in the 2030 Agenda?' in Adams et al. (eds), *Spotlight on Sustainable Development – Report by the Reflection Group on the 2030 Agenda for Sustainable Development* (2016), 80 (83).

[93] And for now, it might be almost four decades; Donald, 'Will inequality get left behind in the 2030 Agenda?' in in Adams et al. (eds), *Spotlight on Sustainable Development – Report by the Reflection Group on the 2030 Agenda for Sustainable Development* (2016), 80 (83); Though, the effectiveness of redistribution on the international scene is controversy, see Knoop, *Understanding Economic Inequality – Bigger Pies and Just Deserts* (2020), 44 ff.

[94] Oestreich, 'SDG 10: Reduce inequality in and among countries' (2018) 37 *Social Alternatives*, 34 (39).

[95] Oestreich, 'SDG 10: Reduce inequality in and among countries' (2018) 37 *Social Alternatives*, 34 (39).

[96] A/HRC/39/51, *Report of the Special Rapporteur on the right to development*, 20 July 2018, para. 21; see further Oestreich, 'SDG 10: Reduce inequality in and among countries' (2018) 37 *Social Alternatives*, 34 (38 f.).

[97] Apel, 'Inequality in development: the 2030 Agenda, SDG 10 and the role of redistribution' (2020) 92 *Real-World Econ. Rev*, 228 (231).

[98] See for economic impact of target 10.5: https://stats.unctad.org/Dgff2016/prosperity/goal10/target_10_5.html.

[99] Cournède and Denk and Hoeller, *Finance and Inclusive Growth – OECD Economic Policy Paper* (2015), 28 f.

[100] CESR, *From Disparity to Dignity – Tackling economic inequality through the Sustainable Development Goals* (2016), 18.

in food and housing markets'.[101] Furthermore, finance markets' regulation by states is ought to prevent global financial crises and their consequences which lead to higher inequality in developing countries including severe human rights violations based on the growing inequalities.[102]

States' extraterritorial obligation to respect and protect human rights based on international law breaks through several globally relevant areas and those need to be tackled on a common and cooperative basis between the states. Examples range from transboundary tax abuse to international tax competition and international trade and trade agreements.[103] In this context, the representation of developing countries within international economic and financial institutions (SDG 10.6)[104] is crucial to enhance the impact on and participation of developing countries in the global economic system. However, there is a lack of accuracy in the concrete implementation and measurement of SDG 10.6.[105]   **49**

Global distortions and inequalities between countries are also a cause for migration and the search of people for a better life in developed countries. Yet, it is necessary to differentiate between various types of migration which can also serve as an instrument for reducing global inequalities, for example by encouraging well-educated workers to migrate to developing countries in order to bring about innovation and economic recovery there.[106] This is one of various possible policy approaches to facilitate orderly, safe, regular and responsible migration as in line with SDG 10.7.[107]   **50**

b. International Trade and Inequality

The omnipresent and large economic differences and inequalities between industrialised and developing countries also have an impact on world trade.[108] The World Trade Organisation (WTO)[109], the members of which are both industrialised and developing countries with different political approaches, offers various instruments for the better integration of developing countries into the world market and thus for the reduction of   **51**

---

[101] CESR, *From Disparity to Dignity – Tackling economic inequality through the Sustainable Development Goals* (2016), 19; see also Art. 10 of the United Nations Guiding Principles on Business and Human Rights.

[102] CESR, *From Disparity to Dignity – Tackling economic inequality through the Sustainable Development Goals* (2016), 19.

[103] CESR, *From Disparity to Dignity – Tackling economic inequality through the Sustainable Development Goals* (2016), 29 ff.

[104] See for the political and economic structure of SDG 10.6: https://stats.unctad.org/Dgff2016/pros perity/goal10/target_10_6.html; Novitz and Pieraccini, 'Agenda 2030 and the Sustainable Development Goals: Responsive, Inclusive, Pariticipatory and Representative Decision-Making?' (2020) in Pieraccini and Novitz (eds), *Legal Perspectives on Sustainability*, 39 (54); https://sdg.humanrights.dk/en/targets2?targ et=10.6.

[105] McNaughton, 'Vertical inequalities: are the SDGs and human rights up to the challenge?' (2017) 21 *Int. J. Hum. Right*, 1050 (1060); see SDG 16.8.

[106] UN, *World Social Report 2020 – Inequality in a rapidly changing world* (2020), 133 ff.; Bastia, 'Migration and Inequality – An introduction' in Bastia (ed), *Migration and Inequality* (2013), 1 (1 ff.); United Nations International Organisation for Migration, *Migration and the Agenda 2030 – A Guide for Practitioners* (2018); ODI and Swiss Agency for Development and Cooperation, *Migration and the 2030 Agenda for Sustainable Development* (2018); https://sdg.humanrights.dk/en/targets2?target=10.7; McGregor, 'Migration, the MDGS and SDGs – Context and complexity' in Bastia and Skeldon (eds), *Routledge Handbook of Migration and Development* (2020), 284 (284 ff.); Milanovic, *Global Inequality – A New Approach for the Age of Globalization* (2016), 118 ff.

[107] UN, *World Social Report 2020 – Inequality in a rapidly changing world* (2020), 130 ff.

[108] Example agreement between developing and developed states: APC-EU Cotonou Partnership Agreement (2000).

[109] WTO, Agreement Establishing the Multilateral Trade Organization (1994).

global inequalities. In line with SDG 10.a, the special and differential treatment clauses in almost all existing WTO agreements are in the foreground. The aim of these clauses is to facilitate the participation of developing countries in global trade.[110] These provisions can be subdivided into those that

(1) grant transitional periods to developing country Members to comply with certain WTO obligations,
(2) allow greater flexibility to developing-country Members in making commitments or using policy instruments,
(3) encourage the granting of technical assistance to developing-country Members,
(4) aim at increasing the trade opportunities for developing-country Members and
(5) provide that developed Members should safeguard the interest of developing-country Members.[111]

52   For the facilitated access of developing countries to markets of developed countries, the '1979 GATT Decision on Differential and More Favorable Treatment, Reciprocity and Fuller Participation of Developing Countries'[112] (Enabling Clause[113]) represents probably the most common special and differential treatment to grant those accesses without violating the most favoured nation (MFN)[114] treatment obligation of Art. I:1 GATT. This clause constitutes one of the strongest instruments within WTO law to facilitate access of developing countries to new markets while not requiring the granting countries to equally grant this simplification directly to all other countries with which they are bound by the agreements under WTO law (principle of MFN treatment).[115] By integrating the enabling clause into the WTO system, WTO members are almost literally invited to derogate from the MFN treatment of Art. I:1 GATT to make use of the special and differential treatment towards developing countries.[116]

53   Other instrumental measures within the WTO framework are the Bali package (2013), seeking the reduction of international trade barriers[117] and the Nairobi package (2015) including

> six Ministerial Decisions on agriculture, cotton and issues related to least-developed countries. These include a commitment to abolish export subsidies for farm exports [...], public stockholding for food security purposes, a special safeguard mechanism for developing countries, [...] measures related to cotton [...] [,] preferential treatment for least developed countries (LDCs) in the area of services and the criteria for determining whether exports from LDCs may benefit from trade preferences.[118] (→ Goal 10 mn. 91)

---

[110] Van den Bossche and Zdouc, *The Law and Policy of the World Trade Organization* (2017), 123 f.

[111] Van den Bossche and Prévost, *Essentials of WTO Law* (2016), 253; see further: Chaisse and Lin, *International Economic Law and Governance – Essays in Honour of Mitsuo Matsushita* (2016).

[112] Van den Bossche and Zdouc, *The Law and Policy of the World Trade Organization* (2017), 321.

[113] Para. 1 of the Enabling Clause: 'Notwithstanding the provisions of Article I of the General Agreement, contracting parties may accord differential and more favourable treatment to developing countries, without according to such treatment to other contracting parties'; further, Art. XX GATT (1994) entails conditions for the use of special and differential treatments insofar its 'chapeau' (Introductory paragraph of Art. XX GATT (1994)) is met.

[114] https://www.wto.org/english/thewto_e/whatis_e/tif_e/fact2_e.htm: 'Under the WTO agreements, countries cannot normally discriminate between their trading partners. Grant someone a special favour (such as a lower customs duty rate for one of their products) and you have to do the same for all other WTO members. [...] It is so important that it is the first article of the General Agreement on Tariffs and Trade (GATT), which governs trade in goods'.

[115] Van den Bossche and Zdouc, *The Law and Policy of the World Trade Organization* (2017), 321 ff.

[116] Van den Bossche and Zdouc, *The Law and Policy of the World Trade Organization* (2017), 322.

[117] https://www.wto.org/english/thewto_e/minist_e/mc9_e/balipackage_e.htm.

[118] https://www.wto.org/english/news_e/news15_e/mc10_19dec15_e.htm.

The Trade and Development Board of the United Nations of the United Nations 54
Conference on Trade and Development (UNCTAD) analyses the impact of trade policies
on inequalities by summing up that

> [t]rade reforms have contributed to reducing income inequality between countries, yet they have
> also been accompanied by polarization in the distribution of income in some places, with significant
> increases in within-country income inequality. The latter is possibly the main cause behind the cur-
> rent reaction against international trade. Trade is a catalyst for economic growth and development.
> Accordingly, to respond to inequality, rather than focusing exclusively on productivity and economic
> growth, policymakers need to focus on encouraging trade and on ensuring that the benefits brought
> by international trade become more inclusive and responsive to the imperatives under the Sustain-
> able Development Goals. Taking as a point of departure a set of guiding questions received from
> member States, this note discusses trade policies and their impact on inequalities.[119]

III. A Specific Look at the Indicators

Before analysing the indicators, it is useful to look at the targets of SDG 10 and 55
their effectiveness in terms of implementation. Regarding SDG 10.1, it is already striking
that, although it aims at the target of income growth for the bottom 40 per cent of
the population, no other income groups are mentioned, such as the top 10 per cent of
the population. Thus, the income growth of the bottom 40 per cent is not related to
other income groups in society. SDG 10.1 is already achieved when the income of the
lower 40 per cent grows faster than the national average, but the inequalities between
the lower income group and higher income groups are disregarded. Accordingly, a
stronger increase in the income of the higher income population ultimately increases
the inequality between these groups within a country despite the demanded growth
for the bottom 40 per cent. Consequently, inequalities in income between groups at
horizontal level are not reduced. Besides, it is questionable how effective SDG 10.1 is
due to its direct link to economic growth, since in the absence of economic growth, the
growth of the income of the bottom 40 per cent also tends towards zero.[120] The indicator
10.1.1 shows a similar approach and does merely feature the growth rates of household
expenditure or income per capita among the bottom 40 per cent of the population as
reference point of measurement.

> Rather than using more precise metrics (such as the Gini coefficient or Palma Ratio) to measure
> unequal economic outcomes, decision-makers led by the World Bank chose the target of boosting the
> income of the bottom 40 per cent faster than the average. Amongst other limitations, this target in
> no way measures income or wealth growth at the top, which is the leading determinant of domestic
> economic inequality.[121]

SDG 10.2 and SDG 10.3 show a similar degree of vagueness in their formulation. 56
These SDGs do not contain any measurable reference points that could represent their
successful implementation.[122] However, it is to be welcomed that SDG 10.2 is a precise

---

[119] UNCTAD, TD/B/66/4, *Trade policies and their impact on inequalities* (2019), Executive Summary.

[120] McNaughton, 'Vertical inequalities: are the SDGs and human rights up to the challenge?' (2017)
21 *Int. J. Hum. Right*, 1050 (1058); McNaughton notes: 'The target is, in fact, concerned with poverty
reduction, rather than reduction of vertical equality. [...] It is in fact a *means* for poverty reduction rather
than a benchmark for a reduction in inequalities.'

[121] CESR, *From Disparity to Dignity – Tackling economic inequality through the Sustainable Development
Goals* (2016), 34.

[122] McNaughton, 'Vertical inequalities: are the SDGs and human rights up to the challenge?' (2017) 21
Int. J. Hum. Right, 1050 (1059); McNaughton notes: 'As a result, it is not clear how progress toward the
target [10.2] can be measured, nor how it can be determined when the target is met. If countries merely
'promote' but do not 'achieve' inclusion, is this sufficient to meet this target?'.

listing of various human characteristics, irrespective of the fact that all people are to be treated equally (irrespective of age, sex, disability, race, ethnicity, origin, religion or economic or other status).

> Yet, the indicator proposed to measure it ([10.2.1] the proportion of people living below 50 per cent of median income, disaggregated by age group, sex and persons with disabilities) does not even list five of the groups in the target and is a very limited measure of 'social, economic and political inclusion'. Meanwhile, the indicator set for Goal 10 neglects to robustly measure economic inequality at all.[123]

57   Moreover, the indicator lacks relevant reference to other groups of people which is required to exactly measure the targeted inequalities and their possible reduction. The mere proportion of people living below 50 per cent of median income classified by age, sex and persons with disabilities has again more to do with poverty than with inequalities.[124]

58   With respect to SDG 10.3, indicator 10.3.1[125] is likewise based on figures concerning the proportion of the population which have reported their experience of discrimination. International human rights law is cited as a reference point for discrimination, which provides a legal framework, but it is questionable to what extent it is effective to record discrimination through personal reporting by the individuals concerned. In countries with severe political discrimination, it is not unlikely that only a small number of those affected will report such discrimination to the relevant authorities.[126]

59   Equally, SDG 10.4 and its indicator 10.4.1 are vague in their formulation and their implementation. There is a complete lack of description of policies and steps to be taken at political level. The mere adoption of 'policies' in the areas of fiscal, wage and social security does not guarantee that the policies are sufficiently implemented and that they ultimately reduce inequality. On the other side, SDG 10.4 is improved by the indicator selected: 'Labor share of GDP, comprising wages and social protection transfers, which measures one aspect of vertical inequality'.[127]

60   Indicator 10.5.1 is rather short and only refers to 'financial soundness indicators' which are provided by the International Monetary Fund 'with aim of supporting analysis and assessing strengths and vulnerabilities of financial systems'.[128]

61   Indicator 10.6.1[129] provides a measurable figure to point out in how far developing countries are represented in international countries. Though, 'it fails to incentivize or pinpoint the steps that specific actors need to take to reach it, and so all can easily absolve themselves of responsibility if progress is disappointing or non-existent'.[130]

---

[123] CESR, *From Disparity to Dignity – Tackling economic inequality through the Sustainable Development Goals* (2016), 34.

[124] McNaughton, 'Vertical inequalities: are the SDGs and human rights up to the challenge?' (2017) 21 *Int. J. Hum. Right*, 1050 (1059).

[125] 10.3.1: 'Proportion of the population reporting having personally felt discriminated against or harassed within the previous 12 months on the basis of a grounds of discrimination prohibited under international human rights law'.

[126] McNaughton, 'Vertical inequalities: are the SDGs and human rights up to the challenge?' (2017) 21 *Int. J. Hum. Right*, 1050 (1059 f.).

[127] McNaughton, 'Vertical inequalities: are the SDGs and human rights up to the challenge?' (2017) 21 *Int. J. Hum. Right*, 1050 (1060).

[128] https://data.imf.org/?sk=51B096FA-2CD2-40C2-8D09-0699CC1764DA; International Monetary Fund, *Financial Soundness Indicators Compilation Guide* (2019); UN STATS.

[129] Indicator 10.6.1: 'proportion of members and voting rights of developing countries in international organizations'; see indicator 16.8.1: 'Proportion of members and voting rights of developing countries in international organizations'.

[130] CESR, *From Disparity to Dignity – Tackling economic inequality through the Sustainable Development Goals* (2016), 34.

SDG 10.7 and indicators 10.7.1 and 10.7.2 do not directly apply to reducing inequali-　62
ties between countries. They rather seem to better fit to SDG 8 and the aim to establish
decent work.[131]

The calculation of the indicator 10.a.1 will allow observing on how many products　63
developing countries and LDCs will have free access to developed countries markets.
Compared to the tariff rates applicable to other countries, this indicator allows an
assessment of the extent to which special and differential treatment has been granted in
import duties. Tariffs are defined to be customs duties on merchandise imports, levied
either on an ad valorem basis (percentage of value) or on a specific basis (e.g. $7 per
100 kg).[132] Tariffs can be used to create a price advantage for similar locally-produced
goods and for raising government revenues. Trade remedy measures and taxes are not
considered to be tariffs.

Indicator 10.c.1 gives a view on the remittance costs as a proportion of the amount　64
remitted to be able to identify if both components of SDG 10.c are fulfilled: Firstly, '3
percent or less of the transaction costs of migrant remittances' must prevail.

> This transaction cost should be intended as "Global average total cost of sending $200 (or equivalent
> in local sending currency) and expressed as % of amount sent". This indicator is readily available
> and published on a quarterly basis by the World Bank in the Remittance Prices Worldwide database,
> which covers 365 country corridors, from 48 sending to 105 receiving countries. The second compo-
> nent is to eliminate corridor where cost is 5% or higher.

Secondly, 'remittance corridors with costs higher than 5 per cent' must be eliminated.　65
International remittance transfer means a

> cross-border person-to-person payment of relatively low value. The transfers are typically recurrent
> payments by migrant workers (who send money to their families in their home country every
> month). In the report, the term "remittance transfer" is used for simplicity (i.e. it is assumed the
> transfer is international).

A money transfer operator (MTO) is defined a　　　　　　　　　　　　　　66

> non-deposit taking payment service provider where the service involves payment per transfer (or
> possibly payment for a set or series of transfers) by the sender to the payment service provider (for
> example, by cash or bank transfer).[133]

C. Interdependences of SDG 10

Long-term effects of the SARS-CoV-2 pandemic on the distribution of income and　67
wealth at this point in time can hardly be determined. 'The stock market plunge in
March 2020 initially led to a huge destruction of wealth that has hit the rich but
recovered quickly after central banks around the world began to inject fresh money
into the economy, driving stock prices back up.'[134] By contrast, the massive job losses
caused by the pandemic and resulting closures are likely to increase levels of inequality
in future which is even more expected by the ILO for workers at small and medium-

---

[131] McNaughton, 'Vertical inequalities: are the SDGs and human rights up to the challenge?' (2017) 21
Int. J. Hum. Right, 1050 (1061); see for indicators 10.a.1, 10.b.1 and 10.c.1: McNaughton, 'Vertical inequalities: are the SDGs and human rights up to the challenge?' (2017) 21 *Int. J. Hum. Right*, 1050 (1061 ff.).

[132] UN Stats: Tariff data for the calculation of this indicator are retrieved from ITC (MacMap), http://w
ww.macmap.org/; WTO (IDB) - http://tao.wto.org - and UNCTAD (TRAINS) databases.

[133] https://w3.unece.org/SDG/en/Indicator?id=126.

[134] Martens and Ellmers and Pokorny on behalf of Global Policy Watch, *COVID-19 and the SDGs, The
impact of the coronavirus pandemic on the global sustainability agenda* (2020), 9.

sized enterprises (SME), precarious workers and day labourers. Socio-economic factors significantly influence how badly individuals are affected by the crisis.[135]

68   Poverty as an expression of extreme inequality reveals the outstanding interlinkage between SDG 10 and SDG 1.[136] This means not only a lack of economic performance but also exclusion from many social areas and a 'deprivation of capabilities and choices'.[137] To achieve equality, poverty must be fought and defeated. At the same time, poverty can only be tackled through equal opportunities.

69   Achieving 'Quality Education' and equal access to education (SDG 4) could be a key driver to achieve SDG 10, which represents an important interconnection between those SDGs.[138] SDG 4 focuses on quality and equality of education[139] and is therefore also more specific than SDG 10. As a lack of education leads to inequalities later in life,[140] education constitutes a powerful factor in the fight against inequality.[141] Education creates human capital, which has a long-term positive impact on income.[142] If this development is faster among previously disadvantaged people, it will contribute to the fight against inequality[143] and can thus contribute to people's empowerment[144] and a means for opportunities for economic and social advancement.[145] However, differences and inequalities in education often exist even within countries. The quality or very existence of educational opportunities most often depends on income or gender.[146]

70   Education is thus in itself a factor in combating inequalities And, at the same time, an indicator of existing inequalities (where it is non-existent or limited). The reduction of inequalities and the provision of education are interdependent and may positively interact.[147]

71   Moreover, SDG 10 is strongly related to SDG 5.[148] While SDG 5 focuses on the equal rights of all women, SDG 10 is not defined in terms of gender. According to UN WOMEN, 'women earn 24 per cent less than men, with varied gaps between countries.

---

[135] See Martens and Ellmers and Pokorny on behalf of Global Policy Watch, *COVID-19 and the SDGs, The impact of the coronavirus pandemic on the global sustainability agenda* (2020), 9.

[136] Van Soest et al., 'Analysing interactions among Sustainable Development Goals with Integrated Assessment Models' (2019) 1 *Global Transitions,* 210 (213).

[137] Food and Agriculture Organization (FAO), Legal measures to eradicate rural poverty 7(2) *Legal Brief For Parliaments in Africa.*

[138] Van Soest et al., 'Analysing interactions among Sustainable Development Goals with Integrated Assessment Models' (2019) 1 *Global Transitions,* 210 (213).

[139] Unterhalter, 'The Many Meanings of Quality Education: Politics of Targets and Indicators in SDG4' (2019) 10 *Global Policy,* 39 (39).

[140] Department of Economic & Social Affairs, *How well are the links between education and other sustainable development goals covered in UN flagship reports? A contribution to the study of the science-policy interface on education in the UN system* (2015), 13.

[141] Department of Economic & Social Affairs, *How well are the links between education and other sustainable development goals covered in UN flagship reports? A contribution to the study of the science-policy interface on education in the UN system* (2015), 13.

[142] World Bank, *World Development Report 2018* (2018), 41.

[143] World Bank, *World Development Report 2018* (2018), 41.

[144] Department of Economic & Social Affairs, *How well are the links between education and other sustainable development goals covered in UN flagship reports? A contribution to the study of the science-policy interface on education in the UN system* (2015), 13.

[145] World Bank, *World Development Report 2018* (2018), 42.

[146] Department of Economic & Social Affairs, *How well are the links between education and other sustainable development goals covered in UN flagship reports? A contribution to the study of the science-policy interface on education in the UN system* (2015), 14.

[147] Van Soest et al., 'Analysing interactions among Sustainable Development Goals with Integrated Assessment Models' (2019) 1 *Global Transitions,* 210 (213).

[148] Van Soest et al., 'Analysing interactions among Sustainable Development Goals with Integrated Assessment Models' (2019) 1 *Global Transitions,* 210 (213).

They are also more likely than men to be in vulnerable employment, with up to 75 per cent of women's jobs being informal or unprotected in developing countries.'[149] Moreover, women make up 83 per cent of domestic workers with no right to a minimum wage.[150] Women are often legally discriminated against, either by denying them rights or by failing to adequately prosecute and punish crimes against them.[151]

As a result, women are mostly economically excluded and frequently are victims of   72 discriminatory laws. The social and economic inclusion of women and the abolition of discriminatory laws therefore leads to a reduction in discrimination against women and girls, resulting in greater equality within countries (SDG 5).[152]

Similarly, it holds an important interrelation with SDG 16, as equality can only be   73 achieved through equality before the law and the administration of justice.[153] The *rule of law* is thus a fundamental factor in the fight against inequality.

D. Jurisprudential Significance of SDG 10

Notwithstanding some perceptible positive evidence of a reduction in inequality   74 'such as reducing relative income inequality in some countries and preferential trade status benefiting lower income countries, inequality still persists in all forms'[154] and is, due to the SARS-CoV-2 pandemic, increasing within and between countries. Besides, international migration 'is a multidimensional reality of major relevance for the development of countries of origin, transit and destination'[155] and is shifting socio-economic structures more and more due to the higher rate of global conflicts , thereby decreasing the freedom and self-determination of many vulnerable groups and individuals.

Transformative pathways that generate a world of more equal opportunities 'requires   75 protection of liberty and other basic freedoms for all and cautioned that denial of civic space makes inequality less visible.' In particular, the participation of women must be fortified to assure the transformation needed. It is remarkable that even today '[r]esilience in LDCs, LLDCs and Africa is threatened by inequality and unemployment across populations and political-economic policies being rolled out to reduce government budget deficits' (→ Goal 8, Goal 1).[156]).

The creation of equal opportunities refers in particular to gender equality and the   76 empowerment of individuals, as well as enabling access to instruments, which is central not only to the Global Agenda 2030 but also to the Addis Ababa Action Agenda (AAAA) and, moreover, concerns not only North-South cooperation (10.b) but also South-South cooperation.

---

[149] United Nations Entity for Gender Equality and the Empowerment of Women, *Women and Sustainable Development*, 20.

[150] United Nations Entity for Gender Equality and the Empowerment of Women, *Women and Sustainable Development*, 20.

[151] UN, Commission on the status of women, E/2016/27-E/CN.6/2016/22, *Report on the sixtieth session* (2016), 10.

[152] United Nations Entity for Gender Equality and the Empowerment of Women, *Women and Sustainable Development*, 20.

[153] Van Soest et al., 'Analysing interactions among Sustainable Development Goals with Integrated Assessment Models' (2019) 1 *Global Transitions*, 210 (213).

· [154] E/2020/xxx, *Progress towards the Sustainable Development Goals, Report of the Secretary-General*, para. 18.

[155] HLPF, A/RES/74/4, *Political declaration of the high-level political forum on sustainable development convened under the auspices of the General Assembly*, 21 October 2019, paras. 20, 21.

[156] HLPF, *Summary by the President of the Economic and Social Council of the high-level political forum on sustainable development convened under the auspices of the Council at its 2020 session*, 8.

I. Jurisdiction on Vision and Objectives

77   As a main instrument for empowering people to participate and overcome inequalities, '[p]eople-centred legal and justice services [that] go beyond a fair and effective justice system to greater objectives such as inclusive growth, equality, poverty-reduction, social justice and social inclusion'[157] is essential. 'Since the core of access to justice is equality and social inclusion in the light of the "leave no one behind" imperative' of the Global Agenda 2030,[158] the inability to access legal and justice services can be both a result as well as a cause of disadvantage, poverty, and inequality in income and employment opportunities, educational attainment and health conditions. Within the judiciary, one of the main issues that is inherent in the very nature of courts and tribunals is the treatment and evaluation of inequalities. As a cross-sectional issue based on the fundamental principles of (balancing/equitable) law, this subject is immensely reflected in a wide variety of considerations at the international, regional and national levels. The following excerpt from case law can therefore, due to its abundance but also due to its political character, hardly capture or depict essential currents, but at least provide a basic understanding of the cornerstones of the inequality as understood by SDG 10.

1. International Jurisdiction

78   Inequality at the international level of jurisdiction occurs not only as substantive, law illuminating issue, but also as a formal requirement. The ICJ Statute, for instance, declares that all are equal before the court, which is at least true for the period after *lis pendens*. Inequality before *lis pendens*, however, is to be seen in a quite different way. Since the ICJ's jurisdiction is dependent on the voluntary submission of claims, this can be assumed an unequal treatment of sovereign states in case one of the State's parties involved (or another State interested) invokes a reservation or does not recognise its jurisdiction at all.[159] The equal treatment of states after *lis pendens* applies due to Art. 35 (2) ICJ Statute[160] as well as to the integrity requirements of the ICJ.[161]

79   Albeit this way of creating equality does not correspond to the targets and indicators of SDG 10 in the actual sense, it does represent the principle that is reflected in the vision and title of SDG 10 'Reduce inequality [...] among countries' on a formal level. On the substantive level, too, this unalterable principle has become international, which may not be violated under any circumstances and which goes hand in hand with the principle of non-interference, manifested in customary international law 'as a logical consequence and a corollary of the principle of the sovereign equality of States' in constant and substantial practice as well as in jurisprudence, even if this principle is repeatedly violated.[162]

---

[157] OECD, *Governance as an SDG Accelerator: Country Experiences and Tools* (2019), XX.

[158] OECD, *Governance as an SDG Accelerator: Country Experiences and Tools* (2019), XX.

[159] Smith-Morris, 'The Problem of Legal Inequality between States: A Case Study of the Marshall Islands' (2019) *Michigan Journal of International Law (MJIL)*, 40 (3) 2019; Kolb, *The International Court of Justice* (2013), 1120 (therein fn 4.); see also Ku, 'International Court of Justice' in Weiss and Daws (eds), *The Oxford Handbook on the United Nations* (2018), 195.

[160] Art. 35(2) Statute of the International Court of Justice: 'but in no case shall such conditions place the parties in a position of inequality before the court'.

[161] Kolb, *The International Court of Justice* (2013), 1120 and therein see fn. 4 and the established case-law, see amongst many: *Case Concerning Military and Paramilitary Activities in and against (Nicaragua v. United States of America)*, 27 June 1986, ICJ, para. 59.

[162] *Case Concerning Military and Paramilitary Activities in and against (Nicaragua v. United States of America)*, 27 June 1986, ICJ, paras. 59, 70, 202 f.

The fundamental acknowledgement does not prevent cross-border enforcement **80** (obligation *erga omnes*) before the ICJ, as could be read, for example, most recently from *The Gambia v. Myanmar*,[163] in which a third country (The Gambia) was required to examine the application or fulfilment of the Genocide Convention relating to the to be assumed genocide of the Rohingya by Myanmar or its failure to protect this Muslim minority in the predominantly Buddhist country. If one takes this case for the interpretation of the meaning of SDG 10.2 and SDG 10.3, it means both an impetus for the recognition of minority rights on a global scale and the possibility of determining claim holders just as globally. The *ratione personae* would thus be considerably expanded. This judgement would also probably fuel the discussion in international law on the maintenance of state immunity during or after international conflict or war crimes.[164]

The ICJ in 2017[165] also determined its substantive jurisdiction (*ratione materiae*) **81** in the event that the parties disagreed on the existence of the legal bases used. With regard to SDG 10.2, the court, referring to ICERD[166] and ICSFT,[167] found a "'policy of cultural erasure" through [...] discrimination against the Crimean Tatar and ethnic Ukrainian population'[168] of irreparable prejudice, which may cause irreparable damage to the minority. Therefore, the Court set provisional measures.[169] Regarding SDG 10.3, the differentiated (or unequal) treatment of 'persons or groups whose situations are objectively different' as otherwise behaviour constitutes discrimination in effect is emphasised by the UN Committee on the Elimination of Racial Discrimination (CERD) to warrant reducing inequalities of outcome.[170]

SDG 10.7 is also touched upon which is revealed by a closer look at the UDHR as **82** the main foundation of ICERD. The UDHR recognises the right to seek asylum from persecution as a human right which is the basis of the Convention Relating to the Status of Refugees (Geneva Convention)[171] adopted by the UN in 1951 'which, with its 1967 Protocol, became the universal standard on the right to asylum'.[172]

Similarly, the IACtHR has strong decision-making powers in the area of discrimina- **83** tion. Two cases show particularly clearly the line the court is taking. In *Norín Catrimán et al. v. Chile*, the indigenous population was deprived of their ancestral land which then was released for investment projects without prior consultation with them. Recognition of their land titles was repeatedly denied by the domestic court. The indigenous protests supported by NGOs and other civil enterprises were criminalised by the establishment

---

[163] *The Gambia v. Myanmar*, Order, 23 January 2020, ICJ; proceedings incl. Separate Opinions, https://www.icj-cij.org/en/case/178.

[164] See ICJ, *Arrest Warrant Case (DR Congo v Belgium)*, 11 April 2000; and more recently: *Ukraine v. Russian Federation*, Provisional Measures, Order, 19 April 2017, I.C.J. Reports (2017), 115, para. 22.

[165] *Ukraine v. Russian Federation*, Order, Provisional Measures, 19 April 2017, I.C.J. Reports (2017), para. 22 (115).

[166] A/RES/21/06 (XX), *International Convention on the Elimination of All Forms of Racial Discrimination, Adopted and opened for signature and ratification by General Assembly resolution 2106 (XX) of 21 December 1965*, entry into force 4 January 1969, in accordance with Art. 19.

[167] A/RES/54/109, *International Convention for the Suppression of the Financing of Terrorism, Adopted by the General Assembly of the United Nations*, 9 December 1999.

[168] *Ukraine v. Russian Federation*, Order, Provisional Measures, 19 April 2017, I.C.J. Reports (2017), para. 91.

[169] *Ukraine v. Russian Federation*, Order, Provisional Measures, 19 April 2017, I.C.J. Reports (2017), paras. 98 f., 102, 106.

[170] CERD/C/GC/32, *General recommendation No. 32 The meaning and scope of special measures in the International Convention on the Elimination of All Forms Racial Discrimination*, 24 September 2009, paras. 21-6.

[171] 2. Convention Relating to the Status of Refugees, 28 July 1951, most notably manifests the fundamental principles of non-discrimination, non-penalisation and non-refoulement.

[172] https://www.coe.int/en/web/compass/migration.

and selective and discriminatory application of the Anti-Terrorist Act. In 2014, the IACtHR ruled that the 'sentences were based on stereotypes and prejudices, in violation of the principles of equality and non-discrimination'. It also found that the right to due process had been violated.[173] The court, moreover, defined the principle of equality and non-discrimination as follows:

> "the notion of equality springs directly from the oneness of the human family, and is linked to the essential dignity of the individual." Thus, any situation is incompatible with this concept that, by considering one group superior to another group, leads to treating it in a privileged way; or, inversely, by considering a given group to be inferior, treats it with hostility or otherwise subjects it to discrimination in the enjoyment of rights that are accorded to those who are not so classified. The Court's case law has also indicated that, at the current stage of the evolution of international law, the fundamental principle of equality and non-discrimination has entered the sphere of jus cogens. It constitutes the foundation for the legal framework of national and international public order and permeate the whole legal system.

> Regarding the concept of discrimination, the definitions contained in Article 1(1) of the International Convention on the Elimination of All Forms of Racial Discrimination and Article 1(1) of the Convention on the Elimination of All Forms of Discrimination Against Women lead to the conclusion that discrimination is any distinction, exclusion, restriction or preference based on the prohibited reasons which has the purpose or effect of nullifying or impairing the recognition, enjoyment or exercise, on an equal footing, of human rights and fundamental freedoms in the political, economic, social, cultural or any other field.[174]

84   This judgment is further reinforced by the recent report of the International Law Commission (ILC) by taking up the reasoning of the IACtHR and endorsing that

> [f]rom a normative and moral perspective, there can be no argument against this call for the prohibition arbitrary discrimination to be accorded jus cogens status. Yet, there is limited explicit opinio juris cogentis regarding the prohibition of discrimination in general (or the more limited, prohibition of gender discrimination).[175]

85   This would allow both SDG 10.2 and SDG 10.3 to become connected to legally binding standardisation in scope, and are even suitable for a qualification beyond a status of entitlement to legally binding standardisation.

---

[173] *Case Of Norín Catrimán et al. (Leaders, Members And Activist Of The Mapuche Indigenous People) v. Chile*, Judgment, Merits, Reparations And Costs, 29 May 2014, IACtHR, para. 269.

[174] *Case Of Norín Catrimán et al. (Leaders, Members And Activist Of The Mapuche Indigenous People) v. Chile*, Judgment, Merits, Reparations And Costs, 29 May 2014, IACtHR Series C, No. 279, para. 197 f.; see also *Yatama v. Nicaragua*, Judgment, Preliminary objections, merits, reparations and costs, 23 June 2005, IACtHR Series C, No. 127, para. 184 ('At the current stage of the evolution of international law, the fundamental principle of equality and non-discrimination has entered the realm of jus cogens'); *Servellón-García et al. v. Honduras*, Judgment, Merits, reparations and costs, 21 September 2006, IACtHR Series C, No. 152, para. 94 ('This Tribunal considers that the fundamental principle of equality and non-discrimination belongs to the realm of jus cogens that, of a peremptory character, entails obligations erga omnes of protection that bind all States and result in effects with regard to third parties, including individuals'); *Expelled Dominicans and Haitians v. Dominican Republic*, Judgment, Preliminary objections, merits, reparations and costs, 28 August 2014, IACtHR Series C, No. 282, para. 264: The Court reiterates that the jus cogens principle of equal and effective protection of the law and non-discrimination requires States, when regulating the mechanisms for granting nationality, to abstain from establishing discriminatory regulations or regulations that have discriminatory effects on different groups of a population when they exercise their rights; all found in ILC, A/CN.4/727, *Fourth report on peremptory norms of general international law (jus cogens) by Dire Tladi, Special Rapporteur*, 31 January 2019, 61 (fn. 412).

[175] ILC, A/CN.4/727, *Fourth report on peremptory norms of general international law (jus cogens) by Dire Tladi, Special Rapporteur*, 31 January 2019, para. 135.

In a similarly systematic way, the IACtHR in *Atala Riffo and daughters v. Chile*[176] **86** found unlawful discrimination on grounds of sexual orientation. The plaintiff, who was deprived of custody of her four children in Chile's national courts because of her overt sexual orientation and cohabitation with her same-sex partner, was to become the first LGBTI case before the IACtHR to be decided in favour. The IACtHR affirmed that 'sexual orientation and gender identity are protected categories' the discrimination of which violates international law. 'The judgment declared that sexual orientation is part of a person's personal life and is not relevant when their suitability as a parent is examined. The Court also stated that the American Convention does not define a limited concept of family. the family unit created between the claimant, her same-sex partner, and the children should not be disturbed, and that separating the children from their family environment in an unjustified manner amounted to an arbitrary interference with and infringement of the children's right to private and family life. It then ruled that separating them from their mother affected the claimants' as well as the children's right to family life.'[177] The *Atala Riffo case* and the *Norín Catrimán case* both are examples of the clear and systematic anti-discrimination programme of the IACtHR.

2. European Jurisdiction

As the EU emerged out of an area of free trade, human rights were not settled in **87** the beginning at all and were not even assumend to be interrupted by this coalescence. When in fact more cases of human rights violations were heard before the ECJ, the court developed a body of judge-made laws,[178] known as the 'general principles' of Community Law. These mostly reflected the national constitutions and human rights treaties, and in particular the European Charter of Human Rights (ECHR). In the subsequent formation of the EU and the revision of the treaties 'human dignity, freedom, democracy, equality, the rule of law and respect for human rights became the Union's founding values, embedded in its treaties and mainstreamed into all its policies and programmes.'

Within the EU, anti-discrimination legislation is settled, since 'equality is one of the **88** fundamental values on which the EU is founded'. Equality is reflected in the Treaty on European Union (TEU), in the Treaty on the Functioning of the European Union (TFEU) as well as in the Charter of Fundamental Rights, which in accordance with and subject to further specification by the EU's (non-discrimination) directives explicitly 'foresee the possibility of positive action'.[179] Thus, the EU has the mandate and

---

[176] *Atala Riffo and daughters v. Chile*, Request for Interpretation of the Judgment on Merits, Reparations and Costs, 21 November 2012, IACtHR Series C no. 254.

[177] *Atala Riffo and daughters v. Chile*, Request for Interpretation of the Judgment on Merits, Reparations and Costs, 21 November 2012, IACtHR Series C no. 254, para. 167; further reading: Fernández and Peña and Smart, *Chile and the Inter-American Human Rights System* (2017).

[178] See amongst others: CJEU, Case 29/69, 12.11.1969, *Erich Stauder v. City of Ulm*, ECLI:EU:C:1969:57; CJEU, Case 11/70, 17.12.1970, *Internationale Handelsgesellschaft mbH v. Einfuhr- und Vorratsstelle für Getreide und Futtermittel*, ECLI:EU:C:1970:114; CJEU, Case 4/73, 14.05.1974, *J. Nold, Kohlen- und Baustoffgroßhandlung v. Commission of the European Communities*, ECLI:EU:C:1974:51; and regarding the principle of non-discrimination CJEU, C-149/77, 5.06.1978, *Gabrielle Defrenne v. Société anonyme belge de navigation aérienne Sabena*, ECLI:EU:C:1978:130.

[179] European Union Agency for Fundamental Rights and Council of Europe, *Handbook on European non-discrimination law, 2018 edition* (2018), 75; examples include Council Directive 2000/43/EC implementing the principle of equal treatment between persons irrespective of racial or ethnic origin, 29 June 2000, Art. 5; Council Directive 2000/78/EC establishing a general framework for equal treatment in employment and occupation, 27 November 2000, Art. 7; Council Directive 2004/113/EC implementing the principle of equal treatment between men and women in the access to and supply of goods and services, 13 December 2004, Art. 6; and with a deviating formulation: Directive 2006/54/EC of the European Par-

responsibility to combat discrimination. Alike to the non-discrimination principle at international level, grounds protected by the EU's non-discrimination law are gender, racial or ethnic origin, religion or belief, disability, age and sexual orientation. However, though not free of criticism,[180] the ECJ sees itself as a body of the EU which protects and preserves equality and which upholds union values and thus, has well-established systematic jurisdiction regarding the principle of equal treatment.[181]

89   The application of this principle, as well as the ECJ's unanimous understanding of it, was clearly illustrated by the *Milkova case*, a preliminary ruling, which was decided in 2017. In this case the dismissal of the claimant, a person with disabilities, on the basis of domestic legislation was discussed in detail. The ECJ clarified in general terms that the aim is 'to achieve substantive, rather than formal, equality by reducing [...] inequalities'[182] and stated in particular that the EU equal treatment legislation,[183] Art. 7(2) must be 'read in the light of the UN Convention and in conjunction with the general principle of equal treatment enshrined in Articles 20 and 21 of the Charter'. It declared that

> [t]he principle of equal treatment is a general principle of EU law, now enshrined in Articles 20 and 21 of the Charter, which requires that comparable situations must not be treated differently and that different situations must not be treated in the same way unless such treatment is objectively justified (judgments of 22 May 2014, Glatzel, C-356/12, EU:C:2014:350, paragraph 43, and of 21 December 2016, Vervloet and Others, C-76/15, EU:C:2016:975, paragraph 74 and the case-law cited). A difference in treatment is justified if it is based on an objective and reasonable criterion, that is, if the difference relates to a legally permitted aim pursued by the legislation in question, and it is proportionate to the aim pursued by the treatment (judgment of 22 May 2014, Glatzel, C-356/12, EU:C:2014:350, paragraph 43 and the case-law cited).[184]

90   Moreover, the application of the principle should not be based on identical situations, but rather on the comparability that can be established 'in a specific and concrete manner in the light of the objective and of the aim of the national legislation creating the distinction at issue'.[185] European case law allows unequal treatment to the extent that equality of outcome is achieved. It thus also corresponds to the meaning and purpose of SDG 10, and specifically of SDG 10.3.

3. Arbitration Proceedings

91   In addition to political and financial regulation goals, SDG 10 contains clear references to the legal framework of the WTO in its means of implementation. Special and differential treatment, which is permitted under certain conditions of the WTO agreements, is to be implemented (SDG 10.a), and ODA and FDI (SDG 10.b) are to be

---

liament and of the Council on the implementation of the principle of equal opportunities and equal treatment of men and women in matters of employment and occupation (recast), 5 July 2006, Art. 3.

[180] European Union Agency for Fundamental Rights and Council of Europe, *Handbook on European non-discrimination law, 2018 edition* (2018), 62 f.

[181] ECJ, C-313/99, 20.06.2002, *Mulligan and Others*, ECLI:EU:C:2002:386, para. 46; CJEU, C-428/07, 16.7.2009, *Horváth*, ECLI:EU:C:2009:458, para. 56; CJEU, C-24/13, 16.1.2014, *Dél-Zempléni Nektár Leader Nonprofit*, ECLI:EU:C:2014:40, para. 17.

[182] ECJ, C-406/15, 9.3.2017, *Petya Milkova v. Izpalnitelen direktor na Agentsiata za privatizatsia i sledprivatizatsionen kontrol*, ECLI:EU:C:2017:198, para. 47; on this issue see also: CJEU, C-395/15, 1.12.2016, *Mohamed Daouidi v. Bootes Plus SL and Others*, ECLI:EU:C:2016:917.

[183] Council Directive 2000/78/EC of 27 November 2000 establishing a general framework for equal treatment in employment and occupation.

[184] ECJ, C-406/15, 9.3.2017, *Petya Milkova v. Izpalnitelen direktor na Agentsiata za privatizatsia i sledprivatizatsionen kontrol*, ECLI:EU:C:2017:198, para. 55.

[185] ECJ, C-406/15, 9.3.2017, *Petya Milkova v. Izpalnitelen direktor na Agentsiata za privatizatsia i sledprivatizatsionen kontrol*, ECLI:EU:C:2017:198, para. 57.

encouraged. The basic legal framework of the WTO is to ensure non-discrimination.[186] However, it allows for deviations from this principle, either through the use of the Enabling Clause[187] which was introduced in the context of the decolonisation processes or by using the exceptions contained in Art. XX GATT (1994), the protective purpose of which was extended after the Bali Ministerial Conference held in 2013 (Bali Package).[188] Customs facilitation and agricultural subsidies in the areas of food security, cotton, preferential rules of origin and further support for Least Developed Countries (LDCs) in the form of a Trade Facilitation Agreement (TFA) should facilitate market access and promote participation in the world (market) economy. In 2015, the Nairobi Package, adopted at the Nairobi Ministerial Conference, supplemented these instruments by the area of services trade for LDCs in order to further increase the participation opportunities for the poorest countries and give priority concerns and interests to LDCs.[189] The implementation of these instruments was demanded not least with the financing instrument of the Global Agenda 2030, the AAAA under the guise of 'aid for trade' and 'trade facilitation', but also subsequently during the implementation process of the SDGs (→ Goal mn. 111).[190]

Within this framework, a number of arbitration proceedings can be found, which 92 primarily deal with the violation of one of these basic principles.

Before the Permanent Court of Arbitration (PCIJ), the question 'whether the tax 93 is an expropriation or whether the tax is discriminatory to the relevant Competent Tax Authority'[191] was examined by applying UNCITRAL rules. In the course of this proceeding, the taxation was found to be a measure setting up inequality and thus to violate one of the basic principles of the WTO (infringement of national treatment) and therefore functions as a means to be discriminatory.[192] Although the PCIJ pointed out that it is not a human rights court, it emphasised that the question of a

> in any way impair[ed] by unreasonable or discriminatory measures [Claimants'] management, maintenance, use, enjoyment or disposal" of its investment, or subjected Claimants' investment to measures having the effect equivalent to an expropriation. In the context of that inquiry, the

---

[186] The basic principle of non-discrimination in Trade of Goods and Services and on FDI is implemented in the regimes covered by the WTO by a) the most-favoured-nation-principle, by which all advantages granted to one state must be equally granted to all other states and b) the principle of national treatment, which states that domestic and foreign goods or investments are not to be treated less favourably (than domestic investment).

[187] Decision of 28 November 1979 (L/4903); Repertory of Appellate Body Reports, Enabling Clause, https://www.wto.org/english/tratop_e/dispu_e/repertory_e/e1_e.htm.

[188] The Bali Package included the Bali Ministerial Declaration (WT/MIN(13)/DEC), Ministerial Conference, Ninth Session, Bali, 3-6 December 2013, the November 2014 General Council decision (WT/L/941) and 15 other decisions on programmes such as Aid for Trade, waivers and other possibilities that allow asymmetries; full overview https://www.wto.org/english/thewto_e/minist_e/mc9_e/bali_texts_combined_e.pdf.

[189] Nairobi Ministerial Declaration (WT/MIN(15)/DEC); Special Safeguard Mechanism for Developing Country Members (WT/MIN(15)/43 — WT/L/978); Public Stockholding for Food Security Purposes (WT/MIN(15)/44 — WT/L/979); Export Competition (WT/MIN(15)/45 — WT/L/980); Cotton (WT/MIN(15)/46 — WT/L/981); Preferential Rules of Origin for Least Developed Countries (WT/MIN(15)/47 — WT/L/917/Add.1) and Implementation of Preferential Treatment in Favour of Services and Service Suppliers of Least Developed Countries and Increasing LDC Participation in Services Trade (WT/MIN(15)/48 — WT/L/982).

[190] Inter-Agency Task Force on Financing for Development (IATF), *Monitoring commitments and actions, Inaugural Report 2016, Inter-agency Task Force on Financing for Development* (2016), 93, 96.

[191] *Hulley Enterprises Limited (Cyprus) v. The Russian Federation*, PCA, Case No. 2005-03/AA226, application of UNCITRAL rules, Final Award, 18.07.2014, para. 114 (5(b) (i)).

[192] *Hulley Enterprises Limited (Cyprus) v. The Russian Federation*, PCA, Case No. 2005-03/AA226, application of UNCITRAL rules, Final Award, 18.07.2014, paras. 1407, 1433-8.

Tribunal will set out the evidentiary record with respect to the alleged "campaign of harassment and intimidation.

94   The arbitral court focused in particular on the underlying motivation for the taxation, but not on the actual designation or action taken, which, according to the PCIJ, would undermine the overall protective purpose. Before the Court of First Instance in The Hague, the dispute, which has been ongoing since 2006, has now been finally terminated by an immediate final judgement.

4. Domestic Jurisdiction

95   Where the principle of equality and non-discrimination is concerned, it is frequently dealt with in connection with other relevant human rights in national legislation. However, the understanding and inclusion of SDG 10 at the national level does not indicate a clear trend on the basis of which a legal derivation appears possible. Considering the human rights instruments mentioned above, ICERD and CRPD, for instance, are recognised by 182 states (12 and 7 states inactive, respectively) and CEDAW by 189 states (6 states inactive).[193] Their common basis, the UDHR, which is recognised as customary international law, is in many cases constitutionally enshrined or is used to interpret human rights or violations thereof at the national level ($\rightarrow$ Goal 16 mn. 57 ff.).[194] The UDHR also serves as a basis for the interpretation of the UN Charter, which is used by domestic judicial bodies as fundamentally valid for determining the meaning of human rights, and represents the 'minimum consensus'[195] that states recognise in its meaning.

96   Against this background, which is identifiable in most of the major legal families, a progressive judgement can only be taken as an example to highlight the principle of using international human rights instruments to interpret national laws.

97   In a case before the German Federal Constitutional Court (FCC),[196] brought by the Higher Social Court of North Rhine-Westphalia, the former Asylum Seekers Benefits Act (§ 3) was found to be incompatible with the German fundamental right to a dignified minimum standard of living, which applies without distinction to all persons residing in Germany. The FCC stated that in particular, the amount of cash benefits paid should not be reduced on the basis of a refugee or asylum seeker status and *a fortiori* should not be determined on the basis of a minimum standard of living in the respective country of origin, but must be based on the standard of the country of residence. In this respect, human dignity may not be relativised by migration-policy considerations. In its ruling, the FCC not only interpreted the context of the minimum of social assistance to be granted under international law and applied it to the living conditions in Germany, but also gave considerable weight to the ICESCR, in that it found the exclusion from cultural life as a result of insufficiently defined social benefits to be incompatible with Art. 15.1.a ICESCR (right to take part in cultural life). In addition, the court held that various rights under the Convention on the Rights of the Child were being violated.[197]

98   As one example of countless more, this judgment illustrates the transition of international law in the contentual sphere of SDG 10 into national law and its effects on the

---

[193] https://indicators.ohchr.org/.

[194] Hannum, 'The UDHR in National and International Law' (1998) 3(2) *Health and Human Rights*, 144 (150).

[195] Hannum, 'The UDHR in National and International Law' (1998) 3(2) *Health and Human Rights*, 144 (153).

[196] German Federal Constitutional Court, 1 BvL 10/10, Judgment of the First Senate of 18 July 2012, ECLI:DE:BVerfG:2012:ls20120718.1bvl001010.

[197] German Federal Constitutional Court, 1 BvL 10/10, Judgment of the First Senate of 18 July 2012, ECLI:DE:BVerfG:2012:ls20120718.1bvl001010, paras. 48 f., 68.

shaping of subsequent legislation. Although the subject matter under consideration can clearly be assigned to the sphere of SDG 10, no direct validity as an indication can be derived. Even though the principles of equality and non-discrimination are repeatedly similar within a wide variety of legal families and systems, their judicial interpretation in the context of specific (secondary) legislation is still too manifold and all the more not (directly) attached (yet) to the principle of sustainable development or, even less, to the Global Agenda 2030. Moreover, the complexity of the subject matter can hardly be grasped legally or specified to a conclusive essence. Rather, the infringement of human rights most often is accompanied by neglecting the principle of equality and non-discrimination. Insofar, reference must be made to the relevant SDG examination in this book.

II. The Enforcement of 'No Inequality'

The content of SDG 10, although given fundamental importance, and its measure- **99** ment within the Global Indicator Framework (GIF) already indicate its vagueness. The jurisdiction and jurisprudential interpretation of the term 'inequality' allow only a loose definition of its meaning in a floating context. It is striking, however, that within the international judicial evaluation at least a tendency to perceive the principles of this SDG – the principle of equality and non-discrimination – finds noticeable legal anchoring. An entitlement to the status of *jus cogens* can be identified which is also encouraged by the ILC. Nevertheless, the enforcement of these principles of SDG 10 remains subject to considerable difficulties ($\rightarrow$ Goal 16 mn. 65).

As can be seen in particular from the human rights background, the principle of **100** equality and non-discrimination are formally established, but it is still difficult to discern a substantive legal significance which would entail binding positive measures (by states) in particular.[198] The proceedings under consideration show a noticeable impairment of the enforcement of the rights invoked on the basis of this principle, both at international and regional level.

III. De Facto Influences on the Jurisdiction

Climate change, one of the most important drivers of our time, aggravates global **101** inequalities. However, whether SDG 10.7 also covers migration and mobility of climate refugees (environmental migration) cannot be read from the wording of SDG 10. Indicator 10.7.4 ('Proportion of the population who are refugees, by country of origin') is the only indicator that suggests that not only migrants but also refugees are to be included in the meaning of SDG 10. With recourse to the Geneva Convention on Refugees, however, climate refugees cannot be granted official refugee status and thus in principle cannot invoke a 'right to seek asylum (from persecution)'. Recent case-law, however, may point to an emerging right or at least to increasing discussion in this respect ($\rightarrow$ Goal 13 mn. 60, 64). But so far, the status and protection of a refugee can only be provided on humanitarian grounds, thus excluding people fleeing the effects of climate change.

UNCTAD as principal organ of the UN General Assembly (UNGA) serves as the fo- **102** cal point within the UN Secretariat for all matters related to FDI and transnational corporations and through its diverse data-collection and annual reports seeks to build inter-

---

[198] Oppenheimer, 'The Ubiquity of Positive Measures for Addressing Systemic Discrimination and Inequality, A Comparative Global Perspective' (2019) 3.3–4 *Comparative Discrimination Law*, 1 (5).

governmental consensus. In particular, the World Investment Report (WIR) is renowned as 'world's leading publication on FDI trends and policies and the development agenda.'[199] Moreover, historically, UNCTAD has exerted considerable influence on the global structures that exist today. In the 1970 s, UNCTAD drafted the criteria for identifying LDCs, thus dividing countries into poor and even poorer ones with the aim of improving the implementation of aid and development assistance. In this context, it also launched the Generalized System of Preferences (GSP), which allowed asymmetrical market access for LDCs. Further developments, such as the Global System of Trade Preferences Among Developing Countries (GSTP) to strengthen South-South cooperation should follow the demand of the UN Member States. UNCTAD's former mandate included 'maximising the ability of economic development to support inclusive development and sustainable growth'.[200] However, its current mandate focuses, amongst others, on the creative industries to achieve the SDGs since these contribute to the 'empowerment of all women and girls, the promotion of a culture of peace and non-violence, global citizenship and the appreciation of cultural diversity and of culture's contribution to sustainable development.'[201] Through its ongoing work, UNCTAD forms a governance factor that should not be neglected. Although it does not directly influence jurisdiction, this agency makes a significant contribution to shaping the realities of life, e.g. by influencing policy-makers and private actors in terms of both equality and inequality.[202]

103   At the European level, too, the systems of Generalised Preferences (Standard GSP; Everything But Arms) or with references to sustainable development and good governance (GSP +) are likely to have even more significant effects, as they are a key feature of all trade and investment agreements concluded by the EU with developing (or emerging) countries.[203] These trade and investment instruments each contain own dispute settlement mechanisms or make use of international dispute settlement tribunals, amongst others UNCITRAL, NAFTA, USMCA or WTO Dispute Settlement.[204] However, the EU GSP System expires on 31 December 2023 and is currently revised. Since the EU Parliament primarily emphasised its benefits,[205] the GSP will prospectively be maintained after a reform that mostly focuses on new eligibility criterias. It remains to be seen to what extent inequality between the EU and other countries will actually be reduced as a result and whether this is compatible with SDG 10.

104   Further influences on jurisdiction are mostly given by the World Bank Group and other development financial institutes such as the Inter-American Development Bank

---

[199] Magraw, 'United Nations Conference on Trade and Development (UNCTAD)' in Cottier and Nadakavukaren Schefer (eds), *Elgar Encyclopedia of International Economic Law* (2017), 74.

[200] Magraw, 'United Nations Conference on Trade and Development (UNCTAD)' in Cottier and Nadakavukaren Schefer (eds), *Elgar Encyclopedia of International Economic Law* (2017), 75, 176.

[201] A/C.2/74/L.16/Rev.1, *International Year of Creative Economy for Sustainable Development, 2021*, 8 November 2019, 3.

[202] See as example of exerting influence: UNCTAD/TC/2015/1/Rev.2, *UNCTAD Toolbox, Delivering Results, Third Edition* (2020); UNCTAD, *World Investment Report 2020, International Production Beyond the Pandemic* (2020).

[203] More information on the EU GSP Schemes: UNCTAD, *Generalized System of Preferences, Handbook on the Scheme of the European Union* (2015).

[204] In fact, the WTO's Dispute Settlement Mechanism (DSB) is being used for the issue of tariff preferences, with disputes extending over immense periods of time; see for instance: *DS246: European Communities — Conditions for the Granting of Tariff Preferences to Developing Countries (EC – India)*; Cuts International, 'GSP Dispute, Winning the battle, losing the war' (2004) 1/2004 *Trade Law Brief*; see similarly: WT/DS246/16/Add.3, *Status Report by the European Communities*, 8 July 2005; *DS242: European Communities — Generalized System of Preferences (EC – Thailand)*.

[205] European Parliament, P8_TA(2019)0207, *Implementation of the Generalised Scheme Preferences (GSP) Regulation European Parliament resolution of 14 March 2019 on the implementation of the GSP Regulation (EU) No 978/2012 (2018/2107(INI))*.

or the Asian Infrastructure Investment Bank (AIIB), as well as initiatives such as the Global Compact or the World Justice Project since these are financially supporting (strategic) litigation or collect and educate on relevant data and / or process them to public indices such as the WJP Rule of Law Index[206] measured by nine factors: 1. Constraints on Government Powers, 2. Absence of Corruption, 3. Open Government, 4. Fundamental Rights, 5. Order and Security, 6. Regulatory Enforcement, 7. Civil Justice, 8. Criminal Justice, 9. Informal Justice or the GINI coefficient (GINI Index) which bases on the 'comparison of cumulative proportions of the population against cumulative proportions of income they receive'.[207]

E. Conclusion on SDG 10

SDG 10 should be considered as one of the most ambitious SDGs laying out a vast   **105** area for political decision making and at the same time just a small field for legal aspects and thoughts. The objectives cover social and economic inclusion, financial markets and institutions, development participation in institutions and benefits in the world trade system through preferential treatment of third countries, as well as ODA and FDI.[208]

A direct legal relevance in the scope of SDG 10 is more difficult to identify than   **106** with other SDGs. SDG 10 refers to targets that entail a wide and systematic range over most difficult issues, which are primarily political in nature and could be achieved by a consensus with other countries, or which are to be generated within the country itself. Sometimes, however, such targets are also independent of the political framework in that the globalised world economy sets the pace. The strength of the economy within a specific given framework based on theoretical considerations (liberal/socialist approach) in a country will set the decisive factor as to whether the income of a country has the chance to increase progressively (SDG 10.1). This outcome is hardly a topic that can be achieved by political consensual resolution but more than that by economic driving factors.

In principle, the targets of SDG 10 are desirable to such an extent that there are hard-   **107** ly any objections to them, but they remain mostly vague as objectives and, in the absence of concrete measures, are hardly suitable for a translation into concrete policies or even a normative setting of laws. The goal of improving the regulation and monitoring of global financial markets and institutions contained in SDG 10.5, accompanied by SDG 10.4, is part of a financial system that has evolved historically and grown out of several crises, and improvements and adjustments are being intensively fought for at numerous levels. Here, the scepticism prevails as to whether the targets generally formulated in SDG 10 can be more than a reminder to link concrete policy with statutory plans of the targets and indicators of SDG 10.

The goal of implementation of planned and well-managed migration policies (SDG   **108** 10.7 implementation of planned and well-managed migration policies) is unlikely to lead to an improvement of the existing different legal systems in practice. The EU can be used as an example to illustrate which different and conflicting interests prevent consistent and necessary successful management in the field of migration policy.

The general formulation of objectives in SDG 10.5 is unlikely to bring about any   **109** change, let alone improvement, in the general public. It is still true that the 'role of international law in financial regulation and supervision cannot be determined by

---

[206] https://worldjusticeproject.org/about-us/overview/what-rule-law.
[207] https://data.oecd.org/inequality/income-inequality.htm.
[208] https://stats.unctad.org/Dgff2016/prosperity/goal10/index.html.

an all-embracing formula'.[209] There are so many different levels, institutions, political reservations, different systems involved. A 'one-size-fits-all approach' is still not in sight concerning the complex finance systems.[210]

110   The same applies to the target of 'fiscal, wage and social protection policies' (SDG 10.4). Here, too, the achievement of the target is unlikely to be successful based on this vague formulation that is not specific. This is all the more true as this is a particularly controversial area.[211]

111   Against the broad background of each target, it is obviously not easy to establish indicators capable of measuring the application of the targets and their outcome. The UN has so far been able to provide 14 indicators for SDG 10 which are more or less clear at first glance but are too vague to reveal a clear picture of whether inequality decreases or not.

112   Since the United Nations Conference on Environment and Development in Rio (1992), sustainable development has been difficult to achieve in particular for many African countries, with poverty being a major challenge as well as desertification, deforestation and climate change. However, it remains to be hoped that SDG 10 will be able to trigger independent improvement or even transitions into legal spheres.

113   Therefore, the main aspects of SDG 10 are touching upon the regulation of migration, the mobility of people and the financing of the participation of states in the global structures of trade and investment in order to create lasting peaceful coexistence and / or cooperation of states and societies. To express it freely according to Montesquieu – if trade crosses borders, soldiers will not, whether they are state or non-state actors.[212]

114   Further content of SDG 10 is largely to be anchored in areas of governance and political discussion but hardly can be assigned to legal structures. Exceptions can be found in jurisdiction mainly at the international level before the IACtHR with a clear systematic approach to eliminate discrimination and within the EU with its principles of non-discrimination and equal treatment which is strictly persecuted by the ECJ. Interestingly, the principle of equality is deemed to be entitled to *jus cogens*. In this respect, the further assessment needs to be closely monitored. However, these developments occur without a remarkable influence of SDG 10 but are generally discussed in international law. A confluence of this SDG and specific legal normativity cannot be assumed at this point of the SDGs' life cycle.

115   Therefore, jurisprudence clearly confirms what can already be deduced from the content of SDG 10 at a theoretical level: SDG 10 is not intended to create equality, but to reduce inequality and melt away its most blatant peaks.

---

[209] Tietje and Lehmann, 'The role and prospects of international law in financial regulation and supervision' (2010) 13(3) *JIEL*, 663-82.

[210] See Jones and Knaack, 'Global Financial Regulation: Shortcomings and Reform Options' (2019) *Glob Policy*, 10.

[211] OECD (ed), *Lessons from the EU-SPS Programme, Implementing Social Protection Strategies* (2019); World Bank, *Resilience, equity, and opportunity: the World Bank's social protection and labour strategy 2012-2022* (2012); https://www.social-protection.org/gimi/gess/ShowTheme.action?id=1321.

[212] Montesquieu, *Vom Geist der Gesetze (De L'esprit des Loix)* (1748).

Goal 11
Make cities and human settlements inclusive, safe, resilient and sustainable

11.1 By 2030, ensure access for all to adequate, safe and affordable housing and basic services and upgrade slums

11.2 By 2030, provide access to safe, affordable, accessible and sustainable transport systems for all, improving road safety, notably by expanding public transport, with special attention to the needs of those in vulnerable situations, women, children, persons with disabilities and older persons

11.3 By 2030, enhance inclusive and sustainable urbanization and capacity for participatory, integrated and sustainable human settlement planning and management in all countries

11.4 Strengthen efforts to protect and safeguard the world's cultural and natural heritage

11.5 By 2030, significantly reduce the number of deaths and the number of people affected and substantially decrease the direct economic losses relative to global gross domestic product caused by disasters, including water-related disasters, with a focus on protecting the poor and people in vulnerable situations

11.6 By 2030, reduce the adverse per capita environmental impact of cities, including by paying special attention to air quality and municipal and other waste management

11.7 By 2030, provide universal access to safe, inclusive and accessible, green and public spaces, in particular for women and children, older persons and persons with disabilities

11.a Support positive economic, social and environmental links between urban, peri-urban and rural areas by strengthening national and regional development planning

11.b By 2020, substantially increase the number of cities and human settlements adopting and implementing integrated policies and plans towards inclusion, resource efficiency, mitigation and adaptation to climate change, resilience to disasters, and develop and implement, in line with the Sendai Framework for Disaster Risk Reduction 2015–2030, holistic disaster risk management at all levels

11.c Support least developed countries, including through financial and technical assistance, in building sustainable and resilient buildings utilizing local materials

Word Count related to 'Cities' and 'Settlement'
A/RES/70/1 - Transforming our world: the 2030 Agenda for Sustainable Development: 'Cities': 6 'Settlement': 5
Instruments mentioned in A/RES/70/1 in the section entitled: 'Sustainable Development Goals and targets':
A/RES/69/313 - Addis Ababa Action Agenda of the Third International Conference on Financing for Development adopted on 27 July 2015: 'Cities': 2 'Settlement': 2
A/RES/66/288 - The future we want (Rio +20 Declaration) adopted on 27 July 2012: 'Cities': 10 'Settlement': 8
A/RES/55/2 - United Nations Millennium Declaration adopted on 8 September 2000: 'Cities': 1 'Settlement': 0

Select Bibliography: Diletta Acuti, Marco Bellucci and Giacomo Manetti, 'Company disclosures concerning the resilience of cities from the Sustainable Development Goals (SDGs) perspective' (2020) 99 *Cities*, 102608; Michael Osei Asibey, Michael Poku-Boansi, Isaac Osei Adutwum, 'Residential segregation of ethnic minorities and sustainable city development. Case of Kumasi, Ghana' (2021) 116 *Cities*, 103297; Helmut Aust and Alejandro Rodiles, 'Cities and Local Governments: International Development from Below?' in Luis Eslava, Ruth M Buchanan and Sundhya Pahuja (eds), *The Oxford Handbook of International Law and Development* (2021) (forthcoming), 13, 17; Helmut Aust, 'Cities as International Legal Authorities-Remarks on Recent Developments and Possible Future Trends of Research' (2020) 4 *JCULP*, 82; Helmut Aust, 'The shifting role of cities in the global climate change regime: From Paris to Pittsburgh and back?' (2019) 28.1 *Review of European, Comparative & International Environmental Law*, 57-66; Yishai Blank, 'International legal personality/subjectivity of cities' in Helmut Aust and Janne Elisabeth Nijman (eds), *Research Handbook on International Law and Cities* (Edward Elgar, 2021) (forthcoming); Tiziana Caponio and Peter Scholten and Ricard Zapata-Barrero, *The Routledge Handbook of the Governance of Migration and Diversity in Cities* (Routledge, London 2018); Catherine Farvacque-Vitkovic and Mihaly Kopanyi, *Better Cities, Better World : A Handbook on Local Governments Self-Assessments* (World Bank, Washington, DC 2019); Billie Giles-Corti, Melanie Lowe and Jonathan Arundel, 'Achieving the SDGs: Evaluating indicators to be used to benchmark and monitor progress towards creating healthy and sustainable cities' (2020) 124 *Health Policy*, 581; Douglas C. Harris, 'Condominium Government and the Right to Live in the City' (2019) 34(3), *Canadian Journal of Law and Society*, 371-392; Jolene Lin, *Governing climate change: global cities and transnational lawmaking* (Cambridge University Press, Cambridge 2018); Nico Moons, *The Right to housing in law and society* (Routledge, New York 2018); Alastair M. Morrison and J. Andres Coca-Stefaniak, *Routledge Handbook of Tourism Cities* (Routledge, London 2020); Caroline O. N. Moser, 'Gender transformation in a new global urban agenda: challenges for Habitat III and beyond' (2016) 29 *IIED*, 221; Janne Elisabeth Nijman and Helmut Aust, 'The Emerging Roles of Cities in International Law - Introductory Remarks on Practice, Scholarship and the Handbook' in Helmut Aust and Janne Elisabeth Nijman (eds), *Research Handbook on International Law and Cities* (Edward Elgar, 2021); Barbara Oomen, Moritz Baumgärtel and Elif Durmus, 'Accelerating cities, constitutional brakes? Exploring the local authorities between global challenges and domestic law' in Ernst Hirsch Ballin, Gerhard van der Schyff, Maarten Stremler and Maartje De Visser (eds), *European Yearbook of Constitutional Law 2020 (Vol. 2)* (T.M.C. Asser Press, The Hague 2021), 260; Adam Ploszka, 'A Homeless Bill of Rights as a New Instrument to Protect the Rights of Homeless Persons' (2020), 16 *European Constitutional Law Review*, 601; Martin Pogačar, Jasna Fakin Bajec, Katarina Polajnar Horvat, Aleš Smrekar and Jernej Tiran, 'Promises and Limits of Participatory Urban Green Development: Experience from Maribor, Budapest, and Krakow' in Janez Nared and David Bole (eds), *Participatory Research and Planning in Practice* (Springer Verlag, Berlin-Heidelberg 2020), 75; Oriana Ramirez-Rubio, Carolyn Daher, Gonzalo Fanjul, Mireia Gascon, Natalie Mueller, Leire Pajín, Antoni Plasencia, David Rojas-Rueda, Meelan Thondoo and Mark J. Nieuwenhuijsen, 'Urban health: an example of a "health in all policies" approach in the context of SDGs implementation' (2019) 15 *Globalization and Health*, 87; Seth Schindler, 'Reflections on the New Urban Agenda' (2017) 39 *International Development Planning Review*, 349; David Simon, *Rethinking Sustainable Cities, Accessible, Green and fair* (Policy Press, Bristol 2016); Victor Udemezue Onyebueke, Julian Walker, Barbara Lipietz, Oliver Ujah, Victoria Ibezim-Ohaeri, 'Evicting the poor in the 'overriding public interest': Crisis of rights and interests, and contestations in Nigerian cities' (2020)

101 *Cities*, 102675; UN Habitat, *World Cities Report 2020: The Value of Sustainable Urbanization* (2020); UNEP, *The ABC for Sustainable Cities: A Glossary for Policy Makers* (2016); World Bank, *Handbook for Gender-Inclusive Urban Planning and Design* (2020); Roland Zinkernagel, James Evans and Lena Neij, 'Applying the SDGs to Cities: Business as Usual or a New Dawn?' (2018) 10 *Sustainability*, 2.

A. Background and Origin of SDG 11

Urban populations have been growing for many decades and building the majority of the world's population since 2007.[1] According to the Department of Economic and Social Affairs, the world population will be 8.5 to 8.6 billion in 2030, 9.4 to 10.1 billion in 2050 and 9.4 to 12.7 billion in 2100,[2] with the assumption that the vast majority of growth will take place in urban areas.[3] By 2060, most likely 68 per cent of the world's population will live in urban areas.[4]   1

Such a continuously increase of population concentrate in cities and urban areas raising questions on where people should live in particular in confined cities. The estimated growth of population in the upcoming decades obviously demonstrate critical/current concerns that need to be addressed urgently such as infrastructure, climate change, food and fresh water supply, security, schools, universities, health, gender equality, protection of historical and cultural sites and museums.[5]   2

Although the UN has observed improvements in the quality of living in cities, including slum and informal-settlement dwellers, since the United Nations Conferences on Human Settlements in Vancouver, Canada, in 1976 and in Istanbul, Turkey, in 1996, and the adoption of the Millennium Development Goals in 2000, hard obstacles persists. Multiple forms of poverty, growing inequalities and environmental degradation remain, amongst others, as the major obstacles with social and economic exclusion and spatial segregation.[6] Overall, cities are becoming increasingly important in connection with the SDGs as a number of researchers have noted that cities and urban activities touch upon the majority of all 17 goals.[7]   3

Worldwide, around 1 billion people live in slums.[8] In many places, this leads to a shortage in the health sector and therefore has an extremely negative impact on the health of those affected.[9] During the SARS-CoV2 pandemic, cities are particularly affected and account for approximately 90 per cent of cases.[10] But even outside of global humanitarian crises such as SARS-CoV-2, residents of urban areas are exposed to particular dangers.[11] For example, they are frequently affected by indoor air pollution   4

---

[1] World Bank, *Urban population (% of total population)*.

[2] UN, ST/ESA/SER.A/42, *World Population Prospects 2019* (2019), 5.

[3] UN, ST/ESA/SER.A/42, *World Population Prospects 2019* (2019), 37.

[4] UN, Department of Economic and Social Affairs, *68% of the world population projected to live in urban areas by 2050, says UN* (2018).

[5] See Aust, 'The shifting role of cities in the global climate change regime: From Paris to Pittsburgh and back?' (2019) 28 *RECIEL*, 57-66.

[6] A/RES/71/256, *New Urban Agenda*, 25 January 2017, Annex, para. 3.

[7] Zinkernagel et al., 'Applying the SDGs to Cities: Business as Usual or a New Dawn?' (2018) 10(9) *Sustainability*, 2.

[8] UN Habitat, *World Cities Report 2020: The Value of Sustainable Urbanization* (2020), 26.

[9] Griggs et al., *A Guide to SDG Interactions: From Science to Implementation* (2017), 107; UN, *Progress towards the Sustainable Development Goals Report of the Secretary-General E/2020/57* (2020) para. 100; For more information on health in cities see: Ramirez-Rubio et al., 'Urban health: an example of a "health in all policies" approach in the context of SDGs implementation' (2019) 15 *Globalization and Health,* 87.

[10] UN, *The Sustainable Development Goals Report 2020* (2020), 46.

[11] For initiatives to improve health in cities see: WHO, 'Shanghai Consensus on Healthy Cities 2016' (2017) 32(4) *Health Promotion International,* 603.

and contaminated drinking water, thereby providing good conditions for infectious diseases due to their confined living spaces.[12]

5   If SDG 11 may be advocated as a 'stand-alone urban goal' or not, cities today and in the future play an important role for the attempts of global development pathways. The manifold issues of urban and local governance must be addressed. The question is how growing cities can be managed and properly planned with all the related questions deriving from people, infrastructure, finance and legal provisions as well as constrains a city has to deal with. To this regard, the New Urban Agenda (NUA)[13] contains a vast array of statements and approaches.[14] To unleash the potential of cities in many ways and in a multi-level legal matrix with different streams of technology, decentralisation and self-assessment of cities are prerequisites to act smart on planning techniques and with investment partners in an increasingly globalised environment.[15]

6   Cities and Communities are particularly affected by emissions of various kinds. Three quarters of the world's CO_2 emissions are emitted in urban areas,[16] meaning that cities also represent a major burden from an environmental point of view.

7   Cities were already addressed by the UN in the 1970 s. At the Stockholm Conference in 1972, the recommendation was made

> that all development assistant agencies [...] give high priority within available resources to requests from governments for assistance in the planning of human settlements, notably in housing, transportation, water, sewerage and public health, the mobilization of human and financial resources, the improvement of transitional urban settlements and the provision and maintenance of essential community services.[17]

8   The World Commission on Environment and Development in Our Common Future (1987) was significantly more comprehensive. In 'The Urban Challenge', it devoted a separate chapter to various aspects of urban growth.[18] According to the commission, the 20th century was the 'century of the urban revolution.'[19] Moreover, many aspects included in SDG 11 have been coherently highlighted:

> Few city governments in the developing world have the power, resources, and trained staff to provide their rapidly growing populations with the land, services, and facilities needed for an adequate human life: clean water, sanitation, schools, and transport. The result is mushrooming illegal settlements with primitive facilities, increased overcrowding, and rampant disease linked to an unhealthy environment.[20]

9   Agenda 21 (1992) also made strong reference to emerging urbanisation. Chapter 7 ('Promoting Sustainable Human Settlement Development') addressed different impacts

---

[12] Griggs et al., *A Guide to SDG Interactions: From Science to Implementation* (2017), 107, 108.

[13] 2016 World Conference on Housing and Sustainable Urban Development (Habitat III) in Quito, Ecuador, from 17–20 October 2016; see Chapter 4 'Way Forward and Perspectives for the Future, Transformative Actions for a New Urban Agenda' in Farvacque-Vitkovic and Kopanyi, *Better Cities, Better World : A Handbook on Local Governments Self-Assessments* (2019).

[14] See http://sdg.iisd.org/commentary/policy-briefs/the-new-urban-agenda-and-the-sustainable-development-goals-synergies-and-challenges-ahead/.

[15] Farvacque-Vitkovic and Kopanyi, *Better Cities, Better World : A Handbook on Local Governments Self-Assessments*, xiv.

[16] UN, *Sustainable Cities: Why They Matter*, 2.

[17] UN, Declaration of the United Nations Conference on the Human Environment, 1st recommendation, Stockholm 1972.

[18] Report of the World Commission on Environment and Development: *Our Common Future* (1987), Chapter 9.

[19] Report of the World Commission on Environment and Development: *Our Common Future* (1987), Chapter 9, para. 3.

[20] Report of the World Commission on Environment and Development: *Our Common Future* (1987), Chapter 9, para. 9.

of urbanisation and elaborated a 'human settlement objective'.[21] This program took many of the aspects contained in Our Common Future and translated them into an action plan, which is reminiscent in parts of SDG11.[22] The Rio Declaration of 1992 also called for improved living conditions in urban areas, although not as directly as in Agenda 21.[23]

Urbanisation was a central issue at the International Conference on Population and **10** Development in Cairo in 1994.[24] A concrete objective was set up to counteract the phenomenon of increasing urbanisation. The approach was mainly to distribute the migrating population groups more evenly,[25] which was called for again in 2008 by the Commission on Population and Development and underlined by more detailed proposals.[26]

Because of the wide range of impacts on people and the environment, the ultimate **11** implementation of the SDGs involved a wide range of proposals. These can be divided into the following three categories: (1) a stand-alone goal for sustainable cities, (2) goals that support sustainable cities, and (3) a generalisation of urbanisation to be able to achieve sustainable development on a global level.[27] In the end, a sizable compromise was reached which attempted to address a variety of different effects and impacts. In the context of the Conference on Sustainable Development, it was noted:

> We recognize that, if they are well planned and developed, including through integrated planning and management approaches, cities can promote economically, socially and environmentally sustainable societies. In this regard, we recognize the need for a holistic approach to urban development and human settlements that provides for affordable housing and infrastructure and prioritizes slum upgrading and urban regeneration. We commit to work towards improving the quality of human settlements, including the living and working conditions of both urban and rural dwellers in the context of poverty eradication so that all people have access to basic services, housing and mobility. We also recognize the need for conservation, as appropriate, of the natural and cultural heritage of human settlements, the revitalization of historic districts and the rehabilitation of city centres.[28]

With the NUA, a global commitment was reaffirmed to a sustainable urban develop- **12** ment as a critical step for realising sustainable development with the participation of all relevant actors, which should contribute to the implementation and localization of the

---

[21] UN, *Agenda 21* (1992), para. 7.4.

[22] See e.g. UN, *Agenda 21* (1992), para. 7.5: a) *Providing adequate shelter for all/* SDG11.1 *By 2030, ensure access for all to adequate, safe and affordable housing and basic services and upgrade slums*; e) *Promoting sustainable energy and transport systems in human settlements*; SDG11.2 *By 2030, provide access to safe, affordable, accessible and sustainable transport systems for all, improving road safety, notably by expanding public transport, with special attention to the needs of those in vulnerable situations, women, children, persons with disabilities and older persons.*

[23] A/CONF.151/26, Principle 5: *All States and all people shall cooperate in the essential task of eradicating poverty as an indispensable requirement for sustainable development, in order to* **decrease the disparities in standards of living** *(emphasis added) and better meet the needs of the majority of the people of the world.*

[24] UN, *Programme Of Action Of The International Conference On Population And Development* (1994).

[25] UN, *Programme Of Action Of The International Conference On Population And Development (1994),* para. 9.2.

[26] UN, Commission on Population and Development, 2008/1, para. 4: 'Calls upon Governments to address the challenges and opportunities of urban growth and internal migration by taking prompt, forward-looking and sustained action to ensure that those phenomena have a positive impact on economic growth, poverty eradication and environmental sustainability and, in doing so, to enable the participation and representation of all relevant stakeholders in planning for an urban future [...]'.

[27] United Nations General Assembly (UNGA) Open Working Group on Sustainable Development Goals, *Compendium of TST Issues Briefs October 2014,* 157.

[28] A/CONF.216/16, 134.

Global Agenda 2030.[29] The efforts of some national and local governments to enshrine this vision, referred to as a 'right to the city', in their legislation, political declarations and charters were noted.[30] The implementation of the agenda takes place within the framework of the Quito implementation plan for the NUA.[31] The next United Nations Conference on Housing and Sustainable Urban Development (Habitat IV) is planned in 2036.[32]

13   According to the NUA, the states envisage cities and human settlements that:

(a) Fulfil their social function, including the social and ecological function of land, with a view to progressively achieving the full realization of the right to adequate housing as a component of the right to an adequate standard of living, without discrimination, universal access to safe and affordable drinking water and sanitation, as well as equal access for all to public goods and quality services in areas such as food security and nutrition, health, education, infrastructure, mobility and transportation, energy, air quality and livelihoods;

(b) Are participatory, promote civic engagement, engender a sense of belonging and ownership among all their inhabitants, prioritize safe, inclusive, accessible, green and quality public spaces that are friendly for families, enhance social and intergenerational interactions, cultural expressions and political participation, as appropriate, and foster social cohesion, inclusion and safety in peaceful and pluralistic societies, where the needs of all inhabitants are met, recognizing the specific needs of those in vulnerable situations;

(c) Achieve gender equality and empower all women and girls by ensuring women's full and effective participation and equal rights in all fields and in leadership at all levels of decision-making, by ensuring decent work and equal pay for equal work, or work of equal value, for all women and by preventing and eliminating all forms of discrimination, violence and harassment against women and girls in private and public spaces;

(d) Meet the challenges and opportunities of present and future sustained, inclusive and sustainable economic growth, leveraging urbanization for structural transformation, high productivity, value-added activities and resource efficiency, harnessing local economies and taking note of the contribution of the informal economy while supporting a sustainable transition to the formal economy;

(e) Fulfil their territorial functions across administrative boundaries and act as hubs and drivers for balanced, sustainable and integrated urban and territorial development at all levels;

(f) Promote age- and gender-responsive planning and investment for sustainable, safe and accessible urban mobility for all and resource-efficient transport systems for passengers and freight, effectively linking people, places, goods, services and economic opportunities;

(g) Adopt and implement disaster risk reduction and management, reduce vulnerability, build resilience and responsiveness to natural and human-made hazards and foster mitigation of and adaptation to climate change;

(h) Protect, conserve, restore and promote their ecosystems, water, natural habitats and biodiversity, minimize their environmental impact and change to sustainable consumption and production patterns.[33]

---

[29] A/RES/71/256, *New Urban Agenda*, 25 January 2017, para. 9; For a survey, offered in English, French, Spanish, and Korean completed by 111 local governments around the world considering seventeen integrated environmental, social, and economic topics, including climate change, waste, ecological diversity, and local economy; see MacDonald et al., 'Multi-stakeholder Partnerships (SDG #17) as a Means of Achieving Sustainable Communities and Cities (SDG #11)' in Leal Filho (ed), *Handbook of Sustainability Science and Research. World Sustainability Series* (2017).

[30] A/RES/71/256, *New Urban Agenda*, 25 January 2017, para. 11; see also: Harris, 'Condominium Government and the Right to Live in the City' (2019) 34(3), *Canadian Journal of Law and Society*, 371-92.

[31] A/RES/71/256, *New Urban Agenda*, 25 January 2017, para. 23.

[32] A/RES/71/256, *New Urban Agenda*, 25 January 2017, para. 174.

[33] A/RES/71/256, *New Urban Agenda*, 25 January 2017, para. 13; For more information on the agenda see: Schindler et al., 'Reflections on the New Urban Agenda' (2017) 39(4) *International Development Planning Review*, 349-74.

B. Scope and Dimensions of SDG 11

More than half of the world's population now lives in cities - and the trend is rising, **14** making their sustainable design all the more necessary. This also means that existing deficits in urban planning must be addressed.

I. Definition of Cities

When attempting to uncover the meaning of 'cities' as the central element of SDG **15** 11, it can first be noted that although various global agendas address the aspect of 'cities', no uniform definition exists.[34] Instead, states use national definitions, which makes international comparison difficult.[35] However, two possible definitions have been established at the global level which take into account its urban extent. Accordingly, a city can be defined 'as an operational entity that incorporates both built-up areas and open spaces, which often extend beyond official/formal administrative boundaries'.[36] A city means a town or settlement incorporated by that name.[37] In its original form, 'this word did not signify a town, but a portion of mankind who lived under the same government', the civitas in the understanding of the Romans and what was described by the Greeks with the word polis.[38]

In a more descriptive way, '[c]ities are hubs for ideas, commerce, culture, science, **16** productivity, social, human and economic development. Urban planning, transport systems, water, sanitation, waste management, disaster risk reduction, access to information, education and capacity-building are all relevant issues to sustainable urban development'.[39] However, in a legal framework, a more normative definition is needed, in particular when the duality of the increasing involvement of cities in the field of international development is brought into focus, e.g. when the World Bank contracts directly with cities or when questions of interdependencies between the Belt and Road Initiative (BRI) and the role of cities are at stake.[40]

A variety of cities invites to classification and distinction such as, amongst others, **17** Smart cities, Megacities, City-regions, Metropolitan areas, Megalopolis equivalent used as super cities (more than one city) or the Free Hanseatic City of Bremen or the Free and Hanseatic City of Hamburg in Germany which are acknowledged constitutionally as both a city-state a municipality within the Federal Republic of Germany. In legal terms, a city is not only a place where people stay and live, but moreover a place which is organised by a framework of laws and regulations fitted in the system of a state constitution the city belongs to and even the question of the subjectivity and international legal personality of cities is raised.[41] Mostly, there are legal bases for substantive rights conferred on a city, as well as formal regulations, e.g. regarding the organisation of an

---

[34] https://ghsl.jrc.ec.europa.eu/degurbaOverview.php.

[35] https://ghsl.jrc.ec.europa.eu/degurbaOverview.php.

[36] UN-Habitat, *SDG Indicator 11.7.1 Training Module: Public Spaces* (2018), 9.

[37] The Free Dictionary, 'City' in Bouvier (ed), *A Law Dictionary: Adapted to the Constitution and Laws of the United States* (1856).

[38] The Free Dictionary, 'City' in Bouvier (ed), *A Law Dictionary: Adapted to the Constitution and Laws of the United States* (1856).

[39] https://sustainabledevelopment.un.org/topics/sustainablecities.

[40] Aust and Rodiles, 'Cities and Local Governments: International Development from Below?' in Eslava and Buchanan and Pahuja (eds), *The Oxford Handbook of International Law and Development* (2021) (forthcoming), 13, 17.

[41] Blank, 'International legal personality/subjectivity of cities' in Aust and Nijman (eds), *Research Handbook on International Law and Cities* (2021), 103 ff.

assembly, the composition of a board of directors, or rule of law provisions according to which a mayor must act. These regulations are internationally and often also within a state inconsistent and have different legal character.

18   Moreover, a city can be defined by its degree of urbanisation, which is a 'classification that indicates the character of an area'.[42] According to this definition, a city is a densely populated area.[43] Several other definitions – although not universally agreed upon – have been developed[44] that include, for instance and in particular, the interactions between international law and cities, which is a fruitful and emerging area of research[45]:

> the "city proper", [which] describes a city according to an administrative boundary. A second approach, termed the "urban agglomeration", considers the extent of the contiguous urban area, or built-up area, to delineate the city's boundaries. A third concept of the city, the "metropolitan area", defines its boundaries according to the degree of economic and social interconnectedness of nearby areas, identified by interlinked commerce or commuting patterns, for example.[46]

II. The Right to Adequate Housing

19   The right to adequate housing is part of the right to an adequate standard of living and is internationally recognised as a human right.[47] Nevertheless, billions of people worldwide are not adequately housed, millions of whom live in conditions that endanger their lives or health, including in overcrowded slums.[48] SDG 11.1 aims to 'ensure access for all to adequate, safe and affordable housing and basic services and upgrade slums' by 2030. It repeats the 'imperative of ensuring basic living conditions for human dignity' that was already part of the MDGs (→ Intro mn. 53 ff.).[49] According to the United Nations Committee on Economic, Social and Cultural Rights (CESCR), the right to adequate housing 'should be seen as the right to live somewhere in security, peace and dignity'.[50] The right applies to all people 'regardless of age, economic status, group or other affiliation or status and other such factors'.[51] The right to adequate housing is enshrined in the Universal Declaration of Human Rights (UDHR) of 1948 and the International Covenant on Economic, Social and Cultural Rights (ICESCR) of 1996. Art. 25(1) of the UDHR states: 'Everyone has the right to a standard of living adequate for the health and well-being of himself and of his family, including [...] housing [...]'. The central instrument concerning the protection of the right to adequate housing is the ICESCR.[52] Art. 11 states that 'the States Parties to the present Covenant recognise the right of everyone to an adequate standard of living for himself and his family, including adequate food, clothing and housing, and to the continuous improvement of living conditions'.

20   The right to adequate housing includes both certain freedoms and entitlements. Freedoms include '[p]rotection against forced evictions and the arbitrary destruction and

---

[42] https://ec.europa.eu/eurostat/web/degree-of-urbanisation/background.

[43] https://ec.europa.eu/eurostat/web/degree-of-urbanisation/background.

[44] Eurostat, *Applying the Degree of Urbanisation, A Methodological Manual To Define Cities, Towns And Rural Areas For International Comparisons, 2021 edition* (2020).

[45] Further reading: Aust and Nijman, *Research Handbook on International Law and Cities* (2021).

[46] Further information: UN DESA, *The World's Cities in 2018, Data Booklet* (2018), 1; further information: UN Habitat, *World Cities Report 2020, The Value of Sustainable Urbanization* (2020).

[47] UN-Habitat, *The Right to Adequate Housing* (2019), 1.

[48] UN-Habitat, *The Right to Adequate Housing* (2019), 1.

[49] Rudd et al, 'The UN, the Urban Sustainable Development Goal, and the New Urban Agenda' in Elmqvist et al. (eds), *Urban Planet: Knowledge towards Sustainable Cities* (2018), 180 (185).

[50] CESCR General Comment No. 4: The Right to Adequate Housing (Art. 11(1) of the Covenant), para. 7.

[51] CESCR General Comment No. 4: The Right to Adequate Housing (Art. 11(1) of the Covenant), para. 6.

[52] UN-Habitat, *The Right to Adequate Housing* (2019), 11.

demolition of one's home; [t]he right to be free from arbitrary interference with one's home, privacy and family; and [t]he right to choose one's residence, to determine where to live and to freedom of movement'.[53] Entitlements include 'security of tenure; housing, land and property restitution; equal and non-discriminatory access to adequate housing; participation in housing-related decision making at the national and community level'.[54] Further, housing must meet certain criteria to be considered adequate.[55] Housing is adequate if it has 'more than four walls and a roof' and meets at least the criteria of legal security, availability of services, materials, facilities and infrastructure, affordability, habitability, accessibility, location and cultural appropriateness.[56]

In addition, there are people who are not housed at all, i.e. homeless, which exposes   **21** them to exclusion with high risks. On a global scale, around 150 million are affected by homelessness.[57] An unusual way to protect the rights of homeless persons is the Model European Homeless Bill of Rights[58] which was adopted by FEANTSA with the aim to countering the criminalisation of homelessness, to be seen as a recent policy trend in various European countries.[59] Yet, the phenomenon of criminalising homelessness can also be observed outside of Europe.[60]

The progress on SDG 11 is measured by the 'proportion of urban population living in   **22** slums, informal settlements or inadequate housing' according to indicator 11.1.1.

1. Forced Eviction

In the context of development and infrastructure projects, forced evictions are car-   **23** ried out by governments with the intention of serving the public interest.[61] However, these forced evictions leave the people affected homeless, landless and in extreme poverty.[62] Therefore, forced evictions violate various internationally recognised civil, cultural, economic, political and social human rights, including the right to adequate housing.[63] In particular, forced evictions are often characterised by a lack of security of tenure.[64] Security of tenure means that 'all persons should possess a degree of security of tenure which guarantees legal protection against forced eviction, harassment and other threats'.[65] Forced eviction can be defined as 'the permanent or temporary removal against the will of individuals, families and / or communities from the homes and / or land which the occupy, without the provision of, and access to, appropriate forms

---

[53] UN-Habitat, *The Right to Adequate Housing* (2019), 3.

[54] UN-Habitat, *The Right to Adequate Housing* (2019), 3.

[55] CESCR General Comment No. 4: The Right to Adequate Housing (Art. 11(1) of the Covenant), para. 8.

[56] UN-Habitat, *The Right to Adequate Housing* (2019), 3 f.

[57] Ploszka, 'A Homeless Bill of Rights as a New Instrument to Protect the Rights of Homeless Persons' (2020), 16(4) *European Constitutional Law Review*, 601 (603).

[58] Ploszka, 'A Homeless Bill of Rights as a New Instrument to Protect the Rights of Homeless Persons' (2020), 16(4) *European Constitutional Law Review*, 601 (602).

[59] Ploszka, 'A Homeless Bill of Rights as a New Instrument to Protect the Rights of Homeless Persons' (2020), 16(4) *European Constitutional Law Review*, 601 (609).

[60] Ploszka, 'A Homeless Bill of Rights as a New Instrument to Protect the Rights of Homeless Persons' (2020), 16(4) *European Constitutional Law Review*, 601 (610).

[61] UN-Habitat, *Forced Evictions* (2014), 1; further reading: Udemezue Onyebueke et al., 'Evicting the poor in the 'overriding public interest': Crisis of rights and interests, and contestations in Nigerian cities' (2020) 101 *Cities*, 102675.

[62] UN-Habitat, *Forced Evictions* (2014), 1.

[63] UN-Habitat, *Forced Evictions* (2014), 5.

[64] UN-Habitat, *Forced Evictions* (2014), 8.

[65] CESCR General Comment No. 4: The Right to Adequate Housing (Art. 11(1) of the Covenant), para. 8(a).

of legal or other protection'.[66] The UN Commission on Human Rights stated that 'the practice of forced eviction constitutes a gross violation of human rights, in particular the right to adequate housing'.[67] Consequently, large-scale evictions are only justified in exceptional circumstances and must remain in harmony with the applicable principles of international law.[68] Governments often justify forced evictions in informal settlements based on the 'lack of title and residency'.[69] In the case of a justified eviction, the eviction must be 'carried out in a lawful, reasonable and proportionate matter and in accordance with international law'.[70] Those affected by eviction should be provided with effective remedies and redress such as compensation.[71] In principle, it is the responsibility of governments to provide legal certainty.[72] The Habitat II Agenda of 1996 stated in this context:

> We further commit ourselves to the objectives of: [...]
> (b) Providing legal security of tenure and equal access to land to all people, including women and those living in poverty; [...]
> (n) Protecting all people from and providing legal protection and redress for forced evictions that are contrary to the law, taking human rights into consideration; when evictions are unavoidable, ensuring, as appropriate, that alternative suitable solutions are provided.[73]

24   The prevention of evictions is also addressed in Habitat III, but rather hidden. It is addressed in the context of promoting 'affordable, sustainable housing options' and in the context of promoting 'the development of adequate and enforceable regulations in the housing sector'.[74] To improve security of tenure, the Special Rapporteur published 'Guiding principles on security of tenure for the urban poor' in 2014.[75] It is essential that forced evictions do not lead to homelessness or human rights violations.[76]

2. Informal Settlements

25   Another challenge of adequate housing are informal settlements. There are many reasons for the emergence of informal settlements and slums, including population growth, lack of affordable housing, weak governance, discrimination as well as displacement.[77] Informal settlements can be defined as 'areas where housing units have been constructed on land that the occupants have no legal right to or/and unplanned settlements where housing is not in compliance with current planning and building regulations'.[78] Due

---

[66] General Comment No. 7: The right to adequate housing (Art. 11.1): forced evictions, para. 3.

[67] E/CN.4/RES/1993/77, para. 1.

[68] UN-Habitat, *The Right to Adequate Housing* (2019), 5.

[69] UN-Habitat, *Forced Evictions* (2014), 9.

[70] UN-Habitat, *The Right to Adequate Housing* (2019), 5.

[71] UN-Habitat, *The Right to Adequate Housing* (2019), 5.

[72] UN-Habitat, *Forced Evictions* (2014), 9.

[73] A/CONF.165/14, Report of the United Nations Conference on Human Settlements (Habitat II)* (Istanbul, 3-14 June 1996).

[74] A/RES/71/256, *New Urban Agenda*, 25 January 2017, paras. 107, 111.

[75] A/HRC/25/54, Report of the Special Rapporteur on adequate housing as a component of the right to an adequate standard of living, and on the right to non-discrimination in this context, Raquel Rolnik, 30 December 2013.

[76] UN-Habitat, *The Right to Adequate Housing* (2019), 5.

[77] UN-Habitat, *Habitat III Issue Paper: 22 – Informal Settlements* (2015), 2.

[78] UNEP, *The ABC for Sustainable Cities: A Glossary for Policy Makers* (2016), 34; On unauthorised buildings in Italy see Esposito and Punziano, 'Abitare la crisi della casa: strategie e significati dell'informalità abitativa in Italia' (2020), No. 15 *Argomenti*; Abbate, 'Processi di edificazione abusiva nel territorio di Agrigento: una questione irrisolta' (2009), *Progettare le Identità del Territorio. Piani e Interventi per uno Sviluppo Locale Autosostenibile nel Paesaggio Agricolo della Valle dei Templi di Agrigento*, 145-64; Cilona, 'Edilizia abusiva a Favara. Analisi dell'insediamento e sviluppo del territorio' (2007) *1 Convegno*

to the poor living conditions that prevail in informal settlements, conditions in these settlements can be considered one of the most pervasive human rights violations.[79] In particular, the state denies the population their right to access basic shelter.[80] Slums represent one such form of an informal settlement.[81] The term 'slum' describes a 'wide range of low-income settlements and / or poor human conditions'[82] which is a 'heavily populated urban area characterized by substandard housing and squalor'.[83] Slums can be divided into slums of hope and slums of despair.[84] Slums of hope are emerging settlements (new, usually self-built structures that are usually illegal), while slums of despair are shrinking neighbourhoods that are going through a process of decay.[85] A slum household is defined by a 2003 UN definition as 'a group of individuals living under the same roof lacking one or more of the following five conditions: (1) access to improved water, (2) access to improved sanitation facilities, (3) sufficient living area - not overcrowded, (4) structural quality/durability of dwellings, and (5) security of tenure'.[86]

III. Public and Sustainable Transport

Barely half of the world's urban population has appropriate access to public trans-   26 port.[87] Therefore, SDG 11.2 aims to 'provide access to safe, affordable, accessible and sustainable transport systems for all, improving road safety, notably by expanding public transport, with special attention to the needs of those in vulnerable situations, women, children, persons with disabilities and older persons' by 2030. Sustainable transport means

the provision of services and infrastructure for the mobility of people and goods— advancing economic and social development to benefit today's and future generations— in a manner that is safe, affordable, accessible, efficient, and resilient, while minimizing carbon and other emissions and environmental impacts.[88]

Public transport can be defined as a 'shared passenger transport services that are available to the general public and which are provided for the public good', like 'cars, buses, trolleys, trams, trains, subways, and ferries that are shared by strangers without prior arrangement'.[89] Access to public transport is considered convenient if the nearest stop of a public transport is within a walking distance of 500 m.[90] While access to transport previously focused on infrastructure development to improve the use of private ve-

---

Internazionale. Scenari dell'abitare abusivo. Strategie per l'intervento di recupero. 1st International Symposium. Scenarios of illegal dwelling. Strategies of building and town recovery.

[79] A/73/310/Rev.1, *Report of the Special Rapporteur on adequate housing as a component of the right to an adequate standard of living, and on the right to non-discrimination in this context*, 18 December 2018, 2 (Summary).

[80] A/73/310/Rev.1, *Report of the Special Rapporteur on adequate housing as a component of the right to an adequate standard of living, and on the right to non-discrimination in this context*, 18 December 2018, para. 12.

[81] UN-Habitat, *The Challenge of Slums: Global Report on Human Settlements 2003* (2003), 9.

[82] UN-Habitat, *The Challenge of Slums: Global Report on Human Settlements 2003* (2003), 8.

[83] UN-Habitat, *The Challenge of Slums: Global Report on Human Settlements 2003* (2003), 8.

[84] UN-Habitat, *The Challenge of Slums: Global Report on Human Settlements 2003* (2003), 9.

[85] UN-Habitat, *The Challenge of Slums: Global Report on Human Settlements 2003* (2003), 9.

[86] UN-Habitat, *Habitat III Issue Paper: 22 – Informal Settlements* (2015), 2.

[87] UN, *The Sustainable Development Goals Report 2020* (2020), 46.

[88] High-level Advisory Group on Sustainable Transport, *Mobilizing Sustainable Transport for Development* (2016), 7.

[89] UN-Habitat, *SDG Indicator 11.2.1 Training Module: Public Transport System* (2018), 8.

[90] UN-Habitat, *SDG Indicator 11.2.1 Training Module: Public Transport System* (2018), 8.

hicles, sustainable transport focused on the quality of life that can be achieved through access by transport, as well as on safety and social equity.[91] The concept of 'access to transport' is directly reflected in SDG 11.2. At an international level, no binding legal instruments on this topic exist.[92] However, non-binding instruments can be found.[93] In the NUA, which was developed in 2017 at the UN Conference on Housing and Sustainable Urban Development and endorsed by the UN General Assembly, the participants stated that they 'envisage cities and human settlements [with] equal access for all to public goods and quality services in areas such as [...] mobility and transportation'.[94] The NUA aims to ensure that the urban population can profit from economic and social chances by having access to safe and suitable transport, taking into account all population groups.[95] Furthermore, this agenda emphasised the importance of sustainable and efficient transport in terms of human health.[96] It aims to support the 'significant increase in accessible, safe, efficient, affordable and sustainable infrastructure for public transport, as well as non-motorized options such as walking and cycling, prioritizing them over private motorized transportation'.[97] The Ashgabat Statement, adopted at the 2016 United Nations World Conference on Sustainable Transport, emphasised the importance of sustainable transport for the implementation of the SDGs.[98] It was reaffirmed that sustainable transport is of great importance for a functioning public life.[99] In particular, it stressed the importance of access to transport for rural populations to enable them to access urban economic as well as social opportunities.[100] Furthermore, mobility can be seen in the light of a human right.[101] In this perspective, mobility is about 'granting access to opportunities and empowering people to fully exercise their human rights'.[102] Since it is generally accepted that political, social, cultural and economic rights can only be exercised if they are made accessible, this also has to apply to mobility.[103] In the course of providing accessibility, social, economic, political and physical barriers need to be overcome.[104] For the aspect of road safety, reference is made to SDG 3.6.

27 The progress of SDG 11.2 is measured by the 'proportion of the population that has convenient access to public transport by sex, age and persons with disabilities' according to indicator 11.2.1.

---

[91] High-level Advisory Group on Sustainable Transport, *Mobilizing Sustainable Transport for Development* (2016), 12.

[92] Sustainable Mobility for All, *A Review of international agreements, conventions and other instrument to achieve sustainable mobility* (2018), 11.

[93] Sustainable Mobility for All, *A Review of international agreements, conventions and other instrument to achieve sustainable mobility* (2018), 15.

[94] A/RES/71/256, *New Urban Agenda*, 25 January 2017, para. 13(a).

[95] Sustainable Mobility for All, *A Review of international agreements, conventions and other instrument to achieve sustainable mobility* (2018), 15.

[96] A/RES/71/256, *New Urban Agenda*, 25 January 2017, para. 54.

[97] A/RES/71/256, *New Urban Agenda*, 25 January 2017, para. 114(a).

[98] Ashgabat Statement on Commitments and Policy Recommendations on the Global Sustainable Transport Conference, para. 3.

[99] Ashgabat Statement on Commitments and Policy Recommendations on the Global Sustainable Transport Conference, para. 5.

[100] Ashgabat Statement on Commitments and Policy Recommendations on the Global Sustainable Transport Conference, para. 12.

[101] UN-Habitat, *Planning and Design for Sustainable Urban Mobility: Global Report on Human Settlements 2013* (2013), 3.

[102] UN-Habitat, *Planning and Design for Sustainable Urban Mobility: Global Report on Human Settlements 2013* (2013), 3.

[103] UN-Habitat, *Planning and Design for Sustainable Urban Mobility: Global Report on Human Settlements 2013* (2013), 3.

[104] UN-Habitat, *Planning and Design for Sustainable Urban Mobility: Global Report on Human Settlements 2013* (2013), 3.

IV. Urban and Territorial Planning

While 26.9 per cent of the world's population lived in cities in 1950, it is projected   **28** that 60 per cent of the world's population will live in cities by 2030.[105] This poses an enormous challenge to the way cities are planned. As a result, SDG 11.3 places an unprecedented focus on urban planning.[106] SDG 11.3 aims to 'enhance inclusive and sustainable urbanization and capacity for participatory, integrated and sustainable human settlement planning and management in all countries' by 2030. Urban planning is an important tool for 'reshaping forms and functions of cities [...] in order to generate endogenous economic growth, prosperity and employment, while addressing the needs of the most vulnerable, marginalized or underserved groups'.[107] Urban and territorial planning can be defined as 'a decision-making process aimed at realizing economic, social, cultural and environmental goals through the development of spatial visions, strategies and plans and the application of a set of policy principles, tools, institutional and participatory mechanisms and regulatory procedure'.[108] Urban planning, in particular, is 'the activity of designing, organising or preparing for the future lay-out and condition of a city or town' and 'consist of a conscious control of growth or change in a city, town, or community, taking into account aesthetics, industry, utilities, transportation, and many other factors that affect the quality of life'.[109] The urban planning aspect is reflected in the NUA which states in the relevant part:

> By addressing the way cities and human settlements are planned, designed, financed, developed, governed and managed, the New Urban Agenda will help to end poverty and hunger in all its forms and dimensions; reduce inequalities; promote sustained, inclusive and sustainable economic growth; achieve gender equality and the empowerment of all women and girls in order to fully harness their vital contribution to sustainable development; improve human health and well-being; foster resilience; and protect the environment.[110]

NUA includes 'planning and managing urban spatial development' as an important   **29** component for implementing the agenda, as well as several references to 'urban and territorial planning'.[111] Furthermore, 'urban and territorial planning and design' is part of UN-Habitat's Action Framework for Implementation of the New Urban Agenda (AFINUA).[112] Moreover, the NUA refers to the International Guidelines on Urban and Territorial Planning[113], which were adopted by the Governing Council of UN-Habitat in 2015. According to these guidelines, urban planning is an 'inclusive and participatory decision-making process', 'which promotes local democracy, participation and inclusion, transparency and accountability'.[114] Those guidelines aim to improve '"policies, plans, designs and implementation processes" for more compact, socially inclusive, better integrated and connected cities and territories that foster sustainable urban development

---

[105] UN-Habitat, *International Guidelines on Urban and Territorial Planning* (2015), 1.

[106] Rudd et al, 'The UN, the Urban Sustainable Development Goal, and the New Urban Agenda' in Elmqvist et al. (eds), *Urban Planet: Knowledge towards Sustainable Cities* (2018), 180 (185).

[107] UN-Habitat, *International Guidelines on Urban and Territorial Planning* (2015), 2.

[108] UN-Habitat, *International Guidelines on Urban and Territorial Planning* (2015), 2.

[109] UNEP, *The ABC for Sustainable Cities: A Glossary for Policy Makers* (2016), 50.

[110] A/RES/71/256, *New Urban Agenda*, 25 January 2017, para. 5.

[111] UN-Habitat, *International Guidelines on Urban and Territorial Planning (IG-UTP) Handbook* (2018), 4.

[112] UN-Habitat, *International Guidelines on Urban and Territorial Planning (IG-UTP) Handbook* (2018), 4.

[113] A/RES/71/256, *New Urban Agenda*, 25 January 2017, para. 93.

[114] UN-Habitat, *International Guidelines on Urban and Territorial Planning* (2015), 8.

and are resilient to climate change'.[115] Public participation has become central to urban planning in the last decades as a reaction to the ineffectiveness of 'dominant top-down models and expert-driven approaches in planning practices'.[116] The term encompasses various activities that concern the involvement of the public in the planning and management process in order to be able to influence policy and action.[117] Yet, urban planning faces a lack of trust in government institutions, as they are seen as too bureaucratic and unable to meet citizens' needs.[118] Therefore, public participation can serve to restore the trust of the citizens.[119] The main methods of participation are public meeting and public hearings[120] which allows different groups to bring in 'their needs, demands and expectation' into the planning process.[121]

30   In addition to sustainable urban planning, development planning should take place that takes into account a wide range of factors. SDG 11.a. aims to 'support positive economic, social and environmental links between urban, peri-urban and rural areas by strengthening national and regional development planning'. Progress is measured by the 'Number of countries that have national urban policies or regional development plans that (a) respond to population dynamics; (b) ensure balanced territorial development; and (c) increase local fiscal space.'

31   Furthermore, SDG 11.c calls to '[s]upport least developed countries, including through financial and technical assistance, in building sustainable and resilient buildings utilising local materials'.

V. Environmental Impacts

32   In order to make cities sustainable, the environmental impacts they generate must be taken into account. Therefore, SDG 11.6 aims to 'reduce the adverse per capita environmental impact of cities, including by paying special attention to air quality and municipal and other waste management' by 2030. Increasing urbanisation poses problems for municipal solid waste management, especially as the need for landfills and wastewater treatment plants increases.[122] A failure to ensure safe disposal and management of waste endangers the environment and human health.[123] This is particularly the case in developing countries where landfill management is either inadequate or non-existent.[124] Municipal waste can be defined as 'waste collected and treated by or for municipalities' which 'covers waste from households, including bulky waste, similar waste from commerce and trade, office buildings, institutions and small businesses,

---

[115] UN-Habitat, *International Guidelines on Urban and Territorial Planning (IG-UTP) Handbook* (2018), 5.

[116] Akbar et al, 'Participatory planning practice in rural Indonesia: A sustainable development goals-based evaluation' (2020), 51 (3) *Community Development*, 243 (243).

[117] Akbar et al, 'Participatory planning practice in rural Indonesia: A sustainable development goals-based evaluation' (2020), 51 (3) *Community Development*, 243 (243).

[118] Åström, 'Participatory Urban Planning: What Would Make Planners Trust the Citizens?' (2020), 5(2) *Urban Planning*, 84 (85).

[119] Åström, 'Participatory Urban Planning: What Would Make Planners Trust the Citizens?' (2020), 5(2) *Urban Planning*, 84 (85).

[120] Akbar et al, 'Participatory planning practice in rural Indonesia: A sustainable development goals-based evaluation' (2020), 51 (3) *Community Development*, 243 (244).

[121] Pogacar et al., 'Promises and Limits of Participatory Urban Green Development: Experience from Maribor, Budapest, and Krakow' in Nared and Bole (eds), *Participatory Research and Planning in Practice* (2020), 75 (78).

[122] UNEP, *Sustainable, Resource Efficient Cities – Making It Happen!* (2012), 16.

[123] UNEP, *Sustainable, Resource Efficient Cities – Making It Happen!* (2012), 16.

[124] UNEP, *Sustainable, Resource Efficient Cities – Making It Happen!* (2012), 32.

as well as yard and garden waste, street sweepings, the contents of litter containers, and market cleansing waste if managed as household waste'.[125] The progress on municipal waste is measured according to indicator 11.6.1 by the 'proportion of municipal solid waste collected and managed in controlled facilities out of total municipal waste generated, by cities'. Another major burden in cities is air pollution, as 70 per cent of GHG emission are caused by cities[126] which can be explained by rapid urbanisation and vehicle emissions.[127] Air pollution means the presence of contaminant or pollutant substances in the air that do not disperse properly and that interfere with human health or welfare, or produce other harmful environmental effects'.[128] In fact, 90 per cent of the world's population lives in areas where air quality limits are exceeded.[129] In 2016, the WTO stated that 'health is one of the most 'effective markers' of the sustainable development of a city, reiterating its 2008 conclusion, that 'health and health equity should be at the heart of city planning'.[130] As a result, it is important to recognise that urban planning will deeply influence the health and well-being of its residents.[131] Nevertheless, a resilient legal framework concerning the prevention of polluted air still has to be developed.[132] The progress on air pollution is measured by 'annual mean levels of fine particulate matter (e.g. $PM_{2.5}$ and PM_{10}) in cities (population weighted)' according to indicator 11.6.2.

VI. Public Spaces

Public space is fundamental to sustainable cities as it improves health and well-being,   **33** facilitates social integration and economic exchange, and as a result improves the quality of life for all.[133] Therefore, SDG 11.7 aims to 'provide universal access to safe, inclusive and accessible, green and public spaces, in particular for women and children, older persons and persons with disabilities' by 2030. According to the Charter of Public Spaces, public spaces can be defined as 'all places publicly owned or of public use, accessible and enjoyable by all for free and without a profit motive'.[134] Four typologies can be distinguished: Streets, public open spaces, public facilities and markets.[135] With NUA, the parties committed themselves:

> to promoting safe, inclusive, accessible, green and quality public spaces as drivers of social and economic development, in order to sustainably leverage their potential to generate increased social

---

[125] https://data.oecd.org/waste/municipal-waste.htm.

[126] Giles-Corti, Lowe and Arundel, 'Achieving the SDGs: Evaluating indicators to be used to benchmarkand monitor progress towards creating healthy and sustainable cities' (2020) 124 (6) *Health Policy*, 581 (581).

[127] UNEP, *The ABC for Sustainable Cities: A Glossary for Policy Makers* (2016), 13.

[128] UNEP, *The ABC for Sustainable Cities: A Glossary for Policy Makers* (2016), 13.

[129] Liang and Gong, 'Urban and air pollution: a multi-city study of long-term effects of urban landscape patterns on air quality trends' (2020) 10 No. 18618 *Scientific Reports*, 1 (1).

[130] Giles-Corti, Lowe and Arundel, 'Achieving the SDGs: Evaluating indicators to be used to benchmarkand monitor progress towards creating healthy and sustainable cities' (2020) 124(6) *Health Policy*, 581 (582).

[131] Giles-Corti, Lowe and Arundel, 'Achieving the SDGs: Evaluating indicators to be used to benchmarkand monitor progress towards creating healthy and sustainable cities' (2020) 124(6) *Health Policy*, 581 (589).

[132] Huck et al., 'The Right to Breathe Clean Air and Access to Justice - Legal State of Play in International, European and National Law' (2021) 13(10) *International Environmental Law (eJournal)*, 1 (21).

[133] https://unhabitat.org/programme/global-public-space-programme.

[134] UN-Habitat, *SDG Indicator 11.7.1 Training Module: Public Spaces* (2018), 9.

[135] UN-Habitat, *SDG Indicator 11.7.1 Training Module: Public Spaces* (2018), 9.

and economic value, including property value, and to facilitate business and public and private investments and livelihood opportunities for all.[136]

34   Progress on SDG 11.7 is measured by the 'average share of the built-up area of cities that is open space for public use for all, by sex, age and persons with disabilities' according to Indicator 11.7.1 and by the 'proportion of persons victim of physical or sexual harassment, by sex, age, disability status and place of occurrence, in the previous 12 months' according to Indicator 11.7.2.

VII. Cultural and Natural Rights

35   Cultural heritage is a 'fragile wealth' that must be preserved and respected so that it is not lost forever.[137] To counteract a loss of cultural heritages, SDG 11.4 aims to 'strengthen efforts to protect and safeguard the world's cultural and natural heritage'. Cultural heritage, which has replaced the concept of cultural property, and its protection are part of international law.[138] Unlike cultural property, cultural heritage is 'considered to be of such value that its safeguarding is necessary because of a public interest, regardless of ownership'.[139] There is no universally accepted definition of cultural heritage.[140] Rather, definitions vary within national and international instruments.[141] Nevertheless, cultural heritage can include 'artefacts, monuments and groups of buildings and sites that have a variety of values, including symbolic, historical, artistic, aesthetic, ethnological or anthropological, scientific and social significance'.[142] Thereby, cultural heritage comprises 'things inherited from the past that are now considered so valuable or significant that individuals and communities wish to pass them on to future generations'.[143] A precise list of which objects are considered cultural heritage can be found in Art. 1 of the World Heritage Convention, which was adopted in 1972. The World Heritage Convention already stated

> that the cultural heritage and the natural heritage are increasingly threatened with destruction not only by the traditional causes of decay, but also by changing social and economic conditions which aggravate the situation with even more formidable phenomena of damage or destruction.[144]

36   Furthermore, Art. 4 of the Convention states:

> Each State Party to this Convention recognizes that the duty of ensuring the identification, protection, conservation, presentation and transmission to future generations of the cultural and natural heritage referred to in Articles 1 and 2 and situated on its territory, belongs primarily to that State.

---

[136] A/RES/71/256, *New Urban Agenda*, 25 January 2017, para. 53.

[137] UNESCO, *Culture for Development Indicators* (2014), 132.

[138] Donders, 'Cultural Heritage and Human Rights' in Francioni and Vrdoljak (eds), *The Oxford Handbook of International Cultural Heritage Law* (2020), 379 (379 f).

[139] Donders, 'Cultural Heritage and Human Rights' in Francioni and Vrdoljak (eds), *The Oxford Handbook of International Cultural Heritage Law* (2020), 379 (380).

[140] A/HRC/17/38, Report of the independent expert in the field of cultural rights, Farida Shaheed, 21 March 2011, 3.

[141] A/HRC/17/38, Report of the independent expert in the field of cultural rights, Farida Shaheed, 21 March 2011, 3.

[142] UNESCO Institute for Statistics, *The 2009 UNESCO Framework for Cultural Statistics* (2009), 25.

[143] A/HRC/17/38, Report of the independent expert in the field of cultural rights, Farida Shaheed, 21 March 2011, 4.

[144] UNESCO, *Convention concerning the protection of the world cultural and natural heritage*, Adopted by the General Conference at its seventeenth session, Paris, 16 November 1972, preamble.

Although, there is no human right to cultural heritage at international level,[145] ap-   37
proaches, however, can be seen for the creation of such a right.[146] On the one hand,
there has been a shift in international law from the protection of 'cultural heritage as
such, based on its historical value to humanity, its uniqueness and its non-renewable
character' to the protection of 'cultural heritage as a crucial value for peoples and
individuals in relation to the (re)construction of their cultural identity'.[147] On the other
hand, a link between cultural heritage and human rights was recognised by states in the
Human Rights Council and affirmed by the UN Special Rapporteur on cultural rights.[148]
The UN Rapporteur stated in his report that '[c]onsidering access to and enjoyment of
cultural heritage as a human right is a necessary and complementary approach to the
preservation/safeguard of cultural heritage'.[149]

Cultural heritage is closely linked to natural heritage.[150] A natural heritage includes   38
'natural features, geological and physiographical formations and delineated areas that
constitute the habitat of threatened species of animals and plants and natural sites of
value from the point of view of science, conservation or natural beauty'.[151] There are
many factors that threaten cultural and natural heritage, such as increasing urbanisation,
inadequate urban planning or disasters.[152] Recent disasters have shown how much
cultural and natural heritage can suffer from disaster events.[153] Yet, the protection of
cultural and natural heritage from disasters is not enshrined in international law.[154]

The progress of SDG 11.4 is measured by the 'total expenditure (public and private)   39
per capita spent on the preservation, protection and conservation of all cultural and
natural heritage' according to indicator 11.4.1.

VIII. Disaster Risk Reduction

In 2020, 389 disasters took place, mainly climate-related in the form of floods and   40
storms, resulting in 15,080 deaths, directly affecting 98 million people, while economic
losses amounted to US$ 17 billion.[155] This clearly shows the dangers that disasters pose
on the human security, especially since rapidly advancing urbanisation as well as the
lack of housing space encourage parts of the population to settle in disaster-prone areas
such as coastal lowlands or floodplains.[156] Therefore, SDG 11.5 seeks o avoid such
harmful events 'by 2030, significantly reduce the number of deaths and the number of

---

[145] Donders, 'Cultural Heritage and Human Rights' in Francioni and Vrdoljak (eds), *The Oxford Hand-book of International Cultural Heritage Law* (2020), 379 (380).

[146] Donders, 'Cultural Heritage and Human Rights' in Francioni and Vrdoljak (eds), *The Oxford Hand-book of International Cultural Heritage Law* (2020), 379 (380).

[147] Donders, 'Cultural Heritage and Human Rights' in Francioni and Vrdoljak (eds), *The Oxford Hand-book of International Cultural Heritage Law* (2020), 379 (380).

[148] Donders, 'Cultural Heritage and Human Rights' in Francioni and Vrdoljak (eds), *The Oxford Hand-book of International Cultural Heritage Law* (2020), 379 (380).

[149] A/HRC/17/38, Report of the independent expert in the field of cultural rights, Farida Shaheed, 21 March 2011, 3.

[150] Donders, 'Cultural Heritage and Human Rights' in Francioni and Vrdoljak (eds), *The Oxford Hand-book of International Cultural Heritage Law* (2020), 379 (385).

[151] UNESCO Institute for Statistics, *The 2009 UNESCO Framework for Cultural Statistics* (2009), 25.

[152] https://whc.unesco.org/en/158/.

[153] Bartolini, 'Cultural Heritage and Disasters' in Francioni and Vrdoljak (eds), *The Oxford Handbook of International Cultural Heritage Law* (2020), 145 (145).

[154] Bartolini, 'Cultural Heritage and Disasters' in Francioni and Vrdoljak (eds), *The Oxford Handbook of International Cultural Heritage Law* (2020), 145 (145).

[155] CRED & UNDRR, *2020: The non-COVID Year in Disaster* (2021), 2.

[156] UNISDR, *How To Make Cities More Resilient: A Handbook For Local Government Leaders* (2017), 10.

people affected and substantially decrease the direct economic losses relative to global gross domestic product caused by disasters, including water-related disasters, with a focus on protecting the poor and people in vulnerable situations'. Disasters are the result of a natural hazard.[157] A disaster is therefore the 'harm arising from the hazard, whether natural or man-made'.[158] There are two approaches for a legal definitions of the concept of 'disaster'.[159] Based on the 'occurrence of an event', a disaster can be defined as a 'calamitous event or series of events resulting in widespread loss of life, great human suffering and distress, mass displacement, or large scale material or environmental damage, thereby seriously disrupting the function of society'.[160] Based on the 'focus on the consequence of the onset of an event', a disaster can be defined as 'a serious disruption of the functioning of society, which poses a significant, widespread threat to human life, health, property of the environment, whether arising from accident, nature or human activity, whether developing suddenly or as the result of long-term processes, but excluding armed conflict'.[161] The state is legally obliged to 'to protect persons on its territory from the effects of the disaster'.[162] To determine the territory, the entire area affected by disasters must be included.[163]

41   The progress of SDG 11.5 is measured according to Indicator 11.5.1 by the 'number of deaths, missing persons and directly affected persons attributed to disasters per 100,000 population' and according to Indicator 11.5.2 by the 'direct economic loss in relation to global GDP, damage to critical infrastructure and number of disruptions to basic services, attributed to disasters'.

42   Another aspect of international disaster law is disaster risk reduction. The duty of a state to reduce disaster risk is reflected in SDG 11.b aims to 'substantially increase the number of cities and human settlements adopting and implementing integrated policies and plans towards inclusion, resource efficiency, mitigation and adaptation to climate change, resilience to disasters, and develop and implement, in line with the Sendai Framework for Disaster Risk Reduction 2015-2030, holistic disaster risk management at all levels' by 2020. The Sendai Framework for Disaster Risk Reduction was adopted during the Third UN World Conference on Disaster Risk Reduction. The objective of the Framework is 'the substantial reduction of disaster risk and losses in lives, livelihoods and health and in the economic, physical, social, cultural and environmental assets of persons, businesses, communities and countries'.[164] In particular, the Framework aims to

> [p]revent new and reduce existing disaster risk through the implementation of integrated and inclusive economic, structural, legal, social, health, cultural, educational, environmental, technological, political and institutional measures that prevent and reduce hazard exposure and vulnerability to disaster, increase preparedness for response and recovery, and thus strengthen resilience.[165]

---

[157] Pronto, 'International Disaster Law' in Geiß and Melzer (eds), *The Oxford Handbook of the international Law of Global Security* (2021), 566 (566).
[158] Pronto, 'International Disaster Law' in Geiß and Melzer (eds), *The Oxford Handbook of the international Law of Global Security* (2021), 566 (566).
[159] Pronto, 'International Disaster Law' in Geiß and Melzer (eds), *The Oxford Handbook of the international Law of Global Security* (2021), 566 (570).
[160] Pronto, 'International Disaster Law' in Geiß and Melzer (eds), *The Oxford Handbook of the international Law of Global Security* (2021), 566 (570).
[161] Pronto, 'International Disaster Law' in Geiß and Melzer (eds), *The Oxford Handbook of the international Law of Global Security* (2021), 566 (570).
[162] Pronto, 'International Disaster Law' in Geiß and Melzer (eds), *The Oxford Handbook of the international Law of Global Security* (2021), 566 (572).
[163] Pronto, 'International Disaster Law' in Geiß and Melzer (eds), *The Oxford Handbook of the international Law of Global Security* (2021), 566 (573).
[164] Sendai Framework for Disaster Risk Reduction 2015-2030, para. 16.
[165] Sendai Framework for Disaster Risk Reduction 2015-2030, para. 17.

Disaster risk can be defined as 'the potential disaster losses, in lives, health status,   **43**
livelihoods, assets and services, which could occur to a particular community or a
society over some specified future time period'.[166] Furthermore, disaster risk reduction
can be defined as 'the concept and practice of reducing disaster risks through systematic
efforts to analyse and manage the causal factors of disasters, including through reduced
exposure to hazards, lessened vulnerability of people and property, wise management of
land and the environment, and improved preparedness for adverse events'.[167] The duty
to reduce disaster risk means the obligation of States to 'reduce the risk of disasters by
taking appropriate measures, including through legislations and regulations to prevent,
mitigate and prepare for disasters'.[168] In this context, it is not a state's duty to completely
prevent or mitigate disasters, but to reduce the risk of potential harm.[169] For disaster risk
reduction, the territorial scope must be broader than just the area directly affected.[170]

The success of SDG 11.b. is measured according to Indicator 11.b.1 by the 'number   **44**
of countries that adopt and implement national disaster risk reduction strategies in line
with the Sendai Framework for Disaster Risk Reduction 2015-2030' and according to
Indicator 11.b.2 by the '[p]roportion of local governments that adopt and implement
local disaster risk reduction strategies in line with national disaster risk reduction strategies'. As of 2020, 85 countries reported that national strategies for disaster risk reduction
have been created that include parts of the Sendai Framework, while six countries have
created national strategies that consider the complete Sendai Framework.[171] As a result,
progress was made, but was not reached.[172]

IX. Women and Girls in Urban Planning

Until now, urban planning has been designed – mostly by men without the participa-   **45**
tion of women – for the interests of men, neglecting the interests of women and girls.[173]
As a result, urban planning does not represent women's daily lives and perspectives.[174]
Urban spaces can restrict the right of women and girls to move freely due to a lack of
security.[175] Moreover, women can be faced with discrimination concerning employment,
property ownership, and services.[176] Without access to public transport, women are
unable to receive proper medical treatment, which can lead to death or infertility.[177]
Insufficient housing conditions, overcrowding and poor hygiene contribute to higher
susceptibility to disease, leaving woman to take on care work.[178] In developing countries,

---

[166] UNISDR, *2009 UNISDR Terminology on Disaster Risk Reduction* (2009), 9 f.

[167] UNISDR, *2009 UNISDR Terminology on Disaster Risk Reduction* (2009), 10 f.

[168] Pronto, 'International Disaster Law' in Geiß and Melzer (eds), *The Oxford Handbook of the international Law of Global Security* (2021), 566 (575).

[169] Pronto, 'International Disaster Law' in Geiß and Melzer (eds), *The Oxford Handbook of the international Law of Global Security* (2021), 566 (576).

[170] Pronto, 'International Disaster Law' in Geiß and Melzer (eds), *The Oxford Handbook of the international Law of Global Security* (2021), 566 (574).

[171] https://unstats.un.org/sdgs/report/2020/progress-summary-for-SDG-targets/.

[172] https://unstats.un.org/sdgs/report/2020/progress-summary-for-SDG-targets/.

[173] World Bank, *Handbook for Gender-Inclusive Urban Planning and Design* (2020), 30.

[174] UN-Habitat, *Gender Issue Guide: Urban Planning and Design* (2012), 15.

[175] https://www.unwomen.org/en/news/in-focus/women-and-the-sdgs/sdg-11-sustainable-cities-comm
unities.

[176] UN-Habitat, *Gender Issue Guide: Urban Planning and Design* (2012), 16.

[177] https://www.unwomen.org/en/news/in-focus/women-and-the-sdgs/sdg-11-sustainable-cities-comm
unities.

[178] https://www.unwomen.org/en/news/in-focus/women-and-the-sdgs/sdg-11-sustainable-cities-comm
unities.

more women than men are forced to live under slum-like conditions, mostly women and girls aged 15 to 49, which means that they do not have full access to clean water, improved sanitation facilities, permanent housing or adequate living space.[179] The NUA addresses the problems women and girls are facing in the area of gender inequality[180] and states in its vision:

> Achieve gender equality and empower all women and girls by ensuring women's full and effective participation and equal rights in all fields and in leadership at all levels of decision-making, by ensuring decent work and equal pay for equal work, or work of equal value, for all women and by preventing and eliminating all forms of discrimination, violence and harassment against women and girls in private and public spaces.[181]

46   Yet, to be successful, a 'more effective agenda' might be needed.[182]

C. Interdependences of SDG 11

47   'More than 3.9 billion people-half the world's population were affected by the lockdown decisions of their governments in April 2020. But for many of them, the appeals to stay at home and keep at physical distance seem cynical. After all, more than 1 billion people worldwide live in densely populated slums or informal settlements.[183] Many live in cramped conditions and often have no access to the most vital public services such as water, sanitation and electricity. Policy and local practise are often exposed to financial constraints, sometimes overcome the challenge of slum with the focus on upgrading, which are not seen as effectively.[184]

48   Slums are an ideal breeding ground for viruses. In refugee camps, the 'demand for physical distancing is a farce, and the risk of a rapid spread of the virus is inevitable.'[185]

49   With over 90 per cent of SARS-CoV-2 cases occurring in urban areas,[186] the pandemic highlights the urgent need to develop new sustainable strategies and the critical role of governments who acts as first responders in crisis response, recovery and rebuilding. As urban economies account for more than 80 per cent of global GDP,[187] governmental measurements to mitigate the further spread of the virus (such as lockdowns, curfews etc.) led and will lead to economic impacts beyond their boundaries, e.g. the loss of an estimated 400 million full-time jobs in the first quarter of 2020.[188] Building or (re)shaping the cities of the future into a more resilient, sustainable, inclusive and safe form could mitigate the outcomes of the SARS-CoV-2 pandemic and prepare cities and communities for future pandemics and other catastrophic events, which reveals that SDG 11 is directly linked to SDG 1, SDG 3, SDG5, SDG 9, SDG 12, SDG 14 and SDG 15, 16 und 17.

---

[179] UN Women/DESA, *Progress on the Sustainable Development Goals, The Gender Snapshot 2019* (2019), 17.

[180] Moser, 'Gender transformation in a new global urban agenda: challenges for Habitat III and beyond' (2016) 29 (1) *IIED*, 221 (234).

[181] A/RES/71/256, *New Urban Agenda*, 25 January 2017, para. 13(c).

[182] Moser, 'Gender transformation in a new global urban agenda: challenges for Habitat III and beyond' (2016) 29 (1) *IIED*, 221 (234).

[183] https://unstats.un.org/sdgs/report/2019/goal-11/.

[184] Croese and Cirolia and Graham, 'Towards Habitat III: Confronting the disjuncture between global policy and local practice on Africa's 'challenge of slums'' (2016) 53 *Habitat International*, 237 (239 ff.).

[185] Martens and Ellmers and Pokorny on behalf of Global Policy Watch, *COVID-19 and the SDGs, The impact of the coronavirus pandemic on the global sustainability agenda*, 6 f.

[186] UN, *The Sustainable Development Goals Report 2020*, 46.

[187] World Bank, *Urban Development* (2020).

[188] ILO, *ILO Monitor: COVID-19 and the world of work. Fifth edition*, 1.

Currently, the pandemic is hitting the most vulnerable persons the hardest, includ- 50
ing the 1 billion residents of the world's densely populated informal settlements and
slums.[189] Many of those residents live without access to on-site water or sanitation,
are overcrowded and often face a constant threat of forced eviction, which makes it
almost impossible for those residents to follow the basic guidelines to prevent the further
spread of the virus, such as social / physical distancing, handwashing and quarantine
possibilities.[190] Ensuring access for all to adequate and safe housing, basic services, and
upgrade slums (SDG 11.1) is directly linked to SDG 1 and also synergises well with
achieving universal and equitable access to safe water (SDG 6.1) and achieving access to
adequate and equitable sanitation and hygiene for all (SDG 6.2).

In densely inhabited slums or other forms of severe housing deprivation, people often 51
lack access to clean water, sanitation and energy, and are also often exposed to air
pollution. In the short term, housing which is free of pollutants and hazards (SDG 3.9)
and which provides adequate temperatures and space to support health and well-being
in general, equipped with an accessible and sustainable transport infrastructure (SDG
11.2) to improve access to health care facilities (SDG 3.8).[191] In addition, ensuring
access to adequate, safe and affordable housing (SDG 11.1) will also help to combat
communicable diseases and future pandemics (SDG 3.3).

SDG 11.2 promotes the access to safe, affordable and sustainable transport systems 52
for, improving road safety by notably expanding public transport with a special attention to the needs of those in vulnerable situations, women, children, persons with
disabilities and older persons. In 2019, only half of the world's urban population had
convenient access to public transport and progress made towards this goal are haltered
or even reversed during the events of the SARS-CoV-2 pandemic.[192] SDG 11.2 could
be achieved by developing quality, reliable, sustainable and resilient infrastructure (SDG
9.1), promoting inclusive and sustainable industrialisation (SDG 9.2), increasing access
of small-scale enterprises in to value chains and markets (SDG 9.3) and upgrading existing infrastructure and retrofit industries to make them sustainable (SDG 9.4). Achieving
SDG 11.2 would also consequently improve air quality, as sustainable transportation
systems will also reduce air pollution and thus this target also synergizes well with SDG
3.9.

Between 2007 and 2050, the urban population is expected to increase as much as 53
it did since 1920, that is, 3.1 billion additional urban dwellers are expected by 2050
(which equals 70 per cent of the world's population).[193] Despite the positive efficiencies
of compactness, cities remain large-scale consumers of water, energy, and natural and
processed products as well as significant generators of GHG emissions and waste, which
often results in overconsumption and inefficiency, as the materials flows in many cities
are linear rather than circular.[194] To effectively reduce the adverse per capita environmental impact of cities (SDG 11.6) it is mandatory, that waste generation is reduced
through the promotion of a circular economy and materials flows (as promoted in SDG
12.5).

---

[189] UN, *The Sustainable Development Goals Report 2020*, 46.
[190] OHCHR, *Covid-19 Guidance Note: Protecting residents of informal settlements*, 1.
[191] Griggs et al., *A Guide to SDG Interactions: From Science to Implementation* (2017), 88.
[192] E/2020/57, *Progress towards the Sustainable Development Goals, Report of the Secretary-General*, 28
April 2020, 15.
[193] UN/POP/EGM-URB/2008/01, *An Overview of Urbanization, Internal Migration, Population Distribution and Development in the World*, 3.
[194] UNGA Open Working Group on Sustainable Development Goals, *Compendium of TST Issues Briefs*,
154.

54   Coasts are a highly attractive zone for human settlement and urban development, often driven by the opportunities for economic activities and natural resources provided by coasts and coastal zones, which is underlined by the fact that 65 per cent of all megacities worldwide are located in coastal areas, and as a result, coastal areas generally show higher population densities, growth and urbanisation trends than inland areas, which implies a direct relationship between ocean sustainability and sustainable cities and communities.[195] Therefore, achieving the targets of SDG 14 influences coastal cities and communities, as amongst others, by preventing and significantly reducing marine pollution of kinds, in particular from land-based activities (SDG 14.1) would improve adequate, safe and affordable housing and basic services and upgrade slums (SDG 11.1), enhance inclusive and sustainable urbanisation processes (SDG 11.3) and reduce the adverse per capita environmental impact of (especially) those cities (SDG 11.6).

D. Jurisprudential Significance of SDG 11

55   SDG 11 with its very different manifestations is clearly borne by governance, cooperation and partnerships (→ Goal 17). Cities, as well as rural regions and communities, have a safeguard role towards their inhabitants, e.g. with regard to the supply of gas, electricity, drinking water (and wastewater management), infrastructure, public goods and quality services (→ Goal 9 mn. 4, 22 f.). As organisational units, they are responsible for providing their residents with easy access and participation to critical services. They are also responsible for establishing and maintaining security and order. If they fail to provide the necessary regulation and / or reliable executive authority, this endangers the organisational unit city or other human settlement and thus the possibility of peaceful coexistence of the population in these areas. In legal terms, this complex interaction of various public and private stakeholders is initially interpreted as 'good urban governance' which is partly seen as a normative guiding function in the SDG agenda.[196] In particular, SDG 11 is shaped by the New Urban Agenda[197] declared at the Habitat III conference in Quito. Although not legally binding, the Habitat III declaration connects the wording of SDG 11 (since it reflects parts of it) with the human rights background to housing. In this regard, Aust denotes the Habitat III declaration as a '*lex specialis* relationship in a loose sense' towards the SDGs.[198] This idea becomes even more important when considering the barely possible inclusion of the most diverse residents and other stakeholders worldwide, who are to be granted participation.

56   The Global Agenda 2030 opens up the horizon of international law and human rights for SDG 11 as well as for every other SDG. Even if the development process was characterised by various coalitions that were not primarily concerned with anchoring

---

[195] Griggs et al., *A Guide to SDG Interactions: From Science to Implementation* (2017), 181.

[196] Aust and Plessis, 'Good urban governance as a global aspiration: on the potential and limits of SDG 11' in French and Kotzé (eds), *Sustainable Development Goals, Law Theory and Implementation* (2018), 201.

[197] The New Urban Agenda acknowledges the 'purposes and principles of the Charter of the United Nations, including full respect for international law. In this regard, the New Urban Agenda is grounded in the Universal Declaration of Human Rights, international human rights treaties, the Millennium Declaration and the 2005 World Summit Outcome. It is informed by other instruments such as the Declaration on the Right to Development' and draws its formulation from the Brundtland definition of sustainable development; see A/RES/71/256*, *New Urban Agenda*, 25 January 2017, paras. 11, 12.

[198] Albeit with the limitation of not being legally binding, Aust and Plessis, 'Good urban governance as a global aspiration: on the potential and limits of SDG 11' in French and Kotzé (eds), *Sustainable Development Goals, Law Theory and Implementation* (2018), 214.

human rights in this context,[199] this does not change the context of interpretation or the reality in which jurisdiction often is reflected.

Of primary relevance is the 'right to (adequate) housing' as a basic human right   57 which is inherent in the meaning of SDG 11.1. Further points of reference are the rights to life, security, and physical integrity, as well as the right to a healthy environment.[200] Yet, other, indirect constellations of connection are plausible as well that fall within the broad scope of SDG 11.

Various 'Sustainable Mega Cities' around the world, which are oriented towards sus-   58 tainability requirements, provide initial insights into what the city or human settlement of the future may look like and which legal and governance challenges are linked to this (necessary) transformation.

The reference to the Sendai Framework for Disaster Risk Reduction 2015-2030 (SDG   59 11.6), as globally agreed by the UN Member States, also illustrates the increasing influ-ence of the effects of climate change on the structural design of cities. In particular, critical infrastructures[201] and basic services[202] are often subject to relevant protection regulations, even if these legal regulations are of domestic nature. In this context, it is questionable what effect and application international and public international law has on cities that act together in global networks, e.g. by financing and investing. In any case, they are not original subjects of international law that are bound by international law.[203]

The Sendai Framework itself calls for regional and international cooperation as well   60 as global partnerships and the identification of responsibilities at the national level. The Sendai Framework thus translates the global theme of SDG 11 into national contexts and clearly shows which instruments must be used and which measurements of success must be carried out. In doing so, the framework leaves the way open to go beyond disaster management laws, the application of which alone would not meet the needs of the different realities of life.[204]

Laws, regulations, and public policies together with strategies and plans as well as   61 standards are instrumental to interpret and translate into national and local contexts the Sendai Framework's guidance, and thus enable its implementation.[205]

I. Jurisdiction on Vision and Objectives

The actions of cities and communities called for by the NUA, which describes the   62 implementation of SDG 11 in more detail, must contribute to the global shift toward a sustainable development that tackles 'poverty, improves health outcomes, expands access to education and reduces carbon emissions, among other societal challenges.'[206] This

---

[199] Dodds and Donoghue and Leiva Roesch, *Negotiating the Sustainable Development Goals, A transfor-mational agenda for an insecure world* (2017), 66.

[200] See ILA, *Conference Report Sydney, Role Of International Law In Sustainable Natural Resource Management For Development* (2018), 44.

[201] E.g. physical structures, facilities, networks and other assets which provide services that are essential to the social and economic functioning of a community or society.

[202] E.g. societal services that are needed to function appropriately such as health and educational facilities or waste management.

[203] Similar thoughts see Aust, 'Shining Cities on the Hill? The Global City, Climate Change, and Inter-national Law' (2015) 26(1) *EJIL*, 270; and on the same topic: Du Plessis, *Climate change law and sustain-able development*, 187 ff.

[204] See UNISDIR, *Reading the Sendai Framework for Disaster Risk Reduction 2015 – 2030*, paras. 97-100.

[205] See UNISDIR, *Reading the Sendai Framework for Disaster Risk Reduction 2015 – 2030*, paras. 99.

[206] UN Habitat, *World Cities Report 2020, The Value of Sustainable Urbanization* (2020), xv.

builds on various processes, such as national urban policies, legislation, spatial planning and local finance frameworks.

63   Inevitably, various tensions are created, especially when objectives of sustainable development and the growth of cities and communities collide with the accompanying transformation of peripheral residential areas, e.g. poorer neighbourhoods or slums. This predominantly affects the poorest and deprived dwellers the harshest. A frequent concern in this regard are forced evictions, which take place in housing tenancies with insecure tenants and / or in informal settlements, quite often initiated for the purpose of sustainable (further) development of the city or community. The Committee on Economic, Social and Cultural Rights (CESR) has emphasised on several occasions that in the case of forced evictions, 'alternative housing to persons who are left homeless as a result of eviction, irrespective of whether the eviction is initiated by its authorities or by private entities such as the owner of the property' must be provided.[207] Moreover, states must 'provide, to the maximum of their available resources, alternative accommodation for evicted persons who need it includes the protection of the family unit, especially when the persons are responsible for the care and education of dependent children' that do not neglect the dignity of the persons. The measures associated with eviction, such as cutting off water or electricity, have been deemed a deprivation of the right to life.[208]

1. International Jurisdiction

64   Translating international law into the concerns of SDG 11 is not readily possible.[209] The applicable law and regulation within cities and municipalities regarding sustainable governance is predominantly domestic. Although the interest on the interdependencies between the consequences of globalisation and the urbanistic sphere has significantly increased,[210] international law and especially human rights obligations are not binding directly on cities and municipalities since these are no subjects of international law, even though some cities may operate as international or even global actors. The contextualisation within the realm of international law (arts, cultural and historic sites, antiterrorism, migrants, Paris Agreement, C40)[211] cannot be overlooked and could lead to a transformative role of cities in the future. Nevertheless, protection requirements for the area of sustainable housing, urban disaster risk management and for the health protection of the population within human settlements can be found at least indirectly in some regional legal instruments of the various legal families.[212]

---

[207] E/C.12/61/D/5/2015, *Ben Djazia and Bellili v. Spain*, 21 July 2017; E/C.12/66/D/37/2018, *López Albán v. Spain*, 27 November 2012.

[208] E/C.12/61/D/5/2015, *Ben Djazia and Bellili v. Spain*, 21 July 2017, paras. 15.2, 15.3.

[209] See ILA, *Conference Report Sydney, Role Of International Law In Sustainable Natural Resource Management For Development* (2018), 44.

[210] HP Aust, 'Shining Cities on the Hill? The Global City, Climate Change, and International Law' (2015) 26 *EJIL*, 255.

[211] Nijman and Aust, 'The Emerging Roles of Cities in International Law - Introductory Remarks on Practice, Scholarship and the Handbook' in Aust and Nijman (eds), *Research Handbook on International Law and Cities* (2021); Nijman, 'The Urban Pushback: International Law as an Instrument of Cities' (2019) 113 *Proceedings of the ASIL Annual Meeting*, 119-23; see also: ILA Study Group on the Role of Cities in International Law; Aust, 'The Shifting Role of Cities in the Global Climate Change Regime: From Paris to Pittsburgh and Back?' (2019) 23 *Review of European, Comparative and International Environmental Law*, 57-66; Layard, 'Researching Urban Law' (2020) 21.7 *German Law Journal*, 1446-63.

[212] For example, in connection with the protection of property in Art. 14 of the African Charter on Human and Peoples' Rights, Art. 1 of Protocol No. 1 to the European Convention on Human Rights, Art. 21 of the American Convention on Human Rights or Art. 15 of the ICESCR, when, amongst others, the possession of land is a prerequisite for the practice of culture, as in the case of indigenous people's land, which is inseparably linked to the very identity of the people and their ancestral practices.

Building sustainable cities and housing in the Americas is being reinforced since the   65
1996 Sustainable Development Summit[213] which yielded in the Plan of Action for the
Sustainable Development of the Americas.[214] In the areas of economic development,
housing, pollution prevention and environmental protection, and sustainable transport
since elaborates the Department of Sustainable Development of the Organization of
American States (OAS-DSD) in close coordination with member states and with a particular focus on an Energy and Climate Partnership of the Americas (ECPA). In addition
to countless other policy prescriptions at member state level and the mutual promotion
of sustainable urban design, the judicial assessment of the IACtHR in particular is
particularly far-reaching.

In its Advisory Opinion 23/17, the IACtHR pointed out the link between the most   66
diverse human rights and the right to an adequate standard of living and the right to
a healthy environment, each of which includes in many forms the right to housing and
the particular social protection associated with it.[215] These would be affected in a special
way by environmental impacts, for example when they lead to 'displacements caused by
environmental deterioration frequently unleash violent conflicts between the displaced
population and the population settled on the territory to which it is displaced'[216] with a
greater intensity for vulnerable groups such as indigenous people, children, people living
in extreme poverty, minorities, people with disabilities and even more disproportionately affecting women.[217] In particular, the geographical location of cities and municipalities must be taken into account in order to adequately consider influencing effects such
as those of climate change.[218] States therefore have risk management obligations that go
hand in hand with a regulatory obligation insofar as the harmful activities are likely to
curtail the right to life and / or the right to personal integrity.[219] This also includes the
duty to supervise and monitor the 'actions of public entities and private individuals' to
ensure effective human rights protection as part of the state's obligation to prevention.[220]

---

[213] First Summit on Sustainable Development in the Americas held in Santa Cruz de la Sierra in
December 1996.

[214] http://www.summit-americas.org/boliviaplan.htm.

[215] IACtHR, Advisory Opinion OC-23/17 of November 15, 2017, Requested by the Republic of Colombia the Environment and Human Rights, para. 66; A/RES/64/255, *Report of the Special Rapporteur on adequate housing as a component of the right to an adequate standard of living, and on the right to non-discrimination in this context*, 6 August 2009, paras. 26, 27 and 30 ff.

[216] IACtHR, Advisory Opinion OC-23/17 of November 15, 2017, Requested by the Republic of Colombia the Environment and Human Rights, para. 66.

[217] See e.g. A/HRC/25/53, *Mapping report of the Independent Expert on the issue of human rights
obligations relating to the enjoyment of a safe, clean, healthy and sustainable environment*, John H. Knox, 30
December 2013, paras. 76 to 78.

[218] IACtHR, Advisory Opinion OC-23/17 of November 15, 2017, Requested by the Republic of Colombia the Environment and Human Rights, para. 67 (fn. 126): In particular, the effects of climate change
may result in saltwater flooding, desertification, hurricanes, erosion and landslides, leading to scarcity of
water supplies and affecting food production from agriculture and fishing, as well as destroying land and
housing.

[219] IACtHR, Advisory Opinion OC-23/17 of November 15, 2017, Requested by the Republic of Colombia the Environment and Human Rights, para. 149.

[220] IACtHR, Advisory Opinion OC-23/17 of November 15, 2017, Requested by the Republic of Colombia the Environment and Human Rights, paras. 152 ff.; see for similar reasoning with respect to natural
heritages (SDG 11.4): IACtHR, *Case of the Kaliña and Lokono Peoples v. Suriname*, Judgment of 25
November 2015, paras. 221 f.; see also ICJ, *Case of Pulp Mills on the River Uruguay (Argentina v. Uruguay)*,
Judgment of 20 April 2010, para. 197.

67   The IACtHR has recognised the link between environmental interventions and human rights violations in several cases.[221] In *La Oroya v. Perú*[222], the court ruled on the design of cities and their economic activities.[223] In the city of La Oroya, a city located in the Andes of Perú, the residents were exposed to lead, arsenic, cadmium, and sulphur dioxide pollution caused by multi-metal smelting activities of the smelter a majority of the residents were employed by. The court, despite being limited in applying the Protocol of San Salvador[224], ruled in the 'first case involving environmental contamination of a non-indigenous community'.[225] Not only builds this case a foundational basis for further petitions before the IACtHR to claim on 'environmental problems that affect the health, life, or the personal integrity of a community, such as pesticide contamination or air pollution' in conjunction with a vast array of human rights bases,[226] but also highlights the many differences that cities face but can be addressed through the human rights context as a measure of sustainability. While not directly referring to cities as such, the Court underlined the special interconnectedness of the adverse impact on the human environment and the human right to life, as regularly affirmed by the Inter-American Commission on Human Rights:

> Respect for the inherent dignity of the person is the principle which underlies the fundamental protections of the right to life and to preservation of physical well-being. Conditions of severe environmental pollution, which may cause serious physical illness, impairment and suffering on the part of the local populace, are inconsistent with the right to be respected as a human being.[227]

68   Linking rights relating to housing, to property or other conceivably relevant rights under SDG 12 also allows, to some extent, for legal consideration before the ECtHR, so that initially a 'potential as a gateway for social justice'[228] could be assumed. The EctHR has ruled on a number of issues relating to the protection of housing rights concerns through a number of Convention rights. Here, the EctHR repeatedly and unequivocally states that it does not recognise a separate right to housing stemming from the European Convention on Human Rights (ECHR), not 'of a particular standard or at all'. The relevant jurisprudence of the EctHR also does not reveal the protection of such a (self-standing) right.[229] In *Balakin*, for instance, the Court stressed that

---

[221] A connection that can be found increasingly frequently; see e.g. ILA, *Conference Report Sydney, Role of International Law in Sustainable Natural Resource Management For Development* (2018), 44.

[222] IACtHR, *Community of La Oroya v. Peru*, IACHR Admissibility Report No. 76/09, 5 August 2009.

[223] IACtHR, *Community of La Oroya v. Peru*, IACHR Admissibility Report No. 76/09, 5 August 2009; further reading: Spieler, 'The La Oroya Case: the Relationship Between Environmental Degradation and Human Rights Violations' (2010) 18(1) *Human Rights Brief*, 19-23.

[224] OAS, *Additional Protocol to the American Convention on Human Rights in the Area of Economic, Social, and Cultural Rights*, 16 November 1999.

[225] IACtHR, *Community of La Oroya v. Peru*, IACHR Admissibility Report No. 76/09, 5 August 2009.

[226] In this case the IACtHR declared the claim admissible on the basis of Arts. 4, 5, 13, 19, 8, and 25 of the American Convention on Human Rights (ACHR), in connection with the obligations established in Arts. 1.1 and 2 ACHR.

[227] OHCHR, *Mapping Human Rights Obligations Relating to the Enjoyment of a Safe, Clean, Healthy and Sustainable Environment, Individual Report on the American Declaration of the Rights and Duties of Man, the American Convention on Human Rights, and the Additional Protocol to the American Convention on Human Rights in the Area of Economic, Social and Cultural Rights, Report No. 13*, paras. 25 f.

[228] Moons, *The Right to housing in law and society* (2018), 97.

[229] ECtHR, *Volkova v. Russia*, App. no. 48758/99, 18 November 2003; ECtHR, *Chapman v. United Kingdom*, App. no. 27238/95, 18 January 2001, para. 99.

even though there is no watertight division separating the sphere of social and economic rights from the field covered by the Convention, the Court considers that [...] [the right to housing] clearly belongs to the realm of socio-economic rights, which is not covered by the Convention.[230]

Nevertheless, some judgments have been made in which related rights are fortified. **69** On the basis of Arts. 6 (fair trial) and 13 (access to justice), the EctHR decided that while a delay or failure to enforce domestic judgments within a reasonable time frame can be justified in certain circumstances. However, a lack of money or housing cannot qualify as permissible excuses for not complying with a judgment. This was confirmed in 2015 in a case against France, in which the *Droit au Logement Opposable* was the subject of EctHR jurisprudence for the first time. Social housing as ordered by a French judge had not been provided within a reasonable time. Therefore, the EctHR found a violation of Art. 6 of the ECHR which means that a right to housing can be protected by the ECHR in case a right to housing is made enforceable at the national level.[231]

However, in some contexts, the EctHR has acknowledged housing as a protectable **70** interest, for instance, in relation to Art. 8 ECHR. This provision proclaims a right to respect private and family life including the home.[232] The peaceful enjoyment of the home has frequently been balanced against other interests of the community (in many cases of an economic nature), e.g. in cases of environmental pollution and noise nuisance. However, a residence may also be protected autonomously on the basis of Article 8 ECHR.[233]

Furthermore, the balancing of environmental protection interests and the right to **71** property on the one hand and the interests of the State on the other must be characterised by proportionality. Regarding the economic well-being of a State, the EctHR has underlined that it is necessary 'to strike a fair balance between the interest of the State or a town's economic well-being and the effective enjoyment by individuals of their right to respect for their home and their private and family life'. 'States have the obligation to evaluate the risks associated with activities that involve danger to the environment, such as mining, and to take adequate measures to protect the right to respect for private and family life, and to allow the enjoyment of a healthy and protected environment'.[234]

In the *Yordanova case* the EctHR added that for particularly vulnerable individuals, **72** exceptional circumstances can even lead to an obligation to secure shelter, but with reference to the fact that the right to housing is generally not given via the ECHR and that only exceptional circumstances could lead to recognition or prevention of homelessness. No eviction must take place if the public authority has not looked for alternative methods for rehousing [...].[235] In this regard, the EctHR 'expanded the meaning of "home" from article 8 to include land, caravans, etc. – basically any specific

---

[230] ECtHR, *Balakin v. Russia*, App. no. 21788/06, 4 July 2013, para. 33; further reading Moons, *The Right to housing in law and society* (2018), 102.

[231] Moons, *The Right to housing in law and society* (2018), 103.

[232] Moons, *The Right to housing in law and society* (2018), 102.

[233] ECtHR, *Fadeyeva v. Russia*, App. no. 55723/00, 9 June 2005; ECtHR, *Lopez-Ostra v. Spain*, App. no. 16798/90, 9 December 1994; ECtHR, *Guerra and others v. Italy*, App. no. 116/1996/735/932, 19 February 1998.

[234] See e.g. EСtHR, *Case of Tătar v. Romania*, No. 67021/01, Judgment of 27 January 2009, para. 107; EСtHR, *Hatton and others v. United Kingdom*, App. no. 36022/97, 8 July 2003; EСtHR, *Moreno Gómez v. Spain*, App. no. 4143/02, 16 November 2004; further reading University of Geneva, Global Studies Institute, *Mapping Human Rights Obligations Relating to the Enjoyment of a Safe, Clean, Healthy and Sustainable Environment, Individual Report on the European Convention on Human Rights and the European Union, Report No. 14* (2013).

[235] EСtHR, *Yordanova and others v Bulgaria*, App. no. 25446/06, 24 April 2012, para. 130; further reading on forced evictions: Onyebueke et al., 'Evicting the poor in the 'overriding public interest': Crisis of rights and interests, and contestations in Nigerian cities' (2020) 101 *Cities*, 102675; Amnesty International, *The Human Cost Of A Megacity, Forced Evictions Of The Urban Poor In Lagos, Nigeria* (2017).

place which a party can prove a sufficient and continuous link with. Even an illegally occupied place or dwelling, whether public or private property, can be considered a home for the purposes of article 8 ECHR.[236] Evictions must be in accordance with law, pursue a legitimate aim and be necessary in a democratic society whereby, as is deeply rooted in the understanding of European judicial assessment, States and State's institutions have a wide margin of appreciation.

73   In *McCann*[237], the EctHR stated that 'the loss of one's home is a most extreme form of interference with the right to respect for the home'[238] and that therefore the proportionality of the measure should be evaluated by an independent tribunal, still in view, of course, of the applicant's personal circumstances.

74   The EctHR stated that particular attention must be paid to consequences of an eviction before deciding whether it is appropriate to proceed, in particular when it could cause homelessness which expresses quite clearly the principle of proportionality in the application and evaluation of law in the continental-European legal family.[239] These evictions are usually accompanied by a violation of the right to property, protected by Art. 1 of the First Protocol to the ECHR. The EctHR ruled in *Stretch v. the UK* that 'possession' can include a tenant's reasonable expectation of continuation of a tenancy:

> Modern societies consider housing of the population to be a prime social need, the regulation of which cannot entirely be left to the play of market forces. The margin of appreciation is wide enough to cover legislation aimed at securing greater social justice in the sphere of people's homes, even where such legislation interferes with existing contractual relations between private parties.[240]

75   In connection with other rights such as Arts. 6 and 8 ECHR, Art. 1 of the First Protocol, or with the fundamental freedoms such as the free movement of persons and capital, a wide margin of appreciation for the States themselves is given which thereby hinders the progressive realisation of the right to adequate housing in terms of pushing State's obligations.

76   Besides the EctHR, the European Committee of Social Rights (ECSR) opens up a further path of justice but only to a limited extent since the ECSR only allows for collective complaints (*actio popularis*). Moreover, the Charter of Social Rights serves as a kind of template, the content of which the ratifying states can opt-out insofar as the nine core obligations are not affected (six of which must be ratified). The right to adequate housing, expressed in Art. 31 ESCR has been accepted by 'a mere nine state parties [for] all paragraphs, another four [accepted] at least one of its paragraphs'.[241] This fact itself restricts the possible *access to justice* considerably.

77   In *FEANTSA v. France*, the ECSR pointed out that housing and social rights measures taken must be practical and effective, rather than purely theoretical in order to effectively protect social rights. States must:

a) Adopt the necessary legal, financial and operational means of ensuring steady progress towards achieving the goals laid down by the Charter;

---

[236] ECtHR, *Buckley v United Kingdom*, App. no. 20348/92, 29 September 1996, paras. 53 f.

[237] ECtHR, *McCann v United Kingdom*, App. no. 19009/04, Judgment, 13 August 2008, para. 50; 'McCann has been used in a judgment that ordered the annulment of a Flemish Housing Code provision that would enable social landlords to terminate a rental agreement without the preceding intervention of a peace judge', Moons, *The Right to housing in law and society* (2018), 109 (Constitutional Court of Belgium, App. no. 101/208, 10 July 2008, B.23.3).

[238] ECtHR, *McCann v United Kingdom*, App. no. 19009/04, Judgment, 13 August 2008, para. 50; see also ECtHR, *Winterstein and Others v. France*, App. no. 27013/07, Judgment, para. 148(δ).

[239] ECtHR, *Winterstein and Others v. France*, App. no. 27013/07, Judgment, paras. 147 and 153 ff.

[240] ECtHR, *James and others v. United Kingdom*, App. no. 8793/79, Judgment, 21 February 1986, para. 47.

[241] Moons, *The Right to housing in law and society* (2018), 100.

b) Maintain meaningful statistics on needs, resources and results;
c) Undertake regular reviews of the impact of the strategies adopted;
d) Establish a timetable and not defer indefinitely the deadline for achieving the objectives of each stage;
e) Pay close attention to the impact of the policies adopted on each of the categories of persons concerned, particularly the most vulnerable.

2. European Jurisdiction

Art. 34 No. 3 European Charter of Fundamental Rights (ECFR)[242] and is also enshrined in Principle 19 of the EU Pillar of Social Rights. Indirect protection of housing: The ECJ evaluates housing-related cases most often pertaining to the 'equal treatment of EU citizens and the free movement of persons, services and capital'.[243] **78**

The only case where the ECJ decided on a case related to Art. 34 ECFR has been the *Kamberaj case*[244], but remained to answer questions around equal treatment of an Albanian citizen with a permanent residence in Italy who had not been granted the same rental subsidy as other EU citizens. Housing rights concerns and the EU Charter did not play a decisive role in the judgment.[245] Since the court was not asked to determine the exact parameters for Art. 34(3) of the EU Charter in this particular case, no conclusion can be drawn on the meaning of the provision on the basis of this judgment. **79**

When looking at the scope of the charter, it becomes apparent that the ECFR is only binding against 'the institutions and the bodies of the Union with due regard for the principle of subsidiarity and to the Member States only when they are implementing Union law', Art. 51 ECFR. Yet, no competence lies with the EU when it comes to housing directly. Although the EU's New Green Deal contains several policy requirements that relate to housing and, in particular, to the sustainable design of housing, the ECJ is unable to give an assessment, at least not as long as Art. 34 ECFR is concerned. Jurisdiction therefore remains with the EU Member States, and the judicial assessment is thus the responsibility of national judges with rights in the area of housing that are often very differently framed. **80**

No eviction without final court decision: The State must put in place a system that allows effective protection of consumers against the risks of eviction from their mortgaged housing until a final court decision has been reached.[246] **81**

The areas further addressed by SDG 11 are anchored in different ways in the basic treaties of the EU. In the area of transport (SDG 11.2), there is shared competence, Art. 4(2) (g) TFEU, which means that the EU can take measures and decisions in these areas. For the area of disaster risk management (SDG 11.5, SDG 11.b), the EU only has a supporting, coordinating or complementary competence, Art. 6(f) TFEU. This means that without action by the individual Member States, the EU cannot adopt measures or assess them judicially. For the maintenance of air quality and waste management, a shared competence could be derived, if necessary, insofar as either environmental as- **82**

---

[242] Art. 34 European Charter of Fundamental Rights (Social security and social assistance) states as follows:

3. In order to combat social exclusion and poverty, the Union recognises and respects the right to social and housing assistance so as to ensure a decent existence for all those who lack sufficient resources, in accordance with the rules laid down by Community law and national laws and practices.

[243] Moons, *The Right to housing in law and society* (2018), 105.

[244] ECJ, C-571/10, *Servet Kamberaj/ Istituto per l'Edilizia sociale della Provincia autonoma di Bolzano (IPES) and others*, 24 April 2012.

[245] Moons, *The Right to housing in law and society* (2018), 105.

[246] CJEU, C-415/11, *Mohamed Aziz v. Catalonia*, 14 March 2013, para. 73.

pects are affected, Art. 4(2) € TFEU, or a unional common safety concern exists in the area of public health, Art. 4(2) (k) TFEU, whereby the EU is again limited to complementary, supporting or promoting measures.[247]

83   The environmental impact of cities and municipalities in the EU is shaped with a particular wealth of regulation, especially within secondary law (→ Goal 13 mn. 34, 81). The EU Green Deal forms the starting point for the further, in part even narrower, framing of the existing legal situation, which is already very comprehensively regulated within the EU, for example with regard to air pollution control (SDG 11.6). The particular gravity of this area of regulation[248] has led to a rich jurisprudential evaluation before the ECJ. Nevertheless, there is no positively formulated right to clean air within the EU to date. Instead, case law suggests a defensive right that can be asserted in the case of long-lasting and severe exposure. It is particularly difficult to achieve *locus standi* before the ECJ, as the court still regularly assesses the individual concern (direct and individual concern criteria) on the basis of settled case law according to the *Plaumann formula*[249], which in particular closes with the higher number of affected persons. All too often, the ECJ refers to national courts, which could then appeal to the ECJ by way of preliminary ruling proceedings. The thus limited access to court denies the fulfilment of the right to (legal) remedy and runs counter to the multilateral obligations entered into by the EU within the framework of the Aarhus Convention[250] which explicitly demands such access to justice. The lack of legal standing of individuals and NGOs before the ECJ remains part of the democratic deficit of the EU.[251]

3. Arbitration Proceedings

84   Investment treaties can affect several urban and rural governance issues such as a change or revision of the host state's legislation in the pre-establishing phase of a treaty which as a result may yield in the redesignation of land, resettlement of the population, densification of residential areas, expropriation of both the investor or the national property holder, as well as environmental impact and / or alteration of ecosystems or (healthy) living environments due to the commissioning and / or operation of the investment enterprise.[252]

85   Many other constellations are conceivable, which in particular evoke conflicts between the economic goals of an investor and the host state and the human rights

---

[247] See Art. 168 TFEU.

[248] European Environment Agency, *Air quality in Europe – 2020 report*, 10: 'Air pollution is a major cause of premature death and disease and is the single largest environmental health risk in Europe [...] responsible for around 400 000 premature deaths per year in the EEA-39 (excluding Turkey) [...].'; see also Stafoggia et al., 'Long-term health effects of air pollution: Results of the European project ESCAPE' (2014) 122 *Environ Health Perspect*, 919 (919 ff.); Varvastian, 'The Revised EU Air Quality Policy and Public Health' in Negri (ed), *Environmental Health in International and EU Law* (2020), 83 (105).

[249] The test demands that 'the alleged infringement must distinguish the applicant individually' whereas 'individual concern' is defined as follows: 'by reason of certain attributes peculiar to them, or by reason of a factual situation which differentiates them from all other persons and distinguishes them individually in the same way as the addressee'; ECJ, Carvalho and Others v Parliament and Council, T-330/18, 8.5.2019, ECLI:EU:T:2019:324, para. 48; thereby referring to its settled case-law: *Arcelor v Parliament and Council*, T-16/04, Judgment, 2 March 2010, EU:T:2010:54, para. 103 and the case-law cited.

[250] UNECE Convention on Access to Information, Public Participation in Decision-making and Access to Justice in Environmental Matters (Aarhus Convention), done at Aarhus, Denmark, on 25 June 1998.

[251] For an overview of the right to clean air: see Huck et al., 'The Right to Breathe Clean Air and Access to Justice - Legal State of Play in International, European and National Law' (2021) 8(22) *International Environmental Law (eJournal)*, 19; further reading: Misonne, 'The emergence of a right to clean air: Transforming European Union law through litigation and citizen science' (2020) 0 *RECIEL*, 1-12.

[252] See IIED, Cotula, *Land rights and investment treaties, Exploring the interface* (2015), 42.

obligations towards the inhabitants/population within cities and settlements, which can be found in jurisdiction to a certain extent.

Under the Chilean-Malaysian Bilateral Investment Treaty (BIT) a dispute between **86** the Chilean authorities and a Malaysian company that had acquired land for the development of real estate in the area of Santiago de Chile arose in 2001. The Chilean Foreign Investment Commission approved the authorisation of the proposed investment without consulting the ministry responsible for housing and urban development. This led to the investor, which had been 'speculating that the policies regarding land use in Chile would be modified in its favor'[253], being rejected by this ministry when approaching for converting the land from agricultural use (exclusive *silvoagropecuario* zone) to residential use. In reasoning that the redesignation of land would not be consistent with the urban development plans in force. The project was stalled. However, the arbitral tribunal found that the Chilean authorities had violated the fair and equitable treatment standard under the applicable investment treaty. The tribunal held that the treatment suffered by the investor did not constitute an indirect expropriation since a state (host country) is not obliged to modify its laws in favour of any investor (right to regulate includes action or omission).[254] However, the tribunal found unfair treatment by the state, which had approved the investment against the existing policy within the state.

Beyond that, there is little or no connection between international legal provisions **87** and spatial planning, which in many cases involves the radical redesignation of land and other urban and rural areas. Precisely the reservations for the protection of the common good, for example, as known in the European legal family, are unknown in other parts of the world and cannot be applied to protect against resettlement, expropriation, land-grabbing, or the degradation of cultural and natural heritages. This means that a proportion of the conceivable constellations only find limited or no access to court and are accordingly not judicially evaluated at all. At a minimum, it would be conceivable that the concerns covered by SDG 11 in the national context would at least be recorded and taken into account as 'beyond border measures' in the context of the further development of law under the guise of WTO law.[255]

4. Domestic Jurisdiction

The wide range of urban concerns to be legally assessed is subject to a multitude of **88** influencing factors such as geographical factors (rural, peri-urban and urban areas from small communities to slums and mega cities of every conceivable state of development). Additionally, the different legal levels (municipal law, national and transnational, regional and international law), which in turn are divided by subject (e.g. redevelopment, green space and spatial planning) and legal field (e.g. planning law, construction law, environmental law, social law, investment law, traffic law, climate protection law), coupled with the unique characters of the respective national legal systems and the different constitutional integration of provincial, rural and urban structures, lead to a complex of interpretations that hardly allows a clear derivation of what can be attributed to SDG 12 in terms of jurisprudence.

As can be seen from its interdependences, SDG 12 is the precursor, means of imple- **89** mentation and resilience target of almost every other SDG of the Global Agenda 2030.

---

[253] International Centre For Settlement Of Investment Disputes (ICSID), *MTD Equity Sdn. Bhd. v. Republic of Chile*, Case No. ARB/01/7, Award, 25 May 2004, para. 122.

[254] ICSID, *MTD Equity Sdn. Bhd. v. Republic of Chile*, Case No. ARB/01/7, Award, 25 May 2004.

[255] See in a similar context: Cottier and Bürgi Bonanomi, 'Land Grabbing, Human Rights and Land Registration Protection' in Cottier and Nadakavukaren Schefer (eds), *Elgar Encyclopedia of International Economic Law* (2017), 640 f.

This leads to the fact that judicial evaluations in each of these areas can also be placed under the umbrella of SDG 12. Innumerable jurisprudence can be found worldwide on the following focal points, among others:

– Degree and Density of Urbanisation
– Health
– Migration[256]
– Educational attainment level and outcomes of education
– Living Conditions and Welfare
– Labour Market
– Tourism[257]
– Digital Economy and Society
– Other Global, International or Transboundary Action

90   However, it must be taken into account that the classification of what constitutes a city is already understood in completely different ways around the world and is consequently also treated differently in legal terms ($\rightarrow$ Goal 11 mn. 15 ff.).[258] A legal integration or classification of national judgments in view of the almost 200 states of this world and the 1,146 cities with at least 500,000 inhabitants[259] appears to be limited in its classification.

91   In general, however, jurisdiction touches on various topics of SDG 11[260] and developments in a human rights context are noticeable[261] and might be used in strategic or public interest litigation in the future.

92   One issue that is likely to be of particular importance globally due to the threats of climate change, and is equally gaining momentum within Europe, is the reduction of CO_2 emissions as well as the reduction of air pollution in general, including particulate matter pollution (in particular PM_{10} and $PM_{2.5}$). Although PM_{10} and $PM_{2.5}$ measurements are regularly collected in many thousands of locations throughout the world, the amount of monitors in different geographical areas vary, with some areas having little or no monitoring at all or with people not gaining access to the relevant data and thus, similarly not gaining access to justice (including redress and remedy) in this context.[262]

---

[256] See e.g. Asibey and Poku-Boansi and Adutwum, 'Residential segregation of ethnic minorities and sustainable city development. Case of Kumasi, Ghana' (2021) 116 *Cities*, 103297; Caponio and Scholten and Zapata-Barrero, *The Routledge Handbook of the Governance of Migration and Diversity in Cities* (2018).

[257] Morrison and Coca-Stefaniak, *Routledge Handbook of Tourism Cities* (2020).

[258] See for an attempt to internationally define cities Eurostat, *Applying the Degree of Urbanisation, A Methodological Manual to Define Cities, Towns and Rural Areas for International Comparisons, 2021 edition* (2021).

[259] According to UN estimates, when figures are calculated for all communities with more than 150,000 inhabitants, the figure is as high as 4,420 cities; UN DESA, *The World's Cities in 2018, Data Booklet* (2018); further information: UN Habitat, *World Cities Report 2020, The Value of Sustainable Urbanization* (2020).

[260] See as general examples of the various considerations, but without evaluating the gravity of the individual cases High Court Of Bombay, *Bombay Environmental Action Group Vs. A R Bharati Deputy Conservator of Forest*, Judgement of 15 September 2003, 2004(3) *Bom.C.R.* 244 (O.S.) (use of space in cities as recreational space).

[261] On SDG 11.1, SDG 11.2 and SDG 11.6: Constitutional Court (South Africa) 4 October 2000, CCT 11/00, *Government of the Republic of South Africa et al. v. Grootboom et al.*, para. 41 (coherent public housing programme directed towards the progressive realisation of the right of access to adequate housing within the state's available means); London Inner South Coroner's Court, Inquest touching the death of Ella Roberta Adoo Kissi-Debrah, Inquest opened on 17 December 2019 (Death due to air pollution).

[262] See Huck et al., 'The Right to Breathe Clean Air and Access to Justice - Legal State of Play in International, European and National Law' (2021) 13(10) *International Environmental Law (eJournal)*.

The Federal Republic of Germany's (Germany) persistent exceeding of the air pollu- 93 tion limit values led to infringement proceedings pursuant to Art. 258 TFEU.[263] The ECJ has upheld the Commission's infringement proceeding against Germany, finding that Germany has failed to fulfil its obligations to maintain ambient air quality,[264] in part systematically and persistently[265] to an extent that were beyond the EU Member State's margin of discretion to take (or omit) measures. In case of continuing non-compliance by Germany's cities, the Commission will be entitled to impose further action and financial sanctions against Germany.

In the cases considered, it is noticeable that various conflicts of objectives arise in 94 the planning and operation of cities, including those aimed at achieving sustainable development, for example between efforts to minimise the CO_2 emissions of cities and the protection of cultural heritage or the well-being of inhabitants.[266]

II. The Enforcement of a 'Right to Sustainable, Safe, Inclusive Housing'?

The jurisprudence and legal realities that fall within the comprehensive scope of 95 SDG 11 show various difficulties in both the development of the actual legal basis and the enforcement of the decisions taken. Against the background of the fact that legally assessing the manifold processes of enforcement in the most diverse legal fields is hardly possible, reference is made at this point to the respective relevant SDGs, each of which provides more detailed information on the legal enforcement of their subject.

III. De Facto Influences on Jurisdiction

As one of the most severe drivers of future supply with water, food, biodiversity, 96 health and well-being and the mitigation or prevention of natural disasters, tackling climate change will be decisive.[267] The Climate change regime and the jurisdiction found in this context will even more exert its influence on the shaping of future cities and the judicial review. As can be seen from the supranational framing of the EU, cities, municipalities and other human settlements are led to the sustainable acting in all their policies and in the sovereign activities of their governments and official entities.

---

[263] ECJ, Case C-635/18, *Commission v Germany (Valeurs limites – NO2)*, judgement of 3 June 2021, ECLI:EU:C:2021:437.

[264] In compliance with Directive 2008/50/EC of the European Parliament and of the Council of 21 May 2008 on ambient air quality and cleaner air for Europe (Air Quality Directive).

[265] ECJ, Case C-635/18, *Commission v Germany (Valeurs limites – NO2)*, Judgment of 3 June 2021, ECLI:EU:C:2021:437, paras. 82 f.; Annual limit value exceedances were found for nitrogen dioxide (NO_2) in 26 of the 89 zones and agglomerations examined from 1 January 2010 up to and including 2016 and hourly limit value exceedance for NO2 in two zones systematically and persistently.

[266] New Zealand Environment Court, *Genesis Power Limited v Franklin District Council* [2005] NZRMA 541 (Awhitu) (Construction of a wind farm on an archaeological site); further reading Krause and Hawkins, 'Viewpoints: Improving cities' implementation of sustainability objectives' (2021) 113 *Cities*, 103167; Trisolini and Zasloff, 'Cities, Land Use and the Global Commons: Genesis and the Urban Politics of Climate Change', in Burns and Osofsky (eds), *Adjudicating Climate Change – State, National and International Approaches* (2009), 72 (87).

[267] See Aust and Du Plessis, 'Good urban governance as a global aspiration: on the potential and limits of SDG 11' in French and Kotzé (eds), *Sustainable Development Goals, Law Theory and Implementation* (2018), 213; see also Aust, 'Shining Cities on the Hill? The Global City, Climate Change, and International Law' (2015) 26(1) *EJIL*, 255-78.

97   Beyond, SDG 11 is driven by a number of coalitions such as the Comunitas coalition which had secured the negotiations on a urban goal from the beginning of the SDG negotiation processes.[268] Several partnerships and networks as *de facto* components of the global environmental governance regime[269] help ignite and implement the notions of SDG 11:

- ICLEI – a coalition of more than 1,500 members build by local Governments for Sustainability (former International Council for Local Environmental Initiatives) is a global network of more than 2500 local and regional governments (of cities, towns and regions) committed to sustainable urban development. ICLEI is active in more than 125 countries and attempts to influence sustainability policy with a focus on 'local action for low emission, nature-based, equitable, resilient and circular development'.[270] With the offered peer exchange, partnerships and capacity building they fulfil the demands of SDG 17 as well.
- C40 Cities Climate Change Leadership Group – an alliance that partners with international organizations such as the World Bank to develop a consistent approach towards climate action plans on the local level. C40 initiated the work on a common standard for the measuring of greenhouse gas emissions to steer investment decisions of the 'Climate Investment Fund' of the World Bank.[271]
- EU 'Covenant of the Mayors' Alliance – a similar alliance to the C40 at the European level set up by the European Commission with 'institutional structures to develop the so-called 'Covenant of Mayors', a scheme under which cities and municipalities in the EU and beyond can sign up to produce 'Sustainable Energy Action Plans'. 'These plans are then monitored by the Commission and – if they are in compliance with the goals of the Covenant – give privileged access to funding by the European Development Bank'.[272]

98   The standard-setting of these and other (emerging) alliances and partnerships will continue to shape the jurisprudential structure in the future, whether in civil law, e.g. in contract interpretation, or in public law, e.g. in the specifications for public procurement ($\rightarrow$ Goal 8 mn. 97, Goal 9 mn. 33, 93 ff.).

99   Another influencing factor is companies, whose role is to be seen in promoting urban resilience, as well as in the (at best sustainable) practices they implement and disclose and thus may develop or make use of strategies to enhance biodiversity, prevention and governance.[273]

E. Conclusion on SDG 11

100   SDG 11 is an example of a particularly illustrative goal of the importance of networks and partnerships. Connecting and coordinating the network of a city, region or human

---

[268] Dodds and Donoghue and Leiva Roesch, *Negotiating the Sustainable Development Goals, A transformational agenda for an insecure world* (2017), 66.

[269] Aust and Du Plessis, 'Good urban governance as a global aspiration: on the potential and limits of SDG 11' in French and Kotzé (eds), *Sustainable Development Goals, Law Theory and Implementation* (2018), 212.

[270] https://iclei.org/.

[271] Aust, 'Shining Cities on the Hill? The Global City, Climate Change, and International Law' (2015) 26(1) *EJIL*, 255 (263).

[272] Aust, 'Shining Cities on the Hill? The Global City, Climate Change, and International Law' (2015) 26(1) *EJIL*, 255 (264).

[273] Acuti and Bellucci and Manetti, 'Company disclosures concerning the resilience of cities from the Sustainable Development Goals (SDGs) perspective' (2020) 99 *Cities*, 102608.

settlement with its numerous population strata, social and political needs.[274] It seems as if there was no other way than to keep this SDG quite loose in order to be able to include all cities and human settlements of this world. The needs seem to depend too much on geographical, socio-economic and political structures. The almost impossibility of definitions in the contexts addressed by SDG 11 also allows all legal concepts, policies and jurisdictions to be subsumed under it, even if it may be the broadest one, and to retreat to the narrowest of meanings in the definition of meaning. It is hard to explain why the human rights background was hardly taken into account either in the wording or in the recital. In any case, the transfer into legal realms seems to be endangered. In their global nature, cities can help shape a democratic, citizen-oriented world society and play a decisive role in shaping issues such as democracy, health, security, climate change, education, knowledge and culture. SDG 11 thus has the function of a transporter for all other SDGs.

The coming population growth and the acceleration of urban growth are remarkably   **101** interrelated, paving a trajectory in speed and size that hardly can be denied. Whether cities can provide the necessary space and build the necessary infrastructure over the years in the face of scarce land resources, water scarcity and rising temperatures in the wake of climate change is questionable for several reasons. The foreseeable developments put cities under tremendous pressure in their respective legal formats. It will be questionable in detail whether the cities and regions will manage to strengthen additionally their efforts to protect and safeguard the world's cultural and natural heritage (SDG 11.4) numerously located in cities.

The financial resources of many cities are not congruent with the expectations they   **102** have to meet. Cities' income depends on a strong and forward-looking economy that provides jobs, innovative products and services that cities need like clean air to breathe. At the same time, climate change, economic transformation, disruption through digitalisation, energy consumption, water and health security, migration, pandemics and the fight against corruption and multiple conflicts in the fight against organised crime will be crucial for the future. Many of those issues are reflected in international law which is to some extent invoked in municipalities to strengthen social justice on a local level.[275]

In the ongoing evolvement of globalisation and driven, among other things, by   **103** climate change and digitisation, cities have been exposed to international norms over the years. These norms, which have a direct impact on cities, have been used as grounds for their increasing participation in international discussions.[276]

The domestic laws and regulations must be strictly enforceable according to an   **104** applicable rule of law principle. In addition, there is the elimination of inequality in living and housing conditions. The expansion of urban settlements will probably not be enough to meet the demand. The legal instruments of cities, some of which are strictly integrated into existing constitutional structures, can only be expanded

---

[274] See Simon, *Rethinking Sustainable Cities, Accessible, green, and fair* (2016), 35.

[275] Oomen and Baumgärtel and Durmus, 'Accelerating cities, constitutional brakes? Exploring the local authorities between global challenges and domestic law' in Ballin et al. (eds), *European Yearbook of Constitutional Law 2020 (Vol. 2)* (2021), 260.

[276] Aust, 'Cities as International Legal Authorities-Remarks on Recent Developments and Possible Future Trends of Research' (2020) 4 *JCULP*, 82; Lin, *Governing climate change: global cities and transnational lawmaking* (2018); Aust, 'The shifting role of cities in the global climate change regime: From Paris to Pittsburgh and back?' (2019) 28.1 *Review of European, Comparative & International Environmental Law*, 57-66; see for further examples emphasising the case of New York City which declared itself in 2018 to be the first city to report directly to the United Nations on the local implementation of the SDGs: Nijman and Aust, 'The Emerging Roles of Cities in International Law - Introductory Remarks on Practice, Scholarship and the Handbook' in Aust and Nijman (eds), *Research Handbook on International Law and Cities* (2021), 5.

on a case-by-case basis and usually in the long term. The path taken by Habitat III may also be criticised as too broad due to the abundance of statements. However, a bottom-up process with 30,000 voices and numerous transparent voting processes is discernible,[277] which culminated consensually in the outcome resolution.[278] As a result, the Global Agenda 2030 and the SDGs are qualified as a central building block on which further planning builds. The chosen path of focusing on participation, transparency and accountability is the right one, at least for urban planning leading to networking and self-assessment as an anchor of a new role for cities facing the impact of climate change and technology development. Respect for human rights and the principle of justice is essential to neutralise the appalling inequalities in current living and health conditions and to maintain segregation and inclusion. Girls and women and young people need to be empowered to participate and have a real opportunity for education and vocational training that could help them in an ability-based policy. Access to education and equity as a general fairness as well as access to water and housing is essential for people. The legal instruments of the cities, some of which are strictly integrated into existing constitutional structures, needs to be expanded for articulating answers in times of challenges of climate change, SDGs, migration and formal and informal expansion of cities not only as a cause of population growth.

---

[277] UN, *Habitat III, A conference of 30.000 voices* (2017).
[278] A/RES/71/256*, *New Urban Agenda*, 25 January 2017.

Goal 12
Ensure sustainable consumption and production patterns

12.1 Implement the 10-Year Framework of Programmes on Sustainable Consumption and Production Patterns, all countries taking action, with developed countries taking the lead, taking into account the development and capabilities of developing countries

12.2 By 2030, achieve the sustainable management and efficient use of natural resources

12.3 By 2030, halve per capita global food waste at the retail and consumer levels and reduce food losses along production and supply chains, including post-harvest losses

12.4 By 2020, achieve the environmentally sound management of chemicals and all wastes throughout their life cycle, in accordance with agreed international frameworks, and significantly reduce their release to air, water and soil in order to minimize their adverse impacts on human health and the environment

12.5 By 2030, substantially reduce waste generation through prevention, reduction, recycling and reuse

12.6 Encourage companies, especially large and transnational companies, to adopt sustainable practices and to integrate sustainability information into their reporting cycle

12.7 Promote public procurement practices that are sustainable, in accordance with national policies and priorities

12.8 By 2030, ensure that people everywhere have the relevant information and awareness for sustainable development and lifestyles in harmony with nature

12.a Support developing countries to strengthen their scientific and technological capacity to move towards more sustainable patterns of consumption and production

12.b Develop and implement tools to monitor sustainable development impacts for sustainable tourism that creates jobs and promotes local culture and products

12.c Rationalize inefficient fossil-fuel subsidies that encourage wasteful consumption by removing market distortions, in accordance with national circumstances, including by restructuring taxation and phasing out those harmful subsidies, where they exist, to reflect their environmental impacts, taking fully into account the specific needs and conditions of developing countries and minimizing the possible adverse impacts on their development in a manner that protects the poor and the affected communities

Word Count related to 'Consumption' and 'Production'
A/RES/70/1 – Transforming our world: the 2030 Agenda for Sustainable Development: 'Consumption': 12 'Production': 14
Instruments mentioned in A/RES/70/1 in the section entitled: 'Sustainable Development Goals and targets':
A/RES/69/313 – Addis Ababa Action Agenda of the Third International Conference on Financing for Development adopted on 27 July 2015: 'Consumption': 8 'Production': 7
A/RES/66/288 – The future we want (Rio +20 Declaration) adopted on 27 July 2012: 'Consumption': 8 'Production': 17
A/RES/55/2 – United Nations Millennium Declaration adopted on 8 September 2000: 'Consumption': 1 'Production': 2

Select Bibliography: David J. Attard, Malgosia Fitzmaurice and Alexandros Ntovas, 'The UN World Tourism Organization and Global Ocean Governance' in David J. Attard, Malgosia Fitzmaurice and Alexandros Ntovas (eds), *The IMLI Treatise On Global Ocean Governance: Volume II: UN Specialized Agencies and Global Ocean Governance* (Oxford University Press, Oxford 2018), 195; Daniel Bodansky and Jessica C. Lawrence, 'Trade and Environment', in Daniel Bethlehem, Isabelle Van Damme, Donald McRae and Rodney Neufeld (eds), *The Oxford Handbook of International Trade Law* (Oxford University Press, Oxford 2009), 505; Branco Manuel Castelo, 'Sustainability Reporting Guidelines' in Samuel O. Idowu, Nicholas Capaldi, Liangrong Zu and Ananda Das Gupta (eds), *Encyclopedia of Corporate Social Responsibility* (Springer Verlag, Berlin/Heidelberg 2013), 2389; Jason Czanezki, Margot Pollans and Sarah M. Main, 'Eco-Labelling' in Emma Lees and Jorge E. Viñuales (eds), *The Oxford Handbook of Comparative Environmental Law* (Oxford University Press, Oxford 2019), 996; European Commission, *Buying Green! A handbook on green public procurement* (2016); FAO, *SDG 12.3.1: Global Food Loss Index* (2018); Martin Hirschnitz-Garbers, Francesca Montevecchi and André Martinuzzi, 'Resource Efficiency' in Samuel O. Idowu, Nicholas Capaldi, Liangrong Zu and Ananda Das Gupta (eds), *Encyclopedia of Corporate Social Responsibility* (Springer Verlag, Berlin/Heidelberg 2013), 2012; Natalie Jones, and Geert van Calster, 'Waste Regulation' in Emma Lees and Jorge E. Viñuales (eds), *The Oxford Handbook of Comparative Environmental Law* (Oxford University Press, Oxford 2019) 607; Jens Martens, Bodo Ellmers and Vera Pokorny, *COVID-19 and the SDGs The impact of the coronavirus pandemic on the global sustainability agenda* (Social Watch/Global Policy Watch/Global Policy Forum, Uruguay/USA/Germany 2020); OECD, *Towards green growth: A summary for policy makers* (2011); María Victoria Lottici, Carlos Galperín and Julia Hoppstock, '"Green Trade Protectionism": An Analysis of Three New Issues that Affect Developing Countries' (2014), 2 No. 2 *Chinese Journal of Urban and Environmental Studies*, 1; Philipp Schreck, 'Disclosure (CSR Reporting)' in Samuel O. Idowu, Nicholas Capaldi, Liangrong Zu and Ananda Das Gupta (eds), *Encyclopedia of Corporate Social Responsibility* (Springer Verlag, Berlin/Heidelberg 2013), 80; Thomas Tsalis, Kyveli E. Malamateniou, Dimitrios Koulouriotis and Ioannis E. Nikolaou, 'New Challenges for corporate sustainability reporting: United Nations' 2030 Agenda for sustainable development and the sustainable development goals' (2020), 27 No. 2 *Corp Soc Responsib Environ Manag.*, 1; UNEP, *Buying for a better world: A Guide on Sustainable Procurement for the UN System* (2011); UNEP, *Decoupling Natural Resource Use and Environmental Impacts from Economic Growth* (2011); UNEP, *Sustainable Consumption and production, A Handbook for Policymakers* (2015); Christina Voigt, 'Principle 8: Sustainable Development through Integratioin' in Jorge E. Viñuales (ed), The Rio Declaration on Environment and Development: A Commentary (Oxford University Press, Oxford 2015), 246.

A. Background and Origin of SDG 12

1   An economic cycle is significantly characterised by the production of goods and their consumption.[1] At the same time, production means a demand for a wide variety of

---

[1] UN, *The Sustainable Development Goals Report 2020* (2020), 48.

resources, which increases as the demand for goods rises. These resources are taken from nature and thus influence the planet in many ways.[2] As the demand for natural resources continues to increase, this results in a growing impact on the environment.[3] The goods produced lead to various types of waste throughout the production process and often represent a burden for the planet after their consumption.

Given the particular importance of ending global hunger, reducing food waste is a central challenge (SDG 12.3) (→ Goal 2 mn. 1 ff.).[4] In 2019, approximately 931 million tonnes of food were wasted, which represents 17 per cent of the global food production.[5]   2

Chemical waste poses a particular threat to humans and nature. The globally increasing production and use of chemicals therefore deserves specific attention (SDG 12.4).[6] In addition, the growing demand for electronic products and the resulting increase in electronic waste cannot be ignored.[7]   3

At the United Nations Conference on the Human Environment in 1972, great importance was attached to the conservation of natural resources with a focus on non-renewable resources.[8] Furthermore, a principle was established to protect the environment from toxic substances.[9] Thus, although the central objectives from SDG 12 were not directly addressed, the principles behind SDG 12 were expressed in a generalised way.   4

The need for a sustainable industry was explicitly addressed in the 1987 Brundtland Report.[10] In addition, various sub-targets from SDG 12 have already been identifiable: 5

> Nations have to bear the costs of any inappropriate industrialization, and many developing countries are realizing that they have neither the resources nor – given rapid technological change – the time to damage their environments now and clean up later. But they also need assistance and information from industrialized nations to make the best use of technology. Transnational corporations have a special responsibility to smooth the path of industrialization in the nations in which they operate.[11]

This clearly shows the value placed on an industry that is compatible with the environment and also emphasises that nations cannot wait until later to address environmental impacts but must do so from the very beginning which is why waste management has already been addressed and required (SDG 12.3, SDG 12.4, SDG 12.5). In addition, the dissemination of necessary knowledge about sustainable technologies (SDG 12.8) and the special responsibility of multinational companies (SDG 12.6) were underlined.   6

Agenda 21 (1992) dealt in detail with a change in production and consumption patterns and dedicated an entire chapter to this topic.[12] In addition to a call for increased   7

---

[2] For example, the demand for different natural resources leads to multiple influences on global forest stocks Schröder et al., 'SDG 12: Responsible Consumption and Production – Potential Benefits and Impacts on Forests and Livelihoods' in Katila et al. (eds), *Sustainable Development Goals: Their Impacts on Forests and People* (2019), 386 (387). For the impact on marine ecosystems see Griggs et al., *A Guide to SDG Interactions: From Science to Implementation* (2017), 203.

[3] UN, *The Sustainable Development Goals Report 2020* (2020), 48.

[4] UNESCO, *(2021-2030) The Science We Need for the Ocean We Want United Nations Decade of Ocean Science for Sustainable Development*.

[5] UNEP, *Food Waste Index Report 2021* (2021), 8.

[6] UNEP, *From Legacies to Innovative Solutions: Implementing the 2030 Agenda for Sustainable Development* (2019), 2.

[7] UN, *The Sustainable Development Goals Report 2020* (2020), 48.

[8] UN, *Report of the United Nations Conference on the human environment 1972*, Principles 2, 3, 5.

[9] UN, *Report of the United Nations Conference on the human environment 1972*, Principle 6.

[10] Report of the World Commission on Environment and Development: *Our Common Future* (1987), Overview by the World Commission on Environment and Development, paras. 66-70.

[11] Report of the World Commission on Environment and Development: *Our Common Future* (1987), Overview by the World Commission on Environment and Development, para. 68.

[12] UN, *Agenda 21* (1992), Chapter 4, paras. 4.1-4.27.

efficiency in production,[13] a necessary research and international dissemination of this knowledge was also widely addressed,[14] which were complemented with several chapters dealing with different types of waste,[15] emphasising their particular importance for sustainable production and consumption.

8   In the same year, the Rio Declaration on Environment and Development emphasised the special importance of sustainable production and consumption patterns as follows: 'To achieve sustainable development and a higher quality of life for all people, States should reduce and eliminate unsustainable patterns of production and consumption and promote appropriate demographic policies.'[16]

9   This created a special significance and link to sustainable development as a whole and a higher quality of life.[17] According to Voigt, 'unsustainable patterns of production and consumption are the major impediment to sustainable development', which is why Principle 8 aims to separate the link between economic growth and environmental contamination[18] as was also highlighted in the 1994 Declaration of Barbados.[19]

10   Within the framework of the Johannesburg Declaration on Sustainable Development from 2002, a change in production and consumption was characterised as central components for sustainable development:

> 'We recognize that poverty eradication, **changing consumption and production patterns** (emphasis added) and protecting and managing the natural resource base for economic and social development are overarching objectives of and **essential requirements for sustainable development** (emphasis added).'

11   With the Johannesburg Plan of Implementation (JPoI) of the World Summit on Sustainable Development, this characterisation was even expanded through comprehensive approaches for sustainable production and consumption.[20] Moreover, approaches for waste management systems were created and specific requirements were set for the handling of chemical and other hazardous waste.[21] Both, the JPoI and 'The future we want' of the Rio+20 Conference in 2012 (Rio+20) 'recognized that "poverty eradication, changing unsustainable patterns of production and consumption and protecting and managing the natural resource base of economic and social development are overarching objectives of, and essential requirements for, sustainable development"'. The JPoI de-

---

[13] See e.g. UN, *Agenda 21* (1992), para. 4.15: 'Achieving the goals of environmental quality and sustainable development will require **efficiency in production** [emphasis added] and changes in consumption patterns in order to emphasize optimization of resource use and minimization of waste'.

[14] UN, *Agenda 21* (1992), Chapter 4, para. 4.10-4.13.

[15] UN, *Agenda 21* (1992), Chapter 19: 'Environmentally sound management of toxic chemicals, including prevention of illegal international traffic in toxic and dangerous products'; UN, *Agenda 21* (1992), Chapter 20: 'Environmentally sound management of hazardous wastes, in hazardous wastes'; UN, *Agenda 21* (1992), Chapter 21: 'Environmentally sound management of solid wastes and sewage-related issues'; UN, *Agenda 21* (1992), Chapter 22: 'Safe and environmentally sound management of radioactive wastes'.

[16] UN, A/CONF.151/26, Report of the United Nations Conference on Environment and Development, 3-14 June 1992, Principle 8.

[17] Voigt, 'Principle 8: Sustainable Development through Integration' in Viñuales (ed), *The Rio Declaration on Environment and Development: A Commentary* (2015), 246 (246).

[18] Voigt, 'Principle 8: Sustainable Development through Integration' in Viñuales (ed), *The Rio Declaration on Environment and Development: A Commentary* (2015), 246 (246).

[19] A/CONF.167/9, Report Of The Global Conference On The Sustainable Development Of Small Island Developing States, 26 April – 6 May 1994, Annex I: *Declaration of Barbados*, Part Two III 3: 'To achieve sustainable development and a higher quality of life for all people, including people of small island developing States, all States should reduce and eliminate unsustainable patterns of production and consumption, and should promote appropriate demographic policies.'

[20] UN, *Plan of Implementation of the World Summit on Sustainable Development* (2002), paras. 14-23.

[21] UN, *Plan of Implementation of the World Summit on Sustainable Development* (2002), paras. 22, 23.

manded the development of a 10-Year Framework of Programmes on Sustainable Consumption and Production Patterns (10YFP) which has then been adopted at Rio+20.[22]

In implementing the Sustainable Development Goals, an approach was ultimately **12** adopted that includes diverse sustainability aspects along a value chain. This is complemented and concretised by the 10-Year Framework of Programmes on Sustainable Consumption and Production Patterns, which in turn refers directly to Agenda 21, the Rio Declaration on Environment and Development and the Johannesburg Plan of Implementation.[23] The goal of the framework is to 'enhance international cooperation and accelerate the shift towards sustainable consumption and production [...] patterns in both developed and developing countries'.[24]

B. Scope and Dimensions of SDG 12

In order to achieve economic growth and sustainable development, human consump- **13** tion patterns as well as the production of goods must change in the future. This requires a consideration of the entire life cycle of a product – from beginning to end – by involving consumers, industries and governments to achieve sustainability. It also requires adequate management of resources and environmentally friendly disposal methods, especially for toxic waste and pollutants.

I. Sustainable Consumption and Production

Current global consumption and production trends confirm the urgent need for **14** sustainable consumption and production (SCP) as an important component for sustainable development.[25] In 1994, the concept of SCP was defined 'the use of services and related products which respond to basic needs and bring a better quality of life while minimising the use of natural resources and toxic materials as well as the emission of waste and pollutants over the life cycle of the service or product so as not to jeopardise the needs of future generations'.[26] A more recent UNEP definition defines SCP as a 'holistic approach to minimising the negative environmental impacts from consumption and production systems while promoting quality of life for all'.[27] Ultimately, it can be stated that SCP 'is about providing goods and services to meet basic needs of the world population without further burdening the already burdened environment and thereby compromising future generations to meet their own needs'.[28] SPC focuses on the life cycle perspective (life cycle thinking).[29] This approach takes into account the entire value chain of a product or service, from its development to its manufacture, distribution

---

[22] UNGA Open Working Group on Sustainable Development Goals, *Compendium of TST Issues Briefs* (2014), 167.

[23] A/CONF.216/5, *Letter dated 18 June 2012 from the Permanent Representative of Brazil to the United Nations addressed to the Secretary-General of the United Nations Conference on Sustainable Development*, 19 June 2012, Annex: *A 10-year framework of programmes on sustainable consumption and production patterns*, para. 1.

[24] High-Level Political Forum On Sustainable Development, *The 10 Year Framework of Programmes on Sustainable Consumption and Production Patterns* (2014), 1.

[25] UNEP, *Sustainable Consumption and production: A Handbook for Policymakers* (2015), 7.

[26] UNEP, *Sustainable Consumption and production: A Handbook for Policymakers* (2015), 10.

[27] UNEP, *Sustainable Consumption and production: A Handbook for Policymakers* (2015), 10.

[28] Voigt, 'Principle 8: Sustainable Development through Integratioin' in Viñuales (ed), *The Rio Declaration on Environment and Development: A Commentary* (2015), 246 (247).

[29] UNEP, *Global Outlook on Sustainable Consumption and Production Policies: Taking action together* (2012), 19; Arcuri and Partiti, 'SDG 12: Ensure Sustainable Consumption and Production Patterns'

and disposal.[30] In the course of this, the focus is also on the use of resources and the resulting emissions, waste water and waste.[31] The life cycle approach requires sustainable and efficient management that takes into account all steps of the value chain and triggers the development of processes that minimise resource consumption and generate less waste, including hazardous substances.[32] Such management is based on a precautionary and preventive approach.[33] The concept of SCP is reflected in SDG 12.1 which states:

> Implement the 10 Year Framework of Programmes on Sustainable Consumption and Production Patterns, all countries taking action, with developed countries taking the lead, taking into account the development and capabilities of developing countries.

15   A global framework for SCP is the 10-Year Framework of Programmes on Sustainable Consumption and Production Patterns (10YFP), which was adopted in 2012 as a result of the Rio+20 conference 'to enhance international cooperation to accelerate the shift towards SCP in both developed and developing countries'.[34] It was noted that

> fundamental changes in the way societies produce and consume are essential to achieve global sustainable development. All countries should promote sustainable consumption and production patterns, with developed countries taking the lead and all countries benefiting from the process [...].[35]

16   The 10YFP aims to 'to develop, replicate and scale up SCP and resource efficiency initiatives, at national and regional levels, decoupling environmental degradation and resource use from economic growth, and thus increase the net contribution of economic activities to poverty eradication and social development'.[36] However, the Framework's programmes are voluntary.[37]

17   At the international level, legal foundations are rather sparse. However, there are a number of multilateral environmental agreements that include efforts to change production and consumption patterns.[38] Although none of the agreements includes the term SCP, basic ideas of this concept can be found in the agreements.[39] The Vienna Convention for the Protection of the Ozone Layer, which entered into force in 1988, although not containing any references to SCP, accompanies the Montreal Protocol on Substances that Deplete the Ozone Layer. It has already led to changes in consumption

---

(2021) *TILEC Discussion Paper, DP 2021-007*, 2 (Forthcoming in Ebbeson and Hay (eds), *The Cambridge Handbook on SDGs and international law*).

[30] UNEP, *Global Outlook on Sustainable Consumption and Production Policies: Taking action together* (2012), 19.

[31] UNEP, *Global Outlook on Sustainable Consumption and Production Policies: Taking action together* (2012), 19.

[32] UNEP, *Global Outlook on Sustainable Consumption and Production Policies: Taking action together* (2012), 19.

[33] UNEP, *Global Outlook on Sustainable Consumption and Production Policies: Taking action together* (2012), 19.

[34] UNEP, *Sustainable Consumption and production: A Handbook for Policymakers* (2015), 52.

[35] A/CONF.216/5, *Letter dated 18 June 2012 from the Permanent Representative of Brazil to the United Nations addressed to the Secretary-General of the United Nations Conference on Sustainable Development,* 19 June 2012, Annex: *A 10-year framework of programmes on sustainable consumption and production patterns,* para 1(a).

[36] UNEP, *Sustainable Consumption and production: A Handbook for Policymakers* (2015), 52.

[37] A/RES/66/288, *The future we want,* 11 September 2012, para. 226.

[38] Voigt, 'Principle 8: Sustainable Development through Integration' in Viñuales (ed), *The Rio Declaration on Environment and Development: A Commentary* (2015), 246 (258).

[39] Voigt, 'Principle 8: Sustainable Development through Integration' in Viñuales (ed), *The Rio Declaration on Environment and Development: A Commentary* (2015), 246 (258).

and production chains in practice[40] and thus is of great importance for the sustainable transition. Another relevant agreement is the 1992 United Nations Framework Convention on Climate Change (UNFCCC). The objective of the Convention can only be achieved by considering an effective SCP.[41] The success of SDG 12.1 is measured by the 'number of countries developing, adopting or implementing policy instruments aimed at supporting the shift to sustainable consumption and production' according to indicator 12.1.1.

Furthermore, developed countries are requested to support developing countries   **18** towards sustainable production and consumption. SDG 12.a states: 'support developing countries to strengthen their scientific and technological capacity to move towards more sustainable patterns of consumption and production'. This is measured according to indicator 12.b.1 by the 'implementation of standard accounting tools to monitor the economic and environmental aspects of tourism sustainability'.

II. Resource Efficiency and Sustainable Management of Natural Resources

A large number of natural resources are needed for modern consumption and pro-   **19** duction.[42] The problem is, however, that not every resource is infinitely available. Therefore, sustainable use of natural resources, i.e. resource efficiency, is crucial. SDG 12.1 aims to 'achieve the sustainable management and efficient use of natural resources' by 2030. The aspect of resource efficiency is part of the SCP concept.[43] Resource efficiency means 'creating more (economic) value with less input of resources [...] and reducing the environmental impacts associated with resource use to break the link between economic growth and the use of nature'.[44] The need for resource efficiency is becoming increasingly urgent as natural resources are consumed to exhaustion.[45]

Next to the efficient use of resources, SDG 12.1 calls for the sustainable management   **20** of natural resources. Natural resource management is about 'the sustainable utilization of major natural resources, such as land, water, air, minerals, forests, fisheries, and wild flora and fauna'.[46] In recent years, progress has been made to secure sustainable management of natural resources in multilateral environmental agreements and other sustainable development treaties.[47] For example, the EU has concluded legally binding bilateral trade agreements with various countries to ensure that only legal timber is imported to the EU.[48] Under this Forest Law Enforcement Governance and Trade (FLEGT)

---

[40] Voigt, 'Principle 8: Sustainable Development through Integration' in Viñuales (ed), *The Rio Declaration on Environment and Development: A Commentary* (2015), 246 (258).

[41] Voigt, 'Principle 8: Sustainable Development through Integration' in Viñuales (ed), *The Rio Declaration on Environment and Development: A Commentary* (2015), 246 (260).

[42] UNEP, *Sustainable Consumption and production: A Handbook for Policymakers* (2015), 12.

[43] UNEP, *Sustainable Consumption and production: A Handbook for Policymakers* (2015), 11.

[44] Hirschnitz-Garbers et. al, 'Resource Efficiency' in Idowu et al. (eds), *Encyclopedia of Corporate Social Responsibility* (2013), 2012 (2013 f.).

[45] UNEP, *Guidelines for National Waste Management Strategies: Moving from Challenges to Opportunities* (2013), 12.

[46] Muralikrishna and Manickam, 'Natural Resource Management and Biodiversity Conservation' in Muralikrishna and Manickam (eds), *Environmental management: Science and Engineering for Industry* (2017), 23.

[47] ILA, *The Role of International Law in Sustainable Natural Resources Management for Development*, Resolution No. 4 (2020), para. 4.3.2.

[48] https://ec.europa.eu/trade/policy/policy-making/sustainable-development/#_environmental-p rotection; Zeitlin and Overdevest, 'Experimentalist Interactions: FLEGT and the Transnational Timber Legality Regime' (2019) *SSRN Electronical Journal*, 10.; on forest and trade see also: Raza et al., *How can*

initiative, voluntary partnership agreements are negotiated.[49] The FLEGT II Program 2013-2016 launched by the EU respected the fact that there is an 'increased pressure on forests due to growing demand for forest products and services' and acknowledges the consequence of 'loss of forest resources'.[50] The new Working Program 2018-2022 has been agreed upon in 2018.[51]

21   Human development has impacts on the surrounding natural environment and its resources. To identify these impacts, there are different types of impact assessments. The best known one is the Environmental Impact Assessment (EIA) tool, which originated in the United States in 1970.[52] It is widely recognised as a key tool for environmental management and is therefore enshrined in national and international environmental law.[53] EIA is an 'analytical process or procedure that systematically examines the possible environmental consequences of a given activity or project' to make sure that inter-related socio-economic, cultural and human health impacts on the environment are considered before the decision-making.[54] This allows to predict environmental impacts at an early stage of the project process as well as a better adaption of the project to the local environment.[55] A related approach is sustainable impact assessment, which focuses on sustainable criteria.[56] The EU uses a Sustainability Impact Assessment (SIA) tool, which was introduced by DG Trade in 1999 to support major EU trade negotiations.[57] SIA has two characteristics: '(i) it is a methodological soft policy instrument for developing integrated policies which take full account of the three sustainable development dimensions and which include cross-cutting, intangible and long-term considerations; and (ii) a process for assessing the likely economic, social and environmental effects of policies, strategies, plans and programmes before they have been formulated'.[58] Therefore, the SIA-Tool provides the Commission with an in-depth analysis of the potential economic, social, human rights, and environmental impacts of the trade agreement under negotiation.[59] Among other aspects, the impact of the agreement on resources as well as waste and waste management is taken into account.[60] Furthermore, the contribution it makes to resource efficiency and how it can promote sustainable consumption and production is considered.[61] Moreover, Research Impact Assessment could be an essential element for

---

international trade contribute to sustainable forestry and the preservation of the world's forests through the Green Deal? (2020).

[49] Zeitlin and Overdevest, 'Experimentalist Interactions: FLEGT and the Transnational Timber Legality Regime' (2019) *SSRN Electronical Journal*, 1 (4).

[50] https://www.enpi-fleg.org/about/about-fleg/.

[51] See *Work Plan 2018-2022 for the Implementation of the Forest Law Enforcement, Governance and Trade Action Plan* (2018).

[52] UNEP, *Environmental Impact Assessment and Strategic Environmental Assessment: Towards and Integrated Approach* (2004), 7; further reading Aung et al., 'Evaluating environmental impact assessment (EIA) in the countries along the belt and road initiatives: System effectiveness and the compatibility with the Chinese EIA' (2020) *Environmental Impact Assessment Review*, 81.

[53] Morgan, 'Environmental impact assessment: the state of the art' (2012) 30 (1) *Impact Assessment and Project Appraisal*, 5 (6).

[54] UNEP, *The ABC for Sustainable Cities: A Glossary for Policy Makers* (2016), 28; https://www.cbd.int/impact/whatis.shtml.

[55] https://www.cbd.int/impact/whatis.shtml.

[56] Morgan, 'Environmental impact assessment: the state of the art' (2012) 30 (1) *Impact Assessment and Project Appraisal*, 5 (7).

[57] European Commission, *Handbook for trade sustainability impact assessment* (2016), 7,8.

[58] OECD, *Guidance on Sustainability Impact Assessment* (2010), 4.

[59] European Commission, *Handbook for trade sustainability impact assessment* (2016), 8.

[60] European Commission, *Handbook for trade sustainability impact assessment* (2016), 23.

[61] European Commission, *Handbook for trade sustainability impact assessment* (2016), 23.

the design of socially responsible research processes that are guided by the responsibility for sustainable development.[62]

Resource efficiency is also linked to the concept of decoupling.[63] Resource decou- **22** pling means reducing the use of primary resources per economic unit, resulting in an efficient use of resources.[64] For sustainable economic growth, economic growth must be decoupled from environmental impacts and poor people, especially in developing countries, must be enabled to meet their basic needs.[65] Impact decoupling is about 'increasing economic output while reducing negative environmental impacts'.[66] Environmental impacts can occur along the entire life cycle of a product – from extraction, production and consumption to its disposal – but can also be unintended side effects of economic activities.[67] In particular, negative environmental impacts occur in the form of greenhouse gases. In summary, decoupling means using 'less resources per unit of economic output and reducing the environmental impact of any resources that are used or economic activities that are undertaken'.[68] Organisations that want to reduce their environmental impacts, can set up an environmental management system (EMS). An environmental management system is a 'a means of ensuring effective implementation of an environmental management plan or procedures and compliance with environmental policy objectives and targets'.[69] It enables public and private organisations to improve their environmental performance.[70] Moreover, organisations using an EMS can require a certification, for the EU under EMAS or EN/ISO 14001.[71] The progress on SDG 12.2 is measured, according to Indicator 12.2.1, by the 'material footprint, material footprint per capita, and material footprint per GDP' and, according to indicator 12.2.2, by the 'domestic material consumption, domestic material consumption per capita, and domestic material consumption per GDP'.

III. Waste and Chemical Management

In recent years, the consumption and production of chemicals has increased world- **23** wide.[72] Several chemicals, products and wastes have adverse health and environmental impacts and require proper handling and disposal.[73] There is no established definition for the term 'waste'.[74] One possible definition of waste defines it as 'substances or objects which are disposed of or are intended to be disposed of or are required to be disposed of by the provisions of national law'.[75] Waste streams can come from different sources,

---

[62] Weißhuhn et al., 'Research impact assessment in agriculture—A review of approaches and impact areas' (2018) 27 (1) *Research Evaluation*, 36 (36).

[63] UNEP, *Decoupling Natural Resource Use and Environmental Impacts from Economic Growth* (2011), 4.

[64] UNEP, *Decoupling Natural Resource Use and Environmental Impacts from Economic Growth* (2011), 4.

[65] UNEP, *Buying for a better world, A Guide on Sustainable Procurement for the UN System* (2011), 11.

[66] UNEP, *Decoupling Natural Resource Use and Environmental Impacts from Economic Growth* (2011), 4.

[67] UNEP, *Decoupling Natural Resource Use and Environmental Impacts from Economic Growth* (2011), 4 f.

[68] UNEP, *Decoupling Natural Resource Use and Environmental Impacts from Economic Growth* (2011), xiii.

[69] https://www.eea.europa.eu/help/glossary/eea-glossary/environmental-management-system.

[70] https://ec.europa.eu/environment/gpp/faq_en.htm#framework1.

[71] https://ec.europa.eu/environment/gpp/faq_en.htm#framework1.

[72] UNEP, *Global Chemicals Outlook II, From Legacies to Innovative Solutions* (2019), 2.

[73] UNEP, *Global Chemicals Outlook II, From Legacies to Innovative Solutions* (2019), 3.

[74] Jones and van Calster, 'Waste Regulation' in Lees and Viñuales (eds), *The Oxford Handbook of Comparative Environmental Law* (2019), 607 (613).

[75] Basel Convention (1989), Art. 2(1).

which in turn can have different impacts on health and the environment.[76] Therefore, waste is classified into hazardous and non-hazardous waste.[77] Hazardous waste can be defined as 'a used or discarded material that can damage human health and the environment' like 'heavy metals, toxic chemicals, medical wastes or radioactive material'.[78] Basically, the concepts of waste management vary from country to country.[79] In general, environmentally sound management of hazardous waste or other waste includes 'all practicable steps to ensure that hazardous wastes or other wastes are managed in a manner which will protect human health and the environment against the adverse effects which may result from such wastes'.[80] Therefore, SDG 12.4 states to 'achieve the environmentally sound management of chemicals and all wastes throughout their life cycle, in accordance with agreed international frameworks, and significantly reduce their release to air, water and soil in order to minimize their adverse impacts on human health and the environment' by 2020. The legal framework for the 'Life Cycle Management of Hazardous Chemicals' is provided by the Basel Convention, the Rotterdam Convention and the Stockholm Convention.[81]

24   In 1989, the Basel Convention on the Control of Transboundary Movements of Hazardous Wastes and their Disposal was adopted. The Parties were aware 'of the risk of harm to human health and the environment caused by hazardous wastes and other wastes and the transboundary movements thereof'.[82] It was further recognised that 'that the most effective way of protecting human health and the environment from the dangers posed by such wastes is the reduction of their generation to a minimum in terms of quantity and/or hazard potential'.[83]

25   In 1989, the focus of the Basel Convention was transboundary movements of hazardous wastes.[84] This focus was expanded in 2000 to include the 'minimization of waste through environmentally sound management that addresses virtually all stages in its production and consumption, including generation, storage, transport, treatment, reuse, recycling, recovery, and final disposal, thereby adopting an integrated life-cycle approach'.[85]

26   The Basel Convention is complemented by the Rotterdam Convention, which was adopted in 1998.[86] The Rotterdam Convention confirms 'the harmful impact on human health and the environment from certain hazardous chemicals and pesticides in international trade'[87] and establishes 'mandatory rules regarding the import and export of

---

[76] UNEP, *Guidelines for National Waste Management Strategies, Moving from Challenges to Opportunities* (2013), 15.

[77] UNEP, *Guidelines for National Waste Management Strategies, Moving from Challenges to Opportunities* (2013), 15.

[78] UNEP, *The ABC for Sustainable Cities: A Glossary for Policy Makers* (2016), 33.

[79] UNEP, *Guidelines for National Waste Management Strategies, Moving from Challenges to Opportunities* (2013), 18.

[80] Basel Convention (1989), Art. 2(8).

[81] UNEP, *Global Outlook on Sustainable Consumption and Production Policies: Taking action together* (2012), 26.

[82] Basel Convention (1989), preamble.

[83] Basel Convention (1989), preamble.

[84] Voigt, 'Principle 8: Sustainable Development through Integration' in Viñuales (ed), *The Rio Declaration on Environment and Development: A Commentary* (2015), 246 (259).

[85] Voigt, 'Principle 8: Sustainable Development through Integration' in Viñuales (ed), *The Rio Declaration on Environment and Development: A Commentary* (2015), 246 (259).

[86] Voigt, 'Principle 8: Sustainable Development through Integration' in Viñuales, (ed) *The Rio Declaration on Environment and Development: A Commentary* (2015), 246 (259).

[87] Rotterdam Convention (1998), preamble.

hazardous chemicals and pesticides, creating mechanisms for information sharing and encouraging the environmentally sound management of permitted chemicals'.[88]

The Stockholm Convention, adopted in 2001, recognised 'the need to take measures **27** to prevent adverse effects caused by persistent organic pollutants at all stages of their life cycle'[89], 'to protect human health and the environment from persistent organic pollutants'[90]. The aim of the Convention is to eliminate or restrict the chemicals listed in the Annex to the Convention for production, use, import and export and to establish the obligation to take measures with regard to the waste and unintentional release of persistent organic pollutants.[91]

The most recent convention is the Minamata Convention on Mercury, which was **28** adopted in 2013. The aim of the convention is 'to protect the human health and the environment from anthropogenic emissions and releases of mercury and mercury compounds'.[92] The convention included, among other aspects, the establishment of control measures to regulate emissions and environmentally sound interim storage and disposal of mercury.[93]

The progress of SDG 12.4 is measured by the 'number of parties to international **29** multilateral environmental agreements on hazardous waste, and other chemicals that meet their commitments and obligations in transmitting information as required by each relevant agreement' (indicator 12.4.1) and according to Indicator 12.4.2 by the '(a) Hazardous waste generated per capita; and (b) proportion of hazardous waste treated, by type of treatment'. Nevertheless, SDG 12.4 to reduce the harmful effects of chemicals and waste by 2020 was not achieved.[94]

1. Waste Reduction and Extended Producer Responsibility

Every year, about 1.3 billion tonnes of solid waste are collected worldwide.[95] This is **30** expected to increase to 2.2 billion tonnes by 2025, with developing countries accounting for the largest share.[96] SDG12.5 has the goal to 'substantially reduce waste generation through prevention, reduction, recycling and reuse' by 2030. Waste reduction is about how to generate less waste, i.e. the prevention of waste.[97] An environmental policy approach to waste prevention is extended producer responsibility, which gives manufacturers long-term environmental responsibility for their products.[98] Extended producer responsibility is based on the polluter-pays-principle, which is already incorporated into different waste management laws.[99] The concept is largely implemented through take-back schemes that require producers to take back and recycle their products after

---

[88] Voigt, 'Principle 8: Sustainable Development through Integration' in Viñuales (ed), *The Rio Declaration on Environment and Development: A Commentary* (2015), 246 (259).

[89] Stockholm Convention (2001), preamble.

[90] Stockholm Convention (2001), Art. 1.

[91] UNEP, *Global Chemicals Outlook II, From Legacies to Innovative Solutions* (2019), 223.

[92] Minamata Convention (2013), Art. 1.

[93] UNEP, *Global Chemicals Outlook II, From Legacies to Innovative Solutions* (2019), 223.

[94] https://unstats.un.org/sdgs/report/2020/progress-summary-for-SDG-targets/.

[95] UNEP, *Guidelines for National Waste Management Strategies: Moving from Challenges to Opportunities* (2013), 13.

[96] UNEP, *Guidelines for National Waste Management Strategies: Moving from Challenges to Opportunities* (2013), 13.

[97] Jones and van Calster, 'Waste Regulation' in Lees and Viñuales (eds), *The Oxford Handbook of Comparative Environmental Law* (2019), 607 (617).

[98] Jones and van Calster, 'Waste Regulation' in Lees and Viñuales (eds), *The Oxford Handbook of Comparative Environmental Law* (2019), 607 (620).

[99] Jones and van Calster, 'Waste Regulation' in Lees and Viñuales (eds), *The Oxford Handbook of Comparative Environmental Law* (2019), 607 (620).

use by consumers or pay fees to entities that collect and recycle products instead of the producer.[100] Progress on SDG12.5 is measured by the 'national recycling rate, tons of material recycled' (indicator 12.5.1).

2. Reduction of Food Waste

31   It is estimated that about one third of the food produced worldwide is lost or wasted.[101] This wasteful use of food not only has a negative impact on the climate and nature, but also contributes to environmental pollution, whereas the actual extent is not yet sufficiently known.[102] Next to the aspect of environmental pollution, the problem of food security plays a major role, as millions of people suffer from hunger while food is thrown away or wasted.[103] Therefore, it is the objective of SDG 12.3 to 'halve per capita global food waste at the retail and consumer levels and reduce food losses along production and supply chains, including post-harvest losses' by 2030. SDG 12.3 has two focal points: while the aspect of 'food loss' is supply-orientated, the aspect of 'food waste' is demand-orientated.[104] Food loss includes 'decrease, at all stages of the food chain prior to the consumer level, in mass, of food that was originally intended for human consumption, regardless of the cause'.[105] Food waste includes 'food appropriate for human consumption being discarded or left to spoil at consumer level-regardless of the cause'.[106] Food loss is measured under the food loss index, while food waste is measured under the food waste index. Both indices are used to measure the progress of SDG 12.3. according to Indicator 12.3.1. The food loss index measures the incurred losses of a country's main commodities along the entire supply chain, while the food waste index measures the incurred waste of food and inedible components at the retail and consumer level.[107] The indexes are designed to make food loss and food waste more transparent in order to make the food supply system more efficient.[108]

IV. Green Economy and Green Growth

32   Sparked by numerous crises, the concept of the 'Green Economy' was created by UNEP in 2008 as part of the Global Green New Deal.[109] A green economy should be achieved by 'improv[ing] human well-being and social equity, while significantly reducing environmental risks and ecological scarcities'.[110] To achieve a green economy, it was proposed, among other things, to apply environmental subsidies and, in this course, to reduce subsidies for environmentally harmful activities – such as subsidies for fossil fuels.[111] It was also proposed to use market-based instruments and taxes to promote

---

[100] Jones and van Calster, 'Waste Regulation' in Lees and Viñuales (eds), *The Oxford Handbook of Comparative Environmental Law* (2019), 607 (620 f.).

[101] UNEP, *Food Waste Index Report 2021* (2021), 20.

[102] UNEP, *Food Waste Index Report 2021* (2021), 7, 20.

[103] HLPE, *Food losses and waste in the context of sustainable food systems* (2014), 19.

[104] FAO, *SDG 12.3.1: Global Food Loss Index* (2018), 7.

[105] HLPE, *Food losses and waste in the context of sustainable food systems* (2014), 22.

[106] HLPE, *Food losses and waste in the context of sustainable food systems* (2014), 22.

[107] UNEP, *Food Waste Index Report 2021* (2021), 21.

[108] FAO, *SDG 12.3.1: Global Food Loss Index* (2018), 2.

[109] UNEP, *Towards a Green Economy: Pathways to Sustainable Development and Poverty Eradication* (2011), 1 f.

[110] UNEP, *Towards a Green Economy: Pathways to Sustainable Development and Poverty Eradication* (2011), 2.

[111] Lottici et al., '"Green Trade Protectionism": An Analysis of Three New Issues that Affect Developing Countries' (2014) 2 No 2 *Chinese Journal of Urban and Environmental Studies*, 1 (9).

green investment and innovation.[112] In addition, the OECD created the 'Green Growth Strategy' in 2009 as part of the Declaration on Green Growth.[113] Green Growth will

> 'foster economic growth and development while ensuring that natural assets continue to provide the resources and environmental services on which our well-being relies. To do this it must catalyse investment and innovation which will underpin sustained growth and give rise to new economic opportunities'.[114]

Here, the role of the state as a central figure in driving green technologies was also   **33** recognised in the form of public procurement and the creation of standards.[115] To achieve Green Growth, it is considered necessary that the economy's environmental efficiency is improved through technological changes and substitutions while governments are able to accelerate this process through appropriate regulations and incentives.[116] Moreover, according to UNEP, 'green growth requires absolute decoupling of GDP from resource use and environmental impact'.[117] Yet, this requirement may not be possible to reach.[118]

1. Trade and Green Protection

In addition to multilateral agreements, international trade agreements play a crucial   **34** role in the SCP.[119] In a globalised world, life cycles cannot only be nationally limited but must also be determined in a global context.[120] The most important international trade agreement is the GATT 1994. Green protectionism as the relevant keyword defines 'various non-tariff measures used to protect or support the growing "green" industry'.[121] It means 'the use of environmental policies in the form of packaging laws, eco-labelling, production methods and much more to restrict access to foreign markets with the intention of protecting the domestic industry, whether organic or synthetic'.[122] In essence, therefore, this is about environmental goods. Those goods can be defined as 'goods [...] used to measure, prevent, limit, minimise or correct environmental damage'.[123] Environmental standards exist in particular for food and agricultural products.[124]

---

[112] Lottici et al., '"Green Trade Protectionism": An Analysis of Three New Issues that Affect Developing Countries' (2014) 2 No 2 *Chinese Journal of Urban and Environmental Studies*, 1 (9).

[113] C/MIN(2009)5/ADD1/FINAL, Declaration On Green Growth, 25 June 2009, para 13.

[114] OECD, *Towards green growth: A summary for policy makers* (2011), 4.

[115] Lottici et al., '"Green Trade Protectionism": An Analysis of Three New Issues that Affect Developing Countries' (2014) 2 No 2 *Chinese Journal of Urban and Environmental Studies*, 1 (9 f.).

[116] Hickel and Kallis, 'Is Green Growth Possible?' (2020) 25 (4) *New Political Economy*, 470; further reading on green growth Belmonte-Ureña et al., 'Circular economy, degrowth and green growth as pathways for research on sustainable development goals: A global analysis and future agenda' (2021) 185 *Ecological Economics*.

[117] Hickel and Kallis, 'Is Green Growth Possible?' (2020) 25 (4) *New Political Economy*, 470.

[118] Hickel and Kallis, 'Is Green Growth Possible?' (2020) 25 (4) *New Political Economy*, 484.

[119] UNEP, *Global Outlook on Sustainable Consumption and Production Policies: Taking action together* (2012), 27.

[120] UNEP, *Global Outlook on Sustainable Consumption and Production Policies: Taking action together* (2012), 27.

[121] Mukherjee, 'Green protectionism: Nuisance or Catalyst for Cross-Border trade (With reference to India)' (2017) 22 No 9 *IOSR-JHSS*, 1 (2).

[122] Mukherjee, 'Green protectionism: Nuisance or Catalyst for Cross-Border trade (With reference to India)' (2017) 22 No 9 *IOSR-JHSS*, 1 (2).

[123] OECD, *Policy Brief: Opening markets for environmental goods and services* (2005), 1.

[124] Mukherjee, 'Green protectionism: Nuisance or Catalyst for Cross-Border trade (With reference to India)' (2017) 22 No 9 *IOSR-JHSS*, 1 (2).

35   Trade-related environmental measures are likely to affect international trade.[125] They are particularly critical because they run counter to Art. XI GATT 1994[126] while it is not necessary for a measure to directly affect trade.[127] On the one hand, different national production standards within the framework of environmental regulations can have a negative impact on global trade.[128] By setting standards, countries are forced to create similar standards when they trade with each other.[129] On the other hand, environmental measures can violate the principle of non-discrimination under Article III GATT.[130] This is a particular challenge for developing countries, which are often unable to meet these standards.[131] This aspect was taken up in the Doha Declaration, which states '[...] to give particular attention to: (i) the effect of environmental measures on market access, especially in relation to developing countries, in particular the least-developed among them [...]'.[132]

36   Green protectionism can be countered by concluding multilateral agreements, as these mitigate the dangers of the unilateral national measures just mentioned.[133] Moreover, the TBT and SPS agreements are relevant for this subject. These two agreements ensure that technical and health standards are not used as non-tariff barriers to trade.[134] However, these two agreements set stricter requirements than trade restrictive measures covered by Art. XX GATT 1994.[135]

2. Sustainable Public Procurement

37   The promotion of sustainable public procurement is a core element in achieving sustainable consumption and production.[136] Globally, there is a positive development in sustainable public procurement practices, not only focusing on energy savings, resource efficiency and climate protection, but also increasing the importance of social aspects.[137] SDG 12.7 has to goal to 'promote public procurement practices that are sustainable, in accordance with national policies and priorities'. Sustainable public procurement is defined as a 'process whereby public organizations meet their needs for goods, services, works and utilities in a way that achieves value for money on a whole life-cycle basis in terms of generating benefits not only to the organization, but also to society and

---

[125] Mukherjee, 'Green protectionism: Nuisance or Catalyst for Cross-Border trade (With reference to India)' (2017) 22 No 9 *IOSR-JHSS*, 1 (4).

[126] Bodansky and Lawrence, 'Trade and Environment' in Bethlehem et al. (eds), *The Oxford Handbook of International Trade Law* (2009), 505 (512).

[127] Bodansky and Lawrence, 'Trade and Environment' in Bethlehem et al. (eds), *The Oxford Handbook of International Trade Law* (2009), 505 (512).

[128] Bodansky and Lawrence, 'Trade and Environment' in Bethlehem et al. (eds), *The Oxford Handbook of International Trade Law* (2009), 505 (513).

[129] Mukherjee, 'Green protectionism: Nuisance or Catalyst for Cross-Border trade (With reference to India)' (2017) 22 No 9 *IOSR-JHSS*, 1 (4).

[130] Bodansky and Lawrence, 'Trade and Environment' in Bethlehem et al. (eds), *The Oxford Handbook of International Trade Law* (2009), 505 (513).

[131] Mukherjee, 'Green protectionism: Nuisance or Catalyst for Cross-Border trade (With reference to India)' (2017) 22 No 9 *IOSR-JHSS*, 1 (4).

[132] WT/MIN(01)/DEC/1, 20 November 2001, para 32.

[133] Bodansky and Lawrence, 'Trade and Environment' in Bethlehem et al. (eds), *The Oxford Handbook of International Trade Law* (2009), 505 (523).

[134] Bodansky and Lawrence, 'Trade and Environment' in Bethlehem et al. (eds), *The Oxford Handbook of International Trade Law* (2009), 505 (519).

[135] Bodansky and Lawrence, 'Trade and Environment' in Bethlehem et al. (eds), *The Oxford Handbook of International Trade Law* (2009), 505 (520).

[136] UNEP, *Building Circularity into our Economies through Sustainable Procurement* (2018), 3.

[137] UNEP, *Building Circularity into our Economies through Sustainable Procurement* (2018), 3.

the economy, whilst significantly reducing negative impacts on the environment'.[138] In 2012, a work programme on sustainable development was adopted at WTO level by the Government Procurement Committee 'noting that Article XXII:8(a) of the Agreement on Government Procurement (Agreement) provides that the Parties shall adopt and periodically review a work programme, including a work programme on sustainable procurement'.[139]

Sustainable public procurement brings a wide range of benefits. In particular, govern- **38** ments can positively influence the market supply due to their high purchasing power if they buy environmentally friendly products and thus trigger innovation processes towards more environmentally friendly products.[140] This is mostly reflected in Green Public Procurement (GPP), a form of SPP, which should be incentivised according to the ILA.[141] GPP is defined as 'a process whereby public authorities seek to procure goods, services and works with a reduced environmental impact throughout their life-cycle when compared to goods, services and works with the same primary function that would otherwise be procured'.[142] Equitable benefit-sharing constitutes a crucial element in the concept of SPP.[143] For example, procurement should ensure that suppliers pay adequate wages and that workers and residents living next to the production site are not harmed.[144] Also, special attention should be paid to minority- and women-owned companies in the procurement process.[145] In addition to these aspects, geographical equity should ensure that public procurement does lead or support negative impacts across borders.[146] Moreover, procedural equity should enable every individual and organisation to participate in public procurement.[147] Overall, an effective SPP should benefit all. To promote sustainable public procurement, the 10YFP Programme on Sustainable Public Procurement was established in 2014 as a global multi-stakeholder umbrella programme of organisations.[148] Furthermore, six Principles of Sustainable Public Procurement were published in 2015 as part of the programme.[149]

Public procurement in the EU is subject to different laws and regulations: **39**

- The Procurement Directives (2014/24/EU and 2014/25/EU)
- The Treaties (Treaty on the Functioning of the EU, Treaty on the EU and their predecessors)
- Case law of the Court of Justice of the European Communities
- Law applying to related areas such as State Aid and Competition

---

[138] UNEP, *Building Circularity into our Economies through Sustainable Procurement* (2018), 5.

[139] GPA/113, 2 April 2012, Appendix 2, Annex E, preamble.

[140] GOV/PGC/ETH(2013)3, *Mapping out good practices for promoting green public procurement, OECD meeting of Leading Practitioners on Public Procurement*, 23 January 2013, para 2.

[141] ILA, *ILA Guidelines on Role of international Law in Sustainable Resource Management for Development* (2020), para. 4.2.2.

[142] European Commission, *Buying Green! A handbook on green public procurement* (2016), 4.

[143] ILA, *ILA Guidelines on Role of international Law in Sustainable Resource Management for Development* (2020), para. 5.2.1.

[144] The Royal Institute of International Affairs, *Public Procurement for sustainable development* (2020), 13.

[145] The Royal Institute of International Affairs, *Public Procurement for sustainable development* (2020), 13.

[146] The Royal Institute of International Affairs, *Public Procurement for sustainable development* (2020), 14.

[147] The Royal Institute of International Affairs, *Public Procurement for sustainable development* (2020), 14.

[148] https://www.oneplanetnetwork.org/sustainable-public-procurement.

[149] UNEP, *10YFP SPP Programme Principles of Sustainable Public Procurement* (2015), 2 f.

40   In addition, several sources support the interpretation of the relevant laws and principles.[150] Nevertheless, to effectively contribute to SPP, clarifications as well as simplifi-
cations of the EU legal framework might be necessary.[151] The progress of SDG 12.7
is measured by the 'degree of sustainable public procurement policies and action plan
implementation' (indicator 12.7.1).

41   Furthermore, SDG 12.c calls to 'rationalize inefficient fossil-fuel subsidies that encourage wasteful consumption by removing market distortions, in accordance with national circumstances, including by restructuring taxation and phasing out those harmful
subsidies, where they exist, to reflect their environmental impacts, taking fully into
account the specific needs and conditions of developing countries and minimizing the
possible adverse impacts on their development in a manner that protects the poor
and the affected communities' which is pivotal because sustainable consumption and
production require the careful use of natural resources.[152] Furthermore, the use of fossil
fuels is harmful to the environment because greenhouse gases are released.[153] Progress is
measured by the 'amount of fossil-fuel subsidies (production and consumption) per unit
of GDP' (indicator 12.c.1).

3. Sustainable Tourism

42   Tourism is one of the world's largest economic sectors and accounts for a large share
of global trade.[154] Therefore, a tourism sector that takes SCP into account can play
an important role towards sustainable change.[155] In this course, SDG 12.b aims to 'develop and implement tools to monitor sustainable development impacts for sustainable
tourism that creates jobs and promotes local culture and products'. Sustainable tourism
can be defined as 'tourism that takes full account of its current and future economic,
social and environmental impacts, addressing the needs of visitors, the industry, the
environment and host communities'.[156] Within the framework of the 10 Year Framework
of Programmes on Sustainable Consumption and Production Patterns (10 YFP), a
programme on sustainable tourism was created, which aims to establish SCP practices
in tourism in order to achieve economic, social and environmental improvements.[157]
Furthermore, at the international level, the United Nations World Tourism Organization
(UNWTO) has a Programme on Sustainable Development of Tourism.[158] The progress

---

[150] For example *Buying Green! A handbook on green public procurement* (2016) and European Commission's Interpretative Communications; https://ec.europa.eu/environment/gpp/what_en.htm; https://ec.eur
opa.eu/environment/gpp/eu_public_directives_en.htm.

[151] Mélon, 'More Than a Nudge? Arguments and Tools for Mandating Green Public Procurement in the
EU' (2020) 12 (3) *Sustainability*, 988 (1004).

[152] UNEP, OECD and IISD, *Measuring Fossil Fuel Subsidies in the Context of the Sustainable Development Goals* (2019), 3.

[153] UN, *The Sustainable Development Goals Report 2020* (2020), 49.

[154] UNWTO, *Sustainable Tourism for Development Guidebook* (2013), 16.

[155] Attard and Fitzmaurice and Ntovas, 'The UN World Tourism Organization and Global Ocean
Governance' in Attard et al. (eds), *The IMLI Treatise On Global Ocean Governance: Volume II: UN
Spezialized Agencies and Global Ocean Governance* (2018), 195 (199).

[156] Attard and Fitzmaurice and Ntovas, 'The UN World Tourism Organization and Global Ocean
Governance' in Attard et al. (eds), *The IMLI Treatise On Global Ocean Governance: Volume II: UN
Spezialized Agencies and Global Ocean Governance* (2018), 195 (202).

[157] Attard and Fitzmaurice and Ntovas, 'The UN World Tourism Organization and Global Ocean
Governance' in Attard et al. (eds), *The IMLI Treatise On Global Ocean Governance: Volume II: UN
Spezialized Agencies and Global Ocean Governance* (2018), 195 (199).

[158] Attard and Fitzmaurice and Ntovas, 'The UN World Tourism Organization and Global Ocean
Governance' in Attard et al. (eds), *The IMLI Treatise On Global Ocean Governance: Volume II: UN
Spezialized Agencies and Global Ocean Governance* (2018), 195 (195, 202).

on SDG 12.b is measured by the 'implementation of standard accounting tools to monitor the economic and environmental aspects of tourism sustainability' (indicator 12.b.1).

4. Corporate Sustainability Reporting

Corporate Social Responsibility (CSR) reporting has steadily increased over the **43** last decades[159] the development of which goes hand in hand with the evolution of the concept of sustainability.[160] To this end, SDG 12.6 aims to 'encourage companies, especially large and transnational companies, to adopt sustainable practices and to integrate sustainability information into their reporting cycle'. While CSR used to focus on environmental aspects, this reporting has evolved into sustainability reporting.[161] In sustainability reporting, companies voluntarily publish information on economic, social and environmental aspects that play a role in the company's activities.[162] This information can be qualitative or quantitative and is intended to inform external stakeholders such as customers, investors and the public.[163] Sustainability reporting is promoted by the Global Reporting Initiative (GRI), which has established guidelines for sustainability reporting.[164] The GRI was founded in 1997 by UNEP and CERES[165] and its GRI guidelines now form the most popular and widely used guide for sustainability reporting worldwide.[166] At EU level, the concept of CSR has so far been integrated into the Non-Financial Reporting Directive (NFRD).[167] In April 2021, The EU Commission adopted a proposal for a Corporate Sustainability Reporting Directive (CSRD), that will amend the reporting requirements set out in the NFRD.[168] The proposal aims to better align EU sustainability reporting standards with the European Green Deal as well as existing legal frameworks such as the Sustainable Finance Disclosure Regulation and the Taxonomy Regulation.[169] The progress of SDG 12.6 is measured by the 'number of companies publishing sustainability reports' (indicator 12.6.1).

---

[159] Castelo, 'Sustainability Reporting Guidelines' in Idowu et al. (eds), *Encyclopedia of Corporate Social Responsibility* (2013), 2389 (2389).

[160] Tsalis et al., 'New Challenges for corporate sustainability reporting: United Nations' 2030 Agenda for sustainable development and the sustainable development goals' (2020) 27 No 2 *Corp Soc Responsib Environ Manag*, 1 (5).

[161] Castelo, 'Sustainability Reporting Guidelines' in Idowu et al. (eds), *Encyclopedia of Corporate Social Responsibility* (2013), 2389 (2389).

[162] Castelo, 'Sustainability Reporting Guidelines' in Idowu et al. (eds), *Encyclopedia of Corporate Social Responsibility* (2013), 2389 (2389).

[163] Castelo, 'Sustainability Reporting Guidelines' in Idowu et al. (eds), *Encyclopedia of Corporate Social Responsibility* (2013), 2389 (2389); Schreck, 'Disclosure (CSR Reporting)' in Idowu et al. (eds), *Encyclopedia of Corporate Social Responsibility* (2013), 801 (801).

[164] Castelo, 'Sustainability Reporting Guidelines' in Idowu et al. (eds), *Encyclopedia of Corporate Social Responsibility* (2013), 2389 (2389).

[165] Castelo, 'Sustainability Reporting Guidelines' in Idowu et al. (eds), *Encyclopedia of Corporate Social Responsibility* (2013), 2389 (2390).

[166] Castelo, 'Sustainability Reporting Guidelines' in Idowu et al. (eds), *Encyclopedia of Corporate Social Responsibility* (2013), 2389 (2390).

[167] Directive 2014/95/EU.

[168] COM(2021) 189 final, *Proposal for a Directive Of The European Parliament And Of The Council amending Directive 2013/34/EU, Directive 2004/109/EC, Directive 2006/43/EC and Regulation (EU) No 537/2014, as regards corporate sustainability reporting*, 21 April 2021; https://ec.europa.eu/info/business-ec onomy-euro/company-reporting-and-auditing/company-reporting/corporate-sustainability-reporting_e n#overview.

[169] COM(2021) 189 final, *Proposal for a Directive Of The European Parliament And Of The Council amending Directive 2013/34/EU, Directive 2004/109/EC, Directive 2006/43/EC and Regulation (EU) No 537/2014, as regards corporate sustainability reporting*, 21 April 2021, 4 f.

5. Consumer Information and Education

44   Consumer information, in the form of accessible, reliable and verifiable sustainability information, can facilitate purchasing sustainable products for the consumer.[170] This can be made possible through eco-labels, voluntary standards and product declarations.[171] Here, eco-labels are a popular option which allow companies and consumers to be informed about the environmental characteristics or hazards of a product (at least to a certain extent).[172] SDG 12.8 states to ensure that 'by 2030 [...] people everywhere have the relevant information and awareness for sustainable development and lifestyles in harmony with nature'. The 10 YFP includes a Consumer Information Programme for Sustainable Consumption and Production, which aims to provide information on the quality of goods and services and to encourage consumers to consume sustainably through effective strategies.[173] Progress on SDG 12.8 is measured by the 'extent to which (i) global citizenship education and (ii) education for sustainable development are mainstreamed in (a) national education policies; (b) curricula; (c) teacher education; and (d) student assessment' (Indicator 12.8.1).

C. Interdependences of SDG 12

45   'The global disruption of supply chains and the closure of shops and restaurants has had a significant impact on consumption and production. On the one hand, long term provisioning and even panic buying of some items became widespread all over the world, which drove up prices for essential goods. At the same time, many food banks received less food for redistribution to people in need, as supermarkets had hardly any goods left to donate. In some countries, agricultural products were destroyed to a considerable extent because the channels to the final consumers were interrupted. In the US, Dairy Farmers of America, the country's largest dairy cooperative, estimated that farmers had to pour away up to 14 million litres of milk every day in April. A single chicken producer destroyed 750,000 unhatched eggs every week.[174] In this respect, it is positive that the downsizing of supply chains and a greater focus on regional products also represent an opportunity for more sustainable consumption and production patterns – provided that these trends survive the crisis (SDG 2).[175]

46   From an estimated 7.7 billion people worldwide in 2019, it is projected that the global population could grow around 8.5 billion in 2030, 9.7 billion in 2050, and 10.9 billion in 2100.[176] To achieve long-term sustainable development, it is mandatory to change the current patterns of unsustainable production and consumption. Changing consumption and production patterns is not only vital for poverty and hunger eradication, but also for protecting and managing the natural resource base and ecosystems, as unsustainable consumption and production patterns are increasing water and air pollution, land and

---

[170] https://www.unep.org/explore-topics/resource-efficiency/what-we-do/sustainable-lifestyles/consumer-information-including.

[171] https://www.unep.org/explore-topics/resource-efficiency/what-we-do/sustainable-lifestyles/consumer-information-including.

[172] Czanezki and Pollans and Main, 'Eco-Labelling' in Lees and Viñuales (eds), *The Oxford Handbook of Comparative Environmental Law* (2019), 996 (996).

[173] https://www.unep.org/explore-topics/resource-efficiency/what-we-do/sustainable-lifestyles/consumer-information-including.

[174] https://www.nytimes.com/2020/04/11/business/coronavirus-destroying-food.html.

[175] Martens and Ellmers and Pokorny on behalf of Global Policy Watch, *COVID-19 and the SDGs, The impact of the coronavirus pandemic on the global sustainability agenda* (2020), 6 f.

[176] UNDESA, *World Population Prospects 2019: Highlights* (2019).

forest degradation, waste generation and the use of harmful chemical substances.[177] Therefore, SDG 12 in its targets is strongly linked to SDG 6, SDG 7, SDG 11, SDG 13 and SDG 15.

As mentioned above, the sustainable production pattern of food is generally leading   **47** to more food waste and food production waste generation, and therefore resources spent to produce such products (especially water) are wasted and lost.[178] Achieving a sustainable management and efficient use of natural resources (SDG 12.2), reducing food waste and post-harvest losses (SDG 12.3), reducing waste generation through prevention, reduction, recycling and reuse (SDG 12.5), and by promoting public procurement practices which are sustainable, in accordance with national policies and priorities are synergizing well with improving water quality (SDG 6.3) and increasing water-use efficiency (SDG 6.4) is mandatory to stop unsustainable practices in food production.

Between 2007 and 2050, the urban population is expected to increase as much as it   **48** did since 1920, that is, 3.1 additional urban dwellers are expected by 2050 (which equals 70 per cent of the world's population) and by an estimate, 80 per cent of the world's GDP is generated by urban areas.[179] Consequently, cities and urban areas are a key driver for waste generation. Achieving SDG 12.5 by substantially reducing waste generation through reduction, recycling and reuse will greatly help to reduce the adverse per capita environmental impact of cities (SDG 11.6).

Reducing waste and pollution, improving resource efficiency, increasing recycling   **49** and reuse, and promoting awareness of more sustainable lifestyles go hand in hand with calls for more efficient use of natural resources. For example, phasing out inefficient, wasteful and market-distorting fossil fuel subsidies could strengthen efforts to deploy renewable energy and energy-efficient technologies and consumption patterns. Thus, sustainable production patterns would be triggered and resource efficiency improved while waste generation would be reduced.[180]

The continuous and increasing conversion of natural ecosystems for agriculture, the   **50** fragmentation of habitats, loss of biodiversity and degradation of various ecosystem services and other unsustainable agricultural practices are leading to many environmental challenges.[181] To escape the increasing pressure from unsustainable consumption and production, SDG 12 promotes the opposite (e.g. a 'waste reduction-circular economy', SDG 12.5) and encourages companies to adopt sustainable practices and to integrate sustainability information into their reporting cycle (SDG 12.6), which synergizes well with SDG 15.1 and SDG 15.2. Although forests are not explicitly mentioned in SDG 12, achieving targets (SDG 12.3, SDG 12.5, SDG 12.b) will result in positive contributions towards forest conservation and support forest-dependent livelihoods.[182]

---

[177] UNGA Open Working Group on Sustainable Development Goals, *Compendium of TST Issues Briefs* (2014), 167.

[178] https://www.npr.org/sections/thesalt/2013/06/06/189192870/when-you-waste-food-youre-wasting-tons-of-water-too?t=1611830325957.

[179] UN/POP/EGM-URB/2008/01, *An Overview of Urbanization, Internal Migration, Population Distribution and Development in the World*, 14 January 2008, 3.

[180] Griggs et al., *A Guide to SDG Interactions: From Science to Implementation* (2017), 134.

[181] UNGA Open Working Group on Sustainable Development Goals, *Compendium of TST Issues Briefs* (2013), 168.

[182] Schröder et al., 'SDG 12: Responsible Consumption and Production – Potential Benefits and Impacts on Forests and Livelihoods' in Katila et al. (eds), *Sustainable Development Goals: Their Impacts on Forests and People* (2019), 386.

D. Jurisprudential Significance of SDG 12

51   SDG 12 represents one of the internal principles of the Global Agenda 2030 ('Planet') and is an essential requirement for sustainable development (→ Intro mn. 140 ff.).[183] While it can be said that the 'existing socio-economic system is the main cause of unsustainable consumption and production patterns', this 'system is [also] shaped and enabled by a cobweb of international law, regulations and governance systems (or lack thereof)'.[184] The international legal system is equipped with strong institutions that primarily protect capital values and promote trade and investment liberalisation.[185] However, mechanisms for the protection and enforcement of environmental and human rights remain relatively weak. Also, the existing protection systems do not induce actual shifts in production and consumption processes or a reallocation of their value.

52   Inclusive governance, based on broad and equal participation, non-discrimination and accountability, is key to achieving SCP patterns as demanded by SDG 12. Beyond these governance-driven notions of decoupling economic growth from resource use and exploitation, enabling access to relevant information[186] (SDG 12.8) is a crucial element of the SCP processes (→ Goal 4 mn. 7, Goal 16 mn. 11).[187]

53   International human rights standards already indicate and accommodate the necessary changes, e.g. by calling for international development cooperation, including the prevention and mitigation of the negative impacts of environmental damage, and demanding participation rights for all people, e.g. in scientific progress and transfer of know-how, and / or promoting fundamental rights such as the right to food, health and water.[188]

54   Both the human rights regime and international law, in their interplay with the effects of the expressions of imperialism and the currently (most often) prevailing system of capitalism,[189] are not the approach that so far addresses the concerns of SDG 12. It is in the context of transnational regulation of private actors, which can hardly be condensed to one legal regime, that the specific address of sustainability in global value and supply chains can be found.

55   Yet, a broader approach is needed that is able to permeate all areas of processes, consider transboundary scenarios[190] (SDG 12.1), respect planetary boundaries and integrate international legal principles such as the principle of common but differentiated respon-

---

[183] UNEP, *10YFP SPP Programme Principles of Sustainable Public Procurement* (2015), 7.

[184] Arcuri and Partiti, 'SDG 12: Ensure Sustainable Consumption and Production Patterns' (2021) *TILEC Discussion Paper, DP 2021-007*, 2 (Forthcoming in Ebbeson and Hay (eds), *The Cambridge Handbook on SDGs and international law*).

[185] Arcuri and Partiti, 'SDG 12: Ensure Sustainable Consumption and Production Patterns' (2021) *TILEC Discussion Paper, DP 2021-007*, 3 (Forthcoming in Ebbeson and Hay (eds), *The Cambridge Handbook on SDGs and international law*).

[186] Instruments are, amongst others, the Minamata Convention on Mercury, the Aarhus Convention, the Paris Agreement or the Escazú Agreement.

[187] UNGA Open Working Group on Sustainable Development Goals, *Compendium of TST Issues Briefs* (2014), 166; European Parliamentary Research Service (EPRS), *Decoupling economic growth from environmental harm* (2020), 1.

[188] UNGA Open Working Group on Sustainable Development Goals, *Compendium of TST Issues Briefs* (2014), 171.

[189] Arcuri and Partiti, 'SDG 12: Ensure Sustainable Consumption and Production Patterns' (2021) *TILEC Discussion Paper, DP 2021-007*, 5 (Forthcoming in Ebbeson and Hay (eds), *The Cambridge Handbook on SDGs and international law*).

[190] UN, *Sustainable Development Report 2021* (2021); further reading O'Neill et al., 'A good life for all within planetary boundaries' (2018) 1(2) *Nature Sustainability*, 88-95; Parrique et al., *Decoupling debunked: Evidence and arguments against green growth as a sole strategy for sustainability* (2019).

sibilities (CBDR) ($\rightarrow$ Intro mn. 141 ff., 158 ff., 217).[191] In this way, different levels of development and national circumstances are recognised and a 'broader, international dimension of equity'[192], which is inherently bound to the principle of sustainable use of natural resources,[193] may be established, which the Global Agenda 2030 recognisably advocates ($\rightarrow$ Intro mn. 35 ff., 184 ff.).[194]

I. Jurisdiction on Vision and Objectives

Noticeably, the overarching vision of SDG 12 cannot be attributed to any jurisdiction **56** directly. Rather, different case law addresses the general concept of sustainable development, a prerequisite of which is sustainable consumption and production patterns, among other things. Legally, particularly in the international sphere, the principle of sustainable use of resources takes on special significance in this context. Furthermore, access to information (SDG 12.8) is a constituent part of an effective and inclusive rule of law and participation in society. The endowment of nature with independent rights, which may lead to harmony with nature (SDG 12.8), can also be derived.[195] Due to a lack of unambiguous cases on sustainable consumption and production patterns, however, a clear indication is discernible that to date SDG 12 is not sufficiently reflected in jurisdiction as a self-standing form of a legal regime and thus shapes the legal landscape too less.

1. International Jurisdiction

Moving towards Sustainable Consumption and Production (SCP) patterns is a mam- **57** moth task which can hardly be borne from any one organisation, sector, region or legal family alone. At the international level, connection points to different legal fields can be found in particular through the 10 YFP[196] (SDG 12.1), harmony with nature (SDG 12.8), and the environmental impact assessments required by international environmental law (SDG 12 b). Further legal fields open up through the embedding of international trade law and the specific protection of vulnerable groups (SDG 12.c).[197]

The main international legal basis for regulating the areas of 'environmentally sound **58** management of chemicals and all wastes throughout their life cycle' addressed in SDG 12.4 can be found in the three instruments: Basel Convention, Rotterdam Convention

---

[191] Des Gasper and Shah and Tankha, 'The Framing of Sustainable Consumption and Production in SDG 12' (2019) 10(Suppl. 1) *Global Policy*, 83 (94).

[192] UNGA Open Working Group on Sustainable Development Goals, *Compendium of TST Issues Briefs* (2014), 5; in 2020, the new Global Commons Stewardship Index (GCSi) has been released which aims to track the domestic and transboundary impacts that countries have on the global commons; further information OECD/EC-JRC, *Understanding the Spillovers and Transboundary Impacts of Public Policies: Implementing the 2030 Agenda for More Resilient Societies* (2021); https://www.unsdsn.org/global-commo ns-stewardship-index-measures-countries-impacts-on-the-environment-beyond-domestic-concerns.

[193] ILA, *The Role of International Law in Sustainable Natural Resources Management for Development,* Resolution No. 4 (2020), preamble.

[194] A/RES/70/1, *Transforming our world: the 2030 Agenda for Sustainable Development,* 21 October 2015, paras. 13, 21; UNEP, *10YFP SPP Programme Principles of Sustainable Public Procurement* (2015).

[195] http://www.harmonywithnatureun.org/rightsOfNature/.

[196] The 10YFP consists of six programmes: Sustainable Public Procurement, Consumer Information for SCP, Sustainable Tourism, Sustainable Lifestyles and Education, Sustainable Buildings and Construction, and Sustainable Food Systems and seeks to achieve resource and impact decoupling.

[197] See e.g. ILA, *The Role of International Law in Sustainable Natural Resources Management for Development,* Resolution No. 4 (2020), paras. 3.1.4., 3.3.3., 3.4.2, 4.2.2., 5.1.3.

and the Stockholm Convention.[198] However, the establishment of SCPs is mostly (still) endangered by the unsustainable production and supply chains that have led to 'chemical and waste globalisation' in many places.[199]

59   The ICJ in *Legality of the Threat or Use of Nuclear Weapons*[200] stated that even during an armed conflict, states are not exempt from the obligation to protect the environment from harmful influences. Although this duty does not limit states in their ability to defend themselves, (military) decisions taken during this state of affairs must be measured against a standard of necessity and proportionality, which includes respect for the environment.[201] With reference to Principle 21 of the Stockholm Declaration, Rio Principles 2 and 24[202] and Arts. 35(3), 55 of the Additional Protocol I (additional protection for the environment), the court underlined that 'these provisions embody a general obligation to protect the natural environment against widespread, long-term and severe environmental damage'.[203] Although the focus of this case was not directly related to SCP, this judicial assessment forms one of the main bases for classifying the production and long-term effects, especially with regard to transboundary harm-producing biological and chemical weapons.[204] In view of the increasing world population and the likewise increasing conflict position of states and societies, this area is also of importance for the implementation of SDG 12, especially since it also opens up access to justice before the ICJ and consequently raises this SDG, which is otherwise mostly characterised by governance and political aspirations, to a legally tangible level.

60   In other cases too, the ICJ has found clear assessments on pollution from chemicals and (air) pollution release, mostly progressively ruled on the protection of the environment and the sustainable use of resources.[205] However, the ICJ does not (usually) make extensive use of its possibilities to interpret the law, but rather regularly points out that it cannot be expected to create or write new law (→ Goal 13 mn. 61, Goal 14 mn. 64 ff., Goal 15 mn. 54).

61   In its jurisdiction, the IACtHR also regularly justifies the sustainable use of resources and the environment in pointing to the obligation of states to implement, protect and promote the right to a healthy environment. This court frequently connects the right

---

[198] UNEP/WG. 190/4, *Basel Convention on the Control of Transboundary Movements of Hazardous Wastes and their Disposal*, 22 March 1989; Stockholm Convention on Persistent Organic Pollutants, 22 May 2001, UNTS, Vol. 2256, 119; Rotterdam Convention on the Prior Informed Consent Procedure for Certain Hazardous Chemicals and Pesticides in International Trade, Rotterdam, 10 September 1998, UNTS, Vol. 2244, 337.

[199] Khan, 'Role of International Law in a Future Detoxified' in Ataputtu and Gonzalez and Seck (eds), *The Cambridge Handbook of Environmental Justice and Sustainable Development* (2021), 255.

[200] ICJ, *Legality of the Threat or Use of Nuclear Weapons*, Advisory Opinion, 8 July 1996.

[201] ICJ, *Legality of the Threat or Use of Nuclear Weapons*, Advisory Opinion, 8 July 1996, para. 31.

[202] ICJ, *Legality of the Threat or Use of Nuclear Weapons*, Advisory Opinion, 8 July 1996, paras. 27, 31; Rio Principle 24 states: 'Warfare is inherently destructive of sustainable development. States shall therefore respect international law providing protection for the environment in times of armed conflict and cooperate in its further development, as necessary.'

[203] ICJ, *Legality of the Threat or Use of Nuclear Weapons*, Advisory Opinion, 8 July 1996, para. 32.

[204] Convention on the Prohibition of the Development, Production and Stockpiling of Bacteriological (Biological) and Toxin Weapons and on their Destruction, 10 April 1972; and the Convention on the Prohibition of the Development, Production, Stockpiling and Use of Chemical Weapons and on Their Destruction, 13 January 1993.

[205] *Trail Smelter case* (United States v. Canada) (1938 and 1941), 3 R.I.A.A., 1905-1982; *Case concerning the Gabčíkovo-Nagymaros Project (Hungary v Slovakia)*, Judgment of 25 September 1997, ICJ; *Certain Activities and Construction of a Road cases (Nicaragua v Costa Rica)*, Judgment of 16 December 2015, ICJ; further reading Kummer and Schechinger, 'Transboundary Movement of Hazardous Waste and Chemicals' in Nollkaemper and Plakokefalos (eds), *The Practice of Shared Responsibility in International Law* (2017); Kindji and Faure, 'Assessing reparation of environmental damage by the ICJ: A lost opportunity?' (2019) 57 *QIL*, 5-33.

to life, the right to personal development and the right to protection of family life as a frequent reasoning for the application of the right to a healthy environment.[206]

Noticeably, particularly vulnerable groups such as indigenous peoples, women and children are especially affected by impacts on the environment, both directly and indirectly (e.g. in the case of forced resettlement in the context of investments or their protection). The IACtHR interprets human rights obligations of states quite extensively in favour of those peoples affected. As a result, the court strengthens the pillar of social justice in particular on the one hand, but also increasingly recognises the close link between environmental protection and human rights and thus strengthens the concerns pursued with SDG 12 (→ Goal 13 mn. 61, Goal 14 mn. 64 ff., Goal 15 mn. 54).[207] 62

Furthermore, the African Commission on Human Rights,[208] after a severe oil spill in the Ogoniland, has linked the 'right to a general satisfactory environment, as guaranteed under Article 24 of the African Charter or the right to a healthy environment' with clear obligations of a government which require to actively take measure 'to prevent pollution and ecological degradation, to promote conservation, and to secure an ecologically sustainable development and use of natural resources'.[209] This case illustrates, as many others, in addition to other profound interconnections with other human rights, the inclusion of the principle of sustainable use of resources in the light of the principle of Permanent Sovereignty Over Natural Resources under international law, which is subject to clear limits. This allows at least a basic classification, which can serve as a precondition for the emergence of sustainable consumption and production patterns. 63

2. European Jurisdiction

The EU policy on sustainable consumption and production mainly builds on the EU Sustainable Development Strategy from 2008 'which reinforces the EU's long-standing commitment to meet the challenges of sustainable development and builds on initiatives and instruments at EU and international level such as the United Nations' Marrakech Process'.[210] 'The EU has established an extensive range of proposals on sustainable consumption and production (SCP), which include an energy- and resource-efficient economy, circular economy, waste prevention and recycling, among others'.[211] The extensive plans are detailed by an immense amount of secondary law.[212] 64

The EU Green Deal adopted in 2020 also contains several components that relate to SCP, such as the Farm to Fork Strategy, which initiates a far-reaching transition of European farmers and fishermen, or the New Industrial Strategy, which is intended to transform the EU economy into a CO_2-neutral circular economy.[213] The focus is also on the framing of a socially just societal transition, in particular the establishment 65

---

[206] Amongst many others: *La Oroya v. Perú*, IACtHR; *Indigenous Community Members of the Lhaka Honhat (Our Land) Association vs. Argentina*, IACtHR; *Pacheco Tineo family v. Bolivia*, IACtHR, para. 143, and *Hernández v. Argentina*, IACtHR, para. 66.

[207] See as proxy: *Requested by the Republic of Colombia the Environment and Human Rights*, Advisory Opinion OC-23/17, 15 November 2017, IACtHR, and the myriad of case-law cited therein.

[208] Further reading: Gwam, 'Toxic Waste Dumping and the Enjoyment of Economic, Social and Cultural Rights in Africa' in Yusuf (ed), *African Yearbook of International Law* (2008), 237-54.

[209] ACommHR, *Social and Economic Rights Action Center & the Center for Economic and Social Rights v. Nigeria*, Communication No. 155/96, 27 May 2002, para. 52.

[210] https://ec.europa.eu/environment/eussd/escp_en.htm.

[211] Pineiro-Villaverde and García-Álvarez, 'Sustainable Consumption and Production: Exploring the Links with Resources Productivity in the EU-28' (2020) 12 *Sustainability*, 1.

[212] Amongst many others: EC, Directive 2008/98/EC of the European Parliament and of the Council of 19 November 2009 on waste and repealing certain Directives, OJ L 312/3, 22 November 2008.

[213] COM(2019) 640 final, *Communication From The Commission To The European Parliament, The European Council, The Council, The European Economic And Social Committee And The Committee Of The*

of the European Pillar of Social Rights.[214] These and future legislative processes and legislative initiatives will be further developed.[215] The aim and purpose are to promote the well-being and health of citizens, make Europe climate-neutral by 2050 and protect, conserve and enhance the EU's natural capital and biodiversity. It is expected that these will also continue to be aligned with the goals of the Global Agenda 2030. However, when looking at the indicators to measure the implementation of the SDGs at the EU level, there is only a partial alignment.[216] These political programmes are accompanied by various funding programmes such as Horizon 2020.[217]

66   Under the EU taxonomy regulation, the EU requires, among other things, sustainable reporting and the greatest possible freedom of access to information for companies and other stakeholders, thereby supporting the achievement of SDG 12.6 and SDG 12.8. The EU taxonomy 'is a classification system, establishing a list of environmentally sustainable economic activities [in order to enable scaling] up sustainable investment and to implement the European Green Deal'.[218]

67   In the area of public procurement (SDG 12.7), which accounts for 19.7 per cent of the gross domestic product of member states within the EU, the EU has developed Green Public Procurement (GPP) criteria to facilitate the inclusion of environmentally friendly requirements in public tender documents. The EU GPP criteria aim to strike a balance between environmental performance, cost considerations, market availability and ease of verification. It is up to the procuring authorities to require all or only certain requirements in their tenders, depending on their needs and requirements.

68   Since the revision of public procurement in 2014, Art. 18(2) Public Procurement Directive anchors social and environmental compatibility/sustainability as a principle in addition to the general prohibition of discrimination and refers to the international social and environmental instruments[219] as follows:

Regions, The European Green Deal, 11 December 2019; see for an overview of policy programmes yielding from the EU Green Deal https://ec.europa.eu/info/strategy/priorities-2019-2024/european-green-deal_en.

[214] This includes, among other things, the establishment of a European minimum wage, increased funding for quality vocational training and employment and social protection and inclusion; COM(2020) 14 final, *Communication From The Commission To The European Parliament, The Council, The European Economic And Social Committee And The Committee Of The Regions, A Strong Social Europe For Just Transitions,* 14 January 2020.

[215] Some initiatives are already in place, such as: EU Taxonomy Climate Delegated Act; Corporate Sustainability Reporting Directive (CSRD); six amending Delegated Acts on fiduciary duties, investment and insurance advice.

[216] However, it is noticeable that a focus is placed on measuring air quality and CO_2 neutrality. In addition, the use of an indicator to measure the share of e-mobility is under discussion, whose sustainable footprint, against the background of the frequently unsustainable production, supply and value chains, might at least be questionable. The connection to climate change mitigation is taken into account by multi-purpose indicators (MPI), whereas as of yet the measurement of food waste is on hold; EC, *EU SDG Indicator set 2021, Result of the review in preparation of the 2021 edition of the EU SDG monitoring report,* Final version of 15/01/2021.

[217] https://ec.europa.eu/programmes/horizon2020/en/home; https://ec.europa.eu/research/participants/docs/h2020-funding-guide/grants/applying-for-funding/find-a-call/h2020-structure-and-budget_en.htm.

[218] https://ec.europa.eu/info/business-economy-euro/banking-and-finance/sustainable-finance/eu-taxonomy-sustainable-activities_en.

[219] Annex X lists as follows: ILO Convention 87 on Freedom of Association and the Protection of the Right to Organise; ILO Convention 98 on the Right to Organise and Collective Bargaining; ILO Convention 29 on Forced Labour; ILO Convention 105 on the Abolition of Forced Labour; ILO Convention 138 on Minimum Age; ILO Convention 111 on Discrimination (Employment and Occupation); ILO Convention 100 on Equal Remuneration; ILO Convention 182 on Worst Forms of Child Labour; Vienna Convention for the protection of the Ozone Layer and its Montreal Protocol on substances that deplete the Ozone Layer; Basel Convention on the Control of Transboundary Movements of Hazardous Wastes and their Disposal (Basel Convention); Stockholm Convention on Persistent Organic Pollutants (Stockholm

> Member States shall take appropriate measures to ensure that in the performance of public contracts economic operators comply with applicable obligations in the fields of environmental, social and labour law established by Union law, national law, collective agreements or by the international environmental, social and labour law provisions listed in Annex X.

This allows 'for environmental requirements, the use of criteria underlying environ-   **69** mental labels, and the option to take into account environmental factors in the production process and life-cycle analysis'.[220] Although the authorities thus have a very broad discretion in determining the subject matter of the contract, they are still bound by the limit of narrowing down competition. It is in this tension that the design of public contracts moves (and thus creates an astonishing synchronisation with the requirements of WTO law (→ Goal 12 mn. 78 ff.).

The European Court of Justice (ECJ) has interpreted public procurement cases in   **70** the EU on many occasions, thereby interpreting relevant primary (TEU, TFEU) and secondary law (regulations, directives) and thus impacts on how public procurement is to be understood and conducted. The following examples reflect the basic orientation and assessment of the ECJ in the field of green public procurement.

The judicial basis for the ECJ's decisions on green public procurement and the estab-   **71** lishment of sustainable consumption and production patterns are cases in which the court examined the eligibility of ecological criteria in tenders. The ECJ has developed test criteria according to which such a link to ecological factors is permissible in principle, whereby these may also be assessed with a high weighting. This is possible insofar as these criteria must be directly linked to the subject matter of the tender. In addition, these must in particular be accompanied by requirements which enable the contracting authority to verify the information submitted regarding compliance with the environmental criteria and

> [...] do not confer an unrestricted freedom of choice on the authority, are expressly mentioned in the contract documents or the tender notice, and comply with all the fundamental principles of Community law, in particular the principle of non-discrimination.[221]

In a tender of the European Environment Agency (EEA), the ECJ clarified the   **72** existing wide margin of discretion of public authorities in the design of their award procedures, also with regard to the determination of the environmental compatibility of a tenderer. The EEA awarded a contract for the provision of IT consultancy services. An unsuccessful bidder challenged the tender, inter alia, because of the use of an award criterion based on environmental policy (10 per cent points for General Environmental Policy of the company). The contract was awarded to a company that had an environmental management system certified by a third party. The ECJ made reference to its

> settled case-law that the contracting authority has a broad discretion in assessing the factors to be taken into account for the purpose of deciding to award a contract following an invitation to tender and that the Court's review must be limited to verifying that there has been no serious and manifest error.[222]

POPs Convention); Convention on the Prior Informed Consent Procedure for Certain Hazardous Chemicals and Pesticides in International Trade (UNEP/FAO) (The PIC Convention) Rotterdam, 10 September 1998, and its 3 regional Protocols.

[220] Pouikli and Kleoniki, 'Towards mandatory Green Public Procurement (GPP) requirements under the EU Green Deal: reconsidering the role of public procurement as an environmental policy tool' (2021) 21 *ERA Forum*, 699 (703).

[221] ECJ, Case C-448/01, 04.12.2003, *EVN AG, Wienstrom GmbH v Republic of Austria*, ECLI:EU:C: 2003:651; see also ECJ, Case C-513/99, 17.09.2002, ECLI:EU:C:2002:495, para. 33; further information https://ec.europa.eu/environment/gpp/case_law_en.htm.

[222] ECJ, Case T-331/06, 08.07.2010, *Evropaïki Dynamiki v European Environment Agency*, para. 61.

73   This case shows how much leeway contracting authorities have in assessing what constitutes 'equivalent' evidence. While third party certification cannot generally be required, it can be considered strong evidence of a company's environmental standards.[223] The appeal was dismissed as well with reference to the faultless exercise of its competence (since it was widely discretionary).[224]

74   In the *Dutch Coffee case*[225], the ECJ decided on the handling of a Dutch seller of fully automatic coffee machines and ingredients, which was criticised by the Commission. The Commission accused the Dutch actors of discrimination in the tender due to the wording of the award criteria, which referred to social and environmental requirements (linkage with organic and fair trade labels). In the Commission's view, this was in particular in breach of obligations under the then Public Procurement Directive (2004/18/EC) in force and also ran counter to the Commission's proposal to further develop the law. The court stated that a direct link to labels was not permissible in principle, but that it must be possible for the tenderer 'to refer to aspects of the production process in contract award criteria, even where these do not form part of the material substance of the goods being purchased'.[226] The court stated that

> [i]t must therefore be accepted that contracting authorities are also authorised to choose the award criteria based on considerations of a social nature, which may concern the persons using or receiving the works, supplies or services which are the object of the contract, but also other persons.[227]

75   However, the 'subject-matter of each contract and the criteria governing its award [must] be clearly defined from the beginning of the award procedure' to being compliant with 'both the principle of equal treatment and the obligation of transparency which flows from it'.[228] The lack of transparency and preciseness ultimately led to the court declaring the Netherlands' tender to be defective.

76   Without question, the inclusion of sustainable considerations in the EU public procurement is permitted and explicitly stipulated by numerous, amended and extended (public procurement) directives and by the case law of the ECJ, consequently resulting in a statutory right of the contracting authority to include sustainability in the public procurement process.[229] However, social considerations and environmental protection are subject to diverging legal resilience within the EU, which is due to the manner in which the general requirements for sustainability are integrated into the EU's primary law. Inter alia, the hinging clause in Art. 11 TFEU requires that '[e]nvironmental protection requirements must be integrated into the definition and implementation of the Union's policies and activities, in particular with a view to promoting sustainable development'. In contrast, the integration of social requirements with reference to sustainability cannot be found in EU primary law and is regarded quite critically.[230] Since the European legis-

---

[223] ECJ, Case T-331/06, 08.07.2010, *Evropaïki Dynamiki v European Environment Agency.*

[224] ECJ, Case C-462/10P, *Evropaïki Dynamiki – Proigmena Systimata Tilepikoinonion Pliroforikis kai Tilematikis AE v EEA*, ECLI:EU:C:2012:14.

[225] ECJ, Case C-368/10, 10.05.2012, *European Commission v Kingdom of the Netherlands*, ECLI:EU:C: 2012:284.

[226] https://ec.europa.eu/environment/gpp/case_law_en.htm.

[227] ECJ, Case C-368/10, 10.05.2012, *European Commission v Kingdom of the Netherlands*, ECLI:EU:C: 2012:284, para. 85.

[228] CJEU, Case C-368/10, 10.05.2012, *European Commission v Kingdom of the Netherlands*, ECLI:EU:C: 2012:284, para. 56.

[229] Critiques state that social consideration contradict economic objectives and allow for the widening of preferential treatment; Andrecka and Peterková Mitkidis, 'Sustainability requirements in EU public and private procurement – a right or an obligation?' (2017) 2017(1) *NJCL*, 57 (77).

[230] Andrecka and Peterková Mitkidis, 'Sustainability requirements in EU public and private procurement – a right or an obligation?' (2017) 2017(1) *NJCL*, 57 (80).

lative acts are subject to regular revision (fitness check and evaluation[231]) and in particular '[l]ife cycle thinking (LCT), life cycle assessment (LCA) and the environmental footprint (the European Product and Organisation Environmental Footprint PEF/OEF)' are increasingly in the focus of evaluation, a different picture could emerge here in the future. In any case, the clear and multiple inclusion of sustainability standards (also with reference to the Global Agenda 2030) in newly enacted legislative initiatives resulting from the EU Green Deal with the purpose of creating a circular economy and enabling sustainable consumption and production patterns speak in favour here. However, it is noticeable that these changes mainly refer to future, but not to currently existing legislation.[232]

Although strategies had already taken up the idea of sustainable use of natural resources[233] beforehand, these are not reflected in European jurisprudence in a traceable way (→ Goal 16 mn. 52 ff.).　　　　**77**

3. Arbitration Proceedings

The WTO is publicly and comprehensibly committed to the implementation of sustainability and the acknowledges the SDGs as well.[234] In addition to the designation of the purpose of sustainability, characterised by the optimal use of the world's resources and demanding the integration of trade in a 'pro-growth and pro-development [manner], and by continuing to foster stable, predictable and equitable trading',[235] WTO law allows for several exceptions and deviations from its established principles, which are generally suitable for promoting sustainable consumption and production patterns and in some cases explicitly focus on sustainable development.[236] Further exceptions that may be relevant for the implementation of SDG 12 are also permitted by the following WTO norms and instruments: Art. XX GATT with its chapeau, Agreement on Technical Barriers to Trade, Agreement on sanitary and phytosanitary measures, WTO Agreement on Subsidies and Countervailing Measures which aims to prevent application of perverse or trade-distorting subsidies), the WTO Agreement on Trade-Related Aspects of Intellectual Property Rights (TRIPS) which provides a framework governing the intellectual property system which positively incentivises innovation and promotes dissemination of green technologies, and the WTO Agreement on Government Procurement which provides for collaboration across the global procurement market and establishment of technical provisions which support green procurement, the Basel Convention and the Kiev Protocol on Pollutant Release and Transfer Registers, insofar as these do not have a trade-distorting effect. The absolute requirement here is any form of discrimination on the one hand and the limit of trade distortion beyond　　　**78**

---

[231] SWD (2017) 50, *Commission Staff Working Document, Better Regulation Guidelines (Chapter VI 'Guidelines on evaluation (including fitness checks))*, 7 July 2017, 50-66.

[232] Sala et al., 'The evolution of life cycle assessment in European policies over three decades' (2021) *Int J Life Cycle Assess*, 6, 11 ff.

[233] COM(2005) 670 final, *Thematic Strategy on the Sustainable Use of Natural Resources*, 21 December 2005 or the Thematic Strategy on Waste Prevention and Recycling; COM(2008) 397 final, *On the Sustainable Consumption and Production and Sustainable Industrial Policy Action Plan*, 16 July 2008.

[234] WTO, *Mainstreaming trade to attain the Sustainable Development Goals* (2018); https://www.wto.org/english/thewto_e/coher_e/sdgs_e/sdgs_e.htm.

[235] https://www.wto.org/english/thewto_e/coher_e/sdgs_e/sdgs_e.htm.

[236] E.g. Special and differential treatment provisions; General System of Preferences (the legal basis of which is the enabling clause); Global System of Trade Preferences (GSTP); further information: WT/COMTD/W/258, Committee on Trade and Development (CTD), *Special And Differential Treatment Provisions In WTO Agreements and Decisions, Note by the Secretariat*, 2 March 2021.

the de minimis limit on the other, which would in each case prevent application of the measure in the dispute.

79 Frequently criticised[237] contradictions between addressing unsustainable consumption patterns and trade can be seen in examples of WTO dispute settlement procedures. In *China-Rare Earths*[238], for example, the national regulation of the pollution policy and the nationally applied measures (export control and production control of minerals[239]), which the defendant had applied as 'relating to the conservation of exhaustible natural resources' under Art. XX(g) GATT, were assessed permissible if they do not apply equally to national and international measures. The Appellate Body (AB) upheld the Panel's previous ruling and pointed out that the measures need not be discriminatory in 'design and structure' and cannot be measured merely in terms of their effect on the market (which were not precluded from considering market effects).[240]

80 Similar arguments can also be found in other assessments of WTO dispute settlement, which in any case prevented the establishment of SCPs.[241] In the tension between the interests of trade and those of sustainability, trade aspects seem to prevail in the existing legal situation. The interpretation of international trade and investment (protection) law does not yet seem to have been given a higher or more sustainable priority.

81 However, additionally, to date there has been no decisive, publicly comprehensible case that has assessed the interpretation of WTO law in favour of sustainability measures and not merely as trade-distorting.[242] Nevertheless, the concerns of SDG 12 will increasingly be reflected in WTO dispute settlement. Various Requests for Consultations have already been conducted and are due to go to settlement in the near future. In *Certain Measures Palm Oil*[243], Malaysia, as one of the largest palm oil producers, demanded consultations after the 'EU adopted legislative measures that, in simple terms, define palm oil as an unsustainable feedstock for the production of biofuel'. The EU argued that palm oil production entails a high risk of indirect land-use change (ILUC). On that basis, the EU did not count oil palm crop-based biofuels to be eligible towards EU renewable energy targets, so that market access for palm oil-based products and fuels has been limited by the EU measures. Malaysia invokes various standards of the TBT Agreement, the SCM Agreement and the GATT to be breached by such measures. Malaysia explicitly argues that it is not the EU's use of sustainability criteria in the context of sustainable energy supply, but the criteria 'sustainability and GHG emission savings criteria in order to be taken into account for the purpose of contributing towards the EU's renewable energy targets and being eligible under the relevant support schemes'

[237] Voigt, 'Sustainable Patterns of Production and Consumption and Demographic Policies' in Viñuales (ed), *The Rio Declaration on Environment and Development, A Commentary* (2015), 264; Hellweg et al., *Global Resources Outlook 2019* (2020), 64-96.

[238] WT/DS431/AB/R, WT/DS432/AB/R, WT/DS433/AB/R, *China — Measures Related to the Exportation of Rare Earths, Tungsten and Molybdenum*, Reports of the Appellate Body, 7 August 2014.

[239] Which included export duties, export quotas, and certain limitations on the enterprises permitted to export the products.

[240] *China — Measures Related to the Exportation of Rare Earths, Tungsten and Molybdenum*, AB Report, paras. 2.115 f.; see also WT/DS394/AB/R, WT/DS395/AB/R, WT/DS398/AB/R, *China - Raw Materials*, Appellate Body Reports, para. 356.

[241] See WT/DS58/23, *United States — Import Prohibition of Certain Shrimp and Shrimp Products (Turtle-Shrimp)*; WT/DS332/19/Add.6, *Brazil — Measures Affecting Imports of Retreaded Tyres (Brazil-Tyres)*.

[242] E.g. the preamble of the Marrakesh Agreement.

[243] WT/DS600/1, G/L/1384, G/TBT/D/54, G/SCM/D131/1, *European Union and Certain Member States - Certain Measures Concerning Palm Oil and Oil Palm Crop-Based Biofuels Request for Consultations by Malaysia*, 19 January 2021 (Panel has been established on 30 July 2021, but no Panel Report or other solution has been adopted or found till late 2021).

(according to which Malaysia's products are classified as ineligible). However, Malaysia's own standard (MSPO) is not recognised by the EU.[244]

This kind of scenario is also reflected in other developing disputes or already decided dispute settlements[245] and highlights a condition that needs to be taken into account in the development of SCP and thus in the implementation of SDG 12. Sustainable actions evolve to varying degrees and degrees and at different times. The systems that emerge in this way are by no means coordinated with each other and generate a wide variety of issues and conflicts in the different legal regimes.   **82**

It can be assumed that in the future these questions will be clearly and recurrently reflected not only politically, but also legislatively (yielding for example from state's green deals) to an increasing extent, so that judicial or, in the context of dispute resolution, arbitral evaluation will (have to) be carried out as well. The development of the law remains in flux and currently reveals a legal (knowledge) situation that mostly understands sustainable measures and regulation in the sense of the SDGs as a distortion of trade (or infringement of investments).   **83**

The integration of SCP into existing trade and investment treaties is particularly difficult. As a rule, a change in the legal situation within a host state, which is accompanied by a complaint by the investor or trader, is accompanied by a claim of violation of legitimate expectations and expropriations. The regulatory chill thus created in the host state can at best be prevented by new agreements or by changing the legal situation in the home state (state of origin) but only to the extent that this has an extraterritorial effect.[246]   **84**

Whether the legal starting position, which is currently inadequate for SDG 12, requires a change in the applicable instruments or whether only a reinterpretation of the existing legal norms must take place here is left to intensive discussion elsewhere. In any case, there are advocates of both positions. In the meantime, it is obvious that new ideas and approaches are needed in order to gain legal ground for the argumentation of SDG 12.   **85**

4. Domestic Jurisdiction

In 2019, the German Federal Constitutional Court (FCC) was addressed with a constitutional complaint[247] as to whether the removal of food waste from a locked (waste) container from the private premises of a supermarket was to be considered theft and whether the principle of proportionality and the *ultima ratio* principle were violated with the criminal law assessment of this offence. The FCC found that the food wastes in waste containers are ownerless ('herrenlos' in a legal sense) and thus foreign objects in the sense of German criminal law, Art. 242 StGB (German Penal Code). On the con-   **86**

---

[244] WT/DS600/6, *European Union and Certain Member States – Certain Measures Concerning Palm Oil and Oil Palm Crop-Based Biofuels, Request for the Establishment of a Panel by Malaysia*, 16 April 2021, paras. 20-2.

[245] WT/DS593/9, *European Union — Certain measures concerning palm oil and oil palm crop-based biofuels*, Request for consultations by Indonesia, 24 March 2020; WT/DS592/1, G/L/1345, G/SCM/D127/1, *Indonesia – Measures Relating To Raw Materials, Request for Consultations by the European Union*, 27 November 2019 (quantitatively restricted market access through the creation of sustainable downstream activity chain); WT/DS511/R/Add.1, *China – Domestic Support For Agricultural Producers Report Of The Panel, Addendum*, ANNEX B-2, Integrated Executive Summary Of The Arguments Of China, 28 February 2019, para. 4 (Exceeding the permissible *De minimis* rule of the Agreement on Agriculture (AoA) through sustainable design of Chinese agricultural policy); WT/DS510/R, *United States — Certain Measures Relating To The Renewable Energy Sector*, Report Of The Panel, 27 June 2019 (Breach of the principle of national treatment by U.S. incentive schemes for renewable energies).

[246] Gehring and Philipps and Shipley, 'SDG 12 on Ensuring Sustainable Consumption and Production Patterns: Contributions of International Law, Policy and Governance' (2016) *UNEP / CISDL Briefs*, 7.

[247] German Federal Constitutional Court, 05.08.2020 – 2 BvR 1985/19, paras. 1-50.

trary, the planned disposal of the contents of the locked containers does not indicate abandonment by the (supermarket) owner. The FCC was in any case unable to derive a violation of 'elementary values of community life' as alleged by the claimants and thus the disproportionate nature of the act of the leap appeal plaintiffs (warning), which had been assessed in the lower court as being punishable under criminal law. Even against the background of the 4.4 million tonnes of food disposed of as waste every year, while there is a food emergency in many places worldwide, the court was unable to do so. The court referred to its function as a supervisor of legal, in this case criminal, regulations with the German constitution, but not as an interpreter of the 'most expedient, reasonable, just' or even desirable solution. This was the task of the legislature, but not of finding the law. Constitutionally, the relevant penal provision was not objectionable; rather, it was precisely the considerations of the claimants that had to yield to the fundamental right to property pursuant to Art. 14 of the German Basic Law. In this context, it was also irrelevant that the legislature could develop the content and limits of property around alternative regulations regarding the handling of disposed food. The decision clearly demonstrates the difficulties involved in transferring the SDG agenda into the legal sphere, especially with regard to SDG 12.3.[248] A large part of the content and the intended objective is still left to political willingness. However, today's necessities are often not reflected in legislation yet. Particularly in the scope of SDG 12, it seems that the legislator is all too often outdated and no longer meets the requirements.

II. The Enforcement of a 'Right to Responsible Consumption and Production'

87   Not just emerging regimes on business and human rights and responsible corporate conduct are notoriously weaker than regimes protecting the liberalisation of international trade and investment. Also, the possibilities for actors pursuing non-economic interests to initiate arbitration, or just to formally complain about non-trade concerns in a trade agreement are much more limited if compared to those available to corporations.[249]

88   On different opportunities, the ILA has stressed rightly the need for public participation accompanying the systems covered by SDG 12.8. Here, the Aarhus Convention[250] and the Escazú Regional Agreement on Access to Information, Participation and Justice in Environmental Matters in Latin America and the Caribbean, adopted on 4 March 2018, entered into force on 22 April 2021 serve as examples for plurilateral, yet regional instrument for increasing participation and facilitating access to information and justice as well. The latter instrument having been initiated during the UNCSD (Rio+20) in 2012 enacts binding provisions for States to equip their citizens with information, judicial corrections and spaces for public participation in environmental matters concerning them.[251]

---

[248] German Federal Constitutional Court, Erfolglose Verfassungsbeschwerde bei einer strafgerichtlichen Verurteilung wegen "Containern" [Unsuccessful constitutional complaint in the case of a criminal conviction for "containerisation"], Press release no. 75/2020 of 18 August 2020.

[249] Ioannou and Serafeim, 'The consequence of mandatory corporate sustainability reporting' (2011) *Harvard Business School Research Working Paper*, 11-100.

[250] Convention on Access to Information, Public Participation in Decision-making and Access to Justice in Environmental Matters, 38 ILM 1 (1999), 517.

[251] Regional Agreement On Access To Information, Public Participation and Justice in Environmental Matters in Latin America and the Caribbean (2018); further reading: Maihold and Reisch, 'Environmental Rights and Conflicts over Raw Materials in Latin America, The Escazú Agreement Is Ready to Come into

> As recognised in the 2012 African Union's Resolution on Human Rights-Based Approach to Natural Resource Governance, transparency, accountability and public participation in the extractive sector is key. The three elements of transparency, accountability and public participation are intricately intertwined and must be present for resource governance programs and policies to be effective at regional, national and local levels, natural resource-driven conflicts [...].[252]

As it prominently stood out in the ILA Guidelines, '[p]ublic Participation and Access **89** to Information and Justice' are cornerstones of the further development in the international but more than that in the whole matrix of the legal framework. The ongoing efforts and the speed gaining pace of digitisation, the development of Artificial Intelligence (AI) and R&D technologies should pave the way to legal questions, accompanied by more options to access and participation, which, however, is still needed.

Additionally, enforcement of responsibilities, as illustrated by the South China Sea **90** Arbitration, which China overtly refused to recognise, is an additional barrier.[253] However, this is also associated with particular difficulties due to the fact that sustainable consumption patterns are still rarely reflected in jurisprudence, either because the existing legal landscape does not integrate such thought and thus does not allow such a reflection yet, or because the instruments that could be used are voluntary in nature limiting possibilities of (executive) enforcement.

III. De Facto Influences on Jurisdiction

With the ILA Sofia Guiding Statements on Sustainable Development Principles,[254] **91** guidance has been set up 'to assist courts of law in applying principles and homogeneous interpretation criteria using a methodically well-founded approach' which may contribute and facilitate in the respective relevant bodies to giving the SDGs 'concrete expression in judicial practice'.[255]

Soft law takes on a particularly significant role for the area of SCP. Even if the **92** different requirements cannot autonomously generate legal bindingness in a positive sense, they frequently are *de facto* followed by relevant actors. The OECD Guidelines for Multinational Enterprises state: 'Companies can also influence suppliers through contractual arrangements such as management contracts, pre-qualification requirements for potential suppliers.' ISO 26000 then works more clearly with contracts as a tool to influence supplier behaviour.

Another effect is the largely voluntary commitment to so-called ESG reporting.[256] **93** ESG reporting 'refers to the disclosure of data related to the environmental, social and corporate governance of the company that monitors the values within an investment strategy or portfolio'. Despite many critics, various ESG tools and reporting require-

---

Force in 2021' (2021) C04 *SWP Comment*; further information: https://www.cepal.org/en/subsidiary-bodi es/acuerdo-regional-acceso-la-informacion-la-participacion-publica-acceso-la-justicia/history-regional-a greement; https://www.unep.org/news-and-stories/story/latin-american-and-caribbean-countries-sign-hi storic-treaty-giving.

[252] ILA, *The Role of International Law in Sustainable Natural Resources Management for Development*, Resolution No. 4 (2020), para. 3.3.4.

[253] Gehring and Philipps and Shipley, 'SDG 12 on Ensuring Sustainable Consumption and Production Patterns: Contributions of International Law, Policy and Governance' UNEP / CISDL Briefs, 9.

[254] 2012 ILA Sofia Guiding Statements, ILA Resolution No. 7/2012.

[255] Huck, 'SDGs and its impact on African, Caribbean and Pacific (ACP) Group of States and CARICOM – soft law on its way through the legal order' in Elias-Roberts and Hardy and Huck, *EU and CARICOM: Dilemmas versus Opportunities on Development, Law and Economics* (2020), 165.

[256] Pollman, 'Corporate Social Responsibility, ESG, and Compliance' in Van Rooij and Sokol (eds), *The Cambridge Handbook of Compliance* (2021), 662-72.

ments are on the rise across a wide range of industries. This development, amongst others, has led to further efforts and even legal adjustments. In the EU, for example, the Taxonomy Regulation was introduced with a focus on environmental aspects in order to direct investments and financial resources to where they are most needed from a sustainable point of view.

94   There is a positive relationship between CSR and employee organisational behaviour (OCB), readable, for example, in a study conducted in Nigeria, which is conducive to the implementation of SDG 12.6.[257]

95   The Global Agenda 2030 acknowledges these efforts of the private (economic) sector 'ranging from micro-enterprises to cooperatives to Multinationals' and calls for 'protecting labour rights and environmental and health standards in accordance with relevant international standards and agreements and other ongoing initiatives in this regard, such as the Guiding Principles on Business and Human Rights […]' (UNGP).[258] In particular, in conjunction with SDG 12.2 (sustainable management and efficient use of natural resources), SDG 12.4 (environmentally sound management of chemicals and all wastes […] to minimise their adverse effects on human health […]), SDG 12.6 (adoption of sustainable practices) and SDG 12.8. (access to relevant information and awareness raising), the UNGPs guide a transformation towards sustainable consumption and production patterns.

96   The UNGPs, in existence since 2011and to be adopted voluntarily,[259] exert influence on corporate behaviour. Historically grown in periods and at first critically scrutinised or neglected,[260] since the 1990 s human rights obligations and CSR have been mainstreamed into corporate and business activities on a voluntary basis (voluntarism). Various voluntary codes of conduct have since emerged, based on individual company or industry initiatives such as the UN Global Compact. The UNGPs can be characterised by an 'institutionalised voluntarism'[261] achieved through the business and human rights framework comprised by the UNGPs. A slight tendency appears to be shifting away from voluntarism, now transitioning to a period of legal obligations through binding due diligence laws.[262]

97   In the EU, in various economic sectors, certain large companies are legally obliged to integrate and disclose sustainability information in their reporting cycle. While SDG

---

[257] Onyishi et al., 'Going the Extra Mile Because My Organization Does: How Does Corporate Social Responsibility Influence Organizational Citizenship in Nigeria?' (2020) 16.1 *Management and Organization Review*, 169 (169).

[258] A/RES/70/1, *Transforming our world: the 2030 Agenda for Sustainable Development*, 21 October 2015, para. 67; A/HRC/17/31, *Report of the Special Representative of the Secretary-General on the issue of human rights and transnational corporations and other business enterprises, John Ruggie Guiding Principles on Business and Human Rights: Implementing the United Nations "Protect, Respect and Remedy" Framework*, 21 March 2011, Annex.

[259] OHCHR, *Guiding Principles on Business and Human Rights, Implementing the United Nations 'Protect, Respect and Remedy' Framework* (2011).

[260] See Ruggie, 'Business and Human Rights: The Evolving International Agenda' (2007) 101(4) *American Journal of International Law*, 819-40: Corporate social responsibility (CSR) in general.

[261] This period also gave rise, for example, to the US Alien Tort Claims Act (ATCA), [or] the emergent 'foreign direct liability' claims then brought predominantly in common law jurisdictions', see Muchlinski, 'The Impact of the UN Guiding Principles on Business Attitudes to Observing Human Rights' (2021) *Business and Human Rights Journal*, 1 (8); see also Muchlinski, *Multinational Enterprises and the Law* (2021).

[262] Developments in this direction exist, for example, with the UK Modern Slavery Act from 2015, the French Loi de vigilance enacted in 2017 or the German Supply Chain Act adopted in 2021, even if – in contrast to the original legislative initiative – the latter only contains few substantive obligations; see also Muchlinski, 'The Impact of the UN Guiding Principles on Business Attitudes to Observing Human Rights' (2021) *Business and Human Rights Journal*, 11 f.

12.6 calls for companies and Transnational Corporations (TNCs) to be encouraged, the practice ostensibly is significantly more ambitious.[263] However, difficulties in implementation exist, such as inadequate or erroneous reporting, or in some cases additional burden due to double reporting.[264] With the Companies Act of 2013, India is one of the few countries in the world to make CSR a legal obligation for Indian companies, regardless of whether they are privately owned or controlled by the government as state-owned enterprises (SOE).[265]

Technological progress towards more efficient, cleaner energy will lead to higher per-   **98** formance with lower emissions (Solar inks and quantum thermodynamics are two of many areas currently being researched). With each disruptive technological breakthrough, standards and / or norms will inevitably be reframed and will necessitate either redefining or reinterpreting them (→ Goal 7 mn. 62 ff.)[266]

E. Conclusion on SDG 12

Sustainable consumption and production as a framework provides sustainable pat-   **99** terns for the use of resources, sustainable infrastructure in management and learning and the applicability of chemicals and waste, and providing access to essential services, green and decent jobs, and the tourism sector.

SDG 12 points to a development within the 10 YFP. The use of natural resources in   **100** the legal field covers a vast area from mining in the outer space, in the deeper seabed, and at the same time forests, water and other resources. Regarding the individual segments of each law in the rules matrix, an overall view is needed, covering many aspects in principle rather than in detail. To be able to grasp these aspects, the 2020 ILA Kyoto Guidelines for Natural Resources Management for Development[267] are most helpful.

---

[263] See EPRS and Zamfir, *Towards a mandatory EU system of due diligence for supply chains* (2020).

[264] A study commissioned by the Federal Environment Agency (UBA) shows that German companies are increasingly reporting on the topics of climate, water, resources and waste, but that there are still considerable gaps, which can be traced back to inadequate legal regulations, among other things. The UBA calls for more detailed reporting at the EU level; see German Environment Agency, *Strengthening environmental and climate protection in corporate reporting obligations Analysis of mandatory corporate sustainability reports shows deficits*, Press Release No 21/2021; see also Lautermann and Young and Hoffmann, *Climate and environmental reporting by German companies, Evaluation of the CSR reporting obligation for the years 2018 and 2019* (2021).

[265] Jumde and Du Plessis, 'Legislated Corporate Social Responsibility (CSR) in India: The Law and Practicalities of its Compliance' (2020) *Statute Law Review*, 1-28; Okoye, 'CSR and a Capabilities Approach to Development: CSR Laws as an Allocative Device?' in Osuji and Ngwu and Jamali (eds), *Corporate Social Responsibility in Developing and Emerging Markets: Institutions, Actors and Sustainable Development* (2019), 31-48.

[266] European Parliamentary Research Service, *Decoupling economic growth from environmental harm* (2020), 2.

[267] International Law Association (ILA), *Resolution No. 4/2020, The Role of International Law in Sustainable Natural Resources Management for Development*, 13 December 2020.

Goal 13
Take urgent action to combat climate change and its impacts[*]

13.1 Strengthen resilience and adaptive capacity to climate-related hazards and natural disasters in all countries

13.2 Integrate climate change measures into national policies, strategies and planning

13.3 Improve education, awareness-raising and human and institutional capacity on climate change mitigation, adaptation, impact reduction and early warning

13.a Implement the commitment undertaken by developed-country parties to the United Nations Framework Convention on Climate Change to a goal of mobilizing jointly $100 billion annually by 2020 from all sources to address the needs of developing countries in the context of meaningful mitigation actions and transparency on implementation and fully operationalize the Green Climate Fund through its capitalization as soon as possible

13.b Promote mechanisms for raising capacity for effective climate change-related planning and management in least developed countries and small island developing States, including focusing on women, youth and local and marginalized communities

Word Count related to 'Climate' and 'Climate Change'

A/RES/70/1 – Transforming our world: the 2030 Agenda for Sustainable Development: 'Climate': 26 and 'Climate Change': 20

Instruments mentioned in A/RES/70/1 in the section entitled: 'Sustainable Development Goals and targets':

A/RES/69/313 – Addis Ababa Action Agenda of the Third International Conference on Financing for Development adopted on 27 July 2015: 'Climate': 28 'Climate Change': 3

A/RES/66/288 – The future we want (Rio +20 Declaration) adopted on 27 July 2012: 'Climate': 26 'Climate Change': 7

A/RES/55/2 – United Nations Millennium Declaration adopted on 8 September 2000: 'Climate': 0

---

[*] Acknowledging that the United Nations Framework Convention on Climate Change is the primary international, intergovernmental forum for negotiating the global response to climate change.

Select Bibliography: Elkanah O. Babatunde, 'Distributive Justice in the Age of Climate Change' (2020) 33 *Canadian Journal of Law & Jurisprudence*, 263; Ayelet Banai, 'Sovereignty over natural resources and its implications for climate justice' (2016) 7 *WIREs Clim Change*, 238; Daniel Bodansky, Jutta Brunnée and Lavanya Rajamani, *International Climate Change Law* (Oxford University Press, Oxford 2017); Christoph Böhringer, 'Kyoto Protocol: A Review and Perspectives' (2003) 19 *Oxford Review of Economic Policy*, 451; Jutta Brunnée, 'The Precautionary Principle and International Law, The Challenge of Implementation' in David Freestone and Ellen Hey (eds), *International Environmental Law and Policy Series, Vol. 31* (Kluwer Law International, The Hague, London, Boston 1996); Heather Colby, Ana Stella Ebbersmeyer, Lisa Marie Heim and Marthe Kielland Røssaak, 'Judging Climate Change: The Role of the Judiciary in the Fight Against Climate Change' (2020) 7(3) *Oslo Law Review*, 168; Marie-Claire Cordonier Segger, 'Commitments to Sustainable Development' in Marie-Claire Cordonier Segger and Christopher G. Weeramantry (eds), *Sustainable Development Principles in the Decisions of International Courts and Tribunals, 1992 – 2012* (Routledge, UK/USA 2017), 71; Marie-Claire Cordonier Segger and Alexandra Harrington, 'Environment and Sustainable Development' in Simon Chesterman, David M. Malone and Santiago Villalpando, *The Oxford Handbook of United Nations Treaties* (Oxford University Press, Oxford 2019), 204; Monica Di Gregorio, Dodik Ridho Nurrochmat, Jouni Paavola, Intan MayaSari, Leandra Fatorelli, Emilia Pramova, Bruno Locatelli, Maria Brockhaus and Sonya Dyah Kusumadewia, 'Climate policy integration in the land use sector: Mitigation, adaptation and sustainable development linkages' (2017) 67 *Environmental Science & Policy*, 35; Anna Dias, Agnieszka Nosowicz and Stéphanie Seeuws, 'EU Border Carbon Adjustment and the WTO: Hand in Hand Towards Tackling Climate Change' (2020) 15 *Global Trade and Customs Journal*, 15; Liz Fisher, 'Challenges for the EU Climate Change Regime' (2020) 21 *German Law Journal*, 5; Francesco Francioni and Ottavio Quirico, 'Untying the Gordian Knot, Towards the human right to a climatically sustainable environment?' in Ottavio Quirico and Mouloud Boumghar (eds), *Climate Change and Human Rights – An internationa and comparative law perspective* (Routledge, UK/USA 2016), 147; Angel Hsu, John Brandt, Oscar Widerberg, Sander Chan and Amy Weinfurter, 'Exploring links between national climate strategies and non-state and subnational climate action in nationally determined contributions (NDCs)' (2020) 20 *Climate Policy*, 443; Intergovernmental Panel on Climate Change (IPCC), *Climate Change 2014: Mitigation of Climate Change* (IPCC, Geneva 2018), Intergovernmental Panel on Climate Change (IPCC), *Global Warming of 1.5°C – An IPCC Special Report on the impacts of global warming of 1.5°C above pre-industrial levels and related global greenhouse gas emission pathways, in the context of strengthening the global response to the threat of climate change, sustainable development, and efforts to eradicate poverty* (IPCC, Geneva 2018); Wolfgang Kahl and Marc-Philippe Weller, 'Liability for Climate Damages – Synthesis and future prospects' in Wolfgang Kahl and Marc-Philippe Weller (eds), *Climate Change Litigation – A Handbook* (C.H. Beck/Hart/Nomos, Munich/Oxford/Baden-Baden 2021), 535; Therese Karlsson Niska, 'Climate Change Litigation and the European Court of Human Rights – A Strategic Next Step?' (2020) 13 *Journal of World Energy Law and Business*, 331; Mia Landauer, Sirkku Juhola, and Johannes Klein, "The role of scale in integrating climate change adaptation and mitigation in cities", (2019) 62 *Journal of Environmental Planning and Management*, 741; Bas Louman, Rodney J. Keenan, Daniela Kleinschmit, Stibniati Atmadja, Almeida A. Sitoe, Isilda Nhantumbo, Ronnie de Camino Velozo and Jean Pierre Morales, 'SDG 13: Climate Action – Impacts on Forests and People' Pia Katila, Carol J. Pierce Colfer, Wil de Jong, Glenn Galloway, Pablo Pacheco and Georg Winkel (eds), *Sustainable Development Goals – Their Impacts on Forests and People* (Cambridge University Press, Cambridge 2019), 419; Lauren Nishimura, 'Climate Change Migrants: Impediments to a Protection Framework and the Need to Incorporate Migration into Climate Change Adaptation Strategies' (2015) 27 *International Journal of Refugee Law,* 107; André Nollkaemper and Laura Burgers, 'A New Classic in Climate Change Litigation: The Dutch Supreme Court Decision in the Urgenda Case' (2020) *EJIL:Talk!*; Deok-Young Park, *Legal Issues on Climate Change and International Trade Law* (Springer, Cham 2016); Tetyana Payosova, 'Climate Change Mitigation and Renewable Energy' in Thomas Cottier and Krista Nadakavukaren Schefer (eds), *Elgar Encyclopedia* of International Economic Law (Edward Elgar Publishing, Cheltenham/Northampton 2017), 625; Mehrdad Payandeh, 'The role of courts in climate protection and the separation of powers' in Wolfgang Kahl and Marc-Philippe Weller (eds), *Climate Change Litigation – A Handbook* (C.H. Beck/Hart/Nomos, Munich/Oxford/Baden-Baden 2021), 62; Brian J. Preston, 'The Influence of the Paris Agreement on Climate Litigation: Legal Obligations and Norms (Part I)' (2020) 33 *Journal of Environmental Law*, 1; Lavanya Rajamani, 'Ambition and differentiation in the 2015 Paris Agreement: Interpretative Possibilities and Underlying Politics', (2016) 65 *International and Comparative Law Quarterly* 493; Mikko Rajavuori, 'The Role of Non-State Actors in Climate Law' in Benoit Mayer and Alexander Zahar (eds), *Debating Climate Law* (Cambridge University Press, UK/USA/Australia/India/Singapore 2021); Jorgen Randers et al., 'Achieving the 17 Sustainable Development Goals within 9 Planetary Boundaries' (2019) 2 *Global Sustainability*, 24; Kendra Sakaguchi, Anil M. Varughese and Graeme Auld, 'Climate Wars? A Systematic Review of Empirical Analyses on the Links between Climate Change and Violent Conflict' (2017) 19 *International Studies Review*, 622.

A. Background and Origin of SDG 13

1   Climate change imposes a particular threat to different aspects of sustainable development. It leads to different kind of impacts from floods, desertification, drowns, food loss, water scarcity leading to migration and potentially wars to the curtailment of human rights.[1] Sustainable development can be set back decades in this way.[2] Since the 1970 s, the UN has been increasingly focusing on the threat posed by this phenomenon. Nevertheless, 50 years later, climate change still poses enormous dangers and has the power to change societies, living conditions, biodiversity, or in brief, to put the natural environment in the Anthropocene under severe and destructive pressure.

2   At the Stockholm Conference in 1972, it was stated that the well-being of humanity is highly dependent on its natural environment.[3] Moreover, the protection and improvement of the environment should also influence economic development and, therefore, be the responsibility of all people and governments.[4] Thus, as early as 1972, the demand was made to treat the environment with respect in order to be able to guarantee human well-being in the long term. It was further recommended '[a]s a general rule, no country should solve or disregard its environmental problems at the expense of other countries.'[5]

3   The 1985 Vienna Convention for the Protection of the Ozone Layer and the 1987 Montreal Protocol on Substances that Deplete the Ozone Layer concretised existing threats to the environment by emphasising the importance of the ozone layer for human health and the environment.[6] The arising dangers should be averted through international cooperation in the field of research and legislation.[7]

4   Also in 1987, the eminent Report of the World Commission on Environment and Development, the so-called 'Brundtland-Report' emphasising the outstanding role of Gro Harlem Brundtland, stated that the risks of climate change 'increase faster than do our abilities to manage them'[8] and that we 'may already be close to transgressing critical thresholds'.[9] In this way, the particular urgency of intervening against climate change became evident.

5   The Intergovernmental Panel on Climate Change (IPCC) was established by the United Nations Environment Programme (UNEP) and the World Meteorological Organization (WMO) in 1988. The establishment of the IPCC was endorsed by UN General Assembly in 1988. Its initial task, as outlined in UN General Assembly Resolution 43/53 of 6 December 1988, was to prepare a comprehensive review and recommendations concerning the state of knowledge of the science of climate change; the social and

---

[1] Nishimura, 'Climate Change Migrants: Impediments to a Protection Framework and the Need to Incorporate Migration into Climate Change Adaptation Strategies' (2015) 27 *International Journal of Refugee Law,* 107 (110); Sakaguchi, Varughese and Auld 'Climate Wars? A Systematic Review of Empirical Analyses on the Links between Climate Change and Violent Conflict' (2017) 19 *International Studies Review,* 622 (640); For more information on the specific significance of global warming of 1.5 degrees, see Bazaz et al., 'Summary for Policymakers' in IPCC, *Special Report Global Warming Of 1.5 °C* (2018).

[2] United Nations General Assembly Open Working Group on Sustainable Development Goals, *Compendium of TST Issues Briefs October 2014* (2014), 175.

[3] UN, *Report of the United Nations Conference on the human environment 1972,* 1st proclaim.

[4] UN, *Report of the United Nations Conference on the human environment 1972,* 2nd proclaim.

[5] UN, *Report of the United Nations Conference on the human environment 1972,* Recommendation 103.

[6] UNEP, *Vienna Convention for the Protection of the Ozone Layer* (1985), preamble; UN, *Montreal Protocol on Substances that Deplete the Ozone Layer* (1987), preamble.

[7] UNEP, *Vienna Convention for the Protection of the Ozone Layer* (1985), Art. 2(2).

[8] Report of the World Commission on Environment and Development: *Our Common Future* (1987), Part I Chapter 1 II, para. 32.

[9] Report of the World Commission on Environment and Development: *Our Common Future* (1987), Part I Chapter 1 II, para. 32.

economic impact of climate change, and potential response strategies and elements for inclusion in a possible future international convention on climate.

In 1992, the United Nations Framework Convention on Climate Change established   6
the following definition for climate change:

> Climate change means a change of climate which is attributed directly or indirectly to human activity that alters the composition of the global atmosphere and which is in addition to natural climate variability observed over comparable time periods.[10]

It has thus been shown that climate change to a great extent is a man-made phe-   7
nomenon. In the same year, Agenda 21 also highlighted the importance of climate change for the marine environment.[11] In this context, various uncertainties about climate change and and its distinct linkage to rising sea levels were acknowledged.[12]

Five years later, the 1997 Kyoto Protocol established the first binding target for   8
greenhouse gas (GHG) emissions.[13] The first period affected was between 2008 and 2012.[14] One of the key targets was to reduce GHG emissions by at least 5 per cent compared to 1990. While the signatory states were allowed to trade emissions among themselves,[15] binding country-specific targets were also included.

The 2002 Johannesburg Declaration on Sustainable Development subsequently stated   9
that multiple climate change impacts are progressing steadily and at an accelerating pace.[16] Additionally, there was a call for global partnerships[17] and institutions to ensure sustainable development: 'To achieve our goals of sustainable development, we need more effective, democratic and accountable international and multilateral institutions' (→ Goal 17 mn. 8).[18]

This approach was further intensified in 2012.[19] The outcome document 'The future   10
we want' also highlighted the global significance of climate change in relation to sustain-

---

[10] UN, *Framework Convention on Climate Change* (1992), Art. 1(2).

[11] United Nations Conference on Environment & Development, *Agenda 21*, 3-14 June 1992, para. 17.96.

[12] United Nations Conference on Environment & Development, *Agenda 21*, 3-14 June 1992, para. 17.97: 'There are many uncertainties about climate change and particularly about sealevel rise. Small increases in sealevel have the potential of causing significant damage to small islands and low-lying coasts'.

[13] Böhringer, 'Kyoto Protocol: A Review and Perspectives' (2003) 19 *Oxford Review of Economic Policy*, 451 (451).

[14] UN, *Kyoto Protocol To The United Nations Framework Convention On Climate Change* (1998), Art. 3(7).

[15] Sales and Sabbag, 'Environmental Requirements and Additionality under the Clean Development Mechanism: A Legal Review under the UNFCCC, the Kyoto Protocol, and the Brazilian Legal Framework on Climate Change' (2006) 16 *Yearbook of International Environmental Law*, 235 (242).

[16] UN, *Johannesburg Declaration on Sustainable Development* (2002), para. 13:
The global environment continues to suffer. Loss of biodiversity continues, fish stocks continue to be depleted, desertification claims more and more fertile land, the adverse effects of climate change are already evident, natural disasters are more frequent and more devastating, and developing countries more vulnerable, and air, water and marine pollution continue to rob millions of a decent life.

[17] Streck, 'The World Summit on Sustainable Development: Partnerships as New Tools in Environmental Governance' (2003) 13 *Yearbook of International Environmental Law*, 63 (65).

[18] UN, *Johannesburg Declaration on Sustainable Development* (2002), para. 31.

[19] A/RES/66/288*, *The future we want* (2012), para. 76(h).

able development.[20] In addition, a demand for better protection against climate-related natural disasters has already been made, as it can be found today in SDG 13.[21]

11   In 2015, the Paris Agreement set a legally binding target for global warming. According to this target, global warming should be at least below 1.5° C above pre-industrial levels.[22] In this way, a first obligation was created for the signatory states to communicate and comply with emission targets[23] thereby emphasising the particular importance of international cooperation.[24] At the same time, the Paris Agreement builds a crucial instrument for achieving SDG 13.[25]

12   All of these conclusions and instruments had been taken into account in the creation and interpretation of SDG 13. Initially, different approaches were sought in the implementation of SDG 13. Climate change most often was thematically combined with other development goals such as energy, water and food security[26] which led to proposals such as 'curb human-induced climate change and ensure sustainable energy' or 'Sustainable Management of the Biosphere, Enabling People and the Planet to Thrive Together'.[27] However, due to the enormous importance of climate change and the associated disasters, it was finally given its own goal.[28]

13   But even today, combating climate change still faces enormous challenges. The global SARS-CoV-2 pandemic has suddenly claimed all conceivable investments, setting back sustainable development by several years.[29] For developing countries in particular, it will become even more difficult in the future to finance sustainable development and thus implement measures to combat climate change.[30]

---

[20] A/RES/66/288*, *The future we want* (2012), para. 25:
We acknowledge that climate change is a cross-cutting and persistent crisis, and express our concern that the scale and gravity of the negative impacts of climate change affect all countries and undermine the ability of all countries, in particular, developing countries, to achieve sustainable development and the Millennium Development Goals, and threaten the viability and survival of nations. Therefore, we underscore that combating climate change requires urgent and ambitious action, in accordance with the principles and provisions of the United Nations Framework Convention on Climate Change.

[21] A/RES/66/288*, *The future we want* (2012), para. 111: '[…] enhancing resilience to climate change and natural disasters'.

[22] *Paris Agreement to the United Nations Framework Convention on Climate Change*, 12 December 2015, T.I.A.S. No. 16-1104, Art. 2(1) (a).

[23] Preston, 'The Influence of the Paris Agreement on Climate Litigation: Legal Obligations and Norms (Part I)' (2020) eqaa20 *Journal of Environmental Law*, 1 (1).

[24] Preston, 'The Influence of the Paris Agreement on Climate Litigation: Legal Obligations and Norms (Part I)' (2020) eqaa20 *Journal of Environmental Law*, 14 (1).

[25] Louman et al., 'SDG 13: Climate Action – Impacts on Forests and People' in Katila et al., *Sustainable Development Goals: Their Impacts on Forests and People* (2019), 419 (419).

[26] United Nations General Assembly Open Working Group on Sustainable Development Goals, *Compendium of TST Issues Briefs October 2014* (2014), 179.

[27] United Nations General Assembly Open Working Group on Sustainable Development Goals, *Compendium of TST Issues Briefs October 2014* (2014), 179.

[28] United Nations General Assembly Open Working Group on Sustainable Development Goals, *Compendium of TST Issues Briefs October 2014* (2014), 175.

[29] Global Center on Adaption, *State and Trends in Adaption Report 2020* (2020), 5.

[30] Global Center on Adaption, *State and Trends in Adaption Report 2020* (2020), 7:
Developing countries face an increasingly steep funding gap for climate adaptation because so much focus has rightly been given to emergency spending, compounded by a decline in tax revenues and global trade. Countries now face dual risks to their sovereign credit ratings: limited fiscal space and increasing awareness of climate impacts, both of which affect their borrowing capacity amid growing debt distress due to Covid-19.

B. Scope and Dimensions of SDG 13

SDG 13 aims to prioritise 'taking urgent action to combat climate change and its 14 impacts'.

Limiting global temperature rise to 1.5 °C as agreed upon under the Paris Agreement 15 is one of the most critical priorities to take coordinated global action in the twenty-first century. However, the UN Sustainable Development Goals Report 2020 has noted that 'the world is way off track to meet the Paris Agreement target, signalling cataclysmic changes ahead'.[31] The report has also shown that 2019 was the second warmest year on record and 2010-2019 was the warmest decade. The Inter-Governmental Panel on Climate Change (IPCC)[32] – the principal scientific body that studies and synthesizes the science of climate change science – noted in its special report in 2018 on the 'impacts of global warming of 1.5 °C above pre-industrial levels and related global greenhouse gas emission pathways' *inter alia* that, limiting global warming to 1.5 °C requires 'rapid and far-reaching transitions in energy, land, urban and infrastructure (including transport and buildings), and industrial systems'.[33] It advocates that sustainable development can support and enable such transitions. Furthermore, the report also provides evidence for climate mitigation action to merit a high level of concern and attention as there are striking differences in consequences with global warming increasing up to 2 °C instead of 1.5 °C.[34] The UNEP Emissions Gap Report 2019 has presented an even more grim reality by finding that 'even if all unconditional Nationally Determined Contributions (NDCs) under the Paris Agreement are implemented, we are still on course for a 3.2 °C temperature rise.'[35] In this context, it is not at all far-fetched to conclude that climate change is one of the most important SDGs and is intrinsically linked, by cause and effect, to every other SDG.

The UN has defined five targets and eight indicators within SDG 13. The targets 16 translate the overall goal, while the indicators provide a statistical reference point which have the task to monitor and measure the performance of a goal. Ideally, the different targets and indicators match perfectly. Sometimes indicators are missing or do not exactly match the targets.

I. Legal Framework and Definitions

1. Climate Change in International Environment Law

The legal framework to climate change law[36] was laid with the legal action to pro- 17 tect the ozone layer. The first convention that addressed this issue was the Vienna

---

[31] UN, *The Sustainable Development Goals Report 2020* (2020), 50.

[32] The Intergovernmental Panel on Climate Change (IPCC) is the UN body for assessing the science related to climate change. It was established by the United Nations Environment Programme (UNEP) and the World Meteorological Organization (WMO) in 1988 to provide political leaders with periodic scientific assessments concerning climate change, its implications and risks, as well as to put forward adaptation and mitigation strategies. It has 195 member states. In the same year, the UN General Assembly endorsed the action by the WMO and UNEP in jointly establishing the IPCC.

[33] Intergovernmental Panel on Climate Change (IPCC), *Special Report: Global Warming of 1.5⊕ C (Summary for Policymakers)* (2018), 15.

[34] Intergovernmental Panel on Climate Change (IPCC), *Special Report: Global Warming of 1.5⊕ C (Summary for Policymakers)* (2018), 15.

[35] United Nations Environment Programme, *Emissions Gap Report 2019* (2019), XIII.

[36] See also International Law Association (ILA), Resolution 2 (2014), Declaration of Legal Principles relating to Climate Change (2014).

Convention for the Protection of the Ozone Layer (Vienna Convention) which took effect in 1988.[37] Later, the Montreal Protocol on Substances that Deplete the Ozone Layer (Montreal Protocol) which is a multi-lateral environmental agreement entered into force in 1989, with the objective of phasing out the production and consumption of ozone-depleting substances.[38] After the enactment of the Montreal Protocol, in the landmark United Nations Conference on Environment and Development (UNCED) in 1992, the UN set out the United Nations Framework Convention on Climate Change (UNFCCC) to address issues pertaining to climate change.

18   The aims of SDG 13 and the legal design of the UNFCCC are set in the background of important principles of international environmental law such as the precautionary principle, cooperation and common but differentiated responsibilities and respective capabilities (CBDR-RC). Interwoven and affected from the discourse on climate change, the precautionary principle was integrated in Principle 15 of the Rio Declaration at the UNCED in 1992 as follows:

> In order to protect the environment, the precautionary approach shall be widely applied by States according to their capabilities. Where there are threats of serious or irreversible damage, lack of full scientific certainty shall not be used as a reason for postponing cost-effective measures to prevent environmental degradation.[39]

19   The preamble to UNFCCC acknowledges the importance of the duty of states to cooperate in the following words:

> the global nature of climate change calls for the widest possible cooperation by all countries and their participation in an effective and appropriate international response, in accordance with their common but differentiated responsibilities and respective capabilities and their social and economic conditions.[40]

20   The principle of CBDR-RC runs through the structure of the UNFCCC, which has near-universal membership today and remains the 'foundation of the UN climate regime'.[41] Under the umbrella of the UNFCCC, the Kyoto Protocol to the UNFCCC was adopted in 1997 (though it did not enter into force before 2005)[42] and the Paris Agreement was adopted in 2015.[43]

21   The scope and the gravity of SDG 13 is difficult to comprehend despite the enormous research regarding climate change and its impact that has taken place in the past few decades. The IPCC defines 'climate' as,

> the average weather, or more rigorously, as the statistical description in terms of the mean and variability of relevant quantities over a period of time ranging from months to thousands or millions of years. The classical period for averaging these variables is 30 years, as defined by the World Meteorological Organization. The relevant quantities are most often surface variables such as temperature, precipitation and wind. Climate in a wider sense is the state, including a statistical description, of the climate system.[44]

---

[37] UNEP, *Vienna Convention for the Protection of the Ozone Layer* (1985).

[38] UN T. S., 1522, 3, *Montreal Protocol on Substances that Deplete the Ozone Layer* (1987).

[39] A/CONF.151/26/Rev.1 (Vol. I), *Report of the United Nations Conference on Environment and Development*, 3-14 June 1992, Principle 15; see Freestone and Hey, *The Precautionary Principle and International Law: The Challenge of Implementation* (1996).

[40] *United Nations Framework Convention on Climate Change* (1992), preamble.

[41] Bodansky, Brunnée Rajamani, *International Climate Change Law* (2017), 43, 51-2, and 118.

[42] *Kyoto Protocol to the United National Framework Convention on Climate Change* (1997).

[43] *Paris Agreement to the United Nations Framework Convention on Climate Change*, 12 December 2015, T.I.A.S. No. 16-1104.

[44] Intergovernmental Panel on Climate Change, *Climate Change 2014: Synthesis Report* (2015), 119.

The UNFCCC defines climate change as 'a change of climate which is attributed **22**
directly or indirectly to human activity that alters the composition of the global atmosphere and which is in addition to natural climate variability observed over comparable
time periods.'[45] It is self-evident from this definition that even the quantification and
measurement of climate change is an enormous scientific task, and enacting policy instruments that address the causality directly and effectively is a significantly complicated
task for policy makers. The UNFCCC makes a distinction between 'climate change'
and 'adverse effects of climate change'. 'Climate change' has been accorded a definition
limited by the UNFCCC only to the measurement of the change in the composition
of the global atmosphere due to human activity. 'Adverse effects of climate change' is
defined separately under the UNFCCC as the 'changes in the physical environment or
biota resulting from climate change which have significant deleterious effects on the
composition, resilience or productivity of natural and managed ecosystems or on the
operation of socio-economic systems or on human health and welfare.' The UNFCCC
calls upon parties to 'take precautionary measures to anticipate, prevent or minimize the
causes of climate change and mitigate its adverse effects'.[46]

The IPCC defines 'climate change' as 'a change in the state of the *climate* that **23**
can be identified (e.g., by using statistical tests) by changes in the mean and / or the
variability of its properties and that persists for an extended period, typically decades
or longer. Climate change may be due to natural internal processes or *external forcings*
such as modulations of the solar cycles, volcanic eruptions and persistent anthropogenic
changes in the composition of the atmosphere or in *land use*.'[47] Unlike the UNFCCC
definition of 'climate change', the IPCC measures climate change irrespective of its cause.

The UNFCCC adopted a hybrid model in its design combining elements of both a **24**
bottom-up and a top-bottom approach. The bottom-up approach allows parties to develop and adopt suitable policy instruments to meet the objectives set out in the framework and a top-bottom approach takes the form of a review mechanism by way of an
obligation to communicate information set out under Art. 12 of the framework. The hybrid approach of the UNFCCC, is also adopted in the Paris Agreement. The bottom-up
approach in the Paris Agreement is embedded in the form of 'nationally determined
contributions'. Art. 4.2 of the Paris Agreement provides that 'each Party shall prepare,
communicate and maintain successive nationally determined contributions that it intends to achieve. Parties shall pursue domestic mitigation measures, with the aim of
achieving the objectives of such contributions'. Thus, it allows countries to set for itself
the scope and form of how and how much it will contribute to action against climate
change through mitigation efforts.[48]

In relation to SDG 13, a bottom-up approach is reflected in SDG 13.2 and SDG 13.3. **25**
SDG 13.2 aims to 'integrate climate change measures into national policies, strategies
and planning' with indicators set tomeasure the '[n]umber of countries with nationally
determined contributions, long-term strategies, national adaptation plans, strategies
as reported in adaptation communications and national communications',[49] and the
'total greenhouse gas emissions per year'.[50] In accordance wit the UNFCCC, parties
submit their GHG inventories to the Climate Change Secretariat as per the reporting

---

[45] *United Nations Framework Convention on Climate Change* (1992), Art. 1, para. 2.
[46] United Nations Framework Convention on Climate Change (1992), Art. 3.
[47] Intergovernmental Panel on Climate Change, *Climate Change 2014: Synthesis Report* (2015), 120.
[48] Bodansky et al., *International Climate Change Law* (2017), 214-5.
[49] A/RES/71/313, E/CN.3/2021/2, *Global Indicator Framework*, Indicator 13.2.1.
[50] A/RES/71/313, E/CN.3/2021/2, *Global Indicator Framework*, Indicator 13.2.2.

requirements laid down.[51] The reporting requirements of non-Annex I countries are less stringent that Annex I countries and this may create gaps in the data collected. Further, the inventory reports are required to be submitted very close to the timing of the SDG progress reports which may impede legitimate analysis of the progress of countries towards the objectives of the Paris Agreement.[52] SDG 13.3 aims to 'improve education, awareness-raising and human and institutional capacity on climate change mitigation, adaptation, impact reduction and early warning'. This target is measured by an assessment of the '[e]xtent to which (i) global citizenship education and (ii) education for sustainable development are mainstreamed in (*a*) national education policies; (*b*) curricula; (*c*) teacher education; and (*d*) student assessment'.[53] This target is in alignment with the UNESCO 'Recommendation concerning Education for International Understanding, Co-operation and Peace and Education relating to Human Rights and Fundamental Freedoms' in 1974 and required countries to report on the recommendation every four years.[54] This will form the data basis for the assessment of indicator 13.3.1 which aims to ensure that learners of all ages are empowered with education regarding the global challenges humanity is facing. Both SDG 13.2 and SDG 13.3 provide flexibility to countries to meet the objectives under the Paris Agreement.

2. Common but Differentiated Responsibilities and Respective Capabilities

26   The principle of CBDR, also referred to as CBDRRC principle, is of high importance in environmental law generally, and has become centre stage in the concerted international efforts to combat climate change.[55]

27   The first time that countries recognised that the 'principle of equity' and CBDR of countries should be the basis of any global response to climate change, developed countries must take the lead' was in the Second World Climate Conference in 1990.[56]

28   Thereafter, the principle found place in the Rio Declaration in 1992[57] and also in the UNFCCC[58] and its Kyoto Protocol[59].

29   The UNFCCC embodied the principle of CBDRRC in *inter alia* Art. 3.1 in the following words:

> The Parties should protect the climate system for the benefit of present and future generations of humankind, on the basis of equity and in accordance with their common but differentiated responsibilities and respective capabilities. Accordingly, the developed country Parties should take the lead in combating climate change and the adverse effects thereof.[60]

30   The Kyoto Protocol adopted the principle with a bifurcation approach that bound only developed countries to reduce their emissions, while the developing countries were required only to report their emissions.[61] The CBDRRC has become a fundamental

---

[51] United Nations Framework Convention on Climate Change (1992), Art. 4.

[52] United Nations Statistics Division, *SDG Indicators: Metadata Repository*, Indicator 13.2.2.

[53] A/RES/71/313, E/CN.3/2021/2, *Global Indicator Framework*, Indicator 13.3.1.

[54] UNESCO, *Recommendation concerning Education for International Understanding, Co-operation and Peace and Education relating to Human Rights and Fundamental Freedoms* (1974).

[55] See Viñuales, *Rio Declaration on Environment and Development: A Commentary* (2015), 28 f.

[56] A/45/696/Add.1, *Progress Achieved in the implementation of resolution 44/207 on protection of global climate for present and future generations of mankind*, 8 November 1990, 16.

[57] A/CONF.151/26/Rev.1 (Vol. I), *Report of the United Nations Conference on Environment and Development*, 3-14 June 1992, Principle 7.

[58] *United Nations Framework Convention on Climate Change* (1992), Art. 3(1) and Art. 4.

[59] UN, *Kyoto Protocol To The United Nations Framework Convention On Climate Change* (1998), Art. 10.

[60] *United Nations Framework Convention on Climate Change* (1992), Art. 3.1.

[61] The Convention includes a list of 43 developed countries in its Annex I. All other countries, mostly the developing countries, are known as non-Annex I Parties.

issue in climate change negotiations[62] and this is evident in the Paris Agreement which adopted an approach that focusses more on the commonalities between the developed and developing countries while also keeping the principle of CBDRRC albeit in light of differing 'national circumstances'.[63]

In context of SDG 13, the principle of CBDRRC is reflected in SDG 13.a and SDG　31
13.b to some extent. SDG 13.a aims to hold developed countries to their commitment under the UNFCCC to mobilise joint financial assistance of $100 billion annually till 2025 to developing countries to enable climate change mitigation efforts by them and operationalize the Green Climate Fund through its capitalisation as soon as possible.

SDG 13.b is aimed at promoting mechanisms for raising capacity for effective climate　32
change-related planning and management in least developed countries and small island developing States. Broadly, SDGs 13.a and 13.b find roots in Arts. 3(2), 3(5), 4(3), 4(4), 4(7), 4(8), 4(9), 6(11) and Art. 11 of the UNFCCC.

The debate regarding whether the obligations and capabilities of countries need to　33
be in tandem for the attainment of SDG 13 remains at the core of climate change mitigation efforts and the extent to which the principle of CBDR-RC will drive climate change negotiations after 2020 may have ramifications for meeting climate change goals. Curiously, when considered within the context of sustainable development which focuses on inter-generational equity, CBDR-RC may be distinguished based on its focus as it aims to achieve intra-generational equity and arguably, its relevance in the discourse on climate change may be questioned in the future.

II. Climate Change Mitigation and Adaptation

The 2018 report of the IPCC presents a grim picture of the future of the planet.[64] The　34
IPCC in its 2014 Synthesis Report refers to climate change adaptation and mitigation as
two complementary strategies for responding to climate change. Adaptation is the process of adjustment to actual or expected climate and its effects in order to either lessen or avoid harm or exploit beneficial opportunities. Mitigation is the process of reducing emissions[65] or enhancing sinks of greenhouse gases (GHGs), so as to limit future climate change.[66]

Many factors can enable adaptation and mitigation strategies such as innovation and investments in clean technology that can help reduce GHG emissions, improving coordination and cooperation in governance, institutional, educational and behavior change or changes in lifestyle and consumption patterns. The importance of integrating both objectives while devising climate policy is starkly visible in areas such as the land use sector as cities need to prepare for the risk and impact of climate change.[67]

---

[62] Winkler and Mantlana and Letete, 'Transparency of action and support in the Paris Agreement' (2017) 17 *Climate Policy* 853 (858).

[63] Rajamani, 'Ambition and differentiation in the 2015 Paris Agreement: Interpretative Possibilities and Underlying Politics' (2016) 65 *International and Comparative Law Quarterly* 493 (507 ff.).

[64] Intergovernmental Panel on Climate Change (IPCC), *Special Report: Global Warming of 1.5⊕ C (Summary for Policymakers)* (2018).

[65] See also *Minamata Convention on Mercury* (2013).

[66] IPCC, *Climate Change 2014: Synthesis Report. Contribution of Working Groups I, II and III to the Fifth Assessment Report of the Intergovernmental Panel on Climate Change* (2014), 151.

[67] See Di Gregorio et al., 'Climate policy integration in the land use sector: Mitigation, adaptation and sustainable development linkages' (2017) 67 *Environmental Science & Policy*, 35-43; Landauer and Juhola and Klein, 'The role of scale in integrating climate change adaptation and mitigation in cities' (2019) 62(5) *Journal of Environmental Planning and Management*, 741 (741 ff.).

1. Climate Change and Disaster Risk Reduction

35   Climate change is impacting and increasing the frequency and intensity of climate related disasters and hazards and impeding attainment of the SDGs.[68] Disaster risk reduction[69] and climate change adaptation might be construed to be two sides of the same coin.

36   Adapting for disaster risk implications of climate change as can be read from SDG 13.1 aims to 'strengthen resilience and adaptive capacity to climate-related hazards and natural disasters in all countries' integrates the measurement of progress by three objectively defined indicators which seek to assess the 'Number of deaths, missing persons and directly affected persons attributed to disasters per 100,000 population'[70]; 'Number of countries that adopt and implement national disaster risk reduction strategies in line with the Sendai Framework for Disaster Risk Reduction 2015–2030'[71]; and 'Proportion of local governments that adopt and implement local disaster risk reduction strategies in line with national disaster risk reduction strategies'[72].

37   Missing people under indicator 13.1.1 are defined as 'the number of people whose whereabouts is unknown since the hazardous event. It includes people who are presumed dead, for whom there is no physical evidence such as a body, and for which an official/legal report has been filed with competent authorities'.[73] Further, people who are 'directly affected' are defined as '[t]he number of people who have suffered injury, illness or other health effects; who were evacuated, displaced, relocated or have suffered direct damage to their livelihoods, economic, physical, social, cultural and environmental assets. Indirectly affected are people who have suffered consequences, other than or in addition to direct effects, over time, due to disruption or changes in economy, critical infrastructure, basic services, commerce or work, or social, health and psychological consequences'.[74]

38   In relation to data collection for indicator 13.1.1, the data provider at national level is appointed Sendai Framework Focal Points. In most countries disaster data are collected by line ministries and national disaster loss databases are established and managed by special purpose agencies including national disaster management agencies, civil protection agencies, and meteorological agencies. The Sendai Framework Focal Points in each country are responsible of data reporting through the Sendai Framework Monitoring System.[75]

39   A key focus of the Sendai Framework for Disaster Risk Reduction 2015–2030 (Sendai Framework) is building resilience to disasters.[76] It describes 'resilience' as '[t]he ability of a system, community or society exposed to hazards to resist, absorb, accommodate, adapt to, transform and recover from the effects of a hazard in a timely and efficient

---

[68] United Nations, *Sendai Framework for Disaster Risk Reduction 2015-2030* (2015), Preamble, para. 4; IPCC, *Managing the Risks of Extreme Events and Disasters to Advance Climate Change Adaptation* (2012), 1-19.

[69] United Nations Office for Disaster Risk Reduction (UNISDR), *Technical Guidance for Monitoring and Reporting on Progress in Achieving the Global Targetsof the Sendai Framework for Disaster Risk Reduction* (2017).

[70] A/RES/71/313, E/CN.3/2021/2, *Global Indicator Framework*, Indicator 13.1.1.

[71] A/RES/71/313, E/CN.3/2021/2, *Global Indicator Framework*, Indicator 13.1.2.

[72] A/RES/71/313, E/CN.3/2021/2, *Global Indicator Framework*, Indicator 13.1.2.

[73] United Nations Statistics Division, SDG Indicators: *Metadata Repository*, Indicator 13.1.1.

[74] United Nations Statistics Division, SDG Indicators: *Metadata Repository*, Indicator 13.1.1.

[75] United Nations Statistics Division, SDG Indicators: *Metadata Repository*, Indicator 13.1.1.

[76] United Nations, *Sendai Framework for Disaster Risk Reduction 2015-2030* (2015).

manner, including through the preservation and restoration of its essential basic structures and functions through risk management.'[77]

The Sendai Framework while identifying climate change as a disaster risk driver,[78] **40** notes that one of the lessons learnt and future challenges identified pursuant to the Hyogo Framework for Action in 2005 is that

> [a]ddressing climate change as one of the drivers of disaster risk, while respecting the mandate of the United Nations Framework Convention on Climate Change,[8] represents an opportunity to reduce disaster risk in a meaningful and coherent manner throughout the interrelated intergovernmental processes.'[79]

As volatility of the environment and uncertainty of the risks posed increase, risk **41** reducing approaches of the UN, governments and UN partners at global, regional and country level should be guided by the UN Common Guidelines on Helping Build Resilient Societies (UN Resilience Framework).[80] The UN Resilience Framework offers a blueprint that will facilitate ongoing efforts to build resilient societies towards achieving the Global Agenda 2030.

2. Building Resilience of Financial Systems

Another instrumental factor to mitigate the risks of climate change is finance and **42** investment. The lessons from the current pandemic make it abundantly clear that countries cannot respond to a global crisis in silos and that it is critically important to invest in crisis prevention and risk reduction.[81] Further, as climate change risks are changing asset valuations, institutional investors are responding to these risks by factoring in performance of companies on sustainability metrics in their investment decisions. In the same vein, there is also an increasing momentum to push companies to make disclosures pertaining to climate related risks.[82] The Network for Greening the Financial System acknowledged that risks posed by climate change are a source of financial risks and that central banks and supervisors need to work towards making the financial system resilient to these risks and in 2019 published guidelines to enable this process.[83] Further, the promotion of green financing to increase investment flows towards attainment of sustainable development goals needs impetus through structural and regulatory frameworks, and public and private investments.[84] The Paris Agreement has recognised the need for climate financing and increasing the flow of finance 'consistent with a pathway towards low greenhouse gas emissions and climate-resilient development'.[85] This priority

---

[77] United Nations Office for Disaster Risk Reduction (UNISDR), *Technical Guidance for Monitoring and Reporting on Progress in Achieving the Global Targets of the Sendai Framework for Disaster Risk Reduction* (2017).

[78] United Nations, *Sendai Framework for Disaster Risk Reduction 2015-2030* (2015), paras. 6, 13.

[79] United Nations, *Sendai Framework for Disaster Risk Reduction 2015-2030* (2015).

[80] United Nations, *Common Guidance on Helping Build Resilient Societies* (2020).

[81] UNEP, *Financing Sustainable Development: Moving from Momentum to Transformation in a Time of Turmoil* (2016).

[82] See Recommendations of the Task Force on Climate-related Financial Disclosures (2017).

[83] Network for Greening the Financial System, *Guide for Supervisors Integrating Climate-Related and Environmental Risks into Prudential Supervision* (2020).

[84] United Nations, *Report of the Inter-agency Task Force on Financing for Development : Financing for Sustainable Development Report 2020* (2020); https://www.un.org/pga/71/wp-content/uploads/sites/40/20 17/02/Financing-Sustainable-Development-in-a-time-of-turmoil.pdf.

[85] *Paris Agreement to the United Nations Framework Convention on Climate Change*, 12 December 2015, T.I.A.S. No. 16-1104, Art. 2(1) (c).

is reflected in SDG 13.a discussed above. However, the efforts to make financial flows aligned with the Paris Agreement is far from adequate.[86]

III. Other Policy Responses to Combat Climate Change

43   Several initiatives have been taken by countries to combat and mitigate the effects of climate change such as commitment to zero carbon dioxide, reduction in GHG emissions, encouraging the use of renewable energy, reducing fossil fuel subsidy, shift to sustainable infrastructure and industrialisation and make use of emissions trading schemes (ETS) (initiative of the EU). Noteworthy are the initiatives taken by the EU which launched the Green Deal[87] in response to a declaration of a climate emergency by the EU Parliament in 2019.[88] The EU Green Deal presents a roadmap of the European Commission's strategy to implement the Global Agenda 2030 and achieve the SDGs and defining its vision to become the first carbon neutral continent by 2050. It includes several ambitious proposals including a proposal for a European Climate Law and an ambition of a zero pollution action plan for air, water and soil, and policy measures such as carbon border adjustment mechanism for certain sectors, promoting sustainable alternative fuels in aviation, electric vehicles and expanding the scope of the EU ETS. The EU ETS works on a 'cap and trade' system and is a market-based policy measure to reduce emissions that caps the total amount of GHG that can be emitted by an installation covered under the system and allowing companies to trade emission allowances (which have a value) with each other.[89] The EU ETS can be seen as a success with a reduction of about 35 per cent in emissions between 2005 and 2019 of the installations covered under the system.

IV. International Trade and Climate Change

44   International trade is one facet of the international multilateral cooperation mechanism and has immense significance to tackle policy problems pertaining to climate change. The Marrakesh Agreement establishing the WTO made a clear link between international trade and sustainable development, emphasising that markets must be opened up while keeping environment and social priorities in sight.[90] Today, even though climate change priorities are at the top of the Global Agenda 2030, it has not found place in the international trade law framework of the WTO yet. Concerns are increasingly being raised regarding the (in)compatibility of climate change efforts and international trade law as it exists.[91] With countries testing new and varied policies to reduce emissions, their policies may often be asymmetric and present counter-incentives for companies to invest in countries with stringent policies or which are less carbon intensive.[92] This may impede climate action by countries as it may become too costly. Moreover, this may not lead to overall reduction of emissions, but simply lead to a

---

[86] UNEP, *Emissions Gap Report 2019* (2019).

[87] European Commission, COM(2019) 640 final, *The European Green Deal*, 11 December 2019.

[88] European Parliament, *European Parliament resolution of 28 November 2019 on the climate and environment emergency* (2019/2930(RSP)).

[89] European Commission, *ETS Handbook for Climate Action* (2015).

[90] Marrakesh Agreement Establishing the World Trade Organization (1994).

[91] https://www.wto.org/english/tratop_e/envir_e/climate_impact_e.htm; The Economist Intelligence Unit, *Climate Change and Trade Agreements: Friends or Foes?* (2019).

[92] See Deok-Young Park, *Legal Issues on Climate Change and International Trade Law* (2016), 1-6.

readjustment of emission levels among countries. Threatened with losing investments and increasing prices, countries are being compelled to consider carbon border adjustments on imports to correct carbon leakage which may conflict with existing General Agreement on Tariffs and Trade (GATT) provisions. Another policy measure that might be enacted by countries could be to ban or restrict imports of goods that are carbon intensive and may not be aligned with the climate policies of the importing country such as reduction of fossil fuels. *Prima facie*, the scope of Art. XX GATT may be considered to include such measures as it allows contracting parties to adopt and enforce measures that are 'necessary to protect human, animal or plant life or health'[93] or that relate to 'conservation of exhaustible natural resources if such measures are made effective in conjunction with restrictions on domestic production or consumption'[94]. However, a deeper consideration shows limited practical application of this exemption and is discussed in greater detail in the next section. Thus, combating climate change requires new and innovative measures and policies which need to be tested against several provisions of the GATT and rules of WTO, and call into question the need for reassessing the adequacy of the current WTO framework for prioritising climate change action by countries in international trade. As it stands today, there is a big need for shift in the legal framework for international trade alongside the current and future needs of development of the WTO.

C. Interdependences of SDG 13

GHG emissions are still influenced by economic performance, despite all political **45** declarations of intent and technical attempts to decouple them. As a result, the closure of entire sectors during the events of the SARS-CoV-2 pandemic led to lower emissions[95] which allowed some countries to unexpectedly reach their national CO_2 emission targets.[96] During the drastic reduction of human activities, the global greenhouse gas emissions dropped by 6 per cent (SDG 13.2).[97]

Over the last 30 years there has been an evolving recognition that climate change **46** mitigation and disaster risk reduction is a prerequisite for achieving sustainable development, as climate change and disasters threaten to roll back decades of development gains.[98] SDG 13 reveals the strongest links to SDG 2, SDG 3, SDG 7, SDG 14 and SDG 15.

The food system and production relying on agriculture underpins that the world's **47** current dietary patterns is responsible for around 21-35 per cent of total greenhouse gas emissions, and thus is a major driver of GHG emissions and other detrimental effects on the environment (SDG 2.1, SDG 2.2).[99] Through rising temperatures, extreme weather events and the reduction of water availability, climate change impacts on food security and food availability (SDG 2.1, SDG 2.4).[100]

---

[93] General Agreement on Tariffs and Trade (1986), Art. XX(b).

[94] General Agreement on Tariffs and Trade (1986), Art. XX(g).

[95] Martens and Ellmers and Pokorny on behalf of Global Policy Watch, *COVID-19 and the SDGs, The impact of the coronavirus pandemic on the global sustainability agenda* (2020), 7.

[96] https://www.klima-warnsignale.uni-hamburg.de/verfehlt-deutschland-sein-klimaziel-2020/.

[97] Nevertheless, this development still misses the annually 7.6 per cent reduction goal, to meet the 1.5 °C – or even the 2 °C – maximum target called for in the Paris Agreement; UN, *The Sustainable Development Goals Report 2020* (2020), 50.

[98] UNGA Open Working Group on Sustainable Development Goals, *Compendium of TST Issues Briefs* (2014), 175.

[99] FAO, *Executive Summary: Food Security and Nutrition Around The World* (2020).

[100] IPCC, *Special Report: Special Report On Climate Change and Land* (2019), 450.

48   A volatile and decreased food security affects the status of health and well-being (SDG 3) and is most likely to exert increasing influence and stimulation of migration flows which is (most often) accompanied by a deprivation of potential fulfilment such as gaining decent jobs (SDG 8.5, SDG 8.6, SDG 8.8), exacerbating social, economic, and political inequalities (SDG 10.2, SDG 10.3) especially against women and girls (SDG 5.1, SDG 5.5), hinders the creation of sustainable consumption and production patterns (SDG 12.2, SDG 12.a, SDG 12.c), and the exclusion from public and societal participation (SDG 16.3, SDG 16.7, SDG 16.10[101]).

49   Global warming and specifically heat waves,[102] and air, water and soil pollution affects health and well-being. The interaction between the reduction of the number of deaths and illnesses from air, water and soil pollution (SDG 3.9) and integrating climate change measures into national policies, strategies and planning (SDG 13.2) is striking, as e.g. the combustion of fossil fuels is largely responsible for local and climate air pollution.[103]

50   Marine as well as land biodiversity and ecosystems are heavily affected by climate change and thus, achieving goals of SDG 13 is highly synergistic with SDG 14 and SDG 15. Due to projected climate change by the mid-21st century and beyond, global marine-species redistribution and marine-biodiversity reduction in sensitive regions will challenge the sustained provision of fisheries productivity and other ecosystem services, while the projected sea level rise lead to additional adverse impacts on coastal systems and low-lying areas such as submergence, coastal flooding and coastal erosion.[104] Strengthening the resilience of ocean and coastal ecosystems, by reducing pollution (SDG 14.1), restoring their health (SDG 14.2), tackling ocean acidification (SDG 14.3), managing fish stocks sustainably (SDG 14.4, 14.6) and protecting coastal and marine areas and biodiversity (SDG 14.5) helps strengthen the overall resilience and adaptive capacity of coastal systems to climate change (SDG 13.1) which needs to be accompanied by the integration of climate change measures into policies and planning (SDG 13.2), climate change-related planning and management (SDG 13.b) and the implementation of commitments on climate mitigation taken under the United Nations Framework Convention on Climate Change (SDG 13.a).[105]

51   Since the pre-industrial period, the land surface air temperature has risen nearly twice as much as the global average temperature. Climate change, including increases in frequency and intensity of extremes, affects terrestrial ecosystems and contributes to desertification, droughts, floods and land degradation in many regions (SDG 15.3).[106] Ensuring the conservation, restoration and sustainable use of terrestrial and inland natural resources and freshwater ecosystems (SDG 15.1, SDG 15.2) will help maintain and stabilise natural habitats and halt the loss of biodiversity (SDG 15.5). Resilience and adaptive capacity to climate-related hazards and natural disasters (SDG 13.1) through the inte-

---

[101] SDG 13 directly refers to the United Nations Framework Convention on Climate Change and indirectly aligns with the aim of the 2015 Paris Agreement.

[102] https://www.who.int/news-room/fact-sheets/detail/climate-change-heat-and-health.

[103] Griggs et al., *A Guide to SDG Interactions: From Science to Implementation* (2017), 114; further reading: Huck et al.,'The Right to Breathe Clean Air and Access to Justice – Legal State of Play in International, European and National Law' (2021) 13(10) *International Environmental Law (eJournal)*, 1 (5); McFarlane et al., 'SDG 3: Good Health and Well-Being – Framing Targets to Maximise Co-Benefits for Forests and People' in Katila et al. (eds), *Sustainable Development Goals: Their Impacts on Forests and People* (2019), 72 (94).

[104] IPCC, *Climate Change 2014: Impacts, Adaptation and Vulnerability – Summary for Policymakers* (2014), 17.

[105] Griggs et al., *A Guide to SDG Interactions: From Science to Implementation* (2017), 207 f.

[106] IPCC, *Climate Change and Land* (2019), 9.

gration of ecosystem and biodiversity values into national and local planning (SDG 15.a) therefore is needed to cope with climate change but all the more is essential to adhere and respond to the principles (5 P) manifested in the Global Agenda 2030 ($\rightarrow$ Intro mn. 122 ff.).[107]

D. Jurisprudential Significance of SDG 13

The Global Agenda 2030 and most of its predecessors classify climate change as **52** the greatest challenge that requires the broadest possible international cooperation to counteract further climate warming, in particular by reducing global greenhouse gas emissions.[108] '[C]limate change is one of the greatest challenges of our time and its adverse effects'[109] undermine the ability of all countries to achieve sustainable development. Therefore, it would be inadequate if the jurisprudential relevance of an anthrophenic event such as climate change could not be reflected in law. A multitude of international and regional environmental law[110] as well as human rights agreements[111] serve as a basic framework for counteracting climate change. Most of them are agreed as cooperative instruments, the breach of which, however, mostly offer a restricted way of legal prosecution. The most far-reaching agreements with direct reference on climate include:

– Vienna Convention on the Protection of the Ozone Layer (1985)
– UN Convention to Combat Desertification in those Countries Experiencing Serious Drought and / or Desertification, Particularly in Africa (1994/1996) (UNCCD)
– United Nations Framework Convention on Climate Change (1992/1994) (UNFCCC)
– Kigali Amendment to the Montreal Protocol on Substances that Deplete the Ozone Layer (2016)

This structure is complemented by the 1987 Kyoto Protocol and above all the 2015 **53** Paris Agreement (196 participating countries[112] – PA), the Conferences of the Parties (CoPs), domestic national authorities and outcomes of various other conferences.[113] Despite their different tasks and functions, these agreements serve as principles and frameworks for scientific collaboration. They give explicit voice to African and Small Island Development States (SIDS). The human rights instruments primarily attribute climate change issues to the 'right to life' and the 'right of everyone to live in a healthy

---

[107] A/RES/70/1, *Transforming our world: the 2030 Agenda for Sustainable Development*, preamble.
[108] A/RES/70/1, *Transforming our world: the 2030 Agenda for Sustainable Development*, 21 October 2015, paras. 191, 14.
[109] A/RES/70/1, *Transforming our world: the 2030 Agenda for Sustainable Development*, 21 October 2015, para. 14.
[110] Convention on Biological Diversity (1992); Nagoya Protocol on Access to Genetic Resources and the Fair and Equitable Sahring of Benefits Arising from the Utilisation of the Convention on Biological Diversity (2011); The Antarctic Treaty in conjunction with Art. 3 of the Protocol on Environmental Protection to the Antarctic Treaty; Convention on Access to Information, Public Participation in Decision-making and Access to Justice in Environmental Matters (Aarhus Convention), 25 June 1998; and many regional, bilateral and unilateral agreements more.
[111] Art. 12(2) ICESCR; Art. 24(2) (c) CRC; Art. 11 San Salvador Protocol; Art. 24 ACHPR in conjunction with Arts. 18, 19 of the 2003 AU Protocol to the ACHPR on the Rights of Women in Africa.
[112] With the US repatriation under the Biden administration, 197 parties participiate in the PA.
[113] Seventeenth session of the Conference of the Parties to the Convention and the seventh session of the Conference of the Parties serving as the Meeting of the Parties to the Kyoto Protocol, held in Durban, South Africa, from 28 November to 9 December 2011.

environment'.[114] According to Francioni and Quirico, the 'right to development' is also an unambiguously decisive legal basis for pursuing 'an ecologically sustainable environment' and has already become established as a principle, at least regionally.[115] However, as a (to date highly contentious) third generation human right its status is uncertain.

54   General principles of international law such as the principle of Common But Differentiated Responsibilities (CBDR)[116], the Polluter Pays Principle[117] and the principle of Permanent Sovereignty Over Natural Resources (PSONR)[118] are considered in climate-relevant jurisprudence and their legal impact in the judicial discussion is prominent.[119]

55   The agreements mentioned are of different binding nature, and are further complemented by the concept of **planetary boundaries** which outlines 'a safe operating space for humanity [...] for innovation, growth and development in the pursuit of human prosperity in an increasingly populated and wealthy world'[120] and harmony with nature[121] which forms a basis to address 'Earth jurisprudence, the 2030 Agenda for Sustainable Development, trends in the implementation of Earth-centred law and a range of initiatives and achievements in law, policy, education and public engagement relating to Earth jurisprudence' (→ Goal 12).[122] Both concepts have already (partly) influenced the negotiations of SDG 13[123] and should help to achieve 'a paradigm shift from a

---

[114] Art. 12(2) ICESCR; Art. 24(2) (c) CRC; Art. 11 San Salvador Protocol; Art. 24 ACHPR in conjunction with Arts. 18, 19 ofthe 2003 AU Protocol to the ACHPR on the Rights of Women in Africa.

[115] Francioni and Quirico, 'Untying the Gordian Knot, Towards the human right to a climatically sustainable environment?' in Quirico and Boumghar (eds), *Climate Change and Human Rights, An international and comparative law perspective* (2016), 147.

[116] *Inuit Petition* (2005), 69; Athabaskan Petition (2013); *Matthews v the United Kingdom*, ECtHR Appl No 24833/94; see also *Greenpeace Southeast Asia and Philippine Rural Reconstruction Movement*, Petition to the Commission on Human Rights of the Philippines Requesting for Investigation of the Responsibility of the Carbon Majors for Human Rights Violations or Threats of Human Rights Violations Resulting from the Impacts of Climate Change; see for a deeper reflection Cordonier Segger, 'Commitments to Sustainable Development' in Cordonier Segger and Weeramantry (eds), *Sustainable Development Principles in the Decisions of International Courts and Tribunals, 1992-2012* (2017), 88.

[117] Primarily understood as a principle of allocating the costs of pollution or environmental measures. In recent European jurisprudence, a broader view of the responsibility of the polluter is gaining acceptance, according to which also measures for prevention and restoration of environmental damage must be taken; ECJ, C-129/16, 13.07.2017, *Túkecej Tejtermelö Kft.*, ECLI:EU:C:2017:547, para. 47; See for a deeper consideration Rehbinder, 'Climate damages and the 'Polluter Pays' Principle' in Kahl and Weller (eds), *Climate Change Litigation* (2021), 1 (45).

[118] See Cordonier Segger, 'Commitments to Sustainable Development' in Cordonier Segger and Weeramantry (eds), *Sustainable Development Principles in the Decisions of International Courts and Tribunals, 1992-2012* (2017), 71 and the jurisdiction cited; see also: Szabó, 'Sustainable Development in the jufgments of the International Court of Justice' in Cordonier Segger and Weeramantry (eds), *Sustainable Development Principles in the Decisions of International Courts and Tribunals, 1992-2012* (2017), 266-80 and the jurisdiction cited.

[119] See Banai, 'Sovereignty over natural resources and its implications for climate justice' (2016) 7 *WIREs Clim Change*, 238-50; Schuppert, 'Introduction: Justice, Climate Change, and the Distribution of Natural Resources' (2016) 22 *Res Publica*, 3-8.

[120] See e.g. Rockström and Sachs with Öhman and Schmidt-Traub, *Sustainable Development and Planetary Boundaries, Background Research Paper*, Submitted to the High Level Panel on the Post-2015 Development Agenda, 3; Randers et al., 'Achieving the 17 Sustainable Development Goals within 9 Planetary Boundaries' (2019) 2 *Global Sustainability* 24.

[121] A/RES/70/1, *Transforming our world: the 2030 Agenda for Sustainable Development*, 21 October 2015, paras. 191, 14, preamble and para. 9; A/RES/74/224, *Resolution adopted by the General Assembly on 19 December 2019 [on the report of the Second Committee (A/74/381/Add.9)]*, *Harmony with Nature*, 17 January 2020; A/72/175, *Harmony with Nature, Report of the Secretary-General*, 19 July 2017; and further Reports A/65/314, A/66/302, A/67/317, A/68/325, A/68/325/Corr.1, A/69/322, A/70/268, A/72/175, A/73/221 and A/74/236.

[122] A/72/175, *Harmony with Nature, Report of the Secretary-General*, 19 July 2017, Summary.

[123] See e.g.: Rockström and Sachs with Öhman and Schmidt-Traub, *Sustainable Development and Planetary Boundaries, Background Research Paper*, Submitted to the High Level Panel on the Post-2015

human-centred to an Earth-centred society in the implementation of the 2030 Agenda for Sustainable Development'.[124] More than 500 Multilateral Environmental Agreements also address environmental issues,[125] thereby influencing climate change law such as from the energy sector which help to curb the sector with the highest emissions of climate-relevant emissions[126] and decouple CO_2 emissions from economic growth ($\rightarrow$ Goal 8 mn. 31, 95).

What can be observed is a constantly evolving basis in environmental and interna-   **56** tional law, which, with the support of the UN, has generated a consensus in the basic discussion, according to which nature can be endowed its own 'subjective rights'. As a result, some form of legal standing has already been established before courts, where specific parts of nature can oppose projects through legal channels.[127] This fundamental framing has so far led to some resilience in terms of enforcement and legal consequences such as omission, instruction to rework policy plans, and occasionally withdrawal of operating licences and payment of damages in the event of non-compliance, depending on the applicable legal basis. The background, although clearly dedicated to international environmental law, is interlinked with and measured against the concept of sustainable development in human rights instruments and jurisprudence. Interconnectedness will be increasingly recognised, including through consideration of intergenerational equity and the legal nesting of humans with their environment through the impacts of climate change.

The pressing aggravation of human environment leads to expanding (strategic)   **57** climate litigation and direct and indirect regulatory impacts driving each other. Humankind is becoming more aware that there is no other option but to adapt to nature and thus adapt its own behaviour by means of legal framing. SDG 13 supports this development, especially as a financing instrument (SDG 13.a) and basis for legal reasoning, while the UNFCCC remains the primary forum for climate action.

I. Jurisdiction on Vision and Objectives

Climate change jurisprudence has gained momentum in recent years. One of the first   **58** cases to link human rights with impacts of climate change has been the *Inuit Petition* to the Inter-American Commission on Human Rights in 2005,[128] thereby revealing the most outstanding obstacles in getting access to justice and thus hindering the possibility of jurisprudential consideration and development.[129]

Development Agenda; further information Randers et al., *Transformation is feasible, How to achieve the Sustainable Development Goals within Planetary Boundaries, A report to the Club of Rome, for its 50 years anniversary*, 17 October 2018; Randers and others, 'Achieving the 17 Sustainable Development Goals within 9 Planetary Boundaries' (2019) 2 *Global Sustainability* 24.

[124] A/75/266, *Harmony with Nature, Report of the Secretary-General*, 28 July 2020, Summary.

[125] Cordonier Segger and Harrington, 'Environment and Sustainable Development' in Chesterman, Malone and Villalpando (eds), *The Oxford Handbook of United Nations Treaties* (2019), 204.

[126] Payosova, 'Climate Change Mitigation and Renewable Energy' in Cottier and Nadakavukaren Schefer (eds), *Elgar Encyclopedia of International Economic Law* (2017), 625.

[127] *Sierra Club v. Morton*, Judgment, 19 April 1972, Supreme Court of the United States, SEC. INT. No. 70-34, 405 U.S. 727; *Lalit Miglani v State of Uttarakhand & others*, Judgment, 30 March 2017, High Court of Uttarakhand at Naintal, Writ Petition (PIL) No.140 of 2015.

[128] Inuit Circumpolar Council Canada, *Petition to the Inter-American Commission on Human Rights Seeking Relief from Violations Resulting from Global Warming Caused by Acts and Omissions of the United States*, 7 December 2005.

[129] Adelman and Lewis, 'Symposium Foreword: Rights-Based Approaches to Climate Change' (2018) 7(1) *Transnational Environmental Law*, 9-15.

59   Since 2020, global movements such as Scientists for Future, Climate Justice, Fridays for Future and Rebellion Extinction attracted increased attention to climate change among the general public[130] which broadened the base of organisations active in climate and environmental protection. Prior to the outbreak of the SARS-CoV-2 pandemic, an increase in strategic climate change lawsuits related to intergenerational justice occurred, aimed at changing the behaviour of large corporations (especially the so-called carbon majors) or at least drawing public and media attention to their behaviour to have the resulting pressure induce them to undertake more climate-friendly ventures. An increasing number of cases targeted the financial sector and based on tort law and concepts of duty of care and duty of vigilance[131] in the form of damage cases (e.g. the liability suits filed by state and local governments in the US), technical disclosure claims, and human rights procedures. The rising number of cases might also have given rise to 'novel arguments' in courts approaches.[132] 'But to be used in courts, law and climate science need to be connected. In an increasing number of climate litigation cases, challenges remain when attributing specific climate-related events to global greenhouse gas emissions or specific emitters'.[133] The extent to which liability damages, climate-relevant behaviour of individual actors (companies) or governments that do not take action against such behaviour can be claimed by individuals with only limited *locus standi* which forms a convoluted starting point for assessing the jurisprudential relevance of the so (vitally) important SDG 13. Difficulties exist in particular in the so far hardly possible provability that they are affected by climate-relevant behaviour of those actors (*causa*), combined with the impossibility of proving which damages have actually and imminently occurred (in scope and at all).

60   Examples for the recognition of 'respect for the environment' as a necessity supported by the common interest of the world community are legion in jurisprudence, e.g. with reference to international and national environmental law, but also beyond in the human rights context. Another important development in climate litigation involves the circumstances of 'climate refugees' – individuals seeking refuge or asylum having fled their home for fear of the threat of climate change impacts to their livelihoods.[134]

1. International Jurisdiction

61   The ICJ, with the well-known jurisprudence of the *Gabčíkovo-Nagymaros*, *Pulp Mills* and *Legality of the Threat of Nuclear Weapons* cases, has adjudicated the erga omnes nature of the obligation to respect the environment and has referred to it as a common good that is important for all humankind.[135] Though climate change is not directly named, these cases form the foundation of a fundamental recognition on international ground.

52   Climate change litigation is recognised as a relatively new, but rapidly growing judicial area framed by environmtal law describing a growing asymmetry between climate

---

[130] See for further information on the work and effects of NGOs Rajavuori, 'The Role of Non-State Actors in Climate Law' in Mayer and Zahar (eds), *Debating Climate Law* (2021); Hsu et al., 'Exploring links between national climate strategies and non-state and subnational climate action in nationally determined contributions (NDCs)' (2020) 20(4) *Climate Policy*, 443-57.

[131] Setzer and Byrnes, *Global trends in climate change litigation: 2020 snapshot, Policy Report* (2020), 18.

[132] Preston, 'The Influence of the Paris Agreement on Climate Litigation: Causation, Corporate Governance and Catalyst (Part II)' (2020) 00 *Journal of Environmental Law*, 1 (29).

[133] Setzer and Byrnes, *Global trends in climate change litigation: 2020 snapshot, Policy Report* (2020), 18.

[134] Setzer and Byrnes, *Global trends in climate change litigation: 2020 snapshot, Policy Report* (2020), 17.

[135] *Gabčíkovo-Nagymaros Project (Hungary Slovakia)*, Judgment of 25 September 1997, ICJ, para. 53; *Pulp Mills on the River Uruguay (Argentina vs. Uruguay)*, Judgment of 20 April 2010, ICJ, para. 76; *Legality of the Threat of Nuclear Weapons (1996)*, Advisory Opinion, 8 July 1996, ICJ, para. 29.

change mitigation and an political outcome perceived in civil society as inadequate against the impact of climate change.

In the last 20 years, the evolution of national, interregional and international law   63 mostly on human rights, consumer protection, private law, administrative and constitutional law have paved the way for the courts to judge on climate change litigation.

The UN Human Rights Committee (HRC), on 7 January 2020, delivered a landmark   64 decision recognising for the first time that the forced repatriation of a person 'to a place where their life is at risk due to the adverse effects of climate change may violate the right to life under Article 6 of the ICCPR.'[136] After exhausting unsuccessfully national legal proceedings aimed at recognising refugee status on climate grounds, the HRC recognised for the first time in *Teitiota v. New Zealand*[137] that sea-level rise due to climate change (as environmental degradation) and the associated harm to human well-being may well constitute a violation of the 'right to life' under Art. 6 ICCPR. *Teitiota* relied upon the principle in international law of states being obliged not to extradite, deport, expel or otherwise remove a person from their territory when there are substantial grounds for believing that there is a real risk of irreparable harm. However, the case was unsuccessful due to the high threshold set by the court and subsequently raised discussions 'on the scope of the right to life, climate migration and how the so-called 'slow violence' of climate change'[138] could be determined and how 'a high threshold for providing substantial grounds to establish that a real risk of irreparable harm exists'[139] that 'satisfies the test of 'imminence' of human rights harms in climate-vulnerable states'[140] should be understoodin contrast, e.g. to the *Urgenda Case* (→ Goal 13 mn. 79 ff.). But so far no mandate exists relating to states' obligations of non-refoulement under the ICCPR for any international organisation.

Before the ECtHR, the first claim related to climate change was filed in September   65 2020 by six Portuguese youth against all 27 EU Member States as well as Norway, Russia, Switzerland, Turkey, the UK and Ukraine.[141] The plaintiffs sought a finding that the defendants had violated human rights by failing to take sufficient measures to address climate change. Calls were made to require them to take more ambitious action to help reduce global greenhouse gas emissions, as they share responsibility for the existing and impending damage caused by global warming and climate change. In addition, the applicants argued extraterritorial jurisdiction over significant transboundary environmental damage and requested the court to determine whether the respondent States are contributing their 'fair share' to efforts to mitigate climate change. Interestingly, the ECtHR went beyond the grounds of the application. While these were based on Art. 2, 8 and 14 ECHR (life and respect for private and family life, non-discrimination), the court extended the requested pleas to Art. 3 ECHR (prohibition of torture and inhuman and degrading treatment) and Art. 1 of Protocol No. 1 to the Convention (right to property).[142] The responses are due by the end of February 2021 and it remains to be seen how the

---

[136] Oxford Human Rights Hub and Sinclair-Blakemore, *Teitiota v New Zealand: A Step Forward in the Protection of Climate Refugees under International Human Rights Law?* (2020).

[137] CCPR/C/127/D/2728/2016, *Ioane Teitiota v. New Zealand* (advance unedited version), 7 January 2020.

[138] Setzer and Byrnes, *Global trends in climate change litigation: 2020 snapshot, Policy Report* (2020), 17.

[139] CCPR/C/127/D/2728/2016, *Ioane Teitiota v. New Zealand* (advance unedited version), 7 January 2020, para. 9.3.

[140] Setzer and Byrnes, *Global trends in climate change litigation: 2020 snapshot, Policy Report* (2020), 17.

[141] ECtHR, Request No. 39371/20, Cláudia DUARTE AGOSTINHO and others against Portugal and 33 other States submitted 7 September 2020; on November 30, 2020, the Court accepted and fast-tracked the case and upheld its decision against the defendant's motion (rejection of April 2, 2021).

[142] The Court thus acted in accordance with the frequently applied principle *jura novit curia*.

ECtHR will rule on the relevant issues of 'victim status, admissibility, shared responsibility, and the interplay between the Strasbourg court and domestic actors'.[143] This type of legal action with the aim to ground *locus standi* is being taken more and more and appears to be a clear trend that can be expected to continue in the future.[144] As great as the aspirations with this case are, there is a danger that it will be rejected on procedural grounds alone. In principle, the ECtHR can only be called upon when the national jurisdictions have been exhausted in each case, which would mean that jurisdiction would first have to be exhausted in all 33 States, possibly meaning the end of the matter for financial reasons alone. If adopted, this case would be the first of its kind to be heard before the ECtHR. Although to date the ECtHR has developed a rich jurisprudence on environmental damages and human rights, certainly partly overlapping in subject matter and context, it has not ruled directly on climate change concerns.[145] Furthermore, both access to justice before the ECtHR and the application of individual rights of the ECHR still appear to be considerably difficult.[146] The link between environmental responsibility and human rights based on the ECHR continues to be in the process of development. However, while the 33 States were called upon to file their defenses, the Council of Europe Commissioner for Human Rights Dunja Mijatović published her third party intervention underscoring the salient human rights impacts of environmental degradation and climate change.[147] She emphasised the many elements of the right to a healthy environment contained in the ECHR and the legal framework that must provide protection for victims of environmental degradation and climate change, which cannot be realised without an effective remedy for all parties concerned. According to Mijatović this case provides a 'unique opportunity' to evolve the law for a more comprehensive implementation of the ECHR and the effective realisation of the right to remedy. Yet, it remains to be seen whether the ECtHR will deliver such a far-reaching decision.

66   Databases with current overviews of climate change legislation and litigation and supporting arguments for litigation can, amongst others, be found at:

- http://climatecasechart.com/climate-change-litigation/
  This website provides two databases of climate change caselaw. Cases in the databases are organised by type of claim and are searchable. In many cases, links are available to decisions, complaints, and other case documents
- https://climate-laws.org/
  Climate Change Laws of the World covers national-level climate change laws, policies, and climate litigation cases globally. It builds on more than decade of data collection by both the Grantham Research Institute at the LSE and the Sabin Center for Climate Change Law at Columbia Law School.

---

[143] Heri, 'The ECtHR's Pending Climate Change Case: What's Ill-Treatment Got To Do With It?' (2020) *EJIL:Talk!*, Blog of the European Journal of International Law, 22.12.2020.

[144] See, by way of example, for the growing body of jurisdiction: Committee on the Rights of the Child, *Sacchi et al v. Argentina, Brazil, France, Germany & Turkey*, Communications n°105/2019 (Brazil), n° 106/2019, (France), n°107/2019 (Germany); United States Court of Appeals for the Ninth Circuit, *Juliana v. United States*, Case No. 18-36082.

[145] Pedersen, 'The European Court of Human Rights and International Environmental Law' in Knox and Pejan (eds), *The Human Right to a healthy environment* (2018), 59 (83-87) [found in Payandeh, 'The role of courts in climate protection and the separation of powers' in Kahl and Weller (eds), *Climate Change Litigation – A Handbook* (2021), Chapter C, mn. 6].

[146] Karlsson Niska, 'Climate Change Litigation and the European Court of Human Rights – A Strategic Next Step?' (2020) 13 *Journal of World Energy Law and Business*, 331 (339 f.).

[147] Council of Europe, *Third party intervention by the Council of Europe Commissioner for Human Rights under Article 36, paragraph 3, of the European Convention on Human Rights*, Application No. 39371/20, *Cláudia Duarte Agostinho and others v. Portugal and 32 other States*, 5 May 2021.

2. European Jurisdiction

The far-reaching anchoring of various established principles, such as the principle of 67
equality in Arts. 20 and 21 of the EU Charter, the unequivocal embedding of the principle of sustainable development in Art. 3 TEU, Art. 11 TFEU and Art. 37 EU Charter of
Fundamental Rights, the EU explicitly takes into account the principles of precaution
and prevention in the formulation and application of its environmental policies in accordance with the 'tackle at the origin' and 'polluter pays' principles, Art. 191 TFEU. This
framework is supplemented by an immense amount of secondary legislation that defines
the handling of environmental and climate-relevant concerns in more detail. It seems
even more astonishing that European jurisdiction has so far failed to comply with this
framework. In particular, access to justice is clearly limited, especially if no *locus standi* is
granted before European system of norm control (→ Goal 16 mn. 9 ff., 22 ff.).

In 2019, the General Court (GC) rejected the so-called *People's Climate Case* as inad- 68
missible. The Court reasserted its established and well-settled case law on legal standing,
known as the 'Plaumann test', and held that the applicants here were not individually
concerned for the purpose of Art. 263(4) TFEU, which sets the standing requirements
before the EU Court of Justice (ECJ). The General Court (GC) stated that

> it is true that every individual is likely to be affected one way or another by climate change, that
> issue is recognised by the European Union and the Member States who have, as a result, committed
> to reducing emissions. However, the fact that the effects of climate change may be different for one
> person than they are for another does not mean that, for that reason, there exists standing to bring an
> action against a measure of general application.[148]

With the concern of creating *locus standi* for all, without having to fulfil the criteria 69
imposed by the Treaty of being individually concerned,[149] the court held instead that
natural and legal persons which cannot challenge EU decisions due to a lack of standing
before the EU courts, are able 'to plead the invalidity of such acts' indirectly under
Art. 277 TFEU or under the procedure of Art. 267 TFEU before domestic courts (preliminary ruling).[150] However, the lack of legal standing of individuals and NGOs before
the ECJ remains part of the democratic deficit of the EU. The ECJ's interpretation of direct and individual concern criteria appears to be a bottleneck for accessing judicial
remedy particularly in cases with more serious damage affecting a higher number of
persons.[151] In this respect, settled jurisdiction excluded any environmental or human
rights NGO and individuals from having standing since 1963.[152] This interpretation led
to a succession of cases[153] in which the Paris Agreement as well as the EU's implementa-

---

[148] ECJ, Case T-330/18, 8.5.2019, *Carvalho and Others v Parliament and Council*, ECLI:EU:T:2019:324,
para. 50.

[149] The test demands that 'the alleged infringement must distinguish the applicant individually'; ECJ,
Case T-330/18, 8.5.2019, *Carvalho and Others v Parliament and Council*, ECLI:EU:T:2019:324, para. 48;
thereby referring to its settled case-law: ECJ, Case T-16/04, 2.3.2010, *Arcelor v Parliament and Council*,
EU:T:2010:54, para. 103 and the case-law cited.

[150] ECJ, Case T-330/18, 8.5.2019, *Carvalho and Others v Parliament and Council*, ECLI:EU:T:2019:324,
para. 53; further reading: Winter, 'Armando Carvalho and Others v. EU: Invoking Human Rights and the
Paris Agreement for Better Climate Protection Legislation' (2020) 9(1) *Transnational Environmental Law*,
37-164; brief summary: https://www.clientearth.org/projects/access-to-justice-for-a-greener-europe/upda
tes/the-general-court-of-the-eu-rejects-the-people-climate-case-as-inadmissible/.

[151] The *Plaumann* formula defines 'individual concern' as follows: 'by reason of certain attributes
peculiar to them, or by reason of a factual situation which differentiates them from all other persons and
distinguishes them individually in the same way as the addressee'.

[152] General Court (GC), Case T-18/10, 6.9.2011, *Inuit Tapiriit Kanatami*, ECLI:EU:T:2011:419, para. 71.

[153] General Court (GC), Case T-18/10, *Inuit Tapiriit Kanatami*, 6.9.2011, ECLI:EU:T:2011:419, para. 71
(see also the cases of *Jégo-Quéré* and *Stichting Greenpeace*).

tion of the Aarhus Convention have been the subject of repeated controversy such as being 'a scandalous refusal of legal protection'.[154] Not at least, the dismissal of the so-called *People's Climate Case* in which the claimants 'sought to oblige the European legislator to set more ambitious climate targets for 2030'[155] illustrated clearly the immanent difficulties in EU jurisdiction by merely referring to the lacking formal aspect of individual concern. Yet another time, a European body of control has positioned itself to the detriment to the intended and politically and legally embedded just and sustainable transition.[156]

70   Overall, environment-related cases are sparse before the ECJ including the GC.[157] Although 'appropriate action, including on the part of the courts'[158] is called for, jurisdiction so far appears not promising. More significant, however, is the respective domestic case law, which in many cases is brought by NGOs, local authorities and individuals before domestic courts throughout the EU (→ Goal 13 mn. 79 ff.).

3. Arbitration Proceedings

71   The WTO as one part of the architecture of multilateral cooperation, going back to the Bretton Woods system, with the creation of the GATT 1947 and the succeeding GATT 1994, provides a framework to facilitate global trade and serves as a forum to negotiate further trade openness.

72   Although sustainable development is mentioned in the preamble of the WTO Agreement, the relationship to climate change and how it possibly alters the provisions and interpretation remain an arena for discussion on the reconciliaton of trade and sustainable development. As the former Director General (DG) of the WTO Lamy in 2008pointed out: 'The issue of climate change, *per se*, is not part of the WTO's ongoing work programme and there are no WTO rules specific to climate change. However, the WTO is relevant because climate change measures and policies intersect with international trade in a number of different ways.'[159]

73   As early as 2008, Lamy emphasised that, '[t]hat the relationship between international trade, the WTO, and climate change, would be best defined by a consensual international accord on climate change.' A global consensus is needed 'to tackle the issue of climate change', and at the same time, 'WTO Members will continue to hold different views on what the multilateral trading system can and must do.' Several other speeches reveal that it is up to 'the WTO Members themselves to deepen their dialouges and to decide what the task of the WTO should be in the field of climate change.'[160]

74   The current WTO deadlock makes its reform likely, but whether and to what extent it will be possible to legally integrate climate protection into the WTO is uncertain.[161]

---

[154] GC, Case T-18/10, *Inuit Tapiriit Kanatami*, 6.9.2011, ECLI:EU:T:2011:419, para. 133.

[155] Klinger, 'Why the Initiative "Everyone" Comes at the Right Time' (2021), *Völkerrechtsblog, International Law & International Legal Thought*, 14.04.2021, https://voelkerrechtsblog.org/time-for-an-update-of-the-eu-charter-of-fundamental-rights/.

[156] ECJ, Case C-565/19, 25.03.2021, *Armando Carvalho and Others v European Parliament and Council of the European Union*, ECLI:EU:C:2021:252, paras. 46-50.

[157] Cases in 2019 before the ECJ: 60 cases out of 1,102 pending cases, and before the GC: 12 cases out of 1,398 pending cases; ECJ, *The year in review, Annual Report 2019* (2020), 55, 59.

[158] ECJ, *The year in review, Annual Report 2019* (2020), preface.

[159] Dias and Nosowicz and Seeuws, 'EU Border Carbon Adjustment and the WTO: Hand in Hand Towards Tackling Climate Change' (2020) 15(1) *Global Trade and Customs Journal*, 15-23; WTO, *Trade and Climate Change* (2009), Introduction.

[160] https://www.wto.org/english/news_e/news20_e/ddgaw_18sep20_e.htm.

[161] Lewis et al. (eds), *A Post-WTO International Legal Order: Utopian, Dystopian and Other Scenarios* (2020); Petersmann, 'A Post-WTO International Legal Order: Utopian, Dystopian and Other Scenarios' (2021) 00 *Journal of International Economic Law*.

According to the WTO's founding Charter, the Marrakesh Agreement, trade is tied 75 to human values and welfare goals such as raising standards of living, optimal use of the world's resources in accordance with the objective of sustainable development, and protection and preservation of the environment.[162] Yet, trade liberalisation and the ambitions for economic growth and human advancement create a tense relationship that brings impacts on climate change with it.[163]

The issue of climate change is not *per se* part of the WTO's ongoing work programme 76 and there are no WTO rules specific to climate change but its relevance for climate change measures and policies grounds on its intersection with international trade in different ways.[164] Theoretically, the Chapeau under Art. XX could constitute a sound basis to develop a climate-sensitive reading of disputed measures under WTO agreements.[165] As a starting point for relevant WTO jurisprudence, the *US-Shrimp* case can be cited, in which the Appellate Body (AB) fundamentally held that 'governments have every right to protect human, animal or plant life and health and to take measures to conserve exhaustible resources'.[166] The AB also referred to the principle of CBDR to conserve and protect the environment and to Principle 12 of the Rio Declaration on Environment and Development, thus emphasising the common, non-discriminatory approach that must be followed and that otherwise (in the case of non-compliance) would lead to the inapplicability of the said right to high environmental standards.[167] The ruling also included the reference that WTO panels may accept 'amicus briefs' (friends of the court submissions) from NGOs or other interested parties.

Dispute settlement conducted within the framework of the Dispute Settlement Un- 77 derstanding (DSU) are particularly fraught with obstacles due to the non-restricted scope of the DSU if the covered (disputed) agreements[168] do not include independent provisions relating to climate or environmentally relevant measures or objects of protection. The purpose of the dispute settlement system is to preserve and clarify the existing agreements but 'cannot add to or diminish the rights and obligations provided' therein, Arts. 3.2, 19 DSU. The decisions and recommendations are thus solely up to the interpretation of the dispute settlement bodies within the framework of the 'customary rules of interpretation of public international law', Art. 3.3 DSU.[169]

There is an ongoing discussion[170] on how trade could positively influence climate 78 change mitigation, with a focus on WTO law, which with its diverse and particular agreements encompasses much of the regulatory content relevant to climate change. Similarly, the clear tension between global trade and climate-relevant regulations and

---

[162] https://www.wto.org/english/tratop_e/envir_e/climate_impact_e.htm.

[163] Further information https://www.wto.org/english/tratop_e/envir_e/climate_impact_e.htm; The Economist Intelligence Unit, *Climate Change and Trade Agreements: Friends or Foes?* (2019).

[164] https://www.wto.org/english/tratop_e/envir_e/climate_intro_e.htm.

[165] See similar thoughts with reference to the Agreement on Subsidies and Countervailing Measures (SCM agreement): Genest, 'The Canada—FIT Case and the WTO Subsidies Agreement: Failed Fact-Finding, Needless Complexity, and Missed Judicial Economy' (2018) 10(2) *McGill International Journal of Sustainable Development Law and Policy / Revue Internationale De Droit Et Politique Du Développement Durable De McGill*, 237 (255); dissenting view: Espa and Durán, 'Renewable Energy Subsidies and WTO Law: Time to Rethink the Case for Reform Beyond Canada – Renewable Energy/Fit Program' (2018) 21(3) *Journal of International Economic Law*, 621-53.

[166] *United States — Import Prohibition of Certain Shrimp and Shrimp Products (Shrimp-Turtle)*, 6 November 1998, WTO case Nos. 58 (and 61), paras. 185 ff.

[167] *United States — Import Prohibition of Certain Shrimp and Shrimp Products (Shrimp-Turtle)*, 6 November 1998, WTO case Nos. 58 (and 61), para. 124.

[168] See WTO Agreement, Annex I.

[169] See also Temmerman, 'Trade in Bulk Water' in Cottier and Schefer (eds), *Elgar Encyclopedia of International Economic Law* (2017), 643 (645).

[170] The Economist Intelligence Unit, *Climate Change and Trade Agreements: Friends or Foes?* (2019), 5.

measures that are capable of being restrictive to trade is obvious. This can be read, for example, in the *Canada-FIT* proceedings, in which so-called feed-in tariffs for renewable energy electricity generators were disputed as market-distorting instruments, the admissibility of which was in any case determined by the AB insofar as they are capable of preventing 'the adverse impact on human health and the environment of fossil fuel energy emissions and nuclear waste disposal' or positively address environmental concerns,[171] thereby overturning the Panel's finding. As yet, this decision is indicative of other climate-relevant measures of market control,[172] the sustainable design of which has not been supported (to a sufficient extent)[173] by WTO jurisprudence and has so far been measured against the standard of non-discrimination within a target market area, but without actually serving the overriding values such as climate protection.[174] In addition, the AB, which is still not open to appeal, excludes further possibilities of review.

4. Domestic Jurisdiction

79   In three recent landmark cases,[175] the claimants asserted that governmental action against climate change is a fundamental human right and the lack of government action would constitute a severe violation of that right.[176]

80   In *Urgenda v The United Kingdom of the Netherlands*[177], the Supreme Court of the Netherlands (SCN) established a positive obligation to take measures for the prevention of climate change by ordering the Netherlands to reduce its greenhouse gas (GHG) emissions with at least 25 per cent by the end of 2020, compared to 1990 levels. Following a decision at first instance still based on Dutch law by reference to the doctrine of hazardous negligence, the arguments in the cross-appeal were based on the protection of the 'right to life' and to 'private and family life' with reference to Arts. 2 and 8 ECHR.[178] In addition, the SCN took into account in its reasoning the UNFCCC, the 2015 Paris Agreement, the obligation to exercise due diligence in preventing significant transboundary harm, and the precautionary principle[179] which are inherent in the Global

---

[171] *Canada — Measures Relating to the Feed-in Tariff Program (Canada-FIT)*, WT/DS412/AB/R; WT/DS426/AB/R, Appellate Body Report, adopted 24 May 2013, para. 5.181.

[172] These include: fiscal measures (e.g. taxreductions, tax credits), aimed at increasing consumption of renewable electricity and facilitating investment in RE technologies; investment support measures (e.g. capital grants, favourable lending conditions, risk-mitigating instruments, re-search and development grants), aimed at reducing the capital costs of installing and deploying RE technologies and price support mechanisms (e.g. feed-in tariffs, feed-in premiums).

[173] Further reading: Espa and Durán, 'Renewable Energy Subsidies and WTO Law: Time to Rethink the Case for Reform Beyond Canada – Renewable Energy/Fit Program' (2018) 21(3) *Journal of International Economic Law*, 621-53.

[174] See also *United States — Standards for Reformulated and Conventional Gasoline*, WTO case Nos. 2 and 4. Ruling adopted on 20 May 1996; *United States — Taxes on Automobiles*, ruling not adopted, circulated on 11 October 1994.

[175] *The State of the Netherlands v Stichting Urgenda*, Judgment of 20 December 2019, Dutch Supreme Court, ECLI:NL:HR:2019:2007; *Friends of the Irish Environment v Ireland*; *Juliana v the United States of America*.

[176] https://www.idunn.no/oslo_law_review/2020/03/judging_climate_change_the_role_of_the_judiciary_in_the_fi.

[177] *The State of the Netherlands v Stichting Urgenda*, Judgement of 20 December 2019, Dutch Supreme Court, ECLI:NL:HR:2019:2007; Summary of the case: Meguro, 'State of the Netherlands v. Urgenda Foundation' (2020) 114(4) *American Journal of International Law*, 729-35; https://www.hogeraad.nl/actuee l/nieuwsoverzicht/2019/december/dutch-state-case-reduce-greenhouse-gas-emissions/.

[178] *The State of the Netherlands v Stichting Urgenda*, 20 December 2019, Dutch Supreme Court, ECLI:NL:HR:2019:2006, paras. 5.6.2 and Summary of the judgment, conclusion.

[179] *The State of the Netherlands v Stichting Urgenda*, 20 December 2019, Dutch Supreme Court, ECLI:NL:HR:2019:2006, paras. 31(c), (d), 4.7, 5.3.2, 5.6.2.

Agenda 2030 and the SDGs (→ Intro mn. 251). The SCN confirmed this view and rejected in full the State's requests to deviate, and also made it clear that the responsibility of individual states can be determined even dissociated from a joint responsibility (partial responsibility), in this case of climate change, of several states.[180] Despite being controversial,[181] this decision subsequently gave rise to a number of lawsuits[182] which unambiguously refer to contents of SDG 13, assuming intergenerational justice as an indispensable prerequisite for the right to life, which thus becomes a right to future (→ Goal 3 mn. 63, 77). In the *Urgenda* case, which for the first time linked climate protection with human rights, demanded a case-law review by national courts, although the issue was not covered by the ECHR. The SCN referred to existing legal foundations as being sufficient for legal assessment.[183] It also confirmed that it was not necessary to identify potential victims of climate change individually, but that the state had obligations towards the general population,[184] and in turning to Art. 47 of the International Law Commission's Articles on Responsibility of States for Internationally Wrongful Acts, held the Netherlands 'individually responsible if it fails to carry out its part to prevent global hazardous effects that impair human rights under ECHR Arts. 2 and 8'.[185]

Similar cases can be found both in Europe[186] and worldwide[187] with varying degrees **81** of success. Within Europe, for example in Germany or in the United Kingdom (UK), courts have frequently rejected actions by people trying to compel their governments

---

[180] *The State of the Netherlands v Stichting Urgenda*, 20 December 2019, Dutch Supreme Court, ECLI: NL:HR:2019:2006, paras. 5.7.1-5.8; see for further information on this case: Noellkaemper and Burgers, 'A New Classic in Climate Change Litigation: The Dutch Supreme Court Decision in the Urgenda Case' (2020) *EJIL Talk*; 'State of the Netherlands v. Urgenda, Foundation Hague Court of Appeal Requires Dutch Government to Meet Greenhouse Gas Emissions Reductions By 2020' (2019), *132 Harv. L. Rev.*, 2090.

[181] See for a comprehensive consideration: Preston, 'The Influence of the Paris Agreement on Climate Litigation: Legal Obligations and Norms (Part I)' (2020) 00 *Journal of Environmental Law*; Preston, 'The Influence of the Paris Agreement on Climate Litigation: Causation, Corporate Governance and Catalyst (Part II)' (2020) 00 *Journal of Environmental Law*.

[182] See e.g.: *Future Generations v. Ministry of the Environment and Others*, Judgment, 5 April 2018, Colombia Supreme Court, Reg. No 11001-22-03-000-2018-00319-00; *Maria Khan et al. v. Federation of Pakistan et al.*, 15 December 2019, Lahore High Court, Writ Petition No.8960 of 2019; also by calling on the IACtHR: Republic of Colombia, Request for an Advisory Opinion from the Inter-American Court of Human Rights Concerning the Interpretation of Art. 1(1), 4(1) and 5(1) of the American Convention on Human Rights, and Advisory Opinion OC-23/17, 15 November 2017.

[183] The Court stated that Contracting States to the ECHR must consider 'international treaties, soft law sources and principles of international law, such as the 'no harm' principle and the precautionary principle' which give 'enough common ground to answer such new questions of law', see Setzer and Higham, *Global trends in climate change litigation: 2021 snapshot* (2021) and Setzer and Byrnes, *Global trends in climate change litigation: 2020 snapshot* (2020), 16.

[184] *The State of the Netherlands v Stichting Urgenda*, 20.12.2019, Dutch Supreme Court, ECLI:NL:HR: 2019:2006, paras. 5.3.1, 5.6.2.

[185] Meguro, 'State of the Netherlands v. Urgenda Foundation' (2020) 114(4) *American Journal of International Law*, 729 (731); see on the issue of applying ECHR rights before domestic courts: Niska, 'Climate Change Litigation and the European Court of Human Rights – A Strategic Next Step?' (2020) 13 *Journal of World Energy Law and Business*, 331-42; Wegener, 'Can the Paris Agreement Help Climate Change Litigation and Vice Versa?' (2020) 9 *Transnational Environmental Law*, 17.

[186] See e.g. *Commune de Grande-Synthe v. France*, Conseil D'Etat (Highest Administrative Court in France), Case N° 427301 (pending, declared admissible).

[187] *Center for Social Justice Studies et al. v. Presidency of the Republic et al.*, Constitutional Court of Colombia, Judgment T-622/16; *Thomas v. EPA*, Supreme Court of Guyana; *McVeigh v. Retail Employees Superannuation Trust*, Federal Court of Australia; *PSB et al. v. Brazil (on deforestation and human rights)*, Federal Supreme Court of Brazil; *Institute of Amazonian Studies v. Brazil*, Federal District Court of Curitiba; *Center for Food and Adequate Living Rights et al. v. Tanzania and Uganda*, East African Court of Justice; *Bushfire Survivors for Climate Action Incorporated v. Environmental Protection Authority*, New South Wales Land and Environment Court.

to take swifter climate action[188] whereas in France, despite underlining that the case was driven by French and European law and not the Paris Agreement (as alleged), the administrative court of Paris reasoned that the Paris Agreement is decisive in the interpretation of national law when determining if a government has failed to reduce greenhouse gas emissions and thus violates domestic and international law, including the European Convention on Human Rights, the Paris Agreement, the French Environmental Code, and the French Environmental Charter. The Court also accepted interventions by NGOs and other interested cities and thus made one of the most progressive climate rulings in the EU so far.[189]

82   In a case before the German Federal Constitutional Court (FCC), this has most recently been assessed differently in favour of climate protection.[190] The German Climate Protection Act, which had been adopted prior to a tightening of European climate protection targets, fell short of the new EU requirements. The FCC then declared central components of the Climate Protection Act to be incompatible with the German Basic Law (Grundgesetz – GG) and based its reasoning on Art. 2(2) sentence 1 GG (protection of life and physical integrity). The FCC emphasised that Art. 2 'includes protection against impairments of fundamental rights by environmental pollution, irrespective of by whom and through what circumstances they are threatened' and clarified the state's obligation to take 'early, transparent measures' to achieve climate neutrality in order not to burden future generations excessively.[191] Shortly afterwards, in a decision that is not yet binding, the Rechtbank Den Haag ordered Royal Dutch Shell to reduce its CO_2 emissions by 45 per cent by 2030 compared to 2019.[192] Even though these cases resemble a burgeoning wave, they still need to be assessed in their respective national contexts. Not every formal process requirement can be fulfilled equally in every member state across Europe. Also, it remains to be seen how soon and by which means the rulings will actually be implemented.

83   Progressive jurisprudence can be found in Latin America, which directly relate to Earth Jurisprudence providing legal status to nature itself, for example, in Columbia where the Constitutional Court held that

> [t]he conservation of biodiversity is not based solely on the protection of species and ecosystems because of their intrinsic value: the survival of human communities is undoubtedly linked to the integrity of their environment [with] indirect benefits of biodiversity, such as regulation of water cycles, carbon, climate and cultural services.[193]

---

[188] https://www.climatechangenews.com/2020/09/03/six-portuguese-youth-file-unprecedented-climate-lawsuit-33-countries/.

[189] Tribunal Administratif De Paris, N°1904967, 1904968, 1904972, 1904976/4-1, *Association Oxfam France Association Notre Affaire À Tous Fondation Pour La Nature Et L'homme Association Greenpeace France*, http://paris.tribunal-administratif.fr/content/download/179360/1759761/version/1/file/190496719 0496819049721904976.pdf.

[190] FCC, Order of the First Senate of 24 March 2021 – 1 BvR 2656/18 –, ECLI:DE:BVerfG: 2021:rs20210324.1bvr265618, paras. 1-270.

[191] FCC, Order of the First Senate of 24 March 2021 – 1 BvR 2656/18 –, ECLI:DE:BVerfG: 2021:rs20210324.1bvr265618, paras. 90, 115 ff.; At EU level, the ECJ ruled in infringement proceedings that the Federal Republic of Germany had failed to fulfil requirements under Directive 2008/50/EC of the European Parliament and of the Council of 21 May 2008 on ambient air quality and cleaner air for Europe ('Air Quality Directive') by failing for many years to take sufficiently effective action against exceedances of limit values for the air pollutant nitrogen dioxide (Case C-635/18).

[192] The Hague District Court, *Vereniging Milieudefensie v Royal Dutch Shell Plc*, C/09/571932 / HA ZA 19-379 (engelse versie), ECLI:NL:RBDHA:2021:5339.

[193] *Center for Social Justice Studies et al. v. Presidency of the Republic et al.* (acción de tutela), Judgment T-622/16, Constitutional Court of Colombia, unofficial English translation, para. 5.3 [76], available at: http://files.harmonywithnatureun.org/uploads/upload838.pdf.

Moreover, the Court underlined the importance of timely legal action for the greatest 84
challenge of climate change and sticked to 'a more extensive interpretation' of the
precautionary principle 'whereby the burden of proof is transferred on the potentially
contaminating agent (be it a State, a company or a citizen), who must demonstrate that
their activity or residues that occur will not significantly affect the environment'.[194]

Besides, *Kim Yujin et al. v. South Korea* 'is the first case of its kind in East Asia 85
and will also provide a precedent for how litigants can bring cases and how courts are
able to manage and hear climate litigation during the COVID-19 era'[195] and thus could
probably serve as the succeeder of the *Urgenda* case.

Whether and to what extent customary international law can also serve as a legal 86
source for judicial proceedings remains questionable. However, customary law foundations can be found in cases that address the law of nature. In Uganda, where the Rights
of Nature were included in the 2019 National Environmental Act, the Buliisa District
Local Government Council signed a Resolution on 22 November 2019 in recognition
of the Customary Laws of the Bagungu Custodian Clans, noting the 'concern of the
Bagungu clan leaders for Butoka (Mother Earth) and for the future generations of all
species of the Earth', and their 'ancestral responsibility to protect the wellbeing of their
land, and of the planet'.

The non-governmental organisation Society for Alternative Learning and Transfor- 87
mation (SALT) has been working with local communities in Tharaka district, Eastern
Kenya, to revitalise their Earth-centred customary laws and indigenous practices, to help
build back resilience in climate-changed times.

The debate on the derivation and form of liability is not only found in public law 88
actions, i.e. against a state or an authority, but is also becoming increasingly prevalent in
private or corporate law actions[196] where human rights responsibility and environmental
responsibility in the form of climate responsibility are about to become a sub-category of
CSR.[197] The recent and still pending *Lliuya case*[198] exemplifies this development. In this
case, a Peruvian citizen claimed a lawsuit against the German energy provider RWE as
being an emittent of heavy amounts of carbon dioxide into the atmosphere. The caused
air pollution severely contributes to GHG in the atmosphere, and thus to temperature
rise which consequently changes the ecosystem in Peru. The claimant Lliuya argued the
melting glaciers of the Peruvian Andes to be a result of RWE's misbehaviour which in
turn led to the desertification of his livelihood. The court of first instance (Essen District
Court) dismissed the claim and reasoned that the amount of pollution in relation to the
heating of Planet Earth would be too low. However, the court of second instance did
not dismiss the case but rather ordered further inspections on site. The case is currently
pending due to the SARS-CoV-2 pandemic. Presumably, this case will culminate into

---

[194] *Center for Social Justice Studies et al. v. Presidency of the Republic et al.* (acción de tutela), Judgment
T-622/16, Constitutional Court of Colombia, unofficial English translation, para. 7.36. [228].

[195] Setzer and Yoshida, 'The Trends and Challenges of Climate Change Litigation and Human Rights'
(2020) 2 *European Human Rights Law Review*, 140-52.

[196] E.g. *Smith v Fonterra Co-operative Group Ltd Hook*, New Zealand High Court, [2020] NZHC 419;
further reading: Maria, Warnock, Allan and Pirini, 'Tort to the Environment: A Stretch Too Far or a
Simple Step Forward? Smith v Fonterra Co-operative Group Ltd and Others [2020] NZHC 419' (2021) 00
Journal of Environmental Law, 1-16.

[197] Kahl and Weller, 'Liability for Climate Damages – Synthesis and future prospects' in Kahl and
Weller, *Climate Change Litigation – A Handbook* (2021), Conclusions, mn. 67.

[198] *Saúl Anannías Luciano Lliuya v RWE AG*, Higher Regional Court Hamm.

a high-profile case 'not only for the climate change regime but also as an indication of what forms of air pollution could be claimed in Germany in the future.'[199]

II. The Enforcement of a 'Right to a Healthy Climate'

89   'The cooperation between the national legislative power and the judicial system is particularly relevant in the case of climate change policies, as climate change narratives grow in importance in the legislative debate, both nationally and internationally.'[200] What is problematic is the recurring influence on jurisprudence or its implementation by 'mandates of the Court being overturned by action or inaction of ministries [...] or being reversed by legislative reform' in different parts of the world.[201] This is compounded by the frequent lack of procedural requirements, which deny access to justice entirely or return it to national jurisdiction, as in the case of the EU courts, for example, and thus only national legal decisions take precedence. In this way, regional or even international decisions are prevented which generates high costs but even more erodes the rule of law and public trust making climate change an environmental and socio-economic issue.[202] Despite an often strong and comprehensive body of environmental policy and regulation, frameworks are not providing the results they should because they are not properly implemented or enforced.

90   In contrast, the *rule of law* concept as a whole is receiving increased attention on the international arena. At the European level, this has led, for example, to the appointment of the Chief Trade Enforcement Officer (CTEO) Mr Denis Redonnet, who will in future accompany the implementation of the EU's multilateral, regional and bilateral trade agreements and shall ensure that commitments under EU FTAs are met, amongst others, 'with focus on tackling climate change, and; the environment'. The EU legislation has hitherto been inconsistent regarding the enforcement of the TSD in the EU's trade agreements. The amended Trade Enforcement Regulation 654/2014 is contrary to the international obligations of the EU in the WTO context and public international law rules and suggests that it will hardly be applied.[203]

91   Moreover, single entry points for submitting complaints, a Complaints Office (which is dedicated to TDI complaints and as such distinct from the Single Entry Point) in order to 'coordinate dispute settlement proceedings between the EU and non-EU countries in the World Trade Organization, and; under EU trade agreements' and ensure 'the availability of effective dispute settlement rules'[204] as well as 'an effective arsenal to enforce EU rights under international agreements (the Enforcement Regulation), to protect itself from coercive actions (the Anti-Coercion Instrument) and has the necessary tools to manage investment disputes (the Regulation on Financial Responsibility).'[205] Neverthe-

---

[199] Huck et al., 'The Right to Breathe Clean Air and Access to Justice – Legal State of Play in International, European and National Law' (2021) 13(10) *International Environmental Law (eJournal)*, 1 (19).

[200] Colby et al., 'Judging Climate Change: The Role of the Judiciary in the Fight Against Climate Change' (2020) 7(3) *Oslo Law Review*, 168 (180).

[201] Setzer and Byrnes, *Global trends in climate change litigation: 2020 snapshot, Policy Report* (2020), 24 f.

[202] https://www.clientearth.org/projects/access-to-justice-for-a-greener-europe/updates/the-general-co urt-of-the-eu-rejects-the-people-climate-case-as-inadmissible/.

[203] Weiß and Furculita, 'The EU in Search for Stronger Enforcement Rules: Assessing the Proposed Amendments to Trade Enforcement Regulation 654/2014' (2020) 23(4) *JIEL*, 865-84.

[204] Through the reform of the WTO Dispute Settlement Understanding, the negotiation and upkeep of bilateral dispute settlement systems and the reform of investment state dispute settlement through the establishment of a multilateral investment court.

[205] https://ec.europa.eu/trade/trade-policy-and-you/contacts/chief-trade-enforcement-officer/; in this context, the use of regional and preferential trade agreements (RTA and PTA) in order to promote

less, access to direct enforcement of decisions at different levels are lacking. Too often, international courts must return their decisions to national courts for implementation (e.g. ECtHR) and are thus left to their assessment and implementation.

III. De Facto Influences on Jurisdiction

SDG 13 is significantly affected by the impact of the global pandemic. Due to **92** the numerous lockdowns and the conversion of all public institutions, and thus also the courts, to electronic or other solutions, there is a decline in processed cases in 2020. In addition, the lack of financial security is likely to have led to a decline in pending cases almost everywhere. Perhaps this development will be reversed after the re-establishment of adapted public structures, if the connection between the outbreak of the global pandemic and man-made climate change is linked, which could ultimately lead to a strengthening of the environmental *rule of law*. 'Another possible source of climate litigation could be challenges to government bailouts of the oil, airline and car industries.'[206] 'Early findings on the links between biodiversity, climate change and the COVID-19 outbreak will be included in the next Panel report, to be issued in 2021.'[207] In addition, SDG 13 received special attention in 2019 in the context of political and social campaigns, e.g. Fridays for Future, Scientists for Future, Extinction Rebellion and many more. These movements are accompanied by the global use of 'high-profile strategic climate litigation' which is used as part of a protesting strategy with a continued focus on human rights and with different strategies used in recent litigation against major private sector emitters (so-called 'Carbon Majors').[208] Certainly, impact will also be exerted by the Environmental Goods Agreement still to be negotiated at WTO level.[209] However, the conclusion of the plurilateral trade agreement which should contribute to environmental protection, climate action, green growth and sustainable development has so far been prevented by failing to define a green good (amongst others). Regionally, at least at the European level, detrimental currents, such as of right-wing populist parties in EU member states, can also be identified,[210] which strongly oppose the very existence of climate change leading to disinformation campaigns on the subject matter. These, should they continue to grow, will certainly influence the further development of jurisprudential interpretation of climate change and the assessment of associated liability obligations.

E. Conclusion on SDG 13

The Global Agenda 2030 stresses that climate change is the main challenge threaten- **93** ing humanity. It is therefore the responsibility of the legislative, executive and judicial branches to address this challenge inernally and externally on different levels. Historical-

---

environment and climate objectives is also likely to affect the climate impacts of global trade relations in the future, thereby opening up further *access to justice*, assumingly in coordination with the International Centre for Trade and Sustainable Development (ICTSD).

[206] See Setzer and Byrnes, *Global trends in climate change litigation: 2020 snapshot, Policy Report* (2020) 13.

[207] A/75/266, *Harmony with Nature, Report of the Secretary-General*, 28 July 2020, para. 13.

[208] Setzer and Byrnes, *Global trends in climate change litigation: 2020 snapshot, Policy Report* (2020).

[209] 18 participants representing 46 WTO members are engaged in negotiations seeking to eliminate tariffs on a number of important environment-related products: https://www.wto.org/english/tratop_e/en vir_e/ega_e.htm.

[210] Fisher, 'Challenges for the EU Climate Change Regime' (2020) 21 *German Law Journal*, 5 (7).

ly, the recognition that climate change is an event that threatens humanity dates back (at least) to the 1970 s. The IPCC provides authoritative and reliable evidence in terms of both research findings and areas for action, and these need to be translated into the policy context and into a legal framework of different sectors like agriculture, energy, transport or water management that can serve as a new basis for affected groups and individuals. The withholding of individual rights and those of groups impacted by direct and indirect effects of climate change must be revised. The changes brought about by climate change and the causes that contribute to it have been widely researched and assessments are available that provide sufficient impetus for the necessary action in national, interregional and international legal frameworks.

94   However, the legal and judicial field suffers from the acceptance of the lack of standing and the difficult question of how to overcome the burden of proof and sufficiently establish causality. At a time that lays bare the human rights dimension of climate change and the appointment of a Special Rapporteur on Climate Change and Human Rights is being discussed, it would be a right step into the future to grant a legal basis that helps to claim compensation for damages caused by climate change, for example.

95   Planetary boundaries (which are, however, variable and not fixed even in terms of geological time) needs to be respected and brought into the focus of Earth jurisprudence. This is another area that partly overlaps with climate change jurisprudence and needs to be systematically placed in an appropriate legal framework.

96   By all means, one aspect can be gleaned from jurisdiction: The discussion and jurisprudential evaluation of climate-relevant measures, interventions and violations of internationally agreed goals can no longer be seen as isolated cases, but are being vigorously pursued in strategic campaigns. This phenomenon can hardly be found in any other field of law to such an extent. The close observation of judicial trends and the development of the legal basis on which judges are able to decide at all is of utmost necessity to further consolidate this globally impacted field, not only for the environmental area of justice, but also for extraterritorial solidarity as well as the expansion of social justice in particular. And yet, climate change litigation and jurisprudence rooted in territorial jurisdiction will hardly solve the global issue of climate change and even more so cannot invoke a separate human right to a healthy climate, albeit every single case might raise increasing awareness in so that legislation and legal resilient frameworks might follow.

97   While SDG 13 aims to maintain planetary boundaries, it also shows clearly what is meant by this in whole: Nature and humans are inextricably intertwined, belonging to the same system that we call Mother Earth. Science shows the measures needed to maintain this system. Humanity inherent in this system develops the means to implement these measures, and legally, human behaviour is increasingly reprimanded to comply with them. The fine weave of decisions results in an overall picture that, to a considerable extent, strives towards the goals of SDG 13, but sometimes even beyond that, aiming for a new and inevitable equitable balance. However, the jurisprudence simultaneously points to the difficulties that need to be overcome in order to remedy the global, cross-border issue of climate change. National jurisdictions may be very progressive, but as far as interregional or international courts only rarely decide on climate mitigation actions, these lack the all-important basis of forming uniform, holistic foundations linked to (environmental) justice, equity and human rights that would provide the necessary global impetus. Aside from the question of (human rights) state liability, it will be particularly important in the future to ensure the traceability and exposure to liability of private actors as well as to shape the enforcement of relevant rulings, opinions and verdicts, which also encounters many difficulties at present. The

overall process must not fall short of the vision of SDG 13 in any way, especially not in the involvement of all levels[211] and the just and shared distribution of responsibility.[212]

---

[211] Similar thoughts: Kahl and Weller, 'Liability for Climate Damages – Synthesis and future prospects' in Kahl and Weller (eds), *Climate Change Litigation – A Handbook* (2021), Conclusions, mn. 69.

[212] Babatunde, 'Distributive Justice in the Age of Climate Change' (2020) 33 *Canadian Journal of Law & Jurisprudence*, 263; see Fisher, 'Challenges for the EU Climate Change Regime' (2020) 21 *German Law Journal*, 5 (7).

Goal 14
Conserve and sustainably use the oceans, seas and marine resources for sustainable development

14.1 By 2025, prevent and significantly reduce marine pollution of all kinds, in particular from land-based activities, including marine debris and nutrient pollution

14.2 By 2020, sustainably manage and protect marine and coastal ecosystems to avoid significant adverse impacts, including by strengthening their resilience, and take action for their restoration in order to achieve healthy and productive oceans

14.3 Minimize and address the impacts of ocean acidification, including through enhanced scientific cooperation at all levels

14.4 By 2020, effectively regulate harvesting and end overfishing, illegal, unreported and unregulated fishing and destructive fishing practices and implement science-based management plans, in order to restore fish stocks in the shortest time feasible, at least to levels that can produce maximum sustainable yield as determined by their biological characteristics

14.5 By 2020, conserve at least 10 per cent of coastal and marine areas, consistent with national and international law and based on the best available scientific information

14.6 By 2020, prohibit certain forms of fisheries subsidies which contribute to over-capacity and overfishing, eliminate subsidies that contribute to illegal, unreported and unregulated fishing and refrain from introducing new such subsidies, recognizing that appropriate and effective special and differential treatment for developing and least developed countries should be an integral part of the World Trade Organization fisheries subsidies negotiation[1]

14.7 By 2030, increase the economic benefits to small island developing States and least developed countries from the sustainable use of marine resources, including through sustainable management of fisheries, aquaculture and tourism

14.a Increase scientific knowledge, develop research capacity and transfer marine technology, taking into account the Intergovernmental Oceanographic Commission Criteria and Guidelines on the Transfer of Marine Technology, in order to improve ocean health and to enhance the contribution of marine biodiversity to the development of developing countries, in particular small island developing States and least developed countries

14.b Provide access for small-scale artisanal fishers to marine resources and markets

14.c Enhance the conservation and sustainable use of oceans and their resources by implementing international law as reflected in the United Nations Convention on the Law of the Sea, which provides the legal framework for the conservation and sustainable use of oceans and their resources, as recalled in paragraph 158 of "The future we want"

Word Count related to 'Marine Resources' and 'fishing/fisheries/fishers' and 'Convention on the Law of the Sea': 2
A/RES/70/1 – Transforming our world: the 2030 Agenda for Sustainable Development: 'Marine Resources': 11 'fishing/fisheries/fishers': 14 'Convention on the Law of the Sea': 2
Instruments mentioned in A/RES/70/1 in the section entitled: 'Sustainable Development Goals and targets':

---

[1] Taking into account ongoing World Trade Organization negotiations, the Doha Development Agenda and the Hong Kong ministerial mandate.

A/RES/69/313 – Addis Ababa Action Agenda of the Third International Conference on Financing for Development adopted on 27 July 2015: 'Marine Resources': 8 'fishing/fisheries/fishers': 10 'Convention on the Law of the Sea': 1
A/RES/66/288 – The future we want (Rio +20 Declaration) adopted on 27 July 2012: 'Marine Resources': 26 'fishing/fisheries/fishers': 37 'Convention on the Law of the Sea': 5
A/RES/55/2 – United Nations Millennium Declaration adopted on 8 September 2000: 'Marine Resources': 0 'fishing/fisheries/fishers': 0 'Convention on the Law of the Sea': 0

Select Bibliography: Aldo E. Chircop, 'The International Maritime Organization' in Donald R. Rothwell, Alex Oude Elferink, Karen Scott and Tim Stephens (eds), *The Oxford Handbook of the Law of the Sea* (Oxford University Press, Oxford 2015), 416; Donald K. Anton, Robert A. Makgill and Cymie R. Payne, 'Seabed Mining—Advisory Opinion on Responsibility and Liability' (2011) 41 *Environmental Policy and Law*, 60; Smiriti Bahety and Julian Mukiibi, *WTO Fisheries Subsidies Negotiations: Main Issues and Interests of Least Developed Countries* (CUTS International, Geneva 2017); David Le Blanc, Clovis Freire and Marjo Vierros, 'Mapping the linkages between oceans and other Sustainable Development Goals: A preliminary exploration' (2017) 149 *DESA Working Paper* (ST/ESA/2017/DWP/149); Neil Boister, *An Introduction to Transnational Criminal Law* (2nd edition, Oxford University Press, Oxford 2018), 202; Alan Boyle, 'Climate Change, Sustainable Development, and Human Rights' in Markus Kaltenborn, Markus Krajewski and Heike Kuhn, *Sustainable Development Goals and Human Rights* (Springer Nature Switzerland AG, Cham 2019), 174; Fanny Chenillat, Thierry Huck, Christophe Maes, Nicolas Grima and Bruno Blanke, 'Fate of floating plastic debris released along the coasts in a global ocean model' (2021) 165 *Marine Pollution Bulletin*, 1; Thomas Cottier, 'Property Rights, Legal Security and Development' in Thomas Cottier and Krista Nadakavukaren Schefer, *Elgar Encyclopedia of International Economic Law* (Edward Elgar Publishing, Cheltenham/Northampton 2017), 516; Daniela Diz, David Johnson, Michael Riddell, Sian Rees, Jessica Battle, Kristina Gjerde, Sebastian Hennige and J. Murray Roberts, 'Mainstreaming marine biodiversity into the SDGs: The role of other effective area-based conservation measures (SDG 14.5)' (2018) 93 *Marine Policy*, 251; Robert A. Duce, James N. Galloway and Peter S. Liss, 'The impacts of atmospheric deposition to the ocean on marine ecosystems and climate' (2009) 58 *WMO Bulletin*, 61; European Parliament, *The environmental impacts of plastics and micro-plastics use, waste and pollution: EU and national measures* (EU, Brussels 2020); Food and Agricultural Organisation, *The State of the World Fisheries and Aquaculture – Sustainability in Action*, (FAO, Rome 2020); David Freestone, 'Advisory Opinion of the Seabed Disputes Chamber' (2011) 15 *ASIL Insights*; Duncan French, 'From the Depths: Rich Pickings of Principles of Sustainable Development and General International Law on the Ocean Floor – the Seabed Disputes Chamber's 2011Advisory Opinion' (2011) 26 *International Journal of Marine and Coastal Law*, 525; Duncan French, 'The Sofia Guiding Statements on sustainable development principles in the decisions of international tribunals' in Marie-Claire Cordonier Segger and H. E. Judge Christopher Gregory Weeramantry, *Sustainable Development Principles in the Decisions of International*

Courts and Tribunals, 1992 – 2012 (Routledge, UK/USA 2017), 202; Daniel A. Friess, Toe Toe Aung, Mark Huxham, Catherine Lovelock, Nibedita Mukherjee and Sigit Sasmito, 'SDG 14: Life below Water – Impacts on Mangroves' in Pia Katila, Carol J. Pierce Colfer, Wil de Jong, Glenn Galloway, Pablo Pacheco and Georg Winkel (eds), *Sustainable Development Goals: Their Impacts on Forests and People* (Cambridge University Press, Cambridge 2019), 445; Markus Gehring and Alexandre Genest, 'Disputes on sustainable development in the WTO regime' in Marie-Claire Cordonier Segger and H. E. Judge Christopher Gregory Weeramantry, *Sustainable Development Principles in the Decisions of International Courts and Tribunals, 1992 – 2012* (Routledge, UK/USA 2017); Gabriele Goettsche-Wanli, 'The Role of the United Nations, including its Secretariat in Global Ocean Governance' in David Joseph Attard, David M. Ong and Dino Kritsiotis, *The IMLI Treatise On Global Ocean Governance: Volume I: UN and Global Ocean Governance* (Oxford University Press, Oxford 2018), 4; Megan L. Grant, Jennifer L. Lavers, Ian Hutton and Alexander L. Bond 4, 'Seabird breeding islands as sinks for marine plastic debris' (2021) 276 *Environmental Pollution*; James Harrison, *Saving the Oceans Through Law – The International Legal Framework for the Protection of the Marine Environment* (Oxford University Press, Oxford 2017); Winfried Huck, 'The UN Sustainable Development Goals and the Governance of Global Public Goods, The Quest for Legitimacy' (2021) in Massimo Iovane, Fulvio M. Palombino, Daniele Amoroso and Giovanni Zarra (eds), *The Protection of General Interests in Contemporary International Law: A Theoretical and Empirical Inquiry* (Oxford University Press, Oxford 2021), 361; Jeffrey A. McNeely, 'Protected Areas, Biodiversity, and the Risks of Climate Change' in Fabrice G. Renaud, Karen Sudmeier-Rieux, Marisol Estrella and Udo Nehren (eds), *Ecosystem-Based Disaster Risk Reduction and Adaptation in Practice, Advances in Natural and Technological Hazards Research* (Springer, Cham 2016), 379; John H. Knox., 'Human Rights, Environmental Protection, and the Sustainable Development Goals' (2015) 24 *Wash. L. Rev.*, 517; Mamadou Hébié, 'principle 6, Special Situation of Developing Countries' in Jorge E. Viñuales (ed), *The Rio Declaration of Environment and Development – A Commentary* (Oxford University Press, Oxford 2015); Essam Yassin Mohammed, Dave Steinbach and Paul Steele, 'Fiscal reforms for sustainable marine fisheries governance: Delivering the SDGs and ensuring no one is left behind' (2018) 93 *Marine Policy*, 262; Mara Ntona and Elisa Morgera, 'Connecting SDG 14 with the other Sustainable Development Goals through marine spatial planning' (2018) 93 *Marine Policy*, 214; OECD, *OECD Review of Fisheries 2020* (OECD Publishing, Paris 2020); Colin T. Reid, 'Protection of Sites' in Emma Lees and Jorge E. Viñuales (eds), *The Oxford Handbook of Comparative Environmental Law* (Oxford University Press, Oxford 2019), 848; Nadia Sánchez Castillo-Winckels, 'How the Sustainable Development Goals promote a new conception of ocean commons governance' in: Duncan French and Louis J. Kotzé (eds), *Sustainable Development Goals – Law, Theory and Implementation* (Edward Elgar Publishing, Cheltenham/Northampton 2018), 117; Judith Schäli, 'Trade, Environment and the Law of the Sea' in Thomas Cottier and Krista Nadakavukaren Schefer, *Elgar Encyclopedia of international Economic Law* (Edward Elgar Publishing, Cheltenham/Northampton 2017), 632; Surya P. Subedi, 'The Role of the Commission on the Limits of the Continental Shelf in the Governance of the Seas and Oceans' (2018) in David Joseph Attard, David M Ong Dino Kritsiotis, *The IMLI Treatise On Global Ocean Governance: Volume I: UN and Global Ocean Governance* (Oxford University Press, Oxford 2018), 94; Tullio Treves, 'Historical Development of the Law of the Sea' in Donald R. Rothwell et al. (eds), *The Oxford Handbook of the Law of the Sea* (Oxford University Press, Oxford 2015).

A. Background and Origin of SDG 14

1   The ocean as the largest ecosystem of the world holds huge number of biodiversity systems such as 'mangroves, coral reefs and wetlands, pelagic waters, seamounts, submarine ridges and the seafloor itself'[2] and interacts in a complex way with the global climate system.[3] According to the IPCC, all people on Earth depend directly or indirectly on the ocean. The global ocean covers 71 per cent of the Earth's surface and contains about 97 per cent of the Earth's water.[4] The state of the ocean and cryosphere interacts with each aspect of sustainability reflected in the SDGs. For example, fish,

---

[2] UNGA Open Working Group on SDGs, *Compendium of TST Issues Briefs* (2014), 185.

[3] United Nations Educational, Scientific and Cultural Organization (UNESCO), *Global Ocean Science Report* (2017), 3; For more detailed information on the interaction between the ocean and the climate system, see Kagan, *Ocean Atmosphere Interaction and Climate Modelling* (1995).

[4] IPCC, 'Summary for Policymakers' in *IPCC Special Report on the Ocean and Cryosphere in a Changing Climate* (2019), 5.

as a resource originating from the ocean, is an important factor for the supply of proteins.[5] Furthermore, the oceans also represent a significant resource from an economic perspective.[6]

However, the oceans and their associated ecosystems and resources are under massive   2
threat, since particularly climate change causes manifold and severe impact to the ocean and the cryosphere. To IPCC it is certain that the global ocean has warmed unabated since 1970 and has taken up more than 90 per cent of the excess heat in the climate system.[7] The current observation and further estimation revealing a serious change of the most crucial systems of the Earth. Currently, the global mean sea level (GMSL) is rising with a higher acceleration in recent decades due to increasing rates of ice loss from the Greenland and Antarctic ice sheets.[8] Extreme sea level events that are historically rare (once per century in the recent past) are projected to occur frequently (at least once per year) at many locations by 2050 in all Representative Concentration Pathway (RCP) scenarios, especially in tropical regions.[9]

Over the 21st century, the ocean is projected to transition to unprecedented condi-   3
tions with increased temperatures, greater upper ocean stratification, further acidification and oxygen decline.[10] Today, climate change, the loss of biodiversity and the state of overfishing play a central role[11] in endangering the food supply of large parts of the population.[12] In addition, increasing pollution of the world's oceans (marine debris) puts at risk a large number of living creatures and thus also significantly interferes with natural ecosystems.[13]

Since humankind has been utilising the ocean, references have been made to the   4
proclamation of sovereign rights to its use, e.g. its navigation and its exploitation of resources. While the *Treaty of Tordesillas*[14] divided the ocean into different legal spheres for the first time in 1494, Grotius' *mare liberum* and the *Peace of Westphalia* in 1648 laid the foundation for the freedom of the seas doctrine and a distinction of the territorial sea and the high seas.[15] Although these developments led to increasing international

---

[5] Griggs et al., *A Guide to SDG Interactions: From Science to Implementation* (2017), 190; UN, *The role of seafood in global food security*, 3.

[6] In 2015, the ocean's asset value was estimated at US $ 24 trillion: WWF, *Reviving the Ocean Economy – The case for action 2015*, 15.

[7] IPCC, 'Summary for Policymakers' *in IPCC Special Report on the Ocean and Cryosphere in a Changing Climate* (2019), 9.

[8] IPCC, 'Summary for Policymakers' *in IPCC Special Report on the Ocean and Cryosphere in a Changing Climate* (2019), 10.

[9] IPCC, 'Summary for Policymakers' *in IPCC Special Report on the Ocean and Cryosphere in a Changing Climate* (2019), 20.

[10] IPCC, 'Summary for Policymakers' *in IPCC Special Report on the Ocean and Cryosphere in a Changing Climate* (2019), 18.

[11] FAO, *The State of World Fisheries and Aquaculture* (2018), 40.

[12] World Bank, *The Potential of the Blue Economy* (2017), 15; Friess et al., 'SDG 14: Life below Water – Impacts on Mangroves' *in Sustainable Development Goals: Their Impacts on Forests and People* (2019), 445 (461); Overfishing also leads to a significant loss of welfare in the fisheries sector: World Bank, *The Sunken Billions Revisited* (2017), 36.

[13] WWF, *Reviving the Ocean Economy – The case for action 2015* (2015), 23.

[14] Davenport, *European Treaties Bearing on the History of the United States and its Dependencies to 1648* (1917): Treaty of Tordesillas of 7 June 1494, Ratified in Arévalo by King Ferdinand II of Aragon and Queen Isabella I of Castile on 2 July 1494 and in Setúbal by the King of Portugal on 5 September 1494, issued by Pope Alexander VI., bull *Inter Caetera* of 4 May 1493: Agreement between the Portuguese and the Spanish Kingdoms to establish a new boundary line between the two crowns. The line is to run from pole to pole, 370 miles west of the Cape Verde Islands; further reading: Díaz-Trechuelo, Lourdes, 'El Tratado de Tordesillas y su proyección en el Pacífico' (1994) 4 *Revista Española del Pacífico*, 11-22.

[15] See Treves, 'Historical Development of the Law of the Sea' in Rothwell et al. (eds), *The Oxford Handbook of the Law of the Sea* (2015), 3-23.

trade on a broad scale (mostly grounded on colonialism and accompanied with slavery, exploitation and disempowerment[16]), it was not until the 21st century that concerns for the conservation and protection of the marine environment and biospheres were raised.

5   A clear reference to marine protection can be found in the 1972 Stockholm Declaration. During the Stockholm Conference, marine protection was established as a central component of environmental protection, created as a stand-alone principle in a first approach to preventing pollution of the world's oceans.[17]

6   In 1982, the United Nations Convention on the Law of the Sea (UNCLOS)[18] created a comprehensive body of law that, amongst others, includes regulations concerning pollution of the oceans and provides a comprehensive definition of the term 'pollution of the maritime environment' which refers to an

> [...] introduction by man, directly or indirectly, of substances or energy into the marine environment, including estuaries, which results or is likely to result in such deleterious effects as harm to living resources and marine life, hazards to human health, hindrance to marine activities, including fishing and other legitimate uses of the sea, impairment of quality for use of sea water and reduction of amenities [...][19]

7   According to Art. 192 UNCLOS, states also have a general obligation to protect and conserve the marine environment. Overall, Part VII of the Convention contains extensive regulations on the 'protection and conservation of the marine environment'.[20] When interpreting the legal background of SDG 14 in its meaning, two aspects are of particular importance: As with the *mare liberum*, UNCLOS also guarantees an area of freedom of the sea in addition to other zones although the premise assumed at the time of Grotius that the sea and its resources are inexhaustible has clearly been refuted (→ Goal 14 mn. 14 ff.). Moreover, UNCLOS does not confer absolute sovereignty rights in the extended zones, but only endows them with certain defensive rights (e.g. customs, fiscal, immigration or sanitary laws). As a result, the sea is subject to shared use and management in all its areas, albeit to varying degrees. This idea of commonship regarding benefits, burden-sharing and the 'further development of specific areas of the law of the sea'[21] is reflected in the development and formulation of SDG 14.

8   The report 'Our Common Future' (Brundtland Report), published in 1987 by the World Commission on Environment and Development, dealt extensively with oceans and their global significance. According to the report, the oceans represent the 'balance of life'.[22] However, this balance is under serious threat due to several central factors such as overexploitation, pollution, and land-based development.[23] To overcome these perils and enable sustainable development, the report also contains a variety of measures for ocean management.[24]

---

[16] See instead of many: Piketty, *Capital and Ideology* (2020).

[17] UN, *Report of the United Nations Conference on the human environment 1972*, Principle 7: 'States shall take all possible steps to prevent pollution of the seas by substances that are liable to create hazards to human health, to harm living resources and marine life, to damage amenities or to interfere with other legitimate uses of the sea'.

[18] United Nations Convention on the Law of the Sea (UNCLOS), Montego Bay, 10 December 1982, 1833 UNTS, 397 (entered into force on 16 November 1994).

[19] UNCLOS, Art. 1 IV.

[20] UNCLOS, Part VII/, Art. 192-273.

[21] UNGA Open Working Group on SDGs, *Compendium of TST Issues Briefs* (2014), 185.

[22] Report of the World Commission on Environment and Development: Our Common Future, Part III Chapter 10 I, para. 1.

[23] Report of the World Commission on Environment and Development: Our Common Future, Part III Chapter 10, para. 9.

[24] Report of the World Commission on Environment and Development: Our Common Future, Part III Chapter 10 I, para 2.

In 1992, the protection of the oceans was also extensively included in Agenda 21.[25]   **9**
The call for ocean management raised in the Brundtland Report was taken up and
further elaborated Such as in the Agenda 21 and the Rio Declaration[26] which already
linked the management of coastal and marine areas,[27] articulated the precautionary and
the ecosystem approaches, and show a structure that is now echoed in SDG 14.2.[28]

Two years later, the aspects contained in Agenda 21 were taken up again in the 1994   **10**
report of the global conference on the sustainable development of Small Island Developing States (SIDS)[29] and expanded to include a comprehensive action programme. The
focus was on SIDS and their particular vulnerability in being ecologically fragile and
sensitive to environmental disasters and the effects of climate change such as hurricanes,
floods, storms and sea level rise which is even aggravated by their small size, limited
resources, and geographic dispersion. The natural isolation from markets and the prevention from economies of scale makes the ocean and coastal environment a strategic
and 'valuable development resource' for SIDS.[30]

In 1995, the 'Agreement for the implementation of the provisions of the United   **11**
Nations Convention on the Law of the Sea of 10 December 1982 relating to the conservation and management of straddling fish stocks and highly migratory fish stocks'
established an approach to the protection of fish stocks.[31] In this context, a first definition of the term 'fish' has been established: 'molluscs and crustaceans except those
belonging to sedentary species as defined in article 77 of the Convention'.[32] Within the
framework of the Johannesburg Declaration on Sustainable Development in 2002, the
special importance of protecting global fish stocks was again emphasised.[33]

In 2012, the UN adopted 'The future we want',[34] a comprehensive concept with   **12**
various aspects of sustainability where oceans and seas were given their own section. All
previous aspects were integrated and at the same time extensively linked to other aspects
of sustainable development. The conservation and sustainable use of the oceans, for
example, contributes to 'poverty eradication, sustained economic growth, food security
and creation of sustainable livelihoods and decent work, while at the same time protecting biodiversity and the marine environment and addressing the impacts of climate

---

[25] United Nations Conference on Environment and Development (UNCED), Rio de Janeiro, Brazil, 3
to 14 June 1992 (Agenda 21), Chapter 17: 'Protection of the oceans, all kinds of seas, including enclosed
and semi-enclosed seas, and coastal areas and the protection, rational use and development of their living
resources'.

[26] UN, *Report of the United Nations Conference on Environment and Development*, Rio de Janeiro, 3–14
June 1992' (Rio Declaration) (n 2), annex I.

[27] UNCED, Rio de Janeiro, Brazil, 3 to 14 June 1992 (Agenda 21), Chapter 17, Programme Area A:
'Integrated management and sustainable development of coastal and marine areas, including exclusive
economic zone'.

[28] Goettsche-Wanli, 'The Role of the United Nations, including its Secretariat in Global Ocean Governance' in Attard and Ong and Kritsiotis, *The IMLI Treatise On Global Ocean Governance: Volume I: UN
and Global Ocean Governance* (2018), 13.

[29] A/CONF.167/9.

[30] Rio Declaration, Principle 6; see also Hébié, 'Principle 6, Special Situation of Developing Countries'
in Viñuales, *The Rio Declaration of Environment and Development, A Commentary* (2015), 217.

[31] A/CONF.164/37, Art. 2: 'The objective of this Agreement is to ensure the long-term conservation and
sustainable use of straddling fish stocks and highly migratory fish stocks through effective implementation
of the relevant provisions of the Convention'.

[32] A/CONF.164/37, Art. 1 c).

[33] A/CONF.199/20, para. 13.

[34] A/RES/66/288, *The future we want*, 11 September 2012.

change.'[35] Furthermore, the signatory states were urged to implement UNCLOS and the 1995 Fish Stock Agreement in a holistic manner.[36]

13   In the final drafting of the SDGs, two different approaches were discussed: On the one hand, goals related to the ocean should be integrated into various other goals.[37] On the other hand, a stand-alone goal with a reference to the sea should be created.[38] In the end, the second approach prevailed, resulting in the creation of SDG 14. From 2021, the UN Decade of Ocean Research for Sustainable Development will be proclaimed to push for and generate more reliable data on the protection and conservation of the marine environment to keep other SDGs on track[39] (→ Goal 13 mn. 46, 50, Goal 15, Goal 8 mn. 81, Goal 2 mn. 60, Goal 14 mn. 46 ff.).

B. Scope and Dimensions of SDG 14

14   Oceans and seas form a vital part of our ecosystem and their health and survival are crucial to the existence of the planet as we know it. With increasing ocean warming, acidification and marine pollution, the habitat and existence of several species is under threat, and with it the livelihoods of many communities that rely on fisheries for their livelihoods.[40]

15   Indicator 14.1.1 a thus includes an Index of Coastal Eutrophication (ICEP) and 14.1.1 b of plastic debris density. Global fish production is expected to reach 200 Mt by 2029 and 90 per cent of the fish produced is projected to be utilised for human consumption.[41] Further, oceans and seas also absorb large amounts of carbon dioxide and have a direct impact on climate change. Thus, a legal framework that aims at conservation and sustainable use of oceans, seas and marine resources is of utmost importance for the economy as well as for preserving biodiversity and the environment. In this regard, SDG 14 with eight targets aims to lay out a framework of various aspects of the marine ecosystem and related economy that needs attention to ensure the conservation and sustainable use of oceans, seas and marine resources.

---

[35] A/RES/66/288, *The future we want*, 11 September 2012, para. 158.

[36] A/RES/66/288, para. 158; UNGA Open Working Group on SDGs, *Compendium of TST Issues Briefs* (2014), 186.

[37] The following two categories can be found: 'Inclusion in SDGs that relate to a healthy and resilient planet and productive ecosystems, environmental sustainability, respect for planetary boundaries and / or the maintenance of the global commons. (2) Inclusion in SDGs that relate to determinants of human well-being, such as food security and good nutrition.' United Nations General Assembly Open Working Group on Sustainable Development Goals, *Compendium of TST Issues Briefs October 2014*, 187.

[38] UNGA Open Working Group on SDGs, *Compendium of TST Issues Briefs* (2014), 186.

[39] UNESCO, *(2021-2030) The Science We Need for the Ocean We Want United Nations Decade of Ocean Science for Sustainable Development*.

[40] IPCC, 'Summary for Policymakers' in Pörtner et al. (eds), *IPCC Special Report on the Ocean and Cryosphere in a Changing Climate* (2019); https://www.ipcc.ch/site/assets/uploads/sites/3/2019/11/03_SR OCC_SPM_FINAL.pdf.

[41] OECD/FAO, *OECD-FAO Agricultural Outlook 2020-2029*, 188, 190.

I. Sustainable use and Conservation of Oceans, Seas and Marine Resources

The framing legal fabric is set by the law of the seas and the 1982 United Nations   **16**
Convention on the Law of the Sea (UNCLOS).[42] UNCLOS governs all activities related
to the seas and the oceans including conservation and sustainable use of marine resources. The implementation of international law as reflected in UNCLOS is embodied
as a specific target under SDG 14 which seeks to protect life under water (SDG 14.c).
The oceans present conflicting challenges – on one hand to conserve and protect marine
biodiversity and ecosystems, and to protect the interests of those who depend on the use
of marine resources for their livelihood on the other.

UNCLOS allows coastal states the right to determine the allowable catch of the living   **17**
resources in its exclusive economic zone, Art. 61 UNCLOS. It further provides that,

> The coastal State, taking into account the best scientific evidence available to it, shall ensure through
> proper conservation and management measures that the maintenance of the living resources in the
> exclusive economic zone is not endangered by over-exploitation. As appropriate, the coastal State
> and competent international organizations, whether subregional, regional or global, shall cooperate
> to this end.

These obligations under the guise of UNCLOS outline the framework of the targets of   **18**
SDG 14 which aim to 'conserve and sustainably use the oceans, seas and marine resources for sustainable development'. The concept of sustainability holds a broad-rang-
ing connotation such as 'sustained yield' or 'sustainable development' but can also mean
'ecological sustainability'[43] with an effective potency that is mainly directed to people
($\rightarrow$ Intro mn. 28, 35 ff., 61). 'Ecological sustainability' presents another dimension to the
concept of 'sustainability', beyond conservation of resources, and protection of biodiversity and can be understood to mean 'the maintenance, in the same place at the same
time, of two interactive "things": culturally selected human economic activities and
ecosystem health.'[44] This definition offers a solution to the challenges posed by SDG 14
which focusses on conserving the marine ecosystem, while at the same time sustainably
using marine resources. The two are contradictory objectives to some extent, compelling
an understanding of sustainability that focusses on the dynamic interaction between
economic activities and the health of the ecosystem.

> Target 14.2 aims to "sustainably manage and protect marine and coastal ecosystems to avoid signifi-
> cant adverse impacts, including by strengthening their resilience, and take action for their restoration
> in order to achieve healthy and productive oceans." The success of the target is assessed by the
> "number of countries using ecosystem-based approaches to managing marine areas.[45]

In the ecological context, ecosystem approaches 'consider the connections between   **19**
living organisms, habitats, physical and chemical conditions within an ecosystem and
focus on the importance of ecological integrity, biodiversity and overall ecosystem
health.'[46] They 'reduce disaster risks while ensuring continued benefits to people from

---

[42] UNCLOS, 1982. As of 2021, 168 member states have ratified the convention; see at a regional level
Convention for the Conservation of the Biodiversity and the Protection of Priority Wilderness Areas in
Central America (1992).

[43] Callicott and Mumford, 'Ecological Sustainability as a Conservation Concept' (1997) 11(1) *Conservation Biology*, 32 (34).

[44] Callicott and Mumford, 'Ecological Sustainability as a Conservation Concept' (1997) 11(1) *Conservation Biology*, 32 (34).

[45] A/RES/71/313, UN Statistical Commission, Indicator 14.2.1.

[46] UN Statistics Division, SDG Indicators: Metadata Repository, Indicator 14.2.1.

ecosystem services' and thus allow for enhancing socio-ecological resilience.[47] This understanding is also reflected in a management context, where ecosystem approaches refer to 'integrated management strategies for socio-ecological systems that consider ecological, social and economic factors and apply principles of sustainable development'.[48] In order to interlink the diverse areas of UNCLOS as fundament of SDG 14 and to ensure an integrated approach to sustainable ocean management, international cooperation and coordination, the Division for Ocean Affairs and the Law of the Sea (DOALOS), a specialized secretariat of the UNGA, provides support at the global level.[49]

20   The meaning and scope of 'conservation' of living resources refers to coastal States having to 'determine the allowable catch of the living resources in its exclusive economic zone', Art. 61. Further, the coastal state must 'ensure through proper conservation and management measures that the maintenance of the living resources in the exclusive economic zone is not endangered by over-exploitation [...]' and that 'such measures shall also be designed to maintain or restore populations of harvested species at levels which can produce the maximum sustainable yield, as qualified by relevant environmental and economic factors, including the economic needs of coastal fishing communities and the special requirements of developing States, and taking into account fishing patterns, the interdependence of stocks and any generally recommended international minimum standards, whether subregional, regional or global'.

21   SDG 14.5 aims at conserving 'at least 10 per cent of coastal and marine areas, consistent with national and international law and based on the best available scientific information' by 2020. One indicator to the target assesses the 'coverage of protected areas in relation to marine areas'.[50] Marine protected areas (MPAs) are crucial to reduce the decline of biodiversity and ensure conservation, restoration and sustainable use of marine resources.[51] They can be described as a 'defined area within or adjacent to the marine environment which has been reserved by legislation or other effective means' to ensure 'that its marine and / or coastal biodiversity enjoys a higher level of protection than its surrounding'.[52]

22   SDG 14.a emphasises the importance of scientific and evidence-based decision making by focussing on increasing scientific knowledge, developing research capacity and transferring marine technology to facilitate development of developing countries, small island developing States (SIDS) and least developed countries.

II. Threats to Oceans

23   Despite the massive impact of climate change to the ocean and human behaviour threats to the oceans as covered by SDG 14 are among others:

---

[47] Takeuchi et al., 'Ecosystem-Based Approaches Toward a Resilient Society in Harmony with Nature' in Renaud et al (eds), *Ecosystem-Based Disaster Risk Reduction and Adaptation in Practice, Advances in Natural and Technological Hazards Research* (2016), 318 f.

[48] UN Statistics Division, SDG Indicators: Metadata Repository, Indicator 14.2.1.

[49] Goettsche-Wanli, 'The Role of the United Nations, including its Secretariat in Global Ocean Governance' in Attard, Ong, Kritsiotis, *The IMLI Treatise On Global Ocean Governance: Volume I: UN and Global Ocean Governance* (2018), 4.

[50] A/RES/71/313, UN Statistical Commission, Indicator 14.5.1.

[51] UN Statistics Division, SDG Indicators: Metadata Repository, Indicator 14.5.1.

[52] OECD, *Marine Protected Areas: Economic, Management and Effective Policy Mixes,* 2017, 13; further reading McNeely, 'Protected Areas, Biodiversity, and the Risks of Climate Change' in Renaud et al. (eds), *Ecosystem-Based Disaster Risk Reduction and Adaptation in Practice, Advances in Natural and Technological Hazards Research, Vol. 42,* 379-400.

1. Marine Pollution

Marine pollution occurs when harmful effects result from the entry into the ocean of   **24**
chemicals, particles, industrial, agricultural and residential waste, noise, or the spread of
invasive organisms. 80 per cent of marine pollution comes from land. Air pollution and
atmospheric alteration are also a contributing factor by carrying off iron, carbonic acid,
nitrogen, silicon, sulphur, pesticides or dust particles into the ocean.[53]

Under the auspices of the International Maritime Organization (IMO),[54] the protec-   **25**
tion of the environment started with the Convention on the Prevention of Marine
Pollution by Dumping of Wastes and Other Matter 1972 ('London Convention'), which
was one of the first global conventions to protect the marine environment from human
activities. Despite this and other agreements aiming to protect the marine environment,
such as MARPOL Annex V (Regulations for the Prevention of Pollution from Ship-gen-
erated Waste), 13 countries were documented to have disposed or dumped nuclear /
radioactive waste in the sea between 1946 and 1993. The waste materials included both
liquids and solids in various containers, as well as reactor vessels with and without spent
or damaged nuclear fuel.[55]

One of the earliest anti-dumping laws was Australia's Beaches, Fishing Grounds and   **26**
Sea Routes Protection Act 1932, which prohibited the discharge of 'garbage, rubbish,
ashes or organic refuse' from 'any vessel in Australian waters' without prior written
permission from the federal government which also required permission for scuttling.[56]

Marine Pollution is addressed by an abundance of international legal instruments and   **27**
provisions.[57] SDG 14.1 aims to 'prevent and significantly reduce marine pollution of all
kinds, in particular from land-based activities, including marine debris and nutrient pollution' by 2025. According to Art. 194 UNCLOS, a state is required to take 'all measures
[...] that are necessary to prevent, reduce and control pollution of the marine environmental from any source.' The two indicators to the SDG 14.1 are the index to coastal eutrophication[58]; and plastic debris density.[59] There are two levels of data proposed to
measure the two indicators with SDG 14.1. Level 1 is 'globally available data from earth
observations and modelling', and level 2 is 'national data which will be collected from
countries.'[60] Eutrophication as mentioned above is defined by the European Commission
as 'the enrichment of water by nutrients, especially compounds of nitrogen and / or
phosphorus, causing an accelerated growth of algae and higher forms of plant life to pro-

---

[53] Duce and Galloway and Liss, 'The impacts of atmospheric deposition to the ocean on marine ecosystems and climate' (2009) 58(1) *WMO Bulletin*, 61-6.

[54] Further reading on the purposes and functions of the IMO: Chircop, 'The International Maritime Organization' in Rothwell et al. (eds), *The Oxford Handbook of the Law of the Sea* (2015), 416 ff.

[55] IAEA-TECDOC-1105, *Inventory of radioactive waste disposals at sea 1999*, Vienna, 14 (Table V.); IAEA-TECDOC-1776, *Inventory of Radioactive Material Resulting from Historical Dumping, Accidents and Losses at Sea for the Purposes of the London Convention 1972 and London Protocol 1996.*

[56] https://www.legislation.gov.au/Details/C1932A00073.

[57] UNEP, *Marine Litter Legislation: A Toolkit for Policymakers*, 2016, 6; Guidelines for the Monitoring and Assessment of Plastic Litter in the Ocean; see e.g. UNEP/GPA/IGR.3/5, Manila Declaration on Furthering the Implementation of the Global Programme of Action for the Protection of the Marine Environment from Land-based Activities (2011); Kuwait Regional Convention for Co-operation on the Protection of the Marine Environment from Pollution (1978) and its Protocol concerning Marine Pollution resulting from Exploration and Exploitation of the Continental Shelf (1989); International Maritime Organization, International Convention for the Prevention of Pollution from Ships (MARPOL) (1973) and its Protocol of 1978; International Maritime Organization, Convention on the Prevention of Marine Pollution by Dumping of Wastes and Other Matter (London Convention) (1972) and its Protocol of 1996.

[58] UN Statistical Commission, A/RES/71/313, Indicator 14.1.1 a.

[59] UN Statistical Commission, A/RES/71/313, Indicator 14.1.1 b.

[60] UN Statistics Division, SDG Indicators: Metadata Repository, Indicator 14.1.1.

duce an undesirable disturbance to the balance of organisms present in the water and to the quality of the water concerned.[61] The definition of Eutrophication from the UN is as follows: 'excess nutrient loading into coastal environments from anthropogenic sources, resulting in excessive growth of plants, algae and phytoplankton.'[62]

28   The gravity of this problematic widespread occurrence is revealed by the US Environmental Protection Agency (EPA), that 'nutrient pollution is one of America's most widespread, costly and challenging environmental problems, and is caused by excess nitrogen and phosphorus in the air and water.'[63]

29   Eutrophication is a big concern for the environment with the potential to cause extreme damage to marine ecosystems. Marine litter, also called marine debris, is 'any persistent, manufactured, or processed solid material that is discarded, disposed of or abandoned in the marine and coastal environment.'[64] Coastal zone is the 'exclusive economic zone' (EEZ) which extends up to 200 nautical miles from the baselines from which the breadth of the territorial sea is measured.[65]

2. Marine Debris

30   The Marine Debris Program of the US National Oceanic and Atmospheric Administration (NOAA) and the United Nations Environment Programme (UNEP) jointly developed a global agenda specifically developed for and aiming at the prevention, reduction and management of marine debris. Known as the Honolulu Strategy,[66] it is a non-legally binding framework for a 'comprehensive and global collaborative effort to reduce the ecological, human health, and economic impacts of marine debris worldwide' to align further efforts such as the Hawaii Marine Debris Action Plan to cope with the 'complex cultural and multi-sectoral problem'.[67]

31   Marine Debris consists at least of '[p]lastic and other solid waste from land-based and at-sea sources, lost cargo, ALDFG, and abandoned or derelict vessels'.[68] The littering with marine debris detrimentally and directly affect 'coastal and marine species and habitats' due to entanglement or ingestion which causes restricted movement, starvation, suffocation, laceration (subsequent) infection and / or mortality. Marine debris is likely to also alter, degrade or destruct habitats through physical interference a result of which is the immediate and chronic threat to aquatic and terrestrial food webs. Especially polychlorinated biphenyls (PCBs), persistent organic pollutants such as dichlorodiphenyltrichloroethane (DDT), polycyclic aromatic hydrocarbons, and aliphatic hydrocarbons remain permanently in the oceans and cannot be dissolved or extracted

---

[61] Directive 91/271/EEC, Art. 2.

[62] https://unstats.un.org/sdgs/metadata/files/Metadata-14-01-01.pdf.

[63] https://www.epa.gov/nutrientpollution/issue.

[64] UNEP, *Marine Litter: A Global Challenge*, 2009, 13; UNEP, *Marine Litter Legislation: A Toolkit for Policymakers*, 2016, 2.

[65] UNCLOS, Art. 57; The baselines as initial point of measuring are to be determined in accordance with UNCLOS, see e.g. Arts. 5, 7, 14, 47.

[66] NOAA and UNEP, *The Honolulu Strategy, A Global Framework for Prevention and Management of Marine Debris* (2016), https://wedocs.unep.org/bitstream/handle/20.500.11822/10670/Honolulu%20strategy.pdf?sequence=1&isAllowed=y.

[67] NOAA and UNEP, *The Honolulu Strategy, A Global Framework for Prevention and Management of Marine Debris* (2016), 4.

[68] NOAA and UNEP, *The Honolulu Strategy, A Global Framework for Prevention and Management of Marine Debris* (2016), 4.

with technical means (yet). This permanent form of alteration also impacts 'economic health, human health and safety, and social values'.[69]

The non-binding character of the Honolulu Strategy calls for the accompaniment of   32 further, in particular positive-legally anchored 'national, municipal, industrial or international organisational activities and is therefore restricted to the will of participating states and stakeholders'.[70]

3. Ocean Acidification

Like climate change, ocean acidification is caused due to absorption of carbon diox-   33 ide or other emissions. Ocean acidification has a profound impact on marine biodiversity and threatens the extinction of many species.[71] SDG 14.3 aims at tackling this issue.[72] Ocean acidification is the 'reduction in the pH of the ocean over an extended period, typically of decades or longer, which is caused primarily by the uptake of carbon dioxide from the atmosphere'.[73] SDG 14.3 aims to 'minimize and address the impacts of ocean acidification, including through enhanced scientific cooperation at all levels'.

The indicator to SDG 14.3 measures the 'average marine acidity (pH) measured at   34 agreed suite of representative sampling stations'[74] and is based on observations that constrain the ocean carbon system and which are required to describe the variability in ocean acidity. The carbon system in this context mainly refers to the four measurable parameters: pH (the concentration of hydrogen ions on a logarithmic scale), DIC (CT; total dissolved inorganic carbon), pCO_2 (carbon dioxide partial pressure), and TA (AT, total alkalinity). Average, as used here, is the equally weighed annual mean.[75]

With ocean acidification, a serious by-product of greenhouse gas emissions is ad-   35 dressed under SDG 14.3. However, several other issues such as sea-level rise, ocean warming and salinity, which have a significant impact on ecosystems and fall into the scope of SDG 14 have not found place in the priorities under SDG 14.[76]

III. Protecting the Economy Surrounding Oceans

1. Sustainable Fisheries

One of the main objectives of UNCLOS has been to conserve and manage fisheries   36 for sustainable use. UNCLOS provides coastal states with the rights and obligations to sustainably use the fisheries in their EEZ, Art. 58 UNCLOS. EEZs contain 90 per cent of the world's fisheries.[77] Art. 6 of the 1995 Agreement for the Implementation of the Provisions of the UNCLOS relating to the Conservation and Management of Straddling Fish

---

[69] NOAA and UNEP, *The Honolulu Strategy, A Global Framework for Prevention and Management of Marine Debris* (2016), 4-10; see also European Parliament, *The environmental impacts of plastics and micro-plastics use, waste and pollution: EU and national measures* (2020), 4-54.

[70] European Parliament, *The environmental impacts of plastics and micro-plastics use, waste and pollution: EU and national measures* (2020), 29.

[71] Sakashita, 'Curbing CO2 Pollution: Using Existing Laws To Address Ocean Acidification' in Abate (ed), *Climate Change Impacts on Ocean and Coastal Law: U.S. and International Perspectives* (2015), 28 ff.

[72] UN Statistics Division, SDG Indicators: Metadata Repository, Indicator 14.3.1.

[73] UN Statistics Division, SDG Indicators: Metadata Repository, Indicator 14.3.1.

[74] UN Statistics Division, SDG Indicators: Metadata Repository, Indicator 14.3.1.

[75] UN Statistics Division, SDG Indicators: Metadata Repository, Indicator 14.3.1.

[76] Blanc and Freire and Vierros, 'Mapping the linkages between oceans and other Sustainable Development Goals: A preliminary exploration' (2017) 149 *DESA Working Paper*, 5.

[77] Food and Agricultural Organisation (FAO), *The State of the World Fisheries and Aquaculture. Sustainability in Action*, 2020, 94.

Stocks and Highly Migratory Fish Stocks (United Nations Fish Stock Agreement, 'UNF-SA') provides for a precautionary approach to conserve, manage and exploit straddling fish stocks and highly migratory[78] fish stocks. Further, states are also required to give access to and share scientific information to enable reliance on scientific advice for developing, adopting and implementing measures to promote fishery conservation and management.[79] In addition, the UNGA resolution also encourages states to 'apply the precautionary approach and an ecosystem approach in adopting and implementing conservation and management measures addressing, inter alia, by-catch, pollution, overfishing, and protecting habitats of specific concern, taking into account existing guidelines developed by the Food and Agriculture Organization of the United Nations'.[80]

37   SDG 14.4 covers similar objectives and aims at effective regulation of harvesting and bringing an end to overfishing, illegal, unreported and unregulated fishing and destructive fishing practices. With SDG 14.4 'science-based management plans, in order to restore fish stocks in the shortest time feasible, at least to levels that can produce maximum sustainable yield as determined by their biological characteristics' shall be implemented by 2020. Indicator 14.4.1 measures the 'proportion of fish stocks within biological sustainable levels'.[81] A fish stock is considered to be biologically sustainable if 'its abundance is at [level] or greater than the level that can produce the maximum sustainable yield'.[82] Further, 'maximum sustainable yield' is defined as 'the greatest amount of catch that can be harvested continuously from a stock under constant and current environmental conditions (e.g. habitat, water conditions, species composition and interactions, and anything that could affect birth, growth, or death rates of the stock) without affecting the long-term productivity of the stock'.[83] Even though the indicator is in conformity with the requirements under UNCLOS,[84] UNFSA[85] and the FAO Code of Conduct for Responsible Fisheries (1995),[86] measuring the sustainable level of fish stock as one that can produce sustainable yield, can be said to be more consumption-oriented rather than (ecological) conservation oriented.

38   In relation to illegal, unregulated and unreported (IUU) fishing, the FAO Agreement on Port State Measures of 2009 (PSMA) is significant as it is the first binding international agreement that specifically addresses this menace. The agreement is built on disincentivising port vessels from engaging in IUU fishing by using port-state mea-

---

[78] See also Convention on the Conservation of Migratory Species of Wild Animals (Convention on Migratory Species (CMS)) (1979); Addis Ababa Principles and Guidelines for the Sustainable Use of Biodiversity (CBD Guidelines) (2004), Principles 3 and 10.

[79] A/CONF.164/37, *Agreement for the Implementation of the Provisions of the United Nations Convention on the Law of the Sea of 10 December 1982 Relating to the Conservation and Management of Straddling Fish Stocks and Highly Migratory Fish Stocks* (1995), Art. 6; see also A/RES/61/105, *Sustainable fisheries, including through the 1995 Agreement for the Implementation of the Provisions of the United Nations Convention on the Law of the Sea of 10 December 1982 relating to the Conservation and Management of Straddling Fish Stocks and Highly Migratory Fish Stocks, and related instruments*, para. 6.

[80] FAO, *Code of Conduct for Responsible Fisheries* (1995); FAO and Committee on World Food Security, *Voluntary Guidelines on the Responsible Governance of Tenure of Land, Fisheries and Forests in the Context of National Food Security* (2012); FAO, *Voluntary Guidelines for Flag State Performance* (2015); FAO, *Voluntary Guidelines for Securing Sustainable Small-Scale Fisheries in the Context of Food Security and Poverty Eradication* (2018).

[81] UN Statistical Commission, A/RES/71/313, Indicator 14.4.1.

[82] UN Statistics Division, SDG Indicators: Metadata Repository, Indicator 14.4.1.

[83] UN Statistics Division, SDG Indicators: Metadata Repository, Indicator 14.4.1.

[84] UNCLOS, Arts. 61(3), 119(1).

[85] A/CONF.164/37, *Agreement for the Implementation of the Provisions of the United Nations Convention on the Law of the Sea of 10 December 1982 Relating to the Conservation and Management of Straddling Fish Stocks and Highly Migratory Fish Stocks* (1995), Art. 5(b).

[86] FAO, *Code of Conduct for Responsible Fisheries* (1995), Art. 7.2.1.

sures[87] (not allowing *inter alia* unauthorised vessels or vessels engaging in IUU fishing from using ports and landing their catches), and thereby preventing the products from such activities from reaching the national and international markets. The PSMA has adopted the definition of IUU fishing from the 2001 FAO International Plan of Action to Prevent, Deter and Eliminate Illegal, Unreported and Unregulated Fishing.[88] The PSMA entered into force in 2016 and has 68 States Parties. The definition of IUU fishing provided by the FAO is very broad. In brief, IUU fishing exists when 'fishing violates the laws and regulations that apply to fisheries in territorial waters, exclusive economic zones, or high sea fisheries.'[89]

One of the major agreements that support the prevention of illegal fishing lies in the **39** important role of flags of vessels. It is important to ensure that a State prevent a 're-flagging', Art. 5 and to strengthen its control over its vessels to ensure compliance with international conservation and management measures. The Agreement to Promote Compliance with International Conservation and Management Measures by Fishing Vessels on the High Seas (Compliance Agreement), aims to enhance the role of flag States and ensure compliance with international measures.[90]

The Agreement for the Implementation of the Provisions of the United Nations **40** Convention on the Law of the Sea of 10 December 1982 relating to the Conservation and Management of Straddling Fish Stocks and Highly Migratory Fish Stocks (UN Fish Stocks Agreement) entered into force on 11 December 2001.

The UN Fish Stocks Agreement aims to ensure the long-term conservation and **41** sustainable use of straddling and highly migratory fish stocks within the framework of UNCLOS. The Agreement also spells out the duties of flag States including those related to registration and records of vessels, authorisations, MCS and compliance and enforcement.[91]

The several international agreements are accompanied by additional Regional Mech- **42** anism serving to combat IUU fishing.[92] However, the US estimated that China, Russia, Mexico, Vietnam, and Indonesia are to be relatively substantial exporters of marine-capture IUU imports to the US.[93]

2. Subsidies contributing to illegal, unreported and unregulated fishing

As another aspect affecting sustainable fisheries, subsidies contribute to overcapacity **43** and overfishing or contribute to illegal, unreported and unregulated fishing. SDG 14.6 attempts to prohibit and / or eliminate such subsidies and to also make special and differential treatment for developing and least developed countries an integral part of the WTO fisheries subsidies negotiation. The only indicator to SDG 14.6 assesses progress by the extent to which international instruments aimed at combating illegal, unreported and unregulated fishing such as UNCLOS, UNFSA, The International Plan of Action to Prevent, Deter and Eliminate Illegal, Unreported and Unregulated Fishing (IPOA-IUU), The 2009 FAO Agreement on Port State Measures to Prevent, Deter and Eliminate

---

[87] FAO, *Agreement on Port State Measures to Prevent, Deter and Eliminate Illegal, Unreported and Unregulated Fishing* (adopted 22 November 2009, entered into force 5 June 2016), Art. 2.

[88] FAO, *International Plan of Action to Prevent, Deter and Eliminate Illegal, Unreported and Unregulated Fishing*, para 3.

[89] Boister, *An Introduction to Transnational Criminal Law* (2nd Edition, 2018), 202.

[90] Agreement to Promote Compliance with International Conservation and Management Measures by Fishing Vessels on the High Seas (The Compliance Agreement) (Rome 1995).

[91] http://www.fao.org/iuu-fishing/international-framework/un-fish-stocks-agreement/en/.

[92] http://www.fao.org/iuu-fishing/regional-mechanisms/en/.

[93] Report of the United States International Trade Commission, *Seafood Obtained via Illegal, Unreported, and Unregulated Fishing: U.S. Imports and Economic Impact on U.S. Commercial Fisheries* (2021), 11.

Illegal, Unreported and Unregulated Fishing (PSMA), The FAO Voluntary Guidelines for Flag State Performance (VG-FSP) and The FAO Agreement to Promote Compliance with International Conservation and Management Measures by Fishing Vessels on the High Seas (Compliance Agreement) are implemented by a state.[94] While SDG 14.6 seems to be specifically about subsidies, the indicator that measures the achievement of SDG 14.6 is broader in scope and assesses the conformity to international instruments in general, and thus, the indicator overlaps with SDG 14.4.

3. Small Scale Fishers

44   Fisheries are the source of livelihood for many impoverished and indigent communities around the world. Small scale fisheries employ more than 90 per cent of people working in fisheries[95] of whom approximately 97 per cent live in developing countries.[96] They are characterised by 'a dynamic and evolving subsector of fisheries employing labour-intensive harvesting, processing and distribution technologies to exploit marine and inland water fishery resources'.[97] SDG 14.b addresses the threat posed to the livelihoods of small small-scale artisanal fishers by strained marine resources by aiming to provide them access to marine resources and markets in line with Rio+20 outcome document which states,

> We commit to observe the need to ensure access to fisheries and the importance of access to markets, by subsistence, small-scale and artisanal fisherfolk and women fish workers, as well as indigenous peoples and their communities, particularly in developing countries, especially small island developing States.[98]

45   Indicator 14.b.1 assesses 'progress by countries in the degree of application of a legal/regulatory/policy/institutional framework which recognizes and protects access rights for small-scale fisheries'. Access right for small-scale fisheries require an enabling environment which comprises 'appropriate legal, regulatory and policy frameworks; specific initiatives to support small-scale fisheries; and related institutional mechanisms which allow for the participation of small-scale fisheries organisations in relevant processes'.[99]

C. Interdependences of SDG 14

46   The oceans contribute to poverty alleviation by providing sustainable livelihoods and decent work, while at the same time being critical to global food security and human health. Moreover, oceans function as the primary regulator of the global climate and an important sink for greenhouse gases as well supplying humanity with water and the oxygen we breathe.[100] As noted above, climate change is causing a variety of impacts on the ocean that relate to all the SDGs.

---

[94] UN Statistics Division, SDG Indicators: Metadata Repository, Indicator 14.6.1.
[95] See also A/RES/73/165, *United Nations Declaration on the Rights of Peasants and Other People Working in Rural Areas*, 21 January 2019, Arts. 13, 17 and 20.
[96] FAO, *The State of the World Fisheries and Aquaculture. Sustainability in Action*, 2020, 133.
[97] FAO, *A research agenda for small-scale fisheries*, 2004, 3.
[98] A/RES/66/288, *The future we want*, para. 175.
[99] UN Statistics Division, SDG Indicators: Metadata Repository, Indicator 14.b.1.
[100] UNGA Open Working Group on SDGs, *Compendium of TST Issues Briefs* (2014), 182 f.; OECD, *OECD Review of Fisheries 2020* (2020).

The ongoing alteration of oceans which harms low-lying islands and coasts (LLIC)   **47**
already today, including SIDS and least developed countries.[101] Disproportionately higher risks are expected in the course of the 21st century. The relationship with SIDS
underlines the wide range of relationships to SDGs 2, 5, 6, 7, 12, 13, 14, 15 and 17 and in
the case of tourism to SDG 8 as well.[102]

The first two years of the SARS-CoV-2 pandemic have led to an enormous increase   **48**
in plastic waste. Hygiene regulations and the falling price of petroleum and the plastics
made from it threaten to reverse progress already made in the prevention and recycling
of plastics, revealing a currently amplified link to SDG 12 (SDG 12.3, 12.4, 12.5).[103]

Through fisheries and marine aquacultures, shipping and shipbuilding, ports,   **49**
tourism, oil, gas, mining and maritime transport industries as well as through actions
of restoration of marine and coastal ecosystems creates workplaces (SDG 8.3, SDG 8.4)
and thus contributes to eradicate poverty (SDG 1.5, SDG 1.b),[104] as 80 per cent of global
trade volume is seaborne.[105] Other net benefits of achieving SDG 14.2 would include
improved revenue from tourism (SDG 8.9, SDG 12.b),[106] enhanced biodiversity and fish
stocks, and increased potential for income from blue carbon markets and coastal habitats protect homes, communities and businesses from extreme climate-related events
such as coastal flooding and storms, which contributes to reduce the vulnerability of
poor people (SDG 1.5) and the associated economic impacts (SDG 1.1, SDG 1.2).[107]

Fish as a key driver for providing food security and meeting nutritional needs in   **50**
many developing and developed countries (SDG 2.1, SDG 2.2, SDG 2.4)[108] accompanied
by effective regulation to end overfishing, IUU and destructive fishing practices and
prohibiting or eliminating certain forms of (fisheries) subsidies which contributes to
overcapacity and overfishing (SDG 14.4, SDG 14.6) directly contributes to achieving safe
nutrition (SDG 2.1) and ending malnutrition in all its forms (SDG 2.2).

However, SDG 14 could also adversely affect the targets of SDG 8, as taking mea-   **51**
surements, to protect, restore and promote marine and coastal ecosystems might entail
restrictions for economic activities and therefore limit its opportunities for economic
growth and job creation (and vice versa).[109] It should be also mentioned, that tourism
may provide a substantial opportunity, especially for SIDS, for economic growth but may
at the same time be harmed by several forms of mass tourism that may cause lasting
damage to the ecosystem of the sea and coastal areas (→ Goal 8 mn. 81).

Since coasts and coastal zones are highly attractive for human settlement and ur-   **52**
ban development, often driven by the economic opportunities and natural resources

---

[101] See Cordonier Segger and Weeramantry, 'Introduction' in Cordonier Segger and Weeramantry, *Sustainable Development Principles in the Decisions of International Courts and Tribunals, 1999-2012* (2017), 2.

[102] https://www.ipcc.ch/srocc/chapter/cross-chapter-box-9-integrative-cross-chapter-box-on-low-lying-islands-and-coasts/.

[103] https://www.ecowatch.com/coronavirus-plastic-waste-2645831072.html; Martens and Ellmers and Pokorny on behalf of Global Policy Watch, COVID-19 and the SDGs, The impact of the coronavirus pandemic on the global sustainability agenda, 6 f.

[104] UNGA Open Working Group on SDGs, *Compendium of TST Issues Briefs* (2014), 182; Griggs et al., *A Guide to SDG Interactions: From Science to Implementation* (2017), 180; insights on shaping decent work in the fisheries sector in the future: FAO, *Joining forces to shape the fishery sector of tomorrow, Promoting safety and decent work in fisheries through the application of international standards* (2020).

[105] UNCTAD, *Review Of Maritime Transport 2018*, 23.

[106] UNEP/CMS/Resolution 12.23, Convention on Migratory Species, Sustainable Tourism and Migratory Species.

[107] Griggs et al., *A Guide to SDG Interactions: From Science to Implementation* (2017), 185.

[108] FAO, *The State Of World Fisheries and Aquaculture 2020*, 67.

[109] Griggs et al., *A Guide to SDG Interactions: From Science to Implementation* (2017), 192.

provided, a direct relationship between ocean sustainability and sustainable cities and communities reveals.[110] Therefore, achieving targets under SDG 14 has influence on coastal cities and communities, such as by preventing and significantly reducing marine pollution of all kinds, in particular from land-based activities (SDG 14.1) would improve adequate, safe and affordable housing and basic services and upgrade slums (SDG 11.1), enhance inclusive and sustainable urbanisation processes (SDG 11.3) and reduce the adverse per capita environmental impact of cities (SDG 11.6) (→ Goal 11 mn. 49, 54).

53   As mentioned above, drastically reducing marine pollution and stop the unsustainable practice of illegal, unreported and unregulated fishing (SDGs 14.1, 14.4 and 14.7) which impacts significantly on life below water as well as on life on land,[111] is mandatory to sustainably preserve and conserve the ocean's biodiversity, and therefore strongly synergises with achieving the sustainable management and efficient use of natural resources (SDG 12.2), reducing food waste (SDG 12.3), achieving the environmentally sound management of chemicals and all wastes throughout their life cycle (SDG 12.4) and promoting to reduce waste generation through prevention, reduction, recycling and reuse (SDG 12.5) and encouraging companies to adopt sustainable practises (SDG 12.6).

54   Oceans and their biodiversity are affected by climate change and thus, achieving goals of SDG 14 is highly synergistic with SDG 13, as among others, strengthening the resilience of ocean and coastal ecosystems, and restoring their health and protect the ocean from further unsustainable practices will greatly contribute to achieve SDG 13 (→ Goal 13 mn. 46, 50). 'Life under water is essential to life on land.'[112] The ocean holds a large part of CO_2. Its health and capacity naturally determine the formation and shaping of terrestrial habitats.

55   Referring to Sánchez Castillo-Winckels, SDG 14 is strongly intertwined with SDG 16 since it is 'highly relevant to ocean stability […], for it aims at building transparent, accountable and effective institutions at all levels.'[113] Moreover, the encouraged public access to information and participation in decision-making as a way of strengthening institutions at all levels supports the implementation of SDG 14 and resembles upon SDG 4, SDG 6, SDG 9 and SDG 12 as well as SDG 7 and SDG 17. Together with SDGs 6, SDG 13 and SDG 15, SDG 14 builds the biosphere basis for all other SDGs.[114]

D. Jurisprudential Significance of SDG 14

56   SDG 14 adds various concepts such as the ecosystem approach, the development approach, and as natural capital or man-made capital. The concepts supported are

---

[110] 65 per cent of all megacities worldwide are located in coastal areas, and as a result coastal areas generally show higher population densities, growth and urbanisation trends than inland areas; Griggs et al., *A Guide to SDG Interactions: From Science to Implementation* (2017), 181.

[111] http://www.unesco.org/new/en/natural-sciences/ioc-oceans/focus-areas/rio-20-ocean/blueprint-fo r-the-future-we-want/marine-pollution/facts-and-figures-on-marine-pollution/; https://www.sciencedire ct.com/topics/earth-and-planetary-sciences/marine-pollution; see on the specific matter of plastic debris: Chenillat et al., 'Fate of floating plastic debris released along the coasts in a global ocean model' (2021) 165 *Marine Pollution Bulletin*; Mucientes and Queiroz, 'Presence of plastic debris and retained fishing hooks in oceanic sharks' (2019) 143 *Marine Pollution Bulletin*, 6-11; Grant et al., 'Seabird breeding islands as sinks for marine plastic debris' (2021) 276 *Environmental Pollution*.

[112] https://www.un.org/press/en/2020/sea2122.doc.htm.

[113] Sánchez Castillo-Winckels, 'How the Sustainable Development Goals promote a new conception of ocean commons governance' (2017) in French and Kotzé (eds), *Sustainable Development Goals, Law, Theory and Implementation*, 117.

[114] Sánchez Castillo-Winckels, 'How the Sustainable Development Goals promote a new conception of ocean commons governance' (2017) in French and Kotzé (eds), *Sustainable Development Goals, Law, Theory and Implementation*, 117.

complemented by the 'do no harm' principle which is anchored in the expression of sustainable management and the restoration of fish stocks, applying equitable burden sharing and benefit sharing, e.g. for Small Island Developing States (SIDS). Under UNCLOS, SDG 14 becomes legally applicable mainly through the jurisdiction of the associated body of judicial control, ITLOS. With its scope over maritime occurrence covering more than 70 per cent of the planet, UNCLOS clarifies 'a State's freedom of navigation and fishing'[115] through the classification of zones that are either subject to state sovereignty (internal waters, 12 nautical miles territorial sea), subject only to limited or shared jurisdiction (max. 24 nautical miles contiguous zone, continental shelf, and 200 nautical miles, EEZ) or are assigned to the seabed of the high seas (the Area[116]), which is seen as common heritage of humankind.[117] The Area as subject to the principle of joint and cooperative exploitation is protected by specific legal regimes such as regulating fishing on the high seas or deep seabed mining. By implementing international law as reflected in UNCLOS, the conservation and sustainable use of oceans and their resources shall be achieved (SDG 14.c).[118] Thus, international water law and international law have a limiting effect on the exercise and acquisition of property rights.[119] Further background of legal interpretation and limitation is set by the international law principle of CBDR, the precautionary principle, the principle of prevention, the ecosystems approach, and the participatory approach. These principles mainly unfold effects on State-to-State legal relations, e.g. when international treaties or other (protective) instruments are developed and must be considered when interpreting UNCLOS.[120] Since UNCLOS indicates which areas (zones) are beyond the jurisdiction of a coastal State, it follows that no single State has overall competence for the protection and preservation of the marine environment. Rather, these areas are deemed 'the global commons' which allow access for every State.[121] This forms context to the question who actually is the (duty) addressee of SDG 14.1, SDG 14.2 and SDG 14.3 and how the burden of conserving and sustainably using the ocean are to be understood and shared. In particular, the principles of precaution and prevention, manifested in a huge amount of marine-protecting instruments and frameworks,[122] reveal the inseparable

---

[115] Schäli, 'Trade, Environment and the Law of the Sea' in Cottier and Nadakavukaren Schefer, *Elgar Encyclopedia of International Economic Law* (2017), 632.

[116] To be understood as the seabed and ocean floor and subsoil thereof, beyond the limits of national jurisdiction, Art. 1(1) UNCLOS.

[117] The Common heritage of mankind include 'the Area' and its resources, Art. 136 UNCLOS; see also UNGA resolution 2749 (XXV) of 17 December 1970, para. 1; other expressions include: 'common heritage of humankind' or 'global environmental commons which is needed for human survival' or 'ocean global commons', see Schrijver, 'Advancements in principles of international law' in Cordonier Segger and Weeramantry (eds), *Sustainable Development Principles in the Decisions of International Courts and Tribunals, 1992–2012* (2017), 105; Independent Group of Scientists appointed by the Secretary-General, *Global Sustainable Development Report 2019: The Future is Now – Science for Achieving Sustainable Development* (2019), 95; Sánchez Castillo-Winckels, 'How the Sustainable Development Goals promote a new conception of ocean commons governance' in French and Kotzé (eds), *Sustainable Development Goals, Law, Theory and Implementation* (2017), 117.

[118] Sánchez Castillo-Winckels, 'How the Sustainable Development Goals promote a new conception of ocean commons governance' in French and Kotzé (eds), *Sustainable Development Goals, Law, Theory and Implementation*, 132.

[119] Cottier, Property Rights, Legal Security and Development' in Cottier and Nadakavukaren Schefer, *Elgar Encyclopedia of International Economic Law* (2017), 516.

[120] Harrison, *Saving the Oceans Through Law: The International Legal Framework for the Protection of the Marine Environment* (2017), 26.

[121] Harrison, *Saving the Oceans Through Law: The International Legal Framework for the Protection of the Marine Environment* (2017), 17 ff.

[122] See e.g. 1971 Treaty on the Prohibition of the Emplacement of Nuclear Weapons and Other Weapons of Mass Destruction on the Sea-bed and the Ocean Floor and in the Subsoil Thereof; 1977 Con-

intertemporal dimension[123] which was given explicit expression with the means of SDG 14.c.

57   In addition to these specific regimes, the commercial use of the ocean, such as the exploitation of fish stocks for trade, transport or energy opens up the sphere of application of world trade law. Further international legal instruments that shape the interpretation of SDG 14 include the 'Straddling Fish Stocks Agreement'[124], the Ramsar Convention[125], the New York Convention[126], and the Helsinki Convention[127] which provide for cooperation and collaboration relating to protection of wetlands, international watercourses or transboundary watercourses'.[128]

58   This legal framework is contrasted with changes in natural conditions such as the increasing marine acidification due to, among other things, increased CO_2 uptake largely attributable to climate change accompanied by ocean temperature rise, the high level of marine pollution from shipping, plastic waste, industrial waste and wastewater, as well as overfishing and the associated destruction of biotopes in the sea. This changing conditions hit coastal regions and SIDS significantly harder due to their geographic location and the ocean being a central element in their culture 'while at the same time being tightly linked to their economies.'[129] Further, not entirely new challenges are becoming more apparent and acute in the not so far future such as environmental or climate refugees and the intertwined[130] phenomenon of sea-level rising (flooding of low-lying islands) or further issues relating to 'the pollution of the oceans, rivers and

---

vention on the Prohibition of Military or Any Other Hostile Use of Environmental Modification Techniques; 1972 Convention on the Prevention of Marine Pollution by Dumping of Wastes and Other Matter; 1974 Convention for the Prevention of Marine Pollution from Land-Based Sources; 1972 Convention for the Prevention of Marine Pollution by Dumping from Ships and Aircraft; 1972 UNESCO Convention for the Protection of the World Cultural and Natural Heritage; 1991 OAU Bamako Convention on the Ban of the Import into Africa and the Control of Transboundary Movement and Management of Hazardous Wastes within Africa (Article 4 (3) (f)), in the 1992 Convention for the Protection of the Marine Environment of the North-East Atlantic (OSPAR Convention, Article 2 (2) (a)), and in the 1992 Convention on the Protection of the Marine Environment of the Baltic Sea Area (Article 3 (1) and (2)), 1992 Convention on Biological Diversity (preamble and Article 3), 1992 United Nations Framework Convention on Climate Change (preamble and Article 3 (3)), and the 1997 Kyoto Protocol to the United Nations Framework Convention on Climate Change (preamble), 2000 Cartagena Protocol on Biosafety (preamble and Arts. 2, 4), 2001 Convention on Persistent Organic Pollutants (POPs Convention) (preamble and Art. 1).

[123] Both principles and their time-independent, intergenerational character are also subject to judicial discussion; see e.g. in the context of common goods: ICJ, *Pulp Mills on the River Uruguay (Argentina v. Uruguay)*, Separate Opinion of Judge Cançado Trindade, 20 April 2010, paras. 89-96.

[124] Agreement for the Implementation of the Provisions of the United Nations Convention on the Law of the Sea of 10 December 1982 relating to the Conservation and Management of Straddling Fish Stocks and Highly Migratory Fish Stocks; Agreement relating to the Implementation of Part XI of the United Nations Convention on the Law of the Sea of 10 December 1982.

[125] Convention on Wetlands of International Importance, 21 December 1975.

[126] UN Convention on the Law of the Non-navigational Uses of International Watercourses, 21 May 1997.

[127] Convention on the Protection and Use of Transboundary Watercourses and International Lakes, 17 March 1992.

[128] CISDL / UNEP, *SDG 14 on Ensuring Conservation and Sustainable Use of Oceans and Marine Resources: Contributions of International Law, Policy and Governance, Issue Brief 2016.*

[129] UNGA Open Working Group on SDGs, *Compendium of TST Issues Briefs* (2014), 183.

[130] Different forms of pollution affecting different spheres of the Earth lead to marine system harm. This important interlinkage has been recognised and is also reflected in the context of the development of law, see e.g. A/73/10, Report of the International Law Commission, Seventieth session (30 April–1 June and 2 July–10 August 2018), paras. 77 f. (general comment), at preamble: 'Acknowledging that the atmosphere is essential for sustaining life on Earth, human health and welfare, and aquatic and terrestrial ecosystems'.

lakes of this world.'[131] Until now, the ocean has bound about 90 per cent of the heat generated by rising greenhouse gas (GHG) emissions in the Earth's system as well as 30 per
cent of carbon emissions.[132] This absorption alters the composition of the ocean and its
ecosystems. The resulting impacts on human beings require marine conservation be
placed at the centre of efforts.[133] The legal profundity offered by SDG 14 cannot be directly recognised or inferred from its wording. However, SDG 14 includes multiple levels
of law that reveal the far-reaching interconnections between environmental law and human rights and not only demand but also enable a holistic legal reasoning.

Human rights agreements were also mentioned during the SDG negotiations as a   **59**
means to ensure that the designation of marine protected areas (MPAs) does not harm
local communities and that the regulation of sea-based economic activities serves to
protect the rights of women and children, indigenous peoples, migrants and refugees,
and other vulnerable and marginalised groups. According to Knox, SDG 14 could be
used to determine 'whether an acceptable balance between environmental protection
and economic development has been achieved.'[134] This would allow to derive whether
states comply with their international human rights obligations and whether they fulfil
their function 'to protect against human rights abuses due to environmental harm.'[135]

I. Jurisdiction on Vision and Objectives

Relevant legal disputes that fall within the sphere of SDG 14 are particularly related   **60**
to the pollution of the oceans and the resulting acidification with its relevance for
climate change, the overfishing and illegal exploitation,[136] the 'unsustainable extraction
of marine non-living resources' such as deep sea mining offshore oil and gas drilling'[137]
as well as delimiting sovereign rights of states, e.g. due to melting polar ice that opening
up new shipping passages and new potential resources, are ongoing issues.

---

[131] Weeramantry, 'Sustainable justice through international law' in Cordonier Segger and Weeramantry
(eds), *Sustainable Development Principles in the Decisions of International Courts and Tribunals, 1992 –
2012* (2017), 111 f.; Behlert, 'A significant opening, On the HRC's groundbreaking first ruling in the case of
a 'climate refugee" (2020) *Völkerrechtsblog* (International Law & Legal Thought, 30/01/2020); https://www.
ohchr.org/EN/NewsEvents/Pages/DisplayNews.aspx?NewsID=25482&LangID=E.

[132] https://unfccc.int/news/urgent-climate-action-is-needed-to-safeguard-the-world-s-oceans.

[133] Further reading on the multi-layered impacts on human social, cultural and economic conditions:
Diz et al., 'Mainstreaming marine biodiversity into the SDGs: The role of other effective area-based
conservation measures (SDG 14.5)' (2018) 93 *Marine Policy*, 251-61; Kenny et al., 'Delivering sustainable
fisheries through adoption of a risk-based framework as part of an ecosystem approach to fisheries
management' (2018) 93 *Marine Policy*, 232-40; Mohammed et al., 'Fiscal reforms for sustainable marine
fisheries governance: Delivering the SDGs and ensuring no one is left behind' (2018) 93 *Marine Policy*,
262-70.

[134] Knox, 'Human Rights, Environmental Protection, and the Sustainable Development Goals' (2015)
24 *Wash. L. Rev.*, 517 (529, 533); Ntona and Morgera, 'Connecting SDG 14 with the other Sustainable
Development Goals through marine spatial planning' (2018) 93 *Marine Policy*, 214-22.

[135] Ntona and Morgera, 'Connecting SDG 14 with the other Sustainable Development Goals through
marine spatial planning' (2018) 93 *Marine Policy*, 214 (215).

[136] Independent Group of Scientists appointed by the Secretary-General, *Global Sustainable Development Report 2019: The Future is Now – Science for Achieving Sustainable Development* (2019), 10, 132.

[137] United Nations General Assembly/Open Working Group on Sustainable Development Goals, *Compendium of TST Issues Briefs* (2014), 183.

1. International Jurisdiction

61   The linkage of life to the world's oceans and the need to protect these fragile entities in international cooperation and solidarity can be read from Art. 197 UNCLOS[138] which requires States to 'cooperate on a global and, if appropriate, on a regional basis [to formulate] standards and practices for the protection and preservation of the marine environment'. The protection and preserving of the marine environment as demanded in Art. 192 UNCLOS leads to states' obligations of all parties to UNCLOS but, moreover, is argued to be of *erga omnes* character which 'owes the international community as a whole.'[139] Such reasoning can be found in the *South China Sea Arbitration*[140], where the Tribunal stated that 'the environmental obligations in Part XII [UNCLOS] apply to States irrespective of where the alleged harmful activities took place' and irrespective from the jurisdiction that 'is not dependent on the question of sovereignty over any particular feature, on a prior determination of the status of any maritime feature, on the existence of an entitlement by China or the Philippines to an exclusive economic zone in the area, or on the prior delimitation of any overlapping entitlements.'[141] The general obligation to apply Part XII is to be interpreted in the context of the sovereign right to exploit their [States'] natural resources incorporated in Art. 193 UNCLOS. UNCLOS thus places environmental concerns in the context of a sustainable management of the marine environment and thus also of economic interests. The resulting balance corresponds to the basic principle of the concept of sustainable development.[142]

62   The ITLOS Seabed Disputes Chamber effectively has compulsory jurisdiction over disputes relating to the exploration and exploitation of the international seabed and ocean floor ('the Area').[143] The Seabed Disputes Chamber can acquire jurisdiction not just by virtue of and over the states involved, but also by a range of actors engaged in activities in the Area (e.g. State Parties, the International Seabed Authority, state enterprises, legal or natural persons and prospective contractors). In addition to provisions of UNCLOS and principles of international law not incompatible with it, the Seabed Disputes Chamber can apply the rules, regulations and procedures of the International Seabed Authority, as well as terms of contracts concerning activities in matters relating to them.

63   Unusually, ITLOS also has jurisdiction to order provisional measures under UNCLOS, even when parties have chosen a different forum to resolve their disputes, in the absence of alternative agreement between the parties, and pending the constitution of the parties chosen forum.[144] This provision has been invoked on a number of occasions.[145]

---

[138] UNCLOS binds States to comply with all aspects of the legal regime and does not allow reservations to any substantive rules in the Convention and, moreover, reflects customary international law; further reading: Harrison, *Saving the Oceans Through Law: The International Legal Framework for the Protection of the Marine Environment* (2017), 17 ff.

[139] Harrison, *Saving the Oceans Through Law: The International Legal Framework for the Protection of the Marine Environment* (2017), 25.

[140] *The South China Sea Arbitration (The Republic of Philippines v. The People's Republic of China)*, PCA Case No. 2013-19.

[141] *The South China Sea Arbitration (The Republic of Philippines v. The People's Republic of China)*, PCA Case No. 2013-19, para. 927.

[142] With Agenda 21 (1992), paras. 17.1.-17.136 the international community already demanded the cautious and balanced interpretation.

[143] https://www.itlos.org/en/main/the-tribunal/chambers/.

[144] https://www.itlos.org/en/main/the-tribunal/chambers/.

[145] Harrington and Robb, 'A complex system of international courts and tribunals' in Cordonier Segger and Weeramantry, *Sustainable Development Principles in the Decisions of International Courts and Tribunals, 1999 – 2012* (2017), 143.

Concurrent jurisdiction can exist, where a treaty provides a range of options for   64
dispute settlement. UNCLOS, for example, allows parties to choose between the ICJ,
various arbitral tribunals and ITLOS in relation to much of the treaty, and thus all of
them would potentially have jurisdiction.[146]

In relation to semi-enclosed seas, the Convention further specifies in Art. 123 that   65
States shall endeavour to coordinate the implementation of their rights and duties with
respect to the protection and preservation of the marine environment. The importance
of cooperation to marine protection and preservation has been recognised by ITLOS
frequently.[147] ITLOS regularly bases its argumentation, inter alia, on the case law of the
ICJ, which in *Pulp Mills on the River Uruguay*[148] acknowledged that 'by co-operating [...]
the States concerned can manage the risks of damage to the environment that might be
created by the plans initiated by one or [the] other of them, so as to prevent the damage
in question' (→ Goal 6).[149] The ICJ stated further that it was exactly the 'interconnectedness between equitable and reasonable utilization of a shared resource and the balance
between economic development and environmental protection that is the essence of sustainable development.'[150] By referring to the *Pulp Mills* case, the ITLOS illustrates that it
follows the guidance on how to find equity and reasonableness in the utilisation of
shared sources and considers it applicable to marine waters as well (→ Intro mn. 176 ff.).

Judge Cançado Trindade in its Separate Opinion in the *Pulp Mills* case stated that the   66
precautionary principle is indispensably 'interwoven with the ineluctable inter-temporal
dimension' which 'is necessarily a long-term one, since the decisions taken by public
authorities of today may have an impact on the living conditions of not only present, but
also future generations'.[151], amongst others, due to the naturally given uncertainties and
complexities as well as limitations in human development.[152] Though this description of

---

[146] Harrington and Robb, 'A complex system of international courts and tribunals' in Cordonier Segger and Weeramantry, *Sustainable Development Principles in the Decisions of International Courts and
Tribunals, 1999 – 2012* (2017), 133.

[147] *The MOX Plant Case (Ireland v. United Kingdom)*, Provisional Measures, Order of 3 December 2001,
ITLOS Reports 2001, para. 82; *Case concerning Land Reclamation by Singapore in and around the Straits of
Johor (Malaysia v. Singapore)*, Provisional Measures, Order of 8 October 2003, ITLOS Reports 2003, para.
92; *Request for an Advisory Opinion Submitted by the Sub-Regional Fisheries Commission (SRFC)*, Advisory
Opinion of 2 April 2015, ITLOS Reports 2015, para. 140; see also *Merits Hearing, Tr. (Day 4)*, 40-41 [found
in: ITLOS, *Arbitration Between the Republic of the Philippines and the People's Republic of China*, PCA Case
No. 2013-19, Award (July 12, 2016), http://www.pca-cpa.org, paras. 984 f.]; ITLOS has moreover established a special Chamber for Marine Environmental Disputes.

[148] *Pulp Mills on the River Uruguay (Argentina v. Uruguay)*, Judgment, ICJ Reports 2010: In this case,
the maintenance of a treaty was weighted against harmful environmental interference into a non-marine
water body.

[149] *Pulp Mills on the River Uruguay (Argentina v. Uruguay)*, Judgment, ICJ Reports 2010, 14, 49,
para. 77; see also *Consequences Arising Out Of Acts Not Prohibited By International Law (Prevention of
Transboundary Harm From Hazardous Activities)*, in Report of the International Law Commission on the
work of its Fifty-third session (23 April-1 June and 2 July-10 August 2001), UN Doc. GAOR A/56/10
(2001).

[150] *Pulp Mills on the River Uruguay (Argentina v. Uruguay)*, Judgment, ICJ Reports 2010, 14, 49, para. 177.

[151] *Pulp Mills on the River Uruguay (Argentina v. Uruguay)*, Judgment, ICJ Reports 2010, 14, 49, para. 90.

[152] Judge Cançado Trindade argues both with the inadequacy of scientific knowledge (scientific uncertainties) and, respectively, due to the limitations of human knowledge and the even more scarcity of human wisdom, which was already recognised by Socrates (Plato, Apology of Socrates [399 BC], 21b-d; 22a-
c; 22 d; 23a-b.). Referring to other philosophers (Erasmus (1465-1536), Rabelais (circa 1488-1553) and
Montaigne (1533-1592)), among others, he goes on to say that humankind 'needs to have conscience of
one's own limits' and links the universal validity of this statement with the difficulty for humans to recognize risks and uncertainties at all, whether they are human-made or natural phenomena. From this development the precautionary principle and later also the general belief that the cultivation of specialized
knowledge was the most adequate path to human safety and even happiness were derived. Human-made
destruction and the pressing need of controlling the uses of scientific knowledge led to thinking and acting

sustainable development might be understood from a wide variety of scholars to lie 'in the realm of natural law thinking',[153] the apparent accuracy and description of the real and factual effects of human impact cannot be denied. Rather, this framing clarifies the if-then prerequisite for the deployment of this dimension of sustainability.

67   With the (pending) case of *Nicaragua v Colombia*, violations of sovereign rights and maritime spaces in the Caribbean Sea have been claimed. While these claims are not directly attributable to any of the targets in SDG 14, the decision of the ICJ on the counter claims raised, underscores the limited admissibility of claims that are relevant to sustainable development. The ICJ found a lack of direct legal connection of the counter claims[154] with which Colombia sought to allege a violation of sovereign rights and maritime spaces in the Caribbean Sea. Colombia grounded its claims on Nicaragua's failure to 'prevent [the Nicaraguan] flag or licensed vessels from fishing in Colombia's waters; [...] from engaging in predatory and unlawful fishing methods in violation of its international obligations; [...] failing to fulfil its international legal obligations with respect to the environment in areas of the Caribbean Sea'.

68   Whereas the first two counterclaims were based on infringements of a duty of due diligence to protect and preserve the marine environment of the south-western Caribbean Sea and to protect the right of the inhabitants to benefit from a healthy, sound and sustainable environment, the third and fourth related to the infringement of customary artisanal fishing rights and international law. The ICJ turned down the first and second counter-claims as being inadmissible as such, thereby not forming part of the current proceedings.[155] The ICJ thus prevented two of the counterclaims on formal grounds, although it recognised 'that Colombia relies on the alleged failure of Nicaragua to protect and preserve the marine environment in the south-western Caribbean Sea' to prevent harmful private vessels flying under the Nicaraguan flag from predatory fishing practices and destroying the marine environment of the south-western Caribbean Sea and, thus, 'preventing the inhabitants [...] from benefiting from a healthy, sound and sustainable environment and habitat'.[156] Nevertheless, the ICJ referred to the different 'legal principles relied upon by the parties'. It thus denied a 'direct connection, either in fact or in law'[157] and prevented the observation and judicial review of conduct adverse to SDG 14.4, SDG 14.6 and SDG 14.7.

69   With ITLOS, an intergovernmental organisation which grounded on the mandate of the Third United Nations Conference on the Law of the Sea, a universal mechanism has been established for the judicial review of conflicts in the sphere of UNCLOS. Since 1982, ITLOS has dealt with 29 cases. Yet, few cases can be deemed contributing to SDG 14 specifically or to sustainable development principles in general. A majority of these cases dealt with several associated principles for managing the environmental impacts of human usage of the oceans (including, *inter alia*, the precautionary principle and

---

with moderation and care (awareness) in the 20th century and gave nascence to 'the formulation of the principles of prevention — to avoid environmental damage — and of precaution, to take action so as to foresee probable and even long-term harmful consequences to the environment, amidst scientific uncertainties' which also opened the door for the recognition of common goods, *Pulp Mills on the River Uruguay (Argentina v. Uruguay)*, Judgement, ICJ Reports 2010, paras. 67-83.

[153] *Pulp Mills on the River Uruguay (Argentina v. Uruguay)*, Judgement, ICJ Reports 2010, 14, 49, para. 90.

[154] *Alleged Violations of Sovereign Rights and Maritime Spaces in the Caribbean Sea (Nicaragua v. Colombia)*, Judgement on 17 March 2016, paras. 34 ff.

[155] *Alleged Violations of Sovereign Rights and Maritime Spaces in the Caribbean Sea (Nicaragua v. Colombia)*, Order, 15 November 2017; ICJ, *Yearbook, 2017 – 2018, pending cases*, 15.

[156] *Alleged Violations of Sovereign Rights and Maritime Spaces in the Caribbean Sea (Nicaragua v. Colombia)*, Order, 15 November 2017, para. 37.

[157] *Alleged Violations of Sovereign Rights and Maritime Spaces in the Caribbean Sea (Nicaragua v. Colombia)*, Order, 15 November 2017, para. 39.

environmental impact assessments). However, ITLOS has a clear mandate to adjudicate on matters of sustainable development.[158]

One of the most prominent cases is the *Seabed Mining Advisory Opinion*[159] of the   **70** Seabed Dispute Chamber[160] which was requested by the International Seabed Authority (ISA) Council following concerns by Nauru about the responsibilities and potential liabilities especially of developing States when sponsoring mining activities in the Area.[161] The *Opinion* addressed questions on the 'legal responsibilities and obligations of States Parties to the Convention with respect to the sponsorship of activities in the Area; extent of liability of a State Party for any failure to comply with the provisions; and what constitutes necessary and appropriate measures that a sponsoring State must take in order to fulfil its responsibilities under the relevant UNCLOS and the 1994 agreement. The Chamber offered observations particularly on the principles of sustainable use of natural resources, the principles of precaution and CBDR, equity and good governance. Although it does not refer to sustainable development, it can be read from the *Opinion* that it homogenously considered and interpreted the International Law Association's (ILA) understanding of sustainable development as set out in the 2002 New Delhi Declaration of Principles of International Law relating to Sustainable Development.[162] It stands out that the Chamber by interpreting the precautionary approach in the context of the Nodules and Sulphides Regulations where this principle has been included 'by express reference to the Rio Declaration'.[163] The opportunity to interpret and give legal meaning to the Rio Declaration is 'highly unusual—if not unique—for a judicial body'. The Chamber linked the precautionary principle not only by its customary nature but also by the 'summation of trends' to be a part of sustainable development through the obligation to fulfil due diligence,[164] thereby referring to the former *Southern Bluefin*

---

[158] Jaeckel and Stephens, 'The interpretation of sustainable development principles in ITLOS' in in Cordonier Segger and Weeramantry (eds), *Sustainable Development Principles in the Decisions of International Courts and Tribunals, 1992–2012* (2017), 339.

[159] ITLOS, *Responsibilities and obligations of States sponsoring persons and entities with respect to activities in the Area*, Request for Advisory Opinion Submitted to the Seabed Disputes Chamber, Advisory Opinion, 1 February 2011.

[160] The Seabed Dispute Chamber builds a further forum within ITLOS and is a legally independent body ('a tribunal within a tribunal') which interprets Part XI of UNCLOS and regulations on the exploration and exploitation of minerals at or beneath the international seabed, 'the Area' beyond the limits of national jurisdiction. Such regulations are adopted by the International Seabed Authority (ISA), which administers the Area 'on behalf of mankind as a whole', Jaeckel and Stephens, 'The interpretation of sustainable development principles in ITLOS' in Cordonier Segger and Weeramantry (eds), *Sustainable Development Principles in the Decisions of International Courts and Tribunals, 1992–2012* (2017), 346 f.

[161] Jaeckel and Stephens, 'The interpretation of sustainable development principles in ITLOS' in in Cordonier Segger and Weeramantry (eds), *Sustainable Development Principles in the Decisions of International Courts and Tribunals, 1992 – 2012* (2017), 346 f.

[162] ITLOS, *Responsibilities and obligations of States sponsoring persons and entities with respect to activities in the Area*, Request for Advisory Opinion Submitted to the Seabed Disputes Chamber, Advisory Opinion, 1 February 2011, paras. 99-150, 170-211, 223-41; see also: French, 'From the Depths: Rich Pickings of Principles of Sustainable Development and General International Law on the Ocean Floor—the Seabed Disputes Chamber's 2011 Advisory Opinion' (2011) 26 *International Journal of Marine and Coastal Law*, 525 (536 ff.); Freestone, 'Advisory Opinion of the Seabed Disputes Chamber' (2011) 15(7) *ASIL Insights*; Anton and Makgill and Payne, 'Seabed Mining—Advisory Opinion on Responsibility and Liability' (2011) 41 *Environmental Policy and Law*, 60-5.

[163] '[T]he Regulations note that States and the Authority "shall apply a precautionary approach, as reflected in Principle 15 of the Rio Declaration"', French, 'From the Depths: Rich Pickings of Principles of Sustainable Development and General International Law on the Ocean Floor—the Seabed Disputes Chamber's 2011 Advisory Opinion' (2011) 26 *International Journal of Marine and Coastal Law*, 525 (548).

[164] ITLOS, *Responsibilities and obligations of States sponsoring persons and entities with respect to activities in the Area*, Request for Advisory Opinion Submitted to the Seabed Disputes Chamber, Advisory Opinion, 1 February 2011, para. 130.

Tuna cases where the link of precaution and due diligence already had been made, albeit with the connotation of prudence and caution.[165] The *Opinion* even ten years back in time and having been developed before the nascence of the SDGs, gives a precious indication on at least three aspects: (1) it shows how interaction with the Area and with marine spheres beyond jurisdictions should be understood legally against the background of precaution and sustainable development, (2) how it is interwoven in international law in a manner that give rise to rights and responsibility (liability) of different actors, and (3) how international jurisprudence might further develop with relevance not only to the Area[166] but to common heritages of humankind in general.

71   The difficulties associated with the questions of illegal, unregulated and unreported (IUU) fishing (SDG 14.4, SDG 14.6) were addressed by ITLOS in the *Camouco*[167], *Monte Confurco*[168], *Volga*[169] and *Juno Trader*[170] cases which all were prompt release cases. The *Camouco, Monte Confurco* and *Volga* cases, which arose from arrests of vessels conducting IUU fishing for Patagonian toothfish in the Southern Ocean near Antarctica. In *Camouco* and *Monte Confurco*, and *Volga*, ITLOS needed to determine if the financial bond and other conditions set by the arresting States were 'reasonable'[171] for the purposes of Arts. 73 (Enforcement of laws and regulations of the coastal State) and 292 (Prompt release of vessels and crews) of UNCLOS. While ostensibly the questions examined are not directly related to the targets of SDG 14, these cases demonstrate the legal issues associated with this SDG. SDG 14, which legally relies on the application of UNCLOS and other regulations within its sphere, can, by logical consequence, hardly stand alone or marginalise areas that are conducive to its implementation and enforcement.

72   The necessary measures, including those of enforcement, to ensure compliance of vessels flying under the flag State can be read from the *SRFC* case where the Tribunal held that

> [t]he flag State, in fulfilment of its obligation to effectively exercise jurisdiction and control in administrative matters under article 94 of the Convention, has the obligation to adopt the necessary administrative measures to ensure that fishing vessels flying its flag are not involved in activities in the exclusive economic zones of the SRFC Member States which undermine the flag State's responsibility under article 192 of the Convention for protecting and preserving the marine environment and conserving the marine living resources which are an integral element of the marine environment. The foregoing obligations are obligations of "due diligence".[172]

2. European Jurisdiction

73   In the EU, the Common Fisheries Policy (CFP) sets the rules on management of the European fishing fleets and conservation of fishing stocks. The CFP aims to mitigate negative impacts and to prevent the degradation of the marine environment. Since its second reform in 2013, the CFP focuses on multispecies multiannual plans which

---

[165] *Southern Bluefin Tuna Cases* (*New Zealand v Japan; Australia v Japan*), Order of 27 August 1999, para. 77.

[166] See French, 'From the Depths: Rich Pickings of Principles of Sustainable Development and General International Law on the Ocean Floor—the Seabed Disputes Chamber's 2011 Advisory Opinion' (2011) 26 *International Journal of Marine and Coastal Law*, 525 (567 f.).

[167] *Camouco (Panama v France)* (prompt release) (2000) 125 ILR 151, (2000) 39 ILM 666.

[168] Monte Confurco (Seychelles v France) (prompt release) (2000) 125 ILR 203.

[169] *Volga (Russian Federation v Australia)* (prompt release) (2003) 42 ILM 159.

[170] *Juno Trader (St Vincent and the Grenadines v Bissau)* (prompt release) (2005) 44 ILM 498.

[171] The criterion of 'reasonableness' was already discussed in the very first case of ITLOS: *M/V Saiga (Saint Vincent and the Grenadines v Guinea)* (prompt release) (1997) 110 ILR 736, Judgment, 4 December 1997, para. 82.

[172] ITLOS, *Request for an Advisory Opinion Submitted by the Sub-Regional Fisheries Commission (SRFC)*, Advisory Opinion, 2 April 2015, para. 219.

point on the Maximum Sustainable Yield (MSY). The EU coastal and marine policy complements the CFP in the area of protection and clean-up of the coasts. The 7th Environment Action Programme covers, among others, marine waters in order to achieve or maintain good environmental status. Beyond its borders, the EU supports the protection of the marine environment and sustainable fisheries management through the European development policy. The EU agenda on International Ocean Governance focuses on securing safe, secure, and sustainable development of the oceans through better and more effective rules as well as through more effective knowledge and research.[173]

3. Arbitration Proceedings

Harmful fisheries subsidies unbalance the fishing industry, incentivising vessels to catch and remove fish faster than stocks can replenish. Bycatch is a threat to ocean life and is especially damaging to endangered species like some dolphins and sea turtles.   **74**

Even though many more fishers are employed by small-scale fisheries than industrial fleets, experts estimate that 81 per cent of governments' fisheries subsidies benefit large industrial fleets. This distorts access to marine resources at the expense of the many artisanal fishers for whom fishing is both a matter of survival and the heart of a rich cultural identity.[174]   **75**

With the 11th Ministerial Conference the Ministerial Decision gave rise for a new mandate to negotiate 'an agreement on comprehensive and effective disciplines that prohibit certain forms of fisheries subsidies that contribute to overcapacity and overfishing, and eliminate subsidies that contribute to IUU-fishing'.[175]   **76**

Despite the deadline set with SDG 14.6 and its importance for limiting the harm of fisheries subsidies having been acknowledged by the WTO,[176] the WTO failed to achieve an agreement on fisheries subsidies[177] till the end of 2021. Negotiations on the intended agreement are still ongoing.[178]   **77**

Under the guise of UNCLOS States parties have the responsibility to ensure compliance and liability for damage caused by exploitative activities in the Area, Art. 139. In the *South China Sea Arbitration*[179], the Arbitral Tribunal, amongst many other issues, examined the question as to whether the People's Republic of China could be held responsible for armed protecting vessels flying under the Chinese flag during their harmful fisheries' activities in the South China Sea within the EEZ of the Philippines. The Tribunal made clear that 'ensure' constitutes an obligation of conduct for the State. In refer-   **78**

---

[173] https://ec.europa.eu/sustainable-development/goal14_en.

[174] See also A/RES/73/165, United Nations Declaration on the Rights of Peasants and Other People Working in Rural Areas, 21 January 2019, Arts. 13, 17 and 20.

[175] WT/MIN(17)/64, WT/L/1031, 18 December 2017, Fisheries Subsidies, Ministerial Decision of 13 December 2017. The topics covered by this agreement were: subsidies contributing to illegal, unreported and unregulated (IUU) fishing, transparency, standstill, special and differential treatment, and institutional issues.

[176] https://www.wto.org/english/thewto_e/minist_e/mc11_e/briefing_notes_e/bffish_e.htm.

[177] https://www.wto.org/english/tratop_e/rulesneg_e/fish_e/fish_e.htm; further reading on fisheries subsidies harm: Bahety and Mukiibi, *WTO Fisheries Subsidies Negotiations: Main Issues and Interests of Least Developed Countries* (2017).

[178] https://www.wto.org/english/tratop_e/rulesneg_e/fish_e/fish_e.htm; https://www.wto.org/english/news_e/news21_e/fish_29oct21_e.htm.

[179] *Arbitration Between the Republic of the Philippines and the People's Republic of China*, PCA Case No. 2013-19, Jurisdiction and Admissibility (Oct. 29, 2015); In referring to *The South China Sea Arbitration (The Republic of Philippines v. The People's Republic of China)*, PCA Case No. 2013-19, Award of 12 July 2016, para. 944.

ring to *Pulp Mills*[180] and the *Seabed Disputes Chamber advisory opinion*[181], the Tribunal underscored that for meeting due diligence requirements 'appropriate rules and measures, but also a certain level of vigilance in their enforcement and the exercise of administrative control' must be set by the State.[182]

79   The Tribunal also ruled on the so-called 9-dash line. This internationally non-recognised territorial boundary in the South China Sea, set by the People's Republic of China that extends partly through Philippine sovereign territory, has been condemned by the Tribunal in the *South China Sea Arbitration*.[183] Although the Tribunal did not rule on the issue of sea boundary limitations, the ruling shows that sovereign rights are unequivocally vested in living and non-living resources belonging only to the exclusive economic zone and the continental shelf of the coastal state. Sovereign rights cannot exist simultaneously over the same resources stored in this area. Rather, with particular regard to the 'continental shelf, the rights of other states are limited to laying cables and pipelines and to the rights and freedoms to which they are otherwise entitled in the superjacent waters.'[184] Nor could this be interrupted by the historical rights asserted by China, which the Tribunal also denied.[185] The tribunal declared the effect of exclusive fisheries zones to be 'a matter of customary law'.[186] The 'nine-dash-line' could naturally not be upheld with regard to UNCLOS as a recognised international body of rules, as this line is diametrically opposed to it.[187] This decision significantly nourishes the meaning of SDG 14.b and SDG 14.c in particular and demonstrates both the strength of judicial interpretation of international law as an instrument of protection for sustainably managed environmental systems such as the ocean, but also reveals the link between conflicts driven by original understandings of sovereignty under international law and the act of sustainable action, today borne out of the content of SDG 14.

80   However, the multi-layered and intricate conflict over fishing grounds, oil and gas resources and the control of a major shipping route in the South China Sea still persists and has recently been subject to increasing tensions and military interventions.[188] The power struggle over resources inevitably affects the shaping of sustainable development and implementation of the SDGs.

81   With regard to the conservation and sustainable use of oceans, the DSB decided very clearly on how states can perform or implement protective (environmental) legislation

---

[180] *Pulp Mills on the River Uruguay (Argentina v. Uruguay)*, Judgment, ICJ Reports 2010, 14.

[181] Request for an *Advisory Opinion Submitted by the Sub-Regional Fisheries Commission (SRFC)*, Advisory Opinion of 2 April 2015, ITLOS Reports 2015, para. 131; quoting *Pulp Mills on the River Uruguay (Argentina v. Uruguay)*, Judgment, ICJ Reports 2010, 14, at 79, para. 197.

[182] *The South China Sea Arbitration (The Republic of Philippines v. The People's Republic of China)*, PCA Case No. 2013-19, Award of 12 July 2016, para. 944.

[183] *Arbitration Between the Republic of the Philippines and the People's Republic of China*, PCA Case No. 2013-19, Jurisdiction and Admissibility (Oct. 29, 2015); In referring to *The South China Sea Arbitration (The Republic of Philippines v. The People's Republic of China)*, PCA Case No. 2013-19, Award of 12 July 2016, para. 944.

[184] *Arbitration Between the Republic of the Philippines and the People's Republic of China*, PCA Case No. 2013-19, 29 October 2015, para. 244.

[185] *Arbitration Between the Republic of the Philippines and the People's Republic of China*, PCA Case No. 2013-19, 29 October 2015.

[186] *Arbitration Between the Republic of the Philippines and the People's Republic of China*, PCA Case No. 2013-19, 29 October 2015, para. 257.

[187] *Arbitration Between the Republic of the Philippines and the People's Republic of China*, PCA Case No. 2013-19, 29 October 2015, para. 278.

[188] https://www.reuters.com/world/asia-pacific/philippines-vows-continue-maritime-exercises-south-china-sea-2021-05-02/.

to not interfere with WTO law. In the *US – Shrimp I*[189] case, the US, in referring to the Convention on International Trade in Endangered Species of Wild Fauna and Flora (CITES), had set import bans on shrimp that that has not been proven to provide a certain degree of protection from bycatch, particularly of the most endangered sea turtles. India, Malaysia, Pakistan and Thailand did not comply with their regulation and practices to this requirement. The DSB first emphasised the importance and relevance of the 'the objective of sustainable development' as included in the preamble of the WTO agreement and further international instruments such as CITES, UNCLOS, the CBD and Agenda 21. The dispute settlement body recognised that the US measures did comply with the legitimate safeguard purpose of Art. XX(g) GATT 1994.[190] Nevertheless, it underlined that

> this measure has been applied by the U. S. in a manner which constitutes arbitrary and unjustifiable discrimination between Members of the WTO, contrary to the requirements of the chapeau of Art. XX. [...] WTO Members are free to adopt their own policies aimed at protecting the environment as long as, in so doing, they fulfill *(sic!)* their obligations and respect the rights of other Members under the WTO Agreement

In particular, the DSB argued that it did not meet the test of Art. XX GATT 1994   **82** and was therefore not justified. With this decision, the DSB in principle granted scope for unilaterally enacted legislation with extraterritorial reach that even implements sustainable development requirements or, with regard to the SDGs currently in place, serves precisely their protective purpose. In any case, international legal instruments, including *soft law*, are permissible in order to interpret WTO law.[191]

An indication on how due diligence is to be understood when preventing 'illegal,   **83** unreported and unregulated fishing and destructive fishing practices' (SDG 14.4) was shown in the *Request for an Advisory Opinion submitted by the Sub-Regional Fisheries Commission (SRFC)* in 2015.[192] ITLOS moreover clarified that the duty of proper acting when sustainably using the ocean and its resources (SDG 14.c) addresses the flag states and the involved international organisations as well. These rights bearers are obliged to fulfil their 'due diligence'

> to ensure that vessels flying their flag do not engage in IUU fishing activities, and that the flag state may be held liable if that obligation of due diligence is breached. In addition, the Tribunal clarified that where fisheries competence has been transferred from a state to an international organization, it is the organization, not the flag state, that may face liability for a failure to have taken adequate measures to prevent IUU fishing.[193]

Finally, the Tribunal confirmed that coastal states have a duty to consult and cooper-   **84** ate[194] with each other in the sustainable management of shared stocks[195] and highly mi-

---

[189] WT/DS58/AB/R, *United States — Import Prohibition of Certain Shrimp and Shrimp Products (US – Shrimp I)*, AB Report, 15 June 2001.

[190] WT/DS58/AB/R, *United States — Import Prohibition of Certain Shrimp and Shrimp Products (US – Shrimp I)*, AB Report, 15 June 2001, para. 132.

[191] Gehring and Genest, 'Disputes on sustainable development in the WTO regime' in Cordonier Segger and Weeramantry, *Sustainable Development Principles in the Decisions of International Courts and Tribunals, 1999 – 2012* (2017), 357 (364 f.).

[192] ITLOS, *Request for an Advisory Opinion submitted by the Sub-Regional Fisheries Commission (SRFC)* (Request for Advisory Opinion submitted to the Tribunal), Advisory Opinion of 2 April 2015.

[193] ITLOS, *Request for an Advisory Opinion submitted by the Sub-Regional Fisheries Commission (SRFC)* (Request for Advisory Opinion submitted to the Tribunal), Advisory Opinion of 2 April 2015, para. 114.

[194] ITLOS, *Request for an Advisory Opinion submitted by the Sub-Regional Fisheries Commission (SRFC)* (Request for Advisory Opinion submitted to the Tribunal), Advisory Opinion of 2 April 2015, para. 199.

[195] 'Shared stocks' are 'stocks occurring within the exclusive economic zones of two or more coastal states or both within the exclusive economic zone and in an area beyond and adjacent to it', Art. 2(12)

gratory species. It further clarified that the meaning of sustainable management is to be guided by Art. 61 UNCLOS as 'the basic framework concerning the conservation and management of the living resources in the exclusive economic zone' with the 'conserv[ing] and develop[ing fish stocks] as a viable and sustainable resource' as the ultimate goal.[196] The tribunal also indicated what constitutes sustainable fisheries management:

> The Tribunal is of the view that the term "development of such stocks" used in article 63, paragraph 1, of the Convention suggests that these stocks should be used as fishery resources within the framework of a sustainable fisheries management regime. This may include the exploitation of non-exploited stocks or an increase in the exploitation of under-exploited stocks through the development of responsible fisheries, as well as more effective fisheries management schemes to ensure the long-term sustainability of exploited stocks. This may also include stock restoration, guided by the requirement under article 61 of the Convention [UNCLOS] that a given stock is not endangered by over-exploitation, thus preserving it as a long-term viable resource.

4. Domestic Jurisdiction

85   In domestic jurisdiction some quite progressive decisions can be found that support a clear utterance with the contents of SDG 14, but moreover give meaning and impetus to the UN approach Harmony with Nature. This approach connects self-standing rights for (parts of) nature (Earth-centred law) indispensably with the human right to a healthy environment since human health and well-being depends on much more than wealth. The 2020 Report of the Secretary-General states:

> With the acceleration of climate change and ecosystems being pushed to collapse, the human right to a healthy environment cannot be achieved without securing Nature's own rights first. More precisely, the human right to life is meaningless if the ecosystems that sustain humankind do not have the legal rights to exist. Furthermore, the rights of each sentient being are limited by the rights of all other beings to the extent necessary for the maintenance of the integrity, balance and health of larger ecological communities.[197]

Convention on the Determination of the Minimal Conditions for Access and Exploitation of Marine Resources within the Maritime Areas under Jurisdiction of the Member States of the Sub-Regional Fisheries Commission (SRFC) (MCA Convention).

[196] ITLOS, *Request for an Advisory Opinion submitted by the Sub-Regional Fisheries Commission (SRFC)* (Request for Advisory Opinion submitted to the Tribunal), Advisory Opinion of 2 April 2015, paras. 189 f.; ITLOS stressed in particular paras. 2, 3 and 4 of Art. 61 UNCLOS:
Conservation of the living resources
2. The coastal State, taking into account the best scientific evidence available to it, shall ensure through proper conservation and management measures that the maintenance of the living resources in the exclusive economic zone is not endangered by over-exploitation. As appropriate, the coastal State and competent international organizations, whether subregional, regional or global, shall cooperate to this end.
3. Such measures shall also be designed to maintain or restore populations of harvested species at levels which can produce the maximum sustainable yield, as qualified by relevant environmental and economic factors, including the economic needs of coastal fishing communities and the special requirements of developing States, and taking into account fishing patterns, the interdependence of stocks and any generally recommended international minimum standards, whether subregional, regional or global.
4. In taking such measures the coastal State shall take into consideration the effects on species associated with or dependent upon harvested species with a view to maintaining or restoring populations of such associated or dependent species above levels at which their reproduction may become seriously threatened.
[197] A/75/266, *Harmony with Nature, Report of the Secretary-General*, para. 41; A/75/266, *Supplement to SG Report on Harmony with Nature*: This special Supplement complements the Report on Harmony with Nature (A/75/266) and includes over 170 cases and developments in Earth Jurisprudence, advances in law and policy, and initiatives in both formal and informal education, learning and public outreach activities worldwide, during the second half of 2019 and the first half of 2020.

The fact that the systematic linking of the human right to a healthy environment   **86**
with the concerns of environmental and climate protection, with special consideration
of the intergenerational equity concept, is not always judicially assertive was shown by
the rejecting decision in *Pandey v. India*. The applicant, citing the UNFCCC and the
Paris Agreement, had sought to expand India's climate change legislation to include
the 'integrity of all ecosystems, including oceans and the protection of biodiversity'[198]
since it otherwise endangers 'the survival and well-being of plants, fish, wildlife, and
biodiversity'.[199] The National Green Tribunal did not accept this application for decision
as it considered the national 1986 Environment (Protection) Act to be sufficient. International agreements such as the Paris Agreement were not considered to add to the
already existing legislation.[200]

However, a decision from the Judicial Committee of the Privy Council[201] from 2017   **87**
does point to the fact that jurisdiction takes up extensive references to principles,
agreements and even voluntary guidelines as well as (planned) instruments as context
for judicial interpretation, which can also be found as cornerstones of the concept of the
Global Agenda 2030 and its underlying principle of sustainable development:

> The Polluter Pays Principle (PPP) is now firmly established as a basic principle of international
> and domestic environmental laws. It is designed to achieve the "internalization of environmental
> costs", by ensuring that the costs of pollution control and remediation are borne by those who cause
> the pollution, and thus reflected in the costs of their goods and services, rather than borne by the
> community at large (see e. g. OECD Council 1972 Recommendation of the Council on Guiding
> Principles concerning International Economic Aspects of Environmental Policies; Rio Declaration
> 1992 Principle 16). Most recently, the Principle has been simply expressed in the Draft Global
> Pact for the Environment, presented by President Macron to the United Nations Assembly on 19
> September 2017.[202]

To read a progression of the law in this legal area and to attribute this to SDG 14   **88**
and its legal history, must at this point be assigned to the respective jurisdiction as there
cannot be established that a clear or common legal orientation already exists.

II. The Enforcement of a 'Right to healthy Oceans, Seas and Marine Resources'

The content of SDG 14 and its embeddedness in UNCLOS and maritime law regimes   **89**
reveals to a certain extent how a sustainably managed ocean or an ecologically sound
marine resource is constituted. UNCLOS and the legal provisions based on it provide a
multitude of principles that that lead to certain state obligations such as taking all mea-

---

[198] National Green Tribunal, Principal Bench, New Delhi, Original Application No. 187/2017, Order of
15 January 2019 (*Pandey v. India*), para. 7.
[199] National Green Tribunal of India, Principal Bench, New Delhi, *Pandey v. India*, Original Application
No. 187/2017, para. vii. (b).
[200] National Green Tribunal, Principal Bench, New Delhi, *Pandey v. India*, Order of 15 January 2019,
para. 3.
[201] The Judicial Committee of the Privy Council is the court of final appeal for the UK overseas
territories and Crown dependencies, and for those Commonwealth countries that have retained the appeal
to Her Majesty in Council or, in the case of Republics, to the Judicial Committee.
[202] Decision from the Judicial Committee of the Privy Council), *Fisherman and Friends of the Sea v. The
Minister of Planning, Housing and the Environment*, 27 November 2017.

sures necessary to prevent, reduce and control pollution of the marine environment from any source, Art. 194(1) UNCLOS.[203]

90   However, this fundament of law holds in itself a number of ambiguities. It is far from clear how a 'right to healthy oceans, seas and marine resources' relating to the continental shelf beyond 200 nautical miles can be shaped and how the addressees of SDG 14 should or must act beyond this point or how it could even be enforced. Further controversies on the legal treatment are likely to occur or worsening in the Arctic and Antarctic regions,[204] the East and South China Sea where competing claims challenges the work of ITLOS or the Commission on the Limits of the Continental Shelf (Commission). The escalating conflicts, some of which are openly being carried out, underline the limited possibilities of enforcement of a decision by ITLOS and the even minor weight of the recommendations of the Commission. They have no independent power to enforce their respective pronouncements. Although monitoring mechanisms exist, compliance still depends on the voluntary submission of states to the decision or recommendations.[205]

91   Nevertheless, this could open up much more far-reaching possibilities. The Chamber's reference to the obligation to protect the marine environment in areas beyond national jurisdiction as an *erga omnes* obligation implied that each State Party may bring a claim. With this assessment, the Chamber accepted, 'in principle, the existence of an actio popularis for environmental harm to global commons.'[206] The Chamber thus became the first international standard-setting body to acknowledge Art. 48 of the ILC Articles on State Responsibility.[207] The *Seabed Mining Advisory Opinion* has lessened existing doubts about the legal status of Art. 48 and solidified its position in international law. This could prove significant in understanding the ability of international courts to enforce environmental obligations and thus, to enforce goals set by SDG 14.

III. De Facto Influences on Jurisdiction

92   In 2016, UNCTAD obtained a new mandate[208] on oceans and seas at the UNCTAD 14 Conference with which the UN agency should seek to support developing countries, in particular SIDS

> in cooperation with other relevant international organizations and other stakeholders [...] in the advancement of Sustainable Development Goal 14 in the design and implementation of regional

---

[203] See A/RES/72/249, *International legally binding instrument under the United Nations Convention on the Law of the Sea on the conservation and sustainable use of marine biological diversity of areas beyond national jurisdiction*, 19 January 2018.

[204] See e.g. Convention on the Regulation of Antarctic Mineral Resource Activities (1988).

[205] Subedi, 'The Role of the Commission on the Limits of the Continental Shelf in the Governance of the Seas and Oceans' (2018) in Attard and Ong and Kritsiotis, *The IMLI Treatise On Global Ocean Governance: Volume I: UN and Global Ocean Governance* (2018), 94 ff.

[206] French, 'The Sofia Guiding Statements on sustainable development principles in the decisions of international tribunals' in Cordonier Segger and Weeramantry (eds), *Sustainable Development Principles in the Decisions of International Courts and Tribunals, 1999 – 2012* (2017), 202.

[207] International Law Commission, *Draft articles on Responsibility of States for Internationally Wrongful Acts, with commentaries* (2001), Art. 48. Invocation of responsibility by a State other than an injured State, Yearbook of the International Law Commission, 2001, Vol. II, Part Two, Report, Supplement No. 10 (A/56/10).

[208] TD/519/Add.2*, *Nairobi Maafikiano, From decision to action: Moving towards an inclusive and equitable global economic environment for trade and development*, 5 September 2016, para. 100(t).

and/or national economic development strategies for the conservation and sustainable use of oceans and their resources [...].[209]

UNCTAD has since translated the mandate into a variety of Oceans Economy   **93**
and Trade Strategies (OETS)[210] which address, amongst others, maritime and coastal tourism, offshore operations such as oil, gas and wind, port activities and fisheries, waste disposal and transportation. Subsidies that contribute to overcapacity and overfishing, as mentioned in SDG 14.6, are of particular concern. Several members supported a ban on such subsidies that contribute to overfishing and overcapacity of a fleet. However, despite a unanimous agreement on the principle, the lacking internationally agreed definition of 'overfishing' or 'overcapacity' has so far prevented an effective rejection of these subsidies policies since such a definition is determinant for classifying which subsidies are in fact harmful. As yet, no such definition could be agreed due to diverging global approaches, although some initial approaches have been made. Special and differential treatment (SDG 14.6) is also being explicitly developed further, with the aim of extending the transition periods, specifically for developing states or 'for implementing prohibitions regarding unreported unregulated fishing [...] in general or for small scale, artisanal and subsistence fishing activities'.[211] The recommended Ocean Economy Classification primarily enables the accurate data collection of 'trade-related and other relevant statistics for the monitoring and analysis of ocean-based sectors, as a whole or by sector, at the national and global levels or from a supply or demand perspective' and thus complements the indicators on SDG 14 and enhances private and governmental standard setting such as policy decisions on the allocation of resources.[212] The found common understanding is likely to result in new standards which will shape the marine-related economy, contributes to SDG 14, and in the (not so far) future may consequently also be reflected in jurisdiction. Further influence is exerted through the FAO which has a crucial role in the promotion of productive and sustainable fisheries and the IMO which is responsible for safety and security for of shipping.

In addition to these institutional influences, the legal framework of SDG 14 implies   **94**
a clear limitation in the emergence, development and application of further jurisdiction. UNCLOS, for instance, as the main framework to be applied, restricts the possibility of judicial review to those parties (duty and /or rights bearers) which originally belong to the sphere of public law. Solely states can make use of this legal recourse. However, cargo owners and shipping companies as some of the main actors in this legal area are excluded from the authority of UNCLOS.[213] As a frequent issue, the interests of vessel owners, cargo owners and shipping companies differ from that of either the flag

---

[209] TD/519/Add.2*, *Nairobi Maafikiano, From decision to action: Moving towards an inclusive and equitable global economic environment for trade and development*, 5 September 2016, para. 100(t).

[210] To name but a few: UNCTAD, *Blue BioTrade: Harnessing Marine Trade to Support, Ecological Sustainability and Economic Equity* (2018); UNCTAD, *Advancing Sustainable Development Goal 14: Sustainable fish, seafood value chains, trade and climate* (2019); UNCTAD, *Towards A Harmonized International Trade Classification For The Development Of Sustainable Ocean-Based Economies* (2021).

[211] UNCTAD, *Advancing Sustainable Development Goal 14: Sustainable fish, seafood value chains, trade and climate* (2019), 29 f.

[212] See UNCTAD, *Towards A Harmonized International Trade Classification For The Development Of Sustainable Ocean-Based Economies* (2021), 38 f.; see on effects of indicators and standard setting: Huck, 'The UN Sustainable Development Goals and the Governance of Global Public Goods, The Quest for Legitimacy' (2021) in Iovane et al. (eds), *The Protection of General Interests in Contemporary International Law: A Theoretical and Empirical Inquiry* (2021), 361-82; see on effects of science and business collaborations: Österblom et al., 'Emergence of a global science-business initiative for ocean stewardship' (2017) 114(34) *Proc Natl Acad Sci U S A*, 9038-43.

[213] See Shaughnessy and Tobin, 'Flags of Inconvenience, Freedom and Insecurity on the High Seas' (2018) 5 *Journal of International Law & Policy*, 10.

state (which must not be the same) or from those of the state in which coastal zone they operate. Whereas the maritime crews technically fall into the scope of UNCLOS and other international agreements, private actors (companies or owners) do not which coincides with the fact that they are hardly regulated in this area.

E. Conclusion on SDG 14

95   Carbon emissions from human activities are causing ocean warming, acidification and oxygen loss with some evidence of changes in nutrient cycling and primary production. The warming ocean is affecting marine organisms at multiple trophic levels, impacting fisheries with implications for food production and human communities. Concerns regarding the effectiveness of existing ocean and fisheries governance have already been reported, highlighting the need for timely mitigation and adaptation responses.

96   The implementation is aggravated by the fact that most indicators for SDG 14 targets are classified as 'Tier 3' which is the lowest-ranking SDG indicator and means that 'no internationally established methodology or standards are yet available for the indicator'. Consequently, the overall progress towards SDG 14 and its reflection in the different jurisdictions can hardly be evaluated as valid. Thus, the extent to which governance and monitoring can be deemed successful considering the 'complicated nature of social and economic systems related to the oceans and the complex ecosystems within them' is difficult to ascertain.[214]

97   SDG 14 unfortunately lacks at first glance participatory elements and does not include the forms of management it needs to be implemented, nor does it directly link to gender equality or human rights. In this respect, it falls *prima vista* behind in the degree of connection, specifically to the human rights background of the Agenda 2030 and the other SDGs contained. SDG 14 related questions and their entanglement with inherent challenges, in particular with the impact of climate change as analysed by the IPCC, shows that participatory elements exist but expressed directly. As mentioned in the introduction of this book, the external systematic leads to the prevalence of concepts related to the general agenda of the SDGs. In the text of the Global Agenda 2030 it has been stated that human rights are fundamental for the understanding and the applicability of the SDGs.[215] Here, the concept of the wrapped SDGs with internal and external systemic relationships reveals their inherent core of human rights ant their participatory approach, which is underlined as well in SDG 17. The SDGs cannot be perceived as an isolated content but are interwoven with the concept of sustainable development in its three dimensions and overarched from the inherent 'planetarian' concept as well. As laid down in the very introduction, particularly the Small Island Developing States (SIDS) through the implementation of the SIDS Accelerated Modalities of Action (SAMOA) help create the SIDS Partnership toolbox, (→ reflecting the urgent demands of affected communities (→ Goal 17)).[216]

98   Adverse to implementation is that the protection of marine ecosystems does not provide guidance on how to relate to states or global waters. Obviously, joint state

---

[214] IIED, Beauchamp and Lucks, *MEL Handbook for SDG 14 – Conserve and sustainably use the oceans, seas and marine resources for sustainable development* (2019), 13.

[215] A/RES/70/1, preamble, paras. 19, 35.

[216] A/RES/74/3, Political declaration of the high-level meeting to review progress made in addressing the priorities of small island developing States through the implementation of the SIDS Accelerated Modalities of Action (SAMOA) Pathway, 10 October 2019.

responsibilities (should logically) prevail in the scope of application of SDG 14[217] since otherwise no effective implementation could be realised. The jurisdiction examined, however, show that this responsibility does not always follow despite being demanded by compulsory legal frameworks. The great variety parts of jurisdiction which range from 'areas of the sea and the sea-bed' to 'ships' and 'navigation and fishing' as well as 'the absence of an 'owner'[218] make even more difficult to identify actual obligations without getting lost in context. Furthermore, the possibilities to also subject private actors to judicial control and actually hold them liable are still very limited. It is likely that this will change in the future with increasing climate change. A clearer assessment must therefore be awaited so far.

The inadequacies already identified in SDG 6, and in particular the lacking link to the global water cycles, including the cryosphere also make the ecosystem approach, at least the one formulated in SDG 14, appear more than questionable. Watercourses, the high seas and marine ecosystems are naturally interconnected. A separate consideration is therefore neither possible nor purposeful. It is surprising that the actual purpose of SDG 14 is then agreed to be the provision of marine resources for human use – albeit for sustainable use. It becomes particularly clear here that the conservation of ecosystems ultimately serves only human development, and that natural capital ultimately serves only as human capital. This might be in line with the anthropocentric approach inherent in the SDGs and the Global Agenda 2030. Thus, although SDG 14 concerns global commons, the preservation of which is already a pursuit in itself, it degrades it to the level of harnessing it for human needs, regardless of any ownership. **99**

If, like Boyle, it is assumed to be true that the SDGs have 'given the concept of sustainable development more concrete content, [...] they may also have under-estimated the seriousness of the environmental problems the world continues to generate on a global scale.'[219] SDG 14 would thus be a very evident example of both the principle of sustainable development as a 'development tool' for humankind (and not as a protective tool of a common vision at all costs) and the lack of coherence and balance in the SDGs in their entirety. **100**

However, it should be noted that the limited scope of SDG 14 does not exclusively aim at the sustainable maintenance and use of the oceans by means of environmental measures, but that original economic measures also accompany this object of protection. **101**

Against this background, it seems more than questionable how SDG 14 can be successfully implemented. The set 2020 deadline for sustainably managing and protecting marine and coastal ecosystems (SDG 14.2), effectively regulating harvesting and over-exploitation of fish stock and yield (SDG 14.4), and restricting fisheries subsidies (SDG 14.6) already expired with SDG 14 not having been satisfactorily achieved. This all the more underscores that the difficulties prevalent in the multilevel legal system also affect the achievement of SDG 14. **102**

The existing international agreements have so far failed to stop illegal fishing and its subsidisation. Without a solid legal basis and a clear enforceability of legal norms by appropriately mandated authorities, it will not be possible to get a grip on the numerous problems, also in the wake of climate change. Describing the problems is one thing, establishing rights is another. If the will in the multilateral sphere is not sufficient, the oceans will not get the protection they need, not even in the interest of the people. **103**

---

[217] And is demanded from UNCLOS.

[218] Reid, 'Protection of Sites' in Lees and Viñuales, *The Oxford Handbook of Comparative Environmental Law* (2019), 848 f.

[219] Boyle, 'Climate Change, Sustainable Development, and Human Rights' in Kaltenborn and Krajewski and Kuhn (eds), *Sustainable Development Goals and Human Rights* (2020), 174.

Goal 15

Protect, restore and promote sustainable use of terrestrial ecosystems, sustainably manage forests, combat desertification, and halt and reverse land degradation and halt biodiversity loss

15.1 By 2020, ensure the conservation, restoration and sustainable use of terrestrial and inland freshwater ecosystems and their services, in particular forests, wetlands, mountains and drylands, in line with obligations under international agreements

15.2 By 2020, promote the implementation of sustainable management of all types of forests, halt deforestation, restore degraded forests and substantially increase afforestation and reforestation globally

15.3 By 2030, combat desertification, restore degraded land and soil, including land affected by desertification, drought and floods, and strive to achieve a land degradation-neutral world

15.4 By 2030, ensure the conservation of mountain ecosystems, including their biodiversity, in order to enhance their capacity to provide benefits that are essential for sustainable development

15.5 Take urgent and significant action to reduce the degradation of natural habitats, halt the loss of biodiversity and, by 2020, protect and prevent the extinction of threatened species

15.6 Promote fair and equitable sharing of the benefits arising from the utilization of genetic resources and promote appropriate access to such resources, as internationally agreed

15.7 Take urgent action to end poaching and trafficking of protected species of flora and fauna and address both demand and supply of illegal wildlife products

15.8 By 2020, introduce measures to prevent the introduction and significantly reduce the impact of invasive alien species on land and water ecosystems and control or eradicate the priority species

15.9 By 2020, integrate ecosystem and biodiversity values into national and local planning, development processes, poverty reduction strategies and accounts

15.a Mobilize and significantly increase financial resources from all sources to conserve and sustainably use biodiversity and ecosystems

15.b Mobilize significant resources from all sources and at all levels to finance sustainable forest management and provide adequate incentives to developing countries to advance such management, including for conservation and reforestation

15.c Enhance global support for efforts to combat poaching and trafficking of protected species, including by increasing the capacity of local communities to pursue sustainable livelihood opportunities

Word Count 'terrestrial ecosystems' and 'forests' and 'desertification' and 'biodiversity': 10
A/RES/70/1 - Transforming our world: the 2030 Agenda for Sustainable Development: 'terrestrial ecosystems': 3 'forests': 7 'desertification': 6 'biodiversity': 10
Instruments mentioned in A/RES/70/1 in the section entitled: 'Sustainable Development Goals and targets':
A/RES/69/313 - Addis Ababa Action Agenda of the Third International Conference on Financing for Development adopted on 27 July 2015: 'terrestrial ecosystems': 1 'forests': 1 'desertification': 3 'biodiversity': 10
A/RES/66/288 - The future we want (Rio +20 Declaration) adopted on 27 July 2012: 'terrestrial ecosystems': 0 'forests': 15 'desertification': 10 'biodiversity': 27
A/RES/55/2 - United Nations Millennium Declaration adopted on 8 September 2000: 'terrestrial ecosystems': 0 'forests': 1 'desertification': 'biodiversity': 0

Select Bibliography: Sumudu Atapattu and Andrea Schapper, *Human Rights and the Environment, Key Issues* (Routledge, UK/USA 2019); Ben Boer and Ian Hannam, 'Land Degradation' in Emma Lees and Jorge E. Viñuales (eds), *The Oxford Handbook of Comparative Environment Law* (Oxford University Press, Oxford 2019), 438; Peter Bridgewater, Mathieu Régnier and Roberto Cruz García, 'Implementing SDG 15: Can large-scale public programs help deliver biodiversity conservation, restoration and management, while assisting human development?' (2015) 39 *Natural Resources Forum*, 214; Antônio Augusto Cançado Trindade, 'Principle 15, Precaution' in Jorge E. Viñuales (ed), *The Rio Declaration on Environment and Development* (Oxford University Press, Oxford 2015), 425; Marie-Claire Cordonier Segger and H. E. Judge Christopher Gregory Weeramantry, *Sustainable Development Principles in the Decisions of International Courts and Tribunals, 1992 – 2012* (Routledge, UK/USA 2017); Thomas Cottier and Bürgi Bonanomi, 'Soil as a Common Concern: Toward Disciplines on Sustainable Land Management' in Thomas Cottier and Krista Nadakavukaren Schefer (eds), *Elgar Encyclopedia of International Economic Law* (Edward Elgar Publishing, UK/USA 2017), 628; Erin Daly, *Human Rights and the Environment, Legality, Indivisibility, Dignity and Geography* (Edward Elgar Publishing, UK/USA 2019); Alan Boyle, 'Human Rights and the Environment: Where Next?' (2012) 23 *EJIL*, 613; Food and Agriculture Organization, *Keeping an eye on SDG 15* (FAO, Rome 2013); Agustín García-Ureta, 'Nature Conservation' in Emma Lees and Jorge E. Viñuales, *The Oxford Handbook on Comparative Environmental Law* (Oxford University Press, Oxford 2019), 460; Antonio G M La Viña and Alaya de Leon, 'Conserving and Enhancing Sinks and Reservoirs of Greenhouse Gases, including Forests (Article 5)' in Daniel R. Klein, María Pía Carazo, Meinhard Doelle, Jane Bulmer and Andrew Higham (eds), *The Paris Agreement on Climate Change: Analysis and Commentary* (Oxford University Press, Oxford 2017), 166; OECD, *The Post-2020 Biodiversity Framework: Targets, indicators and measurability implication at global and national level Interim report, November 2019 Prepared by the OECD* (OECD, Paris 2019); Raina K. Plowright, Jamie K Reaser, Harvey Locke, Stephen J Woodley, Prof Jonathan A Patz, Daniel J Becker, Gabriel Oppler, Prof Peter J Hudson and Gary M Tabor, 'Land use-induced spillover: a call to action to safeguard environmental, animal, and human health' (2021) 5 E237–45 *Lancet Planet Health*; Molly Sargen, *Biological Roles of Water: Why is water necessary for life?*(2019)/; UNODC, *World Wildlife Crime Report, Trafficking in protected species* (United Nations Publication, Vienna/New York 2020); Gus Waschefort, 'Wild Fauna and Flora Protection', in Robin Geiß and Nils Melzer (eds), *The Oxford Handbook of International Law of Global Security* (2021), 610; Burcu Yüksel Ripley, *Covid-19 and Illegal Wildlife Trade: Where does the Law Fail and How Digital Technologies can help?*

A. Background and Origin of SDG 15

According to its title, SDG 15 is dedicated to protecting, restoring and promoting the   1
sustainable use of terrestrial ecosystems, sustainable management of forests, combating

desertification, and halting and reversing land degradation and biodiversity loss. 12 targets and 14 indicators have been set to measure the achievement of this programme linked to nature on land. SDG 15 is to be understood as an objective with an anthropocentric character ($\rightarrow$ Intro mn. 60 ff., 135, 229).

2 Human life is strictly dependent on life on the land, not least because a multitude of different factors influence human well-being. Agriculture, for example, is the central source of nutrients,[1] fresh water sources make human life possible in the first place,[2] forests are important sources of raw materials[3] and at the same time are able to absorb and store large amounts of CO_2.[4] Forests provide ecosystems service and are crucial for the human welfare.[5]

3 However, these factors are under threat and steadily declining, with direct and indirect impacts on human well-being. The world's forest areas, which have shrunk by 100 million hectares since 2000, are particularly at risk.[6] At the same time, this means a massive reduction in the habitats of many animal species and contributes to a loss of biodiversity.[7] Furthermore, the amount of CO^2 absorbed and stored by trees is decreasing and thus also contributes to climate change. At the same time, desertification is steadily progressing, thus also causing a loss of forest areas and at the same time harming agriculture by making more and more land unusable for agriculture.[8] This causes massive soil degradation and poses a threat to many different animal species ($\rightarrow$ Goal 14).[9]

4 Demands for the sustainable use of forests are not merely a phenomenon of the present day because of their special importance for mankind. In Germany, for example, concrete considerations for sustainable forest management can be documented as early as the 18th century.[10]

5 At the UN level, first demands for sustainable management of the environment can be seen at the Stockholm Conference in 1972. The demand for a sustainable management of the Earth's natural resources already exists in Principle 2[11] and, additionally, the protection of biodiversity and its habitats which was also called for.[12] While these demands are broad and general, particular steps to protect specific aspects such as the

---

[1] https://www.undp.org/content/undp/en/home/sustainable-development-goals/goal-15-life-on-land.html.
[2] Sargen, *Biological Roles of Water: Why is water necessary for life?* (2019).
[3] FAO, *2020 State of the World's Forests* (2020), 2.
[4] UN Forum on Forests, *Forests and Climate Change* (2019), 5.
[5] Katila et al, *Sustainable Development Goals: Their Impacts on Forests and People* (2019), 10.
[6] UN, *The Sustainable Development Goals Report 2020* (2020), 55.
[7] UN, *The Sustainable Development Goals Report 2020* (2020), 55.
[8] IPCC, *Special Report Climate Change and Land* (2020), 260.
[9] UN, *The Sustainable Development Goals Report 2020* (2020), 55; see also Convention on the Conservation of Migratory Species of Wild Animals (1979).
[10] See e.g. Hans von Carlowitz, *Sylvicultura Oeconomica* (1713) or Georg Ludwig Hartig, *Anweisung zur Holzzucht für Förster* (1791).
[11] UN, *Report of the United Nations Conference on the human environment 1972*, 2nd principle: The natural resources of the earth, including the air, water, land, flora and fauna and especially representative samples of natural ecosystems, must be safeguarded for the benefit of present and future generations through careful planning or management, as appropriate.
[12] UN, *Report of the United Nations Conference on the human environment 1972*, 4th principle: Man has a special responsibility to safeguard and wisely manage the heritage of wildlife and its habitat, which are now gravely imperilled by a combination of adverse factors. Nature conservation, including wildlife, must therefore receive importance in planning for economic development.

protection of global forest resources can also be found in the recommendations of the conference.[13]

The report Our Common Future, published in 1987 by the World Commission　6 on Environment and Development, dealt extensively with the importance of global forests.[14] It already shows a thematic link between forests, desertification, land degradation, biodiversity and climate change:

> 'There are also environmental trends that threaten to radically alter the planet, that threaten the lives of many species upon it, including the human species. Each year another 6 million hectares of productive dryland turns into worthless desert. Over three decades, this would amount to an area roughly as large as Saudi Arabia. More than 11 million hectares of forests are destroyed yearly, and this, over three decades, would equal an area about the size of India. Much of this forest is converted to low-grade farmland unable to support the farmers who settle it. In Europe, acid precipitation kills forests and lakes and damages the artistic and architectural heritage of nations; it may have acidified vast tracts of soil beyond reasonable hope of repair. The burning of fossil fuels puts into the atmosphere carbon dioxide, which is causing gradual global warming. This 'greenhouse effect' may by early next century have increased average global temperatures enough to shift agricultural production areas, raise sea levels to flood coastal cities, and disrupt national economies.'[15]

In 1992, the protection of the forests was also extensively included in Agenda 21[16] and　7 the connection shown in Our Common Future was repeated[17] and even extended by a call for action for specific management activities in relation to forests.[18]

In the same year, the UN Convention on Biological Diversity drew particular at-　8 tention to the human-induced decline in biodiversity.[19] In this context, the following definition of biodiversity can be found:

> '"Biological diversity" means the variability among living organisms from all sources including, inter alia, terrestrial, marine and other aquatic ecosystems and the ecological complexes of which they are part: this includes diversity within species, between species and of ecosystems.'[20]

In 2002, the Plan of Implementation of the World Summit on Sustainable Develop-　9 ment provided a strong link between sustainable forest management and sustainable development.[21] This was accompanied by a comprehensive catalogue of measures that,

---

[13] UN, *Report of the United Nations Conference on the human environment 1972*, Recommendation 24-8.

[14] The term 'forest' can be found a total of 283 times in the report.

[15] Report of the World Commission on Environment and Development: *Our Common Future* (1987), Part I, para. 7.

[16] The term 'forest' can be found a total of 289 times in the report. With Chapter 11 'combating deforestation', a whole chapter is also dedicated to this topic.

[17] United Nations Conference on Environment & Development, *Agenda 21*, 3-14 June 1992, para. 11.10.

[18] United Nations Conference on Environment & Development, *Agenda 21*, 3-14 June 1992, para.11.13.

[19] A/RES/64/203, *Convention on Biological Diversity*, 14 December 1992, preamble.

[20] A/RES/64/203, *Convention on Biological Diversity*, 14 December 1992, Art. 2.

[21] A/CONF.199/20, *Report of the World Summit on Sustainable Development*, 26 August- 4 September 2002, para. 45:

Forests and trees cover nearly one third of the Earth's surface. Sustainable forest management of both natural and planted forests and for timber and nontimber products is essential to achieving sustainable development as well as a critical means to eradicate poverty, significantly reduce deforestation, halt the loss of forest biodiversity and land and resource degradation and improve food security and access to safe drinking water and affordable energy; in addition, it highlights the multiple benefits of both natural and planted forests and trees and contributes to the well-being of the planet and humanity. The achievement of sustainable forest management, nationally and globally, including through partnerships among interested Governments and stakeholders, including the private sector, indigenous and local communities and non-governmental organizations, is an essential goal of sustainable development [...].

among other concerns, establishes a link to the UN Forum on Forests,[22] which is subordinated to the Department of Economic and Social Affairs and still exists today.[23]

10   In 2012, the UN addressed most of the SDG 15 content extensively in 'The future we want'. This report successively addressed climate change, forests, biodiversity and land degradation[24] and underlined their particular importance for sustainable development.[25]

11   The Millennium Development Goals (MDGs), the predecessors of the SDGs, already linked the protection of forests (MDG 7.A) and biodiversity (MDG 7.B) in terms of content. However, MDG 7.C and 7.D also created a link to drinking water, sanitation and improving the living conditions of slum dwellers.[26]

12   Initially, two different approaches were sought to ultimately implement a forest and land-related stand-alone goal in the SDGs: Forest-specific approaches, which would have given the protection of the global forest stock a stand-alone goal, and an approach to link this protection with other related goals. In the end, the latter approach was chosen due to the links to other content already shown.[27] SDG 15 is an essential part of protecting the planet in the spirit of the Road to Dignity by 2030.[28]

13   In 2020, the International Law Association (ILA) issued a draft resolution[29] which, in Annex I, contains the 2020 ILA Guidelines on the Role of International Law in Sustainable Natural Resources Management for Development.[30] The draft resolution explicitly recognises the far-reaching interconnections 'in the atmosphere-land-water-biodiversity nexus, as well as the need to respect ecological limits and planetary boundaries to avoid tipping points and reduce risks to society and nature' that have received too little or no attention until now and points to their immense impact on 'environmental, animal and human health and well-being' ($\rightarrow$ Goal 3 mn. 29, 60).

B. Scope and Dimensions of SDG 15

14   Human life depends on the earth for food and living. With plants making up 80 per cent of the human food.[31] Furthermore, the majority of terrestrial biodiversity can be found in the forests worldwide. They comprise more than 60 000 different tree species and habitats for 80 per cent of amphibian species, 75 per cent of bird species and 68 per

---

[22] A/CONF.199/20, *Report of the World Summit on Sustainable Development*, 26 August- 4 September 2002, para. 45(b).

[23] For a recent reference see E/RES/2017/4, *United Nations strategic plan for forests 2017–2030 and quadrennial programme of work of the United Nations Forum on Forests for the period 2017–2020*, 7 July 2017; UN Department of Economic and Social Affairs, *Global forest goals and targets of the un strategic plan for forests 2030* (2019).

[24] A/RES/66/288, *The future we want*, 11 September 2012, paras. 190-209.

[25] A/RES/66/288, *The future we want*, 11 September 2012, paras. 190, 193, 197, 205.

[26] https://www.un.org/millenniumgoals/environ.shtml.

[27] For the individual possible advantages and disadvantages of the approaches, see: United Nations General Assembly Open Working Group on Sustainable Development Goals, *Compendium of TST Issues Briefs October 2014* (2014), 194.

[28] A/69/700, *The road to dignity by 2030: ending poverty, transforming all lives and protecting the planet, Synthesis report of the Secretary-General on the post-2015 sustainable development agenda*, 4 December 2014.

[29] ILA, *Draft Resolution No. 4/2020, The Role of International Law in Sustainable Natural Resources Management for Development*, 13 December 2020.

[30] ILA, *Draft Resolution No. 4/2020, The Role of International Law in Sustainable Natural Resources Management for Development*, 13 December 2020, Annex I, where the term 'forest' is mentioned 68 times, 'land' 99 times, 'sustainable use' 39, and 'biodiversity' 33 times.

[31] https://www.undp.org/content/undp/en/home/sustainable-development-goals/goal-15-life-on-land.html.

cent of mammal species.[32] Yet, 10 million hectares of forests are destroyed every year, and more than 2 billion hectares of land are degrading, resulting in the extinction of species.[33] Although the number of protected areas (Key Biodiversity Areas – KBAs[34]) on land has increased, biodiversity is still in danger. Nearly 6,000 animals and plant species have been traded illegally.[35] Wildlife crime not only affects biodiversity and ecosystem health, but also human health, economic development and security.[36] In this context, SDG 15 with its 12 targets aims to lay out a framework of various aspects of the terrestrial ecosystem and its related threats (ecosystem approach[37]).

I. Sustainable Use and Conservation of the Terrestrial Ecosystem

The 1992 United Nations Convention on Biological Diversity (CBD) regulates the   **15** conservation of biodiversity and the sustainable use of its components.[38] Since SDG 15.1 aims at ensuring 'the conservation […] and sustainable use of terrestrial and inland freshwater ecosystems' by 2020, it provides relevant context for interpreting the legal meaning of 'sustainable use'. Sustainable use can be defined as 'the use of components of biological diversity in a way and at a rate that does not lead to the long-term decline of biological diversity, thereby maintaining its potential to meet the needs and aspirations of present and future generations', Art. 2 CBD which then is described in more detail in Art. 10 of the CBD. 'Conservation' as explained in Art. 8(a) of the CBD calls on a state to 'establish a system of protected areas or areas where special measures need to be taken to conserve biological diversity'. The aspect of protected areas[39] as mentioned in the Convention is also reflected in indicator 15.1.2 which measures the 'proportion of important sites for terrestrial and freshwater biodiversity that are covered by protected areas, by ecosystem type'. Protected areas are 'specially dedicated to the protection and maintenance of biological diversity, and of natural and associated cultural resources, and managed through legal or other effective means'.[40] By 2021, the share of protected areas with terrestrial coverage increased to 15,4 per cent.[41]

Indicator 15.1.1 measures 'forest area as a proportion of total land area', thus em-   **16** phasising the important role of forests for biodiversity and its relevance within the conservation process. Forests can be defined as 'land spanning more than 0.5 hectares with trees higher than 5 meters and a canopy cover of more than 10 percent, or trees able to reach these thresholds in situ. It does not include land that is predominantly

---

[32] FAO, *The State of the World's Forests – In Brief* (2020), 4.

[33] UN, *Sustainable Development Report 2020* (2020), 55.

[34] UNEP-WCMC and IUCN and its World Commission on Protected Areas (UNEP-WCMC 2016), WDPA; further reading: García-Ureta, 'Nature Conservation' in Lees and Viñuales (eds), *The Oxford Handbook on Comparative Environmental Law* (2019), 460-88; protectedplanet.net; keybiodeversityareas.org.

[35] UNODC, *World Wildlife Crime Report, Trafficking in protected species* (2020), 9.

[36] UN, *Sustainable Development Report 2020* (2020), 55.

[37] To be understood in the sense of the CBD with the 12 principles and five points of operational guidance; further reading: Bridgewater and Régnier and García, 'Implementing SDG 15: Can large-scale public programs help deliver biodiversity conservation, restoration and management, while assisting human development?' (2015) 39 *Natural Resources Forum*, 214-23.

[38] See also the Addis Ababa Principles and Guidelines for the Sustainable Use of Biodiversity (CBD Guidelines) (2004) and the Convention for the Conservation of the Biodiversity and the Protection of Priority Wilderness Areas in Central America (1992).

[39] UNEP-WCMC and IUCN and its World Commission on Protected Areas (UNEP-WCMC 2016), WDPA, protectedplanet.net; keybiodeversityareas.org.

[40] IUCN, *Defining Protected Areas* (2007), 9.

[41] https://livereport.protectedplanet.net/chapter-2.

under agricultural or urban land use'.[42] Land area means 'the country area excluding area under inland waters and coastal waters'.[43] In 2020, around 700 million ha of forests are in protected areas.[44]

17   In 2010, the Strategic Plan for Biodiversity 2011 – 2020 was adopted to provide the parties of the CBD a guiding framework to promote an effective implementation of the Convention.[45] As a result, 20 targets (Aichi Biodiversity Targets) were defined with five strategic objectives. This Strategic Plan acknowledged the relevance of addressing 'the underlying causes of biodiversity loss' and decreasing 'the direct pressures on biodiversity'.[46] It was recognised, that biodiversity concerns have been insufficiently addressed in policy-making so far.[47] Within the SDGs, SDG 15.9 aims to integrate 'ecosystem and biodiversity values into national and local planning, development process, poverty reduction strategies and accounts' by 2020. This is in line with Aichi Biodiversity Target 2, which is explicitly mentioned in indicator 15.9.1. and measures the 'number of countries that have established national targets in accordance with or similar to Aichi Biodiversity Target 2 of the Strategic Plan for Biodiversity 2011 – 2020 in their national biodiversity strategy and action plans'. As of their expiring date of 2020, none of the Aichi Biodiversity Targets have been achieved, neither was SDG 15.1 and SDG 15.9.[48] The CBD is going to adopt a post-2020 Biodiversity Framework with revised targets.[49]

18   SDG 15.4 focuses on the conservation of mountain ecosystems. This target recognises the importance of the mountain ecosystem as crucial and fragile biodiversity centre, and therefore needs to be protected.[50] The level of conservation is measured by the 'coverage of protected areas of important sites for mountain biodiversity' according to Indicator 15.4.1. The Mountain Green Cover Index (MGCI), as mentioned in indicator 15.4.2 'indicates the conservation status of mountain environments based on the recognition that there is a direct correlation between green cover in mountainous areas and the capacity of those areas to fulfil their ecosystem roles'.[51] In order to achieve sustainable use and conservation, SDG 15.a and SDG 15.b stipulate an increase of financial resources.

---

[42] United Nations Statistics Division, *SDG Indicators: Metadata Repository*, Indicator 15.1.1.

[43] United Nations Statistics Division, *SDG Indicators: Metadata Repository*, Indicator 15.1.1.

[44] FAO, *Global Forest Resources Assessment 2020 - Key Findings* (2020), 7.

[45] UNEP/CBD/COP/DEC/X/2, *Decision Adopted By The Conference Of The Parties To The Convention On Biological Diversity At Its Tenth Meeting*, 29 October 2010, Annex, para. 1.

[46] UNEP/CBD/COP/DEC/X/2, *Decision Adopted By The Conference Of The Parties To The Convention On Biological Diversity At Its Tenth Meeting*, 29 October 2010, Annex, para. 10(a) and (b).

[47] UNEP/CBD/COP/DEC/X/2, *Decision Adopted By The Conference Of The Parties To The Convention On Biological Diversity At Its Tenth Meeting*, 29 October 2010, Annex, para. 5.

[48] CBD, *Global Biodiversity Outlook 5* (2020), 10; https://unstats.un.org/sdgs/report/2020/progress-summary-for-SDG-targets/#fn1.

[49] OECD, *The Post-2020 Biodiversity Framework: Targets, indicators and measurability implication at global and national level* (2019), 5.

[50] UN Statistics Division, *SDG Indicators: Metadata Repository*, Indicator 15.4.2; see also the Protocol for the Implementation of the Alpine Convention of 1991 relating to the Nature Protection and Landscape Conservation (1994) and the Protocol for the Implementation of the 1991 Alpine Convention in the field of Soil Protection (1998).

[51] FAO, *Keeping an eye on SDG 15* (2013), 8.

II. Sustainable Management of Forests

Forests cover 31 per cent of the worldwide land area and provide shelter for most   19
of the Earth's terrestrial biodiversity.[52] Therefore, sustainable forest management (SFM)
plays a crucial role within SDG 15 and is to be achieved by 2020. SDG 15.2 aims
to 'promote the implementation of sustainable management of all types of forest, halt
deforestation, restore degraded forests and substantially increase afforestation and reforestation globally'. The UN recognised 'that forests and trees outside forests provide multiple economic, social and environmental benefits, and emphasiz[ed] that sustainable
forest management contributes significantly to sustainable development and poverty
eradication'.[53] By 2020, around 2 billion hectare (ha) of forest are part of a management
plan.[54]

Sustainable forest management is 'a dynamic and evolving concept, aim[ing] to main-   20
tain and enhance the economic, social and environmental values of all types of forests,
for the benefit of present and future generations'.[55] It was reaffirmed to

> reverse the loss of forest cover worldwide through sustainable forest management, including protec-
> tion, restoration, afforestation and reforestation, and increase efforts to prevent forest degradation
> and contribute to the global effort of addressing climate change.[56]

Indicator 15.2.1 measures progress towards sustainable development through five   21
sub-indicators focusing environmental, social and economic values that are in line with
the UN Resolution.[57] The importance of sustainable forest management is becoming
more urgent as deforestation and forest degradation increases alarmingly and biodiversity decreasing as a result.[58] In this context, the beginning of forest area decline can be
dated back to the 1990 s.[59] To promote sustainable forest management, in 2017, the UN
adopted a Strategic Plan for Forests with six global forest goals and 26 associated targets
to be achieved by 2030.[60] Global forest goal 1 aims to increase forest cover worldwide by
3 per cent.[61] This goal has been missed so far[62] which is unfortunate as extensive forest
restoration has to be done to meet the SDGs and to safeguard biodiversity.[63] The United
Nations Decade on Ecosystem Restoration 2021 – 2030, proclaimed in March 2019, aims
to accelerate action to restore ecosystem worldwide.[64] In addition, the Aichi Biodiversity
Target 5 and the New York Declaration on Forests Goal 1 addresses the issue of forests.[65]
By 2020, SDG 15.2 was not achieved.[66]

---

[52] FAO, *The State of the World's Forests – In Brief* (2020), 7; see also FAO, International Plant Protection
Convention (1997); International Tropical Timber Agreement (1983) and its following agreements ITTA2
(1994) and ITTA3 (2006); Southern African Development Community Protocol on Forestry (2002).

[53] A/RES/62/98, *Non-legally binding instrument on all types of forests*, 31 January 2008, Annex, para. 1.

[54] FAO, *Global Forest Resources Assessment 2020 - Key Findings* (2020), 8.

[55] A/RES/62/98, *Non-legally binding instrument on all types of forests*, 31 January 2008, Annex III, para. 4.

[56] UN, E/RES/2017/4, *United Nations strategic plan for forests 2017–2030 and quadrennial programme of
work of the United Nations Forum on Forests for the period 2017–2020*, 7 July 2017, Global forest goal 1.

[57] United Nations Statistics Division, *SDG Indicators: Metadata Repository*, Indicator 15.2.1.

[58] FAO, *The State of the World's Forests – In Brief* (2020), 9.

[59] FAO, *The State of the World's Forests – In Brief* (2020), 12.

[60] E/RES/2017/4, *United Nations strategic plan for forests 2017–2030 and quadrennial programme of work
of the United Nations Forum on Forests for the period 2017–2020*, 7 July 2017, para. 4.

[61] E/RES/2017/4, *United Nations strategic plan for forests 2017–2030 and quadrennial programme of work
of the United Nations Forum on Forests for the period 2017–2020*, 7 July 2017, para. 27.

[62] FAO, *The State of the World's Forests – In Brief* (2020), 12.

[63] FAO, *The State of the World's Forests – In Brief* (2020), 25.

[64] FAO, *The State of the World's Forests – In Brief* (2020), 25.

[65] FAO, *The State of the World's Forests – In Brief* (2020), 11.

[66] https://unstats.un.org/sdgs/report/2020/progress-summary-for-SDG-targets/#fn.

III. Access and Benefit-Sharing

22   Genetic resources include 'any material of plant, animal, microbial or other origin containing functional units of heredity of actual or potential value'.[67] They represent both a source of information about nature as well as a benefit to humans.[68] Nevertheless, genetic resources are unequally distributed around the world.[69] Therefore, the 'fair and equitable sharing of the benefits arising from the utilization of genetic resources' and access to them, is crucial and can be found in SDG 15.6. The relevant international agreement is the Nagoya Protocol on Access to Genetic Resources and the Fair and Equitable Sharing of Benefits Arising from their Utilization to the Convention on Biological Diversity adopted in 2010. Its objective is the 'fair and equitable sharing of the benefits arising from the utilization of genetic resources' and 'appropriate access to genetic resources'.[70] The utilisation of genetic resources can be defined as 'means to conduct research and development on the genetic and / or biochemical composition of genetic resources'.[71] The Convention recognises 'the importance of genetic resources to food security, public health, biodiversity conservation, and the mitigation of and adaptation to climate change'.[72] Furthermore, it acknowledges 'the potential role of access and benefit-sharing to contribute to the conservation and sustainable use of biological diversity, poverty eradication and environmental sustainability'.[73]

23   The concept of 'access and benefit-sharing' (ABS) encompasses how genetic resources are accessed and how benefits are shared by a person or country providing a resource (provider) with a person or country using it (user).[74] Providers can be natural persons, but may also include governments or civil society bodies.[75] The legal basis for ABS is the CBD, in which access to genetic resources is regulated in Art. 15 CBD. The provider grants the user a prior informed consent and, in addition, both parties negotiate the development of mutually agreed terms.[76] Prior informed consent means 'a permission given by the competent national authority of a provider country to a user prior to accessing genetic resources, in line with an appropriate national legal and institutional framework'.[77] Mutually agreed terms are 'an agreement reached between the providers of genetic resources and users on the conditions of access and use of the resources, and the benefits to be shared between both parties'.[78] The benefits shared can be monetary or non-monetary, as agreed in the material transfer agreement (MTA).[79]

---

[67] A/RES/64/203UN, Convention on Biological Diversity (14 December 1992), Art. 2.

[68] CBD, *Introduction to access and benefit-sharing* (2021), 2.

[69] CBD, *Introduction to access and benefit-sharing* (2021), 2.

[70] Nagoya Protocol on Access to Genetic Resources and the Fair and Equitable Sharing of Benefits Arising from the Utilisation of the Convention on Biological Diversity (2011), Art. 1.

[71] Nagoya Protocol on Access to Genetic Resources and the Fair and Equitable Sharing of Benefits Arising from the Utilisation of the Convention on Biological Diversity (2011), Art. 2(c).

[72] Nagoya Protocol on Access to Genetic Resources and the Fair and Equitable Sharing of Benefits Arising from the Utilisation of the Convention on Biological Diversity (2011), 3.

[73] Nagoya Protocol on Access to Genetic Resources and the Fair and Equitable Sharing of Benefits Arising from the Utilisation of the Convention on Biological Diversity (2011), 2.

[74] CBD, *Introduction to access and benefit-sharing* (2021), 3.

[75] CBD, *Introduction to access and benefit-sharing* (2021), 3.

[76] CBD, *Introduction to access and benefit-sharing* (2021), 3, see also Art. 15(4) and (5) CBD.

[77] CBD, *Introduction to access and benefit-sharing* (2021), 3.

[78] CBD, *Introduction to access and benefit-sharing* (2021), 3.

[79] IUCN, *An Explanatory Guide to the Nagoya Protocol on Access and Benefit-sharing* (2012), 9.

Genetic resources are often found in complex and sensitively balanced ecosystems.[80]   **24**
Therefore, the CBD calls on states to 'adopt measures relating to the use of biological resources to avoid or minimize adverse impacts on biological diversity'.[81]

In addition to the Nagoya Protocol, the FAO's International Treaty on Plant Genetic   **25**
Resources for Food and Agriculture (ITPGRFA), a binding legal agreement from 2001, pursues the same objective of 'equitable sharing of the benefits derived from plant genetic resources for food and agriculture'.[82] The ITPGRFA achieves ABS through a multilateral system of exchange of plant genetic resources for food and agriculture.[83] The process of ABS is similar to that under CBD by requiring a MTA.[84] Progress towards SDG 15.6 is measured by the 'number of countries that have adopted legislative, administrative and policy frameworks to ensure fair and equitable sharing of benefits' (indicator 15.6.1).

IV. Threats to the Terrestrial Ecosystem

1. Desertification and Land Degradation

Land, and thus soil, not only forms the terrestrial foundation for human life, soil is   **26**
also essential for terrestrial biodiversity.[85] Unfortunately, the health of soil and its fertility is declining on a global scale at an unforeseen rate.[86] To address land degradation on a legal basis, the United Nations Convention to Combat Desertification (UNCCD) was adopted in 1994. It is the only 'legally binding international agreement linking environment and development to sustainable land management'.[87] Its objective is 'to prevent and reduce land degradation, rehabilitate partly degraded land, and reclaim desertified land, particularly in countries that experience serious drought'.[88] Land degradation as defined by the Convention means a

> reduction or loss, in arid, semi-arid and dry sub-humid areas, of the biological or economic productivity and complexity of rainfed cropland, irrigated cropland, or range, pasture, forest and woodlands resulting from land uses or from a process or combination of processes, including processes arising from human activities and habitation patterns [...].[89]

---

[80] CBD, *Introduction to access and benefit-sharing* (2021), 2.

[81] CBD, Art. 10(b).

[82] ITPGRFA, Art. 1.1.

[83] ITPGRFA, Art. 10.1.

[84] ITPGRFA, Art. 12.4.

[85] Boer and Hannam, 'Land Degradation' in Lees and Viñuales (eds), *The Oxford Handbook of Comparative Environment Law* (2019), 438 (439).

[86] http://sdg.iisd.org/commentary/guest-articles/kill-not-the-goose-that-lays-the-golden-egg-striving-for-land-degradation-neutrality/; see also FAO, Voluntary Guidelines for Sustainable Soil Management (2017); FAO and Committee on World Food Security, Voluntary Guidelines on the Responsible Governance of Tenure of Land, Fisheries and Forests in the Context of National Food Security (2012); FAO, Revised World Soil Charter (2015).

[87] *United Nations Convention to Combat Desertification* (1994) (UNCCD).

[88] Boer and Hannam, 'Land Degradation' in Lees and Viñuales (eds), *The Oxford Handbook of Comparative Environment Law* (2019), 438 (445).

[89] UNCCD, Art. 1(f).

27   Critical drivers of land degradation are agriculture, forestry, urbanisation, infrastructure development, energy production, mining[90] and quarrying.[91] Desertification as a form of land degradation can be defined as 'land degradation in arid, semi-arid and dry sub-humid areas resulting from various factors, including climatic variations and human activities'.[92]

28   To improve the implementation of the UNCCD, the UNCCD 2018 – 2030 Strategic Framework was adopted. It recognises 'desertification/land degradation and drought (DLDD) as challenges of a global dimension' and 'to the sustainable development of all countries'.[93] The Strategic Framework contains a 'range of provisions with respect to policy and planning and "actions on the ground" but does not specifically include legal requirements to achieve its objectives'.[94] The UNCCD, the Strategic Framework as well as SDG 15 aim to achieve Land Degradation Neutrality (LDN). LDN was designed to promote a two-pronged approach that combines measures to prevent or reduce land degradation with measures to reverse the degradation of already degraded land so that losses are offset by gains to achieve a position where there is no net loss of healthy and productive land.[95] Therefore, SDG 15.3 'strive[s] to achieve a land degradation-neutral world'.[96] LDN can be defined as 'a state whereby the amount and quality of land resources necessary to support ecosystem functions and services and enhance food security remain stable or increase within specified temporal and spatial scales and ecosystems'.[97] Together with rehabilitation and restoration, SLM represents an important mechanism to achieve LDN.[98] Sustainable land management is 'the use of land resources, including soils, water, animals and plants, for the production of goods to meet changing human needs, while simultaneously ensuring the long-term productive potential of these resources and the maintenance of their environmental functions' and can be seen as 'a holistic approach to achieving long-term productive ecosystems by integrating biophysical, socio-cultural and economic needs and values'.[99] In addition

---

[90] Intergovernmental Forum on Mining, Minerals, Metals and Sustainable Development; International Lead and Zinc Study Group; International Nickel Study Group; International Copper Study Group; ILO Convention No. 176 Safety and Health in Mines (1995); International Cyanide Management Code for the Manufacture, Transport and Use of Cyanide in the Production of Gold (2002); Kimberley Process Certification Scheme (2003); The International Network for Acid Prevention, Global Acid Rock Drainage Guide (2009); OECD Due Diligence Guidance for Responsible Supply Chains of Minerals from Conflict-Affected and High-Risk Areas (2013).
[91] Boer and Hannam, 'Land Degradation' in Lees and Viñuales (eds), *The Oxford Handbook of Comparative Environment Law* (2019), 438 (440).
[92] UNCCD, Art. 1(a).
[93] ICCD/COP(13)/L.18, *The future strategic framework of the Convention, Draft decision submitted by the Chair of the Committee of the Whole*, 14 September 2017, Annex, para. 1.
[94] Boer and Hannam, 'Land Degradation' in Lees and Viñuales (eds), *The Oxford Handbook of Comparative Environment Law* (2019), 438 (453).
[95] UNCCD, *Scientific Conceptual Framework for Land Degradation Neutrality, A Report of the Science Policy Interface* (2017), 21.
[96] ICCD/COP(12)/20/Add.1, *Report of the Conference of the Parties on its twelfth session, held in Ankara from 12 to 23 October 2015 Part two: Action taken by the Conference of the Parties at its twelfth session*, 21 January 2016, Decision 3/COP.12: Integration of the Sustainable Development Goals and targets into the implementation of the United Nations Convention to Combat Desertification and the Intergovernmental Working Group report on land degradation neutrality, 8-10.
[97] ICCD/COP(12)/20/Add.1, *Report of the Conference of the Parties on its twelfth session, held in Ankara from 12 to 23 October 2015 Part two: Action taken by the Conference of the Parties at its twelfth session*, 21 January 2016, para. 2.
[98] UNCCD, *Sustainable Land Management contribution to successful land-based climate change adaptation and mitigation, A Report of the Science-Policy Interface* (2017), 30.
[99] UNCCD, *Sustainable Land Management contribution to successful land-based climate change adaptation and mitigation, A Report of the Science-Policy Interface* (2017), 30.

to preventing, mitigating and reversing land degradation, SLM can also help to fight climate change.[100]

2. Climate Change

The terrestrial ecosystem plays a crucial role in climate change. According to the   **29**
IPCC, some events have been observed that underline the nexus between land and climate change. It is projected, that ongoing warming will lead to 'a shift of climate zones'.[101] As a result, ecosystems in affected regions are going to be 'increasingly exposed to temperature and rainfall extremes beyond the climate regimes' to which 'they are currently adapted to'.[102] This can lead to structural, compositional and functional changes of the ecosystem.[103] With regard to the terrestrial ecosystem, it was found, that 'climate change, including increases in frequency and intensity of extremes', has had a negative impact and 'contributed to desertification and land degradation in many regions'.[104] The increase in 'frequency, intensity and duration of heat-related events' such as heatwaves is caused by GHG leading to an increase in droughts.[105]

The land-based ecosystem is, next to the oceans, the main sink of the Earth's green-   **30**
house gases (GHG).[106] Yet, land use and changes in land-use, such as deforestation, contributes to the emission of GHG, which in return affects the regional and global climate.[107] The UNFCCC recognised the importance of the terrestrial ecosystem as the sink and reservoir of GHG as early as 1992.[108] The 2015 Paris Agreement reaffirms 'the importance of the conservation and enhancement, as appropriate, of sinks and reservoirs of the greenhouse gases referred to in the Convention'.[109] A driving factor of climate change is land degradation leading to the emission of GHG[110] which underlines the importance achieving land degradation neutrality ($\rightarrow$ Goal 13 mn. 51).

3. Risk of Extinction

Extinction is the most severe form of biodiversity loss. Currently, 37,400 species are   **31**
endangered with extinction.[111] In this context, the extinction of species not only means the irreversible loss of diversity, but it also has a negative impact on the function, productivity and resilience of ecosystems.[112] SDG 15.5 aims to 'protect and prevent the extinction of threatened species' by 2020. Art. 9 CBD calls on its members to 'adopt measures for the recovery and rehabilitation of threatened species and for their reintroduction into their natural habitats'.

---

[100] UNCCD, *Sustainable Land Management contribution to successful land-based climate change adaptation and mitigation, A Report of the Science-Policy Interface* (2017), 33.

[101] IPCC, *Climate Change and Land* (2019), 8.

[102] IPCC, *Climate Change and Land* (2019), 44.

[103] IPCC, *Climate Change and Land* (2019), 44.

[104] IPCC, *Climate Change and Land* (2019), 7.

[105] IPCC, *Climate Change and Land* (2019), 7, 45.

[106] La Viña and de Leon, 'Conserving and Enhancing Sinks and Reservoirs of Greenhouse Gases, including Forests (Article 5)' in Klein et al. (eds), *The Paris Agreement on Climate Change: Analysis and Commentary* (2017), 166 (166).

[107] La Viña and de Leon, 'Conserving and Enhancing Sinks and Reservoirs of Greenhouse Gases, including Forests (Article 5)' in Klein et al. (eds), *The Paris Agreement on Climate Change: Analysis and Commentary* (2017), 166 (166).

[108] UNFCCC, preamble and Art. 5.

[109] UN Paris Agreement (2015), preamble.

[110] Boer and Hannam, 'Land Degradation' in Lees and Viñuales (eds), *The Oxford Handbook of Comparative Environment Law* (2019), 438 (447).

[111] IUCN 2021, The IUCN Red List of Threatened Species, Version 2021-1.

[112] ECD, *Biodiversity: Finance and the Economic and Business Case for Action* (2019), 24.

32   In 1964, the Red List of Threatened Species was compiled by the International Union of Conservation of Nature (IUCN). It provides data on 'the global extinction risk status of animal, fungus and plant species' and is thus a 'critical indicator of the health of the world's biodiversity'.[113] Nevertheless, the process to prevent the extinction of threatened species as well as the improvement of their conservation is slow.[114] This is also reflected in the fact that SDG 15.5 was not reached by 2020.[115]

4. Illegal Wildlife Trade

33   Wildlife crime has implications for biodiversity, human health, national security and socio-economic development.[116] Nevertheless, it represents one of the most profitable illegal businesses in the world, with most of the trade in mammals (like elephants, pangolins and rhinos) and reptiles.[117] Illegal wildlife trade (IWT) is one aspect of wildlife crime. IWT is a great danger for sustainability, as the illegal capture, killing and trade of protected species harms biodiversity and contributes to its decline.[118] Accordingly, SDG 15.7 recognises poaching and trafficking as a worldwide threat and call on countries to 'take urgent action to end poaching and trafficking of protected species of flora and fauna and address both demand and supply of illegal wildlife products'.

34   The legal basis for regulating wildlife trade at the international level is provided by the United Nation Convention on International Trade in Endangered Species of Wild Fauna and Flora (CITES) of 1975, whose regulations cover legal and illegal trade in wild species of flora and fauna. Illegal wildlife trade can be defined as 'trade in wildlife or wildlife parts that violates either international legal framework of the legislation of one or several of the countries through which a wildlife product has passed'.[119] In the definition of indicator 15.7.1, illegal trade means 'the sum of the value of all CITES/listed specimens seized'.[120] The Convention obliges states to protect their wild flora and fauna.[121] Beyond, it recognises in Art. II that trade in endangered specimens 'must be subject to particularly strict regulation in order not to endanger further their survival and must only be authorized in exceptional circumstances.'

35   In order to prevent illegal wildlife trade, CITES provides a permit scheme which stipulates that im- and export permits and re-export certificates are required.[122] In this regard, legal trade 'is the sum of the value of all shipments made in compliance with the Convention on International Trade in Endangered Species of Wild Fauna and Flora (CITES), using valid CITES permits and certificates'.[123] It is worth noting that CITES, as a convention on trade, does not represent a crime-related convention and therefore

---

[113] https://www.iucnredlist.org/about/background-history.

[114] FAO, *The State of the World's Forests – In Brief* (2020), 12.

[115] https://unstats.un.org/sdgs/report/2020/progress-summary-for-SDG-targets/#fn1; see also Convention on the Conservation of Migratory Species of Wild Animals (1979).

[116] UNODC, *World Wildlife Crime Report: Trafficking in protected species* (2020), 19.

[117] Rosen, *The Evolving War on Illegal Wildlife Trade* (2020), 2; UNODC, *World Wildlife Crime Report: Trafficking in protected species* (2020), 10.

[118] OECD, *The Illegal Wildlife Trade in Southeast Asia: Institutional Capacities in Indonesia, Singapore, Thailand and Viet Nam, Illicit Trade* (2019), 16.

[119] OECD, *The Illegal Wildlife Trade in Southeast Asia: Institutional Capacities in Indonesia, Singapore, Thailand and Viet Nam, Illicit Trade* (2019), 19.

[120] United Nations Statistics Division, *SDG Indicators: Metadata Repository*, Indicator 15.7.1.

[121] *Convention on International Trade in Endangered Species of Wild Fauna and Flora* (CITES), preamble.

[122] Waschefort, 'Wild Fauna and Flora Protection' in Geiß and Melzer (eds), *The Oxford Handbook of International Law of Global Security* (2021), 610.

[123] United Nations Statistics Division, *SDG Indicators: Metadata Repository*, Indicator 15.7.1.

does not oblige countries to make illegal wildlife trade a criminal offence.[124] In fact, an international agreement on wildlife crime is still lacking.[125]

To recognise the danger of illegal wildlife trade, several resolutions on 'tackling illicit   **36** wildlife trafficking' have been adopted by the UN General Assembly which in the resolution of 2019 urged

> Member States to take decisive steps at the national level to prevent, combat and eradicate the illegal trade in wildlife, on the supply, transit and demand sides, including by strengthening their legislation and regulations necessary for the prevention, investigation, prosecution and appropriate punishment of such illegal trade, as well as by strengthening enforcement and criminal justice responses […].[126]

The most recent resolution from 2021 reinforces this call even further.[127]

In addition, SDG 15.c emphasises on the importance of a global support to combat   **37** illegal wildlife trade. To determine the reduction of trafficked wildlife, indicator 15.7.1 measures the proportion of poached or illicitly trafficked traded wildlife. However, more than 35.000 species are unter international protection, making it impracticable to track all poaching.[128] Yet, illegal trade can serve as 'an indirect indicator of poaching'.[129] Wildlife seizures are a specific case of illegal trade, but there is no data available on how large their share of total wildlife crime is.[130]

5. Invasive Alien Species

Invasive alien species have a strong, mostly irreversible impact on native biodiversity,   **38** leading to biodiversity loss and species extinction.[131] The spread of non-native species, accidentally or intentionally, is fuelled by globalisation and the resulting increase in the movement of people and goods through trade and tourism.[132] Invasive alien species (IAS), as mentioned in SDG 15.8, can be defined as 'species whose introduction and / or spread outside their natural past or present distribution threatens biological diversity'.[133] They invade domestic flora and fauna in nearly every ecosystem type and affect all taxonomic groups.[134] The CBD considers invasive alien species as 'one of the primary threats to biodiversity, especially in geographically and evolutionary isolated ecosystems'[135] and therefore calls to 'prevent the introduction of, control or eradicate those alien species which threaten ecosystems, habitats or species', Art. 118 CBD. This wording allows the parties to choose their implementation means freely.[136] In this context the CBD recognised

---

[124] Rosen, *The Evolving War on Illegal Wildlife Trade* (2020), 3.

[125] https://www.theplanetarypress.com/2019/02/do-we-need-a-wildlife-crime-convention/.

[126] A/RES/73/343, *Tackling illicit trafficking in wildlife*, 20 September 2019, para. 4.

[127] A/75/L.116, *Tackling illicit trafficking in wildlife*, 16 July 2021, para. 5.

[128] United Nations Statistics Division, *SDG Indicators: Metadata Repository*, Indicator 15.7.1.

[129] United Nations Statistics Division, *SDG Indicators: Metadata Repository*, Indicator 15.7.1.

[130] United Nations Statistics Division, *SDG Indicators: Metadata Repository*, Indicator 15.7.1.

[131] IUCN, *IUCN Guidelines for the Prevention of Biodiversity Loss Caused by Alien Invasive Species* (2000), 2.

[132] IUCN, *Issue Brief 7: Invasive Alien Species and Sustainable Development* (2018), 1.

[133] https://www.cbd.int/invasive/WhatAreIAS.shtml; United Nations Statistics Division, *SDG Indicators: Metadata Repository*, Indicator 15.8.1.

[134] IUCN, *IUCN Guidelines for the Prevention of Biodiversity Loss Caused by Alien Invasive Species* (2000), 3.

[135] CBD, SBSTTA 6 Recommendation VI/4, Art. 2.

[136] IUCN, *Designing Legal and Institutional Frameworks on Alien Invasive Species* (2000), 14.

the importance of national and regional invasive alien species strategies and action plans, and of international collaboration to address the threats to biodiversity of invasive alien species and the need for funding as a priority to implement existing strategies.[137]

39   The CBD Conference of the Parties (COP) adopted Guiding Principles in 2002 to support the implementation of the Convention's requirements.[138] Those principles consist of a 'three-stage hierarchical approach'.[139] In addition, the prevention and control of IAS is part of the Strategic Plan for Biodiversity 2011 – 2020. Aichi Target 9 states: 'By 2020, invasive alien species and pathways are identified and prioritized, priority species are controlled or eradicated, and measures are in place to manage pathways to prevent their introduction and establishment'. As stated above, this goal was not reached.[140] By calling for action on introduction pathways, Aichi Target 9 places a direct focus on the aspect of identifying the introduction pathways of alien species into a new environment. By identifying the pathways of introduction, it is possible to determine where prevention and management measures need to be applied.[141] Thereby, eradication is considered the best way to counteract the introduction and establishment.[142]

40   The progress of SDG 15.8 is measured by the 'proportion of countries adopting relevant national legislation and adequately resourcing the prevention or control of invasive alien species' (Indicator 15.8.1). SDG 15.8 was to be achieved by 2020, but this goal was not met.[143]

C. Interdependences of SDG 15

41   Conservation of terrestrial ecosystems is not trending towards sustainability: Forest areas continue to decline at an alarming rate, protected areas are not concentrated in sites known for their biological diversity, and species remain threatened with extinction. Moreover, surging wildlife crime, land use changes such as deforestation, and habitat encroachment are primary pathways of transmission for emerging infectious diseases, including SARS-CoV-2.[144] A growing number of ecologists issue warnings that the likelihood of pandemics will increase as ecosystems and biodiversity continue to be destroyed.[145]

42   Forests as the main habitat for plants and animals and the primary source of plant-derived medicines[146], halting desertification processes and restoring degraded land and

---

[137] CBD, COP 6 Decision VI/23, Art. II.

[138] CBD, COP 6 Decision VI/23.

[139] Council of Europe, T-PVS (2003) 7 revised, *European Strategy on Invasive Alien Species*, 5.

[140] CBD, *Global Biodiversity Outlook 5* (2020), 10.

[141] García-Ureta, 'Nature Conservation' in Lees and Viñuales (eds), *The Oxford Handbook of Comparative Environmental Law* (2019), 460 (481).

[142] García-Ureta, 'Nature Conservation' in Lees and Viñuales (eds), *The Oxford Handbook of Comparative Environmental Law* (2019), 460 (482).

[143] https://unstats.un.org/sdgs/report/2020/progress-summary-for-SDG-targets/#fn1.

[144] UN, *The Sustainable Development Goals Report 2020* (2020), 54; see also Martens and Ellmers and Pokorny on behalf of Global Policy Watch, *COVID-19 and the SDGs, The impact of the coronavirus pandemic on the global sustainability agenda* (2020), 8.

[145] Martens and Ellmers and Pokorny on behalf of Global Policy Watch, *COVID-19 and the SDGs, The impact of the coronavirus pandemic on the global sustainability agenda* (2020), 8.

[146] In the last two centuries, humans have cleared or converted 70 per cent of grasslands, 50 per cent of the savannah, 45 per cent of temperate deciduous forests and 27 per cent of tropical forests for agriculture, see UNDP, *UNDP Support to the Implementation of Sustainable Development Goal 15* (2016).

forests[147], as well as protecting biodiversity and natural biotopes, are crucial to achieving sustainable development. Therefore, SDG 15 relates to every other SDG, but shares its strongest interdependences with SDG 2, SDG 6, SDG 7, SDG 12 and SDG 13.

Women, especially poor women living in rural areas, tend to depend on forests   **43** for fuel, animal feed and food. Deforestation therefore means, among other things, a considerable additional burden in securing needs (e.g. longer daily walks). Their frequent limitation of land ownership reduces their ability to adapt to losses or make decisions about land use. While some have extensive knowledge of traditional practices that are inherently sustainable, this is often not recognised when making decisions about sustainable ecosystems.[148]

Agriculture was identified by the Millennium Ecosystem Assessment as the major   **44** cause of land use change, land degradation and desertification; and as such, achieving SDG 15 could constrain efforts of SDG 2 (Zero Hunger, improved nutrition and increased agricultural productivity). However, SDG 15 broadly supports efforts to achieve sustainable agricultural production and genetic diversity.[149] The conservation, restoration and sustainable use of terrestrial and inland freshwater ecosystems (SDG 15.1), the implementation of sustainable management of all types of forests and halting deforestation (SDG 15.2), combating desertification and restoring degraded lands and soils (SDG 15.3), and the conservation of mountain ecosystems (SDG 15.4) link to SDG 2.4.

Another dimension of continuous preservation and restoration of terrestrial ecosys-   **45** tems (SDG 15.1, SDG 15.2) is also ensuring to protect and restore water-related ecosystems, such as mountains, forests, wetlands, rivers, aquifers and lakes (SDG 6.6) and substantially increasing the water-use efficiency across all sectors to especially address water scarcity (SDG 6.4).[150]

Worldwide, forests play a significant role in the supply of energy services. For people   **46** in low- and middle-income countries, where traditional wood fuels dominate the energy portfolio, reliance on biomass for household energy will decline overall in the coming decades, although the absolute number of traditional wood fuel users in sub-Saharan Africa and South and Southeast Asia will grow substantially. However, rapid urbanisation processes in Africa and South and Southeast Asia indicates a potential shift from firewood to charcoal for cooking and heating, which raises concerns about the associated impacts on forests in the absence of introduction of clean fuels.[151]

To escape the increasing pressure from unsustainable consumption and production,   **47** SDG 12 promotes the opposite (e.g. a 'waste reduction-circular economy', SDG 12.5) and encourages companies to adopt sustainable practices and to integrate sustainability information into their reporting cycle (SDG 12.6), which combines well with SDG 15.1 and SDG 15.2.

Since the pre-industrial period, the land surface air temperature has risen nearly   **48** twice as much as the global average temperature. Climate change, including increases in frequency and intensity of extremes, has adversely impacted terrestrial ecosystems as well as contributed to desertification and land degradation in many regions.[152] Healthy and resilient forests play a critical role in climate change mitigation and adaption, as

---

[147] In the last two centuries, humans have cleared or converted 70 per cent of grasslands, 50 per cent of the savannah, 45 per cent of temperate deciduous forests and 27 per cent of tropical forests for agriculture, see UNDP, *UNDP Support to the Implementation of Sustainable Development Goal 15* (2016).

[148] https://www.unwomen.org/en/news/in-focus/women-and-the-sdgs/sdg-15-life-on-land.

[149] Griggs et al., *A Guide to SDG Interactions: From Science to Implementation* (2017), 41.

[150] See also Ramsar Convention on Wetlands of International Importance Especially as Waterfowl Habitat (1971).

[151] Katila et al., *Sustainable Development Goals: Their Impacts on Forests and People* (2019), 206 f.

[152] IPCC, *Climate Change and Land* (2019), 9.

the largest storehouse of carbon after the oceans, forests have the potential to absorb and store about one-tenth of global carbon emissions projected for the first half of this century into their biomass, soils and products[153] (→ Goal 13 mn. 46, 51).

D. Jurisprudential Significance of SDG 15

49   Considered to be the SDG that reflects the fundamental idea of sustainable development as it was mostly understood in its origins on the European continent,[154] SDG 15 fulfils a no less important role in the SDG agenda. Sustaining biodiversity as it is demanded by SDG 15 greatly contributes to human well-being and constitutes a 'critical foundation of the Earth's life support system on which the welfare of current and future generations depend'.[155]

50   SDG 15 is *a fortiori* driven by the increasing demand for food and other resources resulting from the rising world population, to satisfy their equally increasing needs for water, food, a healthy living environment and a corresponding security of supply. However, by its very nature, there is a tension between the availability of natural resources and the possibilities for socio-economic development.[156] The use and utilisation, extraction, alteration and cultivation of land, forests, marshes and other terrestrial ecosystems are thus subject to considerable additional strain, which in many cases leads to environmental and land degradation.[157]

51   Additionally, recent findings show causal links between unsustainable land development, land use and / or exploitation with the impacts of climate change (→ Goal 13 mn. 22 f.) and human health,[158] either through directly affecting changing livelihoods or indirectly through the alteration of the yields that can be harvested from the land (→ Goal 3 mn. 54, 59).[159]

52   In this future-determining conglomeration of issues, few (binding) legal frameworks relate directly and holistically to sustainable conservation and management, apart from some areas of international, regional or national law.[160] In principle, States have the sovereign right to dispose of their own genetic and biological resources (Permanent Sovereignty Over Natural Resources). This principle of international law allows states to exploit resources according to their own national laws and policies, unless other States or extraterritorial territories are affected by harmful activities beyond their own

---

[153] UNGA Open Working Group on Sustainable Development Goals, *Compendium of TST Issues Briefs* (2014), 190.

[154] Von Carlowitz, *Sylvicultura Oeconomica* (1713), 105 f.

[155] UNGA Open Working Group on Sustainable Development Goals, *Compendium of TST Issues Briefs* (2014), 199.

[156] Dickens et al., 'Evaluating the Global State of Ecosystems and Natural Resources: Within and Beyond the SDGs' (2020) 12 *Sustainability*, 7381 (7381).

[157] To name but a few: Brazil, deforestation of the rainforest; Germany, acidification of the soil leads to crop losses and degradation of groundwater; other interventions such as fertilisation, land and river straightening, draining or deepening (e.g. river Weser) lead to changes in animal and plant vegetation; in Africa and Asia, monocultures lead to land degradation, vulnerability of crops, droughts and famines.

[158] See e.g. A/RES/66/288, *The Future We Want*, 11 September 2012, paras. 190-209; Plowright et al., 'Land use-induced spillover: a call to action to safeguard environmental, animal, and human health' (2021) 5(4) E237–45 *Lancet Planet Health* 2021.

[159] To name but a few, these include the increasing infertility of land due to acidification, the impact on livestock farming, the genetic adaptation of crops and fodder plants, the more frequent spread of diseases through spillover, and the promotion of global health risks.

[160] E.g. the Bern Convention on the Conservation of European Wildlife and Natural Habitat (1979) that has been implemented in the EU by the EU Nature Directives.

jurisdiction.[161] However, many aspects contained in SDG 15 fall under the auspices of world trade and investment law, e.g. with regard to fair and equitable benefit sharing (SDG 15.6), environmental economic accounting (SDG 15.9) or the acquisition of official development assistance and other funding (SDG 15.a).[162]

The focus of SDG 15 on the conservation and protection of biodiversity, moreover,   53 leads, as is the case with SDG 13 and SDG 14, to the *principles of prevention and precaution* associated with its legal significance which results from the assessment and interpretation of the Convention on Biological Diversity (CBD)[163] and its 'commonly recognized' direct linkage to sustainable development.[164] In addition, the Rio Declaration[165] and the ILC Draft Articles on Prevention[166] even expand its legal significance.

I. Jurisdiction on Vision and Objectives

The protection of ecosystems is not only based on international environmental law –   54 albeit this may represent the largest share of relevant jurisdiction – but also touches on questions of state sovereignty and also includes, for example, correlative principles and rights to avoid transboundary harm[167] or the fulfilment of human rights.

1. International Jurisdiction

With reference to the rights to life and to personal integrity in relation to environ   55 mental damage, the IACtHR underlined the close interrelationship between human rights and the environment.[168] The court made clear that to the extent that human rights are affected by 'degradation to the environment, including the right to a healthy environment', this must be accompanied by positive duties to be fulfilled by the state immediately:

> States must take the necessary measures to create an appropriate legal framework to deter any threat to the right to life; establish an effective system of justice capable of investigating, punishing and providing redress for any deprivation of life by State agents or private individuals, and safeguard the right of access to the conditions that ensure a decent life, which includes adopting positive measure

---

[161] UNEP/CISDL, Cabrera, Perron-Welch and Pisupati, *SDG 15 on Terrestrial Ecosystems and Biodiversity: Contributions of International Law, Policy and Governance* (Issue Brief 2016), 4.

[162] See UNCTAD, *BioTrade Principles and Criteria* (2007).

[163] The CBD is linked to both the supplementing Cartagena Protocol on Biosafety to the Convention on Biological Diversity, 29 January 2000, Arts. 10(6) and 11(8) and the Nagoya Protocol on Access to Genetic Resources and the Fair and Equitable Sharing of Benefits Arising from the Utilisation of the Convention on Biological Diversity (2011); see further Addis Ababa Principles and Guidelines for the Sustainable Use of Biodiversity (CBD Guidelines) (2004).

[164] Cançado Trindade, 'Principle 15, Precaution' in Viñuales (ed), *The Rio Declaration on Environment and Development* (2015), 425.

[165] A/CONF.151/26 (Vol. I), *Rio Declaration on Environment and Development*, 12 August 1992, Principle 15.

[166] ILC, *Draft Articles On Prevention Of Transboundary Harm From Hazardous Activities* (2001).

[167] ICJ, *Certain activities carried out by Nicaragua in the border area (Costa Rica v. Nicaragua)*, 2 February 2018; *Construction of a road in Costa Rica along the San Juan River (Nicaragua v. Costa Rica)*, Judgment, 16 December 2015, para. 104; ICJ, *Pulp Mills on the River Uruguay case (Argentina v. Uruguay)*, 20 April 2010; ICJ, *Gabčíkovo-Nagymaros Project case (Hungary v. Slovakia)*, 25 September 1997; ICJ, *Advisory opinion on the legality of the threat or use of nuclear weapons*, 8 July 1996; *Lake Lanoux Arbitration (France v. Spain)*, 16 November 1957; ICJ, *Corfu Channel Case (United Kingdom v. Albania)*, 9 April 1949; ICJ, *Trail Smelter*, arbitral sentence, 11 March 1941.

[168] The IACtHR specifically interpreted Arts. 1(1), 4(1) and 5(1) of the American Convention on Human Rights.

to prevent the violation of this right [...] The Court has also included environmental protection as a condition for a decent life.[169]

56   The IACtHR derived 'that health is a state of complete physical, mental and social well-being and not merely the absence of disease or infirmity. Thus, environmental pollution may affect an individual's health' (→ Goal 3 mn. 11, 29, 58 ff.). In its verdict, the court traces the genesis of universal sustainability agreements and the obligations of state due diligence, in particular relating to the duties of prevention, precaution and cooperation.[170] Moreover, it considered in its reasoning the decisions of other judicial bodies such as the European Court of Human Rights, the African Commission on Human and Peoples Rights, and experts such as the UN Special Rapporteur on human rights and the environment.

57   The IACtHR made clear that the right to a healthy environment is a fundamental human right and that environmental degradation, including the negative effects of climate change, impairs the enjoyment of this and other fundamental human rights. Therefore, states are obliged to ensure that their actions (and the actions of those under their effective control) do not affect the enjoyment of these basic rights – including the rights of those living outside their own state borders.[171]

58   The ECtHR regularly establishes links between severe environmental degradation and the health and well-being of individuals as well and considered in particular 'violations of human rights, such as the rights to life,[172] to respect for private and family life,[173] and to property.[174, 175]

2. European Jurisdiction

59   The biodiversity strategy of the EU focuses on three steps: protection, restoration and enforcement using 'policy coherence for sustainable development in all its policies [to] reduce the pressure on biodiversity worldwide'.[176] The EU nature legislation, consisting of the Birds Directive and the Habitats Directive, forms the policy and legal basis for the protection of biodiversity in the EU. At the same time, these build the starting point

---

[169] IACtHR, Advisory Opinion, Requested By The Republic Of Colombia, OC-23/17, 15 November 2017, para. 109.
[170] IACtHR, Advisory Opinion, Requested By The Republic Of Colombia, OC-23/17, 15 November 2017, paras. 108-242.
[171] IACtHR, Advisory Opinion, Requested By The Republic Of Colombia, OC-23/17, 15 November 2017, para. 47; see also: *Case of Kawas Fernández v. Honduras*, Merits, Reparations and Costs, Judgment, 3 April 2009, para. 148; https://www.elaw.org/IACHR_CO2317.
[172] *Öneryildiz v. Turkey* [GS], Judgment, 30 November 2004, ECHR Case No. 48939/99, paras. 71, 89, 90 and 118; *Budayeva and Others v. Russia*, Judgment, 20 March 2008, ECHR Case No. 15339/02, 21166/02, 20058/02, 11673/02 and 15343/02, paras. 128 to 130, 133 and 159, and *M. Özel and Others v. Turkey*, Judgment, 17 November 2015, ECHR Case No. 14350/05, 15245/05 and 16051/05, paras. 170 f. and 200.
[173] *Giacomelli v. Italy*, Judgment, 2 November 2006, ECHR Case No. 59909/00, paras. 76-82, 97 f.; *Tätar v. Romania*, Judgment, 27 January 2009, ECHR Case No. 67021/01, paras. 85-8, 97, 107, 113 and 125; *Di Sarno and Others v. Italy*, Judgment of 10 January 2012, ECHR Case No. 30765/08, paras. 104-10, 113.
[174] *Papastavrou and Others v. Greece*, Judgment, 10 April 2003, ECHR Case No. 46372/99, paras. 33, 36-9; *Öneryildiz v. Turkey* [GS], Judgment, 30 November 2004, ECHR Case No. 48939/99, paras. 124-9, 134-36 and 138; *Turgut and Others v. Turkey*, Judgment, 8 July 2008, ECHR Case No. 1411/03, paras. 86, 90-3.
[175] Found in: IACtHR, Advisory Opinion, Requested by the Republic of Colombia, OC-23/17, 15 November 2017, para. 50; further reading Atapattu and Schapper, *Human Rights and the Environment, Key Issues* (2019); Daly, *Human Rights and the Environment, Legality, Indivisibility, Dignity and Geography* (2019); Boyle, 'Human Rights and the Environment: Where Next?' (2012) 23(3) *EJIL*, 613-42.
[176] COM(2020) 380 final, *Communication From The Commission To The European Parliament, The Council, The European Economic And Social Committee And The Committee Of The Regions, EU Biodiversity Strategy for 2030, Bringing nature back into our lives*, 20 May 2020, 23.

for the network[177] that is permanently expanded and reworked to meet the goals of the EU's own biodiversity strategy for 2030, which as a part of the European Green Deal, is aligned to the Global Agenda 2030 and the SDGs.

The European Court of Justice (ECJ) has registered a record increase in its number of **60** cases in the last three years, which only declined due to the global SARS-CoV-2 pandemic, with the majority of cases being preliminary rulings under Article 263 TFEU.[178] In particular, the number of referrals to the Court concerning liability issues in the case of air pollution, soil pollution or water pollution increased. This considerable increase was related, inter alia, to the rise in climate change-related litigation in the EU Member States and in human health safety concerns ($\rightarrow$ Goal 3 mn. 58 f., $\rightarrow$ Goal 13 mn. 67 ff.). For instance, chemical substances such as Bisphenol A, Glyphosate, Nitrogen and Particulate Matter are being increasingly subject to such lawsuits.

In *PlasticsEurope v ECHA*[179], the ECJ confirmed the classification of Bisphenol A **61** (BPA) in the REACH[180] list of substances of very high concern. In interpreting of Art. 57(f) REACH, the ECJ underlined that the consideration of the standard of proof from a legal perspective does not require 'to establish the probable nature of the serious effects on health or the environment' and that the 'probability' criterion stated in Art. 57(f) REACH is sufficient to determine a risk from a chemical substance being existent.[181] It rejected any further inclusion of criteria such as the applicants claim of 'plausibility' inclusion. The following rejection of the claim yielded obligations for suppliers of products containing Bisphenol A to inform stakeholders in the supply chain and consumers.

In the *Tweedale* case and *Hautala and others v EFSA* the ECJ annulled the decision **62** of the Food Safety Authority (EFSA) refusing access to studies on the toxicity and

---

[177] Convention on International Trade in Endangered Species of Wild Fauna and Flora (CITES); Directive 2009/147/EC of the European Parliament and of the Council of 30 November 2009 on the conservation of wild birds (codified version of Directive 79/409/EEC as amended) (Birds Directive); Council Directive 92/43/EEC of 21 May 1992 on the conservation of natural habitats and of wild fauna and flora (Also available the consolidated version of 1 January 2007 with the latest updates of the annexes) (Habitats Directive); Regulation on Invasive Alien Species: Regulation (EU) No 1143/2014 of the European Parliament and of the Council of 22 October 2014 on the prevention and management of the introduction and spread of invasive alien species (Invasive Alien Species Regulation); Council Directive 1999/22/EC of 29 March 1999 on the keeping of wild animals in zoos (Zoos Directive); Council Regulation (EEC) No 3254/91 of 4 November 1991 prohibiting the use of leghold traps in the Community and the introduction into the Community of pelts and manufactured goods of certain wild animal species originating in countries which catch them by means of leghold traps or trapping methods which do not meet international humane trapping standards (Leghold Traps Regulation); Regulation (EC) No 1007/2009 of the European Parliament and of the Council of 16 September 2009 on trade in seal products (Text with EEA relevance) (Trade in Seal Products Regulation); Council Directive 83/129/EEC of 28 March 1983 concerning the importation into Member States of skins of certain seal pups and products derived therefrom (Seal Pups Directive); Council Regulation (EC) No 338/97 of 9 December 1996 on the protection of species of wild fauna and flora by regulating trade therein.

[178] ECJ, *Annual Report 2020, Judicial Activity, Synopsis of the judicial activity of the Court of Justice and the General Court of the European Union* (2021), 15.

[179] ECJ, T-185/17 and T-636/17, judgments of 11 July 2019 and 20 September 2019, *PlasticsEurope v ECHA*.

[180] The EU REACH regulation has been adopted to provide improved protection of human health and environment from the risks that can be posed by chemicals; Regulation (EC) No 1907/2006 of the European Parliament and of the Council of 18 December 2006 concerning the Registration, Evaluation, Authorisation and Restriction of Chemicals (REACH), establishing a European Chemicals Agency, amending Directive 1999/45/EC and repealing Council Regulation (EEC) No 793/93 and Commission Regulation (EC) No 1488/94 as well as Council Directive 76/769/EEC and Commission Directives 91/155/EEC, 93/67/EEC, 93/105/EC and 2000/21/EC (Text with EEA relevance).

[181] ECJ, T-185/17 and T-636/17, Judgments of 11 July 2019 and 20 September 2019, *PlasticsEurope v ECHA*, paras. 99, 101.

carcinogenicity of glyphosate. Glyphosate is the most widely used chemical product in pesticides/herbicides in the EU and was included on the list of active substances since 2002. The claimants had requested to take insight in the studies mentioned. In both cases, the EFSA refused access to the documents arguing that a disclosure of the relevant information might seriously harm the commercial and financial interests of the company and that no overriding public interest would be justified. The court found that 'the public must have access to information enabling it to ascertain whether the emissions were correctly assessed and must be given the opportunity reasonably to understand how the environment could be affected by those emissions'.[182] Thus, information which 'relates to emissions into the environment […] is deemed to be in the overriding public interest' and is to be weighed of higher value against the 'commercial interests of a particular natural or legal person'. The information to be disclosed include data about 'the emissions as such, but also covers information relating to the effects of those emissions'.[183] The ECJ also referred to the existing European Directive[184] on public access to environmental information that serves to implement the Aarhus Convention.[185] Therefore, it is mandatory to interpret the legal situation in the light of the Aarhus Convention which forms an integral part of the EU legal order.[186] The ECJ stated that the public 'must be given the opportunity reasonably to understand how the environment could be affected by those emissions'.[187]

63   These cases are of high significance, since the disclosure of relevant data forms the starting point for the implementation of plans and measures that enable the conservation, restoration and sustainable use of the land exposed to chemical products (SDG 15.1) and gives weight and recognition to international monitoring instruments and allows action to reduce degradation of natural habitats (SDG 15.5) and moreover, to prevent harm to human health (SDG 3). The interregional Aarhus Convention is particularly relevant because the possibility of extending access to justice in environmental matters is currently being examined in the EU. After having been reprimanded by

---

[182] ECJ, *Anthony C. Tweedale v European Food Safety Agency (EFSA) (Tweedale v EFSA)*, T-716/14 and *Hautala and Others v EFSA*, T-329/17, Judgment of 7 March 2019; a similar linkage of human health and environmental damage with reference to the *precautionary principle* was already acknowledged by the ECJ in *Gowan Comércio Internacional e Serviços Lda v Ministero della Salute*, Case C-77/09, Judgment of 22 December 2010, ECLI:EU:C:2010:803, para. 75 (Restrictions on the use of fenarimol as an active substance).

[183] General Court (GC), T-716/14 and T-329/17, 07.03.2019 *Anthony C. Tweedale v European Food Safety Agency (EFSA) (Tweedale v EFSA)* and *Hautala and Others v EFSA*, ECLI:EU:T:2019:141, paras. 92, 99 f.; see, by analogy, also ECJ, Case C-442/14, 23.11.2016, *Bayer CropScience* and *Stichting De Bijenstichting*, EU:C:2016:890, para. 86; see also General Court of the European Union, Press Release No 25/19, 7 March 2019.

[184] Directive 2003/4/EC of the European Parliament and of the Council of 28 January 2003 on public access to environmental information and repealing Council Directive 90/313/EEC.

[185] Regulation (EC) No 1367/2006 of the European Parliament and of the Council of 6 September 2006 on the application of the provisions of the Aarhus Convention on Access to Information, Public Participation in Decision-making and Access to Justice in Environmental Matters to Community institutions and bodies (Aarhus Regulation), 6 September 2006.

[186] ECJ, *Anthony C. Tweedale v European Food Safety Agency (EFSA) (Tweedale v EFSA)*, T-716/14 and *Hautala and Others v EFSA*, T-329/17, Judgment of 7 March 2019, ECLI:EU:T:2019:141, paras. 94 f.

[187] ECJ, T-716/14 and T-329/17, 07.03.2019 *Anthony C. Tweedale v European Food Safety Agency (EFSA) (Tweedale v EFSA)* and *Hautala and Others v EFSA*, ECLI:EU:T:2019:141, para. 118; Approx. 125,000 cases are being pursued in the US concerning the usage of glyphosate. There, by contrast, claims relate almost exclusively as a matter of compensation due to the impairment of human health caused by the alleged carcinogenic effect of the product 'Round Up'. The adverse effect on biodiversity in soils and waters, however, is not considered in these cases.

the Aarhus Compliance Committee (ACCC),[188] the EU Commission in October 2020 brought a legislative proposal[189] to open the possibility of an 'internal review' not only for NGOs, but also for 'other members of the public', i.e. for issues occurring not only under environmental law and even for those decisions 'not legally binding and external' in their effects, thus opening up the possibility of *actio popularis* (→ Goal 16 mn. 62).[190]

In the judgment in *Commission v Italy*[191], the ECJ decided on an infringement **64** procedure, initiated in 2014, against the Italian Republic for having systematically and persistently exceeded the limit values for particulate matter (PM_{10}) laid down by Directive 2008/50 310 ('Air Quality Directive') in a certain number of zones in Italy. The court upheld the action for failure to fulfil obligations claiming that the Italian Republic had failed to comply with its obligations under EU law by exceeding the limit values applicable to concentrations of PM_{10} particulate matter. The court in its finding stressed that

> it is irrelevant whether the failure to fulfil obligations is the result of intention or negligence on the part of the Member State responsible, or of technical or structural difficulties encountered by it, unless it is established that there were exceptional circumstances whose consequences could not have been avoided despite all the steps taken.[192]

The court made also clear that an extension of deadlines set cannot be exceeded so as **65** to not endanger the *de facto* purpose of protection of the regulations in question.[193]

The ECJ continued to uphold liability, referring in particular to the urgent fulfil- **66** ment of the state's obligation to meet given deadlines for implementation. In the case *Naturschutzbund Deutschland - Landesverband Schleswig-Holstein*[194] in which the court examined various issues concerning the operation of a pumping station for the purpose of draining agricultural land, which had the effect of taking the water level down. The court emphasised in particular the principle of 'normal management of sites'. Normal management must be understood as encompassing any measure which enables good administration or organisation of sites hosting protected species or natural habitats that is consistent, inter alia, with commonly accepted agricultural practices'. With recourse to the *precautionary principle* and the *polluter pays principle*, the court stated that in any

---

[188] ECE/MP.PP/C.1/2017/7, *Findings and recommendations of the Compliance Committee with regard to communication ACCC/C/2008/32 (part II) concerning compliance by the European Union*, 2 June 2017, para. 121: 'fail[ure] to comply with article 9, paragraphs 3 and 4, of the Convention'; The ACCC found it particularly questionable that 'the consequences of applying the Plaumann test to environmental and health issues is that in effect no member of the public is ever able to challenge a decision or a regulation in such case before the ECJ' (→ Goal 13 mn. 67 ff.); ACCC/M/2017/3 (European Union), Advice by the Aarhus Convention Compliance Committee to the European Union concerning the implementation of request ACCC/M/2017/3, para. 36.

[189] COM(2020) 642 final, 2020/0289 (COD), *Proposal for a Regulation of the European Parliament and of the Council on amending Regulation (EC) No 1367/2006 of the European Parliament and of the Council of 6 September 2006 on the application of the provisions of the Aarhus Convention on Access to Information, Public Participation in Decision-making and Access to Justice in Environmental Matters to Community institutions and bodies*, 14 October 2020.

[190] See European Parliament, Halleux, Members' Research Service, *Access to justice in environmental matters* (PE 690.593, May 2021), 1.

[191] ECJ, Case C-644/18, 10.11.2020, EU:C:2020:895.

[192] ECJ, *Annual Report 2020, Judicial Activity, Synopsis of the judicial activity of the Court of Justice and the General Court of the European Union* (2021), 179.

[193] Further information on air pollution in the EU: Huck et al., 'The Right to Breathe Clean Air and Access to Justice - Legal State of Play in International, European and National Law' (2021) 13(10) *International Environmental Law (eJournal)*.

[194] ECJ, Case C-297/19, 9.7.2020, *Naturschutzbund Deutschland – Landesverband Schleswig-Holstein*, EU:C:2020:533; Case C-636/18, 24.10.2019, *Commission v France*, ECLI:EU:C:2019:900; Case C-723/17, 26.06.2019, *Craeynest and Others*, ECLI:EU:C:2019:533.

case, the operation of a site must be considered normal 'only if it complies with the objectives and obligations laid down in' the Habitats Directive and the Birds Directive.[195]

3. Arbitration Proceedings

67   The protection and conservation of biodiversity also plays a role in arbitration proceedings, especially against the background of the exceptions of Art. XX GATT, the TBT Agreement and the SPS Agreement, the protection and conservation of biodiversity. The balancing of the justification of possible measures for environmental and biodiversity protection against the (possible) trade distortion and / or restriction of economic actors (investors, traders, etc.) under the provisions of WTO law and agreed trade and investment agreements depends on the individual case – a precedent does not arise in this respect. However, sustainable management and the principle of sustainable use are becoming increasingly important in recent proceedings, also against the background of the increased inclusion and emphasis in the trade and foreign trade policies of various states.

68   Closely linked to these issues are the principles of prevention and precaution, which lead to various obligations, including environmental impact assessments[196] or sustainability impact assessments (→ Goal 14 mn. 9, 36, 56, 66 ff.).[197] The application of these principles, in particular the precautionary principles, has, however, been discussed in *EC – Hormones* and been reflected against Arts. 3.3, 5.7 and the preamble of the SPS Agreement, the existence and application of which does not affect the Arts. 5.1 and 5.2.[198]

69   The Panel in *China - Rare Earths*, which dealt with China's export quotas for rare earths, molybdenum and tungsten, determined the meaning of 'conservation' to be connotated with

> [...] for the purposes of Article XX(g), [...] a "broad meaning" that strikes an appropriate balance between trade-liberalization, sovereignty over natural resources, and the right to sustainable development.[199]

70   In this context, 'conservation' must be effectively framed, which as relating to a legal instrument is defined as 'in operation at a given time' and understood as 'brought into operation, adopted, or applied'.[200] Also against the background of the related the polluter pays principle, the sustainable design of domestic policy is considered trade-distorting insofar as discriminatory differential treatment[201] can be established.[202] Accordingly, such a measure must be applied to domestic and international actors in order to qualify for an exception under Art. XX(g) GATT.

---

[195] ECJ, Case C-297/19, 9.7.2020, *Naturschutzbund Deutschland - Landesverband Schleswig-Holstein*, EU:C:2020:533, paras. 48 f.

[196] See United Nations Convention on Environmental Impact Assessment in a Transboundary Context (1991).

[197] See on systematic order of the two principles: Cançado Trindade, 'Principle 15, Precaution' in Viñuales (ed), *The Rio Declaration on Environment and Development* (2015), 422 f.

[198] WT/DS26/AB/R, WT/DS48/AB/R, *European Communities — Measures Concerning Meat and Meat Products (Hormones)*, paras. 124 f.; see similarly WT/DS76/AB/R, *Japan - Measures Affecting Agricultural Products*, 19 March 1999, DSR 1999:I, para. 277; *Japan - Measures Affecting the Importation of Apples*, WT/DS245/AB/R, adopted 10 December 2003, DSR 2003:IX, 4391.

[199] WT/DS431/AB/R, WT/DS432/AB/R, WT/DS433/AB/, *China - Rare Earths*, Panel Reports, para. 7.277.

[200] WT/DS394/AB/R WT/DS395/AB/R WT/DS398/AB/R, *China - Measures Related to the Exportation of Various Raw Materials*, 30 January 2012, para. 356 with reference to Garner, *Black's Law Dictionary* (2009).

[201] Which makes the right to regulate recede in any case.

[202] WT/DS394/AB/R, WT/DS395/AB/R, WT/DS398/AB/R, *China - Raw Materials*.

The close connection to the impacts of climate change are recognised in the litera- 71
ture, which calls for a 'need to build a network of supplies offsetting these risks'[203] but a
positional reflection in the WTO procedures is not yet found (→ Goal 13 mn. 71 ff.).

Other subjects covered by SDG 15 such as wildlife trafficking, illegal or unsustainable 72
trade and poaching of protected species and flora and fauna (SDG 15.7 and SDG 15.c)
are not addressed in arbitration proceedings.[204] Although illegal wildlife trade, alongside
deforestation, landscape fragmentation, habitat degradation and destruction, is one of
the biggest threats to the health of ecosystems, these activities are mostly based on
adverse business practices such as corruption of economic actors and / or supply chains
and often fall under the protection provisions of the SPS Agreement.[205]

4. Domestic Jurisdiction

The case of *Thilakan v Circle Inspector of Police, Cherpu Police Station and Oth-* 73
ers[206] involved the business of providing earth for land filling for various development
projects. Although the owner of the land was not obliged to obtain a permission for
the removal of earth from his property, the High Court of India took a position and
formulated a significant principle: '[n]o man can claim absolute right to indulge in
activities resulting in environmental degradation in the land owned by him.' It referred
to the decision in *State of Tamil Nadu v Hind Stone*, where the court endorsed both intra
and inter-generational equity principle:

> Rivers, Forests, Minerals and such other resources constitute a nation's natural wealth. These re-
> sources are not to be frittered away and exhausted by any one generation. Every generation owes a
> duty to all succeeding generations to develop and conserve the natural resources of the nation in the
> best possible way. It is in the interest of mankind. It is in the interest of the nation.

The special nexus of respect for human rights and the preservation of ecological sys- 74
tems has been particularly recognised in India. The decision in *M. C. Mehta v Union of*
India as a starting point in 1988 is still cited in many legal reasonings today. The court
had at that time shut down more than 50,000 industries for their polluting activities
(oleum gas) in the Ganga basin area, which allowed reopening only after controlled pollution. The Supreme Court argued a violation of the constitutional right to life (Art. 21
Indian Constitution) and also established the principle of 'no fault' liability against the
polluting actors. Although this case related to a land-related claim, the court clarified
that human health is dependent on different ecological systems, the protection of which
must be ensured at all times. In particular, the principles of *polluter pays* and *precaution-*
ary approach were given special importance, which were then reflected in the Public
Trust Doctrine. Since then, a monitoring board has accompanied the implementation of
this decision and the decisions that followed as a trend.[207] The court additionally clarified that urgent intervention is necessary in so that the *rule of law* is preserved. Since it

---

[203] Schwartz, 'The Polluter-Pays Principle' in Viñuales (ed), *The Rio Declaration on Environment and*
Development (2015), 433 f.; Cottier und Bonanomi, 'Soil as a Common Concern: Toward Disciplines on
Sustainable Land Management' in Cottier and Nadakavukaren Schefer (eds), *Elgar Encyclopedia of Inter-*
national Economic Law (2017), 628.

[204] DLA Piper, *Empty Threat 2015: Does The Law Combat Illegal Wildlife Trade? A Review Of Legislative*
And Judicial Approaches In Fifteen Jurisdictions (2015).

[205] See Yüksel Ripley, 'Covid-19 and Illegal Wildlife Trade: Where does the Law Fail and How Digital
Technologies can help?' (2020) *U. o. Aberdeen Blog Post*.

[206] *Thilakan v. Circle Inspector of Police, Cherpu Police Station and Others*, Kerala High Court of India,
W. P. (C) No. 24627/2007(F) (2007.10.23).

[207] *M.C. Mehta v. Union of India*, W.P.(C) No.4677 of 1985 (2013) 16 SCC 336, 18 March 2004, and
Order dated 5 April 2002.

otherwise would be impossible to concede the 'source of corruption [...], action is also necessary to check corruption, nepotism and total apathy towards the rights of the citizens' (→ Goal 16 mn. 22 ff.).

75   This pattern can be found in Indian jurisprudence far earlier when in *Vellore Citizens*[208] the Court stated that the precautionary principle in the context of municipal law means:

(i)   Environmental measures must anticipate, prevent and attack the causes of environmental degradation.

(ii) Where there are threats of serious and irreversible damage, lack of scientific certainty should not be used as a reason for postponing measures to prevent environmental degradation.

(iii) The 'onus of proof' is on the actor or the developer/industrialist to show that his action is environmentally benign.

76   Already then the Court stated that protecting biodiversity from harm acknowledged that '[s]ustainable development, and in particular the *polluter pays principle* and the *precautionary principle*, have become part of customary international law'.[209]

77   In this context, at least the decision of the German Federal Constitutional Court (FCC), which was widely respected from a German and European point of view, is noteworthy. The FCC identified a clear constitutional obligation to protect life and health from the numerous effects of the climate-related extreme weather events such as heat waves, forest fires, hurricanes, heavy rainfall, floods, avalanches and landslides. The fundamental right to property under German Grundgesetz (Art. 14(1) GG) also imposes a duty of protection on the state with regard to the property risks caused by climate change such as agricultural land or real estate (e.g. due to rising sea levels or droughts).[210]

78   Similar arguments can also be found with references to the deforestation of rainforests and the desertification of land through monocultures in various places. For example, the Constitutional Tribunal of Peru and the accompanying land-grabbing of territories from indigenous people. The 'unlawful dispossession, destruction and conversion' of land and forests, e.g. for palm oil or cocoa production. This harmful behaviour of private actors under the omission of states acting protective against such behaviour has been strongly condemned by the Constitutional Court which, amongst other things, found that the 'titling of ancestral territories is consistent with the property rights of indigenous peoples'. The court stated that 'any impacts on territorial and environmental rights also brings with it a violation of the right to cultural identity, given the enormous cultural and spiritual significance that the rivers and forests have in their cosmology'. Remarkably, for purposes of speed and efficiency, the court decided autonomously and did not refer the case back to the first instance, as usual in amparo cases (→ Goal 15 mn.

---

[208] Supreme Court of India, *Vellore Citizens' Welfare Forum v Union of India & Ors*, 28 August 1996.

[209] Cordonier Segger and Harrington and Cordon, 'Judicial deliberations and progress on sustainable development' in Cordonier Segger and Weeramantry (eds), *Sustainable Development Principles in the Decisions of International Courts and Tribunals, 1999-2012* (2017), 824.

[210] German Federal Constitutional Court, 24.03.2021, 1 BvR 2656/18, ECLI:DE:BVerfG: 2021:rs20210324.1bvr265618, mn. 1-270; see also: German Federal Constitutional Court, Press release No. 31/2021, 29 April 2021.

81 ff.).[211] This created enormous *access to justice* for indigenous people (→ Goal 16 mn. 64).[212]

In March 2020, an unprecedented judicial settlement was reached in favour of the   **79** Ashaninka people living in the Brazilian Amazon, signed by Brazil's Attorney General Augusto Aras, to make reparations for crimes committed almost 40 years ago against the Ashaninka people, whose land was deforested in the 1980s to supply the European furniture industry.[213] The Federal Ministry of State argued that this environmental damage is incontestable, i.e. cannot be undone, as it falls under the right to life. Setting a statute of limitations thus would deny future generations the right to fight for a healthy environment. This legal reasoning has been accepted by the Superior Court of Justice and the Supreme Court's review of the decision will assume a status of general effect with the result that the ruling will apply to all cases from that point forward. In addition to the financial reparation to the indigenous people of Ashaninka, the logging companies must pay compensation to a human rights fund for the harm caused to society as a whole as well as officially apologising and acknowledging 'Ashaninka people as guardians of the forest, dutiful in the preservation of the environment and in the conservation and dissemination of their customs and culture' for the deforestation. This admission of guilt, in particular, is understood as an indication that such harmful practices will not be repeated in the future.[214]

Moreover, a slight tendency can be seen that parts of nature itself are also endowed   **80** with rights. In June 2020, the Colombian Supreme Court declared the Isla de Salamanca National Park a legal entity to be preserved from rampant deforestation.[215]

II. The Enforcement of a 'Right to Biodiversity'

As the case of the Ashaninka People in Brazil shows, the possibility of conserving bio-   **81** diversity, on the one hand, is accompanied by difficulties when deriving it from human rights obligations. All too often, long periods of time have to be reckoned with. Often, the possibility of obtaining an enforceable judgement is limited, e.g. because of formal obstacles, high procedural costs, the inaccessibility of jurisdictions or substantive-legal chains of causation that are sometimes difficult to prove. Particularly in cases where the public is not involved or funding is secured externally, e.g. through NGOs, a productive output can hardly be traced.

---

[211] 'Peru's supreme court will resolve the case of Shipibo community vs the Peruvian government for restitution of their ancestral lands grabbed for palm oil, A preliminary legal analysis' (2019), 5; see also: https://news.mongabay.com/2020/12/peruvian-court-absolves-cacao-company-of-illegal-amazon-defo restation/; https://www.dw.com/en/indonesia-files-wto-lawsuit-against-eu-over-palm-oil-biofuels/a-5 1688336 (→ Goal 15 mn. 64); further reading: Barthel et al., *Study on the environmental impact of palm oil consumption and on existing sustainability standards For European Commission, DG Environment, Final Report and Appendices* (2018).

[212] 'Peru's Supreme Court will resolve the case of Shipibo community vs the Peruvian government for restitution of their ancestral lands grabbed for palm oil, A preliminary legal analysis' (2019), 6.

[213] A/75/266, *Harmony with Nature, Supplement to SG Report on Harmony with Nature*, 28 July 2020, para. 5; http://files.harmonywithnatureun.org/uploads/upload960.pdf.

[214] https://news.mongabay.com/2020/04/3-million-and-an-official-apology-brazils-ashaninka-get-unpr ecedented-compensation-for-deforestation-on-their-land/.

[215] A/75/266, *Harmony with Nature, Report of the Secretary-General*, 28 July 2020, para. 56(g); *Case of Indigenous Communities Members of the Association Lhaka Honhat (Nuestra Tierra) vs. Argentina*, Judgment, 6 February 2020, Merits, Reparations and Costs, Official Summary Issued by the Inter-American Court; see also: https://www.elespectador.com/noticias/judicial/corte-suprema-declara-sujeto-de-derecho s-a-la-via-parque-isla-salamanca/.

82   On the other hand, linking to environmental law norms is most often also associated with the difficulty of proving an actual liability situation. How should an individual, who at best can sue for the creation of official environmental protection plans before administrative courts, satisfactorily obtain a behavioural change of the actual polluter? In this context, especially in the Continental European legal family, it is often not possible to prove the institute of individual concern, which is, however, needed to open up procedural processes. Although a slight tendency towards opening up can be seen in the case law, the difficulties in proving causal chains, especially with regard to polluting actors, still remain.[216] However, beyond this, cases such as the palm oil cases in Peru and Indonesia show that enforcing rights against investing companies and states alike is not easily accomplished. Even with legally binding judgments, there is frequently non-compliance, non-payment of fines and compensation, non-adaptation of policies or further harmful behaviour still remains.[217] Enforcing environmental criminal law is also still in its infancy worldwide and can hardly be applied efficiently.

83   Concomitantly, in many cases the alteration of ecosystems, habitats and livelihoods is irreversible and restitution cannot be achieved even at great financial effort (→ Goal 13 mn. 91 f., Goal 14 mn. 24, 31, 47).

III. De Facto Influences on Jurisdiction

84   The jurisprudence surrounding SDG 15 clearly shows that cooperation, collaboration and mutual support are of utmost importance in order to achieve an effective level of protection worldwide, both in terms of the legal principles to be applied and the legal and political situation, which is too fragmented and has so far failed to provide sufficient protection.

85   Initial efforts towards integrated regional, transnational and / or global networks have already been launched and will be further developed in the future.[218] Worldwide, policy programmes for green and blue economies are being designed, which will probably ensure more far-reaching environmental and biodiversity protection in the future (→ Goal 6, Goal 13, Goal 14). This means that the judicial evaluation will probably also be stricter in the future. However, the extent to which this will actually benefit the various objectives of SDG 15 remains to be seen. Multilateral and regional efforts, such as the Aarhus Convention or the Escazú Agreement, which entered into force on 22 April 2021, increase access to justice, enshrining a right to sustainable development and point to further possibilities of development in this area.[219]

---

[216] See Huck et al., 'The Right to Breathe Clean Air and Access to Justice - Legal State of Play in International, European and National Law' (2021) 13(10) *International Environmental Law (eJournal)*.

[217] See for issues related to the enforcement amongst many others: https://news.mongabay.com/2020/1 2/peruvian-court-absolves-cacao-company-of-illegal-amazon-deforestation/; https://www.earthsight.or g.uk/news/idm/indonesian-state-court-failing-enforce-twenty-six-million-supreme-court-palm-oil-fine; https://www.greenpeace.org/international/press-release/22030/indonesian-government-actively-blocking -efforts-to-reform-palm-oil-industry/; https://news.mongabay.com/2020/12/an-oil-palm-front-advances -on-an-indigenous-community-in-peru/; https://www.business-humanrights.org/en/latest-news/peru-ind igenous-community-urges-european-banks-to-insist-that-companies-they-invest-in-remove-ocho-sur-p -from-their-palm-oil-supply-chains/.

[218] See for an overview of transnational networks: Heyvaert, 'Transnational Networks' in Lees and Viñuales (eds), *The Oxford Handbook of Comparative Environmental Law* (2019), 769-89.

[219] Further reading: UNECLAC, *Regional Agreement on Access to Information, Public Participation and Justice in Environmental Matters in Latin America and the Caribbean* (2018); https://sdg.iisd.org/news/esca zu-agreement-takes-effect-enshrining-right-to-sustainable-development/.

However, the extent to which the desired changes for the protection of biodiversity   **86**
can be achieved as long as a 'lack of market incentives, insecure land tenure and
resource-use rights' exist, remains questionable at this point in time.[220]

E. Conclusion on SDG 15

SDG 15 is dedicated to diverse aspects of the use of land, forests and other land   **87**
regions, the nexus between climate change and is clearly analysed by the IPCC. Land
provides for agriculture and nutrition to people and animals. Regarding weather effects
on land and the challenges for agriculture shed light to the question how to provide food
for an increasing number of people according to the estimation of UN. This is the point
where STI comes into play (SDG 17.6 and SDG 17.8.).

Multilateralism is one pillar to establish sectors for naturally balanced biodiversity   **88**
systems (→ Intro mn. 169 ff.). The protection of forest should be intensified on an international level to protect rain forests and ancient landscapes against deteriorating effects.
Nature needs more attention and cutting edge sanctions systems under a multilateral
umbrella against those who turn a blind eye to the exploitation of biodiversity, poaching
protected animals and plants. To protect indigenous people in their habitats, the concept
to grant legality to rivers, mountains or other biophysical systems is one example of
granting rights to those communities and at the same time to support the nature itself
against exploitation (→ Intro mn. 141 ff.).[221]

The willingness of sovereign states to combat the illegal trade in animals cannot be   **89**
assessed to be very high. The willingness to enforce might be there, but significantly
more enforcement units are needed in people's communities to tackle the heinous criminal activities. At the same time, there can be little understanding when fully equipped
enforcement units hunt down poachers while criminal organisations keep communities
in fear with the police not being present to provide security.

---

[220] Obersteiner, *Financing Sustainable, Resilient and Inclusive Solutions to attain SDG 15* (2017), 6.
[221] ILA, *Draft Resolution No. 4/2020, The Role of International Law in Sustainable Natural Resources Management for Development*, 13 December 2020, preamble, 1.3.4, 4.1.2.

Goal 16
Promote peaceful and inclusive societies for sustainable development, provide access to justice for all and build effective, accountable and inclusive institutions at all levels

16.1 Significantly reduce all forms of violence and related death rates everywhere

16.2 End abuse, exploitation, trafficking and all forms of violence against and torture of children

16.3 Promote the rule of law at the national and international levels and ensure equal access to justice for all

16.4 By 2030, significantly reduce illicit financial and arms flows, strengthen the recovery and return of stolen assets and combat all forms of organized crime

16.5 Substantially reduce corruption and bribery in all their forms

16.6 Develop effective, accountable and transparent institutions at all levels

16.7 Ensure responsive, inclusive, participatory and representative decision-making at all levels

16.8 Broaden and strengthen the participation of developing countries in the institutions of global governance

16.9 By 2030, provide legal identity for all, including birth registration

16.10 Ensure public access to information and protect fundamental freedoms, in accordance with national legislation and international agreements

16.a Strengthen relevant national institutions, including through international cooperation, for building capacity at all levels, in particular in developing countries, to prevent violence and combat terrorism and crime

16.b Promote and enforce non-discriminatory laws and policies for sustainable development

Word Count related to 'Peace' and 'Justice'

A/RES/70/1 - Transforming our world: the 2030 Agenda for Sustainable Development: 'Peace': 18 'Justice': 5

Instruments mentioned in A/RES/70/1 in the section entitled: 'Sustainable Development Goals and targets':

A/RES/69/313 - Addis Ababa Action Agenda of the Third International Conference on Financing for Development adopted on 27 July 2015: 'Peace': 12 'Justice': 1

A/RES/66/288 - The future we want (Rio +20 Declaration) adopted on 27 July 2012: 'Peace': 1 'Justice': 3 'just': 9

A/RES/55/2 - United Nations Millennium Declaration adopted on 8 September 2000: 'Peace': 17 'Justice': 7

Instruments mentioned in the Global Indicator Framework:

A/RES/48/134 - National institutions for the promotion and protection of human rights adopted on 20.12.1993: 'Peace': 0 'Justice': 0

Select Bibliography: Natasha Affolder, 'The Legal Concept Of Sustainability', submitted to *A Symposium on Environment in the Courtroom: Key Environmental Concepts and the Unique Nature of Environmental Damage*, March 23-24, 2012 (University of Calgary 2012); Nora Arajärvi, 'The Rule of Law in the 2030 Agenda – Rise or Decline' 9/2017 *KFG Working Paper Series* (Berlin Potsdam Research Group, Berlin 2017); Francisco Rojas Aravena, 'Peace, Justice and Effective Institutions' in Helen Ahrens, Horst Fischer, Verónica Gómez and Manfred Nowak (eds), *Equal Access to Justice for All and Goal 16 of the Sustainable Development Agenda: Challenges for Latin America and Europe* (LIT Verlag Zürich 2019); Juan Carlos Botero, Angela Maria Pinzon-Rondon Christine S. Pratt, 'How, when and why do governance, justice and rule of law indicators fail public policy decision making in practice?' (2016), 8 *Hague Journal on the Rule of Law*, 51; Tanja Chopra and Deborah Isser, 'Access to Justice and Legal Pluralism in Fragile States: The Case of Women's Rights' (2012) 4(2) *Hague Journal on the Rule of Law*, 337; European Parliament, *Peace, justice and strong institutions EU support for implementing SDG 16 worldwide, Briefing* (EU, Brussels 2020); Duncan French, 'Sofia Guiding Statements on sustainable developments' (2017) in Marie-Claire Cordonier Segger and Christopher G. Weeramantry (eds), *Sustainable Development Principles in the Decisions of International Courts and Tribunals, 1992 – 2012* (Routledge, UK/USA 2017); Sakiko Fukuda-Parr, 'Sustainable Development Goals' in Thomas G. Weiss and Sam Daws, *The Oxford Handbook on the United Nations* (Oxford University Press, Oxford 2017); Halmai Gábor, 'The Possibility and Desirability of Rule of Law Conditionality' (2018) in 11 *Hague J Rule Law*, 171; Heike Gramckow and Nicholas Menzies, 'Justice Proposed for Sustainable Development Goal, Governance for Development', *Blog*, 9.2.2015; Michèle Griffin, 'The UN's Role in a changing Global Landscape' in Thomas G. Weiss and Sam Daws, *The Oxford Handbook on the United Nations* (Oxford University Press, Oxford 2017); Sarah Hearn, 'Peaceful and Inclusive Societies' in Noha Shawki (ed.), *International Norms, Normative Change, and the UN Sustainable Development Goals* (Lexington Books, Lanham/London 2016); High-Level Political Forum on Sustainable Development, *Review of SDG implementation and interrelations among goals – Discussion on SDG 16 – Peace, justice and strong institutions, Background note* (2019); Winfried Huck, 'The EU and the Global Agenda 2030: Reflection, Strategy and legal implementation' (2020) 2020-1 *C-EENRG Working Papers*; Ingo Keilitz, 'The Trouble with Justice in the United Nations Sustainable Development Goals 2016 – 2030' (2016), 7(2) *William & Mary Policy Review*, 11; Irene Khan, 'How Can the Rule of Law Advance Sustainable Development in a Troubled and Turbulent World?' (2018), 13(2) *MJSDL*, 211; Augusto Lopez-Claros, Arthur L. Dahl and Maja Groff (eds), 'Strengthening the International Rule of Law' in *Global Governance and the Emergence of Global Institutions for the 21st Century* (Cambridge University Press, Cambridge 2020), 208; Jennifer Maaß, 'Die Normativität der Sustainable Development Goals in den internen und externen Politiken Europas' in Winfried Huck (ed), *Schriften zum Internationalen Wirtschaftsrecht* (Dr. Kovac Verlag, Hamburg 2020); Sahar Maranlou (ed), 'Access of Women to Justice and Legal Empowerment' in *Access to Justice in Iran: Women, Perceptions, and Reality* (Cambridge University Press, Cambridge 2014), 123; Constance L. McDermott, Emmanuel Acheampong, Seema Arora-Jonsson, Rebecca Asare, Wil de Jong, Mark Hirons, Kaysara Khatun, Mary Menton, Fiona Nunan, Mahesh Poudyal and Abidah Setyowati, 'SDG 16: Peace, Justice and Strong Institutions – A Political Ecology Perspective' in Pia Katila , Carol J. Pierce Colfer, Wil De Jong, Glenn Galloway, Pablo Pacheco and Georg Winkel (eds), *Sustainable Development Goals: Their Impacts on Forests and People* (Cambridge University Press, Cambridge 2019), 510; André Nollkaemper, 'The Internationalized Rule of Law' (2009) 1(1) *Hague Journal on the Rule of Law*, 77; Michael O'Boyle and Michelle Lafferty, 'General Principles and Constitutions as Sources of Human Rights Laws' in Dinah Shelton (ed), *The Oxford Handbook of International Human Rights Law* (Oxford University Press, Oxford 2015), 197; Stephanie Safdi and Sébastien Jodoin, 'The principle of sustainable development in the practice of UN human rights bodies' in Marie-Claire Cordonier Segger and H. E. Judge Christopher Gregory Weeramantry, *Sustainable Development Principles in the Decisions of International Courts and Tribunals, 1992 – 2012* (Routledge, UK/USA 2017), 450; Amartya Kumaar Sen, *The Idea of Justice* (Cambridge University Press, Cambridge 2009); Niko Soininen, 'Torn by (un)certainty – can there be peace between the rule of law and other Sustainable Development Goals?' in Duncan French and Louis J. Kotzé (eds.), *Sustainable Development Goals, Law Theory and Implementation* (Taylor Francis, Cheltenham/Northampton 2018); Robert Stein, 'Rule of Law: What Does It Mean?' (2009) 18 *MINN. J. INT'L L.*, 293; Brian Z. Tamanaha, 'The History and Elements of the Rule of Law' (2012) 2012 *Singapore Journal of Legal Studies* 232 (233); Victoria Tittle and Akihiro Seita, 'No health without peace: why SDG 16 is essential for health' (2016), 388 *The Lancet*, 2352; United Nations Development Programme, UN Women, UNFPA and ESCWA, *Gender Justice & Equality before the law, Analysis of Progress and Challenges in the Arab States Region* (UNDP, New York 2019).

A. Background and Origin of SDG 16

1   Violence is acknowledged to be one of the leading causes of death in all parts of the world and claims more than 1.6 million deaths annually worldwide.[1] Victims of violence, whether of civilian nature or due to conflict, are most often found in poor social classes. Violence mainly affects the most vulnerable groups of people and thus especially children and women as multiple affected groups. SDG 16 pursues the goal of creating and / or maintaining equal, just and democratic societies and structures, which are a critical foundation and enabler for sustainable development. Its purpose, to create non-discriminatory, safe and financially and economically stable societies and states, equally enables and builds on peace and good governance. This exceeds a significant impact on the well-being of societies.[2] In this sense, argued to be one of the most important SDGs,[3] SDG 16 with an extensive scope addresses indispensable factors of human existence. In the light of the agenda, whose purpose is 'to strengthen universal peace'[4] and 'to foster peaceful, just and inclusive societies which are free from fear and violence',[5] SDG 16 explicitly reflects these core principles.

2   The serious effects and dimensions of this SDG are evident in today's societies all too often and manifest in people lacking legal identity, experiences in psychological aggression or even physical punishment hitting the most vulnerable groups such as children, women or indigenous people the most. It can be observed that victimization in human trafficking and exploitation has been increased and with it, many forms of corruption accompanied by the push back or in some (too many) cases even the killing of human rights defenders erode societies additionally.[6]

---

[1] Krug et al., *Worldreport on violence and health* (2002), 18.

[2] United Nations General Assembly/Open Working Group on Sustainable Development Goals, *Compendium of TST Issues Briefs* (2014), 225-29.

[3] Tittle and Seita, 'No health without peace: why SDG 16 is essential for health' (2016) 388 *The Lancet*, 2352 f.

[4] A/RES/70/1, *Transforming our world: the 2030 Agenda for Sustainable Development*, 21 October 2015, preamble.

[5] A/RES/70/1, *Transforming our world: the 2030 Agenda for Sustainable Development*, 21 October 2015, preamble.

[6] HLPF on Sustainable Development, *Review of SDG implementation and interrelations among goals Discussion on SDG 16 – Peace, justice and strong institutions, Background note* (2019), 3 f.; https://www.undp.org/content/undp/en/home/sustainable-development-goals/goal-16-peace-justice-and-strong-institutions.html; European Parliament, *Peace, justice and strong institutions EU support for implementing SDG 16 worldwide, Briefing* (2020), 4.

I. Human Rights Background of SDG 16

'Sustainable development cannot be realized without peace and security; and peace **3** and security will be at risk without sustainable development.'[7] Considering this precondition, the creation of inclusive societies implies a broad acknowledgement and respect for human rights. The thematic scope of SDG 16 includes the right to development, promoting the effective *rule of law* and good governance at all levels and builds on and maintains transparent, effective and accountable institutions, thereby providing equal access to justice. Factors which give rise to violence, insecurity and injustice, such as inequality, corruption, poor governance and illicit financial and arms flows are addressed.[8] SDG 16 incorporates these basic assumptions and assembles different but interwoven human rights backgrounds,[9] though an obvious connection is only contained in SDG 16.10, which states to 'protect fundamental freedoms'.[10]

Nevertheless, as can be seen from the SDGs examined earlier, numerous human **4** rights instruments are to be applied to the individual targets. Above all, SDG 16 is rooted in the right to life, liberty and security and the right to fair trial and effective remedy, as well as in the right to development. The initial provisions can be found primarily in the Universal Declaration of Human Rights (UDHR), the ICCPR and the ICESCR and are supplemented by further instruments, such as the Convention on the Rights of the Child (CRC), the Convention on the Elimination of All Forms of Discrimination against Women (CEDAW), the Convention on the Rights of Persons with Disabilities (CRPD) as well as in the UN Declaration on the Rights of Indigenous People (UNDRIP), and the respective general comments. Through its permeation in every other goal of the agenda, SDG 16 combines a massive foundation and history of these rights. In this way, the additional rights to health, food, education, water and sanitation, and the right to housing are also accessible through the targets of SDG 16. In this respect as a central requirement, public (social) services must not only be accessible, but also of good quality since this constitutes a principle of all economic and social rights.[11]

II. Nascence of SDG 16 – Visions about Securing the World

Ahead of the negotiation process of SDG 16, the United Nations high level declara- **5** tion on the *rule of law* 2012[12] prepared the way for the inclusion of the *rule of law*

---

[7] A/RES/70/1, *Transforming our world: the 2030 Agenda for Sustainable Development*, 21 October 2015, para. 35.

[8] Independent Group of Scientists appointed by the Secretary-General, *Global Sustainable Development Report 2019: The Future is Now – Science for Achieving Sustainable Development* (2019), 196.

[9] The Danish Institute for Human Rights found that 92 per cent of the 169 SDG targets are linked to international human rights instruments, but hardly referred to in the specific SDG or the accompanying indicator; see also: OHCHR and Center for Economic and Social Rights, *Who Will Be Accountable? Human Rights and the Post2015 Development Agenda* (2013).

[10] European Parliament, *Peace, justice and strong institutions, EU support for implementing SDG 16 worldwide* (2020), 4; Arajärvi, 'The Rule of Law in the 2030 Agenda – Rise or Decline' (2017) 9/2017 *KFG Working Paper Series*.

[11] United Nations General Assembly/Open Working Group on Sustainable Development Goals, *Compendium of TST Issues Briefs* (2014), 139; see also A/RES/41/128, *Declaration on the Right to Development*, 4 December 1986, 'development is an inalienable human right by virtue of which every human person and all peoples are entitled to participate in, contribute to, and enjoy economic, social, cultural and political development, in which all human rights and fundamental freedoms can be fully realized.'

[12] A/RES/67/1, *Declaration of the High-level Meeting of the General Assembly on the Rule of Law at the National and International Levels*, 30 November 2012.

in the SDGs.[13] Since the UN assumed a strong interrelation and mutual reinforcement between (human and economic) development and the *rule of law*, they stressed the importance of its including into the agenda and manifestation as a stand-alone goal[14] in conjunction with ensuring *access to justice* which is broadly recognised.[15] Negotiations were mainly influenced by three informal alliances: the 'Friends of Governance for Sustainable Development', the 'Friends of Children' and the 'Friends of Rule of Law' which intended to foster 'cooperation and system-wide coherence in the UN's rule of law activities'.[16] In addition, the members of the World Bank's Justice, Rights and Public Security (JRPS) explicitly supported the idea to include a goal of justice into the SDGs.[17] But also civil society 'exerted their influence' on governance aspects. Further aspirations by other organisations ensured a wording based on a human rights background.[18] Notwithstanding this, it is obvious that negotiations on SDG 16 were purposely contentious due to the 'competing national priorities'.[19] In this respect, the so-called North-South conflict was decisive in that its contents were agreed upon in an ostensibly inconsistent manner and based on different principles. Developing countries feared the goals being downgraded to an agenda mainly of peacekeeping and thus neglecting other developmental and social goals.[20] In this context, for instance, foreign occupation was omitted from this SDG[21] although there still is reference within the Global Agenda 2030.[22] These difficulties and several diplomatic compromises led to an SDG of ambiguous nature the meaning of which is to be examined in the most sensitive way on the one hand and promises one of the highest and most prolific legal shares within the SDG agenda on the other.

B. Scope and dimensions of SDG 16

6   Against its historical development, the depth of content and different levels of SDG 16 should also be determined. The creation of peaceful and inclusive societies for sustainable development, based on the resilient foundations of the state and on inter-

---

[13] European Parliament, *Peace, justice and strong institutions, EU support for implementing SDG 16 worldwide* (2020), 3.

[14] A/RES/67/1, *Declaration of the High-level Meeting of the General Assembly on the Rule of Law at the National and International Levels*, 30 November 2012, para. 7.

[15] A/RES/67/187, *UN Principles and Guidelines on Access to Legal Aid in Criminal Justice Systems*, 28 March 2013.

[16] Dodds and Donoghue and Leiva Roesch, *Negotiating the Sustainable Development Goals, A transformational agenda for an insecure world* (2017), 50-61.

[17] Gramckow and Menzies, 'Justice Proposed for Sustainable Development Goal, Governance for Development', Blog, 9.2.2015 [found in Keilitz, 'The Trouble with Justice in the United Nations Sustainable Development Goals 2016 – 2030' (2016) 7(2) *William & Mary Policy Review*, 9].

[18] Fukuda-Parr, 'Sustainable Development Goals' in Weiss and Daws (eds), *The Oxford Handbook on the United Nations* (2017), 771.

[19] McDermott et al., 'SDG 16: Peace, Justice and Strong Institutions – A Political Ecology Perspective' in Katila et al. (eds.), *Sustainable Development Goals: Their Impacts on Forests and People* (2019); Dodds and Donoghue and Leiva Roesch, *Negotiating the Sustainable Development Goals, A transformational agenda for an insecure world* (2017), 80; see also Khan, 'How Can the Rule of Law Advance Sustainable Development in a Troubled and Turbulent World?' (2018) 13(2) *MJSDL*, 211 (212).

[20] Hearn, 'Peaceful and Inclusive Societies' in Shawki (ed), *International Norms, Normative Change, and the UN Sustainable Development Goals* (2016), 120 ff.; European Parliament, *Peace, justice and strong institutions, EU support for implementing SDG 16 worldwide* (2020), 2.

[21] Dodds and Donoghue and Leiva Roesch, *Negotiating the Sustainable Development Goals, A transformational agenda for an insecure world* (2017), 46.

[22] A/RES/70/1, *Transforming our world: the 2030 Agenda for Sustainable Development*, 21 October 2015, para. 35.

national and social cooperation, leads to manifold manifestations in its overarching meaning and in the three subject areas it covers.

I. Legal Foundation and tripartite Nature

SDG 16 and the associated indicators show that, depending on its interpretation and implementation, it either focuses on a strong state in the Westphalian sense[23] or is based on a more decentralised approach guided by (good) governance approaches.[24] These diverging assumptions lead to different expressions and evaluations of the scope and dimensions[25] of this SDG and, consequently, of its normative impact and jurisprudential relevance. It is apparent that SDG 16 contains both people- and state-centred content.[26] Deeply rooted in international human rights law, the acronym of SDG 16 already contains three terms which on different levels may be attributed deviating connotations, but which also entail their own particular strands of interoperability. The same applies to its targets and associated indicators, both separately and as a whole, which are subject to interpretation. By sticking to its acronym, the tripartite nature of SDG 16 illustrates the different requirements it attempts to serve and are to be considered in legal reasoning. 7

1. Peace

The basic assumption[27] that '[t]here can be no sustainable development without peace and no peace without sustainable development',[28] the formation of peaceful, just and inclusive societies on justice and respect for human rights,[29] is a focal point on how to reach security and is directly linked to the 'culture of peace' expressed by the UN.[30] Peace, being understood by the UN, albeit its efforts to reform, is highly controversial in itself due to the disintegration of societies and a changing understanding of the nature of states. Organised crime and global terrorism, which are perceived today as greatest threats to societies, can hardly be added to the core understanding of peacekeeping.[31] 8

---

[23] Woyke, *Weltpolitik im Wandel, Revolutionen, Kriege, Ereignisse … und was man daraus lernen kann* (2016), 9-19.

[24] See A/RES/70/1, SDG 16.6, SDG 16.7, SDG 16.8 which reflect principles of good governance, as well as relying on the institutions of global governance; see also McDermott et al., 'SDG 16: Peace, Justice and Strong Institutions – A Political Ecology Perspective' in Katila et al. (eds.), *Sustainable Development Goals: Their Impacts on Forests and People* (2019), 511.

[25] Botero and Pinzon-Rondon and Pratt, 'How, when and why do governance, justice and rule of law indicators fail public policy decision making in practice?' (2016) 8 *Hague Journal on the Rule of Law*, 51 (67, 72).

[26] See Khan, 'How Can the Rule of Law Advance Sustainable Development in a Troubled and Turbulent World?' (2018) 13(2) *MJSDL*, 211 (213, 215).

[27] A/RES/70/1, *Transforming our world: the 2030 Agenda for Sustainable Development*, 21 October 2015, paras. 3, 17, 35.

[28] A/RES/70/1, *Transforming our world: the 2030 Agenda for Sustainable Development*, 21 October 2015, preamble.

[29] A/RES/70/1, *Transforming our world: the 2030 Agenda for Sustainable Development*, 21 October 2015, paras. 3, 17, 35.

[30] A/RES/73/126, *Follow-up to the Declaration and Programme of Action on a Culture of Peace*, 19 December 2018; see also: A/RES/73/1, *Political declaration adopted at the Nelson Mandela Peace Summit*, 3 October 2018; 'A Culture of Peace' and 'interreligious and intercultural dialogue and tolerance, understanding and cooperation for peace' (N. 65/11, 2010, N. 65/138, 2010, N. 66/116, 2011, N. 66/226, 2011, N. 67/104, 2012, N. 67/106, 2012, N. 68/125, 2013, N. 68/126, 2013, N. 69/139, 2014, N. 69/140, 2014, N. 70/19, 2015, N. 70/20, 2015, 71/249, 2015, N. 71/252, 2016 and N. 73/126, 2018, N. 73/129, 2018 and N. 73/328, 2018).

[31] Griffin, 'The UN's Role in a changing Global Landscape' in Weiss and Daws (eds), *The Oxford Handbook on the United Nations* (2017), 834.

Peace, however, in the sense of SDG 16 (based on the concept of sustainable development), reflects and addresses exactly these developments and thus involves much more than the absence of violence. Also the Addis Ababa Action Agenda (AAAA), the SDGs' financing instrument, focuses on precisely that understanding of peace-building[32] and thus avoids the UN's frequent problem of insufficient funding.[33] Since the SDGs are meant to be an anthropocentric expression of how to reach peaceful coexistence and co-operation of peoples, the existential part leading to peace means to guarantee human dignity and preserve an enabling development.[34] The pacification of human societies creates both, individual and societal opportunities for development and contributes to well-being and justice (→ Goal 16 mn. 3 ff.).

2. Justice and Strong Institutions

9   Achieving justice and strong institutions is accompanied with giving people access to judicial infrastructure and to legally empower them. SDG 16 shall strengthen trust and support preventing corruption and mismanagement. Access to compensation and control mechanisms shall be provided which is highly supportive to the implementation of all other SDGs.[35] As an essential factor, justice, if given the right turn, provides the opportunity to achieve policy outcomes such as better health, education, gender equality, employment and housing.[36] However, to suggest an indication of the idea of justice not merely as a formal phrase, but to become aware of its substance, a thought of Amartya Sen illustrates the possible multiple levels of meaning in stating that '[...] justice cannot be indifferent to the lives that people actually live.'[37] This implies that a just interpretation of the same facts means evaluating them differently, taking into account their specific context, which translates into defining the clear meaning being left to the interpretative organs.

10   An inseparable expression of justice and strong institutions has been anchored with the *rule of law* in SDG 16.3. Basically, the *rule of law* shall give clarity, predictability and certainty and therefore 'separates liberty and tyranny'.[38] Again, the governance approach is thus densified since the UN defines it to be 'a principle [...] in which all persons, institutions and entities, public and private, including the State itself, are accountable to laws that are publicly promulgated, equally enforced and independently adjudicated, and which are consistent with international human rights norms and standards.'[39] As a 'core element of the humanitarian and human rights agendas'[40] giving 'the freedom to live in

---

[32] A/RES/69/313, *Addis Ababa Action Agenda of the Third International Conference on Financing for Development*, 27 July 2015, paras. 8, 18, 68.

[33] Griffin, 'The UN's Role in a changing Global Landscape' in Weiss and Daws (eds), *The Oxford Handbook on the United Nations* (2017), 832 f.

[34] Griffin, Michèle, 'The UN's Role in a changing Global Landscape' in Weiss and Daws (eds), *The Oxford Handbook on the United Nations* (2017), 832; see also Safdi and Jodoin, 'The principle of sustainable development in the practice of UN human rights bodies' in Cordonier Segger and Weeramantry (eds), *Sustainable Development Principles in the Decisions of International Courts and Tribunals, 1992 – 2012* (2017), 450; https://www.un.org/ruleoflaw/the-three-pillars/.

[35] OECD, *Governance as an SDG Accelerator Country, Experiences and Tools* (2019), Chapter 6.

[36] OECD, *Governance as an SDG Accelerator Country, Experiences and Tools* (2019), Chapter 6.

[37] Sen, *The Idea of Justice* (2009), 18.

[38] Soininen, 'Torn by (un)certainty – can there be peace between the rule of law and other Sustainable Development Goals?' in French and Kotzé (eds), *Sustainable Development Goals, Law Theory and Implementation* (2018), 251; See these factors to be assumed as a merely tool for economic development: Khan, 'How Can the Rule of Law Advance Sustainable Development in a Troubled and Turbulent World?' (2018) 13(2) *MJSDL*, 211 (213).

[39] https://www.un.org/ruleoflaw/what-is-the-rule-of-law/.

[40] https://www.un.org/ruleoflaw/what-is-the-rule-of-law/.

dignity',[41] the UN stresses the interlinkages of justice, the *rule of law* and human sustainable development.[42] Implementing the *rule of law* leads to stable and transparent legal regimes and furthers economic development. By ensuring equal societal opportunities and equitable access to basic services, it promotes social development ($\rightarrow$ Goal 10, mn. 9 ff., 20 f.). Furthermore, by strengthening the environmental legal framework through a fair, sustainable management of natural resources, it promotes ecological development.[43] In consequence, the *rule of law* is of relevance to the whole concept of sustainable development. Having said this, Soininen points out that its vagueness and context-dependency in an ecological or human rights context does not necessarily constitute a disadvantage. Rather, this opens up the possibility of including further issues in its scope of regulation. In context of the Global Agenda 2030, this suggests that the *rule of law* as a *Grundnorm* of law would thus be shaped in all spheres and scopes of action given by every SDG[44] as substantive (or designing) matter[45] as well as by the extensive foundation of every law and principle inherent or shaping the Global Agenda 2030 such as human rights law, humanitarian law and further principles of international law due to their acknowledgement in the Agenda 2030.

Besides these system-theoretical considerations, it is noticeable that SDG 16.3 uses a   **11** merely different, more narrow definition of the *rule of law* excluding a broader concept as it has been expressed with the 'Declaration of the High-level Meeting of the General Assembly on the Rule of Law at the National and International Levels' in 2012.[46] The 2012 UNGA declaration contains accessibility and responsiveness of justice and security institutions,[47] good governance,[48] impartiality of the judiciary and non-discrimination[49] whereas SDG 16.3 focuses more on individual victims of violence than on structural problems with *rule of law* institutions as a whole.[50] Moreover, in taking corruption as a highly detrimental factor to the successful implementation of the *rule of law* and sustainable development in whole,[51] the definition of corruption appears equivocal since bribery is specified, but other forms of corruption are not. Beyond the targets, which explicitly refer to the need to provide access and participation (SDG 16.3, SDG 16.8, SDG 16.10), the basic requirement for the implementation of SDG 16 in its entirety

---

[41] https://www.un.org/ruleoflaw/the-three-pillars/.

[42] A/68/345, *Promotion of truth, justice, reparation and guarantees of non-recurrence*, 23 August 2013, para. 64.

[43] Khan, 'How Can the Rule of Law Advance Sustainable Development in a Troubled and Turbulent World?' (2018) 13(2) *MJSDL*, 211 (212).

[44] This means each target and each specific indicator should contribute to their interpretation and their limitation as well; see Fukuda-Parr, 'Sustainable Development Goals' in Weiss and Daws (eds), *The Oxford Handbook on the United Nations* (2017), 775.

[45] Soininen, 'Torn by (un)certainty – can there be peace between the rule of law and other Sustainable Development Goals?' in French and Kotzé (eds.), *Sustainable Development Goals, Law Theory and Implementation* (2018), 255; Huck, 'The EU and the Global Agenda 2030: Reflection, Strategy and legal implementation' (2020) 2020-1 *C-EENRG Working Papers*, 4; dissenting view: European Parliament, *Peace, justice and strong institutions, EU support for implementing SDG 16 worldwide* (2020), 4.

[46] A/RES/67/1, *Declaration of the High-level Meeting of the General Assembly on the Rule of Law at the National and International Levels*, 30 November 2012.

[47] A/RES/67/1, *Declaration of the High-level Meeting of the General Assembly on the Rule of Law at the National and International Levels*, 30 November 2012, paras. 11, 14 ff.

[48] A/RES/67/1, *Declaration of the High-level Meeting of the General Assembly on the Rule of Law at the National and International Levels*, 30 November 2012, paras. 12, 35.

[49] A/RES/67/1, *Declaration of the High-level Meeting of the General Assembly on the Rule of Law at the National and International Levels*, 30 November 2012, paras. 12 ff., 16 f.

[50] Aravena, 'Peace, Justice and Effective Institutions' in Ahrens et al. (eds), *Equal Access to Justice for All and Goal 16 of the Sustainable Development Agenda: Challenges for Latin America and Europe* (2019), 34.

[51] European Parliament, *Peace, justice and strong institutions, EU support for implementing SDG 16 worldwide* (2020), 3.

is the creation of participation, which manifests in the principles of access to justice, access to information and the ability to participate in decision-making processes. These principles can already be traced in various instruments of international law, such as the Aarhus Convention,[52] the ILA Principles (No 5)[53] and the Sofia Guiding Principles (No 7) or the UN Convention against corruption.[54] These instruments serve as foundation and embedding of SDG 16 and are mirrored in the purposes of the individual targets[55] or in the interpretation of the background provided by its indicators. Some of these contents either already hold the status of *jus cogens*, 'enjoy some support' or 'may in the future attain the necessary recognition and acceptance of non-derogability'.[56] These include, amongst other norms, the right to due process (SDG 16.3, SDG 16.10, SDG 16.a) or the prohibition of discrimination (SDG 16.7, SDG 16.b).

12   While the meaning of the *rule of law* in SDG 16 can be partially understood, its high degree of contextual dependency makes it difficult to define. It should be noted that it is a principle of governance which relies on 'just, fair and equitable laws and [...] entitles all persons, (public and private) institutions and entities, and States without any discrimination to equal protection of the law'[57] as well as on independence, impartiality and integrity of the judicial system in so that no discrimination in the administration of justice can occur.[58]

II. Elementary Definitions of legally significant Terms

13   Due to its legal substance, SDG 16 contains a number of legally definable terms, some of which are described in various human rights instruments. These include violence and torture against children (SDG 16.2), rule of law (SDG 16.3), accountable institutions (SDG 16.6). For these and other targets of SDG 16, it is remarkable that the meaning would by no means be identical or, as it were, interpretable. As discussed in the preceding SDGs, it is the context and reference system for which a valid or at least applicable description or definition is effective and important. The indicators nourish and / or limit the scope of meaning and application. Some of the expressions used can at least be given approximate thought in an international context shaped by the UN.

1. Abuse, Exploitation, Trafficking, Violence and Torture

14   SDG 16.2 'End abuse, exploitation, trafficking and all forms of violence against and torture of children' is measured by three indicators two of which are further commented: 16.2.1 which includes the proportion of children aged 1-17 years who experienced any

---

[52] Convention on Access to Information, Public Participation in Decision-making and Access to Justice in Environmental Matters (Aarhus Convention), 25 June 1998.

[53] ILA, *New Delhi Declaration of Principles of International Law Relating to Sustainable Development*, Principle 5 and 6.

[54] See also *OECD Convention on Combating Bribery of Foreign Public Officials in International Business Transactions* (1997); OECD/G20 Inclusive Framework on Tax Base Erosion and Profit Shifting.

[55] Affolder, 'The Legal Concept Of Sustainability' in *A Symposium on Environment in the Courtroom: Key Environmental Concepts and the Unique Nature of Environmental Damage*' (2012), 7.

[56] ILC, A/CN.4/727, *Fourth report on peremptory norms of general international law (jus cogens) by Dire Tladi, Special Rapporteur*, 31 January 2019.

[57] A/RES/67/1, *Declaration of the High-level Meeting of the General Assembly on the Rule of Law at the National and International Levels*, 30 November 2012, para. 2.

[58] A/RES/67/1, *Declaration of the High-level Meeting of the General Assembly on the Rule of Law at the National and International Levels*, 30 November 2012, para. 13 [found in: United Nations General Assembly/Open Working Group on Sustainable Development Goals, *Compendium of TST Issues Briefs* (2014), 230].

physical punishment and/or psychological aggression by caregivers in the past month; 16.2.3 which includes the proportion of young women and men aged 18-29 years who experienced sexual violence by age 18.

The protection of children against the harmful practices described in 16.2.1 corre- **15** sponds to the concept of protection of children's rights as set out in the UN Convention on the Rights of the Child, Art. 19 CRC. Violence includes all forms of physical and psychological harm set out in Article 19 CRC: 'physical or mental violence, injury or abuse, neglect or negligent treatment, maltreatment or exploitation, including sexual abuse'. The target thus represents the basic prerequisite for the preservation of survival, dignity, well-being, health and development, participation and non-discrimination of a child.[59] It specifically includes the 'use of violent (physical or verbal) disciplining techniques' as one of 'the most widespread and socially accepted type of violence against children that infringes children's rights and which can result in both immediate effects and long-term consequences that children carry well into adulthood'.[60] *Physical or corporal punishment* are actions intended to cause physical pain or discomfort, but not injuries such as shaking the child, hitting or slapping on the hand, arm or leg, hitting the body with a hard object, spanking or hitting on the bottom with bare hands, hitting or slapping on the face, head or ears, and repeated rough beating. In addition, *psychological aggression* against children is comprised which refers to the actions of shouting, yelling or screaming at a child, and calling a child offensive names such as 'dumb' or 'lazy'.

According to General Comment No. 13, the child is the rights holder that must be **16** 'recognized, respected and protected' and whom are to be equally protected under the law which means that the rule of law is fully applicable to them in the way as to an adult. The accompanying obligations of State parties are related to the national, the provincial as well as the municipal level and include the relations of parents and state institution to children (wards). State obligations are of positive and active nature to 'support and assist parents and other caregivers to secure, within their abilities and financial capacities and with respect for the evolving capacities of the child, the living conditions necessary for the child's optimal development (Arts. 18 and 27).' States parties also must ensure to hold all persons responsible within the context of their work in order to prevent, protect and react to violence against children and to provide accessible justice systems which address the needs and respects the rights of children.[61]

In addition to General Comment No. 13, the interpretation of this target is linked to **17** the wider context of Arts. 5, 9, 18 and 27 of the CRC and the Optional Protocol on the sale of children, child prostitution and child pornography and the Optional Protocol on the involvement of children in armed conflict.

The further indicator 16.2.3 explicitly distinguishes between sexual violence against **18** women and men. This also refers to the description in General Comment no. 13 of *sexual violence against children*. This comprises any sexual activities imposed by an adult on a child against which the child is entitled to protection by criminal law which includes:

1) The inducement or coercion of a child to engage in any unlawful or psychologically harmful sexual activity;
2) The use of children in commercial sexual exploitation;

---

[59] CRC/C/GC/13, *General comment No. 13 (2011), The right of the child to freedom from all forms of violence*, 18 April 2011.

[60] https://unstats.un.org/wiki/display/SDGeHandbook/Goal+16.

[61] CRC/C/GC/13, *General comment No. 13 (2011), The right of the child to freedom from all forms of violence*, 18 April 2011, para. 5.

3) The use of children in audio or visual images of child sexual abuse; and

4) Child prostitution, sexual slavery, sexual exploitation in travel and tourism, trafficking for purposes of sexual exploitation (within and between countries), sale of children for sexual purposes and forced marriage.

5) Sexual activities are also considered as abuse when committed against a child by another child if the offender is significantly older than the victim or uses power, threat or other means of pressure. Consensual sexual activities between children are not considered as sexual abuse if the children are older than the age limit defined by the State Party. 'Sexual violence' is operationally defined in the indicator as sexual intercourse or any other sexual acts that were forced, physically or in any other way.

19   Like the violence held in indicator 16.2.1, the more specific issue of sexual abuse of children as 'one of the gravest forms of violence against children'[62] is associated with a wide array of mental health consequences and adverse behavioural outcomes in adulthood. Experiences of sexual violence in childhood hinder all aspects of physical, psychological, emotional and social development.

20   By now, both indicators lack resilient data that is comparable since different study methodologies and designs, sampling frames and questionnaires are used and deviating definitions of sexual violence exist. Besides, collecting such data is challenged by under-reporting such engraving experiences in childhood, which is especially valid in finding relevant data of boys and men.[63]

21   The proactive prevention of all forms of violence as well as to explicitly prohibit all forms of violence are again included in the States parties obligations. Since the respectful, supportive child-care, guidance and upbringing free from violence in one generation reduces the likelihood of violence in the following generation, SDG 16.2 allows for social progress for decreasing inequalities between children and adults in an existential manner.

2. Rule of Law

22   SDG 16.3 intends to promote the rule of law at national and international level and should ensure equal access to justice for all. Despite not being further elucidated within the official UN Handbook on indicators, the term *rule of law* and equal access to justice are legally coined. Since its origins can be traced back to the ancient Greeks, the main concept of the *rule of* law lies in a separation of powers, as well as in the predictability and superiority of law which jointly characteristically represent the free state.[64] Besides this clear indication of application, the *rule of law* unfolds the most diverse meanings and connotations according to the respective state and the underlying state form, structure and (political) ethics it is formed of. In any understanding of what forms a reliable state, this concept means 'that government officials and citizens are bound by and abide by the law',[65] whatever the specific law may be (→ Goal 16 mn. 7 ff.).

23   Whereas 'justice' may not easily be defined against the background of the Global Agenda 2030 and SDG 16.3, it can at least be understood as a (stable) condition in which

---

[62] https://unstats.un.org/wiki/display/SDGeHandbook/Goal+16.

[63] https://data.unicef.org/resources/briefing-notes-on-sdg-global-indicators-related-to-children/; https://data.unicef.org/topic/child-protection/violence/sexual-violence/.

[64] See Aristotle, *Rhetoric*, 32 (Kennedy trans., 2ⁿᵈ ed. 2007); Hayek, 'The Origins of the Rule of Law' (1960) 162 *The Constitution*, 9 [found in: Stein, 'Rule of Law: What Does It Mean?' (2009) 18 *MINN. J. INT'L L.* 293 (297)].

[65] Tamanaha, 'The History and Elements of the Rule of Law' (2012) 2012 *Singapore Journal of Legal Studies* 232 (233).

injustice is sought to be avoided, mitigated or neutralised and allows to eradicate the most blatant forms of inequality and thus achieve some form of equity ($\rightarrow$ Intro Part A, VII., mn. 68, 176 ff, 184 ff.).[66]

Access to justice constitutes an internal principle of the SDGs and is equally charac-　**24** terised as a fundamental prerequisite for sustainable development, for the implementation of human rights and for societal (or democratic) participation ($\rightarrow$ Intro mn. 184 ff.).[67] 'Access' to justice in this context means the ability to obtain 'just and timely remedy for violations of rights' before official and unofficial dispute resolution mechanisms. Access to justice is characterised in particular by:

> that those seeking relief (1) have knowledge of or can easily find the mechanisms available to them; (2) can utilize these mechanisms without undue delay or prohibitive cost; and (3) can access skilled technical assistance necessary to pursue their claims.[68]

3. Corruption, Bribery and Bribe

According to the UN Convention against Corruption (UNCAC) and with recalling　**25** the Johannesburg Declaration on sustainable development, corruption is 'a threat to the sustainable development of people' leading to societal instability and insecurity, weak institutions and the vanishing of democratic, ethical values and justice which obstructs the rule of law.[69]

Corruption is a driver of conflict in human societies and includes the abolition of ju-　**26** dicial independence and impartiality due to internal or external influences, the absence of accounting and auditing standards in the private sector or the impunity or absence of legal consequences in case of non-compliance, the intentional intransparency of (state) institutions, or the 'misuse of procedures regulating private entities, including procedures regarding subsidies and licences granted by public authorities for commercial activities' or denying the participation of society through hindering their contribution in decision-making processes and / or not allowing (effective) access to information[70] or the absence of law enforcement. That means in brief 'the abuse of public office for private gain' which is the case 'when an official accepts, solicits, or extorts a bribe.'[71]

Bribery is defined a committed intentionally promise, offering or giving to a foreign　**27** public official or an official of a public international organization, directly or indirectly, of an undue advantage, for the official himself or herself or another person or entity, in order that the official act or refrain from acting in the exercise of his or her official duties, in order to obtain or retain business or other undue advantage in relation to the conduct of international business.[72]

---

[66] See Huck and Maaß, 'Gaining a foot in the door: Access to Justice with SDG 16.3?' (2021) 2021-5 *C-EENRG Working Papers*, 11.

[67] A/RES/70/1, paras. 8, 35.

[68] A/HRC/37/25, *Right to access to justice under article 13 of the Convention on the Rights of Persons with Disabilities – Report of the Office of the United Nations High Commissioner for Human Rights*, (2017), para. 3; A/HRC/25/35, *Access to justice for children – Report of the United Nations High Commissioner for Human Rights*, (2013), para. 4; see also UNEP, Environmental Rule of Law, First Global Report (2019).

[69] A/RES/58/4, *United Nations Convention against Corruption*, 31 October 2003.

[70] A/RES/58/4, *United Nations Convention against Corruption*, 31 October 2003, Arts. 11, 12, 13.

[71] The World Bank, *Helping Countries Combat Corruption: The Role of the World Bank, Poverty Reduction and Economic Management* (1997), 8.

[72] A/RES/58/4, *United Nations Convention against Corruption*, 31 October 2003, Art. 16.

4. Participation

28   SDG 16.8 to broaden and strengthen the participation of developing countries in the institutions of global governance ist measured by indicator 16.8.1 which captures the proportion of members and voting rights of developing countries in international organisations. As a global and structural indicator, it determines 'the percentage of members (or voting rights) in international organizations that are (or belong to) developing countries.' It is based on the international law principle of sovereign equality of states, Art. 2 UN Charter and is intended to show the extent to which states are represented in an appropriate and equitable manner in international organisations. 'For institutions where membership and voting rights are different, this indicator observes the percentages separately.' The term 'International organizations' refers to the following multilateral institutions:

(1)   UN General Assembly;
(2)   UN Security Council;
(3)   UN Economic and Social Council;
(4)   International Monetary Fund;
(5)   International Bank for Reconstruction and Development;
(6)   International Finance Corporation;
(7)   African Development Bank;
(8)   Asian Development Bank;
(9)   Inter-American Development Bank;
(10) World Trade Organization; and
(11) Financial Stability Board.

29   There is no established convention for the designation of *developing countries* in the UN system. But, in common practice, developing countries refer to all other countries besides Japan, Canada, the United States of America, Australia, New Zealand and European countries. The aggregation across all institutions is currently done according to the United Nations M.49 statistical standard which includes designation of 'developed regions' and 'developing regions'.

30   As a structural indicator, only small changes will be observed over time which reflect agreement on new States joining as members, suspension of voting rights, membership withdrawal and negotiated voting rights changes. Cross-institutional comparisons need to pay attention to the different memberships of intuitions. Voting rights and memberships in their institutions are agreed to by the member states themselves.[73]

5. Legal Identity

31   Providing legal identity for all, including birth registration is measured by the proportion of children under 5 years of age whose births have been registered with a civil authority, by age (indicator 16.9.1.). Birth registration means 'the continuous, permanent and universal recording, within the civil registry, of the occurrence and characteristics of births in accordance with the legal requirements of a country'.[74]

> 'Children without official identification documents may be denied health care or education. Later in life, the lack of such documentation can mean that a child may enter into marriage or the labour

---

[73] https://unstats.un.org/wiki/display/SDGeHandbook/Goal+16.

[74] A/HRC/27/22, *Birth registration and the right of everyone to recognition everywhere as a person before the law*, 17 June 2014 (Birth registration is a fundamental right, recognised by Art. 24(2) of the International Covenant on Civil and Political Rights (ICCP) and Art. 7 of the Convention on the Rights of the Child (CRC)).

market, or be conscripted into the armed forces before the legal age. In adulthood, birth certificates may be required to obtain social assistance or a job in the formal sector, to buy or prove the right to inherit property, to vote and to obtain a passport.'[75]

In giving legal identity to children secures their recognition before the law and should   **32** safeguard the rights granted to them. The children's right to a name and nationality as enshrined in Art. 7 CRC enables them to access basic services and receive healthcare and education and gives legal basis for age.

6. Capacity

With SDG 16.a as it seeks to '[s]trengthen relevant national institutions, including   **33** through international cooperation, for building capacity at all levels, in particular in developing countries, to prevent violence and combat terrorism and crime' is measured through the finding of the 'existence of independent national human rights institutions in compliance with the Paris Principles'[76] and are based on the rules of procedure of the Global Alliance of National Human Rights Institutions (GANHRI).[77]

'The National Human Rights Institution (NHRI) is an independent administrative   **34** body set up by a country with a constitutional or legislative mandate to promote and protect human rights' which operate independently from the government. They address discrimination in all its forms, and further significantly the protection of civil, political, economic, social and cultural rights handling complaints, educate on human rights and make recommendations on law reform and therefore ensure the effective implementation of human rights standards[78] and thus enhance the capacity to prevent human rights violations and help prevent terrorism and crime. The NHRIs are accredited by GANHRI by the standards set with the Paris Principles.[79] The following institutions connect governments and civil society since they fill the gap between 'the human rights of individuals and the State's obligations under international law':

(1) human rights commissions
(2) human rights ombudsperson institutions
(3) hybrid institutions
(4) consultative and advisory bodies
(5) institutes and centres
(6) multiple institutions

Overall, it is noticeable that the terms chosen in SDG 16 are in some parts defin-   **35** able but the accompanied indicators lack determinacy. Nor can they be assigned to internationally agreed definitions on the one hand or to a reliance on domestic ones on the other hand. On great parts, SDG 16 indicators are blurred[80] or are lacking at all

---

[75] https://unstats.un.org/sdgs/metadata/files/Metadata-16-09-01.pdf.

[76] A/RES/48/134, *National institutions for the promotion and protection of human rights*, 4 March 1994.

[77] GANHRI is the successor of the International Coordinating Committee of National Institutions for the Promotion and Protection of Human Rights or ICC.

[78] A/RES/63/172, *Final Document and Programme of Action of the 1993 World Conference on Human Rights in Vienna*, 20 March 2009; A/RES/64/161, *National institutions for the promotion and protection of human rights*, 12 March 2010; also acknowledged in A/RES/63/169, *The role of the Ombudsman, mediator and other national human rights institutions in the promotion and protection of human rights*, 20 March 2009; HRC/RES/5/1, *Institution-building of the United Nations Human Rights Council*, 18 June 2007.

[79] Further information http://www.ohchr.org/EN/ProfessionalInterest/Pages/StatusOfNationalInstituti ons.aspx; information on the status of accreditation of NHRIs https://www.ohchr.org/Documents/Issues/ HRIndicators/NHRI.pdf.

[80] For instance, by now the promotion and enforcement of non-discriminatory law and policies for sustainable development is measured through the peoples' feeling of having been discriminated. The life

which means that it cannot be measured at all. Other indicators focus on a perceived perception of persons (or groups), are insufficient or only covered by outdated data.

C. Interdependences of SDG 16

36   The interlinkages of SDG 16, touching numerous spheres of life, reveal its enormous relevance within the SDG system (→ Intro mn. 203).[81] Conflict prevention, sustainable development and peace are interdependent and mutually reinforcing.[82] The prevention of armed conflict and organised crime plays a key role in in 'creating conditions conducive to lasting peace and sustainable development',[83] leading to a secure and stable coexistence of people.

37   In particular, access to justice and initiatives to strengthen the rule of law (SDG 16.1, SDG 16.2, SDG 16.3) are necessary elements to achieve policy goals such as health (SDG 3.2, SDG 3.8, SDG 3.d), education (SDG 4.1, SDG 4.2, SDG 4.3), social and gender equality (SDG 5.1, SDG 5.5, SDG 5.c) or employment (SDG 8.5).[84]

38   As '[p]eace is essential— and in fact, non-negotiable— to ensure a healthy, productive global population'[85] (SDG 3.2, SDG 3.8, SDG 3.d), the absence of peace prevents the other 16 SDGs from being realised (SDG 16.1, SDG 16.2, SDG 16.3), and in particular SDG 3. Moreover, justice, understood in its manifold concepts and being far more than the sum of peace and good governance, influences almost every other SDG.[86] Setting up 'infrastructures for peace' that creates space for dialogue within and amongst communities, can address sources of recurring violence, build social cohesion and help address tensions and grievances.[87]

39   An effective implementation and the promotion of the *rule of law*, enforcing antidiscrimination laws and addressing discriminatory social norms to ensure universal and effective *access to justice* for all groups (SDG 16.3), especially between women and men (SDG 16.b), across countries thus helps reducing societal and gender inequalities (SDG 5.3, SDG 5.a, SDG 5.c, SDG 10.3, SDG 10.4).[88]

40   'The average cost of civil war is equivalent to more than 30 years of GDP growth for a medium-sized developing country'[89] and '[p]eople in conflict-affected states are

---

realities of people which in itself are likely to be perceived so differently that the derivation of a valid data situation hardly seems possible.

[81] Harrington, 'Feature – Brief on the World Trade Organization's Dispute Settlement Body and the Sustainable Development Goals' (2020) 15(1) *MJSDL*, 23 (30).

[82] A/55/985, Prevention of armed conflict, 7 June 2001 and Corr.1.

[83] A/RES/57/337, Prevention of armed conflict, 18 July 2003; A/RES/65/283, Strengthening the role of mediation in the peaceful settlement of disputes, conflict prevention and resolution, 28 July 2011.

[84] Soininen, 'Torn by (un)certainty – can there be peace between the rule of law and other Sustainable Development Goals?' in French and Kotzé (eds), *Sustainable Development Goals, Law Theory and Implementation* (2018), 251; see also https://www.un.org/ruleoflaw/what-is-the-rule-of-law/.

[85] Tittle and Seita, 'No health without peace: why SDG 16 is essential for health' (2016) 388 *The Lancet*, 2352-3.

[86] Keilitz, 'The Trouble with Justice in the United Nations Sustainable Development Goals 2016 – 2030' (2016) 7(2) *William & Mary Policy Review*, 11.

[87] United Nations General Assembly/Open Working Group on Sustainable Development Goals, *Compendium of TST Issues Briefs* (2014), 22.

[88] Independent Group of Scientists appointed by the Secretary-General, *Global Sustainable Development Report 2019: The Future is Now – Science for Achieving Sustainable Development* (2019), 128.

[89] The World Bank, *World Development Report 2011, Conflict, Security, and Development (2011)*, 65 [found in: United Nations General Assembly/Open Working Group on Sustainable Development Goals, *Compendium of TST Issues Briefs* (2014), 228].

three times more likely to be undernourished'.[90] Thus, creating secure and stable (state) structures is likely to improve development and opportunities for states and people, while poverty (SDG 1.1, SDG 1.5) and hunger (SDG 2.1, SDG 2.2) are more likely to be alleviated.

During the SARS-CoV-2 pandemic, many countries worldwide had to face unprece-   **41** dented restrictions on fundamental rights and freedoms, many of which were temporary and appropriate. In some countries, however, measures were taken where crisis management (SDG 3.3, SDG 3.8) has only been a guise to curtail the freedom of speech, expression and the press, thereby undermining the *rule of law* (SDG 16.3).[91]

The management and conservation of global environmental commons, ecosystems   **42** and biodiversity (SDG 13.1, SDG 13.2, 13.a, SDG 14.4, SDG 14.5, SDG 14.6, SDG 15.1, SDG 15.7) are inextricably dependent from the realisation of environmental justice (SDG 16.3, SDG 16.6). Earth system recovery and resilience requires anticipating feedback effects to maximise co-benefits and minimise trade-offs, as well as protective regulation at global and local levels.[92] It is difficult to regulate the sustainable use and management of global commons or tackle the threat of climate change on the basis of national law alone. Environmental injustices need to be addressed at least internationally by avoiding inequitable resource use and ensuring liability for damage already caused through access to justice and further participation rights (SDG 16.3, SDG 16.6, SDG 16.7).[93]

To implement the above factors and achieve peace, inclusivity, accountability and   **43** participation, knowledge and skills built through quality education at all levels and for all stakeholders of the SDGs are a key means of implementation (SDG 4.7, SDG 4.c).

D. Jurisprudential Significance of SDG 16

The impact of this SDG is based on the many different ways in which it has been   **44** struck in the conflict-ridden times and its entanglements of today's world. Conflicts, (social) insecurity, weak institutions and the accompanying limited access to justice have a direct detrimental effect on the peaceful coexistence and cooperation of human societies. Against the background that issues such as people fleeing war, persecution and conflict in 2019 exceeded 79.5 million,[94] further illustrates the urgent need for action. In addition, the SARS-CoV-2 pandemic threatens to amplify and exploit fragilities across the globe.

Moreover, the relevance of jurisprudential recognition of the concepts contained in   **45** SDG 16 can be derived from the role played by judicial decision-makers and adjudicators. They are considering norms, principles, and rules bringing together different legal regimes and varying demands and thus, 'bridging the gap between multiple regulatory regimes and actors'.[95] They contribute vastly to the interpretation of sustainable develop-

---

[90] FAO and WFP, *State of Food Insecurity in the World: Addressing Food Insecurity in Protracted Crises* (2010) [found in: United Nations General Assembly/Open Working Group on Sustainable Development Goals, *Compendium of TST Issues Briefs* (2014), 228].

[91] Martens and Ellmers and Pokorny on behalf of Global Policy Watch, *SARS-COV-2 and the SDGs, The impact of the coronavirus pandemic on the global sustainability agenda* (2020), 9.

[92] See Independent Group of Scientists appointed by the Secretary-General, *Global Sustainable Development Report 2019: The Future is Now – Science for Achieving Sustainable Development* (2019), 94.

[93] Independent Group of Scientists appointed by the Secretary-General, *Global Sustainable Development Report 2019: The Future is Now – Science for Achieving Sustainable Development* (2019), 98 f.

[94] UN, *The Sustainable Development Goals Report 2020* (2020), 56.

[95] Khan, 'Trade-Sustainable Development Relationship: The Role of WTO Adjudication in Interpreting and Operationalizing Sustainable Development' (2018)14(1) *MJSDL*, 34 (56).

ment in diverse contexts, including the scope of SDG 16. Retaining the acronym of SDG 16 and the determined content, corresponding jurisprudence can be found to an immeasurable extent on different levels. If this jurisdiction is narrowed to sustainable development-relevant cases, it densifies into a few no less meaningful cases. This section presents a short extract of jurisdiction relevant to this examination and are then placed in the preceding context.

I. Vision and Principles

46   From the overall vision of SDG 16, it can be seen that the structure and governance of states and the creation of peaceful societies specifically affect children and women. They are most often hindered from accessing justice which, however, is key for protecting them from violence and exploitation and / or not drowning them in criminal spheres. 'Poor and marginalized groups are also often penalized through the law by means of criminalization, prosecution and incarceration and excessive regulation and controls (that can include the imposition of heavy fines, unlawful detention of children, disentitlement from social benefits and infringement on individual privacy and autonomy)'.[96] The jurisprudence reflects these serious concerns significantly and shows partly far-reaching decisions and application of principles, which equally emphasises the concept and densification of the SDGs. Albeit the complexity and entanglement can hardly be depicted here in its entirety, the most obvious currents may still be captured by a glimpse into jurisdiction.

1. International Jurisdiction

47   Considering the area of 'peace', the interlinkage to numerous concerns in international human rights and humanitarian rights is apparent. Even if no explicit right to peace can be inferred from the human rights regime of international law, it can be derived implicitly from the right to life, the *ius contra bellum*, which is intended to prevent war; *ius in bello*, which functions as a legal framework during military interventions; and *ius post bellum*, which seeks to re-establish peaceful order in the post-military conflict period.[97] These areas interoperate to ensure collective security, which, as a general prohibition of violence, is also part of customary international law. Thus, the principle of non-use of force as reflected in SDG 16.1 and SDG 16.2 was classified by the International Court of Justice (ICJ) as early as 1984 in *Nicaragua v United States of America* as customary international law, from which, irrespective of the recognition of international legal conventions, which the US had renounced at the time, no deviation is permitted.[98] Two years later, the ICJ reaffirmed this view in the associated appeal proceedings and emphasised that customary international law cannot be defined in more detail by identical contract laws, nor that these have priority in application due to the similarity of content. It further clarified 'that both the Charter and the customary international law flow from a common fundamental principle outlawing the use of

---

[96] Guidance Note of the Secretary–General, *United Nations Approach to Justice for Children* (2008) [found in: United Nations General Assembly/Open Working Group on Sustainable Development Goals, *Compendium of TST Issues Briefs* (2014), 230].

[97] Vitzthum and Proelß, *Völkerrecht* (2019), 596.

[98] *Case concerning Military and Paramilitary Activities and against Nicaragua*, Jurisdiction of the Court and Admissibility of the Application, 26 November 1984, ICJ Reports (1984), para. 73.

force in international relations'.[99] In the more recent jurisdiction of the case *Democratic Republic of the Congo v. Uganda*, the ICJ recalled on this and illustrated the responsibility of 'a party to an armed conflict [being] responsible for all acts by persons forming part of its armed forces'[100] which is accompanied by 'full reparation for the injury caused by that [wrongful] act'.[101] The ICJ moreover affirmed that the protective function of human rights conventions do not loose effect in case of an existing armed conflict. The court also recalled preceding jurisdiction which stated that different fields of law, namely Human Rights Law and Humanitarian Law not only co-exist and produce individually applicable norms, but which in different areas belong to both fields of law and are therefore to be evaluated and applied in both lights.[102]

The area of justice, which is characterised by the application of different governance principles and the creation and strengthening of strong institutions, anchored specifically in SDG 16.3, SDG 16.6, SDG 16.7 and SDG 16.8, can be found in case law in the three areas already mentioned. Jurisdiction that decide on access to justice and access to information and thus on participation can be found in particular in cases before the IACtHR and the ECtHR.[103] In the case *Claude Reyes et al. v Chile*, the need for access to information was based on the technical, financial and social evaluation of the Río Cóndor project and the Trillium company and the associated environmental risk assessment. The IACtHR decided that 'State's actions should be governed by the principles of disclosure and transparency' to enable all persons to effectively participate and to 'exercise democratic control'.[104] Access to information was classified as the basic prerequisite for individuals to being able to decide and participate adequately and sustainable regarding public affairs. In the same decision, access to justice was also granted in that the IACtHR included the decision on costs in the concept of reparations, reasoning that

> the activity deployed by the victim in order to obtain justice at both the national and the international levels entails expenditure that must be compensated when the State's international responsibility is declared in a judgment against it.[105]

Moreover, the court recognised this access to be part of the right to freedom of thought and expression and stated that it

> includes the protection of the right of access to State-held information, which also clearly includes the two dimensions, individual and social, of the right to freedom of thought and expression that must be guaranteed simultaneously by the State.[106]

In addition, the IACtHR, in its further case law *Kawas Fernández v. Honduras*, made it clear that a right to information is a state obligation to combat impunity, which it considered to be one of the greatest detrimental factors affecting human rights and

---

[99] *Case concerning Military and Paramilitary Activities in and against Nicaragua*, Merits, 27 June 1986, Reports of Judgments, Advisory Opinions and Orders, paras. 174-81.

[100] *Armed Activities on the Territory of the Congo*, Judgment, 19 December 2005, ICJ Reports (2005), para. 214.

[101] *Armed Activities on the Territory of the Congo*, Judgment, 19 December 2005, ICJ Reports (2005), para. 259 and the jurisdiction cited.

[102] *Armed Activities on the Territory of the Congo*, Judgment, 19 December 2005, ICJ Reports (2005), para. 216 by reference to *Legal Consequences of the Construction of a Wall in the Occupied Palestinian Territory*, ICJ Reports (2004), para. 106.

[103] French, 'Sofia Guiding Statements on Sustainable Development' in Cordonier Segger and Weeramantry (eds), *Sustainable Development Principles in the Decisions of International Courts and Tribunals, 1992 – 2012* (2017), 217 f.

[104] *Claude Reyes et al. v Chile*, Judgment, Order, 19 September 2006, IACtHR, para. 86.

[105] *Claude Reyes et al. v Chile*, Judgment, Order, 19 September 2006, IACtHR, para. 166.

[106] *Claude Reyes et al. v Chile*, Judgment, Order, 19 September 2006, IACtHR, para. 77.

access to justice in general. States have a responsibility to guarantee structures that allow human rights to be fully exercised. In this respect, it also defined the proper conduct of criminal investigations and proceedings 'within a reasonable period of time' and the provision of information about them as a means of reparation. In any case, states are obliged to 'remove all factual and legal obstacles hindering' so that victims 'are allowed to submit claims, receive information, provide evidence, make arguments and, basically, assert and enforce their interests.' Also the publication and making the public aware of the judicial determination of the facts was evaluated as an additional element of access to justice.[107] These far-reaching obligations can be found in the jurisdictional history of the IACtHR quite frequently.[108]

51   In the case of *Guerra and others v Italy*,[109] the ECtHR linked the right of access to information with the personal right to the integrity of family and private life which is granted in Europe under the European Charter on Human Rights (ECHR). In this case, the state's failure to disclose the release of information concerning potential environmental risks constituted a breach of the state's obligations. This assessment, from which at least 'indirectly a right to access to information' can be derived,[110] was confirmed by the ECtHR in further cases.[111] Moreover, the right to access to justice was decided early on, even before the Permanent Court on International Justice (PCIJ).[112] In 1938, the PCIJ already decided on another aspect of the *rule of law*, namely the principle of *res judicata*, which was stated in the *Trail Smelter case* to be

> [t]hat the sanctity of res judicata attaches to a final decision of an international tribunal is an essential and settled rule of international law. If it is true that international relations based on law and justice require arbitral or judicial adjudication of international disputes, it is equally true that such adjudication must, in principle, remain unchallenged, if it is to be effective to that end.[113]

2. European Jurisdiction

52   Since the promotion of peace is one of the fundamental values of the EU, Art. 3(1) TEU, and moreover considering itself not only a carrier of values, but also committed to contributing to peace, security, global sustainable development, [...] and the protection of human rights, Art. 3(5) TEU, the objectives of SDG 16 may directly be attributed to

---

[107] *Kawas Fernández v. Honduras*, Merits, Reparations and Costs, Judgment, 3 April 2009, IACtHR, paras. 190-4.

[108] *Kawas Fernández v. Honduras*, Merits, Reparations and Costs, Judgment, 3 April 2009, IACtHR, paras. 194 (fn. 228): *Case of the Caracazo v. Venezuela*, Judgment, Reparations and Costs, 29 August 2002. Series C No. 95, para. 118; *Case of Bayarri*, Preliminary Objection, Merits, Reparations and Costs, 30 October 2008supra note 135, para. 176; *Case of Valle-Jaramillo et al.*, Merits, Reparations and Costs, 27 November 2008, supra note 10, para. 233; Case of *Las Palmeras v. Colombia*, Judgment, Reparations and Costs, 26 November 2002, Series C, No. 96, para. 67; *Case of Heliodoro-Portugal*, Preliminary Objections, Merits, Reparations and Costs, 12 August 2008, supra note 123, para. 247; *Goiburú et al. v. Paraguay*, Merits, Reparations and Costs, 22 September 2006, para. 93.

[109] *Guerra v Italy*, Judgment, 19 December 1998, ECtHR ECLI:CE:ECHR:1998:0219JUD001496789, App. no. 116/1996/735/932, para. 58.

[110] French, 'Sofia Guiding Statements on sustainable developments', in Cordonier Segger and Weeramantry (eds), *Sustainable Development Principles in the Decisions of International Courts and Tribunals, 1992 – 2012* (2017).

[111] See *Case of McGinley and Egan v The United Kingdom*, Judgment, 9 June 1998, ECtHR ECLI: CE:ECHR:1998:0609JUD002182593, App. no. 10/1997/794/995-996, paras. 98, 101; *Öneryildiz v Turkey*, Judgment, 30 November 2004, ECtHR ECLI:CE:ECHR:2004:1130JUD0048 93999, App. no. 48939/99, paras. 89-92.

[112] The PCIJ, as an international court attached to the League of Nations, and predecessor of the International Court of Justice, was set up during 1922 and 1946.

[113] PCIJ, Reports Of International Arbitral Awards, *Trail smelter case* (United States, Canada), 16 April 1938 and 11 March 1941, Volume III, 1950-51.

the EU. However, with regard to the creation of an area of freedom, security and justice, as well as in areas of development cooperation and humanitarian aid and other cross-cutting issues of SDG 16, it must be noted that the EU and its member states either have shared competence or the EU holds merely a supporting function, Art. 4(2), (4) TFEU. Additionally, most of the contents of SDG 16 are reflected in the EU Charter of Fundamental Rights.[114]

Despite the EU having expanded its role in preventing conflicts and building peace   **53** outwardly,[115] especially the strengthening of the *rule of law* and upholding the judicial independence is of high priority within the EU.[116] In addition to the political expansion of this issue[117] within the EU, the ECJ decided first final judgment regarding allegations by the EU institutions towards EU Member States for not upholding the rule of law. A recent case of the ECJ directly linked to the issue of judicial independence shows the judicial reasoning of the ECJ in a particularly well illustrated manner. In *Commission v Poland*, the court decided that the lowering of the retirement age of Polish Supreme Court judges, as part of a greater justice reform in Poland, was not justified by a legitimate objective and because of not complying with the proportionality principle diminishes judicial independence and impartiality, a main foundation of EU law. In light of Art. 19(1) TEU subpara. 2 and Art. 47 Charter of Fundamental Rights of the European Union the court found that the improper reorganisation of justice systems led to a restriction of the protection of effective legal remedies, inter alia when courts apply or interpret EU law. As a 'key part of the fundamental right to a fair trial' which is reliant on the permanent nature on judicial activity, Poland was held to breach its obligations as a Member State.[118] Further ECJ decisions confirm that not only direct influences on the independence of the judiciary cannot be justified, but that the overall context must also be taken into account to determine undue interference.[119]

In *Associação Sindical dos Juízes Portugueses*[120], the ECJ holds among others that   **54** Art. 19 TEU, which gives concrete expression to the value of the *rule of law* stated in Art. 2 TEU, entrusts the responsibility for ensuring judicial review in the EU legal order not only to the ECJ but also to national courts and tribunals. The court grounded this decision on the guarantee of independence, which is inherent in the task of adjudication, is not merely required at the level of the ECJ but also at the level of every Member States and its (domestic) courts.

---

[114] See for deeper insights and a detailed overview European Union Agency for Fundamental Rights (FRA), *Fundamental Rights Report 2019* (2019), 13.

[115] Visoka and Doyle, 'Neo-Functional Peace: The European Union Way of Resolving Conflicts' (2016) 54(4) *JCMS 2016*, 862 (862).

[116] Bachmaier, 'Compliance with the Rule of Law in the EU and the Protection of the Union's Budget, Further reflections on the Proposal for the Regulation of 18 May 2018' (2019) 2/2019 *eucrim*, 120 (120).

[117] See amongst others COM(2019) 343 final, *Strengthening the rule of law within the Union, A blueprint for action*, 17 July 2019; COM(2019) 163 final, *Further strengthening the Rule of Law within the Union, State of play and possible next steps*, 3 April 2019.

[118] ECJ, C-619/18, 24.6.2019, *Commission v Poland*, ECLI:EU:C:2019:531, paras. 34-6; C-216/18 PPU, 25.7.2018, *Minister for Justice and Equality (Deficiencies in the system of justice)*, EU:C:2018:586, para. 64 and the case-law cited therein; further information on this case: European Union Agency for Fundamental Rights (FRA), *Fundamental Rights Report 2019* (2019), 203-4; Wahl and Riehle, 'Foundations, Fundamental Rights' (2019) in 2/2019 *eucrim*, 79 (80 ff.).

[119] See (by analogy) C-614/10, 16.10.2012, *Commission v Austria*, EU:C:2012:631, para. 43; C-288/12, 08.4.2014, *Commission v Hungary*, EU:C:2014:237, para. 51 (found in ECJ, C-619/18, 24.6.2019, *Commission v Poland*, ECLI:EU:C:2019:531, para. 112); also to be found in a quite similar context in C-216/18, 25.7.2018, *LM*, Request for a preliminary ruling under Article 267 TFEU from the High Court (Ireland), ECLI:EU:C:2018:586.

[120] C-64/16, *Associação Sindical dos Juízes Portugueses*, 27.2.2018, ECLI:EU:C:2018:117.

3. Arbitration Proceedings

55   In WTO proceedings as well, issues of access to justice[121] *per se* and access to information[122] are raised and decided. Further awards of arbitrations also contain decisions on access to justice and participation. In the NAFTA arbitration *Methanex Corporation v United States of America*, the public right to participate in arbitral proceedings was decided under the guise of the UNCITRAL arbitration rules as a basic prerequisite for democratic systems:

> Legislation in democratic systems involves, by its nature, participation by a wide spectrum of private individuals and interest groups in addition to the members of the legislature and the executive, insofar as its endorsement is also necessary for a bill to become law. While there may be circumstances in which facts would support an inference that one "invisible hand" was lurking behind and controlling a seemingly democratic process which had been elaborately contrived to conceal its machinations, it is clear beyond peradventure that the facts in the record do not warrant such an inference here.[123]

56   An ICSID arbitration case, decided in 2009, clearly illustrated the possibility of considering peremptory norms of general international law (*jus cogens*) to the extent they may be of interest in an investment matter. If so, such norms must prevail over any contrary provision of a BIT, as per the express statement in Art. 53 of the Vienna Convention. Investment law, bilateral investment agreements (BIT) and the ICSID Convention's judicial requirements 'cannot be read and interpreted in isolation from public international law, and its general principles'.[124] The tribunal moreover stated that ICSID protection cannot 'be granted to investments made in violation of the most fundamental rules of protection of human rights, like investments made in pursuance of torture or genocide or in support of slavery or trafficking of human organs'.[125]

4. Domestic Jurisdiction

57   Case law that affect the broader scope of SDG 16 can also be found at the domestic level and in further areas *in extenso*.[126] Within the given limits of this commentary, it hardly seems possible to find a leading line within the case law with regard to the targets of SDG 16. Rather, it appears at this point in time that certain currents of argumentation of international (human rights) courts are being led to strengthen the outlined rights. At best, it is noticeable that the transition from the international to the national level is sometimes associated with difficulties. However, the by nature all too diverse national courts worldwide do not permit the identification of currents to SDG 16, either because they are not in practice, for example in times of conflict (war or conflict tribunals), or because the perception and establishment of the law (legal systems and forms of

---

[121] WT/DS528, *Saudi Arabia—Measures Relating to Trade in Goods and Services, and Trade-Related Aspects of Intellectual Property Rights*; WT/DS527, *Bahrain—Measures Relating to Trade in Goods and Services, and Trade-Related Aspects of Intellectual Property Rights*.

[122] WT/DS525/1, *Ukraine – Measures Relating To Trade In Goods And Services*, Request For Consultations by the Russian Federation, 1 June 2017 paras. 1 f., 6, 9.

[123] *Methanex Corporation v United States of America*, Final Award of the Tribunal on Jurisdiction and Merits, 3 August 2005, NAFTA Arbitration, Matter of an International Arbitration under Chapter 11 of the North American Free Trade Agreement and the UNCITRAL Arbitration Rules, para. 46 (232).

[124] WT/DS2/AB/R, *United States - Standards for Reformulated and Conventional Gasoline (US — Gasoline)*, AB-1996-1, 17 (DSR 1996:I, 3 at 16).

[125] *Phoenix Action, Ltd. v. The Czech Republic*, ICSID/ARB/06/5, para. 78.

[126] To name but a few: *Algix Jamaica v J. Wray and Nephew Ltd*, 25 January 2016, JMCC COMM.2; *Roao Luke Davey v Oxfordshire County Council*: 'If it is neither appropriate nor proportionate then it is unlawful.'; ACCC/C2005/15, Aarhus Convention Compliance Committee; *Case concerning Romania*, 16/4/2008, para. 30; *Bandhua Mukti Morcha v. Union of India & Ors.*, Supreme Court of India (1997) 10 SCC 549.

government or states forms) are too different, for example with regard to state principles or the shaping of the *rule of law*.

Nonetheless, international courts of all kinds interpret the relevant international prin-   58
ciples and foundations as well as the respective national legal provisions. International and regional case law thus at least implicitly includes references to the valuation within national law. However, currents are still widely spread to the extent that an illustration of them is not considered to be useful here.

II. Jurisdiction on Targets and Indicators

Reducing all forms of violence and related deaths everywhere (SDG 16.1) is highly   59
relatable to the serious issue of armed conflict on the one hand, and to the perhaps more mundane, less-attended problem of violence against women, which in the gravest scenario leads to their death (femicide) on the other. More commonly known as honour killings, the murder of a (female) family or clan member by one or more fellow (mostly male) family members, where the murderers (and potentially the wider community) believe the victim to have brought dishonour upon the family, clan, or community.[127] In *Opuz v. Turkey*,[128] the ECtHR dealt with the recurrent physical violence of a husband against his wife (applicant), which ultimately resulted in the shooting of the applicants' mother by the husband. The court, taking into account national, international law as well as human rights law and the inclusion of international (human rights) jurisdiction on a massive scale, also established state responsibility for those areas in which 'private acts relies on state failure to comply with the duty to ensure human rights protection',[129] which applies equally to acts and omissions of private individuals. With the cited international case law and the appreciation of various human rights instruments, the court not only precisely recorded the historical course and development of violence against women and in doing so delimited the 'impossible or disproportionate burden on the authorities', but also applied the anchored principles to the question of whether the violence established could only have occurred on the basis of a possible discrimination of the applicants in their capacity as women. It evaluated the domestic judicial decisions in this case as revealing 'a lack of efficacy and a certain degree of tolerance, and had no noticeable preventive or deterrent effect on the conduct'[130] and also presented 'the existence of a *prima facie* indication that the domestic violence affected mainly women and that the general and discriminatory judicial passivity in Turkey created a climate that was conducive to domestic violence'.[131] This decision, which resulted in (pecuniary and non-pecuniary) compensation, was based in particular on 'the evolution of norms and principles in international law' (→ Goal 5 mn. 71 ff.).

Against the background of Turkey's announcement in 2020 to withdraw from the   60
Istanbul Convention (for the protection of women) and the fact that, as the case law

---

[127] Euromed, *National Situation Analysis Report: Women's Human Rights and Gender Equality, Jordan* (2010), 30; UNDP, *Gender Justice & Equality before the law, Analysis of Progress and Challenges in the Arab States Region* (2019); see also Kulczycki and Windle, 'Honor Killings in the Middle East and North Africa: A Systematic Review of the Literature' (2011) 17(11) *Violence against women*, 1442-64.

[128] *Case of Opuz v. Turkey*, Judgment, 9 June 2009, ECtHR Application no. 33401/02 and the huge amount of case law cited therein.

[129] *Case of Opuz v. Turkey*, Judgment, 9 June 2009, ECtHR Application no. 33401/02, para. 84.

[130] *Case of Opuz v. Turkey*, Judgment, 9 June 2009, ECtHR Application no. 33401/02, para. 170.

[131] *Case of Opuz v. Turkey*, Judgment, 9 June 2009, ECtHR Application no. 33401/02, para. 198; see for similar considerations and judicial reasoning *Gonzalez et al. ("Cotton Field") v Mexico*, Judgment, Preliminary Objection, Merits, Reparations, and Costs, 16 November 2009, IACtHR.

shows, its protection is often not guaranteed under national law or state structures are not effective, the severity of this issue is once again gaining weight (→ Intro mn. 273, 275).

61   Ending abuse, exploitation, trafficking and all forms of violence against and torture of children (SDG 16.2) was given strong expression in the so-called *RUF case* before the Special Court of Sierra Leone, in which, in addition to countless other serious human rights violations, child soldiers were routinely recruited 'by way of conscripting or enlisting children, girls and boys alike, under the age of 15 years into an armed force or group and / or using them to participate actively in hostilities.'[132] This atrocity was deemed a crime under customary international law which entailed individual criminal responsibility prior to the time frame of the Indictment. It also stated that every such abuse (constituted through the children's enrolment in militia) must be understood in a broad sense in so that the participation of children in conflict can effectively be prevented. Besides, the SCSL underscored rape, sexual slavery and any other form of sexual violence or inhumane act constitutes a crime against humanity.

62   Another case is specifically illustrative of the particular vulnerability of children and warded persons. With its third decision,[133] the African Committee of Experts on the Rights and Welfare of the Child (ACERW), decided on a case equally important for SDG 16.2 and SDG 16.3. The decision was effective for more than 100,000 children, who were forced to beg by their educators and guardians in Qu'ran schools in Senegal. Instead of being taught, the children begged for large parts of the day for their educators personal enrichment. Due to the fact that with this ruling the many children were granted as admitted complainants before the law, a lack of *actio popularis* in the Respondent State's (Senegal) legal system was abolished. Moreover, the State was held internationally responsible for the human rights infringement committed by non-state actors as a matter of ensuring the respect for human rights.[134] It was further emphasised 'that states are not merely responsible for providing formal legal protection, but also for ensuring effective implementation of laws.' The application of norms must be discernible in practice since otherwise 'the normative promise of socio-economic rights' could not be transferred in lived reality. Additionally, it was the first decision that was followed by a collaborative approach to find sustainable solutions and thus stands in stark contrast to the tendency of governments to negate such responsibilities.[135]

63   The case of *Kawas Fernández v. Honduras* highly relates to SDG 16.3 and clarifies that the legally prescribed consequences must be effectively enforced to uphold the *rule of law* (→ Goal 16 mn. 50). In order to fulfil its duties, 'states must provide adequate resources, including, without limitation, economic and logistic resources, and the required protection to move the investigation of and proceeding'[136] a case forward which moreover and in fact includes domestic as well as international cooperation. The *Case concerning Armed Activities on the Territory of the Congo* gives an indication

---

[132] *Prosecutor v. Sesay, et al.*, Judgment, Special Court for Sierra Leone (SCSL) RUF Case, SCSL-04-15-T (SCSL TCI, Mar. 02, 2009).

[133] African Committee of Experts on the Rights and Welfare of the Child (ACERWC), *The Centre for Human Rights (University of Pretoria) and La Rencontre Africaine pour la Defense des Droits de l'Homme (Senegal) v Government of Senegal*, Decision No 003/Com/001/2012.

[134] African Committee of Experts on the Rights and Welfare of the Child (ACERWC), *The Centre for Human Rights (University of Pretoria) and La Rencontre Africaine pour la Defense des Droits de l'Homme (Senegal) v Government of Senegal*, Decision: N° 003/Com/001/2012, para. 37.

[135] See https://www.escr-net.org/caselaw/2015/centre-human-rights-university-pretoria-and-rencontre-africaine-pour-defense-droits.

[136] *Kawas Fernández v. Honduras*, Judgment, Merits, Reparations and Costs, 3 April 2009, IACtHR, paras. 190-4.

in dealing with and combating organised crime. The ICJ in this case stated that an omission (of a state behaviour) can already be considered as an act that constitutes a claim for recovery and compensation since this infringes a states' duty of vigilance.[137] However, this entitlement does not apply to (rebel) groups located on the territory of the accused state. These groups cannot be attributed to the state even if they are organised as a criminal organisation for the purpose of exploiting natural resources and human capital.[138]

Innumerable examples of further jurisdiction concerning the indicators of SDG 16 can again be found before the IACtHR. For instance, SDG 16.9 is reflected in many cases of indigenous people, and thereof most often girls and women, not having access to legal identity at all which deprives them of their 'enjoyment of their right to citizenship, the right to move around freely, to vote, to access education and participate in the public affairs of their country' and of recourse to justice.[139] In *Osorio and Family Members v Peru*, for instance, the '[p]rohibition of enforced disappearance', as contained in SDG 16.10.1, is certified 'a blatant rejection of the essential principles that underlie the inter-American system' from an international Human Rights Law perspective, confirming the status of *jus cogens*.[140] The IACtHR has confirmed this status in various proceedings and, in particular, adopted a 'crime against humanity' which, as part of the courts' duty, shall be 'emphasized to preserve historical memory and [...] to ensure that such facts are never repeated.'[141] It thus derived a direct obligation within the meaning of SDG 16.10. In other cases, the IACtHR has also accepted, and thus gives SDG 16.b a rights-enlightening integration, for instance, that 'at the current stage of the evolution of international law, the fundamental principle of equality and non-discrimination has entered the realm of *jus cogens*' which consequently also applies *de jure* or *de facto* 'in the safeguard of other rights and in all domestic laws that it adopts' and thus 'permeates the whole legal system'.[142] In some cases the court confirmed even beyond, 'a peremptory character, [which] entails obligations *erga omnes* of protection that bind all States and result in effects with regard to third parties, including individuals'.[143] These jurisdiction equally underpins and illuminates SDG 16.b in its legal purpose and application to a considerable extent.

64

---

[137] This statement alone is of high interest to many issues and facts that can be found in investment law and finance (law) as well.

[138] *Democratic Republic Of The Congo v. Uganda*, Case concerning Armed Activities on the Territory of the Congo, Judgment, 19 December 2005, ICJ, paras. 246-7.

[139] See amongst many cases *Girls Yean and Bosico v. Dominican Republic*, Preliminary Objections, Merits, Reparations, and Costs, Judgment, 8 September 2005, IACtHR, paras. 237-42 (→ Goal 4 mn. 51); further information: International Work Group For Indigenous Affairs (IWGIA), *The Indigenous World 2019* (2019), 488 [found in: Indigenous Peoples' Major Group for Sustainable Development (IPMG), *Inclusion, Equality, and Empowerment to Achieve Sustainable Development: Realities of Indigenous Peoples* (2019), 9].

[140] *Case of Osorio Rivera and Family Members v Peru*, Judgment, 26 November 2013, IACtHR, para. 112.

[141] *Case of García and family members v Guatemala*, Judgment, 29 November 2012, IACtHR, para. 96; *Case of Goiburú et al. v Paraguay*, Judgment, 22 September 2006, IACtHR, para. 93; see also ILC, A/CN.4/727, *Fourth report on peremptory norms of general international law (jus cogens) by Dire Tladi, Special Rapporteur*, 31 January 2019.

[142] *Yatama v. Nicaragua*, Judgment, Preliminary objections, merits, reparations and costs, 23 June 2005, IACtHR Series C, No. 127, paras. 184-6; *Veliz Franco et al. v. Guatemala*, Judgment (Preliminary objections, merits, reparations and costs), 19 May 2014, IACtHR Series C, No. 277, paras. 205 f.

[143] *Servellón-García et al. v. Honduras*, Judgment, Merits, reparations and costs, 21 September 2006, IACtHR Series C, No. 152, paras. 94 f.

III. The Enforcement of SDG 16

65   'The right to information held by public authorities is an integral aspect of free-dom of expression and serves as a mechanism to support government openness and accountability as well as enhanced empowerment and equality among all social groups. Progress is being made in ensuring this right through policies and binding laws.'[144] But this statement, which has been announced at UN level, takes on greater depth when the application of binding law is examined more closely. Even in the case of political declarations of intent or legislative measure and even more in the case of supposedly sufficient legal norms granting protection (against violence), some results can be observed that are precisely against the purpose of SDG 16. In the EU, inter alia, a number of even adverse effects can be observed.[145] Despite promoting practical measures to strengthen the rights of crime victims and training of practitioners, another reaction lies in accompanying legislative actions such as implementing the Victims' Rights Directive within the EU or the Council of Europe Convention on preventing and combating violence against women and domestic violence (the Istanbul Convention) in 2017. But there also remains strong opposition in some Member States,[146] which shows that supportive non-binding measures as well as legally binding legislation do not (always) result in the intended implementation success.[147] Notwithstanding this, along with access to justice, particularly violence against women remains one of the most urgent issues at the European level that prevents a 'peaceful society' in the sense of SDG 16. In 2018 alone, violence and especially (gang) rape against women could be observed to increase in several member states.[148] The judicial assessment in any case remained either below the respective possible sentence, referring to the physical damage to women being 'not high enough' (to be determined), or to a definition of the normative element of the offence that based on the exercise of violence and not on consent to sexual activities.[149] Thus enforcement fails not primarily because of a denial of access to justice, but rather because of applying the (inadequate) existing laws.[150]

---

[144] UN, *The Sustainable Development Report 2020* (2020), 57.

[145] Halmai, 'The Possibility and Desirability of Rule of Law Conditionality' (2018) 11 *Hague J Rule Law*, 171 (171).

[146] European Union Agency for Fundamental Rights (FRA), *Fundamental Rights Report 2019* (2019), 207.

[147] See European Union Agency for Fundamental Rights (FRA), *Fundamental Rights Report 2019* (2019), 210.

[148] See European Union Agency for Fundamental Rights (FRA), *Fundamental Rights Report 2019* (2019), 211 f.

[149] Denmark, The District court in Herning (Retten i Herning), Dom i nævningesag om blandt andet voldtægt, press release, 14 September 2018; Berlingske, 'Endnu en frifindelse for voldtægt peger på ofres manglende retssikkerhed', 23 September 2018; Portugal, Court of Appeal of Porto (Tribunal da Relação do Porto), 2ª Secção criminal, Proc. n.º 3897/16.9JAPRT, P1, 27 June 2018; The Guardian, "Protests in Spain as five men cleared of teenager's gang rape", 26 April 2018; Europapress, "Remitirán al CGPJ la sentencia condenatoria a Juana Rivas por si hubiera 'violencia institucional'", ("Juana Rivas judgment will be sent to CGPJ for institutional violence"), Press release, 1 August 2018 [found in: European Union Agency for Fundamental Rights (FRA), *Fundamental Rights Report 2019* (2019), 221].

[150] See European Union Agency for Fundamental Rights (FRA), *Fundamental Rights Report 2019* (2019), 211 f.

IV. De Facto Influences on Jurisdiction

Since SDG 16 is a counter-agenda in itself to reduce inequalities and protect minori- **66**
ties and the most vulnerable groups,[151] girls and women as people suffering from
multiple discriminative approaches in legal systems worldwide. An example of women
being denied access to justice can be seen from a recent study of 18 Arab States. It
was found that an exclusion of women demanding their rights is grounded by a lack
of information about their possibilities to engage these. This was due to their illiteracy
and thus their unawareness about their rights. Moreover, the different needs of men
and women in legal processes are most often diminished by untrained officials and a
lack of understanding the sensitivities for instance of gender-based violence and the
gender-adequate application of law. This is exacerbated by the main barrier of costs
of legal services, since women are most often limited to having access to their family's
financial resources which is even amplified by poverty and / or in conflict-struck areas.
In conjunction with existent hazardous gender norms and male-dominated expectancies
to the role of women in society, human rights NGOs can hardly absorb these occurrences, since being frequently insufficiently funded. These system are most often of
conservative or traditional nature which means that these even seeking for consensus,
compromise and the reduction of social shame, solidify patriarchal systems which at
all increases gender bias thereby confirming discriminatory gender roles. Some of these
existing structures are opposed by new developments such as an increasing participation
of women in the judiciary. Quota regulations or, in some cases, presidential decrees are
promoting this development further, so that in future a more just and universal *rule of
law*-compliant design of justice seems possible.[152]

From an environmental perspective, some developments are discernible with regard **67**
to enacted regional instruments that increase public participation and provide new
compliance mechanisms or tools for norm control. Instruments such as the 1998 Aarhus
Convention[153] or the Escazú Agreement[154], which entered into force on 22 April 2021,
increase access to justice, enshrine a right to sustainable development and point to
further opportunities for development in the field of environmental law and human
rights.[155] Notwithstanding the fact that the *rule of law* (SDG 16.3) is, in the sense
of the SDGs, coined by an anthropocentric understanding, it should be noted that
the connections between a healthy environment, especially its biodiversity, and human
health are inextricably interdependent.[156] In recognising that environmental degradation
most often coincides with human rights violations, these instruments, which broaden
access to justice, offer important, forward-looking opportunities to strengthen a rule of

---

[151] United Nations General Assembly/Open Working Group on Sustainable Development Goals, *Compendium of TST Issues Briefs* (2014), 225.

[152] UNDP/UN Women/UNFPA/ESCWA, *Gender Justice & Equality before the law, Analysis of Progress and Challenges in the Arab States Region* (2019), 17 ff.; see also United Nations General Assembly/Open Working Group on Sustainable Development Goals, *Compendium of TST Issues Briefs* (2014), 230.

[153] UNECE, *Convention on Access to Information, Public Participation in Decision-Making and Access to Justice in Environmental Matters*, done at Aarhus, Denmark on 25 June 1998.

[154] Further reading: UNECLAC, *Regional Agreement on Access to Information, Public Participation and Justice in Environmental Matters in Latin America and the Caribbean* (2018); https://sdg.iisd.org/news/esca zu-agreement-takes-effect-enshrining-right-to-sustainable-development/.

[155] Further reading: UNECLAC, *Regional Agreement on Access to Information, Public Participation and Justice in Environmental Matters in Latin America and the Caribbean* (2018); https://sdg.iisd.org/news/esca zu-agreement-takes-effect-enshrining-right-to-sustainable-development/.

[156] ILA, Draft Resolution No. 4 /2020, *The Role of International Law in Sustainable Natural Resources Management for Development*, 14, 21, 26; UNEP, *Environmental Rule of Law, First Global Report* (2019), 192, 226 ff.

law that is understood holistically, as is necessary before the background of the Global Agenda 2030.

V. Evaluation of Jurisprudential Significance

68   This brief insight into the existing jurisdiction not only stresses the manifold manifestations of SDG 16 in various areas of human life. Relying on the fact that international courts not only apply law and general principles of law,[157] but also derive applicable norms 'from national laws of legal systems of the world',[158] this means that the jurisprudence under consideration also reflects to a certain extent 'commonly accepted domestic rules',[159] so that an 'overlap exists between general principles and constitutions'.[160] This connection is apparent since the SDGs in general and SDG 16 in particular incorporate substantive content relating to fundamental human rights and humanitarian law, which became part of the constitutions of the recognising states at the latest[161] with their acknowledgment of the UDHR and constitutionalised further international human rights instruments and standards in the ongoing development.[162] Consequently, SDG 16 is also permeated by legal structures and is distinguished in its content and interpretation only by the fact that it introduces the concept of sustainability into this legal framework and attempts to unify it. As the life cycle of the SDGs progresses, it is to be expected that in future jurisdiction will increasingly adopt this concept. So far, however, there have been at best slight offshoots, but no clear considerations of the concept[163] or a direct application of SDG 16 in jurisdiction. While its normative status may be on the legal periphery up to now,[164] it is precisely these legal structures that should support and simplify the actual transfer into legal fairways.

E. Conclusion on SDG 16

69   The objectives of SDG 16 offering essential concepts on how societies should deploy a stable institutional framework to citizens and companies. The main features of SDG 16 pointing at peace, the *rule of law*, access to justice and governance. These concepts

---

[157] See Art. 38(c) of the Statute of the Permanent Court of International Justice.

[158] Art. 21(1) (c) Rome Statute of the International Criminal Court.

[159] O'Boyle and Lafferty, 'General Principles and Constitutions as Sources of Human Rights Laws' in Shelton (ed), *The Oxford Handbook of International Human Rights Law* (2015), 196.

[160] O'Boyle and Lafferty, 'General Principles and Constitutions as Sources of Human Rights Laws' in Shelton (ed), *The Oxford Handbook of International Human Rights Law* (2015), 197.

[161] The recognition of human rights in various forms can be traced historically much earlier, for instance in the Magna Carta, adopted 1215 by King John or in the English Bill of Rights from 1689. Significantly earlier, however, evidence can also be found in the Corpus Iuris Civilis of 534, initiated by Emperor Justinian.

[162] O'Boyle and Lafferty, 'General Principles and Constitutions as Sources of Human Rights Laws' in Shelton (ed), *The Oxford Handbook of International Human Rights Law* (2015), 197.

[163] Perhaps the proportionality principle of law could be seen as inherent in the concept of sustainability as it also seeks to create balanced solutions. Whether these two elements are congruent or could be merged, however, would be subject of a separate examination.

[164] See Huck, 'Die EU und die Globale Agenda 2030 der Vereinten Nationen: Reflexion, Strategie und rechtliche Umsetzung' (2019) *Europäische Zeitschrift für Wirtschaftsrecht (EuZW)*, 581-7; Huck, 'The EU and the Global Agenda 2030: Reflection, Strategy and legal implementation' (2020) 2020-1 *C-EENRG Working Papers*, 3; Maaß, 'Die Normativität der Sustainable Development Goals in den internen und externen Politiken Europas' in Huck (ed), *Schriften zum Internationalen Wirtschaftsrecht* (2020), 38-9; Huck and Maaß, 'Gaining a Foot in the Door: Giving Access to Justice with SDG 16.3?' (2021) 2021-5 *C-EENRG Working Papers*.

play an inevitable role for every omission or decisive action of a national government or other entities assigned with official power. In particular, when this power affects women and girls, the quality and effectivity of the *rule of law* are a litmus test for the quality of a genuine *rule of law* approach and fair access to justice. The guarantee of peace, the *rule of law* and governance is not a new issue and was already recognised in the Millennium Declaration and reaffirmed at the 2005 World Summit, the 2010 MDG High-level plenary meeting, the Rio+20 conference and many other resolutions on the *rule of law*.[165] The Millennium Declaration underlined the *rule of law* as the all-important framework for advancing human security and prosperity.[166] SDG 16 is a leading orientation for all SDGs. Without the essential functioning, it seems to be unlikely to measure progress in most of all SDGs. Thus, SDG 16 is recognised as a *conditio sine qua non* for all emanations of sustainable development, which cannot be achieved at a national, interregional, transnational or international level without compliance with the *rule of law*. The achievement of almost all SDGs is hardly possible without combating and neutralising violence, corruption and bribery. In dystopian societies, in which organised crime has openly or covertly infiltrated state functions and has permanently dissolved state guarantees and corruption, the concept of sustainable development cannot flourish.

I. Peace

The achievement of peace is recognised as one of the outstanding pillars upholding   70
sustainable development ($\rightarrow$ Intro mn. 160 ff.). Violent conflicts still were and are one of the greatest obstacles to the achievement of sustainable development. During the evolution of the SDGs the OWG has discussed the gap in MDG performance between conflict-affected and other developing countries as large and increasing,[167] and observed that in the recent years' conflicts have evolved from inter-state wars to intra-state conflicts and various forms of violence involving non-state actors, such as armed groups, rebels, gangs and organised crime.[168] The deeper reasons and drivers for violent conflicts are from the viewpoint of the UN often related to inequitable access to social services and weak social welfare systems; absence of decent work (particularly for young adults); poor natural resources management; injustices; human rights violations and abuses; political exclusion (particularly of youth and women).[169]

II. The Rule of Law

The fight against crime is apparently not in any case succeeding, or only insufficiently   71
succeeding, in neutralising organised crime. Corruption and bribery are widespread. For many people, in particular girls' and women's access to justice is insufficient or non-existent. The demand for transparency, accountability and even the establishment

---

[165] Open Working Group on Sustainable Development Goals, *Compendium of TST Issues Briefs, Issues Brief 29* (2014), 225 ff.

[166] A/59/2005, *Follow-up to the outcome of the Millennium Summit, In larger freedom: towards development, security and human rights for all, Report of the Secretary-General*, 21 March 2005, para. 133.

[167] Open Working Group on Sustainable Development Goals, *Compendium of TST Issues Briefs Issues Brief 29* (2014), 226.

[168] Open Working Group on Sustainable Development Goals, *Compendium of TST Issues Briefs Issues Brief 29* (2014), 226.

[169] Open Working Group on Sustainable Development Goals, *Compendium of TST Issues Briefs Issues Brief 29* (2014), 227.

of a legal identity are therefore the foundations, which should enable societies based on the rule of law.

72   The *rule of law* concept as a fundament of SDG 16 delivers a sound basis and for the general concept of access to justice as well. It is hard to accept that mostly girls and women are in certain regions and countries not entitled to grant a birth certificate, what distract them from access to schooling, housing, loans etc.

73   The *rule of law* concept as different as it is in countries is one of the three pillars of the UN for its work in peace and security, development and human rights according the UN Charter.[170] The UN has underlined several times that the *rule of law* is essential for the realisation of sustained economic growth and sustainable development.[171] Nollkaemper observed for instance that '[t]ere may be several explanations for this dichotomy between the rule of law at the international level and the rule of law at the domestic level' according to structural differences between the international and the national legal orders. Moreover, Nollkaemper points out that '[i]n essence, the rule of law means literally, what it says: persons and institutions should be ruled by the law – as a norm and in actual practice.'[172] This roughly outlined definition does not reflect the ingredient of the law itself, whether right or wrong, which should be obeyed, neither any transparency, participation nor accountability. However, the very nucleus of the *rule of law* is not filled and decorated with other content but reducible to the relentless acceptance of the law by all institutions, people and entities irrespective of the source being constituted in domestic, interregional or international law. Nevertheless, it should be noted that the *rule of law* concept refers to a principle of governance in which all persons, institutions and entities, public and private, including the State itself, are accountable to laws that are publicly promulgated, equally enforced and independently adjudicated, and which are consistent with international human rights norms and standards. It requires, as well, measures to ensure adherence to the principles of supremacy of law, equality before the law, accountability to the law, fairness in the application of the law, separation of powers, participation in decision-making, legal certainty, avoidance of arbitrariness and procedural and legal transparency.[173]

74   The concept of the *rule of law* and even this of justice pointing to the protection from fear, peaceful conflict management supported by legal structures and the fair administration of justice.[174] Indeed, there are a lot of deficits to observe. The disappointment of so many deficits in the acceptance of the *rule of law* in so many countries culminated in the following bitter observation:

Although the UN has promoted the establishment of the rule of law procedures and institutions in so many different ways, still myriad deficits remain, like among others: a lack of political will for reform, a lack of institutional independence within the justice sector, a lack of domestic technical capacity, a lack of material and financial resources, a lack of public confidence in Government, a lack of official respect for human rights and, more generally, a lack of peace and security.[175]

---

[170] A/RES/60/1, *2005 World Summit Outcome*, 24 October 2005, para 16; A/68/213/Add.1, *Strengthening and coordinating United Nations rule of law activities, Report of the Secretary-General*, 11 July 2014, paras. 7 ff.

[171] A/RES/74/191, *The rule of law at the national and international levels*, 30 December 2019, preamble.

[172] Nollkaemper, 'The Internationalized Rule of Law' (2009) 1(1) *Hague Journal on the Rule of Law*, 77.

[173] S/2004/616, *The rule of law and transitional justice in conflict and post-conflict societies, Report of the Secretary-General*, 23 August 2004, para. 6.

[174] A/68/213/Add.1, S/2004/616, *The rule of law and transitional justice in conflict and post-conflict societies, Report of the Secretary-General*, 23 August 2004, paras. 2, 5.

[175] S/2004/616, *The rule of law and transitional justice in conflict and post-conflict societies, Report of the Secretary-General*, 23 August 2004, para. 3.

One of the answers of the UN was to establish an Office of Rule of Law and Security　75
Institutions (OROLSI).[176] The OROLSI includes five components: Police Division; Justice and Corrections Service; Disarmament, Demobilization and Reintegration Section; Security Sector Reform Unit; and UN Mine Action Service. The Global Focal Point for the Rule of Law (GFP) is a United Nations platform co-chaired by DPO and UNDP that is designed to strengthen the provision of *rule of law* assistance to address and prevent violent conflict, to protect human rights and to restore justice and security for conflict-affected people.[177]

It has become clear, that corruption has not only a negative effect on economic　76
growth and development, but deeper than that a corrosive impact on legitimacy, the *rule of law*, fair and effective laws, as well as all part of the division of three powers.[178]

With the unanimously adopted SDGS, the UN and its member states committed and　77
renewed to strengthen the 'rule of law' at the international and national levels, across issue areas.[179]

There is also a growing consensus that sustainable development not only requires　78
capable states but also governments that are accountable to their populations. Accountability mechanisms include administrative, political, judicial and quasi-judicial as well as social accountability systems to assure the quality of services. Openness and transparency are also associated with better socio-economic and human development indicators, higher competitiveness in international markets and lower corruption.[180]

In particular, the main features of SDG16 mirror women's empowerment and gender　79
equality. They are strongly connected with good governance and the *rule of law*. Gender equality is an objective in itself ($\rightarrow$ Goal 5 mn. 19 f.). Research shows that where women have access to employment, participate in public decision-making and enjoy equal property and inheritance rights, countries reap the rewards through lower levels of corruption and a lessened propensity to engage in intra and inter-state conflict. It has been observed that in 98 economies equal inheritance rights were related to a higher likelihood of women having formal bank accounts and credit.[181]

III. Concept of Justice

Although the UDHR in Art. 8 states: 'Everyone has the right to an effective remedy by　80
the competent national tribunals for acts violating the fundamental rights granted him by the constitution or by law' – this protection is repeated in many human rights treaties, including the ICCPR (Art. 2(3)) – reality proves to be different. Thus, justice may not to be brought to everybody within legal structures and a fair on the *rule of law* operating judicial system. Probably effective access to fair and adequate justice is one of the prominent tasks to been achieved. To promote access to justice for everyone seems to be a keyway to ensure that assets can be protected and that unfair practices and discrimination can be halted to allow for more significant opportunities for individuals and

---

[176] See https://peacekeeping.un.org/en/office-of-rule-of-law-and-security-institutions.

[177] https://peacekeeping.un.org/sites/default/files/august_2019_gfp_factsheet1.pdf.

[178] Sajdik, 'Delivering justice on the Ground: The Challenges of Fighting corruption at the National and International Levels' (2012), 4/2012 *UN Chronicle* 20.

[179] Lopez-Claros and Dahl and Groff, 'Strengthening the International Rule of Law' (2020) in *Global Governance and the Emergence of Global Institutions for the 21st Century*, 208 (217).

[180] Lopez-Claros and Dahl and Groff, 'Strengthening the International Rule of Law' (2020) in *Global Governance and the Emergence of Global Institutions for the 21st Century*, 208 (234).

[181] Lopez-Claros and Dahl and Groff, 'Strengthening the International Rule of Law' (2020) in *Global Governance and the Emergence of Global Institutions for the 21st Century*, 208 (236).

communities.[182] Nevertheless, access to justice means different things according to a different understanding of justice embedded in different systems to give a proper unified answer.

IV. Rule of Law and Women

81   All of the main principles of the SDGs must be combined with gender equality in the law and its practice.[183] Firstly, knowledge of the law must be guaranteed as one is at the heart of the rule of law and of a democratic state.[184] Information is a prerequisite of political participation and accountability.[185] It would not be recommended to rely in any case on the formal provides systems by the rule of law and justice an ignore parallel in the specific culture rooted alternative systems.[186] Further, it is assumed that women's rights can only be enforced through formal justice institutions, and therefore the role of alternative institutions should be minimised. Chopra and Isser have observed several reasons, why the formal justice approach often fails to serve women[187] because '[i]n many places, judicial personnel send women back to community authorities, where they believe their cases should be handled'.[188] Social pressure as a *Normative Kraft des Faktischen* (G. Jellinek)[189] shows the interconnectedness between cultural behaviour that often supersedes the impact of legalistic (western) systems of positive normativity.[190]

82   Chopra and Isser explain the situation very well, when '[i]n Somalia, for example, local norms prohibit a woman from [...] accessing courts, requiring that she be represented by her husband or a male family member, who may have interests at odds with hers. In Afghanistan, women and girls who act against the wishes of their families often face threats and intimidation. In addition, in Aceh, local leaders actively discourage women from turning to the formal system, as it may upset the community order'.[191]

83   Thus, the failure of a wider penetration of the main features of SDG 16 that is complained by the UN[192] and others[193] must be fixed with a framework and set of tools in order to tackle discrimination to guarantee effectiveness for justice. Once again: accountability of states before international law which can also be used by all citizens regardless of their sex as a universal applicable norm in the realm of international, domestic, interregional law as a global legal binding standard influenced and embedded

---

[182] Guard, 'Justice: What We Need in a Post-2015 World' (2012) XLIX(4) *UN Chronicle*.

[183] UNDP and ESCWA and UNFPA and UN Women, *Gender Justice & Equality before the law, Analysis of Progress and Challenges in the Arab States Region* (2019), 2.

[184] Peruginelli, 'Law Belongs to the People: Access to Law and Justice' (2016) 16(2) *Legal Information Management*, 107 (107).

[185] Peruginelli, 'Law Belongs to the People: Access to Law and Justice' (2016) 16(2) *Legal Information Management*, 107 (108).

[186] Chopra and Isser, 'Access to Justice and Legal Pluralism in Fragile States: The Case of Women's Rights' (2012) 4(2) *Hague Journal on the Rule of Law*, 337–358.

[187] Chopra and Isser, 'Access to Justice and Legal Pluralism in Fragile States: The Case of Women's Rights' (2012) 4(2) *Hague Journal on the Rule of Law*, 337 (341); see additionally Maranlou, 'Access of Women to Justice and Legal Empowerment' (2014) in *Access to Justice in Iran: Women, Perceptions, and Reality* (2014), 123.

[188] Chopra and Isser, 'Access to Justice and Legal Pluralism in Fragile States: The Case of Women's Rights' (2012) 4(2) *Hague Journal on the Rule of Law*, 337 (343).

[189] See Anter, *Die normative Kraft des Faktischen: das Staatsverständnis Georg Jellineks* (2004).

[190] Anter, *Die normative Kraft des Faktischen: das Staatsverständnis Georg Jellineks* (2004), 344.

[191] Anter, *Die normative Kraft des Faktischen: das Staatsverständnis Georg Jellineks* (2004), 344.

[192] See https://peacekeeping.un.org/en/office-of-rule-of-law-and-security-institutions.

[193] See Chopra and Isser, 'Access to Justice and Legal Pluralism in Fragile States: The Case of Women's Rights' (2012) 4(2) *Hague Journal on the Rule of Law*, 337 (341).

with a human rights-based legal framework. On this basis, justice processes at the local level could be positively influenced.[194]

---

[194] Chopra and Isser, 'Access to Justice and Legal Pluralism in Fragile States: The Case of Women's Rights' (2012) 4(2) *Hague Journal on the Rule of Law*, 337 (355).

Goal 17
Strengthen the means of implementation and revitalize the Global Partnership for Sustainable Development

Finance

17.1 Strengthen domestic resource mobilization, including through international support to developing countries, to improve domestic capacity for tax and other revenue collection

17.2 Developed countries to implement fully their official development assistance commitments, including the commitment by many developed countries to achieve the target of 0.7 per cent of gross national income for official development assistance (ODA/GNI) to developing countries and 0.15 to 0.20 per cent of ODA/GNI to least developed countries; ODA providers are encouraged to consider setting a target to provide at least 0.20 per cent of ODA/GNI to least developed countries

17.3 Mobilize additional financial resources for developing countries from multiple sources

17.4 Assist developing countries in attaining long-term debt sustainability through coordinated policies aimed at fostering debt financing, debt relief and debt restructuring, as appropriate, and address the external debt of highly indebted poor countries to reduce debt distress

17.5 Adopt and implement investment promotion regimes for least developed countries

Technology

17.6 Enhance North-South, South-South and triangular regional and international cooperation on and access to science, technology and innovation and enhance knowledge sharing on mutually agreed terms, including through improved coordination among existing mechanisms, in particular at the United Nations level, and through a global technology facilitation mechanism

17.7 Promote the development, transfer, dissemination and diffusion of environmentally sound technologies to developing countries on favourable terms, including on concessional and preferential terms, as mutually agreed

17.8 Fully operationalize the technology bank and science, technology and innovation capacity-building mechanism for least developed countries by 2017 and enhance the use of enabling technology, in particular information and communications technology

Capacity-building

17.9 Enhance international support for implementing effective and targeted capacity-building in developing countries to support national plans to implement all the Sustainable Development Goals, including through North-South, South-South and triangular cooperation

Trade

17.10 Promote a universal, rules-based, open, non-discriminatory and equitable multilateral trading system under the World Trade Organization, including through the conclusion of negotiations under its Doha Development Agenda

17.11 Significantly increase the exports of developing countries, in particular with a view to doubling the least developed countries' share of global exports by 2020

17.12 Realize timely implementation of duty-free and quota-free market access on a lasting basis for all least developed countries, consistent with World Trade Organization decisions, including by ensuring that preferential rules of origin applicable to imports from least developed countries are transparent and simple, and contribute to facilitating market access

Systemic issues

Policy and institutional coherence

17.13 Enhance global macroeconomic stability, including through policy coordination and policy coherence
17.14 Enhance policy coherence for sustainable development
17.15 Respect each country's policy space and leadership to establish and implement policies for poverty eradication and sustainable development

Multi-stakeholder partnerships

17.16 Enhance the Global Partnership for Sustainable Development, complemented by multi-stakeholder partnerships that mobilize and share knowledge, expertise, technology and financial resources, to support the achievement of the Sustainable Development Goals in all countries, in particular developing countries
17.17 Encourage and promote effective public, public-private and civil society partnerships, building on the experience and resourcing strategies of partnerships

Data, monitoring and accountability

17.18 By 2020, enhance capacity-building support to developing countries, including for least developed countries and small island developing States, to increase significantly the availability of high-quality, timely and reliable data disaggregated by income, gender, age, race, ethnicity, migratory status, disability, geographic location and other characteristics relevant in national contexts
17.19 By 2030, build on existing initiatives to develop measurements of progress on sustainable development that complement gross domestic product, and support statistical capacity-building in developing countries

Word Count related to 'Partnership'
A/RES/70/1 – Transforming our world: the 2030 Agenda for Sustainable Development: 23
Instruments mentioned in A/RES/70/1 in the section entitled: 'Sustainable Development Goals and targets':
A/RES/69/313 – Addis Ababa Action Agenda of the Third International Conference on Financing for Development adopted on 27 July 2015: 28
A/RES/66/288 – The future we want (Rio +20 Declaration) adopted on 27 July 2012: 25
A/RES/55/2 – United Nations Millennium Declaration adopted on 8 September 2000: 1

Select Bibliography: Andreas Antoniou and Abbas Berya, *Long-term debt sustainability in developing countries – The HIPC Initiative Revisited* (Commonwealth Secretariat, London 2004); Gro Harlem Brundtland, 'Our Common Future – Call for Action' (1987) 14 *Environmental Conversation*, 291; Marie-Claire

Cordonier Segger, 'Commitments to sustainable development through international law and policy' in Marie-Claire Cordonier Segger and H.E. Judge Christopher Gregory Weeramantry, Sustainable Development Principles in the Decisions of International Courts and Tribunals, 1992-2012 (2017); Alan Desmond, 'A New Dawn for the Human Rights of International Migrants? Protection of Migrants' Rights in Light of the UN's SDGs and Global Compact for Migration' (2020) 16.3 *International Journal of Law in Context*, 222-38; Paolo Esposito and Lucio Dicorato Spiridione, 'Sustainable development, governance and performance measurement in public private partnerships (PPPs): A methodological proposal' (2020) 12.14 *Sustainability*, 5696; Barbara Gray and Jill Purdy, *Collaborating for our future: Multistakeholder partnerships for solving complex problems* (Oxford University Press, Oxford 2018); Lorren Kirsty Haywood, Nikki Funke, Michelle Audouin, Constansia Musvoto and Anton Nahman, 'The Sustainable Development Goals in South Africa: Investigating the need for multi-stakeholder partnerships' (2019) 36(5) *Development Southern Africa*, 555-69; L. Hens and B. Nath, 'The Johannesburg Conference' (2003) 5 *Environment, Development and Sustainability*, 7; Martin W. Holdgate, 'Our Common Future: The Report of the World Commission on Environment and Development' (1987) 14 *Environmental Conversation*, 282; Georg Kell, 'The Global Compact Selected Experiences and Reflections' (2005) 59 *J Bus Ethics*, 69-79; John Lannon and John N. Walsh, 'Project facilitation as an active response to tensions in international development programmes' (2020) 38.8 *International Journal of Project Management*, 486-99; Leigland, 'Public-private partnerships in developing countries: The emerging evidence-based critique' (2018) 33.1 *The World Bank Research Observer*, 103-34; David J. Maurrasse, 'From the MDGs to the SDGs: Cross-Sector Partnerships as Avenues to Development in the UN System' in Margaret Chon, Pedro Roffe, and Ahmed Abdel-Latif (eds), *The Cambridge Handbook of Public-Private Partnerships, Intellectual Property Governance, and Sustainable Development* (Cambridge University Press, Cambridge 2018), 356-75; André Nollkaemper and Dov Jacobs, 'Shared responsibility in international law: a conceptual framework' (2013) 34 *Michigan Journal of International Law*, 360; André Nollkaemper and Ilias Plakokefalos, 'The Practice of Shared Responsibility: A Framework Analysis' in André Nollkaemper and Ilias Plakokefalos (eds), *The Practice of Shared Responsibility in International Law* (Cambridge University Press, Cambridge 2017); Oluwaseun James Oguntuase, 'Role of Transnational Multi-stakeholder Partnerships in Achieving Sustainable Development Goals' in Walter Leal Filho (ed), *Partnerships for the Goals – Encyclopedia of the UN Sustainable Development Goals* (Springer, Cham 2020); Rasche, 'The United Nations Global Compact and the Sustainable Development Goals' in Oliver Laasch, Roy Suddaby, R. E. Freeman and Dima Jamali (eds), Research Handbook of Responsible Management (Edward Elgar Publishing, Cheltenham 2020); John Gerard Ruggie, 'Global-governance.net: The global compact as learning network' (2001) 7 *Global Governance*, 371; Peter H. Sand, 'Principle 27: Cooperation in a Spirit of Global Partnership' in Jorge E. Viñuales, *The Rio Declaration on Environment and Development, A Commentary* (2015), 622; Lisa Sanderink and Naghmeh Nasiritousi, 'How institutional interactions can strengthen effectiveness: The case of multi-stakeholder partnerships for renewable energy' (2020) 141 *Energy Policy*, 111447; Pamela Sloan and David Oliver, 'Building trust in multi-stakeholder partnerships: Critical emotional incidents and practices of engagement' (2013) 34.12 *Organization Studies*, 1835-68; Katharina Spraul and Julia Thaler, 'Partnering for good? An analysis of how to achieve sustainability-related outcomes in public–private partnerships' (2020) 13 *Business Research*, 485; Ayça Tokuç, 'Rio Declaration on Environment and Development (UN)' in Samuel O. Idowu, Nicholas Capaldi, Liangrong Zu and Ananda Das Gupta (eds), *Encyclopedia of Corporate Social Responsibility* (Springer Verlag, Berlin/Heidelberg 2013), 2087; United Nations Department of Economic and Social Affairs, *Partnerships for sustainable Development Goals – A legacy review towards realizing the 2030 Agenda* (UN-DESA, New York 2015); Oliver F. Williams, 'The UN Global Compact: The Challenge and the Promise' (2004) 14.4 Business Ethics Quarterly, 755-74.

A. Background and Origin of SDG 17

1   The 1972 United Nations Conference on the Human Environment in Stockholm elicited an explanatory memorandum which underscored that natural 'problems could only be solved through international co-operation.'[1] In the declaration itself, several forms of partnerships were already considered even though they were not titled like

---

[1] UN Audiovisual Library of International Law, *Declaration of the United Nations Conference on the Human Environment - Procedural History*, 1.

that. Principle 11 acknowledges that 'appropriate steps should be taken by States and international organizations'.[2] Principle 22[3] explicitly indicates that

> [s]tates shall co-operate to develop further the international law regarding liability and compensation for the victims of pollution and other environmental damage caused by activities within the jurisdiction or control of such States to areas beyond their jurisdiction.[4]

However, the subsequent Principle 23 also clarifies that 'the value systems and the   2 extent of applicability of standards prevailing in each country shall be taken into account' and cannot be applied (or only to a limited extent) to developing countries if the social costs are too high. At least three aspects were thus emphasised: (1) the intended partnerships are as rich as possible globally or at least multilaterally; (2) the intended partnerships take into account and allow for differences between the partners; and (3) these partnerships explicitly include an inter-generational contract, which means that an infinite duration of partnership is intended.

Principle 25 then points to the importance of international organisations by express-   3 ing that states should ensure that 'international organizations play a co-ordinated, efficient and dynamic role'.[5]

In 1983, the General Assembly laid the foundation for the World Commission on   4 Environment and Development. The task of the Commission was to prepare a global agenda to reach sustainable development by 2000.[6] Within the framework of the agenda the Commission should 'propose new forms of international cooperation and national action to deal with environmental concerns'.[7] Moreover, it was stated that international cooperation 'will influence policies and events in the direction of needed changes'.[8] Since the aspect of international cooperation was crucial for the preparation of the report, it can be found throughout the whole report. Since the Stockholm Conference, scientific communities as well as non-governmental organisations (NGOs) played an important role to raise public awareness and influence political changes.[9] Even governments started to acknowledge NGOs as precious and experienced partners.[10] Therefore, they are considered essential for sustainable development in the report.[11] During the creation of the report, the Commission already used the expertise of a broad global network of individuals, research institutes and international organisations.[12] In addition, the report stressed that governments cannot act alone but also need the participation of international and private organisations, business communities, trade unions and scien-

---

[2] A/CONF.48/14/Rev.1, *Report of the United Nations Conference on the Human Environment*.

[3] This Principle is emphasised with Principle 24 which demands that 'international matters should be handled in a co-operative spirit by all countries, big and small, on an equal footing [and be realised through] [c]o-operation through multilateral or bilateral arrangements or other appropriate means [...]'.

[4] A/CONF.48/14/Rev.1, *Report of the United Nations Conference on the Human Environment*, Principle 22.

[5] A/CONF.48/14/Rev.1, *Report of the United Nations Conference on the Human Environment*.

[6] Holdgate, 'Our Common Future: The Report of the World Commission on Environment and Development' (1987), *Environmental Conversation Vol. 14 No. 3*, 282.

[7] Holdgate, 'Our Common Future: The Report of the World Commission on Environment and Development' (1987), *Environmental Conversation Vol. 14 No. 3*, 282.

[8] World Commission on Environment and Development, *'Our Common future'* (1987), para. I. 1. 9.

[9] Brundtland, 'Our Common Future – Call for Action' (1987), *Environmental Conversation Vol. 14 No. 4*, 291.

[10] Brundtland, 'Our Common Future – Call for Action' (1987), *Environmental Conversation Vol. 14 No. 4*, 291.

[11] World Commission on Environment and Development, *'Our Common future'* (1987), 16.

[12] Holdgate, 'Our Common Future: The Report of the World Commission on Environment and Development' (1987), *Environmental Conversation Vol. 14 No. 3*, 282.

tists.[13] Chairman Brundtland underscored that especially industries and governments will benefit from cooperation.[14] The report also emphasised the need of international co-operation to also be effective.[15]

5   The United Nations Conference on Environment and Development (Earth Summit) was held in 1992 in Rio de Janeiro (→ Intro mn. 38, 254, 257). During this Conference, the Agenda 21 and the Rio Declaration on Environment and Development were adopted. Agenda 21 is an action plan that has 'to be taken globally, nationally, and locally by organizations of the United Nations System, Governments, and Major Groups in every area in which human impacts on the environment'.[16] Already in the preamble of Chapter 1 it is stated, that a 'global partnership for sustainable development' is needed.[17] It is the first time the term 'global partnership' was used with regard to development. Section III explicitly deals with the strengthening of the roles of major groups like non-governmental organisations, trade unions, business and industry and the scientific and technological industry. Partnerships are repeatedly mentioned throughout the entire Agenda 21 and, moreover, includes 'Capacity-building' in Chapter 37, 'Trade' in Chapter 2, 'Finance' in Chapter 33 as well as 'Scientific and Technological Community' in Chapter 31 which is a telling similarity to SDG 17 of the Global Agenda 2030.

6   The Rio Declaration contains principles 'for the relationship of states to each other and the relationship between states and their citizens in the field of environment and development' (→ Intro mn. 254).[18] The Declarations' intent was to make all stakeholders pursue the 'goal of establishing a new and equitable global partnership through the creation of new levels of cooperation among States, key sectors of societies and people'.[19] But already the Rio+20 Conference and the drafting process of the Rio Declaration attracted 'the attention of thousands of representatives of the UN system and other key groups and resulted in over 700 voluntary commitments, witnessing the formation of new partnerships to advance sustainable development'.[20] The joint work laid the foundation for many other collaborations, especially the demanded public-private partnerships that brought together governments, international organisations, businesses and NGOs to initiate projects to create and implement sustainable development, which is since supported by the leadership of various UN agencies.[21] The UN Global Compact was one of several starting points for joint projects to which companies and institutions can still voluntarily commit to today.[22]

7   The Millennium Declaration was signed during the United Nations Millennium Summit in 2000 (→ Intro mn. 265 f.). The declaration includes eight Millennium Devel-

---

[13] World Commission on Environment and Development, *'Our Common future'* (1987), e.g. para. III 2.1 50., II 5.4 90., II 4.1.

[14] Brundtland, 'Our Common Future – Call for Action' (1987), *Environmental Conversation Vol. 14 No. 4*, 293.

[15] World Commission on Environment and Development, *Our Common future* (1987), 25.

[16] https://sustainabledevelopment.un.org/outcomedocuments/agenda21.

[17] UN, *Agenda 21* (1992), 3.

[18] Tokuç, *Rio Declaration on Environment and Development (UN)* (2013), 2087.

[19] A/CONF.151/26 (Vol.I), *Report of the United Nations Conference on Environment and Development* (1992), 1.

[20] Cordonier Segger, 'Commitments to sustainable development through international law and policy' in Cordonier Segger and Weeramantry, *Sustainable Development Principles in the Decisions of International Courts and Tribunals, 1992-2012* (2017), 54.

[21] Sand, 'Principle 27: Cooperation in a Spirit of Global Partnership' in Viñuales, *The Rio Declaration on Environment and Development, A Commentary* (2015), 622.

[22] Ruggie, 'Global-governance.net: The global compact as learning network' (2001) 7 *Global Governance*, 371; Williams, 'The UN Global Compact: The Challenge and the Promise' (2004) 14.4 *Business Ethics Quarterly*, 755-74; Rasche, 'The United Nations Global Compact and the Sustainable Development Goals' in Laasch et al. (eds), *Research Handbook of Responsible Management* (2020).

opment Goals which should be achieved by 2015. By signing the declaration, the world leaders 'committed their nations to a new global partnership'.[23] The relevant Millennium Development Goal is Goal 8: 'Develop a global partnership for development'. The main subject of MDG 8 are trading and financial system, support for developing countries as well as new technologies. 'Shared responsibility' formed a key for the then demanded transformation and is defined in the Millennium Declaration as 'responsibility for managing worldwide economic and social development, as well as threats to international peace and security, must be shared among the nations of the world and should be exercised multilaterally'.[24] The concept of shared responsibility includes multiple actors like states, international organisations, multinational corporations and individuals.[25] Thereby it has to be distinguished from a collective responsibility, which means that each actor bears only its own responsibility for a certain outcome.[26] However, shared responsibility also includes cases where responsibility is built on various actors contributing to each other's actions and thus to the ultimate outcome.[27]

The Johannesburg Plan of Implementation was the result of the World Summit taking place in Johannesburg in 2002 (→ Intro mn. 267). In Chapter X, the institutional framework for sustainable development was elaborated on explaining the development of national and international institutions needed for implementation, the role of the UN and its institutions, the enhancement of partnerships and the promotion of participation of major groups.[28] Chapter IX described the means of implementation including the areas of finance and trade.[29] Furthermore, the significance of capacity-building as well as the importance of science-based decision making to achieve sustainable development was recognised.[30]   **8**

'The future we want' was the result of the United Nations Conference on Sustainable Development taking place in Rio de Janeiro (→ Intro mn. 276). The relevant contents of SDG 17 such as finance were already considered in this document (paras. 253 to 268) demanding the Member States to 'recognize the need for significant mobilization of resources from a variety of sources and the effective use of financing in order to give strong support to developing countries in their efforts to promote sustainable development'.[31] Technology can be found in paragraph 269 to 276 which is described in more detail in paragraph 272, where it is stated that the member states 'recognize the importance of strengthened national, scientific and technological capacities for sustainable development' to 'help countries, especially developing countries, to develop their own innovative solutions, scientific research and new, environmentally sound technologies,   **9**

---

[23] DESA, *Partnerships for sustainable Development Goals: A legacy review towards realizing the 2030 Agenda* (2015), 4.

[24] A/RES/55/2, *United Nations Millennium Declaration*, 2.

[25] Nollkaemper and Jacobs, 'Shared responsibility in international law: a conceptual framework' (2013), *Michigan Journal of International Law Vol. 34 No 2*, 366.

[26] Nollkaemper and Plakokefalos, 'The Practice of Shared Responsibility in International Law: A Framework for Analysis', *The Practice of Shared Responsibility in International Law* (2017), 4; Maurrasse, 'From the MDGs to the SDGs: Cross-Sector Partnerships as Avenues to Development in the UN System' in Chon and Roffe and Abdel-Latif (eds), *The Cambridge Handbook of Public-Private Partnerships, Intellectual Property Governance, and Sustainable Development* (2018), 356-75.

[27] Nollkaemper and Plakokefalos, 'The Practice of Shared Responsibility in International Law: A Framework for Analysis', *The Practice of Shared Responsibility in International Law* (2017), 4.

[28] Hens and Nath, 'The Johannesburg Conference', *Environment, Development and Sustainability* (2003), 7-39.

[29] A/CONF.199/20, *Plan of Implementation of the World Summit on Sustainable Development*, 41 ff.

[30] https://sdgs.un.org/topics/capacity-development; https://sustainabledevelopment.un.org/topics/science.

[31] A/RES/66/288, *The future we want*, 48.

with the support of the international community'.[32] Additionally, it emphasises 'the need for enhanced capacity-building for sustainable development and for the strengthening of technical and scientific cooperation'.[33] Paragraphs 281 to 282 address how trade contributes to economic growth, specifically pointing to the importance of a multilateral trading system.[34]

10   The Addis Ababa Action Agenda (AAAA) was the result of the Third International Conference on Financing for Development (→ Intro mn. 288 ff.). The AAAA contains 'a new global framework for financing sustainable development' and 'a comprehensive set of policy actions' to achieve the SDGs.[35] The AAAA is integrated in the Global Agenda 2030 and builds a foundation for its implementation.[36] The Global Agenda 2030 speci- fies the relationship between the actions and policies agreed in Addis Ababa and the agenda itself.[37] The Addis Ababa Action Agenda addresses the topics of domestic public resources, domestic and international private business and finance, international devel- opment cooperation, international trade, debt sustainability, systemic issues, science, technology, innovation, capacity building, data and monitoring.[38] Moreover, it includes a 'policy framework to realign financial flows with public goals'.[39]

B. Scope and Dimensions of SDG 17

11   SDG 17 as part of the Agenda 2030 acknowledges 'multi-stakeholder partnerships as important vehicles for mobilizing and sharing knowledge, expertise, technologies and financial resources to support the achievement of the sustainable development goals in all countries, particularly developing countries' and 'seek to encourage and promote effective public, public-private and civil society partnerships, building on the experience and resourcing strategies of partnerships'.[40] The definition of partnership has changed over time.[41] Partnerships in the framework of the MDGs were defined 'by the north giving the south aid, debt relief and trade access'[42] and categorised as *the* task of the private sector to supply the developing countries with medicines, information, and communications technology.[43] In the framework of the SDGs, partnerships should be built 'on mutual terms and on a more equal footing'.[44]

I. SDG 17 in Context of the Global Agenda 2030

12   SDG 17 has a special role within the framework of the Global Agenda 2030, since it connects to each SDG. SDG 17 can be seen as an essential instrument for the implemen- tation of the SDGs, requiring cooperation within and outside the UN to support the

---

[32] A/RES/66/288, *The future we want*, 51.

[33] https://sdgs.un.org/topics/capacity-development.

[34] https://sustainabledevelopment.un.org/topics/trade.

[35] DESA, *A DESA Briefing Note on the Addis Ababa Action Agenda* (2015), 1.

[36] DESA, *A DESA Briefing Note on the Addis Ababa Action Agenda* (2015), 1.

[37] https://sustainabledevelopment.un.org/topics/finance.

[38] DESA, *A DESA Briefing Note on the Addis Ababa Action Agenda* (2015), 4 ff.

[39] DESA, *A DESA Briefing Note on the Addis Ababa Action Agenda* (2015), 1.

[40] https://sustainabledevelopment.un.org/sdinaction.

[41] https://www.oecd.org/dev/development-posts-sdg-global-partnership.htm; see also e.g. the UN Global Compact Strategy 2021-2023 (2021).

[42] https://www.oecd.org/dev/development-posts-sdg-global-partnership.htm.

[43] https://www.oecd.org/dev/development-posts-sdg-global-partnership.htm.

[44] https://www.oecd.org/dev/development-posts-sdg-global-partnership.htm.

fulfilment of all SDGs of the Global Agenda 2030 and to enable global cooperation and partnerships. In line with SDG 17, these need to be implemented in the areas of finance, trade, policy and international institutional coherence in order to implement the SDGs and monitor progress.[45]

II. Means of Implementation

The Means of Implementation (MoI) determine 'the interdependent mix of financial   13
resources, technology development and transfer, capacity-building, inclusive and equitable globalisation and trade, regional integration, as well as the creation of a national
enabling environment required to implement the new sustainable development agenda,
particularly in developing countries.'[46] They can be divided into financial and non-financial means.

III. Financial MoIs

The financial MoIs are about development financing. Especially developing countries   14
must raise more revenues to be able to reach the SDGs.[47]

Official development assistance (ODA), as a financial support for developing coun-   15
tries by a third party, plays an important role to finance development. The implementation of ODAs for developed countries can be found in SDG 17.2. ODA includes
'ODA flows in form of grants, loans and other flows'.[48] ODA flows are defined as 'flows
to countries and territories on the DAC List of ODA Recipients and to multilateral
development institutions which are: (i) provided by official agencies, including state and
local governments, or by their executive agencies; and (ii) each transaction of which:
(a) is administered with the promotion of the economic development and welfare of
developing countries as its main objective; and (b) is concessional in character' and
'conveys a grant element' of 10 to 45 per cent depending on the kind of loan.[49] ODA
flows can come from high-income countries, multilateral development agencies or the
World Bank.[50] In addition, SDG 17.3 expands financial resources beyond the ODA.
Further financial resources can be provided by South-South cooperation, foreign direct
investment (FDI) and philanthropic and private charities.[51] These types of financial
aid need 'to ensure coordination, policy coherence, transparency, and accountability'[52]
which is a complex task and is not sufficiently achievable everywhere.

---

[45] ILA, Kyoto Conference (2020), Resolution No. 4 /2020, *The Role of International Law in Sustainable Natural Resources Management for Development*, para. 3.2.3: National Action Plans as well as through international cooperation and partnerships, including long-term integrated strategies focusing on improved productivity of land, and the rehabilitation, conservation and sustainable management of land and water resources, leading to improved living conditions.

[46] TST, *Issues Brief: Means of Implementation; Global Partnership for achieving sustainable development* (2014), 1.

[47] https://stats.unctad.org/Dgff2016/partnership/goal17/target_17_1.html.

[48] http://www.oecd.org/development/financing-sustainable-development/development-finance-standa rds/officialdevelopmentassistancedefinitionandcoverage.htm.

[49] http://www.oecd.org/development/financing-sustainable-development/development-finance-standa rds/officialdevelopmentassistancedefinitionandcoverage.htm.

[50] https://www.oecd-ilibrary.org/development/official-development-assistance-oda/indicator-group/en glish_5136f9ba-en.

[51] https://stats.unctad.org/Dgff2016/partnership/goal17/target_17_3.html.

[52] https://stats.unctad.org/Dgff2016/partnership/goal17/target_17_3.html.

16   External borrowing can be regarded as a way of financing. SDG 17.4 deals with the topic of long-term sustainable debt. Debt sustainability exists when 'the government is able to meet all its current and future payment obligations without exceptional financial assistance or going into default'.[53] External borrowing is used by developing countries to meet 'the gap in domestic savings and desired investment'.[54] Without long-term debt sustainability there is a risk of rising debt payments for developing countries. Regularly, higher debt payments mean less public spending. To reach the SDGs the public sector needs to investment must increase, not decrease.[55] Therefore, debt relief is crucial because it means public funds can be used for the implementation of SDGs.

17   If a state can use its own resources, it can invest in sustainable development as well as reduce its dependence from international aid.[56] SDG 17.1 deals with the topic of domestic resource mobilisation of developing countries with international support. Domestic Resource Mobilisation is a 'process through which low-income and lower middle-income countries raise and spend their own funds to provide for their people'[57] which, amongst others, makes tax revenue an important factor as it provides governments with an independent source of revenue.[58] Nevertheless, it also brings internal challenges like weak tax administration, low taxpayer morale, corruption, poor governance (weak *rule of law* and political instability), poor tax compliance and difficulties in taxing multinational enterprises'.[59] An external challenge is trade liberalisation, which cuts tariffs on import and export and therefor lessens the tax revenue.[60] The link to trade, as mentioned in SDG 17.10 and SDG 17.11, is evident here. Furthermore, domestic resource mobilisation can be supported by police advice, financial support and technical assistance through multilateral and bilateral institutions.[61] A key role plays fiscal policy, which can – if done effectively – reduce the above mentioned challenges.

18   Investment promotions regimes as mentioned in SDG 17.5 can be defined as 'those instruments that directly aim at encouraging outward or inward foreign investment through particular measures of the home or host countries of investment'.[62] Implementation in this sense means 'that a country has actually started to promote individual investments in developing countries [...] on the basis of the relevant legislation.'[63] In this regard, **foreign direct investment** (FDI) as an international financial flow plays an important role for the sustainable development and the economic growth of LDCs.[64] Without enough funds in the public sector, important investments cannot be made. Therefore, the private sector plays an important role by contributing to those necessary investments. To attract private investors, investment promotion in developing countries is needed. Ways to attract private investors are liberalisation of national policies for inward FDIs, incentives for foreign investors, and entries into investment agreements

---

[53] https://www.imf.org/external/pubs/ft/fandd/2020/09/what-is-debt-sustainability-basics.htm.

[54] Amani, *Long-term debt sustainability in developing countries – The HIPC Initiative Revisited* (2004), 12.

[55] Jones, *Rising Debt Burdens, the Impact on Public Spending, and the Corona Crisis* (2020), 2.

[56] https://stats.unctad.org/Dgff2016/partnership/goal17/target_17_1.html.

[57] https://www.cgdev.org/topics/domestic-resource-mobilization.

[58] OECD, *Development Co-operation Report 2014*, 91.

[59] OECD, *Development Co-operation Report 2014*, 91, 93.

[60] OECD, *Development Co-operation Report 2014*, 94.

[61] https://www.cgdev.org/topics/domestic-resource-mobilization.

[62] https://unstats.un.org/sdgs/metadata/files/Metadata-17-05-01.pdf.

[63] https://unstats.un.org/sdgs/metadata/files/Metadata-17-05-01.pdf.

[64] UN-OHRLLS, *Strengthening Investment Promotions Regimes for Foreign Direct Investment in the Least Developed Countries* (2015), iv; Greeninvest, *Green Foreign Direct Investment in Developing Countries* (2017), 7.

and double taxations treaties.[65] However, incentives in form of tax incentives, have a negative impact on the tax revenue of the country.[66] In addition, regulatory frameworks for investments, including FDIs, are increasing in developing countries.[67]

A major problem in finance is illicit financial flows (IFF), which arise from 'methods, **19** practices and crimes aiming to transfer financial capital out of a country in contravention of national or international law'.[68] Practices in this sense include money laundering, bribery by international companies, tax evasion and trade mispricing.[69] IFFs hits developing countries especially as it strips resources from public finances, destabilises the financial system and the economy.[70] Moreover, it leads to a reduction of public and private domestic expenses and investments.[71]

IV. Non-financial MoIs

Experience has shown, that MoIs are the most effective when financial MoIs are **20** complemented by non-financial MoIs.[72] Non-financial MoIs include policies and institutional measures.[73] Within the framework of SDG 17 the relevant topics are technology, capacity-building, trade, and systemic issues.

SDGs 17.6 to 17.8 deal with the topic of technology. To achieve the SDGs, relevant **21** knowledge and technology must be shared. This can be realised by giving access or by transferring this information. Through an implementation process the existing technology divide can be bridged and digital policies can be reformed.[74] SDG17.6 deals with cooperation on and access to science, technology, innovation, and information.[75] An important tool to access information is the Internet.[76] It can also help to foster and enhance regional and international cooperation.[77] To expand the availability of internet finance as well as partnerships play an important role to make the necessary investments.

Capacity-building is recognised as one of the means of implementation to achieve **22** sustainable development.[78] It can be defined as 'process by which individuals, organizations, institutions and societies develop abilities to perform functions, solve problems and set and achieve objectives'[79] which is manifested in SDG 17.9.

International trade as means of implementation should realise 'sustained, inclusive **23** and sustainable economic growth'.[80] A key role plays the multilateral trading system,

---

[65] UN-OHRLLS, *Strengthening Investment Promotions Regimes for Foreign Direct Investment in the Least Developed Countries* (2015), 5.

[66] OECD, *Development Co-operation Report 2014*, 94.

[67] UN-OHRLLS, *Strengthening Investment Promotions Regimes for Foreign Direct Investment in the Least Developed Countries* (2015), 5.

[68] OECD, *Illicit Financial Flows from Developing Countries: Measuring OECD Responses* (2014), 16.

[69] OECD, *Illicit Financial Flows from Developing Countries: Measuring OECD Responses* (2014), 16.

[70] OECD, *Illicit Financial Flows from Developing Countries: Measuring OECD Responses* (2014), 15.

[71] OECD, *Illicit Financial Flows from Developing Countries: Measuring OECD Responses* (2014), 15.

[72] Bhattacharya and Ali, *The SDGs – What are the "means of implementation"?* (2014), 2.

[73] Bhattacharya and Ali, *The SDGs – What are the "means of implementation"?* (2014), 2.

[74] https://unstats.un.org/sdgs/metadata/files/Metadata-17-08-01.pdf; https://stats.unctad.org/Dgff2016/partnership/goal17/target_17_6.html.

[75] Bhattacharya and Ali, *The SDGs – What are the "means of implementation"?* (2014), 3.

[76] https://stats.unctad.org/Dgff2016/partnership/goal17/target_17_6.html.

[77] https://unstats.un.org/sdgs/metadata/files/Metadata-17-06-01.pdf.

[78] https://sdgs.un.org/topics/capacity-development.

[79] E/C.16/2006/4, *Definition of basic concepts and terminologies in governance and public administration*, 7.

[80] UNCTAD, *Trading into sustainable development: Trade, Market Access, and the Sustainable Development Goals* (2016), 19.

which improves living conditions all around the world.[81] In being essential to the 'economic, social and environmental development in both developed and developing countries' as well as for the achievement of the Sustainable Development Goals,[82] policymakers need to ensure that trade benefits are shared.[83] Major institutional stakeholders are the UNCTAD, WTO, and International Trade Center (ITC), which 'monitor trends, analyse policy, and build analytical capacity'.[84] The World Trade Organization (WTO) is explicitly mentioned in SDG 17.10 and SDG 17.12. According to SDG17.10, a 'promotion of the multilateral trading system under the WTO' is needed. This can be reached by multilateral negotiations and regional trade agreements.[85] The WTO plays a crucial role in achieving the SDGs since it develops and implements trade reforms.[86] Moreover, policy coherence is needed in trade policy.[87] Another important aspect is market access as mentioned in SDG 17.12. Conditions for market access 'in international trade have been determined largely by the height of tariffs'[88] which begs the obvious connection to the General Agreement on Tariffs and Trade 1994 (GATT).

24   The UN defines partnerships as 'voluntary and collaborative relationships between various parties, both State and non-State, in which all participants agree to work together to achieve a common purpose or undertake a specific task and to share risks and responsibilities, resources and benefits'.[89] The strength of a global partnership for sustainable development depends on its quality.[90]

25   Multi-Stakeholder Partnerships, as mentioned in SDG17.6, can be defined as 'voluntary associations between different stakeholders such as civil society organizations, the private sector, philanthropic organizations, and international organizations' that 'provide collective goods', 'solve contemporary global challenges' and share a common vision.[91] They involve in the process of policy decision making and measures on matters of global development.[92] By sharing experience, information, technologies, and financial resources of all partners of a multi-stakeholder partnership mutual solutions can be reached.[93] Therefore, multi-stakeholder partnerships make important contributions to the implementation process and the achievement of the development goals[94] such as for renewable energy.[95]

---

[81] TD/B/C.I/45, *Trade, multilateral cooperation and sustainable development*, 1.

[82] TD/B/C.I/45, *Trade, multilateral cooperation and sustainable development*, 1.

[83] TD/B/C.I/45, *Trade, multilateral cooperation and sustainable development*, 1.

[84] TD/B/C.I/45, *Trade, multilateral cooperation and sustainable development* (2018), 1.

[85] https://unstats.un.org/sdgs/metadata/files/Metadata-17-10-01.pdf.

[86] WTO, *Mainstreaming trade to attain the Sustainable Development Goals* (2018), 4.

[87] UNCTAD, *Trading into sustainable development: Trade, Market Access, and the Sustainable Development Goals* (2016), IX.

[88] UNCTAD, *Trading into sustainable development: Trade, Market Access, and the Sustainable Development Goals* (2016), 19.

[89] https://sustainabledevelopment.un.org/partnerships/about.

[90] https://unstats.un.org/sdgs/metadata/files/Metadata-17-16-01.pdf.

[91] https://www.un.org/en/development/desa/policy/untaskteam_undf/faqs.pdf; Oguntuase, *Role of Transnational Multi-stakeholder Partnerships in Achieving Sustainable Development Goals* (2020).

[92] Oguntuase, *Role of Transnational Multi-stakeholder Partnerships in Achieving Sustainable Development Goals* (2020).

[93] Oguntuase, *Role of Transnational Multi-stakeholder Partnerships in Achieving Sustainable Development Goals* (2020).

[94] https://www.un.org/en/development/desa/policy/untaskteam_undf/faqs.pdf.

[95] Sanderink and Nasiritousi, 'How institutional interactions can strengthen effectiveness: The case of multi-stakeholder partnerships for renewable energy' (2020) 141 *Energy Policy*, 111447; Haywood et al., 'The Sustainable Development Goals in South Africa: Investigating the need for multi-stakeholder partnerships' (2019) 36(5) *Development Southern Africa*, 555-69; Sloan and Oliver, 'Building trust in multi-stakeholder partnerships: Critical emotional incidents and practices of engagement' (2013) 34.12 *Organization Studies*, 1835-68; Gray and Purdy, *Collaborating for our future: Multistakeholder partnerships*

Public Private Partnerships (PPP), as mentioned in SDG 17.17, can be defined as **26**
'a cooperative arrangement between the public and private sectors that involves the
sharing of resources, risks, responsibilities, and rewards with others for the achievement
of joint objectives'.[96] PPP comprise informal or contractual arrangements or 'mixed
public private company foundations'.[97] The relevance of public private partnerships
results from the 'the lack of public funds and inefficiency of public services'.[98] Therefore,
PPP are needed for the implementing process to introduce finances and support the
realisation of necessary investments to achieve the SDGs.[99]

Policy coherence in the sense of SDG 17.14 can be defined as coherence between **27**
domestic and international policies 'in general that cover the dimensions of sustainable
development'.[100] Policy coherence should be ensured by all level of government and offer
coherence within different sectors.[101] As a result, policies should mutually reinforce each
other and be implemented in a sustainable manner.[102] Moreover, it is essential within the
SDGs that domestic policies benefit developing countries.[103] Additionally, the interests
of the stakeholders such as civil society, the private sector, and foundations need to be
considered too.[104] Within the process of policy coherence, monitoring and finance play a
crucial role as well.[105]

SDG 17.18 and SDG 17.19 address data provision, monitoring and accountability, **28**
with the associated targets made measurable with the indicators created by the by
the Inter-agency and Expert Group on SGS Indicators (IAEG-SDGs).[106] This group
consists of UN Member States and is observed by international agencies.[107] The SDGs
were assigned to different international agencies, so-called custodian agencies, bodies
of the UN, that compile, verify and submit country data for SDG indicators to the UN
Statistics Division.[108] Beyond, custodian agencies develop international standards and
recommend methodologies for monitoring, to measure the progress on the SDGs.[109]
The monitoring process strongly depends on the participation of countries.[110] They
must provide national data collected by their national statistical system.[111] Here, the

---

for solving complex problems (2018); Dentoni and Bitzer and Schouten, 'Harnessing wicked problems in
multi-stakeholder partnerships' (2018) 150.2 *Journal of Business Ethics*, 333-56.

[96] Spraul and Thaler, 'Partnering for good? An analysis of how to achieve sustainability-related outcomes in public–private partnerships' (2020) 13 *Bus Res*, 485 (488).

[97] Spraul and Thaler, 'Partnering for good? An analysis of how to achieve sustainability-related outcomes in public–private partnerships' (2020) 13 *Bus Res*, 485 (488).

[98] Spraul and Thaler, 'Partnering for good? An analysis of how to achieve sustainability-related outcomes in public–private partnerships' (2020) 13 *Bus Res*, 485 (488).

[99] Further reading Leigland, 'Public-private partnerships in developing countries: The emerging evidence-based critique' (2018) 33.1 *The World Bank Research Observer*, 103-34; Esposito and Spiridione,
'Sustainable development, governance and performance measurement in public private partnerships
(PPPs): A methodological proposal' 12.14 *Sustainability*, 5696; Stephen Osborne, *Public-private partnerships: Theory and practice in international perspective* (2000).

[100] https://unstats.un.org/sdgs/metadata/files/Metadata-17-14-01.pdf; OECD, Recommendation of the
Council on Policy Coherence for Sustainable Development (2019), 6.

[101] https://unstats.un.org/sdgs/metadata/files/Metadata-17-14-01.pdf.

[102] https://unstats.un.org/sdgs/metadata/files/Metadata-17-14-01.pdf.

[103] https://stats.unctad.org/Dgff2016/partnership/goal17/target_17_14.html.

[104] OECD, *Recommendation of the Council on Policy Coherence for Sustainable Development* (2019), 5.

[105] https://unstats.un.org/sdgs/metadata/files/Metadata-17-14-01.pdf.

[106] https://blogs.worldbank.org/opendata/world-bank-s-role-sdg-monitoring.

[107] https://blogs.worldbank.org/opendata/world-bank-s-role-sdg-monitoring.

[108] https://www.sdg6monitoring.org/activities/roles-and-responsibilities/; https://blogs.worldbank.org/
opendata/world-bank-s-role-sdg-monitoring.

[109] https://www.sdg6monitoring.org/activities/roles-and-responsibilities/.

[110] https://www.sdg6monitoring.org/activities/roles-and-responsibilities/.

[111] https://www.sdg6monitoring.org/activities/roles-and-responsibilities/.

countries decide whether and to what extent they share their national data with custodi-an agencies.[112] In addition to the report on data for the relevant indicators, countries are free to publish additional information by voluntary national reports at the HLPF.[113] SDG 17.18. aims to build capacity to increase data availability. Its implementation process is mainly influenced by national statistical legislation. National statistic legislation can be defined as 'rules, regulation, measures with regard to the organization, management, monitoring and inspection of the statistical activities in a systematic way, strength, effec-tiveness and efficiency to assure the full coverage, accuracy and consistency with facts in order to provide reference for policy direction, socio economic planning, and contribute to the country's development to achieve wealth, culture, well-being and equity'.[114] As a framework for orientation, the UN offers Fundamental Principles of Office Statistics which highly influence the development agenda.[115] These Principles offer statistical information which can be used for fact-based decision making, increase transparency and allow to measure the process on reaching the SDGs.[116]

29   Due to their manifold function in the implementation process of the SDGs, UN bodies and other global actors are of crucial importance. However, their involvement also brings risks. The WHO and the WTO, for instance, strongly depend on the political will of governments. Since the WTO operates on the principle of consensus, it relies on the mutual agreement of all member states. For their funding, the WTO and WHO rely on the financial flows of their member states.[117] As a result, the function of the WTO and WHO can easily be limited if member states are not willing to cooperate, making it difficult to meet their obligations in the implementation process.

C. Interdependences of SDG 17

30   SDG 17 is by its very nature and as a fundamental principle of sustainable devel-opment linked to all other SDGs and thus forms the basis for the implementation of all SDGs. Multi-stakeholder partnerships are stated as the favoured mechanism to implement all other SDGs.[118] Moreover, financing can be seen as an essential part for the means of implementation under each individual SDG.[119] Private investments as mentioned in SDG 17 play a crucial role in the development of infrastructure, health, education, and climate change mitigation activities.[120] The actual SARS-CoV-2 pandem-ic has a strong negative impact on finance for sustainable development.[121] Wealthier countries are pushed into fiscal, monetary and financial stimulus packages, which increases public debt and leaves less room for financing the SDGs.[122] Consequently,

---

[112] https://www.sdg6monitoring.org/activities/roles-and-responsibilities/.

[113] https://www.sdg6monitoring.org/activities/roles-and-responsibilities/.

[114] https://unstats.un.org/sdgs/metadata/files/Metadata-17-18-02.pdf.

[115] A/RES/68/261, Fundamental Principles of Official Statistics (2014), 1.

[116] A/RES/68/261, Fundamental Principles of Official Statistics (2014), 1.

[117] https://www.who.int/about/funding; https://www.wto.org/english/thewto_e/secre_e/budget_e.htm.

[118] Oguntuase, *Role of Transnational Multi-stakeholder Partnerships in Achieving Sustainable Develop-ment Goals* (2020).

[119] https://sustainabledevelopment.un.org/topics/finance.

[120] https://stats.unctad.org/Dgff2016/partnership/goal17/target_17_5.html.

[121] Martens and Ellmers and Pokorny on behalf of Global Policy Watch, *COVID-19 and the SDGs, The impact of the coronavirus pandemic on the global sustainability agenda* (2020), 9.

[122] Martens and Ellmers and Pokorny on behalf of Global Policy Watch, *COVID-19 and the SDGs, The impact of the coronavirus pandemic on the global sustainability agenda* (2020), 9; https://www.unescap.org/blog/financing-sdgs-covid-19.

ODAs from wealthier countries will be lower and domestic resources are drained.[123] The Global South in particular is affected by the impact of the SARS-CoV-2 pandemic, as it relies on external funding and increasing revenue streams from several countries to a higher extent.[124] External private finances decline, as there is a fall in FDI and remittances.[125] The international community, the International Monetary Fund (IMF), regional development banks and UN agencies provided aid programmes, but mostly without support or alignment to the SDGs.[126] Therefore, wealthier countries are urged to offer additional ODA for the countries of the Global South that are in need.[127] The UN in its 2021 Report on Financing for Sustainable Development lists immediate actions to secure financing which contains the suspension of debt payments for poor countries, next to a coordinated stimulus package that includes the reversal of ODAs and the increase of concessional finance to avoid a debt crisis.[128]

The following UN agencies are involved in SDG 17, being custodians of one or **31** several indicators:

- Department of Economic and Social Affairs-Statistics Division (DESA-UNSD)
- International Monetary Fund (IMF)
- International Trade Center (ITC)
- International Telecommunication Union (ITU)
- Organisation for Economic Co-operation and Development (OECD)
- United Nations Development Programme (UNDP)
- United Nations Environmental Programme (UNEP)
- United Nations Environmental Programme-Climate Technology Centre and Network (UNEP-CTCN)
- UNESCO Institute for Statistics (UNESCO-UIS)
- United Nations Conference on Trade and Development (UNCTAD)
- World Bank (WB)
- World Trade Organization (WTO)

Reference is also made to a global technology support mechanism advocated by the **32** G77 countries,[129] but also to public-private partnerships, as well as blended finance at all conceivable levels.[130] Collaboration happens especially between philanthropic actors, governments and other development actors. These multi-stakeholder partnerships, between foundations, NGOs, private donors and private individuals open the door to greater international private financial participation.

---

[123] http://www.oecd.org/newsroom/covid-19-crisis-threatens-sustainable-development-goals-financing .htm; https://www.unescap.org/blog/financing-sdgs-covid-19.

[124] Jens Martens, Bodo Ellmers and Vera Pokorny on behalf of Global Policy Watch, *COVID-19 and the SDGs, The impact of the coronavirus pandemic on the global sustainability agenda* (2020), 10.

[125] http://www.oecd.org/newsroom/covid-19-crisis-threatens-sustainable-development-goals-financing .htm.

[126] Martens and Ellmers and Pokorny on behalf of Global Policy Watch, *COVID-19 and the SDGs, The impact of the coronavirus pandemic on the global sustainability agenda* (2020), 10.

[127] Jens Martens, Bodo Ellmers and Vera Pokorny on behalf of Global Policy Watch, *COVID-19 and the SDGs, The impact of the coronavirus pandemic on the global sustainability agenda* (2020), 10.

[128] UN, Inter-Agency Task Force on Financing for Development, *Financing for Sustainable Development Report 2021* (2021), 133 ff.; https://www.unescap.org/blog/financing-sdgs-covid-19.

[129] A/RES/70/1, SDG 17.6; Thereby the People's Republic of China and the G77 countries mainly stirred the discussion on including a stand-alone goal to resemble partnerships together with means of implementation; Dodds and Donoghue and Leiva Roesch, *Negotiating the Sustainable Development Goals, A transformational agenda for an insecure world* (2017), 41.

[130] Such as North-North-Partnerships, North-South-Partnerships, South-South-Partnerships and, see A/RES/69/313, para. 48.

33   The Development Cooperation Forum of the Economic and Social Council is considered one of the lead agencies. Other relevant fora, such as the Global Partnership for Effective Development Cooperation,[131] the UN Global Compact,[132] and the Global Compact for Migration (GCM)[133] take a more subject-specific approach:

–   Global Environment Facility (GEF) in mainstreaming environmental concerns into development efforts and providing grant and concessional resources to support environmental projects in developing countries.
–   World Health Organization Framework Convention on Tobacco Control
–   Global Alliance for Vaccines and Immunization (Gavi)
–   Global Fund to Fight AIDS, Tuberculosis and Malaria
–   United Nations Framework Convention on Climate Change, and
–   Conference of the Parties (as primary international, intergovernmental forum for negotiating the global response to climate change)
–   Global Financing Facility in support of Every Woman, Every Child
–   Global Partnership for Education

D. Jurisprudential Significance of SDG 17

34   Partnerships, as envisioned by SDG 17, encompass an unlimited number of relationships needed to meet the objectives of the Global Agenda 2030 in all its concerns and in all countries and societies worldwide. Partnerships and collaborations serve as a means for the purpose of building capacity and catalysing, supporting and accelerating the sustainable transformation. Therefore, SDG 17 is in itself a means of implementation and together with the means of implementation anchored in each SDG, the objectives of SDG 17 involve all countries and all stakeholders.[134] Partnership and cooperation are thus to be interpreted in a modern and broad way, encompassing all forms of mutual support[135] 'in the spirit of global partnership and solidarity'[136] to be led by governments.[137]

35   Various focal points were set during the abundantly reluctant negotiation processes towards this SDG. Rapprochement explicitly includes every actor and every legal family, but not only states and their representatives and institutions. The involvement of International Organisations, including as lead coordination units, is explicitly desired in order to achieve coherence.[138]

36   What is astonishing here is the actually limited mandate of the UN, which does not (recognisably) include such a far-reaching stipulation and promotion or action of the UN and its agencies.[139] Beyond state levels, however, also public and private actors are

---

[131] A/RES/69/313, para. 58.

[132] https://www.unglobalcompact.org/.

[133] https://www.iom.int/global-compact-migration; Alan Desmond, 'A New Dawn for the Human Rights of International Migrants? Protection of Migrants' Rights in Light of the UN's SDGs and Global Compact for Migration' (2020) 16.3 *International Journal of Law in Context*, 222-38.

[134] A/RES/70/1, preamble and para. 40.

[135] See A/RES/69/313, para. 76: 'partnerships are effective instruments for mobilizing human and financial resources, expertise, technology and knowledge'.

[136] A/RES/70/1, preamble and paras. 39 f.; A/RES/69/313, paras. 1, 9.

[137] A/RES/69/313, para. 10.

[138] UNGA Open Working Group on Sustainable Development Goals, *Compendium of TST Issues Briefs*, 57.

[139] See Arts. 10-13 UN Charter which mandates the UN with discussions and recommendations on matters in the scope of the Charter.

addressed and, among others, directly and indirectly financed. The UN and its agencies thus provide a formative structure in which new connections emerge which result in standards, political action plans and legislative initiatives, and ultimately in laws. However, the common approach and thrust generated in this way is not aligned to the approach explicitly formulated beforehand in the AAAA which focuses on '[c]ohesive nationally owned sustainable development strategies' and respect for countries' policy space.[140]

The importance of the process and the measurement of implementation and practical   **37** cooperation is particularly incumbent on the High-Level Political Forum (HLPF) and ECOSOC or the inter-agency task team on science, technology and innovation for the Sustainable Development Goals (IATT on STI) which have 'central oversight responsibility and support for their concerns, such as funding coordination, provision of data, and the implementation of the global partnership'.[141]

In addition to the (quite technical) options and means for establishing and / or main-   **38** taining partnerships as explicitly listed in SDG 17, various legal principles play a fundamental role in the relationships between the partners.[142] These principles stem from the very notion and concept of sustainable development law and are closely linked to the right to development. They foremost manifest the duty to co-operate, common but differentiated responsibilities and should realise equity in law. Although these principles primarily bind states, they are not limited to these traditional actors under international law, but also include other relevant actors in accordance with the approach and principle of sustainable development (→ Intro mn. 194 ff., 247) As stated in the ILA New Delhi Declaration, these include at least

> [i]nternational organizations, corporations (including in particular transnational corporations), non-governmental organizations and civil society should co-operate in and contribute to this global partnership. Industrial concerns have also responsibilities pursuant to the polluter pays principle.[143]

Referring to the genesis and history of SDG 17, forming global partnerships is   **39** indispensable to leave no one behind, which empathically gives expression to the overarching goals of 'moral impact and resonance' that emphasises the underlying thought of equity in the Global Agenda 2030.[144] With the concept and principle of sustainable development as understood and coined by the UN and the Global Agenda 2030, a generational contract has emerged which, tentative and non-binding as it may be in the initial resolution, calls upon the trust of societies – for a certain period of time still represented in states – in each other.

---

[140] A/RES/69/313, para. 9.

[141] A/RES/70/1, para. 70; Dodds and Donoghue and Leiva Roesch, *Negotiating the Sustainable Development Goals, A transformational agenda for an insecure world* (2017), 130; further information: https://sdgs.un.org/tfm/interagency-task-team.

[142] ILA, *New Delhi Declaration of Principles of International Law Relating to Sustainable Development* (2002); for deeper insights see Schrijver, 'Advancements in the principles of international law on sustainable development' in Cordonier Segger and H.E. Judge Weeramantry, *Sustainable Development Principles in the Decisions of International Courts and Tribunals, 1992-2012* (2017), 99-102.

[143] ILA, *New Delhi Declaration of Principles of International Law Relating to Sustainable Development* (2002).

[144] Dodds and Donoghue and Leiva Roesch, *Negotiating the Sustainable Development Goals, A transformational agenda for an insecure world* (2017), 130.

40   Trust is reflected in various principles and norms of international law,[145] but also beyond, such as in international environmental law,[146] which are either characterised by their universal recognition or whose disregard cannot be plausibly reasoned due to their handling or regulation of, amongst others, the global commons. In contrast to the principles of state sovereignty,[147] these dilute the rigid legal relationships and gather legal communities across state borders.

E. De Facto Influences on SDG 17

41   The UN, but also other actors, have already brought forth partnerships, initiatives and projects that are geared towards sustainable development and are relevant in a wide range of economic, social or political areas. Addressed stakeholders generally voluntarily commit to these partnerships. Alliances include, amongst innumerable others, the following:

- UN Global Compact (GC) which is the main UN initiative for engagement with the private sector and businesses with the aim to foster disaster risk reduction for sustainable development and resilience.[148]
- Global Reporting Initiative (GRI) which sets standards in the area of climate change, human rights and corruption and is strongly aligned to the SDGs. With the aim of creating business transparency, GRI unites, amongst others, UNEP, GC, OECD, ISO and the Coalition for Environmentally Responsible Economies (CERES).

42   Since the AAAA as implementation and financing instrument of the Global Agenda 2030, being almost identical to the Rio Declaration, calls for 'creating an enabling environment at all levels for sustainable development in the spirit of global partnership and solidarity',[149] it is difficult to discover legally binding efforts alongside the many non-binding (financing) initiatives and projects (→ Goal 17 mn. 5 ff.).

43   In the future, one instrument might be the Global Pact for the Environment (Pact)[150], which has been launched in 2017.[151] This civil society network, so far mainly consisting of legal scholars, lawyers and judges, intends to induce states 'to adopt a text codifying the general principles of the environment'.[152] The draft of the Pact has been launched in 2021 and is planned to become adopted as a multilateral treaty. The treaty grounds on the general principles of environmental rights as recognised by the 1972 Stockholm Declaration, the 1982 'World Charter for Nature, the 1992 Rio Declaration, the IUCN World Declaration on the Environmental Rule of Law, and other instruments to solidify

---

[145] E.g. different expressions of good faith (bona fide, pacta sunt servanda, venire contra factum proprium, estoppel doctrine); further reading Sombra, 'The Duty of Good Faith taken to a New Level: An Analysis of Disloyal Behavior' (2016) 9(1) *J Civ L Stud*, 28-55; the principle of prevention.

[146] Principle of precaution (contentious), principle of common but differentiated responsibilities, polluter-pays-principle.

[147] Such as the principle of non-intervention or the principle of permanent sovereignty over natural resources.

[148] https://www.preventionweb.net/files/43291_sendaiframeworkfordrren.pdf.

[149] A/RES/69/313, para. 1.

[150] Preliminary Draft of the Group of Experts, *Draft Global Pact For The Environment*; further information: A/RES/72/277, *Towards a Global Pact for the Environment*, 14 May 2018; Les Club de Juristes, *White Paper for the Environment, Toward a Global Pact* (2017).

[151] Similar aspirations existed, for instance, with the Earth Charter in 1994, which, however, did not come to fruition; Sand, 'Principle 27: Cooperation in a Spirit of Global Partnership' in Viñuales, *The Rio Declaration on Environment and Development, A Commentary* (2015), 623.

[152] https://globalpactenvironment.org/en/the-pact/origins/.

the environmental rule of law around the world and to achieve the 2030 Agenda for Sustainable Development',[153] but shall apply without distinction to environmental law in its entirety.

The draft of the Pact refers to different principles already known in international   **44** (environmental) law as follows: principle of prevention with related due diligence obligations as well-established rule of customary international law, principle of precaution (albeit its status is not without controversy[154]), the polluter pays principle mainly coined from the continental European legal family, environmental democracy which accommodates elements of public participation, namely access to information, participation in decision-making and access to environmental justice, the principle of cooperation which 'entails an obligation to cooperate in good faith and in a spirit of global partnership'[155], the right to a clean and healthy environment, sustainable development as 'a source of law and policy when addressing treaty implementation and the interpretation of norms', the principle of common but differentiated responsibilities and respective capabilities as an expression of equity in law, and the principle of non-regression and progression which is intended to prevent already set protection standards from reversing their development.[156]

While the principles may not be novel, it is the unifying element and framing of   **45** all regimes and at the same time being initiated through a bottom-up process in civil society, triggered by the UN's plethora of resolutions, conventions and treaties striving for sustainable development. Irrespective of the success (through adoption) of the Pact, this process is a prime example of the partnerships called for by the Global Agenda 2030. Moreover, when adopted, the Pact may serve as a landmark for the evolution of law in the field of sustainable development in the future.

F. Conclusion

Many aspects play a decisive and important role in the implementation process of   **46** the SDGs. Thereby, financial means of implementation and non-financial means of implementation are closely linked. It can be stated that with regard to finances, it is particularly a matter of supporting developing countries. Be it through direct financial flows such as ODAs or the development of domestic financial flows in the form of domestic resource mobilisationThe main objective is to financially equip the public sector to allow for the investments required be made within the framework of the SDGs.. In the context of non-financial MoIs, the relevance of partnerships for trade and the possibility of exchanging technology, knowledge and experience is evident. To this end, policy makers and their political willingness are crucial, as they can play a decisive role in shaping these processes and improving them through the exchange of information. Beyond, the importance of reliable data as well as a controlling monitoring process becomes apparent in order to identify deficits in implementation and to take all targeted measures needed. Moreover, SDG 17 has a special function in the SDG agenda as it forms the core means

---

[153] https://www.iucn.org/commissions/world-commission-environmental-law/resources/wcel-importa nt-documentation/global-pact-environment.

[154] See e.g. Cançado Trindade, 'Principle 15: Precaution' in Viñuales (ed), *The Rio Declaration on Environment and Development* (2015), 403-28.

[155] A/73/419*, *Gaps in international environmental law and environment-related instruments: towards a global pact for the environment, Report of the Secretary-General*, para. 16.

[156] Preliminary Draft of the Group of Experts, *Draft Global Pact For The Environment*; further information A/RES/72/277, *Towards a Global Pact for the Environment*, 14 May 2018; Les Club de Juristes, *White Paper for the Environment, Toward a Global Pact* (2017).

of implementation, building the basis for the implementation processes of all other SDGs. However, as with all other SDGs, the progress made under SDG 17 has been set back by the SARS-CoV-2 pandemic. ODA is being cut back, countries are going into debt, global nationalism instead of internationalism is on the rise, each of which means a struggle for existing partnerships. In conclusion, partnerships and cooperation based on mutual trust, whether financial or non-financial are the indispensable fundament and starting point for any of the implementation processes needed for the aspired global transition.

Epilogue

The struggle for sustainability with its inherent economic, social and environmental 1
dimensions is still ongoing, and sometimes it seems as if the fight against climate change
is the only effort that enjoys a greater (media) attention. However, it should not be
seriously contested that the impact of the SDGs will at the same time be linked to a
profound and comprehensive transformation of societies. This must also include the
legal systems in the different legal families. Rights to a greenhouse gas-free environment
must be enshrined and not merely postulated in a declaratory and thus pointless manner
and, above all, be individually enforceable.

Commitments to the SDGs as a declaratory act of goodwill will not be of help if they 2
are not backed by valid and resilient law, enforced by an independent and well-trained
judiciary, even against state authorities and transnational corporations (TNC), if necessary.

This applies to all of the SDGs. Climate change has been identified in the Global 3
Agenda 2030 as one of the greatest challenges facing humanity, and has been many times
before. However, the UN is, and with good reason, sceptical whether the goals of the
Paris Agreement and thus the limit of 1.5 °C can still be achieved and global greenhouse
gas emissions significantly reduced.

The factual key points of the SDGs which are developing dynamically into the future 4
are diametrically opposed to the goals. The facts include a rising world population and
with it increasing densities of human settlements, changes in agricultural land with
simultaneously higher food demand, a rising energy demand, as well as profound and
far-reaching consequences of the changes caused by climate change as analysed by the
IPCC for land, oceans and the cryosphere.

The Global Agenda 2030, with the SDGs at its heart, proves to be an interwoven 5
construct that theoretically does not allow for the separation of individual SDGs. Rather,
the SDGs are internally linked to each other and are also placed in a larger international
legal context through an external system.

The following findings emerge as a more general distillate from this work. In my 6
work, I have closely followed the text and a systematic approach. Word frequency,
among other aspects, yields indications of the gravity of individual terms and their
embedding environment. The Global Agenda 2030 frames the SDGs, which are not
unconnected but interrelated, in multiple ways. From this internal order, a distinction
must be made to the references of the Global Agenda 2030, which in a sense create
an external dimension. Here, a framework is stretched that radiates onto the SDGs
and charges them in a sometimes factual and sometimes legal sense and, in addition,
also effects the indicators for determining the SDGs. Beyond that, the Global Agenda
2030 contains numerous references that form another surrounding and enveloping layer,
which, in this way, are inextricably linked to the SDGs. It is in this context that the
SDGs themselves are placed, which in turn refer to numerous agreements, principles and
conferences pointing to a variety of arguments.

For the interpretation of the SDGs, a further distinction must be made whether, 7
for example, the targets of an SDG are analysed for their legal relevance in general
or whether a political statement or a legal result is analysed which is based on a
different foundation. Namely, the application of indicators, whose selection and content
are responsible for political assessments and subsequent legal decisions through laws,
resolutions or even regional or international agreements, provides the relevant guidance
here.

Epilogue

8   In numerous legal disputes, direct or indirect reference is made to the SDGs, their respective references or to the concept of sustainable development as one of the parental thoughts of the Global Agenda 2030. This commentary is intended to help provide legal definitions and contexts for direct applicability that can be used as arguments in a judicial or administrative balancing and dispute scenarios in both private and public law in the matrix of law.

9   The foregoing analysis can certainly only provide a glimpse into the life cycle of the SDGs and the Global Agenda 2030. The given in-depth examination in some places is limited in its content either by the concentration on certain legal families and circles, by the speed of change in the areas of law, or the *de facto* circumstances in the various realities of life.

10   Nonetheless, the research carried out shows the far-reaching and many-faceted interconnection of the SDGs and the Global Agenda 2030 within the matrix of the norms and principles in a multi-level system. At the same time, light could be shed on the process of norm creation. The links can be described as tentatively indeterminate, and the developments described suggest that in the future even more influence will be exerted on the formulation of normative concepts and legal foundations on pressing issues such as climate change, loss of biodiversity, disadvantaging girls and women, pollution of water, health impairments and not at least the establishment of the *rule of law*. The SDGs themselves have hardly arrived in jurisprudence yet. In legislative processes and in the drafting of contracts, however, the SDGs are already being referred to in many cases, and their objectives have already been taken up, at least partially, as a basis for regulation or direct law-making as such. Once a distillation of the political, legislative and legal processes has taken place, the jurisdiction will be (even more) enabled to scrutinize and exert their specific judicial opinion on these influences. Indications to this effect can be observed quite frequently in bodies, organisations and entities already today.[1]

11   The richness of the SDGs as well as their basic essence will be captured in the following pages in order to draw a conclusion from the study's extensive, if sometimes pinhead-sized findings. Furthermore, the formulated theses are intended to clarify and consolidate the basic theoretical structure of the new approach as set out in the introduction to this commentary.

12   To this end, the core of each SDG is reproduced to the extent possible, and its meaning is fed into the new approach. In this way, an indication of the legal relevance of the individual SDGs is obtained on an upstream (meta) level, which additionally promotes their acceptance as normatively effective starting positions. Similarly, a conclusive overall assessment is made possible, which should ultimately reveal the degree of legal transition of the SDGs.

I. SDG 1 and the Notion of No Poverty

13   As a gateway to the SDG agenda, the fight against poverty shapes the guiding principle of sustainable development and can thus already be structurally assigned to a fundamental idea that has been included in resolutions, declarations and other pronouncements since at least 1972.[2] Moreover, this is one of the fundamental ideas

---

[1] A/76/10, Report of the International Law Commission, Seventy-second session (26 April–4 June and 5 July–6 August 2021).
[2] The Club of Rome, *Limits to Growth* (1972).

of the United Nations[3] and can also be found in the foundations of ('Westphalian') international law.[4]

However, and this is the *de facto* side of the coin – in contrast to these values, which **14** are valuable in theory – it can be stated that despite the immense importance of this idea, it has not yet been sufficiently implemented or even grown into an independent, positively anchored and thus enforceable right. This is true at least from a universal perspective. Rather, it is clear, and explicitly so in the link to SDG 1 that a successful fight against poverty is 'a quite Herculean task that demands a great deal from institutions, governments, and societies with a specific engagement in multilateralism'.[5]

In applying the Global Agenda's new approach, it becomes apparent that the causes **15** and sheer existence of poverty obviously cannot be solved with court rulings or awards of alternative dispute resolution mechanisms.

Nonetheless, two levels recur consistently: the idea of proportionality and human **16** dignity, the consideration of which provides (peaceful) stability and, at the same time, for the alleviation of poverty.

The question of proportionality of living conditions, which can be (re)balanced by **17** access to at least equitable education, health, housing and justice as cornerstones of an overall framework for poverty reduction, remains open and unresolved as long as the willingness to adapt in member states is underdeveloped nationally and internationally. Therefore, it is necessary to establish fair public participation which qualifies essential to foster sustainable development and good governance free of corruption. As a result, effective protection of human rights is ensured, complemented by an effective accessible judicial or administrative process that ensures impartial and fair investigations, including in cross-border cases.[6]

Thus, at least a starting point can be set to guarantee the social security and disrupt **18** inter-generational poverty as stipulated in numerous human rights conventions, human rights, equality or non-discrimination instruments of many regional bodies and in the constitutions and legislation of many states.[7]

In the future, the focus should be placed on a new approach to obligations. Not **19** only states should be included in the various obligations of the relevant human and other protective rights, but also the currently prevailing design of production, supply and value chains should be redesigned in a compulsory manner, with a focus on both transnational and non-transnational companies.[8]

In order to give expression to a substantive legal equality of value, it is not only **20** necessary to rewrite existing norms or add further political meaningless statements. Additionally, legal instruments must be created that can be applied with global validity

---

[3] Art. 25 UDHR, Arts. 10, 11 ICESCR.

[4] UN Charter, preamble and, amongst others, Arts. 1, 55.

[5] See SDG 1, mn. 106.

[6] ILA, *New Delhi Declaration of Principles of International Law Relating to Sustainable Development*, 2002, mn. 5.1; see ILA New Delhi Declaration of Principles of International Law Relating to Sustainable Development (2002) 2 *International Environmental Agreements: Politics, Law and Economics*, 209-16; Schrijver, 'Advancements in the principle of international law on sustainable development' in Cordonier Segger and Weeramantry (eds), *Sustainable Development Principles in the decisions of International Courts and Tribunals* (2017), 107; see also: Schrijver, *The Evolution of Sustainable Development in International Law: Inception, Meaning and Status* (2008), 257.

[7] De Schutter, *Tackling extreme poverty in times of crisis: Key challenges facing the fight against poverty and thematic priorities for the Special Rapporteur on extreme poverty and human rights*, 1.5.2020.

[8] De Schutter, *Tackling extreme poverty in times of crisis: Key challenges facing the fight against poverty and thematic priorities for the Special Rapporteur on extreme poverty and human rights*, 1.5.2020; A/HRC/WG.2/19/CRP.1 *The international dimensions of the right to development: a fresh start towards improving accountability*, Olivier De Schutter, 22.01.2018.

and effectiveness by everyone and that confer *locus standi*. Sometimes those instruments occur within their specific context but could be grasped as starting point. Instruments such as public interest litigation (PIL)[9] or the tutela as a form of constitutional injunction expand *access to justice* and can (partly only after refinement) considerably relieve the judicial system of a state.[10] They also have the potential to create a form of global consolidation of certain rights through their use in strategic litigation and can thus be actively used to shape global law and interpretation. But other instruments are also conceivable with which the ideas of equity and capability creation can be given substance within the legal systems.

II. Tackling Hunger Everywhere with SDG 2

21   Even more clearly, the fight against hunger depicts a situation that can hardly be addressed from a legal point of view alone. On the one hand, having an abundance of food available that causes people illness with (chronic) disease and, on the other hand, experiencing global famines that claim illness and death as well, point to deep linkages such as social security lines, dysfunctional distribution mechanisms (aphorisms) and, from an economic point of view, inadequately functioning global trade and investment exchanges, food commodity markets and improper benefit sharing of the 'utilization of genetic [seed] resources'.[11] Yet, hunger in its various forms is still rising around the world. Moreover, in view of climate change, human overexploitation of nature combined with the dynamics of a growing population will lead to the assumption of difficult and lamentably devastating consequences for food production, it can no longer be said with certainty that this situation of abundance will remain so. A shift towards infertile soils and non-fruit-bearing aquatic environments is likely to come.

22   These developments need to be countered in at least two ways: On the one hand, principles such as the sustainable use of natural resources and the sustainable management of natural resources are required to become legally enforceable standards in the respective sectors, which means that enforceability must be secured with the right of any individual to take legal action in the event of a violation of the aforementioned principles. On the other hand, a transformation of existing food production systems must take place and a new understanding must be developed on how these can be made more resilient against shock wavers caused by pandemics and other disasters. This is only possible through an approach based on Science, Technology and Innovation (STI), which hold considerable importance in the fight against hunger.

23   However, not the private sector but politics should take the lead and focus on suitable actions across the food supply chains to tackle the costs of nutritious foods and guarantee shared and inclusive access for all. Such actions which normally would be enacted after parliamentary debates by laws and regulations should '[e]nhance efficiencies in

---

[9] Brems and Adekoya, 'Human Rights Enforcement by People Living in Poverty: Access to Justice in Nigeria' (2010) 54(2) *Journal of African Law*, 258 (274 f.).

[10] Further reading: Landau, Dixon and Sen, 'Constitutional Non-Transformation?: Socioeconomic Rights beyond the Poor' in Young (ed), *The Future of Economic and Social Rights* (2019); Merhof, 'Building a bridge between reality and the constitution: The establishment and development of the Colombian Constitutional Court' (2015) in 13(3) *I•CON*, 714-32.

[11] A/RES/70/1, *Transforming our world: the 2030 Agenda for Sustainable Development*, 25 September 2015, SDG 2.5, SDG 2.c.

food storage, processing, packaging, distribution and marketing, while also reducing food losses.'[12]

III. Good Health and Well-Being with SDG 3

Embedding SDG 3 in the wording of the right to health 'including the rights to life, **24** to the enjoyment of the highest attainable standard of physical and mental health, to an adequate standard of living, to adequate food, to housing, to safe drinking water and sanitation and to participation in cultural life, for present and future generations'[13] needs the wrapping in different layers of international law and interpretation.[14] For example, health in the understanding of the WHO and the right to health have a different backgrounds and substance and therefore must be defined to lead to a different scope of understanding and applicability.

However, in a legal field, it remains essential for gaining a people-centred under- **25** standing of development.[15] Beyond its close linkage to the UDHR, where the rights to health and an adequate standard of living are ingrained (Art. 25) and the comprehensive socio-economic background as defined in the ICESCR,[16] however, the right to health remains a nebulous concept.[17] At the least, it must be interpreted to include Global Justice, Universal Health Coverage (UHC), environment, gender and Earth Jurisprudence and cover new diseases and pandemics responses to be effective.

When looking at global health jurisprudence, one becomes aware that not only a **26** human-centric approach is reflected, but also a cross-border status of ecological health and well-being. The innate entanglement between the human rights anchoring of health protection and the protection of the environment is becoming increasingly apparent[18] and is also known in other levels of the multi-level system of law.[19] This contains sharing (of burdens, duties and benefits) and conserving of natural resources or at least doing no irrevocable harm to a humans' environment on the behalf of the well-being for humanity, also detached from a precise temporal frame, but rather with permanent

---

[12] FAO, IFAD, UNICEF, WFP and WHO, *The State of Food Security and Nutrition in the World 2020, Transforming food systems for affordable healthy diets* (2020), 138.

[13] OHCHR, *The right to health*, Factsheet No. 31; and more recently A/HRC/48/L.23/Rev.1, *The human right to a safe, clean, healthy and sustainable environment*, 5 October 2021, 2.

[14] Burci and Cassels, 'Health' in Katz Cogan and Hurd and Johnstone (eds), *The Oxford Handbook of International Organizations* (2016), 450 ff.

[15] See Chapter 1 of the Rio Declaration.

[16] General Comment No. 14 (2000) under para. 1 provides further guidance on how this right is to be understood in legal terms: '[h]ealth is a fundamental human right indispensable for the exercise of other human rights'.

[17] Tobin, *The Right to Health in International Law* (2012).

[18] See amongst others FCCC/CP/2015/10/Add.1, Decision 1/CP.21 (Annex), Paris Agreement under the United Nations Framework Convention on Climate Change, 12 December 2015 (in force 4 November 2016); IACtHR, Advisory Opinion OC 23-17, Environment and Human Rights (2017); A/HRC/37/59, UN Special Rapporteur on Human Rights and the Environment, *Framework Principles on Human Rights and the Environment* (2018); ILA, *Conference Report Sydney, Role Of International Law In Sustainable Natural Resource Management For Development* (2018), 44; ILA, *The Role Of International Law In Sustainable Natural Resources Management For Development*, Resolution No. 4 (2020); A/HRC/48/L.23/Rev.1, *The human right to a safe, clean, healthy and sustainable environment*, 5 October 2021, 2.

[19] See (at least to some degree) Agreement Establishing the World Trade Organisation, preamble; Art. XX(b) GATT; see also the provisions of several FTAs which prohibit 'race to the bottom' regulatory strategies with assets such as health, safety and environmental measures being protected; see ILA, *Conference Report Sydney, Role of International Law in Sustainable Natural Resource Management for Development* (2018), 30 ff.

validity,[20] in which the concepts of sustainable use of natural resources and sustainable management of natural resources in particular are becoming increasingly important.

27   Nevertheless, SDG 3 does not address a primarily individual right to health or the (not existing because not grantable) right to be healthy,[21] but much more a corresponding systemic counterpart of an existing, capable and throughout well-functioning health system, which is eligible to respond to the different objectives. The systemic approach does not mean that the right to health is neglected, but as a right, it must meet with international state obligations where those individual rights can be satisfied by various instruments of the health system provided, maintained and offered on an acknowledged quality level on the basis of equity by the state.

IV. Enabling the Transformation – Education for Sustainable Development with SDG 4

28   As an enabling factor and for raising awareness for all SDGs and the values set in the Global Agenda 2030, quality education is normatively linked to the dignity of every human being in order to support people, including the most vulnerable, in their right to education. Several aspects of the SDGs and constitutional provisions of individual states are interwoven and hardly separable.[22] In this context, an education as understood in SDG 4 and in particular human rights education (HRE) hold a basis for the creation of lifelong opportunities. HRE emphasises the ideals of peace, mutual respect and understanding between peoples,[23] also including sexual education. HRE thus builds a fundamental pillar and useful tool for addressing global challenges, most of which are interconnected, such as violent extremism and conflict[24] and significantly shapes the development of legal norms and systems. However, difficulties exist in terms of enforcement and more generally access to justice,[25] highlighting the arduous process of claiming the right to education before a court or arbitration mechanism. Nevertheless, legal measures play a crucial role in the legal enforcement of the right to education, including the right to be heard by judges, which is not the case everywhere.

29   Education is to be acknowledged as one of the essential SDGs to achieve human rights, dignity and sustainability and make all people capable of achieving prosperity and accomplishing the different columns on which the 5 Ps are built ($\rightarrow$ Intro mn. 122 ff.).

---

[20] See also ILA, *Conference Report Sydney, Role of International Law in Sustainable Natural Resource Management for Development* (2018), 31.

[21] Bantekas and Oette, *International Human Rights Law and Practise* (2016), 428; E/C.12/2000/4, *Substantive Issues Arising In The Implementation of the International Covenant on Economic, Social and Cultural Rights General Comment No. 14 (2000): The right to the highest attainable standard of health (article 12 of the International Covenant on Economic, Social and Cultural Rights)*, 11 August 2000, paras. 8 f.

[22] UNESCO, *Global Education Monitoring Summary Report* (2016), 8 sheds light that all of the 16 SDGs are interconnected with SDG 4.

[23] Already coined in 1965 with A/RES/20/2037, *Declaration on the Promotion Among Youth of the Ideals of Peace, Mutual Respect and Understanding Between Peoples*, 7 December 1965.

[24] A/HRC/35/6, *Panel discussion on the implementation of the United Nations Declaration on Human Rights Education and Training: good practices and challenges*, 27 March 2017, para. 48.

[25] Despite 55 per cent of member states of the UN have a justiciable right to education, where only 27 percent of UN member states dispose of directive principles or aspirational rights to education and 18 percent do not have a state constitutional right to education; UNESCO, *Right to Education handbook* (2019), 243; see in more detail on access to justice: Huck and Maaß, 'Gaining a foot in the door: Giving Access to Justice with SDG 16.3?' 2021-05 *C-EENRG Working Paper Series*.

V. An Imperative of Humankind – Gender Equality with SDG 5 as a conditio sine qua non for Sustainable Development

Empowerment presupposes that international legally binding agreements are trans-　**30**
posed into national binding and enforceable law, where they are accepted above all
by those societies whose cultural, traditional or religious beliefs have made it difficult
or denied women access to participate in society, to draw from an economic and
legal environment, and have directly or indirectly supported sexualised violence or
honour killings.[26] From my perspective gender equality is a *conditio sine qua non* for
the preparedness of a state or any other legal community to embark on the creation of
sustainability in a legal sense. I would go even further and argue that the lack of acceptance of gender equality prevents these countries from the adoption of any sustainability
which could be defined as a normative concept of sustainability. Addressing climate
change without girls and women or accepting the *rule of law* without establishing
gender equality leads to a blatantly cynical approach excluding sustainability rather than
promoting it.

The spectrum of rights denied to women and girls is alarmingly long and in stark　**31**
contrast to the long lists constituting women's rights. Contrary to CEDAW the reality is
a different one. Not only is the gender-based denial of equal opportunities for women
and girls in accessing the respective societies problematic and often unacceptable in
political and economic terms, but it also remains one of the shocking obstacles when the
lives and health of girls and women throughout the world are seriously threatened or
violated.[27]

What can be observed are the significant obstacles to the effective implementation of　**32**
all SDGs and the direct contradiction to SDG 16 in enforcing their human rights embeddedness and the underlying approach of the SDGs if inappropriate or inadequate laws
remain in force. Particularly in areas where access to adequate resources is denied, where
reporting rates for gender-based violence are very low, where institutional barriers exist,
and where patriarchal systems and gender stereotypes prevail in security, police and
judicial institutions,[28] these barriers and their atrocious effects are exacerbated when the
law remains neutral or even excludes the female share of our global population.

According to the UN, states as the main norm addressees should prioritise measures　**33**
that also bring about cultural change in other areas, e.g. to eliminate widespread phenomena such as sexual harassment in the workplace.[29] Establishing legal foundations
that enable all women to access justice in a functioning legal system should therefore
be understood as the main instrument for achieving lasting gender equality and demonstrates the close link between SDG 16 and SDG 5. It is the *rule of law* that remains a
litmus test for humanity and freedom in a society for all people, comprehensive rights
and access to independent courts.

---

[26] A/RES/70/1, *Transforming Our World: The 2030 Agenda For Sustainable Development*, 25 September
2015, preamble: '[T]hey seek to realize the human rights of all and to achieve gender equality and the
empowerment of all women and girls' and paras. 3, 20: '[R]ealizing gender equality and the empowerment
of women and girls will make a crucial contribution to progress across all the Goals and targets'.

[27] https://www.unwomen.org/en/what-we-do/ending-violence-against-women/facts-and-figures.

[28] A/75/274, *Intensification of efforts to eliminate all forms of violence against women and girls, Report of
the Secretary-General*, 30 July 2020, para. 2.

[29] https://www.ilo.org/dyn/normlex/en/f?p=NORMLEXPUB:12100:0::NO::P12100_ILO_CODE:C190;
A/75/274, *Intensification of efforts to eliminate all forms of violence against women and girls, Report of the
Secretary-General*, 30 July 2020, para. 55.

Epilogue

VI. Availability of Clean Water and Sanitation for all with SDG 6

34   The right to water can be traced to a long history that has significantly shaped societies, and in the form of the right to safe drinking water and sanitation,[30] which is reflected in a broader sense in the targets and indicators of SDG 6, can be added to the protective spheres of various human rights. Despite its long history, its inherent necessity and the brilliant arguments of many scholars who advocate for a stand-alone right to water from a legal perspective, a clear, precise set of norms or recognition as customary international law, including indigenous peoples and their ecosystems,[31] is still lacking.

35   The SDGs and the Global Agenda 2030 and their integrated approach[32] call for a fair distribution of water, the growing recognition of which will become a recognised right to water and sanitation in international law as it develops further.[33] This process is accelerating and is fuelled by dynamic occurrences such as population growth and asymmetric population distribution, water scarcity, droughts, agriculture[34] and multiple impacts on water and health caused by climate change.[35]

36   However, the right to water even in the sense of the SDGs should not be understood as lending a right to water supply services that are to be available freely, but rather must be affordable even for those with little or no income.[36]

37   From a legal perspective, the demand for good governance and access to justice must be transformed into the applicability and legal enforcement of the principles of human rights concerning the right to water and sanitation (→ Goal 16 mn. 9, 22 ff.). Adopting a human rights-based approach (HRBA) to development could improve to achieve climate justice concerning water,[37] even when the scientific interrelations of the causality of temperature change, water stress and migration are still not clearly understood.[38]

---

[30] A/RES/70/1, *Transforming our world: the 2030 Agenda for Sustainable Development*, 25 September 2015, para. 7

[31] Macpherson, 'Justifying Indigenous Water Rights: Jurisdiction and Distribution' in Macpherson, *Indigenous Water Rights in Law and Regulation: Lessons from Comparative Experience*, (2019), 17; Eckstein et al., 'Conferring Legal Personality on the World's Rivers: A Brief Intellectual Assessment' (2019) in *Water International* (Texas A&M University School of Law Legal Studies Research Paper No. 19-30); Schromen-Wawrin, 'Representing Ecosystems in Court: An Introduction for Practitioners' (2018) in 31(2) *Tulane Environmental Law Journal*, 279 (279 ff.)

[32] A/RES/70/1, *Transforming our world: the 2030 Agenda for Sustainable Development*, 25 September 2015, paras. 13, 17.

[33] Arden, 'Water for all? Developing a human right to water in national and international law' (2016) 65 *ICLQ*, 771 (789).

[34] See OWG – Session 'Water Supply and Sanitation' (May 23, 2013): 'To grasp the difficulties on managing the topic of water, one should bear in mind that the accessibility of water is linked to external effects. One of an array of occurrences is population: 'In 1950, just 60 years ago, there were only 2.5 billion people in the world, 10 years ago there were 6 billion people on the planet. By 2020 there are expected to be 7.5 billion of us. And, current growth rates, we are projected to reach over 9 billion beyond 2030.' The incremental growth of people creates an urgent demand for water for health and sanitation, agribusiness and many others.'

[35] Population growth, agricultural intensification, urbanisation, industrial production and pollution, are beginning to overwhelm traditional consume and agricultural patterns are to be questioned and in particular against the effects of climate change – and brings new responsibilities with it; Bos, *Manual of the Human Rights to Safe Drinking Water and Sanitation for Practitioners* (2016), 5.

[36] Bos, *Manual of the Human Rights to Safe Drinking Water and Sanitation for Practitioners* (2016), 5.

[37] UNESCO, UN-Water, *2020: United Nations World Water Development Report 2020: Water and Climate Change* (2020), 159.

[38] Wrathall et al., on behold of the Food and Agriculture Organization of the United Nations, *Water stress and human migration: a global, georeferenced review of empirical research* (2018), ix.

Participation is seen, among others, as a critical governance function where planning,   **38**
coordination, regulation, and licensing must be added.[39] In this light, the Paris Agreement and the Human Rights Council (HRC) rightly refer to equity and human rights[40]
which are profoundly linked with SDG 6,[41] despite the fact that water as such has not
yet been explicitly mentioned in international agreements such as the Paris Agreement,
although it is an essential component of almost all strategies to combat climate change.[42]

As a result, the pathway leading to equity also paves the way for climate justice[43]   **39**
as has already been demanded with Principle 10 of the Rio Declaration on Environment and Development, underlining citizen participation in environmental issues. This
principle sets out three fundamental rights: access to information, access to public
participation and access to justice, as key pillars of sound environmental governance.[44]
Putting the arguments together, it appears quite impossible to perceive the content of
SDG 6 outside the sphere of normativity and a broad access for those who suffer from
inadequate supply. Therefore, a legal deep rooted entitlement on access to water must be
developed to underline the deep link to essential prerequisite to (human) life.

VII. Affordable and Clean Energy with SDG 7

With SDG 7, a new level of the approach is set which, however, primarily focuses on   **40**
the sustainable transition of developing and least developed countries. Surprisingly, to
pursue this very focus excludes various judicial decisions and thus also an evolving basis
of legal interpretation in an already underdeveloped area of law.

Even if the necessary teleological interpretation inherent in the SDGs and the Global   **41**
Agenda 2030 as a holistic approach opens up the possibility of considering those areas
of energy policy and law that cannot be located in developing countries. However, these
areas, which are not the focus of SDG 7, can only serve as a moderate basis for argumentation if SDG 7 is attempted to be given legal significance. Why developed countries are
explicitly excluded from the objectives of SDG 7 and are only addressed in the context of
knowledge and technology transfer, facilitation and investment can hardly be explained
against the fact that most of the LDCs are not the main emitters and users of non-clean

---

[39] UNESCO, *UN-Water, 2020: United Nations World Water Development Report 2020: Water and Climate Change* (2020), 6.

[40] UNESCO, *UN-Water, 2020: United Nations World Water Development Report 2020: Water and Climate Change* (2020), 35.

[41] See A/HRC/RES/41/21 of 23 July 2019, stressing the access of persons with disabilities in particular to […] safe drinking water and sanitation, further 'noted the importance for some of the concept of "climate justice" when taking action to address climate change'.

[42] UNESCO, UN-Water, *2020: United Nations World Water Development Report 2020: Water and Climate Change* (2020), 2; A/RES/70/1, *Transforming our world: the 2030 Agenda for Sustainable Development*, 25 September 2015, preamble, subpara. 3, paras. 2, 5, 74 (b) and para. 31: 'We acknowledge that the United Nations Framework Convention on Climate Change (UNFCCC) is the primary international, intergovernmental forum for negotiating the global response to climate change'.

[43] Beck, 'Inside the System, Outside the Box: Palau's Pursuit of Climate Justice and Security at the United Nations) (2014) 3(1) *Transnational Environmental Law*, 17-29. (doi:10.1017/S2047102514000028): 'Palau announced, in 2011, that it would take the issue of climate change to the ICJ', 24; Caney, 'Cosmopolitan Justice, Responsibility, and Global Climate Change' (2005) 18(4) *Leiden Journal of International Law*, 747–75; see https://www.ohchr.org/EN/Issues/HRAndClimateChange/Pages/HRClimateChangeIndex.aspx; see also: Strauss, 'Climate Change Litigation: Opening the Door to the International Court of Justice' (2009) 3 *School of Law Faculty* Publications; Strauss, 'The Legal Option: Suing the United States in International Forums for Global Warming Emissions' (2003) 33 *ELR 10185*.

[44] UNESCO, UN-Water, *2020: United Nations World Water Development Report 2020: Water and Climate Change* (2020), 155.

and non-renewable energies.[45] A debate on this subject cannot be conducted within the scope of this commentary. However, a fundamental reconsideration or reassessment seems worthwhile, especially against the background of noticeable developments in the closely interwoven field of climate protection.

VIII. Decent Work and Economic Growth with SDG 8

42   SDG 8 reveals a clearly limited derivable form of normativity, which is limited to some enshrined concepts such as 'full and productive employment and decent work', which is inclusive, or 'equal pay for work of equal value' (SDG 8.5).

43   And yet, a distinction needs to be made here between the possibilities of intervening in private or public markets and enterprises in a labour law or broader economic sense. For example, it should not be overlooked that a government outside the public sector, SOEs, has only little competencies and capabilities to break with interventions into the demands and offers of a specific market, which is even more difficult, when this market is deemed to be a free one and following the rules of the WTO. A cornerstone for improving working conditions and opening up markets for women and men alike would be a comprehensive, thorough and swift law enforcement against all manifestations of modern slavery, human trafficking and child labour (SDG 8.7), as well as vigorous and consistent application of the rule of law by state agencies, ensured by a well-trained and well-paid judiciary, and the successful fight against corruption (SDG 16).

IX. Science, Technology and Innovation as Transformative Output of SDG 9

44   Building on the provision and use of affordable and clean energy (SDG 7) and the creation of decent work and economic growth (SDG 8), SDG 9 forms the basis for the design of future-oriented industries, innovations and infrastructures. This includes the so-called green and blue technologies to create a (disaster risk) resilient industrialisation, whether this includes transport on all modes, technologies for energy production or innovations in raw material extraction and use. Like with SDG 7 and SDG 8, this requires a stimulating market and public legal environment, which is characterised by a strict *rule of law* concept, enclosing transparent conduct against corruption.

45   The processing and value creation of raw materials as well as the development of structures and the associated interventions in environmental and human rights concerns, which also provide intellectual property and access requirements, must be subordinated to this clear legal conception. In this regard, viable instruments already exist, especially at the international level in private contract and investment law, such as contracts based on common templates and model contracts used in the construction in-dustry (e.g. published by FIDIC or recommended by the World Bank for infrastructure projects). An element of planning at the national and constitutional level is also reflected in national public law, which accompanies the formation phase of start-ups through small and medium-sized enterprises to larger industrial enterprises and clusters.

46   Nevertheless, SDG 9, which thematically situates in public and private law as well as supra-regional and international law, including transnational norms and (private law) regulations, is only a limited legally relevant frame of reference. Rather, it enriches other,

---

[45] Statista, *Largest producers of fossil fuel CO2 emissions worldwide in 2019, by share of emissions.*

legally more unambiguous SDGs with interpretive contexts and points to requirements to be considered in the respective environment.

Institutionally, the current situation of innovation is framed by WTO TRIPS, WIPO, UNCTAD, OECD, EUIPO and other specialised IO and organisations of the UN (IMO, ICAO, WMO). With their support, frontier technologies[46] are enabled to foster innovations in their respective fields and reshape industrialisation. For their part, these new instruments require forward-looking and inclusive regulation in order to avoid inequality and gender inequality and corruption-related loopholes in the regulatory landscape, e.g. in blockchain and legal tech. Therefore, a true opportunity exists to create legislation imbued with genuine sustainability from the very beginning through governments by laws, regulations or political based action.   **47**

X. Reducing Inequalities with SDG 10

SDG 10 should be considered as one of the most ambitious SDGs laying out a vast area for political decision making and at the same time just a small field for legal aspects and thoughts. SDG 10 refers to objectives that entail a wide and systematic range over most difficult issues such as social and economic inclusion, financial markets and institutions, development participation in institutions and benefits in the world trade system through preferential treatment of third countries, as well as ODA and FDI.[47] All of these are primarily political in nature and could only be achieved by a consensus within a country or with other countries. Some objectives, however, are independent of one political framework – may it be liberal or socialist – in that the globalised world economy sets the pace.   **48**

In principle, the objectives of SDG 10 are desirable to such an extent that there are hardly any objections to them, but they remain mostly vague as objectives and, in the absence of concrete measures, are hardly suitable for a translation into concrete policies or even a normative setting of laws. Improving regulation and monitoring of global financial markets and institutions is part of a financial system that has evolved historically and grown out of several crises, and improvements and adjustments are being intensively fought for at numerous levels. Here the scepticism prevails as to whether the targets generally formulated in SDG 10 can be more than a reminder to link concrete policy with statutory plans of the targets and indicators of SDG 10. Similar issues are evident when planning and managing migration policies which make it unlikely to lead to an improvement of the existing different legal systems in practice.   **49**

The general formulation of SDG 10 is unlikely to bring about any change, let alone improvement, in the general public. Too many different levels, institutions, political reservations and different systems are involved and exert their very own influence which naturally neglects 'one-size-fits-all approach', especially facing the complex finance systems.[48] Jurisprudence clearly confirms what can already be deduced from the content of SDG 10 on a theoretical level: SDG 10 is not intended to create equality, but to reduce inequality and melt away its greatest peaks.   **50**

---

[46] UNCTAD (2021), 9: AI, IoT, Big Data, Blockchain, 5G, 3D printing, robotics, drones, gene editing, nanotechnology and solar photovoltaic (Solar PV).

[47] https://stats.unctad.org/Dgff2016/prosperity/goal10/ index.html.

[48] See Jones and Knaack, 'Global Financial Regulation: Shortcomings and Reform Options' (2019) *Glob Policy*, 10.

Epilogue

XI. Partnerships for Sustainable Cities and Communities with SDG 11

51   SDG 11 is an example of a particularly illustrative goal of the importance of networks and partnerships. Connecting and coordinating the network of a city, region or human settlement with its numerous population strata, social and political needs.[49] It seems as if there was no other way than to keep this SDG so loose to be able to include all forms of cities and human settlements as they are highly diverse in geographical, socio-economic and political structures. However, the human rights background is not obviously recognisable in the wording or in the recitals and with the identifiable broad definitions, the transfer into legal realms must be deemed endangered. In their global character, cities, with their shaping of democratic structures and citizen-oriented world societies, play a crucial role in framing issues such as democracy, health, security, climate change, education, knowledge and culture, which makes SDG 11 a conveyor of all other SDGs.

52   In the course of ongoing globalisation, and driven, among other factors, by climate change and digitalisation, energy scarcity and instable water and food supply cities have been exposed to international law over the years. These norms, which directly impact on cities, have been used as grounds for their increasing participation in international discussions.[50] With the path taken by Habitat III, a bottom-up process and numerous transparent voting processes,[51] the Global Agenda 2030 and the SDGs qualify as central building block for further planning, focusing on participation, transparency and accountability. Cities fulfil a new role in applying technologies, setting innovations and tackling the impact of climate change. Obviously, the respect for human rights and access to justice are essential to neutralise the appalling inequalities in current living and health conditions and to end segregation. The legal instruments of cities, however, most often remain in domestic and municipal laws and regulations some of which are strictly integrated into existing constitutional structures. This no longer seems commensurate with the challenges they have to address. Rather, their competences need to be expanded for articulating answers in times of challenges such as climate change, migration and population growth.

XII. Responsible Consumption and Production with SDG 12

53   The considerations of SDG 7, SDG 8, SDG 9 and SDG 11 must be supplemented with the sustainable consumption and production of all stakeholders. The framework of regulation touches upon the use of resources, sustainable infrastructure in management and learning as well as on chemicals and waste management, providing access to essen-

---

[49] See Simon, *Rethinking Sustainable Cities, Accessible, green, and fair* (2016), 35.

[50] Aust, 'Cities as International Legal Authorities-Remarks on Recent Developments and Possible Future Trends of Research' (2020) 4 *JCULP*, 82; Lin, *Governing climate change: global cities and transnational lawmaking* (2018); Aust, 'The shifting role of cities in the global climate change regime: From Paris to Pittsburgh and back?' (2019) 28.1 *Review of European, Comparative & International Environmental Law*, 57-66; see for further examples emphasising the case of New York City which declared itself in 2018 to be the first city to report directly to the United Nations on the local implementation of the SDGs: Nijman and Aust, 'The Emerging Roles of Cities in International Law - Introductory Remarks on Practice, Scholarship and the Handbook' in Aust and Nijman (eds), *Research Handbook on International Law and Cities* (2021), 5.

[51] UN, *Habitat III, A conference of 30.000 voices* (2017) and outcome resolution A/RES/71/256*, New Urban Agenda, 25 January 2017.

tial services, green and decent jobs, and the tourism sector. However, this vast array of endeavours cannot be gathered logically under merely one legal canopy.

The use of natural resources alone covers legal fields from mining in outer space, 54 in the deeper seabed, at the same time, forests, water to many other resources more. Regarding the separated segments of the particular laws in the matrix of rules, SDG 12 calls for a general view covering many aspects in principle than in detail and should be taken into account as a fundamental principle when designing legal structures or in judicial interpretation, similar to the efficiency requirement of law or as is already done with the inclusion of sustainable development in many legal decision-making deliberations.

XIII. Climate Action with SDG 13

Deemed to be the greatest challenge facing humanity, the IPCC provides authorita- 55 tive and reliable evidence in terms of both research findings and areas for action to tackle climate change. However, these facts need to be translated into policies and legal frameworks of different sectors such as agriculture, energy, transport and water manage-ment or as a basis for different affected groups and individuals. Their integration into constitutional law demonstrate that global changes of planetary boundaries placed at risk by climate change need to be reflected and integrated into constitutional principles leading to an expanding individual right basis and expanded tasks for governments to protect life, health and property.[52]

The withholding of individual rights and those of groups impacted by direct and 56 indirect effects of climate change must be revised. It is remarkable, that the legal and judicial areas suffer from the acceptance of the lack of *locus standi* and the difficult question of how to overcome the burden of proof and sufficiently establish causality. At a time when the human rights dimension of climate change is concerned and a Special Rapporteur on Climate and Human Rights is being discussed, a right step into future would be to grant a legal basis for a claim that leads to compensation for damages caused by climate change.

Planetary boundaries (which are, however, variable and not fixed even in geological 57 time) must be respected and get in the focus of earth jurisprudence which as another area that partly overlaps with climate change needs to be systematically brought into an appropriate legal framework.

XIV. Sustaining Life Below Water with SDG 14

Following on from the climate and environmental protection of SDG 13 and SDG 6, 58 SDG 14 raises concerns regarding the effectiveness of existing ocean and fisheries gover-nance, highlighting the need for timely mitigation and adaptation responses. However, since the implementation is aggravated by the fact that most indicators of SDG 14 are classified as 'Tier 3' which is the lowest-ranking SDG indicator,[53] neither the overall progress nor its reflection in the different jurisdictions can be evaluated as valid.

Moreover, SDG 14 lacks at first glance participatory elements, the forms of manage- 59 ment it needs to be implemented or at least directly link to gender equality or human

---

[52] German Federal Constitutional Court, Order of the First Senate of 24 March 2021 – 1 BvR 2656/18, 1 BvR 78/20, 1 BvR 96/20, 1 BvR 288/20 –, ECLI:DE:BVerfG:2021:rs20210324.1bvr265618, paras. 1-270.

[53] This means that 'no internationally established methodology or standards are yet available for the indicator'.

rights. In this respect, it falls *prima vista* behind in the degree of connection, specifically to the human rights background of the Global Agenda 2030 and the other SDGs contained.

60   However, the human rights background bears the fundament for the understanding and the applicability of the SDGs in whole.[54] Here, the concept of the wrapped SDGs with internal and external systemic relationships reveals their inherent core of human rights and their participatory approach, which is underlined as well in SDG 17. The SDGs cannot be perceived as an isolated content but are interwoven with the concept of sustainable development in its three dimensions and overarched from the inherent 'planetarian' concept in the SDGs as well. As laid down in Part A, particularly the Small Island Developing States (SIDS) through the implementation of the SIDS Accelerated Modalities of Action (SAMOA) help create the SIDS partnership toolbox, reflecting the urgent demands of affected communities (→ Goal 17).[55]

61   Adverse to implementation and legal transition is that the protection of marine ecosystems does not provide guidance on how to relate to states or global waters. Obviously, joint state responsibilities (should logically) prevail in the scope of application of SDG 14[56] since otherwise no effective implementation can be realised. The jurisdiction examined, however, show that this responsibility does not always follow despite being demanded by compulsory legal frameworks. The great variety parts of jurisdiction which range from 'areas of the sea and the sea-bed' to 'ships' and 'navigation and fishing' as well as 'the absence of an 'owner'[57] make even more difficult to identify actual obligations without getting lost in context. Furthermore, the possibilities to also subject private actors to judicial control and actually hold them liable are still very limited. It might be assumed that this will change in the future with increasing litigation in the climate change regime. A clearer assessment must therefore be awaited so far.

62   The inadequacies already identified in SDG 6, and in particular the lacking link to the global water cycles, including the cryosphere also make the ecosystem approach, at least the one formulated in SDG 14, appear more than questionable. Watercourses, the high seas and marine ecosystems are naturally interconnected. A separate consideration is therefore neither possible nor purposeful. It is surprising that the actual purpose of SDG 14 is then agreed to be the provision of marine resources for human use – albeit for sustainable use. It becomes particularly evident that the conservation of ecosystems ultimately serves only human development and prosperity, and that natural capital ultimately serves only as human capital. Of course, this is in line with the anthropocentric approach inherent in the SDGs and the Global Agenda 2030. Thus, although SDG 14 concerns global commons, the preservation of which is already a pursuit in itself, it degrades it to the level of harnessing it for human needs, regardless of any ownership.

63   SDG 14 would thus be a very evident example of both the principle of sustainable development as a 'development tool' for humankind (and not as a protective tool of a common vision at all costs) and the lack of coherence and balance in the SDGs in their entirety.

---

[54] A/RES/70/1, *Transforming our world: the 2030 Agenda for Sustainable Development*, 25 September 2015, preamble, paras. 19, 35.

[55] A/RES/74/3, Political declaration of the high-level meeting to review progress made in addressing the priorities of small island developing States through the implementation of the SIDS Accelerated Modalities of Action (SAMOA) Pathway, 10 October 2019.

[56] And is demanded from UNCLOS.

[57] Reid, 'Protection of Sites' in Lees and Viñuales, *The Oxford Handbook of Comparative Environmental Law*, 848 f.

XV. Sustaining Life on Land with SDG 15

Similar issues, albeit related to terrestrial ecological and biophysical systems, are   64
evident in the legal background of the area addressed by SDG 15. Forests, wetlands,
mountains and drylands as well as inland freshwater systems and all species of flora and
fauna cannot be adequately protected if no overarching, at best multilateral, enforceable
protection instruments exist. Nature needs more attention and cutting-edge sanctions
systems under a multilateral umbrella to become effectively sustained and protected.

Possible means of achieving this protection include the use of human-protecting   65
rights such as indigenous peoples' rights in their habitats. The concept to grant legality
to rivers, mountains and further areas of nature (even under cultural aspects) is one
example of granting rights to those communities and at the same time to support
the nature itself against exploitation.[58] In this way, the guardians of knowledge and
preservers of ecosystems are protected and with them the ecosystem itself. The means
of Science, Technology and Innovation (STI) certainly hold further opportunities, but so
far no conclusion can be drawn from a legally reliable context.

XVI. Legal Transition and Dependability – SDG 16 as Enabler for the Sustainable Transformation

As a leading orientation for all SDGs, SDG 16 supports the establishment of stable   66
institutional framework to citizens and companies. Its main features point at peace, the
rule of law, access to justice and good governance and builds the fundament for every
omission or decisive action of any powers of a state and aligned private organisations
and in particular a national government and other entities assigned with official power.
In particular, when this power affects women and girls, the quality and effectivity of
the *rule of law* are a litmus test for the quality of a genuine *rule of law* approach and
fair access to justice[59] which advances human security and prosperity.[60] Without any
doubt, the *rule of law* constitutes a *conditio sine qua non* for all emanations of sustainable
development, which cannot be achieved at a national, interregional, transnational or
international level without complying to this very basis.[61]

The concepts of justice and peaceful relations anchored in SDG 16 as fundamental   67
principles are indispensable for the implementation of the Global Agenda 2030 and its
inherent new approach. Probably effective access to fair and adequate justice is one
of the prominent tasks to achieve. To promote access to justice for everyone seems
to be a keyway to ensure that assets can be protected and that unfair practices and
discrimination can be halted to allow for more significant opportunities for individuals
and communities.[62] Nevertheless, access to justice means different things according to

---

[58] ILA, *The Role of International Law in Sustainable Natural Resources Management for Development*,
Resolution No. 4 (2020), preamble, 1.3.4, 4.1.2.

[59] Millennium Declaration; reaffirmed at the 2005 World Summit, the 2010 MDG High-level plenary
meeting, the Rio+20 conference and many other resolutions on the *rule of law*; Open Working Group on
Sustainable Development Goals, *Compendium of TST Issues Briefs, Issues Brief 29* (2014), 225 ff.

[60] A/59/2005, *Follow-up to the outcome of the Millennium Summit, In larger freedom: towards development, security and human rights for all, Report of the Secretary-General*, 21 March 2005, para. 133;
A/RES/74/191, *The rule of law at the national and international levels*, 30 December 2019, preamble.

[61] A/RES/60/1, *2005 World Summit Outcome*, 24 October 2005, para 16; A/68/213/Add.1, *Strengthening
and coordinating United Nations rule of law activities, Report of the Secretary-General*, 11 July 2014, para.
7 ff.

[62] Guard, 'Justice: What We Need in a Post-2015 World' (2012) XLIX(4) *UN Chronicle*.

a different understanding of justice embedded in different systems to give a proper unified answer. While its essence seems to lie in the creation and maintenance of a states' accountability without discrimination, upholding peaceful societies seems to be more difficult to set up in legal framings, and certainly going beyond the actual mandate of the UN.

68   A shift can be observed that it is no longer only developing and least developed countries that are affected by conflicts. Rather, conflicts that have been simmering for decades are also breaking out in many places in industrialised and emerging countries and are being exacerbated by additional challenges such as the increasingly serious lack of secure food and housing due to climate change, global health crises, slowed prosperity development[63] and other factors such as inequitable access to social services and weak social welfare systems; absence of decent work (particularly for young adults); poor natural resources management; injustices; human rights violations and abuses; political exclusion (particularly of youth and women).[64]

69   The fight against crime is apparently not in any case succeeding. Organised crime, corruption and bribery are widespread. For many people, in particular girls' and women's access to justice is insufficient or non-existent. The demand for transparency, accountability and even the establishment of a legal identity are therefore the foundations, which should enable societies based on the *rule of law*.

70   However, the very nucleus of the *rule of law* is not filled and decorated with other content but reducible to the relentless acceptance of the law by all institutions, people and entities irrespective of the source being constituted in domestic, interregional or international law.[65] A society to thrive obeys the principles of supremacy of law, equality before the law, accountability to the law, fairness in the application of the law, separation of powers, participation in decision-making, legal certainty, avoidance of arbitrariness and procedural and legal transparency.[66]

XVII. Cooperation at the Core of the New Approach with SDG 17

71   Indeed, it can be argued that the new approach of the Global Agenda 2030 has a core that is not necessarily new. The uncovering of each individual objective of each SDG, but also of the accompanying processes laid down in the Global Agenda 2030, inevitably point to a common imperative:

72   It is the reactivation of a global partnership, the joint production and utilisation of harvests/results, which is supported by a spirit of equal responsibility (shared knowledge, shared burden, shared prosperity) – which should make a (more) peaceful and (more) sustainable future possible for all states and societies. However, what is new in this approach of global partnership, which has been understood since the beginnings of tender international legal impulses, is the transparent and participatory approach, which on the one hand led to this agenda in the first place, and on the other hand, despite its

---

[63] Open Working Group on Sustainable Development Goals, *Compendium of TST Issues Briefs Issues Brief 29* (2014), 226.

[64] Open Working Group on Sustainable Development Goals, *Compendium of TST Issues Briefs Issues Brief 29* (2014), 227.

[65] Nollkaemper, 'The Internationalized Rule of Law' (2009) 1(1) *Hague Journal on the Rule of Law*, 77: Nollkaemper points out that '[i]n essence, the rule of law means literally, what it says: persons and institutions should be ruled by the law – as a norm and in actual practice.'

[66] S/2004/616, *The rule of law and transitional justice in conflict and post-conflict societies, Report of the Secretary-General*, 23 August 2004, para. 6.

multiple imprecision and perhaps also inadequacy, nevertheless shows exactly where the bottom line of the global community actually lies (→ Intro mn. 50).

SDG 17, which can be found in its basic idea and in abstract form in international law 73 as a guiding *Grundnorm* as well as in a range of principles, can nevertheless hardly be framed in legal terms in its more precise formulation of objectives, even if areas of law and, in particular, principles of treaty law are clearly recognisable.

At the same time, it is obvious that implementation will only be successful if the pub- 74 lic sector is financially well-equipped so that necessary investments can be made within the framework of the SDGs, allowing policy-making to provide the private sector with room and a framework in the same sense, so that a transformation of the private sector becomes feasible and a worthwhile option. In consequence, the immense underfunding of joint solutions to the common concerns of humankind, but also to almost any form of sustainable transition that a state may devise to follow the proposed path of the SDGs, is the major impediment to the success of this agenda.

SDG 17, like SDG 16, differs from the other SDGs by exerting a more cross-cutting 75 function than the other SDGs. Partnerships and cooperation based on mutual trust, whether financial or non-financial, are the indispensable fundament and starting point for any of the implementation processes needed for the aspired global transition.

XVIII. Conclusion

The Global Agenda 2030 and its SDGs, in the big picture, build on trust, partner- 76 ship and the *rule of law*, which are prerequisites for building and sustaining peace. Considered by some as the 'fourth pillar' for sustainable development,[67] peace is realised through (legal) security or stability. This represents but one of several reasons why the transfer of the Global Agenda 2030 into legal realms is indispensable if its concept is to be rewarded with success.

But why is it necessary at all to achieve the normative appeal or benefit by mapping 77 international law questions onto specific SDGs or the entire SDG agenda? Or perhaps *vice versa*, why is it beneficiary or normatively appealing to use the SDGs to capture or address unresolved questions of international law and legal practice? These and similar questions are repeatedly raised in both academic and practical debates.[68]

Based on the research conducted for this commentary, it has become apparent that 78 a synthesis achieves something that did not previously exist in this holistic form. The SDGs not only have the potential, but have already shown that they are capable of steering, altering and giving new interpretations to law as it is being applied. Overall, the SDGs prepare the most diverse areas of law in a unique format of application, making them understandable for their norm addressees – be they predominantly states, companies, other private actors or individuals – and making them measurable in their ever-so-imperfect form. The SDGs permeate therefore into private and public law at the same time. Consequently, a successful application of the SDGs in practice requires a transfer of transnational norms into the realm of private law-based relationships. By means of the Global Agenda 2030 and the SDGs, political will-forming and implementation are equally pursued and abstract international law and legal principles are disentangled and made understandable for everyone so that, as a result, law can function more responsively and become more easily comprehensible. In its diversity

---

[67] Viñuales, *The Rio Declaration on Environment and Development, A Commentary* (2015), 54.
[68] Rachovitsa and Hesselman (eds), 'Introduction to the Special Issue: International Law for the Sustainable Development Goals' (2020) 2(1) *Brill Open Law*, 1-7.

of subjects and areas of law, the SDGs seem to almost overwhelm and confuse the user due to their many connections and conflicting objectives. It is precisely here that the commentary sets in with its readily digestible and systematically structured format. While the commentary is not to be understood as a complete avenue of integrating law and awakening the normativity of the SDGs, the commentary yet can be a pathfinder to a reasonable, mostly legal interpretation. What is not actually law itself in its formal origin, the resolution A/RES/70/1, is made discernible and revealed in its legal relevance through examples from the various legal families.

79   Remarkably, against the new approach to be understood from the Global Agenda 2030, the main norm addressee of many of the SDGs' objectives often remains the state. But as argued before, private law could contribute decisively to achieving much more than relying only on state responsibility. To engage wider stakeholders, but also to generate context-appropriate pathways and solutions, a teleological interpretation of the SDGs is necessary. But how could the SDGs provide legal certainty if they can (and must) be understood differently in every context, in every form of government, in every reality of private and public life? When everything becomes context-dependent, nothing is dependable at all. What exactly then is the common bottom-line of the global societies anyways? Here, it becomes apparent that the SDGs are more than just a synthesis of principles and, as a flexible norm-forming and norm-affecting instrument, they redefine the future development of law. Therefore, it is to be understood that the SDGs stimulate, initiate and trigger relevant legislation (processes) and thus may emanate into positive law over time.

80   What can also be seen from this commentary and the fundament of scientific data it is built upon is that its specific legal transformation or, to speak in clearer words, reformation lags behind. Moreover, the examined jurisdiction can only provide an insight into the perspective with which law and SDGs could be interpreted (legal elucidation). The different narrow and broader contexts of the SDGs ('clusters') are evident from this study and therefore also lead to the necessary shaping and framing of future emerging norms and protective instruments such as international treaties and agreements or legislative proposals and guidelines, codes of conduct and much more in the sphere of soft law.

81   Consequently, the immense underfunding of joint solutions to the concerns of humanity, but also to almost any form of sustainable transition that a state can design to follow the proposed path of the SDGs, is the major impediment to the success of this agenda.

82   Despite the attempt to circumvent the immense lack of funding with the AAAA by means of an independent funding instrument, it is obvious that due to various factors – first and foremost the SARS-CoV-2 pandemic – the financing for implementation is still insufficient. In some cases, it is not possible to determine whether funding is reaching where it is needed or whether it is actually being used to finance the implementation of the SDGs or rather to initiate funding in a broader sense of some form of sustainable development.

83   However, with the Global Agenda 2030 and the SDGs, a redistribution mechanism or even an actual reallocation has not been created. Despite the required holistic approach and the epistemically broad, above all teleological scope for interpretation, in many places it is precisely not possible to derive legal elements or even to speak of a normative framing. As necessary as the positive legal framing is for achieving the objectives of the SDGs, the approach clearly goes much beyond and illustrates the governance functions and the political, public, but also civil will-building, without which this agenda will not be judged a success in the year 2030.

Yet, in addition to the many areas of regulation that can be assigned a normative **84** content, this agenda is very much an indication that law in its future version will have to be understood differently and in a much more holistic way, and that societies will only thrive and prosper harmoniously once they are (gender) equal, inclusive, transparent, participatory and based on trust and partnership.

Resolution adopted by the General Assembly on 25 September 2015

[without reference to a Main Committee (A/70/L.1)]

70/1.
Transforming our world: the 2030 Agenda for Sustainable Development

The General Assembly

Adopts the following outcome document of the United Nations summit for the adoption of the post-2015 development agenda:

Transforming our world: the 2030 Agenda for Sustainable Development

Preamble

This Agenda is a plan of action for people, planet and prosperity. It also seeks to strengthen universal peace in larger freedom. We recognize that eradicating poverty in all its forms and dimensions, including extreme poverty, is the greatest global challenge and an indispensable requirement for sustainable development.

All countries and all stakeholders, acting in collaborative partnership, will implement this plan. We are resolved to free the human race from the tyranny of poverty and want and to heal and secure our planet. We are determined to take the bold and transformative steps which are urgently needed to shift the world on to a sustainable and resilient path. As we embark on this collective journey, we pledge that no one will be left behind.

The 17 Sustainable Development Goals and 169 targets which we are announcing today demonstrate the scale and ambition of this new universal Agenda. They seek to build on the Millennium Development Goals and complete what they did not achieve. They seek to realize the human rights of all and to achieve gender equality and the empowerment of all women and girls. They are integrated and indivisible and balance the three dimensions of sustainable development: the economic, social and environmental.

The Goals and targets will stimulate action over the next 15 years in areas of critical importance for humanity and the planet.

People

We are determined to end poverty and hunger, in all their forms and dimensions, and to ensure that all human beings can fulfil their potential in dignity and equality and in a healthy environment.

Planet

We are determined to protect the planet from degradation, including through sustainable consumption and production, sustainably managing its natural resources and taking urgent action on climate change, so that it can support the needs of the present and future generations.

Transforming our world: the 2030 Agenda for Sustainable Development

Prosperity

We are determined to ensure that all human beings can enjoy prosperous and fulfilling lives and that economic, social and technological progress occurs in harmony with nature.

Peace

We are determined to foster peaceful, just and inclusive societies which are free from fear and violence. There can be no sustainable development without peace and no peace without sustainable development.

Partnership

We are determined to mobilize the means required to implement this Agenda through a revitalized Global Partnership for Sustainable Development, based on a spirit of strengthened global solidarity, focused in particular on the needs of the poorest and most vulnerable and with the participation of all countries, all stakeholders and all people.

The interlinkages and integrated nature of the Sustainable Development Goals are of crucial importance in ensuring that the purpose of the new Agenda is realized. If we realize our ambitions across the full extent of the Agenda, the lives of all will be profoundly improved and our world will be transformed for the better.

Introduction

1. We, the Heads of State and Government and High Representatives, meeting at United Nations Headquarters in New York from 25 to 27 September 2015 as the Organization celebrates its seventieth anniversary, have decided today on new global Sustainable Development Goals.

2. On behalf of the peoples we serve, we have adopted a historic decision on a comprehensive, far-reaching and people-centred set of universal and transformative Goals and targets. We commit ourselves to working tirelessly for the full implementation of this Agenda by 2030. We recognize that eradicating poverty in all its forms and dimensions, including extreme poverty, is the greatest global challenge and an indispensable requirement for sustainable development. We are committed to achieving sustainable development in its three dimensions – economic, social and environmental – in a balanced and integrated manner. We will also build upon the achievements of the Millennium Development Goals and seek to address their unfinished business.

3. We resolve, between now and 2030, to end poverty and hunger everywhere; to combat inequalities within and among countries; to build peaceful, just and inclusive societies; to protect human rights and promote gender equality and the empowerment of women and girls; and to ensure the lasting protection of the planet and its natural resources. We resolve also to create conditions for sustainable, inclusive and sustained economic growth, shared prosperity and decent work for all, taking into account different levels of national development and capacities.

4. As we embark on this great collective journey, we pledge that no one will be left behind. Recognizing that the dignity of the human person is fundamental, we wish to see the Goals and targets met for all nations and peoples and for all segments of society. And we will endeavour to reach the furthest behind first.

5. This is an Agenda of unprecedented scope and significance. It is accepted by all countries and is applicable to all, taking into account different national realities, capacities

and levels of development and respecting national policies and priorities. These are universal goals and targets which involve the entire world, developed and developing countries alike. They are integrated and indivisible and balance the three dimensions of sustainable development.

6. The Goals and targets are the result of over two years of intensive public consultation and engagement with civil society and other stakeholders around the world, which paid particular attention to the voices of the poorest and most vulnerable. This consultation included valuable work done by the Open Working Group of the General Assembly on Sustainable Development Goals and by the United Nations, whose Secretary-General provided a synthesis report in December 2014.

Our vision

7. In these Goals and targets, we are setting out a supremely ambitious and transformational vision. We envisage a world free of poverty, hunger, disease and want, where all life can thrive. We envisage a world free of fear and violence. A world with universal literacy. A world with equitable and universal access to quality education at all levels, to health care and social protection, where physical, mental and social well-being are assured. A world where we reaffirm our commitments regarding the human right to safe drinking water and sanitation and where there is improved hygiene; and where food is sufficient, safe, affordable and nutritious. A world where human habitats are safe, resilient and sustainable and where there is universal access to affordable, reliable and sustainable energy.

8. We envisage a world of universal respect for human rights and human dignity, the rule of law, justice, equality and non-discrimination; of respect for race, ethnicity and cultural diversity; and of equal opportunity permitting the full realization of human potential and contributing to shared prosperity. A world which invests in its children and in which every child grows up free from violence and exploitation. A world in which every woman and girl enjoys full gender equality and all legal, social and economic barriers to their empowerment have been removed. A just, equitable, tolerant, open and socially inclusive world in which the needs of the most vulnerable are met.

9. We envisage a world in which every country enjoys sustained, inclusive and sustainable economic growth and decent work for all. A world in which consumption and production patterns and use of all natural resources – from air to land, from rivers, lakes and aquifers to oceans and seas – are sustainable. One in which democracy, good governance and the rule of law, as well as an enabling environment at the national and international levels, are essential for sustainable development, including sustained and inclusive economic growth, social development, environmental protection and the eradication of poverty and hunger. One in which development and the application of technology are climate-sensitive, respect biodiversity and are resilient. One in which humanity lives in harmony with nature and in which wildlife and other living species are protected.

Our shared principles and commitments

10. The new Agenda is guided by the purposes and principles of the Charter of the United Nations, including full respect for international law. It is grounded in the Univer-

sal Declaration of Human Rights,[1] international human rights treaties, the Millennium Declaration[2] and the 2005 World Summit Outcome.[3] It is informed by other instruments such as the Declaration on the Right to Development.[4]

11. We reaffirm the outcomes of all major United Nations conferences and summits which have laid a solid foundation for sustainable development and have helped to shape the new Agenda. These include the Rio Declaration on Environment and Development,[5] the World Summit on Sustainable Development, the World Summit for Social Development, the Programme of Action of the International Conference on Population and Development,[6] the Beijing Platform for Action[7] and the United Nations Conference on Sustainable Development. We also reaffirm the follow-up to these conferences, including the outcomes of the Fourth United Nations Conference on the Least Developed Countries, the third International Conference on Small Island Developing States, the second United Nations Conference on Landlocked Developing Countries and the Third United Nations World Conference on Disaster Risk Reduction.

12. We reaffirm all the principles of the Rio Declaration on Environment and Development, including, inter alia, the principle of common but differentiated responsibilities, as set out in principle 7 thereof.

13. The challenges and commitments identified at these major conferences and summits are interrelated and call for integrated solutions. To address them effectively, a new approach is needed. Sustainable development recognizes that eradicating poverty in all its forms and dimensions, combating inequality within and among countries, preserving the planet, creating sustained, inclusive and sustainable economic growth and fostering social inclusion are linked to each other and are interdependent.

Our world today

14. We are meeting at a time of immense challenges to sustainable development. Billions of our citizens continue to live in poverty and are denied a life of dignity. There are rising inequalities within and among countries. There are enormous disparities of opportunity, wealth and power. Gender inequality remains a key challenge. Unemployment, particularly youth unemployment, is a major concern. Global health threats, more frequent and intense natural disasters, spiralling conflict, violent extremism, terrorism and related humanitarian crises and forced displacement of people threaten to reverse much of the development progress made in recent decades. Natural resource depletion and adverse impacts of environmental degradation, including desertification, drought, land degradation, freshwater scarcity and loss of biodiversity, add to and exacerbate the list of challenges which humanity faces. Climate change is one of the greatest challenges of our time and its adverse impacts undermine the ability of all countries to achieve sustainable development. Increases in global temperature, sea level rise, ocean

---

[1] Resolution 217 A (III).

[2] Resolution 55/2.

[3] Resolution 60/1.

[4] Resolution 41/128, annex.

[5] *Report of the United Nations Conference on Environment and Development, Rio de Janeiro, 3–14 June 1992*, vol. I, *Resolutions Adopted by the Conference* (United Nations publication, Sales No. E.93.I.8 and corrigendum), resolution 1, annex I.

[6] *Report of the International Conference on Population and Development, Cairo, 5–13 September 1994* (United Nations publication, Sales No. E.95.XIII.18), chap. I, resolution 1, annex.

[7] *Report of the Fourth World Conference on Women, Beijing, 4–15 September 1995* (United Nations publication, Sales No. E.96.IV.13), chap. I, resolution 1, annex II.

acidification and other climate change impacts are seriously affecting coastal areas and low-lying coastal countries, including many least developed countries and small island developing States. The survival of many societies, and of the biological support systems of the planet, is at risk.

15. It is also, however, a time of immense opportunity. Significant progress has been made in meeting many development challenges. Within the past generation, hundreds of millions of people have emerged from extreme poverty. Access to education has greatly increased for both boys and girls. The spread of information and communications technology and global interconnectedness has great potential to accelerate human progress, to bridge the digital divide and to develop knowledge societies, as does scientific and technological innovation across areas as diverse as medicine and energy.

16. Almost 15 years ago, the Millennium Development Goals were agreed. These provided an important framework for development and significant progress has been made in a number of areas. But the progress has been uneven, particularly in Africa, least developed countries, landlocked developing countries and small island developing States, and some of the Millennium Development Goals remain off-track, in particular those related to maternal, newborn and child health and to reproductive health. We recommit ourselves to the full realization of all the Millennium Development Goals, including the off-track Millennium Development Goals, in particular by providing focused and scaled-up assistance to least developed countries and other countries in special situations, in line with relevant support programmes. The new Agenda builds on the Millennium Development Goals and seeks to complete what they did not achieve, particularly in reaching the most vulnerable.

17. In its scope, however, the framework we are announcing today goes far beyond the Millennium Development Goals. Alongside continuing development priorities such as poverty eradication, health, education and food security and nutrition, it sets out a wide range of economic, social and environmental objectives. It also promises more peaceful and inclusive societies. It also, crucially, defines means of implementation. Reflecting the integrated approach that we have decided on, there are deep interconnections and many cross-cutting elements across the new Goals and targets.

The new Agenda

18. We are announcing today 17 Sustainable Development Goals with 169 associated targets which are integrated and indivisible. Never before have world leaders pledged common action and endeavour across such a broad and universal policy agenda. We are setting out together on the path towards sustainable development, devoting ourselves collectively to the pursuit of global development and of "win-win" cooperation which can bring huge gains to all countries and all parts of the world. We reaffirm that every State has, and shall freely exercise, full permanent sovereignty over all its wealth, natural resources and economic activity. We will implement the Agenda for the full benefit of all, for today's generation and for future generations. In doing so, we reaffirm our commitment to international law and emphasize that the Agenda is to be implemented in a manner that is consistent with the rights and obligations of States under international law.

19. We reaffirm the importance of the Universal Declaration of Human Rights, as well as other international instruments relating to human rights and international law. We emphasize the responsibilities of all States, in conformity with the Charter of the United Nations, to respect, protect and promote human rights and fundamental freedoms for

all, without distinction of any kind as to race, colour, sex, language, religion, political or other opinion, national or social origin, property, birth, disability or other status.

20. Realizing gender equality and the empowerment of women and girls will make a crucial contribution to progress across all the Goals and targets. The achievement of full human potential and of sustainable development is not possible if one half of humanity continues to be denied its full human rights and opportunities. Women and girls must enjoy equal access to quality education, economic resources and political participation as well as equal opportunities with men and boys for employment, leadership and decision-making at all levels. We will work for a significant increase in investments to close the gender gap and strengthen support for institutions in relation to gender equality and the empowerment of women at the global, regional and national levels. All forms of discrimination and violence against women and girls will be eliminated, including through the engagement of men and boys. The systematic mainstreaming of a gender perspective in the implementation of the Agenda is crucial.

21. The new Goals and targets will come into effect on 1 January 2016 and will guide the decisions we take over the next 15 years. All of us will work to implement the Agenda within our own countries and at the regional and global levels, taking into account different national realities, capacities and levels of development and respecting national policies and priorities. We will respect national policy space for sustained, inclusive and sustainable economic growth, in particular for developing States, while remaining consistent with relevant international rules and commitments. We acknowledge also the importance of the regional and subregional dimensions, regional economic integration and interconnectivity in sustainable development. Regional and subregional frameworks can facilitate the effective translation of sustainable development policies into concrete action at the national level.

22. Each country faces specific challenges in its pursuit of sustainable development. The most vulnerable countries and, in particular, African countries, least developed countries, landlocked developing countries and small island developing States, deserve special attention, as do countries in situations of conflict and post-conflict countries. There are also serious challenges within many middle-income countries.

23. People who are vulnerable must be empowered. Those whose needs are reflected in the Agenda include all children, youth, persons with disabilities (of whom more than 80 per cent live in poverty), people living with HIV/AIDS, older persons, indigenous peoples, refugees and internally displaced persons and migrants. We resolve to take further effective measures and actions, in conformity with international law, to remove obstacles and constraints, strengthen support and meet the special needs of people living in areas affected by complex humanitarian emergencies and in areas affected by terrorism.

24. We are committed to ending poverty in all its forms and dimensions, including by eradicating extreme poverty by 2030. All people must enjoy a basic standard of living, including through social protection systems. We are also determined to end hunger and to achieve food security as a matter of priority and to end all forms of malnutrition. In this regard, we reaffirm the important role and inclusive nature of the Committee on World Food Security and welcome the Rome Declaration on Nutrition and the Frame-work for Action.[1] We will devote resources to developing rural areas and sustainable agriculture and fisheries, supporting smallholder farmers, especially women farmers, herders and fishers in developing countries, particularly least developed countries.

---

[1] World Health Organization, document EB 136/8, annexes I and II.

25. We commit to providing inclusive and equitable quality education at all levels – early childhood, primary, secondary, tertiary, technical and vocational training. All people, irrespective of sex, age, race or ethnicity, and persons with disabilities, migrants, indigenous peoples, children and youth, especially those in vulnerable situations, should have access to life-long learning opportunities that help them to acquire the knowledge and skills needed to exploit opportunities and to participate fully in society. We will strive to provide children and youth with a nurturing environment for the full realization of their rights and capabilities, helping our countries to reap the demographic dividend, including through safe schools and cohesive communities and families.

26. To promote physical and mental health and well-being, and to extend life expectancy for all, we must achieve universal health coverage and access to quality health care. No one must be left behind. We commit to accelerating the progress made to date in reducing newborn, child and maternal mortality by ending all such preventable deaths before 2030. We are committed to ensuring universal access to sexual and reproductive health-care services, including for family planning, information and education. We will equally accelerate the pace of progress made in fighting malaria, HIV/AIDS, tuberculosis, hepatitis, Ebola and other communicable diseases and epidemics, including by addressing growing anti-microbial resistance and the problem of unattended diseases affecting developing countries. We are committed to the prevention and treatment of non-communicable diseases, including behavioural, developmental and neurological disorders, which constitute a major challenge for sustainable development.

27. We will seek to build strong economic foundations for all our countries. Sustained, inclusive and sustainable economic growth is essential for prosperity. This will only be possible if wealth is shared and income inequality is addressed. We will work to build dynamic, sustainable, innovative and people-centred economies, promoting youth employment and women's economic empowerment, in particular, and decent work for all. We will eradicate forced labour and human trafficking and end child labour in all its forms. All countries stand to benefit from having a healthy and well-educated workforce with the knowledge and skills needed for productive and fulfilling work and full participation in society. We will strengthen the productive capacities of least developed countries in all sectors, including through structural transformation. We will adopt policies which increase productive capacities, productivity and productive employment; financial inclusion; sustainable agriculture, pastoralist and fisheries development; sustainable industrial development; universal access to affordable, reliable, sustainable and modern energy services; sustainable transport systems; and quality and resilient infrastructure.

28. We commit to making fundamental changes in the way that our societies produce and consume goods and services. Governments, international organizations, the business sector and other non-State actors and individuals must contribute to changing unsustainable consumption and production patterns, including through the mobilization, from all sources, of financial and technical assistance to strengthen developing countries' scientific, technological and innovative capacities to move towards more sustainable patterns of consumption and production. We encourage the implementation of the 10-Year Framework of Programmes on Sustainable Consumption and Production Patterns. All countries take action, with developed countries taking the lead, taking into account the development and capabilities of developing countries.

29. We recognize the positive contribution of migrants for inclusive growth and sustainable development. We also recognize that international migration is a multidimensional reality of major relevance for the development of countries of origin, transit and destination, which requires coherent and comprehensive responses. We will cooperate internationally to ensure safe, orderly and regular migration involving full respect for human

rights and the humane treatment of migrants regardless of migration status, of refugees and of displaced persons. Such cooperation should also strengthen the resilience of communities hosting refugees, particularly in developing countries. We underline the right of migrants to return to their country of citizenship, and recall that States must ensure that their returning nationals are duly received.

30. States are strongly urged to refrain from promulgating and applying any unilateral economic, financial or trade measures not in accordance with international law and the Charter of the United Nations that impede the full achievement of economic and social development, particularly in developing countries.

31. We acknowledge that the United Nations Framework Convention on Climate Change[2] is the primary international, intergovernmental forum for negotiating the global response to climate change. We are determined to address decisively the threat posed by climate change and environmental degradation. The global nature of climate change calls for the widest possible international cooperation aimed at accelerating the reduction of global greenhouse gas emissions and addressing adaptation to the adverse impacts of climate change. We note with grave concern the significant gap between the aggregate effect of parties' mitigation pledges in terms of global annual emissions of greenhouse gases by 2020 and aggregate emission pathways consistent with having a likely chance of holding the increase in global average temperature below 2 degrees Celsius, or 1.5 degrees Celsius above pre-industrial levels.

32. Looking ahead to the twenty-first session of the Conference of the Parties in Paris, we underscore the commitment of all States to work for an ambitious and universal climate agreement. We reaffirm that the protocol, another legal instrument or agreed outcome with legal force under the Convention applicable to all parties shall address in a balanced manner, inter alia, mitigation, adaptation, finance, technology development and transfer and capacity-building; and transparency of action and support.

33. We recognize that social and economic development depends on the sustainable management of our planet's natural resources. We are therefore determined to conserve and sustainably use oceans and seas, freshwater resources, as well as forests, mountains and drylands and to protect biodiversity, ecosystems and wildlife. We are also determined to promote sustainable tourism, to tackle water scarcity and water pollution, to strengthen cooperation on desertification, dust storms, land degradation and drought and to promote resilience and disaster risk reduction. In this regard, we look forward to the thirteenth meeting of the Conference of the Parties to the Convention on Biological Diversity to be held in Mexico.

34. We recognize that sustainable urban development and management are crucial to the quality of life of our people. We will work with local authorities and communities to renew and plan our cities and human settlements so as to foster community cohesion and personal security and to stimulate innovation and employment. We will reduce the negative impacts of urban activities and of chemicals which are hazardous for human health and the environment, including through the environmentally sound management and safe use of chemicals, the reduction and recycling of waste and the more efficient use of water and energy. And we will work to minimize the impact of cities on the global climate system. We will also take account of population trends and projections in our national rural and urban development strategies and policies. We look forward to the upcoming United Nations Conference on Housing and Sustainable Urban Development to be held in Quito.

---

[2] United Nations, *Treaty Series*, vol. 1771, No. 30822.

35. Sustainable development cannot be realized without peace and security; and peace and security will be at risk without sustainable development. The new Agenda recognizes the need to build peaceful, just and inclusive societies that provide equal access to justice and that are based on respect for human rights (including the right to development), on effective rule of law and good governance at all levels and on transparent, effective and accountable institutions. Factors which give rise to violence, insecurity and injustice, such as inequality, corruption, poor governance and illicit financial and arms flows, are addressed in the Agenda. We must redouble our efforts to resolve or prevent conflict and to support post-conflict countries, including through ensuring that women have a role in peacebuilding and State-building. We call for further effective measures and actions to be taken, in conformity with international law, to remove the obstacles to the full realization of the right of self-determination of peoples living under colonial and foreign occupation, which continue to adversely affect their economic and social development as well as their environment.

36. We pledge to foster intercultural understanding, tolerance, mutual respect and an ethic of global citizenship and shared responsibility. We acknowledge the natural and cultural diversity of the world and recognize that all cultures and civilizations can contribute to, and are crucial enablers of, sustainable development.

37. Sport is also an important enabler of sustainable development. We recognize the growing contribution of sport to the realization of development and peace in its promotion of tolerance and respect and the contributions it makes to the empowerment of women and of young people, individuals and communities as well as to health, education and social inclusion objectives.

38. We reaffirm, in accordance with the Charter of the United Nations, the need to respect the territorial integrity and political independence of States.

Means of implementation

39. The scale and ambition of the new Agenda requires a revitalized Global Partnership to ensure its implementation. We fully commit to this. This Partnership will work in a spirit of global solidarity, in particular solidarity with the poorest and with people in vulnerable situations. It will facilitate an intensive global engagement in support of implementation of all the Goals and targets, bringing together Governments, the private sector, civil society, the United Nations system and other actors and mobilizing all available resources.

40. The means of implementation targets under Goal 17 and under each Sustainable Development Goal are key to realizing our Agenda and are of equal importance with the other Goals and targets. The Agenda, including the Sustainable Development Goals, can be met within the framework of a revitalized Global Partnership for Sustainable Development, supported by the concrete policies and actions as outlined in the outcome document of the third International Conference on Financing for Development, held in Addis Ababa from 13 to 16 July 2015. We welcome the endorsement by the General Assembly of the Addis Ababa Action Agenda,[1] which is an integral part of the 2030 Agenda for Sustainable Development. We recognize that the full implementation of the Addis Ababa Action Agenda is critical for the realization of the Sustainable Development Goals and targets.

---

[1] The Addis Ababa Action Agenda of the Third International Conference on Financing for Development (Addis Ababa Action Agenda), adopted by the General Assembly on 27 July 2015 (resolution 69/313, annex).

Transforming our world: the 2030 Agenda for Sustainable Development

41. We recognize that each country has primary responsibility for its own economic and social development. The new Agenda deals with the means required for implementation of the Goals and targets. We recognize that these will include the mobilization of financial resources as well as capacity-building and the transfer of environmentally sound technologies to developing countries on favourable terms, including on concessional and preferential terms, as mutually agreed. Public finance, both domestic and international, will play a vital role in providing essential services and public goods and in catalysing other sources of finance. We acknowledge the role of the diverse private sector, ranging from micro-enterprises to cooperatives to multinationals, and that of civil society organizations and philanthropic organizations in the implementation of the new Agenda.

42. We support the implementation of relevant strategies and programmes of action, including the Istanbul Declaration and Programme of Action,[2] the SIDS Accelerated Modalities of Action (SAMOA) Pathway[3] and the Vienna Programme of Action for Landlocked Developing Countries for the Decade 2014–2024,[4] and reaffirm the importance of supporting the African Union's Agenda 2063 and the programme of the New Partnership for Africa's Development,[5] all of which are integral to the new Agenda. We recognize the major challenge to the achievement of durable peace and sustainable development in countries in conflict and post-conflict situations.

43. We emphasize that international public finance plays an important role in complementing the efforts of countries to mobilize public resources domestically, especially in the poorest and most vulnerable countries with limited domestic resources. An important use of international public finance, including official development assistance (ODA), is to catalyse additional resource mobilization from other sources, public and private. ODA providers reaffirm their respective commitments, including the commitment by many developed countries to achieve the target of 0.7 per cent of gross national income for official development assistance (ODA/GNI) to developing countries and 0.15 per cent to 0.2 per cent of ODA/GNI to least developed countries.

44. We acknowledge the importance for international financial institutions to support, in line with their mandates, the policy space of each country, in particular developing countries. We recommit to broadening and strengthening the voice and participation of developing countries – including African countries, least developed countries, land-locked developing countries, small island developing States and middle-income countries – in international economic decision-making, norm-setting and global economic governance.

45. We acknowledge also the essential role of national parliaments through their enactment of legislation and adoption of budgets and their role in ensuring accountability for the effective implementation of our commitments. Governments and public institutions will also work closely on implementation with regional and local authorities, subregional institutions, international institutions, academia, philanthropic organizations, volunteer groups and others.

46. We underline the important role and comparative advantage of an adequately resourced, relevant, coherent, efficient and effective United Nations system in supporting the achievement of the Sustainable Development Goals and sustainable development. While stressing the importance of strengthened national ownership and leadership at the country level, we express our support for the ongoing dialogue in the Economic

---

[2] *Report of the Fourth United Nations Conference on the Least Developed Countries, Istanbul, Turkey, 9–13 May 2011* (A/CONF.219/7), chaps. I and II.

[3] Resolution 69/15, annex.

[4] Resolution 69/137, annex II.

[5] A/57/304, annex.

and Social Council on the longer-term positioning of the United Nations development system in the context of this Agenda.

Follow-up and review

47. Our Governments have the primary responsibility for follow-up and review, at the national, regional and global levels, in relation to the progress made in implementing the Goals and targets over the coming 15 years. To support accountability to our citizens, we will provide for systematic follow-up and review at the various levels, as set out in this Agenda and the Addis Ababa Action Agenda. The high-level political forum under the auspices of the General Assembly and the Economic and Social Council will have the central role in overseeing follow-up and review at the global level.

48. Indicators are being developed to assist this work. Quality, accessible, timely and reliable disaggregated data will be needed to help with the measurement of progress and to ensure that no one is left behind. Such data is key to decision-making. Data and information from existing reporting mechanisms should be used where possible. We agree to intensify our efforts to strengthen statistical capacities in developing countries, particularly African countries, least developed countries, landlocked developing countries, small island developing States and middle-income countries. We are committed to developing broader measures of progress to complement gross domestic product.

A call for action to change our world

49. Seventy years ago, an earlier generation of world leaders came together to create the United Nations. From the ashes of war and division they fashioned this Organization and the values of peace, dialogue and international cooperation which underpin it. The supreme embodiment of those values is the Charter of the United Nations.

50. Today we are also taking a decision of great historic significance. We resolve to build a better future for all people, including the millions who have been denied the chance to lead decent, dignified and rewarding lives and to achieve their full human potential. We can be the first generation to succeed in ending poverty; just as we may be the last to have a chance of saving the planet. The world will be a better place in 2030 if we succeed in our objectives.

51. What we are announcing today – an Agenda for global action for the next 15 years – is a charter for people and planet in the twenty-first century. Children and young women and men are critical agents of change and will find in the new Goals a platform to channel their infinite capacities for activism into the creation of a better world.

52. "We the peoples" are the celebrated opening words of the Charter of the United Nations. It is "we the peoples" who are embarking today on the road to 2030. Our journey will involve Governments as well as parliaments, the United Nations system and other international institutions, local authorities, indigenous peoples, civil society, business and the private sector, the scientific and academic community – and all people. Millions have already engaged with, and will own, this Agenda. It is an Agenda of the people, by the people and for the people – and this, we believe, will ensure its success.

53. The future of humanity and of our planet lies in our hands. It lies also in the hands of today's younger generation who will pass the torch to future generations. We have mapped the road to sustainable development; it will be for all of us to ensure that the journey is successful and its gains irreversible.

Transforming our world: the 2030 Agenda for Sustainable Development

Sustainable Development Goals and targets

54. Following an inclusive process of intergovernmental negotiations, and based on the proposal of the Open Working Group on Sustainable Development Goals,[1] which includes a chapeau contextualizing the latter, set out below are the Goals and targets which we have agreed.

55. The Sustainable Development Goals and targets are integrated and indivisible, global in nature and universally applicable, taking into account different national realities, capacities and levels of development and respecting national policies and priorities. Targets are defined as aspirational and global, with each Government setting its own national targets guided by the global level of ambition but taking into account national circumstances. Each Government will also decide how these aspirational and global targets should be incorporated into national planning processes, policies and strategies. It is important to recognize the link between sustainable development and other relevant ongoing processes in the economic, social and environmental fields.

56. In deciding upon these Goals and targets, we recognize that each country faces specific challenges to achieve sustainable development, and we underscore the special challenges facing the most vulnerable countries and, in particular, African countries, least developed countries, landlocked developing countries and small island developing States, as well as the specific challenges facing the middle-income countries. Countries in situations of conflict also need special attention.

57. We recognize that baseline data for several of the targets remains unavailable, and we call for increased support for strengthening data collection and capacity-building in Member States, to develop national and global baselines where they do not yet exist. We commit to addressing this gap in data collection so as to better inform the measurement of progress, in particular for those targets below which do not have clear numerical targets.

58. We encourage ongoing efforts by States in other forums to address key issues which pose potential challenges to the implementation of our Agenda, and we respect the independent mandates of those processes. We intend that the Agenda and its implementation would support, and be without prejudice to, those other processes and the decisions taken therein.

59. We recognize that there are different approaches, visions, models and tools available to each country, in accordance with its national circumstances and priorities, to achieve sustainable development; and we reaffirm that planet Earth and its ecosystems are our common home and that "Mother Earth" is a common expression in a number of countries and regions.

Sustainable Development Goals	
Goal 1.	End poverty in all its forms everywhere
Goal 2.	End hunger, achieve food security and improved nutrition and promote sustainable agriculture
Goal 3.	Ensure healthy lives and promote well-being for all at all ages
Goal 4.	Ensure inclusive and equitable quality education and promote lifelong learning opportunities for all
Goal 5.	Achieve gender equality and empower all women and girls

---

[1] Contained in the report of the Open Working Group of the General Assembly on Sustainable Development Goals (A/68/970 and Corr.1; see also A/68/970/Add.1–3).

Sustainable Development Goals
Goal 6. Ensure availability and sustainable management of water and sanitation for all
Goal 7. Ensure access to affordable, reliable, sustainable and modern energy for all
Goal 8. Promote sustained, inclusive and sustainable economic growth, full and productive employment and decent work for all
Goal 9. Build resilient infrastructure, promote inclusive and sustainable industrialization and foster innovation
Goal 10. Reduce inequality within and among countries
Goal 11. Make cities and human settlements inclusive, safe, resilient and sustainable
Goal 12. Ensure sustainable consumption and production patterns
Goal 13. Take urgent action to combat climate change and its impacts[*]
Goal 14. Conserve and sustainably use the oceans, seas and marine resources for sustainable development
Goal 15. Protect, restore and promote sustainable use of terrestrial ecosystems, sustainably manage forests, combat desertification, and halt and reverse land degradation and halt biodiversity loss
Goal 16. Promote peaceful and inclusive societies for sustainable development, provide access to justice for all and build effective, accountable and inclusive institutions at all levels
Goal 17. Strengthen the means of implementation and revitalize the Global Partnership for Sustainable Development

Goal 1.
End poverty in all its forms everywhere

1.1 By 2030, eradicate extreme poverty for all people everywhere, currently measured as people living on less than $1.25 a day

1.2 By 2030, reduce at least by half the proportion of men, women and children of all ages living in poverty in all its dimensions according to national definitions

1.3 Implement nationally appropriate social protection systems and measures for all, including floors, and by 2030 achieve substantial coverage of the poor and the vulnerable

1.4 By 2030, ensure that all men and women, in particular the poor and the vulnerable, have equal rights to economic resources, as well as access to basic services, ownership and control over land and other forms of property, inheritance, natural resources, appropriate new technology and financial services, including microfinance

1.5 By 2030, build the resilience of the poor and those in vulnerable situations and reduce their exposure and vulnerability to climate-related extreme events and other economic, social and environmental shocks and disasters

1.a Ensure significant mobilization of resources from a variety of sources, including through enhanced development cooperation, in order to provide adequate and predictable means for developing countries, in particular least developed countries, to implement programmes and policies to end poverty in all its dimensions

---

[*] Acknowledging that the United Nations Framework Convention on Climate Change is the primary international, intergovernmental forum for negotiating the global response to climate change.

1.b Create sound policy frameworks at the national, regional and international levels, based on pro-poor and gender-sensitive development strategies, to support accelerated investment in poverty eradication actions

Goal 2.
End hunger, achieve food security and improved nutrition and promote sustainable agriculture

2.1 By 2030, end hunger and ensure access by all people, in particular the poor and people in vulnerable situations, including infants, to safe, nutritious and sufficient food all year round

2.2 By 2030, end all forms of malnutrition, including achieving, by 2025, the internationally agreed targets on stunting and wasting in children under 5 years of age, and address the nutritional needs of adolescent girls, pregnant and lactating women and older persons

2.3 By 2030, double the agricultural productivity and incomes of small-scale food producers, in particular women, indigenous peoples, family farmers, pastoralists and fishers, including through secure and equal access to land, other productive resources and inputs, knowledge, financial services, markets and opportunities for value addition and non-farm employment

2.4 By 2030, ensure sustainable food production systems and implement resilient agricultural practices that increase productivity and production, that help maintain ecosystems, that strengthen capacity for adaptation to climate change, extreme weather, drought, flooding and other disasters and that progressively improve land and soil quality

2.5 By 2020, maintain the genetic diversity of seeds, cultivated plants and farmed and domesticated animals and their related wild species, including through soundly managed and diversified seed and plant banks at the national, regional and international levels, and promote access to and fair and equitable sharing of benefits arising from the utilization of genetic resources and associated traditional knowledge, as internationally agreed

2.a Increase investment, including through enhanced international cooperation, in rural infrastructure, agricultural research and extension services, technology development and plant and livestock gene banks in order to enhance agricultural productive capacity in developing countries, in particular least developed countries

2.b Correct and prevent trade restrictions and distortions in world agricultural markets, including through the parallel elimination of all forms of agricultural export subsidies and all export measures with equivalent effect, in accordance with the mandate of the Doha Development Round

2.c Adopt measures to ensure the proper functioning of food commodity markets and their derivatives and facilitate timely access to market information, including on food reserves, in order to help limit extreme food price volatility

Goal 3.
Ensure healthy lives and promote well-being for all at all ages

3.1 By 2030, reduce the global maternal mortality ratio to less than 70 per 100,000 live births

3.2 By 2030, end preventable deaths of newborns and children under 5 years of age, with all countries aiming to reduce neonatal mortality to at least as low as 12 per 1,000 live births and under-5 mortality to at least as low as 25 per 1,000 live births

3.3 By 2030, end the epidemics of AIDS, tuberculosis, malaria and neglected tropical diseases and combat hepatitis, water-borne diseases and other communicable diseases

3.4 By 2030, reduce by one third premature mortality from non-communicable diseases through prevention and treatment and promote mental health and well-being

3.5 Strengthen the prevention and treatment of substance abuse, including narcotic drug abuse and harmful use of alcohol

3.6 By 2020, halve the number of global deaths and injuries from road traffic accidents

3.7 By 2030, ensure universal access to sexual and reproductive health-care services, including for family planning, information and education, and the integration of reproductive health into national strategies and programmes

3.8 Achieve universal health coverage, including financial risk protection, access to quality essential health-care services and access to safe, effective, quality and affordable essential medicines and vaccines for all

3.9 By 2030, substantially reduce the number of deaths and illnesses from hazardous chemicals and air, water and soil pollution and contamination

3.a Strengthen the implementation of the World Health Organization Framework Convention on Tobacco Control in all countries, as appropriate

3.b Support the research and development of vaccines and medicines for the communicable and non-communicable diseases that primarily affect developing countries, provide access to affordable essential medicines and vaccines, in accordance with the Doha Declaration on the TRIPS Agreement and Public Health, which affirms the right of developing countries to use to the full the provisions in the Agreement on Trade-Related Aspects of Intellectual Property Rights regarding flexibilities to protect public health, and, in particular, provide access to medicines for all

3.c Substantially increase health financing and the recruitment, development, training and retention of the health workforce in developing countries, especially in least developed countries and small island developing States

3.d Strengthen the capacity of all countries, in particular developing countries, for early warning, risk reduction and management of national and global health risks

Goal 4.
Ensure inclusive and equitable quality education and promote lifelong learning opportunities for all

4.1 By 2030, ensure that all girls and boys complete free, equitable and quality primary and secondary education leading to relevant and effective learning outcomes

4.2 By 2030, ensure that all girls and boys have access to quality early childhood development, care and pre-primary education so that they are ready for primary education

4.3 By 2030, ensure equal access for all women and men to affordable and quality technical, vocational and tertiary education, including university

4.4 By 2030, substantially increase the number of youth and adults who have relevant skills, including technical and vocational skills, for employment, decent jobs and entrepreneurship

4.5 By 2030, eliminate gender disparities in education and ensure equal access to all levels of education and vocational training for the vulnerable, including persons with disabilities, indigenous peoples and children in vulnerable situations

4.6 By 2030, ensure that all youth and a substantial proportion of adults, both men and women, achieve literacy and numeracy

4.7 By 2030, ensure that all learners acquire the knowledge and skills needed to promote sustainable development, including, among others, through education for sustainable development and sustainable lifestyles, human rights, gender equality, promotion of a culture of peace and non-violence, global citizenship and appreciation of cultural diversity and of culture's contribution to sustainable development

4.a Build and upgrade education facilities that are child, disability and gender sensitive and provide safe, non-violent, inclusive and effective learning environments for all

4.b By 2020, substantially expand globally the number of scholarships available to developing countries, in particular least developed countries, small island developing States and African countries, for enrolment in higher education, including vocational training and information and communications technology, technical, engineering and scientific programmes, in developed countries and other developing countries

4.c By 2030, substantially increase the supply of qualified teachers, including through international cooperation for teacher training in developing countries, especially least developed countries and small island developing States

Goal 5.
Achieve gender equality and empower all women and girls

5.1 End all forms of discrimination against all women and girls everywhere

5.2 Eliminate all forms of violence against all women and girls in the public and private spheres, including trafficking and sexual and other types of exploitation

5.3 Eliminate all harmful practices, such as child, early and forced marriage and female genital mutilation

5.4 Recognize and value unpaid care and domestic work through the provision of public services, infrastructure and social protection policies and the promotion of shared responsibility within the household and the family as nationally appropriate

5.5 Ensure women's full and effective participation and equal opportunities for leadership at all levels of decision-making in political, economic and public life

5.6 Ensure universal access to sexual and reproductive health and reproductive rights as agreed in accordance with the Programme of Action of the International Conference on Population and Development and the Beijing Platform for Action and the outcome documents of their review conferences

5.a Undertake reforms to give women equal rights to economic resources, as well as access to ownership and control over land and other forms of property, financial services, inheritance and natural resources, in accordance with national laws

5.b Enhance the use of enabling technology, in particular information and communications technology, to promote the empowerment of women

5.c Adopt and strengthen sound policies and enforceable legislation for the promotion of gender equality and the empowerment of all women and girls at all levels

Goal 6.
Ensure availability and sustainable management of water and sanitation for all

6.1 By 2030, achieve universal and equitable access to safe and affordable drinking water for all

6.2 By 2030, achieve access to adequate and equitable sanitation and hygiene for all and end open defecation, paying special attention to the needs of women and girls and those in vulnerable situations

6.3 By 2030, improve water quality by reducing pollution, eliminating dumping and minimizing release of hazardous chemicals and materials, halving the proportion of untreated wastewater and substantially increasing recycling and safe reuse globally

6.4 By 2030, substantially increase water-use efficiency across all sectors and ensure sustainable withdrawals and supply of freshwater to address water scarcity and substantially reduce the number of people suffering from water scarcity

6.5 By 2030, implement integrated water resources management at all levels, including through transboundary cooperation as appropriate

6.6 By 2020, protect and restore water-related ecosystems, including mountains, forests, wetlands, rivers, aquifers and lakes

6.a By 2030, expand international cooperation and capacity-building support to developing countries in water- and sanitation-related activities and programmes, including water harvesting, desalination, water efficiency, wastewater treatment, recycling and reuse technologies

6.b Support and strengthen the participation of local communities in improving water and sanitation management

Goal 7.
Ensure access to affordable, reliable, sustainable and modern energy for all

7.1 By 2030, ensure universal access to affordable, reliable and modern energy services

7.2 By 2030, increase substantially the share of renewable energy in the global energy mix

7.3 By 2030, double the global rate of improvement in energy efficiency

7.a By 2030, enhance international cooperation to facilitate access to clean energy research and technology, including renewable energy, energy efficiency and advanced and cleaner fossil-fuel technology, and promote investment in energy infrastructure and clean energy technology

7.b By 2030, expand infrastructure and upgrade technology for supplying modern and sustainable energy services for all in developing countries, in particular least developed countries, small island developing States and landlocked developing countries, in accordance with their respective programmes of support

Goal 8.
Promote sustained, inclusive and sustainable economic growth, full and productive employment and decent work for all

8.1 Sustain per capita economic growth in accordance with national circumstances and, in particular, at least 7 per cent gross domestic product growth per annum in the least developed countries

8.2 Achieve higher levels of economic productivity through diversification, technological upgrading and innovation, including through a focus on high-value added and labour-intensive sectors

8.3 Promote development-oriented policies that support productive activities, decent job creation, entrepreneurship, creativity and innovation, and encourage the formalization and growth of micro-, small- and medium-sized enterprises, including through access to financial services

8.4 Improve progressively, through 2030, global resource efficiency in consumption and production and endeavour to decouple economic growth from environmental degradation, in accordance with the 10-Year Framework of Programmes on Sustainable Consumption and Production, with developed countries taking the lead

8.5 By 2030, achieve full and productive employment and decent work for all women and men, including for young people and persons with disabilities, and equal pay for work of equal value

8.6 By 2020, substantially reduce the proportion of youth not in employment, education or training

8.7 Take immediate and effective measures to eradicate forced labour, end modern slavery and human trafficking and secure the prohibition and elimination of the worst forms of child labour, including recruitment and use of child soldiers, and by 2025 end child labour in all its forms

8.8 Protect labour rights and promote safe and secure working environments for all workers, including migrant workers, in particular women migrants, and those in precarious employment

8.9 By 2030, devise and implement policies to promote sustainable tourism that creates jobs and promotes local culture and products

8.10 Strengthen the capacity of domestic financial institutions to encourage and expand access to banking, insurance and financial services for all

8.a Increase Aid for Trade support for developing countries, in particular least developed countries, including through the Enhanced Integrated Framework for Trade-related Technical Assistance to Least Developed Countries

8.b By 2020, develop and operationalize a global strategy for youth employment and implement the Global Jobs Pact of the International Labour Organization

Goal 9.
Build resilient infrastructure, promote inclusive and sustainable industrialization and foster innovation

9.1 Develop quality, reliable, sustainable and resilient infrastructure, including regional and transborder infrastructure, to support economic development and human well-being, with a focus on affordable and equitable access for all

9.2 Promote inclusive and sustainable industrialization and, by 2030, significantly raise industry's share of employment and gross domestic product, in line with national circumstances, and double its share in least developed countries

9.3 Increase the access of small-scale industrial and other enterprises, in particular in developing countries, to financial services, including affordable credit, and their integration into value chains and markets

9.4 By 2030, upgrade infrastructure and retrofit industries to make them sustainable, with increased resource-use efficiency and greater adoption of clean and environmentally sound technologies and industrial processes, with all countries taking action in accordance with their respective capabilities

9.5 Enhance scientific research, upgrade the technological capabilities of industrial sectors in all countries, in particular developing countries, including, by 2030, encouraging innovation and substantially increasing the number of research and development workers per 1 million people and public and private research and development spending

9.a Facilitate sustainable and resilient infrastructure development in developing countries through enhanced financial, technological and technical support to African countries, least developed countries, landlocked developing countries and small island developing States

9.b Support domestic technology development, research and innovation in developing countries, including by ensuring a conducive policy environment for, inter alia, industrial diversification and value addition to commodities

9.c Significantly increase access to information and communications technology and strive to provide universal and affordable access to the Internet in least developed countries by 2020

Goal 10.
Reduce inequality within and among countries

10.1 By 2030, progressively achieve and sustain income growth of the bottom 40 per cent of the population at a rate higher than the national average

10.2 By 2030, empower and promote the social, economic and political inclusion of all, irrespective of age, sex, disability, race, ethnicity, origin, religion or economic or other status

10.3 Ensure equal opportunity and reduce inequalities of outcome, including by eliminating discriminatory laws, policies and practices and promoting appropriate legislation, policies and action in this regard

10.4 Adopt policies, especially fiscal, wage and social protection policies, and progressively achieve greater equality

10.5 Improve the regulation and monitoring of global financial markets and institutions and strengthen the implementation of such regulations

10.6 Ensure enhanced representation and voice for developing countries in decision-making in global international economic and financial institutions in order to deliver more effective, credible, accountable and legitimate institutions

10.7 Facilitate orderly, safe, regular and responsible migration and mobility of people, including through the implementation of planned and well-managed migration policies

10.a Implement the principle of special and differential treatment for developing countries, in particular least developed countries, in accordance with World Trade Organization agreements

10.b Encourage official development assistance and financial flows, including foreign direct investment, to States where the need is greatest, in particular least developed countries, African countries, small island developing States and landlocked developing countries, in accordance with their national plans and programmes

10.c By 2030, reduce to less than 3 per cent the transaction costs of migrant remittances and eliminate remittance corridors with costs higher than 5 per cent

Goal 11.
Make cities and human settlements inclusive, safe, resilient and sustainable

11.1 By 2030, ensure access for all to adequate, safe and affordable housing and basic services and upgrade slums

11.2 By 2030, provide access to safe, affordable, accessible and sustainable transport systems for all, improving road safety, notably by expanding public transport, with special attention to the needs of those in vulnerable situations, women, children, persons with disabilities and older persons

11.3 By 2030, enhance inclusive and sustainable urbanization and capacity for participatory, integrated and sustainable human settlement planning and management in all countries

11.4 Strengthen efforts to protect and safeguard the world's cultural and natural heritage

11.5 By 2030, significantly reduce the number of deaths and the number of people affected and substantially decrease the direct economic losses relative to global gross domestic product caused by disasters, including water-related disasters, with a focus on protecting the poor and people in vulnerable situations

11.6 By 2030, reduce the adverse per capita environmental impact of cities, including by paying special attention to air quality and municipal and other waste management

11.7 By 2030, provide universal access to safe, inclusive and accessible, green and public spaces, in particular for women and children, older persons and persons with disabilities

11.a Support positive economic, social and environmental links between urban, peri-urban and rural areas by strengthening national and regional development planning

11.b By 2020, substantially increase the number of cities and human settlements adopting and implementing integrated policies and plans towards inclusion, resource efficiency, mitigation and adaptation to climate change, resilience to disasters, and develop and implement, in line with the Sendai Framework for Disaster Risk Reduction 2015–2030, holistic disaster risk management at all levels

11.c Support least developed countries, including through financial and technical assistance, in building sustainable and resilient buildings utilizing local materials

Goal 12.
Ensure sustainable consumption and production patterns

12.1 Implement the 10-Year Framework of Programmes on Sustainable Consumption and Production Patterns, all countries taking action, with developed countries taking the lead, taking into account the development and capabilities of developing countries

12.2 By 2030, achieve the sustainable management and efficient use of natural resources

12.3 By 2030, halve per capita global food waste at the retail and consumer levels and reduce food losses along production and supply chains, including post-harvest losses

12.4 By 2020, achieve the environmentally sound management of chemicals and all wastes throughout their life cycle, in accordance with agreed international frameworks, and significantly reduce their release to air, water and soil in order to minimize their adverse impacts on human health and the environment

12.5 By 2030, substantially reduce waste generation through prevention, reduction, recycling and reuse

12.6 Encourage companies, especially large and transnational companies, to adopt sustainable practices and to integrate sustainability information into their reporting cycle

12.7 Promote public procurement practices that are sustainable, in accordance with national policies and priorities

12.8 By 2030, ensure that people everywhere have the relevant information and awareness for sustainable development and lifestyles in harmony with nature

12.a Support developing countries to strengthen their scientific and technological capacity to move towards more sustainable patterns of consumption and production

12.b Develop and implement tools to monitor sustainable development impacts for sustainable tourism that creates jobs and promotes local culture and products

12.c Rationalize inefficient fossil-fuel subsidies that encourage wasteful consumption by removing market distortions, in accordance with national circumstances, including by restructuring taxation and phasing out those harmful subsidies, where they exist, to reflect their environmental impacts, taking fully into account the specific needs and conditions of developing countries and minimizing the possible adverse impacts on their development in a manner that protects the poor and the affected communities

Goal 13.
Take urgent action to combat climate change and its impacts[*]

13.1 Strengthen resilience and adaptive capacity to climate-related hazards and natural disasters in all countries

13.2 Integrate climate change measures into national policies, strategies and planning

13.3 Improve education, awareness-raising and human and institutional capacity on climate change mitigation, adaptation, impact reduction and early warning

13.a Implement the commitment undertaken by developed-country parties to the United Nations Framework Convention on Climate Change to a goal of mobilizing jointly $100 billion annually by 2020 from all sources to address the needs of developing countries in the context of meaningful mitigation actions and transparency on implementation and fully operationalize the Green Climate Fund through its capitalization as soon as possible

13.b Promote mechanisms for raising capacity for effective climate change-related planning and management in least developed countries and small island developing States, including focusing on women, youth and local and marginalized communities

---

[*] Acknowledging that the United Nations Framework Convention on Climate Change is the primary international, intergovernmental forum for negotiating the global response to climate change.

Goal 14.
Conserve and sustainably use the oceans, seas and marine resources for sustainable development

14.1 By 2025, prevent and significantly reduce marine pollution of all kinds, in particular from land-based activities, including marine debris and nutrient pollution

14.2 By 2020, sustainably manage and protect marine and coastal ecosystems to avoid significant adverse impacts, including by strengthening their resilience, and take action for their restoration in order to achieve healthy and productive oceans

14.3 Minimize and address the impacts of ocean acidification, including through enhanced scientific cooperation at all levels

14.4 By 2020, effectively regulate harvesting and end overfishing, illegal, unreported and unregulated fishing and destructive fishing practices and implement science-based management plans, in order to restore fish stocks in the shortest time feasible, at least to levels that can produce maximum sustainable yield as determined by their biological characteristics

14.5 By 2020, conserve at least 10 per cent of coastal and marine areas, consistent with national and international law and based on the best available scientific information

14.6 By 2020, prohibit certain forms of fisheries subsidies which contribute to overcapacity and overfishing, eliminate subsidies that contribute to illegal, unreported and unregulated fishing and refrain from introducing new such subsidies, recognizing that appropriate and effective special and differential treatment for developing and least developed countries should be an integral part of the World Trade Organization fisheries subsidies negotiation[1]

14.7 By 2030, increase the economic benefits to small island developing States and least developed countries from the sustainable use of marine resources, including through sustainable management of fisheries, aquaculture and tourism

14.a Increase scientific knowledge, develop research capacity and transfer marine technology, taking into account the Intergovernmental Oceanographic Commission Criteria and Guidelines on the Transfer of Marine Technology, in order to improve ocean health and to enhance the contribution of marine biodiversity to the development of developing countries, in particular small island developing States and least developed countries

14.b Provide access for small-scale artisanal fishers to marine resources and markets

14.c Enhance the conservation and sustainable use of oceans and their resources by implementing international law as reflected in the United Nations Convention on the Law of the Sea, which provides the legal framework for the conservation and sustainable use of oceans and their resources, as recalled in paragraph 158 of "The future we want"

---

[1] Taking into account ongoing World Trade Organization negotiations, the Doha Development Agenda and the Hong Kong ministerial mandate.

Goal 15.
Protect, restore and promote sustainable use of terrestrial ecosystems, sustainably manage forests, combat desertification, and halt and reverse land degradation and halt biodiversity loss

15.1 By 2020, ensure the conservation, restoration and sustainable use of terrestrial and inland freshwater ecosystems and their services, in particular forests, wetlands, mountains and drylands, in line with obligations under international agreements

15.2 By 2020, promote the implementation of sustainable management of all types of forests, halt deforestation, restore degraded forests and substantially increase afforestation and reforestation globally

15.3 By 2030, combat desertification, restore degraded land and soil, including land affected by desertification, drought and floods, and strive to achieve a land degradation-neutral world

15.4 By 2030, ensure the conservation of mountain ecosystems, including their biodiversity, in order to enhance their capacity to provide benefits that are essential for sustainable development

15.5 Take urgent and significant action to reduce the degradation of natural habitats, halt the loss of biodiversity and, by 2020, protect and prevent the extinction of threatened species

15.6 Promote fair and equitable sharing of the benefits arising from the utilization of genetic resources and promote appropriate access to such resources, as internationally agreed

15.7 Take urgent action to end poaching and trafficking of protected species of flora and fauna and address both demand and supply of illegal wildlife products

15.8 By 2020, introduce measures to prevent the introduction and significantly reduce the impact of invasive alien species on land and water ecosystems and control or eradicate the priority species

15.9 By 2020, integrate ecosystem and biodiversity values into national and local planning, development processes, poverty reduction strategies and accounts

15.a Mobilize and significantly increase financial resources from all sources to conserve and sustainably use biodiversity and ecosystems

15.b Mobilize significant resources from all sources and at all levels to finance sustainable forest management and provide adequate incentives to developing countries to advance such management, including for conservation and reforestation

15.c Enhance global support for efforts to combat poaching and trafficking of protected species, including by increasing the capacity of local communities to pursue sustainable livelihood opportunities

Goal 16.
Promote peaceful and inclusive societies for sustainable development, provide access to justice for all and build effective, accountable and inclusive institutions at all levels

16.1 Significantly reduce all forms of violence and related death rates everywhere

16.2 End abuse, exploitation, trafficking and all forms of violence against and torture of children

16.3 Promote the rule of law at the national and international levels and ensure equal access to justice for all

16.4 By 2030, significantly reduce illicit financial and arms flows, strengthen the recovery and return of stolen assets and combat all forms of organized crime

16.5 Substantially reduce corruption and bribery in all their forms

16.6 Develop effective, accountable and transparent institutions at all levels

16.7 Ensure responsive, inclusive, participatory and representative decision-making at all levels

16.8 Broaden and strengthen the participation of developing countries in the institutions of global governance

16.9 By 2030, provide legal identity for all, including birth registration

16.10 Ensure public access to information and protect fundamental freedoms, in accordance with national legislation and international agreements

16.a Strengthen relevant national institutions, including through international cooperation, for building capacity at all levels, in particular in developing countries, to prevent violence and combat terrorism and crime

16.b Promote and enforce non-discriminatory laws and policies for sustainable development

Goal 17.
Strengthen the means of implementation and revitalize the Global Partnership for Sustainable Development

Finance

17.1 Strengthen domestic resource mobilization, including through international support to developing countries, to improve domestic capacity for tax and other revenue collection

17.2 Developed countries to implement fully their official development assistance commitments, including the commitment by many developed countries to achieve the target of 0.7 per cent of gross national income for official development assistance (ODA/GNI) to developing countries and 0.15 to 0.20 per cent of ODA/GNI to least developed countries; ODA providers are encouraged to consider setting a target to provide at least 0.20 per cent of ODA/GNI to least developed countries

17.3 Mobilize additional financial resources for developing countries from multiple sources

17.4 Assist developing countries in attaining long-term debt sustainability through coordinated policies aimed at fostering debt financing, debt relief and debt restructuring, as appropriate, and address the external debt of highly indebted poor countries to reduce debt distress

17.5 Adopt and implement investment promotion regimes for least developed countries

Technology

17.6 Enhance North-South, South-South and triangular regional and international cooperation on and access to science, technology and innovation and enhance knowledge sharing on mutually agreed terms, including through improved coordination among existing mechanisms, in particular at the United Nations level, and through a global technology facilitation mechanism

17.7 Promote the development, transfer, dissemination and diffusion of environmentally sound technologies to developing countries on favourable terms, including on concessional and preferential terms, as mutually agreed

17.8 Fully operationalize the technology bank and science, technology and innovation capacity-building mechanism for least developed countries by 2017 and enhance the use of enabling technology, in particular information and communications technology

Capacity-building

17.9 Enhance international support for implementing effective and targeted capacity-building in developing countries to support national plans to implement all the Sustainable Development Goals, including through North-South, South-South and triangular cooperation

Trade

17.10 Promote a universal, rules-based, open, non-discriminatory and equitable multilateral trading system under the World Trade Organization, including through the conclusion of negotiations under its Doha Development Agenda

17.11 Significantly increase the exports of developing countries, in particular with a view to doubling the least developed countries' share of global exports by 2020

17.12 Realize timely implementation of duty-free and quota-free market access on a lasting basis for all least developed countries, consistent with World Trade Organization decisions, including by ensuring that preferential rules of origin applicable to imports from least developed countries are transparent and simple, and contribute to facilitating market access

Systemic issues

Policy and institutional coherence

17.13 Enhance global macroeconomic stability, including through policy coordination and policy coherence

17.14 Enhance policy coherence for sustainable development

17.15 Respect each country's policy space and leadership to establish and implement policies for poverty eradication and sustainable development

Multi-stakeholder partnerships

17.16 Enhance the Global Partnership for Sustainable Development, complemented by multi-stakeholder partnerships that mobilize and share knowledge, expertise, technology and financial resources, to support the achievement of the Sustainable Development Goals in all countries, in particular developing countries

17.17 Encourage and promote effective public, public-private and civil society partnerships, building on the experience and resourcing strategies of partnerships

Data, monitoring and accountability

17.18 By 2020, enhance capacity-building support to developing countries, including for least developed countries and small island developing States, to increase significantly the availability of high-quality, timely and reliable data disaggregated by income, gender, age, race, ethnicity, migratory status, disability, geographic location and other characteristics relevant in national contexts

17.19 By 2030, build on existing initiatives to develop measurements of progress on sustainable development that complement gross domestic product, and support statistical capacity-building in developing countries

Means of implementation and the Global Partnership

60. We reaffirm our strong commitment to the full implementation of this new Agenda. We recognize that we will not be able to achieve our ambitious Goals and targets without a revitalized and enhanced Global Partnership and comparably ambitious means of implementation. The revitalized Global Partnership will facilitate an intensive global engagement in support of implementation of all the Goals and targets, bringing together Governments, civil society, the private sector, the United Nations system and other actors and mobilizing all available resources.

61. The Agenda's Goals and targets deal with the means required to realize our collective ambitions. The means of implementation targets under each Sustainable Development Goal and Goal 17, which are referred to above, are key to realizing our Agenda and are of equal importance with the other Goals and targets. We shall accord them equal priority in our implementation efforts and in the global indicator framework for monitoring our progress.

62. This Agenda, including the Sustainable Development Goals, can be met within the framework of a revitalized Global Partnership for Sustainable Development, supported by the concrete policies and actions outlined in the Addis Ababa Action Agenda, which is an integral part of the 2030 Agenda for Sustainable Development. The Addis Ababa Action Agenda supports, complements and helps to contextualize the 2030 Agenda's means of implementation targets. It relates to domestic public resources, domestic and international private business and finance, international development cooperation, international trade as an engine for development, debt and debt sustainability, addressing systemic issues and science, technology, innovation and capacity-building, and data, monitoring and follow-up.

63. Cohesive nationally owned sustainable development strategies, supported by integrated national financing frameworks, will be at the heart of our efforts. We reiterate that each country has primary responsibility for its own economic and social development and that the role of national policies and development strategies cannot be overemphasized. We will respect each country's policy space and leadership to implement policies for poverty eradication and sustainable development, while remaining consistent with relevant international rules and commitments. At the same time, national development efforts need to be supported by an enabling international economic environment, including coherent and mutually supporting world trade, monetary and financial systems, and strengthened and enhanced global economic governance. Processes to develop and facilitate the availability of appropriate knowledge and technologies globally, as well as capacity-building, are also critical. We commit to pursuing policy coherence and an enabling environment for sustainable development at all levels and by all actors, and to reinvigorating the Global Partnership for Sustainable Development.

64. We support the implementation of relevant strategies and programmes of action, including the Istanbul Declaration and Programme of Action, the SIDS Accelerated Modalities of Action (SAMOA) Pathway and the Vienna Programme of Action for Landlocked Developing Countries for the Decade 2014–2024, and reaffirm the importance of supporting the African Union's Agenda 2063 and the programme of the New Partnership for Africa's Development, all of which are integral to the new Agenda. We recognize the major challenge to the achievement of durable peace and sustainable development in countries in conflict and post-conflict situations.

65. We recognize that middle-income countries still face significant challenges to achieve sustainable development. In order to ensure that achievements made to date are sustained, efforts to address ongoing challenges should be strengthened through the

exchange of experiences, improved coordination, and better and focused support of the United Nations development system, the international financial institutions, regional organizations and other stakeholders.

66. We underscore that, for all countries, public policies and the mobilization and effective use of domestic resources, underscored by the principle of national ownership, are central to our common pursuit of sustainable development, including achieving the Sustainable Development Goals. We recognize that domestic resources are first and foremost generated by economic growth, supported by an enabling environment at all levels.

67. Private business activity, investment and innovation are major drivers of productivity, inclusive economic growth and job creation. We acknowledge the diversity of the private sector, ranging from micro-enterprises to cooperatives to multinationals. We call upon all businesses to apply their creativity and innovation to solving sustainable development challenges. We will foster a dynamic and well-functioning business sector, while protecting labour rights and environmental and health standards in accordance with relevant international standards and agreements and other ongoing initiatives in this regard, such as the Guiding Principles on Business and Human Rights[1] and the labour standards of the International Labour Organization, the Convention on the Rights of the Child[2] and key multilateral environmental agreements, for parties to those agreements.

68. International trade is an engine for inclusive economic growth and poverty reduction, and contributes to the promotion of sustainable development. We will continue to promote a universal, rules-based, open, transparent, predictable, inclusive, non-discriminatory and equitable multilateral trading system under the World Trade Organization, as well as meaningful trade liberalization. We call upon all members of the World Trade Organization to redouble their efforts to promptly conclude the negotiations on the Doha Development Agenda.[3] We attach great importance to providing trade-related capacity-building for developing countries, including African countries, least developed countries, landlocked developing countries, small island developing States and middle-income countries, including for the promotion of regional economic integration and interconnectivity.

69. We recognize the need to assist developing countries in attaining long-term debt sustainability through coordinated policies aimed at fostering debt financing, debt relief, debt restructuring and sound debt management, as appropriate. Many countries remain vulnerable to debt crises and some are in the midst of crises, including a number of least developed countries, small island developing States and some developed countries. We reiterate that debtors and creditors must work together to prevent and resolve unsustainable debt situations. Maintaining sustainable debt levels is the responsibility of the borrowing countries; however we acknowledge that lenders also have a responsibility to lend in a way that does not undermine a country's debt sustainability. We will support the maintenance of debt sustainability of those countries that have received debt relief and achieved sustainable debt levels.

70. We hereby launch a Technology Facilitation Mechanism which was established by the Addis Ababa Action Agenda in order to support the Sustainable Development Goals. The Technology Facilitation Mechanism will be based on a multi-stakeholder collaboration between Member States, civil society, the private sector, the scientific community, United Nations entities and other stakeholders and will be composed of a United Nations inter-agency task team on science, technology and innovation for the Sustainable

---

[1] A/HRC/17/31, annex.
[2] United Nations, *Treaty Series*, vol. 1577, No. 27531.
[3] A/C.2/56/7, annex.

Transforming our world: the 2030 Agenda for Sustainable Development

Development Goals, a collaborative multi-stakeholder forum on science, technology and innovation for the Sustainable Development Goals and an online platform.

- The United Nations inter-agency task team on science, technology and innovation for the Sustainable Development Goals will promote coordination, coherence and cooperation within the United Nations system on science, technology and innovation-related matters, enhancing synergy and efficiency, in particular to enhance capacity-building initiatives. The task team will draw on existing resources and will work with 10 representatives from civil society, the private sector and the scientific community to prepare the meetings of the multi-stakeholder forum on science, technology and innovation for the Sustainable Development Goals, as well as in the development and operationalization of the online platform, including preparing proposals for the modalities for the forum and the online platform. The 10 representatives will be appointed by the Secretary-General, for periods of two years. The task team will be open to the participation of all United Nations agencies, funds and programmes and the functional commissions of the Economic and Social Council and it will initially be composed of the entities that currently integrate the informal working group on technology facilitation, namely, the Department of Economic and Social Affairs of the Secretariat, the United Nations Environment Programme, the United Nations Industrial Development Organization, the United Nations Educational, Scientific and Cultural Organization, the United Nations Conference on Trade and Development, the International Telecommunication Union, the World Intellectual Property Organization and the World Bank.
- The online platform will be used to establish a comprehensive mapping of, and serve as a gateway for, information on existing science, technology and innovation initiatives, mechanisms and programmes, within and beyond the United Nations. The online platform will facilitate access to information, knowledge and experience, as well as best practices and lessons learned, on science, technology and innovation facilitation initiatives and policies. The online platform will also facilitate the dissemination of relevant open access scientific publications generated worldwide. The online platform will be developed on the basis of an independent technical assessment which will take into account best practices and lessons learned from other initiatives, within and beyond the United Nations, in order to ensure that it will complement, facilitate access to and provide adequate information on existing science, technology and innovation platforms, avoiding duplications and enhancing synergies.
- The multi-stakeholder forum on science, technology and innovation for the Sustainable Development Goals will be convened once a year, for a period of two days, to discuss science, technology and innovation cooperation around thematic areas for the implementation of the Sustainable Development Goals, congregating all relevant stakeholders to actively contribute in their area of expertise. The forum will provide a venue for facilitating interaction, matchmaking and the establishment of networks between relevant stakeholders and multi-stakeholder partnerships in order to identify and examine technology needs and gaps, including on scientific cooperation, innovation and capacity-building, and also in order to help to facilitate development, transfer and dissemination of relevant technologies for the Sustainable Development Goals. The meetings of the forum will be convened by the President of the Economic and Social Council before the meeting of the high-level political forum under the auspices of the Council or, alternatively, in conjunction with other forums or conferences, as appropriate, taking into account the theme to be considered and on the basis of a collaboration with the organizers of the other forums or conferences. The meetings of the forum will be co-chaired by two Member States

and will result in a summary of discussions elaborated by the two co-Chairs, as an input to the meetings of the high-level political forum, in the context of the follow-up and review of the implementation of the post-2015 development agenda.

–   The meetings of the high-level political forum will be informed by the summary of the multi-stakeholder forum. The themes for the subsequent multi-stakeholder forum on science, technology and innovation for the Sustainable Development Goals will be considered by the high-level political forum on sustainable development, taking into account expert inputs from the task team.

71. We reiterate that this Agenda and the Sustainable Development Goals and targets, including the means of implementation, are universal, indivisible and interlinked.

Follow-up and review

72. We commit to engaging in systematic follow-up and review of the implementation of this Agenda over the next 15 years. A robust, voluntary, effective, participatory, transparent and integrated follow-up and review framework will make a vital contribution to implementation and will help countries to maximize and track progress in implementing this Agenda in order to ensure that no one is left behind.

73. Operating at the national, regional and global levels, it will promote accountability to our citizens, support effective international cooperation in achieving this Agenda and foster exchanges of best practices and mutual learning. It will mobilize support to overcome shared challenges and identify new and emerging issues. As this is a universal Agenda, mutual trust and understanding among all nations will be important.

74. Follow-up and review processes at all levels will be guided by the following principles:

(a)   They will be voluntary and country-led, will take into account different national realities, capacities and levels of development and will respect policy space and priorities. As national ownership is key to achieving sustainable development, the outcome from national-level processes will be the foundation for reviews at the regional and global levels, given that the global review will be primarily based on national official data sources.

(b)   They will track progress in implementing the universal Goals and targets, including the means of implementation, in all countries in a manner which respects their universal, integrated and interrelated nature and the three dimensions of sustainable development.

(c)   They will maintain a longer-term orientation, identify achievements, challenges, gaps and critical success factors and support countries in making informed policy choices. They will help to mobilize the necessary means of implementation and partnerships, support the identification of solutions and best practices and promote the coordination and effectiveness of the international development system.

(d)   They will be open, inclusive, participatory and transparent for all people and will support reporting by all relevant stakeholders.

(e)   They will be people-centred, gender-sensitive, respect human rights and have a particular focus on the poorest, most vulnerable and those furthest behind.

(f)   They will build on existing platforms and processes, where these exist, avoid duplication and respond to national circumstances, capacities, needs and priorities. They will evolve over time, taking into account emerging issues and the development of new methodologies, and will minimize the reporting burden on national administrations.

(g) They will be rigorous and based on evidence, informed by country-led evaluations and data which is high-quality, accessible, timely, reliable and disaggregated by income, sex, age, race, ethnicity, migration status, disability and geographic location and other characteristics relevant in national contexts.

(h) They will require enhanced capacity-building support for developing countries, including the strengthening of national data systems and evaluation programmes, particularly in African countries, least developed countries, small island developing States, landlocked developing countries and middle-income countries.

(i) They will benefit from the active support of the United Nations system and other multilateral institutions.

75. The Goals and targets will be followed up and reviewed using a set of global indicators. These will be complemented by indicators at the regional and national levels which will be developed by Member States, in addition to the outcomes of work undertaken for the development of the baselines for those targets where national and global baseline data does not yet exist. The global indicator framework, to be developed by the Inter-Agency and Expert Group on Sustainable Development Goal Indicators, will be agreed by the Statistical Commission by March 2016 and adopted thereafter by the Economic and Social Council and the General Assembly, in line with existing mandates. This framework will be simple yet robust, address all Sustainable Development Goals and targets, including for means of implementation, and preserve the political balance, integration and ambition contained therein.

76. We will support developing countries, particularly African countries, least developed countries, small island developing States and landlocked developing countries, in strengthening the capacity of national statistical offices and data systems to ensure access to high-quality, timely, reliable and disaggregated data. We will promote transparent and accountable scaling-up of appropriate public-private cooperation to exploit the contribution to be made by a wide range of data, including earth observation and geospatial information, while ensuring national ownership in supporting and tracking progress.

77. We commit to fully engage in conducting regular and inclusive reviews of progress at the subnational, national, regional and global levels. We will draw as far as possible on the existing network of follow-up and review institutions and mechanisms. National reports will allow assessments of progress and identify challenges at the regional and global level. Along with regional dialogues and global reviews, they will inform recommendations for follow-up at various levels.

National level

78. We encourage all Member States to develop as soon as practicable ambitious national responses to the overall implementation of this Agenda. These can support the transition to the Sustainable Development Goals and build on existing planning instruments, such as national development and sustainable development strategies, as appropriate.

79. We also encourage Member States to conduct regular and inclusive reviews of progress at the national and subnational levels which are country-led and country-driven. Such reviews should draw on contributions from indigenous peoples, civil society, the private sector and other stakeholders, in line with national circumstances, policies and priorities. National parliaments as well as other institutions can also support these processes.

Regional level

80. Follow-up and review at the regional and subregional levels can, as appropriate, provide useful opportunities for peer learning, including through voluntary reviews, sharing of best practices and discussion on shared targets. We welcome in this respect the cooperation of regional and subregional commissions and organizations. Inclusive regional processes will draw on national-level reviews and contribute to follow-up and review at the global level, including at the high-level political forum on sustainable development.

81. Recognizing the importance of building on existing follow-up and review mechanisms at the regional level and allowing adequate policy space, we encourage all Member States to identify the most suitable regional forum in which to engage. United Nations regional commissions are encouraged to continue supporting Member States in this regard.

Global level

82. The high-level political forum will have a central role in overseeing a network of follow-up and review processes at the global level, working coherently with the General Assembly, the Economic and Social Council and other relevant organs and forums, in accordance with existing mandates. It will facilitate sharing of experiences, including successes, challenges and lessons learned, and provide political leadership, guidance and recommendations for follow-up. It will promote system-wide coherence and coordination of sustainable development policies. It should ensure that the Agenda remains relevant and ambitious and should focus on the assessment of progress, achievements and challenges faced by developed and developing countries as well as new and emerging issues. Effective linkages will be made with the follow-up and review arrangements of all relevant United Nations conferences and processes, including on least developed countries, small island developing States and landlocked developing countries.

83. Follow-up and review at the high-level political forum will be informed by an annual progress report on the Sustainable Development Goals to be prepared by the Secretary-General in cooperation with the United Nations system, based on the global indicator framework and data produced by national statistical systems and information collected at the regional level. The high-level political forum will also be informed by the *Global Sustainable Development Report*, which shall strengthen the science-policy interface and could provide a strong evidence-based instrument to support policymakers in promoting poverty eradication and sustainable development. We invite the President of the Economic and Social Council to conduct a process of consultations on the scope, methodology and frequency of the global report as well as its relation to the progress report, the outcome of which should be reflected in the ministerial declaration of the session of the high-level political forum in 2016.

84. The high-level political forum, under the auspices of the Economic and Social Council, shall carry out regular reviews, in line with General Assembly resolution 67/290 of 9 July 2013. Reviews will be voluntary, while encouraging reporting, and include developed and developing countries as well as relevant United Nations entities and other stakeholders, including civil society and the private sector. They shall be State-led, involving ministerial and other relevant high-level participants. They shall provide a platform for partnerships, including through the participation of major groups and other relevant stakeholders.

85. Thematic reviews of progress on the Sustainable Development Goals, including cross-cutting issues, will also take place at the high-level political forum. These will be supported by reviews by the functional commissions of the Economic and Social Coun-

cil and other intergovernmental bodies and forums which should reflect the integrated nature of the Goals as well as the interlinkages between them. They will engage all relevant stakeholders and, where possible, feed into, and be aligned with, the cycle of the high-level political forum.

86. We welcome, as outlined in the Addis Ababa Action Agenda, the dedicated follow-up and review for the financing for development outcomes as well as all the means of implementation of the Sustainable Development Goals which is integrated with the follow-up and review framework of this Agenda. The intergovernmentally agreed conclusions and recommendations of the annual Economic and Social Council forum on financing for development will be fed into the overall follow-up and review of the implementation of this Agenda in the high-level political forum.

87. Meeting every four years under the auspices of the General Assembly, the high-level political forum will provide high-level political guidance on the Agenda and its implementation, identify progress and emerging challenges and mobilize further actions to accelerate implementation. The next high-level political forum under the auspices of the General Assembly will be held in 2019, with the cycle of meetings thus reset, in order to maximize coherence with the quadrennial comprehensive policy review process.

88. We also stress the importance of system-wide strategic planning, implementation and reporting in order to ensure coherent and integrated support to the implementation of the new Agenda by the United Nations development system. The relevant governing bodies should take action to review such support to implementation and to report on progress and obstacles. We welcome the ongoing dialogue in the Economic and Social Council on the longer-term positioning of the United Nations development system and look forward to taking action on these issues, as appropriate.

89. The high-level political forum will support participation in follow-up and review processes by the major groups and other relevant stakeholders in line with resolution 67/290. We call upon those actors to report on their contribution to the implementation of the Agenda.

90. We request the Secretary-General, in consultation with Member States, to prepare a report, for consideration at the seventieth session of the General Assembly in preparation for the 2016 meeting of the high-level political forum, which outlines critical milestones towards coherent, efficient and inclusive follow-up and review at the global level. The report should include a proposal on the organizational arrangements for State-led reviews at the high-level political forum under the auspices of the Economic and Social Council, including recommendations on voluntary common reporting guidelines. It should clarify institutional responsibilities and provide guidance on annual themes, on a sequence of thematic reviews, and on options for periodic reviews for the high-level political forum.

91. We reaffirm our unwavering commitment to achieving this Agenda and utilizing it to the full to transform our world for the better by 2030.

4th plenary meeting
25 September 2015

Instruments mentioned in the section entitled
"Sustainable Development Goals and targets"

World Health Organization Framework Convention on Tobacco Control (United Nations, *Treaty Series*, vol. 2302, No. 41032)

Sendai Framework for Disaster Risk Reduction 2015–2030 (resolution 69/283, annex II)

United Nations Convention on the Law of the Sea (United Nations, *Treaty Series*, vol. 1833, No. 31363)

"The future we want" (resolution 66/288, annex)

Index

Bold numbers refer to Goals, normal ones to margin numbers.

Index

Index

Index

Index

Index

Index